Volume 2 • 2011

WHAT DO I READ NEXT?

A Reader's Guide to Current Genre Fiction

- Fantasy
- Popular Fiction
- Popular Romances
- Horror
- Mystery
- Science Fiction
- Historical
- Inspirational

ISSN 1052-2212

Volume 2 • 2011

WHAT DO I READ NEXT?

A Reader's Guide to Current Genre Fiction

- Fantasy
- Popular Fiction
- Popular Romances
- Horror
- Mystery
- Science Fiction
- Historical
- Inspirational

DANIEL S. BURT

DON D'AMMASSA

HOLLY HIBNER

MARY KELLY

ANGIE KIESLING

CLAIR LAMB

KRISTIN RAMSDELL

GALE
CENGAGE Learning

Detroit • New York • San Francisco • New Haven, Conn • Waterville, Maine • London

What Do I Read Next 2011, Volume 2

Project Editors: Dana Ferguson, Michelle
Kazensky

Composition and Electronic Prepress: Gary
Leach, Evi Seoud

Manufacturing: Rita Wimberley

Gale
27500 Drake Rd.
Farmington Hills, MI, 48331-3535

LIBRARY OF CONGRESS CONTROL NUMBER 82-15700

ISBN-13: 978-1-4144-8763-2
ISBN-10: 1-4144-8763-0

ISSN: 1052-2212

Printed in Mexico
1 2 3 4 5 6 7 15 14 13 12 11

Contents

Introduction

Thousands of books are published each year intended for devoted fans of genre fiction. Dragons, outlaws, lovers, murderers, monsters, and aliens abound on our own world or on other worlds, throughout time—all featured in the pages of fantasy, romance, mystery, horror, science fiction, historical, inspirational, and popular fiction. Given the huge variety of titles available each year, added to the numbers from previous years, readers can be forgiven if they're stumped by the question "What do I read next?" And that's where this book comes in.

Designed as a tool to assist in the exploration of genre fiction, *What Do I Read Next?* guides the reader to both current and classic recommendations in eight widely read genres: Mystery, Romance, Fantasy, Horror, Science Fiction, Historical, Inspirational, and Popular Fiction. *What Do I Read Next?* allows readers quick and easy access to specific data on recent titles in these popular genres. Plus, each entry provides alternate reading selections, thus coming to the rescue of librarians and booksellers, who are often unfamiliar with a genre, yet must answer the question frequently posed by their patrons and customers, "What do I read next?"

Details on Titles

Volume 2 of this year's edition of *What Do I Read Next?* contains entries for titles published primarily in the first half of 2011. These entries are divided into sections for Mystery, Popular Romances, Fantasy, Horror, Science Fiction, Historical, Inspirational, and Popular Fiction. Experts in each field compile the entries for their respective genres. The experts also discuss topics relevant to their genres in essays that appear at the beginning of each section.

The criteria for inclusion of specific titles vary somewhat from genre to genre. In genres such as Romance and Mystery, where large numbers of titles are published each year, the inclusion criteria are more selective, with the experts attempting to select the recently published books that they consider best. In genres such as Horror, where the amount of new material is relatively small, a broader range of titles is represented, including many titles published by small or independent houses and some young adult books.

The entries are listed alphabetically by main author in each genre section. Most provide the following information:

- **Author or editor's** name and real name if a pseudonym is used. Co-authors, co-editors, and illustrators are also listed where applicable.
- **Book title.**
- **Date and place of publication; name of publisher.**
- **Series name.**
- **Story type:** Specific categories within each genre, identified by the compiling expert. Definitions of these types are listed in the "Key to Genre Terms" section.
- **Subject(s):** Gives the subject matter covered by the title.
- **Major character(s):** Names and brief descriptions of up to three characters featured in the title.
- **Time period(s):** Tells when the story takes place.
- **Locale(s):** Tells where the story takes place.
- **What the book is about:** A brief plot summary.
- **Where it's reviewed:** Citations to reviews of the book, including the source of the review, date of the source, and the page on which the review appears. Reviews are included from genre-specific sources such as *Locus* and *Affaire de Coeur*, as well as more general reviewing sources such as *Booklist* and *Publishers* Weekly.
- **Other books by the author:** Titles and publication dates of other books the author has written, useful for those wanting to read more by a particular author.
- **Other books you might like:** Titles by other authors written on a similar theme or in a similar style. These titles further the reader's exploration of the genre.

Indexes Answer Readers' Questions

The nine indexes in *What Do I Read Next?* used separately or in conjunction with each other, create many pathways to the featured titles, answering general questions or locating specific titles. For example:

"Are there any new Maisie Dobbs books?"

The SERIES INDEX lists entries by the name of the series of which they are a part.

"I like Regency Romances. Can you recommend any new ones?"

The GENRE INDEX breaks each genre into story types or more specialized areas. In the Romance genre for example, there is a story type heading "Regency." For the definitions of story types, see the "Key to Genre Terms."

"I'm looking for a story set in Paris."

The GEOGRAPHIC INDEX lists titles by their locale. This can help readers pinpoint an area in which they may have a particular interest, such as their home town, another country, or even Cyberspace.

"Do you know of any science fiction stories set during the 22nd century?"

The TIME PERIOD INDEX is a chronological listing of the time settings in which the main entry titles take place.

"What books are available that feature teachers?"

The CHARACTER DESCRIPTION INDEX identifies the major characters by occupation (e.g. Accountant, Editor, Librarian) or persona (e.g. Cyborg, Noble woman, Stowaway).

"Has anyone written any new books with Sherlock Holmes in them?"

The CHARACTER NAME INDEX lists the major characters named in the entries. This can help readers who remember some information about a book, but not an author or title.

"What has Laurell K. Hamilton written recently?"

The AUTHOR INDEX contains the names of all authors featured in the entries and those listed under "Other books you might like."

The TITLE INDEX includes all main entry titles and all titles recommended under "Other books by the author" and "Other books you might like" in one alphabetical listing. Thus a reader can find a specific title, new or old, then go to that entry to find out what new titles are similar.

"I'm interested in books that depict military life."

The SUBJECT INDEX is an alphabetical listing of all the subjects covered by the main entry titles.

The indexes can also be used together to narrow down or broaden choices. A reader interested in Mysteries set in New York during the 19th century would consult the TIME PERIOD INDEX and GEOGRAPHIC INDEX to see which titles appear in both. Time Travel is a common theme in Science Fiction but occasionally appears in other genres such as Fantasy and Romance. Searching for this theme in other genres would enable a reader to cross over into previously unknown realms of reading experiences. And with the AUTHOR and TITLE indexes, which include all books listed under "Other books by the author" and "Other books you might like," it is easy to compile an extensive list of recommended reading, beginning with a recently published title or a classic from the past.

Also Available Online

The entries in this book can also be found online in Gale's *Books & Authors* database. This electronic product encompasses over 172,500 books, including genre fiction, mainstream fiction, and nonfiction. All the books included in the online version are recommended by librarians or other experts, award winners, or appear on bestseller lists. The user-friendly functionality allows users to refine their searching by using several criteria, while making it easy to identify similar titles for further research and reading. *Books & Authors* is updated with new information weekly. For more information about *Books & Authors*, please visit Gale online at gale.cengage.com.

Suggestions Are Welcome

The editors welcome any comments and suggestions for enhancing and improving *What Do I Read Next?* Please address correspondence to the Editor, *What Do I Read Next?*, at the following address:

Gale, Cengage Learning

27500 Drake Rd.

Farmington Hills, MI 48331-3535

Phone: 248-699-GALE

Toll-free: 800-347-GALE

Fax: 248-699-8054

About the Genre Experts

Daniel S. Burt (Historical Fiction) Burt is a writer and college professor who has taught undergraduate courses at Trinity College and graduate literature courses at Wesleyan University, where he was a dean for nine years. He is the author of *The Chronology of American Literature* (Houghton Mifflin, 2004), *What Historical Novel Do I Read Next?* Volumes 1-3 (Gale, 1997-2003), *The Novel 100* (Facts on File, 2003), *The Literary 100* (Facts on File, 2001), *The Biography Book* (Greenwood/Oryx, 2001), *Drama 100* (Facts on File, 2007). He is the academic director for an annual series of educationally-based workshops held in Ireland (www.discoverytours.ws). When not teaching and traveling to Ireland, he lives with his wife on Cape Cod, Massachusetts.

Don D'Ammassa (Science Fiction, Horror, and Fantasy) D'Ammassa was the book reviewer for *Science Fiction Chronicle* for almost thirty years. He has had fiction published in fantastic magazines and anthologies and has contributed essays to a variety of reference books dealing withfantastic literature. D'Ammassa is the author of the novels *Blood Beast* (Windsor, 1988), *Servants of Chaos* (Leisure, 2002), *Scarab* (Five Star, 2004), *Haven* (Five Star, 2004), *Narcissus* (Five Star, 2007), and the nonfiction works *Encyclopedia of Science Fiction* (Facts on File, 2005), the *Encyclopedia of Fantasy and Horror* (Facts on File, 2006), and the *Encyclopedia of Adventure Fiction* (Facts on File, 2008).

Holly Hibner (Popular Fiction) Holly manages the Adult Services department at a public library in Michigan. She received an MLIS degree from Wayne State University in 1999. Since that time, she has published and spoken on a variety of topics, and received the 2007 Loleta Fyan award from the Michigan Library Association for innovation in library service. She loves all things techie and the challenge of a good reference question. Together with Mary Kelly, Holly created the popular blog "Awful Library Books," which led to an appearance on *Jimmy Kimmel Live,* and has also co-authored the book *Making a Collection Count: A Holistic Approach to Library Collection Management.*

Mary Kelly (Popular Fiction) Mary is a Youth Services Librarian at the Lyon Township Public Library in Michigan. She has worked in a variety of library jobs for more than ten years. Mary has published and presented on topics such as computer instruction, reader's advisory, and providing tech support. She received both an MBA and an MLIS from Wayne State University. Mary is passionate about collection quality and technology. Together with Holly Hibner, Mary created the popular blog "Awful Library Books," *which led to an appearance on Jimmy Kimmel Live,* and has also co-authored the book *Making a Collection Count: A Holistic Approach to Library Collection Management.*

Angie Kiesling (Inspirational) Angie Kiesling has worked in the publishing industry since 1985 as a writer and editor, authoring numerous books along the way, including the novel *Skizzer.* She has worked as a magazine staff editor, website editor, and small press editorial manager, and she formerly covered religion and spirituality trends for Publishers Weekly. A fiction judge for a national awards contest, today she works as a freelance writer/editor, author consultant, and writing retreat leader.

Clair Lamb (Mystery) is a writer, editor and researcher whose clients include award-winning, bestselling authors and first-time novelists. She is a regular contributor to *Crimespree* magazine, has written The Mystery Bookstore http://www.mystery-bookstore.com 's weekly and monthly newsletters since 2000, and maintains a personal blog at www.answergirlnet.blogspot.com http://www.answergirlnet.blogspot.com.

Kristin Ramsdell (Romance Fiction) Ramsdell is a librarian at California State University, East Bay and is a nationally known speaker and consultant on the subject of romance fiction. Besides writing articles about the romance genre, she writes a romance review column for *Library Journal* and is the author of *Romance Fiction: A Guide to the Genre* (Libraries Unlimited, 1999) and its predecessor, *Happily Ever After: A Guide to Reading Interests in Romance Fiction* (Libraries Unlimited, 1987). She was named Librarian of the Year by Romance Writers of America in 1996 and received in 2007 the Melinda Helfer Fairy Godmother Award from *Romantic Times* Magazine.

John Charles (Romance Fiction) Charles, a reference librarian and retrospective fiction selector for the Scottsdale

Public Library, was named 2002 Librarian of the Year by the Romance Writers of America. Charles reviews books for *Library Journal, Booklist*, the *Chicago Tribune*, and *VOYA(Voice of Youth Advocates)* and co-authors VOYA's annual "Clueless: Adult Mysteries with Young Adult Appeal" column. John Charles is co-author of *The Mystery Readers' Advisory: The Librarian's Clues to Murder and Mayhem* (ALA, 2001). Along with co-author Shelley Mosley, Charles has twice been the recipient of the Romance Writers of America's Veritas Award.

Shelley Mosley (Romance Fiction) Retired library manager Shelley Mosley has co-authored several non-fiction books: The Suffragists in Literature for Youth; Romance Today: An A-to-Z Guide to Contemporary American Romance Writers; The Complete Idiot's Guide to the Ultimate Reading List;and Crash Course in Library Supervision. With John Charles, she has won two Romance Writers of America's Veritas awards. Mosley, Romance Writers of America's 2001 Librarian of the Year, reviews books for both Booklist and Library Journal. She also writes romantic comedies with Deborah Mazoyer under the pen name Deborah Shelley. Their novels have been published by Kensington and, most recently, Avalon Books.

Key to Genre Terms

The following is a list of terms used to classify the story type of each novel included in What Do I Read Next? along with brief definitions of the terms. To find books that fall under a particular story type heading, see the Genre Index.

Action/Adventure ▮ Minimal detection; not usually espionage, but can contain rogue police or out of control spies.

Adult ▮ Fiction dealing with adult characters and mature, developed ideas.

Adventure ▮ The character(s) must face a series of obstacles, which may include monsters, conflict with other travelers, war, interference by supernatural elements, interference by nature, and so on.

Alternate History ▮ A story dealing with how society might have evolved if a specific historical event had happened differently, e.g., if the South had won the American Civil War.

Alternate Intelligence ▮ Story featuring an entity with a sense of identity and able to self-determine goals and actions. The natural or manufactured entity results from a synergy, generally unpredictable, of individual elements. This subgenre frequently involves a computer-type intelligence.

Alternate Universe ▮ More accurately, in most cases, alternate history, in which the South won the Civil War, the Nazis triumphed, etc. The idea is a venerable one in SF.

Alternate World ▮ The story starts out in the everyday world, but the main character is transported to an alternate/parallel world by supernatural means.

Amateur Detective ▮ Detective work is performed by a non-professional rather than by police or a private detective.

Americana ▮ A romance set in the present that features themes that are particularly American; often focuses on small-town life.

Ancient Evil Unleashed ▮ The evils may take familiar forms, like vampires undead for centuries, or malevolent ancient gods released from bondage by careless humans, or ancient prophecies wreaking havoc on today's world. The so-called *Cthulhu Mythos* originated by H.P. Lovecraft, in which *Cthulhu* is prominent among a pantheon of ancient evil gods, is a specific variation of this.

Anthology ▮ A collection of short stories by different authors, usually sharing a common theme.

Apocalyptic Horror ▮ Traditionally, horrors that signal or presage the end of the world, or the world of the characters, and the establishment of a new, possibly very sinister order.

Arts ▮ Fiction that incorporates some aspect of the arts, whether it be music, painting, drama, etc.

Biblical Fiction ▮ Novels that take their plots or characters from the Bible.

Black Magic ▮ Magic directed toward malevolent ends, as distinct from white magic, which is directed toward benevolent ends. Witchcraft is commonly thought of as a black art. Voodoo consists of mysterious rites and practices, including sorcery, magic and conjuration, and often has evil goals.

Carnival-Circus Horror ▮ Derived from its setting, especially the freakish world of the sideshow, in which the distorted or horrific is the norm and is sometimes used as a distorting mirror to reveal hidden selves.

Chase ▮ A traditional Western in which the action of the plot is based on some form of pursuit.

Child-in-Peril ▮ The innocence of childhood is often used to heighten the intensity and unpredictability of evil.

Collection ▮ A book of short stories by a single author.

Coming-of-Age ▮ A story in which the primary character is a young person, usually a teenager. The growth of maturity is chronicled.

Contemporary ▮ A story set in the present.

Contemporary/Exotic ▮ Set in the present but with an especially unusual or exotic setting, e.g., the tent of a desert sheik or a boat on the Amazon.

Contemporary/Fantasy ▮ A contemporary story that makes use of fantasy or supernatural elements.

Contemporary/Innocent ▮ Story set in the present that contains little or no sex.

Contemporary/Mainstream ▮ A story set in the present that would be more properly categorized as general fiction rather than a work in a specific genre.

Contemporary Realism ▮ An accurate representation of characters, settings, ideas, themes in the present day. Not idealistic in nature.

Cozy Mystery ▮ Most often "gentle" reads that frequently downplay graphic violence, profanity, and sex.

Curse ▮ Words said when someone wishes evil or harm on someone or something, such as a witch's or prophet's curse.

Cyberpunk ▌ Usually applied to the stories by a group of writers who became prominent in the mid-1980s, such as William Gibson and his *Necromancer* (1984). The "cyber" is derived from cybernetics, nominally the study of control and communications in machines. These books also feature a downbeat, punk sensibility reminiscent of the hardboiled school of detective fiction writers.

Disaster ▌ A tale recounting some event or events seriously disruptive of the social fabric but not as serious as a holocaust.

Domestic ▌ Fiction relating to household and family matters. Concerned with psychological and emotional needs of family members.

Doppelganger ▌ A double or alter ego, popularized in the works of E.T.A. Hoffmann, Edgar Allan Poe, and Robert Louis Stevenson.

Dystopian ▌ The antonym of utopian, sometimes called anti-utopian, in which traditionally positive utopian themes are treated satirically or ironically and the mood is downbeat or satiric.

End of the World ▌ A story that concerns the last events following some sort of disaster.

Erotic Horror ▌ Sexuality and horror are often argued to be inextricably linked, as in Bram Stoker's *Dracula* and Sheridan Le Fanu's "Carmilla," although others have argued that they are antithetical. Sexuality became increasingly explicit in the 1980s, sometimes verging on the pornographic, as in Brett Easton Ellis' *American Psycho*.

Espionage ▌ Involving the CIA, KGB, or other organizations whose main focus is the collection of information from the other side. Can be either violent or quiet.

Espionage Thriller ▌ Plot contains a high level of action and suspense relating to espionage.

Ethnic ▌ A work in which the ethnic background of the characters is integral to the story. Usually the focus is on an American ethnic minority group (e.g., African American, Asian American, Native American, Latino) and the two main characters are members of this group.

Evil Children ▌ The presumed innocence of a child is replaced with adult-like malevolence and cunning, contradicting the reader's usual expectations.

Family Saga ▌ Stories focusing on the problems or concerns of a family; estrangement and reunion are common themes.

Fantasy ▌ A story that contains some fantasy or supernatural elements.

Femme Fatale ▌ A seductress for whom men abandon careers, families, and responsibilities and who feels no pity or compunction in return; a common figure in history and literature.

First Contact ▌ Any story about the initial meeting or communication of humans with extraterrestrials or aliens. The term may take its name from the eponymous 1945 story by Murray Leinster.

Future Shock ▌ A journalistic term derived from Alvin Toffler's 1970 book and which refers to the alleged disorientation resulting from rapid technological change.

Futuristic ▌ A story with a science fiction setting. Often these stories are set on other planets, aboard spaceships or space stations, or on Earth in an imaginary future or, in some cases, past.

Gay/Lesbian Fiction ▌ Stories portraying homosexual characters or themes.

Generation Starship ▌ If pseudoscientific explanations involving faster-than-light drives are rejected, then the time required for interstellar travel will encompass many human generations.

Genetic Manipulation ▌ Sometimes called genetic engineering, this assumes that the knowledge exists to shape creatures, human or otherwise, using genetic means, as in *Brave New World* (1932).

Ghost Story ▌ The spirits of the dead, who can be benevolent, as in Charles Dickens, or malevolent, as in the tales of M.R. James.

Gothic ▌ A story with a strong mystery suspense plot that emphasizes mood, atmosphere, and/or supernatural or paranormal elements. Unexplained events, ancient family secrets, and a general feeling of impending doom often characterize these tales. These stories are most often set in the past.

Gothic Family Chronicle ▌ A story often covering several generations of a family, many of whose members are typically evil, perverted, or loathsome, and in which family violence is common. The family may live in a decaying mansion suggestive of those in 18th century Gothic novels.

Hard Science Fiction ▌ Stories in which the author adheres with varying degrees of rigor to scientific principles believed to be true at the time of writing, principles derived from hard (physical, biological) rather than soft (social) sciences.

Haunted House ▌ Literally, a house visited by ghosts, usually with evil intentions in horror fiction, but sometimes the subject of comedy.

Historical ▌ Set in an earlier time frame than the present.

Historical/American Civil War ▌ Set during the American Civil War, 1861-1865.

Historical/American Revolution ▌ Set during the American Revolutionary period.

Historical/American West ▌ Set in the Western portion of the United States, usually during the second half of the 19th century. Stories often involve the hardships of pioneer life (Indian raids, range wars, climatic disasters, etc.) and the main characters (most often the hero) can be of Native American extraction.

Historical/American West Coast ▌ Set in the American Far West (California, Oregon, Washington, or Alaska). Stories often focus on the Gold Rush and the tension between Spanish Land Grant families and immigrants from the Pacific Rim, usually China.

Historical/Americana ▌ A story dealing with themes unique to the American experience.

Historical/Ancient Egypt ▌ A novel set during the time of the pharaohs from the fourth century B.C. to the first century A.D. and the absorption of Egypt into the Roman Empire.

Historical/Ancient Greece ∎ Set during the flowering of the ancient Greek civilization, particularly during the age of Pericles in the 5th century B.C.

Historical/Ancient Rome ∎ Covering the history of Rome from its founding and the Roman Republic before Augustus through the decline and fall of the Roman Empire in the fifth century.

Historical/Antebellum American South ∎ Set in the American Old South (prior to the Civil War).

Historical/Canadian West ∎ Set in the western or frontier portions of Canada, usually during the 19th century. Stories most often revolve around the hardships of frontier life.

Historical/Colonial America ∎ Set in America before the American Revolution, 1620-1775. Stories featuring the Jamestown Colony, the Salem Witch Trials, and the French and Indian Wars are especially popular.

Historical/Depression Era ∎ Set mainly in America during the period of economic hardship brought on by the 1929 Stock Market Crash that continued throughout the 1930s.

Historical/Edwardian ∎ Set during the reign of Edward VII of England, 1901-1910.

Historical/Eighteenth Century ∎ A work of fiction set during the eighteenth century.

Historical/Elizabethan ∎ A novel set during the reign of Elizabeth I of England (1558-1603). There is some overlap with the last part of the Historical Renaissance category but the emphasis is British.

Historical/Exotic ∎ Setting is an unusual or exotic place.

Historical/Fantasy ∎ A historical work that makes use of fantasy or supernatural elements.

Historical/French Revolution ∎ Set during the French Revolution, 1789-1795.

Historical/Georgian ∎ Set during the reigns of the first three "Georges" of England. Roughly corresponds to the 18th century. Stories often focus on the Jacobite Rebellions and the escapades of Bonnie Prince Charlie.

Historical/Mainstream ∎ Historical fiction that would be more properly categorized as fiction rather than a specific genre.

Historical/Medieval ∎ Set during the Middle Ages, approximately the fifth through the fifteenth centuries. Stories feature battles, raids, crusades, and court intrigues; plotlines associated with the Battle of Hastings (1066) are especially popular.

Historical/Napoleonic Wars ∎ Set between 1803-1815 during the wars waged by and against France under Napoleon Bonaparte.

Historical/Post-American Civil War ∎ Set in the years following the Civil War/War Between the States, generally from 1865 into the 1870s.

Historical/Post-American Revolution ∎ Set in the years immediately following the Civil War, 1865-1870s.

Historical/Post-French Revolution ∎ Set during the years immediately following the French Revolution; stories usually take place in France or England.

Historical/Pre-History ∎ Set in the years before the Middle Ages.

Historical/Regency ∎ A novel that is set during the Regency period (1811-1820).

Historical/Renaissance ∎ Novel set in the years of the Renaissance in Europe, generally lasting from the 14th through the 17th centuries.

Historical/Roaring Twenties ∎ Usually has an American setting and takes place in the 1920s.

Historical/Russian Revolution ∎ These stories are set around and during the 1917 Russian Revolution.

Historical/Seventeenth Century ∎ A work of fiction set during the 17th century. Stories of this type often center around the clashes between the Royalists and the Cromwellians and the Restoration.

Historical/Tudor Period ∎ A novel set during the Tudor dynasty in England (1485-1603). Roughly corresponds to the Renaissance, but the emphasis is British. Overlaps with the Elizabethan period, which is marked by the reign of Elizabeth Tudor.

Historical/Victorian ∎ Set during the reign of Queen Victoria, 1837-1901. This designation does not include works with a predominately American setting.

Historical/Victorian America ∎ Set in America, usually the Eastern part, during the Victorian Period, 1837-1901.

Historical/War of 1812 ∎ Set during the British-U.S. conflict which lasted from 1812 to 1814.

Historical/World War I ∎ Set during the First World War, 1914-1918.

Historical/World War II ∎ Set in the years of the Second World War, 1939-1945.

Holiday Themes ∎ Fiction that focuses on or is set during a particular holiday or holiday season (e.g., Christmas, Valentine's Day, Mardi Gras).

Horror ∎ Refers to stories in which interest in the events, the intellectual puzzle characteristic of much of SF, is subordinated to a feeling of terror or horror by the reader, which could result from a variety of causes, including a disaster or an invasion of earth.

Humor ∎ Story with an amusing story line.

Immortality ∎ Usually includes extreme longevity, resulting from fountains of youth, elixirs, or something with a pseudoscientific basis.

Indian Culture ∎ These novels center on the lives, customs, and cultures of characters who are American Indians or who lived among the Indians.

Indian Wars ∎ Often traditional Westerns, these stories are set during the period of the Indian wars and rely on this warfare for plots, characters, and themes.

Inspirational ∎ A novel with an uplifting, often Christian theme, and usually considered "innocent."

Invasion of Earth ∎ An extremely common theme, often paralleling historical events and reflecting fears of the time. Most invasions are depicted as malign, only occasionally benign.

Legal ∎ Main focus is on a lawyer, though it does not always involve courtroom action.

Legend ▌ A story based on a legend, myth, or fairy tale that has been rewritten.

Lesbian/Contemporary ▌ A story with lesbian protagonists set in the present.

Lesbian/Historical ▌ Historical fiction with lesbian protagonists.

Light Fantasy ▌ There is a great deal of humor throughout the story and it is almost guaranteed to have a happy ending.

Literary ▌ Relates to the nature and knowledge of literature; can be applied to setting or characters.

Lost Colony ▌ Stories centering around a colony on another world that loses contact with or is abandoned by its parent civilization and the type of society that evolves under those conditions. Conflict usually arises when contact is re-established between the colony and its home world.

Magic Conflict ▌ The main conflict of the story stems from magical interference. Protagonists may be caught in the middle of a conflict between sorcerers or may themselves be engaged in conflict with other sorcerers.

Magic Realism ▌ A style of prose fiction writing in which the author blends the realism of describing ordinary places and incidents with fantastic, dreamlike, or mythical events and does not differentiate between the real and the magical.

Man Alone ▌ A lone man, alienated from the society that would normally support him, faces overwhelming dangers.

Medical ▌ Stories in which medical themes are dominant.

Military ▌ Stories have a military theme; may deal with life in the armed forces or military battles.

Modern ▌ Reflection of the present time period.

Mountain Man ▌ Any story in which the principal characters are mountain men and women, living in mountain areas remote from civilization and depending upon their own resourcefulness for survival.

Multicultural ▌ A romance in which the ethnic background of the characters is integral to the story.

Mystery ▌ Usually a story where a crime occurs or a puzzle must be solved.

Mystical ▌ Fiction dealing with spiritual elements. Miraculous or supernatural characteristics of events, characters, settings, and themes.

Nature in Revolt ▌ Tales in which normally docile plants or animals suddenly turn against humankind, sometimes transformed (giant crabs resulting from radioactivity, predatory rats, plagues, blobs that threaten London or Miami, etc.).

Occult ▌ An adjective suggesting fiction based on a mystical or secret doctrine, but sometimes referring to supernatural fiction generally. Implies that there is a reality beyond the perceived world that only adepts can penetrate.

Paranormal ▌ Novel contains supernatural elements. Story may include ghosts, UFOs, aliens, demons, and haunted houses among other unexplained phenomenon.

Parody ▌ A narrative that follows the form of the original but usually changes its sense to nonsense, thus making fun of the original or its ideas.

Police Procedural ▌ A story in which the action is centered around a police officer.

Political ▌ The novel deals with political issues that are skewed by the use and presence of fantastic elements.

Possession ▌ Domination, usually of humans, by evil spirits, demons, aliens, or other agencies in which one's own volition is replaced by an outside force.

Post-Disaster ▌ Story set in a much degraded environment, frequently involving a reduction in population and the resulting loss of access to processes, resources, technology, etc.

Post-Holocaust ▌ The events following a world-wide disaster, often the result of human folly rather than natural events (collision with a meteor, etc.).

Post-Nuclear Holocaust ▌ The events following a world-wide nuclear disaster.

Private Detective ▌ Usually detection, involving a professional for hire.

Psychic Powers ▌ Parapsychological or paranormal powers.

Psychological ▌ Fiction dealing with mental or emotional responses.

Psychological Suspense ▌ Tales in which the psychological exploration and quirks of characters generate suspense and plot.

Quest ▌ The central characters are on a journey filled with dangers to reach some worthwhile goal.

Ranch Life ▌ The basic cowboy story, in which the plot and characters are inextricably bound up in the workings of a ranch.

Regency ▌ A light romance involving the British upper classes, set during the Regency Period, 1811-1820. During this time, the Prince of Wales acted as Prince Regent because of the incapacity of his father, George III. In 1820, "Prinny" became George IV. These stories, in the style of Jane Austen, are essentially comedies of manners and the emphasis is on language, wit, and style. Georgette Heyer set the standard for the modern version of this genre. This designation is also given to stories of similar type that may not fit precisely within the Regency time period.

Reincarnation ▌ A tale in which the horror arises in connection with the reincarnation of one of the characters.

Religious ▌ Religion of any sort plays a primary role in the plot.

Revenge ▌ A character who has suffered an unjust loss returns to take vengeance. This is one of the most common traditional themes.

Robot Fiction ▌ From the Jewish Golem to the traditional clanking bucket of bolts to the human-like android, robots in various guises have been among us for centuries. The term comes from Karl Capek's play, *R.U.R.*, which stands for Rossum's Universal Robots. Robots are often surrogates for humans and may be treated seriously or comically.

Romance ▌ Stories involving love affairs and love stories; deals with the emotional attachments of the characters.

Romantic Suspense ❚ Romance with a strong mystery suspense plot. This is a broad category including works in the tradition of Mary Stewart, as well as the newer women-in-jeopardy tales by writers such as Mary Higgins Clark. These stories usually have contemporary settings but some are also set in the past.

Saga ❚ A multi-generational story that usually centers around one particular family and its trials, tribulations, successes, and loves.

Satanism ❚ Suggests worship of evil rather than benevolent gods, the antithesis of conventional theism, whether Christianity or other religions. Evil demons are Satan writ small and usually lack the awful majesty of their parent.

Satire ❚ Fiction written in a sarcastic and ironic way to ridicule human vices or follies; usually using an exaggeration of characteristics to stress a point.

Science Fantasy ❚ A somewhat vague term in which there are "rational" elements from SF and "magical" or "fanciful" elements from fantasy, which hopefully cohere in a plausible story.

Science Fiction ❚ Although the story has been classified in another genre, there are strong elements of science fiction.

Serial Killer ❚ A multiple murderer, going back to Bluebeard and up to Ed Gein, who inspired Robert Bloch's *Psycho*.

Series ❚ A number of books united either by continuing characters and situations or by a common theme. Series books may appear under a single author's name or each book in the series may be by a different author.

Small Town Horror ❚ The coziness and intimacy of a small community is disrupted by some sort of horrific happening, suggesting an unjustified placidity and complacency on the part of the citizens.

Space Colony ❚ A permanent space station, usually orbiting Earth but in principal located in deep space or near other planets or stars.

Space Opera ❚ Intergalactic adventures; westerns in space; a specialized form of the genre type Adventure.

Steampunk ❚ Genre fiction typically set in Britain in the 1900s when steam power was prevalent and prior to the broad use of electricity. The location can be anywhere, however, including North America. Steampunk usually encompasses alternate history elements and fantastical inventions powered by steam or other more anachronistic energy sources for the time period.

Supernatural Vengeance ❚ Punishment inflicted by God or a godlike creature, whether justly or capriciously.

Sword and Sorcery ❚ Often a muscle-bound swordsman, who is innocent of thought and common sense, up against evil sorcerers and sorceresses, who naturally lose in the end because they are evil.

Techno-Horror ❚ Suggests a catastrophe with horrific elements resulting from a scientific miscalculation or technological hubris; Victor Frankenstein's unnamed monster or a plague resulting from a laboratory mishap.

Techno-Thriller ❚ Stories in which a technological development, such as an invention, is linked to a series of suspenseful (thrilling) events.

Theological ❚ Stories in which religion or religious belief plays an important role.

Time Travel ❚ A story in which characters from one time are transported either literally or in spirit to another time period. The time shifts are usually between the present and another historical period.

Traditional ❚ Traditional stories may deal with virtually any time period or situation, but they are related by shared conventions of setting and characterization.

Trail Drive ❚ Any story in which a cattle drive (or, more rarely, a drive of sheep or horses) is a major plot component.

UFO ❚ Unidentified Flying Objects, literally, although sometimes used more generally to refer to any object of mysterious origin or intent.

Urban ❚ Stories set in large cities; usually the tone of the novel is gritty and realistic and may involve issues such as drugs and gangs.

Utopia ❚ A large, often influential, story type that takes its name from Thomas More's 1516 book. Usually refers to a society considered better by the author, even if not perfect. Aldous Huxley's *Island* (1962) is a utopia, whereas his more famous *Brave New World* (1932) is a dark twin, a dystopia.

Vampire Story ❚ Based on mythical bloodsucking creatures possessing supernatural powers and various forms, both animal and human. The concept can be traced far back in history, long before Bram Stoker's famous novel, *Dracula*.

Wagon Train ❚ A book that deals with wagon trains traveling across the American West.

Werewolf Story ❚ Were is Old English for man, suggesting the ancient lineage of a creature that once dominated a world in which witches and sorcerers were equally feared. Sometimes used to refer to any shape shifter, whether wolves or other animals.

Wild Talents ❚ The phrase comes from Charles Fort's writings and usually refers to parapsychological powers such a telepathy, psychokinesis, and precognition, collectively called psychic or psi phenomena.

Witchcraft ❚ Characters either profess to be or are stigmatized as witches or warlocks, and practitioners of magic associated with witchcraft. This can include black magic or white magic (e.g., Wicca).

Young Adult ❚ A marketing term for publishers; one or more of the central characters is a teenager often testing his or her skills against adversity to achieve a greater degree of maturity and self-awareness. A category used by librarians to shelve books of likely appeal to teenage readers.

Young Readers ❚ A novel with characters, plot, and vocabulary primarily aimed at juveniles.

Zombie ❚ A creature that is typically a reanimated corpse or a human being who is being controlled by someone else by use of magic or voodoo.

Award Winners

Romance Awards
by Kristin Ramsdell

As romance fiction has attained increased recognition as a legitimate literary genre, various publications, organizations, and groups have developed to support the interests of its writers and readers. As part of this mission, a number of these offer awards to recognize the accomplishments of the practitioners. Some awards are juried and are presented for excellence in quality and style of writing; others are based on popularity; some are based on sales. Usually awards are given for a particular work by a particular writer; however, some awards are presented for a body of work produced over a number of years (a type of career award) and others are given for various types of contributions to romance fiction in general. The included categories may change over time to reflect the changing nature of the genre. The Romance Writers of America and the *RT Book Reviews* (formerly called *Romantic Times*) are the sponsors of most of the awards listed below.

Romance Writers of America Awards: These awards for excellence in romance fiction writing were presented by the Romance Writers of America at the annual RWA conference in New York City in July, 2011.

RITA Awards for Published Novels: These awards are presented by the Romance Writers of America for the best romance novel published during 2010. Named for Rita Clay Estrada, RWA's first president, RITAs for published works are given in a number of categories, some of which have changed over the years. The 2011 winners in selected categories are as follows:

First Book: *Pieces of Sky* by Kaki Warner

Contemporary Series Romance: *Welcome Home, Cowboy* by Karen Templeton

Contemporary Series Romance: Suspense/Adventure: *The Moon That Night* by Helen Brenna

Young Adult Romance: *The Iron King* by Julie Kagawa

Historical Romance: *His at Night* by Sherry Thomas

Regency Historical Romance: *The Mischief of the Mistletoe* by Lauren Willig

Paranormal Romance: *Unchained: The Dark Forgotten* by Sharon Ashwood

Romantic Suspense: *Silent Scream* by Karen Rose

Contemporary Single Title: *Simply Irresistible* by Jill Shalvis

Inspirational: *In Harm's Way* by Irene Hannon

Novella: "Shifting Sea" by Virginia Kantra (Included in the anthology *Burning Up*)

Novel with Strong Romantic Elements: *Welcome to Harmony* by Jodi Thomas

Golden Heart Awards: Presented by the Romance Writers of America for the best romance novel manuscript by an unpublished writer. Golden Hearts are given in a number of categories, some of which have changed over the years. The 2011 winners in selected categories are as follows:

Contemporary Series Romance: "Lost and Found" by Jo Anne Banker

Contemporary Series Romance: Suspense/Adventure: "Stolen Lullaby" by Robin Lynn Perini

Historical Romance: "The Dark Lady" by Maire Shelley

Regency Historical Romance: "The Proper Miss's Guide to Bad Behavior" by Anne Barton

Paranormal: "The Blood Sworn King" by Trisza Ray

Romantic Suspense: "Spy in the Mirror" by Diana Van Dyke

Contemporary Single Title Romance: "The Sinners" by Lisa Connelly

Inspirational Romance: "At His Command" by Ruth Kaufman

Young Adult Romance: "Irresistible" by Suzanne Kaufman Kalb

Novel with Strong Romantic Elements: "Nearly Departed in Deadwood" by Ann Charles

Readers' Crown Awards: Chosen by romance readers and presented at the second annual RomCon, a reader/

author event, in Denver on August 7, 2011. The 2011 winners in selected categories are as follows:

Best First Romance: *Backstage Pass* by Olivia Cunning

Best Long Contemporary Romance: *Something About You* by Julie James

Best Long Historical Romance: *The Chief* by Monica McCarty

Best Paranormal Romance: *A Highlander's Destiny* by Melissa Mahue

Best Long Romantic Suspense (tie): *White Heat* by Brenda Novak and *Risk No Secrets* by Cindy Gerard

Best Mainstream Women's Fiction: *Sleep No More* by Susan Crandall

Best Romantic Novella: "No Ordinary Man" by Abby Gaines in *One in a Million*

Best Sci-Fi/Futuristic/Time Travel Romance: *Body Master* by C.J. Barry

Best Short Contemporary Romance: *A One-of-a-Kind Family* by Holly Jacobs

Best Short Historical Romance: *To Tempt a Saint* by Kate Moore

Best Short Romantic Suspense: *Along Came a Husband* by Helen Brenna

RT Bookclub Reviewer's Choice Awards: Presented by *RT Bookclub Magazine* for outstanding romances published in the previous year. Selection is done by the *RT* romance reviewers and the categories may vary from year to year. The awards for books published in 2010 were announced at the Awards Ceremony at the *RT* Booklovers Convention in Los Angeles in April, 2011. The 2011 winners in selected categories are as follows:

Best First Series Romance: *Da Silva's Mistress* by Tina Duncan

Best Harlequin American: *Miracle Baby* by Laura Bradford

Best Harlequin Blaze: *Claimed!* by Vicki Lewis Thompson

Best Harlequin Intrigue: *Mystery Lover* by Lisa Childs

Best Harlequin Presents: *The Virgin's Proposition* by Anne McAllister

Best Harlequin Presents Extra: *The Konstantos Marriage Demand* by Kate Walker

Best Harlequin Romance: *Hired: Sassy Assistant* by Nina Harrington

Best Harlequin Superromance: *Until He Met Rachel* by Debra Salonen

Best Kimani Romance: *Recipe for Temptation* by Maureen Smith

Best Silhouette Nocturne: *Lord of the Desert* by Nina Bruhns

Best Silhouette Desire: *To Tame a Sheikh* by Olivia Gates

Best Silhouette Romantic Suspense: *Her Hero in Hiding* by Rachel Lee

Best Silhouette Special Edition: *A Thunder Canyon Christmas* by RaeAnne Thayne

Best Steeple Hill Love Inspired Suspense: *Betrayal in the Badlands* by Dana Mentink

Best Steeple Hill Love Inspired: *Their First Noel* by Annie Jones

Best Steeple Hill Love Inspired Historical: *Her Healing Ways* by Lyn Cote

Best Inspirational Romance: *Here Burns My Candle* by Liz Curtis Higgs

Best Inspirational Novel: *Rooms* by James L. Rubart

Best Inspirational Mystery/Suspense/Thriller: *The Bishop* by Steven James

Historical Romance of the Year: *Barely a Lady* by Eileen Dreyer

Best First Historical Romance: *When Harry Met Molly* by Kieran Kramer

Best Historical Love & Laughter: *Mad About the Duke* by Elizabeth Boyle

Most Innovative Historical Romance: *Seven Nights to Forever* by Evangeline Collins

Best British Isle-Set Historical Romance: *When Marrying a Scoundrel* by Kathryn Smith

Best Regency-Set Historical Romance: *One Dance with a Duke* by Tessa Dare

Best Scotland-Set Historical Romance: *Taming the Highland Bride* by Lynsay Sands

Best Historical Fantasy/Paranormal: *The Time Weaver* by Shana Abé

Best Historical Romantic Adventure: *The Forbidden Rose* by Joanna Bourne

Best Sensual Historical Romance: *Ruthless* by Anne Stuart

Best Historical Fiction: *The Winter Sea* by Susanna Kearsley

Best Historical K.I.S.S. Hero: Armand Harcourt, comte de Valére from *The Making of a Gentleman* by Shana Galen

Best Erotic Romance: *Coming Undone* by Lauren Dane

Best Erotica Fiction: *Control* by Kayla Perrin

Best Paranormal/Fantasy/Sci-Fi Erotic Romance: *Dane* by Elizabeth Amber

Best Futuristic Romance: *Enemy Within* by Marcella Burnard

Best Science Fiction Novel: *Who Fears Death* by Nnedi Okorafor

Best Fantasy Novel: *The Broken Kingdoms* by N.K. Jemisin

Best Urban Fantasy Novel: *Magic Bleeds* by Ilona Andrews

Best Urban Fantasy Protagonist: Gin Blanco in *Spider's Bite* by Jennifer Estep

Best Epic Fantasy Novel: *Passion Play* by Beth Bernobich

Best Contemporary Romance: *Crush on You* by Christie Ridgway

Best Romantic Suspense: *Last Chance* by Christy Reece

Best Vampire Romance: *Eternal Kiss of Darkness* by Jeaniene Frost

Best Shapeshifter Romance: *Play of Passion* by Nalini Singh

Best Paranormal Romance: *The Iron Duke* by Meljean Brook

Best Paranormal Romantic Suspense: *Skin Tight* by Ava Gray

Best Paranormal Fiction: *Nice Girls Don't Live Forever* by Molly Harper

Best Multicultural Romance: *Heart's Secret* by Adrianne Byrd

Best Multicultural Fiction Novel: *A Second Helping* by Beverly Jenkins

Best Small Press Paranormal/Fantasy/Futuristic: *Jabril* by D.B. Reynolds

Best Small Press Romance: *Long Time Gone* by Meg Benjamin

Best Small Press Erotic Romance/Fiction: *Branded as Trouble* by Lorelei James

Best Young Adult Novel *Return to Paradise* by Simone Elkeles

Best Young Adult Paranormal/Fantasy Novel: *Radiant Shadows* by Melissa Marr

Best Contemporary Mystery: *Crooked Letter, Crooked Letter* by Tom Franklin

Best Historical Mystery: *Royal Blood* by Rhys Bowen

Best First Mystery: *Murder at Mansfield Park* by Lynn Shepherd

Best Suspense/Thriller Novel: *One Grave Less* by Beverly Connor

Best Amateur Sleuth Novel: *Bone Appetit* by Carolyn Haines

Best Mainstream Fiction: *Winter Garden* by Kristin Hannah

RT Bookclub Career Achievement Awards: Presented by *RT Bookclub Magazine* for outstanding career achieve-

ment. Awards were announced at the *RT Booklovers Convention* in Los Angeles in April, 2011. The 2011 winners in selected categories are as follows:

Historical Romance: Lisa Kleypas

Contemporary Romance: Robyn Carr

Paranormal Romance: MaryJanice Davidson

Sci-Fi/Fantasy: Sharon Shinn

Urban Fantasy: Rachel Caine

Romantic Suspense: Jayne Ann Krentz

Mystery, Suspense, and Thriller: Catherine Coulter and Carole Nelson Douglas

Inspirational Romance: Terri Blackstock

Young Adult: Caroline B. Cooney

Series Romance: Brenda Jackson

Erotica: Kate Douglas

Mainstream: Fern Michaels

Awards information courtesy of the Romance Writers of America, RomCon and the Romantic Times Publishing Group.

Fantastic Fiction Awards by Don D'Ammassa
Various awards for science fiction, fantasy, and horror fiction are presented by several professional and fan organizations, usually on an annual basis, sometimes with open balloting, sometimes confining the final decision to a group of judges. These awards typically cover short fiction of varying lengths, dramatic presentations, and other categories in addition to those involving a specific book. Since these awards are all presented retroactively, the individual titles below will have been covered in earlier editions of *What Do I Read Next?*. The final ballots for some of these are listed below, with the winners to be presented later in the year.

Hugo Awards: The Hugo Awards are named in honor of Hugo Gernsback for his pioneering work in creating science fiction magazines. They are presented at the World Science Fiction convention, which took place on August 20, 2011, in Reno, Nevada. This is fantastic fiction's oldest continuing award originating in 1953 and awarded every year since with one lapse. Anyone who purchases a membership is entitled to nominate and vote in all categories. The 2011 winners in selected categories are as follows:

Best Novel: *Blackout/All Clear* by Connie Willis

Best Related Book: *Chicks Dig Time Lords: A Celebration of Doctor Who by the Women Who Love It* edited by Lynne M. Thomas and Tara O'Shea

Best Graphic Novel: *Girl Genius, Volume 10: Agatha Heterodyne & the Guardian Misuse* by Kaja and Phil Foglio; Art by Phil Foglio; Colours by Cheyenne Wright

Nebula Awards: The Nebula Awards are presented by the Science Fiction and Fantasy Writers of America at their annual meeting. Only full members are entitled to vote for

the final selection. The award has been presented annually since 1965. The winners for 2010 in selected categories are as follows:

Best Novel: *Blackout/All Clear* by Connie Willis

Andre Norton Award: *I Shall Wear Midnight* by Terry Pratchett

Bram Stoker Awards: This award is presented by the Horror Writers of America at their annual meeting, which took place on June 18, 2011. All members can nominate but only full members can vote on the final ballot. The award is named after the author of *Dracula* and has been presented since 1987. The 2010 winners in selected categories are as follows:

Best Novel: *A Dark Matter* by Peter Straub

Best First Novel (tie): *Black and Orange* by Benjamin Kane Ethridge and *Castle of Los Angeles* by Lisa Morton

Best Collection: *Full Dark, No Stars* by Stephen King

Best Anthology: *Haunted Legends* edited by Ellen Datlow and Nick Mamatas

Best Non-Fiction: *To Each Their Darkness* by Gary A. Braunbeck

Best Poetry Collection: *Dark Matters* by Bruce Boston

The Shirley Jackson Awards: These awards are selected by a panel of editors and writers to reward outstanding achievement in psychological suspense and horror. The winners were announced July 17th 2011, at Readercon 22, Conference on Imaginative Literature, in Burlington, Massachusetts. The 2010 winners in selected categories are as follows:

Best Novel: *Mr. Shivers* by Robert Jackson Bennett

Best Single-Author Collection: *Occultation* by Laird Barron

Best Anthology: *Stories: All New Tales* edited by Neil Gaiman and Al Sarrantonio

Arthur C. Clarke Awards: This is a British award given for the best science fiction novel published in the UK during the previous year. The award was presented on April 27, 2011 at Sci-Fi London 10.

2011 winner: *Zoo City* by Lauren Beukes

2011 Popular Fiction Awards by Holly Hibner and Mary Kelly

Pulitzer Prize for Fiction: Established in 1917, this award is given annually to an American author for a work of fiction about American life.

2011 winner: *A Visit from the Goon Squad* by Jennifer Egan

Man-Booker Prize: The Man Booker Prize, Great Britain's major literary prize, is awarded annually to the author of a full-length novel. The prize was established in 1968 by Booker PLC, an international food company, and

the Book Trust and Publishers Association. The Man Group took over sponsorship for the prize in 2002. The 2011 short-list titles are as follows:

The Sense of an Ending by Julian Barnes

Menagerie by Carol Birch Jamrach

The Sisters Brothers by Patrick deWitt

Half Blood Blues by Esi Edugyan

Pigeon English by Stephen Kelman

Snowdrops by A.D. Miller

National Book Critic Circle Award: Each year this award is given by the National Book Critics Circle, an organization of approximately 700 book reviewers, to the best work of fiction for the previous year.

2010 winner: *A Visit from the Goon Squad* by Jennifer Egan

2011 Pen Faulkner Awards: The PEN/Faulkner Award for Fiction was founded in 1980 by National Book Award winner Mary Lee Settle. Her goal was to establish a national prize that would recognize literary fiction of excellence, an award juried by writers for writers, free of commercial concerns. The prize was named for William Faulkner, who used his Nobel Prize funds to establish an award for younger writers, and PEN, the international writers' organization.

2011 Winner: The Collected Stories of Deborah Eisenberg by Deborah Eisenberg

O. Henry Awards for Short Stories: This prize is given annually specifically for short stories. It is funded by the Society of Arts and Sciences. Twenty short stories are chosen by the editor of the O. Henry Prize Stories. The stories are given to three appointed jurors, who each choose their favorite to comment on.

2011 Juror Favorites:

"Your Fate Hurtles Down at You" by Jim Shepard

"Sunshine" by Lynn Freed

"Something You Can't Live Without" by Matthew Neill Null

2010 Juror Favorites:

"A Spoiled Man" by Daniyal Mueenudin

"Oh, Death" by James Lasdun

"The Woman of the House" by William Trevor

Inspirational Awards by Angie Kiesling

The Christy Awards: Since 2000, the Christy Awards have been presented to honor inspirational novels released by Christian publishing houses. The awards were named in honor of Christy, a 1967 novel by Catherine Marshall that marked a turning point in religious fiction and served as the inspiration for a television series that ran from 1994-1995.

Christy Awards entries are submitted by publishers, and a panel of independent judges narrows the field to the top three nominees in each category. The winners in each category were announced in July prior to the International Christian Retail Show. The 2010 winners in selected categories are as follows:

Contemporary Romance: *Sworn to Protect* by DiAnn Mills

Contemporary Series, Sequels, and Novellas: *The Reluctant Prophet* by Nancy Rue

Contemporary Standalone: *Almost Heaven* by Chris Fabry

First Novel: *Heartless* by Anne Elisabeth Stengl

Historical: *While We're Far Apart* by Lynn Austin

Historical Romance: *The Girl in the Gatehouse* by Julie Klassen

Suspense: *The Bishop* by Steven James

Visionary: *To Darkness Fled* by Jill Williamson

Young Adult: *Motorcycles, Sushi, and One Strange Book* by Nancy Rue

ECPA Christian Book Awards: Since 1978 the Evangelical Christian Publishers Association has recognized quality and encouraged excellence by presenting the ECPA Christian Book Awards (formerly known as Gold Medallion) each year. After a rigorous judging process, five finalists are selected in each of six categories. Out of 226 entries of books and Bibles, five finalists in six categories were chosen to represent Christian publishing's finest books and Bibles for 2011. Among them were four titles appearing in the past year on the New York Times bestseller list, and the winner of the 2011 Christian Book of the Year award also took first prize in the Non-fiction category: Bonhoeffer: Pastor, Martyr, Prophet, Spy by Eric Metaxas (Thomas Nelson). The 2011 winners in selected categories are as follows:

Christian Book of the Year: *Bonhoeffer: Pastor, Martyr, Prophet, Spy* by Eric Metaxas

Bibles: *HCSB Study Bible* Jeremy Royal Howard and Ed Blum, General Editors

Fiction: *Almost Heaven* by Chris Fabry

Children: *The Action Bible*, Sergio Cariello, Illustrator; Doug Mauss, General Editor

Inspiration: *You Changed My Life* by Max Lucado

Bible Reference: *Zondervan Illustrated Bible Backgrounds Commentary*, John H. Walton, General Editor

Non-fiction: *Bonhoeffer: Pastor, Martyr, Prophet, Spy* by Eric Metaxas

Christian Small Publisher Book of the Year Award: The Christian Small Publisher Book of the Year Award annually honors books released by member houses of the Christian Small Publishers Association (CSPA). Awards are presented in eight categories, including fiction. The 2011 winners in selected categories are as follows:

Biography: *I Can See the Shore: Growing Up Yanomamo Today* by Mike Dawson

Bible Study/Theology: *Real Mothers: A Bible Study About Mothers for Mothers* by Joyce Long

Fiction: *The Master's Wall* by Sandi Rog

Children's 4-8: *With My Rifle by My Side: A Second Amendment Lesson* by Kimberly Jo Simac, Desta Garrett - Managing Editor, Emily Kirk Phillips and Donna Goeddaeus

Children's 8-12: *10 Things Every Kid Should Know About God* by Tina V. Bryson and Mykle Lee

Family Relationships: *Raising Real Men: Surviving, Teaching, and Appreciating Boys* by Hal Young and Melanie Young

Christian Living: *Why God Matters: How to Recognize Him in Daily Life* by Karina Lumbert Fabian and Deacon Steven Lumbert

Young Adult: *The Awakening* by Cliff Warden

The Audies Awards: Winners of the Audio Publishers Association's annual Audies Awards for spoken word entertainment were announced in May at The TimesCenter in New York City. Awards were presented in 28 categories, including Inspirational/Faith-Based Fiction. The winner in the Inspirational/Faith-Based Fiction category is:

Fireflies in December by Jennifer Erin Valent, narrated by Kate Forbes

Mystery Awards 2011 by Clair Lamb, for Bookreporter.com

The Anthony Awards: These awards are presented annually at Bouchercon, the World Mystery Convention. They are named after Anthony Boucher, a founder of Mystery Writers of America and the first mainstream literary critic to consider mysteries as serious literature. Books are nominated and voted on by conference participants. The awards were presented at Bouchercon XLII in St. Louis on September 18, 2011. The 2011 winners in selected categories are as follows:

Best Novel: *Bury Your Dead* by Louise Penny

Best First Novel: *The Damage Done* by Hilary Davidson

Best Paperback Original: *Expiration Date* by Duane Swierczynski

Best Short Story: "Swing Shift" by Dana Cameron, from *Crimes by Moonlight: Mysteries from the Dark Side*

Best Graphic Novel: *The Chill* by Jason Starr

The Barry Awards: These awards are presented annually at Bouchercon, the World Mystery Convention, by the editors of . They are named after fan reviewer Barry Gardner. Between 2007 and 2009, the Barrys were presented jointly by the editors of *Deadly Pleasures* and *Mystery News*

(now defunct). The awards were presented at Bouchercon XLII in St. Louis on September 18, 2011. The 2011 winners in selected categories are as follows:

Best Novel: *The Lock Artist* by Steve Hamilton

Best First Novel: *The Poacher's Son* by Paul Doiron

Best British Novel: *The Woodcutter* by Reginald Hill

Best Paperback Original: *Fever at the Bone* by Val McDermid

Best Thriller: *Thirteen Hours* by Deon Meyer

Best Short Story: "The List" by Loren D. Estleman, from *Ellery Queen's Mystery Magazine*

The Macavity Awards: These awards are presented annually at Bouchercon, the World Mystery Convention, by the members of Mystery Readers International. The Macavity Award is named for the "mystery cat" of T.S. Eliot's Old Possum's Book of Practical Cats. The awards were presented at Bouchercon XLII in St. Louis on September 18, 2011. The 2011 winners in selected categories are as follows:

Best Mystery Novel: *Bury Your Dead* by Louise Penny

Best First Mystery: *Rogue Island* by Bruce DeSilva

Best Mystery Short Story: "Swing Shift" by Dana Cameron, from *Crimes by Moonlight: Mysteries from the Dark Side*

Sue Feder Memorial Historical Mystery: *City of Dragons* by Kelli Stanley

The Shamus Awards: These awards are presented annually by the Private Eye Writers of America (PWA) for excellence in writing about private eyes. The PWA defines a "private eye" as any mystery protagonist who is a professional investigator, but not a police officer or government agent. The Shamus Awards are presented at a banquet, generally held in conjunction with Bouchercon, the World Mystery Convention. The awards were presented in St. Louis on September 18, 2011. The 2011 winners in selected categories are as follows:

Best Hardcover: *No Mercy* by Lori Armstrong

Best First P.I. Novel: *In Search of Mercy* by Michael Ayoob

Best Paperback Original: *Asia Hand* by Christopher G. Moore

Best Short Story: "The Lamb Was Sure to Go" by Gar Anthony Haywood, from *Alfred Hitchcock's Mystery Magazine*

Historical Fiction
by
Holly Hibner

Historical fiction is any story based in a time that has passed. Often the stories are about significant events or people throughout history. Sometimes, though, historical fiction is simply about common folk in a particular time period, or how they react to a significant historical event. One distinction to make is that they are not meant to be novels written in the author's lifetime. A novel written in and about the 1920s, and read today, is not truly historical fiction. By my own definition, historical fiction is at least a generation removed from the author's lifetime. However, reading books that were written during the time of a historical fiction novel do make nice accompaniments to them, to compare accuracy. Historical fiction provides a relaxing, engaging way to learn about history while enjoying the drama and creativity of fiction. This essay will explore common themes in historical fiction, discuss the appeal factors of this genre, and outline some popular historical fiction novels and authors.

Common Themes in Historical Fiction

One of the common themes in historical fiction is exploration. Westward expansion in the United States (roughly the early 1800s to the early 1900s), the dust bowl (1930s), the Age of Discovery (Europe, beginning in the fifteenth century), and even the early days of space exploration (late 1950s) are examples of events that could fit into this category. The idea of searching for something, such as knowledge or land, that will improve the characters' ways of life is the prevailing idea in these novels. Some titles that fit in this category include:

Ines of My Soul by Isabel Allende, 2006 Ines Suarez, a real person in history, travels from Spain to the New World to find her husband.

The Egyptologist by Arthur Phillips, 2004 An egyptologist risks his reputation and his fiancee's fortune to find the tomb of a pharaoh.

Beyond the Divide by Kathryn Lasky, 1983 In 1849 a 14-year-old Amish girl leaves Pennsylvania with her father to join a wagon train to the west.

The Devil's Paintbox by Victoria McKernan, 2009 Two teens try to survive by leaving Kansas on the Oregon Trail after their parents die.

The search for freedom from persecution is another common theme in historical fiction. Characters try to escape from situations such as slavery, religious persecution, or political rule. Events such as civil war, the holocaust, and various revolutions and rebellions throughout history are examples of settings for historical fiction in this category. Titles with this theme include:

The Book Thief by Markus Zusak, 2006 In Germany during the holocaust, Liesel steals books and learns to read while her family hides a Jewish man in their basement.

Song of Slaves in the Desert by Alan Cheuse, 2011 A Jewish boy from New York, Nathaniel Periera is sent to his uncle's plantation, where he sees the realities of slavery and falls in love with a beautiful slave woman.

Fall of Giants by Ken Follett, 2010 Follows five inter-related families in various countries as they struggle through World War I, the Russian Revolution, and women's sufferage.

A third common theme in historical fiction is choices and responsibilities. Where a problem or difficult situation arises, will the character emerge triumphant? The situation itself, as well as the rules of the time or historical setting can make it seem impossible for the character to make a choice that will get him or her out of trouble. In modern times, we think of ourselves as having free choice, but the cultural expectations and mores of different time periods limit the choices the characters in those settings might consider. For example, in a regency romance novel, marriage or the nunnery are among the very few choices a woman is presented with. To avoid scandal and remain proper, she must conform. When faced with marrying a man she does not love, or giving up an "unsuitable" marriage prospect, what choice will she make? Will love prevail? Another example is in wartime: Will a young man go to war, even if it means fighting against his neighbors, his family, and his friends?

Will he be brave enough to go to war at all, stubborn enough to stand up against his enemies and for his beliefs? He has to choose, and in historical times, young men went to war, stood up for their family, and abandoned their dreams. Examples of books in this category include:

That Perfect Someone by Johanna Lindsey, 2010 Richard Allen dodges a marriage set up by his father by escaping to the high seas. Upon a brief return, he finds himself back on an ocean voyage with the fiancee to escape his angry father.

Gifts of War by Mackenzie Ford, 2009 A soldier returns home to England after being wounded in World War I and falls in love with his friend's girlfriend.

White Doves at Morning by James Lee Burke, 2004 Two young men join the confederate army, despite their lack of conviction in what the confederates stand for.

Appeal Factors

As one can see from the examples given above, historical fiction covers the spectrum of sub-genres. There are historical mysteries, historical romances, and even alternate histories that fall under science fiction and fantasy. Each sub-genre has its own appeal factors.

Let's start with regency romances, which are very popular among romance readers. The appeal factors there include an exotic setting, complete with castles and foreign lands. The women wear huge gowns and fancy dresses, so the fashion of the time holds appeal, too. They attend balls and ride in horse-drawn carriages. These details are all accurate to the time period and the place, but seem exotic and interesting to contemporary readers.

Historical mysteries fall into yet more categories, such as cozy mysteries that are gentle and usually less violent, hard boiled mysteries that involve police or detectives as they solve a crime, and amateur sleuth mysteries where an unsuspecting layperson gets involved. These are just a few examples. Any of these types of mysteries can also be historical. An example of a a cozy historical mystery is the Amelia Peabody series by Elizabeth Peters. Spinster Amelia Peabody's visit to Egypt resulted in an archaeology puzzle, and she's been solving them ever since: The first title in the series is *Crocodile on the Sandbank*. Historical fiction is any story based in a time that has passed. Often the stories are about significant events or people throughout history. Sometimes, though, historical fiction is simply about common folk in a particular time period, or how they react to a significant historical event. One distinction to make is that they are not meant to be novels written in the author's lifetime. A novel written in and about the 1920s, and read today, is not truly historical fiction. By my own definition, historical fiction is at least a generation removed from the author's lifetime. However, reading books that were written during the time of a historical fiction novel do make nice accompaniments to them, to compare accuracy. Historical fiction provides a relaxing, engaging way to learn about history while enjoying the drama and creativity of fiction. This essay will explore common themes in historical fiction, discuss the appeal factors of this genre, and outline some popular historical fiction novels and authors.

An important historical event is, at its face, noteworthy and interesting. The outline of the story is already in place. The author uses that drama and personalizes it as one person's experience of the event. The appeal is in the human factor. It's one thing to read about historical figures, but they are even more interesting when they interact with their environment: their families, their friends, and their home towns. When put into a fictional story based on a real story, we get more details about their daily lives. When the story is about a "commoner's" reaction to a historical event, we can relate to that character's situation. We can almost see ourselves in the same situation, and are fascinated with the decisions the character makes. In *Mount Vernon Love Story*, by Mary Higgins Clark (2002), for instance, George Washington's life after his presidency is described in detail, as well as his relationship with his wife, Martha. And in *My Name is Mary Sutter* by Robin Oliveira (2010), historical figures such as Dorothea Dix and Abraham Lincoln come to life as they interact with civil war nurse, Mary Sutter.

Another appeal factor in historical fiction is the charm of "olden days." The lack of modern conveniences, and how the characters cope with situations in their primitive environment is interesting. We learn how things were done in times gone by, and the tools and procedures that were used to get by. Something as simple as preparing food or driving to church becomes remarkable. This is especially true in prehistoric fiction such as Jean Auel's Earth's Children series, where the characters are so ancient and primal, and where they don't yet have any sort of technology to get by in daily life.

The level of realism in these details is itself an appeal factor. Readers may appreciate true, gritty details of the implements of war or of ancient religious rituals, or, as Sarah Johnson points out in her book *Historical Fiction: A Guide to the Genre*, they may "prefer a more romanticized version of history, one that emphasizes the glory and heroism of past eras" (2005, p.7).

The way historical fiction shows us values and attitudes that are different from our own allows us to escape into what feels like a different world. We connect with the characters, enlightening our own idea of what is right and wrong and how we came to those conclusions. As Susan Vreeland said, "Each time we enter imaginatively into the life of another, it's a small step upwards in the elevation of the human race. When there is no imagination of others' lives, there is no human connection. Where there is no human connection, there is no compassion. Without compassion, community, commitment, lovingkindness, human understanding, peace-- all shrivel. Individuals become isolated, the isolated turn cruel, and the tragic hovers. Historical fiction is an antidote to that." (retrieved from http://www.svreeland. com/historical-fiction.html)

This brings us to one more appeal factor in historical fiction, specific to international historical fiction: cultures. It is interesting to read about the history and people in different countries. World history put to fiction makes for exotic, diverse reading. Consider Lisa See's Shanghai Girls, which is set in late 1930s Shanghai. The story talks about rickshaw pullers, the foods they bought from street vendors, and the older generation of women with bound feet. The Japanese invasion of Shanghai feels personal, as places are bombed that we have come to picture in our minds and characters are killed that we have come to know. When we come to understand other people, in different places and times, we become more compassionate and peaceful with more worldly, community-oriented values.

Historical Fiction Authors to Know About

Reader's advisory for this genre is easier to do when you are familiar with the popular authors in the category. Because historical fiction includes various genres and covers practically all known history, there are "best of" authors in each of those categories. When performing reader's advisory in historical fiction, one can start with what time period the reader is interested in. That can narrow down which authors to look for, as many historical fiction authors tend to write largely of one time period (Johanna Lindsey, for example, writes romances in the regency era. Jean Auel writes of prehistoric times. Michael Dobbs writes about Winston Churchill and World War II.)

Another strategy for historical fiction reader's advisory is to look for books by type of character. If the reader interested in the idea of a famous person as the main character, suggest books like Chang and Eng by Darin Strauss (2000), about the famous conjoined twins of early 1800s China. Another interesting choice is Rasputin's Daughter by Robert Alexander (2006), which is about how Rasputin's daughter Maria tries to save his reputation even as he tries to save the Tsarevich Alexei from death by hemophilia. His methods are unusual, and people have begun to think he is crazy, and that the Russian government lacks judgement for believing in him. For a reader more interested in a book about how an average citizen gets by in a historical time, suggest something like The Endless Forest by Sarah Donati, which is about a family's challenges during an 1824 flood in a New York village. Another choice is Walking to Gatlinberg by Howard Frank Mosher (2010), which chronicles the journey of a teenager who tries to find his brother, who has been missing since the battle at Gettysburg.

Each of these examples is also different in terms of tone, pace, themes, and character types—all factors that can be used to match readers to books they may enjoy.

Recommendations

Here are a few first-time, upcoming authors to watch for in historical fiction:

Nancy Horan, *Loving Frank*, 2007 A fictional representation of the relationship between Frank Lloyd Wright and Mamah Cheney. A bestseller, popular with book clubs

Paula McLain, *The Paris Wife*, 2011 Ernest Hemingway's first wife navigates 1920s Paris. Widely, favorably reviewed.

Wayson Choy, *The Jade Peony*, 2011 A Chinese family in Canada remembers their childhood in Vancouver in the 1930s and 1940s. Selected for the 2010 Canada Reads, a program of the CBC.

Claudia Long, *Josefina's Sin*, 2011 Josefina is a 17th century Mexican landowner's wife who becomes pregnant after an affair with a Bishop, and then studies under an educated nun. Widely, favorably reviewed.

Jenna Blum, *Those Who Save Us*, 2011 A love story between a Jewish doctor and a non-Jewish woman during the holocaust. Widely, favorably reviewed.

Conclusion

It was said best on the web site HistoricalNovels.info: "The worlds to which historical fiction carries us may seem utterly different from our own - but they really existed. A deep understanding of the past can help us understand our own time and our own motivations better. And by blending history and fiction, a novel lets us do more than simply read history: it lets us participate in the hopes, fears, passions, mistakes and triumphs of the people who lived it." Historical fiction is hugely popular. The best part is that authors of this genre will never run out of material, as history is created every day!

Popular Fiction

1

DIANA ABU-JABER

Birds of Paradise

(New York: W.W. Norton & Company, 2011)

Story type: Family Saga
Subject(s): Family; Missing persons; Interpersonal relations
Major character(s): Felice Muir, 18-Year-Old, Daughter (of Brian and Avis), Sister (of Stanley); Stanley Muir, Store Owner, Brother (of Felice), Son (of Brian and Avis); Avis Muir, Spouse (of Brian), Mother (of Stanley and Felice), Cook (pastry chef); Brian Muir, Father (of Stanley and Felice), Spouse (of Avis), Lawyer
Locale(s): Miami, Florida

Summary: *Birds of Paradise* is a novel by author Diana Abu-Jaber. Five years ago, at the age of 13, Avis and Brian Muir's daughter Felice vanished without a trace. Now it is Felice's 18th birthday and Avis and Brian, along with their son Stanley, still wonder if she is okay or even if she is still alive. Meanwhile, Felice is living an alternative lifestyle of raves, tattoos, and piercings. Yet she continues to protect the reason that she ran away in the first place. As each family member copes with his or her own emotions about Felice's disappearance, the Muirs struggle to keep their family intact. Abu-Jaber is also the author of *The Language of Baklava*, *Origin*, and *Crescent*.

Where it's reviewed:
Booklist, August 1, 2011, page 18
Marie Claire, September 2010, page 212
Publishers Weekly, June 4, 2011, page 45

Other books by the same author:
Origin, 2007
The Language of Baklava, 2005
Crescent, 2003

Other books you might like:
Sarah Braunstein, *The Sweet Relief of Missing Children*, 2011
Chang-Rae Lee, *The Surrendered*, 2010
Jacquelyn Mitchard, *The Deep End of the Ocean*, 1996
Kyung-Sook Shin, *Please Look After Mom*, 2011
William Trevor, *The Story of Lucy Gault*, 2002

2

THELMA ADAMS

Playdate

(New York: Thomas Dunne Books, 2011)

Story type: Contemporary
Subject(s): Marriage; Infidelity; Interpersonal relations
Major character(s): Lance, Spouse (of Darlene); Darlene, Spouse (of Lance); Alec, Spouse (of Wren); Wren, Spouse (of Alec)
Time period(s): 21st century; 2010s
Locale(s): Encinitas, California

Summary: Thelma Adams's *Playdate* is set in a picture-perfect California community, where the manicured lawns and immaculate tract housing hide a seamier side of life. Beneath the well-groomed facade, two couples go about their daily business—unaware they are walking an emotional tightrope. Lance is a stay-at-home dad who is married to Darlene, an unapologetic workhorse who doesn't have the time for her husband or child. Alec is a businessman working with Darlene on her latest venture, while his wife, Wren, teaches Lance a few yoga moves. Soon the relationships of these couples come crashing together, and nothing will remain in the same in this quiet California suburb.

Where it's reviewed:
Booklist, December 15, 2010, page 20
Publishers Weekly, October 18, 2010, page 24

Other books you might like:
Emily Giffin, *Heart of the Matter*, 2010
Herve Le Tellier, *Enough About Love*, 2011
Caroline Leavitt, *Pictures of You*, 2011
Leah Stewart, *Husband and Wife: A Novel*, 2010
Emily Woof, *The Whole Wide Beauty: A Novel*, 2010

3

SARAH ADDISON ALLEN

The Peach Keeper

(New York: Bantam, 2011)

Story type: Contemporary
Subject(s): Family history; Murder; Mysticism

Major character(s): Willa Jackson, Young Woman; Paxton Osgood, Friend (of Willa)
Time period(s): 21st century; 2010s
Locale(s): Walls of Water, North Carolina

Summary: Sarah Addison Allen's *The Peach Keeper* follows Willa Jackson, a young woman who has struggled for years with the dubious legacy of her once-grand Southern family. When old friend Paxton Osgood purchases and restores the Jackson's crumbling manor home, a body is discovered on the property. This mysterious find impels Willa and Paxton to embark on an investigation into the story behind the body—and what they learn unearths long-buried family secrets and the mystical connections binding a small Southern town.

Where it's reviewed:
Booklist, March 1, 2011, page 27
Library Journal, October 15, 2010, page S5
Publishers Weekly, March 7, 2011, page 46

Other books by the same author:
The Girl Who Chased the Moon, 2009
The Sugar Queen, 2008
Garden Spells, 2007

Other books you might like:
Brunonia Barry, *The Lace Reader: A Novel*, 2008
Laura Esquivel, *Swift as Desire*, 2001
Kristin Hannah, *Winter Garden*, 2010
Alice Hoffman, *The Red Garden*, 2011
Rebecca Wells, *The Crowning Glory of Calla Lily Ponder*, 2009

4

CHRIS ADRIAN

The Great Night

(New York: Farrar, Straus and Giroux, 2011)

Story type: Contemporary
Subject(s): Fantasy; Shakespeare, William; Adventure
Major character(s): Titania, Royalty (queen of the fairies), Spouse (of Oberon); Oberon, Royalty (king of the fairies)
Time period(s): 21st century; 2010s
Locale(s): San Francisco, California

Summary: Chris Adrian's *The Great Night* is set in Buena Vista Park in the heart of San Francisco, where lives a very surprising family. King Oberon, Queen Titania, and the entire royal court of Shakespeare's *A Midsummer Night's Dream* calls the park home, and a trio of strangers—drawn together by their respective heartbreaks—are pulled into the world of Shakespeare's sprightly players. But the world of Titania and Oberon has changed drastically since *Midsummer Night*, and the threesome must contend with Titania's wrath—which could spell the end of the world as they know it.

Where it's reviewed:
Booklist, April 15, 2011, page 28
Esquire, May 2011, page 46
New York Times Book Review, May 8, 2011, page 13(L)
Publishers Weekly, March 7, 2011, page 40

Other books by the same author:
A Better Angel, 2008
The Children's Hospital, 2006
Gob's Grief, 2000

Other books you might like:
Anne Fortier, *Juliet*, 2010
Myrlin A. Hermes, *The Lunatic, the Lover, and the Poet*, 2010
John Marsden, *Hamlet: A Novel*, 2009
Arthur Phillips, *The Tragedy of Arthur*, 2011
Tania Roxborogh, *Banquo's Son*, 2009

5

CECELIA AHERN

The Book of Tomorrow

(London: HarperCollins, 2011)

Subject(s): Love; Death; Magic
Major character(s): Tamara Goodwin, Young Woman
Time period(s): 21st century; 2000s
Locale(s): Dublin, Ireland; Kilkenny, Ireland

Summary: In Cecelia Ahern's *The Book of Tomorrow*, readers meet Tamara Goodwin, a young woman who lives in the moment. She was born into a wealthy family and had everything she's ever wanted handed to her. From her own private beach, designer clothes, the perfect bedroom with her own bathroom, she's never had to do without anything. All that changes when her father dies leaving her mother with nothing but grief. They are forced to sell their home and move in with Tamara's aunt and uncle. Tamara soon finds herself in a world of loneliness. One day she discovers a book at a fair and is intrigued by it. The book is covered in leather and padlocked shut. With a lot of trouble, she manages to pry the book open. What she discovers inside changes her life forever.

Where it's reviewed:
Kirkus Reviews, November 15, 2010, page 1119
Library Journal, November 1, 2010, page 53
Publishers Weekly, November 22, 2010, page 41
School Library Journal, December 1, 2010, page 22

Other books by the same author:
The Gift, 2009
Thanks for the Memories, 2009
There's No Place Like Here, 2008
If You Could See Me Now, 2006
P.S. I Love You, 2004

Other books you might like:
Maeve Binchy, *Minding Frankie*, 2011
Mary Janice Davidson, *Me, Myself, and Why?*, 2010
Marian Keyes, *The Brightest Star in the Sky*, 2009
Sophie Kinsella, *Twenties Girl*, 2009
Audrey Niffenegger, *The Time Traveler's Wife*, 2003

6

ELLEN AIRGOOD

South of Superior

(New York: Riverhead Books, 2011)

Story type: Contemporary
Subject(s): Friendship; Family; Community relations
Major character(s): Madeline Stone, Caregiver; Gladys, Aged Person, Friend (of Madeline); Arbutus, Aged Person, Friend (of Madeline)
Time period(s): 21st century; 2010s
Locale(s): Upper Peninsula, Michigan

Summary: *South of Superior* is the debut novel of author Ellen Airgood. When Madeline Stone left Michigan's Upper Peninsula many years ago, she never thought she'd be back. After being shunned by her grandfather and left behind by her mother, she made Chicago her new home. Yet when an aging friend of her grandfather's needs a caretaker she returns to her old hometown to help out, hoping to clear the air once and for all with her estranged grandparent. Once she's back, she begins to learn the importance of kinship and camaraderie in a town where everyone knows one another, and everyone sticks together. Soon Madeline realizes that it doesn't matter where she's been, because this may be exactly where she belongs. First novel.

Where it's reviewed:
Booklist, April 15, 2011, page 25
Kirkus Reviews, June 1, 2011, page 897
Publishers Weekly, April 4, 2011, page 33

Other books you might like:
Steve Amick, *The Lake, the River and the Other Lake*, 2005
Barbara Taylor Bradford, *Three Weeks in Paris*, 2002
Pearl Cleage, *What Looks Like Crazy on an Ordinary Day*, 1997
Monica McInerney, *The Alphabet Sisters*, 2005
Kristina Riggle, *The Life You've Imagined*, 2010

7

SUSAN WITTIG ALBERT

Mourning Gloria

(New York: Berkley Prime Crime, 2011)

Series: China Bayles Series. Book 19
Story type: Amateur Detective; Series
Subject(s): Detective fiction; Murder; Arson
Major character(s): China Bayles, Herbalist, Detective— Amateur, Friend (of Ruby), Aunt (of Caitlin); Ruby Wilcox, Friend (of China); Caitlin, 11-Year-Old, Niece (of China); Sheila Dawson, Police Officer (chief); Blackie Blackwell, Lawman (sheriff); Jessica Nelson, Journalist (newspaper intern)
Time period(s): 21st century; 2010s
Locale(s): Pecan Springs, Texas

Summary: In *Mourning Gloria*, Susan Wittig Albert's 19th China Bayles mystery, herbalist-amateur detective China investigates another case of murder in the town of Pecan Springs, Texas. When China comes upon a burning mobile home, a woman is still inside crying out for help. China is unable to save the trapped woman and realizes that she has just witnessed a murder. As China investigates the disturbing case, she consults professionally with local law-enforcement officers Sheila Dawson and Blackie Blackwell, and relies on her friend Ruby and niece Caitlin for assistance. The case takes an unexpected turn when Jessica Nelson, a newspaper intern covering the story, goes missing. *Mourning Gloria* is interspersed with herbal tips and recipes including "China's Cosmetic Vinegar" and "Ruby's Calming Fragrance Blend."

Where it's reviewed:
Booklist, April 1, 2011, page 33
Publishers Weekly, Feb 28, 2011, page 38

Other books by the same author:
The Darling Dahlias and the Naked Ladies, 2011
Holly Blues, 2010
Wormwood, 2009
Nightshade, 2008
Spanish Dagger, 2007

Other books you might like:
Diane Mott Davidson, *Crunch Time*, 2011
Earlene Fowler, *Spider Web*, 2011
Sarah Graves, *Knockdown*, 2011
Carolyn Haines, *Bones of a Feather*, 2011
Elaine Viets, *Pumped for Murder: A Dead-End Job Mystery*, 2011

8

MONICA ALI

Untold Story

(New York: Scribner, 2011)

Story type: Contemporary
Subject(s): Identity; Royalty; Interpersonal relations
Major character(s): Diana/Lydia, Royalty (Princess of Wales)
Time period(s): 21st century; 2000s
Locale(s): United States

Summary: In *Untold Story: A Novel*, acclaimed author Monica Ali imagines what Princess Diana's life might have been like had she survived the fatal car crash. In this sensitive rendering, Diana flees public life and builds a quiet life for herself in a small town in the Midwestern United States. She goes by the name Lydia and spends her days going swimming and doing charity work. She yearns to see the children she abandoned when the world thought she had died. Then one day, Lydia is spotted by a member of the paparazzi, and she wonders if the new life she has built for herself will come crashing down around her.

Where it's reviewed:
Booklist, May 15, 2011, page 19
Maclean's, April 25, 2011, page 82
New York Times Book Review, June 26, 2011, page 1(L)
Publishers Weekly, May 2, 2011, page 37
Specator, April 16, 2011, page 35

Other books by the same author:
In the Kitchen, 2009
Alentejo Blue, 2006
Brick Lane, 2003

Other books you might like:
Daisy Goodwin, *The American Heiress*, 2011
Ann Napolitano, *A Good Hard Look*, 2011
Susan Sellers, *Vanessa and Virginia*, 2009
Curtis Sittenfeld, *American Wife*, 2008
James Tipton, *Annette Vallon: A Novel of the French Revolution*, 2007

9

KEVIN J. ANDERSON

The Key to Creation

(New York: Orbit, 2011)

Series: Terra Incognita Series. Book 3
Subject(s): Sea stories; Sailing; Ships
Major character(s): Saan, Sailor, Stepson (of Omra); Omra, Leader (of Uraba); Queen Anjine, Royalty; Criston Vora, Sailor

Summary: *The Key to Creation* is the third book in author Kevin J. Anderson's Terra Incognita trilogy. In this final book, the great sailor Criston Vora, along with Saan, the stepson of Omra of Uraba, finally seeks out the lost land of Terravitae. Both have been sent there as saviors for their own land. Saan looks for the legendary Key to Creation, an artifact that may be used to defend Uraba against opposing forces. Criston has other plans however, seeking revenge against a monster that nearly cost him everything. Meanwhile, Queen Anjine and Omra of Uraba continue warring in their homeland. Yet secretly, the Saedran race works to finish the Map of All Things, which will bring back God and hopefully end the war.

Where it's reviewed:
Library Journal, April 15, 2011, page 86
Publishers Weekly, May 9, 2011, page 38

Other books by the same author:
The Map of All Things, 2010
Moobase Crisis, 2010
The Edge of the World, 2009
The Ashes of Worlds, 2008
Metal Swarm, 2007

Other books you might like:
Kathryn Lasky, *Watch Wolf*, 2011
George R.R. Martin, *Dance With Dragons: A Song of Ice and Fire*, 2011
Andre Norton, *Elvenborn*, 2002
Michael A. Stackpole, *The New World*, 2007
Tad Williams, *Shadowheart*, 2010

10

MARY KAY ANDREWS

Summer Rental

(New York: St. Martin's Press, 2011)

Story type: Contemporary
Subject(s): Friendship; Summer; Beaches
Major character(s): Ellis, Friend (of Julia and Dorie); Julia, Friend (of Ellis and Dorie); Dorie, Friend (of Ellis and Julia); Ty Bazemore, Landlord; Maryn Shackleford, Runaway
Time period(s): 21st century; 2010s
Locale(s): Outer Banks, North Carolina

Summary: *Summer Rental* is a best-selling novel by author Mary Kay Andrews. Best friends Ellis, Julia, and Dorie are ready for a necessary summer vacation. Ellis has recently lost her job, Dorie has recently lost the man she loves, and Julia has lost all of her confidence. A month-long stay along the beaches of the Outer Banks in North Carolina could be just the recipe to get these women back on track. Yet once at their summer rental, each woman begins to learn something new about not only her friends but herself. Meanwhile, Ellis fights her growing attraction to their landlord, Ty, as the women take in a mysterious woman named Maryn. Andrews is also the author of *Hissy Fit*, *Blue Christmas*, and *Savannah Breeze*.

Where it's reviewed:
Booklist, May 15, 2011, page 18
Library Journal, May 1, 2011, page 78
Publishers Weekly, April 18, 2011, page 30

Other books by the same author:
The Fixer Upper, 2009
Deep Dish, 2008
Blue Christmas, 2006
Savannah Breeze, 2006
Hissy Fit, 2004

Other books you might like:
Jennifer Crusie, *Maybe This Time*, 2010
Emily Giffin, *Heart of the Matter*, 2010
Jane Heller, *An Ex to Grind*, 2005
Sophie Kinsella, *Remember Me?*, 2008
Jennifer Weiner, *Fly Away Home*, 2011

11

KATE ATKINSON

Started Early, Took My Dog

(New York: Little, Brown, and Company, 2011)

Series: Jackson Brodie Series. Book 4
Story type: Mystery
Subject(s): Missing persons; Detective fiction; Actors
Major character(s): Jackson Brodie, Detective—Private; Tracy Waterhouse, Detective—Police (retired); Tilly Squires, Actress
Time period(s): 21st century; 2010s
Locale(s): Leeds, United Kingdom

Summary: Detective Jackson Brodie has come back to his hometown to investigate the case of a young woman looking for her biological parents. As he hits dead end after dead end, retired police detective Tracy Waterhouse suddenly finds herself embroiled in the case of a young child placed in her care. Figuring into these disparate cases is Tilly Squires, an aging actress who is descending into dementia. Kate Atkinson's *Started Early, Took My Dog* is the fourth installment in a series starring PI Jackson Brodie.

Where it's reviewed:
Booklist, January 1, 2011, page 52
Library Journal, January 2011, page 76
New York Times, March 17, 2011, page C1(L).
Publishers Weekly, January 17, 2011, page 26
Spectator, August 21, 2010, page 30

Other books by the same author:
When Will There Be Good News?: A Novel, 2008
One Good Turn, 2006
Not the End of the World, 2003
Emotionally Weird, 2000
Human Croquet, 1997
Case Histories, 1996
Behind the Scenes at the Museum, 1995

Other books you might like:
Alafair Burke, *Long Gone*, 2011
Gillian Flynn, *Sharp Objects*, 2006
Tana French, *In the Woods*, 2007
Jennifer Haigh, *Faith*, 2011
Laura Lippman, *What the Dead Know*, 2007
Rosamund Lupton, *Sister*, 2011
Ann Patchett, *State of Wonder*, 2011
S.J. Watson, *Before I Go To Sleep*, 2011

12

JEAN M. AUEL

The Land of Painted Caves
(New York: Random House, 2011)

Series: Earth's Children Series. Book 6
Subject(s): Prehistoric peoples; Epics; Women
Major character(s): Ayla, Prehistoric Human; Jondalar, Prehistoric Human, Lover (of Ayla); Jonayla, Baby, Daughter (of Ayla and Jondalar); Balderan, Hunter; Marona, Prehistoric Human
Locale(s): Zelandoni, France

Summary: In *The Land of Painted Caves*, author Jean Auel concludes the saga of Cro-Magnon woman Ayla and her experiences in prehistoric France. Ayla and her mate, Jondalar, have produced a daughter and have joined a clan of healers. As Ayla trains to be a shaman, she makes several discoveries that broaden her way of thinking. In painted caves she learns the beauty of art. After consuming a mind-altering plant, she formulates the notion of committed love. Dangers abound in their Ice Age world, and Ayla and Jondalar must deal with fierce beasts and natural disasters to ensure the survival of their young family. *The Land of Painted Caves* is the sixth book in the Earth's Children series.

Where it's reviewed:
Booklist, February 15, 2011, page 57
Kirkus Reviews, February 15, 2011, page 258
Library Journal, February 1, 2011, page 50
Publishers Weekly, January 24, 2011, page 24

Other books by the same author:
Shelters of Stone, 2002
Plains of Passage, 1990
Mammoth Hunters, 1985
Valley of Horses, 1982
Clan of the Cave Bear, 1980

Other books you might like:
Piers Anthony, *Climate of Change*, 2011
Stephen Baxter, *Stone Spring*, 2010
Bill Fawcett, Editor, *Exiled: Clan of the Claw*, 2011
Dorothy Hearst, *Secrets of the Wolves*, 2011
Kathleen O'Neal Gear, *The Dawn Country*, 2011

13

DAVID BALDACCI

One Summer
(New York: Grand Central Publishing, 2011)

Story type: Contemporary
Subject(s): Family; Grief; Interpersonal relations
Major character(s): Jack Armstrong, Widow(er), Father; Bonnie, Mother (mother-in-law of Jack); Lizzie, Spouse (of Jack), Mother
Time period(s): 21st century; 2010s
Locale(s): Ohio, United States; South Carolina, United States

Summary: In David Baldacci's *One Summer*, Jack Armstrong is a devoted family man who has learned he is dying. After his wife is killed in a car accident, Jack's mother-in-law shuttles Jack's three kids off to various relatives and relegates Jack to a hospice center. But when his health takes a turn for the better, Jack reclaims his children and relocates to his late wife's hometown. As they attempt to resettle into life as a family, his mother-in-law once again interferes, suing Jack for custody of the kids.

Where it's reviewed:
Booklist, March 1, 2011, page 27
Publishers Weekly, February 28, 2011, page 31

Other books by the same author:
No Rest for the Dead, 2011
The Sixth Man, 2011
Zero Day, 2011
Deliver Us from Evil, 2010
First Family, 2009

Other books you might like:
Ellyn Bache, *The Art of Saying Goodbye*, 2011
Erica Bauermeister, *Joy for Beginners*, 2011
Kevin Canty, *Everything: A Novel*, 2010
Scott Heim, *We Disappear: A Novel*, 2008
Mary Alice Monroe, *Sweetgrass*, 2005

14

J.G. BALLARD

Millennium People

(New York: W.W. Norton & Company, 2011)

Subject(s): Terrorism; Cults; Social class
Major character(s): David Markham, Psychologist; Richard Gould, Cult Member
Locale(s): London, England

Summary: *Millennium People* is a novel by author J.G. Ballard. After terrorists set off a bomb at Heathrow Airport in London, psychologist David Markham is shocked to learn that the culprits are not linked with Al Qaeda, but are members of a London-based movement. The group's purpose is to incite protest amongst the English middle class, and Markham decides that he will go undercover to pose as one of their own. Yet the more Markham gets to know members of the group, particularly its leader Richard Gould, the more he is drawn in to their goals and purpose. London has become a powder keg as its citizens become enraged with the trappings of the middle class. That powder keg is about to ignite.

Where it's reviewed:
Library Journal, June 15, 2011, page 72.
Publishers Weekly, June 15, 2011, page 72

Other books by the same author:
Super Cannes, 2000
Cocaine Nights, 1998
Rushing to Paradise, 1995
Kindness of Women, 1991
Running Wild, 1989

Other books you might like:
Bret Easton Ellis, *Imperial Bedrooms*, 2010
Adam Levin, *The Instructions*, 2010
Chuck Palahniuk, *Damned*, 2011
Ransom Riggs, *Miss Peregrine's Home for Peculiar Children*, 2011
Daniel H. Wilson, *Robopocalypse*, 2010

15

NEVADA BARR

Burn

(New York: Minotaur Books, 2011)

Series: Anna Pigeon Series. Book 16
Subject(s): Suspense; Voodooism; Crime
Major character(s): Anna Pigeon, Ranger, Detective—Amateur; Geneva, Friend (of Anna), Singer; Jordan, Young Man (tenant of Geneva)
Time period(s): 21st century; 2010s
Locale(s): New Orleans, Louisiana

Summary: In *Burn,* the 16th novel in the Anna Pigeon Mysteries series, Anna heads to New Orleans to alleviate the stresses of the last several weeks. There she meets an old friend, Geneva, and soon meets Jordan, an unsettling young man who rents a room from Geneva. Shortly thereafter, Anna comes upon a voodoo doll made in her likeness. Now she must figure out if someone wants her dead, and if so, who? Is it the bizarre Jordan? Or perhaps another of the questionable characters walking around Geneva's neighborhood? Anna is determined to find out.

Where it's reviewed:
Booklist, July 15, 2010, page 639
Bookmarks, Nov/Dec 2010, page 42
Kirkus Reviews, July 15, 2010, page 639
Publishers Weekly, June 1, 2010, page 29

Other books by the same author:
13 1/2, 2009
Borderline, 2009
Winter Study, 2008
Hard Truth, 2005

Other books you might like:
Tess Gerritsen, *Ice Cold*, 2010
Barbara Hambly, *Graveyard Dust*, 1999
Tony Hillerman, *The Shape Shifter*, 2006
Lisa Jackson, *Malice*, 2009
Barbara Kingsolver, *Prodigal Summer*, 2000

16

ELIZABETH BASS

Miss You Most of All

(New York: Kensington Publishing Company, 2011)

Story type: Contemporary
Subject(s): Ranch life; Sisters; Stepfamilies
Major character(s): Rue Anderson, Rancher, Sister (of Laura), Stepsister (of Heidi); Laura Anderson, Sister (of Rue), Stepsister (of Heidi); Heidi Bogue, Stepsister (of Laura and Rue)
Time period(s): 21st century; 2010s
Locale(s): Texas, United States

Summary: *Miss You Most of All* is the debut novel written by author Elizabeth Bass. In it, the author tells the story of two sisters who run a ranch home for vacationers in Texas. As Rue and Laura Anderson work to make Sassy Spinster Farm a success, Rue also works to bring up her daughter by herself. Then Rue and Laura get a surprise when a person from their past shows up. Heidi, their one-time stepsister who lived with them for several years until Heidi's mother left their father suddenly one night, has shown up needing help. Rue still considers Heidi family and, despite Laura's protestations, welcomes Heidi at Sassy Spinster Farm. Yet Heidi has a secret reason for being there, and needs Laura and Rue's sisterhood more than ever.

Where it's reviewed:
Publishers Weekly, March 1, 2010, page 36

Other books by the same author:
Wherever Grace Is Needed, 2011

Other books you might like:
Poppy Adams, *The Sister*, 2008
Christine Feehan, *Magic in the Wind*, 2005
Sarah Jio, *The Violets of March*, 2011
Rosamund Lupton, *Sister*, 2011
Rebecca Rasmussen, *The Bird Sisters*, 2011

17

ERICA BAUERMEISTER

Joy for Beginners
(New York: Putnam, 2011)

Story type: Contemporary
Subject(s): Women; Cancer; Friendship
Major character(s): Kate, Cancer Patient (survivor); Caroline, Friend (of Kate); Daria, Friend (of Kate); Marion, Sister (of Daria), Friend (of Kate); Sara, Friend (of Kate); Hadley, Friend (of Kate); Ava, Friend (of Kate)
Time period(s): 21st century; 2010s
Locale(s): Seattle, Washington

Summary: *Joy for Beginners* by author Erica Bauermeister is the story of a group of women who decide to conquer their fears and meet life head on. When Kate announces that her cancer has gone into remission, the group of friends meets for a celebratory supper. It is then that Kate also announces her plans to take a whitewater rafting trip with her daughter down the Colorado River. In response to Kate's announcement, each woman vows to embark on a journey of her own in order to accomplish something she's never done. After Kate chooses an adventure for each woman, they all launch their own quests for self-discovery. Bauermeister is also the author of *The School of Essential Ingredients*.

Where it's reviewed:
Booklist, May 15, 2011, page 16
Publishers Weekly, April 18, 2011, page 31

Other books by the same author:
The School of Essential Ingredients, 2009

Other books you might like:
Ellyn Bache, *The Art of Saying Goodbye*, 2011
David Baldacci, *One Summer*, 2011
Eleanor Brown, *The Weird Sisters*, 2011
Barbara Delinsky, *While My Sister Sleeps*, 2009
Janet Tronstad, *The Sisterhood of the Dropped Stitches*, 2007

18

AIMEE BENDER

Particular Sadness of Lemon Cake
(New York: Doubleday, 2011)

Subject(s): Magic; Family; Self awareness
Major character(s): Rose Edelstein, 9-Year-Old
Time period(s): 21st century; 2010s
Locale(s): United States

Summary: Aimee Bender's *The Particular Sadness of Lemon Cake* tells the enchanted tale of nine-year-old Rose Edelstein, who learns she possesses a very special ability. When she takes a bite of her mother's homemade cake, she finds that she not only tastes the sweet perfection of the dessert but also the emotions of the person who baked it. She is shocked to find the cake is filled with her mother's discontentment and unhappiness. This unusual sensory ability leads Rose on a journey of discovery—discovery about her family, herself, and the secretive, suffering nature of humanity.

Where it's reviewed:
Booklist, May 1, 2010, page 72
O, The Oprah Magazine, July 2010, page 111
Publishers Weekly, April 12, 2010, page 29
USA Today, July 1, 2010, page 4D
Vanity Fair, June 2010, page 78

Other books by the same author:
Willful Creatures, 2005
An Invisible Sign of My Own, 2000
The Girl in the Flammable Skirt, 1998

Other books you might like:
Sarah Addison Allen, *The Peach Keeper*, 2011
Kirsten Bakis, *Lives of the Monster Dogs*, 1997
Judy Budnitz, *If I Told You Once*, 1999
Jonathan Safron Foer, *Extremely Loud and Incredibly Close*, 2005
Alice Hoffman, *The Red Garden*, 2011
Alice McDermott, *After This: A Novel*, 2006
Ann Packer, *Swim Back to Me*, 2010

19

ELIZABETH BERG

Once Upon a Time There Was You
(New York: Random House, 2011)

Story type: Contemporary
Subject(s): Divorce; Parent-child relations; Family life
Major character(s): John Marsh, Spouse (former, of Irene); Irene Marsh, Spouse (former, of John); Sadie Marsh, 18-Year-Old, Daughter (of John and Irene); Ron, Boyfriend (of Sadie)
Time period(s): 21st century; 2010s
Locale(s): California, United States; Minnesota, United States

Summary: In *Once upon a Time, There Was You* by Elizabeth Berg, the relationship of a divorced couple bound together by their love for their daughter is tested by tragedy. Eighteen-year-old Sadie lives with her mother, Irene, in California, but spends time with her father, John, in Minnesota. Irene and John, now in their 50s, have ventured back into the dating world; Sadie has found love with a young man named Ron. When Sadie is abducted, John and Irene are united by their grief and resolve to save their daughter. Once freed, Sadie abruptly marries Ron, leaving John and Irene to examine the shared history that brought them to this troubling point in their lives.

Where it's reviewed:
Booklist, April 1, 2011, page 26
Kirkus Reviews, May 15, 2011, page 807

Other books by the same author:
The Last Time I Saw You, 2010
Home Safe, 2009
The Day I Ate Whatever I Wanted: and other small acts of liberation, 2008
Dream When You're Feeling Blue, 2007

Popular Fiction

The Handmaid and the Carpenter, 2006

Other books you might like:
Barbara Delinsky, *Coast Road*, 1998
Gail Godwin, *The Odd Woman*, 1974
Sandra Kring, *Thank You for All Things*, 2008
Elizabeth Lowell, *The Wrong Hostage: A Novel*, 2006
Karen White, *Color of Light*, 2005

20

MAEVE BINCHY

Minding Frankie

(New York: Alfred A. Knopf, 2011)

Story type: Family Saga
Subject(s): Family; Love; Alcoholism
Major character(s): Noel, Father (of Frankie), Alcoholic, Friend (of Lisa), Cousin (of Emily); Frankie, Baby, Daughter (of Noel); Lisa, Friend (of Noel); Emily, Cousin (of Noel)
Time period(s): 21st century; 2010s
Locale(s): Dublin, Ireland

Summary: A man struggling with alcoholism learns that he's a father in *Minding Frankie*. Although Noel has always had trouble taking care of himself, he vows to change his ways when he learns that a former girlfriend is pregnant with his child and suffering from a deadly illness. However, raising Frankie soon proves to be more difficult than he could ever imagine. That's when Noel's friend, Lisa, and his cousin, Emily, step in to give him a hand. But trouble brews when a social worker hears about the situation and decides that little Frankie would be better off living with a real family. Noel won't give up his daughter without a fight. Now, the makeshift family must prove that they're fit to care for Frankie.

Where it's reviewed:
Booklist, December 15, 2010, page 20
Bookmarks, Mar/Apr 2011, page 5
Library Journal, January 2011, page 80
Publishers Weekly, November 29, 2010, page 27

Other books by the same author:
Heart and Soul, 2009
Whitethorn Woods, 2007
Nights of Rain and Stars, 2004
Quentins, 2002
Scarlet Feather, 2001

Other books you might like:
Elizabeth Berg, *Home Safe*, 2009
Dorothea Benton Frank, *Full of Grace: A Novel*, 2006
Rosamunde Pilcher, *Winter Solstice*, 2000
Jeanne Ray, *Eat Cake*, 2003

21

MARIE BOSTWICK

Threading the Needle

(New York: Kensington Publishing Company, 2011)

Story type: Contemporary
Subject(s): Sisters; Friendship; Economic depressions

Major character(s): Tess Woodruff, Store Owner, Friend (of Madelyn); Madelyn Beecher, Friend (of Tess)
Locale(s): New Bern, Connecticut

Summary: *Threading the Needle* is a novel from Marie Bostwick's Cobbled Court series. In this book, the author tells the story of two women who turn to a quilting class in order to find the strength to survive various issues in their life. Tess Woodruff's business—the very one she convinced her husband to leave Boston for and invest all their money in—is failing miserably, and Tess's marriage has also taken a turn for the worse. Meanwhile, a childhood friend, Madelyn Beecher, returns to town after her husband is jailed for embezzlement and fraud. Now Tess and Madelyn must lean on one another as well as the women from the Cobbled Court Quilt Shop to get through these tough times. Bostwick is also the author of *A Single Thread*, *A Thread So Thin*, and *Threaded the Truth*.

Where it's reviewed:
Publishers Weekly, April 11, 2011, page 30

Other books by the same author:
A Thread So Thin, 2010
A Thread of Truth, 2009
A Single Thread, 2008
On Wings of the Morning, 2007
Fields of Gold, 2005

Other books you might like:
Elizabeth Buchan, *Separate Beds*, 2011
Carol Edgarian, *Three Stages of Amazement*, 2011
Joe Meno, *The Great Perhaps*, 2009
Eric Puchner, *Model Home: A Novel*, 2010
Lynn Schnurnberger, *The Best Laid Plans*, 2011

22

ANN BRASHARES

Sisterhood Everlasting

(New York: Random House, 2011)

Story type: Contemporary; Young Adult
Subject(s): Women; Friendship; Love
Major character(s): Bridget, Friend (of Carmen, Lena, and Tibby); Carmen, Friend (of Bridget, Lena, and Tibby); Lena, Friend (of Bridget, Carmen, and Tibby); Tibby, Friend (of Bridget, Carmen, and Lena)
Time period(s): 21st century; 2010s
Locale(s): United States

Summary: In *Sisterhood Everlasting*, best-selling author Ann Brashares presents a sequel to her runaway smash *The Sisterhood of the Traveling Pants*. This outing takes place ten years after the first novel and finds Bridget, Carmen, Lena, and Tibby having gone their separate ways. Now full-grown women with lives and dreams of their own, the ladies have understandably grown apart. But the prospect of a reunion rekindles old feelings, and soon the quartet is once again brought together and dealing with the ups and downs of life, love, and friendship.

Where it's reviewed:
Library Journal, April 1, 2011, page 84
Publishers Weekly, April 11, 2011, page 26

Other books by the same author:
My Name Is Memory, 2010
3 Willows: The Sisterhood Grows, 2009
Forever in Blue, 2007
The Last Summer (of You and Me), 2007
Girls in Pants, 2005

Other books you might like:
Mary Kay Andrews, *Summer Rental*, 2011
David Baldacci, *One Summer*, 2011
Judy Blume, *Summer Sisters*, 1998
Dorothea Benton Frank, *Folly Beach*, 2010
Kristin Hannah, *Night Road*, 2011
Elin Hilderbrand, *Silver Girl*, 2011
J. Courtney Sullivan, *Maine*, 2011
Nancy Thayer, *Heat Wave*, 2011
Jennifer Weiner, *Best Friends Forever*, 2009
Jennifer Weiner, *Then Came You*, 2011

23

LIBBA BRAY

Beauty Queens

(New York: Scholastic, 2011)

Story type: Young Adult
Subject(s): Beauty contests; Adolescent interpersonal relations; Humor
Major character(s): Taylor, Beauty Pageant Contestant
Time period(s): 21st century; 2010s

Summary: In *Beauty Queens*, prize-winning author Libba Bray tells the witty, insightful tale of a group of teenage beauty pageant contestants caught up in the most dangerous—and hilarious—of circumstances. When their plane goes down on a remote tropical island, it's every beauty queen for herself. Suddenly, the competition is no longer about winning a pretty, bejeweled crown—but about staying alive. As the girls struggle to survive the trying circumstances, allegiances are made and broken, unexpected challenges arise, and their respective abilities to express poise under pressure are put to the ultimate test.

Where it's reviewed:
Booklist, May 15, 2011, page 46
New York Times Book Review, May 15, 2011, page 19
Publishers Weekly, March 21, 2011, page 78

Other books by the same author:
Going Bovine, 2009
Vacations from Hell, 2009
The Sweet Far Thing, 2007
Rebel Angels, 2005
A Great and Terrible Beauty, 2003

Other books you might like:
Suzanne Collins, *Hunger Games Trilogy*, 2008
Cornelia Funke, *Reckless*, 2010
Margaret Peterson Haddix, *Claim to Fame*, 2009
Tamora Pierce, *Melting Stones*, 2008
Scott Westerfeld, *Uglies*, 2005

24

ALBERT BROOKS

2030: The Real Story of What Happens To America

(New York: St. Martin's Press, 2011)

Story type: Future Shock; Satire
Subject(s): Earthquakes; Dystopias; Aging (Biology)
Major character(s): President Matthew Bernstein, Government Official (U.S. President); Kathy Bernard, Young Woman; Sam Mueller, Scientist
Time period(s): 21st century; 2030s (2030)
Locale(s): Los Angeles, California

Summary: In *2030: The Real Story of What Happens To America*, legendary actor Albert Brooks creates a novel set in the not-too-distant future, in an America thrown into a moral and practical chaos by a sudden Los Angeles earthquake. The government went bankrupt long ago and no longer has the ability to financially sustain its citizenry, and now it's every man for himself as repercussions from the quake spread across the country, affecting the lives of all men, women, and children. One of the main conflicts involves the country's first Jewish president, President Bernstein, who must decide how to respond when China offers to rebuild Los Angeles in exchange for ownership of half the land in Southern California.

Where it's reviewed:
Booklist, April 15, 2011, page 21
Kirkus Reviews, March 15, 2011, page 441
Library Journal, April 1, 2011, page 76
Publishers Weekly, March 28, 2011, page 32

Other books you might like:
Cormac McCarthy, *The Road*, 2006
L.E. Modesitt, *The Eternity Artifact*, 2005
Philip Reeve, *Mortal Engines*, 2001
Neal Shusterman, *Unwind*, 2007
Sheri S. Tepper, *Six Moon Dance*, 1998

25

GERALDINE BROOKS

Caleb's Crossing

(New York: Viking, 2011)

Subject(s): Friendship; Cultural identity; Universities and colleges
Major character(s): Bethia Mayfield, Young Woman; Caleb, Young Man (Native American), Friend (of Bethia)
Time period(s): 17th century; 1660s (1665)
Locale(s): Martha's Vineyard, Massachusetts

Summary: In *Caleb's Crossing*, Pulitzer Prize-winning author Geraldine Brooks tells the story of the first Native American to receive a college degree from Harvard, as told through the eyes of a minister's daughter. It is 1665, and Bethia Mayfield comes of age in a small Great Harbor community, where she meets a local Native-

Popular Fiction

American boy named Caleb. Both youngsters possess a passion for knowledge, and a string of fateful events leads Bethia more deeply into Caleb's orbit. She soon witnesses his acceptance to college and the limitations placed upon her own life as a woman yearning for education.

Where it's reviewed:
Booklist, March 15, 2011, page 27
Kirkus Reviews, April 15, 2011, page 627
Library Journal, March 15, 2011, page 106
New York Times Book Review, March 15, 2011, page 16
Publishers Weekly, March 14, 2011, page 47

Other books by the same author:
People of the Book, 2008
March, 2005
Year of Wonders: A Novel of the Plague, 2001

Other books you might like:
Connie Briscoe, *A Long Way from Home*, 1999
Michel Faber, *The Crimson Petal and the White*, 2002
Nancy Horan, *Loving Frank: A Novel*, 2007
Lisa See, *Shanghai Girls*, 2009
Lee Smith, *On Agate Hill*, 2006

26

RITA MAE BROWN

Hiss of Death

(New York: Bantam, 2010)

Series: Mrs. Murphy Series. Book 19
Subject(s): Detective fiction; Cancer; Murder
Major character(s): Mary Minor "Harry" Haristeen, Detective—Amateur, Cancer Patient; Paula Benton, Nurse, Crime Victim; Mrs. Murphy, Cat
Time period(s): 21st century; 2010s
Locale(s): Crozet, Virginia

Summary: Mary Minor "Harry" Haristeen and her sleuthing pets return in the 19th installment of Rita Mae Brown's Mrs. Murphy Mysteries series. *Hiss of Death* finds Harry dealing with a breast cancer diagnosis. Just before she is to take part in a charity walk, Harry comes upon the body of a beloved local nurse. Paula Benton seems to have died from a hornet sting, but upon closer inspection, Harry and her animal crew discover the nurse may have been murdered—and may have had more than one enemy who wished her dead.

Where it's reviewed:
Publishers Weekly, Feb 7, 2011, page 38

Other books by the same author:
Cat of the Century, 2010
A Nose For Justice, 2010
The Purrfect Murder, 2008
The Sand Castle, 2008
Santa Clawed, 2008

Other books you might like:
Blaize Clement, *Cat Sitter Among the Pigeons*, 2010
Carole Nelson Douglas, *Cat in an Ultramarine Scheme*, 2010
Rebecca M. Hale, *How to Wash a Cat*, 2008

Shirley Rousseau Murphy, *Cat Coming Home: A Joe Grey Mystery*, 2010
Leann Sweeney, *The Cat, the Lady and the Liar: A Cats in Trouble Mystery*, 2011

27

VICTORIA BROWN

Minding Ben

(New York: Hyperion-Voice, 2011)

Story type: Contemporary
Subject(s): Child care; Wealth; Emigration and immigration
Major character(s): Grace Caton, 18-Year-Old, Child-Care Giver; Sylvia, Immigrant, Guardian (to Grace); Miriam, Wealthy, Employer (of Grace)
Time period(s): 20th century; 1990s
Locale(s): New York, New York

Summary: *Minding Ben* is a thought-provoking novel from author Victoria Brown. At the age of 18, Grace Caton leaves behind her tropical homeland of Trinidad for a new life in New York City, but Crown Heights, Brooklyn is a stark departure from the magical and opportunistic place of Grace's dreams. When her guardian disappears, Grace finds herself living with Sylvia, a fellow Trinidadian with little money, three children, and a lazy boyfriend. During the week, Grace spends her days nannying for a wealthy, demanding, and self-involved family in Manhattan, where her duties range from snapping nude pregnant photos of mom Miriam to serving seder supper at Passover in a maid's uniform. When Grace uncovers shocking secrets about her employers, she learns a great deal about herself, the strange new world she's inhabiting, and the future.

Where it's reviewed:
Booklist, March 1, 2011, page 26
Library Journal, March 1, 2011, page 68
Publishers Weekly, January 31, 2011, page 27

Other books by the same author:
Debut Novel

Other books you might like:
Liane Moriarty, *What Alice Forgot*, 2011
Tea Obreht, *The Tiger's Wife*, 2011
Ann Patchett, *State of Wonder*, 2011
Josh Ritter, *Bright's Passage*, 2011
Meg Wolitzer, *The Uncoupling*, 2011

28

ELIZABETH BUCHAN

Separate Beds

(New York: Viking, 2011)

Story type: Contemporary
Subject(s): Marriage; Family; Money
Major character(s): Tom, Spouse (of Annie); Annie, Spouse (of Tom)
Time period(s): 21st century

Locale(s): United States

Summary: A financial catastrophe plays a major role in saving a marriage in Elizabeth Buchan's *Separate Beds*. Though Tom and Annie have grown children and are enjoying a relatively prosperous life, their marriage is far from ideal. When the economic downturn hits, Tom is fired from his job and both the couple's son and Tom's mother are forced to move in with the couple. Suddenly Tom and Annie are forced to make this unorthodox situation work, leading them to unexpected results that bring them back to one another.

Where it's reviewed:
Booklist, December 1, 2010, page 27
Kirkus Reviews, October 1, 2010, page 952
Library Journal, November 1, 2010, page 53
Publishers Weekly, October 18, 2010, page 24

Other books by the same author:
The Second Wife, 2006
Wives Behaving Badly, 2006
Everything She Thought She Wanted, 2005
The Good Wife Strikes Back, 2004
Revenge of the Middle-Aged Woman, 2003
Perfect Love, 1999
Daughters of the Storm, 1997

Other books you might like:
A. Manette Ansay, *Good Things I Wish You: A Novel*, 2009
Carol Edgarian, *Three Stages of Amazement*, 2011
Helen Fielding, *Olivia Joules and the Overactive Imagination*, 2004
Joe Meno, *The Great Perhaps*, 2009
Eric Puchner, *Model Home: A Novel*, 2010
Lynn Schnurnberger, *The Best Laid Plans*, 2011
Haywood Smith, *Waking Up in Dixie*, 2010
Jess Walter, *The Financial Lives of the Poets*, 2009
Karen White, *The Beach Trees*, 2011

▮29▮

JAN BURKE

Disturbance

(New York: Simon and Schuster, 2011)

Series: Irene Kelly Series. Book 11
Subject(s): Journalism; Serial murders; Newspapers
Major character(s): Irene Kelly, Journalist; Nick Parrish, Serial Killer
Time period(s): 21st century; 2010s
Locale(s): California, United States

Summary: *Disturbance* is an installment from author Jan Burke's mystery series featuring Irene Kelly. Journalist Irene Kelly is back, but this time she is barely keeping it together as the newspaper she works at stays afloat. Then Irene receives some truly disturbing news: Nick Parrish, a convicted serial killer whom Irene helped put away through her investigative journalism work, has escaped from prison. Worse yet, Nick has a cadre of bizarre fans known as the Moths, who consider him to be some type of idol. Irene is getting threats from all sides, and her life may be at stake. Unfortunately she can't be sure

which threats are simply the fruits of idle hero worship, and which ones could be from the serial killer himself.

Where it's reviewed:
Booklist, May 1, 2011, page 20
Publishers Weekly, April 25, 2011, page 113

Other books by the same author:
Messenger, 2008
Kidnapped, 2006
Bloodlines, 2005
Nine, 2002
Flight, 2001

Other books you might like:
C.J. Box, *Cold Wind*, 2010
J.A. Jance, *Betrayal of Trust*, 2011
Perri O'Shaughnessy, *Dreams of the Dead*, 2011
John Sandford, *Buried Prey*, 2011
Erica Spindler, *Watch Me Die*, 2011

▮30▮

ROBERT OLEN BUTLER

A Small Hotel

(New York: Grove Press, 2011)

Story type: Contemporary
Subject(s): Marriage; Divorce; Love
Major character(s): Kelly Hays, Spouse (of Michael); Michael Hays, Spouse (of Kelly)

Summary: *A Small Hotel* is a novel by author Robert Olen Butler. After being together for nearly 25 years, Michael Hays and his wife Kelly have decided to separate and file for divorce. Just as the divorce is about to be finalized, Kelly decides to skip the hearing and instead drives to a small hotel on the French Quarter in New Orleans. It was at this very hotel where Kelly and Michael first fell in love. As Kelly reflects on the life they had together, she tries to remember when those feelings ended. Now it's up to Kelly to decide if she wants to save the marriage for the sake of love and family.

Where it's reviewed:
Booklist, April 1, 2011, page 26
Publishers Weekly, March 14, 2011, page 46

Other books by the same author:
Hell, 2009
Intercourse, 2008
Severance: Stories, 2008
Had a Good Time: Stories from American Postcards, 2004
A Good Scent from a Strange Mountain, 2001

Other books you might like:
Louise Erdrich, *Tales of Burning Love*, 1996
Valerie Laken, *Dream House: A Novel*, 2009
Diane Meier, *The Season of Second Chances: A Novel*, 2010
Joe Meno, *The Great Perhaps*, 2009
Austin McGiffert Wright, *Tony and Susan*, 2011

31

MEG CABOT

Overbite

(New York: William Morrow, 2011)

Story type: Vampire Story
Subject(s): Vampires; Supernatural; Romances (Fiction)
Major character(s): Meena Harper, Writer (soap operas), Psychic; Lucien Antonescu, Vampire, Son (of Dracula)

Summary: *Overbite* is the sequel to Meg Cabot's vampire romance novel *Insatiable*, which follows soap opera script writer Meena Harper as she is conscripted by the Vatican to help fight vampires and other supernatural creatures. Meena has unique psychic abilities that make her the ideal ally in a war against evil. Meena also has a deep, dark secret though: she has a soft spot for one of the creatures. Lucien Antonescu, the son of Dracula, is her ex-boyfriend, after all, and she's still in love with him, even if she denies it to herself sometimes. Can Meena overcome her emotions and heed her true calling, or should she follow her heart? Cabot is also the author of the Princess Diaries series of young adult novels.

Where it's reviewed:
Publishers Weekly, May 15, 2011, page 34

Other books by the same author:
Abandon, 2011
Insatiable, 2010

Other books you might like:
Lara Adrian, *Midnight Breed Series*, 2007
MaryJanice Davidson, *Betsy Taylor Undead Series*, 2004
Charlaine Harris, *A Touch of Dead*, 2009
Amy Plum, *Die for Me*, 2011
Kiersten White, *Paranormalcy*, 2011

32

JOHN CASEY

Compass Rose

(New York: Knopf, 2011)

Story type: Family Saga
Subject(s): Family sagas; Fishing (Recreation); Interpersonal relations
Major character(s): Elsie Buttrick, Naturalist (natural resources warden); Dick Pierce, Fisherman, Lover (of Elsie); Rose, Daughter (of Elsie and Dick); May Pierce, Spouse (of Dick)
Time period(s): 20th century-21st century; 1990s-2010s
Locale(s): Sawtooth Point, Rhode Island

Summary: In *Compass Rose*, author John Casey revisits the cast of characters he introduced in his 1989 novel, *Spartina*. Elsie Buttrick's family is trying to transform its small estuary community of Sawtooth Point, Rhode Island, into a vacation spot for the rich. Elsie, a wildlife warden, opposes her family's ideology with choices in her professional and her personal life. As the new mother of a baby girl fathered by local fisherman Dick Pierce,

Elsie has added to the controversies swirling in Sawtooth Point. But as little Rose grows into a young woman, the relationships in town adapt just as the coastal environment endures change.

Where it's reviewed:
Bookmarks, Mar/Apr 2011, page 31
Entertainment Weekly, October 22, 2010, page 118
The Houston Chronicle, November 21, 2010, page 17
New York Times Book Review, November 7, 2010, page 14
Publishers Weekly, July 12, 2010, page 24

Other books by the same author:
The Half-Life of Happiness, 1998
Spartina, 1989
South Country, 1988
Testimony and Demeanor, 1979
An American Romance, 1977

Other books you might like:
Louise Erdrich, *Shadow Tag: A Novel*, 2010
Julia Glass, *I See You Everywhere*, 2008
Ian McEwan, *On Chesil Beach*, 2007
Joyce Carol Oates, *Give Me Your Heart: Tales of Mystery and Suspense*, 2011
Marge Piercy, *Sex Wars*, 2005
Marilynne Robinson, *Home*, 2008
Richard Russo, *Empire Falls*, 2001
Rose Tremain, *Trespass*, 2010

33

MARK CHILDRESS

Georgia Bottoms

(New York: Little, Brown, and Company, 2011)

Story type: Contemporary
Subject(s): Southern United States; Humor; Wealth
Major character(s): Georgia Bottoms, Southern Belle
Time period(s): 21st century; 2010s
Locale(s): Six Points, Alabama

Summary: Mark Childress's *Georgia Bottoms* tells the story of the title heroine, a stunning Southern belle in the grandest sense of the term. But Georgia Bottoms is harboring a shocking secret: she is flat broke, her family fortune having run dry long ago. Determined to keep up the uber-rich facade, the publicly pious Georgia begins being "kept" by a number of different suitors, one of whom is the married minister of the local church. Her plan hits a snag when the minister decides to come clean to the community about his affair, and now Georgie must do what it takes to stop him from exposing her.

Where it's reviewed:
Booklist, February 1, 2011, page 28
Kirkus Reviews, December 1, 2010, page 1176
Library Journal, January 2011, page 82
Publishers Weekly, December 13, 2010, page 37

Other books by the same author:
One Mississippi, 2006
Crazy in Alabama, 1999
Gone for Good, 1998

V for Victor, 1998
A World Made of Fire, 1998

Other books you might like:
Fannie Flagg, *I Still Dream About You*, 2010
John Green, *Looking for Alaska: A Novel*, 2005
Nick Hornby, *Juliet, Naked*, 2009
Joshilyn Jackson, *Gods in Alabama*, 2005
Lee Smith, *The Last Girls*, 2002

34

KATE CHRISTENSEN

The Astral

(New York: Random House, 2011)

Story type: Contemporary
Subject(s): Men; Aging (Biology); Marriage
Major character(s): Harry Quirk, Spouse (of Luz), Writer (poet), Father (of Karina and Hector); Luz Quirk, Spouse (of Harry), Mother (of Karina and Hector); Karina Quirk, Activist, Daughter (of Luz and Harry); Hector Quirk, Cult Member, Son (of Luz and Harry)
Time period(s): 21st century; 2010s
Locale(s): New York, New York

Summary: *The Astral* is a novel by author Kate Christensen. Harry and Luz Quirk have lived in the Astral, an aging Brooklyn apartment building, since the beginning of their marriage three decades earlier. Yet after discovering a cache of romantic poems, Luz suspects Harry of having an extramarital affair, and Harry finds himself out on the street. As Harry tries desperately to win Luz back, he looks to reconnect with the neighborhood and people he once knew so well, including his daughter Karina, a hippie who searches restaurant dumpsters for discarded food, and his son Hector, the member of a Christian cult. Now, Harry must face up to the man he has become if he ever wants his life—and Luz—back.

Where it's reviewed:
Booklist, May 15, 2011, page 14
New York Times Book Review, July 31, 2011, page 14(L)
People, June 20, 2011, page 63
Publishers Weekly, April 15, 2011, page 1

Other books by the same author:
Trouble: A Novel, 2009
The Great Man, 2007
The Epicure's Lament, 2004
Jeremy Thrane, 2001
In the Drink, 1999

Other books you might like:
Kate Christensen, *The Great Man*, 2007
Susan Fales-Hill, *One Flight Up: A Novel*, 2010
Joshua Ferris, *The Unnamed*, 2010
Helen Schulman, *This Beautiful Life*, 2011
Joanna Trollope, *The Other Family: A Novel*, 2010

35

MEG WAITE CLAYTON

The Four Ms. Bradwells

(New York: Ballantine Books, 2010)

Story type: Contemporary
Subject(s): Women; Friendship; Abuse
Major character(s): Mia, Friend (of Lainey, Betts, and Ginger); Lainey, Friend (of Mia, Betts, and Ginger); Betts, Friend (of Mia, Lainey, and Ginger); Ginger, Friend (of Mia, Lainey, and Betts)
Time period(s): 21st century; 2010s
Locale(s): United States

Summary: Meg Waite Clayton's *The Four Ms. Bradwells* centers on the relationship between a quartet of female friends who come together after decades apart. As Betts is awaiting an appointment to the Supreme Court, each woman looks back on her life, the bond she shares with the other women in the group, and the dark secret that has held them all hostage.

Where it's reviewed:
Publishers Weekly, December 6, 2010, page 27

Other books by the same author:
The Wednesday Sisters, 2008
The Language of Light, 2003

Other books you might like:
Mary Kay Andrews, *Summer Rental*, 2011
Eleanor Brown, *The Weird Sisters*, 2011
Robyn Carr, *A Summer in Sonoma*, 2010
Beth Kendrick, *Second Time Around*, 2010
Sarah Strohmeyer, *Kindred Spirits*, 2011

36

JENNIFER CLOSE

Girls in White Dresses

(New York: Knopf Doubleday Publishing Group, 2011)

Story type: Romance
Subject(s): Women; Romances (Fiction); Weddings
Major character(s): Isabella, Young Woman, Businesswoman; Mary, Lawyer, Spouse, Mother; Lauren, Waiter/Waitress
Time period(s): 21st century; 2010s
Locale(s): New York, New York

Summary: Author Jennifer Close's *Girls in White Dresses* is the story of three New York City girlfriends trapped in a seemingly never-ending loop of bridal showers and weddings as nearly all of their friends take the plunge. On top of that, each of the girls is also forced to deal with the myriad of troubles they encounter within their personal lives. Isabella, who works for a mailing-list company, struggles with the stress of a busy workday and an overly demanding boss. Mary, a married lawyer with two kids, has to deal with her husband, a mama's boy who is virtually incapable of doing anything for himself. Lauren is a waitress fiercely determined not to fall in love with a bartender whose talent with a drink and good looks make avoiding him nearly impossible.

Close follows the three friends as they negotiate their complicated lives and romantic escapades.

Where it's reviewed:
Booklist, July 1, 2011, page 24
Marie Claire, August 2011, page 110
Publishers Weekly, May 30, 2011, page 44

Other books you might like:
Candace Bushnell, *Sex and the City*, 2002
Katie Fforde, *Wedding Season*, 2010
Joanna Smith Rakoff, *A Fortunate Age*, 2009
Jennifer Weiner, *Then Came You*, 2011
Lauren Weisberger, *The Devil Wears Prada*, 2003

37

LEAH HAGER COHEN

The Grief of Others

(New York: Riverhead Press, 2011)

Story type: Contemporary
Subject(s): Death; Grief; Family
Major character(s): John Ryrie, Spouse (of Ricky), Father (of Biscuit and Paul); Ricky Ryrie, Mother (of Biscuit and Paul), Spouse (of John); Biscuit Ryrie, Daughter (of Ricky and John), Sister (of Paul); Paul Ryrie, Son (of Ricky and John), Brother (of Biscuit)

Summary: *The Grief of Others* is a novel written by author Leah Hager Cohen. In this book, the author tells the story of a married couple struggling to come to terms with the recent death of their child, who lived to be barely three days old. The wife, Ricky Ryrie, knew a strong possibility existed that the child would not survive, but kept this information from her husband John in hopes that a new baby would hold their marriage together. Meanwhile the Ryrie's older children—Biscuit, 11, and Paul, 13—react in a variety of ways to the loss of their baby sibling. When a secret from John's past appears on the Ryrie's doorstep, it could either tear their family apart or give them exactly what they need to hold it together.

Where it's reviewed:
Publishers Weekly, July 18, 2011, page 129

Other books by the same author:
House Lights, 2007
Heart, You Bully, You Punk, 2003
Heat Lightning, 1998

Other books you might like:
A. Manette Ansay, *Blue Water*, 2006
Helen Dunmore, *Mourning Ruby*, 2003
Jane Hamilton, *A Map of the World*, 1994
Alice Sebold, *The Lovely Bones*, 2002
Anne Tyler, *The Accidental Tourist*, 1985

38

EOIN COLFER

Plugged

(London: Headline, 2011)

Subject(s): Organized crime; Murder; Crime
Major character(s): Lincoln McEvoy, Bouncer, Boyfriend (of Connie); Connie, Girlfriend (of Lincoln), Crime Victim
Time period(s): 21st century; 2010s
Locale(s): New Jersey, United States

Summary: *Plugged* is a novel by author Eoin Colfer. When Lincoln McEvoy, an Irish bouncer employed at a New Jersey casino, finds his girlfriend Connie dead in the parking lot, he never imagines that he would soon be on the run for his own life. Yet soon he is, as mobsters and cops on the take all think he is involved in the same dirty dealings as Connie. Now McEvoy must deal with people who want him dead as well as the voices in his own head, which he blames on his recent hair plugs. Can he avoid trouble long enough to stop the voices and figure out what these underground crime thugs want from him?

Where it's reviewed:
Booklist, July 1, 2011, page 35
The Financial Times, May 28, 2011, page 13
Kirkus Reviews, April 15, 2011, page 4
Library Journal, June 15, 2011, page 74
Publishers Weekly, June 6, 2011, page 25

Other books by the same author:
Artemis Fowl: The Atlantis Complex, 2010
And Another Thing—: Douglas Adams's Hitchhiker's Guide to the Galaxy, Part Six of Three, 2009
Airman, 2008
Artemis Fowl: The Time Paradox, 2008
Benny and Omar, 2007
The Opal Deception, 2005
The Eternity Code, 2003
The Arctic Incident, 2002

Other books you might like:
Anthony Horowitz, *The Switch*, 1997
Juliet Marillier, *Seer of Sevenwaters*, 2010
James Patterson, *Angel: A Maximum Ride Novel*, 2011
Darren Shan, *Birth of a Killer*, 2010
Jeff Smith, *Bone: Crown of Horns*, 2004

39

CLAIRE COOK

Best Staged Plans

(New York: Voice/Hyperion, 2011)

Story type: Contemporary
Subject(s): Decorative arts; Real estate; Family
Major character(s): Sandy Sullivan, Interior Decorator, Mother
Time period(s): 21st century; 2010s
Locale(s): Atlanta, Georgia; Boston, Massachusetts

Summary: In best-selling author Claire Cook's *Best Staged Plans*, Sandy Sullivan's career as a home stager has made her an expert at de-cluttering homes for sale, but her own life is packed full of messy situations. Sandy desires to sell her family's suburban Boston home, but first she needs to convince her reluctant husband and grown son who recently moved back home to live in the basement. When Sandy is offered a job in Atlanta by her best friend's boyfriend to stage a small hotel, she's eager

college and formed a bond so tight that it overshadowed all other relationships and romances. It was Cat who finally broke up the threesome, choosing marriage to her boyfriend Jason and moving out of her friends' shared apartment. Apart for six years but still very much in one another's thoughts, Pen and Will respond to Cat's surprising request for a reunion at their college. When they arrive at school they are welcomed by Jason, who reveals that Cat, grieving over her father's death, has gone missing.

Where it's reviewed:
Kirkus Reviews, April 15, 2011, page 5
Library Journal, May 15, 2011, page 61
Publishers Weekly, May 2, 2011, page 32

Other books by the same author:
Belong to Me, 2008
Love Walked In, 2005

Other books you might like:
Katie Fforde, *Love Letters*, 2011
Kristan Higgins, *My One and Only*, 2011
Rona Jaffe, *The Best of Everything*, 2005
Nicholas Sparks, *Safe Haven*, 2010
Danielle Steel, *44 Charles Street*, 2011

46

JEFFERY DEAVER

The Edge

(London: Hodder & Stoughton, 2011)

Subject(s): Suspense; Crime; Murder
Major character(s): Corte, Agent (Strategic Protection Department); Henry Loving, Bounty Hunter; Ryan Kessler, Police Officer
Time period(s): 21st century; 2010s
Locale(s): Washington, District of Columbia

Summary: *Edge* is a novel written by author Jeffrey Deaver. When a cop named Ryan Kessler is hunted by a ruthless shakedown artist, it's up to Strategic Protection Agent Corte to watch Kessler's back. Corte is part of a secret government organization whose job it is to protect people just like Kessler: people who have been marked for crime or murder. Now Henry Loving, a so-called "lifter" who is hired to torture people in order to get information from them, is after Kessler. Corte does not know why Kessler has been targeted, and he does not re- ally care. His only mission is to keep Kessler safe while trying to find out who Loving works for, and how to stop him.

Where it's reviewed:
Booklist, October 15, 2010, page 24
Library Journal, October 15, 2010, page 64
Publishers Weekly, September 6, 2010, page 23

Other books by the same author:
Burning Wire, 2010
Roadside Crosses, 2009
Broken Window, 2008
The Sleeping Doll, 2007
The Cold Moon, 2006

Other books you might like:
David Baldacci, *The Sixth Man*, 2011
Jonathan Kellerman, *Mystery*, 2010
John T. Lescroart, *Damage*, 2011
John Sandford, *Buried Prey*, 2011
Taylor Stevens, *The Informationist*, 2011
Peter Turnbull, *Aftermath*, 2011

47

BARBARA DELINSKY

Escape

(New York: Doubleday, 2011)

Story type: Contemporary
Subject(s): Self awareness; Family; Self esteem
Major character(s): Emily Aulenbach, Lawyer
Locale(s): New Hampshire, United States

Summary: In *Escape*, the author tells the story of Emily Aulenbach, a 30-year-old attorney whose hectic pace and lifestyle have stopped her from being the person whom she thought she would become. Once upon a time, her goal was to champion idealistic causes, but instead she now works for a firm that represents a bottled-water company in a lawsuit. Worse yet, her family life seems foreign to her, and the only close relationships she seems to have are with her electronic devices. In an effort to regain her former self, Emily escapes to a New Hamp- shire mountain town, where she is determined to learn whom she really should be and how to become that person.

Where it's reviewed:
Booklist, June 1, 2011, page 34
Library Journal, June 15, 2011, page 74
Publishers Weekly, May 16, 2011, page 50

Other books by the same author:
Not My Daughter, 2010
While My Sister Sleeps, 2009
The Secret Between Us, 2008
Family Tree, 2007
Looking for Peyton Place, 2005

Other books you might like:
Elizabeth Berg, *Once Upon a Time There Was You*, 2011
Cassandra King, *Queen of Broken Hearts*, 2007
Elinor Lipman, *The Family Man*, 2009
Jodi Picoult, *Sing You Home*, 2011
Rebecca Wells, *The Crowning Glory of Calla Lily Ponder*, 2009

48

SARAH DESSEN

What Happened to Goodbye

(New York: Random House, 2011)

Story type: Contemporary; Young Adult
Subject(s): Divorce; Identity; High schools

Major character(s): McLean Sweet, 17-Year-Old, Girl; Mr. Sweet, Father (of McLean); Dave, Friend (of McLean)
Time period(s): 21st century; 2010s
Locale(s): United States

Summary: In *What Happened to Goodbye* by Sarah Dessen, 17-year-old McLean Sweet struggles to find herself in the aftermath of her mother's betrayal and her parents' divorce. McLean's mother's extramarital affair with a basketball coach has shocked their community and left their family in a shambles. After the divorce, McLean moves in with her father—but her father is always moving. A restaurant consultant, Mr. Sweet must relocate often. At first, the arrangement suits McLean well. In each town she creates a new identity for herself. After playing the roles of cheerleader and actress, McLean and her father move again. This time, McLean wants to stop pretending to be someone else, but she will need the help of her new neighbor, Dave, to discover the person she has become.

Where it's reviewed:
Booklist, May 1, 2011, page 85
Kirkus Reviews, April 15, 2011, page 28
Publishers Weekly, February 21, 2011, page 134

Other books by the same author:
Along for the Ride, 2011
That Summer, 2006
Truth About Forever, 2006
Dreamland, 2004
Someone Like You, 2004

Other books you might like:
Joan Bauer, *Hope Was Here*, 2000
Rachel Cohn, *Gingerbread*, 2002
Susane Colasanti, *Waiting for You*, 2009
Julie Halpern, *Into the Wild Nerd Yonder*, 2009
Jenny Han, *The Summer I Turned Pretty*, 2009

49

HEATHER DIXON

Entwined

(New York: Greenwillow Books, 2011)

Story type: Fantasy; Young Adult
Subject(s): Royalty; Dance; Father-daughter relations
Major character(s): Azalea, Royalty (princess)
Locale(s): Eathesbury, Fictional Location

Summary: In the young adult novel *Entwined* by Heather Dixon, Azalea is the eldest daughter of the king of the enchanted world of Eathesbury. After her mother succumbs to an illness, Azalea and her 11 other sisters are required to mourn for a given period of time. Then they uncover a magical location just beyond the castle walls, a place where they can dance in their mother's memory. The dancing place is controlled by an enigmatic man named Keeper, who seems not to have the sisters' best interests in mind. Will Azalea fall prey to this mysterious man's plans? This book is based on the Grimm fairytale "The Twelve Dancing Princesses," also known as "The Worn-Out Dancing Shoes." First novel.

Where it's reviewed:
Booklist, February 1, 2011, page 68
Horn Book, May/June 2011, page 87
Publishers Weekly, February 28, 2011, page 58

Other books you might like:
Margaret Peterson Haddix, *Palace of Mirrors*, 2008
Lindsey Leavitt, *The Royal Treatment*, 2011
Robin McKinley, *Deerskin*, 1993
Ellis O'Neal, *The False Princess*, 2011
Vivian Vande Velde, *The Conjurer Princess*, 1997
Suzanne Weyn, *The Night Dance*, 2005

50

JENNIFER EGAN

A Visit from the Goon Squad

(New York: Knopf, 2011)

Story type: Contemporary; Literary
Subject(s): Family; Travel; Friendship
Major character(s): Sasha, Young Woman, Thief (kleptomaniac), Mentally Ill Person, Artist; Bennie Salazar, Musician, Father, Traveler
Time period(s): 20th century-21st century; 1970s-2010s
Locale(s): San Francisco, California; Naples, Florida; New York, United States

Summary: In *A Visit from the Goon Squad*, the settings and time periods change with every point of view. This novel is split between Sasha and Bennie, two people whose lives cross paths numerous times, but never long enough for them to get to know one another. Sasha's story first comes to life as she sits in her therapist's office, reflecting on the events of her past and her current struggles to supress the urge to steal. Throughout the novel, Sasha flashes back to her childhood—her parents' tragic marriage, her best friend's bouts with depression and suicide—and dwells on the relationship she attempted to form with her uncle. Bennie, an aging rock star, also plays a key role in this novel. The book moves from his stardom in the 1970s to the birth of his son to his unhappy marriages. As he moves across the world, the setting changes, his life changes, and oddly enough, so does Sasha's.

Where it's reviewed:
The New York Times, June 21, 2010, page C4
New York Times Book Review, July 11, 2010, page 1
People, June 28, 2010, page 55
Publishers Weekly, March 22, 2010, page 46
Time, June 28, 2010, page 56

Other books by the same author:
The Keep, 2006
Look at Me, 2001
Emerald City, 1996
The Invisible Circus, 1994

Other books you might like:
Emma Donaghue, *Room*, 2010
Tana French, *Faithful Place*, 2011
Pagan Kennedy, *The Exes*, 1998
Donna Leon, *Drawing Conclusions*, 2011
Rosamund Lupton, *Sister*, 2011

Popular Fiction

Tom Perrotta, *The Wishbones*, 1997
S.J. Watson, *Before I Go To Sleep*, 2011

51

JANET EVANOVICH

Smokin' Seventeen

(New York: Bantam, 2011)

Series: Stephanie Plum Series. Book 17
Subject(s): Detective fiction; Serial murders; Love
Major character(s): Stephanie Plum, Bounty Hunter; Joe
  Morelli, Police Officer, Boyfriend (of Stephanie);
  Ranger, Security Officer
Time period(s): 21st century; 2010s
Locale(s): New Jersey, United States

Summary: *Smokin' Seventeen* is the 17th installment in Janet Evanovich's best-selling Stephanie Plum series. This
episode finds dead bodies turning up left and right in a
local construction area, and Stephanie appears to be on
the killer's to-do list. As she grapples with this latest
mystery, an onslaught of personal dramas starts to
interfere. Can Stephanie choose between the two men in
her life? Should she follow her mother's advice and
hook up with a high-school friend? And, most importantly, can she make the right decision while fending off
a serial killer?

Where it's reviewed:
Library Journal, January 1, 2011, page 60

Other books by the same author:
Sizzling Sixteen, 2010
Finger Lickin Fifteen, 2009
Fearless Fourteen, 2008
Lean, Mean Thirteen, 2007
Twelve Sharp, 2006

Other books you might like:
Tori Carrington, *Love Bites*, 2011
Harlan Coben, *Live Wire*, 2011
Diane Mott Davidson, *Crunch Time*, 2011
Susan Isaacs, *As Husbands Go*, 2010
Heather Webber, *Deeply, Desperately*, 2010

52

RICHARD PAUL EVANS

Miles to Go

(New York: Simon & Schuster, 2011)

Series: Walk Series. Book 2
Story type: Literary; Series
Subject(s): Identity; Psychology; Travel
Major character(s): Alan Christoffersen, Advertising
  (former executive); Angel, Friend (of Alan)
Time period(s): 21st century; 2010s
Locale(s): Spokane, Washington

Summary: In *Miles to Go*, author Richard Paul Evans
continues the story of Alan Christoffersen's soul-
searching odyssey begun in *The Walk*. After losing

everything important in his life, Alan had set out on a
backpacking journey from his home in Bellevue,
Washington to Key West, Florida. But Alan doesn't get
far when an unprovoked knife attack lands him in a
Spokane hospital. With a long convalescence looming,
the former advertising executive worries that he has no
place to live and no one to care for him. Then he meets
a woman named Angel who offers friendship and
support. *Miles to Go* is the second book in *The Walk*
series.

Where it's reviewed:
Booklist, April 15, 2011, page 25

Other books by the same author:
Promise Me, 2010
The Walk, 2010
Christmas List, 2009
Grace, 2008
The Gift, 2007

Other books you might like:
Emily Giffin, *Heart of the Matter*, 2010
Debbie Macomber, *A Turn in the Road*, 2010
Nicholas Sparks, *Safe Haven*, 2010
Dan Walsh, *The Unfinished Gift: A Novel*, 2008
Jason F. Wright, *The Wednesday Letters*, 2007

53

KATIE FFORDE

Love Letters

(London: Century, 2011)

Story type: Contemporary
Subject(s): Romances (Fiction); Books; Carnivals
  (Amusements)
Major character(s): Laura, Clerk (bookstore); Eleanora,
  Agent (literary); Dermot Flynn, Writer
Time period(s): 21st century; 2000s
Locale(s): England; Ireland

Summary: *Love Letters* is a novel by author Katie Fforde.
Twenty-six year old Laura works in a bookstore that will
soon close, and as a final farewell she plans one last
author appearance for her store. There, she meets
Eleanora, a literary agent who asks Laura to come work
for her in planning a book festival. Laura is determined
to impress Eleanora, so she attempts to book bestselling
author Dermot Flynn, a reclusive writer who lives in
Ireland. Laura flies off to the Emerald Isles to meet with
the popular author, and when they meet sparks fly. Can
Laura use her feminine wiles to convince Dermot to
come out of exile and meet his adoring fans?

Where it's reviewed:
Kirkus Reviews, December 1, 2010, page 1177

Other books by the same author:
Wedding Season, 2010
Practically Perfect, 2008
Bidding for Love, 2007
Restoring Grace, 2006
Paradise Fields, 2004

Other books you might like:
Sarah Addison Allen, *The Peach Keeper*, 2011

Helen Fielding, *Olivia Joules and the Overactive Imagination*, 2004
Emily Giffin, *Heart of the Matter*, 2010
Sophie Kinsella, *Twenties Girl*, 2009
Debbie Macomber, *Twenty Wishes*, 2008

54

FANNIE FLAGG

I Still Dream About You

(New York: Random House, 2010)

Story type: Mystery
Subject(s): Southern United States; Humor; Mystery
Major character(s): Maggie Fortenberry, Real Estate Agent, Friend (of Brenda Peoples); Brenda Peoples, Friend (of Maggie); Ethel Clipp, Manager (of real estate office)
Locale(s): Birmingham, Alabama

Summary: In *I Still Dream About You*, bestselling author Fannie Flagg tells the story of Maggie Fortenberry, a former beauty queen and charm school graduate who now works as a real estate agent for Red Mountain Realty. When business starts plummeting at the agency, Maggie comes up with the perfect plan to boost home sales. Unfortunately, she'll still have to contend with her rival, Babs Bingington, who is determined to put Red Mountain Realty out of business. Can Maggie rely on her good friend Brenda Peoples, and her loyal office manager Ethel Clipp, to get her through this? Flagg is also the author of *Daisy Fay and the Miracle Man* and *Fried Green Tomatoes at the Whistle Stop Cafe*, which was adapted into the Academy Award-nominated film *Fried Green Tomatoes*.

Where it's reviewed:
Booklist, October 15, 2010, page 20
Publishers Weekly, October 4, 2010, page 29

Other books by the same author:
Can't Wait to Get to Heaven, 2006
A Redbird Christmas, 2004
Standing in the Rainbow, 2002
Welcome to the World, Baby Girl!, 1998
Daisy Fay and the Miracle Man, 1992

Other books you might like:
Mark Childress, *Georgia Bottoms*, 2011
Abby Drake, *The Secrets Sisters Keep*, 2010
Fannie Flagg, *Welcome to the World, Baby Girl!*, 1998
Beth Hoffman, *Saving CeeCee Honeycutt: A Novel*, 2010
Alexander McCall Smith, *No. 1 Ladies' Detective Agency Series*, 1998

55

THERESE FOWLER

Exposure

(New York: Ballantine Books, 2011)

Story type: Contemporary
Subject(s): Adolescence; Sexual behavior; Sex crimes

Major character(s): Anthony Winter, Boyfriend (of Amelia); Amelia Wilkes, Girlfriend (of Anthony)
Time period(s): 21st century; 2010s
Locale(s): New York, New York

Summary: *Exposure*, a novel by Therese Fowler, deals with a problem that is unique to the digital generation: sexting, or sending obscene pictures or messages between digital devices. Many teenagers may consider this harmless fun, but in *Exposure*, it leads to serious repercussions. In this novel, Anthony Winter and his girlfriend Amelia Wilkes are getting along fine despite their parents' reluctance toward their relationship. However, when Anthony sends pornographic pictures to Amelia—and Amelia's father finds them—the real trouble begins. Anthony is pegged as a sexual offender and Amelia faces judgment and punishment as well. Suddenly the teens regret their foray into sexting.

Where it's reviewed:
Library Journal, April 1, 2011, page 80
Publishers Weekly, Feb 7, 2011, page 33
USA Today, April 28, 2011, page 04D

Other books by the same author:
Reunion, 2009
Souvenir, 2008

Other books you might like:
Jennifer Haigh, *Faith*, 2011
Kristin Hannah, *Night Road*, 2011
Liane Moriarty, *What Alice Forgot*, 2011
Jodi Picoult, *Sing You Home*, 2011

56

DOROTHEA BENTON FRANK

Folly Beach

(New York: William Morrow, 2010)

Story type: Contemporary
Subject(s): Beaches; Southern United States; Infidelity
Major character(s): Cate Cooper, Widow(er)
Time period(s): 21st century; 2010s
Locale(s): Folly Beach, South Carolina

Summary: *Folly Beach* is a humorous novel from author Dorothea Benton Frank's best-selling Lowcountry series. After the death of her husband, Cate Cooper realizes the magnitude of his financial deception and emotional infidelity. Widowed, homeless, and without a penny to her name, Cate's only option is to return to Folly Beach, the small South Carolina town where she spent her childhood. Surrounded by a group of eccentric individuals, Cate slowly begins to warm to the idea of starting over. Drawing from the memories of her past, she begins to find the confidence and hope she needs for a bright new future.

Other books by the same author:
Low Country Summer, 2010
Return to Sullivans Island, 2009
Bulls Island, 2008
The Christmas Pearl, 2007
Land of Mango Sunsets, 2007

Other books you might like:
Mary Kay Andrews, *Summer Rental*, 2011
Maeve Binchy, *Minding Frankie*, 2011
Fannie Flagg, *I Still Dream About You*, 2010
Ann Patchett, *State of Wonder*, 2011
Anita Shreve, *Rescue*, 2010

57

JONATHAN FRANZEN

Freedom

(New York: Farrar, Straus, and Giroux, 2011)

Story type: Contemporary
Subject(s): Family; Marriage; Social conditions
Major character(s): Patty Berglund, Spouse (of Walter);
    Walter Berglund, Spouse (of Patty)
Time period(s): 21st century; 2010s
Locale(s): St. Paul, Minnesota

Summary: In *Freedom*, award-winning author Jonathan
Franzen offers an incisive study of a modern-day
marriage. To all outward appearances, Patty and Walter
Berglund have the ideal marriage; they are two politically evolved, socially conscious citizens with a solid
family and a strong position in the community. But under
the surface lurks a series of problems that threaten to
boil over at any minute. From Walter's ethically
questionable new job to their son's vehement Republican-
ism, from Patty's outsized anger to an old adversary
who refuses to leave their lives, the Berglunds world is
about to come crashing down around them.

Where it's reviewed:
Booklist, July 1, 2010, page 7
Entertainment Weekly, August 6, 2010, page 12
Library Journal, August 2010, page 68
The New York Times, August 16, 2010, page C1
Publishers Weekly, July 5, 2010, page 25

Other books by the same author:
The Discomfort Zone, 2006
How to Be Alone, 2002
The Corrections, 2001
Desperate Characters, 1999
Strong Motion, 1992
The Twenty-Seventh City, 1988

Other books you might like:
Jennifer Egan, *A Visit from the Goon Squad*, 2011
Joyce Carol Oates, *Little Bird of Heaven*, 2009
Ann Patchett, *State of Wonder*, 2011
Eric Puchner, *Model Home: A Novel*, 2010
Richard Russo, *That Old Cape Magic*, 2009
Anne Tyler, *Noah's Compass: A Novel*, 2010

58

JULIA GLASS

Widower's Tale

(New York: Pantheon Books, 2011)

Story type: Contemporary
Subject(s): Family; Love; Cults

Major character(s): Percy Glass, Retiree, Father (of
    Clover), Grandfather (of Robert); Clover, Teacher,
    Daughter (of Percy); Robert, Student—College, Cult
    Member, Grandson (of Percy); Ira, Teacher,
    Homosexual; Celestino, Immigrant, Gardener
Time period(s): 21st century; 2010s
Locale(s): Boston, Massachusetts

Summary: In *The Widower's Tale*, award-winning author
Julia Glass tells the story of a family going through a
profound transformation. Seventy-year-old patriarch
Percy Glass has no idea that renting his barn to a
preschool will change his life so completely. His
daughter Clover takes a job at the school, while Percy's
adored grandson Robert falls in with a cult. Percy himself
starts a relationship with a much younger teacher at the
preschool as the paths of two men—another teacher and
an immigrant gardener—begin to collide with those of
Percy and his family.

Where it's reviewed:
Entertainment Weekly, September 3, 2010, page 77
Good Housekeeping, October 2010, page 222
O, The Oprah Magazine, September 2010, page 158
People, September 20, 2010, page 63
Self, October 2010, page 40

Other books by the same author:
I See You Everywhere, 2008
The Whole World Over, 2006
Three Junes, 2002

Other books you might like:
Michael Cunningham, *The Hours*, 1998
Lily King, *Father of the Rain: A Novel*, 2010
Yann Martel, *Life of Pi*, 2001
Ian McEwan, *Solar*, 2010
Sue Miller, *The Senator's Wife*, 2008
Alice Sebold, *The Almost Moon*, 2007
Mark Spragg, *Bone Fire*, 2010
Anne Tyler, *Noah's Compass: A Novel*, 2010

59

FRANCISCO GOLDMAN

Say Her Name

(New York: Grove Press, 2011)

Story type: Contemporary
Subject(s): Grief; Death; Love
Major character(s): Francisco Goldman, Squirrel (of
    Aura), Writer; Aura, Spouse (of Francisco), Accident
    Victim
Time period(s): 21st century; 2010s
Locale(s): Mexico; New York, United States

Summary: Francisco Goldman's *Say Her Name: A Novel*
tells a fictionalized account of the author's grief and
recovery over the loss of his wife, Aura. He recounts
their meeting and courtship, as well as the tragic events
that led to her death while vacationing in Mexico. Aura's
mother attempts legal action against the author, all while
he battles with his suffocating grief. Slowly, Francisco
comes to terms with the loss of his beloved wife and
learns to live in a world without her.

Where it's reviewed:
Booklist, March 1, 2011, page 28
Maclean's, May 2, 2011, page 91
New York Times Book Review, April 10, 2011, page 1(L)
Publishers Weekly, February 14, 2011, page 36

Other books by the same author:
The Divine Husband, 2004
The Ordinary Seaman, 1997
The Long Night of White Chickens, 1992

Other books you might like:
Travis Holland, *The Archivist's Story*, 2007
Sue Miller, *The Lake Shore Limited*, 2010
Nicole Mones, *The Last Chinese Chef*, 2007
Jacques Roubaud, *The Loop*, 2009
Elizabeth Winthrop, *Fireworks*, 2006

60

DAVID GOODWILLIE

American Subversive

(New York: Scribner, 2011)

Story type: Contemporary
Subject(s): Terrorism; Journalism; Politics
Major character(s): Paige Roderick, Terrorist; Aidan Cole, Journalist
Time period(s): 21st century; 2010s
Locale(s): New York, New York

Summary: In *American Subversive: A Novel*, author David Goodwillie tells the story of two people thrust together by the volatile landscape of politics and revolution. Paige Roderick is still grieving the death of her brother in the Iraq War when she becomes involved with a small-time organization of American terrorists. A bomb planted by Paige causes blogger/aspiring journalist Aidan Cole to track her down, whereupon the two discover they have more in common than either could have ever dreamed.... First novel.

Where it's reviewed:
Booklist, February 1, 2010, page 31
New York Times Book Review, May 9, 2010, page 16
Publishers Weekly, January 25, 2010, page 22
Publishers Weekly, Jan 4, 2010, page 27
USA Today, April 29, 2010, page 5D

Other books by the same author:
Seemed Like a Good Idea at the Time, 2006

Other books you might like:
Alex Berenson, *Secret Soldier*, 2011
Justin Cronin, *The Passage*, 2010
Jennifer Egan, *Look at Me*, 2001
Mohsin Hamid, *The Reluctant Fundamentalist*, 2007
Hannu Rajaniemi, *The Quantum Thief*, 2011
Daniel Suarez, *Freedom: A Novel*, 2010
Brad Thor, *Foreign Influence: A Thriller*, 2010
John Updike, *Terrorist*, 2006

61

LORNA GRAHAM

The Ghost of Greenwich Village

(New York: Ballantine Books, 2011)

Story type: Contemporary - Fantasy
Subject(s): Ghosts; Interpersonal relations; Mother-daughter relations
Major character(s): Eve Weldon, Writer; Donald, Writer, Supernatural Being
Locale(s): New York, New York

Summary: In *The Ghost of Greenwich Village*, author Lorna Graham tells the story of Eve Weldon, a young female writer who decides to move to Greenwich Village in pursuit of an artistic lifestyle. Throughout her life, Eve has heard her mother tell tales of the Village in the 1960s and the hippie and Beat movements that characterized the neighborhood. Now Eve wants a similar adventure of her own, but all she gets is a job writing news segments for a morning magazine show and an apartment that is haunted by a grouch named Donald who gives the term "ghost writer" a whole new meaning. Will Eve find her own flair in this legendary Village, or has the artsy lifestyle that once existed in the neighborhood left for good?

Where it's reviewed:
Booklist, July 1, 2011, page 23
Publishers Weekly, April 25, 2011, page 115

Other books you might like:
Paul Auster, *Sunset Park*, 2010
Bertice Berry, *The Haunting of Hip Hop*, 2001
Francesca Lia Block, *Missing Angel Juan*, 1993
Marjorie Kernan, *The Ballad of West Tenth Street*, 2009
Sarah Schulman, *Rat Bohemia*, 1995

62

HELEN GRANT

Glass Demon

(New York: Bantam Books, 2011)

Subject(s): Supernatural; Demons; Archaeology
Major character(s): Lin Fox, Teenager, Daughter (of Oliver); Oliver Fox, Archaeologist, Father (of Lin)
Locale(s): Germany

Summary: *The Glass Demon* is a young adult fantasy novel by author Helen Grant. Lin Fox's father is on a journey to recover a stained-glass relic thought to be lost forever. His expedition brings the father and daughter to Germany, where the item was last seen. Yet, as Lin and her father get closer to solving the mystery of where the object might be, strange events begin happening. People who may be linked to the ancient relic are turning up dead, surrounded by shattered stained glass. Lin begins to realize that supernatural forces may be at work, and if she doesn't get to the bottom of what or who they are, her father may be their next victim.

Where it's reviewed:
Booklist, May 15, 2011, page 24

Library Journal, May 1, 2011, page 73
Publishers Weekly, April 11, 2011, page 34

Other books by the same author:
The Vanishing of Katharina Linden, 2010

Other books you might like:
Lars Kepler, *The Hypnotist*, 2011
Dean Koontz, *What the Night Knows*, 2011
Ransom Riggs, *Miss Peregrine's Home for Peculiar Children*, 2011
Karin Slaughter, *Fallen*, 2011

63

SARA GRUEN

Ape House

(New York: Spiegel & Grau, 2011)

Story type: Contemporary
Subject(s): Animals; Science; Television
Major character(s): Isabel Duncan, Scientist; John Thigpen, Journalist
Time period(s): 21st century; 2010s
Locale(s): United States

Summary: *Ape House* by writer Sara Gruen, tells the story of six bonobos, a type of ape that has the ability to understand and reason with human beings. These particular six apes have also mastered American Sign Language. Isabel Duncan, the scientist who works with the bonobos, has an incredibly close relationship with the animals. When an audacious reporter breaks into the Great Ape Language Lab to get a story, an accident occurs. The six apes escape the lab, while Isabel is left for dead. Later, the apes reappear on a reality show that quickly garners the attention of the American public. When the apes use their communicating abilities to beg Isabel for help, she promises to get them back.

Where it's reviewed:
Booklist, August 1, 2010, page 22
Bookmarks, Nov/Dec 2010, page 40
Kirkus Reviews, August 1, 2010, page 694
Library Journal, August 2010, page 68
Publishers Weekly, July 5, 2010, page 24

Other books by the same author:
Water for Elephants, 2006
Flying Changes, 2005
Riding Lessons, 2004

Other books you might like:
Russell Banks, *The Darling*, 2004
Geraldine Brooks, *Caleb's Crossing*, 2011
Laurence Gonzales, *Lucy: A Novel*, 2010
Benjamin Hale, *Evolution of Bruno Littlemore*, 2011
Barbara Kingsolver, *The Lacuna: A Novel*, 2009
Ann Littlewood, *Did Not Survive*, 2010
Yann Martel, *Life of Pi*, 2001

64

JENNIFER HAIGH

Faith

(New York: Random House, 2011)

Story type: Religious
Subject(s): Catholicism; Sexual abuse; Family sagas
Major character(s): Shelia McGann, Sister (of Art); Arthur "Art" Breen, Religious (priest), Crime Suspect
Time period(s): 21st century; 2000s (2002)
Locale(s): Boston, Massachusetts

Summary: In *The Land of Painted Caves*, author Jean Auel concludes the saga of Cro-Magnon woman Ayla and her experiences in prehistoric France. Ayla and her mate, Jondalar, have produced a daughter and have joined a clan of healers. As Ayla trains to be a shaman, she makes several discoveries that broaden her way of thinking. In painted caves she learns the beauty of art. After consuming a mind-altering plant, she formulates the notion of committed love. Dangers abound in their Ice Age world, and Ayla and Jondalar must deal with fierce beasts and natural disasters to ensure the survival of their young family. *The Land of Painted Caves* is the sixth book in the Earth's Children series.

Where it's reviewed:
Booklist, April 1, 2011, page 24
Kirkus Reviews, March 15, 2011, page 444
Library Journal, December 2010, page 84

Other books by the same author:
The Condition, 2008
Baker Towers, 2005
Mrs. Kimble, 2003

Other books you might like:
Simon Mawer, *The Glass Room*, 2009
Sue Miller, *The Lake Shore Limited*, 2010
Rose Tremain, *Trespass*, 2010
Adriana Trigiani, *Very Valentine: A Novel*, 2009
Sarah Woodhouse, *My Summer with Julia*, 2000

65

BARBARA HAMBLY

The Shirt on His Back

(London: Severn House Publishers, 2011)

Series: Benjamin January Series. Book 10
Subject(s): Detective fiction; Murder; Western fiction
Major character(s): Benjamin January, Detective, Doctor, Musician
Time period(s): 19th century
Locale(s): United States

Summary: Former slave Benjamin January returns for his tenth investigative escapade in Barbara Hambly's *The Shirt on His Back*. Benjamin desperately needs to escape his native New Orleans for a little getaway, and the infamous Mountain Rendezvous—a month of parties with fur trappers, hunters, and the like—seems the perfect escape. But shortly after the festivities begin, a

body is discovered, and it's up to Benjamin to harness his considerable talents and find the person responsible.

Where it's reviewed:
Booklist, May 1, 2011, page 38
Publishers Weekly, April 25, 2011, page 119

Other books by the same author:
Blood Maidens, 2011
Dead and Buried, 2010
Homeland, 2009
Patriot Hearts: A Novel of the Founding Mothers, 2007
Renfield: Slave of Dracula, 2006

Other books you might like:
Barbara Hamilton, *The Ninth Daughter*, 2009
Laurie R. King, *Pirate King*, 2011
Anne Perry, *Treason at Lisson Grove*, 2011
Charles Todd, *A Bitter Truth*, 2011
Jacqueline Winspear, *A Lesson in Secrets*, 2010

66

STEVE HAMILTON

Misery Bay

(New York: Minotaur Books, 2011)

Series: Alex McKnight Series. Book 8
Story type: Contemporary
Subject(s): Detective fiction; Murder; Suspense
Major character(s): Alex McKnight, Detective
Time period(s): 21st century; 2010s
Locale(s): Paradise, Michigan

Summary: In the icy waters of Lake Superior, a man commits suicide by hanging himself from a tree. Investigator Alex McKnight thinks the death is a self-inflicted act, but the more he learns of the lurid details surrounding the young man's life and death, the more he begins to suspect foul play. *Misery Bay* is the eighth novel in Steve Hamilton's Alex McKnight mystery series.

Where it's reviewed:
Booklist, May 1, 2011, page 33
Publishers Weekly, April 4, 2011, page 33

Other books by the same author:
Lock Artist, 2010
A Stolen Season, 2006
Ice Run, 2004
Blood is the Sky, 2003
North of Nowhere, 2002

Other books you might like:
Lawrence Block, *A Drop of the Hard Stuff*, 2010
C.J. Box, *Cold Wind*, 2010
Tana French, *Faithful Place*, 2011
Jo Nesbo, *The Snowman*, 2011
John Sandford, *Buried Prey*, 2011

67

KRISTIN HANNAH

Night Road

(New York: Macmillan, 2011)

Story type: Coming-of-Age; Psychological
Subject(s): Foster children; Family relations; Parenthood
Major character(s): Jude Farraday, Mother; Mia Farraday, Daughter (of Jude), Twin (of Zach); Zach Farraday, Son (of Jude), Twin (of Mia); Lexi Baill, Foster Child; Eva Lang, Aunt (of Lexi)
Time period(s): 21st century; 2010s
Locale(s): Port George, Washington

Summary: In *Night Road* by Kristin Hannah, Jude Farraday has no idea that the new student her twin son and daughter have befriended is about to shatter their world. Lexi Baill has come to Port George, Washington, to live with a long-lost aunt after a stint in foster care. Her classmate, Mia Farraday, invites Lexi home where she is welcomed by Lexi's mother. Their new friendship is complicated by a romance that develops between Lexi and Mia's twin, Zach. With high school graduation and college on the horizon, Jude hopes her children will stay sensible and safe. But one night the three teenagers make a disastrous choice beyond Jude's control.

Where it's reviewed:
Library Journal, Feb 1, 2011, page 53
Publishers Weekly, Jan 3, 2011, page 30

Other books by the same author:
Winter Garden, 2010
True Colors, 2009
Firefly Lane, 2008
Magic Hour, 2006
Things We Do For Love, 2004

Other books you might like:
Ann Brashares, *Sisterhood Everlasting*, 2011
Barbara Delinsky, *Escape*, 2011
Dorothea Benton Frank, *Folly Beach*, 2010
Mary Alice Monroe, *The Butterfly's Daughter*, 2011
Jeannette Walls, *Half Broke Horses: A True-Life Novel*, 2009

68

CHAD HARBACH

The Art of Fielding

(New York: Little, Brown and Company, 2011)

Story type: Literary
Subject(s): Baseball; College environment; Romances (Fiction)
Major character(s): Henry Skrimshander, Baseball Player, Student—College; Owen Dunne, Baseball Player, Roommate (of Henry), Homosexual; Guert Affenlight, Administrator (college president), Single Father (to Pella); Pella Affenlight, Daughter (of Guert), Divorced Person; Mike Schwartz, Baseball Player, Friend (of Henry)

Time period(s): 21st century; 2010s
Locale(s): Wisconsin, United States

Summary: *The Art of Fielding* is a novel from debut author Chad Harbach. College shortstop Henry Skrimshander seems poised to start a major league baseball career following his graduation from Westish College, but one bad play leads to disastrous results for five individuals. Henry's time at the quaint Wisconsin school is coming to a close, but a crisis of self-doubt might prevent him from achieving the goals he's always dreamed of. College president and longtime bachelor, Guert Affenlight, has fallen madly in love with little regard to the consequences. Henry's best friend and team captain, Mike Schwartz, has devoted too much time to Henry's future and not enough to his own, while Henry's gay roommate, Owen Dunne, is nursing an injury and a dangerous affair. Meanwhile, Guert's adult daughter Pella has returned to Westish after a heartbreaking divorce and she has her sights set on two baseball players. First novel.

Where it's reviewed:
Publishers Weekly, July 25, 2011, page 28

Other books you might like:
Louis Begley, *Matters of Honor*, 2007
Mark Harris, *The Southpaw*, 1953
Sam Lipsyte, *The Ask*, 2010
Micah Nathan, *Losing Graceland*, 2011
Justin Torres, *We the Animals*, 2011

69

BETH HARBISON

Always Something There to Remind Me

(New York: St. Martin's Press, 2011)

Story type: Romance
Subject(s): Romances (Fiction); Love; Psychology
Major character(s): Erin Edwards, Young Woman; Nate Lawson, Boyfriend (of Erin, former)
Time period(s): 21st century; 2010s
Locale(s): United States

Summary: In *Always Something There to Remind Me* by Beth Harbison, Erin Edwards was sure that her first love would be her only love. She planned on spending the rest of her life with Nate Lawson. But their relationship came to an abrupt end when Erin did something Nate couldn't forgive. Twenty years later, Erin is a successful single mother in love with a wonderful guy. She is completely over Nate—or is she? When her boyfriend proposes, Erin can only think of Nate and the once-in-a-lifetime relationship they shared. As memories of the past invade Erin's thoughts, she must make important decisions about her future.

Where it's reviewed:
Library Journal, May 1, 2011, page 78
Library Journal, February 15, 2011, page 85
Publishers Weekly, March 7, 2011, page 40

Other books by the same author:
Thin, Rich, Pretty, 2010

Hope in a Jar, 2009
Secrets of a Shoe Addict, 2008
Shoe Addicts Anonymous, 2007
Drive Me Wild, 2002

Other books you might like:
Richard Paul Evans, *Grace*, 2008
Marian Keyes, *The Brightest Star in the Sky*, 2009
Nora Roberts, *Reunion*, 2004
Adriana Trigiani, *The Queen of the Big Time*, 2004
Lauren Weisberger, *Chasing Harry Winston*, 2008

70

DEBORAH HARKNESS

A Discovery of Witches

(New York: Viking, 2011)

Story type: Paranormal; Vampire Story
Subject(s): Witchcraft; Witches; Vampires
Major character(s): Diana Bishop, Historian, Witch; Matthew Clairmont, Vampire
Locale(s): England

Summary: *A Discovery of Witches* is a novel by author Deborah Harkness. In this story, Harkness tells the story of Diana Bishop, a Yale historian who has come to Oxford to complete research on the ancient art of alchemy. There she stumbles upon a mysterious document that appears to have special powers. Soon she finds herself dodging the attentions of all sorts of demonic creatures, and she must turn to a vampire named Matthew Clairmont for protection. Diana soon learns that she has secrets of her own to protect, however, as she learns more about her family's heritage.

Where it's reviewed:
Booklist, December 1, 2010, page 36
Chatelaine, February 2011, page 110
Library Journal, December 2010, page 102
Publishers Weekly, November 8, 2010, page 40
USA Today, March 3, 2011, page 03D

Other books you might like:
Catherine Coulter, *Wizard's Daughter*, 2007
Jennifer Crusie, *The Unfortunate Miss Fortunes*, 2007
Elizabeth Kostova, *The Historian*, 2005
Karen Marie Moning, *Shadowfever*, 2011
Lauren Willig, *The Secret History of the Pink Carnation*, 2004

71

CHARLAINE HARRIS

Dead Reckoning

(New York: Ace Books, 2011)

Series: Sookie Stackhouse Series. Book 11
Subject(s): Vampires; Southern United States; Fires
Major character(s): Sookie Stackhouse, Waiter/Waitress, Telepath; Eric Northman, Vampire; Sam Merlotte, Shape-Shifter

Time period(s): 21st century; 2010s
Locale(s): Bon Temps, Louisiana

Summary: Sookie Stackhouse, Eric Northman, and the whole gang return in *Dead Reckoning*, the 11th novel in Charlaine Harris's Sookie Stackhouse series. This outing finds Merlotte's, the bar where Sookie works, burned to ash—creating a new mystery for the waitress to solve. As she looks into the possible arson, which she suspects may have something to do with the bar owner being a shape-shifter, Sookie is sucked into another dangerous situation: her boyfriend Eric is planning to kill his vampire master.

Where it's reviewed:
Booklist, May 1, 2011, page 18

Other books by the same author:
Dead in the Family, 2010
Dead and Gone, 2009
From Dead to Worse, 2008
All Together Dead, 2007
Definitely Dead, 2006

Other books you might like:
MaryJanice Davidson, *Undead and Undermined*, 2011
Carolyn Haines, *Bones of a Feather*, 2011
Molly Harper, *How to Flirt with a Naked Werewolf*, 2011
Victoria Laurie, *Ghouls Just Haunt to Have Fun*, March 3, 2009
Chloe Neill, *Some Girls Bite*, 2009

72

CAROLYN G. HART

Dead by Midnight

(New York: William Morrow, 2010)

Series: Death on Demand Series. Book 21
Subject(s): Detective fiction; Murder; Books
Major character(s): Annie Darling, Store Owner (bookseller), Detective—Amateur; Pat Merridew, Crime Victim; Glen Jamison, Crime Victim; Max, Spouse (of Annie)
Time period(s): 21st century; 2010s
Locale(s): Broward's Rock, South Carolina

Summary: Annie Darling is a part-time amateur sleuth and full-time proprietress of the Death on Demand bookstore. After one of her employees, Pat Merrdiew, commits suicide, Annie immediately suspects foul play. She noses around Pat's other job at a local law firm for answers—but when Pat's old boss at the firm is shot and killed, Annie now has two murders to solve. *Dead by Midnight* is the 21st book in Carolyn G. Hart's Death on Demand series.

Where it's reviewed:
Booklist, Feb 15, 2011, page 54
Publishers Weekly, Feb 7, 2011, page 38

Other books by the same author:
Ghost in Trouble, 2010
Laughed 'til He Died, 2010
Dare to Die, 2009
Merry Merry Ghost, 2009

Death Walked In, 2008

Other books you might like:
Susan Wittig Albert, *Mourning Gloria*, 2011
Joanne Fluke, *Devil's Food Cake Murder*, 2011
Sarah Graves, *Knockdown*, 2011
Hannah Reed, *Mind Your Own Beeswax*, 2011
Elaine Viets, *Pumped for Murder: A Dead-End Job Mystery*, 2011

73

ELEANOR HENDERSON

Ten Thousand Saints

(New York: Ecco, 2011)

Story type: Literary
Subject(s): Drug abuse; Teenage parents; Pregnancy
Major character(s): Jude Keffy-Horn, 16-Year-Old; Eliza Urbanski, Pregnant Teenager
Time period(s): 20th century; 1980s
Locale(s): Vermont, United States

Summary: *Ten Thousand Saints* is a debut novel from author Eleanor Henderson. As teenagers in Vermont during the 1980s, Teddy and Jude are best friends, obsessed with doing drugs and the idea of moving to New York City someday. An overdose claims Teddy's life, and nearly kills Jude, too, leaving the latter more intent than ever to fulfill their dream of living in Manhattan. Before Teddy's death, his one sexual encounter with Eliza resulted in her pregnancy, causing Jude to feel the responsibility to look after her. Jude and Eliza befriend Teddy's older brother, Johnny, a punk musician with a strong stance against drug use. Together, the three teens navigate the challenges of the 80s and the complex relationships with their eccentric parents as they try to break free from their small New England town. First novel.

Where it's reviewed:
Booklist, May 1, 2011, page 68
New York Times Book Review, June 19, 2011, page 1(L)
The New Yorker, July 11, 2011, page 95
Publishers Weekly, February 7, 2011, page 32

Other books you might like:
Francesca Lia Block, *Weetzie Bat Series*, 1989
Douglas Coupland, *Hey Nostradamus!: A Novel*, 2003
Meg Mitchell Moore, *The Arrivals*, 2011
Dana Spiotta, *Stone Arabia*, 2011
Jean Thompson, *The Year We Left Home*, 2010

74

JACK HIGGINS

Judas Gate

(New York: G. P. Putnam's Sons, 2010)

Story type: Military
Subject(s): Wars; Suspense; Betrayal
Major character(s): Sean Dillon, Agent

Time period(s): 21st century; 2010s
Locale(s): Afghanistan; England; United States

Summary: World-renowned author Jack Higgins presents another suspenseful thriller in *The Judas Gate*. During a battle in Afghanistan, a group of American soldiers and British medical aids are killed. A tape recording documenting the entire massacre makes its way into the hands of British and American government officials. The chatter on the recording picks up the voices of the Afghani Taliban responsible for the murders, but government agents are shocked to hear that the Taliban commander has an Irish accent. Horrified that the vicious act could be the doing of one of their own men, the U.S. and British governments assign Sean Dillon the task of locating the traitor and bringing him to justice.

Where it's reviewed:
Publishers Weekly, Nov 29, 2010, page 30

Other books by the same author:
Darker Place, 2009
Wolf at the Door, 2009
Rough Justice, 2008
Killing Ground, 2007
Without Mercy, 2005

Other books you might like:
Alex Berenson, *Secret Soldier*, 2011
Clive Cussler, *The Kingdom*, 2010
Cynthia Harrod-Eagles, *The Abyss*, 1995
Eric Van Lustbader, *Blood Trust*, 2011
Patrick Robinson, *The Delta Solution*, 2011

75

ELIN HILDERBRAND

Silver Girl

(New York: Reagan Arthur Books, 2011)

Story type: Contemporary
Subject(s): Friendship; Forgiveness; Women
Major character(s): Meredith Martin Delinn, Friend (of Connie); Constance "Connie" Flute, Friend (of Meredith); Toby, Brother (of Connie)
Time period(s): 21st century; 2010s
Locale(s): Nantucket Island, Massachusetts

Summary: Elin Hilderbrand's *Silver Girl* takes place on Nantucket Island during a single fateful summer that changes two friends' lives forever. Meredith Martin Delinn is still reeling from her husband's deceptions and the shady business dealings that have ended both his career and, now, his marriage. Meredith retreats to Nantucket with old friend Connie Flute, who has been dealing with personal turmoil of her own. As the two women attempt to put together the pieces of their shattered lives, new opportunities for second chances present themselves, and the women are empowered to make the choices that will move them toward forgiveness, peace, and wholeness.

Other books you might like:
Elizabeth Berg, *Once Upon a Time There Was You*, 2011
Anna Maxted, *Rich Again*, 2010

J. Courtney Sullivan, *Maine*, 2011
Nancy Thayer, *Heat Wave*, 2011
Jennifer Weiner, *Then Came You*, 2011

76

CATHY HOLTON

Summer in the South

(New York: Ballantine Books, 2011)

Story type: Contemporary
Subject(s): Family; Family history; Writers
Major character(s): Ava Drabrowski, Writer; Will, Friend (of Ava); Jake, Cousin (of Will)
Time period(s): 21st century; 2010s
Locale(s): Tennessee, United States

Summary: In Cathy Holton's *Summer in the South*, writer Ava Drabrowski has just lost her mother and decides to spend the season in Tennessee with her old friend Will's aging aunts. She wants to take the opportunity to finally start her novel, but as she gets to know Will's family, she is drawn into their rich history. Only one family member—Will's cousin Jake—seems to want to share the dark details of the family's past, and Ava finds herself undeniably attracted to him. But as she learns the secrets buried in the family history, Ava is suddenly forced to confront her own past.

Where it's reviewed:
Booklist, June 1, 2011, page 37
Publishers Weekly, February 7, 2011, page 32

Other books by the same author:
The Fixer Upper, 2009
Deep Dish, 2008
Savannah Breeze, 2006
Hissy Fit, 2004
Little Bitty Lies, 2003

Other books you might like:
Mary Kay Andrews, *Summer Rental*, 2011
Claire Cook, *Best Staged Plans*, 2011
Dorothea Benton Frank, *Folly Beach*, 2010
Anne Rivers Siddons, *Burnt Mountain*, 2011
Susan Straight, *Take One Candle, Light a Room*, 2010

77

J.A. JANCE

Fatal Error

(New York: Simon and Schuster, 2011)

Series: Ali Reynolds Series. Book 6
Subject(s): Detective fiction; Law enforcement; Murder
Major character(s): Ali Reynolds, Detective—Private, Police Officer; Brenda Riley, Journalist (former)
Time period(s): 21st century
Locale(s): Arizona, United States

Summary: *Fatal Error* is a novel written by mystery author J.A. Jance, who is also the author of *Cruel Intent* and *Queen of the Night*. Ali Reynolds's dreams of

becoming a law-enforcement official seem short-lived when, upon completing police academy training, she is laid off by her department. Desperate to stay in the game, not to mention pay her bills, Ali accepts a private assignment from Brenda Riley, a former television reporter whose fiance has gone missing. Ali finds Brenda's fiance a little too late, because a killer has gotten to him first. Now Ali has even more of a mystery on her hands as she tries to get to the bottom of who killed him, and whether or not that person will strike again.

Where it's reviewed:
Booklist, December 15, 2010, page 22
Library Journal, February 1, 2011, page 47
Publishers Weekly, November 29, 2010, page 27

Other books by the same author:
Betrayal of Trust, 2011
Queen of the Night, 2010
Fire and Ice, 2009
Trial by Fire, 2009
Cruel Intent, 2008

Other books you might like:
Mary Higgins Clark, *Just Take My Heart*, 2009
Chris Jordan, *Trapped*, 2007
Stefan Petrucha, *Lurker*, 2007
Bill Pronzini, *Savages: A Nameless Detective Novel*, July 10, 2007
Kate White, *Hush*, 2010

78

SARAH JIO

The Violets of March
(New York: Plume Publishing, 2011)

Story type: Contemporary
Subject(s): Writers; Marriage; Family
Major character(s): Emily Wilson, Writer, Niece (of Aunt Bee); Aunt Bee, Aunt (of Emily)
Locale(s): Bainbridge Island, Washington

Summary: *The Violets of March* is the debut novel for author Sarah Jio. Emily Wilson was once a best-selling novelist whose writing career was something to be marveled at. That was a decade ago, however, and now she is beginning to lose it all as she struggles to come up with another novel and her husband divorces her. In an effort to help Emily forget her troubles, her Aunt Bee asks her to vacation at Bee's beach cottage on Bainbridge Island in Washington. As Emily begins to heal, she finds an old journal kept during the 1940s, and begins to learn a little bit more about whom she is and where she came from. First novel.

Where it's reviewed:
Publishers Weekly, March 28, 2011, page 33
Redbook, May 2011, page 194

Other books by the same author:
The Bungalow, 2011

Other books you might like:
Elizabeth Bass, *Miss You Most of All*, 2011
Cathy Holton, *Summer in the South*, 2011
Leah Stewart, *Husband and Wife: A Novel*, 2010

Irving Weinman, *Wolf Tones*, 2009
Austin McGiffert Wright, *Tony and Susan*, 2011

79

CRAIG JOHNSON

Hell is Empty
(New York: Viking, 2011)

Series: Sheriff Walt Longmire Series. Book 7
Story type: Western
Subject(s): Murder; Adventure; Criminals
Major character(s): Walt Longmire, Police Officer (sheriff); Raynaud Shade, Murderer; White Buffalo, Crime Victim
Time period(s): 21st century; 2010s
Locale(s): Absaroka County, Wyoming

Summary: Raynaud Shade has confessed that he murdered a young boy a decade earlier. After he is put away, Shade and a group of fellow inmates manage a harrowing escape into Wyoming's Cloud Peak Wilderness Area. Fast on their trail is Sheriff Walt Longmire, who will stop at nothing to track down Shade and the body of the murdered boy. Craig Johnson's *Hell Is Empty* is the seventh book in the Walt Longmire Mysteries series.

Where it's reviewed:
Booklist, April 1, 2011, page 31
Publishers Weekly, April 25, 2011, page 109

Other books by the same author:
Junkyard Dog, 2010
Dark Horse, 2009
Another Man's Mocassins, 2008
Kindness goes Unpunished, 2007
Death without Company, 2006

Other books you might like:
Nevada Barr, *Borderline*, 2009
Steve Hamilton, *Misery Bay*, 2011
Jonathon Kellerman, *Mystery*, 2011
Marcia Muller, *Coming Back*, 2010
Dana Stabenow, *Though Not Dead*, 2011

80

WYNONNA JUDD

Restless Heart
(New York: New American Library, 2011)

Subject(s): Romances (Fiction); Country music; Entertainment industry
Major character(s): Destiny Hart, Singer, Waiter/Waitress, Lover (of Seth); Seth Caldwell, Lover (of Destiny)
Time period(s): 21st century; 2010s
Locale(s): Nashville, Tennessee

Summary: *Restless Heart* is the debut novel from country singer Wynonna Judd. When Destiny Hart set out from her small Kentucky town to make it big as a country western singer in Nashville, she never imagined that she would get a job working at the famous Back in the

Saddle saloon. Unfortunately Destiny isn't singing at the bar, but is employed as a waitress. Everyone back in her hometown thinks that she is already well on her way to becoming a famous singer, and Destiny isn't about to tell them the truth. Then she finally gets her chance to sing onstage, on the same evening that her former lover Seth Caldwell is in town. Destiny and Seth begin to fall in love again but as Destiny's star begins to rise, can Seth cope with her sudden fame? First novel.

Where it's reviewed:
Library Journal, January 2011, page 5
Publishers Weekly, February 14, 2011, page 52

Other books you might like:
Susan Anderson, *Coming Undone*, 2010
Elizabeth Lowell, *Forget Me Not*, 1984
LaVyrle Spencer, *Small Town Girl*, 1997
Christine Townsend, *Sweet Desire*, 2004

81

JONATHAN KELLERMAN

Mystery
(New York: Ballantine Books, 2010)

Series: Alex Delaware Series. Book 26
Story type: Mystery
Subject(s): Mystery; Psychology; Crime
Major character(s): Alex Delaware, Psychologist; Robin Castagna, Spouse (of Alex); Milo Sturgis, Detective—Police; Mystery, Prostitute; Markham McReynolds, Client (of Mystery)
Time period(s): 21st century; 2010s
Locale(s): Los Angeles, California

Summary: In *Mystery* by Jonathan Kellerman, psychologist Alex Delaware and his wife, Robin, visit the Fauborg Hotel on its last night of operation to have drinks and reminisce. Among the downhearted customers is a young woman who sits alone, apparently waiting for someone who never arrives. In a few days, Alex's friend Milo Sturgis of the LAPD calls on Alex to help with a murder case. The savagely murdered victim is the woman from the Fauborg, whose identity remains a mystery until an unexpected lead surfaces. The implication of a powerful family in the crime puts Alex and Milo in danger. *Mystery* is the 26th book in the Alex Delaware series.

Where it's reviewed:
Booklist, Jan 1, 2011, page 49
Library Journal, Feb 1, 2011, page 54
Publishers Weekly, Feb 14, 2011, page 37

Other books by the same author:
Deception, 2010
Evidence, 2009
Compulsion, 2008
Bones, 2007
Obsession, 2007

Other books you might like:
Charles Cumming, *The Trinity Six*, 2011
Clive Cussler, *The Kingdom*, 2010
Jeffery Deaver, *Edge: A Novel*, 2010

Joseph Finder, *Buried Secrets*, 2010
Steve Hamilton, *Misery Bay*, 2011

82

SHERRILYN KENYON

Retribution
(New York: St. Martin's Press, 2011)

Series: Dark-Hunter Series. Book 20
Story type: Contemporary - Fantasy; Paranormal
Subject(s): Fantasy; Parapsychology; Romances (Fiction)
Major character(s): William Jessup Brady, Gunfighter (Dark-Hunter); Abigail Yager, Adoptee (vampire family)
Time period(s): 21st century; 2010s
Locale(s): New Orleans, Louisiana

Summary: In *Retribution* by Sherrilyn Kenyon, the paths of a woman raised among vampires and a Dark-Hunter intersect with grave implications for both of their races. Abigail Yager, who has lived with vampires since she was a child, has been taught to blame Jessup Brady for the deaths of her family members. Though Jess is an avowed Dark-Hunter who has killed many, he knows that Abigail's parents are not among his victims. As the Dark-Hunter chases down vampires, the surrogate vampire pursues the Dark-Hunter—both believing that their causes are just. Meanwhile, a newly surfaced evil threatens them all. *Retribution* is the 20th book in the Dark-Hunter series.

Where it's reviewed:
Library Journal, March 15, 2011, page 100

Other books by the same author:
Born of Shadows, 2011
Invincible, 2011
Infinity: Chronicles of Nick, 2010
Night Embrace, 2010
No Mercy, 2010

Other books you might like:
Kelley Armstrong, *Spell Bound*, 2011
Christine Feehan, *Dark Predator*, 2011
Laurell K. Hamilton, *Hit List*, 2011
Kim Harrison, *Pale Demon*, 2011
Linda Howard, *Prey*, 2011

83

KARLEEN KOEN

Before Versailles
(New York: Crown, 2011)

Subject(s): French (European people); Scandals; Royalty
Major character(s): Louis XIV, Royalty (King of France); Henriette, Lover (of Louis); Nicolas Fouquet, Government Official (Minister of Finance)
Time period(s): 17th century
Locale(s): France

Summary: In *Before Versailles: A Novel of Louis XIV*, author Karleen Koen offers a fictionalized account of the legendary king's early years. At the tender age of 22,

Louis takes the helm as leader of France. He also takes Henriette, his brother's wife, as his lover, establishing a reputation for scandal that will follow him throughout his life. As he carries on his affair with Henriette, Louis must contend with an array of adversaries who wish to usurp his power and discredit him at every turn.

Where it's reviewed:
Booklist, May 15, 2011, page 23
Library Journal, April 1, 2011, page 82
Publishers Weekly, March 7, 2011, page 40

Other books by the same author:
Dark Angels, 2006
Now Face to Face, 1996
Through a Glass Darkly, 1986

Other books you might like:
Margaret George, *Elizabeth I*, 2011
Philippa Gregory, *The Red Queen*, 2010
Michelle Moran, *Madame Tussaud: A Novel of the French Revolution*, 2011
Sharon Kay Penman, *Lionheart*, 2011
Anne Perry, *Treason at Lisson Grove*, 2011

84

DEAN KOONTZ

What the Night Knows

(New York: Bantam, 2011)

Subject(s): Ghosts; Murder; Mystery
Major character(s): John Calvino, Investigator, Father, Spouse
Time period(s): 21st century; 2010s

Summary: In Dean Koontz's *What the Night Knows: A Novel*, John Calvino is about to discover that, sometimes, even death cannot stand between a murderer and his desire for blood. When John was a child, he ended the life of a serial murderer who killed his family. Years later, John is a detective with a family of his own. He soon learns that more families are being murdered, and the killings are nearly identical to the ones John witnessed as a young boy. Now, John fears for his family's safety and wonders if the man he killed so many years ago has actually returned to try to finish the job.

Where it's reviewed:
Booklist, November 15, 2010, page 27
Kirkus Reviews, December 1, 2010, page 1180
Library Journal, November 15, 2010, page 60
Publishers Weekly, October 25, 2010, page 26

Other books by the same author:
Lost Souls, 2010
Breathless, 2009
Dead and Alive, 2009
Relentless, 2009
Your Heart Belongs to Me, 2008

Other books you might like:
Jim Butcher, *Storm Front*, 2000
Stephen King, *Duma Key*, 2008
Jeff Mariotte, *Missing White Girl*, 2007

John Saul, *Black Creek Crossing*, 2004
Carlene Thompson, *Last Whisper*, 2006

85

MICHAEL KORYTA

The Ridge

(New York: Little, Brown & Co., 2011)

Story type: Horror
Subject(s): Good and evil; Animals; Human-animal relationships
Major character(s): Kevin Kimble, Lawman (deputy sheriff); Audrey Clark, Businesswoman (owner of large-cat sanctuary), Animal Lover; Wyatt French, Lighthouse Keeper; Roy Darmus, Journalist
Time period(s): 21st century; 2010s
Locale(s): Blade Ridge, Kentucky

Summary: *The Ridge* by Michael Koryta focuses on a series of strange events that unfold in the wooded mountains of Kentucky. On Blade Ridge, far from the ocean, stands a wooden lighthouse built by Wyatt French, a local character. When Wyatt commits suicide at the lighthouse, deputy sheriff Kevin Kimble investigates the case, which seems to have ties to his own past. Not far from the site, Audrey Clark is moving dozens of lions, tigers, and other big cats to a refuge established by her late husband, who died on Blade Ridge. Audrey and Kevin suspect that a dark presence is at work in the forest—a suspicion that is confirmed by the cats' anxious behavior.

Where it's reviewed:
Booklist, May 15, 2011, page 21
Library Journal, June 1, 2011, page 90
New York Times Book Review, June 5, 2011, page 47(L).
Publishers Weekly, April 25, 2011, page 106

Other books by the same author:
The Cypress House, 2011
So Cold the River, 2010
The Silent Hour, 2009
Envy the Night, 2008
Tonight I Said Goodbye, 2004

Other books you might like:
John Connolly, *Bad Men*, 2004
Michael Gruber, *Night of the Jaguar*, 2006
Sara Gruen, *Ape House*, 2011
Carolyn Parkhurst, *The Dogs of Babel*, 2003
Stuart Woods, *Under the Lake*, 1987

86

JEN LANCASTER

If You Were Here

(New York: NAL Hardcover, 2011)

Story type: Contemporary; Humor
Subject(s): Home remodeling; Humor; Marriage

Major character(s): Mia, Writer, Spouse (of Mac); Mac, Spouse (of Mia)
Time period(s): 21st century; 2010s
Locale(s): Chicago, Illinois

Summary: Jen Lancaster's *If You Were Here* chronicles the home-renovating adventures of married couple Mia and Mac. After buying a house in the Chicago suburbs, Mia and Mac set out to renovate the lackluster property. They don't, however, plan on the series of disasters that await them—or the unforgettable people they will have to encounter in their quest to restore their dream house.

Where it's reviewed:
Booklist, March 15, 2011, page 15
Publishers Weekly, March 28, 2011, page 36

Other books you might like:
Jennifer Crusie, *Maybe This Time*, 2010
Nick Hornby, *Juliet, Naked*, 2009
Sophie Kinsella, *Remember Me?*, 2008
Chuck Palahniuk, *Tell-All*, 2010
Allison Pearson, *I Think I Love You*, 2011

87

ALICE LAPLANTE

Turn of Mind
(New York: Atlantic Monthly Press, 2011)

Story type: Psychological
Subject(s): Mental disorders; Murder; Crime
Major character(s): Jennifer White, Doctor, Crime Suspect; Amanda, Neighbor (of Jennifer), Crime Victim

Summary: *Turn of Mind* is a novel by author Alice LaPlante. In this book, LaPlante tells the story of Dr. Jennifer White, a once-brilliant orthopedic surgeon who now suffers from dementia. Despite her failing mind, Jennifer has occasional lucid days, and one day wakes up to discover herself as the primary suspect in the murder of her best friend and neighbor, Amanda. Yet how can Jennifer offer the police an alibi if she herself doesn't even know where she has been? LaPlante tells the story through Jennifer's voice as she attempts to lift the veil of dementia in order to clear her name. First novel.

Where it's reviewed:
Booklist, May 1, 2011, page 38
Library Journal, March 1, 2011, page 70
Publishers Weekly, May 9, 2011, page 31

Other books you might like:
Megan Abbott, *The End of Everything*, 2011
Alafair Burke, *Long Gone*, 2011
Jennifer Haigh, *Faith*, 2011
Rosamund Lupton, *Sister*, 2011
S.J. Watson, *Before I Go To Sleep*, 2011

88

DEBORAH LAWRENSON

The Lantern
(New York: HarperCollins, 2011)

Story type: Ghost Story
Subject(s): Mystery; Romances (Fiction); Murder
Major character(s): Eve, Lover (of Dom); Dom, Lover (of Eve)
Time period(s): 21st century; 2010s
Locale(s): Provence, France

Summary: *The Lantern* is a novel written by author Deborah Lawrenson. In it, the author tells the story of Eve, a woman who meets a lover named Dom. Dom immediately sweeps Eve off her feet, and they retreat to the countryside splendor of Provence, France. There, they purchase an old home with the intention of remodeling it back to its former glory. Meanwhile, a woman who lived generations before in that very same house begins telling her own story about her life in the old home. Soon Eve's life intermingles with the former owner's as she begins to unravel the mystery of the house and the horrible secrets that occurred there.

Where it's reviewed:
Booklist, July 1, 2011, page 25
Publishers Weekly, June 13, 2011, page 31

Other books by the same author:
The Moonbathers, 2008
Songs of Blue and Gold, 2008
The Art of Falling, 2005
Idle Chatter, 1995
Hot Gossip, 1994

Other books you might like:
Daphne du Maurier, *Rebecca*, 1938
Henry James, *The Turn of the Screw*, 1898
Serena Mackesy, *Hold My Hand*, 2008
Bernie McGill, *The Butterfly Cabinet*, 2011
Amanda Eyre Ward, *Close Your Eyes*, 2011

89

JOHN LE CARRE

Our Kind of Traitor
(New York: Viking Adult, 2010)

Subject(s): Mystery; Money; Crime
Major character(s): Perry Makepiece, Professor; Gail Perkins, Lawyer, Girlfriend (of Perry); Dmitri "Dima" Vladimirovich Krasnov, Businessman (money launderer)
Time period(s): 21st century; 2010s
Locale(s): Antigua and Barbuda

Summary: In *Our Kind of Traitor* by John Le Carre, Perry Makepiece, an Oxford professor, and his girlfriend Gail Perkins, a lawyer, are vacationing in Antigua where they meet and befriend Russian businessman Dmitri "Dima" Vladimirovich Krasnov, who turns out to be a famous Russian money launderer. Dima asks Perry to deliver a

message to MI6: He wants to defect from Russia. Perry and Gail are then immediately summoned for a debriefing when they get back to Oxford. Dima has information about certain British agents who were working with the Russian mob and using the money to save themselves during the collapse of the economy. The people who want to keep this information secret will stop at nothing to hide the truth, and now Dima, Perry, and Gail are all in grave danger.

Where it's reviewed:
Bookmarks, Nov/Dec 2010, page 46
Kirkus Reviews, August 15, 2010, page 753
Library Journal, September 1, 2010, page 102
Publishers Weekly, August 9, 2010, page 29

Other books by the same author:
A Most Wanted Man, 2008
The Mission Song, 2006
Absolute Friends, 2004
A Small Town in Germany, 2002
The Constant Gardener, 2000

Other books you might like:
Ted Allbeury, *Spirit of Liberty*, 2007
Len Deighton, *Funeral in Berlin*, 1965
Alan Furst, *Spies of the Balkans: A Novel*, 2010
Graham Greene, *Our Man in Havana*, 2007
Daniel Silva, *The Rembrandt Affair*, 2010

90

CAVANAUGH LEE

Save as Draft

(New York: Simon and Schuster, 2011)

Story type: Contemporary
Subject(s): Women; Interpersonal relations; Computers
Major character(s): Peter, Boyfriend (of Izzy); Izzy Chin, Girlfriend (of Peter), Lover (of Martin); Martin, Lover (of Izzy)
Time period(s): 21st century; 2010s

Summary: *Save As Draft* is a novel written by Cavanaugh Lee. In this book, the author tells the story of a relationship between a woman and her best friend. When Izzy Chin finally learns of her friend Peter's feelings for her, she breaks up with Martin, the man she is seeing, and Peter and Izzy begin a fast romance. Yet Peter is a workaholic whose job gets in the way of the relationship. As Peter works harder and harder, Izzy returns to Martin's arms. Lee tells the story through the format of electronic mail, text messaging, instant messaging, and other electronic correspondence.

Where it's reviewed:
Publishers Weekly, December 20, 2010, page 31

Other books you might like:
Alison Espach, *The Adults*, 2011
Stephanie Fletcher, *E-Mail: A Love Story*, 1996
Xiaolu Guo, *A Concise Chinese-English Dictionary for Lovers*, 2007
David Levithan, *The Lover's Dictionary*, 2011
Gary Shteyngart, *Super Sad True Love Story*, 2010

91

LINDA FRANCIS LEE

Emily and Einstein

(New York: St. Martin's Press, 2011)

Story type: Contemporary
Subject(s): Dogs; Deception; Marriage
Major character(s): Emily Barlow, Widow(er); Einstein, Dog
Time period(s): 21st century; 2010s
Locale(s): New York, New York

Summary: Emily and Sandy seem to have it all: a loving marriage, successful careers, a prosperous bank account. But whe n Sandy is killed in a car accident, Emily's world turns upside down. She's on the brink of being kicked out of her Upper West Side apartment and it turns out that Sandy has been living a life of deception. Determined to find out the truth about her deceased husband, Emily begins an investigation into his life, nudged along by her adopted pup, Einstein. As Emily struggles to make sense of the past and figure out the future, she can't ignore the sense that Einstein is sending her messages that might be coming from beyond the grave.

Where it's reviewed:
Booklist, February 1, 2011, page 27
People, March 14, 2011, page 51
Publishers Weekly, December 20, 2010, page 27

Other books by the same author:
The Ex-Debutante, 2008
The Devil in the Junior League, 2006
The Wedding Diaries, 2003
The Ways of Grace, 2002
Nightingale's Gate, 2001

Other books you might like:
Ann Brashares, *My Name Is Memory*, 2010
W. Bruce Cameron, *A Dog's Purpose*, 2010
Andrew Davidson, *The Gargoyle*, 2008
M.J. Rose, *The Reincarnationist*, 2007
Suzanne Weyn, *Reincarnation*, 2008

92

DONNA LEON

Drawing Conclusions

(New York: Atlantic Monthly Press, 2011)

Series: Guido Brunetti Series. Book 20
Subject(s): Detective fiction; Crime; Murder
Major character(s): Guido Brunetti, Detective—Police; Costanza Altavilla, Widow(er)
Locale(s): Venice, Italy

Summary: *Drawing Conclusions* is the 20th novel in author Donna Leon's detective series featuring Commissario Guido Brunetti. When a widow is found dead in her apartment, Venice's medical examiner rules the cause of death to be a heart attack. Brunetti, however, is not so sure. After finding clothing of several different sizes in

the widow's closet and interviewing neighbors who knew her, Brunetti soon learns that the widow Costanza Altavilla was operating a safe haven for battered women. Was the murderer a husband or lover enraged by Altavilla's interference, or could it have been one of the women she sheltered? Brunetti isn't sure, but he's ready to get to the bottom of the mystery.

Where it's reviewed:
Library Journal, Feb 15, 2011, page 103(1).
New York Times Book Review, April 10, 2011, page 23(L)
Publishers Weekly, Feb 14, 2011, page 40

Other books by the same author:
A Question of Belief, 2010
About Face, 2009
The Girl of His Dreams, 2008
Suffer the Little Children, 2007
Through a Glass, Darkly, 2006

Other books you might like:
David Baldacci, *The Sixth Man*, 2011
Harlan Coben, *The Woods*, 2007
Justin Cronin, *The Passage*, 2010
Stieg Larsson, *The Girl with the Dragon Tattoo*, 2008
Rosamund Lupton, *Sister*, 2011

93

LAURA LIPPMAN

I'd Know You Anywhere

(New York: HarperCollins, 2011)

Subject(s): Prisoners; Rape; Murder
Major character(s): Eliza Benedict, Crime Victim, Spouse, Mother; Walter Bowman, Kidnapper, Prisoner, Murderer
Time period(s): 21st century; 2010s
Locale(s): Washington, District of Columbia

Summary: In Laura Lippman's *I'd Know You Anywhere*, housewife Eliza Benedict moves with her husband, daughter, and son from England back to her hometown of Washington, D.C. One day she receives a letter that shakes her world. It's from Walter Bowman, the man who kidnapped her when she was 15 years old. Eliza remembers the horrific experience, and the memories bring back the pain she's kept hidden deep inside for more than two decades. Bowman, a rapist and murderer, held her hostage but eventually set her free. Others weren't so lucky. Now he's contacted her just weeks before he is set to be put to death for his crimes. At first Eliza feels fear and tries to ignore the letter. But then her curiosity gets the best of her: Why did he let her live all those years ago? She makes the fateful decision to contact him.

Where it's reviewed:
Booklist, May 1, 2010, page 30
New York Times Book Review, September 19, 2010, page 23
O, The Oprah Magazine, September 2010, page 160
People, August 30, 2010, page 45
Publishers Weekly, August 2, 2010, page 31

Other books by the same author:
Girl in the Green Raincoat, 2011
Life Sentences, 2009
Another Thing to Fall, 2008
Hardly Knew Her, 2008
What the Dead Know, 2008
The Power of Three, 2005
Every Secret Thing, 2003

Other books you might like:
Kate Atkinson, *When Will There Be Good News?: A Novel*, 2008
Mary Higgins Clark, *I'll Walk Alone*, 2011
Emma Donoghue, *Room*, 2010
Gillian Flynn, *Dark Places*, 2009
Tana French, *Faithful Place*, 2011
Iris Johansen, *Eve*, 2011
Lesley Kagen, *Whistling in the Dark*, 2007
Stewart O'Nan, *Snow Angels: A Novel*, 1994
Jodi Picoult, *Vanishing Acts*, 2005

94

LAURA LIPPMAN

The Most Dangerous Thing

(New York: William Morrow, 2011)

Story type: Mystery
Subject(s): Death; Mystery; Friendship
Major character(s): Gordon Halloran, Friend (of Gwen and Mickey), Accident Victim; Mickey Wickham, Friend (of Gordon and Gwen); Gwen Robison, Friend (of Gordon and Mickey)
Time period(s): 20th century; (1970s); 21st century; 2010s
Locale(s): Baltimore, Maryland

Summary: *The Most Dangerous Thing* by Laura Lippman is about a dark mystery that reunites a group of friends after many years. The story begins in 1977, when a group of five friends begin spending time together. Among these friends are Gordon Halloran, Gwen Robison, and Mickey Wickham. They share many good times until a mysterious act of violence takes place in their forest hideaway. Much later, as adults, the group is drawn together again by the bizarre story of Gordon's shocking death. The friends reunite to explore the past and try to understand the present in *The Most Dangerous Thing*.

Where it's reviewed:
Booklist, June 1, 2011, page 42
Library Journal, July 2011, page 72
Library Journal, March 15, 2011, page 100
Publishers Weekly, June 27, 2011, page 133

Other books by the same author:
I'd Know You Anywhere, 2010
Life Sentences, 2009
What the Dead Know, 2007
To the Power of Three, 2005
Every Secret Thing, 2003

Other books you might like:
Marisa de los Santos, *Falling Together*, 2011
Lisa Jackson, *Most Likely to Die*, 2007

Stephen King, *It*, 1986
Donna Tartt, *The Secret History*, 1992
Kevin Wignall, *Among the Dead*, 2002

95

ERIC VAN LUSTBADER

Blood Trust

(New York: Forge Books, 2011)

Series: Jack McClure Mystery Series. Book 3
Story type: Contemporary
Subject(s): Adventure; Murder; Terrorism
Major character(s): Alli Carson, FBI Agent; Jack Mc-
   Clure, Political Figure (National Security Advisor);
   Henry Carson, Wealthy, Uncle (of Alli)
Time period(s): 21st century; 2010s
Locale(s): Washington, District of Columbia

Summary: Eric Van Lustbader's *Blood Trust* is the third
novel in the Jack McClure-Alli Carson series of political
mysteries. In this outing, Alli is undergoing rigorous
training to become one of the top agents in her elite sector of the FBI. Jack McClure, the nation's National
Security Advisor, is Alli's friend and mentor throughout
her intense training. When a murder rocks her team of
choice FBI agents, Alli turns out to be the number one
suspect. She comes to Jack for help, and the two embark
upon a labyrinthine adventure that takes them into a
dangerous web of politics, corruption, and terrorism.

Where it's reviewed:
Library Journal, May 1, 2011, page 74
Publishers Weekly, March 28, 2011, page 32

Other books by the same author:
Last Snow, 2010
Robert Ludlum's The Bourne Objective, 2010
Robert Ludlum's The Bourne Deception, 2009
First Daughter, 2008
Robert Ludlum's The Bourne Sanction, 2008

Other books you might like:
Tom Clancy, *Against All Enemies*, 2011
Vince Flynn, *American Assassin: A Thriller*, 2010
Richard North Patterson, *In the Name of Honor*, 2010
Joel Rosenberg, *The Twelfth Imam: A Novel*, 2010
Brad Thor, *Full Black*, 2011

96

DEBBIE MACOMBER

A Turn in the Road

(New York: Mira, 2010)

Story type: Contemporary; Family Saga
Subject(s): Family; Love; Voyages and travels
Major character(s): Bethanne Hamlin, Mother (of Annie),
   Divorced Person; Annie, Daughter (of Bethanne);
   Ruth, Mother (mother-in-law of Bethanne),
   Widow(er)
Time period(s): 21st century; 2010s
Locale(s): United States

Summary: Debbie Macomber's *A Turn in the Road*
chronicles a life-changing road trip undertaken by Bethanne, her daughter Annie, and her mother-in-law Ruth.
On the way to Ruth's high-school reunion, each woman
is dealing with her own romantic woes. Bethanne's ex-
husband wants to reconcile, while Annie is determined
to get over a bad breakup with her boyfriend. Ruth hopes
to meet and rekindle the flame with her first love. But on
their cross-country trek, surprises await, and suddenly
each woman is forced to reevaluate what she wants for
herself and her future.

Where it's reviewed:
Publishers Weekly, March 14, 2011, page 55

Other books by the same author:
Call Me Mrs. Miracle, 2010
Hannah's List, 2010
The Perfect Christmas, 2009
Summer on Blossom Street, 2009
Cedar Cove Christmas, 2008

Other books you might like:
Kristin Hannah, *Night Road*, 2011
Joan Medlicott, *The Three Mrs Parkers*, 2005
Luanne Rice, *Silver Boat*, 2011
Anita Shreve, *Rescue*, 2010
Jeannette Walls, *Half Broke Horses: A True-Life Novel*,
   2009

97

SUSAN MALLERY (Pseudonym of Susan Macias Redmond)

Already Home

(Don Mills, Ontario,Canada: Mira Books, 2011)

Subject(s): Cooking; Family; Divorce
Major character(s): Jenna Stevens, Cook, Store Owner
Time period(s): 21st century; 2010s
Locale(s): Georgetown, Texas

Summary: *Already Home* is a novel by author Susan
Mallery. After going through an intense divorce from a
husband who never knew her true worth, Jenna Stevens
finds herself wanting more from life. Despite her culinary
training, Jenna's been wiling away as a sous chef at a local restaurant. Then Jenna sees a store front for rent, and
begins to plan a new life as a cooking store owner. Jenna
finally begins to feel successful and comfortable in her
new life when in walks her birth parents, looking to
form a relationship with her. Can Jenna find it in her
heart to love her real parents as much as she loves her
adoptive parents?

Where it's reviewed:
Booklist, April 15, 2011, page 26
Library Journal, May 1, 2011, page 79
Romantic Times, April 2011, page 51

Other books by the same author:
The Knitting Diaries, 2011
Almost Perfect, 2010
The Best of Friends, 2010
Chasing Perfect, 2010
Finding Perfect, 2010
Summer Brides, 2010

Tempting, 2010
Hot on Her Heels, 2009
Someone Like You, 2004

Other books you might like:
Elizabeth Berg, *Once Upon a Time There Was You*, 2011
Jennifer Crusie, *Maybe This Time*, 2010
Susan Elizabeth Phillips, *Call Me Irresistible*, 2011
Nora Roberts, *Vision in White*, 2009
Nicholas Sparks, *Safe Haven*, 2010

98

HENNING MANKELL

Troubled Man

(New York: Knopf, 2011)

Series: Kurt Wallander Series. Book 10
Subject(s): Detective fiction; Missing persons; Espionage
Major character(s): Kurt Wallander, Detective, Father; Hakan von Enke, Military Personnel (naval officer), Retiree, Kidnap Victim
Time period(s): 21st century; 2010s
Locale(s): Stockholm, Sweden

Summary: *The Troubled Man* is a mystery novel from best-selling author Henning Mankell. The book is the tenth installment in the Kurt Wallander series about a melancholy detective. *The Troubled Man* begins with the mysterious disappearance of Hakan von Enke, a retired prominent naval officer, while on a walk in Stockholm. The investigation is being run by the Stockholm police, but Wallander has a personal connection to the case so he won't let it go. Wallander's daughter is slated to marry von Enke's son, pulling the detective into the investigation, regardless of the risk. Wallander makes some shocking and confusing discoveries, possibly linking the disappearance to Cold War espionage and making him question his own hidden past.

Where it's reviewed:
Booklist, January 1, 2011, page 53
Bookmarks, Mar/Apr 2011, page 6
Library Journal, February 1, 2011, page 55
New Yorker, April 25, 2011, page 85
Publishers Weekly, January 17, 2011, page 29

Other books by the same author:
Daniel, 2010
The Man from Beijing, 2010
Italian Shoes, 2009
Shadow of the Leopard, 2009
The Pyramid, 2008

Other books you might like:
Arnaldur Indridason, *Jar City*, 2005
John Le Carre, *Our Kind of Traitor*, 2010
Jo Nesbo, *The Redbreast*, 2007
Hakan Nesser, *Mind's Eye*, 2008
Ian Rankin, *The Complaints*, 2009

99

GEORGE R.R. MARTIN

Dance With Dragons: A Song of Ice and Fire

(New York: Bantam, 2011)

Series: Song of Ice and Fire Series. Book 5
Subject(s): Dragons; Adventure; Magic
Major character(s): Daenerys Targaryen, Ruler; Jon Snow, Warrior
Time period(s): Indeterminate
Locale(s): Seven Kingdoms, Fictional Location

Summary: The fate of the Seven Kingdoms is on shaky ground. The eastern part of the empire is ruled by Daenerys Targaryen and her trio of dragons, but enemies known and unknown are out to overthrow her. In the north, the beings that live beneath the ice are about to challenge warrior Jon Snow—and the future of the Kingdoms. As these dramas play out, even more threats are revealed, leading to an epic showdown that could make or break the destiny of the entire empire. George R.R. Martin's *A Dance with Dragons* is the fifth book in the Song of Ice and Fire series.

Where it's reviewed:
Publishers Weekly, May 30, 2011, page 52

Other books by the same author:
Feast for Crows, 2005
Storm of Swords, 2000
Clash of Kings, 1999
Game of Thrones, 1996

Other books you might like:
Terry Brooks, *Bearers of the Black Staff*, 2010
Jim Butcher, *Blood Rites*, 2004
Jacqueline Carey, *Kushiel's Mercy*, 2008
Raymond E. Feist, *A Kingdom Besieged: Book One of the Chaoswar Saga*, 2011
Gail Z. Martin, *The Sworn*, 2011

100

STEVE MARTIN

An Object of Beauty

(New York: Grand Central Publishing, 2011)

Story type: Contemporary
Subject(s): Art; Social class
Major character(s): Lacey Yeager, Art Dealer
Time period(s): 20th century-21st century; 1990s-2000s
Locale(s): New York, New York

Summary: Actor and writer Steve Martin paints a detailed picture of the New York City art scene during the end of the 20th century in his novel *An Object of Beauty*. Lacey Yeager uses her extreme ambition to climb to the peak of New York City society. She uses her allure to get the best jobs, the most useful friends, and the richest lovers. However, as the country's economy begins to decline, Lacey finds herself scrambling to recapture the success that once came so easily. Martin is also the author of a

collection of short stories and a well-received novella titled *Shopgirl*, which was made into a film.

Where it's reviewed:
Entertainment Weekly, November 26, 2010, page 74
The Houston Chronicle, November 21, 2010, page 14
The New York Times, November 29, 2010, page C1
New York Times Book Review, November 28, 2010,
    page 9
USA Today, December 7, 2010, page 3D

Other books by the same author:
Late for School, 2010
The Pleasure of My Company, 2003
The Pleasure of My Company, 2003
Shopgirl, 2000
Pure Drivel, 1998

Other books you might like:
Barbara Taylor Bradford, *Playing the Game*, 2010
Kate Christensen, *The Great Man*, 2007
Fannie Flagg, *I Still Dream About You*, 2010
Danielle Ganek, *Lulu Meets God and Doubts Him*, 2007
Allan Gurganus, *Plays Well with Others*, 1997
Robert Hughes, *Late and Soon*, 2005
Claire Messud, *The Emperor's Children*, 2006
Samantha Peale, *The American Painter Emma Dial*,
    2009
Danielle Steel, *Impossible*, 2005
Lauren Weisberger, *Chasing Harry Winston*, 2008

101

TERRY MCMILLAN

Getting to Happy

(New York: Viking, 2011)

Story type: Contemporary
Subject(s): African Americans; Women; Friendship
Major character(s): Savannah, Spouse; Bernadine, Addict; Robin, Single Mother; Gloria, Spouse
Time period(s): 21st century; 2010s
Locale(s): Phoenix, Arizona

Summary: In *Getting to Happy*, author Terry McMillan presents the sequel to her smash hit bestseller *Waiting to Exhale*. This volume revisits the ups and downs of four female African-American friends living in Phoenix, Arizona. Savannah is struggling with the uncertain fate of her marriage. Bernadine has become an addict in the wake of a painful divorce and an unfulfilling second marriage. Robin is a single mother who still can't find Mr. Right. And Gloria has settled into a comfortable rut from which she is about to be painfully ejected. As the drama of their lives plays out, the four women find strength, solace, and support in their friendship with one another.

Where it's reviewed:
Booklist, July 1, 2010, page 7
Bookmarks, Nov/Dec 2010, page 37
Entertainment Weekly, August 6, 2010, page 12
Library Journal, July 2010, page 76
Publishers Weekly, July 5, 2010, page 24

Other books by the same author:
The Interruption of Everything, 2005
A Day Late and a Dollar Short, 2001
Disappearing Acts, 1999
How Stella Got Her Groove Back, 1996
Waiting to Exhale, 1992
Mama, 1987

Other books you might like:
Connie Briscoe, *Money Can't Buy Love*, 2011
Elizabeth Buchan, *Revenge of the Middle-Aged Woman*,
    2003
Pearl Cleage, *Just Wanna Testify*, 2011
Eric Jerome Dickey, *Tempted by Trouble*, 2010
Olivia Goldsmith, *The First Wives Club*, 1992
Joanna Trollope, *Friday Nights: A Novel*, 2008
Omar Tyree, *The Last Street Novel*, 2007

102

TOM MCNEAL

To Be Sung Underwater

(New York: Little, Brown & Co., 2011)

Story type: Contemporary
Subject(s): Family; Marriage; Imagination
Major character(s): Judith Whitman, Editor (film), Spouse (of Malcolm), Lover (former, of Willy); Malcolm Whitman, Spouse (of Judith); Willy Blunt, Lover (former, of Judith), Carpenter; Camille, Daughter (of Judith and Malcolm)
Time period(s): 21st century; 2010s
Locale(s): Los Angeles, California; Nebraska, United States

Summary: *To Be Sung Underwater* is a novel by author Tom McNeal. Judith Whitman is a middle-aged woman who appears to be living the good life. A movie editor, she lives with her husband and teenage daughter in Los Angeles. Yet her marriage and career feel stale and stagnant, and Judith longs for more. When her husband comes home with a new bedroom suite for her daughter, Judith's life begins to take a bizarre turn. She rents a storage unit and decorates it with her daughter's former bedroom set, which was hers as a teen. As she sits inside the unit, she is mentally transported to her own teenagehood, when life was simpler and her heart belonged to a boy named Willy. Judith wonders what it might be like to reconnect with the lover of her past, and whether or not the grass is always greener on the other side.

Where it's reviewed:
Booklist, April 15, 2011, page 24
Library Journal, May 1, 2011, page 77
Publishers Weekly, April 4, 2011, page 30

Other books by the same author:
Decoding of Lana Morris, 2007
Crushed, 2006
Zipped, 2003
Crooked, 1999
Goodnight, Nebraska, 1998

Other books you might like:
Fannie Flagg, *I Still Dream About You*, 2010

Lauren Grodstein, *A Friend of the Family*, 2009
Jennifer Haigh, *Faith*, 2011
Mary Alice Monroe, *The Butterfly's Daughter*, 2011
Jodi Picoult, *Sing You Home*, 2011

103

STEFAN MERRILL BLOCK

The Storm at the Door

(New York: Random House, 2011)

Subject(s): Mental disorders; Family; Marriage
Major character(s): Katharine Merrill, Spouse (of Frederick); Frederick Merrill, Mentally Ill Person, Spouse (of Katharine)
Time period(s): 20th century-21st century
Locale(s): United States

Summary: Inspired by the story of his grandparents, author Stefan Merrill Block crafts a tale of love, madness, and heartbreak in *The Storm at the Door*. Katharine Merrill wants to believe that her husband Frederick is normal and that their life together is a healthy one. But after he returns from World War II, Frederick is battling his own demons—a battle that erects invisible walls between himself and his wife and daughters. When her husband's bouts with depression, mania, and addiction become too much, Katharine commits him to a mental institution. This single act forces her to reexamine her relationship with her husband, her own powerful denial, and the things she needs to do to secure a happy future for her family.

Where it's reviewed:
Library Journal, June 1, 2011, page 90
Publishers Weekly, March 21, 2011, page 48

Other books by the same author:
The Story of Forgetting, 2009

Other books you might like:
Robert Crais, *The Sentry*, 2011
Jonathon Kellerman, *Mystery*, 2011
Alice LaPlante, *Turn of Mind*, 2011
Rosamund Lupton, *Sister*, 2011
Ransom Riggs, *Miss Peregrine's Home for Peculiar Children*, 2011

104

ROLAND MERULLO

The Talk-Funny Girl

(New York: Crown, 2011)

Story type: Psychological
Subject(s): Self knowledge; Serial murders; Rural life
Major character(s): Marjorie Richards, Abuse Victim; Marjorie, Aunt (of Marjorie); Sands Ivers, Employer (of Marjorie)
Time period(s): 21st century; 2010s
Locale(s): New Hampshire, United States

Summary: In the novel *Talk Funny Girl* by Roland Merullo, a victim of abuse—now a grown woman and mother—recalls her bizarre upbringing in the New Hampshire woods. Marjorie Richards focuses on the year she turned 17 and she was sent out into the world to find work. Though she attended school, Marjorie had lived in isolation in a cabin where she and her parents spoke a muddled dialect of her father's invention. Ridiculed at school and mistreated by her parents, Marjorie gradually gained self-esteem through the intervention of her aunt and her employment with a builder. The life-changing year was also defined by a case of serial murders that gripped Marjorie and her town in fear. Marjorie's narrative reveals the strength and hope that delivered her from a horrific childhood.

Where it's reviewed:
Booklist, June 1, 2011, page 38
Publishers Weekly, May 16, 2011, page 51

Other books by the same author:
American Savior, 2008
Fidel's Last Days, 2008
Breakfast with Buddha, 2007
Golfing with God, 2005
A Little Love Story, 2005

Other books you might like:
Emma Donoghue, *Room*, 2010
Mark Dunn, *Under the Harrow*, 2010
Chris Fabry, *Almost Heaven*, 2010
Lesley Kagen, *Tomorrow River*, 2010

105

FERN MICHAELS

Home Free

(New York: Kensington Publishing Company, 2011)

Series: Sisterhood Series. Book 20
Story type: Series
Subject(s): Friendship; Espionage; Politics
Major character(s): Myra Routledge Martin, Leader (of The Sisterhood); Martine Connor, Political Figure (U.S. President)
Time period(s): 21st century; 2010s
Locale(s): United States

Summary: *Home Free* is the 20th and final novel in author Fern Michaels's series The Sisterhood. Members of the Sisterhood, a crime-fighting group dedicated to protecting democracy and freedom, face the challenge of their lives after U.S. President Martine Connor requests that they join a new agency called the CIC. Their first assignment: to discover who has been embezzling money directly from the U.S. government. Their task isn't something they haven't faced before, but the problem is that some members of the Sisterhood want to quit the job and return to civilian life. Can Sisterhood leader Myra Rutledge Martin keep her girls together long enough to tackle this final mission?

Where it's reviewed:
Publishers Weekly, February 14, 2011, page 39

Other books by the same author:
Cross Roads, 2010

Deja Vu, 2010
Exlusive, 2010
Holiday Magic, 2010
Return to Sender, 2010

Other books you might like:
Catherine Coulter, *Split Second*, 2011
Elizabeth Lowell, *Death Echo*, 2010
Luanne Rice, *Silver Boat*, 2011
Karen Robards, *Shattered*, 2010
Nora Roberts, *Chasing Fire*, 2011

106

KEVIN ALAN MILNE

Sweet Misfortune

(New York: Hachette Book Group, 2011)

Story type: Contemporary; Romance
Subject(s): Family; Grief; Love
Major character(s): Sophiah Jones, Orphan, Store Owner (chocolatier); Garret, Boyfriend (ex, of Sophia)
Time period(s): 21st century; 2010s

Summary: *Sweet Misfortune* is a novel written by author Kevin Alan Milne. Sophia Jones knows heartbreak. At the young age of nine, her parents were killed in an automobile accident. Twenty years later, the love of Sophia's life leaves her just as she is making their wedding plans. Determined to live only for herself, Sophia opens her own chocolate shop and comes up with the idea of misfortune cookies—cookies which, in her mind, tell people the bitter truth about life. Then her ex-boyfriend Garret comes back to town, and begs Sophia for forgiveness. Sophia issues an ultimatum: she will only speak to him if he places a classified advertisement in the local newspaper, and receives 100 responses from people who can define happiness. As the letters begin to pour in, Sophia begins to heal and learn more about the ups and downs of life.

Where it's reviewed:
Booklist, May 1, 2010, page 72
Publishers Weekly, April 19, 2010, page 35

Other books by the same author:
The Final Note, 2011
The Nine Lessons: A Novel of Love, Fatherhood, and Second Chances, 2009
The Paper Bag Christmas, 2006

Other books you might like:
Katie Fforde, *Second Thyme Around*, 2001
Christie Hodgen, *Elegies for the Brokenhearted: A Novel*, 2010
Frances Mayes, *Under the Tuscan Sun: At Home in Italy*, 1996
Kevin Alan Milne, *The Final Note*, 2011
Melissa Senate, *The Love Goddess' Cooking School*, 2010

107

JACQUELYN MITCHARD

Second Nature

(New York: Random House, 2011)

Story type: Contemporary
Subject(s): Accidents; Surgery; Family
Major character(s): Sicily Coyne, Young Woman
Time period(s): 21st century; 2010s

Summary: *Second Nature* is a novel by author Jacquelyn Mitchard. When she was only 13 years old, Sicily Coyne watched as her father perished in a schoolhouse fire. The fire left Sicily permanently disfigured, until more than a decade later when a plastic surgeon offers to perform radical reconstructive surgery. Sicily refuses because she is secure in who she is, until a secret comes to light that could change her life forever. Determined to remake herself entirely, Sicily agrees to the surgery. Yet her new appearance and her quest for a new life could lead to even more complications. Mitchard is also the author of *The Deep End of the Ocean* and *No Time to Wave Goodbye*.

Where it's reviewed:
Booklist, July 1, 2011, page 26
Publishers Weekly, July 25, 2011, page 27

Other books by the same author:
Watch for Me by Moonlight, 2010
Look Both Ways, 2009
No Time to Wave Goodbye, 2009
The Midnight Twins, 2008
Still Summer, 2007

Other books you might like:
Patty Friedmann, *A Little Bit Ruined*, 2007
Ellen Hart, *The Lost Women of Lost Lake*, 2011
Caroline Leavitt, *Pictures of You*, 2011
Laura Lippman, *The Most Dangerous Thing*, 2011
Michele Young-Stone, *The Handbook for Lightning Strike Survivors: A Novel*, 2010

108

KAREN MARIE MONING

Shadowfever

(New York: Delacorte Press, 2011)

Series: Fever Series. Book 5
Story type: Contemporary
Subject(s): Magic; Ireland; Epics
Major character(s): MacKayla "Mac" Lane, Warrior
Time period(s): Indeterminate
Locale(s): Ireland

Summary: The fifth book in the Fever series, Karen Marie Moning's *Shadowfever* continues the mystical adventures of MacKayla Lane, who has returned to Ireland to avenge her sister's death. However, Mac receives much more than she bargained for when she unearths the magical secrets of her own unusual heritage. Caught up in the war between the human and Fae populations, she will

Popular Fiction

stop at nothing to get her hands on an elusive book called *The Sinsar Dubh*, which possesses great powers. Now, Mac must decide how far she's willing to go to achieve her goals.

Other books by the same author:
Dreamfever, 2009
Faefever, 2008
Bloodfever, 2007
Darkfever, 2006
Spell of the Highlander, 2005

Other books you might like:
Christine Feehan, *Dark Preditor*, 2011
Heather Graham, *Phantom Evil*, 2011
Laurell K. Hamilton, *Hit List*, 2011
Linda Howard, *Prey*, 2011
Sherrilyn Kenyon, *Invincible*, 2011

109

LIANE MORIARTY

What Alice Forgot

(New York: Amy Einhorn Books/Putnam, 2011)

Story type: Contemporary
Subject(s): Memory disorders; Family; Interpersonal relations
Major character(s): Alice Love, Amnesiac
Time period(s): 20th century; (1990s); 21st century; 2000s (2008)
Summary: *What Alice Forgot* by Liane Moriarty is the story of a woman suffering from memory loss and trying to discover what has happened to the past ten years of her life. Alice Love is 29-years-old, married to the love of her life, and ready to give birth to her first child. Suddenly, she wakes up in a hospital bed and learns that not only is it ten years later, but also that her life has completely changed. Now Alice must figure out whom she has become and, more importantly, why. Can Alice regain the joy she once felt in life? Moriarty is also the author of *The Last Anniversary* and *Three Wishes*.

Where it's reviewed:
Booklist, May 1, 2011, page 69
Publishers Weekly, March 14, 2011, page 46

Other books by the same author:
The Last Anniversary, 2006
Three Wishes, 2004

Other books you might like:
Christina Berry, *The Familiar Stranger*, 2009
Alice LaPlante, *Turn of Mind*, 2011
Marcus Sakey, *The Two Deaths of Daniel Hayes*, 2011
Anne Tyler, *Noah's Compass: A Novel*, 2010
S.J. Watson, *Before I Go To Sleep*, 2011

110

MARY MCGARRY MORRIS

Light from a Distant Star

(New York: Crown Publishing Group, 2011)

Subject(s): Adolescence; Family life; Murder
Major character(s): Nellie Peck, 13-Year-Old; Benjamin Peck, Father; Henry Peck, Boy, Brother; Max Devaney, Convict; Bucky Saltonstall, Grandson; Dolly Bedelia, Stripper
Locale(s): Springvale, United States

Summary: In author Mary McGarry Morris's *Light From a Distant Star*, Nellie Peck is a 13-year-old girl whose life is turned upside down after she witnesses a brutal murder in her own home. At the outset of the story, Nellie is a typical pre-adolescent girl dealing with all the expected troubles of becoming a young woman. Things begin to change, however, when a group of strangers, including ex-con Max Devaney and stripper Dolly Bedelia, suddenly become a part of her life. Before long, violence erupts, Dolly ends up dead, and only Nellie knows whom the real killer is. Though she is the lone eyewitness, Nellie is so shocked by what she's seen that she's afraid to tell the truth. When she eventually finds herself taking the stand in court with a man's life at stake, she must endure the most difficult trial of her life.

Where it's reviewed:
Booklist, September 1, 2011, page 45

Other books by the same author:
The Last Secret, 2009
The Lost Mother, 2005
A Hole in the Universe, 2004
Fiona Range, 2000
Songs in Ordinary Time, 1995

Other books you might like:
James Lee Burke, *Feast Day of Fools: A Novel*, 2011
Carla Cassidy, *Without a Sound*, 2006
John Grisham, *The Client*, 1993
Jonathan Kellerman, *Billy Straight*, 1998
Richard North Patterson, *Eyes of a Child*, 1994

111

WALTER MOSLEY

Last Days of Ptolemy Grey

(New York: Riverhead Books, 2011)

Story type: Psychological
Subject(s): Aging (Biology); African Americans; Old age
Major character(s): Ptolemy Grey, Aged Person; Robyn Small, 17-Year-Old, Caregiver (to Ptolemy); Reggie, Nephew (great-grand nephew)
Time period(s): 21st century; 2010s
Locale(s): Los Angeles, California

Summary: In *The Last Days of Ptolemy Grey* by Walter Mosley, an elderly dementia patient faces a decision that could change his life while ending it early. At 91, Ptolemy Grey spends his days in solitude in his L.A. apartment. Though he has been abandoned by most of his relatives, a great-grand nephew, Reggie, helps Ptolemy with the grocery shopping. When Reggie is murdered, Ptolemy's emotional and physical situation grows more fragile. Then the appearance of a teenager, Robyn, who visits and tidies his apartment, provides some hope for the old man. But when he learns of a new medical treatment, he must choose between a few months of clarity followed by death or an indefinite decline into dementia.

Where it's reviewed:
Bookmarks, Mar/Apr 2011, page 33
Library Journal, March 15, 2011, page 89
Library Journal, October 1, 2010, page 70
New York Times Book Review, November 21, 2010, page 26
Publishers Weekly, September 13, 2010, page 22

Other books by the same author:
When the Thrill is Gone, 2011
Known to Evil, 2010
The Long Fall, 2009
The Right Mistake, 2008
The Tempest Tales, 2008

Other books you might like:
James Ellroy, *The Black Dahlia*, 1987
Barbara Hambly, *Dead and Buried*, 2010
Dashiell Hammett, *The Maltese Falcon*, 1930
Laurie R. King, *The God of the Hive*, 2010
Kris Nelscott, *Days of Rage*, 2006

112

JO NESBO

The Snowman

(New York: Knopf, 2011)

Series: Harry Hole Series. Book 7
Subject(s): Serial murders; Detective fiction; Suspense
Major character(s): Harry Hole, Detective—Police; The Snowman, Serial Killer
Time period(s): 20th century; 1980s
Locale(s): Oslo, Norway

Summary: In *The Snowman*, author Jo Nesbo tracks the investigations of Norwegian Detective Hole, who is the on the hunt for a serial killer. Known only as The Snowman, the killer leaves behind mementos of victims as adornments to snowmen, and Hole is determined to crack this increasingly violent case. There's just one problem: The Snowman is as diabolical as they come, and his crafty maneuverings may push Hole over the edge. This volume, translated by Don Bartlett, is the seventh novel in the Harry Hole series.

Where it's reviewed:
Booklist, March 1, 2011, page 33
Library Journal, April 1, 2011, page 83
Newsweek, May 30, 2011, page 82.
Publishers Weekly, March 28, 2011, page 32

Other books by the same author:
The Devil's Star, 2010
Nemisis, 2009
The Redbreast, 2007

Other books you might like:
Stieg Larsson, *The Girl with the Dragon Tattoo*, 2008
Donna Leon, *Drawing Conclusions*, 2011
Henning Mankell, *Troubled Man*, 2011
Liza Marklund, *Red Wolf*, 2011
Anders Roslund, *Three Seconds*, 2010

113

ANN PACKER

Swim Back to Me

(New York: Knopf, 2010)

Subject(s): Family; Interpersonal relations; Short stories
Summary: Ann Packer's *Swim Back to Me* contains a collection of the author's short stories as well as two novellas. The tales of this volume follow characters undergoing monumental emotional changes, from the sensitive relationship between two teenagers to a woman coming to terms with her missing husband. Titles in this volume include "Molten," "Dwell Time," "Her First Born," and "Walk for Mankind."

Where it's reviewed:
Booklist, March 1, 2011, page 28
Bookmarks, Mar/Apr 2011, page 5
Library Journal, January 2011, page 92
Publishers Weekly, December 13, 2010, page 34

Other books by the same author:
Songs without Words, 2007
The Dive from Clausen's Pier, 2002
Mendocino and Other Stories, 1994

Other books you might like:
Raymond Carver, *What We Talk about When We Talk about Love: Stories*, 1981
Brett Lott, *A Song I Knew By Heart*, 2004
Sue Miller, *The Lake Shore Limited*, 2010
Jacquelyn Mitchard, *No Time to Wave Goodbye*, 2009
Joyce Carol Oates, *Sourland: Stories*, 2010
Jodi Picoult, *House Rules*, 2010
Anita Shreve, *Rescue*, 2010
Jennifer Weiner, *The Guy Not Taken: Stories*, 2006

114

CHUCK PALAHNIUK

Damned

(New York: Doubleday, 2011)

Story type: Literary
Subject(s): Hell; Devil; Futuristic society
Major character(s): Madison, Teenager; Satan, Demon
Time period(s): 21st century; 2010s
Locale(s): Hell

Summary: *Damned* is a novel by author Chuck Palahniuk. Madison is only a teenager, but she is already facing the underworld when she dies after a drug overdose. She ends up in Hell, the worst place of all, and she can't quite figure out how she got there. The only thing she can think of—other than the overdose, of course—is that she is being punished forever because she is fat. Madison is in good company, however; other teenagers are there with her, including an athlete, a popular cheerleader, a dork, and a punk, none of whom understand why they have been damned for all eternity. In a quest to find out why they are in Hell, the teens head off to challenge Satan. After all, what's the worst that could happen?

Where it's reviewed:
Booklist, June 1, 2011, page 32
Library Journal, May 15, 2011, page 62
Publishers Weekly, May 2, 2011, page 32

Other books by the same author:
Tell-All, 2010
Pygmy, 2009
Snuff, 2008
Rant, 2007
Haunted, 2005

Other books you might like:
Max Brooks, *World War Z: An Oral History of the Zombie War*, 2006
Douglas Coupland, *Player One: What Is to Become of Us*, 2010
Justin Cronin, *The Passage*, 2010
Bret Easton Ellis, *Imperial Bedrooms*, 2010
Patricia Highsmith, *The Black House*, 2004
Christopher Moore, *Bite Me: A Love Story*, 2010
Jo Nesbo, *The Snowman*, 2011
Tim O'Brien, *July, July*, 2002
Kurt Vonnegut, *God Bless You, Dr. Kevorkian*, 2000
Daniel H. Wilson, *Robopocalypse*, 2010

115

ROBERT B. PARKER

Sixkill

(New York: G. P. Putnam's Sons, 2011)

Series: Spenser Series. Book 39
Subject(s): Murder; Mystery; Detective fiction
Major character(s): Spenser, Detective—Private; Zebulon Sixkill, Indian, Football Player (former), Bodyguard (of Jumbo); Jumbo Nelson, Actor, Crime Suspect
Time period(s): 21st century; 2010s
Locale(s): Boston, Massachusetts

Summary: *Sixkill* is the 39th, and final, installment in Robert B. Parker's best-selling Spenser series about a tough Boston private detective. While filming a movie in Boston, actor Jumbo Nelson, known for his hard party-ing ways, is accused of raping and murdering a young woman. The investigation seems sketchy from the get-go so the Boston police department calls on private investigator Spenser for assistance. Spenser's sleuthing leads him to Zebulon Sixkill, a brawny Native American ex-athlete-turned-bodyguard with a tough exterior but a great deal of hidden potential. Spenser takes Sixkill under his wing and together, the two men uncover the truth about what really happened to the victim and Nelson's involvement with the crime.

Where it's reviewed:
Booklist, March 15, 2011, page 26
Kirkus Reviews, April 1, 2011, page 536
Library Journal, May 1, 2011, page 75
Publishers Weekly, March 21, 2011, page 50

Other books by the same author:
Blue-Eyed Devil, 2010
Painted Ladies, 2010

Split Image, 2010
Brimstone, 2009
The Professional, 2009

Other books you might like:
James Lee Burke, *Glass Rainbow*, 2010
Harlan Coben, *Live Wire*, 2011
Robert Crais, *The Sentry*, 2011
Dennis Lehane, *Moonlight Mile*, 2010

116

S.J. PARRIS

Prophecy

(New York: Doubleday, 2011)

Series: Giordano Bruno Series. Book 2
Subject(s): British history, 1066-1688; Murder; Mystery
Major character(s): Giordano Bruno, Detective; John Dee, Astrologer; Elizabeth, Royalty (Queen of England), Historical Figure
Time period(s): 16th century; 1580s (1583)
Locale(s): England

Summary: *Prophecy* is the second book featuring Detective Giordano Bruno from author S.J. Parris. It's 1583 and tensions are rising in England as a rare astrological occurrence is nearing, bringing with it dark predictions about what lies ahead for Queen Elizabeth. When several of the Queen's maids are savagely murdered, she calls on Detective Giordano Bruno and astrologer John Dee to solve the crimes. Dee seeks supernatural guidance in the investigation, but Bruno suspects the murderer is someone living and working within the palace walls. The Queen refuses to believe her life is in danger, forc-ing Bruno to play a risky game of wait-and-see with the killer.

Where it's reviewed:
Booklist, May 1, 2011, page 36
Kirkus Reviews, March 15, 2011, page 450
Library Journal, October 15, 2010, page S6.
Publishers Weekly, March 21, 2011, page 50

Other books by the same author:
Heresy, 2010

Other books you might like:
Simon Beaufort, *A Dead Man's Secret*, 2011
Susanna Gregory, *The Body in the Thames*, 2011
C.S. Harris, *Where Shadows Dance*, 2011
Ian Morson, *Falconer and the Death of Kings*, 2011
C.J. Sansom, *Revelation*, 2008

117

ANN PATCHETT

State of Wonder

(New York: Harper, 2011)

Story type: Medical
Subject(s): Medicine; Research; Indigenous peoples
Major character(s): Marina Singh, Researcher

(pharmaceutical), Doctor; Annick Swenson, Researcher (pharmaceutical), Doctor; Anders Eckman, Investigator

Time period(s): 21st century; 2010s

Locale(s): United States

Summary: *State of Wonder* is a medical thriller from award-winning author Ann Patchett. After making a huge mistake during her residency, Marina Singh has given up her dreams of being a doctor to pursue a career in pharmacology research. Marina's employer, Vogel pharmaceutical company, has been quietly working on a new fertility drug deep in the Amazonian jungles. The team, led by the intimidating Dr. Swenson, has been unaccountable for two years, prompting an investigation by Marina's dear friend, Anders Eckman. When Marina receives word that Anders is dead, she's determined to find out the truth about what's going on with Vogel, even if it means taking a hazardous journey to the jungle.

Where it's reviewed:
Booklist, Feb 1, 2011, page 31
Library Journal, April 1, 2011, page 84
Newsweek, June 20, 2011, page 75.
Publishers Weekly, April 4, 2011, page 30

Other books by the same author:
What Now?, 2008
Run, 2007
Truth and Beauty: A Friendship, 2004
Bel Canto, 2001
Patron Saint of Liars, 1992

Other books you might like:
Jennifer Haigh, *Faith*, 2011
Rosamund Lupton, *Sister*, 2011
Tom McNeal, *To Be Sung Underwater*, 2011
Meg Mitchell Moore, *The Arrivals*, 2011
S.J. Watson, *Before I Go To Sleep*, 2011

118

JAMES PATTERSON
MICHAEL LEDWIDGE, Co-Author

Now You See Her

(New York: Little, Brown, and Co., 2011)

Subject(s): Suspense; Murder; Memory

Major character(s): Nina Bloom, Lawyer (defending wrongly accused man), Crime Victim

Time period(s): 21st century

Locale(s): Key West, Florida; New York, New York

Summary: *Now You See Her* is a novel of mystery and suspense by James Patterson and Michael Ledwidge. In this novel, Nina Bloom is a New York legal expert with a lifetime of trauma she's trying to hide. Long ago, in Key West, Nina had a great life with a loving husband and their first child on the way. Suddenly, she encountered an evil that destroyed all she had. After fleeing to New York, Nina tried to rebuild her life only to have her horrible past resurface. Now, while defending a man wrongly accused of murder, Nina realizes she has to delve back into her own troubled past to save him.

Where it's reviewed:
Booklist, May 1, 2011, page 34(2)

Other books by the same author:
10th Anniversary, 2011
Tick Tock, 2011
Toys, 2011
Cross Fire, 2010
Don't Blink, 2010

Other books you might like:
Lee Child, *Worth Dying For*, 2010
Harlan Coben, *The Woods*, 2007
Greg Iles, *The Devil's Punchbowl*, 2009
Ridley Pearson, *In Harm's Way*, 2010
John Sandford, *Buried Prey*, 2011

119

RICHARD NORTH PATTERSON

Devil's Light

(New York: Scribner, 2011)

Story type: Contemporary

Subject(s): Terrorism; Adventure; Spies

Major character(s): Brooke Chandler, Agent (CIA); Amer Al Zaroor, Terrorist

Time period(s): 21st century; 2010s (2011)

Locale(s): United States

Summary: *The Devil's Light* by Richard North Patterson is set on the eve of the tenth anniversary of the September 11 attacks. Brooke Chandler is a CIA operative who is convinced that al-Qaeda member Amer Al Zaroor is planning another catastrophic attack somewhere in the world. With his superiors unsupportive of his suspicions, Brooke sets off on his own to nab Al Zaroor—and stop the next 9/11.

Where it's reviewed:
Booklist, Feb 1, 2011, page 35
Library Journal, Feb 1, 2011, page 56
Publishers Weekly, March 7, 2011, page 41

Other books by the same author:
In the Name of Honor, 2010
Eclipse, 2009
The Spire, 2009
Exile, 2007
The Race, 2007

Other books you might like:
Justin Cronin, *The Passage*, 2010
David Goodwillie, *American Subversive*, 2011
John Sandford, *Buried Prey*, 2011
Daniel Silva, *Portrait of a Spy*, 2011
Taylor Stevens, *The Informationist*, 2011

120

TOM PERROTTA

The Leftovers

(New York: St. Martin's Press, 2011)

Story type: Literary

Subject(s): Family; Missing persons; Middle class

Major character(s): Kevin Garvey, Leader, Political Figure (mayor), Father; Nora Durst, Widow(er)
Time period(s): 21st century
Locale(s): Mapleton, United States

Summary: *The Leftovers* is a novel from author Tom Perrotta. Three years ago on October 14th, the small town of Mapleton lost 87 of its residents to the Sudden Disappearance, an inexplicable phenomenon that resulted in the abrupt vanishing of millions of people worldwide. Although so much time has passed, the people of Mapleton are still struggling to make sense of the tragedy and put the pieces of their lives back together. Despite the fact that his family has fallen apart, new mayor Kevin Garvey is trying to help lead Mapleton into a season of hope and happiness. But his quest to bring healing to others is failing him at home, where his wife has taken a vow of silence as part of her new cult, his son has dropped out of college to follow a mysterious prophet, and his former straight-A daughter has become distant and odd. Meanwhile, Kevin is secretly harboring feelings for Nora Durst, a woman who lost her entire family and feebly awaits their return.

Where it's reviewed:
Booklist, July 1, 2011, page 25
New York Times Book Review, August 28, 2011, page 1(L)
Publishers Weekly, June 6, 2011, page 22

Other books by the same author:
The Abstinence Teacher, 2007
Little Children, 2004
Joe College, 2000
Election, 1998
The Wishbones, 1997

Other books you might like:
William Giraldi, *Busy Monsters*, 2011
Erin Morgenstern, *The Night Circus*, 2010
Tom Perrotta, *The Abstinence Teacher*, 2007
Ian Sansom, *Mr. Dixon Disappears*, 2007
Kevin Wilson, *Tunneling to the Center of the Earth: Stories*, 2009

121

NANCY PICKARD

The Scent of Rain and Lightning

(New York: Ballantine Books, 2011)

Story type: Mystery
Subject(s): Murder; Family; Mystery
Major character(s): Jody Linder, Teacher; Billy Crosby, Murderer; Collin Crosby, Lawyer, Son (of Billy)
Time period(s): 21st century; 2000s
Locale(s): Rose, Kansas

Summary: In *The Scent of Rain and Lightning* by Nancy Pickard, the quiet town of Rose, Kansas, holds the scars of a 23-year-old murder case. Jody Linder, now a high school English teacher, was just a baby when her mother vanished and her father was shot dead by drunken Billy Crosby. When Jody's three uncles bring Jody the news of Billy's impending release—and his new trial, Jody dreads the inevitable encounter with the man who ruined

her family and her life. Though Jody resents the attempts of Billy's lawyer son, Collin, to clear his father's name, she gradually realizes that they have more in common than she ever imagined.

Where it's reviewed:
Booklist, March 15, 2011, page 25
Publishers Weekly, March 8, 2010, page 32

Other books by the same author:
The Virgin of Small Plains, 2006
The Truth Hurts, 2002
Ring of Truth, 2001
The Secret Ingredient Murders, 2001
The Whole Truth, 2000

Other books you might like:
Carol Higgins Clark, *Mobbed*, 2011
Michael Connelly, *Echo Park*, 2006
Ian McEwan, *Atonement*, 2002
Mary McGarry Morris, *A Hole in the Universe*, 2004
Walter Mosley, *Always Outnumbered, Always Outgunned*, 1998

122

DBC PIERRE

Lights Out in Wonderland

(New York: W.W. Norton & Company, 2011)

Story type: Contemporary
Subject(s): Suicide; Travel; Self love
Major character(s): Gabriel Brockwell, Young Man

Summary: *Lights Out in Wonderland* is a novel written by author D.B.C. Pierre. In this book, the author tells the story of Gabriel Brockwell, a nihilistic young adult with plans to commit suicide. Before he does so, however, he wants to find the ultimate act of self-indulgence. He travels around the world, to cities which include Berlin, Tokyo, and London, in an effort to find the ultimate soiree. Along the way he looks to break a friend out of jail, and he begins to learn more about the person he has become. Pierre is also the author of *Vernon God Little* and *Ludmila's Broken English*.

Where it's reviewed:
Booklist, August 1, 2011, page 22
Publishers Weekly, May 9, 2011, page 30

Other books by the same author:
Ludmila's Broken English, 2006
Vernon God Little: A 21st Century Comedy in the Presence of Death, 2003

Other books you might like:
Preston L. Allen, *Jesus Boy*, 2010
Chris Cleave, *Little Bee: A Novel*, 2009
Tatiana de Rosnay, *Sarah's Key*, 2007
DBC Pierre, *Vernon God Little: A 21st Century Comedy in the Presence of Death*, 2003
Abraham Verghese, *Cutting for Stone: A Novel*, 2009

123

ISMET PRCIC

Shards

(New York: Grove Press, 2011)

Story type: Contemporary
Subject(s): Wars; Autobiographies; Family
Major character(s): Ismet Prcic, Refugee; Mustafa, Military Personnel
Locale(s): Bosnia and Herzegovina; California, United States

Summary: *Shards* is the debut novel written by author Ismet Prcic. In it, the author tells the semi-autobiographical story of a man who shares the same name and his trek from his homeland of Bosnia to the United States. As Ismet works to construct a new life in California, he also grapples with the shame he feels over having to leave his family behind. Ismet tells his story through correspondence to his mother, who stays behind in Bosnia. Meanwhile, a man named Mustafa remains in Bosnia to fight in the war, and Mustafa and Ismet's stories contrast with one another. First novel.

Where it's reviewed:
Publishers Weekly, August 8, 2011, page 24

Other books you might like:
Slavenka Drakulic, *S: A Novel about the Balkans*, 2000
Steven Galloway, *The Cellist of Sarajevo*, 2008
Aleksandar Hemon, *Nowhere Man*, 2002
Yann Martel, *Life of Pi*, 2001
Margaret Mazzantini, *Twice Born*, 2011

124

AMANDA QUICK

Quicksilver

(New York: Penguin, 2011)

Series: Arcane Society Series. Book
Subject(s): Psychics; Detective fiction; Mystery
Major character(s): Virginia Dean, Psychic (glasslight reader); Owen Sweetwater, Investigator
Time period(s): 19th century
Locale(s): England

Summary: This is the second chapter in the "Arcane Society: Looking Glass Trilogy" - the first chapter, *In Too Deep*, was a contemporary tale released by Jayne Ann Krentz (Amanda Quick is one of Krentz's pen names). *Quicksilver* continues her tales of looking-glass psychics, but moves the time period back to Victorian England. In this story, psychic glasslight reader Virginia Dean is caught up with a strange murder, and she must team up with skeptic investigator Owen Sweetwater to find the real murderer and figure out who has been killing other glasslight readers.

Where it's reviewed:
Library Journal, April 15, 2011, page 77
Library Journal, November 15, 2010, page 44

Other books by the same author:
Burning Lamp, 2010
The Perfect Poison, 2009
The Third Circle, 2008
The River Knows, 2007
Sedond Sight, 2006

Other books you might like:
Julie Garwood, *Sizzle: A Novel*, 2009
Linda Howard, *Veil of Night*, 2010
Iris Johansen, *Quinn*, 2011
Jane Anne Krentz, *In Too Deep*, 2010
Elizabeth Peters, *A River in the Sky*, 2010

125

KATHY REICHS

Flash and Bones

(New York: Scribner, 2011)

Series: Temperance Brennan Series. Book 14
Story type: Contemporary
Subject(s): Murder; Mystery; Automobile racing
Major character(s): Temperance "Tempe" Brennan, Anthropologist (forensic anthropologist); Cale Lovette, Boyfriend (of Cindi), Gang Member (right-wing extremist); Cindi Gamble, Girlfriend (of Cale), Crime Victim (possible murder victim)
Time period(s): 21st century
Locale(s): Charlotte, North Carolina

Summary: *Flash and Bones: A Novel* is the 14th novel by Kathy Reichs to feature a quirky, clever forensic investigator named Dr. Temperance Brennan, a character also featured in the television show *Bones*. In this novel, NASCAR fans find a corpse hidden in a barrel full of asphalt just outside a busy speedway in Charlotte, North Carolina. Dr. Brennan is called to investigate the grisly discovery, and she quickly finds some disturbing clues. Her research leads to several possible culprits including a group of paramilitary extremists and a laboratory worker who might use stolen chemicals to kill. Brennan will have to use all her skills to solve this deadly puzzle.

Where it's reviewed:
Library Journal, March 15, 2011, page 101
Publishers Weekly, June 20, 2011, page 33

Other books by the same author:
206 Bones, 2009
Devil Bones, 2008
Bones to Ashes, 2007
Break No Bones, 2006
Cross Bones, 2005

Other books you might like:
Michael Connelly, *Fifth Witness*, 2011
Patricia Cornwell, *Port Mortuary*, 2010
Tess Gerritsen, *Silent Girl*, 2010
Iris Johansen, *Quinn*, 2011
Perri O'Shaughnessy, *Dreams of the Dead*, 2011

126

KATHY REICHS

Spider Bones

(New York: Scribner, 2010)

Series: Temperance Brennan Series. Book 13
Subject(s): Serial murders; Vietnam War, 1959-1975; Detective fiction
Major character(s): Temperance "Tempe" Brennan, Anthropologist (forensic anthropologist); Andrew Ryan, Detective
Time period(s): 21st century; 2010s
Locale(s): Quebec, Canada; Honolulu, Hawaii; North Carolina, United States

Summary: In *Spider Bones*, the thirteenth book in Kathy Reichs's Temperance Brennan series, the forensic anthropologist is investigating the death of John Lowery, who may or may not have accidentally drowned. But after Tempe positively identifies the body, she learns that John Lowery died over 40 years ago—or so says his death certificate, historical records, and the man's grave. This odd discovery propels Tempe on the most exciting case of her career, reconnecting her with her old beau, Detective Andrew Ryan.

Where it's reviewed:
Booklist, May 15, 2010, page 6
Library Journal, July 2010, page 78
Publishers Weekly, June 21, 2010, page 30

Other books by the same author:
206 Bones, 2009
Bones to Ashes, 2007
Break No Bones, 2006
Cross Bones, 2005
Monday Mourning, 2004

Other books you might like:
Patricia Cornwell, *The Scarpetta Factor*, 2009
Tess Gerritsen, *Silent Girl*, 2010
Iris Johansen, *Eve*, 2011
David L. Lindsey, *The Face of the Assassin*, 2004
Douglas Preston, *Impact*, 2010

127

LUANNE RICE

Silver Boat

(New York: Pamela Dorman Books, 2011)

Story type: Family Saga
Subject(s): Sisters; Family; Ireland
Major character(s): Dar, Sister (to Delia and Rory), Artist; Delia, Sister (to Dar & Rory), Mother; Rory, Sister (to Dar & Delia), Single Mother, Divorced Person
Time period(s): 21st century; 2010s
Locale(s): Ireland; Martha's Vineyard, Massachusetts

Summary: *The Silver Boat* is an emotional novel about family and sisterhood from best-selling author Luanne Rice. After the death of their mother, adult siblings, Dar, Delia, and Rory, return to their childhood home on Mar-

tha's Vineyard. Unable to afford the outlandish property taxes or the home's upkeep, the sisters have decided to sell the house, despite the fact that it has been in their family line since colonial times. As they pack up the home's contents and ruminate on the wonderful memories shared there, the ladies stumble upon a stack of letters filled with the truth about their long-absent father and his ill-advised mission to Ireland years prior. Determined to uncover the entire truth about their father, their past, and their futures, the three sisters embark on a journey of their own to the Emerald Isle that's filled with heartache, joy, and self-discovery.

Where it's reviewed:
Booklist, Feb 1, 2011, page 31
Library Journal, Dec 2010, page 108
Publishers Weekly, Jan 3, 2011, page 28

Other books by the same author:
Deep Blue See for Beginners, 2009
The Geometry of Sisters, 2009
The Letters, 2008
What Matters Most, 2007
Sandcastles, 2006

Other books you might like:
Barbara Delinsky, *Escape*, 2011
Kristin Hannah, *Night Road*, 2011
Elin Hilderbrand, *Silver Girl*, 2011
Jodi Picoult, *Sing You Home*, 2011
Heidi Jon Schmidt, *The House on Oyster Creek*, 2010

128

RANSOM RIGGS

Miss Peregrine's Home for Peculiar Children

(Philadelphia: Quirk Books, 2011)

Subject(s): Fear; Children; Adventure
Major character(s): Jacob Portman, 16-Year-Old
Time period(s): 21st century; 2010s
Locale(s): Wales, United Kingdom

Summary: In *Miss Peregrine's Home for Peculiar Children*, author Ransom Riggs tells the story of a ramshackle old house and the eerie inhabitants who just may still be alive. Circumstances force 16-year-old Jacob Portman to take to the seas, where he happens upon an isolated island near the coast of Wales. There he finds the ruins of Miss Peregrine's Home for Peculiar Children, but the more information he unearths about the home's strange residents, the more he is haunted by the idea that they may be alive—and they may be after him. First novel.

Where it's reviewed:
Booklist, May 15, 2011, page 17
Publishers Weekly, April 25, 2011, page 139

Other books you might like:
Ying Chang Compestine, *A Banquet for Hungry Ghosts*, 2009
Lev Grossman, *The Magicians*, 2009
Darren Shan, *Cirque Du Freak Series*, 2000

Lemony Snicket, *Unfortunate Events Series*, 1999
Anne Spollen, *Light Beneath Ferns*, 2010

129

JOSH RITTER

Bright's Passage
(New York: Dial, 2011)

Subject(s): Death; World War I, 1914-1918; Angels
Time period(s): 20th century; 1910s-1930s

Summary: *Bright's Passage* is a debut novel by author Josh Ritter. In it, Ritter tells the story of Henry Bright, a veteran of the Great War who comes back from France to his home in West Virginia to find his life in shambles. His horse talks to him, and his actions are led by angels that only he can see. After abducting a girl and impregnating her, he finds himself with an infant son to care for when the girl dies in childbirth. Now the girl's father is after him, and he must race across West Virginia in an attempt to get away. The novel follows Henry as he flees with his baby to escape the girl's father as well as a wildfire that he set, all the while remembering the horrors that he saw at war.

Where it's reviewed:
Booklist, May 15, 2011, page 14
Library Journal, June 1, 2011, page 93
Publishers Weekly, April 11, 2011, page 26

Other books you might like:
Neil Abramson, *Unsaid*, 2011
Bonnie Jo Campbell, *Once Upon a River*, 2011
Daisy Goodwin, *The American Heiress*, 2011
Tea Obreht, *The Tiger's Wife*, 2011
Helen Simonson, *Major Pettigrew's Last Stand*, 2011

130

NAN PARSON ROSSITER

The Gin & Chowder Club
(New York: Kensington Publishing Company, 2011)

Story type: Contemporary
Subject(s): Family; Romances (Fiction); Friendship
Major character(s): Samuel Coleman, Father (of Asa and Isaac), Spouse (of Sarah), Friend (of Nate and Noelle); Sarah Coleman, Mother (of Asa and Isaac), Spouse (of Samuel), Friend (of Nate and Noelle); Asa Coleman, Brother (of Isaac), Son (of Samuel and Sarah), Lover (of Noelle); Noelle Shepherd, Lover (of Asa), Spouse (of Nate); Nate Shepherd, Spouse (of Noelle), Friend (of Samuel and Sarah); Isaac Coleman, Brother (of Asa), Son (of Samuel and Sarah)
Time period(s): 21st century; 2010s
Locale(s): Cape Cod, Massachusetts

Summary: *The Gin & Chowder Club* is a novel by author Nan Parson Rossiter. In it, the author tells the story of two families, the Colemans and the Shepherds, who spend their summers as next-door neighbors to one another along the shores of Cape Cod. The Coleman family—which includes father Samuel, mother Sarah, and sons Isaac and Asa—have stood by their friend Nate Shepherd during the death of his wife and then encouraged him as he fell in love with and married Noelle, a younger woman. As Asa comes of age, he and Noelle fight a growing attraction to one another. Yet soon they embark on a secret affair that threatens a decades-long friendship between the families. Parson Rossiter is also the author of *Making Spirits Bright* and *Words Get in the Way*.

Other books by the same author:
Words Get In the Way, 2012

Other books you might like:
Nancy Clark, *July and August*, 2008
Deborah Cloyed, *The Summer We Came to Life*, 2011
J. Courtney Sullivan, *Commencement*, 2009
J. Courtney Sullivan, *Maine*, 2011
Jennifer Weiner, *Fly Away Home*, 2011

131

MARY DORIA RUSSELL

Doc
(New York: Random House, 2011)

Subject(s): Law enforcement; Murder; United States history, 1865-1901
Major character(s): Wyatt Earp, Lawman; John Henry "Doc" Holliday, Doctor; Johnnie Sanders, Crime Victim; Maria Katarina Harony, Prostitute
Time period(s): 19th century; 1870s (1878)
Locale(s): Dodge City, Kansas

Summary: Mary Doria Russell's *Doc* takes place in 1878 Dodge City, Kansas, where famed lawman Wyatt Earp and Dr. John Henry "Doc" Holliday join forces to solve the murder of a half-breed boy. Doc has come to Dodge City in hopes of making money, and he finds a willing partner in Earp, who needs a ruthless seeker like Doc—now working as a dentist—to find out what happened to Johnnie Sanders on that fateful night. Their investigation sets the stage for the legendary adventures of the two most famous lawmen in the Old West.

Where it's reviewed:
Booklist, April 15, 2011, page 32
Kirkus Reviews, March 1, 2011, page 362
Library Journal, October 15, 2010, page S6
Library Journal, May 1, 2011, page 77
Publishers Weekly, March 21, 2011, page 51

Other books by the same author:
Dreamers of the Day, 2008
A Thread of Grace, 2005
Children of God, 1998
The Sparrow, 1996

Other books you might like:
Rita Cleary, *River Walk*, 2000
Jane Candia Coleman, *The Silver Queen*, 2008
John Crowley, *Four Freedoms*, 2009
Michael Flynn, *Up Jim River*, 2010
Sharon Lee, *Carousel Tides*, 2010

132

SAPPHIRE

The Kid

(New York: Penguin USA, 2011)

Story type: Coming-of-Age
Subject(s): Poverty; Family; Grief
Major character(s): Abdul Jones, 9-Year-Old, Son (of Precious), Artist; Precious, Mother (of Abdul)
Locale(s): Mississippi, United States; New York, New York

Summary: *The Kid*, a novel by Sapphire, is the follow-up to the author's 1996 best-seller *Push*. This novel introduces readers to Abdul Jones, the son of *Push*'s main character, Precious, as he attends his mother's funeral. The author follows Abdul as he scrambles from a life of abject poverty, is shipped to a Catholic orphanage where he must fight to survive, and then eventually discovers his true passion: art. As Abdul hones his craft, he also fights to learn more about himself and who he truly is. Sapphire is also the author of the poetry anthologies *American Dreams* and *Black Wings and Blind Angels*. In 2009, *Push* was adapted into the feature film *Precious*, which was awarded an Oscar for Best Screenplay and Best Supporting Actress.

Where it's reviewed:
Publishers Weekly, May 2, 2011, page 33

Other books by the same author:
Push, 1996

Other books you might like:
Connie Briscoe, *Money Can't Buy Love*, 2011
Victoria Brown, *Minding Ben*, 2011
Pearl Cleage, *Just Wanna Testify*, 2011
E. Lynn Harris, *In My Father's House: A Novel*, 2010
Rachel Simon, *The Story of Beautiful Girl*, 2011

133

HELEN SCHULMAN

This Beautiful Life

(New York: HarperCollins, 2011)

Story type: Family Saga; Literary
Subject(s): Family; Internet; Wealth
Major character(s): Jake Bergamot, Student—High School; Daisy, 8th Grader
Time period(s): 21st century; 2010s
Locale(s): New York, New York

Summary: The Bergamot family is new to Manhattan's wealthy and privileged Upper West Side. Shy and kindhearted Jake is still trying to figure out life at the private school he now attends when he receives a sexually explicit email from a much younger admirer. Daisy, an 8th grader, wants Jake to give her a chance, despite their age difference, so she sends him a risque home video of herself. Shocked, confused, and a little arrogant about the video, Jake forwards the email onto a friend. Almost instantly, the video goes viral, spreading around the city and the world, and the Bergamots' world is turned upside down. Jake is suspended from school, his father's job is on the line, and his mother's social standing is at risk. *This Beautiful Life* is the tale of how one family comes together while their world is torn apart.

Where it's reviewed:
Booklist, August 1, 2011, page 24
Marie Clair, August 2011, page 110
New York Times Book Review, July 31, 2011, page 1(L)
The New Yorker, August 15, 2011, page 93
Publishers Weekly, April 11, 2011, page 25

Other books by the same author:
A Day at the Beach, 2007
P.S.: A Novel, 2001

Other books you might like:
Rosellen Brown, *Before and After*, 1992
Debra Galant, *Cars from a Marriage*, 2010
Chad Harbach, *The Art of Fielding*, 2011
Jodi Picoult, *House Rules*, 2010
Kevin Wilson, *The Family Fang*, 2011

134

JOHN BURNHAM SCHWARTZ

Northwest Corner

(New York: Random House, 2011)

Story type: Literary
Subject(s): Father-son relations; Conduct of life; Interpersonal relations
Major character(s): Dwight Arno, Convict (former), Father (of Sam); Sam, Student—College, Son (of Dwight), Baseball Player
Time period(s): 21st century; 2010s
Locale(s): California, United States

Summary: In the novel *Northwest Corner* by John Burnham Schwartz, a father and son are united by their mutual flaws and search for redemption. Dwight Arno is a 50-year-old ex-con who has left behind life in prison for a quiet existence in California. He is seeing a woman he doesn't know well and running a sporting-goods shop while trying to forget the incident that all but ruined his life. When Dwight's son Sam comes to visit unexpectedly, the college baseball player has a serious problem of his own—a barroom brawl has effectively ended his career. Together, the two men try to resolve the mistakes of the past and reconcile their troubled history with the women in their lives.

Where it's reviewed:
Booklist, May 1, 2011, page 67
New York Times Book Review, August 7, 2011, page 8(L)
Publishers Weekly, March 21, 2011, page 48

Other books by the same author:
Northwest Corner, 2011
The Commoner, 2008
Claire Marvel, 2002
Reservation Road, 1998
Bicycle Days, 1997

Other books you might like:
Louise Dean, *The Old Romantic*, 2011
Jim Harrison, *Returning to Earth*, 2007
Belinda McKeon, *Solace*, 2011
Richard Russo, *Nobody's Fool*, 1993
Evie Wyld, *After the Fire, a Still Small Voice*, 2009

135

LISA SCOTTOLINE

Save Me

(New York: St. Martin's Press, 2011)

Story type: Contemporary
Subject(s): Bullying; Suspense; Children
Major character(s): Rose McKenna, Mother (to Melly), Volunteer (lunch mom); Amanda, Bully, Child, Accident Victim; Melly, Bullied Child, Daughter (of Rose)
Time period(s): 21st century; 2010s
Locale(s): United States

Summary: Rose McKenna took a volunteer position as a lunch mom at her daughter Melly's elementary school to keep an eye on the young girl, who has lately been the victim of class bully Amanda. One afternoon, Rose witnesses a rift between the two girls that sends Melly tearfully running to the restroom. Moments later, an explosion rocks the cafeteria, forcing Rose to make a split-second decision between rescuing her own daughter or her tormentor. Rose hurriedly tries to do both, leading Amanda and others to safety before racing to save Melly, but unbeknownst to Rose, Amanda rushes back into the building and sustains major injuries. Within hours, Rose is vilified by the administration, students, and press. She's soon facing legal action from Amanda's mother as her marriage begins crumbling and Melly's life is made worse at school. With no one to depend on, Rose must put together the pieces of what really happened on that fateful day if she hopes to save her marriage, her daughter, and her future.

Where it's reviewed:
Library Journal, Feb 15, 2011, page 102
New York Times Book Review, April 24, 2011, page 6(L)
Publishers Weekly, Jan 31, 2011, page 26

Other books by the same author:
Think Twice, 2010
Look Again, 2009
Lady Killer, 2008
Daddy's Girl, 2007
Killer Smile, 2004

Other books you might like:
Emma Donoghue, *Room*, 2010
Tana French, *Faithful Place*, 2011
Jennifer Haigh, *Faith*, 2011
Rosamund Lupton, *Sister*, 2011
Tom McNeal, *To Be Sung Underwater*, 2011

136

RACHEL SIMON

The Story of Beautiful Girl

(New York: Random House, 2011)

Subject(s): Love; Interracial dating; Deafness
Major character(s): Lynnie, Mentally Challenged Person, Mother (of Julia); Homan, Deaf Person, Father (of Julia); Martha, Retiree, Widow(er); Julia, Daughter (of Lynnie and Homan)
Time period(s): 20th century-21st century; 1960s-2000s
Locale(s): United States

Summary: Rachel Simon's *The Story of a Beautiful Girl* charts the experiences of Lynnie, a white woman with mental challenges, and Homan, a deaf black man, who are institutionalized in the same care facility in late-1960s America. The two residents fall in love and escape to the safety of Martha, a kindly widow who hides them in her home. Lynnie eventually gives birth to a baby named Julia, but when the couple is apprehended and returned to the institution, Martha is given the child to hide away and raise. The lives of these four individuals are chronicled in this story of love, race, and the ties that bind a family.

Where it's reviewed:
Booklist, March 1, 2011, page 27
Library Journal, December 2010, page 84
Library Journal, April 1, 2011, page 85

Other books by the same author:
The Magic Touch, 1994
Little Nightmares, Little Dreams, 1990

Other books you might like:
Jo Ann Beard, *In Zanesville*, 2011
Sally Gunning, *The Widow's War*, 2006
Jacquelyn Mitchard, *Twelve Times Blessed*, 2003
Scott Spencer, *A Ship Made of Paper*, 2003
Richard Vasquez, *Chicano*, 1970

137

HELEN SIMONSON

Major Pettigrew's Last Stand

(New York: Random House, 2011)

Story type: Contemporary
Subject(s): Rural life; Retirement; Love
Major character(s): Ernest Pettigrew, Retiree; Jasmina Ali, Widow, Store Owner
Time period(s): 21st century; 2010s
Locale(s): St. Mary, Sussex, United Kingdom

Summary: In *Major Pettigrew's Last Stand: A Novel*, author Helen Simonson charts the unlikely romance between a retired English nobleman and a poor Pakistani shopkeeper. Major Ernest Pettigrew leads an uneventful life in the small town of St. Mary, but his well-ordered exsistence is thrown into turmoil after his brother's death. The tragic incident leads Pettigrew to local store owner Mrs. Jasmina Ali, who has recently lost her husband.

Grief brings the two strangers together—but will their forbidden love tear them apart? First novel.

Where it's reviewed:
Booklist, February 15, 2010, page 37
Bookmarks, May/June 2010, page 4
Library Journal, February 15, 2010, page 28
Publishers Weekly, January 4, 2010, page 1

Other books you might like:
Muriel Barbery, *The Elegance of the Hedgehog*, 2008
Carrie Brown, *Lamb in Love: A Novel*, 1999
Michael Malone, *The Last Noel*, 2002
Ian McEwan, *On Chesil Beach*, 2007
Kathryn Stockett, *The Help*, 2009

138

ALEXANDER MCCALL SMITH

The Saturday Big Tent Wedding Party

(New York: Pantheon Books, 2011)

Series: No. 1 Ladies' Detective Agency Series. Book 12
Subject(s): Mystery; Women; Weddings
Major character(s): Precious Ramotswe, Detective; Grace Makutsi, Secretary
Time period(s): 21st century; 2010s
Locale(s): Botswana

Summary: *The Saturday Big Tent Wedding Party* is a lighthearted mystery novel, the twelfth installment in the No. 1 Ladies' Detective Agency series about a group of friends who run the only all-female detective agency in Botswana. Precious Ramotswe can't escape dreams of driving her old white van, while Grace Makutsi has nightmares that the high grade she earned on the Botswana Secretarial College exam wasn't really hers. When Precious rediscovers her old van, Grace fears that her dream might be true as well. Meanwhile, Phuti Radiphuti's apprentice impregnated a girl and fled, leaving the gang to try to fix the couple's issues, and Precious is hired to investigate strange cattle poisonings.

Where it's reviewed:
Booklist, March 15, 2011, page 26
Kirkus Reviews, March 15, 2011, page 457
Publishers Weekly, February 28, 2011, page 37

Other books by the same author:
The Charming Quirks of Others, 2010
Corduroy Mansions, 2010
The Double Comfort Safari Club, 2010
The Unbearable Lightness of Scones, 2010
La's Orchestra Saves the World, 2009

Other books you might like:
Agatha Christie, *The Mirror Crack'd*, 1962
Harrison Geillor, *The Zombies of Lake Woebegotten*, 2010
Jon Hassler, *The New Woman*, 2005
Ann B. Ross, *Miss Julia Rocks the Cradle*, 2011
James Thurber, *The 13 Clocks*, 1950

139

ALI SMITH

There But for The

(New York: Pantheon, 2011)

Story type: Contemporary
Subject(s): Interpersonal relations; Entertaining; Friendship
Major character(s): Miles Garth, Mentally Ill Person
Locale(s): Greenwich, England

Summary: *There But For The* is a novel written by author Ali Smith. In this book, the author tells the story of a man named Miles Garth, who excuses himself from the table in the middle of a social gathering and barricades himself in a bedroom. As Miles declines to come out of the room, the rest of the party attempts to piece together what happened. The story is told from the perspective of four separate acquaintances of Miles, and none can agree on the true reason for the man's actions. Smith is also the author of *The Accidental* and *Hotel World*.

Where it's reviewed:
Publishers Weekly, July 25, 2011, page 29
Spectator, July 9, 2011, page 42

Other books by the same author:
The First Person and Other Stories, 2010
The Accidental, 2005
The Whole Story and Other Stories, 2003
Hotel World, 2002
Like, 1998

Other books you might like:
Ryonosuke Akutagawa, *Rashomon and Seventeen Other Stories*, 2001
Mark Haddon, *The Curious Incident of the Dog in the Night-Time*, 2003
Stephen Kelman, *Pigeon English*, 2011
Arthur Phillips, *The Tragedy of Arthur*, 2011
Ali Smith, *The First Person and Other Stories*, 2008

140

NICHOLAS SPARKS

The Best of Me

(New York: Grand Central, 2011)

Story type: Romance
Subject(s): Romances (Fiction); Love; Reunions
Major character(s): Amanda Collier, Girlfriend (ex of Dawson); Dawson Cole, Boyfriend (ex of Amanda)
Time period(s): 21st century; 2000s
Locale(s): Oriental, North Carolina

Summary: In the novel *The Best of Me* by Nicholas Sparks, the death of a mutual friend reunites former sweethearts Amanda Collier and Dawson Cole. Decades have passed since they fell in love for the first time. Although back then their disparate backgrounds seemed to doom their relationship, time has not lessened the passion they share. Now that an old friend who played a significant role in their romance has passed away, they

have returned to their small town to pay their respects, remember the past, and decide what lies ahead. Nicholas Sparks is also the author of *The Notebook*, *Safe Haven*, and *A Walk to Remember*.

Other books by the same author:
Safe Haven, 2010
Saying Goodbye, 2010
The Last Song, 2009
The Choice, 2008
The Lucky One, 2008

Other books you might like:
Elizabeth Berg, *The Last Time I Saw You*, 2010
Randy Sue Coburn, *Owl Island*, 2006
Jennifer Crusie, *Maybe This Time*, 2010
Jancee Dunn, *Don't You Forget About Me*, 2008
Nicholas Sparks, *A Walk to Remember*, 1999

141

ERICA SPINDLER

Watch Me Die

(New York: St. Martin's Press, 2011)

Subject(s): Artists; Murder; Suspense
Major character(s): Mira Gallier, Artist, Crime Suspect; Spencer Malone, Detective—Police
Time period(s): 21st century; 2010s
Locale(s): New Orleans, Louisiana

Summary: In *Watch Me Die*, author Erica Spindler tells the story of Mira Gallier, a stained-glass restoration expert who lost her husband in Hurricane Katrina. It's taken years for Mira to put the pain of that loss behind her, but now she's finally ready to move on. Someone, however, is determined to stop her. A series of cryptic messages show up on her stained-glass displays around the city, the priest who cares for them is brutally killed, and a string of murders soon follows. Suddenly Mira doesn't know where to turn—and the cops, headed by detective Spencer Malone, aren't so sure Mira is innocent.

Where it's reviewed:
Publishers Weekly, May 2, 2011, page 39

Other books by the same author:
Blood Vines, 2010
Break Neck, 2009
Last Known Victim, 2007
Copy Cat, 2006
Killer Takes All, 2005

Other books you might like:
Alafair Burke, *Long Gone*, 2011
Lisa Jackson, *Born to Die*, 2011
Iris Johansen, *Quinn*, 2011
Perri O'Shaughnessy, *Dreams of the Dead*, 2011
Karin Slaughter, *Fallen*, 2011

142

DANA SPIOTTA

Stone Arabia

(New York: Scribner, 2011)

Story type: Contemporary
Subject(s): Music; Musicians; Family
Major character(s): Denise Kranis, Sister (of Nik), Advisor (to Nik); Nik Kranis, Brother (of Denise), Musician, Recluse
Time period(s): 21st century; 2010s
Locale(s): Los Angeles, California

Summary: *Stone Arabia* is a novel by Dana Spiotta that explores one eccentric family's relationship with music and memory. The Kranis siblings, Denise and Nik, have always been close. Since their childhood in 1970s Los Angeles, the two have been inseparable. Denise knew Nik as a great musical writer and performer, and he always took joy in performing in public and testing new material with his band. As he gets older, however, Nik becomes reclusive. He continues writing music but does not perform it publicly; in fact, he seems to hide away from the world. Denise tries to encourage his talents as well as help him stay a part of the world, but there are many complications. Denise faces repeated tragedies and the siblings' mother is quickly aging and losing her mental capabilities. Denise must try to keep the family together.

Where it's reviewed:
Booklist, June 1, 2011, page 37
New York Times Book Review, July 10, 2011, page 9(L)
Publishers Weekly, April 4, 2011, page 28

Other books by the same author:
Eat the Document, 2006
Lightning Field, 2001

Other books you might like:
Eleanor Henderson, *Ten Thousand Saints*, 2011
Nick Hornby, *A Long Way Down*, 2005
Marjorie Kernan, *The Ballad of West Tenth Street*, 2009
Bart Yates, *The Distance Between Us*, 2008

143

DANIELLE STEEL

44 Charles Street

(New York: Delacorte Press, 2011)

Story type: Contemporary; Romance
Subject(s): Women; Family life; Interpersonal relations
Major character(s): Francesca Thayer, Art Dealer; Eileen Flanders, Teacher; Chris Harley, Single Father, Divorced Person; Marya Davis, Cook (chef), Widow(er); Ian Harley, 7-Year-Old, Son (of Chris)
Time period(s): 21st century; 2010s
Locale(s): New York, New York

Summary: In *44 Charles Street* by Danielle Steel, a Manhattan art gallery owner has lost her long-time boyfriend but is determined to hold on to her West Village home. Francesca Thayer cannot afford the expensive

property on her own, so she transforms it into a boarding house. Assembled at 44 Charles Street are Francesca; Eileen Flanders, a teacher; Chris Harley, a recently divorced father; and Marya Davis, a chef and cookbook author who has lost her husband. As romance grows between Francesca and Chris, Eileen and Marya experience varying degrees of luck in love. Meanwhile, the aging house's ailments keep landlord Francesca busy.

Where it's reviewed:
Booklist, Feb 1, 2011, page 27
Library Journal, Feb 15, 2011, page 102
Publishers Weekly, Feb 7, 2011, page 42

Other books by the same author:
Big Girl, 2010
Family Ties, 2010
Legacy, 2010
Matters of the Heart, 2009
Southern Lights, 2009

Other books you might like:
Fern Michaels, *Southern Comfort*, 2011
Ann Patchett, *State of Wonder*, 2011
Anita Shreve, *Rescue*, 2010
Mariah Stewart, *Home Again*, 2010
Sherryl Woods, *Driftwood Cottage*, March 29, 2011

144

TAYLOR STEVENS

The Informationist

(New York: Shaye Areheart Books, 2011)

Story type: Contemporary
Subject(s): Mystery; Detective fiction; Missing persons
Major character(s): Vanessa Michael Munroe, Detective—Private; Kate Breeden, Consultant (marketing), Friend (of Vanessa); Miles Bradford, Security Officer; Richard Burbank, Businessman (oilman); Emily Burbank, Daughter (of Richard, adopted); Francisco Beyard, Boyfriend (of Vanessa, former)
Time period(s): 21st century; 2010s
Locale(s): Africa; Texas, United States

Summary: In *The Informationist* by Taylor Stevens, a missing-persons case draws Vanessa Michael Munroe back to the treacherous region of Africa she escaped as a teenager. While living with her missionary parents in Cameroon, Vanessa ran off with a shady gun-runner before giving up her risky lifestyle for a job in the States. Working as an informationist in Texas, Vanessa gathers intelligence for prominent clients. When a wealthy businessman, Richard Burbank, needs help locating his missing daughter in Africa, Vanessa agrees to return. Back in Africa, Vanessa meets up with her ex, Francisco Beyard, and confronts the dangers she left behind. First novel.

Where it's reviewed:
Booklist, Febraury 1, 2011, page 36
Library Journal, February 1, 2011, page 57
Library Journal, February 1, 2011, page 57

Publishers Weekly, January 3, 2011, page 34

Other books you might like:
Jeffery Deaver, *Carte Blanche*, 2011
Joy Fielding, *Now You See Her*, 2011
Ken Follett, *Triple*, 1979
Jonathan Kellerman, *True Detectives*, 2009
Kyung-Sook Shin, *Please Look After Mom*, 2011

145

STEPHANIE STILES

Take it Like a Mom

(New York: New American Library, 2011)

Story type: Contemporary
Subject(s): Parent-child relations; Mothers; Women
Major character(s): Annie Fingardt Forster, Mother, Spouse
Time period(s): 21st century; 2010s

Summary: *Take It Like a Mom* is a novel by author Stephanie Stiles. Annie Fingardt Forster was a high-powered attorney who dressed in business suits and fit the profile of a career woman. Then she had children, quit her job, and became a housewife. Annie and her husband became accustomed to their nuclear family until her husband lost his job. Now Annie is unsure what will become of their family, which includes a toddler and a baby on the way. Can Annie navigate the treacherous seas of 21st-century motherhood while keeping her head above water? First novel.

Where it's reviewed:
Publishers Weekly, May 23, 2011, page 30

Other books you might like:
Elizabeth Buchan, *Separate Beds*, 2011
Carol Edgarian, *Three Stages of Amazement*, 2011
Sophie Kinsella, *Mini Shopaholic*, 2010
Belinda McKeon, *Solace*, 2011
Lynn Schnurnberger, *The Best Laid Plans*, 2011

146

SARAH STROHMEYER

Kindred Spirits

(New York: Dutton, 2011)

Story type: Contemporary
Subject(s): Friendship; Women; Death
Major character(s): Mary Kay, Friend (of Lynne, Beth, and Carol); Beth, Friend (of Lynne, Mary Kay, and Carol); Carol, Friend (of Beth, Lynne, and Mary Kay); Lynne, Friend (of Mary Kay, Beth, and Carol)
Time period(s): 21st century; 2010s
Locale(s): United States

Summary: *Kindred Spirits* is a novel by Sarah Strohmeyer. Stay-at-home moms Lynne, Mary Kay, Beth, and Carol forge a friendship over their young motherhood and their love for martinis. Calling themselves The Ladies' Society for the Conservation of Martinis, they convene every month to talk about their lives and, of course, gossip.

Unforeseen events bring the meetings to a halt, however, and the women grow apart over the course of two years. Then Lynne dies, and as her last wish she asks that the Ladies look through her possessions. There they find an item that will force them to take stock in their own lives and stop taking things—particularly each other's friendship—for granted.

Where it's reviewed:
Booklist, June 1, 2011, page 35
Publishers Weekly, April 4, 2011, page 28

Other books by the same author:
The Penny Pinchers Club, 2009
Sweet Love, 2009
Sweet Love, 2008
The Sleeping Beauty Proposal, 2007
The Cinderella Pact, 2006

Other books you might like:
Marie Bostwick, *A Single Thread*, 2008
Emily Chenoweth, *Hello Goodbye*, 2011
Helen Garner, *The Spare Room: A Novel*, 2009
Elin Hilderbrand, *Barefoot*, 2007
Sherryl Woods, *Seaview Inn*, 2008

147

ELIZABETH STUCKEY-FRENCH

Revenge of the Radioactive Lady

(New York: Doubleday, 2011)

Story type: Revenge
Subject(s): Science experiments (Education); Cancer; Nuclear physics
Major character(s): Marylou Ahearn, Aged Person
Locale(s): Tallahassee, Florida

Summary: *Revenge of the Radioactive Lady* is a novel by Elizabeth Stuckey-French. At over 70 years of age, former schoolteacher Marylou Ahearn has one thing left to do—murder Dr. Wilson Spriggs. In the 1950s, Dr. Spriggs dosed an expecting Marylou with radioactive drugs, which later led to the early death of her 8-year-old child. Marylou tracks Dr. Spriggs down to Tallahassee, Florida, and assumes the identity of Nancy Archer—the same name as the character from *Attack of the 50-foot Woman*. Marylou soon finds that she might not be cut out for murder, but that she can certainly mess with Dr. Spriggs' life. The only problem is, the more she gets to know the Spriggs family, the more she likes them. Will she ever get the revenge she feels she so richly deserves?

Where it's reviewed:
Booklist, January 1, 2011, page 42
Library Journal, February 1, 2011, page 57
Publishers Weekly, December 13, 2010, page 36

Other books by the same author:
Mermaids on the Moon, 2002
The First Paper Girl in Red Oak, Iowa and other stories, 2000

Other books you might like:
Jonathan Franzen, *Freedom*, 2011
Carl Hiaasen, *Star Island*, 2010

Christopher Moore, *Bite Me: A Love Story*, 2010
Haywood Smith, *Waking Up in Dixie*, 2010
Kurt Vonnegut, *God Bless You, Dr. Kevorkian*, 2000

148

J. COURTNEY SULLIVAN

Maine

(New York: Random House, 2011)

Story type: Family Saga
Subject(s): Family; Sisters; Beaches
Major character(s): Alice Kelleher, Grandmother (of Maggie), Mother (of Kathleen), Mother (in-law, of Ann Marie); Maggie Kelleher, Daughter (of Kathleen), Granddaughter (of Alice), Writer; Kathleen Kelleher, Daughter (of Alice), Mother (of Maggie), Sister (in-law, of Ann Marie); Ann Marie Kelleher, Daughter (in-law, of Alice), Sister (in-law, of Kathleen)
Locale(s): Maine, United States

Summary: In *Maine*, author J. Courtney Sullivan tells the story of the Kellehers, a group representing three generations of women. As summer begins, the women congregate at the family cottage in coastal Maine; once there, they must learn to deal with one another as they juggle a host of secrets. Maggie is unmarried and pregnant, and unsure of what her next step will be in life, while her mother Kathleen must try to put up with the very family she once tried to escape. Daughter-in-law Ann Marie masks her discontent as a homemaker through an obsession with dolls, and maternal figure Alice prepares to give the cottage away once and for all to her church parish. Can these women learn to support one another as they make some of the most important decisions of their lives?

Where it's reviewed:
Booklist, June 1, 2011, page 36
Library Journal, April 15, 2011, page 89
Publishers Weekly, March 14, 2011, page 46

Other books by the same author:
Commencement, 2009

Other books you might like:
Mary Kay Andrews, *Summer Rental*, 2011
Ann Brashares, *Sisterhood Everlasting*, 2011
Dorothea Benton Frank, *Folly Beach*, 2010
Elin Hilderbrand, *Silver Girl*, 2011
Cassandra King, *The Same Sweet Girls*, 2005
Nancy Thayer, *Heat Wave*, 2011

149

ELLEN SUSSMAN

French Lessons

(New York: Ballantine Books, 2011)

Story type: Contemporary
Subject(s): Friendship; Interpersonal relations; French (European people)

Major character(s): Josie, Teacher; Riley, Expatriate; Jeremy, Vacationer
Locale(s): Paris, France

Summary: In *French Lessons*, author Ellen Sussman tells the story of three Americans touring Paris, France. Josie, a teacher, has recently ended a relationship, and she hopes that a trip to the world's most romantic city will help mend her shattered heart. Riley, an expatriate living with a native Frenchmen, hopes that a tour of the city will help her feel closer to her new homeland. Jeremy, the husband of a famous actress, feels disconnected from his wife's life of glamour and glitz and longs to find his place in her world. As each person embarks on a tour of the City of Light with his or her individual tour guide, they also embark on adventures of self-discovery that could change their lives forever.

Where it's reviewed:
Booklist, June 1, 2011, page 35
People, July 11, 2011, page 45
Publishers Weekly, May 30, 2011, page 48

Other books by the same author:
On a Night Like This, 2005

Other books you might like:
Maeve Binchy, *Evening Class*, 1996
Susan Fales-Hill, *One Flight Up: A Novel*, 2010
Anna Gavalda, *Hunting and Gathering*, 2007
Diane Johnson, *Le Mariage*, 2000
Tom Rachman, *The Imperfectionists: A Novel*, 2010

150

WILLIAM G. TAPPLY

The Nomination

(New York: Skyhorse Publishing, 2011)

Story type: Psychological Suspense
Subject(s): Suspense; Law enforcement; Politics
Major character(s): Jesse Church, Police Officer; Thomas Larrigan, Judge
Time period(s): 21st century; 2010s
Locale(s): Massachusetts, United States

Summary: *The Nomination* is a novel written by author William G. Tapply. As the President of the United States begins the process of nominating a Massachusetts state justice to the bench of the Supreme Court, a group of interconnected mysteries emerges. Judge Thomas Larrigan is considered to be the best candidate for the job—a squeaky clean family man who is a Vietnam veteran. Larrigan has a long-hidden secret, however, and it could not only keep him from being confirmed but also cost him his career. The only person who stands in his way is an old film actress who is currently writing her memoirs. When former police detective Jesse Church finds her own life threatened, she begins to see that she may be connected to this powerful man and the aging actress who once loved him. Now it's up to Jesse to uncover her past before it is too late.

Where it's reviewed:
Booklist, November 1, 2010, page 32
Publishers Weekly, November 29, 2010, page 29

Other books by the same author:
Outwitting Trolls, 2010
Dark Tiger, 2009
Hell Bent, 2008
One-Way Ticket, 2007
Third Strike, 2007

Other books you might like:
Lincoln Child, *Fever Dream*, 2010
Barry Eisler, *Killing Rain*, 2005
James Grippando, *Money to Burn*, 2010
John T. Lescroart, *Damage*, 2011
Elizabeth Lowell, *Always Time to Die*, 2005

151

ANN TATLOCK

Promises to Keep

(Bloomington, Minnesota: Bethany House Publishing, 2011)

Subject(s): Christian life; Abuse; Family
Major character(s): Roz Anthony, 11-Year-Old, Friend (of Mara); Mara Nightingale, Friend (of Roz); Tillie Monroe, Aged Person
Time period(s): 20th century; 1960s
Locale(s): Mills River, Illinois

Summary: *Promises to Keep* is a novel by author Ann Tatlock. When Roz Anthony's mother makes the decision to finally leave their abusive father, she takes her family to Mills River, Illinois in an effort to leave that life behind. As the Anthonys begin making their new house a home, they find the house's former owner Tillie Monroe sitting on the front porch. Tillie was taken by her family to a convalescent home to live out her last days, but instead she wants to die in the house she's lived in her whole life. As the family welcomes Tillie in as a new member, and Roz makes a new best friend in Mara Nightingale, danger lurks as news that their father is tracking them down reaches the Anthonys.

Where it's reviewed:
Booklist, February 15, 2011, page 57
Publishers Weekly, December 6, 2010, page 33

Other books by the same author:
The Returning, 2008
Things We Once Held Dear, 2006
I'll Watch the Moon, 2003
All the Way Home, 2002
A Place Called Morning, 1998

Other books you might like:
Terri Blackstock, *Intervention*, 2009
Andrew M. Greeley, *The Cardinal Virtues*, 1990
Judith Pella, *Bachelor's Puzzle*, 2007
Francine Rivers, *Her Mother's Hope*, 2010
Lauraine Snelling, *On Hummingbird Wings*, 2011

152

NANCY THAYER

Heat Wave

(New York: Ballantine Books, 2011)

Story type: Family Saga; Romance
Subject(s): Family; Grief; Death
Major character(s): Carley Winsted, Widow(er), Mother (of Cisco and Margaret); Cisco Winsted, 12-Year-Old, Daughter (of Carley); Margaret Winsted, Daughter (of Carley), 5-Year-Old; Wyatt Anderson, Lawyer, Friend (of Carley's late husband)
Locale(s): Nantucket, Massachusetts

Summary: In *Heat Wave*, Nancy Thayer tells the story of Carley Winsted, a young wife who must endure unexpected grief after her husband dies from a heart attack. As she fights to keep herself and her two daughters afloat, Carley decides to turn her large Nantucket house into an inn. As she opens up her house, she also begins to open up her heart to a host of friends. Unfortunately, some of these friends want her to keep a devastating secret. In the meantime, Carley finds herself growing more and more attracted to Wyatt Anderson, her dead husband's best friend. But will the decision to succumb to her emotions further devastate her daughters as well as her husband's parents?

Other books you might like:
Ann Brashares, *Sisterhood Everlasting*, 2011
Zoe Heller, *The Believers: A Novel*, 2009
Elin Hilderbrand, *Silver Girl*, 2011
Debbie Macomber, *A Turn in the Road*, 2010
Liz Rosenberg, *Home Repair*, 2009

153

JEAN THOMPSON

The Year We Left Home

(New York: Simon & Schuster, 2010)

Story type: Literary
Subject(s): Family; Childhood; Identity
Major character(s): Anita, Young Woman, Sister (of Ryan); Ryan, Young Man, Brother (of Anita); Audrey, Mother (of Anita and Ryan); Chip, Cousin (of Anita and Ryan), Veteran (Vietnam)
Time period(s): 20th century-21st century; 1960s-2000s
Locale(s): Granada, Iowa

Summary: *The Year We Left Home* by Jean Thompson is set in a Granada, Iowa household that deals with many problems, both everyday and serious, over the course of three decades. The eldest daughter, a beauty with high hopes for life, gets married, only to find disillusionment with her husband and her fate. One son rebels against his bucolic hometown and tries to become a big-city intellectual only to regret the move, miss his home, and come to admire the conservative Iowans. Meanwhile, a cousin enlists in the army to fight in Vietnam—a choice that would seriously shake the course of his life. After returning from his tour of duty, he is left an uncertain wanderer. Thompson shows many slices of life to give readers a sense of a fairly average family's struggles over time.

Where it's reviewed:
Publishers Weekly, Jan 31, 2011, page 26

Other books by the same author:
Throw Like a Girl, 2007
City Boy, 2004
Wide Blue Yonder, 2003
Who Do You Love, 1999

Other books you might like:
Jennifer Haigh, *Faith*, 2011
Laura Lippman, *I'd Know You Anywhere*, 2011
Tom McNeal, *To Be Sung Underwater*, 2011
Ann Packer, *Swim Back to Me*, 2010
Lisa Scottoline, *Save Me*, 2011

154

LILY TUCK

I Married You for Happiness

(New York: Grove/Atlantic, Inc., 2011)

Story type: Romance
Subject(s): Death; Love; Marriage
Major character(s): Philip, Professor (Mathematics), Spouse; Nina, Artist, Spouse; Louise, Daughter
Time period(s): Multiple Time Periods
Locale(s): Paris, France; Massachusetts, United States

Summary: In *I Married You for Happiness*, author Lily Tuck tells the story of an unlikely couple through the memories that resurface as their relationship comes to an end. As the story opens, Nina returns home to find her husband, Phillip, lying motionless. He is dead. In her shock, Nina quickly finds herself drifting backwards in time, reliving the long, 42-year relationship she shared with her late husband. As a young artist and a university mathematics professor respectively, Nina and Phillip had little in common and were unlikely to have ever even met. Fate did bring them together, however, and Nina fondly remembers both the sweet and bitter details of their courtship, subsequent marriage, the eventual birth of their daughter.

Where it's reviewed:
Publishers Weekly, June 6, 2011, page 1

Other books by the same author:
Interviewing Matisse: Or the Woman Who Died Standing Up, 2006
The News from Paraguay, 2004
Limbo, and Other Places I Have Lived, 2002
Siam: Or the Woman Who Shot a Man, 1999

Other books you might like:
River Jordan, *Saints in Limbo*, 2009
Wendy Markham, *If Only in My Dreams*, 2006
David Nicholls, *One Day*, 2009
Audrey Niffenegger, *The Time Traveler's Wife*, 2003
Allison Winn Scotch, *Time of My Life*, 2008

155

PETER TURNBULL

Aftermath

(New York: Severn House Publishers, 2011)

Story type: Police Procedural; Series
Subject(s): Detective fiction; Mystery; Murder
Major character(s): John Seers, Lawyer; Hennessey, Detective—Police; Yellich, Detective—Police
Locale(s): Yorkshire, England

Summary: *Aftermath* is an installment from author Peter Turnbull's Hennessey and Yellich mystery series. When a wealthy elderly man passes away after a lengthy illness, solicitor John Seers arrives at the dead man's mansion to take stock of the estate. In the garden, Seers makes a gruesome discovery: five corpses chained together, all decomposing at different rates. Seers calls in Yorkshire police detectives Hennessey and Yellich to investigate. With the help of their team, these two detectives find themselves searching for a shared link between the five bodies in order to figure out how they got there and who killed them. Turnbull is also the author of *Informed Consent*, *Deliver Us from Evil*, and *False Knight*.

Where it's reviewed:
Booklist, December 15, 2010, page 21
Library Journal, February 1, 2011, page 47
Publishers Weekly, December 13, 2010, page 40

Other books by the same author:
Deliver Us From Evil, 2010
Improving the Silence, 2010
Informed Consent, 2009
No Stone Unturned, 2008
Turning Point, 2008

Other books you might like:
Michael Connelly, *Nine Dragons*, 2009
Patricia Cornwell, *Port Mortuary*, 2010
Jeffery Deaver, *The Edge*, 2011
Jonathan Kellerman, *Evidence*, 2009
Kathy Reichs, *Spider Bones*, 2010

156

HARRY TURTLEDOVE

The War That Came Early: The Big Switch

(New York: Del Rey, 2011)

Series: War that Came Early Series. Book 3
Subject(s): World War II, 1939-1945; Politics; Military science
Major character(s): Winston Churchill, Historical Figure, Political Figure (British Prime Minister); Peggy Druce, Young Man, Activist; Pete McGill, Military Personnel (soldier)
Time period(s): 20th century; 1940s (1941)
Locale(s): England; France; Poland; Russia; Spain; United States

Summary: In *The Big Switch*, the third book in The War that Came Early series, author Harry Turtledove continues his alternate history in which World War II has gotten underway before the Nazis are fully prepared for their campaign. Because Neville Chamberlain defied rather than backed down from Hitler in 1938, the Third Reich leader set his plan in motion prematurely. As a result, military outcomes and political alliances have shifted. Adding to the atmosphere of uncertainty is the unexpected death of a key political figure. The multifaceted story is revealed from the perspectives of American activist Peggy Druce, wounded soldier Pete McGill, and characters throughout affected European and Asian countries.

Where it's reviewed:
Booklist, May 15, 2011, page 26
Library Journal, June 15, 2011, page 83
Publishers Weekly, May 2, 2011, page 41

Other books by the same author:
Give Me Back My Legions!, 2009
Hitler's War, 2009
United States of Atlantis, 2008
Valley-Westside War, 2008
Opening Atlantis, 2007

Other books you might like:
Taylor Anderson, *Rising Tides: Destroyermen*, 2011
Robert Conroy, *Red Inferno: 1945: A Novel*, 2010
W.E.B. Griffin, *Victory and Honor*, 2011
S.D. Hildebrand, *The Approaching Sun*, 2010
Douglas W. Jacobson, *Night of Flames*, 2007

157

LISA UNGER

Darkness, My Old Friend

(New York: Crown Publishers, 2011)

Story type: Psychological
Subject(s): Missing persons; Psychics; Suspense
Major character(s): Jones Cooper, Police Officer (former); Eloise Montgomery, Psychic; Michael Holt, Explorer (caver); Ray Muldune, Detective—Private; Willow Graves, 15-Year-Old, Girl
Time period(s): 21st century; 2010s
Locale(s): The Hollows, New York

Summary: In *Darkness, My Old Friend*, a follow-up to author Lisa Unger's 2010 novel *Fragile*, Jones Cooper has left The Hollows police force, only to be drawn into a criminal investigation by the man who replaced him. A spelunker, Michael Holt, has come to the upstate-New York town to explore the region's caves and hunt for clues in his mother's 25-year-old disappearance. Assisting Holt in his investigation are private detective Ray Muldune and Eloise Montgomery, a psychic whom Cooper knows from a previous case. Montgomery warns Cooper to stay away from the investigation, citing ominous premonitions she's had. Meanwhile, Holt's activities have attracted the attention of Willow Graves, a troubled teenager new to The Hollows.

Where it's reviewed:
Publishers Weekly, June 13, 2011, page 30

Other books by the same author:
Fragile, 2010
Die for You, 2009
Black Out, 2008
Sliver of Truth, 2007
Beautiful Lies, 2006

Other books you might like:
Megan Abbott, *The End of Everything*, 2011
Jonathan Kellerman, *Mystery*, 2010
Liane Moriarty, *What Alice Forgot*, 2011
John Sandford, *Buried Prey*, 2011
S.J. Watson, *Before I Go To Sleep*, 2011

158

URBAN WAITE

Terror of Living

(New York: Little, Brown and Co., 2011)

Story type: Contemporary
Subject(s): Crime; Drugs; Smuggling
Major character(s): Phil Hunt, Rancher, Convict (former), Spouse (of Nora), Smuggler (drugs); Nora Hunt, Spouse (of Phil); Bobby Drake, Lawman (chasing Phil)
Time period(s): 21st century
Locale(s): Auburn, Washington

Summary: *The Terror of Living: A Novel* is the debut novel of Urban Waite. In this story, Phil and Nora Hunt live quietly on a horse farm in Auburn, Washington. Phil is an ex-convict who tries to do the right thing—mostly—but he still gets mixed up in crime. Specifically, he helps drug runners by carrying their illegal cargo through the mountains. This seems like a good way to bring in needed money, but it puts Phil in a crossfire of danger. Determined lawman Bobby Drake finds out about Phil's work and vows to bring him to justice. At the same time, the drug runners send a killer to get Phil before he has a chance to inform on them.

Where it's reviewed:
Library Journal, February 15, 2011, page 102.
Publishers Weekly, December 20, 2010, page 32

Other books you might like:
Kate Atkinson, *Started Early, Took My Dog*, 2011
Robert Crais, *The Sentry*, 2011
Steve Hamilton, *Misery Bay*, 2011
Craig Johnson, *Hell is Empty*, 2011
Henning Mankell, *Troubled Man*, 2011

159

DAVID FOSTER WALLACE

The Pale King

(New York: Little, Brown and Company, 2011)

Story type: Contemporary; Literary
Subject(s): Work environment; Interpersonal relations; Taxation

Time period(s): 20th century; 2010s

Summary: *The Pale King* is the final novel written by the late author David Foster Wallace. The story centers on a group of IRS employees working in a small Midwestern office, where they encounter personal drama and professional pitfalls as they take on the unique challenges of their jobs.

Where it's reviewed:
Kirkus Reviews, April 1, 2011, page 540
Library Journal, April 1, 2011, page 540
New York Times, April 1, 2011, page C27
New York Times Book Review, April 17, 2011, page 1

Other books by the same author:
Infinite Jest, 2006
The Broom of the System, 2004
Oblivion: Stories, 2004
Brief Interviews with Hideous Men, 1999
Girl with Curious Hair, 1989

Other books you might like:
Thomas Pynchon, *Inherent Vice*, 2009
George Saunders, *The Very Persistent Gappers of Frip*, 2000
John Sayles, *A Moment in the Sun*, 2011
Hunter S. Thompson, *The Rum Diary: the long lost novel*, 1998
Kurt Vonnegut, *Welcome to the Monkey House*, 1968

160

JOSEPH WAMBAUGH

Hollywood Hills

(New York: Little, Brown and Company, 2010)

Story type: Mystery
Subject(s): Mystery; Theft; Movie industry
Major character(s): Nate Weiss, Police Officer (LAPD); Raleigh Dibble, Criminal (ex-con); Nigel Wickland, Art Dealer (for Leona Bruger); Rudy Ressler, Director, Fiance(e) (of Leona); Leona Brueger, Fiance(e) (of Rudy)
Time period(s): 21st century; 2010s
Locale(s): Hollywood, California

Summary: In *Hollywood Hills: A Novel*, author Joseph Wambaugh reveals the underbelly of Hollywood neighborhoods. Nate Weiss has always been eager to be on the big screen in a Hollywood production. When he meets director Rudy Ressler, Nate is on his best behavior, hoping his day has finally come. Instead, Nate gets wrangled into house-sitting Rudy's mansion in the Hollywood Hills while Rudy and his fiance, Leona Brueger, are away. Along with Nate, Raleigh Dibble is also on guard duty; Raleigh is an ex-criminal who is eager to start over. However, Nigel Wickland, Leona's art dealer, aims to steal some paintings from the mansion while the couple is away. Nate and Raleigh's job, as well as Nigel's grand scheme, are about to get thrown out of whack as a teenage gang targets the mansions in the Hollywood Hills.

Where it's reviewed:
Booklist, November 15, 2010, page 24

Bookmarks, Mar/Apr 2011, page 41
Kirkus Reviews, November 15, 2010, page 1130
Publishers Weekly, October 25, 2010, page 31

Other books by the same author:
Hollywood Moon, 2009
Hollywood Crows, 2008
Hollywood Station, 2006
Floaters, 1996
Finnegan's Week, 1993

Other books you might like:
Lawrence Block, *A Drop of the Hard Stuff*, 2010
Michael Connelly, *Fifth Witness*, 2011
Robert Crais, *The Sentry*, 2011
John Sandford, *Buried Prey*, 2011
Stuart Woods, *Bel-Air Dead*, 2011

161

JENNIFER WEINER

Fly Away Home

(New York: Atria Books, 2011)

Story type: Contemporary
Subject(s): Marriage; Politics; Mother-daughter relations
Major character(s): Sylvie Woodruff, Spouse (of Richard Woodruff); Richard Woodruff, Political Figure (senator); Lizzie Woodruff, Daughter (of Sylvie and Richard), Addict; Diana Woodruff, Daughter (of Sylvie and Richard), Doctor
Time period(s): 21st century; 2010s
Locale(s): Minnesota, United States; New York, United States

Summary: In *Fly Away Home* by Jennifer Weiner, a politician's wife and her adult daughters escape their complicated lives for the comfort of a house on the beach. Sylvie Serfer Woodruff has been playing the role of sophisticated spouse to New York Senator Richard Woodruff according to plan when he throws their marriage off course by having an affair. Daughters Lizzie, a 24-year-old former addict, and Diana, a doctor, wife, and mother, are dealing with stresses of their own. After the three women endure a press conference regarding Richard's infidelity, they travel together to a vacation home that offers sanctuary and healing.

Where it's reviewed:
Bookmarks, Nov/Dec 2010, page 36
Entertainment Weekly, July 9, 2010, page 78
People, July 26, 2010, page 51
Publishers Weekly, June 28, 2010, page 110
USA Today, July 13, 2010, page 1D

Other books by the same author:
Best Friends Forever, 2009
Certain Girls, 2008
The Guy Not Taken: Stories, 2006
Goodnight Nobody, 2005
American Girls About Town, 2004
Little Earthquakes, 2004
In Her Shoes, 2002
Good in Bed, 2001

Other books you might like:
Cecelia Ahern, *The Book of Tomorrow*, 2011
Jane Green, *Promises to Keep*, 2010
Sophie Kinsella, *Twenties Girl*, 2009
Emma McLaughlin, *Dedication*, 2007
Allison Winn Scotch, *Time of My Life*, 2008
Jill Smolinski, *The Next Thing on My List*, 2007
Lauren Weisberger, *Last Night at Chateau Marmont*, 2010

162

KAREN WHITE

The Beach Trees

(New York: New American Library, 2011)

Story type: Contemporary
Subject(s): Missing persons; Grief; Natural disasters
Major character(s): Julie Holt, Friend (of Monica), Guardian (of Beau); Beau, 5-Year-Old, Son (of Monica); Monica, Friend (of Julie), Mother (of Beau)
Time period(s): 21st century; 2010s
Locale(s): Biloxi, Mississippi

Summary: *The Beach Trees* is a novel written by author Karen White. Julie Holt receives a surprise when she learns that her deceased friend Monica has named her as the caretaker to Monica's young boy, Beau. Monica also leaves Julie her Gulf Coast beach house, which has been lost in the aftermath of Hurricane Katrina. As Julie travels through the unfamiliar territory of Biloxi, Mississippi, looking for Beau's remaining family, she unearths secrets about herself, including the remaining grief over the loss of her young sister decades before. White is also the author of *On Folly Beach*, *The House on Tradd Street*, and *Falling Home*.

Where it's reviewed:
Publishers Weekly, March 28, 2011, page 38

Other books by the same author:
The Strangers on Montagu Street, 2011
On Folly Beach, 2010
The Girl on Legare Street, 2009
The Lost Hours, 2009
The Memory of Water, 2008

Other books you might like:
Elizabeth Buchan, *Separate Beds*, 2011
Dorothea Benton Frank, *Folly Beach*, 2010
Elin Hilderbrand, *Silver Girl*, 2011
Nicholas Sparks, *Nights in Rodanthe*, 2002
Lenora Worth, *Lacey's Retreat*, 2002

163

DAVID WHITEHOUSE

Bed

(New York: Scribner, 2011)

Subject(s): Conduct of life; Depression (Mood disorder); Mother-son relations

Major character(s): Malcolm "Mal" Ede, Young Man;
Lou, Girlfriend
Time period(s): 21st century; 2010s

Summary: In *Bed*, author David Whitehouse introduces
readers to Malcolm "Mal" Ede, a serial nonconformist
who, at only 25 years of age, has decided to rebel against
the preconceived notion of adult life as a never-ending
routine of work, bills, and family by going to bed—for
the rest of his life. As a result of the extremely sedentary
lifestyle his protest entails, Mal becomes morbidly obese
and is eventually declared the fattest man on the planet.
Mal's journey is documented by his younger brother,
who thoughtfully keeps tabs as Mal's lifelong protest
evolves and impacts the lives of those around him,
including their parents and Lou, Mal's devoted, but
largely discarded girlfriend. Over time, Mal becomes
something of a pseudo-celebrity and everyone, from the
media and curious onlookers to Mal's own friends and
family all find themselves asking the same question:
"Why?"

Where it's reviewed:
Maclean's, August 29, 2011, page 79
New York Times Book Review, August 21, 2011, page
26(L)
Publishers Weekly, May 2, 2011, page 2

Other books you might like:
William Giraldi, *Busy Monsters*, 2011
Peter Hedges, *What's Eating Gilbert Grape?*, 1993
John Irving, *The World According to Garp*, 1978
N.M. Kelby, *Whale Season*, 2006
John Kennedy Toole, *A Confederacy of Dunces*, 1980

164

DANIEL H. WILSON

Robopocalypse

(New York: Doubleday, 2010)

Subject(s): Robots; Robotics; Suspense
Major character(s): Archos, Artificial Intelligence;
Nicholas Wasserman, Scientist; Cormac Wallace,
Photojournalist; Takeo Nomura, Technician; Mikiko,
Android; Lurker, Computer Expert (Hacker)
Time period(s): Indeterminate Future
Locale(s): Afghanistan; Tokyo, Japan; New York, New
York; Oklahoma, United States

Summary: Daniel H. Wilson's *Robopocalypse* is set in the
not-too-distant future, a future where the day-to-day
lives of most humans are aided in some way by robotic
technology - be they miniature servant robots, smart
phones, companion androids, self-driving automobiles,
etc. The tech-aided status quo comes to an end when a
scientist named Nicholas Wasserman creates a powerful
artificial intelligence named Archos. The AI construct,
upon realizing that its creator wants to delete it, escapes
Wasserman's lab and spreads itself across the globe, taking control of almost every electronic device, machine,
and robot in the world and declaring a full-on war against
humanity. The story of "Zero Hour" and the robot uprising is told by Cormac Wallace, a photographer-turned-
human resistance fighter, who discovers Archos' archived

history of the conflict - a collection of oral transcripts,
first-person accounts, security footage, and other historical documents recounting the conflict.

Where it's reviewed:
Booklist, May 15, 2011, page 34
Library Journal, March 1, 2011, page 72
Publishers Weekly, March 14, 2011, page 54

Other books by the same author:
A Boy and His Bot, 2011

Other books you might like:
Vince Flynn, *American Assassin: A Thriller*, 2010
David Goodwillie, *American Subversive*, 2011
Eric Van Lustbader, *Blood Trust*, 2011
Brad Meltzer, *Inner Circle*, 2010
James Rollins, *The Doomsday Key*, 2009

165

JENNY WINGFIELD

The Homecoming of Samuel Lake

(New York: Random House, 2011)

Story type: Family Saga
Subject(s): Religious life; Rural life; Family
Major character(s): Swan Lake, 11-Year-Old, Daughter (of
Willadee and Samuel); Samuel Lake, Religious
(preacher), Spouse (of Willadee); Willadee Lake,
Daughter (of John Moses), Spouse (of Samuel Lake),
Mother (of Swan); John Lake, Grandfather (of
Swan), Father (of Willadee)
Locale(s): Arkansas, United States

Summary: In *The Homecoming of Samuel Lake*, author
Jenny Wingfield tells the story of a preacher's family
and their process of coming to terms with loss. Each
year, the Moses family looks forward to the family
reunion and the attendance of their daughter, Willadee,
along with her husband, the preacher Samuel Lake. The
Lakes enjoy the reunion as well; it is a change of pace
for their three children, and a chance for Willadee to see
her mother and father. Then Willadee's father dies just
as the reunion begins, sending the family into a spiral of
grief and despair exacerbated by Samuel's loss of his
longtime congregation. Only one person can act as the
bond to hold them together: 11-year-old Swan. As Swan
works to help her family through their grief, she also
meets a young boy who needs her protection. Through
strength and love, Swan soon proves to her family that
comfort can come from the most unlikely of places. First
novel.

Where it's reviewed:
Booklist, June 1, 2011, page 45
Publishers Weekly, May 9, 2011, page 33

Other books you might like:
Fannie Flagg, *Can't Wait to Get to Heaven*, 2006
Fannie Flagg, *Daisy Fay and the Miracle Man*, 1992
Anna Jean Mayhew, *The Dry Grass of August*, 2011
Colum McCann, *Let the Great World Spin*, 2009
Timothy Schaffert, *The Coffins of Little Hope*, 2011

166

STUART WOODS

Strategic Moves

(New York: G.P. Putnam's Sons, 2011)

Series: Stone Barrington Series. Book 19
Subject(s): Detective fiction; Adventure; Middle East
Major character(s): Stone Barrington, Detective, Lawyer; Ewrin Gelbhardt, Convict
Time period(s): 21st century; 2010s
Locale(s): United States

Summary: Lawyer and detective, Stone Barrington is recruited to escort a notorious, recently captured convict from Europe to America. But as Stone gets to know Erwin Gelbhardt, he learns the man he is watching over knows the whereabouts of Osama bin Laden. Stone grows determined to both help Gelbhardt negotiate a deal with the American government and, if he plays his cards right, track down the elusive bin Laden. *Strategic Moves* is the 19th installment in Stuart Woods's Stone Barrington series.

Where it's reviewed:
Booklist, November 1, 2010, page 32
Kirkus Reviews, October 15, 2010, page 1028
Publishers Weekly, October 18, 2010, page 23

Other books by the same author:
Bel-Air Dead, 2011
Lucid Intervals, 2010
Santa Fe Edge, 2010
Hothouse Orchid, 2009
Kisser, 2009

Other books you might like:
Jeffrey Archer, *And Thereby Hangs a Tale: Short Stories*, 2010
David Baldacci, *The Sixth Man*, 2011
Stephen J. Cannell, *The Prostitutes' Ball*, 2010
Harlan Coben, *Live Wire*, 2011
John Grisham, *The Confession*, 2010

Popular Fiction

The Mega-Series in Fantasy
by
Don D'Ammassa

There has always been a tendency toward very long books or a series of books in fantasy. Four of the classic fantasy writers—J.R.R. Tolkien, C.S. Lewis, E.R. Eddison, and James Branch Cabell—all wrote primarily in this mode, although the structure varies among them. The Lord of the Rings by Tolkien, for example, is basically one novel in three volumes, a continuous story whose individual components are not complete in themselves. The Hobbit is separate but related, as is the recent reconstruction, The Children of Hurin. Lewis wrote seven volumes in the Narnia series, but although there are recurring characters the books stand alone and one could presumably read them in any order. Eddison's Zimiamvian trilogy is similar, although together they create a much more textured look at his imaginary world than separately. His classic, The Worm Ouroboros, is vaguely related. Cabell's Biography of Manuel also consists of multiple separate volumes, which vary greatly in tone and subject manner.

The same variations exist within the modern fantasy series, although we also have cycles within series. Terry Pratt's Discworld novels, for example, contain standalone novels and separate strands of recurring characters. It is even possible to have trilogies of trilogies, or to jump back and forth on the timeline, or in the case of Michael Moorcock, to have apparently separate series eventually overlap. The appeal of the series novel is obvious from its popularity: Many readers enjoy returning to old characters and situations. They don't have to do the mental work of learning and understanding a new fantasy world, In some cases the author has also established what is essentially a series of cliffhangers to ensure our interest remains at a high level. This latter usually requires regular publication although George R.R. Martin has recently proven that readers will wait several years if necessary for the next installment.

Martin had been highly regarded even before publication of the first volume in his epic fantasy series, A Game of Thrones (1996). The series is one continuous story and the individual volumes should not be read out of sequence. By using a large cast of characters and by making his villains more than simple personifications of evil, he introduced his readers to a large and intricate world beset by numerous problems, factions, and minicultures. Four of the projected eight titles have appeared to date with another due out this year following a six-year hiatus. It seems unlikely that the conclusion will appear before 2020, but the recent cable television series based on the books is likely to help keep readers focused on the various separate story lines.

Robert Jordan's Wheel of Time series started with The Eye of the World (1990), which was also more or less one continuous story. It was initially supposed to end after three volumes but Jordan kept extending the proposed sequence and finally passed away before completing the series. Brandon Sanderson was selected to write the three closing volumes. As with Martin's series, there are several distinct though overlapping story lines involving different subsets of the characters. Jordan's extension of the series from its originally conceived length necessitated slowing the pace of events in later volumes. Like most epic fantasy, the series draws upon a variety of mythologies. Sanderson is a relative newcomer to fantasy—his first novel Elantris appeared in 2005—and is writing his own epic fantasy series, starting with Mistborn, whose fourth installment is scheduled to appear in 2011.

L.E. Modesitt Jr. is one of the more prolific fantasy writers. His Recluce series debuted with The Magic of Recluce in 1991 and has seen more than a dozen sequels, as well as a second series with many similarities, the Spellsong Saga, and other sequences including the Imager books and the Corean Chronicles that vary more noticeably. The Recluce books are generally self contained but most of the other books tend to be more integrated into a single story line. The Recluce books were not written in chronological order and in fact have generally tended to move further backward in time.

There is a very different tone in the Xanth novels by Piers Anthony, which began with A Spell for Chameleon (1977) and saw volume thirty-two, Knot Gneiss, in 2010. The first novel was a pleasantly light fantasy adventure whose protagonist was apparently the only person in his

world who could not perform magic. The series saw a steady succession of different protagonists and occasional variances in tone, but eventually became formulaic and the later volumes are generally far less interesting than the early ones.

Michael Moorcock is almost a special case. He originally became popular for the Elric stories, collections of short tales rather than novels, involving an exiled prince and a cursed, essentially living sword. Moorcock then wrote several other sequences of fantasy adventures featuring Corum, Dorian Hawkmoon, the Von Bek family, and John Daker. Some of these were a single story stretched over multiple volumes while others were a true series of standalone novels. At some point Moorcock decided that his various protagonists were all manifestations of a single personality—the Eternal Champion—tying them all loosely together and even including his science fiction novels in the mix. Although he continues to write occasional stories about Elric, his most popular creation, the newer tales are very different in tone and even style from the original series. The older Elric stories have been collected and recollected in different groupings but with the same or similar titles, so it is difficult to read them chronologically.

Katharine Kerr's Deverry novels can be grouped into subsets, most of which have separate casts of characters with only the setting in common. The first of these began with *Daggerspell* (1986) and the most recent debuted with *The Silver Mage* (2009), which was designed to be the final segment in the series. The entire sequence consists of fifteen books grouped into four cycles. Kerr makes frequent use of flashbacks and jumps back and forth in time even within a single book, which gives her work an unusual texture.

Michelle West was first published as Michelle Sagara, but it is as West that her two major series appeared. The first of these is the Sun Sword sequence starting with *The Broken Crown* (1997) and ending with *The Sun Sword* (2004). The series is related to her earlier two-book sequence, The Sacred Hunt. West is currently writing a new series set in that same universe beginning with *The Hidden City* (2008), with three titles published and two more planned. The individual novels have grown progressively longer and more detailed as she develops her setting and characters.

Steven Erikson is a Canadian novelist who devised the setting for his Malazan Book of the Fallen series with Ian Esslemont as the basis for a role playing game. The first novel in the series was *Gardens of the Moon* (1999) and the most recent is *The Crippled God* (2011). Erikson mixes standalone novels with trilogies within the greater context of the entire series. Esslemont has also written two novels in the same setting. Raymond Feist's fantasy falls mostly into the Riftwar sequence, starting with *Magician* (1982). The saga consists of several separate multi-volume stories set in different eras in his fantasy realm. His imagined world consists of two separate planets whose magicians are able to create

gateways to one another, usually with violent and disastrous consequences.

Terry Brooks is perhaps the most conscious imitator of J.R.R. Tolkien among current fantasy writers, specifically his Shannara books, although the latter ones have explored somewhat different territory. The series began with *The Sword of Shannara* (1977) and has been extended to more than twenty volumes, most of which can be grouped into separate trilogies. Brooks has also written the Magic Kingdom of Landover series, which is considerably lighter in tone.

David Eddings began to list his wife Leigh as co-author late in his career but he acknowledged that she had also written significant portions of some of his earlier books. His first novel was *Pawn of Prophecy* (1982) which introduced the Belgariad series. There are five books in the original sequence, plus a second set of five that take place later, as well as two prequels. He also wrote the Elenium and Tamuli trilogies, which are related to one another. The Eddings used fairly standard fantasy tropes—quests, prophecies, the coming of age of the protagonist, and the throne in peril. Except for the two prequels, none of the books are complete stories except in combination with the other titles in the same sub-series.

Robin Hobb began writing fantasy as Megan Lindholm in the 1980s but created her new persona for the first of the Farseer trilogy, *Assassin's Apprentice* (1995), a much more traditional heroic fantasy than her earlier work. Her novels since then have almost all been set in the Realm of the Elderlings and consist of three trilogies complete unto themselves and a new series, the Rain Wilds Chronicles, which is still in progress. She is also the author of another, unrelated series known as the Soldier Son trilogy.

Terry Goodkind attracted considerable attention with the first volume of the Sword of Truth series, *Wizard's First Rule* (1994) but the later novels in the series became mildly controversial because of their sado-masochistic sexual undertones and ethically challenged protagonists. The last published novel in the series was *Confessor* (2007) although there have been hints that Goodkind might return to this setting in the near future.

There are of course many other writers who produce similar books, but generally they are in shorter sequences and have a definite ending, after which the author moves to a different setting for his or her next work. Among the better authors working this particular vein of fantasy are Jennifer Fallon, Jacqueline Carey, Tad Williams, Dennis L. McKiernan, Sara Douglass, Mark Chadbourn, Chaz Brenchley, Mercedes Lackey, Kate Elliott, Fiona Patton, Dave Duncan, and Sherwood Smith.

There are advantages for the author as well as the reader in writing series novels. Preparation work is reduced because settings, rules of magic, and usually the characters are already established. Publishers prefer multi-book contracts and in most cases the first book in a series establishes a market that is at least somewhat

committed to buy the next. Some critics express concern that series novels stifle creativity and point to Piers Anthony—who was considered a promising and innovative writer who might shake up science fiction when he first began to be published. But as long as readers reward publishers and authors by preferring the familiar to the new, the system discourages experimentation.

Recommended Titles

The year 2011 has not shown much overall change in theme and treatment from the past few years and the largest single block of titles still falls into the urban fantasy category. Adrian Tchaikowsky, Steven Brust, and Steven Erikson all added to their well established fantasy adventure series and some newer series have also seen further volumes. Probably the most anticipated title this year was the second novel by Patrick Rothfuss and the new novel by George R.R. Martin, scheduled to be in print before the year ends. Catherynne Valente and Alex Bledsoe both produced some of their best work in 2011

as well. M.K. Hobson is the most promising of the newer writers to appear during the past two years.

Dark Jenny by Alex Bledsoe

Tiassa by Steven Brust

When the Saints by Dave Duncan

The Crippled God by Steven Erikson

The Hidden Star by M.K Hobson

The Curious Case of the Clockwork Man by Mark Hodder

The Rise of the Iron Moon by Stephen Hunt

Late Eclipses by Seanan McGuire

The Wise Man's Fear by Patrick Rothfuss

The Scarab Path by Adrian Tchaikowsky

Deathless by Catherynne M. Valente

Among Others by Jo Walton

Fantasy Fiction

167

BEN AARONOVITCH

Midnight Riot

(New York: Del Rey, 2011)

Series: Peter Grant Series. Book 1
Story type: Fantasy
Subject(s): Fantasy; Supernatural; Crime
Major character(s): Peter Grant, Police Officer (constable), Supernatural Being (can speak with the dead); Thomas Nightingale, Police Officer (Chief Investigator)
Time period(s): 21st century
Locale(s): London, England

Summary: *Midnight Riot* by Ben Aaronovitch is an urban-based fantasy novel that combines a murder mystery with a secret world of magic. Set in London, the story revolves around a constable, Peter Grant. Grant has high hopes of promotion and stimulating work, but he keeps on getting the least interesting assignments—that is, until he realizes he has a special ability to speak with the dead. Grant is able to interview witnesses and victims after they die, giving him an unprecedented source of information for cracking cases. But his insight into the supernatural has a dark side, too, and Grant finds himself in the midst of many scary happenings ranging from ghost infestations to the misdeeds of magical monsters such as vampires.

Where it's reviewed:
Locus, January 2011, page 18
Publishers Weekly, December 6, 2010, page 34

Other books by the same author:
Moon Over Soho, 2010
The Also People, 1995
Transit, 1992
Remembrance of the Daleks, 1990

Other books you might like:
Alex Bledsoe, *Dark Jenny*, 2011
Jim Butcher, *White Night*, 2007
Glen Cook, *Cruel Zinc Melodies: A Garrett, P.I. Novel*, 2008
Charles de Lint, *Mulengro: A Romany Tale*, 1985
Simon R. Green, *Ghost of a Chance*, 2010

168

BEN AARONOVITCH

Moon Over Soho

(New York: Random House, 2011)

Series: Peter Grant Series. Book 2
Story type: Contemporary; Series
Subject(s): Fantasy; Mystery; Jazz
Major character(s): Peter Grant, Police Officer (constable), Apprentice (wizard); Thomas Nightingale, Detective—Police (chief inspector), Wizard; Cyrus Wilkins, Musician (drummer), Crime Victim; Simone Fitzwilliam, Expert (jazz)
Time period(s): 21st century; 2010s
Locale(s): London, England

Summary: In the fantasy novel *Moon Over Soho* by Ben Aaronovitch, constable Peter Grant is learning the skills of his trade from Thomas Nightingale—a detective chief inspector who is also a licensed wizard. When Grant reports to the scene of his latest case, he realizes that his apprentice wizard talents will prove useful. The jazz musician Cyrus Wilkins is decidedly dead, but the strains of "Body and Soul" continue to sound from his corpse. When other mysterious deaths occur under similar circumstances, Grant calls on Simone Fitzwilliam's jazz expertise and Nightingale's powers of magic. *Moon Over Soho* is the second book in the Peter Grant series.

Where it's reviewed:
Locus, April 2011, page 45

Other books by the same author:
Midnight Riot, 2011
The Also People, 1995
Transit, 1992
Remembrance of the Daleks, 1990

Other books you might like:
Glen Cook, *Gilded Latten Bones*, 2010
Simon R. Green, *Hell to Pay*, 2007
China Mieville, *The City and the City*, 2009
Mike Resnick, *Stalking the Unicorn*, 1987
Michelle Sagara, *Cast in Fury*, 2008

169

ALEX ARCHER

Restless Soul

(Don Mills, Ontario, Canada: Gold Eagle, 2011)

Series: Rogue Angel Series. Book 28
Story type: Adventure; Series
Subject(s): Adventure; Archaeology; Magic
Major character(s): Annja Creed, Archaeologist, Adventurer
Time period(s): Indeterminate Future
Locale(s): Thailand

Summary: Archaeologist Annja Creed has come to Thailand for a little rest and relaxation. She soon finds, however, that the country has a trove of mystical mysteries just waiting to be solved, and she is pulled into the perplexing case of the infamous Spirit Cave. As she and her team explore the strange locale, Annja takes heed of the voices living there to help her solve an ancient mystery. *Restless Soul* is the 28th book in Alex Archer's Rogue Angel series.

Other books by the same author:
The Bone Conjurer, 2010
The Dragon's Mark, 2010
The God Catcher, 2010
Phantom Prospect, 2010
Eternal Journey, 2009

Other books you might like:
Martin Caidin, *Indiana Jones and the White Witch*, 1994
John DeChancie, *Talons*, 2002
James Alan Gardner, *Lara Croft Tomb Raider: The Man of Bronze*, 2005
E.E. Knight, *Lara Croft Tomb Raider: The Lost Cult*, 2004
Mike Resnick, *The Amulet of Power*, 2003

170

JENNIFER ASHLEY

Primal Bonds

(New York: Berkley, 2011)

Series: Shifters Unbound Series. Book 1
Subject(s): Love; Suspense; Murder
Major character(s): Kim Fraser, Shape-Shifter (half-shape-shifter, half-fae), Lawyer; Liam Morrissey, Shape-Shifter
Time period(s): Indeterminate Future
Locale(s): Austin, Texas

Summary: Attorney Kim Fraser is part shape-shifter, part fae. When she finds herself having to represent a shape-shifter suspected of murder, she needs help in figuring out the details of the case. Her investigation takes her into the heart of Shiftertown, where she enlists the aid of feline shape-shifter Liam Morrissey. As her search for answers deepens, she unearths some startling truths about Shiftertown—and some surprising feelings of her own

regarding Liam. Jennifer Ashley's *Primal Bonds* is the first novel in the Shifters Unbound series.

Where it's reviewed:
Publishers Weekly, January 24, 2011, page 138
Romantic Times, March 2011, page 92

Other books by the same author:
Wild Cat, 2012
The Many Sins of Lord Cameron, 2011
Lady Isabella's Scandalous Marriage, 2010
Pride Mates, 2010
The Madness of Lord Ian Mackenzie, 2009
The Calling, 2007
The Gathering, 2007
The Mad, Bad Duke, 2006
The Pirate Hunter, 2004

Other books you might like:
Doranna Durgin, *Dun Lady's Jess*, 1994
Sharon Green, *The Hidden Realms*, 1993
Constance O'Day-Flannery, *Shifting Love*, 2004
Jennifer Roberson, *The Lion Throne*, 2001
Sharon Shinn, *The Thirteenth House*, 2006

171

ANYA BAST

Dark Enchantment

(New York: Berkley Sensation, 2011)

Series: Dark Magick Series. Book 3
Story type: Series; Urban
Subject(s): Fantasy; Dreams; Fairies
Major character(s): Charlotte Bennett, Accountant, Human; Kieran Aimhrea, Mythical Creature (fae)
Locale(s): Piefferburg, Fictional Location

Summary: *Dark Enchantment*, a steamy and suspenseful fantasy novel, is the third installment in the Dark Magick series from author Anya Bast. When Charlotte Bennett begins having unusual and erotic dreams about a beautiful man, she has no idea that indulging in them will have real-life consequences far more serious than she could imagine. The man in her dreams is Kieran Aimhrea, a fae and dream wraith who is seducing Charlotte into helping him to liberate his people. Through the sexy dreams, Kieran lures Charlotte to the city of Piefferburg to help him free a band of deadly fae who've been locked up by the government. But if she complies, she could be unleashing mortal danger on the human population.

Where it's reviewed:
Publishers Weekly, February 28, 2011, page 41

Other books by the same author:
Cruel Enchantment, 2010
Jeweled, 2010
Wicked Enchantment, 2010
Witch Blood, 2008
Witch Fire, 2007

Other books you might like:
Brett Davis, *The Faery Convention*, 1995
Diane Duane, *Stealing the Elf-King's Roses*, 2002

Laurell K. Hamilton, *Mistral's Kiss*, 2006
Karen Marie Moning, *Faefever*, 2008
Judith Tarr, *House of War*, 2003

172

ELIZABETH BEAR

The Sea Thy Mistress

(New York: Tor, 2011)

Series: Edda of Burdens Series. Book 3
Story type: End of the World; Series
Subject(s): Fantasy; Sea stories; Immortality
Major character(s): Muire, Angel, Lover (of Cathoair), Mother (to Cathmar); Cathoair, Immortal, Lover (of Muire), Father (of Cathmar); Cathmar, Teenager, Son (of Cathoair and Muire); Heythe, Villain, Time Traveler
Locale(s): Valdyrgard, Fictional Location

Summary: *The Sea Thy Mistress*, a suspenseful fantasy novel, is the sequel to *All the Windcracked Stars* by award-winning author Elizabeth Bear. The malevolent goddess Heythe carefully plotted the destruction of the world, but when she travels forward in time to gloat over her victory, she's stunned to discover a thriving planet. The world of Valdyrgard owes its preservation to the selfless sacrifice of the angelic Muire who gave up her celestial status to become the Bearer of Burdens, forfeiting her shot at happiness with lover, Cathoair, and their son, Cathmar. When Heythe realizes her plans have failed, she develops a new plot for total annihilation, one that will cost Muire everything precious to her. *The Sea Thy Mistress* is the third book in the Edda of Burdens series.

Where it's reviewed:
Library Journal, January 2011, page 86
Publishers Weekly, January 3, 2011, page 38

Other books by the same author:
By the Mountain Bound, 2009
Hell and Earth, 2008
The Chains That You Refuse, 2007
New Amsterdam, 2007
Whiskey and Water, 2007

Other books you might like:
Jennifer Fallon, *The Immortal Prince*, 2008
Maggie Furey, *The Heart of Myrial*, 1999
Simon R. Green, *The God Killer*, 1991
L. Jagi Lamplighter, *Prospero Lost*, 2009
R.A. Salvatore, *The Demon Awakens*, 1997

173

BRADLEY BEAULIEU

The Winds of Khalakovo

(San Francisco, California: Night Shade, 2011)

Story type: Alternate World
Subject(s): Fantasy; Civil war; Islands
Major character(s): Nikandr, Royalty (prince)

Time period(s): Indeterminate
Locale(s): Khalakovo, Fictional Location

Summary: *The Winds of Khalakovo* is a suspenseful fantasy novel from debut author Bradley Beaulieu. The future is uncertain for Khalakovo, an archipelago of seven islands that stands at the center of the world's trading industry. Civil war has broken out between the ruling race known as the Landed, the indigenous people known as the Aramahn, and the rebellious tribe called the Maharraht, and a deadly disease is rapidly wiping out the population. Khalakovo's only hope for a promising future rests on the outcome of a meeting between the Nine Dukes. Things are off to a terrible start when an elemental spirit attacks and kills Grand Duke Stasa Bolgravya before he even arrives. Khalakovo's Prince Nikandr must hold off the vengeful retaliation of the other dukes long enough to track down an autistic savant who can release the islands from an ominous curse and reverse their fate. First novel.

Where it's reviewed:
Library Journal, March 15, 2011, page 110
Publishers Weekly, February 21, 2011, page 119

Other books you might like:
Stephen Deas, *The Adamantine Palace*, 2010
Kate Elliott, *Crown of Stars*, 2006
Patrick Rothfuss, *The Name of the Wind*, 2007
Adrian Tchaikovsky, *The Scarab Path*, 2011
Tad Williams, *Shadowmarch: Volume 1*, 2004

174

AMBER BENSON

Serpent's Storm

(New York: Ace Books, 2011)

Series: Calliope Reaper-Jones Series. Book 3
Story type: Humor; Series
Subject(s): Fantasy; Death; Sisters
Major character(s): Calliope Reaper-Jones, Young Woman, Daughter (of Death)
Time period(s): 21st century; 2010s
Locale(s): New York, New York

Summary: *Serpent's Storm*, a humorous and supernatural fantasy novel, is the third installment in the Calliope Reaper-Jones series from author Amber Benson. Callie is trying desperately to live the life of a normal girl hoping to make it big in Manhattan, despite the fact that she's Death's Daughter and the rightful heir to the family business, Death Inc. While Callie's working hard to ignore her birthright, her sister is fighting to steal it. After getting out of prison, Callie's sister makes a deal with the Devil to take over Death Inc. and Heaven. The only thing standing in their way is Callie and they have no problem eliminating her, unless she decides to confront her destiny and take hold of it for good.

Other books by the same author:
Cat's Claw, 2010
Death's Daughter, 2009

Other books you might like:
Rachel Caine, *Gale Force*, 2008
Holly Lisle, *Sympathy for the Devil*, 1996

Terry Pratchett, *Good Omens: The Nice and Accurate Prophecies of Agnes Nutter, Witch*, 1990
Terry Pratchett, *Mort*, 1987
Lilith Saintcrow, *Working for the Devil*, 2006

175

CAROL BERG

The Soul Mirror

(New York: Roc, 2011)

Series: Collegia Magica Series. Book 2
Story type: Magic Conflict; Series
Subject(s): Magic; Sisters; Adventure
Major character(s): Anna de Vernase, Young Woman
Time period(s): Indeterminate Past
Locale(s): Merona, Fictional Location

Summary: Anna de Vernase is the poverty-stricken daughter of a once-illustrious family. She is a firm proponent of science and is leery of anything magical. After her sister's death, Anna ventures into the world her sister inhabited—a world populated by mysticism, magic, and all things fantastical. As she becomes more deeply enmeshed in her late sister's life, Anna unearths a dark magic holding a city hostage. And now she just might be the only one to set the city free of the mystical danger that threatens to destroy it. *The Soul Mirror* is the second novel in Carol Berg's Collegia Magica series.

Where it's reviewed:
Library Journal, January 2011, page 86
Locus, April 2011, page 25
Publishers Weekly, November 22, 2010, page 46

Other books by the same author:
The Spirit Lens, 2010
Breath and Bone, 2008
Flesh and Spirit, 2007
Daughter of Ancients, 2005
Guardians of the Keep, 2004

Other books you might like:
Lynn Abbey, *Rifkind's Challenge*, 2006
Anne Bishop, *Belladonna*, 2007
Jacqueline Carey, *Naamah's Kiss*, 2009
Elizabeth Haydon, *Requiem for the Sun*, 2002
Mindy L. Klasky, *The Glasswright's Apprentice*, 2000

176

ANNE BISHOP

Twilight's Dawn

(New York: Roc, 2010)

Series: Black Jewels Series. Book 9
Subject(s): Magic; Supernatural; Adventure
Locale(s): Black Jewels Universe, Alternate Universe

Summary: In *Twilight's Dawn*, best-selling author Anne Bishop presents a collection of novellas set in a fantastical alternative universe. The pieces of this volume center on the characters of Bishop's Black Jewels series. Among

them are Lucivar Yaslana, who must expose the plot of a traitor and the dangerous plans he has laid, and Lucivar's brother, warlord prince Sadi, who must confront the travails of the holidays. Titles in this volume include "Shades of Honor," "The High Lord's Daughter," and "Family."

Where it's reviewed:
Publishers Weekly, January 10, 2011, page 35

Other books by the same author:
Shalador's Lady, 2010
The Shadow Queen, 2009
Tangled Webs, 2008
Sebastian, 2006
Shadows and Light, 2002

Other books you might like:
Carol Berg, *The Soul Mirror*, 2011
Sara Douglass, *Hades' Daughter*, 2003
Jennifer Fallon, *The Lion of Senet*, 2004
Sarah Monette, *Melusine*, 2005
Diana L. Paxson, *The Golden Hills of Westria*, 2006

177

ANNETTE BLAIR

Vampire Dragon

(New York: Berkley, 2011)

Series: Works Like Magick Series. Book 3
Story type: Romance
Subject(s): Romances (Fiction); Fantasy; Vampires
Major character(s): Bronte McBride, Vampire, Lover (of Darkwyn); Darkwyn Dragonelli, Military Personnel (Roman soldier (2,000 years old)), Vampire, Dragon; Killian the Crone, Wizard
Time period(s): 21st century
Locale(s): Salem, Massachusetts

Summary: *Vampire Dragon* is a supernatural fantasy romance novel by Annette Blair and the third entry in Blair's Works Like Magick series. In this book, Darkwyn Dragonelli is a 2,000-year-old Roman legionnaire who was turned into a dragon by an evil wizard. Now, the only way to restore his humanity is to find true love. He visits Earth and falls in love with the beautiful Bronte McBride, a fugitive from numerous enemies, who happens to be a vampire. Darkwyn must protect her, adapt to the ways of the modern world, and find a way to return permanently to his human form in *Vampire Dragon*.

Other books by the same author:
Bedeviled Angel, 2010
Death by Diamonds, 2010
Larceny and Lace, 2009
Gone with the Witch, 2008
My Favorite Witch, 2005

Other books you might like:
Cat Adams, *Blood Song*, 2010
Kresley Cole, *A Hunger Like No Other*, 2006
MaryJanice Davidson, *Derik's Bane*, 2005
Christine Feehan, *Fever*, 2006
Laurell K. Hamilton, *Blue Moon*, 1998

178

ALEX BLEDSOE

Dark Jenny

(New York: Tor, 2011)

Series: Eddie LaCrosse Series. Book 3
Story type: Historical; Mystery
Subject(s): Mystery; Murder; Fantasy
Major character(s): Eddie LaCrosse, Detective
Time period(s): Indeterminate Past
Locale(s): Grand Bruan, Fictional Location

Summary: *Dark Jenny*, a historical fantasy mystery, is the third installment in the Eddie LaCrosse series from author Alex Bledsoe. Eddie LaCrosse, a hired sword/detective, is hired by a woman to investigate her suspicions that her husband is cheating on her. LaCrosse's sleuthing leads him to a royal ball just in time to witness a murder. A newly minted knight is poisoned to death after taking a bite from an apple intended for Queen Jennifer. The fact that LaCrosse doesn't have an invitation to the ball makes him a prime suspect in the poisoning. Fortunately, the persuasive detective convinces the authorities of his innocence, only to find himself wrangled into tracking down the real culprit.

Where it's reviewed:
Booklist, March 1, 2011, page 37
Library Journal, March 15, 2011, page 110
Publishers Weekly, February 21, 2011, page 118

Other books by the same author:
The Girls with Games of Blood, 2010
Blood Groove, 2009
Burn Me Deadly, 2009
The Sword-Edged Blonde, 2007

Other books you might like:
John DeChancie, *Castle Murders*, 1991
Dave Duncan, *The Crooked House*, 2000
Randall Garrett, *Too Many Magicians*, 1966
Melisa Michaels, *Cold Iron*, 1997
John Maddox Roberts, *Murder in Tarsis*, 1996

179

KRISTEN BRITAIN

Blackveil

(New York: Penguin USA, 2011)

Series: Green Rider Series. Book 4
Story type: Magic Conflict
Subject(s): Royalty; Fantasy; Magic
Major character(s): Karigan G'ladheon, Courier

Summary: *Blackveil* is the fourth book in author Kristen Britain's Green Rider series of fantasy novels. In this novel, Karigan G'ladheon has earned the coveted title of Green Rider, a member of a legion of royal messengers entrusted by the king. Yet as evil forces loom, Karigan must accept an assignment like no other, as she goes up against magic from the dreaded Blackveil Forest.

Britain's series includes *Green Rider*, *First Rider's Call*, and *The High King's Tomb*.

Where it's reviewed:
Locus, April 2011, page 25

Other books by the same author:
The High King's Tomb, 2007
First Rider's Call, 2003
Green Rider, 1998

Other books you might like:
Anne Bishop, *Shalador's Lady*, 2010
Mercedes Lackey, *Joust*, 2003
L.E. Modesitt Jr., *Lady-Protector*, 2011
Jean Rabe, *The Finest Creation*, 2004
Patrick Rothfuss, *The Name of the Wind*, 2007

180

ANDREW BROMFIELD
ALEXEY PEHOV, Co-Author

Shadow Chaser

(New York: Tor, 2011)

Series: Chronicles of Siala Series. Book 2
Story type: Alternate World
Subject(s): Elves; Monsters; Wars
Major character(s): Shadow Harold, Thief, Hero
Time period(s): Indeterminate Past
Locale(s): Siala, Fictional Location

Summary: In book 2 of the Chronicles of Siala trilogy, *Shadow Chaser*, readers join Shadow Harold once again as he continues his quest to save the land of Siala from the Nameless One. His journey now takes him to Hrad Spein, an ancient burial ground for powerful beings. The area is still surrounded by magic, making Shadow's journey ever more dangerous, but Shadow must retrieve a long-lost horn in order to save Siala from the Nameless One. Trouble is following Shadow everywhere he goes. Will he be able to find the ancient horn and save his homeland from destruction? Or will Hrad Spein's magic and evils lead to his demise?

Where it's reviewed:
Booklist, May 1, 2011, page 72
Library Journal, March 15, 2011, page 111

Other books by the same author:
Shadow Prowler, 2010

Other books you might like:
Fritz Leiber, *Ill Met in Lankhmar*, 1995
Juliet E. McKenna, *The Thief's Gamble*, 1999
Mickey Zucker Reichert, *The Legend of Nightfall*, 1993
Michael Shea, *A'rak*, 2000
Lawrence Watt-Evans, *Touched by the Gods*, 1997

181

STEVEN BRUST

Tiassa

(New York: Tor, 2011)

Series: Vlad Taltos Series. Book 18
Subject(s): Adventure; Mystery; Antiques

Major character(s): Vlad Taltos, Assassin; Khaavren, Military Personnel (imperial guard captain)
Time period(s): Indeterminate

Summary: In *Tiassa*, author Steven Brust presents the 18th installment in the Dragaera/Vlad Taltos series and continues the adventures of assassin Vlad. This episode centers on a highly coveted artifact known as the Tiassa, which Vlad's archenemy Khaavren is desperate to get his hands on. Vlad, too, wants the Tiassa for his own personal gain, and he sets out to nab the artifact at any cost, even if that means another confrontation with his age-old nemesis.

Where it's reviewed:
Booklist, May 1, 2011, page 72
Library Journal, April 15, 2011, page 86
Locus, May 2011, page 23
Publishers Weekly, February 14, 2011, page 42

Other books by the same author:
The Book of Dragon, 2011
Iorich, 2010
Jhegaala, 2008
Dzur, 2006
The Paths of the Dead, 2002

Other books you might like:
Robin Wayne Bailey, *Swords Against the Shadowlands*, 1998
Dave Duncan, *Paragon Lost: Tales of the King's Blades*, 2002
Simon R. Green, *Beyond the Blue Moon*, 2000
Fritz Leiber, *The Second Book of Lankhmar*, 2001
Michael Moorcock, *Elric: To Rescue Tanelorn*, 2008

182

COL BUCHANAN

Farlander

(New York: Tor, 2011)

Series: Heart of the World Series. Book 1
Story type: Occult; Series
Subject(s): Cults; Fantasy; Murder
Major character(s): Sasheen, Leader (of the Holy Empire of Mann); Ash, Assassin; Nico, Apprentice (to Ash), Assassin
Locale(s): Khos, Fictional Location

Summary: *Farlander*, a suspenseful fantasy novel, is the first installment in the Heart of the World series from debut author Col Buchanan. For five decades, the anarchist cult turned religious empire, the Holy Empire of Mann, has been growing in power. Holy Matriarch Sasheen, the empire's leader, uses a predatory staff of followers known as Diplomats to do her bidding and conquer nation after nation. On the island of Khos, the Roshun is a group of elite assassins who avenge wrongful murders. Ash and his apprentice, Nico, are forced to reckon with the Holy Empire of Mann when Sasheen's son deliberately murders a woman under the Roshun's protection, causing a conflict of epic proportions between the two powerful entities. Originally published in 2010 in the United Kingdom. First novel.

Where it's reviewed:
Booklist, December 15, 2010, page 29
Library Journal, December 2010, page 106
Publishers Weekly, November 8, 2010, page 47

Other books you might like:
Alan Campbell, *God of Clocks*, 2009
Steven Erikson, *The Bonehunters*, 2007
Ian R. MacLeod, *The Light Ages*, 2003
China Mieville, *Iron Council*, 2004
Michael Swanwick, *The Dragons of Babel*, 2008

183

ORSON SCOTT CARD

Lost Gate

(New York: Tor, 2011)

Series: Mither Mages Series. Book 1
Story type: Series
Subject(s): Magic; Adventure; Adolescent interpersonal relations
Major character(s): Danny North, Magician (gate-mage); Wad, Magician (gate-mage)
Time period(s): 21st century; 2010s
Locale(s): Westil, Fictional Location; United States

Summary: Danny North is a mage who lives in exile from his native land. As he uncovers his abilities as a gate-mage, Danny realizes he can unite his people with their homeland. Gate-mages, however, don't tend to live long, and when Danny finds his life in danger, he runs away. His journey takes him on a mystical odyssey that impels him to attempt to open a Great Gate for the first time in hundreds of years. As Danny's story unfolds, another gate-mage, Wad, who lives in the land of Westil, embarks upon a journey of his own—a journey that reveals his true destiny. *The Lost Gate* is the first book in Orson Scott Card's Mither Mages series.

Where it's reviewed:
Kirkus Reviews, November 15, 2010, page 1135
Library Journal, January 2011, page 86
Locus, January 2011, page 25
Publishers Weekly, November 8, 2010, page 47

Other books by the same author:
Ender's Game, 2010
Pathfinder, 2010
Ender's Shadow: Battle School, 2009
Hidden Empire, 2009
Ender in Exile, 2008
The Crystal City, 2003
Heartfire, 2001
Enchantment, 1999
Magic Mirror, 1999
Alvin Journeyman, 1995

Other books you might like:
Craig Shaw Gardner, *Dragon Sleeping*, 1994
Paul Park, *A Princess of Roumania*, 2005
Mickey Zucker Reichert, *The Beasts of Barakhai*, 2001
Roger Zelazny, *Nine Princes in Amber*, 1970

184

JACQUELINE CAREY

Naamah's Blessing

(New York: Grand Central Publishing, 2011)

Series: Naamah Trilogy. Book 3, Naamah's Trilogy; Book 9, Kushiel's Legacy

Series: Kushiel Series. Book 3, Naamah's Trilogy; Book 9, Kushiel's Legacy

Story type: Series; Sword and Sorcery

Subject(s): Royalty; Family; Alternative worlds

Major character(s): Moirin, Witch; King Daniel, Royalty; Prince Thierry, Royalty, Son (of King Daniel); Princess Desiree, 3-Year-Old, Royalty; Queen Jehanne, Royalty, Spirit

Summary: *Naamah's Blessing* is the third novel in author Jacqueline Carey's series Kushiel's Legacy. In this installment, Moirin has come back to Terre d'Ange to learn that the king and his family have been devastated. Queen Jehanne has died, and King Daniel is so wrought with sorrow that he cannot watch over his kingdom. Meanwhile, Prince Thierry has embarked on a journey thousands of miles away. King Daniel begs Moirin to watch over Desiree, the king and queen's toddler daughter, who the Royal Crown's enemies would love to capture. As Moirin swears to give Desiree her protection, Queen Jehanne's ghost visits Moirin and asks her to make one last sacrifice.

Where it's reviewed:
Library Journal, June 1, 2011, page 96
Publishers Weekly, April 11, 2011, page 33

Other books by the same author:
Naamah's Curse, 2010
Naamah's Kiss, 2009
Kushiel's Mercy, 2008
Kushiel's Justice, 2007
Godslayer, 2005

Other books you might like:
Stephen R. Donaldson, *The Mirror of Her Dreams*, 1986
Kate Elliott, *Spirit Gate*, 2006
Katharine Kerr, *The Gold Falcon*, 2006
Melanie Rawn, *The Mageborn Traitor*, 1997
Michelle Sagara, *House Name*, 2011

185

STEVE CASH

The Remembering

(New York: Ballantine Books, 2011)

Series: Meq Series. Book 3

Story type: Historical; Series

Subject(s): Fantasy; History; Immortality

Major character(s): Zianno Zezen, Aged Person (one of the "Meq"); Opari, Steward (carrier of the Stone of Blood)

Time period(s): 20th century; 1940s-1990s

Locale(s): Japan; Russia; United States

Summary: In the fantasy novel *The Remembering* by Steve Cash, the third and final book of The Meq series, the events of the 20th century coincide with a magical quest for missing stones. The Meq is a race of mystical beings that has coexisted with man for centuries. They appear as 12-year-old children; they have the gift of almost perfect immortality. Some also have magical powers bestowed on them by five sacred stones. When atomic bombs are dropped on Hiroshima and Nagasaki in 1945, Zianno Zezen, an aged Meq, faces the possible loss of his fellow Meq. In the decades that follow, Zezen assembles a group of allies, and world powers seek to exploit the Meq as the event known as the Remembering draws near.

Where it's reviewed:
Booklist, March 1, 2011, page 38
Publishers Weekly, January 24, 2011, page 136

Other books by the same author:
Time Dancers, 2006
The Meq, 2005

Other books you might like:
Robert R. McCammon, *The Wolf's Hour*, 1989
Tim Powers, *Declare*, 2001
Judith Reeves-Stevens, *Nighteyes*, 1989
Wen Spencer, *Tinker*, 2003
Chet Williamson, *Siege of Stone*, 1999

186

MARK CHADBOURN

The Scar-Crow Men

(Amherst, New York: Pyr, 2011)

Series: Swords of Albion Trilogy. Book 2

Story type: Alternate History; Series

Subject(s): Missing persons; Magic; Supernatural

Major character(s): Will Swyfte, Spy; Christopher Marlowe, Missing Person, Writer (playwright), Friend (of Will)

Time period(s): 16th century; 1590s (1593)

Locale(s): United Kingdom

Summary: It is 1593, and the plague has hit England with a vengeance. In the midst of the outbreak, Christopher Marlowe's new play is about to debut, but on the eve of the premiere, Marlowe vanishes. Now it's up to the playwright's friend, the flamboyant spy Will Swyfte, to battle the forces of evil and solve the mystery of Marlowe's disappearance. *The Scar-Crow Men* is the second novel in Mark Chadbourn's Swords of Albion series.

Where it's reviewed:
Kirkus Reviews, January 1, 2011, page 23
Library Journal, February 15, 2011, page 104
Locus, February 2011, page 16

Other books by the same author:
The Devin in Green, 2010
Darkest Hour, 2009
Lord of Silence, 2009
The Silver Skull, 2009
Jack of Ravens, 2006

Queen of Sinister, 2004
World's End, 1999

Other books you might like:
Chaz Brenchley, *The Devil in the Dust*, 2003
David Gemmell, *Hero in the Shadows: Waylander the Slayer Stalks an Ancient Evil*, 2000
Paul Kearney, *The Ten Thousand*, 2008
Sam Sykes, *Tome of the Undergates*, 2010
Adrian Tchaikovsky, *Empire in Black and Gold*, 2008

187

BLAKE CHARLTON

Spellbound

(New York: Tor, 2011)

Series: Spellwright Series. Book 2
Story type: Magic Conflict; Series
Subject(s): Magic; Wizards; Fantasy
Major character(s): Nicodemus Weal, Apprentice, Wizard; Francesca, Friend (of Nicodemus)

Summary: In the fantasy novel *Spellbound* by Blake Charlton, Nicodemus Weal continues the problematic wizard's apprenticeship he began in *Spellwright*. In order to succeed as a wizard, Nicodemus must be able to deliver his spells accurately, but his inability to spell words correctly often causes grave errors in his magic. The evil demon who cursed Nicodemus isn't satisfied with watching the young wizard's failed spells; he has devised a plot that will endanger not only the young wizard, but all of humanity as well. Nicodemus fears that even his nearest friends will be corrupted by the demon's power. *Spellbound* is the second book in Charlton's Spellwright series.

Other books by the same author:
Spellwright, 2010

Other books you might like:
Mindy L. Klasky, *The Glasswright's Apprentice*, 2000
China Mieville, *Kraken*, 2010
L.E. Modesitt Jr., *Imager*, 2009
Mel Odom, *The Rover*, 2001
Jack Vance, *Tales of the Dying Earth*, 2000

188

CHRIS D'LACEY

Fire World

(London: Orchard Books, 2011)

Series: Last Dragon Chronicles. Book 6
Story type: Series; Young Adult
Subject(s): Dragons; Adventure; Human-animal relationships
Major character(s): David, 12-Year-Old; Rosanna, 12-Year-Old
Locale(s): Copernica, Fictional Location

Summary: Twelve-year-olds David and Rosanna have just arrived in the world of Copernica, where they find fire-birds housed within a primeval museum. After inadvertently hurting one of the creatures, David and Rosanna are drawn into an epic battle between good and evil. As they ally themselves with the firebirds, they hear tell of dragons—dragons that just might come to their aid and help them battle the forces of darkness. *Fire World* is the sixth installment in Chris D'Lacey's Last Dragon Chronicles series.

Other books by the same author:
Dark Fire, 2010
The Dragons of Wayward Crescent, 2009
The Fire Eternal, 2007
Fire Star, 2007
Ice Fire, 2006

Other books you might like:
Gillian Bradshaw, *The Land of Gold*, 1992
Wayland Drew, *Dragonslayer*, 1981
Richard A. Knaak, *Children of the Drake*, 1991
Naomi Novik, *His Majesty's Dragon*, 2006
Christopher Rowley, *Bazil Broketail*, 1992

189

MARYJANICE DAVIDSON

Undead and Undermined

(New York: Berkley Sensation, 2011)

Series: Betsy Taylor Undead Series. Book 10
Story type: Vampire Story
Subject(s): Fantasy; Fashion; Fashion design
Major character(s): Betsy Taylor, Royalty (Vampire Queen), Expert (on fashion), Vampire
Time period(s): 21st century
Locale(s): United States

Summary: *Undead and Undermined* is the tenth installment of MaryJanice Davidson's series of lighthearted fantasy novels about a quirky vampire queen. This vampire queen is Betsy Taylor and she's about as unlikely an undead monarch as they come: she's beautiful, blonde, and obsessed with fashion. Still, she knows that she has special powers and believes herself to be immortal. She starts to question this, however, when she ends up at the morgue like some expired mortal. Davidson's novels about Betsy Taylor have seen the undead diva in all sorts of adventures, such as fighting enemies and time-traveling, but she hasn't yet faced a foe like death itself.

Other books by the same author:
Undead and Unfinished, 2010
Undead and Unwelcome, 2009
Undead and Unworthy, 2008
Undead and Unpopular, 2006
Undead and Unemployed, 2004

Other books you might like:
Gerry Bartlett, *Real Vampires Don't Diet*, 2009
Molly Harper, *Nice Girls Don't Date Dead Men*, 2009
Victoria Laurie, *Ghouls, Ghouls, Ghouls*, 2010
Katie MacAlister, *In the Company of Vampires*, 2010
Kerrelyn Sparks, *Be Still My Vampire Heart*, 2007

190

STEPHEN DEAS

The King of the Crags

(London: Gollancz, 2010)

Series: Memory of Flames Series. Book 2
Story type: Alternate World; Series
Subject(s): Dragons; Adventure; Human-animal relationships
Major character(s): Snow, Dragon; Zafir, Royalty (queen); Jehal, Royalty (prince); Jaslyn, Royalty (princess); Hyrkallen, Leader (dragonmaster)

Summary: Stephen Deas's *The King of the Crags* is the second novel in The Memory of Flames series. This sophomore volume is set in a fantasy world where the upper classes keep dragons as pets. Little do these noblemen and noblewomen know that their dragons are highly evolved, exceptionally bright creatures who resent their role as pampered pets. One dragon named Snow has escaped, and it is her mission to liberate her fellow dragons. Meanwhile, the aristocracy of the realms partakes in a monumental soap opera of ever-shifting allegiances and affections.

Where it's reviewed:
Publishers Weekly, December 13, 2010, page 42

Other books by the same author:
The Adamantine Palace, 2010

Other books you might like:
Joanne Bertin, *Dragon and Phoenix*, 1999
Carol Dennis, *Dragon's Queen*, 1991
Mercedes Lackey, *The River's Gift*, 1999
Naomi Novik, *His Majesty's Dragon*, 2006
Michael Swanwick, *The Dragons of Babel*, 2008

191

LISA DESROCHERS

Original Sin

(New York: Tor, 2011)

Series: Personal Demons Series. Book 2
Story type: Series; Young Adult
Subject(s): Demons; Heaven; Hell
Major character(s): Luc Cain, Demon; Frannie Cavanaugh, Magician; Gabe, Angel
Locale(s): Heaven

Summary: *Original Sin*, a suspenseful fantasy novel for young adult readers, is the follow-up to *Personal Demons* from author Lisa Desrochers. Luc Cain has traded in his hellish life as a demon to live on earth as a human alongside the beautiful and captivating Frannie Cavanaugh, but Lucifer isn't ready to let him go so easily. Luc's former demonic pals are after him and Frannie on orders from the Prince of Darkness himself. In an effort to save himself and protect Frannie, Luc does the unthinkable: takes her to Heaven to hide out under the watchful eye of angel Gabe. Unfortunately, Frannie's powers are so strong that she begins to lead Gabe astray, forcing him to remove himself from the situation and let Frannie and Luc fend for themselves against a legion of dark forces.

Other books by the same author:
Personal Demons, 2010

Other books you might like:
Amber Benson, *Death's Daughter*, 2009
Steven Brust, *To Reign in Hell*, 1984
Holly Lisle, *Sympathy for the Devil*, 1996
Lilith Saintcrow, *Working for the Devil*, 2006
Roger Zelazny, *Lord Demon*, 1999

192

DAVID DRAKE

Out of the Waters

(New York: Tor, 2011)

Series: Books of the Elements Series. Book 2
Story type: Quest; Series
Subject(s): Fantasy; Questing; End of the world
Major character(s): Gaius Alphenus Saxa, Political Figure (senator); Varus, Son (of Saxa); Alphena, Daughter (of Saxa); Hedia, Spouse (of Saxa), Stepmother (of Varus and Alphena)
Locale(s): Carce, Fictional Location

Summary: In the fantasy novel *Out of the Waters* by David Drake, Gaius Alphenus Saxa, a ruler in the ancient land of Carce, has arranged the performance of a religious play for his people. Throngs gather to witness the fantastic drama, but the spectacle takes a strange turn when the audience also sees images of a watery beast terrorizing the city. The public believes the monster is part of the show but Saxa and his family know that they have shared a vision of Carce's future. Varus, Alphena, and Hedia must stop the forces from the deep if they are to save Carce. *Out of the Waters* is the second book in Drake's Books of Elements series.

Where it's reviewed:
Booklist, May 15, 2011, page34
Publishers Weekly, May 9, 2011, page 38
Publishers Weekly, May 9, 2011, page 38

Other books by the same author:
The Legions of Fire, 2010
The Gods Return, 2008
Balefires, 2007
The Fortress of Glass, 2006
Master of the Cauldron, 2004

Other books you might like:
Ed Greenwood, *The Kingless Land*, 2000
George R.R. Martin, *A Game of Thrones*, 1996
R.A. Salvatore, *The Bear*, 2010
Paula Volsky, *The Gates of Twilight*, 1996
Lawrence Watt-Evans, *Night of Madness*, 2000

Fantasy

193

DAVE DUNCAN

When the Saints

(New York: Tor, 2011)

Series: Brothers Magnus Series. Book 2
Story type: Alternate History
Subject(s): Magic; Fantasy; Middle Ages
Major character(s): Anton Magnus, Warrior; Wulfgang Magnus, Supernatural Being (Speaker), Brother (of Anton); Madlenka, Noblewoman (countess), Spouse (of Anton)
Time period(s): 15th century
Locale(s): Cardice, Fictional Location

Summary: In the fantasy novel *When the Saints* by Dave Duncan, the sequel to *Speak to the Devil*, brothers Anton and Wulfgang Magnus continue their adventures in an alternate 15th-century Europe. In this time and place, people suspected of communicating with demons and saints are known as Speakers. They are both reviled and revered for their power. Wulfgang Magnus is a Speaker on a mission with his brother Anton to protect the castle at Cardice. It is hoped that his relationship with hellish and heavenly forces will increase their chances of success. But Wulfgang is distracted by the earthly woman named Madlenka who is the wife of his brother.

Other books by the same author:
Speak to the Devil, 2010
The Alchemist's Pursuit, 2009
The Alchemist's Code, 2008
The Alchemist's Apprentice, 2007
Children of Chaos, 2006

Other books you might like:
David Drake, *The Fortress of Glass*, 2006
Raymond E. Feist, *Wrath of a Mad God*, 2008
David Gemmell, *Legend*, 1984
J.V. Jones, *Watcher of the Dead*, 2010
Lawrence Watt-Evans, *The Wizard Lord*, 2006

194

ROBERT EARL

Broken Honour

(Nottingham, United Kingdom: Black Library, 2011)

Story type: Historical
Subject(s): Fantasy; Wars; History
Major character(s): Eriksson, Military Personnel
Time period(s): Indeterminate Past
Locale(s): Hochland, Fictional Location

Summary: *Broken Honour*, a suspenseful fantasy novel, is part of the Warhammer and Empire Army series from author Robert Earl. The province of Hochland is barely surviving, its prosperity and safety being destroyed by the attacking beastmen. In one last-ditch effort to save Hochland, Mercenary Captain Eriksson decides to create a free army, made up of criminals and villains, to fight for freedom. Eriksson purchases the freedom of a group of prisoners to put them to work on the battlefield. The men are thrilled to be free, but they must sacrifice their lives for the greater good, fighting against the beastman in a series of horrifying and redemptive battles.

Other books by the same author:
The Adventures of Florin & Lorenzo, 2009
Ancient Blood, 2008
The Corrupted, 2006
The Burning Shore, 2004
Wild Kingdoms, 2004

Other books you might like:
Troy Denning, *Faces of Deception*, 1998
Nick Kyme, *Honourkeeper*, 2009
Nathan Long, *Zombieslayer*, 2010
Anthony Reynolds, *Knight Errant*, 2008
Steven Savile, *Dominion*, 2006

195

STEVE ENGLEHART

The Plain Man

(New York: Tor, 2011)

Series: Max August Series. Book 3
Story type: Political; Series
Subject(s): Fantasy; Wizards; Politics
Major character(s): Max August, Scientist (alchemist)
Time period(s): 21st century; 2010s
Locale(s): United States

Summary: *The Plain Man*, a suspenseful and supernatural fantasy novel, is the third installment in the Max August series from author Steve Englehart. During his long career in alchemy, Max August earned a magical gift that prevents him from ever aging, regardless of how much time goes by. Max must put his magical abilities to the test to thwart the plans of a powerful right-wing organization known as the FRC. The FRC has infiltrated every facet of society, from politics to wizardry, in an attempt to dictate every move of the United States. Max devises a top-secret plan to gain information about the FRC and use it against them, but a catastrophic incident at a nearby nuclear waste facility is the FRC's way of sending Max a strong message to stay out of their lives if he wants to keep enjoying his own.

Where it's reviewed:
Publishers Weekly, April 11, 2011, page 34

Other books by the same author:
The Long Man, 2009
The Point Man, 1981

Other books you might like:
Dave Duncan, *The Alchemist's Code*, 2008
Mark Frost, *The List of Seven*, 1993
Sarah Monette, *The Virtu*, 2006
Talbot Mundy, *The Nine Unknown*, 1923
Michael Scott, *The Alchemyst: The Secrets of the Immortal Nicholas Flamel*, 2007

196

STEVEN ERIKSON

The Crippled God

(New York: Tor Books, 2011)

Series: Malazan Book of the Fallen Series. Book 10
Story type: Alternate Universe; Series
Subject(s): Supernatural; Fantasy; Apocalypse
Major character(s): Kilmandros, Supernatural Being; Errastas, Supernatural Being; Sechul Lath, Supernatural Being; Tavore Paran, Leader (of the Bonehunters)
Locale(s): Kolanse, Fictional Location

Summary: *The Crippled God* is the 10th and final novel in author Steven Erikson's series The Malazan Book of the Fallen. In this book, all races in this alternate universe come together at the Glass Desert in a final clash for the control, or destruction, of the Universe. The Elder Gods—Kilmandros, Errastas, and Sechul Lath—plan to set free a monstrous creature that will decimate the world, ushering in the return of the dragons. Meanwhile, a ragtag army led by Adjunct Tavore Paran marches toward the battle, but rebellion threatens to split their ranks at every turn. Will the battle favor good, or will evil finally prevail and destroy the entire world?

Other books by the same author:
Dust of Dreams, 2010
Reaper's Gale, 2008
Toll the Hounds, 2008
Midnight Tides, 2007
Memories of Ice, 2005

Other books you might like:
Jennifer Fallon, *The Lion of Senet*, 2004
Raymond E. Feist, *Shadow of a Dark Queen*, 1994
David Gemmell, *Ironhand's Daughter: A Novel of the Hawk Queen*, 1995
Brandon Sanderson, *Mistborn*, 2006
Tad Williams, *Shadowmarch: Volume 1*, 2004

197

JENNIFER FALLON

The Chaos Crystal

(New York: Tor Books, 2011)

Series: Tide Lords Series. Book 4
Story type: Alternate World; Series
Subject(s): Fantasy; Immortality; Alternative worlds
Major character(s): Cayal, Immortal, Lover (former, of Arkady); Jaxyn, Immortal, Kidnapper; Lady Arkady, Lady, Human, Kidnap Victim, Lover (former, of Cayal)
Locale(s): Amyrantha, Fictional Location

Summary: *The Chaos Crystal*, a suspenseful fantasy novel, is the fourth and final installment in the Tide Lords series from author Jennifer Fallon. The magical Tide has finally turned, granting the Immortal Lords full access to their powers. With the changing tide comes news that the Chaos Crystal has been discovered. The crystal, an ancient artifact over a millennium old, is rumored to be

powerful enough to grant the Immortal Lords their every wish. Cayal is hoping to use the crystal to end his life, while Jaxyn has a different purpose in mind altogether. Things come to a head when Jaxyn kidnaps Cayal's former lover, Lady Arkady, a mortal woman determined to find the crystal herself and save the world from the destruction it will surely cause.

Where it's reviewed:
Booklist, April 15, 2011, page 28
Library Journal, April 15, 2011, page 87
Publishers Weekly, March 7, 2011, page 49

Other books by the same author:
The Palace of Impossible Dreams, 2010
The Gods of Amyrantha, 2009
Warlord, 2007
Warrior, 2006
Medalon, 2004

Other books you might like:
Dave Duncan, *Children of Chaos*, 2006
Raymond E. Feist, *Exile's Return*, 2004
Barbara Hambly, *Dragonsbane*, 1985
Katharine Kerr, *The Gold Falcon*, 2006
L.E. Modesitt Jr., *Arms-Commander*, 2010

198

CHRISTINE FEEHAN

Dark Predator

(New York: Berkley Books, 2011)

Series: Carpathian Series. Book 22
Story type: Fantasy
Subject(s): Vampires; Fantasy; Supernatural
Major character(s): Zacarias De La Cruz, Hunter (of vampires)
Time period(s): Indeterminate
Locale(s): Carpathian Mountains, Europe; Peru

Summary: Throughout history, the Carpathian Mountains have been the source of many tales of the supernatural. Christine Feehan uses them as the setting in her Carpathian Novel series that combines fantasy, romance, and the supernatural. In *Dark Predator: A Carpathian Novel*, Feehan tells the story of Zacarias De La Cruz, a Peruvian vampire hunter. De La Cruz has been hunting and killing these supernatural creatures for hundreds of years and now he feels his career is wrapping up. There are not enough vampires to search for now, and De La Cruz ponders retirement. It will not be so easy, though—back in Peru, his old lover has turned on him and is preparing a deadly trap.

Other books by the same author:
Ruthless Game, 2011
Burning Wild, 2009
Dark Curse, 2009
Conspiracy Game, 2006
Dark Demon, 2006

Other books you might like:
L.A. Banks, *The Bitten*, 2004
Dakota Cassidy, *The Accidental Human*, 2009
Susan Krinard, *Prince of Dreams*, 1995

Michelle Rowen, *Niight shade*, 2011
Susan Squires, *The Companion*, 2005

199

DANIEL FOX

Hidden Cities

(New York: Ballantine Books, 2011)

Series: Moshui Series. Book 3
Story type: Alternate History; Series
Subject(s): Fantasy; Dragons; Magic
Major character(s): Ping Wen, Assistant (to the emperor); Tien, Healer; Han, Boy
Locale(s): China

Summary: In the fantasy novel *Hidden Cities* by Daniel Fox, an alternate version of feudal China is a mysterious realm of magic and dragons. Santung, a city on the coast, has just survived an attack by invaders and the emperor dispatches staff member Ping Wen to rule there while he tends to his expectant lover. Han, a young boy who has a mystical relationship with a dragon, uses his imposing companion to flee. In Santung, Ping Wen discovers information that has been hidden away for ages—information that could determine the future of the empire. *Hidden Cities* is the third and final book in Fox's Moshui, the Books of Stone and Water series.

Where it's reviewed:
Booklist, April 1, 2011, page 37
Locus, April 2011, page 16
Publishers Weekly, February 7, 2011, page 40

Other books by the same author:
Jade Man's Skin, 2010
Dragon in Chains, 2009

Other books you might like:
Ernest Bramah, *Kai Lung's Golden Hours*, 1928
Kara Dalkey, *The Heavenward Path*, 1998
Lian Hearn, *Across the Nightingale Floor*, 2002
Barry Hughart, *Bridge of Birds*, 1984
Eric Van Lustbader, *The Sunset Warrior*, 1989

200

YASMINE GALENORN

Blood Wyne

(New York: Berkley Books, 2011)

Series: Sisters of the Moon Series. Book 9
Story type: Paranormal; Series
Subject(s): Fantasy; Vampires; Serial murders
Major character(s): Menolly D'Artigo, Human (half), Mythical Creature (half-fae), Agent
Time period(s): 21st century; 2010s
Locale(s): New York, New York

Summary: *Blood Wyne*, a suspenseful paranormal thriller, is the ninth installment in the Sisters of the Moon series from bestselling author Yasmine Galenorn. The half-human, half-fae D'Artigo sisters are turning in their badges to the Otherworld Intelligence Agency and going into business for themselves as free agents. Their first assignment seems clear as a vampire serial killer is on the loose in Manhattan, brutally murdering a string of prostitutes. The trio tracks the murderer through the city, but stops short of catching him when their hunt is disrupted by the presence of powerful poltergeists. Menolly recruits the help of Roman, a sexy ancient vampire, but he demands a hefty price to do her bidding.

Other books by the same author:
Bone Magic, 2010
Demon Mistress, 2009
Dragon Wytch, 2008
Changeling, 2007
Darkling, 2007

Other books you might like:
Patricia Briggs, *Bone Crossed*, 2009
Laurell K. Hamilton, *Micah*, 2006
Nancy Holder, *Blood and Fog*, 2003
Anton Strout, *Dead to Me*, 2008
Rob Thurman, *Nightlife*, 2006

201

TERRY GOODKIND

The Omen Machine

(New York: Tor, 2011)

Series: Sword of Truth Series. Book 12
Story type: Futuristic; Series
Subject(s): Fantasy; Prophecy; Mystery
Major character(s): Zeddicus, Wizard

Summary: *The Omen Machine*, a suspenseful fantasy thriller, is the 12th installment in the Sword of Truth series from bestselling author Terry Goodkind. A mysterious machine is discovered underground that offers predictions about what the future will hold. The prophecies seem harmless and amusing at first, but Zeddicus has a terrible feeling about the enigmatic device and feels that it should be destroyed immediately. Before Zedd has a chance to carry out his plans of destruction, the machine makes a chilling and terrifying prediction about the future that will forever impact Richard and Kahlan, unless they can stop it from happening.

Other books by the same author:
Confessor, 2007
Phantom, 2006
Chainfire, 2004
Naked Empire, 2003
The Pillars of Creation, 2001

Other books you might like:
Susanna Clarke, *Jonathan Strange & Mr. Norrell*, 2004
Storm Constantine, *The Crown of Silence*, 2000
Dave Duncan, *The Alchemist's Apprentice*, 2007
Sarah Monette, *Corambis*, 2009
Mel Odom, *The Rover*, 2001

202

RODERICK GORDON
BRIAN WILLIAMS, Co-Author

Closer
(New York: Scholastic, 2011)

Series: Tunnels Series. Book 4
Story type: Young Adult
Subject(s): Fantasy; Archaeology; Suspense
Major character(s): Will, Teenager, Son (of Dr. Burrows);
  Dr. Burrows, Archaeologist, Father (of Will)
Time period(s): 21st century; 2010s
Locale(s): London, England

Summary: *Closer*, a suspenseful fantasy novel for young adults, is the fourth installment in the best-selling *Tunnels* series from authors Brian Williams and Roderick Gordon. When Will and Chester started digging tunnels in search of Will's archaeologist father, Dr. Burrows, the two teens never expected to discover an exciting and dangerous subterranean world below London. They've managed to outsmart the malevolent Styx for now, but the mysterious villains are eager to track down the boys and recover a deadly virus intended to wipe out the human race. While Will, Dr. Burrows, and the renegade girl, Elliott, are working on excavating pyramids underground, a sinister army is rising up and hoping to hunt them down.

Where it's reviewed:
Booklist, March 15, 2011, page 56
Voice of Youth Advocates, April 2011, page 80

Other books by the same author:
Freefall, 2010
Deeper, 2009
Tunnels, 2007

Other books you might like:
Charlie Fletcher, *Stoneheart*, 2007
Alan Garner, *The Weirdstone of Brisingamen*, 1960
Peter Garrison, *The Changeling War*, 1999
Rick Riordan, *The Red Pyramid: The Kane Chronicles,
  Book One*, 2010
Brandon Sanderson, *Alcatraz Versus the Evil Librarians*,
  2007

203

SIMON R. GREEN

A Hard Day's Knight
(New York: Ace Books, 2011)

Series: Nightside Series. Book 12
Story type: Contemporary; Series
Subject(s): Legends; Adventure; Magic
Major character(s): John Taylor, Detective—Private;
  Shotgun Suzie, Sidekick (of John)
Time period(s): 21st century; 2010s
Locale(s): London, United Kingdom

Summary: John Taylor is a private eye who patrols the Nightside, a part of London plagued by dark magic and mysticism. Now John and his sidekick Shotgun Suzie come up against their most formidable foe yet, one straight out of the annals of history. The famed sword Excalibur shows up on John's doorstep, and when he and Suzie attempt to find out exactly how it came to be there, they land themselves in a series of battles with knights, elves, Merlin, and many other characters from Arthurian legend. *A Hard Day's Knight* is the 12th novel in Simon R. Green's Nightside series.

Where it's reviewed:
Booklist, January 1, 2011, page 57
Publishers Weekly, November 15, 2010, page 44

Other books by the same author:
From Hell with Love, 2010
Ghost of a Chance, 2010
The Good, the Bad, and the Uncanny, 2010
Just Another Judgment Day, 2009
The Man with the Golden Torc, 2007

Other books you might like:
Alex Bledsoe, *Dark Jenny*, 2011
Glen Cook, *Angry Lead Skies*, 2002
Michael Kurland, *A Study in Sorcery*, 1989
Mercedes Lackey, *Four & Twenty Blackbirds*, 1997
Mike Resnick, *Stalking the Dragon: A Fable of Tonight*,
  2009

204

ALYXANDRA HARVEY

Out for Blood
(New York: Walker, 2010)

Series: Drake Chronicles Series. Book 3
Story type: Vampire Story
Subject(s): Fantasy; Vampires; Adolescence
Major character(s): Hunter Wild, Student, Teenager,
  Hunter (of vampires); Helena Drake, Vampire
Time period(s): 21st century
Locale(s): United States

Summary: *Out for Blood* by Alyxandra Harvey is a young adult fantasy novel and part of Harvey's Drake Chronicles about cool high-school vampires. In *Out for Blood*, the main character is teenage vampire hunter Hunter Wild. Hunter attends a school for vampire hunters called Helios-Ra Academy, but at the same time she makes friends with some of the supernatural ghouls including Helena Drake and Quinn Drake. While falling for Quinn, Hunter realizes that many of her classmates are suddenly falling ill and she suspects a plot to destroy the vampire-hunting teens at Helios-Ra Academy. Hunter has to save her classmates as well as her new vampire friends in *Out for Blood*.

Where it's reviewed:
Booklist, March 1, 2011, page 58
Voice of Youth Advocates, April 2011, page 81

Other books by the same author:
Haunting Violet, 2011
Blood Feud, 2010
My Love Lies Bleeding, 2010
Hearts at Stake, 2009

Fantasy

Other books you might like:
L.A. Banks, *Bite the Bullet*, 2008
Christine Feehan, *Dark Predator*, 2011
Chris Marie Green, *The Path of Razors*, 2009
Charlaine Harris, *Definitely Dead*, 2006
Cherie Priest, *Bloodshot*, 2011

205

ALYXANDRA HARVEY

Haunting Violet

(New York: Walker, 2011)

Story type: Ghost Story
Subject(s): Ghosts; Supernatural; Extrasensory perception
Major character(s): Violet Willoughby, Teenager, Friend (of Colin), Psychic (able to speak with dead); Colin, Friend (of Violet)
Time period(s): 21st century

Summary: *Haunting Violet* by Alyxandra Harvey is a young adult novel about a girl, Violet Willoughby, who discovers she has amazing extrasensory powers. At first she is skeptical, and with good reason: Violet's mother is a scam artist who pretends to communicate with the dead. Violet has seen through her act and does not believe that anyone could accomplish such a feat. However, to her amazement, Violet realizes that she is a true medium, and a ghost begins to communicate with her. The ghost isn't looking to torment or terrify her, though. On the contrary, it's looking for help, and it brings a message of warning about a killer who is still on the loose and looking for more victims.

Where it's reviewed:
Booklist, May 1, 2011, page 42
Publishers Weekly, May 23, 2011, page 46

Other books by the same author:
Out for Blood, 2011
Blood Feud, 2010
My Love Lies Bleeding, 2010
Hearts at Stake, 2009

Other books you might like:
Rick Hautala, *Dark Silence*, 1992
Shirley Jackson, *The Haunting of Hill House*, 1959
Graham Masterton, *The House That Jack Built*, 1996
A.J. Matthews, *The White Room*, 2001
Peter Straub, *Ghost Story*, 1979

206

BARB HENDEE

J.C. HENDEE, Co-Author

Of Truth and Beasts

(New York: Roc, 2011)

Series: Noble Dead Series. Book 9
Story type: Quest; Series
Subject(s): Adventure; Magic; History
Major character(s): Wynn Hygeorht, Traveler (Journeyor); Lord of Slaughter, Murderer; Chane, Reanimated Dead; Shade, Wolf
Locale(s): Guild of Sagecraft, Fictional Location

Summary: Journeyor Wynn Hygeorht has discovered ancient texts from the Forgotten History, but her find is quickly taken for analysis and the young adventurer is thrust into another assignment. She is on the hunt for the Orb of the Spirit, a relic from the Forgotten History, but her search turns into a dangerous cat and mouse game when she realizes she's being trailed by the Lord of Slaughter, one of the History's most deadly figures. *Of Truth and Beasts* is the ninth novel in Barb and J.C. Hendee's Noble Dead series.

Where it's reviewed:
Publishers Weekly, November 29, 2010, page 34

Other books by the same author:
In Shade and Shadow, 2009
Child of a Dead God, 2008
Rebel Fay, 2007
Sister of the Dead, 2005
Through Stone and Sea, 201

Other books you might like:
Steven Brust, *Taltos*, 1988
Christie Golden, *Vampire of the Mists*, 1991
Tanith Lee, *The Blood of Roses*, 1991
Meredith Ann Pierce, *The Pearl of the Soul of the World*, 1990
Nora Roberts, *Morrigan's Cross*, 2006

207

C.J. HENDERSON

Central Park Knight

(New York: Tor, 2011)

Series: Piers Knight Series. Book 2
Story type: Adventure; Series
Subject(s): Dragons; Fantasy; End of the world
Major character(s): Piers Knight, Professor, Archaeologist, Magician; Tian Lu, Lover (former, of Piers), Agent (Chinese government)
Time period(s): 21st century; 2010s
Locale(s): New York, New York

Summary: *Central Park Knight* is a suspenseful fantasy novel from author C.J. Henderson. At his job for the Brooklyn Museum, Professor Piers Knight specializes in lost civilizations, esoteric cultures, and the history of magic and mysticism. But unbeknownst to his esteemed colleagues, Knight possesses some supernatural skills of his own—namely the use of magical artifacts—and is hiding a pretty lofty secret. Several years ago, Knight and his then-lover, Chinese agent Tian Lu, made a horrific discovery during a routine archaeological dig when they came face-to-face with a real fire-breathing dragon. Now, the world is facing a greater threat than anyone could imagine. Lu sends Knight an urgent message notifying him that more dragons are beginning to awaken earlier than anticipated, forcing these former romantic lovers to unite in an effort to save mankind from dragon domination. *Central Park Knight* is the second book in the Piers Knight series.

Where it's reviewed:
Publishers Weekly, January 10, 2011, page 35

Other books by the same author:
Brooklyn Knight, 2010
Degrees of Fear and Others, 2008
The Occult Detectives of C.J. Henderson, 2003

Other books you might like:
Jim Butcher, *Small Favor: A Novel of the Dresden Files*, 2008
Charlie Fletcher, *Stoneheart*, 2007
Esther M. Friesner, *New York by Knight*, 1987
Graham Masterton, *Blind Panic*, 2010
Warren Murphy, *The Forever King*, 1992

208

LISA HENDRIX

Immortal Champion

(New York: Berkley Sensation, 2011)

Series: Immortal Brotherhood Series. Book 3
Story type: Historical - Medieval; Romance
Subject(s): Fantasy; History; Vikings
Major character(s): Gunnar, Viking, Mythical Creature (were-creature); Lady Eleanor de Neville, Lady
Time period(s): 15th century

Summary: *Immortal Champion*, a historical paranormal romance, is the third installment in the Immortal Brotherhood series from author Lisa Hendrix. For two centuries, Gunnar the Red has lived under a horrific curse. Cwen the sorceress put the Viking, along with his entire crew, under a spell, forcing him to roam the earth as a were-creature. His only hope of breaking the curse is finding his one true love, but given that half of each day is spent in the form of a bull, Gunnar doesn't anticipate a romantic run-in with his soul mate. When he saves Lady Eleanor de Neville from a tragic death, he's shocked to discover an intense passion brewing inside him, but upon learning that she is betrothed to another, Gunnar escapes into the forest, unsure if he can trust her with his shocking secret.

Where it's reviewed:
Romantic Times, January 2011, page 35

Other books by the same author:
Immortal Outlaw, 2009
Immortal Warrior, 2008
Runaway Bay, 2002
Razzle Dazzle, 1999
To Marry an Irish Rogue, 200

Other books you might like:
Doranna Durgin, *Changespell*, 1997
Lora Leigh, *Coyote's Mate*, 2009
Jennifer Roberson, *Shapechangers*, 1984
Anne Stuart, *A Dark and Stormy Night*, 1997
Thomas Burnett Swann, *Day of the Minotaur*, 1966

209

DARIUS HINKS

Sigvald

(Nottingham, England: Games Workshop, 2011)

Story type: Adventure; Series
Subject(s): Fantasy; Adventure; Questing
Major character(s): Sigvad the Maginficent, Royalty (prince)
Locale(s): Warhammer Universe, Alternate Universe

Summary: In the fantasy novel *Sigvald* by Darius Hinks, a prince's unrelenting desire for pleasure and power threatens to destroy him. Prince Sigvald the Magnificent is so defenseless against his physical cravings that he has made a perilous bargain with the Slaanesh. The Slaaneshi leaders have promised Sigvald the Brass Skull, a relic that will quench his thirst for depravity, as a prize if he emerges victorious from battle. Sigvald embarks on a terrifying journey through the Chaos Wastes that leads him to a dangerous encounter and a devastating realization. *Sigvald* is the fourth book in the Warhammer Heroes series.

Other books by the same author:
Warrior Priest, 2010

Other books you might like:
Dan Abnett, *Fell Cargo*, 2006
Paul Kidd, *The Rats of Aconar*, 2000
Richard A. Knaak, *The Eye of Charon*, 2006
Douglas Niles, *The Druid Queen*, 1993
Chris Wraight, *Sword of Justice*, 2010

210

M.K. HOBSON

The Hidden Goddess

(New York: Spectra, 2011)

Story type: Historical
Subject(s): Witches; Adventure; Marriage
Major character(s): Emily Edwards, Witch; Dreadnought Stanton, Warlock, Fiance(e) (of Emily)
Time period(s): 20th century; 1900s
Locale(s): New York, New York

Summary: In M.K. Hobson's *The Hidden Goddess*, the sequel to 2010's *The Native Star*, spirited witch Emily Edwards lands in New York City at the turn of the 20th century, where she must contend with a new round of enemies out to thwart her at every turn. Emily is newly engaged to warlock Dreadnought Stanton, but she had no idea that her upcoming marriage would cause such upheaval, making her the center of an abundance of negative attention. Not only does Dreadnought's mother want Emily out of the picture, but all the ghosts, ghouls, and evildoers of the city seem to want the exact same thing.

Other books you might like:
Emma Bull, *Territory*, 2007
Alan Dean Foster, *Mad Amos*, 1996

Elizabeth Ann Scarborough, *The Drastic Dragon of Draco, Texas*, 1986
Mark Sumner, *Devil's Engine*, 1997
Logan Winters, *Silverado*, 1981

211

MARK HODDER

The Curious Case of the Clockwork Man

(Oxford, England: Snowbooks, 2011)

Series: Burton and Swinburne Series. Book 2
Story type: Series; Steampunk
Subject(s): Steampunk; History; Time
Major character(s): Richard Francis Burton, Agent (to the king); Algernon Swinburne, Writer (poet), Assistant (to Burton); Roger Tichborne, Heir (Tichborne estate)
Time period(s): 19th century; 1860s (1862)
Locale(s): Australia; England

Summary: In the fantasy novel *The Curious Case of the Clockwork Man* by Mark Hodder, royal agent Sir Richard Francis Burton and his assistant Algernon Swinburne investigate a case involving missing gems and lost time. In 1862, the course of world history is shifted by the appearance of a brass clockwork man in London. Burton recognizes the time rift and searches for a solution as he and Swinburne also hunt for a cache of stolen diamonds. Meanwhile, a nobleman who had been missing for years, Sir Roger Tichborne, has returned seeking his inheritance, but Burton has doubts about his true identity. *The Curious Case of the Clockwork Man* is the second book in the Burton and Swinburne series.

Where it's reviewed:
Library Journal, March 15, 2011, page 110

Other books by the same author:
The Strang Affair of Spring Heeled Jack, 2010

Other books you might like:
James P. Blaylock, *Homunculus*, 1986
Esther M. Friesner, *Druid's Blood*, 1988
K.W. Jeter, *Infernal Devices: A Mad Victorian Fantasy*, 1987
Andrew Mayer, *The Falling Machine*, 2011
S.M. Peters, *Whitechapel Gods*, 2008

212

ERIN HOFFMAN

Sword of Fire and Sea

(Amherst, New York: Pyr, 2011)

Series: Chaos Knight Series. Book 1
Story type: Adventure
Subject(s): Fantasy; Magic; Pirates
Major character(s): Vidarian Rulorat, Sea Captain; Ariadel, Supernatural Being (fire priestess)
Time period(s): Indeterminate

Summary: *Sword of Fire and Sea*, a suspenseful and adventurous fantasy novel, is the first installment in the Chaos Knight series from author Erin Hoffman. Thanks to the socially unacceptable marriage between his great-grandfather and a fire priestess three generations ago, Captain Vidarian Rulorat is legally bound to do the bidding of the High Temple of Kara'zul, the domain of the fire priestesses. As the last surviving member of the Rulorat clan, Vidarian is required to uphold the Breakwater Agreement, a 70-year-old alliance signed by his great-grandfather, and transport a young fire priestess named Ariadel across pirate-infested seas to a water temple. As if the pirates weren't threatening enough, Vidarian also has to protect Ariadel from the Vkortha, a gang of dangerous telepathic magicians who are desperate to silence the young fire priestess forever.

Where it's reviewed:
Publishers Weekly, April 25, 2011, page 119

Other books you might like:
Jennifer Fallon, *The Immortal Prince*, 2008
Ari Marmell, *The Conqueror's Shadow*, 2010
Andre Norton, *Three Hands for Scorpio*, 2005
Joel Shepherd, *Haven*, 2011
Jon Sprunk, *Shadow's Son*, 2010

213

MORGAN HOWELL

The Iron Palace

(New York: Del Rey, 2011)

Series: Shadowed Path Trilogy. Book 3
Story type: Quest; Series
Subject(s): Adventure; Family history; Magic
Major character(s): Froan, 17-Year-Old, Son (of Yim and Lord Bahl); Yim, Slave (former), Mother (of Froan); Lord Bahl, Royalty (avatar of the Devourer), Father (of Froan); Honus, Friend (of Yim)
Locale(s): Grey Fens, Fictional Location

Summary: *The Iron Palace* is the third installment in Morgan Howell's The Shadowed Path series. This outing follows the adventures of 17-year-old Froan, the son of former slave Yim and the evil Lord Bahl. Though Froan knows virtually nothing of his father or the mystical circumstances surrounding his birth, he cannot ignore the penchant for dark magic surging in his veins. With determination and courage, he sets out to discover the truth of his heritage—prompting Yim to prevent his quest at any cost.

Other books by the same author:
Candle in the Storm, 2009
A Woman Worth Ten Coppers, 2008
Clan Daughter, 2007
King's Property, 2007
Royal Destiny, 2007

Other books you might like:
Kristen Britain, *Blackveil*, 2011
Jennifer Fallon, *The Immortal Prince*, 2008
Maggie Furey, *Aurian*, 1994
Gail Z. Martin, *The Summoner*, 2007
R.A. Salvatore, *The Orc King*, 2007

214

KERRIE HUGHES
RACHEL CAINE, Co-Editor

Chicks Kick Butt

(New York: Tor Books, 2011)

Story type: Collection
Subject(s): Women; Short stories; Fantasy

Summary: *Chicks Kick Butt* is a collection of short stories compiled by editors Rachel Caine and Kerrie Hughes. This book contains short stories from 13 popular female authors of the fantasy genre. Among the authors included in this collection are Lilith Saintcrow, author of "Monsters;" P.N. Elrod, author of "Vampires Prefer Blondes;" and Cheyenne McCray, author of "Double Dead." An excerpt from Caine's bestselling series "Weather Wardens" is also included. These stories feature extraordinary women slaying vampires, chasing monsters, warding off demons, and otherwise fighting against evil. Caine is also the author of the Morganville Vampires series, the Revivalist series, and the Outcast Season series.

Other books by the same author:
Undone, 2009
Gale Force, 2008
Thin Air, 2007
Firestorm, 2006
Heat Stroke, 2004

Other books you might like:
L.A. Banks, *Cursed to Death*, 2009
Jenna Black, *The Devil You Know*, 2008
Laurell K. Hamilton, *Skin Trade*, 2009
Lilith Saintcrow, *Redemption Alley*, 2009
Elizabeth Vaughan, *Destiny's Star*, 2010

215

DOUGLAS HULICK

Among Thieves

(New York: Roc, 2011)

Story type: Urban
Subject(s): Fantasy; Crime; Criminals
Major character(s): Drothe, Criminal, Troubleshooter, Smuggler
Time period(s): Indeterminate

Summary: *Among Thieves* is a suspenseful and action-packed fantasy novel from author Douglas Hulick. As an employee of a ruthless crime lord, Drothe's co-workers include a band of unsavory thieves, murderers, and villains. For years, Drothe has earned a living troubleshooting for his malevolent boss, while running a small, secretive side business as a smuggler of rare and ancient relics. Drothe can handle his own among the most unscrupulous of villains, but his life is put in jeopardy when he gains possession of a powerful relic that's capable of bringing down emperors. Everyone in the criminal underworld wants to take hold of Drothe's recent find and they'll stop at nothing to obtain it.

Where it's reviewed:
Library Journal, April 15, 2011, page 88

Other books you might like:
Peter David, *Sir Apropos of Nothing*, 2001
Fritz Leiber, *Ill Met in Lankhmar*, 1995
Juliet E. McKenna, *The Assassin's Edge*, 2002
Mickey Zucker Reichert, *Shadow Climber*, 1988
Michael Shea, *Nifft the Lean*, 1982

216

STEPHEN HUNT

The Rise of the Iron Moon

(London: Harper Voyager, 2009)

Series: Jackelian Series. Book 3
Story type: Series; Steampunk
Subject(s): Steampunk; Fantasy; Wars
Major character(s): Purity Drake, Orphan, Prisoner
Locale(s): Kingdom of Jackals, Fictional Location

Summary: *The Rise of the Iron Moon*, a suspenseful steampunk science fantasy novel, is part of the Jackelian series from author Stephen Hunt. Lonely orphan Purity Drake, a prisoner of the Royal Breeding House, manages to escape a life of captivity after inadvertently killing one of her guards. Rescued by an enigmatic drifter, Purity soon finds herself on the run alongside this mysterious stranger, but they face far greater danger than they realize. The Kingdom of Jackals is being invaded by a dark and powerful force known as the Army of Shadows, a vicious band of enemies who will stop at nothing to destroy the nation. Purity soon finds herself torn between her disgust for the Jackelian government and her loyalty to her people. Can this young orphan find the strength needed to stop an entire army of darkness?

Where it's reviewed:
Booklist, April 1, 2011, page 72
Library Journal, March 1, 2011, page 72
Publishers Weekly, January 24, 2011, page 136

Other books by the same author:
Jack Cloudie, 2011
Secrets of the Fire Sea, 2010
The Kingdom Beyond the Waves, 2009
The Court of the Air, 2007
For the Crown and the Dragon, 1997

Other books you might like:
Alan Campbell, *Scar Night*, 2007
Jay Lake, *Green*, 2009
China Mieville, *The Scar*, 2002
Madeleine E. Robins, *The Stone War*, 1999
Catherynne M. Valente, *Palimpsest*, 2009

217

KAMERON HURLEY

God's War

(San Francisco, California: Night Shade, 2011)

Story type: Futuristic
Subject(s): Fantasy; Wars; Futuristic society

Fantasy

Major character(s): Nyx, Government Official, Bounty Hunter
Time period(s): Indeterminate Future

Summary: *God's War* is a suspenseful fantasy thriller from author Kameron Hurley. On a distant planet established by Muslims, a violent holy war has been raging for centuries. The planet is contaminated and on the brink of destruction as mercenaries, soldiers, and magicians draw out the long, bloody battle. Nyx, a former government agent, now earns a living as a bounty hunter, cutting off people's heads for a hefty price. When the government gets duped during an attempt to end the war, Nyx is recruited to clean up the mess. She has to bring home the head of an off-worlder who possesses the power and ability to end the war, but with a gang of foreign agents and other bounty hunters coming after her, it won't be an easy task.

Where it's reviewed:
Publishers Weekly, December 20, 2010, page 39

Other books you might like:
Piers Anthony, *Blue Adept*, 1981
C.S. Friedman, *Black Sun Rising*, 1991
Irene Radford, *The Last Battlemage*, 1998
Christopher Stasheff, *Warlock and Son*, 1991
Lawrence Watt-Evans, *Out of This World*, 1994

218

HANNAH JAYNE

Under Wraps

(New York: Kensington Books, 2011)

Series: Underworld Detection Agency Chronicles. Book 1
Story type: Mystery
Subject(s): Fantasy; Supernatural; Serial murders
Major character(s): Sophie Lawson, Administrator (for the Underworld Detection Agency), Human; Parker Hayes, Detective
Time period(s): 21st century; 2010s
Locale(s): San Francisco, California

Summary: *Under Wraps*, a humorous and suspenseful fantasy thriller, is the first installment in the Underworld Detection Agency Chronicles from author Hannah Jayne. Thanks to her immunity to magic, Sophie Lawson is the only human on staff with the Underworld Detection Agency, an organization catering to the needs of San Francisco's supernatural creatures. As a UDA employee, Sophie has worked with everyone—and everything— from angry vampires to cantankerous fairies to infatuated trolls, but a series of grisly murders has this wisecracking administrative assistant shaking in her boots. When her sexy werewolf boss goes missing, Sophie has to team up with equally hot detective Parker Hayes, who may or may not be telling her the truth about the investigation.

Where it's reviewed:
Publishers Weekly, January 24, 2011, page 136

Other books by the same author:
Under Attack, 2011

Other books you might like:
Ben Aaronovitch, *Moon Over Soho*, 2011
Jes Battis, *A Flash of Hex*, 2009
Jim Butcher, *Death Masks*, 2003
Mark Del Franco, *Unfallen Dead*, 2009
Seanan McGuire, *Late Eclipses*, 2011

219

CELIA JEROME

Night Mares in the Hamptons

(New York: Penguin, 2011)

Series: Willow Tate Series. Book 2
Story type: Psychic Powers; Series
Subject(s): Fantasy; Epics; Horses
Major character(s): Willow Tate, Writer (graphic novels), Psychic; Ty Farraday, Horse Trainer (horse whisperer)
Time period(s): 21st century; 2010s
Locale(s): Paumanok Harbor, New York

Summary: In the fantasy novel *Night Mares in the Hamptons* by Celia Jerome, Willow Tate is a graphic novelist whose artistic and psychic talents have opened a passage between the world of fairies and the world of humans. Willow travels to Paumanok Harbor in The Hamptons from Manhattan on an assignment for the Department of Unexplained Events. She is charged with finding a lost magic pony with help from horse whisperer Ty Farraday. To complete her task, Willow must face threats from the mortal and magical realm as well as Ty's romantic advances. *Night Mares in the Hamptons* is the second book in the Willow Tate series.

Other books by the same author:
Trolls in the Hamptons, 2010

Other books you might like:
Emma Bull, *War for the Oaks*, 1987
Brett Davis, *The Faery Convention*, 1995
Kristine Grayson, *Utterly Charming*, 2000
Mindy L. Klasky, *How Not to Make a Wish*, 2009
Thorne Smith, *The Stray Lamb*, 1929

220

MARILYN KAYE

Speak No Evil

(New York: Kingfisher, 2011)

Series: Gifted Series. Book 6
Story type: Young Adult
Subject(s): Gifted children; Fantasy; Suspense
Major character(s): Carter Street, Student—Middle School
Time period(s): 21st century; 2010s
Locale(s): United States

Summary: *Speak No Evil*, a fantasy novel for young adults, is the sixth installment in the Gifted series from bestselling author Marilyn Kaye. In Meadowbrook Middle School, the Nine appear to be students just like everyone else, but each member is hiding a shocking secret. Each

Fantasy

of the Nine is gifted, possessing a supernatural skill, gift, or talent. Each of the Nine is a mystery, but Carter Street is especially mysterious. He doesn't speak at all to anyone, not even to reveal what his real name is, yet the other students sense there's something more powerful going on behind his silent exterior. The Nine are about to discover the truth about Carter Street—the dark and ominous truth.

Other books by the same author:
Finders Keepers, 2010
Better Late Than Never, 2009
Here Today, Gone Tomorrow, 2009
Like Father, Like Son, 2001
In Search of Andy, 2000

Other books you might like:
K.A. Applegate, *The Illusion*, 1999
Rachel Caine, *The Dead Girls' Dance*, 2007
Diana G. Gallagher, *Mist and Stone*, 2003
Kathryn Lasky, *May*, 2011
John C. Wright, *Orphans of Chaos*, 2005

221

KATHARINE KERR

License of Ensorcell

(New York: Penguin, 2011)

Story type: Contemporary
Subject(s): Fantasy; Werewolves; Psychics
Major character(s): Nola O'Grady, Psychic, Agent (secret government agency); Ari Nathan, Agent (Interpol)
Time period(s): 21st century; 2010s
Locale(s): San Francisco, California

Summary: In the fantasy novel *License to Ensorcell* by Katharine Kerr, Nola O'Grady's job has brought her back to her hometown of San Francisco. An agent for an ultra-secret government organization, O'Grady uses her psychic skills to track unusual criminals. Her latest case involves a serial murderer whose weapon of choice is a gun loaded with silver bullets. The gunman claims that he is exterminating werewolves, and Nola and her new partner, Interpol agent Ari Nathan, must determine if he's telling the truth. Ari is skeptical but Nola is a believer. Her werewolf brother Patrick was killed by a shooter with a silver bullet.

Other books by the same author:
The Spirit Stone, 2007
The Gold Falcon, 2006
The Shadow Isle, 2002
The Fire Dragon, 2001
The Black Raven, 1998

Other books you might like:
Jim Butcher, *Fool Moon*, 2001
Deborah Harkness, *A Discovery of Witches*, 2011
Simon Hawke, *The Wizard of Santa Fe*, 1991
Tanya Huff, *Smoke and Shadows*, 2004
Celia Jerome, *Trolls in the Hamptons*, 2010

222

NICK KYME
GAV THORPE, Co-Author

Dwarfs

(Nottingham, England: Games Workshop, 2011)

Story type: Collection
Subject(s): Fantasy; Epics; Dwarfs

Summary: In *Dwarfs*, authors Nick Kyme and Gav Thorpe collect three novels set in the Warhammer Universe. Each fantastic adventure focuses on the fierce fighters and skilled artisans of ages past known as the dwarfs. *Grudgebearer*, by Thorpe, chronicles a quest for vengeance undertaken by the son of a slain dwarf king. In *Oathbreaker*, by Kyme, a force of brave dwarfs sets out to reclaim a land that they had lost. *Honourkeeper*, also by Kyme, tells the tale of an epic war waged between the dwarfs and their despised enemies, the elves.

Other books by the same author:
Fall of Damnos, 2011
Firedrake, 2010
Grimblades, 2010
Honourkeeper, 2009
Oathbreaker, 2008

Other books you might like:
Richard Lee Byers, *The Black Bouquet*, 2003
Troy Denning, *The Sorcerer*, 2002
Graham McNeill, *Heldenhammer*, 2008
Mel Odom, *The Black Road*, 2002
Gav Thorpe, *Caledor*, 2011

223

M.D. LACHLAN

Wolfsangel

(London: Gollancz, 2010)

Series: Craw Trilogy. Book 1
Story type: Historical; Series
Subject(s): Fantasy; Werewolves; Brothers
Major character(s): Vali, Brother (of Feileg), Heir (of King Authun); Feileg, Brother (of Vali), Werewolf; Gullveig, Witch; Authun, Royalty (King), Viking
Time period(s): Indeterminate Past

Summary: *Wolfsangel* is a suspenseful historical fantasy novel from author M.D. Lachlan. Viking King Authun and his men embark on a dangerous mission to find an heir to the throne, following the prophecy of a witch named Gullveig. The king kidnaps two infant twin brothers, Vali and Feilig. Vali, a smart and strategic young man, is raised as the king's son, while the brother he never knew grows up as the werewolf bodyguard to Gullveig. These two boys and their lives are as different as can be, but they're both drawn together by their mutual love for Adisla, a farmer's daughter. When Adisla is kidnapped, the two men join together on a supernatural and dangerous quest, bound together by their brotherhood and love for Adisla. *Wolfsangel* is the first book in the Craw Trilogy.

Where it's reviewed:
Publishers Weekly, January 17, 2011, page 34

Other books you might like:
James Barclay, *Cry of the Newborn*, 2005
Patricia Briggs, *Masques*, 1993
Jennifer Fallon, *Wolfblade*, 2006
Jane M. Lindskold, *Through Wolf's Eyes*, 2001
Sam Sykes, *Black Halo*, 2011

224

MERCEDES LACKEY
ROSEMARY EDGHILL, Co-Author

Conspiracies

(New York: Tor, 2011)

Series: Shadow Grail Series. Book 2
Story type: Series; Young Adult
Subject(s): Fantasy; Magic; Boarding schools
Major character(s): Spirit, Orphan, Student—Boarding School; Mark Rider, Magician, Security Officer
Time period(s): 21st century; 2010s
Locale(s): United States

Summary: *Conspiracies*, a suspenseful fantasy mystery for young adult readers, is the second book in the Shadow Grail series from bestselling authors, Mercedes Lackey and Rosemary Edghill. Spirit and her friends at Oakhurst Academy, an elite boarding school for magically gifted orphans, feel as though they've earned a well-deserved break. They did, after all, eliminate a malevolent force that's been murdering students for four decades. But just when the teens begin to relax, a new wave of unexplainable attacks begin. The administration has hired alumnus Mark Rider to provide security on the campus, but Spirit suspects there's something far more powerful at work that Mark's methods won't be able to contain.

Other books by the same author:
Intrigues, 2010
Foundation, 2008
Reserved for the Cat, 2007
One Good Knight, 2006
Sanctuary, 2005

Other books you might like:
Diana Wynne Jones, *Charmed Life*, 1977
J.K. Rowling, *Harry Potter and the Sorcerer's Stone*, 1998
E. Rose Sabin, *A School for Sorcery*, 2002
Caroline Stevermer, *A Scholar of Magics*, 2004
John C. Wright, *Orphans of Chaos*, 2005

225

L. JAGI LAMPLIGHTER

Prospero Regained

(New York: Tor, 2011)

Series: Prospero's Daughter Series. Book 3
Story type: Magic Conflict; Series

Subject(s): Magicians; Hell; Fantasy
Major character(s): Prospero, Sorcerer; Miranda, Daughter (of Prospero)
Time period(s): 21st century; 2010s
Locale(s): Hell

Summary: In the fantasy novel *Prospero Regained*, L. Jagi Lamplighter concludes her Prospero's Daughter trilogy. Prospero, the protagonist of William Shakespeare's play *The Tempest* who survived banishment by his brother, has survived into the 21st century with his daughter, Miranda. Unknown to Earth's humans, Prospero serves as guardian of the world while Miranda manages their business enterprise, Prospero, Inc. When Prospero is taken captive by the minions of the underworld, there is much more at stake than the sorcerer's existence. Miranda and her siblings must brave the forces of Hell and overcome ancient family rivalries if they are to free their father.

Other books by the same author:
Prospero in Hell, 2010
Prospero Lost, 2009

Other books you might like:
Michael Ayrton, *The Maze Maker*, 1967
Sarah A. Hoyt, *All Night Awake*, 2002
Jane M. Lindskold, *The Pipes of Orpheus*, 1995
Thomas Burnett Swann, *The Forest of Forever*, 1971
Tad Williams, *Caliban's Hour*, 1994

226

KATHRYN LASKY

May

(New York: Scholastic, 2011)

Series: Daughters of the Sea Series. Book 2
Story type: Young Adult
Subject(s): Mermaids; Romances (Fiction); Fantasy
Major character(s): May, 15-Year-Old, Supernatural Being (mermaid); Rudd, Boy (suitor); Hugh, Student
Time period(s): Indeterminate

Summary: *May*, a supernatural fantasy romance novel for young adults, is the second installment in the Daughters of the Sea series from author Kathryn Lasky. As her 15th birthday approaches, May is overcome with discontentment and curiosity. She longs to be nearer to the sea and to lose herself in books, but her parents forbid her from swimming and think her literary inquisitiveness is odd. Meanwhile, Rudd won't give up on his attempts to woo her and break her wild spirit. Shortly after her birthday, May is shocked to discover a secret that will change her forever: she's a mermaid! Her newfound freedom overwhelms her with joy and catches the eye of astronomy student Hugh, but Rudd is determined to have May to himself...or not let anyone have her at all.

Where it's reviewed:
Booklist, May 1, 2011, page 86

Other books by the same author:
Hannah, 2009
The Golden Tree, 2007
The Capture, 1993

Shadows in the Water, 1992
Double Trouble Squared, 1991

Other books you might like:
Susan Cooper, *The Dark Is Rising*, 1973
Mollie Hunter, *Kelpie's Pearls*, 1964
Nancy Springer, *Plumage*, 2000
Vivian Vande Velde, *Never Trust a Dead Man*, 1999
Jane Yolen, *White Jenna*, 1989

227

MIKE LEE

Nagash Immortal

(Nottingham, England: Games Workshop, 2011)

Series: Time of Legends: Nagash Trilogy. Book 3
Story type: Series; Sword and Sorcery
Subject(s): Fantasy; Adventure; Epics
Major character(s): Nagash, Magician (necromancer),
    Ruler; Alcadizzar, Warrior
Locale(s): Nehekhara, Fictional Location

Summary: In the fantasy novel *Nagash Immortal* by Mike
Lee, the evil ruler Nagash prepares to face the adversary
that threatens his control of the ancient land of the
undead. The skaven seem to be formidable opponents
until Nagash convinces them to join forces with him in
his quest for Nehekhara. Nagash's newly formed army is
capable of great devastation, but Nehekhara still possess
one mighty defender—the fierce warrior Alcadizzar. As
Nagash and Alcadizzar ready themselves for battle, the
future of their world hangs in the balance. *Nagash Immortal* is the third book in Lee's Time of Legends series.

Other books by the same author:
Fallen Angels, 2009
Nagash the Unbroken, 2009
Nagash the Sorcerer, 2008

Other books you might like:
Elaine Cunningham, *Silver Shadows*, 1996
Michael Jan Friedman, *The Seeker and the Sword*, 1985
Thomas M. Reid, *The Fractured Sky*, 2008
Steven Savile, *Inheritance*, 2006
C.L. Werner, *The Grey Seer*, 2009

228

STINA LEICHT

Of Blood and Honey

(San Francisco, California: Night Shade, 2011)

Series: Fey and the Fallen Series. Book 1
Story type: Historical; Series
Subject(s): Supernatural; Fantasy; Fairies
Major character(s): Liam, Bastard Son (of a fey)
Time period(s): 20th century; 1970s
Locale(s): Derry, Ireland

Summary: *Of Blood and Honey* is a historical and political fantasy novel from debut author Stina Leicht. Set
during the English-Irish turmoil of the 1970s, *Of Blood*

and Honey imagines another layer of supernatural
conflict to the political unrest. Liam grew up without a
father and absolutely no information about him. The
town of Derry assumed he was a Protestant, but Liam is
about to discover that his heritage is far worse. As political divisiveness carries on all around him, Liam soon
discovers there's another conflict raging in the supernatural realm. The fallen and the fey have been fighting for
centuries and Liam is about to be pulled into the battle,
unaware that he's a direct descendant of a powerful fey
who also happens to be his only hope. *Of Blood and
Honey* is the first book in the Fey and the Fallen series.
First novel.

Where it's reviewed:
Library Journal, February 15, 2011, page 104
Publishers Weekly, January 3, 2011, page 38

Other books you might like:
Emma Bull, *War for the Oaks*, 1987
Laurell K. Hamilton, *A Kiss of Shadows*, 2000
Karen Marie Moning, *Dreamfever*, 2009
Kristine Kathryn Rusch, *The Sacrifice: The First Book
    of the Fey*, 1995
Sarban, *Ringstones*, 1951

229

JOHN LEVITT

Play Dead

(New York: Ace Books, 2011)

Series: Dog Days Series. Book 4
Story type: Black Magic; Series
Subject(s): Magic; Fantasy; Theft
Major character(s): Mason, Agent (Enforcer); Lou, Dog;
    Jessica Alexander, Magician
Time period(s): 21st century; 2010s
Locale(s): San Francisco, California

Summary: *Play Dead*, a suspenseful urban fantasy novel,
is the fourth installment in the Dog Days series from
author John Levitt. As an enforcer, Mason was entrusted
with keeping magic practitioners in line, even when they
didn't want to be. These days, Mason has left the magical world for a normal one, wasting away his days
alongside his paranormal pooch, Lou. When Mason's in
need of some extra cash to pay the bills and fix up his
truck, he reluctantly accepts a job from Jessica Alexander, a dark practitioner in search of something that
was stolen from her. As Mason hunts down Jessica's
mystery object, he learns the truth about what she's
searching for: an ancient grimoire that every magical being longs to possess.

Other books by the same author:
Unleashed, 2009
New Tricks, 2008
Dog Days, 2007

Other books you might like:
Emma Bull, *Finder: A Novel of the Borderlands*, 1994
Jim Butcher, *Dead Beat*, 2005
Jerry Jay Carroll, *Top Dog*, 1996
Simon R. Green, *A Hard Day's Knight*, 2011

230

NATHAN LONG

Bloodforged

(Nottingham, England: Games Workshop, 2011)

Series: Ulrika the Vampire Series. Book 2
Story type: Horror; Series
Subject(s): Fantasy; Horror; Vampires
Major character(s): Ulrika, Vampire
Locale(s): Praag, Fictional Location

Summary: In the fantasy novel *Bloodforged* by Nathan Long, Ulrika, still new to her existence as a vampire, has abandoned her attempt to join Lahmian society. The independent-minded young woman sets out for Praag, where dark forces reign but Ulrika's old allies remain. Ulrika discovers that Praag has suffered greatly in the Chaos incursions, but she is pleased to find its residents steadfast in their defense of their city. Ulrika knows that evil is a resourceful power and soon she finds herself facing mounting threats posed by a Slaaneshi cult. *Bloodforged* is the second book in the Ulrika the Vampire series.

Other books by the same author:
Bloodborn, 2010
Elfslayer, 2008
Manslayer, 2007
Orcslayer, 2006
The Broken Lance, 2005

Other books you might like:
Richard A. Knaak, *The God in the Moon*, 2006
Nick Kyme, *Oathbreaker*, 2008
Gav Thorpe, *Shadow King: A Tale of the Sundering*, 2010
C.L. Werner, *Temple of the Serpent*, 2011

231

MARI MANCUSI

Blood Ties

(New York: Berkley Books, 2011)

Series: Blood Coven Series. Book 6
Story type: Fantasy
Subject(s): Romances (Fiction); Supernatural; Vampires
Major character(s): Sunny McDonald, Vampire, Teenager, Sister (of Rayne); Rayne McDonald, Vampire, Teenager, Sister (of Sunny); Jayden, Human (who saved Sunny)
Time period(s): 21st century
Locale(s): Tokyo, Japan

Summary: *Blood Ties* by Mari Mancusi is a novel about romance and schemes among teenage vampires. An entry in Mancusi's Blood Coven series, *Blood Ties* deals with vampire teen twins Sunny and Rayne McDonald. Sunny and Rayne have to settle out their love lives before they confront a group of dangerous vampire slayers called Slayer, Inc. The Slayers are gathering in Tokyo and making plans to kill all the vampires, and that includes the McDonald twins! Sunny and Rayne, along with their boyfriends and romantic interests, have to travel the world, dodging and fighting Slayers. Mari Mancusi also wrote *Night School* about the McDonald twins.

Other books by the same author:
Night School, 2011
Bad Blood, 2010
Girls That Growl, 2007
Boys That Bite, 2006
Stake That!, 2006

Other books you might like:
Karen Chance, *Touch the Dark*, 2006
Casey Daniels, *Don of the Dead*, 2006
Alyxandra Harvey, *Out for Blood*, 2010
Chloe Neill, *Some Girls Bite*, 2009
Cassie Ryan, *Seducing the Succubus*, 2010

232

ARI MARMELL

The Goblin Corps

(Amherst, New York: Pyr, 2011)

Subject(s): Fantasy; Wars; Good and evil
Major character(s): Morthul, Villain, Royalty (Charnel King); Dororam, Royalty (King)
Time period(s): Indeterminate

Summary: *The Goblin Corps* is a suspenseful and action-packed fantasy novel from author Ari Marmell. Morthul, the malevolent Charnel King, has spent centuries within the walls of the Iron Keep devising a foolproof plot to expand his empire. Unfortunately, thanks to a band of bumbling so-called heroes, Morthul has been outsmarted and his plans have been thwarted. The only consolation Morthul has is the knowledge that he took the life of Princess Amalia, the Shauntville family's only heir. Her father, King Dororam, is outraged by her murder and vows to avenge her death by training an army to overtake Morthul. If the Dark Lord hopes to survive, he'll have to gather every goblin on the Brimstone Mountains for a ruthless battle to the death.

Other books by the same author:
The Warlord's Legacy, 2011
Agents of Artifice, 2009
The Conqueror's Shadow, 2009
Gehenna: The Final Night, 2004

Other books you might like:
Glen Cook, *Lord of the Silent Kingdom*, 2007
Jim C. Hines, *Goblin Hero*, 2007
Carl Miller, *The Goblin Plain War*, 1991
Stan Nicholls, *Orcs: First Blood: Bodyguard of Lightning*, 1998
David Sherman, *Onslaught*, 2002

233

ARI MARMELL

The Warlord's Legacy

(New York: Spectra/Ballantine Books, 2011)

Series: Corvis Rebaine Series. Book 2
Story type: Sword and Sorcery

Subject(s): Fantasy; Epics; Magic
Major character(s): Corvis Rebaine, Warrior (former); Baron Jassion, Warrior; Kaleb, Sorcerer; Mellorin, Daughter (of Rebaine)
Locale(s): Imphallion, Fictional Location

Summary: In the fantasy novel *The Warlord's Legacy* by Ari Marmell, the sequel to *The Conqueror's Shadow*, Corvis Rebaine—once the feared warrior known as the "Terror of the East"—has become the victim of an imposter. Wearing Rebaine's imposing suit of armor and wielding a devilish axe, the mysterious man is on a murderous rampage across the lands of Imphallion for which Rebaine will be blamed. But the once mighty warrior has been humbled by grief and loss. He has become prey to a band of enemies that includes his daughter, Mellorin. With his country under threat of invasion and his own life at risk, Corvis Rebaine considers taking up his axe once again.

Where it's reviewed:
Library Journal, February 15, 2011, page 105

Other books by the same author:
The Goblin Corps, 2011
Agents of Artifice, 2009
The Conqueror's Shadow, 2009
Gehenna: The Final Night, 2004

Other books you might like:
David Gemmell, *Knights of Dark Renown*, 1989
Robert E. Howard, *The Coming of Conan the Cimmerian*, 2002
R.A. Salvatore, *The Highwayman*, 2004
Brandon Sanderson, *The Hero of Ages*, 2008
Tad Williams, *The Dragonbone Chair*, 1988

234

J.M. MCDERMOTT

Never Knew Another

(San Francisco, California: Night Shade, 2011)

Series: Dogsland Trilogy series. Book 1
Story type: Historical - Medieval; Series
Subject(s): Demons; Prejudice; Fantasy
Major character(s): Rachel Nolander, Demon, Refugee, Impoverished; Jona, Demon, Guard
Time period(s): Indeterminate Past
Locale(s): Dogsland, Fictional Location

Summary: *Never Knew Another*, a suspenseful fantasy novel, is the first installment in the Dogsland trilogy from author J.M. McDermott. In the city of Dogsland, a quasi-medieval land, the wealthy and the poor live vastly different lifestyles but they're all united in their hatred for demon children. Anyone who has demon blood in his heritage, as evidenced by physical deformities, acidic tears, blood, or sweat, and the ability to spread illness with a mere touch, is ruthlessly hunted down. Rachel Nolander is new to Dogsland, supported by her brother, and lives in desperate fear that her demon heritage will be discovered. Meanwhile, Jona is a former lord who works as a noble's guard, unconcerned about whether his demonic ancestry will be discovered as he flaunts himself around town. A series of shocking events bring

these two together as the Walkers begin hunting them down and threatening their very existence.

Where it's reviewed:
Publishers Weekly, January 31, 2011, page 35

Other books by the same author:
The Last Dragon, 2011

Other books you might like:
Raymond E. Feist, *Flight of the Nighthawks*, 2006
David Gemmell, *Ghost King*, 1988
Mercedes Lackey, *The Eagle and the Nightingales*, 1995
Jennifer Roberson, *Children of the Lion*, 2001
R.A. Salvatore, *The Demon Awakens*, 1997

235

SEANAN MCGUIRE

Late Eclipses

(New York: DAW, 2011)

Series: October Daye Series. Book 4
Story type: Mystery; Series
Subject(s): Fantasy; Mystery; Supernatural
Major character(s): October "Toby" Daye, Mythical Creature (half-human, half-fae), Detective; Lily, Friend (of October); Queen of the Mists, Royalty, Ruler
Time period(s): 21st century; 2010s
Locale(s): San Francisco, California

Summary: In the fantasy novel *Late Eclipses* by Seanan McGuire, October "Toby" Daye is a private detective in San Francisco who has a unique background—she's half-human and half-fairy. Criminal mysteries in the magical world abound, and Toby's professional and personal lives often collide. When Toby is made a countess, she knows that the gesture is part of a scheme hatched by the Queen of the Mists. The sudden illness of Toby's friend Lily and other cases of sickness reveal the queen's plot—she's trying to frame Toby for murder. *Late Eclipses* is the fourth book in the October Daye series.

Where it's reviewed:
Library Journal, March 15, 2011, page 110
Locus, May 2011, page 23
Publishers Weekly, January 31, 2011, page 35

Other books by the same author:
An Artificial Night, 2010
A Local Habitation, 2010
Rosemary and Rue, 2009

Other books you might like:
Emily Drake, *The Magickers*, 2001
Laurell K. Hamilton, *A Kiss of Shadows*, 2000
Karen Marie Moning, *Faefever*, 2008
Will Shetterly, *Elsewhere*, 1991
Rob Thurman, *Blackout*, 2011

236

GRAHAM MCNEILL

Sons of Ellyrion

(Nottingham, England: Games Workshop, 2011)

Story type: Sword and Sorcery
Subject(s): Fantasy; Epics; Adventure
Major character(s): Imrik, Royalty (prince); Tyrion, Royalty (prince); Morathi, Leader (druchii army); Issyk Kul, Leader (druchii army)
Locale(s): Ulthuan, Fictional Location

Summary: In the fantasy novel *Sons of Ellyrion* by Graham McNeill, elven wars have devastated the realm of Ulthuan. Dark elves and high elves are engaged in struggles that will determine who will control the regions of Lothern and Averlorn. Issyk Kul and Morathi, commanders of a dark elvish army, have brought their troops to Tor Elyr. There, the conflict is about more than the possession of territory. Morathi wants to undo the force that binds all of Ulthuan. If he succeeds, Chaos will reign and the high elves will be destroyed.

Other books by the same author:
God King, 2011
Empire, 2009
Defenders of Ulthuan, 2008
Heldenhammer, 2008
The Ambassador, 2003

Other books you might like:
Robert E. Howard, *The Coming of Conan the Cimmerian*, 2002
Paul S. Kemp, *Shadowbred*, 2008
Nick Kyme, *Grimblades*, 2010
Nathan Long, *Bloodborn*, 2010
R.A. Salvatore, *The Pirate King*, 2008

237

GRAHAM MCNEILL

God King

(Nottingham, United Kingdom: Games Workshop, 2010)

Series: Time of Legends: Sigmar Trilogy. Book 3
Story type: Adventure; Series
Subject(s): Adventure; Wars; Magic
Major character(s): Sigmar, Royalty (emperor)
Time period(s): Indeterminate Future
Locale(s): Warhammer Universe, Alternate Universe

Summary: Sigmar has ascended from mere clan leader to god-king of The Empire. Now he must rally all his skill, cunning, and courage to secure his place as leader and take on the forces that threaten to dethrone him. Set in the Warhammer universe, Graham McNeill's *God King* is the third novel in the Time of Legends series.

Other books by the same author:
Sons of Ellyrion, 2011
Empire, 2009
Defenders of Ulthuan, 2008
Heldenhammer, 2008

The Ambassador, 2003

Other books you might like:
Robert Earl, *Broken Honour*, 2011
Mike Lee, *Nagash Immortal*, 2011
Anthony Reynolds, *The Bounty Hunter*, 2010
Anthony Reynolds, *Dark Creed*, 2010
Chris Wraight, *Iron Company*, 2009

238

RICHELLE MEAD

Iron Crowned

(London: Bantam, 2011)

Story type: Mystical
Subject(s): Fantasy; Wars; Mysticism
Major character(s): Eugenie Markham, Shaman, Royalty (queen); Dorian, Mythical Creature (fairy king); Kiyo, Shape-Shifter, Boyfriend (former, of Eugenie)
Time period(s): Indeterminate
Locale(s): Thorn Land, Fictional Location

Summary: *Iron Crowned* is a suspenseful and action-packed fantasy novel from author Richelle Mead. Eugenie Markham, queen of Thorn Land and shaman-for-hire, has always excelled at thwarting mystical entities from interfering with the mortal realm, but Thorn Land is under attack and Eugenie struggles to end the violent war from destroying her kingdom. The only hope for regaining power and ending the destruction is to obtain the Iron Crown, a powerful artifact that is feared throughout the land. Eugenie needs to find the Iron Crown, but she's unsure whom she can trust to locate it and bring it back to Thorn Land. The fairy king Dorian has ulterior motives for wanting to help and Eugenie's former lover, shape-shifter Kiyo, would betray her in a heartbeat. Eugenie's only hope is to go after the Iron Crown herself, facing a dangerous mission that could threaten the existence of both the mystical and mortal realms.

Other books by the same author:
Thorn Queen, 2009
Frostbite, 2008
Storm Born, 2008
Succubus Dreams, 2008
Succubus on Top, 2008

Other books you might like:
Catherine Asaro, *The Charmed Sphere*, 2004
Laurell K. Hamilton, *Divine Misdemeanors*, 2009
Larissa Ione, *Pleasure Unbound*, 2008
Mercedes Lackey, *One Good Knight*, 2006
Michelle Sagara, *Cast in Shadow*, 2005

239

L.E. MODESITT JR.

Lady-Protector

(New York: Tor, 2011)

Series: Corean Chronicles. Book 8
Story type: Magic Conflict; Series

Subject(s): Adventure; Magic; Wars
Major character(s): Mykella, Ruler
Locale(s): Corus, Fictional Location

Summary: Mykella may now be the ruler of the land, but she is faced with a series of challenges that threaten to derail her reign before it even begins. Not only is war looming on the horizon, but her country is nearly penniless. Fortunately, there is an ancient magic revealing itself to Mykella, and she must harness its power if she is to successfully govern. The only problem is that the emerging magic means a daunting adversary will be unleashed, putting Mykella in the fight of her life in order to save her country. *Lady-Protector* is the eighth installment in L.E. Modesitt Jr.'s Corean Chronicles series.

Where it's reviewed:
Library Journal, March 15, 2011, page 110

Other books by the same author:
Arms-Commander, 2010
Imager's Intrigue, 2010
Imager, 2009
Imager's Challenge, 2009
The Lord Protector's Daughter, 2008

Other books you might like:
Dave Duncan, *Impossible Odds*, 2003
Leigh Eddings, *Crystal Gorge*, 2005
Mercedes Lackey, *Foundation*, 2008
Andre Norton, *Three Hands for Scorpio*, 2005
Lawrence Watt-Evans, *The Wizard Lord*, 2006

240

SARAH MONETTE
ELIZABETH BEAR, Co-Author

The Tempering of Men
(New York: Tor, 2011)

Series: Iskryne World Series. Book 2
Story type: Alternate World; Series
Subject(s): Fantasy; Wolves; Epics
Major character(s): Isolfr, Brother (of Viradechtis), Wolf; Viradechtis, Wolf (queen wolf), Sister (of Isolfr); Skjaldwulf, Human; Skjaldwulf, Human
Locale(s): Iskryne, Fictional Location

Summary: In the fantasy novel *The Tempering of Men* by Sarah Monette and Elizabeth Bear, the frozen land of Iskryne is populated with wolfcarls and trellwolves. Viradechtis, the queen wolf, and her brother, Isolfr, hold high positions in their complex society of wolves and humans. The pack is enjoying a respite from the recent battles against the Trolls, but a new threat will arrive in Iskryne soon. This time it is a force of humans on a mission to claim the northern territory for their own. *The Tempering of Men* is the second book in the Iskryne World series.

Other books by the same author:
Corambis, 2009
A Companion of Wolves, 2007
The Mirador, 2007
The Virtu, 2006

Melusine, 2005

Other books you might like:
Elaine Cunningham, *The Wizardwar*, 2002
Ed Greenwood, *Dark Warrior Rising*, 2007
Oliver Johnson, *The Forging of the Shadows*, 1996
Stan Nicholls, *Orcs*, 2004
R.A. Salvatore, *The Orc King*, 2007

241

LUCY MONROE

Moon Burning
(New York: Berkley Sensation, 2011)

Series: Children of the Moon Series. Book 3
Story type: Romantic Suspense; Series
Subject(s): Fantasy; Romances (Fiction); Suspense
Major character(s): Sabrine, Shape-Shifter; Barr, Werewolf, Laird

Summary: *Moon Burning*, a suspenseful and supernatural romance novel, is the third installment in the Children of the Moon series from author Lucy Monroe. Shape-shifter Sabrine will do anything to save her people, even if it means putting her life at risk and infiltrating the enemy's clan. That's exactly what she does when she pretends to have amnesia so a member of the Donegal clan will rescue her and nurse her back to health. Sabrine believes the key to her people's survival is the retrieval of a sacred moonstone, which the Donegal clan stole. The task, although dangerous, seems simple enough, but Sabrine didn't plan on falling in love with a Donegal laird. The intense passion between her and Barr is undeniable, but following her heart means sacrificing her people.

Where it's reviewed:
Romantic Times, February 2011, page 37

Other books by the same author:
Moon Craving, 2010
Moon Awakening, 2007
His Royal Love-Child, 2006
The Greek's Innocent Virgin, 2005
The Sheikh's Bartered Bride, 2005

Other books you might like:
Jennifer Ashley, *Primal Bonds*, 2011
Sarah A. Hoyt, *Draw One in the Dark*, 2006
Larissa Ione, *Ecstasy Unveiled*, 2010
Sheri S. Tepper, *The True Game*, 1985
Freda Warrington, *The Obsidian Tower*, 2001

242

JEN NADOL

The Vision
(New York: Bloomsbury Children's Books, 2011)

Story type: Romance
Subject(s): Fantasy; Adolescence; Supernatural
Major character(s): Cassie Renfield, Teenager, Supernatural Being (able to sense oncoming death);

Demetria, Teenager, Supernatural Being (has power of the Fates)
Time period(s): 21st century
Locale(s): United States

Summary: *The Vision* by Jen Nadol is a supernatural novel for young adults. It is the follow-up to *The Mark*, a story about a girl named Cassie Renfield who learns that she has a special mark that allows her to determine if a person is about to die. In *The Vision*, Cassie continues learning about her special powers and trying to use them wisely. She finds herself in many new developments, such as dealing with Demetria, another girl in her neighborhood who has special powers, and dating her new boyfriend. In the end, Cassie realizes that her powers entail great responsibility when she is forced to make life-and-death decisions.

Other books by the same author:
The Mark, 2010

Other books you might like:
Kate Cann, *Consumed*, 2011
Jackie Morse Kessler, *Rage*, 2011
Stephen King, *Pet Sematary*, 1983
Dean R. Koontz, *The Vision*, 1977
Rachel Ward, *Numbers*, 2010

243

PATI NAGLE

Heart of the Exiled

(New York: Random House, 2011)

Story type: Magic Conflict
Subject(s): Fantasy; Elves; Vampires
Major character(s): Eliani, Young Woman, Warrior; Turisan, Lover (of Eliani); Shalar, Leader (of Clan Darkshore)

Summary: In the fantasy novel *Heart of the Exiled* by Pati Nagle, Eliani is a warrior of the elven clan whose telepathic abilities are about to play a key role in her people's battle for survival. The elven have seen their numbers diminished and now need to unite if they are to defeat the vicious kobalen. When the governor of Fireshore fails to join the other elven governors at a meeting at Glenhallow, Eliani is dispatched to Fireshore to learn the reason for the governor's absence. But Eliani is not the only one trying to reach Fireshore. The region once belonged to a clan that was banished long ago and is now led by the ruthless Shalar.

Other books by the same author:
The Immortal, 2011
The Betrayal, 2009

Other books you might like:
Elaine Cunningham, *The Blood Red Harp*, 2006
Barb Hendee, *Of Truth and Beasts*, 2011
Oliver Johnson, *The Forging of the Shadows*, 1996
Richard A. Knaak, *Ruby Flames*, 1999
Meredith Ann Pierce, *A Gathering of Gargoyles*, 1984

244

GARTH NIX
SEAN WILLIAMS, Co-Author

Troubletwisters

(New York: Scholastic Press, 2011)

Story type: Young Readers
Subject(s): Fantasy; Good and evil; Twins
Major character(s): Jaide Shield, Twin, Child, Ward; Jack Shield, Twin, Ward, Child
Time period(s): 21st century; 2010s

Summary: *Troubletwisters* is a suspenseful and action-packed fantasy novel for young readers from best-selling authors Sean Williams and Garth Nix. Unbeknownst to twin siblings Jaide and Jack Shield (and most of the human population), the Evil has been trying desperately to infiltrate the human world and take over the planet for ages. The Evil's only way to enter the mortal dimension is through specific portals across the globe that are strictly guarded by Wardens. Jaide and Jack are in for a shock when they discover that their father and Grandma X have been serving as Wardens for decades and that the twins are actually troubletwisters, future Wardens whose powers are beginning to develop.

Where it's reviewed:
Publishers Weekly, March 7, 2011, page 64

Other books by the same author:
Lord Loss, 2010
Lady Friday, 2007
Grim Tuesday, 2004
Keys to the Kingdom, 2003
Into Battle, 2001

Other books you might like:
Charlie Fletcher, *Stoneheart*, 2007
Alan Garner, *The Weirdstone of Brisingamen*, 1960
Roderick Gordon, *Closer*, 2011
Rick Riordan, *The Red Pyramid: The Kane Chronicles, Book One*, 2010
Brandon Sanderson, *Alcatraz Versus the Evil Librarians*, 2007

245

PETER ORULLIAN

The Unremembered

(New York: Tor, 2011)

Series: Vault of Heaven Series. Book 1
Story type: Alternate World; Series
Subject(s): Demons; Fantasy; Suspense
Major character(s): Than Junell, Hunter
Locale(s): Bourne, Fictional Location

Summary: *The Unremembered* is a suspenseful paranormal thriller from author Peter Orullian. In addition to creating the worlds, the gods are meant to maintain order and balance among their creations, but one god goes too far in crafting a world filled with terrifying demonic creatures. As punishment, his world and minions are

condemned to the distant land of Bourne to live for eternity behind a veil. As the years pass, the threat of this violent world is downplayed and dismissed as mere rumors, weakening the veil that protects the human world from the beastly creatures. When dreadful troops begin escaping from Bourne and wreaking havoc on the living world, it's up to three young orphans to intervene and protect humankind. *The Unremembered* is the first book in the Vault of Heaven series.

Where it's reviewed:
Library Journal, March 15, 2011, page 110
Publishers Weekly, February 14, 2011, page 42

Other books you might like:
Dave Duncan, *Lord of the Fire Lands*, 1999
Dennis L. McKiernan, *City of Jade*, 2008
Fiona Patton, *The Silver Lake*, 2005
Jennifer Roberson, *Karavans*, 2006
Lawrence Watt-Evans, *Blood of a Dragon*, 1991

246

JOSHUA PALMATIER
PATRICIA BRAY, Co-Editor

After Hours: Tales from the Ur-Bar
(New York: DAW Books, 2011)

Story type: Collection; Science Fiction
Subject(s): Science fiction; Fantasy; Bars (Drinking establishments)

Summary: Edited by Joshua Palmatier and Patricia Bray, *After Hours: Tales from the Ur-Bar* is a collection of short fantasy and science-fiction stories from several authors. The anthology includes fifteen short stories, each of which relies on a bar as its primary setting. The magical and mythical creatures range from zombies to demon hunters and Vikings to time travelers. In one tale, a bouncer learns the importance of keeping out unwanted guests after hours when he faces off against zombies. Another tale follows the adventures of a samurai and water vampire at a bar in Japan. The authors featured in this collection include Jennifer Dunne, D.B. Jackson, Benjamin Tate, and Avery Shade.

Other books you might like:
Poul Anderson, *A Midsummer Tempest*, 1974
Steven Brust, *Cowboy Feng's Space Bar and Grille*, 1990
Arthur C. Clarke, *Tales from the White Hart*, 1957
L. Sprague de Camp, *Tales from Gavagan's Bar*, 1953
Spider Robinson, *Callahan's Crosstime Saloon*, 1977

247

FIONA PATTON

The Shining City
(New York: DAW Books, 2011)

Series: Warriors of Estavia Series. Book 3
Story type: Alternate World
Subject(s): Fantasy; Prophecy; Alternative worlds

Major character(s): Spar, Religious (chief priest), Psychic; Graize, Psychic; Brax, Warrior
Time period(s): Indeterminate
Locale(s): Anavatan, Fictional Location

Summary: *The Shining City*, an action-packed fantasy epic, is the third installment in the Warriors of Estavia series from author Fiona Patton. Seers Spar and Graize and the warrior Brax, three children of prophecy, have grown into young adults and have gone their separate ways. Spar is now serving as the chief priest to the young god Hisar, while Brax is loyally committed to the war god Estavia. As Hisar begins to rise in power and sets out to stake more of a claim in Anavatan, danger threatens in both the spiritual and mortal realms. A gang of malevolent spirits is hoping to destroy Hisar, while an invasion fleet is sailing toward Anavatan. The only hope of protection is if Spar and Graize can put aside their differences and serve together as Hisar's priests.

Other books by the same author:
The Golden Tower, 2008
The Silver Lake, 2005
The Golden Sword, 2001
The Granite Shield, 1999
The Painter Knight, 1998

Other books you might like:
Sharon Green, *Convergence*, 1996
Mercedes Lackey, *Brightly Burning*, 2000
Juliet Marillier, *The Well of Shades*, 2007
Ari Marmell, *The Warlord's Legacy*, 2011
Jennifer Roberson, *Karavans*, 2006

248

PIERRE PEVEL

The Alchemist in the Shadows
(London: Gollancz, 2010)

Story type: Alternate History
Subject(s): Fantasy; Dragons; Spies
Major character(s): La Fargue, Military Personnel (captain); Saint-Lucq, Dragon (half-dragon); Richelieu, Religious (cardinal), Leader; La Donna, Spy
Time period(s): 17th century; 1630s (1633)
Locale(s): Paris, France

Summary: In the fantasy novel *Alchemist in the Shadows* by Pierre Pevel, the sequel to *The Cardinal's Blades*, Cardinal Richelieu and rival dragon forces vie for power in an alternate 17th-century France. The threats against Richelieu and his country are many. An enemy, whose identity is known to the Italian spy La Donna, is scheming to overtake the throne. The Black Claw, a clandestine organization of dragon forces from Spain, is also planning an attack on France that could be devastating. The fate of France lies in the hands of Captain la Fargue and The Cardinal's Blades, a select team that includes a handful of men, one woman, and a half-dragon named Saint-Lucq.

Where it's reviewed:
Booklist, May 15, 2011, page 26
Library Journal, March 15, 2011, page 111
Locus, February 2011, page 17

Publishers Weekly, February 28, 2011, page 38

Other books by the same author:
The Cardinal's Blades, 2010

Other books you might like:
Ann Chamberlin, *The Merlin of the Oak Wood*, 2001
Sara Douglass, *The Nameless Day*, 2004
Thomas Harlan, *The Shadow of Ararat*, 1999
Marie Jakober, *The Black Chalice*, 2001
Naomi Novik, *Tongues of Serpents*, 2010

249

J.A. PITTS

Honeyed Words

(New York: Tor, 2011)

Series: Sarah Beauhall Series. Book 2
Story type: Series; Urban
Subject(s): Fantasy; Urban life; Dragons
Major character(s): Sarah Beauhall, Blacksmith, Heroine; Skella, Sister (of Sarah); Gletts, Brother (of Sarah); Anzeka, Teacher (mentor of Sarah)
Time period(s): 21st century; 2010s
Locale(s): United States

Summary: In the fantasy novel *Honeyed Words* by J.A. Pitts, Sarah Beauhall, a blacksmith and props manager, takes on the new job of savior of the human race. Sarah has recently learned that the mortal world is ruled by shape-shifting dragons and inhabited by all manner of magical folk and beast. Much to her surprise, she also discovered that a sword she made is a powerful replica of an ancient weapon. Now, with the help of her mentor, Anzeka, and a newly found brother and sister, Sarah must keep the sword from those who want it and use the weapon to defend the mortal realm. *Honeyed Words* is the second book in the Sarah Beauhall series.

Other books by the same author:
Black Blade Blues, 2010

Other books you might like:
Jennifer Ashley, *Primal Bonds*, 2011
Doranna Durgin, *Changespell*, 1997
Lisa Hendrix, *Immortal Champion*, 2011
Stephanie Rowe, *Must Love Dragons*, 2006
Freda Warrington, *The Sapphire Throne*, 2000

250

JEAN RABE
MARTIN H. GREENBERG, Co-Editor

Boondocks Fantasy

(New York: DAW, 2011)

Story type: Collection
Subject(s): Short stories; Fantasy

Summary: The American South is the setting for the 20 short stories that comprise *Boondocks Fantasy*. Editors Jean Rabe and Martin H. Greenberg gather a collection of fantastical tales involving all manner of ghoulish creatures, from vampires and werewolves to evil elves and trolls. Stories in this volume include "The Devil Is a Gentleman," "Cat People," and "The Horned Man."

Other books by the same author:
The Finest Challenge, 2006
The Finest Choice, 2005
The Finest Creation, 2004
Downfall, 2000
The Day of the Tempest, 1997

Other books you might like:
Tom Deitz, *Landslayer's Law*, 1997
Jay Lake, *American Sorrows*, 2004
Edward Lee, *The Backwoods*, 2005
Manly Wade Wellman, *The Valley So Low*, 1986
Gene Wolfe, *Innocents Aboard*, 2004

251

IRENE RADFORD

Thistle Down

(New York: DAW Books, 2011)

Story type: Romance
Subject(s): Fantasy; Romances (Fiction); Fairies
Major character(s): Dusty Carrick, Young Woman; Thistle Down, Mythical Creature (pixie), Exile
Time period(s): 21st century; 2010s
Locale(s): Skene Falls, Oregon

Summary: *Thistle Down* is a paranormal romance from author Irene Radford. In the small town of Skene Falls, Oregon, the local children pass their days playing with "imaginary" pixie pals in the Ten Acre Woods. Like all of her friends, Dusty Carrick passed away her childhood enjoying the pixie company, never realizing the pixies were real and that Ten Acre Woods was their home. With the woods in danger, the pixies might lose their home—and their lives—forever. Thistle Down, an exiled pixie trapped in human form, is their last hope. It's up to Thistle to convince Dusty and her friends that the pixies are real and desperately need their help before it's too late.

Where it's reviewed:
Publishers Weekly, April 25, 2011, page 120

Other books by the same author:
Guardian of the Freedom, 2005
Guardian of the Promise, 2003
Guardian of the Vision, 2001
The Loneliest Magician, 1996
The Perfect Princess, 1995

Other books you might like:
Peter S. Beagle, *A Fine and Private Place*, 1960
James P. Blaylock, *Land of Dreams*, 1987
Jonathan Carroll, *The Land of Laughs*, 1980
Pamela Dean, *The Secret Country*, 1985
Richard Grant, *Kaspian Lost*, 1999

252

ANTHONY REYNOLDS

Knights of Bretonnia

(Nottingham, United Kingdom: Black Library, 2011)

Story type: Black Magic
Subject(s): Fantasy; Knights; Suspense
Major character(s): Calard, Knight, Warrior; Chlod, Servant (of Calard)
Locale(s): Bretonnia, Fictional Location

Summary: *Knights of Bretonnia* is a suspenseful fantasy novel from author Anthony Reynolds. In the magical land of Bretonnia, a conflict between good and evil has been raging for generations. In the shadowy forests lives a legion of creatures, under the rule of the Dark Gods. The only hope of peace and protection lies with the Knights of Bretonnia, a group of faithful servants committed to fighting against evil. Calard, a noble young man with huge aspirations, is determined to not only become a knight, but to earn the highest title of all: Grail Knight. With the help of his servant Chlod, Calard must be willing to give up everything and fight the dangerous villains lurking in his own village if he hopes to attain legendary status.

Other books by the same author:
Dark Creed, 2009
Knight of the Realm, 2009
Empire in Chaos, 2008
Knight Errant, 2008
Mark of Chaos, 2006

Other books you might like:
Ben Counter, *Crimson Tears,* 2005
Robert Earl, *Broken Honour,* 2011
Richard A. Knaak, *The Black Talon,* 2007
Gav Thorpe, *Malekith,* 2009
C.L. Werner, *Wulfrik,* 2010

253

MICHELLE SAGARA

House Name

(New York: DAW, 2011)

Series: House Wars Series. Book 3
Story type: Magic Conflict; Series
Subject(s): Wars; Magic; Orphans
Major character(s): Jewel, Orphan
Locale(s): Essalieyan Empire, Fictional Location

Summary: The young orphan Jewel struggles to grow up on the streets of Averalaan. To further complicate her plight, she must also do battle with the dangers of the Undercity. Eventually Jewel becomes a major player in the Essalieyan Empire, and throughout it all, she bears witness to some of the most tragic and triumphant events in the Empire's history. *House Name* is the third novel in Michelle West's House of War series.

Other books by the same author:
City of Night, 2010

The Hidden City, 2008
The Sun Sword, 2004
The Riven Shield, 2003
Speaking with Angels, 2003

Other books you might like:
Elaine Cunningham, *Daughter of the Drow,* 1995
Kate Elliott, *Spirit Gate,* 2006
Katharine Kerr, *The Gold Falcon,* 2006
China Mieville, *Iron Council,* 2004
Diana L. Paxson, *The Jewel of Fire,* 1992

254

STEVEN SAVILE

The Black Chalice

(Oxford, UK: Abaddon Books, 2011)

Story type: Legend
Subject(s): Fantasy; Legends; Epics
Major character(s): Alymere, Knight
Locale(s): England

Summary: In the fantasy novel *The Black Chalice* by Steven Savile, a knight who is attempting to earn a place at the Round Table is drawn into a dark and dangerous quest. While searching for the Holy Grail, Sir Alymere discovers that an evil counterpart to the Lord's cup also exists—the Black Chalice. There is also a Devil's Bible, authored by a madman, which Alymere will use to guide his journey. Sir Alymere is prepared to face the frightening challenges that await him on the path to the Black Chalice. But as he attempts to prove himself a worthy knight, Alymere may sacrifice more than his life.

Other books by the same author:
Curse of the Necrarch, 2008
Vampire Wars, 2008
Retribution, 2007
Dominion, 2006
Inheritance, 2006

Other books you might like:
Richard A. Knaak, *Legacy of Blood,* 2001
Graham McNeill, *Defenders of Ulthuan,* 2008
Michael Moorcock, *Elric in the Dream Realms,* 2009
Karl Edward Wagner, *The Book of Kane,* 1985
C.L. Werner, *Runefang,* 2008

255

LISA SHEARIN

Con & Conjure

(New York: Ace Books, 2011)

Series: Raine Benares Series. Book 5
Story type: Series; Urban
Subject(s): Fantasy; Elves; Theft
Major character(s): Raine Benares, Supernatural Being (seeker)

Summary: *Con & Conjure,* a suspenseful fantasy novel, is the fifth installment in the Raine Benares series from

author Lisa Shearin. Raine Benares earns her keep as a seeker, finding things and people otherwise lost. Her power was made even stronger by the presence of Saghred, a soul-stealing stone that has granted her endless power. Unfortunately for Raine, there are a lot of unsavory characters that wish to get their hands on Saghred and use its power for themselves. With a gang of baddies in hot pursuit, including a goblin thief and her assassin elf ex-fiance, Raine must rely on her criminal family for safety, protection, and support.

Other books by the same author:
Bewitched & Betrayed, 2010
The Trouble with Demons, 2009
Armed & Magical, 2008
Magic Lost, Trouble Found, 2008

Other books you might like:
Lynn Abbey, *Rifkind's Challenge*, 2006
Emma Bull, *Finder: A Novel of the Borderlands*, 1994
Diane Duane, *Stealing the Elf-King's Roses*, 2002
Mindy L. Klasky, *The Glasswright's Master*, 2004
Juliet Marillier, *Wildwood Dancing*, 2007

256

JOEL SHEPHERD

Haven

(Amherst, New York: Pyr, 2011)

Series: Trial of Blood and Steel Series. Book 4
Story type: Alternate World
Subject(s): Fantasy; Wars; Brothers and sisters
Major character(s): Sasha Lenayin, Sister (to Damon); Damon Lenayin, Royalty (king), Brother (to Sasha)
Time period(s): Indeterminate
Locale(s): Saalshen, Fictional Location

Summary: *Haven*, an action-packed fantasy epic, is the fourth installment in the Trial of Blood and Steel series from author Joel Shepherd. As the Army of the Regent Arosh closes in on the serrin land of Saalshen and their allies, the serrin people's only hope of survival is to cross the River Ipshaal and enter the city of Jahnd, the only human city in all of Saalshen. Unfortunately, the Regent Army is moving in swiftly, accompanied by the Army of Lenayin, eliminating opportunities of escape for the serrin people. Sasha, sister of the newly appointed king of Lenayin, no longer supports the army's cause, resulting in division between she and her brother. Sasha makes a desperate move to protect the serrin people and, in the process, is forced to make an impossible decision between loyalty to her nation and loyalty to her brother.

Other books by the same author:
Petrodor, 2010
Tracato, 2010
Sasha, 2009
Killswitch, 2004
Breakaway, 2003

Other books you might like:
Rowena Cory Daniells, *The King's Bastard*, 2010
Gail Z. Martin, *Dark Lady's Chosen*, 2009
Dennis L. McKiernan, *Into the Forge*, 1997

L.E. Modesitt, *Legacies*, 2002
Adrian Tchaikovsky, *Empire in Black and Gold*, 2008

257

NALINI SINGH

Archangel's Consort

(New York: Berkley Sensation, 2011)

Series: Guild Hunter Series. Book 3
Story type: Series; Supernatural Vengeance
Subject(s): Angels; Natural disasters; Fantasy
Major character(s): Elena Deveraux, Vampire Hunter, Angel, Lover (of Raphael); Raphael, Angel, Son (of Caliane), Lover (of Elena); Caliane, Mother (of Raphael), Immortal, Mentally Ill Person
Time period(s): 21st century; 2010s
Locale(s): New York, New York

Summary: *Archangel's Consort*, a suspenseful fantasy novel, is the third installment in the Guild Hunter series from author Nalini Singh. Elena Deveraux, a vampire hunter turned angel, has returned to New York City alongside her lover, archangel Raphael, and is greeted by surprise and disbelief at her new angel status. The couple barely has time to settle in when several bizarre events begin taking place, including a series of natural disasters. Elena and Raphael suspect that someone—or something—is causing the strange phenomena, but why? Could Raphael's mother Caliane, a powerful immortal overcome with madness, be awakening from Sleep and stirring up trouble? There is only one reason Caliane would return to New York: to reclaim Raphael and force him away from his one true love.

Other books by the same author:
Bonds of Justice, 2010
Blaze of Memory, 2009
Branded by Fire, 2009
Hostage to Pleasure, 2009
Mine to Possess, 2008

Other books you might like:
Cherie Bennett, *Angel Kisses*, 1996
Meljean Brook, *Demon Angel*, 2007
Sherrilyn Kenyon, *Daemon's Angel*, 1995
Thomas E. Sniegoski, *A Kiss Before the Apocalypse*, 2009
Nancy Springer, *Metal Angel*, 1994

258

JON SPRUNK

Shadow's Lure

(Amherst, New York: Pyr, 2011)

Story type: Quest
Subject(s): Adventure; Magic; Good and evil
Major character(s): Caim, Assassin
Locale(s): The North, Fictional Land

Summary: Caim is an assassin on a quest for answers. Desperate to find out why his parents were murdered, he

leaves his homeland of Othir and ventures into a strange new world. Soon, the forces of the Dark Side are pulling at Caim, offering him enticements that become harder and harder to resist. In order to do so, however, Caim will have to rally all his skill and cunning and take on the forces of the Shadow. John Sprunk's *Shadow's Lure* is the sequel to 2010's *Shadow's Son*.

Where it's reviewed:
Library Journal, May 15, 2011, page 79

Other books by the same author:
Shadow's Son, 2010

Other books you might like:
Chaz Brenchley, *Bridge of Dreams*, 2006
Erin Hoffman, *Sword of Fire and Sea*, 2011
Sam Sykes, *Corvus*, 2010
Sam Sykes, *Tome of the Undergates*, 2010
Adrian Tchaikovsky, *Empire in Black and Gold*, 2008

259

ANTON STROUT

Dead Waters

(New York: Ace Books, 2011)

Series: Simon Canderous Series. Book 4
Story type: Mystery; Series
Subject(s): Mystery; Fantasy; Supernatural
Major character(s): Simon Canderous, Agent (Department of Extraordinary Affairs)
Time period(s): 21st century; 2010s
Locale(s): New York, New York

Summary: *Dead Waters*, a mysterious and suspenseful urban fantasy novel, is the fourth installment in the Simon Canderous series from author Anton Strout. As an agent for the Department of Extraordinary Affairs, Simon Canderous is accustomed to encountering vampires, ghosts, and zombies on a regular basis. His supernatural sleuthing often leads to some unusual and bizarre cases, but nothing prepares him for the death of a local professor. The NYPD is stumped over the strange circumstances surrounding the death of Professor Mason Redfield so they call in Simon and his supernaturally gifted friends to unravel the mystery before more victims are claimed.

Other books by the same author:
Dead Matter, 2010
Deader Still, 2009
Dead to Me, 2008

Other books you might like:
Yasmine Galenorn, *Demon Mistress*, 2009
Laurell K. Hamilton, *Bullet*, 2010
Marjorie M. Liu, *Tiger Eye*, 2005
Seanan McGuire, *Rosemary and Rue*, 2009
Rob Thurman, *Madhouse*, 2008

260

SAM SYKES

Black Halo

(Amherst, New York: Prometheus Books, 2011)

Series: Aeons' Gate Series. Book 2
Story type: Adventure; Series
Subject(s): Fantasy; Sea stories; Islands
Major character(s): Lenk, Sailor, Adventurer, Leader

Summary: *Black Halo*, a dark and suspenseful fantasy novel, is the second installment in the Aeons' Gate series from author Sam Sykes. Lenk, along with five adventurous associates, takes to the sea to retrieve a cursed artifact from the Kraken Queen. Unfortunately, after weeks at sea, the men have begun to turn on one another—a situation that's made direr when their boat develops a leak, leaving the men stranded on a dangerous haunted island. The six men soon find themselves facing bloodthirsty warriors, underwater monsters, egomaniacal wizards, and other fantastical beasts, but the greatest danger lies within their own hearts and minds as they confront the demons of their pasts.

Other books by the same author:
Tome of the Undergates, 2010

Other books you might like:
David Gemmell, *The Hawk Eternal*, 1996
Paul Kearney, *The Mark of Ran*, 2005
Juliet E. McKenna, *Southern Fire*, 2005
R.A. Salvatore, *The Pirate King*, 2008

261

K.J. TAYLOR

Dark Griffin

(New York: Ace Books, 2011)

Series: Fallen Moon Series. Book 1
Story type: Black Magic; Series
Subject(s): Fantasy; Good and evil; Suspense
Major character(s): Arren Cardockson, Slave (heritage), Companion (to a griffin)
Locale(s): Cymria, Fictional Location

Summary: *Dark Griffin*, a suspenseful fantasy novel, is the first installment in the Fallen Moon series from author K.J. Taylor. Despite his Northern upbringing as a Blackrobe, Arren Cardockson was chosen as a young boy to be a griffin's companion in the southern nation of Cymria. Arren has worked hard to climb the ranks, earning the title of Master of Trade, but he's unable to escape prejudice against his background or heritage as a slave. After racking up a sizable debt, Arren accepts a risky and nearly impossible mission from the Master of Law to track down an unusual and incredibly dangerous black griffin, unaware that there are dark forces at work that will do anything to make Arren fail.

Where it's reviewed:
Publishers Weekly, November 29, 2010, page 33

Other books by the same author:
The Griffin's War, 2011
The Griffin's Flight, 2010

Other books you might like:
Dave Duncan, *The Jaguar Knights*, 2004
Paul Kearney, *Century of the Soldier*, 2010
Mercedes Lackey, *Aerie*, 2006
Gail Z. Martin, *Dark Lady's Chosen*, 2009
Juliet E. McKenna, *Irons in the Fire*, 2009

262

K.J. TAYLOR

The Griffin's Flight

(New York: Ace Books, 2011)

Series: Fallen Moon Series. Book 2
Story type: Black Magic; Series
Subject(s): Fantasy; Magic; Death
Major character(s): Arren Cardockson, Companion (to a griffin), Slave (heritage); Skandar, Magician

Summary: *The Griffin's Flight*, a suspenseful fantasy novel, is the second installment in the Fallen Moon series from author K.J. Taylor. Despite being a Northerner and having the heritage of a slave, Arren Cardockson was chosen to be a griffin's companion in the southern nation of Cymria. Unfortunately, the prejudice against him ultimately resulted in his betrayal and death. Now, Arren's been brought back to life by a supernatural power, but there are still plenty who want him dead. Alongside a dark human-eating griffin named Skandar, Arren embarks on a perilous journey back to the North to find sanctuary and lift the curse thrust upon him.

Where it's reviewed:
Publishers Weekly, December 13, 2010, page 41

Other books by the same author:
The Griffin's War, 2011
Dark Griffin, 2009

Other books you might like:
Jennifer Fallon, *Medalon*, 2000
Raymond E. Feist, *King of Foxes*, 2004
David Gemmell, *Midnight Falcon*, 1999
Mercedes Lackey, *Storm Warning*, 1994
Naomi Novik, *Throne of Jade*, 2006

263

K.J. TAYLOR

The Griffin's War

(New York: Ace Books, 2011)

Series: Fallen Moon Series. Book 3
Story type: Magic Conflict; Series
Subject(s): Magic; Adventure; Human-animal relationships
Major character(s): Arenadd Taranisai, Warrior; Skandar, Mythical Creature (griffin)
Time period(s): Indeterminate

Summary: Warrior Arenadd Taranisai is confined to a dungeon, where he is slowly losing his grip on sanity. After vowing his loyalty to the Night God, Arenadd acquires a mystical gift: the ability to become invisible when cloaked in shadow. Now the determined warrior joins forces with the dark griffin Skandar and sets off to liberate his people from those who oppress them. *The Griffin's War* is the third novel in K.J. Taylor's The Fallen Moon Trilogy.

Where it's reviewed:
Publishers Weekly, January 17, 2011, page 34

Other books by the same author:
The Griffin's Flight, 2011
Dark Griffin, 2009

Other books you might like:
Mercedes Lackey, *Joust*, 2003
Anne McCaffrey, *The Skies of Pern*, 2001
R.A. Salvatore, *The Demon Awakens*, 1997
Lawrence Watt-Evans, *Touched by the Gods*, 1997
Janny Wurts, *Grand Conspiracy*, 2000

264

ADRIAN TCHAIKOVSKY

The Scarab Path

(Amherst, New York: Pyr, 2011)

Series: Shadows of the Apt Series. Book 5
Story type: Science Fantasy
Subject(s): Fantasy; Insects; Wars
Major character(s): Thalric, Spy; Cheerwell Maker, Warrior; Seda, Villain, Leader (Empress)
Time period(s): Indeterminate
Locale(s): Khanaphes, Fictional Location

Summary: *The Scarab Path*, a suspenseful and imaginative fantasy novel, is the fifth installment in the Shadows of the Apt series from author Adrian Tchaikovsky. The war between the Wasp Empire and Collegium has come to a deadlock as each army is severely wounded yet unwilling to surrender. The Empress Seda will do anything to regain her power over the cities that have rebelled against her. The source of her power is more terrifying than anyone could imagine. The only person privy to Seda's secrets is her partner, Thalric, but the Empress will stop at nothing to keep him silent. When Seda unleashes her assassins on Thalric, he escapes to the ancient city of Khanaphes where he encounters his former nemesis, Cheerwell Maker who is wrestling with secrets of her own.

Other books by the same author:
Blood of the Mantis, 2010
Dragonfly Falling, 2010
Empire in Black and Gold, 2010
Salute the Dark, 2010

Other books you might like:
Chaz Brenchley, *Bridge of Dreams*, 2006
Paul Kearney, *Hawkwood and the Kings*, 2010
Richard A. Knaak, *Moon of the Spider*, 2006
Joel Shepherd, *Sasha*, 2009
Sam Sykes, *Black Halo*, 2011

265

GAV THORPE

Caledor

(Nottingham, United Kingdom: Games Workshop, 2011)

Series: Time of Legends Series. Book 3
Story type: Alternate World; Series
Subject(s): Elves; Civil war; Fantasy
Major character(s): Malekith, Traitor; Caledor, Leader, Royalty (prince Imrik)
Locale(s): Ulthuan, Fictional Location

Summary: *Caledor*, a dark and suspenseful fantasy novel, is the final installment in The Sundering trilogy from author Gav Thorpe. The land of Ulthuan is facing complete annihilation as a brutal civil war rages. The Drucchii have risen in power under the dictatorial leadership of the Witch King and will stop at nothing to destroy the high elves, resulting in an intervention from the mighty dragons. When Prince Imrik is betrayed by Malekith and his court is killed, he assumes the name and identity of his late grandfather, Caledor, and rises to the challenge of protecting Ulthuan from the malicious elves. The fate of the nation rests on Caledor's back and will be determined during a final showdown between him and his former pal, Malekith.

Other books by the same author:
Path of the Warrior, 2010
Malekith, 2009
Grudge Bearer, 2005
The Heart of Chaos, 2004
The Blades of Chaos, 2003

Other books you might like:
Richard Lee Byers, *The Enemy Within*, 2007
Darius Hinks, *Sigvald*, 2011
Graham McNeill, *God King*, 2010
Andrew J. Offutt, *The Iron Lords*, 1979
C.L. Werner, *Forged by Chaos*, 2009

266

ROB THURMAN

Blackout

(New York: Roc, 2011)

Series: Cal Leandros Series. Book 6
Story type: Paranormal; Series
Subject(s): Fantasy; Memory; Mystery
Major character(s): Cal Leandros, Mythical Creature (half-human, half-monster); Niko Leandros, Brother (of Cal)
Time period(s): 21st century; 2010s
Locale(s): New York, New York

Summary: In the fantasy novel *Blackout* by Rob Thurman, Cal Leandros—half-human, half-monster—deals with the paranormal every day. Since Cal and his brother Niko moved to New York, their detective work has brought them into close contact with the mystical creatures that populate the city, unseen by their human neighbors. Though Cal's current circumstances seem dire, he remains surprisingly unconcerned. He is lying on a beach, surrounded by the dead bodies of murdered monsters. He knows he is responsible for the carnage but he doesn't remember what happened or whom he is. *Blackout* is the sixth book in the Cal Leandros series.

Other books by the same author:
The Grimrose Path, 2010
Deathwish, 2009
Madhouse, 2008
Moonshine, 2007
Nightlife, 2006

Other books you might like:
Marie Brennan, *Witch and Warrior*, 2006
Yasmine Galenorn, *Dragon Wytch*, 2008
Laurell K. Hamilton, *The Killing Dance*, 1997
Charlaine Harris, *Living Dead in Dallas*, 2002
Anton Strout, *Dead to Me*, 2008

267

CATHERYNNE M. VALENTE

Deathless

(New York: Tor, 2011)

Story type: Historical
Subject(s): Fantasy; Marriage; History
Major character(s): Koschei, Villain, Immortal, Kidnapper; Marya Morevna, Kidnap Victim, Bride (of Koschei), Human; Ivan Nikolayevich, Human
Time period(s): 20th century
Locale(s): Buyan, Fictional Location; Russia

Summary: *Deathless* is a historical fantasy thriller from author Catherynne M. Valente. The novel offers a fresh spin on the Russian folklore tale of Koschei the Deathless, a malevolent villain who kidnaps the wives of heroes. In *Deathless*, Koschei has fallen in love with a human woman named Marya Morevna. Hoping to make Marya his bride, Koschei whisks her away to his home in Buyan where she must complete three tasks in order to be worthy of his love. Over time, Marya begins to become more like her otherworldly betrothed, until she encounters Ivan Nikolayevich, a man who fights to help her regain her humanity.

Where it's reviewed:
Library Journal, February 15, 2011, page 105
Locus, May 2011, page 21
Publishers Weekly, February 21, 2011, page 117

Other books by the same author:
The Habitation of the Blessed, 2010
Under the Mere, 2010
Palimpsest, 2009
In the Cities of Coin and Spice, 2007
In the Night Garden, 2006

Other books you might like:
James Branch Cabell, *Jurgen*, 1919
C.J. Cherryh, *Rusalka*, 1989
Leah R. Cutter, *Paper Mage*, 2003
Kara Dalkey, *Genpei*, 2001
Richard A. Lupoff, *Sword of the Demon*, 1976

268

CARRIE VAUGHN

Kitty's Greatest Hits
(New York: Tor, 2011)

Series: Kitty Norville series
Story type: Collection; Series
Subject(s): Fantasy; Short stories; Occultism

Summary: In *Kitty's Greatest Hits*, author Carrie Vaughn presents a collection of short stories relating to her best-selling Kitty Norville novels. Kitty, a radio-show personality and werewolf, stars in Vaughn's urban fantasy series as the witty defender of goodness in the paranormal realm. These stories, some previously published, others appearing in print for the first time, describe more of Kitty's paranormal exploits and provide background on other popular series characters. The collection includes "A Princess of Spain," "The Book of Daniel," "The Temptation of Robin Green," "Kitty and the Mosh Pit of the Damned," "You're on the Air," and other tales.

Where it's reviewed:
Library Journal, March 15, 2011, page 101

Other books by the same author:
After the Golden Age, 2011
Discord's Apple, 2010
Kitty Goes to War, 2010
Kitty Raises Hell, 2009
Kitty and the Silver Bullet, 2008

Other books you might like:
Ilona Andrews, *Magic Bites*, 2007
Alice Borchardt, *The Silver Wolf*, 1998
Patricia Briggs, *Moon Called*, 2006
Lucy Monroe, *Moon Awakening*, 2007
Irene Radford, *Guardian of the Promise*, 2003

269

CARRIE VAUGHN

After the Golden Age
(New York: Tor, 2011)

Subject(s): Adventure; Magic; Mythology
Major character(s): Celia West, Accountant (forensic accountant); Destructor, Criminal
Time period(s): Indeterminate Future
Locale(s): Commerce City

Summary: In *After the Golden Age*, author Carrie Vaughn tells the story of Celia West, a forensic accountant who happens to be the daughter of two world-famous superheroes. A high-profile tax-evasion case requires Celia to look into the past of the evil Destructor, but she is in no way prepared for what she finds. Her investigation turns up shocking revelations about her own family history, the city, and the future of humankind.

Other books by the same author:
Kitty's Greatest Hits, 2011
Discord's Apple, 2010

Kitty Goes to War, 2010
Kitty Raises Hell, 2009
Kitty and the Silver Bullet, 2008

Other books you might like:
Michael Bishop, *Count Geiger's Blues*, 1992
Emma Bull, *Finder: A Novel of the Borderlands*, 1994
Tom De Haven, *Joe Gosh*, 1988
Caitlin Kittredge, *Black and White*, 2009

270

JO WALTON

Among Others
(New York: Tor, 2011)

Story type: Coming-of-Age
Subject(s): Magic; Fantasy; Mother-daughter relations
Major character(s): Morwenna Phelps, Teenager, Student—Boarding School, Handicapped
Time period(s): 20th century; 1970s
Locale(s): England

Summary: *Among Others* is a thrilling and suspenseful fantasy novel from award-winning author Jo Walton. The coming-of-age tale follows Morwenna Phelps, a Welsh teen trying to escape the clutches of her insane mother. As a child, Morwenna found solace among the magical spirits near her home and in her science fiction novels. When her mother began practicing dark magic, Morwenna was forced to confront her and their horrific battle resulted in the death of her twin sister and her own physical handicap. Fleeing to England, Morwenna seeks safety with the father she barely knows, a man who swiftly sends her off to boarding school. In an attempt to find magically minded friends, Morwenna begins casting spells of her own, a foolish act that summons her mother and results in an unavoidable confrontation of wills.

Where it's reviewed:
Booklist, January 1, 2011, page 59
Locus, January 2011, page 16
Publishers Weekly, November 15, 2010, page 44
Voice of Youth Advocates, April 2011, page 87

Other books by the same author:
Lifelode, 2009
Half a Crown, 2008
Ha'penny, 2007
Farthing, 2006
Tooth and Claw, 2003
The King's Peace, 2000

Other books you might like:
Piers Anthony, *Knot Gneiss*, 2010
Michael Chabon, *The Yiddish Policemen's Union: A Novel*, 2007
Raymond E. Feist, *A Kingdom Besieged: Book One of the Chaoswar Saga*, 2011
Diana Wynne Jones, *Charmed Life*, 1977
Juliet Marillier, *Seer of Sevenwaters*, 2010
Terry Pratchett, *Nation*, 2008
Nancy Springer, *Fair Peril*, 1996

John C. Wright, *Orphans of Chaos*, 2005
Jane Yolen, *Briar Rose*, 1992
Mary Frances Zambreno, *Journeyman Wizard*, 1994

271

JULES WATSON

The Raven Queen
(New York: Spectra, 2011)

Story type: Historical - Medieval
Subject(s): Legends; Ireland; Adventure
Major character(s): Maeve, Royalty (The Raven Queen); Conor, Spouse (of Maeve)
Locale(s): Ireland

Summary: Jules Watson's *The Raven Queen* chronicles the extraordinary adventures of a courageous young heroine named Maeve. Set in the Middle Ages and based upon a much-loved tale of Irish legend, this volume follows Maeve from girlhood to young adulthood. At first, she is used as a wager in her father's nefarious schemes to secure his land. Then, after she is married off to Conor, she must put up with her husband's constant manipulations and plotting. When her father dies, Maeve realizes that her native land is now susceptible to a variety of powerful invaders (including her husband's), and she sets out to save her beloved homeland from the tyranny of those who wish to conquer it.

Other books by the same author:
The Swan Maiden, 2009
The Song of the North, 2008
The Dawn Stag, 2006
The White Mare, 2005

Other books you might like:
Risa Aratyr, *Hunter of the Light*, 1995
S.L. Farrell, *Holder of Lightning*, 2003
Kenneth C. Flint, *Isle of Destiny*, 1988
Morgan Llywelyn, *The Isles of the Blest*, 1989
Juliet Marillier, *Daughter of the Forest*, 2000

272

MARTHA WELLS

The Cloud Roads
(San Francisco, California: Night Shade, 2011)

Story type: Alternate World
Subject(s): Fantasy; Identity; Good and evil
Major character(s): Moon, Shape-Shifter, Orphan
Time period(s): Indeterminate

Summary: *The Cloud Roads* is a suspenseful and imaginative fantasy novel from author Martha Wells. Orphaned at a young age, Moon has spent a lifetime trying to understand his identity. As a shape-shifter with the power to turn into a winged creature, Moon is unsure which tribe he truly belongs to and since his skills reflect similarities to the ominous and malevolent Fell, Moon has to keep his shape-shifting a secret, lest people get the wrong idea about him. When yet another tribe uncov-

ers Moon's secret and expels him, he's grateful to discover his own people, the Raksura, but little does he know, the Raksura have great plans for him that could threaten the balance of power in the world and put the entire tribe at risk.

Where it's reviewed:
Library Journal, February 15, 2011, page 105
Locus, May 2011, page 23
Publishers Weekly, January 17, 2011, page 435

Other books by the same author:
The Ships of Air, 2004
The Wizard Hunters, 2003
Wheel of the Infinite, 2000
The City of Bones, 1995
The Element of Fire, 1993

Other books you might like:
Mercedes Lackey, *Aerie*, 2006
Todd McCaffrey, *Dragonheart*, 2008
Kristine Kathryn Rusch, *The Black Queen*, 1999
Jo Walton, *Tooth and Claw*, 2003
Sarah Zettel, *The Firebird's Vengeance*, 2004

273

MIKE WILD

The Twilight of Kerberos: Trials of Trass Kathra
(Oxford, UK: Abaddon Books, 2011)

Series: Twilight of Kerberos Series. Book 8
Story type: Adventure
Subject(s): Fantasy; Islands; Suspense
Major character(s): Kali Hooper, Warrior
Time period(s): Indeterminate
Locale(s): Trass Kathra, Fictional Location

Summary: *The Twilight of Kerberos: Trials of Trass Kathra* is a suspenseful and action-packed fantasy epic from author Mike Wild. This novel picks up a year after *Engines of the Apocalypse* ended when Kali Hooper overcame the Pale Lord. An enigmatic force known as Hel'ss propels forward toward Twilight, predicting the Ascension of the Final Faith. Kali and her friends recognize the danger that Hel'ss brings with it, but their voices and concern go unheard. The Order of the Swords of Dawn and the Eyes of The Lord are hunting Kali and her pals after deeming them outlaws. Kali's only hope is to travel to Trass Kathra, a mythical island where she must face the Trials of Four in an effort to uncover her destiny and the fate of Twilight.

Other books by the same author:
Crucible of the Dragon God, 2010
Engines of the Apocalypse, 2010

Other books you might like:
Stephen Deas, *The Adamantine Palace*, 2010
Robin Hobb, *Shaman's Crossing*, 2005
J.V. Jones, *A Cavern of Black Ice*, 1999
Peter Orullian, *The Unremembered*, 2011
R.A. Salvatore, *The Ancient*, 2008

274

ALAYNA WILLIAMS

Rogue Oracle

(New York: Pocket Books, 2011)

Series: Delphic Oracle series. Book 2
Story type: Mystery
Subject(s): Missing persons; Mystery; Fantasy
Major character(s): Tara Sheridan, Psychologist (forensic), Criminologist; Harry Li, Agent, Lover (of Tara)
Time period(s): 21st century; 2010s
Locale(s): Russia; United States

Summary: *Rogue Oracle*, a dark and suspenseful fantasy thriller, is the second installment in the Delphic Oracle series from author Alayna Williams. As a criminal profiler, Tara Sheridan has used her training in forensic psychology and her gift for Tarot card reading to earn a reputation as the best in her field. Her new assignment, however, is going to put her to the test like nothing before. When her on-again, off-again lover Agent Harry Li assigns her to a mysterious case involving missing Cold War operatives, Tara suspects a dark force is at work. When the operatives, working together on a top-secret mission to track the disposal of Russian nuclear weapons, begin vanishing without a trace, Harry suspects the disappearances have to do with an illegal weapons operation, but Tara's foreboding dreams and card readings suggest a much more sinister explanation.

Other books by the same author:
Dark Oracle, 2010

Other books you might like:
Jes Battis, *Night Child*, 2008
Alex Bledsoe, *Burn Me Deadly*, 2009
Steve Cash, *The Meq*, 2005
Louise Cooper, *The Book of Paradox*, 1973
Seanan McGuire, *An Artificial Night*, 2010

275

CHRIS WRAIGHT

Sword of Vengeance

(Nottingham, United Kingdom: Games Workshop, 2011)

Series: Warhammer 40,000: Space Marine Battles Series. Book 3
Story type: Adventure; Series
Subject(s): Adventure; Magic; Rebellion
Major character(s): Kurt Helborg, Military Personnel (Grand Marshal of the Reiksguard); Volkmar, Leader (spiritual leader); Schwarzhelm, Warrior; Pieter Verstohlen, Spy
Time period(s): Indeterminate Future
Locale(s): Warhammer Universe, Alternate Universe; Averland, Fictional Location

Summary: Chris Wraight's *Sword of Vengeance* is the sequel to *Sword of Justice* and an installment in the Warhammer Heroes series of novels. This outing continues the adventures of Kurt Helborg, Grand Marshal of the Reiksguard, who just may be the only man able to prevent the total destruction of Averland. The realm is in chaos, prompting several determined individuals to try to stop the domain's further decimation. But it is only Helborg who holds the power to truly end the madness once and for all as he takes on the dark powers ravaging Averland.

Other books by the same author:
Battle of the Fang, 2011
Sword of Justice, 2010
Dark Storm Gathering, 2009
Iron Company, 2009
Masters of Magic, 2008

Other books you might like:
Darius Hinks, *Warrior Priest*, 2010
Nick Kyme, *Grimblades*, 2010
Graham McNeill, *Sons of Ellyrion*, 2011
Gav Thorpe, *The Heart of Chaos*, 2004
C.L. Werner, *Forged by Chaos*, 2009

The Year in Historical Fiction
by
Daniel S. Burt

During the run-up to the tenth anniversary of the 9/11 attacks, we have all been asked to consider time past—the decade that now divides our present from that past event. In countless articles and television specials, we have been invited to reflect on that past decade: what our world was like before September 11, 2001 and what itis like now in 2011. The 9/11 date has joined other annual triggers of remembrance and reflection: July 4, November 11 (though the last World War I combat veteran died this year and the Armistice Day of the Great War has been amalgamated into a more generic Veteranis Day, commemorating all the subsequent wars), and December 7 (the original 9/11). Other great days in our nationis history have faded from our recollections: the birthdays of Washington and Lincoln are now forgotten and replaced by a nonspecific Presidentis Day; November 22nd, the anniversary of John Kennedyis assassination mostly goes unremarked now, though it once loomed large annually. Other dates—April 12th (the firing on Fort Sumter and the opening of the Civil War), May 8th (V-E Day), and August 15th (V-J Day), for example—have all largely passed out of our annual remembrances. This anniversary of 9/11 has included many exhortations, well-intentioned and genuinely meant, that we will never forget, but history suggests that we will, perhaps not by those who lived through that awful day, but by those who didnit. The past to stay present needs to be actively and continually considered to live in our collective consciousness, to retain its power and significance.

To a large extent, thatis exactly the work of both historians and historical novelists. For each, history is not about anniversaries but about a continual and visible relevance in which today is always a reflection of yesterday in some important way. It may seem audacious to equate the work of a historian with a historical novelist. One deals with the verifiable; the other with the imagined, but both play comparable roles in bringing the past back to life and relevance. Sure, the historical novelist trades mainly in entertainment over instruction, but it would be wise to consider Ezra Poundis famous definition of literature: "Literature is news that stays news." Beyond the specifics of the past, the greatest historical novelists are looking for universals, aspects of history that bridge the gaps of time, restoring the human connections that animate a date or a period detail and bring an era, a historical figure, or a time and a place, back from oblivion to relevance.

Ultimately, only in writing—in a history or historical fiction—is the past guaranteed remembrance and a hearing. Memories fade and fail, but a book retains its capacity to let the dead speak and the past live again. That is fundamentally what the mission of historical fiction is: the continual remembrance of crucial moments and indispensable people who are no longer with us.

Selection Criteria

Since Sir Walter Scott in the early nineteenth century first treated the historical past as if it were the recognizable present, historical fiction has dominated bestseller lists and annual selections of the best works of fiction. The historical past remains irresistible and, apparently, inexhaustible as a literary resource. The formis attraction, however, is even more remarkable because historical fiction is surely one of the most difficult and demanding narrative forms. Historical novelists must serve two contradictory masters: verifiability and invention. The historical novelist must balance the demands of representing the historical record accurately and telling a good story and often imaginatively compensating for gaps and deficiencies in that record. Take too much latitude with the facts of history and the illusion of authenticity is shattered; take too little and the data of history never come to life.

More so than any other fictional genre, it is necessary to define exactly what constitutes a historical novel to justify my selections. All novels deal with the past, except science fiction that is set in the future, or most fantasy novels set in an imagined, alternative world outside historical time. Yet not all novels are truly historical. Central to any workable definition of historical fiction is the degree to which the writer attempts not to recall the past but to recreate it. In some cases the time frame, setting, and customs of a novelis era are

merely incidental to its action and characterization. In other cases, period details function as little more than a colorful backdrop for characters and situations that could as easily be played out in a different era with little alteration. So-called historical "costume dramas" could to a greater or lesser degree work as well with a change of costume in a different place and time. The novels that we can identify as truly historical, however, attempt much more than incidental period surface details or interchangeable historical eras. What justifies a designation as a historical novel is the writeris efforts at providing an accurate and believable representation of a particular historical era. The writer of historical fiction shares with the historian a verifiable depiction of past events, lives, and customs. In historical fiction, the past itself becomes as much a subject for the novelist as the characters and action.

Most of us use the phrase "historical novel" casually, never really needing an exact definition to make ourselves understood. We just know it when we see it. This listing, however, requires a set of criteria to determine whatis in and whatis out. Otherwise the list has no boundaries. If the working definition of historical fiction is too loose, every novel set in a period before the present qualifies, and nearly every novel becomes a historical novel immediately upon publication. If the definition is so strict that only books set in a time before the authoris birth, for example, make the cut, then countless works that critics, readers, librarians, and the authors themselves think of as historical novels would be excluded.

The challenge here, therefore, has been to fashion a definition or set of criteria flexible enough to include novels that pass what can be regarded as the litmus test for historical fiction: Did the author use his or her imagination—and often quite a bit of research—to evoke another and earlier time than the authoris own? Walter Scott, who is credited with "inventing" the historical novel in English during the early nineteenth century provides a useful criterion in the subtitle of *Waverley*, his initial historical novel, the story of Scottish life at the time of the Jacobite Rebellion of 1745: "eTis Sixty Years Since." This supplies a possible formula for separating the created past from the remembered past. What is unique and distinctive about the so-called historical novel is its attempt to imagine a distant period of time before the novelistis lifetime. Scottis sixty-year span between a novelis composition and its imagined era offers an arbitrary but useful means to distinguish between the personal and the historical past. The distance of two generations or nearly a lifetime provides a necessary span for the past to emerge as history and forces the writer to rely on more than recollection to uncover the patterns and textures of the past. I have, therefore, adopted Scottis formula but adjusted it to fifty years, including those books in which the significant portion of their plots is set in a period fifty years or more before the novel was written.

Because a rigid application of this fifty-year rule might disqualify quite a few books intended by their authors and regarded by their readers to be historical novels, another test has been applied to books written about more recent eras: did the author use actual historical figures and events while setting out to recreate a specific, rather than a general or incidental, historical period? Although it is, of course, risky to speculate about a writeris intention, it is possible by looking at the bookis approach, its use of actual historical figures, and its emphasis on a distinctive time and place that enhances the readeris knowledge of past lives, events, and customs to detect when a book conforms to what most would consider a central preoccupation of the historical novel.

I have tried to apply these criteria for the historical novel thoughtfully, and have allowed some exceptions when warranted by special circumstances. I hope I have been able to anticipate what most readers would consider historical novels, but I recognize that I may have overlooked some worthy representations of the past in the interest of dealing with a manageable list of titles. Finally, not every title in the Western, historical mystery, or historical romance genres has been included to avoid unnecessary duplication with the other sections of this book. I have included those novels that share characteristics with another genre—whether fantasy, Western, mystery, or romance—that seem to put the strongest emphasis on historical interest, detail, and accuracy.

Historical Fiction Highlights in the First Half of 2011

What better to document the claim that historical fiction continues to retain its popular and critical appeal than the fact that two of the novels collected here are by an award winning film director (John Sayles) and an award winning singer-songwriter (Steve Earle). Historical fiction must be something special if it attracts these two luminaries.

Otherwise, the novels selected here continue to advance former trends in the genre that have been apparent over several years, namely, the dominance of series, the increased popularity of historical fantasy, the predominance of historical mystery and fictional biography, and especially a remarkably wide range of historical eras and events, defying the notion that there is nothing new under the historical fiction sun.

The health of a genre can be measured in two ways: in the continuing work of major literary talents and stalwarts in the form and in the debut of first-time novelists. Both are well represented in this listing. Among the literary lights are Peter Brooks (*The Emperoris Body*), Bobbie Ann Mason (*The Girl in the Blue Beret*), and Joseph OiConnor (*Ghost Light*). The stalwarts are represented by such usual suspects as Margaret George (*Elizabeth I*) Cecelia Holland (*The Kingis Witch*), Anne Perry (*Treason at Lisson Grove*), and Jeff Shaara (*Fall of Giants*). Special mention needs to made of the doyen of prehistory, Jean M. Auel, who with *The Land*

of Painted Caves brings to an end her epic Earthis Children series that began six novels ago with The Clan of the Cave Bear in 1980. Auel, more than anyone, is directly responsible for opening up prehistory for imaginative treatment, and the many novelists who have followed her in bringing to live our first human ancestors owe a great debt to the pioneering Auel.

First-time historical novelists demonstrate clearly that interesting new subjects and original takes on familiar subjects can be found. There are debut novels in the established sub-genres of the form: historical mystery (Carol K. Carris India Black, set in a Victorian brothel with the madam as sleuth) and Bernadette Pajeris A Spark of Death, set in 1901 Seattle); and fictional biography (Peter Carrollis Queen of Misfortune, about Lady Jane Grey; Mazal Alouf-Mizrahiis The Silent Sister, recreating the lost diary of Margot Frank, Anne Frankis sister; and Peter Prangeis The Philosopheris Kiss, about Denis Diderot and Sophie Volland). There are also several intriguing inaugural works that either open up new historical territory or provide novel slants on familiar historical subjects, such as ninth-century Baghdad in Howard Andrew Jonesis The Desert of Souls, a turn-of-the century Indian coffee plantation in Sarita Mandannais Tiger Hills, a retelling of the Robin Hood legend from the perspective of Alan Dale in Angus Donaldis Outlaw, and Cleopatra and vampires in Maria Dahvana Headleyis Queen of Kings. In these works, and several more collected here, the vitality of the form seems guaranteed for the foreseeable future.

Historical Mysteries

For a considerable time now, historical mysteries have remained the single largest sub-genre of historical fiction, and the novels collected here range widely in time and place and find new historical situations and figures to feature sleuthing. There are investigations taking place at the 1893 Columbian Exposition (Steve Hockensmithis Worldis Greatest Sleuth), during a 1919 wheat harvest (Richard A. Thompsonis Big Wheat), during the Spanish Civil War (Jonathan Rabbis The Second Son), around Puget Sound in the nineteenth century (Steven F. Havillis Comes a Time for Burning), and around the Round Table, involving King Arthur and his knights (Tony Haysis The Beloved Dead).

Some of the very best of the historical mystery form are represented, including Charles Todd (A Lonely Death), Jason Goodwin (An Evil Eye), Jacqueline Winspear (A Lesson in Secrets), Rhys Bowen (Bless the Bride), Simon Beaufort (A Dead Manis Secret), Ian Morson (Falconer and the Death of Kings), C.S. Harris (Where Shadows Dance), Philip Kerr (Field Gray), P.C. Doherty (Nightshade), I.J. Parker (The Fires of the Gods), and Phillip Gooden (The Durham Deception).

Several historical mysteries take on a distinctly literary tone, employing literary figures as sleuths or crime victims. There is another installment of the mystery series re-employing Dorothy L. Sayers classic sleuths—

Lord Peter Wimsey and Harriet Vane—in Jill Paton Walshis The Attenbury Emerals. Hemingway is an investigator in Craig McDonaldis One True Sentence. Muckraking journalist Nelly Bly collides with novelist Jules Verne in Carol McClearyis The Illusion of Murder. Oscar Wilde takes up the scent in Gyles Brandrethis Oscar Wilde and the Vampire Murders. The Harlem Renaissance of the 1920s is the locale for Persia Walkeris Black Orchid Blues, and heretical philosopher Giordano Bruno investigates in S.J. Parrisis Prophecy.

Some other intriguing sites for mystery and suspense include Bath during the Roman period in Kelli Stanleyis The Curse-Maker, the Victorian Orkney Islands in Alanna Knightis The Seal King Murders, World War Iis Battle of the Somme in Andrew Martinis Somme Stations, the Zulu Wars in 1879 in Garry Kilworthis Dragoons, the Solomon Islands in the 1960s in Graeme Kentis Devil-Devil, and the film industry in 1913 in Irene Flemingis The Brink of Fame.

Surely with changes of venues and new detective recruits like these, we can expect historical mystery to continue its popularity and dominance in delivering the historical past with the twists of suspense and mysteries.

Fictional Biographies

Fictional biography—the imaginative reconstruction of a historical figureis life in full or in part—remains a perennially popular sub-genre of historical fiction, and the list has biographical treatments of both the famous and the obscure, with a particular emphasis on the literary.

The well-known include Genghis Khan in Sam Djangis two-volume biographical treatment Genghis Khan: The World Conqueror, Napoleon (at least after death) in Peter Brooksis The Emperoris Body, Vincent Van Gogh in Carol Wallaceis Leaving Van Gogh, Elizabeth I in Margaret Georgeis novel of the same name, and the Borgias in Sarah Boweris Sins of the House of Borgia. Lesser known figures include genius inventor Nikola Tesla in Jean Echenozis Lightning, Madame Tussaud (of the famous waxworks) in Michelle Moranis Madame Tussaud, war criminal Victor Capesius in Dieter Schlesakis The Druggist of Auschwitz, Aaron Burris daughter, Theodosia, in Michael Parkeris The Watery Part of the World, Western gambler and gunfighter Doc Holliday in Mary Doria Russellis Doc, and famed New Orleans Voodoo Queen Marie Laveau in Jewell Parker Rhodesis Hurricane.

Literary subjects include Hemingwayis marriage to his first wife Hadley Richardson in the bestselling and well-received The Paris Wife by Paula McLain, Edgar Allan Poeis marriage to Virginia Clemm in Lenore Hartis The Ravenis Bride, Irish playwright John Millington Syngeis relationship with Abbey Theater actress Molly Allgood in Joseph OiConnoris Ghost Light, and French novelist George Sand (and her relationship with many famous men) in Rosalind Brackenburyis Becoming George Sand.

Finally, in my previous list, I reported how even a famous dog gets biographical treatment: Marilyn Monroeis dog in Andrew OiHaganis *The Life and Opinions of Maf the Dog, and His Friend Marilyn Monroe*. Now Winston Churchill is captured from the perspective of his "black dog depression" that takes the form of a real dog in Rebecca Huntis *Mr. Chartwell*. Too few to suggest a trend, but consider the possibilities: Cleopatrais asp? Caligula and his senator horse? Jeffersonis pet mockingbird named Dick? Any historical figure with a monkey on his back transformed into a real monkey?

Historical Fantasy

Huntis inventiveness, suffusing biography with the imagined, echoes a burgeoning sub-genre of historical fiction: historical fantasy. Another way of looking at this trend is that fantasy writers have increasingly discovered history as a venue for their imaginings. Vampires probably lead the list in historical fantasy. There is the aforementioned Cleopatra and vampires in Headleyis *Queen of Kings*, vampires in fifteenth-century Venice in Jon Courtenay Grimwoodis *The Fallen Blade*, vampires in seventeenth-century Bohemia in Chelsea Quinn Yarbrois (*An Embarrassment of Riches* (Yarbro has been a pioneer of historical fantasy for several decades now), and vampires being hunted down by Queen Elizabeth I in Lucy Westonis *The Secret History of Elizabeth Tudor, Vampire Slayer*.

Westonis novel is the latest of the popular literary-historical fantasy mash-up pioneered by Seth Grahame-Smith in *Pride and Prejudice and Zombies* and *Abraham Lincoln: Vampire Hunter*. To be added is Worm Milleris *A Zombieis History of the United States*. Alternate takes on history are also featured in Alice Hoffmanis Civil War-era fantasy *The Red Garden*, Eric Flintis inventive *1636: The Saxon Uprising*, Richard Mathesonis World War 1-era fantasy *Other Kingdoms*, and Bill Jamesis alternative history of World War II, titled definitely *World War Two Will Not Take Place*.

Thereis a lot more history to be changed and the time/space continuum to be altered, so itis assured that fantasy and history—two seemingly incompatibles—will continue to be conjoined.

Historical Fact

Having mentioned historical fantasy, the exception, letis end with the rule, historical fact and more precisely the unusual that continues to enliven and invigorate historical fiction. An actual 1920s terrorist attack on Wall Street is the subject for Jed Rudenfeldis *The Death Instinct*. The Dreyfus Affair inspires Kate Tayloris *A Man in Uniform*. Victorian Egypt is the setting for Kate Pullingeris *The Mistress of Nothing*. Indian life on the Olympic Peninsula in 1889 is depicted in Jonathan Evisonis *West of Here*. Spiritualism in the 1920s is the subject of Paul Elworkis *The Girl Who Would Speak for the Dead*. Jews in the Antebellum South are depicted in Alan Cheuseis *Song of Slaves in the Desert*.

Other intriguing aspects of history that form the backdrop of novels are the famous horse race in Siena, Italy, in the eighteenth-century in Marina Fioratois *The Daughter of Siena*; Lake Superior in 1622, 1902, and 2000 in Danielle Sosinis *The Long-Shining Waters*; Americais first female military pilots in Karl Friedrichis *Wings: A Novel of World War II Flygirls*; and the first Native American to graduate from Harvard in 1665 in Geraldine Brooksis *Calebis Crossing*.

Having started with John Sayles and Steve Earle, letis end with them as well. Both, like the other novelists in this section, have found interesting angles in history to view the world. John Saylesis *A Moment in the Sun* tackles the panorama of American history from the perspective of 1897 and the Spanish American War. Steve Earleis *Iill Never Get out of This World Alive* imagines the life of the physician who administered the fatal morphine overdose to Country Music giant Hank Williams. Both find something new and interesting to say, stimulated by the undiscovered country of the past that deserves remembrance.

Recommendations

Here are my selections of the 25 most accomplished and intriguing historical novels for the second half of 2010:

The Land of Painted Caves by Jean M. Auel

Calebis Crossing by Geraldine Brooks

The Emperoris Body by Peter Brooks

Song of Slaves in the Desert by Alan Cheuse

The Matchmaker of Kenmare by Frank Delaney

Being Polite to Hitler by Robb Forman Dew

Potsdam Station by David DowningS

Iill Never Get Out of This World Alive by Steve Earle

Elizabeth I by Margaret George

An Evil Eye by Jason Goodwin

Children and Fire by Ursula Hegi

The Kingis Witch by Cecelia Holland

The Desert of Souls by Howard Andrew Jones

TField Gray by Philip Kerr

Tiger Hills by Sarita Mandanna

The Girl in the Blue Beret by Bobbie Ann Mason

The Paris Wife by Paula McLain

Madame Tussaud by Michelle Moran

Ghost Light by Joseph OiConnor

Doc by Mary Doria Russell

A Moment in the Sun by John Sayles

Dreams of Joy by Lisa See

Fall of Giants by Jeff Shaara

You Think Thatis Bad by Jim Shepard

A Lesson in Secrets by Jacqueline Winspear

For More Information about Historical Fiction

Lynda G. Adamson, *American Historical Fiction: An Annotated Guide to Novels for Adults and Young Adults*. Phoenix: Oryx Press, 1999.

Lynda G. Adamson, *World Historical Fiction: An Annotated Guide to Novels for Adults and Young Adults*. Phoenix: Oryx Press, 1999.

Daniel S. Burt, *What Historical Fiction Do I Read Next?* Detroit: Gale, Vols. 1-3, 1997-2003.*

Daniel S. Burt, *The Biography Book*. Westport: Oryx/ Greenwood Press, 2001.

Mark C. Carnes, *Novel History: Historians and Novelists Confront Americais Past (and Each Other)*. New York: Simon & Schuster, 2001.

Donald K Hartman, *Historical Figures in Fiction*. Phoenix: Oryx Press, 1994.

The Historical Novel Society (http//www.historicalnovel society.org). Includes articles, interviews, and reviews of historical novels.

Of Ages Past: The Online Magazine of Historical Fiction (http://www.angelfire.com/il/ofagespast/). Includes novel excerpts, short stories, articles, author profiles, and reviews.

Soonis Historical Fiction Site (http://uts.cc.utexas.edu/ ~soon/histfiction/). A rich source of information on the historical novel genre, including links to more specialized sites on particular authors and types of historical fiction.

Historical Fiction

276

KAREN LYNN ALLEN

Beaufort 1849

(San Francisco, California: Cabbages and Kings Press, 2011)

Story type: Historical - Antebellum American South
Subject(s): Southern United States; Slavery; Romances (Fiction)
Major character(s): Jasper Wainwright, Traveler; Cara Randall, Musician (pianist); Henry Birch, Cousin (of Jasper)
Time period(s): 19th century; 1840s (1849)
Locale(s): Beaufort, South Carolina

Summary: After traveling the world, Jasper Wainwright finally returns home to Beaufort, South Carolina in 1849. Thanks to a rise in slavery and cotton, Beaufort has grown into a wealthy Southern city, but Jasper's intolerance with their secessionist attitudes indicates this will be a very short trip. His cousin, Henry Birch, attempts to play matchmaker, setting Jasper up with Cara Randall, a beautiful and spirited pianist who gives Jasper pause about leaving so quickly. When a series of anonymous letters begin showing up in the Charleston Courier, Jasper suspects there are some residents of Beaufort who might be ready to change and he's just the man to convince them to do it.

Other books you might like:
Ava Dianne Day, *Cut to the Heart*, 2002
E.L. Doctorow, *The March*, 2005
John Jakes, *North and South*, 1982
Steve R. Pieczenik, *State of Emergency*, 1997
Anthony Weller, *The Siege of Salt Cove*, 2004

277

MAZAL ALOUF-MIZRAHI

The Silent Sister: The Diary of Margot Frank

(Bloomington, Indiana: Authorhouse, 2011)

Story type: Historical - World War II
Subject(s): Antisemitism; Holocaust, 1933-1945; Jewish history

Major character(s): Margot Frank, Young Woman, Sister (of Anne Frank); Peter van Pels, Young Man; Anne Frank, Sister (of Margot), Historical Figure
Time period(s): 20th century; 1930s-1940s
Locale(s): Amsterdam, Netherlands

Summary: In *The Silent Sister: The Diary of Margot Frank*, author Mazal Alouf-Mizrahi provides a fictional account of the life of Anne Frank's older sister, Margot. Millions have read the journal kept by Anne Frank during her family's harrowing experience as they hid in an office building annex during Germany's occupation of the Netherlands. In this book, Alouf-Mizrahi provides Margot's perspective, including the letter to Margot that served as forewarning for the Franks to seek shelter, her secret romance with Peter, and the events leading up to the Franks' capture by the Nazis. First novel.

Other books you might like:
Ellen Feldman, *The Boy Who Loved Anne Frank*, 2005
Pam Jenoff, *The Diplomat's Wife*, 2008
David Liss, *The Coffee Trader*, 2003
Richard Lourie, *A Hatred for Tulips*, 2007
Stav Sherez, *The Devil's Playground*, 2004

278

KEN BABBS

Who Shot the Water Buffalo?

(New York: Overlook Press, 2011)

Story type: Contemporary
Subject(s): Vietnam War, 1959-1975; Military life; Armed forces
Major character(s): Tom Huckelbee, Pilot (helicopter), Military Personnel (Marine), 21-Year-Old; Mike Cochran, Pilot (helicopter), Military Personnel (Marine), 21-Year-Old
Time period(s): 20th century; 1960s
Locale(s): Vietnam

Summary: *Who Shot the Water Buffalo?* by Ken Babbs is a novel about the early days of American involvement in the Vietnam conflict. Based loosely on Babbs's own experiences as a Marine helicopter pilot, *Who Shot the Water Buffalo?* follows the lives of two young pilots, Tom Huckelbee and Mike Cochran. At first, Tom and Mike are little more than kids looking for fun—and sometimes trouble. They love drinking too much and

playing pranks, and they don't take their military duties very seriously. When they are shipped to Vietnam, they know little about what to expect and think of it as an adventure. Quickly, reality sets in and the young men are tested, hardened, and made into veterans.

Where it's reviewed:
Booklist, March 15, 2011, page 23

Other books by the same author:
Last Go Round, 1995

Other books you might like:
James Lee Burke, *In the Moon of Red Ponies*, 2004
Layne Heath, *The Blue Deep*, 1993
Denis Johnson, *Tree of Smoke: A Novel*, 2007
Karl Marlantes, *Matterhorn: A Novel of the Vietnam War*, 2010
Bobbie Ann Mason, *In Country*, 1985

279

SIMON BEAUFORT

A Dead Man's Secret
(Surrey, England: Severn House, 2011)

Series: Sir Geoffrey Mappestone Series. Book 8
Subject(s): Mystery; Suspense; Letters (Correspondence)
Major character(s): Geoffrey Mappestone, Knight, Detective
Time period(s): 12th century
Locale(s): England

Summary: *A Dead Man's Secret*, a suspenseful historical mystery, is the eighth installment in the Sir Geoffrey Mappestone Mystery series from author Simon Beaufort. Crusader knight-turned-detective Geoffrey Mappestone's latest assignment from King Henry includes delivering a stack of confidential letters to southern Wales and investigating the seven-year-old murder of a noble Welshman. The secrecy surrounding the letters is heightened when their scribe is mysteriously murdered days before Mappestone's journey. When one of Mappestone's companions is also murdered en route to Wales, the sleuth is desperate to uncover the truth about the letters' contents and their connection to the Welshman's death before more innocent victims are killed.

Where it's reviewed:
Booklist, March 1, 2011, page 30
Kirkus Reviews, February 1, 2011, page 67
Publishers Weekly, January 3, 2011, page 36

Other books by the same author:
The Bloodstained Throne, 2010
Deadly Inheritance, 2009
The Bishop's Brood, 2003
A Head for Poisoning, 1999
Murder in the Holy City, 1998

Other books you might like:
Valerie Anand, *The Proud Villeins*, 1990
Alys Clare, *Music of the Distant Stars*, 2010
Pat McIntosh, *A Pig of Cold Poison*, 2010
Ian Morson, *Falconer and the Death of Kings*, 2011
Joan Wolf, *No Dark Place*, 1999

280

RHYS BOWEN

Bless the Bride
(New York: Minotaur Books, 2011)

Series: Molly Murphy Series. Book 10
Subject(s): Mystery; Detective fiction; Irish Americans
Major character(s): Molly Murphy, Detective—Private; Daniel Sullivan, Police Officer (NYPD captain), Fiance(e) (of Molly); Lee Sing Tai, Businessman
Time period(s): 20th century; 1900s (1903)
Locale(s): New York, New York

Summary: In *Bless the Bride* by Rhys Bowen, Molly Murphy's approaching marriage to Daniel Sullivan—Captain of the New York Police Department—may mean the end of her career as a private detective. Though she told her husband-to-be that her crime-solving days will end once they are married, Molly gets drawn into another case even as she prepares her trousseau. Lee Sing Tai, a Chinese businessman, needs her assistance in tracking down a piece of jade and his new wife. When Lee dies under suspicious circumstances, Molly hunts for his killer as well. *Bless the Bride* is the tenth book in the Molly Murphy series.

Where it's reviewed:
Booklist, February 1, 2011, page 34
Kirkus Reviews, January 1, 2011, page 16
Library Journal, February 1, 2011, page 47
Publishers Weekly, January 3, 2011, page 36

Other books by the same author:
The Last Illusion, 2010
In Like Flynn, 2005
For the Love of Mike, 2003
Death of Riley, 2002
Murphy's Law, 2001

Other books you might like:
Kevin Baker, *Paradise Alley*, 2002
Lisa Carey, *The Mermaids Singing*, 1998
Myla Goldberg, *Wickett's Remedy*, 2005
Robin Lee Hatcher, *In His Arms*, 1998
Lou Jane Temple, *The Spice Box*, 2005

281

SARAH BOWER

Sins of the House of Borgia
(Naperville, Illinois: Sourcebooks, Inc., 2011)

Story type: Romance
Subject(s): Italian history; Catholicism; Religion
Major character(s): Esther Sarfati, Servant (of Lucrezia); Lucrezia Borgia, Daughter (of Pope Alexander VI), Fiance(e) (of Alfonso), Sister (of Cesare); Cesare Borgia, Brother (of Lucrezia), Son (of Pope Alexander VI); Alfonso d'Este, Fiance(e) (of Lucrezia), Nobleman; Pope Alexander VI, Father (of Lucrezia and Cesare), Religious (Pope)

Time period(s): 15th century-16th century
Locale(s): Spain

Summary: *Sins of the House of Borgia* is a novel by author Sarah Bower. Esther Sarfati is a Jewish girl hired to serve Lucrezia Borgia, daughter of Pope Alexander VI of the legendary Borgia Papal family, but first she must be baptized in the Roman Catholic faith. When a marriage is arranged between Lucrezia and Alfonso d'Este, the Duke of Ferrara, Esther finds herself a pawn in a series of mind games between the two families. Meanwhile, she harbors a secret love for Lucrezia's brother, Cesare, and she is willing to forgo even her own dignity to make him love her back. Bower is also the author of *The Needle in the Blood* and *The Book of Love*.

Where it's reviewed:
Kirkus Reviews, February 1, 2011, page 153
Publishers Weekly, January 24, 2011, page 133

Other books by the same author:
The Book of Love, 2008
The Needle in the Blood, 2007

Other books you might like:
Jean Briggs, *The Flame of the Borgias*, 1974
John Faunce, *Lucrezia Borgia*, 2003
F.W. Kenyon, *The Naked Sword: The Story of Lucretia Borgia*, 1968
Jean Plaidy, *Madonna of the Seven Hills*, 1958
Sara Poole, *Poison*, 2010

282

ALAN BRADLEY

A Red Herring Without Mustard: A Flavia de Luce Mystery

(New York: Delacorte Press, 2011)

Series: Flavia de Luce Mystery Series. Book 3
Subject(s): Detective fiction; Adolescence; Family
Major character(s): Flavia de Luce, 11-Year-Old, Detective—Amateur
Time period(s): 20th century; 1950s
Locale(s): England

Summary: *A Red Herring Without Mustard* is an installment from author Alan Bradley's Flavia de Luce mystery series. Flavia is a precocious 11-year-old girl whose curiosity has helped her solve mysteries on more than one occasion. This time, her family is threatened as her father faces losing everything and must sell off the family's belongings. But that doesn't stop Flavia from getting involved in a few mysteries: she must also figure out who assaulted a gypsy and who murdered a thief. Can Flavia solve the puzzle of how it is all connected? This series also includes *The Sweetness at the Bottom of the Pie* and *The Weed that Strings the Hangman's Bag*.

Where it's reviewed:
Booklist, February 1, 2011, page 38
Library Journal, January 1, 2011, page 66
Publishers Weekly, December 6, 2010, page 33

Other books by the same author:
The Weed that Strings the Hangman's Bag, 2010

The Sweetness at the Bottom of the Pie, 2009
Other books you might like:
Clare Boylan, *Emma Brown*, 2004
Galaxy Craze, *By the Shore*, 1999
Jane Gardam, *Faith Fire*, 2003
Martha Grimes, *The Winds of Change*, 2004
Andrew Taylow, *The Judgement of Strangers*, 1998

283

GYLES BRANDRETH

Oscar Wilde and the Vampire Murders

(New York: Simon & Schuster, 2011)

Series: Oscar Wilde Murder Mysteries
Subject(s): Murder; Vampires; Mystery
Major character(s): Oscar Wilde, Writer, Detective—Amateur; Arthur Conan Doyle, Writer, Detective—Amateur; Rex LaSalle, Vampire (self-proclaimed), Murderer (suspect)
Time period(s): 19th century; 1890s (1890)
Locale(s): London, England

Summary: *Oscar Wilde and the Vampire Murders* is a historical novel by Gyles Brandreth and part of Brandreth's Oscar Wilde Murder Mysteries series. In this series, flamboyant writer Oscar Wilde constantly finds himself in the center of bizarre scenarios of murder and madness. In this installment, Oscar is attending a ball with British royalty—and one real oddball, a supposed vampire named Rex LaSalle. When a party goer turns up dead with vampire-like neck bites, Oscar and his sidekick Arthur Conan Doyle launch an investigation. Their search leads them to secrets at the heart of the British monarchy.

Where it's reviewed:
Booklist, April 1, 2011, page 34
Kirkus Reviews, February 1, 2011, page 154
Publishers Weekly, March 7, 2011, page 47

Other books by the same author:
Oscar Wilde and the Dead Man's Smile, 2009
Oscar Wilde and a Death of No Importance, 2008
Oscar Wilde and a Game Called Murder, 2008

Other books you might like:
Peter Ackroyd, *The Last Testament of Oscar Wilde*, 1983
Russell Brown, *Sherlock Holmes and the Mysterious Friend of Oscar Wilde*, 1988
Louis Edwards, *Oscar Wilde Discovers America*, 2003
Carol McCleary, *The Alchemy of Murder*, 2010
Robert Reilly, *The God of Mirrors*, 1986

284

PETER BROOKS

The Emperor's Body

(New York: W.W. Norton & Company, 2011)

Story type: Political
Subject(s): Napoleonic Wars, 1800-1815; French

(European people); History

Major character(s): Phillipe de Rohan-Chabot, Diplomat; Henri Beyle, Writer; Amelia Curial, Noblewoman

Time period(s): 19th century; 1840s (1840)

Locale(s): France

Summary: *The Emperor's Body* is a historical novel by author Peter Brooks. In it, Brooks tells the story of the French expedition to retrieve Napoleon Bonaparte's body from St. Helena, the site of his exile, and take it to Les Invalides in Paris. The diplomat entrusted with the task is Phillipe de Rohan-Chabot, whose adversary, Henri Beyle, is a biographer of the late emperor. Meanwhile, both men fall for Amelia Curial, a noblewoman who seeks to release herself from her family's expectations of propriety. As the frigate Belle-Poule draws near France with Napoleon's body aboard, another revolution threatens to break out in opposition to the monarchy.

Where it's reviewed:

Library Journal, October 15, 2010, page 63

New York Times Book Review, November 19, 2011, page 30

Other books by the same author:

World Elsewhere, 1999

Other books you might like:

F.W. Kenyon, *The Emperor's Lady: A Novel Based on the Life of the Empress Josephine*, 1952

Jerry Labriola, *The Strange Death of Napoleon Bonaparte*, 2008

W. G. Sebald, *Vertigo*, 2000

Kay Nolte Smith, *A Tale of the Wind: A Novel of 19th Century France*, 1991

Carol Wallace, *Leaving Van Gogh*, 2011

285

PETER CARROLL

Queen of Misfortune

(Greenfield, Massachusetts: Copperhill Media Corporation, 2011)

Story type: Historical

Subject(s): English (British people); Monarchs; Royalty

Major character(s): Lady Jane Grey, 16-Year-Old, Royalty (Queen of England), Lover (of John Aylmer); John Aylmer, Tutor (of Jane Grey), Lover (of Jane Grey)

Time period(s): 16th century

Locale(s): London, England

Summary: *Queen of Misfortune* by Peter Carroll is a historical novel based on one of the most unusual characters in the history of the British monarchy. This woman, and the unfortunate queen of the title, was Lady Jane Grey. Carroll fashions a novel to answer some of the questions that surround her life. Although only 16, Grey survived an abusive childhood, fell prey to a scheming duke, faced imprisonment in the Tower of London, and reigned as Queen of England for nine days—only to be beheaded for treason! Using a blend of fact and fiction, Carroll examines this remarkable and tragic life through the eyes of John Aylmer, Grey's tutor, and, Carroll believes, her secret lover.

Other books you might like:

Alice Harwood, *The Lily and the Leopards*, 1949

Susan Meissner, *Lady in Waiting: A Novel*, 2010

Margaret Mullally, *A Crown in Darkness: A Novel about Lady Jane Grey*, 1975

A.C.H. Smith, *Lady Jane*, 1985

Alison Weir, *Innocent Traitor: A Novel of Lady Jane Grey*, 2007

286

DONIS CASEY

Crying Blood

(Scottsdale, Arizona: Poisoned Pen Press, 2011)

Story type: Mystery

Subject(s): Mystery; Murder; Native Americans

Major character(s): Shaw Tucker, Hunter, Spouse (of Alafair); Alafair Tucker, Spouse (of Tucker), Mother, Detective—Amateur

Time period(s): 20th century; 1910s (1915)

Locale(s): Oklahoma, United States

Summary: In the fall of 1915, Shaw Tucker and his brother take their boys on a routine quail-hunting trip on their stepfather's Oklahoma land, but their excursion is cut short when the skeleton of a murdered man is discovered. That night, Shaw is certain someone is watching his tent and calling out his name in the darkness. His suspicions are proven correct when he returns home and discovers a young Indian boy named Crying Blood has followed him. The boy is hoping to find clues about the identity of the white man who killed his father, but before Shaw has a chance to get more answers, Crying Blood is murdered as well. Shaw and his wife, Alafair, set out to uncover the killer's true identity before he strikes again.

Where it's reviewed:

Publishers Weekly, November 8, 2010, page 44

Other books by the same author:

The Sky Took Him, 2009

The Drop Edge of Yonder, 2007

Hornswoggled, 2006

The Old Buzzard Had It Coming, 2005

Other books you might like:

Dee Brown, *Creek Mary's Blood*, 1980

Dorothy Garlock, *A Place Called Rainwater*, 2003

Elmore Leonard, *The Hot Kid*, 2005

Billie Letts, *Shoot the Moon*, 2004

Toni Morrison, *Paradise*, 1998

287

ELIZABETH CHADWICK

To Defy a King

(Naperville, Illinois: Sourcebooks, Inc., 2011)

Series: William Marshall Series. Book 4

Story type: Historical - Medieval; Romance

Subject(s): Royalty; British history, 1066-1688; Women

Major character(s): Mahelt Marshal, Spouse (of Hugh), Daughter (of William); William Marshal, Knight,

Father (of Mahelt); Hugh Bigod, Spouse (of Mahelt); King John, Royalty
Time period(s): 13th century; 1200s
Locale(s): England

Summary: *To Defy a King* is a historical novel by author Elizabeth Chadwick. Mahelt Marshal is the daughter of William Marshal, King John of England's most favored knight. Mahelt is engaged to Hugh Bigod, son of the Earl of Norfolk, and at the age of 15 they begin their life together and build a family. Their happiness is soon threatened, however, as King John begins feuding with the people closest to him, including Mahelt's father, William. Now it's up to Mahelt to ensure the safety of her husband and four children, as all of the people she has known her whole life weave a web of deceit around the king. *To Defy a King* is the fourth book in Chadwick's William Marshal series.

Where it's reviewed:
Booklist, February 15, 2011, page 35

Other books by the same author:
Lady of the English, 2011
The Winter Mantle, 2003
The Love Knot, 1999
The Champion, 1998
The Conquest, 1997

Other books you might like:
Pamela Bennetts, *The Barons of Runnymede*, 1974
Julie Garwood, *Shadow Music*, 2007
James Goldman, *Myself as Witness*, 1979
Pamela Kaufman, *The Prince of Poison*, 2006
Jean Plaidy, *The Prince of Darkness*, 1978

288

ALAN CHEUSE

Song of Slaves in the Desert

(Naperville, Illinois: Sourcebooks, Inc., 2011)

Story type: Literary
Subject(s): Civil rights; Slavery; Antebellum period, 1820-1861
Major character(s): Nathaniel Pereira, Entrepreneur
Time period(s): 19th century
Locale(s): South Carolina, United States

Summary: *Song of Slaves in the Desert* is a historical novel by author Alan Cheuse. When a Jewish man named Nathaniel Pereira arrives in South Carolina from New York City in an attempt to rebuild a relative's crumbling plantation, he is shocked to witness the practice of slavery. As he struggles to reconcile how people of his own faith could own slaves after enduring centuries of oppression themselves, he also finds himself falling in love with a slave named Liza. Meanwhile, a narrative describing the enslavement of multiple generations of African women fills out the story. Cheuse is also the author of *To Catch the Lightning* and *The Light Possessed*.

Where it's reviewed:
Booklist, February 1, 2011, page 41

Kirkus Reviews, January 15, 2011, page 78
Library Journal, February 1, 2011, page 51
Publishers Weekly, December 20, 2010, page 27

Other books by the same author:
To Catch the Lightning, 2008
Lost and Old Rivers, 1998
The Sound of Writing, 1991
The Light Possessed, 1990
The Tennessee Waltz, 1990

Other books you might like:
Gwen Bristow, *Deep Summer*, 1937
Wesley Brown, *Darktown Strutters*, 1994
Austin Clarke, *The Polished Hoe*, 2002
Sherley Anne Williams, *Dessa Rose*, 1986
Stephen Wright, *The Amalgamation Polka: A Novel*, 2006

289

CASSANDRA CLARK

The Law of Angels

(New York: Minotaur Books, 2011)

Series: Abbess of Meaux. Book 3
Story type: Mystery; Series
Subject(s): Nuns; Artists; British history, 1066-1688
Major character(s): Abbess Hildegard, Religious (nun)
Time period(s): 14th century; 1380s (1385)
Locale(s): England

Summary: *The Law of Angels* is the third novel in author Cassandra Clark's Abbess of Meaux mystery series. The abbess has installed a secret religious enclave in Deepdale, England, yet when two of her charges are assailed she realizes Deepdale may not be so secret after all. After the English Peasant's Revolt three years before, no one of religious persuasion is safe, and it's up to Abbess Hildegard to protect an artifact very important to her faith—Constantine's Cross. But when assassins start searching for the cross, its protector, and anyone else associated with it, Hildegard begins to fear for her own life.

Where it's reviewed:
Booklist, March 15, 2011, page 24
Kirkus Reviews, April 15, 2011, page 635

Other books by the same author:
Hangman Blind, 2009
The Red Velvet Turnshoe, 2009

Other books you might like:
Peter Ackroyd, *The Clerkenwell Tales*, 2004
Valerie Anand, *The Ruthless Yeomen*, 1991
P.C. Doherty, *A Haunt of Murder: A Mystery*, 2002
Margaret Frazer, *The Reeve's Tale*, 1999
Joanne Harris, *Holy Fools*, 2004

290

CAROLYN COOKE

Daughters of the Revolution

(New York: Knopf Publishing, 2011)

Subject(s): Civil rights; Rebellion; Revolutions
Major character(s): Goddard "God" Byrd, Principal (headmaster, Goode School); Heck, Graduate (of Goode School), Spouse (of Mei-Mei), Father (of EV); Mei-Mei, Spouse (of Heck), Mother (of EV); EV, Daughter (of Heck and Mei-Mei); Rebozos, Friend (of Heck); Carole, Student (Goode School)
Time period(s): 20th century-21st century; 1960s-2000s (1968-2005)
Locale(s): Cape Wilde, Massachusetts

Summary: *Daughters of the Revolution*, by author Carolyn Cooke, is a historical novel set in 1960s New England at an all-boys boarding school. It is 1968, and just as in much of the United States, things are beginning to change in Cape Wilde, Massachusetts. The Goode School, an all-boys school, is feeling pressure from the community to begin admitting women. Of course there are holdouts, including Goode's own headmaster, Goddard "God" Byrd. Yet after a series of unfortunate events, as well as a typo on a student's transcript, a black female student from the West Indies is admitted to the school. Now the school must deal with its own dramatic changes at a time of rebellion and social upheaval. First novel.

Where it's reviewed:
Booklist, May 1, 2011, page 65
Marie Claire, June 2011, page 130
New York Times Book Review, June 26, 2011, page 19(L)
The New Yorker, July 4, 2011, page 76
Publishers Weekly, April 4, 2011, page 30

Other books by the same author:
The Bostons, 2001

Other books you might like:
Devery Freeman, *Father Sky: A Novel*, 1979
John Irving, *The Cider House Rules*, 1985
Walter Mosley, *Cinnamon Kiss*, 2005
Kathryn Stockett, *The Help*, 2009
Glenn Taylor, *The Marrowbone Marble Company: A Novel*, 2010

291

THOMAS RAY CROWEL

Cry Uncle, Sumbody

(Highland, Indiana: Success Press, 2011)

Story type: Historical - American Civil War
Subject(s): Diaries; United States Civil War, 1861-1865; Military life
Major character(s): David Longenecker, Military Personnel (soldier), Writer
Time period(s): 19th century; 1860s
Locale(s): United States

Summary: *Cry Uncle, Sumbody* is a gripping historical novel about the Civil War from author Thomas Ray Crowel. With the Civil War underway and the U.S. government guaranteeing it will be over within 100 days, David Longenecker enlists to serve in the Union Army. He soon finds himself immersed into the dangers, perils, and horrors of war with no viable way of escape. As he and his company engage in violent battles with the Confederate Army, are ultimately captured by their enemies, and are forced to live out their time in a miserable and disgusting prison, David's only solace comes in the form of his diary where he documents the atrocities of war and the lonely ache in his heart with raw honesty.

Other books by the same author:
The Passerby, 2008
Scattered Harvest, 2006

Other books you might like:
Geraldine Brooks, *March*, 2004
Charles Frazier, *Cold Mountain*, 1997
MacKinlay Kantor, *Andersonville*, 1954
Jeff Shaara, *The Last Full Measure*, 1998
Robert Penn Warren, *Wilderness: A Tale of the Civil War*, 1961

292

SANDRA DALLAS

The Bride's House

(New York: St. Martin's Press, 2011)

Subject(s): Women; Housing; Love
Major character(s): Nealie Bent, Young Woman; Pearl, Young Woman; Susan, Young Woman
Time period(s): 19th century-21st century
Locale(s): Georgetown, Colorado

Summary: In *The Bride's House*, author Susan Dallas tells the stories of three very different women, living in three different generations, who find their lives forever affected by a beautiful Victorian house in rural Colorado. In the 19th century, Nealie Bent is torn between two devoted suitors. Decades pass and Pearl comes of age in The Bride's House, where she lives with her father: the man who never got over his unrealized love for Nealie. In the modern era, Susan embraces the tumultuous past of her ancestral home and draws on the strength of Nealie and Pearl to empower her.

Where it's reviewed:
Publishers Weekly, March 14, 2011, page 48

Other books by the same author:
Prayers for Sale, 2009
Tallgrass, 2007
The Chili Queen, 2002
Alice's Tulips, 2000
The Persian Pickle Club, 1995

Other books you might like:
Tamera Alexander, *Beyond This Moment*, 2009
Mona Hodgson, *Too Rich for a Bride*, 2011
Earl Murray, *In the Arms of the Sky*, 1998
Ann Parker, *Leaden Skies*, 2009
Arundhati Roy, *The God of Small Things*, 1997

293

ANGELA DAVIS-GARDNER

Butterfly's Child

(New York: Dial Press, 2011)

Subject(s): Identity; Coming of age; Family
Major character(s): Benji, Son (of Frank); Benjamin "Frank" Franklin Pinkerton, Military Personnel, Father (of Benji), Spouse (of Kate); Kate, Stepmother (of Benji), Spouse (of Frank)
Time period(s): 19th century; 1890s
Locale(s): San Francisco, California; Illinois, United States

Summary: In *Butterfly's Child*, author Angela Davis-Gardner offers an inventive sequel to Puccini's classic opera *Madame Butterfly*. This volume opens with Benji, the illegitimate child of an American serviceman and a recently deceased geisha, returning with his father to a remote corner of Illinois farmland. There Benji must deal with a series of challenges, including hardscrabble life on the land, his isolation from the local community, and the discovery of the secrets of his heritage.

Where it's reviewed:
Booklist, March 15, 2011, page 20
Kirkus Reviews, January 15, 2011, page 79
Library Journal, February 1, 2011, page 51
Publishers Weekly, January 17, 2011, page 24

Other books by the same author:
Plum Wine, 2006
Forms of Shelter, 1991
Felice, 1982

Other books you might like:
S.E. Hinton, *Hawkes Harbor*, 2004
Karen Kingsbury, *Oceans Apart*, 2004
Barbara Kingsolver, *The Lacuna: A Novel*, 2009
Fern Michaels, *Crown Jewel*, 2003
Anne Tyler, *Ladder of Years*, 1995

294

ANNA DEAN

A Gentleman of Fortune: Or, the Suspicions of Miss Dido Kent

(New York: Minotaur Books, 2011)

Series: Dido Kent Series. Book 2
Story type: Mystery
Subject(s): Mystery; Murder; History
Major character(s): Dido Kent, Detective—Amateur, Vacationer, Cousin (of Flora); Flora Beaumont, Cousin (of Dido)
Time period(s): 19th century; 1800s (1806)
Locale(s): Richmond, England

Summary: *A Gentleman of Fortune: Or, the Suspicions of Miss Dido Kent*, a suspenseful historical mystery, is the second installment in the Dido Kent series from author Anna Dean. Miss Dido Kent is spending the summer of 1806 on a holiday to Richmond where she's visiting her cousin, Flora Beaumont. Her relaxing vacation takes a sinister turn when one of Flora's neighbors is dead and the wealthy townsfolk suspect foul play. As an outsider, Dido is in a prime position to play sleuth and dig up dirt on the residents of Richmond, but she's not quite prepared for the slew of dirty secrets and shocking scandals that are unearthed by her impromptu investigation.

Where it's reviewed:
Library Journal, February 15, 2011, page 102
Publishers Weekly, February 21, 2011, page 116

Other books by the same author:
A Woman of Consequence, 2010
Bellfield Hall, 2008
A Moment of Silence, 2008

Other books you might like:
Nancy Atherton, *Aunt Dimity Takes a Holiday*, 2003
A.S. Byatt, *The Children's Book*, 2009
Laurie R. King, *Justice Hall*, 2002
Sophie Kinsella, *The Undomestic Goddess*, 2005
Anne Perry, *A Christmas Visitor*, 2004

295

FRANK DELANEY

The Matchmaker of Kenmare

(New York: Random House, 2011)

Story type: Historical - World War II
Subject(s): Irish history; Missing persons; Interpersonal relations
Major character(s): Kate Begley, Matchmaker, Spy, Spouse (of Charles); Charles Miller, Military Personnel; Ben McCarthy, Spy
Time period(s): 20th century; 1930s-1940s
Locale(s): Kenmare, Kerry

Summary: *The Matchmaker of Kenmare* is the sequel to author Frank Delaney's novel *Venetia Kelly's Traveling Show*. Ben McCarthy is first introduced to Kate Begley, the village matchmaker, as World War II ravages much of Europe. Despite Ireland's desire to remain uninvolved, the nation still cannot help but feel the aftershocks of the battles in England and on the Continent. Then U.S. Intelligence Officer Charles Miller requests Kate and Ben's help with a covert mission to France. Kate and Charles fall in love and are wed upon Kate's return, but Kate cannot deny a connection with Ben, who has become a dear friend. When Charles vanishes during a mission of his own, Kate must enlist Ben's help in finding him. Delaney is also the author of *Ireland: A Novel*.

Where it's reviewed:
Booklist, December 15, 2010, page 26
Kirkus Reviews, January 1, 2011, page 2
Library Journal, October 15, 2010, page S4
Publishers Weekly, December 20, 2010, page 28

Other books by the same author:
Venetia Kelly's Traveling Show, 2010
Shannon, 2009
Tipperary, 2007
Ireland, 2005

Other books you might like:
Elaine Crowley, *The Ways of Women*, 1993
Jeanine Cummins, *The Outside Boy*, 2010
Roddy Doyle, *The Dead Republic*, 2010
Marian Keyes, *This Charming Man: A Novel*, 2008
Colm Toibin, *Brooklyn*, 2009

296

P.T. DEUTERMANN

Pacific Glory

(New York: St. Martin's Press, 2011)

Story type: Historical - World War II
Subject(s): United States. Navy; World War II, 1939-1945; Love
Major character(s): Glory Hawthorne, Nurse (Navy), Widow(er); Mick McCarty, Pilot, Alcoholic; Marsh Vincent, Military Personnel (ship officer)
Time period(s): 20th century; 1930s-1940s
Locale(s): United States

Summary: *Pacific Glory* is an action-packed historical war novel from author P.T. Deutermann. During their time at the naval academy, Marsh Vincent, Mick McCarty, and Tommy Lewis were best friends, roommates, and in love with the same girl, Glory Hawthorne. Tommy won Glory's affection and her hand in marriage after graduation, and the men each went their separate ways, until the attack on Pearl Harbor brought them together again in the worst possible way. Tommy's death at Pearl Harbor leaves Glory as a widowed Navy nurse; Marsh, now a ship officer, finds himself in combat from Guadalcanal; and Mick, a fighter pilot, hopes to redeem himself after his own mistakes cost him everything.

Where it's reviewed:
Booklist, January 1, 2011, page 56
Library Journal, December 1, 2010, page 102
Publishers Weekly, November 22, 2010, page 40

Other books by the same author:
Nightwalkers, 2009
The Moonpool, 2008
Spider Mountain, 2007
The Cat Dancers, 2005
Firefly, 2003
Darkside, 2002
Hunting Season, 2001
The Edge of Honor, 1994

Other books you might like:
James Bassett, *Commander Prince, USN: A Novel of the Pacific War*, 1971
Edward Beach, *Run Silent, Run Deep*, 1955
John J. Gobbell, *When Duty Whispers Low*, 2002
Thomas Heggen, *Mister Roberts*, 1946

297

ROBB FORMAN DEW

Being Polite to Hitler

(New York: Little, Brown, and Company, 2010)

Series: Scofield Trilogy. Book 3
Subject(s): Self knowledge; Women; History
Major character(s): Agnes Scofield, Widow(er), Teacher
Time period(s): 20th century; 1950s-1970s (1953-1973)
Locale(s): Washburn, Ohio

Summary: In *Being Polite to Hitler*, award-winning author Robb Forman Dew presents the third and final installment in a trilogy centered on the denizens of the Scofield family. Set in the small Ohio town of Washburn from the 1950s through the 1970s, this volume follows 70-something Agnes Scofield as she both looks back on the eras she's lived through and deals with the shifting winds of the current times. As the world around her changes, Agnes's perspective of the past is altered as well, and she finds new meaning in the host of unusual circumstances in which she has found herself throughout her life.

Where it's reviewed:
Good Housekeeping, January 2011, page 171
New York Times, January 3, 2011, page C4
New York Times Book Review, January 16, 2011, page 7
People, January 20, 2011, page 47
Publishers Weekly, October 18, 2010, page 24

Other books by the same author:
The Truth of the Matter, 2005
The Evidence Against Her, 2004
Fortunate Lives, 1993
The Time of Her Life, 1984
Dale Loves Sophie to Death, 1982

Other books you might like:
Lisa Genova, *Left Neglected*, 2010
Allison Winn Scotch, *Time of My Life*, 2008
Anne Rivers Siddons, *Off Season*, 2008
Chevy Stevens, *Still Missing*, 2010
Kim Wright, *Love in Mid Air*, 2010

298

SAM DJANG

Genghis Khan Vol. 1: The World Conqueror

(Far Hills, New Jersey: New Horizon Books, 2011)

Story type: Historical
Subject(s): Mongol Empire, 1206-1502; Mongols; Biographies
Major character(s): Temujin, Young Man (who would become Genghis Khan), Nomad
Time period(s): 13th century
Locale(s): Mongolia

Summary: *Genghis Khan Vol. 1: The World Conqueror* by Sam Djang is a historical novel and the first of a two-

part set dealing with the life and times of one of the greatest conquerors in world history, Genghis Khan. This novel is based almost entirely on historical facts Djang found during eight years of research throughout Asia and Europe. In this volume, readers can follow the rise of the young Genghis Khan, known at birth as Temujin. He faces the bleak and hostile conditions of Mongolia that lead him and his countrymen to exciting but dangerous lives of nomadic riding, hunting, and warfare.

Other books by the same author:
Genghis Khan Vol. 2: The World Conqueror, 2011

Other books you might like:
Taylor Caldwell, *The Earth Is the Lord's: A Tale of the Rise of Genghis Khan*, 1941
Don Dandrea, *Orlok*, 1986
Homeric, *The Blue Wolf*, 2003
Conn Iggulden, *Genghis: Birth of an Empire*, 2007
Pamela Sargent, *Ruler of the Sky: A Novel of Genghis Khan*, 1993

299

SAM DJANG

Genghis Khan Vol. 2: The World Conqueror

(Far Hills, New Jersey: New Horizon Books, 2011)

Story type: Historical
Subject(s): Mongol Empire, 1206-1502; Mongols; Wars
Major character(s): Genghis Khan, Leader (of Mongol Empire), Nomad, Warrior
Time period(s): 13th century
Locale(s): Europe; Asia, Mongolia

Summary: *Genghis Khan Vol. 2: The World Conqueror* by Sam Djang is a historical novel and the second and final entry in a set dealing with the life and times of Genghis Khan, one of history's greatest leaders and fiercest conquerors. Djang based his novels almost entirely on historical facts he discovered in Europe and Asia during eight years of research on the famous Mongol. In *Genghis Khan Vol. 2*, readers see the adult Genghis building an empire that spans the known world—only to divide it among his sons and grandsons just prior to his death. Genghis Khan's legacy rides on in Djang's historical novels.

Other books by the same author:
Genghis Khan Vol. 1: The World Conqueror, 2011

Other books you might like:
Hans Baumann, *Sons of the Steppe: The Story of How the Conqueror Genghis Khan Was Overcome*, 1957
John Clou, *A Caravan to Camul*, 1954
Conn Iggulden, *Genghis: Bones of the Hills*, 2009
Conn Iggulden, *Genghis: Lords of the Bow*, 2008
Robert Sproat, *Chinese Whispers*, 1988

300

ANGUS DONALD

Outlaw

(New York: St. Martin's Griffin, 2011)

Story type: Historical - Medieval
Subject(s): Vigilantes; Burglary; Crime
Major character(s): Alan Dale, Young Man, Vigilante (running from the law); Robin Hood, Fugitive, Leader (of vigilante band)
Time period(s): 12th century
Locale(s): England

Summary: *Outlaw* by Angus Donald is a historical novel that takes a new look at the timeless legend of Robin Hood. In this novel, Alan Dale is a young man who fell out of favor with the law. Forced to flee his home and live on the lam, Alan encounters Robin Hood and joins his camp. Robin's followers are not all merry men. In this novel, many, including Robin himself, inhabit a gray area between hero and villain. Many fight for morals and some do not, and few can trust one another. Alan's journey into the heart of this vigilante organization takes readers on a quest into troubled medieval England and its many heroes, monsters, and marauders.

Where it's reviewed:
Booklist, March 1, 2011, page 36
Publishers Weekly, November 29, 2010, page 27

Other books you might like:
Nicholas Chase, *Locksley*, 1983
Parke Godwin, *Sherwood*, 1991
Steve Lawhead, *Hood*, 2011
Jennifer Roberson, *Lady of the Forest*, 1992
Elsa Watson, *Maid Marian*, 2004

301

DAVID DOWNING

Potsdam Station

(New York: Soho Publishing, 2011)

Series: John Russell Series. Book 4
Subject(s): World War II, 1939-1945; Germans; Anti-semitism
Major character(s): John Russell, Journalist, Spy, Boyfriend (of Effi), Father (of Paul); Effi Koenen, Girlfriend (of John); Paul Russell, Son (of John)
Time period(s): 20th century
Locale(s): Berlin, Germany

Summary: *Potsdam Station* is and the fourth book in author David Downing's John Russell series of historical novels centered on World War II. As this novel opens, the year is 1945 and Hitler's reign is finally coming to a halt, yet his stronghold on Berlin remains—for now. As bombs fall on the city, John Russell must figure out a way to get communication through to his son Paul and his lover Effi, neither of whom he has seen since 1941. Despite the falling Nazi Empire, John detects a new threat on the horizon in the form of the Soviet Republic. Now he is determined to get Paul and Effi out of Berlin

at all costs, even if it means going behind enemy lines himself.

Where it's reviewed:
Booklist, March 1, 2011, page 34
Kirkus Reviews, March 1, 2011, page 352
New York Times Book Review, April 24, 2011, page 15
Publishers Weekly, February 7, 2011, page 36
Publishers Weekly, February 7, 2011, page 36

Other books by the same author:
Sealing their Fate, 2009
Stettin Station, 2009
Silesian Station, 2008
Zoo Station, 2007

Other books you might like:
Ken Follett, *Hornet Flight*, 2002
Jack Higgins, *The Eagle Has Landed*, 1975
Scott Turow, *Ordinary Heroes*, 2005
Leon Uris, *QB VII*, 1970
Herman Wouk, *War and Remembrance*, 1978

302

STEVE EARLE

I'll Never Get Out of This World Alive

(Boston: Houghton Mifflin Harcourt, 2011)

Subject(s): Addiction; Abortion; Ghosts
Major character(s): Doc Ebersole, Doctor, Addict; Hank Williams, Musician, Spirit; Graciela, Pregnant Teenager
Time period(s): 20th century; 1960s
Locale(s): San Antonio, Texas

Summary: *I'll Never Get Out of This World Alive* is a novel by author and country singer-songwriter Steve Earle. In this book, Earle tells the story of Doc Ebersole, a black market abortion doctor in 1960s Texas. Ebersole operates his illegal clinic in San Antonio, and practices medicine in between shots of morphine and other illicit drugs. Meanwhile, the ghost of Hank Williams visits Doc, allegedly because Doc was the last man to see Hank alive. When a Mexican girl called Graciela comes to Doc's clinic, Doc witnesses miraculous events that he can only attribute to her. Now Graciela has become somewhat of a local celebrity, and Doc must keep her shielded from those who might take advantage of her. This is the first novel for Earle, who is also the author of the short story collection *Doghouse Roses*.

Where it's reviewed:
Booklist, May 15, 2011, page 16
Library Journal, May 15, 2011, page 74
Publishers Weekly, March 21, 2011, page 51

Other books by the same author:
Doghouse Roses, 2001

Other books you might like:
Harlan Coben, *Tell No One*, 2001
Gerald Green, *The Last Angry Man*, 1956
Pete Hamill, *North River*, 2007

Ha Jin, *Waiting*, 1999
Valerie Martin, *Mary Reilly*, 1990

303

DAVID L. EARLS

Kilroy: The Friendship Behind the Legacy

(Bloomington, Indiana: AuthorHouse, 2011)

Story type: Historical - World War II
Subject(s): World War II, 1939-1945; Cartoons; Wars
Major character(s): William Markowski, Military Personnel (soldier), Friend (of Killian), Artist (creator of Kilroy); Killian Pomelroy, Military Personnel, Friend (of William)
Time period(s): 20th century; 1930s-1940s

Summary: *Kilroy: The Friendship Behind the Legacy* by David L. Earls is a historical novel that presents an explanation for one of the enduring images of World War II: the Kilroy cartoon. During the conflict, Allied soldiers often scrawled an image of a big-nosed man peeking over a wall with the message "Kilroy was here." That graffiti spread across Europe, bringing humor and hope to the Allies and foreboding and confusion to their foes. In *Kilroy*, Earls posits that the iconic cartoon came from a tragic friendship. Soldiers William Markowski and Killian Pomelroy became fast friends on the battlefields of Europe. When Pomelroy was killed in action, Markowski decided to memorialize him with a cartoon version—the image that became Kilroy.

Other books you might like:
Stephen D. Becker, *Dog Tags*, 1973
John Katzenbach, *Hart's War*, 1999
Michel Quint, *In Our Strange Gardens*, 2001
Edwin Howard Simmons, *Dog Company Six*, 2000
Adam Thorpe, *Pieces of Light*, 2000

304

JEAN ECHENOZ

Lightning

(New York: New Press, 2011)

Story type: Literary
Subject(s): History; Biographies; Inventors
Major character(s): Gregor, Inventor; Thomas Edison, Historical Figure, Inventor, Employer (of Gregor); J.P. Morgan, Financier (of Gregor)
Time period(s): 19th century-20th century; 1850s-1940s
Locale(s): United States

Summary: French author Jean Echenoz provides a fictional account of the life of inventor Nikola Tesla in the novel *Lightning*. Here, Tesla is cast as the character Gregor, a young man who travels from Eastern Europe to the United States to work with the brilliant Thomas Edison. In some ways, Gregor's genius surpasses that of Edison. His inventions reveal his uncanny anticipation of future technologies. But Gregor's business naivete and his

personal eccentricities cost him the financial success enjoyed by his peers. A recluse plagued by strange obsessions and anxieties, Gregor chooses to spend time with Central Park's pigeons and Colorado's lightning rather than his fellow human beings.

Where it's reviewed:
Booklist, May 15, 2011, Page 24
Kirkus Reviews, April 1, 2011, page 534
Publishers Weekly, April 25, 2011, page 114

Other books by the same author:
Ravel, 2007
Piano, 2004
I'm Gone, 2001
Big Blondes, 1997
Cherokee, 1987

Other books you might like:
Ad Hudler, *All This Belongs to Me*, 2006
Samantha Hunt, *The Invention of Everything Else*, 2008
Toni Jordan, *Addition: A Comendy that Counts*, 2008
Mona Simpson, *A Regular Guy*, 1996
Tad Wise, *Tesla*, 1994

305

PAUL ELWORK

The Girl Who Would Speak for the Dead

(New York: Amy Einhorn Books/Putnam, 2011)

Story type: Paranormal
Subject(s): Death; Grief; Ghosts
Major character(s): Emily Stewart, 13-Year-Old, Twin (of Michael); Michael Stewart, 13-Year-Old, Twin (of Emily)
Time period(s): 20th century; 1920s (1925)
Locale(s): Philadelphia, Pennsylvania

Summary: In the novel *The Girl Who Would Speak for the Dead* by Paul Elwork, Emily and Michael Stewart are 13-year-old twins living in 1925 Philadelphia. The twins long for their father, an Army doctor who died during the Great War. Their mother regales them with stories about their father's heroism both at home and abroad, but Emily and Michael yearn for some greater connection. When Emily discovers she can make strange knocking sounds with her ankles, she and her brother begin fooling their classmates into believing in ghosts. Then news of Emily's talent as a "medium" gets out into the community, and those who desire a connection to the people they've lost reach out to Emily for help with their grief. First novel.

Where it's reviewed:
Booklist, March 1, 2011, page 36
Library Journal, April 1, 2011, page 78
Publishers Weekly, February 21, 2011, page 111

Other books by the same author:
The Tea House, 2007

Other books you might like:
Gabriel Brownstein, *The Man from Beyond*, 2005
Dorothy Cannell, *Bridesmaids Revisited*, 2000

Arthur Phillips, *Angelica*, 2007
Peter Straub, *In the Night Room*, 2004
Christopher Wilson, *Cotton*, 2005

306

JONATHAN EVISON

West of Here

(New York: Algonquin Books, 2011)

Subject(s): Time; Family; Americana
Time period(s): 19th century; (1890s); 21st century; 2000s
Locale(s): Port Bonita, Washington

Summary: In *West of Here*, novelist and social networker extraordinaire Jonathon Evison tells a story that contrasts the lives of the founders of a small Pacific Northwestern town and the founders' descendents, who one hundred years later are still dealing with the repercussions of their ancestors' actions. The differences between the two settings and groups of characters make a bold comment on just how far society has come since the days of frontier life. The novel's narration staggers between the 1890s and 2006. *West of Here* is described as epic in its storytelling and praised for its evocative description of the Pacific Northwest. Jonathan Evison is also the author of the highly praised novel *All About Lulu*.

Where it's reviewed:
Kirkus Reviews, January 1, 2011, page 4
Library Journal, October 1, 2010, page 66
New York Times Book Review, February 20, 2011, page 13
Publishers Weekly, November 1, 2010, page 1

Other books by the same author:
All About Lulu, 2008

Other books you might like:
Peter Bacho, *Cebu*, 1991
Philip Haldeman, *Shadow Coast*, 2007
Mitch Luckett, *To Kill a Common Loon*, 2001
Marjorie Reynolds, *The Civil Wars of Jonah Moran*, 1999
Naomi Stokes, *The Tree People*, 1995

307

PATRICIA FALVEY

The Linen Queen

(New York: Center Street Publishing, 2011)

Story type: Historical - World War II
Subject(s): World War II, 1939-1945; Ireland; Irish (European people)
Major character(s): Sheila McGee, Beauty Pageant Contestant; Joel Solomon, Military Personnel
Time period(s): 20th century
Locale(s): Ireland

Summary: *The Linen Queen* is a novel written by author Patricia Falvey. In it, the author tells the story of Sheila McGee, a young Irish woman who lives an oppressive

life working at the local mill and caring for her overbearing mother. When the yearly Linen Queen Pageant competition seems to be in the bag for Sheila, she begins making plans to get out of Ireland and start a new life in England. Then the second World War begins, and limitations on oversea journeys keep her at home. Sheila's last chance may be to seduce an American army officer, but the closer she gets to Officer Joel Solomon, the more she begins to realize what is at stake in the fight against Hitler's Germany.

Where it's reviewed:
Booklist, February 1, 2011, page 40
Publishers Weekly, January 10, 2011, page 31

Other books by the same author:
The Yellow House, 2010

Other books you might like:
James R. Benn, *Evil for Evil*, 2009
Seamus Deane, *Reading in the Dark*, 1997
Anne Doughty, *Shadow on the Land*, 2010
Mary Gordon, *Pearl*, 2005
Brian Moore, *The Emperor of Ice-Cream*, 1965

308

MARINA FIORATO

The Daughter of Siena
(New York: St. Martin's Press, 2011)

Story type: Mystery
Subject(s): Italian history; Royalty; Marriage
Major character(s): Violante de Medici, Governess (of Siena); Pia, Young Woman
Time period(s): 18th century; 1720s (1723)
Locale(s): Tuscany, Siena

Summary: *The Daughter of Siena* is a historical novel by author Marina Fiorato. The year is 1723, and the annual tradition of the Palio di Siena is underway in the Tuscan province of Siena. This horse race determines which Contrade has bragging rights for the remainder of the year, but it also determines the fate of two women: Pia, the fiancee of a cruel and brutal man competing in the race, and Violante, the ruling governess of Siena and daughter of the Medici dynasty. This may be Pia's last chance to rid herself of her evil husband-to-be, and Violante's last chance to unearth a conspiracy against her. Fiorato is also the author of *The Madonna of the Almonds* and *The Botticelli Secret*.

Other books by the same author:
The Botticelli Secret, 2010
The Glassblower of Murano, 2009
The Madonna of the Almonds, 2009

Other books you might like:
Anne Fortier, *Juliet*, 2010
David Hewson, *The Sacred Cut*, 2005
Pauline Holdstock, *A Rare and Curious Gift*, 2005
Valerie Martin, *Italian Fever: A Novel*, 1999
April Smith, *White Shotgun*, 2011

309

IRENE FLEMING

The Brink of Fame
(New York: Minotaur Books, 2011)

Story type: Mystery; Series
Subject(s): Detective fiction; Movie industry; Missing persons
Major character(s): Emily Daggett Weiss, Director (film), Detective—Amateur, Spouse (of Adam); Adam Weiss, Spouse (of Emily), Lover (Agnes Gelert); Agnes Gelert, Actress, Lover (of Adam); Holbert Bruns, Detective—Private; Howie Kazanow, Businessman (film company owner); Carl Laemmle, Filmmaker; Ross McHenry, Actor (missing person)
Time period(s): 20th century; 1910s (1914)
Locale(s): Flagstaff, Arizona; Hollywood, California

Summary: *The Brink of Fame*, the second book in Irene Fleming's Emily Daggett Weiss series, finds film director and amateur sleuth Emily on the trail of her philandering husband and a missing actor. Emily and her husband Adam own Melpomene Moving Picture Studios in Fort Lee, New Jersey, and have set their next project in the Arizona desert. Adam heads off to Flagstaff first, and by the time Emily arrives he has run south of the border with actress Agnes Gelert. Worse, he has lost their business in a poker game. Emily's friend, private detective Holbert Bruns, lines her up with Hollywood filmmaker Carl Laemmle. But employment with Laemmle comes with a catch: Emily must first find leading man Ross McHenry. When the missing-persons case becomes a murder case, Emily finds herself with a cast of suspects.

Where it's reviewed:
Kirkus Reviews, March 15, 2011, page 445
Publishers Weekly, May 9, 2011, page 36

Other books by the same author:
The Edge of Ruin, 2010

Other books you might like:
Jeff Abbott, *Panic*, 2005
Laura Childs, *The Silver Needle Murder*, 2008
Susan Isaacs, *Magic Hour*, 1991
Elmore Leonard, *Get Shorty*, 1990
Susan Wilson, *The Fortune Teller's Daughter*, 2002

310

ERIC FLINT

1636: The Saxon Uprising
(Riverdale, New York: Baen Books, 2011)

Series: Assiti Shards Series. Book 13
Story type: Alternate History; Time Travel
Subject(s): Time travel; Wars; Riots
Major character(s): Mike Stearns, Political Figure (former Prime Minister), Military Personnel (general); Gustavus Adolphus, Royalty (King of Sweden); Gretchen, Friend (of Mike)
Time period(s): 17th century; 1630s (1636)

Locale(s): Germany

Summary: *1636: The Saxon Uprising*, a historical science-fiction novel, is the 13th installment in the 1632 Universe series from best-selling author Eric Flint. The inhabitants of modern-day Grantville, West Virginia, have been catapulted throughout time and history to 17th-century Germany. The people, led by Mike Stearns, have joined forces with Swedish king Gustavus Adolphus in the United States of Europe. After losing the Prime Minister reelection, Stearns has been serving as a general in Adolphus's army, gearing up to take action against Saxony after rioting and violence breaks out. General Baner, Saxony's vicious leader, has arrested Gretchen and plans to execute her, forcing Stearns to take stronger action than Adolphus had planned.

Other books by the same author:
1634: The Baltic War, 2007
1635: The Cannon Law, 2006
1824: The Arkansas War, 2006
The Rivers of War, 2005
1634: The Galileo Affair, 2004

Other books you might like:
Robert Harris, *Fatherland*, 1992
Cherie Priest, *Boneshaker*, 2009
Kim Stanley Robinson, *The Years of Rice and Salt*, 2002
Whitley Strieber, *Warday*, 1984
Harry Turtledove, *Ruled Britannia*, 2002

311

KARL FRIEDRICH

Wings: A Novel of World War II Flygirls

(Ithaca, New York: McBooks Press, 2011)

Story type: Historical - World War II
Subject(s): Airplanes; Military life; Women
Major character(s): Sally Ketchum, Pilot, Military Personnel; Dixie Ray Beaumont, Pilot, Military Personnel, Model
Time period(s): 20th century; 1930s-1940s

Summary: *Wings: A Novel of World War II Flygirls* is a historical novel written by first-time author Karl Friedrich. In it, the author tells the story of Sally Ketchum, a female pilot in eastern Texas. When Sally's boyfriend dies in an aircraft accident, Sally vows to find a way to remember him. She discovers the perfect homage after her father's death several years later, when she finally has the courage to sign up for the Women Airforce Service Pilot program. Entrusted with the task of international military flights, the WASP program attracts attention from Congress and other officials who feel that women have no place in the Air Force. But Sally, fellow pilot Dixie Ray Beaumont, and the rest of the WASPs are determined to prove them wrong.

Where it's reviewed:
Publishers Weekly, January 10, 2011, page 28

Other books you might like:
Ben Bova, *The Rock Rats*, 2002

Patrick Sheane Duncan, *Courage under Fire*, 1996
Dee Henderson, *True Valor*, 2002
Michael Malone, *The Four Corners of the Sky*, 2009
Nora Roberts, *Northern Lights*, 2004

312

W. MICHAEL GEAR
KATHLEEN O'NEAL GEAR, Co-Author

Fire the Sky

(New York: Gallery Books, 2011)

Series: Contact: The Battle for America
Story type: Historical - Colonial America
Subject(s): Native North Americans; Native Americans; Native American relocation
Major character(s): Black Shell, Leader (of Native Americans), Spouse (of Pearl Hand); Pearl Hand, Spouse (of Black Shell); Hernando de Soto, Leader (of European colonists)
Time period(s): 16th century
Locale(s): Florida, United States

Summary: *Fire the Sky* by W. Michael Gear and Kathleen O'Neal Gear is a historical novel and an installment in the authors' Contact: The Battle for America series. In this novel, a band of Native Americans faces the 1539 invasion of European colonists led by Hernando de Soto. Leading the natives is Black Shell and his wife, Pearl Hand. They are among the few of their tribe to survive recent battles and massacres and they feel it is their spiritual duty to defy de Soto and his men. However, dirty politics and backstabbing among the native factions threaten to derail their efforts. *Fire the Sky* is a follow-up to 2010's *Coming of the Storm*.

Where it's reviewed:
Booklist, January 1, 2011, page 56
Publishers Weekly, December 20, 2010, page 40

Other books by the same author:
Coming of the Storm, 2010
People of the Longhouse, 2010
People of the Thunder, 2009
People of the Weeping Eye, 2008
People of the Nightland, 2007

Other books you might like:
Hal Borland, *When the Legends Die*, 1963
Dee Brown, *Creek Mary's Blood*, 1980
Charles Frazier, *Thirteen Moons: A Novel*, 2006
Faye Kellerman, *Moon Music*, 1998
Susan Power, *The Grass Dancer*, 1994

313

MARGARET GEORGE

Elizabeth I

(New York: Viking, 2011)

Story type: Historical - Renaissance
Subject(s): History; Biographies; England

Major character(s): Elizabeth I, Royalty (Queen of England); Lettice Knollys, Cousin (of Elizabeth); Robert Dudley, Spouse (of Lettice); Robert Devereaux, Son (of Lettice); Francis Bacon, Historical Figure; Walter Raleigh, Historical Figure; Francis Drake, Historical Figure; William Shakespeare, Historical Figure

Time period(s): 16th century-17th century; 1580s-1600s

Locale(s): England

Summary: In *Elizabeth I: A Novel* by Margaret George, the story of the Virgin Queen's reign is told from the perspective of the monarch herself and that of her cousin and opponent in love, Lettice Knollys. For Elizabeth, love of England comes above all else, though she maintains an affection for Robert Dudley, Earl of Leicester, even after he weds Lettice. As the two women face midlife and the premature death of Dudley, their contentious relationship wears on. Elizabeth remains steadfast in her devotion to her country. For Lettice, the throne—coveted by her son Robert Devereaux, the Earl of Essex—promises personal gain.

Where it's reviewed:
Booklist, February 1, 2011, page 40
Library Journal, February 1, 2011, page 53
Publishers Weekly, January 10, 2011, page 27

Other books by the same author:
Helen of Troy, 2006
Mary, Called Magdalene, 2002
The Memoirs of Cleopatra, 1997
Mary Queen of Scotland and the Isles, 1992
The Autobiography of Henry VIII, 1986

Other books you might like:
Carolly Erickson, *Rival to the Queen*, 2010
Philippa Gregory, *The Virgin's Lover*, 2004
Victoria Holt, *My Enemy the Queen*, 1978
Susan Kay, *Legacy*, 1985
Alison Weir, *The Lady Elizabeth: A Novel*, 2008

314

GOLDIE GOLDBLOOM

The Paperbark Shoe

(New York: Picador, 2011)

Story type: Historical - World War II

Subject(s): Italian history; Prisoners of war; Australian history

Major character(s): Gin Boyle, Spouse (of Agrippas), Musician; Agrippas Toad, Spouse (of Gin); Antonio, Prisoner; John, Prisoner

Time period(s): 20th century; 1940s (1941-1948)

Locale(s): Wyalketcham, Australia

Summary: *The Paperbark Shoe* is a novel written by author Goldie Goldblum. In it, the author tells the story of 1940s Australia and the history of Italian prisoner farm camps. Gin Boyle is an albino and a pianist who faces much ridicule in her Australian farming community. Then she meets Agrippas Toad, a diminutive man who faces similar ridicule because of his penchant for women's clothing. Mr. Toad marries Gin, and together they face the watchful, judgmental eyes of their neighbors. Then two Italian prisoners of war are sent to live on the Toads' farm. Soon both Gin and Mr. Toad are drawn to the newcomers, and they learn something about life, love, and what it means to truly be accepted.

Where it's reviewed:
Kirkus Reviews, February 1, 2011, page 156
Library Journal, April 15, 2011, page 82

Other books you might like:
Anita Brookner, *Falling Slowly*, 1998
Elizabeth Jolley, *The Well*, 1986
Colleen McCullough, *The Thorn Birds*, 1977
Margaret Pemberton, *The Last Goodbye*, 2007
Carrie Tiffany, *Everyman's Rules for Scientific Living*, 2006

315

ADRIAN GOLDSWORTHY

True Soldier Gentlemen

(New York: George Weidenfeld & Nicholson Publishing, 2011)

Series: Napoleonic Wars Series. Book 1

Story type: Military; Series

Subject(s): Napoleonic Wars, 1800-1815; Peninsular War, 1808-1814; Peninsular War, 1808-1814

Major character(s): Hamish Williams, Military Personnel

Time period(s): 19th century

Locale(s): England; France; Portugal

Summary: *True Soldier Gentleman* is a historical novel by Adrian Goldsworthy about Hamish Williams, a volunteer with the British Army's 106th foot regiment. Williams holds the awkward position of being part of the infantry yet quartered with ranked officials because of his volunteer status. Because of this, few people in his regiment truly trust him. When his regiment is called to duty to fight in the Peninsular Wars against Napoleon, Williams must quickly learn a way to obtain the faith and respect of his fellow soldiers. *True Soldier Gentleman* is the first book in the Napoleonic Wars series.

Where it's reviewed:
History Today, March 2011, page 63

Other books you might like:
Hilary Bonner, *No Reason to Die*, 2004
Bernard Cornwell, *Sharpe's Escape*, 2004
Richard Howard, *Bonaparte's Horsemen*, 2002
Sheelagh Kelly, *Family of the Empire*, 2001
Patrick Rambaud, *The Retreat*, 2003

316

DAISY GOODWIN

The American Heiress

(New York: St. Martin's Press, 2011)

Story type: Romance

Subject(s): Wealth; Marriage; History

Major character(s): Cora Cash, Wealthy, Daughter (of flour tycoon); Duke of Wareham, Nobleman

Time period(s): 19th century; 1890s
Locale(s): England; United States

Summary: *The American Heiress* is a historical romance from debut author Daisy Goodwin. Cora Cash is beautiful, wealthy, and spoiled, growing up as the daughter of a millionaire flour tycoon in the late 19th century, but she's desperate to escape the watchful eye of her overbearing mother. Fortunately for Cora, there seems to be a way out of her misery: simply marry a noble Brit. Cora's mother hatches the plan to find an aristocratic husband for her daughter and Cora, eager to be free from her parents' meddling, submissively agrees, traveling to England and winning the heart of the ninth Duke of Wareham. But it doesn't take long for Cora to see that marriage, even marriage to a nobleman, doesn't equal freedom or happiness, especially when she spends her days and nights locked in a mysterious castle with an unusual and secretive husband. First novel.

Where it's reviewed:
Booklist, May 15, 2011, page 23
Library Journal, April 1, 2011, page 80.
Publishers Weekly, April 25, 2011, page 109

Other books you might like:
Juliet Nicolson, *The Perfect Summer: England 1911, Just Before the Storm*, 2007
Tea Obreht, *The Tiger's Wife*, 2011
Helen Simonson, *Major Pettigrew's Last Stand*, 2011
Penny Vincenzi, *Windfall: A Novel*, 2009

317

JASON GOODWIN

An Evil Eye

(New York: Farrar, Straus, and Giroux, 2011)

Series: Yashim the Eunuch Series. Book 4
Subject(s): Mystery; Detective fiction; Turkish history
Major character(s): Yashim, Detective; Fevzi Pasha, Military Personnel (admiral)
Time period(s): 19th century; 1840s
Locale(s): Istanbul, Turkey

Summary: In *An Evil Eye* by Jason Goodwin, Yashim, a eunuch, investigates the defection of his mentor, Fevzi Pasha. To Yashim, the Ottoman fleet's admiral, Pasha, seems an unlikely traitor to the empire. Yashim recalls him as a brutal but steadfast follower of the sultan—a man who trained Yashim well in the art of detection. Yashim's investigation into Pasha's background leads him to the sultan's palace—a mysterious world inhabited by family members, servants, and the harem. As the eunuch detective soon realizes, it is sultan's seductive and dangerous household that holds the key to Fevzi Pasha's shocking actions. *An Evil Eye* is the fourth book in the Yashim the Eunuch series.

Where it's reviewed:
Booklist, April 1, 2011, page 30
New York Times Book Review, April 10, 2011, page 23
Publishers Weekly, February 21, 2011, page 110

Other books by the same author:
The Bellini Card, 2008
The Snake Stone, 2007

The Janissary Tree, 2006
Lords of the Horizons, 1998

Other books you might like:
Michael David Lukas, *The Oracle of Stamboul*, 2011
Barbara Nadel, *Deadly Web*, 2005
Anne Perry, *The Sheen on the Silk: A Novel*, 2010
Mehmet Murat Somer, *The Prophet Murders*, 2008
Jenny White, *The Abyssinian Proof*, 2008

318

DOLORES GORDON-SMITH

Off the Record

(New York: Severn House Publishers, 2011)

Story type: Historical
Subject(s): Mystery; Murder; Inventions
Major character(s): Jack Haldean, Writer (of detective fiction), Detective—Amateur; William Rackham, Detective—Police; Charles Otterbourne, Crime Victim (murdered), Businessman, Philanthropist
Time period(s): 20th century; 1920s (1924)
Locale(s): Stoke Horam, England

Summary: *Off the Record* by Dolores Gordon-Smith is a historical novel of murder and mystery that centers on the adventures of the ingenious, eccentric writer Jack Haldean. Set in Stoke Horam, England in 1924, the story begins with shocking news: a philanthropic businessman and inventor, Charles Otterbourne, has been murdered! Suspects, theories, and motives abound. Scotland Yard's Detective William Rackham thinks the killing may have been inspired by a new invention, an electric sound recorder, being marketed by Otterbourne. Rackham asks his old friend, crime writer Jack Haldean, to ponder the case—and true to his reputation, Haldean is soon in the center of the action!

Where it's reviewed:
Booklist, February 15, 2011, page 56
Kirkus Reviews, January 15, 2011, page 93
Publishers Weekly, February 7, 2011, page 93

Other books by the same author:
A Hundred Thousand Dragons, 2010
As If by Magic, 2009
Mad about the Boy?, 2008
A Fete Worse than Death, 2007

Other books you might like:
Jo Bannister, *Flawed*, 2007
Dorothy Cannell, *She Shoots to Conquer*, 2009
William Gibson, *Pattern Recognition*, 2003
Laurie R. King, *The Language of Bees*, 2009
Jacqueline Winspear, *A Lesson in Secrets*, 2010

319

C.W. GORTNER

The Tudor Secret

(New York: St. Martin's Press, 2011)

Series: The Elizabeth I Spymaster Chronicles. Book 1
Story type: Espionage; Series

Subject(s): England; Royalty; Family
Major character(s): Brendan Prescott, Orphan, Spy; King Edward, Royalty; Elizabeth I, Royalty; Lady Jane Grey, Royalty; Mary, Royalty
Time period(s): 16th century
Locale(s): England

Summary: *The Tudor Secret* is the first book in author C.W. Gortner's The Elizabeth I Spymaster Chronicles. Set during the Tudor dynasty, this book tells the story of Brendan Prescott, an orphan taken in by the Dudley family, the reigning Tudor family. King Edward is dying, and the issue of his rightful successor is called into question. Vying for the throne is Elizabeth I, her sister Mary, and Lady Jane Grey. Soon Brendan finds himself trapped in the midst of political and royal posturing, as the Dudleys and other families fight for their right to the English throne. Gortner is also the author of *The Last Queen* and *The Confessions of Catherine de Medici*.

Where it's reviewed:
Library Journal, November 15, 2010, page 59
Publishers Weekly, November 8, 2010, page 40

Other books by the same author:
The Confessions of Catherine de Medici, 2010
The Last Queen, 2008
The Secret Lion, 2006

Other books you might like:
Patricia Finney, *Firedrake's Eye*, 1992
Philippa Gregory, *The Virgin's Lover*, 2004
Karen Harper, *The Thorne Maze*, 2003
Phil Rickman, *The Bones of Avalon*, 2011
Alison Weir, *The Lady Elizabeth: A Novel*, 2008

320

JON COURTENAY GRIMWOOD

The Fallen Blade

(New York: Hachette Book Group, 2011)

Series: Vampire Assassin Trilogy. Book 1
Story type: Series; Vampire Story
Subject(s): Supernatural; Alternative worlds; Fantasy
Major character(s): Atilo, Guard; Tycho, Vampire
Time period(s): 15th century
Locale(s): Venice, Italy

Summary: *The Fallen Blade* is the first book in The Vampire Assassin Trilogy, which is written by author Jon Courtenay Grimwood. In 15th century Venice, the Renaissance means more than just a rebirth of education and culture—it also means the birth of supernatural forces that populate the city. Venice is ruled by a family that claims Marco Polo as an ancestor. When a cousin of the Duke is abducted, the family calls out Atilo, leader of the the Assassini, a secret service of guards entrusted to protect them. As Atilo tracks down the missing cousin, he meets up with a vampire named Tycho, whom he enlists as an ally.

Where it's reviewed:
Booklist, December 15, 2010, page 29
Kirkus Reviews, November 15, 2010, page 1135

Other books by the same author:
End of the World Blues, 2007
Felaheen, 2006
Stamping Butterflies, 2006
Effendi, 2005
Pashazade, 2005

Other books you might like:
Malcolm J. Bosse, *Captives of Time*, 1987
Judith Lennox, *The Italian Garden*, 1993
Elle Newmark, *The Book of Unholy Mischief*, 2008
Daniel Silva, *The Mark of the Assassin*, 1998
Gloria Skurzynski, *Manwolf*, 1981

321

NIKOLAI GROZNI

Wunderkind

(New York: Free Press, 2011)

Subject(s): Communism; Music; Musicians
Major character(s): Konstatin, 15-Year-Old, Musician
Time period(s): 20th century; 1940s-1980s
Locale(s): Bulgaria

Summary: *Wunderkind* is a novel written by author Nikolai Grozni. In this book, the author tells the story of a 15-year-old child prodigy who plays piano at a school for gifted students in the Eastern Bloc country of Bulgaria. It is the final decade of the Cold War, and although Communism still holds countries behind the Iron Curtain in its icy grip, signs of the political movement's failure are beginning to show. Meanwhile Konstatin, a teenage pianist, studies at the Sofia Music School for the Gifted, hoping that his talent and skill in playing classical piano will someday help him get out of the country and flee to a freer land. Grozni is also the author of *Turtle Feet*.

Where it's reviewed:
Publishers Weekly, June 6, 2011, page 22

Other books by the same author:
Turtle Feet, 2009

Other books you might like:
Nina Berberova, *The Book of Happiness*, 1999
Rana Dasgupta, *Solo*, 2009
Milan Kundera, *The Unbearable Lightness of Being*, 1984
Andrei Makine, *The Music of a Life*, 2002
Gary Shteyngart, *The Russian Debutante's Handbook*, 2002

322

DAVID HALPERIN

Journal of a UFO Investigator

(New York: Viking, 2011)

Subject(s): Supernatural; Extraterrestrial life; Monsters
Major character(s): Danny Shapiro, Teenager, Investigator (of the paranormal)

Time period(s): 20th century; 1960s
Locale(s): Philadelphia, Pennsylvania

Summary: *Journal of a UFO Investigator: A Novel* by David Halperin is a story about aliens and alienation. In this novel, teenage loner Danny Shapiro feels like he has hit rock bottom. His mother is very ill and his father is distant. He has no friends at school and, being Jewish, feels isolated in his predominately Christian neighborhood. Danny escapes into his imagination, creating a complex fantasy life involving aliens and "Men in Black" who try to hide them. In addition, Danny's world is populated by beautiful maidens and dangerous sea monsters. The adventures in his imagination soon threaten to derail his grasp on reality—but could there be fact within his fantasies?

Where it's reviewed:
Booklist, January 1, 2011, page 41
Library Journal, January 1, 2011, page 53
Publishers Weekly, November 22, 2010, page 41

Other books you might like:
Christopher Buckley, *Little Green Men*, 1999
Rebecca Hunt, *Mr. Chartwell*, 2011
George P. Pelecanos, *The Night Gardener*, 2006
Jean Thompson, *The Year We Left Home*, 2010
E. Duke Vincent, *The Camelot Conspiracy*, 2011

323

STEPHEN HARRIGAN

Remember Ben Clayton

(New York: Knopf, 2011)

Subject(s): Fathers; Family; World War I, 1914-1918
Major character(s): Francis "Gil" Gilheaney, Artist (sculptor); Maureen, Daughter (of Gil), Assistant (to Gil); Lamar Clayton, Rancher
Time period(s): 20th century; 1920s
Locale(s): Texas, United States

Summary: Stephen Harrigan's *Remember Ben Clayton* is set in Texas a few years after the end of the First World War. There Gil Gilheaney and his grown daughter Maureen lead relatively uneventful lives. Gil is a sculptor and Maureen his assistant, but beneath the daily routines of father and daughter are buried secrets and Maureen's desire to become an artist in her own right. Meanwhile, Gil is commissioned by local rancher Lamar Clayton to create a statue honoring his son, a soldier killed in the war. Slowly Lamar's story is revealed, and he too is harboring secrets of his own that mirror those of Gil.

Where it's reviewed:
Booklist, April 15, 2011, page 37
Library Journal, May 15, 2011, page 75
Publishers Weekly, March 14, 2011, page 49

Other books by the same author:
Challenger Park, 2006
The Gates of the Alamo, 2000
Jacob's Well, 1984
Aransas, 1980

Other books you might like:
Doris Lessing, *Alfred and Emily*, 2008

Peter Pouncey, *Rules for Old Men Waiting*, 2005
Linda Sole, *Tears Will Not Save Them*, 2011
Dalton Trumbo, *Johnny Got His Gun*, 1939
Louisa Young, *My Dear I Wanted to Tell You*, 2011

324

C.S. HARRIS (Pseudonym of Candace Proctor)

Where Shadows Dance

(New York: Obsidian, 2011)

Series: Sebastian St. Cyr Series. Book 6
Subject(s): Mystery; Murder; History
Major character(s): Sebastian St. Cyr, Detective—Police; Paul Gibson, Doctor (surgeon); Hero Jarvis, Fiance(e) (of Sebastian)
Time period(s): 19th century; 1810s (1812)
Locale(s): London, England

Summary: In *Where Shadows Dance* by C.S. Harris, a London physician calls on Detective Sebastian St. Cyr when he realizes that a cadaver in his laboratory did not die from natural causes. St. Cyr soon learns that the corpse, a diplomat with the foreign office, was stabbed and that he is not to be the only victim in a politically motivated spree. In 1812, the atmosphere in London is tense as Napoleon has extended his reach to Russia. The case becomes personal when the killer sets his sights on St. Cyr's fiance, Hero Jarvis. *Where Shadows Dance* is the sixth book in the Sebastian St. Cyr series.

Where it's reviewed:
Publishers Weekly, January 24, 2011, page 135

Other books by the same author:
What Remains of Heaven, 2009
Where Serpents Sleep, 2008
Why Mermaids Sing, 2007
When Gods Die, 2006
What Angels Fear, 2005

Other books you might like:
Bernard Cornwell, *Gallows Thief*, 2002
David Liss, *A Conspiracy of Paper*, 2000
Anne Perry, *Death of a Stranger*, 2002
Graham Swift, *The Light of Day*, 2003
Will Thomas, *Some Danger Involved*, 2004

325

LENORE HART

The Raven's Bride

(New York: St. Martin's Press, 2011)

Story type: Romance
Subject(s): Literature; Writers; Love
Major character(s): Virginia Clemm, Spouse (of Edgar Allen Poe); Edgar Allen Poe, Writer
Time period(s): 19th century; 1820s-1840s
Locale(s): United States

Summary: *The Raven's Bride* is a historical novel by Lenore Hart that provides a fictional account of the true

romance between literary figure Edgar Allen Poe and his cousin, Virginia Clemm. Told through the eyes of Virginia, the book describes the relationship between her and Poe, beginning with their meeting when she was only seven years old and progressing through the consummation of their relationship when she was only 13 to their subsequent marriage. As Poe grapples with mood swings, poverty, and addiction to alcohol, Virginia—aka Sissy—remains his faithful and true supporter. Hart is also the author of *Waterwoman, Ordinary Springs,* and *Becky: The Life and Loves of Becky Thatcher.*

Where it's reviewed:
Booklist, February 1, 2011, page 40
Library Journal, November 15, 2010, page 59
Publishers Weekly, December 20, 2010, page 59

Other books by the same author:
Becky: The Life and Loves of Becky Thatcher, 2008
Ordinary Springs, 2005
Waterwoman, 2002

Other books you might like:
Bernhardt J. Hurwood, *My Savage Muse: The Story of My Life: Edgar Allan Poe, an Imaginative Work,* 1980
David Madsen, *Black Plume: The Suppressed Memoirs of Edgar Allan Poe,* 1980
Stephen Marlowe, *The Lighthouse at the End of the World,* 1995
Paula McLain, *The Paris Wife,* 2011
Barbara Moore, *The Fever Called Living,* 1976

326

STEVEN F. HAVILL

Comes a Time for Burning

(Scottsdale, Arizona: Poisoned Pen Press, 2011)

Series: Dr. Thomas Parks Series. Book 2
Story type: Medical
Subject(s): Diseases; Medical care; History
Major character(s): Thomas Parks, Doctor, Father, Spouse
Time period(s): 19th century; 1890s (1892)
Locale(s): Port McKinney, Washington

Summary: *Comes a Time for Burning,* a historical novel, is the second installment in the Dr. Thomas Parks Series from author Steven F. Havill. In the spring of 1892, Dr. Thomas Parks devotes most of his time in the quiet logging community of Port McKinney, Washington, to treating lumberjack injuries, but his medical savvy and strength under pressure is about to be put to the ultimate test. When Dr. Parks treats an incredibly ill prostitute, he is shocked to discover that she's actually afflicted with Asian Cholera. The outbreak spreads like wildfire, claiming its victims in a day or less. Torn between his desire to protect his family and his need to understand the contagion, Dr. Parks dedicates himself to uncovering the source of the outbreak, which may be closer than he thinks.

Where it's reviewed:
Booklist, December 1, 2010, page 33
Library Journal, December 1, 2010, page 91

Publishers Weekly, December 6, 2010, page 34

Other books by the same author:
The Fourth Time Is Murder, 2008
Final Paymen, 2007
A Discount for Death, 2003
Leadfire, 1985
The Worst Enemy, 1984

Other books you might like:
Laura Kalpakian, *Educating Waverley,* 2002
David Long, *The Inhabited World,* 2006
Jim Lynch, *The Highest Tide: A Novel,* 2005
Anne Richardson Rolphe, *An Imperfect Lens,* 2006
Susan R. Sloan, *An Isolated Incident,* 1998

327

MARIA DAHVANA HEADLEY

Queen of Kings

(New York: Dutton, 2011)

Story type: Fantasy
Subject(s): Royalty; Vampires; Egyptian history, to 642 (Ancient period)
Major character(s): Cleopatra, Royalty (Queen of the Nile), Vampire; Marc Antony, Lover (of Cleopatra)
Locale(s): Egypt

Summary: In *Queen of Kings,* author Maria Dahvana Headley reimagines the life, loves, and adventures of the legendary Queen of the Nile...with a twist. From Cleopatra's ascent to the throne and her dubious utilization of the power in her possession to her love affair with Marc Antony, this volume follows Cleopatra's journey—with one startling difference. In order to be reunited with her dead love Antony, she agrees to become a vampire in order to walk the earth as a *true* immortal. First novel.

Where it's reviewed:
Booklist, April 15, 2011, page 38
Kirkus Reviews, March 15, 2011, page 445
Library Journal, March 15, 2011, page 75

Other books you might like:
Gillian Bradshaw, *Cleopatra's Heir,* 2002
Karen Essex, *Kleopatra,* 2001
Colin Falconer, *When We Were Gods,* 2000
Margaret George, *The Memoirs of Cleopatra,* 1997
Colleen McCullough, *Antony and Cleopatra,* 2007

328

URSULA HEGI

Children and Fire

(New York: Scribner, 2011)

Subject(s): Germanic peoples; Teachers; History
Major character(s): Thekla Jansen, Teacher
Time period(s): 20th century; 1930s (1934)
Locale(s): Burgdorf, Germany

Summary: Ursula Hegi's *Chlidren and Fire* centers on schoolteacher Thekla Jansen, who heads a small class of fourth graders as Hitler begins to take power. Thekla finds the best way to handle the children's questions about the Fuhrer is to simply do whatever Hitler requires of his countrymen. But this tactic doesn't last long—especially when a long-buried secret from Thekla's history threatens to emerge.

Where it's reviewed:
Booklist, April 15, 2011, page 29
Kirkus Reviews, March 15, 2011, page 445
Library Journal, April 1, 2011, page 80
Publishers Weekly, February 28, 2011, page 32

Other books by the same author:
The Worst Thing I've Done, 2007
Sacred Time, 2003
The Vision of Emma Blau, 2000
Salt Dancers, 1995
Stones from the River, 1994

Other books you might like:
Jeffery Deaver, *Garden of Beasts*, 2004
Gila Lustiger, *The Inventory*, 2001
Mara Rostov, *Eroica*, 1977
J.N. Stroyar, *The Children's War*, 2001
Markus Zusak, *The Book Thief*, 2006

329

DAVID HEWSON

The Fallen Angel

(New York: Delacorte Press, 2011)

Series: Nic Costa & Gianni Peroni Series. Book 9
Subject(s): Mystery; Murder; Suspense
Major character(s): Nic Costa, Detective; Mina Gabriel, 17-Year-Old, Daughter
Time period(s): 21st century; 2010s
Locale(s): Rome, Italy

Summary: *The Fallen Angel* is the ninth book in the Nic Costa series from author David Hewson. Nic Costa's summer holiday in Rome ends abruptly with a bloodcurdling scream and a dead body. Costa discovers the bloody corpse of Malise Gabriel, an unconventional scholar, lying in the middle of the Via Beatrice Cenci after allegedly stepping on some weak scaffolding and accidentally falling to his death. Malise's beautiful teenage daughter, Mina, is also at the scene, huddling over her father's body. At first glance, the death seems to be an unfortunate accident, but the more Costa digs around, the sketchier the details become. The case shows shocking parallels to a centuries-old crime involving a sexually assaulted young woman who murdered her father in 1599. As Costa deepens his investigation, he senses a dark and sinister force at work in the lives of Mina and her family that could destroy them all.

Where it's reviewed:
Kirkus Reviews, March 15, 2011, page 446
Publishers Weekly, March 7, 2011, page 42

Other books by the same author:
The Garden of Evil, 2008

The Seventh Sacrament, 2007
The Lizard's Bite, 2006
The Sacred Cut, 2006
Lucifer's Shadow, 2004

Other books you might like:
Mary Gordon, *The Love of My Youth*, 2011
Susanne Kircher, *A Roman Scandal*, 1976
Frederic Prokosch, *A Tale for Midnight*, 1955
Morris L. West, *Eminence*, 1998
Thornton Wilder, *The Eighth Day*, 1967

330

FRANCES HILL

Deliverance from Evil

(New York: Overlook Press, 2011)

Subject(s): Witches; Trials; Marriage
Major character(s): Mary Cheever, Spouse (of George); George Burroughs, Religious, Spouse (of Mary); Peter White, Friend (of George)
Time period(s): 17th century; 1690s
Locale(s): Wells, Maine; Salem, Massachusetts

Summary: The real-life events of the Salem Witch Trials serve as the backdrop for Frances Hill's *Deliverance from Evil*. In rural Maine, Reverend George Burroughs saves Mary Cheever from a Native American attack, and the two eventually wed. But a few hundred miles to the south, in Salem, Massachusetts, rumors of witches are rampant, and George is named as a potential supplicant to the devil. He is arrested, and Mary sets out to prove her husband's innocence and clear his name. She is unprepared, however, for the hysteria gripping Salem Village—and just what it will take to save George.

Where it's reviewed:
Booklist, February 15, 2011, page 57
Library Journal, March 1, 2011, page 69
Publishers Weekly, January 3, 2011, page 33

Other books by the same author:
Such Men Are Dangerous: The Fanatics of 1692 and 2004, 2004
Hunting for Witches: A Visitor's Guide to the Salem Witch Trials, 2002
The Salem Witch Trials Reader, 2000
A Delusion of Satan: The Full Story of the Salem Witch Trials, 1995
Out of Bounds, 1985

Other books you might like:
Shirley Barker, *Peace, My Daughters*, 1949
Megan Chance, *Susannah Morrow*, 2002
Maryse Conde, *I, Tituba, Black Witch of Salem*, 1992
Katherine Howe, *The Physick Book of Deliverance Dane*, 2009
Kathleen Kent, *The Heretic's Daughter*, 2008

331

STEVE HOCKENSMITH

World's Greatest Sleuth!

(New York: Minotaur Books, 2011)

Series: Holmes on the Range Mystery Series. Book 5
Subject(s): World's Columbian Exposition, Chicago, Illinois, 1893; Mystery; Murder
Major character(s): Gustav "Old Red" Amlingmeyer, Detective, Brother (of Otto); Otto "Big Red" Amlingmeyer, Brother (of Gustav), Detective
Time period(s): 19th century; 1890s (1893)
Locale(s): Chicago, Illinois

Summary: *World's Greatest Sleuth!*, a humorous historical mystery, is the fifth installment in the Holmes on the Range Mystery series from award-winning author Steve Hockensmith. For the Amlingmeyer brothers, Gustav (aka Old Red) and Otto (aka Big Red), a detective contest at the World's Columbian Exposition in Chicago is the prime opportunity to win $10,000, justify their claims of being the best sleuths in the world, and make their hero, Sherlock Holmes, proud. The brothers have barely arrived from Montana when the competition turns deadly serious. When one of the contest's organizers, Armstrong B. Curtis, is killed, the competing detectives must work together to piece together a real murder investigation.

Where it's reviewed:
Booklist, December 15, 2010, page 26
Kirkus Reviews, November 1, 2010, page 1085
Library Journal, November 15, 2010, page 66
Publishers Weekly, November 15, 2010, page 43

Other books by the same author:
Dawn of the Dreadfuls, 2010
The Crack in the Lens, 2009
The Black Dove, 2008
On the Wrong Track, 2007
Holmes on the Range, 2006

Other books you might like:
Carol Cox, *Ticket to Tomorrow*, 2006
Barbara Croft, *Moon's Crossing*, 2003
Grace Mark, *The Dream Seekers*, 1992
Alec Michod, *The White City*, 2004
Robert W. Walker, *City for Ransom*, 2005

332

CECELIA HOLLAND

The King's Witch

(New York: Berkley Books, 2011)

Story type: Historical - Medieval
Subject(s): History; Occultism; Crusades
Major character(s): Richard, Royalty (King of England), Son (of Eleanor); Eleanor, Royalty (Queen Mother), Mother (of Richard); Edythe, Healer
Time period(s): 12th century; 1190s
Locale(s): England

Summary: *The King's Witch* by Cecelia Holland is set during the late 12th century, at a time when England is engaged abroad in the Crusades and at home in battles against sickness and famine. But the court of King Richard the Lionheart contains a young woman who may protect the monarch from the diseases that plague the kingdom. Edythe, a healer of remarkable skill, was brought to the court by Queen Mother Eleanor. Although Richard is at first suspicious of the young woman's presence, her ability to cure a serious illness earns her a position of favor. But is Edythe a woman of medicine, or is she a witch?

Where it's reviewed:
Booklist, April 15, 2011, page 37

Other books by the same author:
Kings of the North, 2010
The Secret Eleanor, 2010
The High City, 2009
The Witches' Kitchen, 2004
Pillar of the Sky, 1985

Other books you might like:
Elizabeth Chadwick, *To Defy a King*, 2011
Susan Higginbotham, *The Queen of Last Hopes: The Story of Margaret of Anjou*, 2011
Helen Hollick, *I Am the Chosen King*, 2011
Pamela Kaufman, *Shield of Three Lions*, 1983
Sharon Kay Penman, *Lionheart*, 2011

333

BABETTE HUGHES

The Hat

(Santa Fe, New Mexico: Sunstone Books, 2011)

Story type: Psychological Suspense
Subject(s): Organized crime; Prohibition; Economic depressions
Major character(s): Kate Brady, Young Woman, Spouse (of Ben), Lover (of Bobby); Bobby Keane, Accountant, Lover (of Kate); Ben Gold, Bootlegger, Spouse (of Kate)
Time period(s): 20th century
Locale(s): Cleveland, Ohio

Summary: In the novel *The Hat*, author Babette Hughes tells the story of a chain of events leading up to the horrific murder of an organized crime boss. Kate Brady is a young woman living through America's Great Depression, when a sudden firing from her job at a bakery leaves her worrying about her future. Her luck seems to change, however, when she is swept up in a swift romance with Ben Gold. After they are married, Kate begins to notice Ben's comings and goings at all hours of the night. As it turns out, Ben is a bootlegger during Prohibition. When Kate meets Ben's accountant, Bobby Keane, she finds herself falling for him—but can either of them ever escape the hold that Ben has over them? First novel.

Other books you might like:
Matt Bondurant, *The Wettest County in the World: A Novel Based on a True Story*, 2008
Dorothy Garlock, *High on a Hill*, 2002

Craig Holden, *The Jazz Bird*, 2002
Lee Irby, *7,000 Clams*, 2004
Harold Livingston, *Ride a Tiger*, 1987

334

REBECCA HUNT

Mr. Chartwell

(New York: Dial Press, 2011)

Subject(s): Depression (Mood disorder); Dogs; Fantasy
Major character(s): Esther Hammerhans, Librarian, Widow(er); Winston Churchill, Political Figure (British Prime Minsiter), Historical Figure; Mr. Chartwell, Dog
Time period(s): 20th century; 1960s (1964)
Locale(s): London, United Kingdom

Summary: In *Mr. Chartwell*, author Rebecca Hunt examines the effects of depression on two very different individuals: statesman Winston Churchill and widowed librarian Esther Hammerhans. Both are leading lives of quiet desperation in London when a large talking dog named Mr. Chartwell shows up on Esther's doorstep. He is the same animal that goaded her husband into suicide months earlier, and now he has come for Esther. During the days, Mr. Chartwell pays visits to Churchill, who is waging his own war with the illness. First novel.

Where it's reviewed:
Booklist, November 1, 2010, page 33
The Financial Times, October 16, 2010, page 15
Library Journal, November 1, 2010, page 55
Publishers Weekly, November 15, 2010, page 35
Spectator, January 1, 2011, page 29

Other books you might like:
Michael Dobbs, *Never Surrender*, 2007
Brian Garfield, *The Paladin: A Novel Based on Fact*, 1979
Leo Kessler, *The Churchill Papers*, 1998
Glenn Meade, *The Sands of Sakkara*, 1999
Mary Doria Russell, *Dreamers of the Day*, 2008

335

DOUGLAS W. JACOBSON

The Katyn Order

(Ithaca, New York: McBooks Press, 2011)

Story type: Historical - World War II
Subject(s): World War II, 1939-1945; Massacres; Polish history
Major character(s): Adam Nowak, Resistance Fighter; Natalia, Spy
Time period(s): 20th century; 1930s-1940s (1939-1940)
Locale(s): Warsaw, Poland

Summary: In the historical novel *The Katyn Order*, author Douglas W. Jacobsen tells the story of the Katyn Forest massacre, during which the Soviet secret police killed approximately 22,000 Polish nationals after the Soviets invaded Poland. The story begins as the Warsaw Upris-ing threatens Nazi Germany's stronghold on Poland. American Resistance fighter Adam Nowak is embedded in Poland as the uprising begins, but after two months the cause seems lost. Then he meets Natalia, a Polish woman who works as a Polish secret agent. Soon rumors of an order to the Soviet secret police reach Adam and Natalia, and they rush to stop the possible murder of thousands of people.

Where it's reviewed:
Booklist, May 1, 2011, page 32
Library Journal, March 1, 2011, page 69
Publishers Weekly, March 14, 2011, page 49

Other books by the same author:
Night of Flames, 2007

Other books you might like:
David Downing, *Potsdam Station*, 2011
Ilona Karmel, *An Estate of Memory*, 1969
Philip Kerr, *Field Gray*, 2011
Jerzy Kosinski, *The Painted Bird*, 1965
W.S. Kuniczak, *The Thousand Hour Day*, 1968

336

BILL JAMES

World War Two Will Not Take Place

(New York: Severn House Publishers, 2011)

Story type: Alternate History
Subject(s): World War II, 1939-1945; History; Espionage
Major character(s): Marcus Mount, Agent (British SIS); Toumlin, Spy (German double-agent); Andreas Valk, Military Personnel (German major)
Time period(s): 20th century; 1930s (1938)
Locale(s): England; Germany

Summary: In *World War Two Will Not Take Place*, author Bill James creates an alternate version of 1938 in which the British Prime Minister seems to have brought Europe back from the brink of war. To verify the Germans' intentions, British SIS agent Marcus Mount travels to Berlin where double agent Toumlin may hold vital information. As Mount tries to determine the status of the relationship between Germany and Russia, his mission grows increasingly complicated and Toumlin goes missing. Meanwhile, Major Andreas Valk travels to England in advance of Hitler's visit, but the true goal of his mission is to catch the British government in a compromising position.

Where it's reviewed:
Booklist, May 1, 2011, page 40
Kirkus Reviews, March 15, 2011, page 447

Other books by the same author:
Full of Money, 2009
Letters from Carthage, 2007
Wolves of Memory, 2006
Top Banana, 1996
Roses, Roses, 1993

Other books you might like:
William Boyd, *Restless: A Novel*, 2006
Alex Dryden, *Red to Black*, 2010

Ken Follett, *Jackdaws*, 2001
Robert Harris, *Enigma*, 1995
Greg Iles, *Black Cross*, 1995

337

HOWARD ANDREW JONES

The Desert of Souls

(New York: Thomas Dunne Books, 2011)

Story type: Mystery
Subject(s): Middle East; Mystery; Royalty
Major character(s): Jaffar, Royalty; Asim, Guard; Dabir, Scholar
Time period(s): 8th century
Locale(s): Baghdad, Iran

Summary: *The Desert of Souls* is a novel by author Howard Andrew Jones. Asim is the captain of the guard of Jaffar, a royal master in 8th century Iran. When Jaffar's beloved pet parrot dies, Asim suggests a fateful trip to the marketplace. There, Jaffar discovers a priceless object with a mysterious message engraved upon it, and he enlists Asim and his friend Dabir, a scholar, with the task of deciphering the words. As they work to uncover the object's powers, the trio encounters fantastical Arabian elements in the desert. Jones is also the author of the Plague of Shadows series and a coauthor of the Complete Cossack Adventures series.

Where it's reviewed:
Booklist, January 1, 2011, page 47
Library Journal, January 1, 2011, page 86
Publishers Weekly, January 3, 2011, page 38

Other books you might like:
Eli Amir, *The Dove Flyer*, 2010
Ted Chiang, *The Merchant and the Alchemist's Gate*, 2007
C.J. Illinik, *Najila*, 2007
Elif Shafak, *The Forty Rules of Love: A Novel of Rumi*, 2010
Barry Unsworth, *Land of Marvels: A Novel*, 2009

338

WARD JUST

Rodin's Debutante

(Boston, Massachusetts: Houghton Mifflin Harcourt, 2011)

Story type: Coming-of-Age
Subject(s): Art; Sex crimes; Wealth
Major character(s): Tommy Ogden, Wealthy, Hunter; Lee Goodell, Student—High School, Wealthy, Artist; Magda Serra, Student—High School, Crime Victim
Time period(s): 20th century
Locale(s): Chicago, Illinois

Summary: In the beginning of the 20th century, wealthy Chicagoan, Tommy Ogden, tries to make a statement to his art-obsessed wife and affluent friends by turning his inherited estate into a private school for boys. Years later, Lee Goodell, an aspiring sculptor from an influen-

tial family, is sent to Ogden Hall School for Boys after tragedy strikes in his small town. A woman is murdered and one of Lee's fellow students, Magda Serra, is the victim of a brutal sexual assault. Lee's father, the town's judge, works with local leaders to cover up the crimes and then leaves the city, along with his family. Lee enjoys his education at Ogden Hall School, learning a lot about his dreams and passions, but when Magda arrives, desperate for answers about what really happened to her, Lee learns a great deal about himself.

Where it's reviewed:
Booklist, February 1, 2011, page 41
Library Journal, February 1, 2011, page 54
New York Times Book Review, March 27, 2011, page 8
Publishers Weekly, January 3, 2011, page 31

Other books by the same author:
Exiles in the Garden, 2009
Forgetfulness, 2008
An Unfinished Season, 2004
A Dangerous Friend, 1999
Echo House, 1997

Other books you might like:
Clare Boylan, *Emma Brown*, 2004
Joanne Harris, *Gentlemen and Players*, 2006
Francine Prose, *Goldengrove*, 2008
Marjane Satrapi, *Persepolis: The Story of a Childhood*, 2003
Anita Shreve, *Testimony*, 2008

339

PHILIP KERR

Field Gray

(New York: G. P. Putnam's Sons, 2011)

Series: Bernie Gunther Series. Book 7
Story type: Mystery; Series
Subject(s): Mystery; History; World War II, 1939-1945
Major character(s): Bernie Gunther, Investigator, Military Personnel, Prisoner
Time period(s): 20th century; 1950s (1954)
Locale(s): Cuba; Germany; United States

Summary: *Field Gray*, a historical novel of war, is the seventh installment in the Bernie Gunther series from award-winning author Philip Kerr. It's 1954 and an anti-Nazi private investigator has managed to survive the Nazi regime. These days he's employed by a seedy crime boss in Cuba, but when one of his jobs gets him entangled with the United States Navy, he finds himself in jail at Guantanamo. Transferred to an army prison in New York City, a rough interrogation results in painful flashbacks about Bernie's service during World War II. Bernie finds himself transferred yet again, this time to the same German prison where Hitler was held in 1923. As Bernie faces violent interrogations from a slew of governments and authorities and wrestles internally with horrific memories of war, he manages to stay one step ahead of the investigators and dispenses only the information of his choosing.

Where it's reviewed:
Booklist, April 1, 2011, page 30

Library Journal, March 15, 2011, page 108
Library Journal, November 15, 2010, page 44
New York Times Book Review, April 24, 2011, page 15
Publishers Weekly, February 21, 2011, page 110

Other books by the same author:
If the Dead Rise Not, 2010
A Quiet Flame, 2009
The One from the Other, 2006
Hitler's Peace, 2005
The Second Angel, 1999
A Five Year Plan, 1998
A Philosophical Investigation, 1993

Other books you might like:
Peter Hogg, Crimes of War, 2001
Charles Kenney, The Last Man, 2001
Brian Moore, The Statement, 1996
Daniel Silva, A Death in Vienna, 2004
Steve Thayer, Wolf Pass, 2003

340

GARRY KILWORTH

Dragoons

(Sutton, Surrey, England: Severn House, 2011)

Story type: Mystery
Subject(s): Mystery; History; Military life
Major character(s): Sebastian Early, Military Personnel
Time period(s): 19th century; 1870s (1879)
Locale(s): South Africa

Summary: Although no gentleman longs to be a military-police officer, Ensign Sebastian Early is working hard to make the most of his newfound post. As provost-marshal in the Anglo-Zulu war in South Africa, Sebastian has an opportunity to use his position for a worthy cause. When he discovers an unidentified body, he sets to work to solve the crime. The corpse belongs to a military lieutenant who seems to have lost his life in an illegal duel, but when Sebastian attempts to investigate, he is thwarted at every turn. The strong opposition from higher-ups leads Sebastian to believe that someone in the British army doesn't want Sebastian digging around in this unsolved mystery.

Other books by the same author:
Scarlet Sash, 2010
Kiwi Wars, 2008
Rogue Officer, 2007
Attack on Redan, 2003
The Winter Soldiers, 2003

Other books you might like:
Steven Barnes, Zulu Heart, 2003
Ronald Bassett, The Tune that They Play, 1973
Peter Bowen, Yellowstone Kelly Series, 1987
Michael Horbach, The Lionness, 1978
William Moore, Bush War!, 1975

341

ALANNA KNIGHT

The Seal King Murders

(London: Allison & Busby, 2011)

Series: Jeremy Faro Series. Book 16
Story type: Mystery; Series
Subject(s): Detective fiction; Crime; Swimming
Major character(s): Inspector Faro, Detective—Police
Time period(s): 19th century; 1860s (1861)
Locale(s): Orkney, England

Summary: The Seal King Murders is the 16th book in author Alanna Knight's mystery series featuring Inspector Faro. The cousin of a former colleague of Faro drowns while swimming, and Faro has been called upon to investigate. Since the victim was a world-class swimmer, the circumstances surrounding his death seem suspect. As Faro arrives in the English town of Orkney, however, he finds himself distracted by ancient myths and relics—and his very first lover. Can Faro stay focused long enough to get to the bottom of the crime? Knight is also the author of the Rose McQuinn series.

Other books by the same author:
Killing Cousins, 1992
Deadly Beloved, 1990
Enter Second Murderer, 1988
Estella, 1986
Castle of Foxes, 1981

Other books you might like:
Quintin Jardine, Skinner's Rules, 1993
Juliet Marillier, Wolfskin, 2003
William Paul, Sleeping Dogs, 1995
Ian Rankin, The Naming of the Dead, 2006
Irvine Welsh, Crime, 2008

342

ROSALIND LAKER

The House by the Fjord

(New York: Severn House Publishers, 2011)

Story type: Historical - World War II
Subject(s): World War II, 1939-1945; Death; Family
Major character(s): Anna, Widow(er); Ingrid, Householder
Time period(s): 20th century; 1940s (1946)
Locale(s): Norway

Summary: The House by the Fjord is a novel written by author Rosalind Laker. In it, Laker tells the story of the widow of a Norwegian World War II pilot and her trek to his country to meet his family. Anna is convinced that she will not stay long when she arrives in Norway, yet the loveliness of the country captivates her. Then she learns that she has inherited a house through her husband's death. Reluctant to live in a place so foreign to her, Anna changes her mind when her father-in-law gives to her a diary kept by the former owner of the house. As Anna learns more about the owner, named Ingrid, she begins to recover from her grief and tries to find love again.

Where it's reviewed:
Booklist, May 1, 2011, page 70

Other books by the same author:
The Sugar Pavilion, 1995
The Venetian Mask, 1993
The Golden Tulip, 1991
Circle of Pearls, 1990
To Dance with Kings, 1988

Other books you might like:
Elizabeth Gill, *The Secret*, 2007
Ursula Hegi, *Children and Fire*, 2011
Thomas Keneally, *The Widow and Her Hero*, 2007
Rosalind Noonan, *One September Morning*, 2009
Christine Weton, *The Dark Wood*, 1946

343

SARITA MANDANNA

Tiger Hills

(New York: Grand Central Publishing, 2011)

Story type: Romance
Subject(s): History; Romances (Fiction); Epics
Major character(s): Devi, Girl; Devanna, Boy; Machu, Cousin (of Devanna)
Time period(s): 19th century
Locale(s): India

Summary: In *Tiger Hills* by Sarita Mandanna, 19th-century India provides the setting for a story of friendship, love, and heartache. Devi is born into a life of privilege, a beloved daughter in a family dominated by males. Her childhood friend, Devanna, has no immediate family to speak of. His mother abandoned him and his father killed himself. Through the years, Devanna's feelings for Devi grow from friendship to romance, but Devi has lost her heart at an early age to Devanna's cousin Machu—a famed tiger hunter. Devanna goes to university to study medicine but abruptly returns home, desperate to be with Devi. First novel.

Where it's reviewed:
Booklist, February 15, 2011, page 50
Kirkus Reviews, January 1, 2011, page 7
Library Journal, March 15, 2011, page 109
Publishers Weekly, December 6, 2010, page 28

Other books you might like:
Thalassa Ali, *Companions of Paradise*, 2007
Carol K. Carr, *India Black*, 2011
Amitav Ghosh, *Sea of Poppies*, 2008
Deanna Raybourn, *Dark Road to Darjeeling*, 2010
Rebecca Ryman, *The Veil of Illusion*, 1995

344

ANDREW MARTIN

Somme Stations

(London: Faber & Faber, 2011)

Series: Jim Stringer Series. Book 7
Subject(s): Railroads; World War I, 1914-1918; Military life

Major character(s): Jim Stringer, Detective, Military Personnel
Time period(s): 20th century; 1910s
Locale(s): France

Summary: *The Somme Stations* is the seventh novel in author Andrew Martin's Jim Stringer detective series. When the Great War becomes a reality for much of England, railway station policeman Jim Stringer decides to enlist in the North Eastern Railway Battalion. Soon Stringer is headed for the Somme front on a mission to transport military equipment when enemy bullets force him and his battalion to take cover. But when a member of the group is mysteriously killed, Stringer is more worried about dying at the hands of his own men. Now he must solve the murder before the entire group breaks down under enemy fire.

Other books by the same author:
The Last Train to Scarborough, 2009
Murder at Deviation Junction, 2009
Death on a Branch Line, 2008
The Lost Luggage Porter, 2008
The Necropolis Railway, 2006

Other books you might like:
Rennie Airth, *River of Darkness*, 1999
Sebastian Faulks, *Birdsong*, 1993
John Harris, *Covenant with Death*, 1994
Kevin Major, *No Man's Land*, 1995
Frederic Manning, *The Middle Parts of Fortune*, 1977
Richard Matheson, *Other Kingdoms*, 2011

345

BOBBIE ANN MASON

The Girl in the Blue Beret

(New York: Random House, 2011)

Story type: Historical - World War II
Subject(s): World War II, 1939-1945; Airplanes; Wars
Major character(s): Marshall Stone, Pilot, Military Personnel

Summary: *The Girl in the Blue Beret* is a historical novel by author Bobbie Ann Mason. In it, Mason tells the story of Marshall Stone, a U.S. fighter pilot based in England during World War II. After being shot and forced to crash-land over enemy lines, Marshall meets a group of Resistance members who help him escape Nazi capture. Marshall returns to the scene of his crash-land years later, looking to thank those who helped him for their bravery and sacrifice, particularly a girl in a blue beret who he cannot get out of his head decades later. Mason is also the author of *In Country* and *Clear Springs: A Family Story*.

Where it's reviewed:
Booklist, April 15, 2011, page 35
Kirkus Reviews, March 15, 2011, page 448
New York Times Book Review, July 24, 2011, page 13
Publishers Weekly, March 14, 2011, page 47

Other books by the same author:
Feather Crowns, 1993
Love Life, 1989

Spence + Lila, 1988
In Country, 1985
Shiloh and Other Stories, 1982

Other books you might like:
Martin Caidin, *The Last Dogfight*, 1974
Sebastian Faulks, *Charlotte Gray*, 1998
Richard Grant, *Another Green World*, 2006
R.J. Pineiro, *The Eagle and the Cross*, 2008
Danielle Steel, *Echoes*, 2004

346

FERENC MATE

Sea of Lost Dreams

(New York: Albatross Books, 2011)

Series: Dugger and Nello Series. Book 2
Story type: Adventure; Series
Subject(s): Sea stories; Sailing; Natural disasters
Major character(s): Dugger, Shipowner; Nello, Sailor;
   Kate, Lover (of Dugger)
Time period(s): 20th century; 1920s (1921)
Locale(s): French Polynesia; Mexico

Summary: *Sea of Lost Dreams* is the second novel in
author Ferenc Mate's Dugger and Nello series. After being imprisoned in Mexico, Nello, Captain Dugger, and
Dugger's romantic interest, Kate, break free and sail
toward the island of Tahiti. Yet soon they discover two
stowaways aboard: one, a young Irish woman escaped
from a convent, and the other a French spy searching for
a rebel leader. Both spell trouble for the trio, but the
storm-tossed seas prove an even more dangerous foe.
The adventure does not end once the crew reaches
French Polynesia, however, as a jungle filled with cannibals and revolutionaries tests Dugger and Nello's
courage. Mate is also the author of *Ghost Sea*.

Where it's reviewed:
Booklist, March 15, 2011, page 27
Publishers Weekly, March 7, 2011, page 46

Other books by the same author:
Ghost Sea, 2007

Other books you might like:
Carol Birch, *Jamrach's Menagerie*, 2011
Nicholas Griffin, *The Requiem Shark: A Novel*, 2000
Gene Hackman, *Wake of the Perdido Star*, 1999
Carsten Jensen, *We, the Drowned*, 2011
Matthew Kneale, *English Passengers: A Novel*, 2000

347

ANNA JEAN MAYHEW

The Dry Grass of August

(New York: Kensington Books, 2011)

Subject(s): Segregation; Racism; Family
Major character(s): Jubie Watts, Sister (of Stell, Puddin,
   and Davie), 13-Year-Old, Girl; Stell, Sister (of Jubie,
   Puddin, and Davie); Davie, Brother (of Jubie, Stell,

and Puddin), Baby; Puddin, Sister (of Jubie, Stell,
and Davie); Mary Luther, Housekeeper (black maid);
Mrs. "Mama" Watts, Mother (of Stell, Jubie, Puddin,
and Davie)
Time period(s): 20th century; 1950s (1954)
Locale(s): Charlotte, North Carolina

Summary: In *The Dry Grass of August* by Anna Jean Mayhew, the Watts family sets out from North Carolina in
1954 for a vacation in Florida, but their journey takes a
terrible turn. The family's black housekeeper, Mary
Luther, accompanies 13-year-old Jubie, her older sister
Stell, younger siblings Puddin and Davie, and their
mother in a relative's Packard that's loaded with their
belongings. Though their route will take them through
Ku Klux Klan territory, Mrs. Watts is confident that their
trip will be a safe one. When the unthinkable happens,
Jubie must reconsider the feelings she has for Mary, the
woman who cared for her like a mother, and her parents,
whose true characters have come to light. First novel.

Where it's reviewed:
Booklist, February 1, 2011, page 40
Publishers Weekly, January 10, 2011, page 28

Other books you might like:
Pat Cunningham Devoto, *The Summer We Got Saved*,
   2005
Allan Gurganus, *Good Help*, 1988
David Haynes, *The Full Matilda*, 2004
Lee Martin, *Quakertown*, 2001
Alice Randall, *Rebel Yell*, 2009

348

CAROL MCCLEARY

The Illusion of Murder

(New York: Forge, 2011)

Series: Nellie Bly Series. Book 2
Subject(s): Mystery; History; Murder
Major character(s): Nellie Bly, Historical Figure, Journal-
   ist, Detective; Sarah Bernhardt, Historical Figure,
   Actress, Magician; Frederick Selous, Historical
   Figure, Explorer, Magician
Time period(s): 19th century; 1880s (1889)
Locale(s): Asia; Egypt; England; United States

Summary: In *The Illusion of Murder*, author Carol Mc-
Cleary creates a fictional account of the exploits of
Victorian journalist and feminist Nellie Bly. It is 1889
and Bly has set out to reenact the global circumnaviga-
tion described in Jules Verne's *Around the World in 80
Days*. The adventure turns deadly when Bly witnesses
the murder of an Englishman in Egypt. As Bly continues
her journey to Asia and North America, she realizes that
she is being followed by the killer she observed in
northern Africa. Sarah Bernhardt and Frederick Selous
aid Bly in her investigation of the mystery. *The Illusion
of Murder* is the second book in the Nellie Bly series.

Where it's reviewed:
Booklist, April 1, 2011, page 32
Kirkus Reviews, March 15, 2011, page 456
Library Journal, March 1, 2011, page 60
Publishers Weekly, February 21, 2011, page 116

Historical

Other books by the same author:
The Alchemy of Murder, 2010

Other books you might like:
Carole Nelson Douglas, *Spider Dance*, 2004
Joe R. Lansdale, *Flaming London*, 2006
Anna Quindlen, *Rise and Shine: A Novel*, 2006
C.S. Richardson, *The End of the Alphabet*, 2007
Anita Shreve, *The Weight of Water*, 1997

349

CRAIG MCDONALD

One True Sentence

(New York: Minotaur Books, 2011)

Series: Hector Lassiter Series. Book 4
Subject(s): Mystery; Writers; Murder
Major character(s): Hector Lassiter, Writer, Detective—
Amateur; Brinke Devlin, Writer, Detective—
Amateur, Lover (of Hector)
Time period(s): 20th century; 1920s (1924)
Locale(s): Paris, France

Summary: *One True Sentence* is the fourth installment in
the Hector Lassiter series from award-winning author
Craig McDonald. The story, set in Paris in 1924, follows
aspiring crime writer turned amateur sleuth, Hector
Lassiter. When a number of magazine editors are
murdered, Gertrude Stein assembles a group of mystery
writers to solve the crimes. Hector teams up with sexy
novelist, Brinke Devlin, both in the bedroom and on the
investigation. As the investigation intensifies, Hector
suspects that a group of writers might be responsible for
the deaths, causing him to question the motives of
everyone around him and fear for his own safety.

Where it's reviewed:
Booklist, January 1, 2011, page 51
Kirkus Reviews, January 1, 2011, page 19
Publishers Weekly, December 6, 2010, page 33

Other books by the same author:
Print the Legend, 2010
Toros & Torsos, 2008
Wolf, 2008
Head Games, 2007

Other books you might like:
Michael Atkinson, *Hemingway Deadlights*, 2009
William McCranor Henderson, *I Killed Hemingway*,
1993
Paula McLain, *The Paris Wife*, 2011
Dan Simmons, *The Crook Factory*, 1999
Shay Youngblood, *Black Girl in Paris*, 2000

350

JAMES MCGEE

Rebellion

(New York: HarperCollins, 2011)

Story type: Historical - War of 1812
Subject(s): War of 1812; Napoleonic Wars, 1800-1815;
Revolutions

Major character(s): Henry Brooke, Agent (of Secret
Service); Matthew Hawkwood, Police Officer, Agent
(sent to make peace treaty); Napoleon Bonaparte,
Ruler (dictator of France)
Time period(s): 19th century; 1810s (1812)
Locale(s): Paris, France

Summary: *Rebellion* by James McGee is a historical novel
based on the turmoil in Europe in the later years of the
Napoleonic Wars. In October, 1812, Napoleon's armies
are clashing with Russia; France, Britain, and Spain are
full of conflict; and France seems to be tottering on the
edge of a new revolution. Who can stop the chaos? The
British Secret Service has devised a cunning plan to end
the war by negotiating a secret treaty. They send Henry
Brooke to enlist Matthew Hawkwood for the job. Hawkwood, a police officer, is dispatched to Paris with little
information but his assignment: to broker a secret peace
deal with the French, or suffer the consequences of
failure!

Other books by the same author:
Rapscallion, 2008
Resurrectionist, 2007
Ratcatcher, 2006

Other books you might like:
Bernard Cornwell, *Sharpe's Devil*, 1992
Linda Donn, *The Little Balloonist*, 2006
Sandra Gulland, *The Last Great Dance on Earth*, 2000
Patrick O'Brian, *The Hundred Days*, 1998
Patrick Rambaud, *The Battle*, 2000

351

BETTY MCINNES

Lady on the Loch

(New York: Severn House Publishers, 2011)

Story type: Historical
Subject(s): Scotland; Scots (British people); Scottish his-
tory
Major character(s): Lachlan Gilmore, Young Man, Rescuer
(of Annabel), Brother (of Christina); Christina
Gilmore, Sister (of Lachlan), Seamstress; Annabel
Erskine, Seamstress (to Mary Stuart); Mary Stuart,
Royalty (Queen of Scots)
Time period(s): 16th century; 1500s (1567)
Locale(s): Castle Island, Lochleven

Summary: In *Lady on the Loch*, a historical novel by Betty
McInnes, a young Scot doing a good deed finds himself
stuck in a web of political machinations and deadly
dangers. In 1567, Lachlan Gilmore finds a carriage stuck
in a ditch and stops to help its occupant, Lady Annabel
Erskine. He is surprised to discover that Annabel is a
seamstress given the task of preparing royal apparel for
Mary Stuart, the Queen of Scots. The queen is being
held captive by political enemies at nearby Castle Island.
Lachlan and his sister Christina, also a seamstress,
become embroiled in this situation which quickly
escalates into a dangerous battle for power over Scotland.

Where it's reviewed:
Booklist, April 1, 2011, page 34

Other books by the same author:
The Longest Journey, 2010
The Balfour Twins, 2006
Collar of Pearls, 2003
MacDougal's Luck, 2003
All the Days of Their Lives, 2002

Other books you might like:
Fiona Buckley, *The Fugitive Queen*, 2003
Carolly Erickson, *The Memoirs of Mary Queen of Scots*, 2009
Margaret George, *Mary, Queen of Scotland and the Isles*, 1992
Philippa Gregory, *The Other Queen*, 2008
Reay Tannahill, *Fatal Majesty: A Novel of Mary, Queen of Scots*, 1999

352

PAULA MCLAIN

The Paris Wife

(New York: Ballantine Books, 2011)

Story type: Literary; Romance
Subject(s): Marriage; Writers; Voyages and travels
Major character(s): Hadley Richardson Hemingway, Spouse (of Ernest); Ernest Hemingway, Spouse (of Hadley), Writer
Time period(s): 20th century
Locale(s): Europe

Summary: Paula McLain's *The Paris Wife* brings to life the often-overlooked adventures of Ernest Hemingway's devoted spouse, Hadley Richardson Hemingway. Injured as a child, Hadley never thought she had many prospects in the way of marriage, but when she meets a charismatic Ernest Hemingway, her entire life changes. The two travel the world together and gather research for Hemingway's novels, though it is Hadley who takes center stage in this story of a woman who, though eventually spurned, provided great love and support to one of the greatest writers of the 20th century.

Where it's reviewed:
Booklist, February 1, 2011, page 40
Kirkus Reviews, January 15, 2011, page 82
Library Journal, November 15, 2010, page 60
Publishers Weekly, December 6, 2010, page 27
Publishers Weekly, December 6, 2010, page 27

Other books by the same author:
A Ticket to Ride, 2008

Other books you might like:
James Aldridge, *One Last Glimpse*, 1977
Clancy Carlile, *The Paris Pilgrims*, 1999
Julien Green, *The Apprentice Writer*, 1993
Bernice Kert, *The Hemingway Women*, 1983
Craig McDonald, *One True Sentence*, 2011

353

MICHAEL MCMENAMIN
PATRICK MCMENAMIN, Co-Author

The Parsifal Pursuit

(New York: Enigma Books, 2011)

Series: Winston Churchill Trilogy. Book 2
Story type: Political
Subject(s): German Republic, 1918-1933; Journalism; Antisemitism
Major character(s): Adolf Hitler, Historical Figure; Mattie McGary, Journalist; Winston Churchill, Godfather (of Mattie), Historical Figure, Political Figure (British Prime Minister); Bourke Cochran Jr., Spy; Kaiser Wilhelm II, Royalty
Time period(s): 20th century; 1930s (1931)
Locale(s): Germany

Summary: *The Parsifal Pursuit* is the second book in the Winston Churchill trilogy by Michael McMenamin and Patrick McMenamin. In it, the authors tell the story of events leading up to Hitler's reign over Nazi Germany and his quest for world domination. The year is 1931, and a plot is uncovered in Germany that pits the supporters of President Hindenburg against those of Kaiser Wilhelm II. Soon Winston Churchill, along with his goddaughter, journalist Mattie McGary, and her boyfriend, Bourke Cochran Jr., are racing against time to stop the plot from developing. When an ancient artifact, the Spear of Destiny—the very spear used to kill Jesus Christ—goes missing, the trio must rush to recover it before Hitler or the Kaiser get their hands on it.

Other books by the same author:
The DeValera Deception, 2010

Other books you might like:
James R. Benn, *Evil for Evil*, 2009
David Dowling, *Potsdam Staton*, 2011
Douglas W. Jacobson, *The Katyn Order*, 2011
Joseph Kanon, *Stardust*, 2009
Philip Kerr, *Field Gray*, 2011

354

WORM MILLER

A Zombie's History of the United States: From the Massacre at Plymouth Rock to the CIA's Secret War on the Undead

(Berkeley, California: Ulysses Press, 2011)

Story type: Parody
Subject(s): United States history; Zombies; Humor

Summary: In *A Zombie's History of the United States: From the Massacre at Plymouth Rock to the CIA's Secret War on the Undead*, author Worm Miller creates a parody of American history that purportedly reveals the role of zombies in pivotal events. Claiming to have researched declassified government documents, Worm casts the un-

dead in five centuries of historic happenings—sometimes as victim, more often as enemy. According to this re-imagined chronicle, zombies were in part responsible for the attacks on the Jamestown colonists and the Alamo, Meriwether Lewis and Audie Murphy were both zombies, and NASA has used zombies in space flights. Zombies, Worm explains, remain an unrecognized segment of American society, whose contributions to U.S. history have been concealed for far too long.

Where it's reviewed:
Booklist, January 1, 2011, page 57

Other books you might like:
Jane Austen, *Pride and Prejudice and Zombies*, 2009
Max Brooks, *World War Z: An Oral History of the Zombie War*, 2006
Cherie Priest, *Boneshaker*, 2009
Paul Theroux, *World's End and Other Stories*, 1980
Lucy Weston, *The Secret History of Elizabeth Tudor, Vampire Slayer*, 201
1

355

LARRY MILLETT

The Magic Bullet

(Minneapolis, Minnesota: University of Minnesota Press, 2011)

Story type: Mystery; Series
Subject(s): Detective fiction; Literature; Politics
Major character(s): Sherlock Holmes, Detective—Private; Shadwell Rafferty, Bartender, Detective—Amateur; Artemus Dodge, Financier
Time period(s): 20th century; 1920s
Locale(s): St. Paul, Minnesota

Summary: *The Magic Bullet* is the sixth book in author Larry Millett's Minnesota Mysteries series. When one of St. Paul's wealthiest entrepreneurs, Artemus Dodge, is shot in cold blood, Shadwell Rafferty and Sherlock Holmes must not only find out the culprit but also how someone could enter Dodge's private, locked office. The Minnesota Public Safety Commission blames anti-political protesters for the crime, but Rafferty suspects something more at work. Can the detectives—one professional, one amateur—cut through the political red tape to find out who really killed Dodge? Millett is also the author of *Sherlock Holmes and the Red Demon*, *Sherlock Holmes and the Ice Palace Murders*, and *Sherlock Holmes and the Secret Alliance*.

Where it's reviewed:
Booklist, April 1, 2011, page 32
Publishers Weekly, February 21, 2011, page 116

Other books by the same author:
The Disappearance of Sherlock Holmes, 2002
Sherlock Holmes and the Secret Alliance, 2001
Sherlock Holmes and the Rune Stone Mystery, 1999
Sherlock Holmes and the Ice Palace Murders, 1998
Sherlock Holmes and the Red Demon, 1996

Other books you might like:
Caleb Carr, *The Italian Secretary*, 2005
Michael Chabon, *The Final Solution*, 2004

Mitch Cullin, *A Slight Trick of the Mind*, 2005
Steve Hockensmith, *World's Greatest Sleuth!*, 2011
Laurie R. King, *Locked Rooms*, 2005

356

DANIEL MILLS

Revenants: A Dream of New England

(United Kingdom: Chomu Press, 2011)

Story type: Historical - Colonial America
Subject(s): United States history, 1600-1775 (Colonial period); Missing persons; Social conditions
Major character(s): Reverend Bellringer, Religious; Ruth, Young Woman; James, Young Man
Time period(s): 17th century; 1680s (1689)

Summary: In Daniel Mills's historical novel *Revenants: A Dream of New England*, the year 1689 has brought alarm and suspicion to the Massachusetts Bay Colony village of Cold Marsh. Surrounded by the dense New England forest, the town has recently lost two of its members—young women who vanished without a trace. Adding to the colonists' anxiety is the assertion by Reverend Bellringer that Satan is responsible for the disappearances. When another young woman goes missing, the townsmen venture into the woods to search for the lost girls. Instead, they find the site where some of their own had slaughtered the members of a Native American community years ago. Their exposed shame compounds their fears for the lost women. First novel.

Where it's reviewed:
Booklist, February 1, 2011, page 41

Other books you might like:
Geraldine Brooks, *Caleb's Crossing*, 2011
Sally Gunning, *The Widow's War*, 2006
Katherine Howe, *The Physick Book of Deliverance Dane*, 2009
Kathleen Kent, *The Heretic's Daughter*, 2008
Anya Seton, *The Winthrop Woman*, 1958

357

GEORGE ROBERT MINKOFF

The Leaves of Fate

(Kingston, New York: McPherson & Company Publishing, 2011)

Series: In the Land of Whispers Series. Book 3
Story type: Historical - Seventeenth Century; Series
Subject(s): Colonialism; United States history, 1600-1775 (Colonial period); Native Americans
Major character(s): Captain John Smith, Settler
Time period(s): 17th century; 1610-1630
Locale(s): Jamestown, Virginia

Summary: *The Leaves of Fate* is the third and final novel in author George Robert Minkoff's In the Land of Whispers trilogy, which features Captain John Smith and the settlement of Jamestown, Virginia. In this novel,

Captain Smith has been banished from the Jamestown settlement and sent back to England. As he looks back on his life in the New World, he thinks of his time with his lover Pocahontas, his efforts to colonize America, and his battles against invading Indian tribes, the Spanish, and the elements. Minkoff is also the author of *The Weight of Smoke* and *The Dragons of the Storm*.

Where it's reviewed:
Publishers Weekly, September 13, 2010, page 22

Other books by the same author:
The Dragons of the Storm, 2007
The Weight of Smoke, 2006

Other books you might like:
John Clarke Bowman, *Powhatan's Daughter*, 1973
Karleen Koen, *Now Face to Face*, 1995
Elizabeth Massie, *1609: Winter of the Dead: a Novel about the Founding of Jamestown*, 2000
William T. Vollmann, *Argall*, 2001
Burton Wohl, *Soldier in Paradise*, 1977

358

ALY MONROE

Washington Shadow

(London: John Murray, 2011)

Story type: Espionage; Series
Subject(s): Espionage; Conspiracy; Politics
Major character(s): Peter Cotton, Agent (British intelligence); John Maynard Keynes, Economist; Harry Truman, Historical Figure, Government Official (U.S. President)
Time period(s): 20th century; 1940s (1945)
Locale(s): United States

Summary: Set in 1945, *Washington Shadow*, the second book in Aly Monroe's Peter Cotton series, focuses on the delicate relations between the United States and England in the aftermath of World War II. British Army vet and intelligence agent Peter Cotton travels to Washington, D.C. with economist John Maynard Keynes to seek financial assistance from the Truman administration. Cotton is also charged with learning the details surrounding the Americans' post-war intelligence operations, which include the dissolution of the OSS and the sharing of intelligence responsibilities by the U.S. Departments of War and State. As Cotton uncovers a plot involving U.S. and English officials, he also discovers his growing attraction to a State Department staffer.

Where it's reviewed:
Booklist, anuary 1, 2011, page 53
Publishers Weekly, November 1, 2010, page 28

Other books by the same author:
Icelight, 2011
The Maze of Cadiz, 2008

Other books you might like:
John Altman, *A Game of Spies*, 2002
Ted Bell, *Warlord*, 2010
David Ignatius, *The Increment*, 2009
John Lawton, *Old Flames*, 1996
Stella Rimington, *Secret Asset*, 2006

359

MICHELLE MORAN

Madame Tussaud: A Novel of the French Revolution

(New York: Crown Publishers, 2011)

Story type: Historical - French Revolution
Subject(s): French Revolution, 1789; French Revolutionary Wars, 1792-1799; French (European people)
Major character(s): Marie Tussaud, Artist (wax sculptor)
Time period(s): 18th century; 1780s-1790s
Locale(s): Paris, France

Summary: At the height of the French Revolution, a remarkable woman used the art of wax sculpting to capture the likenesses of the great leaders—and the unfortunate victims—of the era. *Madame Tussaud: A Novel of the French Revolution* by Michelle Moran is a historical novel based on the colorful life of Madame Marie Tussaud. Moran begins the story with Tussaud's youth in Paris, where she learned how to create lifelike figures of wax. Her skill at that striking art form gained the attention of the royal family. Meanwhile, the French Revolution puts the monarchy—and its supporters—at risk. Tussaud must deal with both sides as she continues pursuing her passion for sculpture.

Where it's reviewed:
Booklist, February 15, 2011, page 58
Kirkus Reviews, February 1, 2011, page 160
Library Journal, October 15, 2010, page 86

Other books by the same author:
Cleopatra's Daughter, 2009
The Heretic Queen, 2008
Nefertiti, 2007

Other books you might like:
Kate Berridge, *Madame Tussaud: A Life in Wax*, 2006
Sylvia Martin, *I, Madame Tussaud*, 1957
Marge Piercy, *City of Darkness, City of Light*, 1996
Christine Trent, *A Royal Likeness*, 2011
Dorrit Willumsen, *Marie*, 1986

360

CLARENCE L. MORRISON

The Grits Eaters

(Tallahassee, Florida: Father & Son Publishing, 2011)

Story type: Historical - American Civil War
Subject(s): Confederate States of America. Army; American Reconstruction, 1865-1877; United States Civil War, 1861-1865
Major character(s): Arch Morrison, Military Personnel
Time period(s): 19th century; 1860s

Summary: *The Grits Eaters* is a novel written by author Clarence L. Morrison, based on the true story of his grandfather, Arch Morrison. At the age of 19, Arch enlisted in the Confederate Army, where he was quickly promoted through the ranks. Yet the end of the war saw him placed in federal prison for treason because he

refused to acknowledge the United States government. After his release, Arch and two other former Confederate soldiers must walk back to their home state of Florida, during which they fall prey to bandits, remaining Union soldiers, and the elements. When Arch finally returns to Florida, he learns that his father has died and that he must become the man of the family. This story tells of Arch's journey through the Reconstruction south, and his struggles that remained once he arrived home.

Other books you might like:
Thomas Ray Crowel, *Cry Uncle, Sumbody*, 2011
Charles Frazier, *Cold Mountain*, 1997
MacKinlay Kantor, *Andersonville*, 1954
Jeff Shaara, *The Last Full Measure*, 1998
Robert Penn Warren, *Wilderness: A Tale of the Civil War*, 1961

361

IAN MORSON

Falconer and the Death of Kings

(Sutton, Surrey, England: Severn House, 2011)

Series: William Falconer Series. Book 8
Story type: Mystery
Subject(s): Mystery; Heretics; British history, 1066-1688
Major character(s): William Falconer, Scholar, Detective; Roger Bacon, Friend (of Falconer), Religious (friar), Prisoner; Thomas Symon, Student (of Falconer)
Time period(s): 13th century; 1270s (1273)
Locale(s): Oxford, England; Paris, France

Summary: *Falconer and the Death of Kings*, a suspenseful medieval mystery, is the eighth installment in the William Falconer series from author Ian Morson. Regent Master William Falconer is called away from the comfy confines of Oxford University at the behest of an old friend, Friar Roger Bacon, who has invited him to Paris. When Falconer arrives, he discovers that Bacon has been imprisoned for his heretical teachings, leaving the daunting task of saving and transferring his scientific teachings to Falconer and his former student, Thomas Symon. Things are compounded for the scholarly detective when King Edward calls on him for an unusual and challenging case that will test him far more than any investigation in history.

Where it's reviewed:
Publishers Weekly, February 14, 2011, page 40

Other books by the same author:
Falconer's Trial, 2009
Falconer and the Ritual of Death, 2008
Falconer and the Face of God, 1996
Falconer's Judgement, 1996
Falconer's Crusade, 1995

Other books you might like:
Simon Beaufort, *A Dead Man's Secret*, 2011
Pamela Bennetts, *A Dragon for Edward*, 1975
James Blish, *Doctor Mirabilis: A Novel*, 1964
Alys Clare, *Music of the Distant Stars*, 2010
P.C. Doherty, *Satan in St. Mary's*, 1986

362

KATE MOSSE

The Winter Ghosts

(New York: Penguin, 2011)

Subject(s): World War I, 1914-1918; French (European people); Mental health
Major character(s): Freddie Watson, Mentally Ill Person, Brother (of George); George Watson, Brother (of Freddie)
Locale(s): French Pyrenees, France

Summary: *The Winter Ghosts* is a novel by author Kate Mosse. Upon learning that his brother George went missing during the Great War, Freddie Watson suffered a mental breakdown and was subsequently institutionalized. Now, a decade later, Freddie is released from the mental hospital. He makes his way to France to find closure for his brother's disappearance, but when a car wreck leaves him stranded in a rural village, he begins to lose hope. Salvation comes to him in the form of a woman named Fabrissa, with whom he spends the night. Yet the following morning, upon awakening, Freddie finds himself in the midst of a centuries-old mystery. Mosse is also the author of *Sepulchre* and *Labyrinth*.

Where it's reviewed:
Booklist, January 1, 2011, page 57
Library Journal, December 2010, page 105
Publishers Weekly, November 15, 2010, page 34

Other books by the same author:
Sepulchre, 2007
Labyrinth, 2005

Other books you might like:
John Dos Passos, *1919*, 1932
Emma Drummond, *Some Far Elusive Dawn*, 1988
Cynthia Harrod-Eagles, *The Dancing Years*, 2011
Richard Marius, *After the War*, 1992
Nicola Thorne, *The House by the Sea*, 2003

363

ANN NAPOLITANO

A Good Hard Look

(New York: Penguin Press, 2011)

Story type: Literary
Subject(s): Writers; Romances (Fiction); History
Major character(s): Flannery O'Connor, Historical Figure, Writer; Cookie Himmel, Southern Belle, Spouse (of Melvin); Melvin Whiteson, Spouse (of Cookie), Friend (of Flannery), Wealthy; Lona Waters, Seamstress
Time period(s): 20th century; 1950s
Locale(s): Milledgeville, Georgia

Summary: *A Good Hard Look* is a historical novel re-imagining the life of author Flannery O'Connor from author Ann Napolitano. Twenty-five years old and suffering from lupus, author O'Connor is forced to leave the bright lights of New York City and return to her

small, Southern hometown of Milledgeville, Georgia. Years pass as Flannery carries on her lonely existence, writing novels and caring for peacocks, until her mother takes her to the wedding of Southern belle, Cookie Himmel, and her wealthy fiance, Melvin Whiteson. Melvin is immediately drawn to the enigmatic and lively writer and the pair forms a secret, unlikely friendship. Meanwhile, Cookie tries to overcome her insecurities by creating a beautiful home with the help of the town's seamstress, Lona Waters, a lonely woman in a loveless marriage, who takes great risks to rediscover the excitement of life.

Where it's reviewed:
Booklist, May 1, 2011, page 65
Publishers Weekly, May 9, 2011, page 31

Other books by the same author:
Within Arms Reach, 2004

Other books you might like:
Michael Cunningham, *The Hours*, 1998
Rebecca Hunt, *Mr. Chartwell*, 2011
Syrie James, *The Lost Memoirs of Jane Austen*, 2007
Susan Sellers, *Vanessa and Virginia*, 2009
James Tipton, *Annette Vallon: A Novel of the French Revolution*, 2007

364

CYNTHIA G. NEALE

Norah: The Making of an Irish-American Woman in 19th Century New York

(Athens, Ohio: Lucky Press, 2011)

Story type: Historical
Subject(s): Irish (European people); Irish Americans; Ireland
Major character(s): Norah McCabe, Immigrant (from Ireland), Activist (for women's rights), Activist (for Irish politics), Businesswoman
Time period(s): 19th century
Locale(s): New York, New York

Summary: *Norah: The Making of an Irish-American Woman in 19th Century New York* by Cynthia G. Neale is a historical novel about Irish immigrants newly arrived in the United States. In truth, most Irish immigrants faced fierce discrimination and filthy living conditions— but Neale's heroine, Norah McCabe, is an astonishing exception to that rule. Norah explores all the positive and exciting aspects of Irish-American life, as well as a few of its dangers. She becomes a protester promoting women's rights, a fashion designer, a business owner, and a political reformer, and she enters a racy affair with an eccentric writer.

Other books you might like:
Nicholas Delbanco, *What Remains*, 2000
Nelson DeMille, *Cathedral*, 1981
Colum McCann, *Let the Great World Spin*, 2009
Alice McDermott, *Charming Billy*, 1998
Donna Jo Napoli, *The King of Mulberry Street*, 2005

365

ELLE NEWMARK

The Sandalwood Tree

(New York: Atria Books, 2011)

Subject(s): History; Marriage; Indian history
Major character(s): Martin Mitchell, Historian, Veteran (World War II); Evie Mitchell, Spouse (of Martin); Billy Mitchell, Son (of Martin and Evie)
Time period(s): 20th century; 1940s (1947)
Locale(s): India

Summary: In *The Sandalwood Tree* by Elle Newmark, Evie Mitchell sees her husband Martin's Fullbright Fellowship as a means to heal her struggling family. Martin's absence during World War II has hurt their marriage. Fearing that his assignment to cover India's partition will further deteriorate their relationship, Evie decides that she and their son Billy will tag along. In India, Martin is busy with his work and Evie feels culturally adrift. When violence forces the family to take refuge in a Himalayan house, Evie finds a collection of old letters that provides an intriguing distraction. As Evie searches for the story behind the century-old letters, her own life suffers another blow.

Where it's reviewed:
Booklist, March 1, 2011, page 36
Kirkus Reviews, February 1, 2011, page 161
Library Journal, January 1, 2011, page 89
Publishers Weekly, March 7, 2011, page 36

Other books by the same author:
The Book of Unholy Mischief, 2009
Bones of the Dead, 2007
The Chef's Apprentice, 2001

Other books you might like:
Julia Gregson, *East of the Sun*, 2008
Gita Mehta, *Raj*, 1989
Anuradha Roy, *An Atlas of Impossible Longing*, 2011
Paul Scott, *Raj Quartet*, 1966
Baldwin Singh, *What the Body Remembers*, 1999

366

JOSEPH O'CONNOR

Ghost Light

(New York: Farrar, Straus, and Giroux, 2010)

Story type: Historical - Edwardian
Subject(s): Acting; Actors; Romances (Fiction)
Major character(s): Molly Allgood, Actress, Lover (of John); John Synge, Writer (of plays), Lover (of Molly)
Time period(s): 20th century; 1900s-1940s (1907-1945)
Locale(s): London, England; Dublin, Ireland

Summary: *Ghost Light* by Joseph O'Connor is a historical novel that tells a love story through generations of change, both personal and societal. In 1907, aspiring actress Molly Allgood, a bright-eyed girl of 18, joins the Abbey Theater in Dublin in hopes of becoming a star.

What she finds is different, but equally compelling: Irish playwright John Synge. Molly is drawn to John even though he is much older and is as quiet and reserved as she is fiery and passionate. The two fall in love and have an unlikely affair. Decades later in London, Molly, now well past her prime and drinking too much, recalls her youth and her memorable years with Synge.

Where it's reviewed:
Booklist, January 1, 2011, page 56
Library Journal, January 1, 2011, page 89
New York Times Book Review, February 6, 2011, page 11
Publishers Weekly, November 1, 2010, page 25

Other books by the same author:
Redemption Falls, 2007
Star of the Sea, 2002
Inishowen, 2000
The Salesman, 1999
Desperadoes, 1994

Other books you might like:
Christine Balint, *Ophelia's Fan*, 2004
Dermot Healy, *A Goat's Song*, 1994
Neil Jordan, *The Past*, 1980
Judith Michael, *Acts of Love*, 1997
Jude Morgan, *Symphony*, 2007

367

KATHLEEN O'NEAL GEAR
W. MICHAEL GEAR, Co-Author

The Dawn Country
(New York: Forge, 2011)

Story type: Indian Culture
Subject(s): Native American captivities; Native Americans; Pre-Columbian civilizations
Major character(s): Koracoo, Leader (War Chief), Spouse (of Gonda), Mother (of Wrass); Gonda, Spouse (of Koracoo), Father (of Wrass); Wrass, Son (of Gonda and Koracoo), Captive; Gannajero, Kidnapper, Witch
Time period(s): 15th century
Locale(s): United States

Summary: *The Dawn Country* is the second novel in the People of the Longhouse series, which is written by husband-and-wife authors W. Michael Gear and Kathleen O'Neal Gear. Wrass and many other children of the Yellowtail have been captured, and when Koracoo and Gonda discover who has taken the children of their tribe they are horrified. Their captor is Gannajero, a rival Iroquois who is rumored to be a witch, and who plans to enslave the children for profit. With the help of a former Mohawk War Chief and a Dawnland Healer, Koracoo and Gonda hope to save the children that have been taken from their village—but can they do it before Gannajero hatches her evil plan?

Where it's reviewed:
Booklist, March 15, 2011, page 27

Other books by the same author:
Fire the Sky, 2011
People of the Longhouse, 2010

People of the Mist, 2007
People of the Nightland, 2007
People of the River, 1992

Other books you might like:
Jean M. Auel, *The Land of Painted Caves*, 2011
Sue Harrison, *Song of the River*, 1997
Linda Lay Shuler, *Let the Drum Speak: A Novel of Ancient America*, 1996
Elizabeth Marshall Thomas, *Reindeer Moon*, 1987
Barbara Wood, *Sacred Ground*, 2001

368

PAMELA OLDFIELD

The Penningtons
(New York: Severn House Publishers, 2011)

Story type: Psychological
Subject(s): Suspense; Family; England
Major character(s): Miss Dutton, Housekeeper; Daisy, Servant; Montague "Monty" Pennington, Householder
Time period(s): 20th century; 1900s (1902)
Locale(s): Bath, England

Summary: In *The Penningtons*, a novel by Pamela Oldfield set in turn-of-the-century Bath, England, a young maid named Daisy is thrust into service when the keeper of the house, Miss Dutton, quits. Daisy is only 17, and her master's family doubts her ability to care for the house master, Montague "Monty" Pennington. Monty is bedridden and difficult to deal with, but he and Daisy soon form a friendship of sorts. Yet unbeknownst to Daisy, the Pennington family has many secrets—as does young Daisy. Oldfield is also the author of *The Boat House*, *Great Plague*, and *Jack's Shadow*.

Where it's reviewed:
Booklist, April 1, 2011, page 33

Other books by the same author:
The Boat House, 2010
Truth Will Out, 2009
The Fairfax Legacy, 2008
Fatal Voyage, 2007
Jack's Shadow, 2006

Other books you might like:
Jamaica Kincaid, *Lucy*, 1990
Valerie Martin, *Mary Reilly*, 1990
Kate Morton, *The House at Riverton: A Novel*, 2008
Thrity Umrigar, *The Space between Us: A Novel*, 2006
Lori Wick, *Just Above a Whisper*, 2005

369

CORY PAMELA

Hassie Calhoun
(Minneapolis, Minnesota: Scarletta Press, 2011)

Story type: Coming-of-Age; Series
Subject(s): Entertainment industry; Singing; Romances (Fiction)

Major character(s): Hassie Calhoun, 17-Year-Old, Singer, Girlfriend (of Jake); Jake Contrata, Boyfriend (of Hassie), Manager (nightclub); Frank Sinatra, Entertainer
Time period(s): 20th century; 1960s
Locale(s): Las Vegas, Nevada

Summary: In *Hassie Calhoun*, the first book in a trilogy by Pamela Cory, dreams of stardom call the 17-year-old title character to leave her small Texas hometown for Las Vegas. In Sin City, Hassie quickly discovers that she will need more than talent and looks to win her big break. She takes a job as a waitress at The Sands, and takes general manager Jake Contrata as her lover. When Frank Sinatra brings his act to the Copa Room, Hassie sleeps with the influential entertainer as well. Her high-stakes gamble eventually pays off when she is hired to perform at The Tropicana. Hassie has learned the laws of Las Vegas survival, but have her choices compromised her character?

Where it's reviewed:
Kirkus Reviews, March 15, 2011, page 443
Publishers Weekly, February 7, 2011, page 32

Other books you might like:
James Ellroy, *The Cold Six Thousand*, 2001
Faye Kellerman, *Moon Music*, 1998
Elizabeth Lowell, *Running Scared*, 2002
Terry McMillan, *A Day Late and a Dollar Short*, 2001
Larry McMurtry, *The Desert Rose*, 1985

370

MICHAEL PARKER

The Watery Part of the World
(New York: Algonquin Books, 2011)

Subject(s): Islands; Race relations; Love
Major character(s): Theodosia Burr, Daughter (of vice-president); Woodrow, Fisherman (seaman); Maggie, Sister (of Whaley); Whaley, Sister (of Maggie)
Time period(s): 19th century; (1810s); 20th century; 1970s (1970)
Locale(s): Nag's Head Island, North Carolina

Summary: In Michael Parker's *The Watery Part of the World*, the story of an island is told through inhabitants living in very different eras. In 1813, the daughter of the vice president is stranded on Nag's Head Island, where she is brought back to health and begins a relationship with a former slave. In 1970, two Caucasian sisters and an African American man are living together on the island, and their unusual living arrangement has made them the subject of much gossip and myth. The stories of these characters converge against the rolling tides of Nag's Head.

Where it's reviewed:
Booklist, March 1, 2011, page 28
Kirkus Reviews, January 1, 2011, page 109
Library Journal, March 15, 2011, page 109
Publishers Weekly, January 10, 2011, page 27

Other books by the same author:
Don't Make Me Stop Now, 2007
If You Want Me to Stay, 2005

Towns Without Rivers, 2001
The Geographical Cure, 1994
Hello Down There, 1993

Other books you might like:
Diane Chamberlain, *Kiss River*, 2003
Homer Hickam, *The Keeper's Son*, 2003
David Payne, *Gravesend Light*, 2000
Anya Seton, *My Theodosia*, 1941
Anne Rivers Siddons, *Outer Banks*, 1991

371

ANNE PERRY

Treason at Lisson Grove
(New York: Ballantine Books, 2011)

Series: Thomas and Charlotte Pitt Series. Book 26
Story type: Historical - Victorian; Mystery
Subject(s): Mystery; Murder; British history, 1815-1914
Major character(s): Thomas Pitt, Government Official (Special Branch officer), Spouse (of Charlotte); Victor Narraway, Employer (of Thomas); Charlotte Pitt, Spouse (of Thomas)
Time period(s): 19th century
Locale(s): England; France

Summary: *Treason at Lisson Grove*, a Victorian-era mystery novel, is the 26th installment in the Thomas and Charlotte Pitt series from best-selling author Anne Perry. Thomas Pitt, British Special Branch officer, is scheduled to meet with a top-secret informant carrying details about a devastating plot against the British empire, but by the time Pitt arrives, the man has been fatally wounded and dies in Pitt's arms before revealing his secrets. Pitt sets out on a wild goose chase to find the killer that leads him all across London and to the French coast. Meanwhile, Pitt's boss, Narraway, is facing slanderous charges of embezzlement. With Pitt traveling across France, Narraway seeks help from Thomas's wife, Charlotte, who agrees to pose as Narraway's sister to help him track down the person responsible for spreading false accusations against him. Little do Narraway and Charlotte realize, they're stepping into a dangerous trap that could destroy them and the entire British government.

Where it's reviewed:
New York Times Book Review, Review, April 24, 2011, page 15

Other books by the same author:
A Christmas Odyssey, 2010
Execution Dock, 2009
Buckingham Palace Gardens, 2008
Angels in the Gloom, 2005
Long Spoon Lane, 2005
Seven Dials, 2003
Death of a Stranger, 2002
Southampton Row, 2002
The Whitechapel Conspiracy, 2001

Other books you might like:
Carole Nelson Douglas, *Spider Dance*, 2004
Elizabeth George, *A Traitor to Memory*, 2001
P.D. James, *Original Sin*, 1994

Historical

Faye Kellerman, *Street Dreams*, 2003
Carol McCleary, *The Illusion of Murder*, 2011

372

JOHN PILKINGTON

After the Fire

(London, England: Robert Hale, 2011)

Story type: Mystery
Subject(s): Mystery; British history, 1066-1688; Serial murders
Major character(s): Betsy Brand, Actress, Detective—Amateur
Time period(s): 17th century; 1670s (1670)
Locale(s): London, England

Summary: It's 1670 and London is slowly being restored and rebuilt after the Great Fire when a series of violent and mysterious murders rattles the city. Each of the killings is somehow connected to the Dorset Gardens Theatre, a new production house where Betsy Brand is starring in William Shakespeare's *Macbeth*. The murders have left the authorities baffled, but Betsy suspects that they're somehow linked to the Salamander, an enigmatic villain who caused trouble during the Fire. As the police come up empty-handed, Betsy decides to take it upon herself to do a little undercover investigating, unaware that she's putting her life at risk.

Other books by the same author:
The Muscovy Chain, 2007
The Jingler's Luck, 2006
The Maiden Bell, 2005
The Mapmaker's Daughter, 2005
A Ruinous Wind, 2003

Other books you might like:
Edward Bewley, *The Italian Potion*, 2010
Philip Gooden, *Alms for Oblivion*, 2003
Susanna Gregory, *A Murder on London Bridge*, 2009
Paul Lawrence, *The Sweet Smell of Decay*, 2009
Fidelis Morgan, *The Rival Queens*, 2002

373

STEFANIE PINTOFF

Secret of the White Rose

(New York: Minotaur Books, 2011)

Series: Simon Zeile Series. Book 3
Subject(s): Detective fiction; Murder; Crime
Major character(s): Simon Ziele, Detective; Theodore Bingham, Police Officer (Commissioner); Al Drayson, Crime Suspect, Defendant; Alistair Sinclair, Criminologist; Hugo Jackson, Crime Victim
Time period(s): 20th century; 1900s (1906)
Locale(s): New York, New York

Summary: *Secrets of the White Rose* is the third novel in author Stephanie Pintoff's Simon Ziele detective series. The year is 1906, and when the judge of a high profile trial is murdered, the entire New York Police Depart-ment sets its sights on the trial's defendant. Al Drayson is accused of bombing a wedding featuring the prominent Carnegie family, and jailing Drayson means the new police commissioner, Theodore Bingham, will win public favor with New York's high society. But when Detective Ziele and his colleague, Columbia University criminologist Alistair Sinclair, find evidence pointing in another direction, they must not only contend with a murderer determined to avoid being caught, but also a police department unwilling to consider any other suspects. Will Ziele and Sinclair catch the right man, or will political posturing put the wrong man in jail?

Where it's reviewed:
Booklist, April 1, 2011, page 34
New York Times Book Review, May 22, 2011, page 22

Other books by the same author:
A Curtain Falls, 2010
In the Shadow of Gotham, 2009

Other books you might like:
Rhys Bowen, *Naughty in Nice*, 2010
Anne Perry, *Treason at Lisson Grove*, 2011
Deanna Raybourn, *The Dark Enquiry*, 2011
J.D. Robb, *Memory in Death*, 2006
Victoria Thompson, *Murder on Sisters' Row*, 2011

374

D. M. PIRRONE

No Less in Blood

(Waterville, Maine: Five Star, 2011)

Story type: Mystery
Subject(s): Adoption; Family; Inheritance and succession
Major character(s): Rachel Connolly, Adoptee, Writer; Luke Chapman, Murderer, Father (of Linnet); Linnet Chapman, 12-Year-Old, Daughter (of Luke)
Time period(s): 21st century; (2010s)
Locale(s): Birch Falls, Minnesota

Summary: In the novel *No Less in Blood* by D.M. Pirrone, Rachel Connolly's search for her birth mother leads her on a mysterious journey into her family's past. Rachel travels to Birch Falls, Minnesota, where she believes relatives of her biological mother may have information about her family. At the Schlegel estate, she meets caretaker Jackson Schlegel and his 12-year-old grand-daughter, Linnet. Rachel soon learns that the estate houses many secrets. Linnet is on the run from her father, who murdered her mother back in Chicago. A diary discovered in the attic reveals that another runaway, Mary Anne Schlegel, sought refuge at the estate in the 1890s, but disappeared mysteriously. Eventually Linnet's mother's murder, Rachel's quest, and the fate of long-deceased Mary Anne converge in a contest for a sizable inheritance.

Where it's reviewed:
Booklist, February 1, 2011, page 38
Kirkus Reviews, November 1, 2010, page 1085
Publishers Weekly, December 6, 2010, page 34

Other books you might like:
William Diehl, *Reign in Hell*, 1997

Judith Michael, *The Real Mother*, 2005
Jacquelyn Mitchard, *The Deep End of the Ocean*, 1996
Sara Paretsky, *Blacklist*, 2003
Scott Turow, *Pleading Guilty*, 1993

375

PETER PRANGE

The Philosopher's Kiss

(New York: Simon and Schuster, 2011)

Story type: Literary
Subject(s): Philosophy; Enlightenment (Cultural movement); Social history
Major character(s): Sophie Volland, Waiter/Waitress; Denis Diderot, Historical Figure, Philosopher
Time period(s): 18th century
Locale(s): Paris, France

Summary: *The Philosopher's Kiss*, a novel by Peter Prange, tells the story of Sophie Volland, a young woman living in 18th century France. After Sophie's mother is executed amidst accusations of witchery, Sophie moves to Paris to work in the legendary Cafe Procope. There she meets French philosopher Denis Diderot. Sophie is intrigued by the intellectual, but his married status prevents them from being together. Meanwhile, Diderot goes to work creating the *Encyclopedie*, a compilation of scientific and intellectual discoveries throughout history. His work attracts negative attention from the Church and the French Monarchy, both of whom will do anything to stop him from publishing the work.

Where it's reviewed:
Kirkus Reviews, March 1, 2011, page 362
Library Journal, February 1, 2011, page 56
Publishers Weekly, January 17, 2011, page 25

Other books you might like:
Stephane Audeguy, *The Only Son*, 2008
Malcolm Bradbury, *To the Hermitage*, 2001
Andrew Crumey, *D'Alembert's Principle*, 1998
Tibor Fischer, *The Thought Gang*, 1994
Karleen Koen, *Through a Glass Darkly*, 1986

376

KATE PULLINGER

The Mistress of Nothing

(New York: Touchstone Publishing, 2009)

Story type: Historical - Exotic
Subject(s): Middle East; Social class; Orphans
Major character(s): Sally Naldrett, Servant; Lady Duff "Lucie" Gordon, Noblewoman, Designer; Omar, Guide
Time period(s): 19th century
Locale(s): Egypt; England

Summary: *The Mistress of Nothing* is a historical novel written by author Kate Pullinger. Sally Naldrett is an orphaned English girl who, along with her sister, has been sent to work as a servant girl for members of the upper-class nobility. After working various menial, low-ranking maid jobs, Sally finally has been given the opportunity to serve Lady Duff Gordon, an English noblewoman and fashion designer. When Lady Duff Gordon, aka Lucie, becomes consumed with tuberculosis, both she and Sally must travel to Egypt for drier weather. Yet Sally's devotion to her lady is called into question when she falls in love with, and gets pregnant by, an interpreter named Omar. This book was awarded the Governor General's Literary Award in Canada in 2009.

Where it's reviewed:
Library Journal, November 15, 2010, page 61
Publishers Weekly, November 1, 2010, page 27

Other books by the same author:
A Little Stranger, 2009
Weird Sister, 1999
The Piano, 1994
Where Does Kissing End?, 1992
Tiny Lies, 1988

Other books you might like:
Andrea Barrett, *The Air We Breathe*, 2007
Michael Cox, *The Glass of Time*, 2008
Jane Jakeman, *The Egyptian Coffin*, 1997
Robert Sole, *The Photographer's Wife*, 1999
Anne Worboys, *Shifting Sands*, 1999

377

JULIA QUINN (Pseudonym of Julie Cotler Pottinger)
ELOISA JAMES, Co-Author
CONNIE BROCKWAY, Co-Author

The Lady Most Likely

(New York: HarperCollins, 2011)

Story type: Historical - Regency
Subject(s): Social class; Romances (Fiction); Marriage
Major character(s): Hugh Dunne, Nobleman, Brother (of Carolyn); Carolyn, Noblewoman, Sister (of Hugh)
Time period(s): 19th century; 1810s
Locale(s): England

Summary: *The Lady Most Likely* is a novel written in three parts by authors Connie Brockway, Julia Quinn, and Eloisa James. After a horse-riding mishap forces nobleman Hugh Dunne, the Earl of Briarly, to face his mortality, he decides that he wants to settle down, get married, and have children. Unfortunately, lifelong bachelor Hugh has no idea how to woo a woman for keeps. His sister Carolyn has the perfect solution: she will act as matchmaker and invite their social circle's most eligible women to a party. She also invites two other noblemen, ensuring that no one goes home "empty-handed." Carolyn is sure that her plan cannot fail—or can it? Brockway, Quinn, and James are all past winners of the Romance Writers of America's RITA Award.

Where it's reviewed:
Booklist, December 15, 2010, page 28
Library Journal, December 2010, page 96
Publishers Weekly, November 29, 2010, page 35
Romantic Times, January 2011, page 35

Other books by the same author:
Just Like Heaven, 2011
Ten Things I Love About You, 2010
What Happens in London, 2009
The Lost Duke of Wyndham, 2008
Mr. Cavendish, I Presume, 2008

Other books you might like:
Mary Balogh, *Then Comes Seduction*, 2009
Lisa Kleypas, *Love in the Afternoon*, 2010
Stephanie Laurens, *The Reckless Bride*, 2010
Johanna Lindsey, *That Perfect Someone*, 2010
Karen Robards, *Shameless*, 2010

378

JONATHAN RABB

Second Son

(New York: Farrar, Straus, and Giroux, 2011)

Story type: Mystery
Subject(s): Antisemitism; World War II, 1939-1945;
Olympics
Major character(s): Sascha Hoffner, Son (of Nikolai);
Georg Hoffner, Son (of Nikolai), Journalist; Nikolai
Hoffner, Detective—Police (former), Father (of
Sascha and Georg)
Time period(s): 20th century; 1930s (1936)
Locale(s): Germany; Spain

Summary: *The Second Son* is the third and final book in
author Jonathan Rabb's Berlin Trilogy. In this book,
Chief Inspector Nikolai Hoffner has been terminated
from his post as police detective when his superiors
learn that his mother, who recently died, was Jewish. As
World War II looms in the not-so-distant future, anti-
Semitism spreads across Hitler's new Germany. Making
matters more complicated is the fact that Hoffner's older
son, Sascha, has joined the Nazi party, while his younger
son, Georg, a journalist, has journeyed to Barcelona to
report on the upcoming People's Olympics in protest of
the Berlin Olympics held by Hitler that same year. When
civil war erupts in Spain, Hoffner must rush to the war-
ravaged country to search for his second son.

Where it's reviewed:
Booklist, February 15, 2011, page 56
Library Journal, December 1, 2010, page 108
New York Times Book Review, February 13, 2011, page
13
Publishers Weekly, December 20, 2010, page 28

Other books by the same author:
Shadow and Light, 2009
Rosa, 2005
The Book of Q, 2001
The Overseer, 1998

Other books you might like:
Lluis-Anton Baulenas, *For a Sack of Bones*, 2008
Jose Maria Gironella, *Peace After War*, 1969
John Harvey, *Far Cry*, 2010
Jo Nesbo, *The Redbreast*, 2007
Johan Theorin, *Echoes from the Dead*, 2008

379

JEWELL PARKER RHODES

Hurricane

(New York: Washington Square Press, 2011)

Subject(s): Voodooism; Mystery; Murder
Major character(s): Marie Laveau, Doctor (emergency
room), Supernatural Being (voodoo queen), Detec-
tive—Amateur; Deet Malveaux, Lawman (deputy of
DeLaire); Aaron Malveaux, Lawman (sheriff of De-
Laire); Nana, Supernatural Being (voodoo queen)
Time period(s): 21st century; 2000s
Locale(s): New Orleans, Louisiana

Summary: *Hurricane* by Jewell Parker Rhodes continues
the saga of Marie Laveau, a *voodooiene*—a voodoo
practitioner—and her supernaturally empowered descen-
dants in New Orleans. In this novel, Dr. Marie Laveau is
an emergency-room physician, a part-time amateur
sleuth, and a woman sensitive to the powers of voodoo.
On an otherwise regular day, Marie is struck by a chilling nightmare and then witnesses the scene of a grisly
triple murder. After reporting the crime to the police,
Marie realizes that she's next on the murderer's hit list!
She will have to use her extrasensory powers to solve
the crime before she becomes the next victim. Other
books by Rhodes about the Laveau family include *Voodoo Dreams*, *Voodoo Season*, and *Yellow Moon*.

Where it's reviewed:
Booklist, February 15, 2011, page 55
Kirkus Reviews, February 1, 2011, page 164
Publishers Weekly, February 7, 2011, page 40

Other books by the same author:
Yellow Moon, 2008
Voodoo Season, 2005
Douglass' Women, 2002
Magic City, 1997
Voodoo Dreams, 1993

Other books you might like:
Barbara Hambly, *Fever Season*, 1998
Francine Prose, *Marie Laveau*, 1977
Kathy Reichs, *Devil Bones*, 2008
Robert Tallant, *The Voodoo Queen*, 1956
Thomas Wheeler, *The Arcanum*, 2004

380

ANTHONY RICHES

Fortress of Spears

(London: Hodder & Stoughton, 2011)

Series: Empire. Book 3
Story type: Historical
Subject(s): Roman Empire, 30 BC-476 AD; Rome
(Ancient state); Romans
Major character(s): Marcus Aquila, Military Personnel
(Roman soldier), Vigilante (impersonating Centurion
Corvus); Calgus, Chieftain (of Northern Tribes)
Locale(s): United Kingdom

Summary: *Fortress of Spears* by Anthony Riches is a historical novel and the third installment in Riches's Empire series. Like other titles in the series, *Fortress of Spears* presents a tale set in the Roman Empire, specifically the Roman Legions pressing for dominance in the British Isles. Among the Roman troops, a mysterious centurion known as Corvus—whose real identity is Marcus Aquila—wants to exact revenge on the Romans for killing his best friend. Meanwhile, he and the other soldiers are ordered to hunt down tribal leader Calgus, who continues to defy Roman domination of his homeland.

Other books you might like:

William Dietrich, *Hadrian's Wall*, 2004

Pauline Gedge, *The Eagle and the Raven*, 1978

Conn Iggulden, *Emperor: The Field of Swords*, 2005

Simon Scarrow, *Under the Eagle*, 2001

Manda Scott, *Dreaming the Eagle*, 2003

381

IMOGEN ROBERTSON

Island of Bones

(New York: Headline Library, 2011)

Story type: Historical - Georgian

Subject(s): England; English (British people); Murder

Major character(s): Gabriel Crowther, Scientist (anatomist), Detective—Amateur, Friend (of Harriet); Harriet Westerman, Noblewoman, Detective—Amateur, Friend (of Gabriel)

Time period(s): 18th century; 1780s (1783)

Locale(s): Cumbria, England

Summary: *Island of Bones* by Imogen Robertson is a murder mystery set in Georgian England in 1783. The reclusive anatomist Gabriel Crowther returns to his home in Cumbria to investigate the bizarre mystery that first drove him into seclusion. Long ago, his family discovered a historic tomb on their land—but inside the tomb was a much more recent murder victim! Gabriel fled the scene, but 30 years later he returns to solve the crime and gain closure. Accompanying him is his unlikely partner, daring noblewoman Harriet Westerman. This pair was introduced in Robertson's previous novel *Instruments of Darkness*.

Other books by the same author:

Instruments of Darkness, 2011

Anatomy of Murder, 2010

Other books you might like:

Greg Iles, *Third Degree*, 2007

Stephen King, *Lisey's Story: A Novel*, 2006

Ann Patchett, *Run*, 2007

John Sandford, *Bad Blood*, 2010

Lisa See, *Shanghai Girls*, 2009

382

IMOGEN ROBERTSON

Instruments of Darkness

(New York: Viking, 2011)

Story type: Historical - Georgian

Subject(s): English (British people); England; Mystery

Major character(s): Gabriel Crowther, Scientist (anatomist), Detective—Amateur, Friend (of Harriet); Harriet Westerman, Friend (of Gabriel), Noblewoman, Detective—Amateur

Time period(s): 18th century

Locale(s): West Sussex, England

Summary: *Instruments of Darkness* by Imogen Robertson is a detective story set in 1780s England. Gabriel Crowther is an anatomist with a shadowy past, living alone and trying to escape his memories. He is surprised to find straight-shooting noblewoman Harriet Westerman summoning him and asking for help with a puzzling murder mystery. Harriet, daughter of a powerful Sussex family, found a dead body near her home. The unfortunate soul carried a ring belonging to the Thornleigh family, an ancient estate with dwindling, but still significant, power in the community. Gabriel and Harriet investigate only to find a deep and deadly plot over the heir to the Thornleigh fortune.

Where it's reviewed:

Library Journal, February 1, 2011, page 56

New York Times Book Review, March 6, 2011, page 8

Publishers Weekly, December 13, 2010, page 36

Other books by the same author:

Anatomy of Murder, 2010

Other books you might like:

Philip Kerr, *Dark Matter*, 2002

Deryn Lake, *Death at St. James's Palace*, 2002

David Liss, *A Conspiracy of Paper*, 2000

Fidelis Morgan, *Unnatural Fires*, 2000

Iain Pears, *An Instance of the Fingerpost*, 1998

383

JED RUBENFELD

The Death Instinct

(New York: Riverhead Books, 2011)

Subject(s): Terrorism; Adventure; Physicians

Major character(s): Stratham Younger, Doctor, Veteran; James Littlemore, Police Officer; Colette Rosseau, Scientist

Time period(s): 20th century; 1920s

Locale(s): Vienna, Austria; New York, New York

Summary: In *The Death Instinct*, bestselling author Jed Rubenfeld tells the story of a devastating terrorist attack on New York City in 1920 and the varied personalities who set out to untangle the mystery surrounding the event. As a response to the assault, Dr. Stratham Younger and NYPD officer Captain James Littlemore team up with French scientist Colette Rosseau to discover the cause and culprits behind the bombing. Their inquiry

takes them across the globe, and, as Colette becomes the victim of a string of violent assaults, Younger and Littlemore must work against the clock to find those responsible.

Where it's reviewed:
Booklist, December 1, 2010, page 29
Library Journal, November 15, 2010, page 64

Other books by the same author:
The Interpretation of Murder, 2006

Other books you might like:
Emily Benedek, *Red Sea*, 2007
Richard E. Crabbe, *Suspension*, 2000
Nelson DeMille, *Cathedral*, 1981
Joseph Finder, *The Zero Hour*, 1996
Vince Flynn, *Pursuit of Honor*, 2009

384

ESMERALDA SANTIAGO

Conquistadora

(New York: Alfred A. Knopf, 2011)

Story type: Historical - Exotic
Subject(s): History; Spain; Puerto Ricans
Major character(s): Ana Larragoity Cubillas, 18-Year-Old; Ramon, Spouse (of Ana); Inocente, Twin (of Ramon)
Time period(s): 19th century; 1840s
Locale(s): Puerto Rico; Spain

Summary: In *Conquistadora* by Esmeralda Santiago, 19th-century Puerto Rico promises a romantic escape for a young woman living in Spain. Ana Larragoity Cubillas has become enchanted with the island by reading old journals. She secures herself passage there by marrying Ramon, heir to a Puerto Rican plantation. Ramon, his new wife Ana, and his twin Inocente move to Puerto Rico and take up residence at Hacienda los Gemelos. The living and working conditions are harder than Ana expected, but she initially revels in her new life. As the repercussions of America's Civil War reach Puerto Rican shores, a wave of change impacts the hacienda's owners and slaves.

Where it's reviewed:
Booklist, April 15, 2011, page 36
New York Times Book Review, July 17, 2011, page 8(L)
Publishers Weekly, March 21, 2011, page 48

Other books by the same author:
America's Dream, 1996
When I Was Puerto Rican, 1993

Other books you might like:
Oscar Hijuelos, *Beautiful Maria of My Soul*, 2010
Oscar Hijuelos, *The Mambo Kings Play Songs of Love*, 1989
Mayra Montero, *The Messenger*, 1999
Debra Spark, *Coconuts for the Saints*, 1994
Ana Lydia Vega, *True and False Romances*, 1994

385

JOHN SAYLES

A Moment in the Sun

(San Francisco: McSweeney's, 2011)

Subject(s): Adventure; United States history; Picaresque literature
Major character(s): Royal Scott, Military Personnel; Mark Twain, Writer; Diosdado Concepcion, Revolutionary
Time period(s): 19th century-20th century
Locale(s): Philippines; United States

Summary: In *A Moment in the Sun*, revered filmmaker John Sayles presents a voluminous tale of American life at the turn of the 20th century. This detailed account opens in 1897 and follows a variety of characters through their lives as the defining events of the era sweep them up. Among them are Royal Scott, a black soldier; beloved author Mark Twain; and Filipino revolutionary Diosdado Concepcion. Through their adventures, the story of a new century unfolds in magnificently detailed splendor.

Where it's reviewed:
Booklist, April 15, 2011, page 36
New York Times Book Review, June 12, 2011, page 8
Publishers Weekly, March 21, 2011, page 51

Other books by the same author:
Los Gusanos, 1991
Union Dues, 1977

Other books you might like:
Peter Bowen, *Imperial Kelly*, 1992
Henry Castor, *The Year of the Spaniard*, 1950
Douglas C. Jones, *Remember Santiago*, 1988
Elmore Leonard, *Cuba Libre*, 1998
Daniel Lynch, *Yellow: A Novel*, 1992

386

DIETER SCHLESAK

The Druggist of Auschwitz

(New York: Farrar, Straus, and Giroux, 2011)

Story type: Historical - World War II
Subject(s): Concentration camps; Drugs; Holocaust, 1933-1945
Major character(s): Adam Salmen, Guard; Victor Capesius, Pharmacist
Time period(s): 20th century; 1960s (1964)
Locale(s): Poland

Summary: *The Druggist of Auschwitz* is a historical novel written by author Dieter Schlesak and translated into English by John Hargraves. The book tells the story of Victor Capesius, an apothecary who worked as the director of the dispensary at Auschwitz, a network of concentration camps created by Nazi Germany during the Holocaust. Adam Salmen, commander of a Jewish Special Action Squad, is given the arduous task of chronicling the results of gas chamber and cremation oven use in the concentration camp. Though he is fol-

lowing orders, Salmen cannot believe the horrors of Auschwitz and he records all that he sees as proof against his Nazi superiors. Schelasak uses both fictional narrative as well as documented transcripts and interviews with survivors as background for this story.

Where it's reviewed:
Booklist, March 15, 2011, page 27
Kirkus Reviews, February 15, 2011, page 268
Library Journal, March 15, 2011, page 112
Publishers Weekly, February 14, 2011, page 37

Other books you might like:
John Boyne, *The Boy in the Striped Pajamas*, 2006
Kirk Douglas, *Dance with the Devil*, 1990
Erich Maria Remarque, *Spark of Life*, 1952
Stella Rodway, *Night*, 1958
Hampton Sides, *Ghost Soldiers: The Forgotten Epic Story of World War II's Most Dramatic Mission*, 2001

387

MONTE SCHULZ

The Last Rose of Summer

(Seattle, Washington: Fantagraphics Books, 2011)

Story type: Literary
Subject(s): Economic depressions; Family; Women
Major character(s): Rachel Hennessey, Daughter (of Maude); Maude Hennessey, Mother (of Rachel); Marie, Daughter (in-law, of Maude)
Time period(s): 20th century; 1920s (1929)
Locale(s): Texas, United States

Summary: *The Last Rose of Summer* is a novel by author Monte Schulz. In it, the author tells the story of three women: Maude Hennessey, the mother and leader of the family; Rachel, her privileged daughter; and Marie, Maude's daughter-in-law. As the Great Depression begins to take hold of the American economy, all three women hunker down in the same Texas homestead. Maude clearly does not want Marie there and she often corrects Marie's manner; meanwhile, Marie begins to question her marriage as she falls for another man. When the town is shocked by a mysterious murder, the identity of the suspect—a black man and veteran of the Great War—pulls the three women in different directions.

Other books by the same author:
This Side of Jordan, 2009
Down by the River, 1991

Other books you might like:
Jim Black, *River Season*, 2003
Paulette Jiles, *The Color of Lightning: A Novel*, 2010
Joe R. Lansdale, *The Bottoms*, 2000
Hobie Mills, *The Song Comes Native*, 1981
Lane Von Herzen, *The Copper Crown*, 1991

388

LISA SEE

Dreams of Joy

(New York: Random House, 2011)

Story type: Family Saga
Subject(s): Sisters; Chinese (Asian people); Communism
Major character(s): Mary, Sister (of Pearl); Pearl, Sister (of Mary); Joy, Daughter (of Pearl); Z.G., Father (of Joy), Artist; Tao, Farmer
Time period(s): 20th century; 1950s
Locale(s): Shanghai, China

Summary: In *Dreams of Joy*, best-selling author Lisa See presents a sequel to 2010's *Shanghai Girls*. Sisters Mary and Pearl are still dealing with the emotional repercussions of the revelation of long-buried family secrets, and Joy flees to the big city to take up with an artist both girls were once infatuated with. There she meets up with the rising communist faction and becomes inextricably involved in its powerful plot to take over the country. Meanwhile, Pearl is concerned for her sister's safety, and she too flees to Shanghai, but her reunion with her sister is cut short by one of China's most tragic and unexpected events.

Where it's reviewed:
Booklist, April 15, 2011, page 32
Library Journal, May 15, 2011, page 80
Publishers Weekly, April 4, 2011, page 35

Other books by the same author:
Shanghai Girls, 2009
Peony in Love, 2007
Snow Flower and the Secret Fan, 2005
Dragon Bones, 2003
The Interior, 1999
Flower Net, 1997
On Gold Mountain, 1995

Other books you might like:
Pearl S. Buck, *Dragon Seed*, 1942
Mimi Chan, *All the King's Women*, 2000
Robert S. Elegant, *From a Far Land*, 1987
Bette Bao Lord, *The Middle Heart*, 1996
Anchee Min, *Becoming Madame Mao*, 2000

389

JEFF SHAARA

The Final Storm

(New York: Ballantine Books, 2011)

Story type: Historical - World War II
Subject(s): World War II, 1939-1945; Japanese (Asian people); Military science
Major character(s): Clay Adams, Military Personnel (marine); Chester Nimitz, Military Personnel (admiral); Simon Bolivar Buckner Jr., Military Personnel (commander), Son (of Civil War veteran); Mitsura Ushijima, Military Personnel (Japanese general)

Time period(s): 20th century; 1940s (1945)
Locale(s): Okinawa, Japan

Summary: *The Final Storm: A Novel of the War in the Pacific* is a historical novel from author Jeff Shaara. After the invasion of Normandy, the United States military shifts their attention to defeating the Japanese. The spring of 1945 brings about one final, massive assault against the island of Okinawa. Shaara recounts the strategy, bloodshed, and turmoil of this three-month battle through the perspective of soldiers on both sides of the skirmish: Private Clay Adams is a young marine, living in his brother's shadow, Admiral Chester Nimitz works hard to build unity between the army and marines, General Simon Bolivar Buckner, Jr. fights to live up to his father's Civil War legacy, and General Mitsura Ushijima is a Japanese general tasked with protecting Okinawa. As the war rages on, the secret development of a powerful weapon is about to change the course of history forever.

Where it's reviewed:
Booklist, May 1, 2011, page 69

Other books by the same author:
No Less than Victory, 2010
The Steel Wave, 2008
The Rising Tide, 2006
To the Last Man, 2004
The Glorious Cause, 2002
The Last Full Measure, 1998

Other books you might like:
Thomas Fleming, *Time and Tide*, 1987
Homer Hickam, *The Far Reaches*, 2007
Jim Lehrer, *Oh, Johnny: A Novel*, 2009
Norman Mailer, *The Naked and the Dead*, 1948
John Shors, *Beside a Burning Sea*, 2008

390

LINDA SOLE

Tears Will Not Save Them

(New York: Severn House Publishers, 2011)

Story type: Historical - World War I
Subject(s): World War I, 1914-1918; Mother-daughter relations; Nursing
Major character(s): Jane Shaw, Nurse
Time period(s): 20th century; 1910s
Locale(s): England; France

Summary: *Tears Will Not Save Them* is a novel by author Linda Sole. Jane Shaw is a young English woman who takes care of her mentally disabled brother under the critical and angry eye of her abusive mother. When her brother passes away, Jane decides she will no longer endure the ridicule and contempt of her mother, and leaves home to work as a governess. Then the Great War begins, and Jane finds herself drawn to a call of duty. She enlists as a volunteer nurse serving injured military men in France, where she finds a greater purpose in her life despite the dreadfulness of war.

Where it's reviewed:
Booklist, April 1, 2011, page 35

Other books by the same author:
A Different Kind of Justice, 2008
Justice Is Served, 2007
A Rose in Winter, 2002
The Last Summer of Innocence, 1992
The Shadow Players, 1992

Other books you might like:
Joy Fielding, *Whispers and Lies*, 2003
Stephen Harrigan, *Remember Ben Clayton*, 2011
Doris Lessing, *Alfred and Emily*, 2008
Peter Pouncey, *Rules for Old Men Waiting*, 2005
Charles Todd, *An Impartial Witness*, 2010

391

DANIELLE SOSIN

The Long-Shining Waters

(Minneapolis, Minnesota: Milkweed Editions, 2011)

Story type: Literary
Subject(s): United States history; Women; Dreams
Major character(s): Grey Rabbit, Indian; Berit Kleiven, Spouse (of Gunnar); Gunnar Kleiven, Spouse (of Berit); Nora Truneau, Bartender (bar owner)
Time period(s): 17th century-21st century
Locale(s): Lake Superior, At Sea

Summary: *The Long-Shining Waters*, Danielle Sosin's debut novel, tells the story of three women living near Lake Superior, all of whom live during different centuries and eras. Grey Rabbit is a Native American woman from the Ojibwe tribe who mistrusts the white settlers who have come to her region during the 17th century. Nearly three hundred years later Berit Kleiven and her husband Gunnar suffer the devastating loss of their unborn child, only to find themselves experiencing resurgence in sexual desire. Then, at the turn of the 21st century, Nora Truneau uses the lake as a source of comfort after the tavern she owns burns to the ground. First novel.

Where it's reviewed:
Booklist, April 15, 2011, page 38
Publishers Weekly, February 28, 2011, page 33

Other books by the same author:
Garden Primitives, 2000

Other books you might like:
Alexander Binning, *The Devil's Chair*, 2003
Geraldine Brooks, *Caleb's Crossing*, 2011
Louise Erdrich, *The Game of Silence*, 2005
Ann Patchett, *State of Wonder*, 2011
Scott Sigler, *Ancestor*, 2009

392

ELIZABETH SPELLER

The Return of Captain John Emmett

(Boston: Houghton Mifflin Harcourt, 2011)

Subject(s): World War I, 1914-1918; Detective fiction; Murder

Major character(s): Laurence Bartram, Veteran, Detective—Amateur; John Emmett, Crime Victim, Veteran; Mary, Sister (of John); Charles, Sidekick (of Laurence)
Time period(s): 20th century; 1920s (1920)
Locale(s): London, United Kingdom

Summary: Elizabeth Speller's *The Return of Captain John Emmett* tells the story of a World War I veteran dealing with an unspeakable misfortune. Ready to retreat from the world and nurse his emotional wounds, Laurence is summoned to help Mary figure out why her brother John, another WWI vet, committed suicide. As he dips his toes in this bizarre investigation, Laurence makes some shocking revelations about the lingering effects of war, the bonds of family, and the question of whether John Emmett committed suicide...or was murdered. First novel.

Where it's reviewed:
Kirkus Reviews, March 15, 2011, page 457
Publishers Weekly, May 9, 2011, page 36

Other books you might like:
Rennie Airth, *River of Darkness*, 1999
Pat Barker, *Life Class: A Novel*, 2008
Barbara Cleverly, *Tug of War*, 2007
Charles Todd, *Search the Dark*, 1999
Jacqueline Winspear, *Among the Mad*, 2009

393

JOHN STACK

Master of Rome

(London: HarperCollins UK, 2011)

Series: Master of the Sea Series. Book 3
Story type: Historical
Subject(s): Roman Empire, 30 BC-476 AD; Romans; Greeks
Major character(s): Atticus, Military Personnel (captain of Roman naval ships), Leader
Time period(s): 3rd century

Summary: *Master of Rome* by John Stack is a historical novel and the third installment in Stack's Master of the Sea series about the naval forces of ancient Rome. In this novel, a Greek sailor named Atticus has risen to a position of power in the Roman navy. He quickly finds himself in dire straights, however—his forces are trapped by Carthaginians and then slammed by a treacherous sea storm. Hundreds of sailors perish and Atticus barely escapes with his life. He soon realizes that the dead may be luckier since he now has to answer for the loss of so many ships and men to the Roman authorities. These rulers are prone to backstabbing and scandal and yet they look down on the brave captain simply because he is Greek. The previous novels in this series are *Ship of Rome* and *Captain of Rome*.

Other books by the same author:
Captain of Rome, 2010
Ship of Rome, 2009

Other books you might like:
Jesse Browner, *The Uncertain Hour*, 2007
Colin Falconer, *When We Were Gods*, 2000

Robert Harris, *Lustrum*, 2007
Conn Iggulden, *Emperor: The Gods of War*, 2006
Simon Scarrow, *The Eagle's Prophecy*, 2006

394

KELLI STANLEY

The Curse-Maker

(New York: Minotaur Books, 2011)

Series: Roman Noir Series. Book 2
Subject(s): Roman Empire, 30 BC-476 AD; Murder; Mystery
Major character(s): Arcturus, Doctor, Detective—Amateur
Time period(s): 1st century
Locale(s): England

Summary: *The Curse-Maker* is the second installment in the award-winning Roman Noir series from author Kelli Stanley. Set in Roman Britain, the book follows the adventures of Arcturus, a governor's doctor turned amateur sleuth. Arcturus and his wife travel to Bath for a relaxing getaway, only to uncover a spooky murder with lasting ramifications. The body of Rufus Bibax is found floating in the spring with an inscribed piece of lead in his mouth. Arcturus learns that Bibax was a curse-maker whose haunting hexes repeatedly came true. As a series of grisly murders follows, Arcturus is unsure if a copycat killer is on the loose or another curse is at work.

Where it's reviewed:
Booklist, January 1, 2011, page 48
Kirkus Reviews, January 1, 2011, page 21
Library Journal, January 1, 2011, page 66
Publishers Weekly, November 29, 2010, page 32

Other books by the same author:
City of Dragons, 2010
A Long Night for Sleeping, 2008

Other books you might like:
Gillian Bradshaw, *Island of Ghosts*, 1998
Lindsey Davis, *A Body in the Bathhouse*, 2001
William Dietrich, *Hadrian's Wall*, 2004
Manda Scott, *Dreaming the Eagle*, 2003
Jules Watson, *The White Mare*, 2005

395

JUNE TATE

Born to Dance

(New York: Severn House Publishers, 2011)

Story type: Coming-of-Age
Subject(s): History; Dance; Romances (Fiction)
Major character(s): Bonny Burton, 18-Year-Old, Dancer, Lover (of Mickey); Shirley, Friend (of Bonny); Rob Andrews, Dancer (choreographer); Mickey O'Halleran, Boxer, Lover (of Bonny)
Time period(s): 20th century; 1930s (1934)
Locale(s): Southampton, England

Summary: Set in 1934 Southampton, England, June Tate's *Born to Dance* follows the personal and professional life of 18-year-old dancer Bonny Burton. When Bonny lands a spot in the chorus at the Palace of Varieties, she finds friendship with Shirley and a valuable mentor in choreographer Rob Andrews. A talent scout who sees Bonny and Rob perform launches the pair's career with an engagement in the West End. But as Bonny's love for dance fires her growing stardom, her romantic relationship with boxer Mickey O'Halleran threatens to sabotage her future. Bonny must learn to navigate Southampton's perilous world of fame, fortune, and crime. First novel.

Where it's reviewed:
Booklist, February 1, 2011, page 39

Other books by the same author:
The Reluctant Sinner, 2010
A Family Affair, 2008
When Somebody Loves You, 2006
To Be a Lady, 2005
Every Time You Say Goodbye, 2004

Other books you might like:
Evan Fallenberg, *When We Danced on Water*, 2011
Elizabeth Lord, *All That We Are*, 2010
Pamela Oldfield, *The Great Betrayal*, 2011
Linda Sole, *All My Sins*, 2010
Laura Wilson, *An Empty Death*, 2011

396

KATE TAYLOR

A Man in Uniform

(New York: Crown Publishers, 2011)

Story type: Mystery
Subject(s): Law; Mystery; French (European people)
Major character(s): Francois Dubon, Lawyer
Time period(s): 19th century; 1890s
Locale(s): Paris, France

Summary: *A Man in Uniform* is a historical mystery from award-winning author Kate Taylor. Set in the late 19th century in Paris, the novel focuses on middle-aged and middle-class attorney Francois Dubon, a man who has found contentment in his trite life through a marriage to an aristocratic wife and daily flings with a scintillating mistress. When an enigmatic widow arrives in his office, eager to hire him to investigate a treason ruling, Dubon is intrigued. The captivating client wants Dubon to head up an appeals trial for Army captain Alfred Dreyfus, a man she claims was wrongfully convicted and sent to Devil's Island. When Dubon uncovers proof of Dreyfus's innocence, he becomes obsessed with the case, neglecting his wife and mistress to don a fake identity and infiltrate the nation's military ranks to see that justice is served.

Where it's reviewed:
Booklist, December 15, 2010, page 26
Library Journal, December 1, 2010, page 109
Publishers Weekly, October 25, 2010, page 27

Other books by the same author:
Madame Proust and the Kosher Kitchen, 2003

Other books you might like:
Michael Hardwick, *Prisoner of the Devil*, 1979
Irene Nemirovsky, *The Dogs and Wolves*, 2009
Iain Pears, *The Dream of Scipio*, 2002
Chana Stasky Rubin, *Tomorrow May Be Too Late*, 1995
Leonard Wolf, *Traitor*, 2006

397

JOHN MILLIKEN THOMPSON

The Reservoir

(New York: Other Press, 2011)

Story type: Mystery
Subject(s): Murder; Mystery; History
Major character(s): Daniel Cincinnatus Richardson, Police Officer; Tommie, Lawyer, Crime Suspect, Brother (of Willie); Willie, Farmer, Crime Suspect, Brother (of Tommie)
Time period(s): 19th century; 1880s (1885)
Locale(s): Richmond, Virginia

Summary: Based on a true story, *The Reservoir* is a gripping historical mystery from debut author John Milliken Thompson. In Richmond, Virginia in the late 19th century, the body of a young pregnant white woman is discovered floating in the city's reservoir. Immediate clues point to suicide, but as more evidence is gathered, soon-to-be-retired police officer Daniel Cincinnatus Richardson suspects foul play. When the woman is identified as Lillian Madison, Richardson begins to uncover a slew of dark family secrets, involving Lillian's questionable relationship with her two cousins, Tommie and Willie. Tommie, an ambitious young lawyer, and Willie, a humble farmer, were both in love with Lillian, but did one of these brothers have a reason to murder her? First novel.

Where it's reviewed:
Kirkus Reviews, April 1, 2011, page 39
Library Journal, April 15, 2011, page 90
Publishers Weekly, April 11, 2011, page 28

Other books you might like:
V.C. Andrews, *Rain*, 2000
Patricia Cornwell, *Isle of Dogs*, 2001
Anna Dean, *A Gentleman of Fortune: Or, the Suspicions of Miss Dido Kent*, 2011
Kay Hooper, *Haunting Rachel*, 1998
Sophie Kinsella, *The Undomestic Goddess*, 2005

398

RICHARD THOMPSON

Big Wheat

(Scottsdale, Arizona: Poisoned Pen Press, 2011)

Subject(s): Mystery; History; Serial murders
Major character(s): Windmill Man, Murderer (serial killer); Charlie Krueger, Young Man; Mabel Boysen, Girlfriend (of Charlie); Jim Avery, Worker (machinist)

Time period(s): 20th century; 1910s (1919)
Locale(s): North Dakota, United States

Summary: In *Big Wheat* by Richard Thompson, threshing season arrives in 1919 North Dakota, bringing promise, prosperity, and fear as a psychotic killer hunts the plains. On the night that Charlie Krueger is ditched by his longtime girlfriend, the young man finally leaves his abusive father to seek work with the wheat harvesters. When Charlie sees a dark figure digging in an exposed field, he doesn't realize that the man is burying his beloved Mabel Boysen, or that he will soon be a suspect in her murder. The killer, who calls himself the Windmill Man, sets his sights on Charlie, whom he believes is the only witness to his crime.

Where it's reviewed:
Booklist, December 1, 2010, page 28
New York Times Book Review, January 30, 2011, page 21
Publishers Weekly, October 4, 2010, page 30

Other books by the same author:
Frag Box, 2009
Fiddle Game, 2008

Other books you might like:
Michael Connelly, *Echo Park*, 2006
Jeffery Deaver, *The Cold Moon*, 2006
Louise Erdrich, *The Beet Queen*, 1986
Susan Power, *The Grass Dancer*, 1994
Carrie Young, *The Wedding Dress: Stories from the Dakota Plains*, 1992

399

CHARLES TODD (Pseudonym of Caroline Todd and Charles Todd)

A Lonely Death

(New York: William Morrow, 2011)

Series: Ian Rutledge Series. Book 13
Subject(s): Detective fiction; Murder; Suspense
Major character(s): Ian Rutledge, Detective—Police
Time period(s): 20th century; 1920s (1920)
Locale(s): Surrey, United Kingdom

Summary: The 13th book in the Inspector Ian Rutledge Mystery series, Charles Todd's *A Lonely Death* focuses on the PI's attempts to find the person responsible for three deaths in a small English village. It is 1920, and Rutledge is determined to unlock the mystery surrounding the killing of the three men, all of whom were veterans of World War I. Shortly after his arrival in the village, another man is killed, putting pressure on Rutledge to solve the crimes before he himself becomes the next victim.

Where it's reviewed:
Booklist, December 15, 2010, page 24
Entertainment Weekly, January 7, 2011, page 73
New York Times Book Review, January 9, 2011, page 22
Publishers Weekly, November 22, 2010, page 45
The Washington Times, January 14, 2011, page B07

Other books by the same author:
The Red Door, 2010

Legacy of the Dead, 2000
Search the Dark, 1999
Wings of Fire, 1998
A Test of Wills, 1996

Other books you might like:
Jonathan Hull, *Losing Julia*, 2000
Laurie R. King, *Touchstone*, 2007
Dawn Clifton Tripp, *The Season of Open Water*, 2005
Marianne Wiggins, *Evidence of Things Unseen*, 2003
Jacqueline Winspear, *Among the Mad*, 2009

400

SIMON TOLKIEN

The King of Diamonds

(New York: Minotaur Books, 2010)

Subject(s): Mystery; Murder; History
Major character(s): William Trave, Detective, Divorced Person; David Swain, Crime Suspect, Prisoner; Katya Osman, Crime Victim, Girlfriend (former, of David), Niece (of Titus); Titus Osman, Uncle (of Katya), Jeweler
Time period(s): 20th century; 1960s (1960)
Locale(s): Oxford, England

Summary: *The King of Diamonds* is a suspenseful historical mystery novel from author Simon Tolkien. Two years earlier, in 1958, Oxford Detective Inspector William Trave's testimony leads to the murder conviction and life sentence of David Swain, a man who allegedly murdered the new lover of his former flame, Katya Osman. Now, Swain has escaped from prison and Katya's been murdered. All signs point to Swain as the killer, but Trave grows increasingly suspicious of Katya's uncle, Titus Osman, a wealthy and overbearing diamond dealer. Since Trave's ex-wife has taken up with Titus, the detective's suspicions are written off by his colleagues as jealous accusation, but Trave is so convinced of Titus's guilt that he starts a rogue investigation of his own.

Where it's reviewed:
Library Journal, February 1, 2011, page 58
Publishers Weekly, January 3, 2011, page 33

Other books by the same author:
The Inheritance, 2010

Other books you might like:
Melanie Benjamin, *Alice I Have Been*, 2010
Colin Dexter, *The Remorseful Day*, 2000
Patricia Hall, *Skeleton at the Feast*, 2002
Jane Langton, *Dead as a Dodo*, 1996
Barbara Pym, *Crampton Hodnet*, 1985

401

AMOR TOWLES

Rules of Civility

(New York: Viking, 2011)

Story type: Literary
Subject(s): Social class; Women; Wealth

Major character(s): Katy Kontent, Young Woman, Secretary; Evelyn Ross, Young Woman, Roommate (of Katy)
Time period(s): 20th century; 1930s (1938)
Locale(s): New York, New York

Summary: *Rules of Civility* is a dramatic historical novel from debut author Amor Towles. In 1938, 25-year old Katy Kontent and her best friend, Evelyn Ross, leave behind their small town for the bright lights of New York City. A chance meeting with a wealthy and handsome banker has Katy reconsidering her station in life. Eager for more of what life has to offer, Katy begins desperately trying to work her way up the social ladder. She leaves behind her secretarial job in search of a more promising career among Manhattan's elite, but as Katy infiltrates the top tier of New York's high society, she gets a firsthand glimpse at the manipulation, insecurity, and treachery that often guides the wealthy. First novel.

Where it's reviewed:
Booklist, July 1, 2011, page 39
New York Times Book Review, August 14, 2011, page 20(L)
Publishers Weekly, March 14, 2011, page 46

Other books you might like:
Susan Fales-Hill, *One Flight Up: A Novel*, 2010
Henry James, *Daisy Miller: A Study*, 1878
Henry James, *The Wings of the Dove*, 1902
Bobbie Ann Mason, *The Girl in the Blue Beret*, 2011
Paula McLain, *The Paris Wife*, 2011

402

LUDMILA ULITSKAYA

Daniel Stern, Interpreter: A Novel in Documents

(New York: Overlook Press, 2011)

Story type: Inspirational
Subject(s): World War II, 1939-1945; Jews; Christianity
Major character(s): Daniel Stein, Survivor (Holocaust), Religious (Carmelite brother)
Time period(s): 20th century
Locale(s): Belarus; Israel

Summary: In *Daniel Stein, Interpreter: A Novel in Documents*, author Ludmila Ulitskaya tells the fictional story of a Holocaust survivor based on the true story of Oswald Rufeisen. In the novel, Polish Jew Daniel Stein escapes death in the concentration camps by agreeing to serve as an interpreter for the Nazis. While he appears to aid the Nazis, Stein also helps to secure safety for hundreds of Jews. After the war, Stein converts to Catholicism and joins the Carmelite Order, eventually moving to Israel where he continues to help people in need regardless of their ethnicity or religion. Stein's remarkable story is told through a series of writings, articles, and other documents.

Other books by the same author:
Sonechka, 2005
Medea and Her Children, 2002
The Funeral Party, 2001

403

JUAN GABRIEL VASQUEZ

The Secret History of Costaguana

(New York: Riverhead Books, 2011)

Story type: Literary
Subject(s): Writers; Literature; Biographies
Major character(s): Joseph Conrad, Historical Figure, Writer; Jose Altamirano, Immigrant
Time period(s): 19th century-20th century; 1820s-1920s
Locale(s): Colombia; England

Summary: *The Secret History of Costaguana* is a novel by author Juan Gabriel Vasquez. In it, Vasquez depicts the life of British novelist Joseph Conrad, author of the contemporary classic *Heart of Darkness*, as he begins writing a novel at the turn of the 20th century. Conrad intends to set the novel in South America, and therefore enlists the help of a Colombian man named Jose Altamirano. Jose's story helps tremendously, and Conrad soon publishes one of his greatest novels, *Nostromo*. Yet upon reading the book, Jose is devastated by what Conrad has written. This book is told through Jose's eyes as he charges the literary great with destroying the fabric of his life. Vasquez is also the author of *The Informers*.

Where it's reviewed:
Booklist, April 15, 2011, page 37
Kirkus Reviews, April 15, 2011, page 633

Other books by the same author:
The Informers, 2009

Other books you might like:
Geraldine Brooks, *Caleb's Crossing*, 2011
Joseph Conrad, *Nostromo*, 1904
Gabriel Garcia Marquez, *Love in the Time of Cholera*, 1988
Sergio Ramirez, *Margarita, How Beautiful the Sea*, 2007
John Sayles, *A Moment in the Sun*, 2011

404

E. DUKE VINCENT

The Camelot Conspiracy

(New York: The Overlook Press, 2011)

Story type: Alternate History
Subject(s): Assassination; Presidents (Government); United States history
Major character(s): Dante Amato, Organized Crime Figure; Sam Giancana, Organized Crime Figure
Time period(s): 20th century; 1950s-1960s (1959-1963)
Locale(s): Cuba; United States

Summary: *The Camelot Conspiracy: A Novel of the Kennedys, Castro and the CIA* opens in 1959. Communist leader Fidel Castro has taken over control of Cuba after overthrowing Fulgencio Batista. After Eisenhower's failed invasion attempts, three very distinct groups seek to take matters into their own hands and assassinate Castro. The Mafia is eager to eliminate the

dictator to gain control of the casinos, the CIA wants to eliminate the Soviet ally, and the anti-Castro factions hope to regain control of their nation. As the years pass by and Castro remains in power, Dante Amato, a Mobster with CIA ties, and his boss, Sam Giancana, shift their sights to US President John F. Kennedy and plot his assassination instead.

Where it's reviewed:
Booklist, May 1, 2011, page 16
Publishers Weekly, March 28, 2011, page 37

Other books by the same author:
The $trip, 2009
Black Widow, 2008
Mafia Summer, 2005

Other books you might like:
George Bernau, *Promises to Keep*, 1988
Don DeLillo, *Libra*, 1988
Stephen W. Frey, *The Legacy*, 1998
Tim Kring, *Shift: Gate of Orpheus Trilogy, Book 1*, 2010
D.M. Thomas, *Flying into Love*, 1992

405

CAROL WALLACE

Leaving Van Gogh

(New York: Spiegel & Grau, 2011)

Subject(s): Artists; Mental disorders; History
Major character(s): Vincent van Gogh, Artist, Mentally Ill Person, Historical Figure; Paul Gachet, Doctor
Time period(s): 19th century; 1890s (1890)
Locale(s): Auvres, France

Summary: *Leaving Van Gogh* is a historical novel from author Carol Wallace. Relying on historical research, Wallace tells the story of Vincent van Gogh's final months through the eyes of his physician, Paul Gachet. In the spring of 1890, after Vincent decides to travel to Auvres, France, to paint and relax, his younger brother, Theo, approaches Paul, a doctor specializing in mental illness, about accompanying Vincent for the summer. Paul, intrigued by Vincent's incredible talent and troubling emotional ailments, agrees. As Vincent slips further into a dark mental and emotional abyss, Paul struggles to diagnose the artist's illness and works feverishly to remedy him before it's too late.

Where it's reviewed:
Booklist, March 1, 2011, page 36
Kirkus Reviews, January 1, 2011, page 15
Library Journal, January 2011, page 91
Publishers Weekly, January 17, 2011, page 24

Other books by the same author:
That Doggone Calf, 2009
Bub, Snow, and the Burly Bear Scare, 2003
Chomps, Fela, and Gray Cat (That's Me!), 2001
The Flying Flea, Callie, and Me, 1999
That Furball Puppy and Me, 1999

Other books you might like:
Andrew Chapman, *Beyond the Silence*, 2003

Joost Poldermans, *Vincent: A Novel Based on the Life of Van Gogh*, 1962
Alyson Richman, *The Last Van Gogh*, 2006
Irving Stone, *Lust for Life*, 1934
Frederic Tuten, *Van Gogh's Bad Cafe: A Love Story*, 1997

406

JILL PATON WALSH

The Attenbury Emeralds

(New York: Minotaur Books, 2011)

Subject(s): Murder; Detective fiction; Suspense
Major character(s): Lord Peter Wimsey, Detective—Private, Spouse (of Harriet); Harriet Vane, Detective—Private, Writer, Spouse (of Peter); Bunter, Servant; Lord Attenbury, Nobleman
Time period(s): 20th century
Locale(s): United Kingdom

Summary: Jill Paton Walsh's finds Lord Peter and his mystery-writer wife reflecting on Wimsey's inaugural case some 30 years prior. Peter, recovering from a breakdown, investigates a wealthy family's missing jewels. Now, one of the surviving family members wants to pawn the emeralds—and Lord Peter and Harriet unearth a whole new mystery surrounding the precious gems.

Where it's reviewed:
Booklist, December 1, 2010, page 29
The Financial Times, September 25, 2010, page 19
The Guardian, October 23, 2010, page 10
Publishers Weekly, November 8, 2010, page 44
The Times of London, October 16, 2010, page 12

Other books by the same author:
Debts of Dishonor, 2006
A Presumption of Death, 2003
Thrones, Dominations, 1998
A Piece of Justice, 1995
The Wyndham Case, 1993

Other books you might like:
Agatha Christie, *Curtain: Hercule Poirot's Last Case*, 1975
David Liss, *A Conspiracy of Paper*, 2000
Anne Perry, *Death of a Stranger*, 2002
Dorothy L. Sayers, *The Nine Tailors*, 1934
Dorothy L. Sayers, *Strong Poison*, 1930

407

CIJI WARE

A Race to Splendor

(Naperville, Illinois: Sourcebooks Landmark, 2011)

Story type: Romance
Subject(s): United States history; Earthquakes; Architecture
Major character(s): Amelia Bradshaw, Architect; J.D.

Thayer, Hotel Owner; Julia Morgan, Architect
Time period(s): 20th century; 1900s (1906)
Locale(s): San Francisco, California

Summary: In *A Race to Splendor* by Ciji Ware, architect Amelia Bradshaw returns to her home city of San Francisco after the devastating earthquake of 1906. She intends to rebuild her grandfather's hotel near Chinatown, even though as a woman she has no property rights. When Amelia learns that ownership of the beautiful Bay View Hotel was transferred to J.D. Thayer in a poker game, she tries to win the building back in court. Then Amelia takes a position with Julia Morgan's architecture firm and finally gets her chance to work on the Bay View. But the project also brings her into close contact with Thayer, with whom she shares professional ambitions and a growing personal attraction.

Where it's reviewed:
Kirkus Reviews, February 2, 2011, page 271
Library Journal, March 1, 2011, page 72
Publishers Weekly, February 14, 2011, page 36

Other books by the same author:
A Light on the Veranda, 2001
Midnight on Julia Street, 1999
A Cottage by the Sea, 1997
Wicket Company, 1992
Island of the Swans, 1989

Other books you might like:
Linda Barlow, *Intimate Betrayal*, 1995
Anthony Flacco, *The Last Nightingale*, 2007
Daniel Hecht, *Bones of the Barbary Coast: A Cree Black Novel*, 2006
Laurie R. King, *Locked Rooms*, 2005
Jean Stubbs, *The Golden Crucible*, 1976

408

LAUREN WILLIG

The Orchid Affair

(New York: Dutton, 2011)

Series: Pink Carnation Series. Book 8
Story type: Romance; Series
Subject(s): Espionage; Romances (Fiction); French (European people)
Major character(s): Andre Jaouen, Police Officer (deputy minister of police); Lauren "Silver Orchid" Grey, Spy; Pink Carnation, Spy
Time period(s): 1790s-1810s
Locale(s): France

Summary: *The Orchid Affair* is the eighth book in author Lauren Willig's Pink Carnation series. This book centers on Lauren Grey, aka the Silver Orchid, a newly trained spy who is sent to France during the reign of Napoleon. Her mission is to act as a servant to Andre Jaouen, the deputy to Napoleon Bonaparte's ministry of police, in order to uncover a possible plot against the emperor. She soon learns, however, that she and Jaouen may be on the same side. When a rival discovers that Jaouen is behaving as a double agent, it is up to the Pink Carnation to save both him and the Silver Orchid.

Where it's reviewed:
Booklist, December 15, 2010, page 28

Other books by the same author:
The Betrayal of the Blood Lily, 2010
The Seduction of the Crimson Rose, 2008
The Deception of the Emerald Ring, 2006
The Secret History of the Pink Carnation, 2005
The Temptation of the Night Jasmine, 2004

Other books you might like:
William Boyd, *Restless: A Novel*, 2006
Helen Fielding, *Olivia Joules and the Overactive Imagination*, 2004
Dorothy Gilman, *Mrs. Pollifax and the Whirling Dervish*, 1990
Neal Stephenson, *The Confusion*, 2004

409

LAURA WILSON

An Empty Death

(New York: Minotaur Books, 2011)

Series: Ted Stratton Series. Book 2
Subject(s): Mystery; World War II, 1939-1945; Deception
Major character(s): Ted Stratton, Detective, Inspector; Duncan Reynolds, Doctor, Crime Victim
Time period(s): 20th century; 1940s (1944)
Locale(s): London, England

Summary: *An Empty Death* is the second installment in the award-winning Ted Stratton series from author Laura Wilson. As World War II wages on, Scotland Yard Detective Inspector Ted Stratton continues to throw himself into his work, desperate for a respite from his war-torn country. His latest case has him baffled as he tries to make sense of the death of Duncan Reynolds, a physician at Middlesex Hospital. Reynolds's body was found near the site of a bombing, but his injuries suggest that he might've been dead before the bomb struck. As Stratton investigates the possible murder, he uncovers a great deal of secrets among the hospital's staff including adulterous affairs, hidden identities, and dangerous obsession.

Where it's reviewed:
Booklist, February 1, 2011, page 36
Library Journal, January 2011, page 66
Publishers Weekly, January 3, 2011, page 33

Other books by the same author:
The Man Who Wasn't There, 2008
Stratton's War, 2007
My Best Friend, 2001
Dying Voices, 2000
A Little Death, 1999

Other books you might like:
Rennie Airth, *The Dead of Winter*, 2009
James R. Benn, *Rag and Bone*, 2010
Sebastian Faulks, *Charlotte Gray*, 1998
Jill Paton Walsh, *A Presumption of Death*, 2003
Sarah Waters, *The Night Watch*, 2006

410

JACQUELINE WINSPEAR

A Lesson in Secrets

(New York: HarperCollins, 2010)

Series: Maisie Dobbs Series. Book 8
Subject(s): Murder; Mystery; England
Major character(s): Maisie Dobbs, Psychologist, Investigator, Nurse (former), Spy
Time period(s): 20th century; 1930s (1932)
Locale(s): Cambridge, England

Summary: *A Lesson in Secrets* is the eighth book in the best-selling Maisie Dobbs historical mystery series by author Jacqueline Winspear. In the summer of 1932, psychologist and investigator, Maisie Dobbs is given a top-secret assignment by the British Secret Service. She goes undercover as a junior philosophy lecturer at a private Cambridge university to observe activities that might seem contrary to the government's best interest. When Greville Liddicote, the college's notorious founder, is murdered, Maisie is ordered to stay out of the investigation. It doesn't take long for Maisie to connect Greville's murder with other peculiar behavior going on with the faculty and students and to note a shocking connection with the Nazi Party's growing power in England.

Where it's reviewed:
Booklist, February 1, 2011, page 36
Kirkus Reviews, February 1, 2011, page 166
Library Journal, February 15, 2011, page 106
New York Times Book Review, March 27, 2011, page 23
Publishers Weekly, January 31, 2011, page 27

Other books by the same author:
The Mapping of Love and Death, 2010
Mapping of Love and Death, 2010
Among the Mad, 2009
An Incomplete Revenge, 2008
Message of Truth, 2006
Pardonable Lies, 2005
Birds of a Feather, 2004
Maisie Dobbs, 2003

Other books you might like:
Jo Bannister, *Flawed*, 2007
Dorothy Cannell, *She Shoots to Conquer*, 2009
William Gibson, *Pattern Recognition*, 2003
P.D. James, *The Skull Beneath the Skin*, 1983
Laurie R. King, *The Language of Bees*, 2009

411

JANET WOODS

Paper Doll

(New York: Severn House Publishers, 2011)

Story type: Historical - Roaring Twenties
Subject(s): History; Toys; Dolls
Major character(s): Julia Howard, Wealthy, Socialite; Latham Miller, Businessman; Martin Lee-Trafford, Businessman, Doctor
Time period(s): 20th century; 1910s-1920s
Locale(s): United States

Summary: *Paper Doll* by Janet Woods is a story about cheating, loss, and sex during the Roaring 1920s. In this novel, Julia Howard is the spoiled daughter of a famous toy manufacturer. Much like the heiresses of the 21st century, Julia felt free to do as she pleased and her father—who modeled his paper dolls after her—did nothing to restrain her. Julia's fiance dies in World War I, taking away her last link to a legitimate, conventional lifestyle. She becomes a party girl, slowing down only briefly to marry her father's business partner, Latham Miller. When this marriage goes sour, Julia promptly disposes of Latham and continues a life of meaningless sex and glamour.

Where it's reviewed:
Booklist, February 1, 2011, page 43

Other books by the same author:
Salting the Wound, 2009
Edge of Regret, 2008
Without Reproach, 2008
The Coal Gatherer, 2007
Cinnamon Sky, 2006

Other books you might like:
Barbara Taylor Bradford, *Unexpected Blessings*, 2005
Jodi Picoult, *The Tenth Circle*, 2006
Marilynne Robinson, *Home*, 2008
Richard Russo, *Empire Falls*, 2001
Jane Smiley, *A Thousand Acres*, 1991

412

LOUISA YOUNG

My Dear I Wanted to Tell You

(New York: HarperCollins, 2011)

Story type: Historical - World War I
Subject(s): World War I, 1914-1918; Interpersonal relations; Family
Major character(s): Julia Locke, Spouse (of Peter); Peter Locke, Spouse (of Julia); Riley, Spouse (of Nadine); Nadine, Spouse (of Riley)
Time period(s): 20th century; 1900s-1910s
Locale(s): England

Summary: *My Dear I Wanted to Tell You*, by author Louisa Young, is a novel about two young couples torn apart by the strains of World War I. The year is 1918, and the Great War has begun erupting all around Europe. Peter and Julia Locke, a middle class British couple, find their previous marital bliss disturbed as the war forces changes in society. Meanwhile, Riley, a blue-collar worker, and Nadine, a member of high society, find their ill-matched love less of an issue as the war begins leveling the class structure in Europe. Can these two marriages endure the ever-changing social landscape during a most turbulent historical period?

Where it's reviewed:
Booklist, May 1, 2011, page 69

Library Journal, March 15, 2011, page 112

Other books by the same author:
Tree of Pearls, 2000
Desiring Cairo, 1999
Baby Love, 1997

Other books you might like:
A.S. Byatt, *The Children's Book*, 2009
Louis De Bernieres, *Birds Without Wings*, 2004
Ken Follett, *Fall of Giants*, 2010
Anne Perry, *We Shall Not Sleep*, 2007
Jeff Shaara, *To the Last Man*, 2004

Why Aren't Horror Movies Made from Books?
by
Don D'Ammassa

Prose and film are two very different types of media and it's not surprising that they overlap less often than not. A good many movies rely on visual effects that do not work as well when described by words alone, and it is very difficult to translate the atmosphere and literary feel of a book to the screen, particularly if a work of fiction involves significant insights into the thoughts and feelings of its characters. The two major science fiction film franchises—*Star Wars* and *Star Trek*—were not based on books, and most movies that were adapted, such as *Starship Troopers*, *The Puppet Masters*, or *Do Androids Dream of Electric Sheep?* (aka *Bladerunner*) have been only moderately successful at making the transition. Fantasy presently seems to be an exception, with Harry Potter and Lord of the Rings leading the way, but one might well argue that these are not so much adaptations of fantasy novels as they are adaptations of bestsellers.

The situation in the horror genre is even more pronounced. Admittedly there has been asteady parade of movies based on Stephen King stories—although most of the films were not nearly as memorable as the originals—and a few even less successful inspired by the work of Dean R. Koontz—but their selection probably has more to do with the name recognition of their bestselling creators than with their actual suitability for the screen. The vast majority of horror movies are not only original screenplays but in many cases are so formulaic and subliterate that they could not possibly have been published in book form except by a vanity press. The plot holes, impossibilities, contradictions, and lapses of logic or fact would not get past even the most undiscriminating editor. It is no surprise that even those horror films that are very successful—the Scream series, the Saw franchise, and others—are not only original scripts but did not even lead to novelizations.

The yawning chasm between horror films and books is in part due to the very different objectives of their creators. A movie director usually wants to startle the audience with a few quick jabs—the supposedly dead villain returning to life, the killer jumping out of the closet, or whatever. The horror novelist is more likely to want to develop the atmosphere of the story incremen-tally, introducing the suspense gradually to create a feeling of accelerating tension. The writer is concerned primarily with the emotions of the protagonist. The director wants to stimulate the emotions of the audience. Writers know that the things that we don't see are usually far more terrifying than what is Visible. The director, by the nature of the media, almost always has to show us everything and hope that the effect is satisfactory.

If we take the subset of horror movies based on published fiction, and then eliminate those drawn from the works of bestselling authors, we have a much smaller list. That eliminates twenty or so by Stephen King alone, plus several by Dean R. Koontz. We should probably also delete *Ghost Story* (1981) based on the Peter Straub novel, because it was a bestseller. Two of the most important horror movies in the genre, *Rosemary's Baby* (1968) and *The Exorcist* (1973) were also based on very popular recent novels by Ira Levin and William Peter Blatty respectively. Significantly none of Straub's subsequent novels were snatched up by Hollywood. This criterion also eliminates two movies based on Anne Rice novels, *Interview with the Vampire* (1995) and *Queen of the Damned* (2002). A couple of non-fantastic horror novels also fall into this category, *The Silence of the Lambs* (1991) based on Thomas Harris' novel, and *Psycho* (1960) and its various sequels and remakes, based on Robert Bloch's novel.

Then we need to separate out all of those movies that were drawn from classics of literature that happened to be horror stories, a kind of special case of the bestseller. This eliminates the various renditions of Dracula and Frankenstein, along with *The Portrait of Dorian Gray*, *Dr. Jekyll and Mr. Hyde*, *The Turn of the Screw*, and *The Legend of Sleepy Hollow*. The various reinterpretations of the work of Edgar Allan Poe fall into the same category. One could argue that the handful of movies based on the works of H.P. Lovecraft should also be eliminated, although most of these make only a nodding reference to the actual stories and simply use Lovecraft's name as a marketing ploy. Two notable exceptions to this are *Dagon* (2001) and *The Resurrected* (1992, aka

Shatterbrain), the latter of which is based on *The Case of Charles Dexter Ward*. The results are a list of about twenty horror movies—though I've probably missed a few—that started life on the printed page.

The earliest on my list is *The Undying Monster* (1942) based very loosely on the 1922 novel by Jessie Douglas Kerruish. It's a gothic novel involving a family curse, a detective specializing in the occult, and has a touch of the werewolf in it, which became more prominent in the lackluster film version. It was not until the early 1960s that a brief but occasionally successful effort was made to draw from literary horror. The two most noteworthy of these were Alfred Hitchcock's *The Birds* (1963) based on the 1952 novelette by Daphne Du Maurier, and *The Haunting* (1962), derived from *The Haunting of Hill House* (1959) by Shirley Jackson. The first is only a reasonable approximation of the original story, but the second was a much more faithful rendition, although that doesn't hold true for the more recent and very disappointing remake. Although not as popular, *Burn Witch Burn* (1962), based on Fritz Leiber's *Conjure Wife* (1952) also stuck close to its source material as it told the story of a college professor who discovers that his wife is a witch. It was remade as *Witches' Brew* in 1980 without even crediting the author.

There were a handful of horror novels adapted during the 1970s but with very limited success. James Blish's short novel *There Shall Be No Darkness* (1950) provides the basic plot of *The Beast Must Die* (1974) but a clever and fairly light hearted story was turned into a dreary and slow paced disaster. And *Now the Screaming Starts* (1973) is based on David Case's story of a family curse and ghostly assaults, *Fengriffen* (1970), but it was designed mostly as a vehicle for Peter Cushing and never rose above obscurity. *The Legend of Hell House* (1973) was one of the brighter spots, in large part because screenwriter Richard Matheson was adapting his own 1971 novel, but it was inevitably compared to *The Haunting*, and not favorably.

Two of the horror novels brought to the screen in the 1970s were based on bestselling novels by authors who were otherwise minor figures in horror fiction. Robert Marasco's *Burnt Offerings* (1973) was a modification of the haunted house story that appeared as a movie in 1976 to generally favorable reviews, but as with Stephen King it owed more to its bestseller status than to its content. The same is true of Jeffrey Konvitz's *The Sentinel* (1974) about a woman who is fated to guard the gates of hell through the end of her life. The 1977 film followed the original plot quite closely, probably because Konvitz produced his own novel, but a sequel, *The Guardian* (1979) never made it to the screen.

Dennis Wheatley's 1953 novel *To the Devil—A Daughter* (1953) became a movie in 1976 but it was more of an adventure story than horror and none of the other novels in that series were adapted. A great disappointment was *The Manitou* (1978), based on Graham Masterton's 1975 novel, a very effective and suspenseful novel that became a silly low budget failure as a film. It

is significant that while Masterton remains a prolific and well established horror writer with more than forty novels published, none of his other novels have been adapted despite many of them having very cinematic qualities.

The 1980s started off well with *Wolfen* (1981) and *The Hunger* (1983), both based on Whitley Strieber novels from a couple of years earlier. Properly speaking these fall into the category of bestsellers but it did appear that Hollywood was at least briefly interested in discovering what properties the horror field might provide. Gary Brandner's *The Howling* (1977) was a paperback original and hardly a major literary success but the 1981 screen version of a hidden werewolf colony was popular enough to spawn several sequels, not based on books. Unfortunately, the trend collapsed abruptly and the only other prose derived horror films during that decade were two inspired by Clive Barker stories, *Rawhead Rex* (1987) and *Hellraiser* (1988), the latter of which also spawned a number of sequels. Perhaps the best of horror movies based on novels from the 1980s is *Something Wicked This Way Comes*, from Ray Bradbury's 1962 novel of a mysterious carnival's visit to a small town. One other film from this period, *The Lair of the White Worm* (1988) is theoretically based on a novel, Bram Stoker's obscure 1911 version, but there is very little similarity to the text.

Hollywood's recourse to printed horror fiction since then has been little more than a footnote. Richard Matheson's *A Stir of Echoes* (1958) became a film in 1999, but Matheson's long standing connections with the film industry may explain this exception. With the waning popularity of horror as a literary genre—always excepting Stephen King—there has been only one bestseller to attract the film industry's attention since the 1980s. The exception is *The Ruins<* (2008) based on the 2006 novel about predatory plants in Mexico by Scott Smith. This was another case where the author wrote the screenplay, so the adaptation is quite faithful. Matthew J. Costello's *Beneath Still Waters* (1989), the story of a drowned town and the things that live there, became a very cheaply made Italian movie in 2005 and F. Paul Wilson's 1990 novella of a world conquered by vampires, *Midnight Mass*, became an unwatchable disaster in 2003.

One could fill several pages describing horror novels that have the potential to be first rate movies. *Black Easter* (1968) by James Blish describes a world dominated by Hell following the death of God. Christopher Fowler's *Rune (1990)*, Charles L. Grant's *The Nestling* (1982), Barbara Hambly's *Those Who Hunt the Night* (1988), Brian Lumley's Necroscope novels, *The Wolf's Hour* (1989) by Robert R. McCammon, *The Chosen Child* (1997) by Graham Masterton, and *Declare* (2001) by Tim Powers all come immediately to mind. A short lived cable anthology series, *The Hunger*, drew heavily on short horror fiction but unfortunately with limited success, possibly because the individual episodes tended to be very much alike. The explanation for this failure is probably that the primary audience for horror movies re-

ally isn't interested in anything innovative or unconventional or that requires some effort to follow. They are more interested in routine slasher fare with perhaps a hint of sex but never the faintest trace of originality or forethought. But if that's what Hollywood provides, then there is no reason for the audience to expect anything more.

Recommended Titles

The year 2011 has been comparative low key in the horror field. The blurred line between horror and urban fantasy continues. Historical settings appear to be growing more popular. The fad of mixing new supernatural text with classic 19th-century novels seems to have abated although there were still some novels featuring alternate lives of historical figures in which they battled vampires or demons. The expected wave of zombie novels has not been as overwhelming as originally anticipated and many of those that did appear are spoofs or satires. The demise of Leisure books has ended the only regular horror publishing program in mass market editions.

Those across the River by Christopher Buehlman

By These Ten Bones by Clare B. Dunkle

Waking Nightmares by Christopher Golden

Thirteen Years Later by Jasper Kent

The Dead Town by Dean R. Koontz

Bloodshot by Cherie Priest

Crossroads by Jeanne C. Stein

The Dark at the End by F. Paul Wilson

An Embarrassment of Riches by Chelsea Quinn Yarbro

Horror Fiction

413

CAT ADAMS

Demon Song
(New York: Tor, 2011)

Series: Blood Singer Series. Book 3
Story type: Paranormal; Series
Subject(s): Demons; Magicians; Occultism
Major character(s): Celia Graves, Supernatural Being (part vampire, part Siren, part human), Bodyguard
Time period(s): 21st century; 2010s
Locale(s): California, United States

Summary: In the novel *Demon Song* by Cat Adams (a pseudonym for C.T. Adams and Cathy Clamp), the third book in the Blood Singer series, bodyguard Celia Graves faces challenges in the mortal and supernatural realms. Her bloodline has made her a Siren, a thwarted vampire attack has made her part-vampire, and a curse she's carried all her life has brought her years of bad luck. But Celia's unique and ever-evolving powers give her an important role in the ongoing battle between good and evil. When a portal opens between a dangerous realm and the natural world, Celia takes great risks to keep the demons at bay.

Where it's reviewed:
Publishers Weekly, January 24, 2011, page 136

Other books by the same author:
Blood Song, 2010
Serpent Moon, 2010
Siren Song, 2010
Cold Moon Rising, 2009
Howling Moon, 2007

Other books you might like:
Patricia Briggs, *Blood Bound*, 2007
Chris Marie Green, *A Drop of Red*, 2009
Laurell K. Hamilton, *Bullet*, 2010
Charlaine Harris, *All Together Dead*, 2007
Kat Richardson, *Vanished*, 2009

414

STEPHEN L. ANTCZAK
JAMES C. BASSETT, Co-Editor
MARTIN H. GREENBERG, Co-Editor

Zombiesque
(New York: DAW, 2011)

Story type: Collection; Zombies
Subject(s): Short stories; Zombies; Horror

Summary: In *Zombiesque*, editors Stephen Antczak, James Bassett, and Martin Greenberg present a collection of 16 stories that explore the unique circumstances of zombie existence. Populated with zombie cheerleaders, zombie vacationers, rookie zombies, and vengeful zombies, the stories featured in *Zombiesque* include "At First Only Darkness" by Nancy Collins, "Do No Harm" by Tim Waggoner, "Into That Good Night" by Robert Sommers, "You Always Hurt the One You Love" by G.K. Hayes, "A Distant Sound of Hammers" by S. Boyd Taylor, "Zombie Zero" by Nancy Holder, and others.

Other books by the same author:
Daydreams Undertaken, 2004
The Z-Files, 2004

Other books you might like:
Amelia Beamer, *The Loving Dead*, 2010
Ken Eulo, *Manhattan Heat*, 1991
Brian Keene, *The Rising*, 2003
Philip Nutman, *Wet Work*, 1993
Joan Frances Turner, *Dust*, 2010

415

GERRY BARTLETT

Real Vampires Don't Wear Size Six
(New York: Berkley Books, 2011)

Story type: Fantasy; Romance
Subject(s): Romances (Fiction); Supernatural; Weight loss
Major character(s): Glory St. Clair, Vampire, Lover (of Jeremy); Jeremy Blade, Lover (of Glory)
Time period(s): 21st century
Locale(s): United States

Summary: *Real Vampires Don't Wear Size Six* is a supernatural romance novel by Gerry Bartlett. In this novel, female vampires fret about their body shapes and boyfriends. Main character Glory St. Clair is a vampire with many supernatural issues to deal with, including fending off demons and making deals with the devil—but her primary concern is that she feels overweight. Glory believes she needs to be thin because she wants to win back her boyfriend Jeremy Blade. Now she wonders what lengths she would go to in order to become a size six again.

Other books by the same author:
Real Vampires Hate Their Thighs, 2010
Real Vampires Have More to Love, 2010
Real Vampires Make Waves, 2009
Real Vampires Get Lucky, 2008
Real Vampires Have Curves, 2007

Other books you might like:
MaryJanice Davidson, *Undead and Unwelcome*, 2009
Molly Harper, *Nice Girls Don't Have Fangs*, 2009
Victoria Laurie, *Ghouls, Ghouls, Ghouls*, 2010
Katie MacAlister, *In the Company of Vampires*, 2010
Kerrelyn Sparks, *Be Still My Vampire Heart*, 2007

416

JES BATTIS

Infernal Affairs

(New York: Ace Books, 2011)

Story type: Paranormal
Subject(s): Demons; Occultism; Detective fiction
Major character(s): Tess Corday, Detective (OSI); Derrick, Detective (OSI); Miles, Detective (OSI); Lucian, Detective (OSI); Ru, Demon, Boy; Basuram, Demon

Summary: *Infernal Affairs* is a novel from author Jes Battis's OSI series featuring Occult Special Investigator Tess Corday. When the body of a young boy washes ashore on a beach, OSI detectives Tess, Derrick, Miles, and Lucian are on the case. Previously believed to be dead, the boy is in fact a demon who has fled the Underworld. The boy, who is called Ru, is being pursued by an adult demon named Basuram, who admits that even he doesn't know why Ru is being hunted. Now it is up to the OSI to protect Ru and keep him from harm's way, at least until they can figure out whom he really is and where he really belongs. Battis is also the author of *Night Child* and *Inhuman Resources*.

Other books by the same author:
A Flash of Hex, 2009
Night Child, 2008

Other books you might like:
Lyn Benedict, *Gods and Monsters*, 2011
Jim Butcher, *Small Favor: A Novel of the Dresden Files*, 2008
Laurell K. Hamilton, *Guilty Pleasures*, 1993
Nancy Holder, *Blood and Fog*, 2003
Yvonne Navarro, *Paleo*, 2000

417

LYN BENEDICT

Gods and Monsters

(New York: Ace Books, 2011)

Series: Shadow Inquiries Series. Book 3
Story type: Mystery
Subject(s): Supernatural; Zombies; Detective fiction
Major character(s): Sylvie Lightner, Detective—Private
Locale(s): The Everglades, Florida

Summary: *Gods and Monsters* is the third book in author Lyn Benedict's Shadows Inquiries series featuring paranormal private investigator Sylvie Lightner. This time, Sylvia must investigate a series of murders deep in the swamps of the Florida Everglades. At first she believes these crimes are just the work of a run-of-the-mill human serial killer, and she decides to leave the investigation to the police. Then the bodies of the women who were murdered come back to life, killing the cops who were working on the case. Now it's up to Sylvie to figure out not only who or what killed these women, but what types of supernatural forces are possessing them.

Other books by the same author:
Ghosts & Echoes, 2010
Sins & Shadows, 2009

Other books you might like:
Amber Benson, *Cat's Claw*, 2010
Patricia Briggs, *Cry Wolf*, 2008
Yasmine Galenorn, *Harvest Hunting*, 2010
Charlaine Harris, *Grave Secret*, 2009
Lilith Saintcrow, *Redemption Alley*, 2009

418

PATRICIA BRIGGS

River Marked

(New York: Ace Books, 2011)

Series: Mercy Thompson Series. Book 6
Subject(s): Adventure; Romances (Fiction); Supernatural
Major character(s): Mercy Thompson, Shape-Shifter, Mechanic; Adam, Lover (of Mercy), Werewolf
Time period(s): 21st century; 2010s
Locale(s): United States

Summary: Mercy Thompson is an auto mechanic by day and a shape-shifter by night. With her lover Adam at her side, she learns of an ancient evil force rising from the waters of a local river. Now it's up to Mercy and Adam to stop this evil from taking over the world—but first they will have to discover its ties to Mercy's father and his heritage. *River Marked* is the sixth book in Patricia Briggs's Mercy Thompson series.

Where it's reviewed:
Locus, April 2011, page 25

Other books by the same author:
Bone Crossed, 2009
Silver Borne, 2009
Cry Wolf, 2008

Dragon Blood, 2003
Dragon Bones, 2002

Other books you might like:
Marie Brennan, *Doppelganger*, 2006
Jim Butcher, *Blood Rites*, 2004
Karen Chance, *Claimed by Shadow*, 2007
Yasmine Galenorn, *Bone Magic*, 2010
Diana Rowland, *Mark of the Demon*, 2009

419

CHRISTOPHER BUEHLMAN

Those Across the River

(New York: Ace Books, 2011)

Story type: Small Town Horror
Subject(s): Southern United States; Family; Memory
Major character(s): Frank Nichols, Writer, Spouse (of Eudora); Eudora Nichols, Spouse (of Frank)
Locale(s): Whitbrow, Georgia

Summary: *Those Across the River* is a novel by author Christopher Buehlman. When Frank Nichols's aunt bequeaths to him the family plantation, she does so while adding a warning to sell the property immediately and never look back. Still, Frank believes it is the perfect time to return back to Whitbrow, Georgia. He settles into the estate with his wife, Eudora, and begins writing a chronicle of his family's legacy. But the horrors that occurred on the plantation, and in rural Whitbrow itself, many years before are about to repeat themselves as supernatural forces go to work to seek out vengeance.

Other books you might like:
James P. Blaylock, *The Rainy Season*, 1999
Jonathan Carroll, *The Marriage of Sticks*, 1999
Stephen King, *Bag of Bones*, 1998
A.J. Matthews, *Looking Glass*, 2004
Robert R. McCammon, *Boy's Life*, 1991

420

KATE CANN

Consumed

(New York: Point, 2011)

Story type: Young Adult
Subject(s): Supernatural; Good and evil; Dating (Social customs)
Major character(s): Rayne Peters, 16-Year-Old, Worker (Morton's Keep); St. John, Leader (cult); Miss Skelton, Manager (Morton's Keep); Ethan, Friend (of Rayne)
Time period(s): 21st century; 2010s
Locale(s): England

Summary: In the young adult novel *Consumed* by Kate Cann, the sequel to *Possessed*, Rayne Peters continues her struggle against the sinister forces that reside at Morton's Keep. Sixteen-year-old Rayne came to the country estate in order to escape her monotonous life in London. But while working at Morton's Keep, Rayne has come

to realize that the old manor conceals dangerous secrets. Local pagan Ethan seems to have subdued the cult leader called St. John, but all is not calm at the Keep. A new manager, Miss Skelton, has arrived and a girl has died at one of Ethan's ritual locations.

Where it's reviewed:
Booklist, May 1, 2011, page 88
The Horn Book Guide, Fall 2010, page 362

Other books by the same author:
Possessed, 2010
Sink or Swim, 2009
Mediterranean Holiday, 2007

Other books you might like:
Clare B. Dunkle, *By These Ten Bones*, 2005
Marilyn Kaye, *Here Today, Gone Tomorrow*, 2009
L.J. Smith, *The Power*, 1992
Lili St. Crow, *Betrayals: A Strange Angels Novel*, 2009
F. Paul Wilson, *Jack: Secret Vengeance*, 2011

421

LEE CARROLL

The Watchtower

(New York: Tor, 2011)

Series: Black Swan Rising Series. Book 2
Story type: Fantasy; Series
Subject(s): Fantasy; Vampires; Fairies
Major character(s): Garet James, Jeweler; Will Hughes, Vampire
Time period(s): 21st century; 2010s
Locale(s): Paris, France; New York, New York

Summary: In the novel *The Watchtower* by Lee Carroll (the pseudonym of Carol Goodman and Lee Slonimsky), New York jewelry designer Garet James continues her journey into the paranormal world she began in *Black Swan Rising*. Garet now knows that she is a member of The Watchtower, an organization responsible for defending the world from evil. She enters into a romantic relationship with Will Hughes, a centuries-old vampire, and follows him to France when he flees with a magical box. As Garet searches for the realm known as the Summer Country, she encounters a gnome, an enchanted tree, a nymph, and other mystical creatures in Paris.

Other books by the same author:
Black Swan Rising, 2010

Other books you might like:
Alex Bledsoe, *Blood Groove*, 2009
Nancy A. Collins, *Darkest Heart*, 2002
P.N. Elrod, *A Chill in the Blood*, 1998
Tanya Huff, *Blood Debt*, 1997
Lee Killough, *Blood Games*, 2001

422

CHRISTINE CODY

Bloodlands

(New York: Ace Books, 2011)

Series: Bloodlands Series. Book 1
Story type: Vampire Story

Subject(s): Apocalypse; Vampires; Supernatural
Major character(s): Mariah, Frontierswoman; Gabriel, Vampire

Summary: *Bloodlands* is the first novel in author Christine Cody's Bloodlands trilogy. In a post-disaster world, where most of America has been transformed into a wasteland, humans seek refuge in technocratic metropolises. Yet these cities cannot shield one from Big Brother's watchful eye, and that's exactly what Mariah wants—to live a free life without interference. She lives in the New Badlands, a territory populated by others like her, who seek independence from the technocracy. But their independence comes at a price, because the Badlands—now called the Bloodlands—are the realm of supernatural creatures like vampires. When Gabriel comes to Mariah's door to find safety, she reluctantly grants him shelter. Yet Gabriel might be just the type of creature Mariah should avoid.

Other books by the same author:
Blood Rules, 2011

Other books you might like:
Stephen King, *The Stand*, 1978
Richard Matheson, *I Am Legend*, 1954
Robert R. McCammon, *They Thirst*, 1981
John Steakley, *Vampire$*, 1990
Lois Tilton, *Vampire Winter*, 1990

423

CHRISTINE CODY

Blood Rules

(New York: Ace Books, 2011)

Series: Bloodlands Series. Blood 2
Story type: Paranormal
Subject(s): Vampires; Supernatural; Apocalypse
Major character(s): Mariah Lysander, Frontierswoman, Werewolf; Gabriel, Vampire; Johnson Stamp, Agent, Vampire Hunter

Summary: *Blood Rules* is the second novel in author Christine Cody's Bloodlands trilogy. In the post-apocalyptic dystopia of the Bloodlands, Mariah Lysander is beginning to feel her inner werewolf emerge more and more. To make matters worse, Gabriel now knows it was she who killed his lover, and he may never be able to forgive her. In an effort to find solace as well as a way to quash the beast within, Mariah sets off on a journey across the wasted landscape. There, she encounters the dreaded Stamp, a former government agent whose only purpose is to eradicate all supernatural beings from the face of the Earth.

Other books by the same author:
Bloodlands, 2011

Other books you might like:
Yasmine Galenorn, *Blood Wyne*, 2011
Tanya Huff, *Blood Pact*, 1993
Cherie Priest, *Bloodshot*, 2011
Dianne Sylvan, *Shadowflame*, 2011
Chelsea Quinn Yarbro, *A Candle for D'Artagnan*, 1989

424

ELLEN CONNOR (Pseudonym of Carrie Lofty)

Nightfall

(New York: Berkley Sensation, 2011)

Series: Dark Age Dawning Series. Book 1
Story type: Fantasy; Romance
Subject(s): Fantasy; Supernatural; Apocalypse
Major character(s): Jenna, Girl (saved by Mason); Mason, Military Personnel (ex-Marine), Rescuer (of Jenna)
Time period(s): 21st century
Locale(s): United States

Summary: *Nightfall* is a post-apocalyptic fantasy romance novel by Ellen Connor and the first entry in Connor's *A Dark Age Dawning* series. In this book, civilization has collapsed and one of the few survivors is beautiful Jenna. Mason is a handsome and mysterious ex-Marine who chooses to rescue her from certain doom. Mason had been a friend of Jenna's father, who had warned him of the coming apocalypse. Now, Mason and Jenna live together in the Pacific Northwest where they fall in love while fending off mutant wolves. Jenna begins adapting to the brutal new "dark age" and learns survival skills from Mason as they prepare for their first winter together.

Where it's reviewed:
Romantic Times, June 2011, page 82

Other books by the same author:
Daybreak, 2011
Midnight, 2011

Other books you might like:
Robert Calder, *The Dogs*, 1976
James Herbert, *Lair*, 1979
Thomas Page, *The Hephaestus Plague*, 1973
Donald Porter, *The Day of the Animals*, 1977
V.M. Thompson, *Deadly Nature*, 1988

425

E.J. COPPERMAN

An Uninvited Ghost

(New York: Penguin, 2011)

Series: Haunted Guesthouse Series. Book 2
Story type: Contemporary; Series
Subject(s): Mystery; Ghosts; Haunted houses
Major character(s): Alison Kerby, Innkeeper, Mother (of Melissa); Melissa, 10-Year-Old, Daughter (of Alison); Scott MacFarlane, Spirit; Maxie, Spirit; Paul, Spirit
Time period(s): 21st century; 2010s
Locale(s): New Jersey, United States

Summary: In the supernatural mystery novel *An Uninvited Ghost* by E.J. Copperman, Alison Kerby has transformed a rundown house into a charming inn at the New Jersey seaside. Recently divorced, Alison lives at the inn with her 10-year-old daughter, Melissa, and the house's resident spirits, Maxie and Paul. Alison has a knack for solving mysteries, but when another ghost, Scott MacFarlane, reports a crime, it is solved easily—the woman

he thought he had killed is alive. But only temporarily. As Alison investigates a case of murder at the guesthouse, a television crew arrives to film the reality show *Down the Shore* on site. *An Uninvited Ghost* is the second book in Copperman's Haunted Guesthouse Mystery series.

Other books by the same author:
Night of the Living Deed, 2010

Other books you might like:
Annette Blair, *Death by Diamonds*, 2010
Casey Daniels, *The Chick and the Dead*, 2007
P.N. Elrod, *Bloodcircle*, 1990
Victoria Laurie, *Ghouls, Ghouls, Ghouls*, 2010

426

CASEY DANIELS

A Hard Day's Fright

(New York: Penguin, 2011)

Series: Pepper Martin Series. Book 7
Story type: Contemporary; Series
Subject(s): Mystery; Detective fiction; Ghosts
Major character(s): Pepper Martin, Guide (cemetery); Lucy Pasternak, Teenager, Spirit
Time period(s): 21st century; 2010s
Locale(s): Cleveland, Ohio

Summary: In the novel *A Hard Day's Fright*, Pepper Martin gives cemetery tours to the living and uses her skills of detection to help the residents of the spirit world. In this case, Pepper comes to the aid of a teenage spirit who longs to receive proper burial. Lucy Pasternak disappeared in 1966 while on her way home from a Beatles concert at the Cleveland Municipal Stadium. Though her fate now is obvious, her body has never been found. Pepper wants to help Lucy rest gently in the afterlife, but the almost 50-year-old case will be her most challenging yet. *A Hard Day's Fright* is the seventh book in Daniels' Pepper Martin Mystery series.

Other books by the same author:
Tomb with a View, 2010
Dead Man Talking, 2009
Night of the Loving Dead, 2009
The Chick and the Dead, 2007
Tombs of Endearment, 2007

Other books you might like:
Annette Blair, *Larceny and Lace*, 2009
E.J. Copperman, *An Uninvited Ghost*, 2011
C.J. Henderson, *The Occult Detectives of C.J. Henderson*, 2003
Victoria Laurie, *Death Perception*, 2008
Mary Stanton, *Avenging Angels*, 2010

427

J.N. DUNCAN

Deadworld

(New York: Kensington Publishing Company, 2011)

Series: Jackie Rutledge Series. Book 1
Story type: Supernatural Vengeance

Subject(s): Detective fiction; Psychics; Vampires
Major character(s): Jackie Rutledge, FBI Agent; Laurel, FBI Agent; Nick Anderson, Detective—Private
Locale(s): Chicago, Illinois

Summary: *Deadworld* is a novel written by author J.N. Duncan. Jackie Rutledge is an FBI agent trying to solve a string of murders plaguing Chicago. Along with her partner Laurel, Jackie must figure out who is killing people and draining them of their blood. They could use all the help they can get, so they turn to private investigator Nick Anderson. Nick is a vampire, though, and could be one of the prime suspects for the killings. With the help of ghosts, vampires, and other things that go bump in the night, Jackie, Laurel, and Nick must attempt to track down the real killer and try to make Chicago a little bit safer.

Other books by the same author:
The Vengeful Dead, 2011

Other books you might like:
Patricia Briggs, *River Marked*, 2011
Yasmine Galenorn, *Bone Magic*, 2010
Marjorie M. Liu, *Darkness Calls*, 2009
Nalini Singh, *Archangel's Kiss*, 2010
Anton Strout, *Dead Matter*, 2010

428

J.N. DUNCAN

The Vengeful Dead

(New York: Kensington Publishing Company, 2011)

Series: Jackie Rutledge Series. Book 2
Story type: Paranormal
Subject(s): Detective fiction; Occultism; Fantasy
Major character(s): Jackie Rutledge, FBI Agent

Summary: *The Vengeful Dead* is the second book in author J.N. Duncan's Deadworld series. After the death of her partner, FBI agent Jackie Rutledge finds herself plagued by guilt, as well as her partner's spirit. When a new supernatural mystery rears its head in the form of a being that can possess and murder humans, Jackie finds herself suddenly a suspect. Now Jackie must not only solve the case, but also prove that she isn't the culprit. The only problem is, Jackie's newfound powers—a result of Deadworld contact—may make her capable of even worse.

Other books by the same author:
Deadworld, 2011

Other books you might like:
Jes Battis, *A Flash of Hex*, 2009
Laurell K. Hamilton, *The Lunatic Cafe*, 1996
Frank Lauria, *Blue Limbo*, 1991
Gary McMahon, *Pretty Little Dead Things*, 2011
Jory Sherman, *The Phoenix Man*, 1980

Horror

429

CHRISTOPHER FARNSWORTH

The President's Vampire

(New York: G.P. Putnam's Sons, 2011)

Series: Nathaniel Cade Series. Book 2
Story type: Historical; Series
Subject(s): Vampires; Horror; Presidents (Government)
Major character(s): Nathaniel Cade, Vampire, Assistant (to president); Zach Barrows, Assistant (to Cade); Graves, Military Personnel (colonel)
Time period(s): 21st century; 2010s
Locale(s): United States

Summary: In the novel *The President's Vampire* by Christopher Farnsworth, Nathaniel Cade is a most unusual presidential aide. Since the 1860s the vampire has served America as a secret agent capable of fighting off mortal and immortal foes. In the 21st century, the world is plagued by sinister threats as it has been for generations. The case at hand for Cade and his human assistant Zach Barrows involves military contracts and espionage. But there is a paranormal factor as well. The Snakeheads, an intelligent race of reptiles, engage Cade in battle while Barrows deals with the human aspects of the investigation. *The President's Vampire* is the second book in the Nathaniel Cade series.

Where it's reviewed:
Library Journal, April 15, 2011, page 81
Publishers Weekly, March 7, 2011, page 49

Other books by the same author:
Blood Oath, 2010

Other books you might like:
Mario Acevedo, *X-Rated Bloodsuckers*, 2006
Nancy A. Collins, *In the Blood*, 1991
P.N. Elrod, *Song in the Dark*, 2005
Lucius Shepard, *The Golden*, 1993
F. Paul Wilson, *The Keep*, 1981

430

CHRISTOPHER FARNSWORTH

Blood Oath

(New York: G. P. Putnam's Sons, 2010)

Series: Nathaniel Cade Series. Book 1
Story type: Vampire Story
Subject(s): Horror; Vampires; Occultism
Major character(s): Nathaniel Cade, Vampire, Assistant (to president); Zach Barrows, Assistant (to Cade); William Griffin, Agent; Johann Konrad, Doctor
Time period(s): 21st century; 2010s
Locale(s): United States

Summary: In *Blood Oath* by Christopher Farnsworth, the U.S. president's inner sanctum includes an impossibly powerful and aged protector, vampire Nathaniel Cade. In the 1830s, Cade took a vow to guard President Andrew Jackson and every president thereafter. But the vampire requires an assistant to see to his needs. When current handler William Griffen retires, Zach Barrows is tapped

for the job. Working in the deepest levels of government secrecy, Barrows faces a formidable opponent—Cade's long-time rival, Dr. Johann Konrad. Konrad is working to build a force of mutant troops, and Cade and Barrows must stop his hazardous experiment. First novel.

Other books by the same author:
The President's Vampire, 2011

Other books you might like:
Alex Bledsoe, *Blood Groove*, 2009
Simon Clark, *London under Midnight*, 2006
Mick Farren, *The Time of Feasting*, 1996
Ray Garton, *Night Life*, 2007
Dan Simmons, *Carrion Comfort*, 1989

431

CHRISTINE FEEHAN

Ruthless Game

(New York: Jove Books, 2011)

Series: GhostWalker Series. Book 9
Subject(s): Pregnancy; Adventure; Fantasy
Major character(s): Rose Patterson, Lover (of Kane Cannon), Adventurer (GhostWalker); Kane Cannon, Lover (of Rose Patterson), Adventurer (GhostWalker)
Time period(s): 21st century; 2010s
Locale(s): Mexico

Summary: *Ruthless Game* is the ninth book in Christine Feehan's GhostWalker series. In this installment, Ghost-Walker Rose Patterson is on the run in Mexico. She is hiding in what she thinks is a safe place when her ex-lover and fellow GhostWalker Kane Cannon strolls back into her life. Once Kane discovers Rose is carrying his child, he knows he can't turn his back on her. The two go on the run together and find comfort in each other's arms again. They know they must protect each other and their child.

Other books by the same author:
Dark Peril, 2010
Burning Wild, 2009
Dark Curse, 2009
Conspiracy Game, 2006
Dark Demon, 2006

Other books you might like:
Amber Benson, *Serpent's Storm*, 2011
William Hallahan, *The Search for Joseph Tully*, 1974
Roger Manvell, *The Dreamers*, 1958
Graham Masterton, *Death Dream*, 1988
Jeffrey Thomas, *The Fall of Hades*, 2009

432

MICHAEL THOMAS FORD

Jane Goes Batty

(New York: Random House, 2011)

Series: Jane Bites Series. Book 2
Story type: Vampire Story

Subject(s): Literature; Vampires; Supernatural
Major character(s): Jane Austen, Writer, Vampire;
    Charlotte Bronte, Writer, Vampire
Locale(s): Brakestone, New York

Summary: *Jane Goes Batty* is the second novel in Michael Thomas Ford's series featuring Jane Austen as a centuries-old vampire. Jane now lives in New England, not old England, and owns a bookstore in the small village of Brakestone in upstate New York. She writes a best-selling novel and finally has all the fame and celebrity she craved in her former life. Life in the spotlight has its price, though, as Jane struggles to keep secret her vampire side as well as the truth about whom she really is. Then she finds out that an old enemy, Charlotte Bronte, has come to town, and Charlotte wants to end Jane once and for all!

Where it's reviewed:
Library Journal, December 2010, page 107
Publishers Weekly, December 13, 2010, page 41

Other books by the same author:
Jane Bites Back, 2009
Full Circle, 2007
Looking for It, 2005
Last Summer, 2004

Other books you might like:
Jane Austen, *Sense and Sensibility and Sea Monsters*,
    2009
Charlotte Bronte, *Jane Slayre*, 2010
Steve Hockensmith, *Dreadfully Ever After*, 2011
A.E. Moorat, *Henry VIII, Wolfman*, 2010
Lucy Weston, *The Secret History of Elizabeth Tudor,
    Vampire Slayer*, 2011

433

RHIANNON FRATER

The First Days

(New York: Tor, 2011)

Series: As the World Dies Trilogy. Book 1
Story type: Series; Zombies
Subject(s): Zombies; Horror; Friendship
Major character(s): Katie, Lawyer; Jenni, Housewife
Time period(s): Indeterminate Future
Locale(s): Texas, United States

Summary: In the horror novel *The First Days*, the first book in Rhiannon Frater's Zombie Trilogy, a sudden zombie plague brings two women together in a struggle for survival. On a morning like any other, Jenni prepares for her daily routine as a homemaker and mother. When she finds that her husband has become a zombie, and that he is feeding on the flesh of their child, she realizes that she has been thrown into a nightmare. Jenni is protected from the escalating zombie attacks by Katie, a lawyer who has left a scene of horror in her own home that morning. As Jenni and Katie battle zombies and try to stay alive, they meet other survivors and begin to plan for their very uncertain future. First novel.

Where it's reviewed:
Publishers Weekly, May 16, 2011, page 60

Other books by the same author:
The Tale of the Vampire Bride, 2009
Pretty When She Dies, 2008

Other books you might like:
Ray Garton, *Zombie Love*, 2003
Mira Grant, *Feed*, 2010
Brian Keene, *Dead Sea*, 2007
Jonathan Maberry, *Patient Zero*, 2009
Joe McKinney, *Apocalypse of the Dead*, 2010

434

CHRISTOPHER FULBRIGHT

The Bone Tree

(Anaheim, California: Bad Moon Books, 2011)

Story type: Paranormal
Subject(s): Childhood; Ghosts; Supernatural
Major character(s): Kevin, Boy (friend of Bobby); Bobby,
    Boy, Friend (of Kevin); Tom Plecker, Boy
Time period(s): 20th century; 1970s (1978)
Locale(s): Texas, United States

Summary: In the horror novel *The Bone Tree* by Christopher Fulbright, two boys in 1970s rural Texas find their idyllic childhood shattered by a supernatural presence. Kevin and Bobby are reading comic books in their tree house on a Friday after school when they see a boy with blond hair running in terror through the woods below. They soon see what has frightened little Tom Plecker so badly—a tree whose branches have contorted into a writhing skeleton. The Bone Tree is not the only horror that the boys must face. The shadow men pay a visit as well, drawing Kevin and Bobby into a battle against a paranormal enemy. Illustrated by Jill Bauman.

Other books by the same author:
Of Wolf and Man, 2009

Other books you might like:
Stephen King, *It*, 1986
Robert R. McCammon, *Boy's Life*, 1991
Cherie Priest, *Wings to the Kingdom*, 2006
Dan Simmons, *Summer of Night*, 1991
Peter Straub, *Lost Boy Lost Girl*, 2003

435

BILL GAUTHIER

Alice on the Shelf

(Anaheim, California: Bad Moon Books, 2011)

Story type: Fantasy
Subject(s): Fantasy; Fairy tales; Alternative worlds
Major character(s): Brad, Friend (of Miranda); Miranda,
    Friend (of Brad)
Time period(s): 21st century; 2010s

Summary: In the novel *Alice on the Shelf* by Bill Gauthier, a young man named Brad finds himself in a modern-day version of Lewis Carroll's imaginary world when his friend Miranda goes missing. When Brad begins search-

ing for Miranda at her home, he instead finds a stranger there who has lost his pocket watch. Though Brad is familiar with the adventures of literature's famed Alice, he is surprised by what he finds in the realm beyond the rabbit hole. The atmosphere there is malevolent and Brad's quest to find his beloved Miranda will be difficult and dangerous. Illustrated by Frank Walls.

Other books you might like:
James P. Blaylock, *The Rainy Season*, 1999
Jonathan Carroll, *The Land of Laughs*, 1980
Graham Masterton, *Picture of Evil*, 1985
Robert R. McCammon, *Usher's Passing*, 1984
John Skipp, *The Emerald Burrito of Oz*, 2000

436

CHRISTOPHER GOLDEN

Waking Nightmares
(New York: Penguin, 2011)

Series: Shadow Saga series. Book 5
Story type: Ancient Evil Unleashed; Series
Subject(s): Horror; Fantasy; Good and evil
Major character(s): Peter Octavian, Vampire (former), Sorcerer
Time period(s): 21st century; 2010s
Locale(s): Montreal, Quebec

Summary: In the horror novel *Waking Nightmares* by Christopher Golden, former vampire and current mage Peter Octavian lives in a world populated by both humans and vampires. The immortal race includes traditional vampires as well as Shadows—those that can feed on blood without destroying the host's life. An uneasy balance exists in the world's complex social structure, but outside forces threaten to destroy the peace. Evil beings from a realm beyond the natural world have found a way in and Octavian must try to stop the darkness from entering. *Waking Nightmares* is the fifth book in Golden's Shadow Saga.

Other books by the same author:
The Lost Ones, 2008
The Borderkind, 2007
The Myth Hunters, 2006
King of the Dead, 2001
Of Saints and Shadows, 1994

Other books you might like:
Jim Butcher, *Blood Rites*, 2004
Jeffrey Konvitz, *The Guardian*, 1979
Brian Lumley, *Necroscope*, 1986
Graham Masterton, *Blind Panic*, 2010
F. Paul Wilson, *The Dark at the End*, 2011

437

AVA GRAY (Pseudonym of Ann Aguirre)

Skin Heat
(New York: Penguin, 2011)

Series: Skin Series. Book 3
Story type: Romance; Series

Subject(s): Horror; Romances (Fiction); Animals
Major character(s): Geneva Harper, Veterinarian; Zeke Noble, Assistant (to Geneva)
Time period(s): 21st century; 2010s
Locale(s): United States

Summary: In the novel *Skin Heat* by Ava Gray, Geneva Harper has chosen a career as a veterinarian over the life of wealth her family had planned. Fiercely independent, Geneva is surprised by the attraction she feels for her new employee, Zeke Noble. She's intrigued by his wild ways, but Zeke's animal magnetism is real—he has been genetically altered and is now only part human. As Zeke tries to adjust to his new existence and find his place in the human world, he also must protect Geneva from a serial killer's attack. *Skin Heat* is the third book in Gray's Skin series.

Where it's reviewed:
Romantic Times, January 2011, page 72

Other books by the same author:
Skin Dive, 2011
Skin Tight, 2010
Skin Game, 2009

Other books you might like:
Cat Adams, *Siren Song*, 2010
John Coyne, *Fury*, 1989
John Farris, *All Heads Turn When the Hunt Goes By*, 1977
Sarah McCarty, *Reaper's Justice*, 2010
Donna Lee Simpson, *Awaiting the Fire*, 2007

438

WALTER GREATSHELL

Xombies: Apocalypso
(New York: Penguin, 2011)

Series: Xombies Series. Book 3
Story type: Series; Zombies
Subject(s): Horror; Zombies; Apocalypse
Major character(s): Lulu Pangloss, Teenager (zombie)
Time period(s): Indeterminate Future
Locale(s): United States

Summary: In the horror novel *Xombies: Apocalypso* by Walter Greatshell, a Xombie virus has left America a battleground between the flesh-eating undead and those who remain uninfected. Lulu Pangloss, a teenager who has become a Xombie, is traveling the waters around the United States aboard the *USS No-Name*, a nuclear sub. Lulu and her crew are trying to increase the Xombie ranks by preying on mortal victims. But some humans, though infected with Agent X, don't become Xombies. Their blood may hold the secret to survival for the living and the undead. *Xombies: Apocalypso* is the third book in Greatshell's Xombies series.

Other books by the same author:
Mad Skills, 2011
Xombies: Apocalypticon, 2010
Xombies, 2004

Other books you might like:
Max Brooks, *World War Z: An Oral History of the Zombie War*, 2006
Mira Grant, *Feed*, 2010
Brian Keene, *The Rising*, 2003
Joe McKinney, *Flesh Eaters*, 2011
David Wellington, *Monster Island*, 2006

439

DARYL GREGORY

Raising Stony Mayhall

(New York: Del Rey Books, 2011)

Story type: Zombies
Subject(s): Apocalypse; Zombies; Supernatural
Major character(s): Stony Mayhall, Supernatural Being; Wanda Mayhall, Mother (adoptive, of Stony)

Summary: *Raising Stony Mayhall* is a novel by author Daryl Gregory. When an infectious disease turns its victims into zombies, Wanda Mayhall and her daughters stumble across a dead young mother lying in the snow. In the young woman's arms lies a baby boy, whom at first appears to be dead but is then discovered to have the zombie illness. Reluctant to kill an infant, Wanda instead hides the baby from anyone who would cause him harm and the boy—now named Stony—begins to grow up. Against his adoptive mother's wishes, Stony wanders off their farm and discovers a world where the living dead are treated like second-class citizens and must fight for their own survival.

Other books by the same author:
The Devil's Alphabet, 2009
Pandemonium, 2008

Other books you might like:
Amelia Beamer, *The Loving Dead*, 2010
Mira Grant, *Deadline*, 2011
Isaac Marion, *Warm Bodies*, 2011
Kim Paffenroth, *Dying to Live: A Novel of Life Among the Undead*, 2008
Joan Frances Turner, *Dust*, 2010

440

JUSTIN GUSTAINIS

Sympathy for the Devil

(Oxford, UK: Solaris, 2011)

Story type: Paranormal
Subject(s): Political campaigns; Supernatural; Demons
Major character(s): Quincey Morris, Detective (of the supernatural); Libby Chastain, Witch; Howard Stark, Political Figure (senator); Sargatanas, Demon

Summary: *Sympathy for the Devil* is an installment from author Justin Gustainis's Morris and Chastain supernatural detective series. This time, occult detective Quincey Morris and his partner Libby Chastain, a witch, find themselves in the middle of a political tempest. Senator Howard Stark, a US presidential candidate, is determined to win the election—especially since he is possessed by a powerful demon. Holding the highest position in the United States will provide the demon Sargatanas the perfect vantage point from which he can open up the gates of Hell. Morris and Chastain must stop this demon, but the US Secret Service cannot see the supernatural forces at hand; all they see is a security threat. The clock is ticking, and Morris and Chastain must work hard and fast if they are going to save the world.

Other books by the same author:
Hard Spell, 2011
Those Who Fight Monsters, 2011
Evil Ways, 2009
Black Magic Woman, 2008

Other books you might like:
P.N. Elrod, *Quincey Morris, Vampire*, 2001
Stephen King, *The Dead Zone*, 1979
Thomas Luke, *The Hell Candidate*, 1980
Thomas F. Monteleone, *The Resurrectionist*, 1995
Seabury Quinn, *The Devil's Bride*, 1976

441

JUSTIN GUSTAINIS

Those Who Fight Monsters

(Calgary, Alberta: Edge, 2011)

Story type: Collection
Subject(s): Vampires; Werewolves; Occultism

Summary: *Those Who Fight Monsters* is a short-fiction collection edited by Justin Gustainis, author of the novels *The Hades Project* and *Black Magic Woman*. This book includes 14 stories from popular urban fantasy detective series and novels. Among the characters included in this collection are Laura Ann Gilman's Danny Hendrickson, from the Cosa Nostradamus series; Pete Caldecott, from the Black London series by Caitlin Kittredge; Chris Marie Green's Dawn Madison, from the author's Vampire Babylon series; Lilith Saintcrow's Jill Kismet, from the series by the same name; and Jessi Hardin, from the Kitty Norville series by Carrie Vaughn.

Other books by the same author:
Hard Spell, 2011
Sympathy for the Devil, 2011
Evil Ways, 2009
Black Magic Woman, 2008

Other books you might like:
Chris Marie Green, *A Drop of Red*, 2009
C.J. Henderson, *Brooklyn Knight*, 2010
William Hope Hodgson, *Carnacki, the Ghost Finder*, 1910
Lilith Saintcrow, *Hunter's Prayer*, 2008
Carrie Vaughn, *Kitty's Greatest Hits*, 2011

Horror

442

NANCY HADDOCK

Always the Vampire

(New York: Berkley Books, 2011)

Story type: Fantasy
Subject(s): Fantasy; Vampires; Weddings
Major character(s): Cesca Marinelli, Vampire, Girlfriend (of Deke Saber); Deke Saber, Boyfriend (of Cesca Marinelli), Supernatural Being (suffering from the Void spell)
Time period(s): 21st century
Locale(s): Florida, United States

Summary: *Always the Vampire* by Nancy Haddock is a fantasy novel about the ups and downs of being a vampire in the modern world. Cesca Marinelli is a centuries-old vampire in the form of a regular woman. She doesn't like the taste of blood; she likes visiting Florida beaches and shopping at Wal-Mart. Cesca is happy to be the maid of honor in her best friend's wedding, but suddenly supernatural forces intervene. A magic spell called the Void strikes her supernatural friends, including her boyfriend and her ex-boyfriend. Cesca realizes she must fully embrace her vampire ways if she wants to save her loved ones from suffering the Void.

Other books by the same author:
Last Vampire Standing, 2009
La Vida Vampire, 2008

Other books you might like:
Karen Chance, *Midnight's Daughter*, 2008
MaryJanice Davidson, *Undead and Unworthy*, 2008
Charlaine Harris, *Dead to the World*, 2004
Victoria Laurie, *Ghouls Gone Wild*, 2010
Kerrelyn Sparks, *Secret Life of a Vampire*, 2009

443

TATE HALLAWAY

Almost Final Curtain

(New York: New American Library, May 3, 2011)

Series: Vampire Princess of St. Paul Series. Book 2
Story type: Young Adult
Subject(s): Adolescent interpersonal relations; Vampires; Witches
Major character(s): Ana Parker, Vampire, Witch, Teenager
Locale(s): St. Paul, Minnesota

Summary: *Almost Final Curtain* is an installment from the Vampire Princess of St. Paul series by Tate Hallaway. Anastasija "Ana" Parker was born into supernatural royalty. Her mother is a powerful witch, and her father is king of the vampires. Yet all Ana really wants is to live like a normal teen, and she thinks the key to doing that is to score a part in the upcoming high-school musical. When a magical charm is taken from the Minnesota Historical Society, Ana must skip play practice to make sure that the charm isn't used to enslave her. Can she stop whomever stole the charm in time to make her musical debut?

Other books by the same author:
Almost to Die For, 2010
Dead If I Do, 2009
Dead Sexy, 2007
Tall, Dark & Dead, 2006

Other books you might like:
Rachel Caine, *Ghost Town*, 2010
MaryJanice Davidson, *Undead and Undermined*, 2011
Charlaine Harris, *Dead in the Family*, 2010
Cherie Priest, *Bloodshot*, 2011
Whitley Strieber, *Lilith's Dream: A Tale of the Vampire Life*, 2002

444

LAURELL K. HAMILTON

Hit List

(New York: Berkley Books, 2011)

Series: Anita Blake: Vampire Hunter Series. Book 20
Subject(s): Fantasy; Horror; Vampires
Major character(s): Anita Blake, Vampire Hunter
Time period(s): 21st century; 2010s
Locale(s): Tacoma, Washington

Summary: In *Hit List* by Laurell K. Hamilton, vampire hunter Anita Blake travels to Tacoma, Washington to investigate a rash of weretiger killings. Anita quickly discovers that the murders are being carried out by mystical paid killers known as the Harlequin. Worse, she believes that the Harlequin are under the control of a vampire queen who has been searching for Anita. The local police are more hindrance than help. Anita's sexual appetite, an inherent aspect of her paranormal existence, keeps her on a constant hunt for new partners. *Hit List* is the 20th book in the Anita Blake, Vampire Hunter series.

Where it's reviewed:
Publishers Weekly, April 25, 2011, page 120

Other books by the same author:
Bullet, 2010
Flirt, 2010
Skin Trade, 2010
Blood Noir, 2008
The Harlequin, 2007
Danse Macabre, 2006
Cerulean Sins, 2003
Guilty Pleasures, 1993

Other books you might like:
Patricia Briggs, *Hunting Ground*, 2009
Jim Butcher, *Changes*, 2010
Charlaine Harris, *Dead and Gone*, 2009
Kat Richardson, *Labyrinth*, 2010
Anton Strout, *Dead Waters*, 2011

445

LORI HANDELAND

Moon Cursed

(New York: St. Martin's Paperbacks, March 1, 2011)

Series: Nightcreature Series. Book 10
Story type: Contemporary; Series
Subject(s): Horror; Fantasy; Romances (Fiction)
Major character(s): Kristin Daniels, Television Personality; Liam Grant, Friend (of Kristin)
Time period(s): 21st century; 2010s
Locale(s): Scotland

Summary: In the novel *Moon Cursed* by Lori Handeland, Kristin Daniels has arrived in Scotland to investigate the celebrated Loch Ness Monster. In her career as host of the TV program *Hoax Hunters*, Kristin has debunked many legends around the world. As she tries to learn the truth about Nessie, Kristin instead finds a mysterious man named Liam Grant. Kristin quickly falls for the handsome man as they make their way through Scotland's ancient ruins. But has Kristin found true love or has she been enchanted by the Highland moon? *Moon Cursed* is the 10th book in Handeland's Nightcreature series.

Where it's reviewed:
Romantic Times, March 2011, page 93

Other books by the same author:
Marked by the Moon, 2010
Apocalypse Happens, 2009
Doomsday Can Wait, 2009
Any Given Doomsday, 2008
Crescent Moon, 2006

Other books you might like:
C.T. Adams, *Cold Moon Rising*, 2009
Christina Dodd, *Touch of Darkness*, 2007
Susan Krinard, *Secret of the Wolf*, 2001
Jennifer St. Giles, *Kiss of Darkness*, 2009
Eileen Wilks, *Blood Challenge*, 2011

446

CHARLAINE HARRIS
TONI L.P. KELNER, Co-Editor

Home Improvement: Undead Edition

(New York: Ace Books, 2011)

Story type: Collection
Subject(s): Short stories; Supernatural; Suspense

Summary: *Home Improvement: Undead Edition*, edited by Charlaine Harris and Toni L.P. Kelner, is a compilation of 14 short stories. The stories in this anthology are urban fantasies with a humorous take on do-it-yourself and home-improvement guides. The book begins with a story by Harris featuring her popular heroine Sookie Stackhouse and ends with a short story by Kelner. This collection also features stories from Patricia Griggs, Heather Graham, James Grady, Melissa Marr, and more.

Harris is also the author of *Dead Reckoning* and *A Touch of Dead*; Kelner is also the author of *Many Bloody Returns* and *Death's Excellent Vacation*.

Other books by the same author:
Dead in the Family, 2010
Dead and Gone, 2009
Grave Secret, 2009
From Dead to Worse, 2008
Definitely Dead, 2006

Other books you might like:
Ilona Andrews, *Hexed*, 2011
Patricia Briggs, *Bone Crossed*, 2009
Ellen Datlow, *Naked City*, 2011
Charlaine Harris, *A Touch of Dead*, 2009
George R.R. Martin, *Down These Strange Streets*, 2011

447

GWEN HAYES

Falling Under

(New York: New American Library, 2011)

Story type: Young Adult
Subject(s): Horror; Supernatural; Dreams
Major character(s): Theia Alderson, 17-Year-Old, Student—High School; Haden Black, Classmate (of Theia)
Time period(s): 21st century; 2010s
Locale(s): Serendipity Falls, California

Summary: In the young adult horror novel *Falling Under* by Gwen Hayes, 17-year-old Theia Alderson enjoys a quiet life in Serendipity Falls, California—until the good-looking guy who has become a recurring figure in her dreams shows up at her high school. Haden Black is a new student, as alluring in the flesh as he is in Theia's nighttime fantasies. Their relationship is complicated, marked with intense attraction and cautious hesitation. As Theia is pulled closer to Haden, she is also drawn into a supernatural realm that holds devastating secrets. She can make things right again, but not without the assistance of her mortal friends.

Where it's reviewed:
Publishers Weekly, January 24, 2011, page 155

Other books you might like:
Amelia Atwater-Rhodes, *Demon in My View*, 2000
Rachel Caine, *Glass Houses*, 2006
P.C. Cast, *Dragon's Oath*, 2011
Melissa de la Cruz, *Blue Bloods*, 2006
Stephenie Meyer, *Twilight*, 2005

448

JOEY W. HILL

Vampire Instinct

(New York: Heat, 2011)

Series: Vampire Queen Series. Book 7
Story type: Fantasy; Romance

Horror

Subject(s): Fantasy; Romances (Fiction); Supernatural
Major character(s): Elisa, Servant (of Lady Daniela), Lover (of Malachi); Lady Daniela, Vampire, Leader (of Elisa); Malachi, Animal Lover (who runs animal shelter), Vampire
Time period(s): 21st century
Locale(s): United States

Summary: *Vampire Instinct* by Joey W. Hill is a an entry in Hill's Vampire Queen series. In this book, Elisa is a servant of a powerful vampire named Lady Daniela. Elisa has served her for some time as a guardian of a group of vampire children. Unexpectedly, Lady Daniela orders Elisa to kill the children. Elisa is unwilling to obey her mistress's evil orders. She takes the children to the home of Malachi, an American Indian who runs an animal shelter and who is also a vampire. As Malachi turns his shelter into a vampire-child refuge, Elisa begins to fall in love with him. But she knows that Lady Daniela will look for the missing children and may seek revenge on her disobedient servant.

Other books by the same author:
Vampire Mistress, 2010
Vampire Trinity, 2010
Beloved Vampire, 2009
A Vampire's Claim, 2009
Mark of the Vampire Queen, 2008

Other books you might like:
Christine Cody, *Blood Rules*, 2011
Kresley Cole, *A Hunger Like No Other*, 2006
Cherie Priest, *Hellbent*, 2011
Whitley Strieber, *The Last Vampire*, 2001
Dianne Sylvan, *Shadowflame*, 2011

449

JEANNIE HOLMES

Blood Secrets

(New York: Bantam, July 5, 2011)

Series: Alexandra Sabian Series. Book 2
Subject(s): Fantasy; Horror; Romances (Fiction)
Major character(s): Alexandra "Alex" Sabian, Vampire, Detective; Varik Baudelaire, Vampire, Fiance(e) (former, of Alex), Detective; Dollmaker, Murderer
Time period(s): 21st century; 2010s
Locale(s): Jefferson, Mississippi

Summary: In the horror novel *Blood Secrets* by Jeannie Holmes, vampire Alexandra Sabian is at odds with her superiors at the Federal Bureau of Preternatural Investigation. In order to redeem herself, Alex agrees to work on a case with Varik Baudelaire—a fellow vampire who was once her co-worker and lover. Their assignment involves a missing college student and a deranged criminal who leaves handmade dolls at his crime scenes. As the detectives track the Dollmaker, their journey leads them into a dangerous world where Alex becomes the killer's target. *Blood Secrets* is the second book in the Alexandra Sabian series.

Other books by the same author:
Blood Law, 2010

Other books you might like:
Rhiannon Frater, *Pretty When She Dies*, 2008
Cherie Priest, *Bloodshot*, 2011
Michelle Rowen, *Nightshade*, 2011
Thomas E. Sniegoski, *A Hundred Words for Hate*, 2011
Eileen Wilks, *Blood Magic*, 2010

450

NANCY HOLZNER

Bloodstone

(New York: Ace Books, 2011)

Series: Deadtown Series. Book 2
Story type: Zombies
Subject(s): Werewolves; Zombies; Demons
Major character(s): Vicky Vaughn, Hunter (of demons)
Locale(s): Boston, Massachusetts

Summary: *Bloodstone* is the second book in Nancy Holzner's Deadtown series. Deadtown is a section of Boston cordoned off from the rest of the city; it is the place where supernatural beings live, removed from society to keep the living from harm. Fortunately, demon hunter Vicky Vaughn is around to enforce order among both the dead and undead. When the Back Bay becomes plagued by a series of murders, all of Boston suspects that one of Deadtown's residents is to blame—after all, this swanky part of town doesn't usually attract a criminal element. Now it's up to Vicky to find the perpetrator in order to calm the turmoil brewing between the human and supernatural residents; otherwise, the entire city could explode in chaos.

Other books by the same author:
Hellforged, 2011
Deadtown, 2010

Other books you might like:
Charlaine Harris, *From Dead to Worse*, 2008
Faith Hunter, *Blood Cross*, 2010
Kelly Meding, *As Lie the Dead*, 2010
Ellen Schreiber, *Vampire Kisses 8: Cryptic Cravings*, 2011
Shiloh Walker, *Hunter's Need*, 2009

451

DEL HOWISON
JEFF GELB, Co-Editor

Dark Delicacies III: Haunted

(Philadelphia: Running Press, 2009)

Story type: Collection
Subject(s): Horror; Fantasy; Short stories

Summary: In *Dark Delicacies III: Haunted*, editors Del Howison and Jeff Gelb present a collection of 21 tales of terror dealing with hauntings. The anthology includes the short stories "Mist on the Bayou" by Heather Graham, "How to Edit" by Richard Christian Matheson, "A Haunting" by John Connolly, "Food of the Gods," by Simon R. Green, "Fetch" by Chuck Palahniuk, "And So

with Cries" by Clive Barker, "Do Sunflowers Have a Fragrance" by Del James, "One Last Bother" by Del Howison, and others. Each story was written specifically for this collection.

Other books by the same author:
When Werewolves Attack, 2010
Dark Delicacies, 2007
Dark Delicacies II, 2007

Other books you might like:
Clive Barker, *In the Flesh*, 1986
Ellen Datlow, *The Best Horror of the Year Volume 3*, 2011
Rick Hautala, *Four Octobers*, 2006
Richard Matheson, *Barking Sands*, 1999
David Morrell, *Nightscape*, 2004

452

LARISSA IONE

Eternal Rider

(New York: Grand Central Publishing, 2011)

Series: Lords of Deliverance Series. Book 1
Story type: Paranormal; Series
Subject(s): Horror; Romances (Fiction); Brothers
Major character(s): Ares, Mythical Creature (one of the Four Horsemen of the Apocalypse); Cara Thornhart, Lover (of Ares)
Time period(s): 21st century; 2010s
Locale(s): United States

Summary: In the horror novel *Eternal Rider* by Larissa Ione, the Four Horsemen of the Apocalypse—War, Famine, Pestilence, and Death—have arrived on Earth to carry out their ancient mission. Possessing the power of good and evil inherited from their parents at birth, the Horsemen can choose to stop the end of the world or allow the Apocalypse to unfold. Ares, the second of the Horsemen and the embodiment of War, struggles with his fated role and the deceit of one of his siblings. Cara Thornhart, a mortal with extraordinary powers of her own, can help Ares but only at great personal risk. *Eternal Rider* is the first book in Ione's Lords of Deliverance series.

Other books by the same author:
Ecstasy Unveiled, 2010
Sin Undone, 2010
Desire Unchained, 2009
Passion Unleashed, 2009
Pleasure Unbound, 2008

Other books you might like:
Charles L. Grant, *Symphony*, 1997
Emma Holly, *Courting Midnight*
Allyson James, *Shadow Walker*, June 7, 2011
Jackie Morse Kessler, *Rage*, 2011
Nalini Singh, *Slave to Sensation*

453

MICHAEL KELLY

Chilling Tales: Evil I Did Dwell; Lewd I Did Live

(Calgary, Alberta: Hades Publications, 2011)

Story type: Collection
Subject(s): Short stories; Horror; Fantasy

Summary: *Chilling Tales: Evil I Did Dwell; Lewd I Did Live* is a collection of horror stories compiled by editor Michael Kelly, who is also the author of *Scratching the Surface* and *Undertow and Other Laments*. The book includes 18 short stories by favorite Canadian horror and fantasy authors. In "The Needle's Eye," author Suzanne Church tells the story of a devastating virus that can blind those who are afflicted by it, but the only known cure may be even worse. "Sympathy for the Devil" by Nancy Kilpatrick is the story of a man who is the catalyst of a devastating car crash; now sinister forces are determined to make sure he pays. Barbara Rogers's "404" features a mysterious company whose office workers seem to vanish into thin air, one by one, while "Stay" by Leah Bobet revolves around themes of greed and mythology. Other authors featured in this collection include Claude Lalumiere, Brett Alexander Savory, Robert J. Wiersema, Richard Gavin, and Barbara Roden.

Other books you might like:
Donald R. Burleson, *Beyond the Lamplight*, 1996
Nancy Kilpatrick, *Cold Comfort*, 2001
Tim Lebbon, *Fears Unnamed*, 2004
Scott Nicholson, *Scattered Ashes*, 2008
Al Sarrantonio, *Toybox*, 2000

454

JASPER KENT

Thirteen Years Later

(London: Bantam, 2010)

Series: Danilov Quintet. Book 2
Story type: Historical; Series
Subject(s): Fantasy; Horror; Russian history
Major character(s): Aleksei Ivanovich Danilov, Military Personnel (colonel, Russian army); Alexander, Leader (czar), Historical Figure; Dimitry, Son (of Aleksei)
Time period(s): 19th century; 1820s (1825)
Locale(s): Russia

Summary: In the horror novel *Thirteen Years Later* by Jasper Kent, the second book in the Danilov Quintet, Aleksei Ivanovich Danilov is a colonel in the Russian army who is enjoying a brief respite in the years following the Napoleonic wars. But in 1825, a spirit of unrest is taking hold in the country and revolution is on the horizon. Danilov's own son, Dimitry, has followed his father into the military, but he is also an agent of the revolution. As Danilov knows, soldiers and politicians aren't the only factors that will determine the fate of

Horror

Russia. Ancient pacts and supernatural forces will also come into play.

Where it's reviewed:
Booklist, February 15, 2011, page 60
Library Journal, February 15, 2011, page 104
Publishers Weekly, January 3, 2011, page 38

Other books by the same author:
Twelve, 2010

Other books you might like:
Barbara Hambly, *Those Who Hunt the Night*, 1988
Mike Mignola, *Baltimore, or, the Steadfast Tin Soldier and the Vampire*, 2007
Anne Rice, *Blood and Gold*, 2001
Michael Romkey, *The London Vampire Panic*, 2001
Chelsea Quinn Yarbro, *Borne in Blood*, 2007

455

JACKIE MORSE KESSLER

Rage

(New York: Houghton Mifflin Harcourt, 2011)

Series: Horsemen of the Apocalypse Series. Book 2
Story type: Young Adult
Subject(s): Self mutilation; Family; High schools
Major character(s): Missy, Teenager, Girlfriend (ex, of Adam); Death, Supernatural Being; Adam, Boyfriend (ex, of Missy)

Summary: *Rage* is the second book from the Horsemen of the Apocalypse series by Jackie Morse Kessler. Missy is a teenage outsider who endures endless torment from her classmates, just for being a little bit different and unpopular. When she fell in love with Adam, she believed everything would change, until he dumped her and humiliated her in front of the entire school. Now Missy cuts herself to find relief from the pain, a pain that even Death himself can feel. When Death offers Missy the chance to become War, one of the Four Horsemen of the Apocalypse, she takes it. And despite the darkness of her new, supernatural powers, she may finally find the light she has always needed in her life.

Where it's reviewed:
Voice of Youth Advocates, April 2011, page 82

Other books by the same author:
Black and White, 2010
Hunger, 2010
Shades of Gray, 2010
Hell's Belles, 2007

Other books you might like:
Charles L. Grant, *Symphony*, 1997
Emma Holly, *Courting Midnight*
Larissa Ione, *Eternal Rider*, 2011
Allyson James, *Shadow Walker*, June 7, 2011
Nalini Singh, *Slave to Sensation*

456

J. ROBERT KING

Death's Disciples

(Nottingham, UK: Angry Robot, 2011)

Story type: Psychic Powers
Subject(s): Ghosts; Terrorism; Aircraft accidents
Major character(s): Sharon Gardner, Survivor, Amnesiac

Summary: *Death's Disciples* is a novel by author J. Robert King. When Sharon Gardner wakes up in a hospital, she cannot even remember who she is, let alone the circumstances that led to her being there. Soon the pieces begin coming together, though: Sharon is the sole survivor of an aircraft explosion perpetrated by a terrorism group known as Death's Disciples. Sharon cannot figure out why she was the only one to survive, or why the ghosts of her fellow passengers are haunting her. Soon she learns that they have a message for her, though—Death's Disciples know that she is still alive, and they won't rest until their job is done.

Other books by the same author:
Angel of Death, 2009
Legions, 2003
Onslaught, 2002
Lancelot Du Lethe, 2001
Invasion, 2000

Other books you might like:
Alex Johnson, *Wipeout*, 2006
Dean R. Koontz, *Sole Survivor*, 1997
Rebecca Levene, *End of the Line*, 2005
Natasha Rhodes, *Dead Reckoning*, 2005
Steven A. Roman, *Dead Man's Hand*, 2005

457

GLENN KLEIER

The Knowledge of Good & Evil

(New York: Tor, 2011)

Story type: Adventure
Subject(s): Horror; Fantasy; Adventure
Major character(s): Ian Baringer, Religious (former priest), Paranormal Investigator, Fiance(e) (of Angela Weber); Angela Weber, Psychologist, Fiance(e) (of Ian Baringer)
Time period(s): 21st century; 2010s
Locale(s): United States

Summary: In the novel *The Knowledge of Good and Evil* by Glenn Kleier, Ian Baringer is a paranormal investigator and former priest seeking proof of the existence of an afterlife. His search began with the loss of his parents in a plane accident. He first searched for comfort in religion until his doubts spurred him to turn to the field of parapsychology. Now, armed with the diary of a priest who claimed to have visited the afterlife, Ian and his fiancee, psychologist Angela Weber, set off on a global quest for answers to the Universe's greatest secret. But a covert religious group will take any measures necessary to stop them.

Where it's reviewed:
Publishers Weekly, May 16, 2011, page 53

Other books by the same author:
The Last Day, 1998

Other books you might like:
Jeffrey Konvitz, *The Sentinel*, 1974
Dean R. Koontz, *Sole Survivor*, 1997
Rebecca Levene, *End of the Line*, 2005
David A. McIntee, *Destination Zero*, 2005
Douglas Preston, *Blasphemy*, 2008

458

ANGELA KNIGHT

Master of Shadows

(New York: Berkley Books, 2011)

Story type: Paranormal
Subject(s): Vampires; Supernatural; Werewolves
Major character(s): La Belle Couer, Vampire; Tristan,
    Knight; King Arthur, Royalty
Locale(s): England

Summary: *Master of Shadows* is a novel by author Angela
Knight. La Belle Coeur is a centuries-old vampire, and a
seducer of fledgling vampires to help usher them into
their new way of life. Then she meets Tristan, one of
King Arthur's most favored Knights of the Round Table.
Together, she and Tristan must thwart the efforts of a
werewolf wizard and a band of vampires, both of whom
have the potential to ignite a war between the supernatural races and both of whom are among King Arthur's
most dreaded enemies. Knight is also the author of *Blood
& Steel*, *Hot Blooded*, and *Beyond the Dark*.

Other books by the same author:
Master of Fire, 2010
Master of Wolves, 2006
Master of the Moon, 2005
Jane's Warlord, 2004
Master of the Night, 2004

Other books you might like:
Karen Chance, *Midnight's Daughter*, 2008
Chris Marie Green, *Night Rising*, 2007
Nancy Holzner, *Bloodstone*, 2011
Jeanne C. Stein, *Blood Drive*, 2007
Eileen Wilks, *Bloodlines*, 2007

459

DEAN KOONTZ

The Dead Town

(New York: Bantam Books, 2011)

Series: Dean Koontz's Frankenstein Series. Book 5
Story type: Horror
Subject(s): Horror; Supernatural; Monsters
Major character(s): Victor Frankenstein, Scientist (mad),
    Leader (of army of monsters)
Time period(s): 21st century

Locale(s): Rainbow Falls, Montana

Summary: *The Dead Town* is a novel by Dean Koontz and
the fifth entry in his Dean Koontz's Frankenstein series.
In this series, Koontz places the famous monster-maker
Victor Frankenstein in modern-day America. There, in
Rainbow Falls, Montana, the mad scientist has grown
even madder and wants to use an undead army to take
over the world. Instead of making just one reanimated
corpse creature, he makes many—and instructs them to
make war upon the living! In *The Dead Town*, Koontz
finishes the series with the end of the war against
Frankenstein's multiple monsters and the continuing
struggle for the future of humankind.

Other books by the same author:
Dead and Alive, 2009
The Darkest Evening of the Year, 2007
The Good Guy, 2007
The Face, 2003
Seize the Night, 1999

Other books you might like:
Brian W. Aldiss, *Frankenstein Unbound*, 1973
Christopher Isherwood, *Frankenstein: The True Story*,
    1973
Theodore Roszak, *The Memoirs of Elizabeth
    Frankenstein*, 1995
Mary Shelley, *Frankenstein: The Modern Prometheus*,
    1818
F. Paul Wilson, *The Dark at the End*, 2011

460

VICTORIA LAURIE

Ghouls, Ghouls, Ghouls

(New York: Signet, 2010)

Series: Ghost Hunter Mysteries Series. Book 5
Story type: Contemporary; Series
Subject(s): Horror; Supernatural; Mystery
Major character(s): M.J. Holliday, Television Personality;
    Peter "Gopher" Gophner, Producer (television)
Time period(s): 21st century; 2010s
Locale(s): Ireland

Summary: In the novel *Ghouls, Ghouls, Ghouls* by Victoria Laurie, M.J. Holliday and the crew of the television
program *Ghoul Getters* have arrived in Ireland to
investigate the haunted happenings at Dunlow castle.
According to legend, the island castle holds ancient
treasure as well as a very protective ghost. The rocky
coast and sea surrounding Dunlow are dangerous. When
Peter "Gopher" Gophner, the show's producer, disappears, are Dunlow's natural hazards or supernatural
threats to blame? As Holliday and her ghost busters try
to locate Gopher and the treasure, Dunlow's spirit resists
their intrusion. *Ghouls, Ghouls, Ghouls* is the fifth book
in Laurie's Ghost Hunter Mysteries series.

Other books by the same author:
Ghouls Gone Wild, 2010
A Glimpse of Evil, 2010
Doom with a View, 2009
Ghouls Just Want to Have Fun, 2009

Horror

Death Perception, 2008

Other books you might like:
Casey Daniels, *Dead Man Talking*, 2009
Christopher Golden, *Dark Times*, 2001
Alice Henderson, *Night Terrors*, 2005
Nancy Holder, *Carnival of Souls*, 2006
Yvonne Navarro, *Broken Sunrise*, 2004

461

DAVID LUBAR

Attack of the Vampire Weenies: And Other Warped and Creepy Tales

(New York: Starscape, 2011)

Story type: Collection; Young Adult
Subject(s): Short stories; Horror; Adolescence

Summary: In *Attack of the Vampire Weenies and Other Warped and Creepy Tales*, author David Lubar presents 33 humorous horror stories for children and young adults. The victims in these tales are unlucky adolescents who face a range of monstrous challenges from vampires, amusement-park rides, angry insects, mad inventors, ghosts, cooties, and more. The collection includes "Get Out of Gym for Free," "Ghost in the Well," "It's Only a Game," "The Pyramid Man," "A Cure for an Uncommon Vampire," "Cloudy with a Chance of Message," and others. The author discusses the source of his story ideas in "A Word about These Stories."

Other books by the same author:
The Big Stink, 2010
Dead Guy Spy, 2010
Goop Soup, 2010
My Rotten Life, 2009
Flip, 2003

Other books you might like:
Jim Butcher, *Blood Lite: An Anthology of Humorous Horror Stories Presented by the Horror Writers Association*, 2008
Bruce Coville, *The Ghost in the Third Row*, 1987
R.L. Stine, *Claws!*, 2011
Vivian Vande Velde, *All Hallows' Eve: 13 Stories*, 2006
Jane Yolen, *Here There Be Ghosts*, 1998

462

DAVID LUBAR

Enter the Zombie

(New York: Tom Doherty Associates, 2011)

Series: Nathan Abercrombie: Accidental Zombie Series. Book 5
Story type: Series; Young Adult
Subject(s): Zombies; Schools; Spies
Major character(s): Nathan Abercrombie, 5th Grader, Supernatural Being (zombie), Spy; Rodney, Bully; Abigail, Friend (of Nathan); Mookie, Friend (of Nathan)
Time period(s): 21st century; 2010s
Locale(s): Fictional Location

Summary: In *Enter the Zombie*, the fifth book in author David Lubar's Nathan Abercrombie, Accidental Zombie series, fifth-grader and secret agent Nathan Abercrombie continues his adventures as a reluctant member of the undead race. His body odor is worse than that of most adolescents and his decomposing body is threatening to fall apart, but at least Nathan can rely on friends Mookie and Abigail. When an evil plot is uncovered at Belgosi Upper Elementary School, Nathan is called into action by the Bureau of Useful Misadventures (BUM). As Nathan works to take down the head of RABID (Raise Anarchy By Inciting Disorder), he risks revealing that he is a zombie.

Other books by the same author:
The Big Stink, 2010
Dead Guy Spy, 2010
Goop Soup, 2010
My Rotten Life, 2009
Flip, 2003

Other books you might like:
MaryJanice Davidson, *Dead and Loving It*, 2006
Harrison Geillor, *The Zombies of Lake Woebegotten*, 2010
Lori Handeland, *Shakespeare Undead*, 2010
A. Lee Martinez, *Gil's All Fright Diner*, 2005
E. Van Lowe, *Never Slow Dance with a Zombie*, 2009

463

MARI MANCUSI

Night School

(New York: Berkley Books, 2011)

Series: Blood Coven Series. Book 5
Story type: Fantasy
Subject(s): Fantasy; Vampires; Schools
Major character(s): Rayne McDonald, Vampire, Student, Sister (of Sunny); Sunny McDonald, Vampire, Student, Sister (of Rayne)
Time period(s): 21st century
Locale(s): Switzerland

Summary: *Night School* is a young adult fantasy novel by Mari Mancusi and the fifth entry in her Blood Coven series about teenage drama and high-school relationships—for a group of vampires. In *Night School*, vampire teen twins Rayne and Sunny McDonald find out that their hip vampire family has a secret: they are part fairy. This realization leads to all sorts of problems including an attempt on their lives. Rayne and Sunny must leave their vampire boyfriends and go to a vampire school hidden in the Swiss Alps. There, they realize the lessons aren't about reading, writing, and arithmetic, but about killing vampires.

Where it's reviewed:
Library Journal, January 2011, page 87

Other books by the same author:
Blood Ties, 2011

Bad Blood, 2010
Girls That Growl, 2007
Boys That Bite, 2006
Stake That!, 2006

Other books you might like:
Jenna Black, *Hungers of the Heart*, 2008
Rachel Caine, *Carpe Corpus*, 2009
Tate Hallaway, *Almost to Die For*, 2010
Alyxandra Harvey, *Hearts at Stake*, 2010
Chloe Neill, *Friday Night Bites*, 2009

464

ISAAC MARION

Warm Bodies

(New York: Simon and Schuster, 2011)

Story type: Zombies
Subject(s): Supernatural; Romances (Fiction); Fantasy
Major character(s): R., Supernatural Being (zombie); Julie, Human, Young Woman
Time period(s): Indeterminate Future

Summary: *Warm Bodies* is the debut novel of author Isaac Marion. R. is one of the undead, a zombie making his way through life in a post-apocalyptic USA where society is in chaos and few humans remain. Despite his lack of humanity, R. still feels a very human need to love and be loved. One day, while eating the brain of a teenager, he begins to feel the same emotions that the young man felt toward his girlfriend. As R. seeks to win the love of this girl, named Julie, he begins a transformation that could alter all of zombie-kind. First novel.

Where it's reviewed:
Publishers Weekly, March 21, 2011, page 52

Other books you might like:
Brian Keene, *The Rising*, 2003
Jonathan Maberry, *The Dragon Factory*, 2010
Kim Paffenroth, *Dying to Live: A Novel of Life Among the Undead*, 2008
Del Stone Jr., *Dead Heat*, 1996
Tim Waggoner, *Nekropolis*, 2010

465

RICHARD MATHESON

Other Kingdoms

(New York: Tor, 2011)

Story type: Romantic Suspense
Subject(s): Horror; Fantasy; Romances (Fiction)
Major character(s): Alex White, 18-Year-Old, Veteran (World War I); Magda, Witch; Ruthana, Mythical Creature (fairy)
Time period(s): 20th century; 1910s (1918)
Locale(s): Gatford, England

Summary: In the novel *Other Kingdoms* by Richard Matheson, 18-year-old Alex White comes to Gatford, England to recover from the horrors he witnessed fight-ing in the Great War. Gatford seems a peaceful community, despite the rumors of an otherworldly presence in the nearby forest. Alex doesn't believe in spirits until he falls under the spell of two local women. Magda, a witch with red hair, enchants Alex and warns him of the dangerous fairies that live in the woods. Of course Magda's cautions only make Alex more eager to discover the wonders of the fairy world. Soon Alex's heart is divided as he chooses between two women from the supernatural realm.

Where it's reviewed:
Booklist, March 1, 2011, page 37
Library Journal, March 1, 2011, page 72
Locus, March 2011, page 17
Publishers Weekly, January 17, 2011, page 28

Other books by the same author:
Visions of Death, 2007
The Link, 2006
Offbeat, 2002
Seven Steps to Midnight, 1993
I Am Legend, 1954

Other books you might like:
Jonathan Carroll, *The Land of Laughs*, 1980
Stephen King, *Bag of Bones*, 1998
Dean R. Koontz, *Hideaway*, 1992
Dan Simmons, *Summer of Night*, 1991
Peter Straub, *In the Night Room*, 2004

466

SEAN MCCABE

Uprising

(New York: Penguin, 2011)

Series: Vampire Federation Series. Book 1
Story type: Series; Vampire Story
Subject(s): Horror; Vampires; Fantasy
Major character(s): Joel Solomon, Detective (inspector); Alexandra Bishop, Vampire, Agent (Vampire Federation)
Time period(s): 21st century; 2010s
Locale(s): England

Summary: In the horror novel *Uprising* by Sean McCabe, the Vampire Federation is responsible for policing the activities of its members around the world. Agent Alex Bishop works hard to ensure that her fellow vampires follow the Federation's laws, but a faction of vampires wants to resort to the old ways of their race. Their revolt against the Federation would bring an outbreak of bloodshed and horror. When Detective Inspector Joel Solomon investigates a grisly crime scene in Oxford-shire, he recognizes it as the work of vampires. As Joel prepares for an increase in vampire violence, Alex struggles to control the uprising among her race. *Uprising* is the first book in McCabe's Vampire Federation series.

Other books by the same author:
The Cross, 2011

Other books you might like:
Simon Clark, *Vampyrrhic*, 2002

Barbara Hambly, *Renfield: Slave of Dracula*, 2006
Brian Lumley, *Blood Brothers*, 1992
Michael Romkey, *The London Vampire Panic*, 2001

467

SEAN MCCABE

The Cross

(New York: Signet, 2011)

Series: Vampire Federation Series. Book 2
Story type: Vampire Story
Subject(s): Vampires; Supernatural; Detective fiction
Major character(s): Gabriel Stone, Vampire; Joel Solomon, Detective (inspector), Vampire; Alexandra Bishop, Agent (Vampire Federation), Vampire

Summary: *The Cross* is an installment from Sean McCabe's Vampire Federation series. The Vampire Federation is a group of vampires sworn to protect the boundaries between the human and vampire world. Gabriel Stone, a sinister vampire and enemy of the Federation, wants nothing more than to end humans' reign over vampires. When he hears of the discovery of the Cross of Ardaich, an ancient artifact that gives vampires ultimate power over the world, he swears he will find it. Now it is up to Detective Joel Solomon and agent Alexandra Bishop of the Federation to stop him before it is too late, not just for traditional vampires but for the entire planet.

Other books by the same author:
Uprising, 2011

Other books you might like:
Gherbod Fleming, *Brujah*, 2000
Stefan Petrucha, *Assamite*, 2002
Adrian Phoenix, *A Rush of Wings*, 2007
Jeanne C. Stein, *Retribution*, 2009
Shiloh Walker, *Hunting the Hunter*, 2006

468

JOE MCKINNEY

Flesh Eaters

(New York: Pinnacle, 2011)

Story type: Contemporary
Subject(s): Zombies; Adventure; Survival
Major character(s): Eleanor Norton, Police Officer (Emergency Ops)
Time period(s): 21st century; 2010s
Locale(s): Houston, Texas

Summary: Joe McKinney's *Flesh Eaters* is a terrifying tale of the undead—and the lone woman out to stop their maniacal feeding. In Houston, Texas, torrents of rain are causing the city streets to flood. Along with the flood waters come legions of zombies, on the rampage for human flesh. Eleanor Norton is an emergency worker now facing the biggest challenge of her career. She not only must save the innocent and struggling citizens of Houston, but she must take on the forces of the undead.

When the feeding commences, Eleanor must work against the clock to get a small group of survivors to a section of the city that remains free of the ravenous flesh eaters.

Other books by the same author:
Apocalypse of the Dead, 2010
Quarantined, 2009
Dead City, 2006

Other books you might like:
Max Brooks, *World War Z: An Oral History of the Zombie War*, 2006
Brian Keene, *Dead Sea*, 2007
Kim Paffenroth, *Dying to Live: A Novel of Life Among the Undead*, 2008
John Russo, *Return of the Living Dead*, 1997
David Wellington, *Monster Island*, 2006

469

GARY MCMAHON

Pretty Little Dead Things

(Nottingham, UK: Angry Robot, 2011)

Series: Thomas Usher Series. Book 1
Story type: Psychic Powers
Subject(s): Accidents; Death; Psychics
Major character(s): Thomas Usher, Psychic

Summary: *Pretty Little Dead Things* is the first book in author Gary McMahon's Thomas Usher series. Thomas Usher is a regular family man until a devastating car wreck claims the lives of his wife and child. Shattered by grief, Thomas still must pick up the pieces and move on with his own life. Then he begins to see them: ghosts, wandering among the living, looking for a way to cross over into the afterlife. They need Thomas's help, and he hopes that by helping them he will once again meet up with his family. But when Thomas is asked to help with an investigation into the death of an organized-crime boss's daughter, his powers become more real than he ever imagined they could.

Where it's reviewed:
Publishers Weekly, November 8, 2010, page 46

Other books you might like:
Jes Battis, *Infernal Affairs*, 2011
Laurell K. Hamilton, *Bloody Bones*, 1996
Charlaine Harris, *Dead as a Doornail*, 2005
Kat Richardson, *Underground*, 2008
Jory Sherman, *Vegas Vampire*, 1980

470

A.E. MOORAT

Henry VIII, Wolfman

(London: Hodder & Stoughton, 2010)

Story type: Historical; Werewolf Story
Subject(s): Werewolves; Horror; British history, 1066-1688

Major character(s): Henry VIII, Royalty (king of England), Historical Figure, Werewolf; Anne Boleyn, Spouse (of Henry), Werewolf, Historical Figure; Thomas Moore, Historical Figure, Werewolf (accused); Jane Seymour, Spouse (of Henry), Hunter (of werewolves), Historical Figure
Time period(s): 16th century
Locale(s): England

Summary: In the horror novel *Henry VIII, Wolfman*, author A.E. Moorat creates an alternate account of one of England's most notorious rulers, portraying the king as a ferocious werewolf. Attacked by a werewolf while trying to protect his son, Henry VIII adapts well to his new existence. In fact, lycanthropy suits the sovereign's innate appetite for excesses. Of course his condition affects his spousal relationships. Like her husband, Anne Boleyn embraces the lycanthropic lifestyle while Jane Seymour becomes a werewolf hunter. The resulting tale is even more bloody than Henry VIII's true reign. Moorat is also the author of *Queen Victoria, Vampire Hunter*.

Where it's reviewed:
Publishers Weekly, May 23, 2011, page 33

Other books by the same author:
Queen Victoria, Demon Hunter, 2010

Other books you might like:
Gary Brandner, *The Howling*, 1977
Michael Cadnum, *Saint Peter's Wolf*, 1991
Ray Garton, *Ravenous*, 2008
Rick Hautala, *Moondeath*, 1981
Thomas Tessier, *The Nightwalker*, 1979

471

JESSE PETERSEN

Flip This Zombie

(New York: Orbit, 2011)

Series: Living with the Dead Series. Book 2
Story type: Series; Zombies
Subject(s): Horror; Fantasy; Zombies
Major character(s): Sarah, Spouse (of David), Businesswoman (ZombieBusters); David, Spouse (of Sarah), Businessman (ZombieBusters)
Time period(s): Indeterminate Future
Locale(s): Arizona, United States

Summary: In the novel *Flip this Zombie* by Jesse Petersen, married couple David and Sarah make the most of the recent Zombie Apocalypse by launching a business that will guarantee them plenty of customers. As the proprietors of Zombiebusters Exterminators Inc., the resourceful entrepreneurs offer a range of zombie-removal services. Traveling south in their vintage van to sunny Arizona, David and Sarah accept a client with an unusual request—he wants his zombies taken alive so he can use them as scientific test subjects. Can the zombie-slaying couple succeed as zombie catchers? *Flip this Zombie* is the second book in Petersen's Living with the Dead series.

Where it's reviewed:
Publishers Weekly, November 1, 2010, page 31

Other books by the same author:
Eat Slay Love, 2011
Married with Zombies, 2010

Other books you might like:
Bob Fingerman, *Pariah*, 2010
Harrison Geillor, *The Zombies of Lake Woebegotten*, 2010
Mira Grant, *Feed*, 2010
David Lubar, *My Rotten Life*, 2009
E. Van Lowe, *Never Slow Dance with a Zombie*, 2009

472

JESSE PETERSEN

Eat Slay Love

(New York: Hachette Book Group, 2011)

Series: Living with the Dead Series. Book 3
Story type: Zombies
Subject(s): Supernatural; Apocalypse; Zombies
Major character(s): Sarah, Spouse (of Dave); Dave, Spouse (of Sarah)
Locale(s): United States

Summary: *Eat Slay Love* is the third book in author Jesse Petersen's Living with the Dead series. Sarah and her husband, Dave, are still on the run after the zombie apocalypse and are searching for a rumored safe haven built by the government at the beginning of the outbreak. The Midwest Wall supposedly keeps the rest of the United States safe from the zombie attacks that have plagued the western part of the country, but Sarah and Dave can't be sure that the Wall even exists. Still, they will take their chances, because they have a small vial of a potential cure for zombie-ism. Unfortunately, a band of backwoods renegades have stopped the duo in their tracks, and now Sarah and Dave must figure out a way not only to thwart the onslaught of zombies but also anyone else who might get in their way.

Where it's reviewed:
Publishers Weekly, May 16, 2011, page 60

Other books by the same author:
Flip This Zombie, 2011
Married with Zombies, 2010

Other books you might like:
Harrison Geillor, *The Zombies of Lake Woebegotten*, 2010
David Lubar, *My Rotten Life*, 2009
A. Lee Martinez, *Gil's All Fright Diner*, 2005
John Russo, *Return of the Living Dead*, 1997
E. Van Lowe, *Never Slow Dance with a Zombie*, 2009

473

ADRIAN PHOENIX

Black Heart Loa

(New York: Simon and Schuster, 2011)

Story type: Supernatural Vengeance
Subject(s): Voodooism; Werewolves; Southern United States

Major character(s): Kallie Riviere, Young Woman; Devlin Daniels, Werewolf
Locale(s): Louisiana, United States
Summary: *Black Heart Loa* is the sequel to the novel *Black Dust Mambo*, both of which were written by author Adrian Phoenix. Deep in the heart of Cajun country, aspiring voodoo priestess Kallie Riviere uncovers a plot to disable the magic protecting Louisiana. When a powerful storm forms off the Gulf Coast and heads straight for New Orleans and certain devastation, Kallie must figure out a way to put the voodoo back in place. Soon she learns, however, that she might be the one undoing the magic after all. Meanwhile, a werewolf named Devlin comes to Kallie's aid—but is he a friend or foe?

Other books by the same author:
Etched in Bone, 2011
Beneath the Skin, 2010
Black Dust Mambo, 2010
In the Blood, 2008
A Rush of Wings, 2007

Other books you might like:
Jan Alexander, *Darkwater*, 1975
Hugh B. Cave, *The Restless Dead*, 2003
James Herbert, *Portent*, 1996
James Osier, *Covenant at Coldwater*, 1983
Douglas Preston, *Cemetery Dance*, 2009

474

ADRIAN PHOENIX

Etched in Bone

(New York: Pocket Books, 2011)

Series: Maker's Song Series. Book 4
Story type: Contemporary; Series
Subject(s): Horror; Fantasy; Supernatural
Major character(s): Dante Baptiste, Vampire, Musician (rock star), Lover (of Heather); Heather Wallace, FBI Agent, Lover (of Dante)
Time period(s): 21st century; 2010s
Locale(s): New Orleans, Louisiana

Summary: In *Etched in Bone*, the fourth book in Adrian Phoenix's Maker's Song series, Dante Baptiste and his band Inferno have come to New Orleans. Dante's looks and stardom make him the object of much adoration, but he is also greatly desired by three very different organizations. A vampire and the offspring of a fallen angel, Dante is wanted by his undead brethren as a pawn and by the Fallen as a leader. Humans want him, too, so they can harness his power. Heather Wallace, an FBI agent and Dante's mortal lover, has become the vampire's ally. But as Dante chooses his destiny, another adversary may emerge who's very close to Heather.

Other books by the same author:
Black Heart Loa, 2011
Beneath the Skin, 2010
Black Dust Mambo, 2010
In the Blood, 2008
A Rush of Wings, 2007

Other books you might like:
Christine Feehan, *Dark Peril*, 2010
Yasmine Galenorn, *Blood Wyne*, 2011
Chris Marie Green, *The Path of Razors*, 2009
Cherie Priest, *Bloodshot*, 2011
Lilith Saintcrow, *Night Shift*, 2008

475

ALEX PRENTISS

Dark Waters

(New York: Bantam Books, 2011)

Story type: Fantasy
Subject(s): Supernatural; Fantasy; Murder
Major character(s): Rachel Matre, Cook, Businesswoman (owns diner), Detective—Amateur (trying to save a supernatural lake)
Time period(s): 21st century
Locale(s): Madison, Wisconsin

Summary: *Dark Waters* is a novel by Alex Prentiss about a supernatural lake that one woman loves and shadowy villains are willing to kill for. Known to her neighbors as "Lady of the Lake," Rachel Matre is a chef in Madison, Wisconsin. Her unusual nickname comes from the fact that every night she swims naked in Lake Mendota, where spirits fill her with a feeling of understanding and fantastic pleasure. But there is trouble lurking nearby. A money-grubbing land developer wants to buy the lake, and soon a killer is on the loose nearby. Matre loves the lake and decides to get to the bottom of the crime and save the lake before she becomes the next victim.

Other books by the same author:
Night Tides, 2010

Other books you might like:
Christopher Buehlman, *Those Across the River*, 2011
Jonathan Carroll, *Voice of Our Shadow*, 1983
John Coyne, *Child of Shadows*, 1990
John Farris, *Son of the Endless Night*, 1985
Tim Powers, *The Stress of Her Regard*, 1989

476

CHERIE PRIEST

Hellbent

(New York: Spectra, 2011)

Series: Cheshire Red Reports Series. Book 2
Story type: Fantasy
Subject(s): Fantasy; Supernatural; Vampires
Major character(s): Raylene Pendle, Vampire, Thief (cat burglar); Adrian DeJesus, Military Personnel (former Navy SEAL and drag queen); Ian Stott, Vampire, Blind Person
Time period(s): 21st century
Locale(s): Seattle, Washington

Summary: *Hellbent* by Cherie Priest is a fantasy novel about supernatural crime, mystery, and cross-dressing. The main character, Raylene Pendle, is a sneaky vampire

who takes a job that involves tracking down and stealing ancient artifacts of great power. This mission is dangerous enough, but Raylene has more to worry about than just keeping herself safe. She also finds a partner-in-crime called Adrian DeJesus, who was once a Navy SEAL and is now a tough-as-nails drag queen. Raylene and Adrian have to find the artifacts while fighting evil wizards and helping a blind vampire named Ian Stott who is next on an assassin's hit list.

Where it's reviewed:
Publishers Weekly, June 6, 2011, page 28

Other books by the same author:
Bloodshot, 2011
Fathom, 2008
Dreadful Skin, 2007
Nor Flesh Nor Feathers, 2007
Wings to the Kingdom, 2006

Other books you might like:
Meljean Brook, *Demon Forged*, 2009
Lee Killough, *Blood Hunt*, 1987
Jonathan Nasaw, *Shadows*, 1997
Jeanne C. Stein, *Legacy*, 2008
S.A. Swiniarski, *Raven*, 1996

477

CHERIE PRIEST

Bloodshot

(New York: Spectra-Ballantine Books, 2011)

Series: Cheshire Red Reports Series. Book 1
Story type: Fantasy; Series
Subject(s): Vampires; Urban life; Fantasy
Major character(s): Raylene Pendle, Thief (cat burglar), Vampire; Ian Stott, Vampire, Blind Person
Time period(s): 21st century; 2010s
Locale(s): United States

Summary: In the novel *Bloodshot* by Cherie Priest, vampire Raylene Pendle makes her living as a thief, stealing art, jewelry, and other items desired by her well-paying clients. Her latest case may be her strangest—and most dangerous—yet. Ian Stott, a fellow vampire, wants Raylene to obtain a stash of secret medical files. Ian was blinded during experiments conducted by the government and he believes that the documents hold the secret to restoring his sight. But the government doesn't want Raylene or Ian to get their hands on the "Bloodshot" project files. As agents and scientists tail her, Raylene is joined by a transvestite who also has a personal interest in the case. *Bloodshot* is the first book in the Cheshire Red Reports series.

Where it's reviewed:
Booklist, February 1, 2011, page 41
Library Journal, January 2011, page 87
Publishers Weekly, December 6, 2010, page 35

Other books by the same author:
Dreadnought, 2010
Fathom, 2008
Dreadful Skin, 2007
Nor Flesh Nor Feathers, 2007

Wings to the Kingdom, 2006

Other books you might like:
Meljean Brook, *Demon Blood*, 2010
Lee Killough, *Blood Hunt*, 1987
Robert R. McCammon, *The Wolf's Hour*, 1989
Jeanne C. Stein, *The Becoming*, 2006
S.A. Swiniarski, *Raven*, 1996

478

JOSEPH S. PULVER SR.

Sin & Ashes

(New York: Hippocampus Press, 2011)

Story type: Collection
Subject(s): Short stories; Horror

Summary: In *Sin and Ashes*, author Joseph S. Pulver, Sr. presents more than 50 tales of horror. Dark, grim, and lyrically written, Pulver's short stories explore the terrors that reside in the supernatural realm and the human spirit. In "She's Waiting," Pulver brings readers into the world of the werewolf, where they experience the excruciating process of lycanthropic transformation. "As the Sun Still Burns Away" finds a deceased witch seeking revenge on the residents of her community. "Caligari, Again" revisits the strange world created in the 1920s silent German film, *The Cabinet of Dr. Caligari*. Horror and fantasy author Laird Barron provides the collection's introduction.

Other books by the same author:
Blood Will Have Its Season, 2009

Other books you might like:
Donald R. Burleson, *Wait for the Thunder: Stories for a Stormy Night*, 2010
Charles L. Grant, *Tales from the Nightside*, 1981
Brian Keene, *Unhappy Endings*, 2009
David Morrell, *Nightscape*, 2004
Jeffrey Thomas, *Nocturnal Emissions*, 2010

479

EILEEN RENDAHL

Dead on Delivery

(New York: Berkley Trade, 2011)

Series: Messenger Series. Book 2
Subject(s): Good and evil; Murder; Supernatural
Major character(s): Melina Markowitz, Detective—Amateur, Psychic (Messenger)
Time period(s): 21st century; 2010s
Locale(s): Sacramento, California

Summary: Paranormal messenger Melina Markowitz returns in the second installment of Eileen Rendahl's Messenger series. *Dead on Delivery* finds Melina faced with her most perplexing case yet. Two men, each of whom were recipients of messages she herself delivered, have suddenly turned up dead. As she launches her own investigation into the unexplained deaths, Melina

unearths some shocking commonalities between the two men. The forces of evil at work in Sacramento take notice, too, and Melina soon realizes she will have to duke it out with these malevolent forces if she's going to solve the mysteries at hand.

Other books by the same author:
Don't Kill the Messenger, 2010
Un-Bridaled, 2008
Un-Veiled, 2007
Balancing in High Heels, 2005
Do Me, Do My Roots, 2004

Other books you might like:
Rachel Caine, *Thin Air*, 2007
Lisa Cantrell, *Boneman*, 1992
Hugh B. Cave, *Legion of the Dead*, 1979
Maggie Davis, *Forbidden Objects*, 1986
Graham Masterton, *Night Wars*, 2006

480

MICHELLE ROWEN

Nightshade

(New York: Berkley, 2011)

Series: Nightshade Series. Book 1
Story type: Series; Vampire Story
Subject(s): Horror; Vampires; Romances (Fiction)
Major character(s): Jillian "Jill" Conrad, Office Worker, Vampire Hunter; Declan Reyes, Vampire
Time period(s): 21st century; 2010s
Locale(s): San Diego, California

Summary: In the novel *Nightshade* by Michelle Rowen, an office worker at a California investment firm goes out for a dose of coffee and is injected with anti-vampire serum instead. When Jill Conrad receives the shot of vampire poison from a mysterious man, she is sickened immediately. The serum has made her blood both desirable and deadly to vampires. Declan Reese, a half-vampire, kills Jill's attacker but he is also susceptible to the powers of the serum pulsing through the young woman's veins. Declan takes Jill to a secret laboratory for treatment, but the bond between mortal and immortal is overwhelming. This novel is the first book in Rowen's Nightshade series.

Where it's reviewed:
Booklist, February 1, 2011, page 43
Publishers Weekly, December 20, 2010, page 40

Other books by the same author:
The Demon in Me, 2010
Something Wicked, 2010
Lady and the Vamp, 2008
Fanged and Fabulous, 2007
Bitten and Smitten, 2006

Other books you might like:
Chris Marie Green, *Deep in the Woods*, 2010
Angela Knight, *Master of Fire*, 2010
Marjorie M. Liu, *A Wild Light*, 2010
Kat Richardson, *Vanished*, 2009
Eileen Wilks, *Mortal Sins*, 2009

481

MICHELLE ROWEN

Bloodlust

(New York: Berkley, 2011)

Series: Nightshade Series. Book 2
Story type: Contemporary; Series
Subject(s): Vampires; Adventure; Violence
Major character(s): Jillian "Jill" Conrad, Vampire Hunter; Declan, Vampire
Time period(s): 21st century; 2010s
Locale(s): United States

Summary: Michelle Rowen's *Bloodlust* is the second installment in the Nightshade series and continues the adventures of Jillian "Jill" Conrad, a young woman whose blood is lethal to vampires—and to herself. Now that she has eliminated the king of the vamps, Jill takes it upon herself to protect his baby daughter from the ravenous bloodsuckers who want them both dead. Sympathetic vampire Declan is out to save Jill and her charge from the marauding masses, but even he cannot stand up to the terrifying adversary who is about to rise up and go after Jill and the vampire king's young daughter.

Where it's reviewed:
Booklist, May 15, 2011, page 26

Other books by the same author:
The Demon in Me, 2010
Something Wicked, 2010
Lady and the Vamp, 2008
Fanged and Fabulous, 2007
Bitten and Smitten, 2006

Other books you might like:
Laurell K. Hamilton, *Danse Macabre*, 2006
Nancy Holzner, *Bloodstone*, 2011
Devon Monk, *Magic to the Bone*, 2008
Chloe Neill, *Twice Bitten*, 2010
Dianne Sylvan, *Queen of Shadows*, 2010

482

DIANA ROWLAND

My Life as a White Trash Zombie

(New York: DAW Books, 2011)

Series: White Trash Zombie Series. Book 1
Story type: Zombies
Subject(s): Supernatural; Accidents; Zombies
Major character(s): Angel Crawford, Supernatural Being
Locale(s): Louisiana, United States

Summary: *My Life as a White Trash Zombie* is the first book in author Diana Rowland's White Trash Zombie series. Angel Crawford is the epitome of white trash: she lives deep in the bayou of Louisiana, has a rap sheet as long as her arm, dropped out of school, and her only true loves are drugs and booze. Then she wakes up in a hospital bed after an accident with no memory of what happened or who she was before. At the same time, a se-

rial killer who leaves victims without their heads sparks Angel's attention. For once, Angel is inspired to do some good and get to the bottom of who is committing these crimes. Now if only she could shake her craving for brains.

Where it's reviewed:
Publishers Weekly, May 23, 2011, page 34

Other books by the same author:
Secrets of the Demon, 2011
Blood of the Demon, 2010
Mark of the Demon, 2009

Other books you might like:
Harrison Geillor, *The Zombies of Lake Woebegotten*, 2010
David Lubar, *The Big Stink*, 2010
A. Lee Martinez, *Gil's All Fright Diner*, 2005
Jesse Petersen, *Married with Zombies*, 2010
E. Van Lowe, *Never Slow Dance with a Zombie*, 2009

483

DIANA ROWLAND

Secrets of the Demon

(New York: Bantam Books, 2011)

Series: Kara Gillian Series. Book 3
Story type: Fantasy; Romantic Suspense
Subject(s): Occultism; Demons; Detective fiction
Major character(s): Kara Gillian, Detective—Police, Psychic
Locale(s): New Orleans, Louisiana

Summary: *Secrets of the Demon* is the third book in author Diana Rowland's series featuring supernatural detective Kara Gillian. This time, Kara has left her hometown of Beaulac, Louisiana, for the Big Easy to work on a case with the FBI's supernatural-crimes division. When a goth-rock singer is threatened by a soul-eater, it's up to Kara to protect the star. The singer disappears anyway, but this time the culprit is no supernatural force that Kara has ever seen. Then the murders begin, and Kara must race against the clock to figure out how these serial killings are connected to the New Orleans goth-rock scene.

Other books by the same author:
My Life As a White Trash Zombie, 2011
Blood of the Demon, 2010
Mark of the Demon, 2009

Other books you might like:
Patricia Briggs, *Iron Kissed*, 2008
Karen Chance, *Curse the Dawn*, 2009
Laurell K. Hamilton, *Flirt*, 2010
Charlaine Harris, *Dead in the Family*, 2010
Adrian Phoenix, *Black Dust Mambo*, 2010

484

CASSIE RYAN (Pseudonym of Tina Gerow)

The Demon and the Succubus

(New York: Berkley Trade, 2011)

Series: Sisters of Darkness Series. Book 2
Subject(s): Supernatural; Sexual behavior; Sexuality
Major character(s): Amalya, Supernatural Being (succubus), Prostitute; Lilith, Royalty (queen of Amalya)
Time period(s): Indeterminate
Locale(s): Nevada, United States

Summary: *The Demon and the Succubus* is a novel by Cassie Ryan and an entry in her Sisters of Darkness series. In *The Demon and the Succubus*, a succubus called Amalya works in a brothel where her supernatural mistress, Lilith, forces her to seduce men and bring them into her wicked ways. When she falls in love with one of her clients, however, Amalya's job is on the line and Lilith won't allow her to leave. When Amalya tries to escape, Lilith and a demon try to stop her. Cassie Ryan tells all about supernatural sex and scheming in *The Demon and the Succubus*.

Where it's reviewed:
Romantic Times, April 2011, page 100

Other books by the same author:
Seducing the Succubus, 2010
Trio of Seduction, 2009
Vision of Seduction, 2008
Ceremony of Seduction, 2007

Other books you might like:
Rick Hautala, *Winter Wake*, 1989
Larissa Ione, *Eternal Rider*, 2011
Tim Powers, *The Stress of Her Regard*, 1989
Ray Russell, *Incubus*, 1975
J.R. Ward, *Lover Unleashed*, 2011

485

STEVEN C. SCHLOZMAN

The Zombie Autopsies: Secret Notebooks from the Apocalypse

(New York: Grand Central Publishing, 2011)

Story type: Zombies
Subject(s): Zombies; Medicine; Humor
Major character(s): Steven C. Schlozman, Doctor
Time period(s): Indeterminate

Summary: *The Zombie Autopsies: Secret Notebooks from the Apocalypse* is a fictitious medical journal written by the fictional neurobiologist Steven C. Schlozman, M.D. Schlozman is an expert on zombies, who are afflicted with a disorder he has coined Ataxic Neurodegenerative Satiety Deficiency Syndrome. This illness is responsible for the vacuous stares and staggerings, as well as the constant hunger for brains, which are characteristics of zombie nature. As a member of the 75 percent who have this disorder, Schlozman is determined to study it and reveal his findings. This notebook tells the story of

Horror

Schlozman and his team as they search for a cure for the disorder before it is too late.

Other books you might like:
Alden Bell, *The Reapers Are the Angels*, 2010
J.L. Bourne, *Day by Day Armageddon: Beyond Exile*, 2010
Jonathan Maberry, *Patient Zero*, 2009
Joe McKinney, *Flesh Eaters*, 2011
Del Stone Jr., *Black Tide*, 2007

486

ELLEN SCHREIBER

Vampire Kisses 8: Cryptic Cravings

(New York: HarperCollins, 2011)

Series: Vampire Kisses. Book 8
Subject(s): Fantasy; Vampires; Adolescence
Major character(s): Raven, Teenager, Girlfriend (of Alexander); Alexander, Vampire, Boyfriend (of Raven); Jagger, Vampire, Manager (of nightclub)
Time period(s): 21st century; 2010s
Locale(s): Dullsville, Fictional Location

Summary: *Vampire Kisses 8: Cryptic Cravings* by Ellen Schreiber is an adolescent melodrama novel about high-school vampires fretting about their social and sex lives. In this story, Dullsville teen Raven has a vampire boyfriend named Alexander. Raven wonders what Alexander thinks of her and whether he will try to make her a vampire, too. Then they hear about another vampire, Jagger, who wants to open a nightclub called the Crypt. Raven has her own vision of this new nighttime hot spot and hopes that Jagger lets her help with the design. *Cryptic Cravings* is the eighth installment in the Vampire Kisses series.

Other books by the same author:
Once in a Full Moon, 2010
The Coffin Club, 2009
Dance with a Vampire, 2009
Kissing Coffins, 2005
Vampire Kisses, 2003

Other books you might like:
Karen Chance, *Embrace the Night*, 2008
Christine Feehan, *Dark Celebration*, 2006
Faith Hunter, *Blood Cross*, 2010
Michelle Rowen, *Bloodlust*, 2011
Eileen Wilks, *Bloodlines*, 2007

487

THOMAS E. SNIEGOSKI

A Hundred Words for Hate

(New York: ROC, 2011)

Series: Remy Chandler Series. Book 4
Story type: Fantasy; Series
Subject(s): Angels; Occultism; Mystery

Major character(s): Remy Chandler, Angel, Detective—Private
Time period(s): 21st century; 2010s
Locale(s): Boston, Massachusetts

Summary: In *A Hundred Words for Hate* by Thomas E. Sniegoski, Remy Chandler is a private detective in Boston with a unique perspective on human nature. Years ago, Remy lived in heaven as an angel named Remiel. Now earthbound by choice, Remy combines his powers of divine intervention with his investigative skills to solve unusual cases. His latest assignment, proposed by the Sons of Adam, is to locate the missing key to the gates of the Garden of Eden. But other immortals believe that the gates should remain locked to contain the evil hidden inside. *A Hundred Words for Hate* is the fourth book in Sniegoski's Remy Chandler series.

Where it's reviewed:
Publishers Weekly, January 17, 2011, page 34

Other books by the same author:
Where Angels Fear to Tread, 2010
Dancing on the Head of a Pin, 2009
The Fallen, 2003
Leviathan, 2003
Soul Trade, 2001

Other books you might like:
P.N. Elrod, *Cold Streets*, 2003
William Hjortsberg, *Falling Angel*, 1978
Tanya Huff, *Blood Debt*, 1997
Nalini Singh, *Angels' Blood*, 2009
Marvin Werlin, *The Savior*, 1978

488

JASON STARR

The Pack

(New York: Ace Books, 2011)

Story type: Paranormal
Subject(s): Suspense; Fathers; Parenthood
Major character(s): Simon Burns, Spouse (of Alison), Father (of Jeremy); Alison Burns, Spouse (of Simon), Mother (of Jeremy); Jeremy Burns, 3-Year-Old, Son (of Simon and Alison)
Locale(s): New York, New York

Summary: *The Pack* is a novel written by author Jason Starr. After being let go from his high-powered position at a New York City firm, Simon Burns must embark on the humiliating task of acting as stay-at-home father to his son while his wife Alison earns the family's sole income. Then he meets a group of stay-at-home dads who are in the same boat. Finally, Simon begins to feel as if he belongs again—until he awakens after a late-night bender alone, naked, and far away from his house. News of his boss's death soon reaches Simon, and all reports indicate that the man was killed by some type of animal. Soon Simon begins to suspect something that can't possibly be true—that he may have transformed into a werewolf.

Where it's reviewed:
Publishers Weekly, April 18, 2011, page 32

Other books by the same author:
Panic Attack, 2009
The Follower, 2008
Hard Feelings, 2002
Cold Collar, 1998

Other books you might like:
Gary Brandner, *The Howling*, 1977
P.D. Cacek, *Canyons*, 2000
John Farris, *High Bloods*, 2009
Ray Garton, *Bestial*, 2009
Dean R. Koontz, *Midnight*, 1989

489

JEANNE C. STEIN

Crossroads

(New York: Ace Books, 2011)

Series: Anna Strong Series. Book 7
Story type: Vampire Story
Subject(s): Supernatural; Vampires; Fantasy
Major character(s): Anna Strong, Vampire; Max, FBI Agent

Summary: *Crossroads* is the seventh novel by author Jeanne C. Stein featuring bounty hunter-turned-vampire Anna Strong. Anna is still reeling from the demise of her vampire mentor when her ex-boyfriend Max comes to her for help. Max is an FBI agent, and the last mortal to love and leave Anna. Anna must put her feelings aside, however, and help Max deal with the case at hand: a bunch of bodies have been found along the US-Mexico border, and all of them have been exsanguinated. Now Anna must figure out if the culprit is human or vamp and what should be done about it.

Other books by the same author:
Chosen, 2010
Retribution, 2009
Legacy, 2008
The Becoming, 2006
Blood Drive, 2006

Other books you might like:
Christine Cody, *Blood Rules*, 2011
Nancy A. Collins, *A Dozen Black Roses*, 1996
Cherie Priest, *Hellbent*, 2011
Whitley Strieber, *The Last Vampire*, 2001
Dianne Sylvan, *Shadowflame*, 2011

490

R.L. STINE

Weirdo Halloween

(New York: Scholastic Inc., 2011)

Story type: Holiday Themes; Young Adult
Subject(s): Halloween; Extraterrestrial life; Suspense
Major character(s): Chris, Twin (of Meg), Brother (of Meg); Meg, Sister (of Chris), Twin (of Chris); Bim the Weirdo, Alien

Summary: *Weirdo Halloween* is the sixteenth book in author R.L. Stine's Goosebumps Horrorland series. Horrorland is an amusement park dedicated to the scariness of Halloween; the only problem is, sometimes things get a little too scary in Horrorland. This time, twin brother and sister Chris and Meg meet up with a strange trick-or-treater who everyone picks on. After defending him, Chris and Meg find out that he isn't wearing a costume after all—he is, in fact, an alien. Now he won't leave Chris and Meg alone, and worse yet, he's invited a bunch of his fellow aliens to come to earth so they can meet Chris and Meg. Will the siblings be able to stop the alien invasion in time?

Other books by the same author:
Claws!, 2011
The Five Masks of Dr. Screem, 2011
The Horror at Chiller House, 2011
Night of the Giant Everything, 2011
Heads, You Lose!, 2010

Other books you might like:
Bruce Coville, *Monster of the Year*, 1989
Damien Graves, *Blood and Sand*, 2005
David Lubar, *The Big Stink*, 2010
Christopher Pike, *The Deadly Past*, 1996
Thadd L. Wolfe, *Digger*, 1999

491

R.L. STINE

The Five Masks of Dr. Screem

(New York: Scholastic Inc., 2011)

Story type: Holiday Themes; Young Adult
Subject(s): Horror; Humor; Halloween
Major character(s): Monica Anderson, 12-Year-Old, Sister (of Peter); Peter Anderson, 10-Year-Old, Brother (of Monica); Dr. Screem, Villain

Summary: *The Five Masks of Dr. Screem* is the third book in R.L. Stine's Goosebumps: Hall of Horrors series. Monica Anderson and her little brother Peter, who is two years younger yet one foot taller than her, are out trick-or-treating one Halloween night. When they attempt to get a treat from an eerie old house, the woman inside instead begs them for help in protecting five magical masks. These masks can control the world, and if they fall into the wrong hands it could mean certain doom for everyone. When a sinister man named Dr. Screem steals all five masks, it's up to Monica and Peter to retrieve them and save the world!

Other books by the same author:
Claws!, 2011
The Horror at Chiller House, 2011
Night of the Giant Everything, 2011
Weird Halloween, 2011
Heads, You Lose!, 2010

Other books you might like:
Tony Abbott, *The Red House*, 2009
Damien Graves, *The Deadly Catch*, 2007
David Lubar, *Invasion of the Road Weenies and Other Warped and Creepy Tales*, 2005

Horror

Christopher Pike, *The Evil House*, 1997
Tom B. Stone, *The Spider Beside Her*, 1999

492

R.L. STINE

Night of the Giant Everything
(New York: Scholastic, 2011)

Series: Goosebumps: Hall of Horrors Series. Book 2
Story type: Series; Young Adult
Subject(s): Horror; Humor; Supernatural
Major character(s): Steven Sweeney, 11-Year-Old; Ava, Friend (of Steven); Courtney, Friend (of Steven)
Time period(s): 21st century; 2010s
Locale(s): United States

Summary: In *Night of the Giant Everything* by R.L. Stine, 11-year-old Steven Sweeney is thrown into a daytime nightmare when his classmates play a practical joke on him. Steven had always enjoyed playing tricks on his friends Ava and Courtney. But after one of his silly-string sneezes ruins Ava's sweater, the girls retaliate by creating a concoction that makes Steven shrink. As Steven grows smaller and smaller, the objects in his everyday world seem bigger—and much more menacing. Animals, dust bunnies, and telephones become obstacles that threaten Steven's chance of survival. *Night of the Giant Everything* is the second book in Stine's Goosebumps: Hall of Horrors series.

Other books by the same author:
Claws!, 2011
The Five Masks of Dr. Screem, 2011
The Horror at Chiller House, 2011
Weird Halloween, 2011
Heads,You Lose!, 2010

Other books you might like:
Tony Abbott, *Bayou Dogs*, 2009
M.T. Coffin, *The Dead Kid Did It*, 1996
David Lubar, *Attack of the Vampire Weenies: And Other Warped and Creepy Tales*, 2011
Christopher Pike, *The Cold People*, 1996
Tom B. Stone, *Don't Tell Mummy*, 1997

493

R.L. STINE

Claws!
(New York: Scholastic, 2011)

Series: Goosebumps: Hall of Horrors Series. Book 1
Story type: Series; Young Adult
Subject(s): Monsters; Felidae; Horror
Major character(s): Mickey, Friend (of Amanda), Boy; Amanda, Friend (of Mickey), Girl
Time period(s): 21st century; 2010s
Locale(s): United States

Summary: In *Claws!* by R.L. Stine, best friends Mickey and Amanda face some fierce felines when their cat-sitting job doesn't go as planned. Taking care of Bella, a neighbor's pet cat, isn't supposed to be hard. Mickey and Amanda only have to feed her and keep her from messing up the house. Unfortunately, Bella outsmarts her sitters, runs into traffic, and is killed. They try to buy a replacement cat at Cat Heaven, a store with a cat that bears an uncanny resemblance to Bella. But when they can't purchase the cat, Mickey and Amanda attempt to steal it instead—and that's when the real trouble starts. *Claws!* is the first book in Stine's Goosebumps: Hall of Horrors series.

Other books by the same author:
The Five Masks of Dr. Screem, 2011
The Horror at Chiller House, 2011
Night of the Giant Everything, 2011
Weird Halloween, 2011
Heads,You Lose!, 2010

Other books you might like:
Tony Abbott, *City of the Dead*, 2009
M.T. Coffin, *The Monster Channel*, 1997
David Lubar, *My Rotten Life*, 2009
Christopher Pike, *The Secret Path*, 1996
Thadd L. Wolfe, *Weird Walter*, 1999

494

R.L. STINE

The Horror at Chiller House
(New York: Scholastic, 2011)

Series: HorrorLand Series. Book 18
Story type: Young Readers
Subject(s): Adventure; Amusement parks; Supernatural
Major character(s): Jonathan Chiller, Store Owner (souvenir shop owner)
Time period(s): 21st century; 2010s
Locale(s): United States

Summary: The 18th book in R.L. Stine's Goosebumps HorrorLand series, *The Horror at Chiller House* finds a group of children summoned to the supernatural amusement park called HorrorLand. They have been invited by the enigmatic Jonathan Chiller to take part in a scavenger hunt. But this is no ordinary game. The kids are trapped, and the only way they can escape is by locating a red chest that leads them to a portal home. Along the way, they'll face some of the most terrifying characters from the series' previous installments.

Other books by the same author:
Claws!, 2011
The Five Masks of Dr. Screem, 2011
Night of the Giant Everything, 2011
Weird Halloween, 2011
Heads,You Lose!, 2010

Other books you might like:
Tony Abbott, *The Ghost Road*, 2009
M.T. Coffin, *Pet Store*, 1996
David Lubar, *Attack of the Vampire Weenies: And Other Warped and Creepy Tales*, 2011
Christopher Pike, *The Little People*, 1996
Tom B. Stone, *Little School of Horrors*, 1998

495

HELEN STRINGER

The Midnight Gate

(New York: Feiwel and Friends, 2011)

Story type: Ghost Story; Young Adult
Subject(s): Supernatural; Ghosts; Orphans
Major character(s): Belladonna Johnson, Teenager; Steve, Friend (of Belladonna); Queen of the Abyss, Supernatural Being

Summary: *The Midnight Gate* is the sequel to author Helen Stringer's novel *Spellbinder*. Now that Belladonna Johnson knows about her special powers as the Spellbinder, she has to figure out what exactly she should do with her new abilities. Then a shadowy specter seeks out Belladonna and her mate Steve and presents them with a strange map. The map may just be the answer that Belladonna needs, but the person the map leads to—the Queen of the Abyss—may not be someone that Belladonna wants to see. Will anyone tell Belladonna the truth about her missing ghost parents or the key to her new magical powers?

Where it's reviewed:
Booklist, May 15, 2011, page 57
School Library Journal, May 2011, page 125

Other books by the same author:
Spellbinder, 2011

Other books you might like:
Kate Cann, *Possessed*, 2010
Caroline B. Cooney, *Night School*, 1995
Clare B. Dunkle, *By These Ten Bones*, 2005
Gwen Hayes, *Falling Under*, 2011
Marilyn Kaye, *Now You See Me*, 2010

496

DIANNE SYLVAN

Shadowflame

(New York: Ace Books, 2011)

Series: Shadow World Series. Book 2
Story type: Vampire Story
Subject(s): Vampires; Fantasy; Royalty
Major character(s): Miranda, Spouse (of David), Royalty (Queen of Vampires); David Solomon, Spouse (of Miranda), Royalty (vampire Prime of the South)
Locale(s): Austin, Texas

Summary: *Shadowflame* is the second novel in author Dianne Sylvan's Shadow World series. Miranda is finally settling down with her new husband David, the prime vampire of the South, and is beginning to learn her duties as queen. Meanwhile, David feels himself torn by his loyalty toward Miranda and his true feelings for someone else. As the pair try to reconcile their emotions, they must also do battle with a mysterious murderer who is trying to kill everyone they know and love, even themselves. Sylvan is also the author of *Queen of Shadows* as well as the nonfiction titles *The Body Sacred* and *The Circle Within*.

Other books by the same author:
Queen of Shadows, 2010

Other books you might like:
Christine Cody, *Bloodlands*, 2011
Nancy A. Collins, *Sunglasses After Dark*, 1989
MaryJanice Davidson, *Undead and Unwed*, 2004
Lee Killough, *Blood Games*, 2001
Cherie Priest, *Bloodshot*, 2011

497

KARIN TABKE

Blood Law

(New York: Heat, 2011)

Series: Blood Moon Trilogy. Book 1
Story type: Fantasy; Romance
Subject(s): Fantasy; Romances (Fiction); Supernatural
Major character(s): Rafael, Werewolf (Lycan), Leader (of Lycan group); Falon, Werewolf (Lycan who kills other Lycans), Lover (of Rafael)
Time period(s): 21st century

Summary: In this story, groups of Lycans—humans by day and wolves at night—try to settle a conflict among them while their leader, Rafael, sets out to find a mate. Rafael chooses a female named Falon, genetically Lycan as well as Slayer, a type of creature that kills Lycans. Rafael's interest in Falon threatens the safety of not only himself, but also his entire pack of Lycans. And, as if this danger wasn't enough, all of the Lycans are awaiting the Blood Moon, a time when the creatures will go to war. Two packs, led by Rafael and his brother, poise for a battle.

Other books by the same author:
Master of Craving, 2009
Master of Surrender, 2008
Master of Torment, 2008

Other books you might like:
L.A. Banks, *Bad Blood*, 2008
Christine Feehan, *Dark Predator*, 2011
Mari Mancusi, *Blood Ties*, 2011
Michelle Rowen, *Something Wicked*, 2010
Cassie Ryan, *The Demon and the Succubus*, 2011

498

ALLISON VAN DIEPEN

The Vampire Stalker

(New York: Scholastic Inc., 2011)

Story type: Vampire Story; Young Adult
Subject(s): Vampires; Literature; Friendship
Major character(s): Amy, Teenager; Alexander Banks, Vampire Hunter; Vigo, Vampire

Summary: *The Vampire Stalker* is a young adult novel written by author Allison Van Diepen. Alexander Banks is the sexy male protagonist of the Otherworld series, a series of novels in which Alexander is a vampire hunter.

Horror

Teenager Amy is a voracious reader of the Otherworld series, and she longs to find a guy just like Alexander. One night she meets Alexander himself, who has been transported into reality to track down a sinister vampire called Vigo. Now Amy is living a life she never imagined in her wildest dreams, but what happens when Alexander must return to his fictitious world? Van Diepen is also the author of *Snitch* and *Street Pharm*.

Other books by the same author:
The Oracle of Dating, 2010
Raven, 2010
Snitch, 2007
Street Pharm, 2006

Other books you might like:
Carmen Adams, *Song of the Vampire*, 1996
Rachel Caine, *Glass Houses*, 2006
P.C. Cast, *Tempted*, 2009
Melissa de la Cruz, *Masquerade: A Blue Bloods Novel*, 2007
L.J. Smith, *Dark Reunion: The Vampire Diaries, Book 4*, 1992

499

TOBY VENABLES

The Viking Dead

(Oxford, UK: Abaddon Books, 2011)

Story type: Historical
Subject(s): Vikings; Legends; Mythology
Major character(s): Bjolf, Viking, Leader (of the Raven)

Summary: *The Viking Dead* by Toby Venables is a Tomb of the Dead book from Abaddon Books publishing company. The great Viking ship the Raven embarks on an invasion when the captain, Bjolf, suddenly demands a withdrawal from battle. In their haste to flee, the Viking men are lost in a forestland wrought with horrors, not the least of which are inexplicable legendary creatures called Draugr. As Bjolf leads his men through a domain filled with supernatural, undead beings, he must encourage their bravery if they are going to survive. The Viking gods cannot save them now, and only one man can lead them to safety. First novel.

Other books you might like:
Paul Finch, *Stronghold*, 2010
Rebecca Levene, *Anno Mortis*, 2009
Weston Ochse, *Empire of Salt*, 2010
Matthew Smith, *The Words of Their Roaring*, 2009
Matthew Sprange, *Death Hulk*, 2006

500

TIM WAGGONER

Dark War

(Nottingham, UK: Angry Robot, June 28, 2011)

Series: Matt Richter Series. Book 3
Subject(s): Detective fiction; Supernatural; Zombies

Major character(s): Matt Richter, Supernatural Being, Detective—Private; Devona, Vampire, Detective—Private

Summary: *Dark War* is the third book in author Tim Waggoner's Matt Richter series. Richter is a private detective who investigates crimes on the streets of Nekropolis, a city populated by the undead. He is also a zombie, which helps him relate to the vampires, were-creatures, shapeshifters, and other supernatural creatures of the city. With the help of his sexy partner, half-vampire Devona, Richter is usually able to solve any case. This time, however, a battle is brewing in Nekropolis, and Richter cannot be certain how to stop it—or even if he should. Waggoner is also the author of *Nekropolis* and *Dead Streets*.

Other books by the same author:
Nekropolis, 2009
Darkness Wakes, 2006
Pandora Drive, 2006
Like Death, 2005
Protege, 2005

Other books you might like:
Amelia Beamer, *The Loving Dead*, 2010
Bob Fingerman, *Pariah*, 2010
Laurell K. Hamilton, *Bloody Bones*, 1996
Jonathan Maberry, *Patient Zero*, 2009
Kat Richardson, *Underground*, 2008

501

RACHEL WARD

The Chaos

(New York: Scholastic Inc., 2011)

Series: Numbers Series. Book 2
Story type: Young Adult
Subject(s): Psychics; Adolescent interpersonal relations; Grandmothers
Major character(s): Adam, Psychic, Grandson (great, of Val); Val, Grandmother (great, of Adam)
Time period(s): 21st century; 2020s (2026-2027)
Locale(s): London, England

Summary: *The Chaos* is the second novel in author Rachel Ward's Numbers series. Since he was a young boy, Adam has had the ability to see when others were going to die. Not only does Adam have the ability to see the exact date of their death, but also the circumstances and anguish surrounding it. As the Atlantic Ocean begins to rise in the year 2026, Adam and his great-grandmother Val must evacuate their coastal home and take refuge in London. Everywhere around him, though, Adam can see people who will die on January 1, 2027. Can Adam stop a worldwide tragedy, or is his number up as well?

Where it's reviewed:
Booklist, April 15, 2011, page 56

Other books by the same author:
Numbers, 2010

Other books you might like:
Nancy A. Collins, *Looks Could Kill*, 2006
Lee Duigon, *Precog*, 1989

Rebecca Levene, *End of the Line*, 2005
David A. McIntee, *Destination Zero*, 2005
Natasha Rhodes, *Dead Reckoning*, 2005

502

PHAEDRA WELDON

Grimoire

(Freeland, Washington: Caldwell Press, 2011)

Story type: Ghost Story
Subject(s): Psychics; Ghosts; Supernatural
Major character(s): Dags McConnell, Psychic; Allard Bonville, Leader (of Ceremonial Magic group)

Summary: *Grimoire* is a novel by author Phaedra Weldon. Darren "Dags" McConnell possesses the unique gift of being able to see ghosts. When he joins an occult group, a set of symbols marked upon his hand only intensifies his psychic abilities. Unfortunately, these abilities attract the attention of Ceremonial Magic group leader Allard Bonville, who has less than pure intentions. Allard plans to retrieve his wife's ghost by using Dags's powers, an act that will certainly kill Dags. But when his incantations go awry, a series of portals open up through Dags's marks. These portals lead to both the hellish Abysmal plane and the heavenly Ethereal plane, and the only thing that can close these doorways to the nether realm is a magical grimoire.

Other books by the same author:
Revenant, 2011
Phantasm, 2009
Spectre, 2008
Wraith, 2007

Other books you might like:
Jim Butcher, *Turn Coat*, 2009
Laurell K. Hamilton, *Blue Moon*, 1998
Kim Harrison, *Black Magic Sanction*, 2010
Mary Stanton, *Defending Angels*, 2008
Rob Thurman, *Blackout*, 2011

503

DAN WELLS

I Don't Want to Kill You

(New York: Tor, 2011)

Series: John Cleaver Series. Book 3
Story type: Series; Supernatural Vengeance
Subject(s): Demons; Horror; Suspense
Major character(s): John Wayne Cleaver, Murderer
Time period(s): 21st century; 2010s
Locale(s): United States

Summary: In the horror novel *I Don't Want to Kill You* by Dan Wells, John Wayne Cleaver continues his battle against evil begun in *I Am Not a Serial Killer* and *Mr. Monster*. Although Cleaver possesses special abilities that have enabled him to fight against the evil forces threatening his community, his dealings with the supernatural have taken their toll. Cleaver must face another monster, this time on his own terms. Having honed his killing skills, Cleaver summons the demon to battle—but his mysterious town may hold more than one enemy. *I Don't Want to Kill You* is the third book in Wells's John Cleaver series.

Where it's reviewed:
Booklist, April 1, 2011, page 35
Publishers Weekly, February 7, 2011, page 36

Other books by the same author:
I Am Not a Serial Killer, 2010
Mr. Monster, 2010

Other books you might like:
Robert Bloch, *Lori*, 1989
John Farris, *The Axman Cometh*, 1989
Stephen King, *Bag of Bones*, 1998
Joe R. Lansdale, *The Nightrunners*, 1987
John Saul, *Black Lightning*, 1995

504

LUCY WESTON

The Secret History of Elizabeth Tudor, Vampire Slayer

(New York: Gallery Books, 2011)

Story type: Historical
Subject(s): Horror; History; Fantasy
Major character(s): Elizabeth, Royalty (queen of England), Vampire Hunter, Historical Figure, Daughter (of Anne Boleyn); Mordred, Vampire; Anne Boleyn, Historical Figure, Mother (of Elizabeth), Spirit
Time period(s): 16th century; 1550s (1559)
Locale(s): England

Summary: In the novel *The Secret History of Elizabeth Tudor, Vampire Slayer* by Lucy Weston, the newly crowned queen of England must protect her country from foes both mortal and immortal. Just before her ascension to the throne in 1559, Elizabeth learns from the spirit of her mother, Anne Boleyn, that she is a vampire slayer. Furthermore, the most dangerous vampire in history—Mordred, illegitimate son of King Arthur—wants Elizabeth for his bride. Mordred's vision of an England dominated by vampires would mean death to Elizabeth's subjects but would ensure eternal youth for the queen. The Virgin Queen is both repulsed and enticed by the vampire's proposal. First novel.

Where it's reviewed:
Booklist, January 1, 2011, page 57
Library Journal, December 2010, page 108
Publishers Weekly, November 15, 2010, page 44

Other books you might like:
Seth Grahame-Smith, *Abraham Lincoln: Vampire Hunter*, 2010
Sarah Gray, *Wuthering Bites*, 2010
Lori Handeland, *Shakespeare Undead*, 2010
A.E. Moorat, *Henry VIII, Wolfman*, 2010
Adam Rann, *Emma and the Werewolves*, 2010

Horror

505

EILEEN WILKS

Blood Challenge

(New York: Penguin, 2011)

Series: World of the Lupi Series. Book 7
Story type: Contemporary; Paranormal
Subject(s): Horror; Werewolves; Romances (Fiction)
Major character(s): Lily Yu, FBI Agent (Magical Crimes Division), Fiance(e) (of Rule Turner); Rule Turner, Werewolf, Fiance(e) (of Lily Yu)
Time period(s): 21st century; 2010s
Locale(s): California, United States; Tennessee, United States

Summary: In the novel *Blood Challenge* by Eileen Wilks, Lily Yu is an agent with the FBI's Magical Crimes Division. Her job is to police the werewolf population that became part of San Diego's demographic after the Turning. Rule Turner, a werewolf of high status in his community, has become Lily's lover. Now he is about to make her his wife. News of Lily and Rule's wedding plans brings unrest to both the humans and werewolves. The repercussions of the couple's shocking decision begin with a series of werewolf killings in Tennessee. *Blood Challenge* is the seventh book in Wilks's The World of the Lupi series.

Where it's reviewed:
Romantic Times, January 2011, page 94

Other books by the same author:
Blood Magic, 2010
Mortal Sins, 2009
Blood Lines, 2007
Mortal Danger, 2005
Tempting Danger, 2004

Other books you might like:
Christine Feehan, *Dark Curse*, 2008
Chris Marie Green, *Night Rising*, 2007
Angela Knight, *Master of the Night*, 2004
Susan Krinard, *Prince of Dreams*, 1995
Lynn Viehl, *Dreamveil: A Novel of the Kyndred*, 2010

506

EILEEN WILKS

Death Magic

(New York: Berkley Books, 2011)

Series: World of the Lupi Series. Book 8
Story type: Werewolf Story
Subject(s): Ghosts; Werewolves; Supernatural
Major character(s): Lily Yu, FBI Agent (Magical Crimes Division), Fiance(e) (of Rule Turner); Rule Turner, Werewolf
Locale(s): San Diego, California

Summary: *Death Magic* is the eighth book in author Eileen Wilks's series World of the Lupi. In this book, Lily Yu is invited to link up with an alliance of ghosts created by her boss. While Rule Turner has no compunction about joining this coalition, Lily cannot bring herself to put aside her belief in justice. Then a government official turns up dead, and the spirits seem to be the only ones who can provide information as well as protection. Now it's up to Lily to either put her principles aside or face the consequences. Wilks is also the author of *Lover Beware, Bloodlines, Meeting at Midnight, Mortal Danger, Mortal Sins*, and *Tempting Danger*.

Other books by the same author:
Blood Magic, 2010
Mortal Sins, 2009
Blood Lines, 2007
Mortal Danger, 2005

Other books you might like:
C.T. Adams, *Timeless Moon*, 2008
Christina Dodd, *Scent of Darkness*, 2007
Jacquelyn Frank, *Elijah*, 2007
Lori Handeland, *Blue Moon*, 2004
Susan Krinard, *Call of the Wolf*, 2006

507

F. PAUL WILSON

The Dark at the End

(New York: Tor Books, 2011)

Series: Repairman Jack Series. Book 14
Story type: Fantasy
Subject(s): Alternative worlds; Mystery; Horror
Major character(s): Jack, Repairman; Dawn Pickering, Mother; Glaeken, Immortal

Summary: *The Dark at the End* is the 14th and final novel in F. Paul Wilson's Repairman Jack series. Jack is preparing for a final confrontation against the evil forces that have plagued him for so long—a decision that goes directly against all of his promises to Glaeken. Jack feels that things are different now though, especially since he seems to be transforming into an immortal. As if his impending final face-off wasn't enough, however, Jack also must help Dawn Pickering locate her child. Dawn was told the child is dead, but Dawn isn't sure about that. Now it is up to Jack to not only save Dawn's baby, but also reality as he knows it.

Other books by the same author:
Jack: Secret Vengeance, 2011
Jack: Secret Histories, 2010
Ground Zero, 2009
Infernal, 2005
Hosts, 2001

Other books you might like:
James Blish, *Black Easter*, 1968
Edward Lee, *City Infernal*, 2001
Thomas F. Monteleone, *The Reckoning*, 1999
Madeleine E. Robins, *The Stone War*, 1999
John Shirley, *Demons*, 2002

508

F. PAUL WILSON

Jack: Secret Vengeance

(New York: Tor, 2011)

Series: Repairman Jack Series. Book 3
Story type: Series; Young Adult
Subject(s): Horror; Fantasy; High schools
Major character(s): Jack "Repairman Jack", Teenager, Detective—Amateur; Weezy, Friend (of Jack); Carson Toliver, Student—High School, Football Player
Time period(s): 20th century; 1980s
Locale(s): Johnson, New Jersey

Summary: In the young adult novel *Jack: Secret Vengeance* by F. Paul Wilson, Jack is a high-school student with the ability to solve mysteries and resolve problems. Set in 1980s New Jersey, this case pits Jack against a formidable foe—quarterback Carson Toliver. The popular senior seems like a good guy until Jack's friend Weezy recounts his violent actions on a recent date. When Weezy is too afraid to report the crime and Carson threatens to ruin her reputation, Jack calls on the residents of the nearby Pine Barrens to help him exact revenge. *Jack: Secret Vengeance* is the third book in the Young Repairman Jack series, which serves as a prequel to Wilson's Repairman Jack novels for adults.

Where it's reviewed:
Voice of Youth Advocates, April 2011, page 88

Other books by the same author:
The Dark at the End, 2011
Jack: Secret Histories, 2010
Ground Zero, 2009
Infernal, 2005
Hosts, 2001

Other books you might like:
Tony Abbott, *Bayou Dogs*, 2009
Bruce Coville, *Amulet of Doom*, 1985
Simon Lake, *Something's Watching*, 1993
Joseph Locke, *Game Over*, 1993
Dan Wells, *I Am Not a Serial Killer*, 2010

509

CHELSEA QUINN YARBRO

An Embarrassment of Riches

(New York: Tor, 2011)

Series: Chronicles of Saint-Germain. Book 24
Story type: Historical; Series
Subject(s): Vampires; Horror; Fantasy
Major character(s): Rakoczy "Saint-Germain" Ferncsi, Vampire, Jeweler, Nobleman (count); Kunigunde, Royalty (queen of Bohemia); Rozsa, Courtier (lady-in-waiting); Imbolya, Teenager; Iliska, Young Woman
Time period(s): 17th century
Locale(s): Bohemia, Prague

Summary: In the novel *An Embarrassment of Riches* by Chelsea Quinn Yarbro, the 3,200-year-old vampire Count Saint-Germain settles in the court of Bohemia's Queen Kunigunde. It is the 17th century, and Saint-Germain—or Rakoczy Ferncsi, as the count is known—plans to bide his time in Prague as a jeweler. Though the queen is pleased with his creations, other women in the court are more interested in his physical attributes. Soon, Saint-Germain's hopes of avoiding undo attention falter. As three women from Kunigunde's court each plot to win the handsome jewelry maker for her own, Saint-Germain risks an unpleasant encounter with Catholic church officials. *An Embarrassment of Riches* is the 24th book in Yarbro's Saint-Germain series.

Where it's reviewed:
Booklist, February 15, 2011, page 58
Publishers Weekly, January 17, 2011, page 34

Other books by the same author:
Burning Shadows, 2009
Roman Dusk, 2006
Dark Is the Sun, 2004
A Feast in Exile, 2001
Mansions of Darkness, 1996

Other books you might like:
Les Daniels, *Yellow Fog*, 1986
Barbara Hambly, *Traveling with the Dead*, 1995
Jasper Kent, *Thirteen Years Later*, 2010
Anne Rice, *Vittorio the Vampire*, 1999
Michael Romkey, *The Vampire Papers*, 1994

Horror

Inspirational Fiction: Fall 2011
Written by Angie Kiesling, for FaithfulReader.com

As autumn whirls in on the backs of falling leaves, readers' minds turn toward the approach of the holiday season, and as usual book publishers are one step ahead of them. This fall is replete with Christmas-themed titles that evoke visions of crackling fires, sumptuous food, festive company—and cryptic notes that hint at long-buried family secrets. That's the theme of just one of this season's tantalizing tales: *The Christmas Note* by Donna VanLiere. Noted for her bestselling The Christmas Hope series, VanLiere weaves a new inspirational novel about an unlikely friendship between two women, but one that will change each of their lives forever.

Other noteworthy titles among this year's bumper crop of Yuletide novels include two that marry the popular Amish romance genre with the magic of a good Christmas story well told: *The Christmas Singing: A Romance* from the Heart of Amish Country by Cindy Woodsmall and *Christmas in Sugarcreek* by Shelley Shepard Gray. Woodsmall's story explores themes of lost love, heartache, and the promise of restoration after a broken engagement on Christmas Eve, while Gray's heroine, against her best intentions, falls for the returned prodigal and "bad boy" of the Sugarcreek community—who's hoping for a new beginning and a chance to win the lady's heart.

Melody Carlson wields her storytelling prowess in a novel that combines the best of Christmas books—an intangible mixture of nostalgia, joy, and a little bit of magic—in *The Christmas Shoppe*, this year's offering in her annual Christmas novella category. The townsfolk of Parrish Springs recoil at the sight of Matilda Honeycutt, a strange woman with scraggly hair and jangling jewelry who opens a new shop on the town's quaint Main Street. When rumors start to fly about what might be going on behind the papered-up windows and locked door, the residents start looking for a way to get this woman and her wares out of their town before Christmas. But Matilda Honeycutt has a little something for each one of them sitting on those cluttered shelves, just waiting to be discovered.

From Steeple Hill's Love Inspired Historical imprint comes The *Captain's Christmas Family* by Deborah Hale, and Berkley Hardcover debuts *Christmas Treasures* by Thomas Kinkade (with Katherine Spencer), the latest installment in the Cape Light series about Reverend Ben. *Paper Angels: A Novel* by country music singer Jimmy Wayne (with Travis Thrasher) is spun off the title of one of Wayne's tear-jerking songs and tells the story of Kevin Morrell, a man whose life is changed by the Salvation Army's Angel Tree Project. Through his encounter with a fifteen-year-old boy from a broken home, Kevin learns the true meaning of Christmas.

Among the heavy-hitters to debut this Christmas season is Glenn Beck's *The Snow Angel*, a beautifully poignant tale about family, forgiveness, and the freedom to live a future free of the past. Best known for being a nationally syndicated radio and Fox News television show host, Beck is also a prolific author whose titles include *An Inconvenient Book*, *Glenn Beck's Common Sense*, and *The Christmas Sweater*, which is also available in a children's book version.

Of all the Christmas novels to be released this fall, however, one stands out as a true original and instant classic: *A Marriage Carol*. Master storyteller and talk radio host Chris Fabry (*Almost Heaven*) partners with marriage expert Gary Chapman (*The 5 Love Languages*) to weave a magical tale of a marriage almost lost but still worth saving—and all the action happens in a single night that will bring transformation and a new beginning. Like the Ebenezer that flowed from Dickens's pen over 150 years ago, Marlee and Jacob Ebenezer have allowed old grievances to seep into their bones and twist their character into unlovely shapes.

Married in a snowstorm twenty years ago, on this Christmas Eve they are on the brink of divorce, their marriage as cold and icy as the winter roads they're traveling en route to the lawyer's office. They take a shortcut on a slippery side road and wind up slamming into a bank of snow, spinning out of control. Marlee trudges up the hill for help and knocks on the door of a house that looks like a bed and breakfast inn. Inside the

house, three golden pots sit on the hearth where a fire crackles. The old man who lives there claims they are used to restoring marriages. Marlee laughs—and begins a journey through her past, present, and future that will test how she views her lifelong love.

Mad about (Vintage) Love

Authors—and apparently readers—continue their love affair with vintage tales of love in another era, as the season's list of new books contains plenty. Among them are *Love on the Line* by Deeanne Gist, *A Lasting Impression* by Tamera Alexander, *The Colonel's Lady* by Laura Frantz, *Tall, Dark, and Determined* by Kelly Eileen Hake, *A Heart Revealed: A Novel* by Julie Lessman, *Belonging* by Robin Lee Hatcher, *A Most Unsuitable Match* by Stephanie Grace Whitson, *Wonderland Creek* by Lynn Austin, *Forsaking All Others* by Allison Pittman, and *A Sound among the Trees* by Susan Meissner, to name a few.

Another blockbuster destined to secure instant readership is *Longing*, book three in the wildly popular Bailey Flanigan Series by Karen Kingsbury, which hits shelves in November. *Longing* picks up where *Learning ended*, and *Loving*, the fourth and final book in the series, is set for a March 2012 release. Meanwhile, Terri Blackstock continues to surprise readers (and her large following of loyal fans) with *Shadow in Serenity*, a September release billed as a modern-day Music Man featuring a small-town girl caught in the web of a smooth-talking man from out of town.

Recommended Titles:

Dangerous Mercy: A Novel by Kathy Herman (Suspense)

The Sweetest Thing by Elizabeth Musser (Historical)

A Sound among Trees by Susan Meissner (Historical Romance)

Torrent: A Novel by Lisa T. Bergren (Speculative)

A Marriage Carol by Chris Fabry and Gary Chapman (Contemporary)

Water's Edge by Robert Whitlow (Mystery)

The Christmas Singing by Cindy Woodsmall (Amish)

Inspirational Fiction

510

CHRISTA ALLAN

The Edge of Grace

(Nashville, Tennessee: Abingdon Press, 2011)

Story type: Family Saga
Subject(s): Homosexuality; Family; Christianity
Major character(s): Caryn Becker, Widow(er), Single Mother, Sister (of David), Religious; David, Brother (of Caryn), Homosexual
Time period(s): 21st century; 2010s
Locale(s): United States

Summary: *The Edge of Grace* is a thought-provoking inspirational novel about family, faith, and conviction from author Christa Allan. As a widowed single mother, Caryn Becker already has enough on her plate to deal with, but she's completely shell-shocked when yet another bomb is dropped on her: her brother, David, is a homosexual. Intolerant and disapproving of his lifestyle, Caryn disowns David and cuts him out of her life, focusing instead on the trials and challenges that dwell in her everyday existence. But Caryn is forced to face David and his sexual orientation eventually. When he's attacked and nearly killed, Caryn must reevaluate her beliefs, her convictions, and her stance on family.

Other books by the same author:
Walking on Broken Glass, 2010

Other books you might like:
C.J. Darlington, *Bound by Guilt*, 2011
Sibella Giorello, *The Mountains Bow Down*, 2011
Meg Moseley, *When Sparrows Fall: A Novel*, 2011
Sheila Walsh, *Sweet Sanctuary*, 2011

511

J. MARK BERTRAND

Pattern of Wounds

(Minneapolis, Minnesota: Bethany House, 2011)

Series: Roland March Series. Book 2
Story type: Mystery; Series
Subject(s): Serial murders; Mystery; Suspense
Major character(s): Roland March, Detective
Time period(s): 21st century; 2010s
Locale(s): Houston, Texas

Summary: *Pattern of Wounds*, a suspenseful and thrilling inspirational mystery, is the second installment in the Roland March Mystery series from author J. Mark Bertrand. A new murder investigation has Detective Roland March confronting the dark past and a mistake he may have made a decade ago. Ten years ago, one of March's cases was the topic for a bestselling true-crime book. Now, a young woman has been stabbed to death in Houston and the details surrounding her death are eerily similar to the famed investigation. As more bodies begin piling up, March must figure out if a copycat killer is on the loose or if he put the wrong man behind bars all those years ago.

Other books by the same author:
Back on Murder, 2010
Beguiled, 2010

Other books you might like:
Davis Bunn, *Lion of Babylon*, 2011
Julie Cave, *Pieces of Light*, 2011
Noel Hynd, *Hostage in Havana*, 2011
Mark Mynheir, *The Corruptible: A Ray Quinn Mystery*, 2011
Travis Thrasher, *Gravestone*, 2011

512

RESHONDA TATE BILLINGSLEY

Say Amen, Again

(New York: Gallery Books, 2011)

Story type: Religious
Subject(s): Christianity; Religion; Infidelity
Major character(s): Rachel Jackson Adams, Spouse (of Pastor Lester); Mary Richardson, Religious; Lester Adams, Religious (pastor), Spouse (of Rachel)
Time period(s): 21st century; 2010s
Locale(s): United States

Summary: *Say Amen, Again*, a thought-provoking inspirational novel, is the follow-up to *Let the Church Say Amen* and *Everybody Say Amen* from bestselling author ReShonda Tate Billingsley. There's more drama and church-wide controversy at Zion Hill, and Pastor Lester Adams' extremely pregnant wife, Rachel Jackson Ad-

ams, is at the forefront. Eight months pregnant with Lester's baby, Rachel must contend with her husband's former mistress and fellow congregant, Mary Richardson, who also happens to be expecting. The baby may or may not be Lester's, causing Mary to stir up dissension among the church and anger within Rachel. As the accusations reach a fever pitch, Rachel is forced to decide between her call to forgiveness and her desire for vengeance.

Other books by the same author:
A Good Man Is Hard to Find, 2011
Holy Rollers, 2010
Everybody Say Amen, 2009
Can I Get a Witness?, 2008
Let the Church Say Amen, 2004

Other books you might like:
Cheryl Faye, *Who Said It Would Be Easy?: A Story of Faith*, 2011
Vanessa Davis Griggs, *Redeeming Waters*, 2011
E.N. Joy, *Trying to Stay Saved*, 2011
Kendra Norman-Bellamy, *Upon This Rock*, 2011
Pat Simmons, *Crowning Glory*, 2011

513

T.C. BOYLE

When the Killing's Done

(New York: Viking, 2011)

Subject(s): Biology; Business; Ecology
Major character(s): Alma Boyd Takesue, Scientist (biologist); Dave LaJoy, Businessman; Anise Reed, Singer, Lover (of Dave); Rita, Mother (of Anise)
Time period(s): 21st century; 2010s
Locale(s): Santa Barbara, California

Summary: In *When the Killing's Done* by T.C. Boyle, the Channel Islands off the coast of Santa Barbara, California were once home to a diverse range of animals species. National Park Service biologist Alma Boyd Takesue has seen the native species compromised by the introduction of rats and feral pigs into the islands' ecosystem. In an attempt to protect the now-endangered native animals, Alma promotes the killing of the rats, pigs, and other invasive species. Businessman Dave LaJoy and his girlfriend Anise Reed protest the killing of any animals on the islands. As the Channel Island animals struggle for survival, Alma, Dave, and Anise fight for dominance in the human arena.

Where it's reviewed:
Booklist, December 1, 2010, page 27
Kirkus Reviews, December 15, 2010, page 1228
Library Journal, January 2011, page 80
New Yorker, March 21, 2011, page 69
Publishers Weekly, December 20, 2010, page 27

Other books by the same author:
Wild Child: And Other Stories, 2010
The Women, 2009
Talk Talk, 2006
Tooth and Claw, 2005
The Inner Circle, 2004

Other books you might like:
Edward Abbey, *The Monkey Wrench Gang*, 1975
William Bernhardt, *Dark Justice*, 1999
Christopher A. Bohjalian, *Water Witches*, 1995
Anastasia Hobbet, *Pleasure of Believing: A Novel*, 1997
Kim Stanley Robinson, *Antarctica*, 1998

514

SIGMUND BROUWER

The Canary List

(Colorado Springs, Colorado: WaterBrook Press, 2011)

Story type: Contemporary
Subject(s): Suspense; Good and evil; Religion
Major character(s): Jaimie Piper, 12-Year-Old, Orphan, Foster Child, Student (of Crockett); Crockett Grey, Teacher
Time period(s): 21st century; 2010s
Locale(s): Santa Monica, California

Summary: *The Canary List* is a suspenseful inspirational novel from author Sigmund Brouwer. Tomboyish outsider Jaimie Piper has spent her life bouncing between foster homes and running for her life, supernaturally sensing a dark and foreboding evil that compels her to flee. The 12-year-old girl is experiencing a new kind of terror at her latest home in Santa Monica, California and the only person she trusts to help her is Crockett Grey, the grieving teacher of her Adaptive Behavior Class. When she shows up at his house late one night, terrified and begging for help, Crockett agrees, if only because Jaimie reminds him of the daughter he lost. But Crockett soon finds himself in a horrifying web of deception, religious intrigue, and witchcraft that threatens his and Jaimie's lives.

Other books by the same author:
Flight of Shadows: A Novel, 2010

Other books you might like:
Ted Dekker, *The Priest's Graveyard*, 2011
Tim Downs, *Nick of Time*, 2011
Steven James, *The Queen: A Patrick Bowers Thriller*, 2011
Lee Strobel, *The Ambition*, 2011
Robert Whitlow, *Water's Edge*, 2011

515

DAVIS BUNN

Lion of Babylon

(Minneapolis, Minnesota: Bethany House, 2011)

Story type: Contemporary
Subject(s): Kidnapping; Middle East; Suspense
Major character(s): Marc Royce, Widow(er), Agent (U.S. intelligence)
Time period(s): 21st century; 2010s
Locale(s): Iraq

Summary: *Lion of Babylon* is a suspenseful inspirational thriller from bestselling and award-winning author T.

Davis Bunn. Since losing his wife and his job, former intelligence agent Marc Royce's life has felt empty and meaningless. But with one phone call from his old boss, he's renewed with a fresh sense of purpose. The Taliban has kidnapped two CIA operatives in Iraq in an effort to stir up turmoil and anger in the area. Two more individuals have gone missing: a well-connected Iraqi civilian and an American humanitarian worker. Traveling to the Middle East on a top-secret mission, Marc must find out if and how the disappearances are connected and who is responsible for the crimes.

Other books by the same author:
The Damascus Way, 2011
The Centurion's Wife, 2010
The Hidden Flame, 2010
All Through the Night, 2008

Other books you might like:
Randy Alcorn, *Courageous*, 2011
Jason Elam, *Inside Threat*, 2011
Jerry B. Jenkins, *The Brotherhood*, 2011
Robin Parrish, *Vigilante*, 2011
Joel C Rosenberg, *The Tehran Initiative*, 2011

516

SANDRA BYRD

To Die For: A Novel of Anne Boleyn

(Nashville, Tennessee: Howard Books, 2011)

Story type: Historical
Subject(s): Friendship; Faith; British history, 1066-1688
Major character(s): Anne Boleyn, Historical Figure, Friend (of Meg), Neighbor (of Meg), Royalty; Meg Wyatt, Friend (of Anne), Neighbor (of Anne)
Time period(s): 16th century
Locale(s): England

Summary: *To Die For: A Novel of Anne Boleyn* is a fictionalized account of Anne Boleyn and her former neighbor, Meg Wyatt, from author Sandra Byrd. Since childhood, neighbors Anne Boleyn and Meg Wyatt have been the best of friends, so committed to one another that when Meg begins to fall in love with a local boy destined to become a clergyman, she turns her back on him to tend to Anne. As Anne rises in power and fame, Meg is by her side, enjoying the extravagance of life in King Henry VIII's court. But when Anne gets herself into irreversible trouble, she might take Meg down with her. Wrestling with her commitment to Anne, her faith in God, and her desire for true love, Meg is forced to make an impossible decision that will impact her future forever.

Other books by the same author:
Asking for Trouble, 2010
Don't Kiss Him Good-bye, 2010
Piece de Resistance: A Novel, 2009
Bon Appetit, 2008
Let Them Eat Cake, 2007

Other books you might like:
Colleen Coble, *The Lightkeeper's Ball*, 2011
Liz Curtis Higgs, *Mine Is the Night*, 2011

Julie Klassen, *The Girl in the Gatehouse*, 2011
Julie Lessman, *A Heart Revealed*, 2011
Susan Meissner, *Lady in Waiting: A Novel*, 2010

517

JAMIE CARIE

Pirate of My Heart

(Nashville, Tennessee: B&H Books, 2011)

Story type: Historical; Romance
Subject(s): Romances (Fiction); History; Sailing
Major character(s): Lady Kendra Townsend, Lady, Orphan, Passenger (on cargo ship); Dorian Colburn, Sea Captain, Widow(er)
Time period(s): 18th century; 1790s
Locale(s): England

Summary: *Pirate of My Heart: A Novel* is a historical inspirational romance novel from author Jamie Carie. Following her father's death, the newly orphaned Lady Kendra Townsend is forced by her ruthless and greedy uncle to make a terrible choice: marry a man she could never love or sail off for America to live with relatives she's never known. Unwilling to marry for any reason other than love and confident that God has a plan for her life, Kendra boards a cargo ship and sets sail for the United States. While aboard the ship, she's surprised to meet Captain Dorian Colburn, a ruggedly handsome man whose wariness of women is almost tangible. Dorian has been hurt by women before and is careful not to get too close to the beautiful Kendra. But when she is put in danger, he must risk his life, and his heart, to save her.

Other books by the same author:
Angel's Den: A Novel, 2010
The Snowflake, 2010
Wind Dancer, 2009
The Duchess and the Dragon, 2008
Snow Angel: A Novel, 2007

Other books you might like:
Jamie Carie, *The Duchess and the Dragon*, 2008
Marylu Tyndall, *The Restitution*, 2007
Susan May Warren, *My Foolish Heart*, 2011
Linda Windsor, *Thief: A Novel*, 2011
Karen Witemeyer, *A Tailor-Made Bride*, 2010

518

MELODY CARLSON

The Christmas Shoppe

(Grand Rapids, Michigan: Revell, 2011)

Story type: Holiday Themes
Subject(s): Christmas; Shopping; Outcasts
Major character(s): Matilda Honeycutt, Aged Person, Store Owner
Time period(s): 21st century; 2010s
Locale(s): Parrish Springs, United States

Summary: *The Christmas Shoppe* is a heartwarming and moving inspirational novel from award winning author

Inspirational

Melody Carlson. The townspeople in the quaint community of Parrish Springs are already unsure about Matilda Honeycutt, the mysterious old woman who looks and acts like a gypsy, but when she purchases the old Barton Building on Main Street, they're downright outraged. With Christmas fast approaching, the Parrish Springs residents are worried that Matilda will turn the shop into an uninviting and unsuccessful junk store. But as townsfolk begin investigating what's going on behind the papered-up windows of the old storefront, they're shocked to find that Matilda's shelves house magic and memories for them all.

Other books by the same author:
Christmas at Harrington's, 2010
The Christmas Dog, 2009
All I Have to Give: A Christmas Love Story, 2008
Back Home Again, 2006
Recipes & Wooden Spoons, 2006

Other books you might like:
Irene Brand, *Love Finds You Under the Mistletoe*, 2010
Greg Kincaid, *Christmas with Tucker*, 2010
Karen Kingsbury, *Leaving*, 2011
Karen Kingsbury, *Take Three*, 2010
Francine Rivers, *Her Daughter's Dream*, 2010

519

VANNETTA CHAPMAN

Falling to Pieces

(Grand Rapids, Michigan: Zondervan, 2011)

Series: Shipshewana Amish Mystery Series. Book 1
Story type: Mystery; Series
Subject(s): Amish; Mystery; Murder
Major character(s): Deborah, Detective—Amateur; Callie, Detective—Amateur
Time period(s): 21st century; 2010s
Locale(s): Shipshewana, Indiana

Summary: *Falling to Pieces*, an inspirational mystery novel, is the first installment in the Shipshewana Amish Mystery series from author Vannetta Chapman. In the cozy Amish community of Shipshewana, two unlikely women come together to organize an online quilt auction and bond over a murder. Deborah and Callie are as opposite as can be, but both women work hard to make the best of their newfound partnership working on a digital quilt sale. After all, it's only a temporary situation. That is, until a horrific murder, shocking suspect, challenging detective, and a widespread panic force them to band together and root out the killer hiding among them.

Other books by the same author:
A Simple Amish Christmas, 2010

Other books you might like:
Melanie Dobson, *The Silent Order*, 2010
Suzanne Woods Fisher, *The Search: A Novel*, 2011
Kathleen Fuller, *The Secrets Beneath*, 2010
Marta Perry, *Vanish in Plain Sight*, 2011
Gayle Roper, *A Secret Identity*, 2010

520

DIANNE L CHRISTNER

Something Old

(Uhrichsville, Ohio: Barbour Publishing, 2011)

Series: Plain City Series. Book 1
Story type: Romance; Series
Subject(s): Mennonites; Christian life; Romances (Fiction)
Major character(s): Katy Yoder, Religious (Mennonite); Jake Byler, Boyfriend (former, of Katy)
Time period(s): 21st century; 2010s
Locale(s): Plain City, Ohio

Summary: *Something Old*, an inspirational romance novel, is part of the Plain City series from author Dianne L. Christner. Katy Yoder is just a young Mennonite woman from Plain City, Ohio struggling to live a life that pleases the Lord and reflects His work in her life. When Katy accepts a new job working for "outsiders," she's confronted with temptations she never expected. Most notably is the return of her former love, Jake Byler, whom she views as nothing more than "spoiled goods." But despite her best efforts and strict moral code, Katy is having a hard time living up to the standards she's set for herself and she soon learns a valuable lesson about the dangers of being judgmental and legalistic.

Other books by the same author:
Keeper of Hearts, 2002
Storm, 2000

Other books you might like:
Barbara Cameron, *A Time to Love*, 2010
Tricia Goyer, *Beside Still Waters*, 2011
Laura V. Hilton, *Patchwork Dreams*, 2011
Beverly Lewis, *The Mercy*, 2011
Emma Miller, *Miriam's Heart*, 2011

521

MARY CONNEALY

Out of Control

(Minneapolis, Minnesota: Bethany House, 2011)

Series: Kincaid Brides Series. Book 1
Story type: Romance; Series
Subject(s): Romances (Fiction); Caves; Ranch life
Major character(s): Rafe Kincaid, Rancher; Julia Gilliland, Writer, Archaeologist, Adventurer, Neighbor (of Rafe)
Time period(s): 19th century
Locale(s): Colorado, United States

Summary: *Out of Control*, an inspirational romance, is the first installment in The Kincaid Brides series from author Mary Connealy. Since being abandoned by his younger brothers as soon as they were old enough to leave, Rafe Kincaid has quietly run his family's Colorado cattle ranch, keeping to himself and trying to block out painful memories. Hoping to put the past behind him, Rafe visits an isolated cave on the far reaches of his property that holds bad memories, but he's surprised to find the beautiful Julia Gilliland trapped inside. Unbeknownst to Rafe,

the adventurous woman has been frequenting the cave, scoping out fossils and researching for her book. Wildly attracted to Julia from this initial meeting, Rafe struggles to come to terms with her fascination with the place he hates most and how it might affect his chance to reconcile with his estranged brothers.

Other books by the same author:
Deep Trouble, 2011
Sharpshooter in Petticoats, 2011
The Husband Tree, 2010
Gingham Mountain, 2009
Petticoat Ranch, 2007

Other books you might like:
Margaret Brownley, *A Vision of Lucy*, 2011
Colleen Coble, *The Lightkeeper's Ball*, 2011
Mona Hodgson, *Too Rich for a Bride*, 2011
Tracie Peterson, *To Have and to Hold*, 2011
Karen Witemeyer, *Head in the Clouds*, 2010

522

KAYE DACUS

Ransome's Quest

(Eugene, Oregon: Harvest House Publishers, 2011)

Series: Ransome Trilogy. Book 3
Story type: Historical; Series
Subject(s): Sea stories; Kidnapping; Pirates
Major character(s): William Ransome, Sea Captain, Spouse (of Julia), Brother (of Charlotte); Charlotte Ransome, Sister (of William), Kidnap Victim; Julia Ransome, Spouse (of William), Kidnap Victim
Time period(s): 19th century; 1810s
Locale(s): Caribbean

Summary: *Ransome's Quest*, a historical inspirational novel, is the third and final installment in the Ransome Trilogy from author Kaye Dacus. Set on the high seas during the early 19th century, *Ransome's Quest* follows Captain William Ransome as he sails the Caribbean Sea in search of his missing sister, Charlotte, who has reportedly been kidnapped by a villain named Salvadore. Compounding the situation is news that Ransome's wife, Julia, has been kidnapped as well by the dreaded pirate, Shaw. Ransome and his crew race to rescue the two most important women in his life. When they recover Charlotte, they're shocked to learn the truth about Salvadore's identity and his eagerness to help locate Julia. Is Ransome desperate enough to find his wife that he's willing to accept help from a known enemy?

Other books by the same author:
The Art of Romance, 2011
Love Remains, 2010
Ransome's Crossing, 2010
Ransome's Honor, 2009
Stand-in-Groom, 2009

Other books you might like:
Andrea Boeshaar, *Undaunted Faith*, 2011
Kelly Eileen Hake, *Tall, Dark and Determined*, 2011
Cara Lynn James, *Love By the Book*, 2011

Delia Parr, *Hidden Affections*, 2011
Tracie Peterson, *Hope Rekindled*, 2011

523

ANNALISA DAUGHETY

Love Finds You in Lancaster County, Pennsylvania

(Minneapolis, Minnesota: Summerside Press, 2011)

Story type: Romance
Subject(s): Amish; Love; Friendship
Major character(s): Lydia Ann Raber, Friend (of Caroline); Caroline DeMarco, Friend (of Lydia); Simon Zook, Carpenter; Michael Landis, Journalist
Time period(s): 21st century; 2010s
Locale(s): Lancaster County, Pennsylvania

Summary: In *Love Finds You in Lancaster County, Pennsylvania*, author Annalisa Daughety tells a story of love and friendship centering on two very different women, united by the painful losses they've suffered in their lives. Lydia Ann Raber, an Amish woman, and Caroline DeMarco, a transplant from the American South, come together and open a quaint gift shop in the Amish haven of Lancaster County. There Lydia meets Amish carpenter Simon Zook, who presents another opportunity for the heartbroken Lydia to find true love. Meanwhile, Caroline is smitten with journalist Michael Landis—but exactly how much does Michael know about Caroline's shadowy past?

Other books by the same author:
Love Is Grand, 2010
Love Is Monumental, 2010
Love Finds You in Charm, Ohio, 2009
Love Is a Battlefield, 2009

Other books you might like:
Melody Carlson, *Love Finds You in Martha's Vineyard, Massachusetts*, 2011
Melanie Dobson, *Love Finds You in Amana, Iowa*, 2011
Miralee Ferrell, *Love Finds You in Sundance, Wyoming*, 2011
Janice Hanna, *Love Finds You in Groom, Texas*, 2011

524

SUSAN PAGE DAVIS

Captive Trail

(Chicago: Moody Publishers, 2011)

Story type: Historical - American West; Series
Subject(s): Love; Native Americans; Christian life
Major character(s): Taabe Waipu, Indian; Ned Bright, Driver (of mail wagon)
Time period(s): 19th century
Locale(s): Texas, United States

Summary: Taabe Waipu is a young Comanche woman who has fled her village and is attempting to make her way through the uncharted Texas frontier. When an ac-

Inspirational

cident leaves her near death, she is rescued by mail carrier Ned Bright, who nurses her back to health. Ned grows determined to find the identity of this mysterious young woman, and when he does just that, he sets out to bring Taabe Waipu back to her family. Instead, he meets opposition from the Comanche, and an epic battle ensues, testing the bond that has developed between Ned and Taabe Waipu.

Other books by the same author:
The Blacksmith's Bravery, 2010
The Crimson Cipher, 2010
The Sheriff's Surrender, 2009
Frasier Island, 2007
The Prisoner's Wife, 2006

Other books you might like:
Lori Copeland, *The One Who Waits for Me*, 2011
Sharon Gillenwater, *Emily's Chance: A Novel*, 2010
Marcia Gruver, *Raider's Heart*, 2011
DiAnn Mills, *Under a Desert Sky*, 2011
Karen Witemeyer, *To Win Her Heart*, 2011

525

ATHOL DICKSON

The Opposite of Art

(Nashville, Tennessee: Howard Books, 2011)

Story type: Literary
Subject(s): Art; Artists; Pilgrimages
Major character(s): Sheridan Ridler, Artist, Traveler
Time period(s): 21st century; 2010s

Summary: *The Opposite of Art: A Novel* is a supernatural and thought-provoking novel about life, death, and art from award-winning author Athol Dickson. When renowned artist Sheridan Ridler is the victim of a hit-and-run driver and is flung into the Harlem River, he has a life-changing epiphany that propels him on a worldwide quest for knowledge. Thought to be dead by everyone who knew him, Sheridan embarks on a decades-long journey to gain a greater understanding of art and eternity from holy men around the planet. After 25 years, word begins to spread that Sheridan may still be alive, prompting surprise visits from the daughter he never knew and the man who tried to kill him.

Other books by the same author:
Lost Mission: A Novel, 2009
Winter Haven, 2009
The Cure, 2008
River Rising, 2006
They Shall See God, 2002

Other books you might like:
Terri Blackstock, *Predator: A Novel*, 2010
Brandilyn Collins, *Deceit*, 2010
Ted Dekker, *The Bride Collector*, 2010
Ted Dekker, *The Priest's Graveyard*, 2011
Tim Downs, *Ends of the Earth: A Bug Man Novel*, 2009

526

SHARON EWELL FOSTER

The Resurrection of Nat Turner, Part 1: The Witnesses

(Nashville, Tennessee: Howard Books, 2011)

Series: Resurrection of Nat Turner Series. Book 1
Story type: Historical; Series
Subject(s): Slavery; Abolition of slavery; United States history
Major character(s): Nat Turner, Slave, Leader, Historical Figure
Time period(s): 19th century; 1830s
Locale(s): Virginia, United States

Summary: The first book in the Witnesses series, *The Resurrection of Nat Turner: A Novel* is a historical novel based on the life of abolitionist hero, Nat Turner, from award winning author Sharon Ewell Foster. Nat Turner, an Ethiopian man turned American slave, is a man on a mission. Determined to set the slaves free, Nat tries his best to reason with those in power. When that doesn't work, he bands together an army of captives and stages an insurrection resulting in the death of 50 white men, the execution of over 100 slaves, and a powerful national debate about the ethics of slavery. In *The Resurrection of Nat Turner*, Foster sheds light on this historic moment, the events leading up to it, and its far-reaching consequences.

Other books by the same author:
Abraham's Well: A Novel, 2006
Riding Through Shadows, 2006
Ain't No Mountain, 2004
Passing Into Light, 2003
Ain't No River, 2001

Other books you might like:
Victoria Christopher Murray, *Sins of the Mother: A Novel*, 2010
Andrea Smith, *Friday Night at Honeybee's*, 2004
Andrea Smith, *The Sisterhood of Blackberry Corner*, 2007
Karen Young, *Lie for Me*, 2011

527

LAURA FRANTZ

The Colonel's Lady

(Grand Rapids, Michigan: Revell, 2011)

Story type: Historical - American Revolution
Subject(s): American Revolution, 1775-1783; Romances (Fiction); Faith
Major character(s): Roxanna Rowan, Gentlewoman, Secretary (to Colonel McLinn); Cassius McLinn, Military Personnel (colonel)
Time period(s): 18th century; 1770s (1779)
Locale(s): Kentucky, United States

Summary: *The Colonel's Lady: A Novel* is a historical inspirational romance from author Laura Frantz. The

year is 1779 and the refined Roxanna Rowan is leaving her lavish home in Virginia on a brave adventure through the harsh frontier. After being dumped by her betrothed, Roxanna is venturing to a remote fort in Kentucky to reunite with her father. When Roxanna arrives, she's devastated to learn that her father has been killed in the line of duty. Out of options and resources, Roxanna accepts a job working for her father's former boss, Colonel Cassius McLinn. As Roxanna and the Colonel spend increasing amounts of time together, rumors are whirling around the fort about the nature of their relationship and the secret that the Colonel is keeping about Roxanna's father's death.

Other books by the same author:
Courting Morrow Little: A Novel, 2010
The Frontiersman's Daughter: A Novel, 2009

Other books you might like:
Laurie Alice Eakes, *Lady in the Mist*, 2011
Julie Klassen, *The Girl in the Gatehouse*, 2011
Julie Lessman, *A Heart Revealed*, 2011
Siri Mitchell, *A Heart Most Worthy*, 2011
Catherine Richmond, *Spring for Susannah*, 2011

528

KATHLEEN FULLER

Hide and Secret

(Nashville, Tennessee: Thomas Nelson, 2011)

Series: Mysteries of Middlefield Series. Book 3
Story type: Mystery; Series
Subject(s): Mystery; Money; Friendship
Major character(s): Anna Mae Shetler, Child, Friend (of Jeremiah & Amos), Detective—Amateur; Jeremiah, Child, Friend (of Anna Mae & Amos); Amos, Child, Friend (of Anna Mae & Jeremiah)
Time period(s): 19th century
Locale(s): Middlefield, Ohio

Summary: *Hide and Secret*, a suspenseful inspirational mystery, is the third novel in the Mysteries of Middlefield series from author Kathleen Fuller. Anna Mae and her two best pals, Jeremiah and Amos, are playing together in the woods when they make a shocking discover that stirs up age-old secrets, betrayals, and wounds. When the floorboard in their tree house breaks, the kids are stunned to discover an old diary and a metal box full of cash hidden beneath it. Determined to crack the mystery surrounding their strange find, the trio begins sleuthing and uncovers some surprising secrets about their families and their long histories together. When the money goes missing, Anna Mae, Jeremiah, and Amos must learn if their friendship can withstand this test or if they'll end up as distant as their grandparents have become.

Other books by the same author:
Treasuring Emma, 2011
A Hand to Hold, 2010
An Honest Love, 2010
The Secrets Beneath, 2010
A Man of His Word, 2009

Other books you might like:
Mindy Starns Clark, *Secrets of Harmony Grove*, 2010
Patricia Davids, *The Farmer Next Door*, 2011
Melanie Dobson, *The Silent Order*, 2010
Marta Perry, *Murder in Plain Sight*, 2010
Marta Perry, *Vanish in Plain Sight*, 2011

529

ANN H. GABHART

The Blessed

(Grand Rapids, Michigan: Revell, 2011)

Series: Shaker Series. Book 4
Story type: Historical; Series
Subject(s): Shakers (Protestants); Romances (Fiction); History
Major character(s): Lacey Bishop, Young Woman, Bride
Time period(s): 19th century; 1840s (1844)
Locale(s): Kentucky, United States

Summary: *The Blessed: A Novel*, a historical inspirational romance, is the fourth installment in the Shaker series from author Ann H. Gabhart. Since the age of 16, Lacey Bishop has been working for her preacher and his wife, caring for the young baby that was left on their doorstep. When the preacher is widowed, Lacey's commitment to the child outweighs her own feelings and she agrees to marry the man who is twice her age. Lacey soon finds herself living among the Shakers, an odd religious sect with strict rules about marriage and family. Separated from her husband and her daughter, Lacey wrestles with her emotions daily, especially when she meets a recently widowed man and is immediately drawn to him. In a strange community where love is forbidden, Lacey finds herself falling more deeply in love with a mysterious man who isn't her husband.

Other books by the same author:
Angel Sister, 2011
The Seeker: A Novel, 2010
The Believer: A Novel, 2009
The Outsider: A Novel, 2008
The Scent of Lilacs, 2005

Other books you might like:
Mindy Starns Clark, *The Amish Nanny*, 2011
Jerry S. Eicher, *A Baby for Hannah*, 2011
Shelley Shepard Gray, *The Protector: Families of Honor, Book Two*, 2011
Ruth Reid, *The Promise of an Angel*, 2011
Cindy Woodsmall, *The Harvest of Grace*, 2011

530

LINDA GOODNIGHT

The Nanny's Homecoming

(New York: Love Inspired, 2011)

Story type: Romance
Subject(s): Romances (Fiction); Faith; Love
Major character(s): Brooke Clayton, Young Woman,

Child-Care Giver; Gabe Wesson, Widow(er),
Wealthy, Businessman, Single Father
Time period(s): 21st century; 2010s
Locale(s): Colorado, United States

Summary: *The Nanny's Homecoming* is an inspirational
romance novel from award-winning author Linda
Goodnight. After a failed romance and a cancelled wedding, Brooke Clayton's only real prospect is to move
home to her small Colorado town. Strangely enough,
lasting in the town for one year will result in a sufficient
payday for the young woman, per the bizarre arrangements in her late grandfather's will. Desperate for work,
Brooke discovers that the wealthy and recently widowed
businessman next door is in need of a nanny for his
young daughter. Brooke is happy to accept the job from
Gabe, but their new arrangement has them both troubled
with memories of their pasts and longings for the future.

Other books by the same author:
A Place to Belong, 2011
The Lawman's Christmas Wish, 2010
The Wedding Garden, 2010
A Season for Grace, 2008
A Very Special Delivery, 2006

Other books you might like:
Patricia Davids, *The Farmer Next Door*, 2011
Jillian Hart, *Wyoming Sweethearts*, 2011
Arlene James, *The Sheriff's Runaway Bride*, 2011
Deb Kastner, *Phoebe's Groom*, 2011
Kit Wilkinson, *Mom in the Making*, 2011

531

SHAWN GRADY

Falls Like Lightning

(Minneapolis, Minnesota: Bethany House, 2011)

Story type: Romance
Subject(s): Suspense; Fires; Romances (Fiction)
Major character(s): Silas Kent, Fire Fighter; Elle West-
more, Single Mother, Pilot
Time period(s): 21st century; 2010s

Summary: *Falls Like Lightning* is a suspenseful and
inspirational romance novel from author Shawn Grady.
Silas Kent's career has finally reached the big time, or
so he thinks, when he's assigned his very own fire crew.
But before the team even has a chance to train together,
they're thrown into one of the most dangerous forest
fires in recent history. Lightning has sparked a vicious
outbreak in the Sierra Nevadas and it's up to Silas and
the gang to parachute in and stop the flames' progress.
Flying them into the blaze is single mom Elle Westmore,
who is forced to stage an emergency landing after a
suspicious engine explosion. On the ground, Silas realizes the real danger is not the flames surrounding them
but the betrayal of the men he considers his team.

Other books by the same author:
Tomorrow We Die, 2010
Through the Fire, 2009

Other books you might like:
Terri Blackstock, *Vicious Cycle*, 2011

Irene Hannon, *Fatal Judgment*, 2011
Steven James, *The Bishop*, 2010
Ronie Kendig, *Nightshade*, July 1, 2010
Richard L. Mabry, *Code Blue*, 2010

532

ROBIN JONES GUNN

Canary Island Song

(Nashville, Tennessee: Howard Books, 2011)

Story type: Romance
Subject(s): Love; Grief; Christian life
Major character(s): Carolyn, Widow(er); Bryan Spencer,
Boyfriend (former, of Carolyn)
Time period(s): 21st century; 2010s
Locale(s): Canary Islands, Spain; San Francisco,
California

Summary: In *Canary Island Song*, author Robin Jones
Gunn tells the story of Carolyn, a middle-aged widow
who gets a second chance at life and love. At the urging
of her adult daughter, Carolyn returns to her native
Canary Islands to pay her mother a visit on the occasion
of the latter woman's 70th birthday. Once arrived in her
hometown, Carolyn runs into an old flame, Bryan
Spencer, and she is suddenly forced to confront the reality of her situation. She is desperately lonely, growing
older, and still grieving her late husband. It's time, Carolyn decides, to move forward with her life, and Bryan
just might be the man to help her accomplish her goal.

Other books by the same author:
Under a Maui Moon: A Novel, 2010
Coming Attractions, 2009
The Sisterchicks Series, 2003-2009

Other books you might like:
Tamara Leigh, *Restless in Carolina*, 2011
Deborah Raney, *Forever After*, 2011
Gayle Roper, *Shadows on the Sand: A Seaside Mystery*,
2011
Susan May Warren, *My Foolish Heart*, 2011

533

PATRICIA HALEY

Broken

(New York: Gallery Books, 2011)

Story type: Family Saga
Subject(s): Family; Business; Forgiveness
Major character(s): Don Mitchell, Businessman, Brother
(to Joel & Tamara), Religious; Joel Mitchell, Brother
(to Don & Tamara), Businessman; Tamara Mitchell,
Sister (to Don & Joel)
Time period(s): 21st century; 2010s
Locale(s): United States

Summary: *Broken* is an inspirational novel about family,
forgiveness, and reconciliation from bestselling and
award-winning author Patricia Haley. When Don Mitchell's younger half-brother, Joel, resigns from his post as

CEO of their father's company, Don sees an opportunity to bring his fragmented family back together again. Don steps in as head of DMI, the multimillion-dollar ministry, and tries to right all of the wrongs that Joel committed. His first order of business is to convince older sister, Tamara, to return to the family, but once she's back, she uses any means necessary to carve out a place for herself in the family's business. Meanwhile, Joel is regretting his decision to step down, forcing Don to figure out a way to simultaneously save the business and save his family without causing collateral damage to either.

Other books by the same author:
Chosen, 2009
No Regrets, 2007
Still Waters, 2007
Let Sleeping Dogs Lie, 2006
Blind Faith, 2003

Other books you might like:
Sheila M. Gross, *Delilah*, 2011
Vanessa Miller, *Promise of Forever Love*, 2011
Nikita Lynette Nichols, *Crossroads*, 2011
Kendra Norman-Bellamy, *Upon This Rock*, 2011
Pat Simmons, *Crowning Glory*, 2011

534

YVONNE L HARRIS

A River to Cross

(Minneapolis, Minnesota: Bethany House, 2011)

Story type: Historical; Romance
Subject(s): Romances (Fiction); United States history, 1865-1901; Kidnapping
Major character(s): Jake Nelson, Ranger; Elizabeth Madison, Kidnap Victim, Daughter (of U.S. senator), Journalist
Time period(s): 19th century; 1880s
Locale(s): Mexico; Texas, United States

Summary: *A River to Cross* is a historical and inspirational romance novel from award-winning author Yvonne L. Harris. Texas Ranger Jake Nelson takes his job guarding the U.S.-Mexico border very seriously, doing his best to protect Americans against Mexican outlaws, bandits, and thieves. Jake and his men are in for a mighty fight when Manuel Diego launches a revolt against the U.S. government, killing a senator's son and kidnapping his daughter. Elizabeth Madison, an aspiring journalist, is strong and beautiful, and when Jake finally rescues her, the natural chemistry and passionate sparks between them come as a surprise. But Diego won't give up so easily, making Elizabeth a target in his violent game, and forcing Jake to risk everything to protect the woman who has stolen his heart.

Other books by the same author:
The Vigilante's Bride, 2010

Other books you might like:
Rosslyn Elliott, *Fairer Than Morning*, 2011
Marcia Gruver, *Bandit's Hope*, 2011
Janice Hanna, *Love Finds You in Groom, Texas*, 2011
Martha Rogers, *Summer Dream*, 2011
Kim Vogel Sawyer, *A Whisper of Peace*, 2011

535

JODY HEDLUND

The Doctor's Lady

(Minneapolis, Minnesota: Bethany House, 2011)

Story type: Historical; Romance
Subject(s): Romances (Fiction); Faith; Missionaries
Major character(s): Priscilla White, Young Woman, Religious; Eli Ernest, Doctor, Young Man, Religious
Time period(s): 19th century
Locale(s): United States

Summary: *The Doctor's Lady* is a historical inspirational romance from author Jody Hedlund. Unlike other women her age, Priscilla White has no interest in becoming a wife or a mother. Instead, her heart's desire is to serve God overseas as a missionary in India. Dr. Eli Ernest, a single man himself, is also solely devoted to his mission work. He's in town on a brief visit to educate others on the importance of missions when he receives a surprising message from the mission board: single men and women are no longer allowed to minister in the field. Stunned and disappointed, Priscilla and Eli begin to realize they are one other's only hope. Marrying in name alone seems like a simple enough task, until a challenging journey out west forces them to reexamine their hearts and confront their growing mutual attraction.

Other books by the same author:
The Preacher's Bride, 2010

Other books you might like:
Andrea Boeshaar, *Undaunted Faith*, 2011
Cara Lynn James, *Love By the Book*, 2011
Deborah Raney, *Forever After*, 2011
Kim Vogel Sawyer, *A Whisper of Peace*, 2011
Marylu Tyndall, *Surrender the Night*, 2011

536

DENISE HILDRETH JONES

The First Gardener

(Carol Stream, Illinois: Tyndale House, 2011)

Story type: Contemporary
Subject(s): Grief; Friendship; Gardening
Major character(s): Jeremiah Williams, Gardener; Mackenzie London, Spouse (of Gray); Gray London, Government Official (governor of Tennessee), Spouse (of Mackenzie)
Time period(s): 21st century; 2010s
Locale(s): Tennessee, United States

Summary: In *The First Gardener*, author Denise Hildreth Jones tells the story of Jeremiah Williams, a mild-mannered gardener who cares for the grounds of the Tennessee governor's mansion. He watches as the governor and his wife, Mackenzie, first struggle to have a child, only to be overjoyed at the eventual birth of their daughter. But then tragedy hits the family, and Mackenzie is left floating in a sea of loss. Jeremiah is greatly affected by Mackenzie's situation, and he gingerly makes his way into her life, helping her come

Inspirational

to terms with her grief and urging her to give life a second chance.

Other books by the same author:
Hurricanes in Paradise, 2010
Flies on the Butter, 2007
The Will of Wisteria, 2007
Savannah by the Sea, 2006
Savannah Comes Undone, 2005

Other books you might like:
Sibella Giorello, *The Mountains Bow Down*, 2011
Neta Jackson, *Who Is My Shelter?*, 2010
Tamara Leigh, *Leaving Carolina*, 2009
Jodi Picoult, *Sing You Home*, 2011
Marybeth Whalen, *She Makes It Look Easy: A Novel*, 2011

537

GINA HOLMES

Dry as Rain

(Carol Stream, Illinois: Tyndale House, 2011)

Story type: Romance
Subject(s): Marriage; Divorce; Accidents
Major character(s): Kyra Yoshida, Spouse (of Eric), Amnesiac; Eric Yoshida, Spouse (of Kyra)
Time period(s): 21st century; 2010s
Locale(s): United States

Summary: *Dry as Rain* is a thought-provoking inspirational novel from bestselling author Gina Holmes. Despite being married for 20 years, Eric and Kyra Yoshida are facing an impending divorce. Like many relationships, theirs has slowly deteriorated over the two decades they've been together, barely hanging on at the time that Eric committed adultery. Just as the couple is about to part ways for good, Kyra is involved in a horrific car accident that results in partial amnesia, wiping her mind clean of the struggles of their marriage. With a newfound love for his wife and commitment to make their relationship work, Eric hides his guilt and pretends that everything is blissful between them. He hopes that Kyra's memory won't return and shatter their chances at love and happiness.

Other books by the same author:
Crossing Oceans, 2010

Other books you might like:
Nicole Bart, *Summer Snow*, 2008
Chris Fabry, *Almost Heaven*, 2010
Jan Karon, *In the Company of Others*, 2010
Elizabeth Musser, *The Sweetest Thing*, 2011
Jennifer Erin Valent, *Catching Moondrops*, 2010

538

SERITA JAKES

The Crossing

(Colorado Springs, Colorado: WaterBrook Press, 2011)

Story type: Mystery
Subject(s): Mystery; Violence; Murder

Major character(s): Claudia Campbell, Spouse (of Assistant District Attorney); Casio Hightower, Crime Victim, Police Officer, Football Player (former)
Time period(s): 21st century; 2010s
Locale(s): Texas, United States

Summary: *The Crossing: A Novel* is a suspenseful inspirational mystery from author Serita Jakes. It's been 10 years since a masked gunman opened fire on a high school bus, but the residents of the tiny Texas town where it happened still relive the horror like it was yesterday. For Claudia Campbell, the assault meant the death of her close friend, cheerleading coach B.J. Remington. For Casio Hightower, former high school football star, the shooting meant the end of a dream and the destruction of his future. After a decade, the killer remains at large but Claudia's assistant district attorney husband, along with Officer Hightower, is determined to find him and finally bring justice to this tormented town, regardless of how painful the investigation is.

Other books you might like:
Robbie Cheuvront, *The Guardian*, 2011
Mary Nealy, *Ten Plagues*, 2011
Gayle Roper, *Shadows on the Sand: A Seaside Mystery*, 2011
Alison Strobel, *Composing Amelia: A Novel*, 2011
Kim Cash Tate, *Cherished*, 2011

539

CHRISTINE JOHNSON

The Matrimony Plan

(New York: Love Inspired, 2011)

Story type: Romance
Subject(s): Romances (Fiction); Social class; Faith
Major character(s): Felicity Kensington, Wealthy, Debutante, Fiance(e) (of Robert); Robert Blevins, Engineer, Fiance(e) (of Felicity), Wealthy; Gabriel Meeks, Religious
Time period(s): 20th century; 1920s
Locale(s): Pearlman, Michigan

Summary: *The Matrimony Plan* is a historical inspirational romance from author Christine Johnson. Despite the fact that Felicity Kensington barely knows Robert Blevins, the well-to-do civil engineer that her father recently hired, it hasn't stopped her from planning their lavish and extravagant wedding. After all, a high society girl like Felicity needs a well-connected husband. Meanwhile, Gabriel Meeks escaped New York and its silly societal ways to settle in Pearlman, Michigan as the town's new preacher. What he never expected was to fall head-over-heels in love with a high-society debutante like Felicity. With her marriage to the engineer on the horizon but her heart longing for the poor pastor, Felicity must make a tough choice about her life, her love, and her future.

Other books you might like:
Winnie Griggs, *Second Chance Family*, 2011
Mary Moore, *The Aristocrat's Lady*, 2011
Regina Scott, *The Irresistible Earl*, 2011
Debra Ullrick, *The Unexpected Bride*, 2011
Lacy Williams, *Marrying Miss Marshal*, 2011

540

RONIE KENDIG

Wolfsbane

(Uhrichsville, Ohio: Barbour Publishing, 2011)

Series: Discarded Heroes Series. Book 3
Story type: Romance; Series
Subject(s): Adventure; Love; Christian life
Major character(s): Danielle "Dani" Roark, Military Personnel (demolitions expert); Canyon Metcalfe, Military Personnel
Time period(s): 21st century; 2010s
Locale(s): Venezuela

Summary: Danielle Roark is a demolitions specialist who has just fled captivity from a ruthless South American military general. Once in America, her story is all but dismissed by the United States government, and she bravely sets off again for the jungles of Venezuela, hoping to find more solid proof of her claims. Accompanying her is Special Forces agent Canyon Metcalfe, for whom Dani is secretly pining. What she doesn't know is that Canyon is harboring a secret—a secret so deadly it could imperil their entire jungle mission. Ronie Kendig's *Wolfsbane* is the third novel in the Discarded Heroes series.

Other books by the same author:
Dead Reckoning, 2010
Nightshade, 2010

Other books you might like:
Brandilyn Collins, *Over the Edge*, 2011
Lynette Eason, *A Killer Among Us: A Novel*, 2011
Irene Hannon, *Deadly Pursuit: A Novel*, 2011
Kristen Heitzmann, *Indelible*, 2011

541

TAMARA LEIGH

Restless in Carolina

(Colorado Springs, Colorado: Multnomah Books, 2011)

Series: Southern Discomfort Series. Book 3
Story type: Romance; Series
Subject(s): Romances (Fiction); Christian life; Architecture
Major character(s): Bridget Pickwick-Buchanan, Widow(er), Environmentalist; J.C. Dirk, Architect (developer)
Time period(s): 21st century; 2010s
Locale(s): Atlanta, Georgia; North Carolina, United States

Summary: *Restless in Carolina: A Novel*, a humorous inspirational romance novel, is the third installment in the Southern Discomfort series from author Tamara Leigh. At 33 years old, Bridget Pickwick-Buchanan is a die-hard environmentalist and a widow. It's been five years since her husband's death and Bridget is finally ready to move on, if only she can find a handsome, eco-friendly man to sweep her off her feet. When Bridget is forced to sell her family's expansive property and mansion, she's determined to find a buyer who will use the

land for "green" purposes. Enter J.C. Dirk, an Atlanta-based environmentally conscious developer. He's uninterested in Bridget and the job, until she bursts in on one of his meetings and convinces him otherwise.

Other books by the same author:
Nowhere, Carolina: A Novel, 2010
Leaving Carolina, 2009
Faking Grace, 2008
Splitting Harriett, 2007
Stealing Adda: A Novel, 2006

Other books you might like:
Kristin Billerbeck, *A Billion Reasons Why*, 2011
Kaye Dacus, *The Art of Romance*, 2011
Rachel Hauck, *Dining with Joy*, 2010
Erynn Mangum, *Cool Beans*, 2010
Susan May Warren, *My Foolish Heart*, 2011

542

BONNIE LEON

Wings of Promise

(Grand Rapids, Michigan: Revell, 2011)

Series: Alaskan Skies Series. Book 2
Story type: Romance; Series
Subject(s): Romances (Fiction); Airplanes; Faith
Major character(s): Kate Evans, Pilot; Paul Anderson, Doctor; Mike Conlin, Friend (of Kate), Pilot
Time period(s): 21st century; 2010s
Locale(s): Alaska, United States

Summary: *Wings of Promise: A Novel*, an inspirational romance, is part of the Alaskan Skies series from bestselling author Bonnie Leon. Kate Evans has finally found success as a bush pilot in Alaska, but making her way in a profession dominated by men seems easy compared to navigating her way through romance. Working alongside handsome doctor Paul Anderson, Kate has begun to have more than friendly feelings for her coworker. But a new boss with a fiery attitude forces her closer to best pal and fellow pilot, Mike Conlin, who has her thinking twice about where her heart belongs. Kate struggles with a difficult decision until a horrifying tragedy seems to determine her course.

Other books by the same author:
Touching the Clouds: A Novel, 2010
Enduring Love: A Novel, 2009
Longings of the Heart, 2008
To Love Anew, 2007
When the Storm Breaks, 2006

Other books you might like:
Loree Lough, *Unbridled Hope*, 2011
Vickie McDonough, *Finally a Bride*, 2011
Tracie Peterson, *A Promise for Tomorrow*
Susan May Warren, *My Foolish Heart*, 2011
Kathleen Y'Barbo, *Anna Finch and the Hired Gun: A Novel*, 2010

Inspirational

543

JULIE LESSMAN

A Heart Revealed

(Grand Rapids, Michigan: Revell, 2011)

Series: Winds of Change Series. Book 2
Story type: Romance; Series
Subject(s): Romances (Fiction); Abuse; Love
Major character(s): Emma Malloy, Divorced Person, Abuse Victim, Religious; Sean O'Connor, Friend (of Emma)
Time period(s): 20th century; 1920s
Locale(s): Boston, Massachusetts

Summary: *A Heart Revealed: A Novel*, an inspirational romance novel, is the second installment in the Winds of Change series from author Julie Lessman. It's been 10 years since Emma Malloy ran away from her abusive husband in Dublin and started a new life in Boston. Although her physical scars have faded over the past decade, there are some wounds that will never fully heal. When Emma begins falling for her friend's handsome brother, Sean O'Connor, a well of other emotions resurfaces alongside her newfound love. Sean seems like a wonderful person, but is Emma truly deserving of this kind of love? As shame and fear begin to overwhelm her, Emma must make a painful choice about the past and the future.

Other books by the same author:
A Hope Undaunted: A Novel, 2010
A Passion Denied, 2009
A Passion Most Pure, 2008
A Passion Redeemed, 2008

Other books you might like:
Robin Lee Hatcher, *Belonging*, 2011
Karen Kingsbury, *Learning*, June 21, 2011
Julie Klassen, *The Girl in the Gatehouse*, 2011
Dorothy Love, *Beyond All Measure*, 2011
Allison Pittman, *Lilies in Moonlight*, 2011

544

CHRISTINE LINDSAY

Shadowed in Silk

(Cumberland, Maryland: WhiteFire Publishing, 2011)

Story type: Historical - World War I
Subject(s): World War I, 1914-1918; Abuse; Indians (Asian people)
Major character(s): Abby Fraser, Spouse (of Nick), Mother (of Cam), Abuse Victim; Nick Fraser, Military Personnel, Father (to Cam), Spouse (to Abby); Cam Fraser, 3-Year-Old, Son (of Abby and Nick); Geoff Richards, Military Personnel, Friend (of Abby)
Time period(s): 20th century; 1910s
Locale(s): India

Summary: *Shadowed in Silk* is a historical inspirational novel from author Christine Lindsay. It's been four long years since Abby Fraser has seen her husband, Nick.

While he was fighting in World War I, she gave birth to their son, Cam, whom Nick has never met. Overwhelmed with anticipation and excitement, Abby and Cam embark on a journey to India, her childhood home, to reunite with Nick, but when they arrive things are not as she expected. Nick seems like a complete stranger to Abby, cruel to their son and dismissive to her. Abby's only refuge is with Major Geoff Richards, a grieving war hero and faithful man who has quickly progressed from being a stranger on the train to a close friend—and possibly something more.

Other books you might like:
Tessa Afshar, *Pearl in the Sand*, 2010
Liz Curtis Higgs, *Mine Is the Night*, 2011
Julie Lessman, *A Passion Redeemed*, 2008
Sandi Rog, *The Master's Wall*, 2010

545

SHARLENE MACLAREN

Livvie's Song

(New Kensington, Pennsylvania: Whitaker House, 2011)

Series: River of Hope Series. Book 1
Story type: Romance; Series
Subject(s): Romances (Fiction); Cooking; Christianity
Major character(s): Olivia Beckman, Single Mother, Widow(er), Restaurateur; Will Taylor, Cook, Prisoner (former)
Time period(s): 21st century; 2010s
Locale(s): Wabash, Indiana

Summary: *Livvie's Song*, an inspirational romance novel, is the first installment in the River of Hope series from author Sharlene MacLaren. In Wabash, Indiana, business is going from bad to worse for single mom, Olivia Beckman. Her restaurant, Livvie's Kitchen, is a favorite among the locals, but money is sparse and things are about to get even tighter when the cook resigns, leaving Livvie in the lurch. Fortunately, as if an answer from God himself, Will Taylor shows up with ten years of cooking experience looking for a job. Little does Livvie know, Will spent the past decade cooking in the prison cafeteria where he was an inmate. But Will is a changed man, converted to Christianity behind bars, and he's ready for a fresh start and maybe a side of romance.

Other books by the same author:
Tender Vow, 2010
Maggie Rose, 2009
Hannah Grace, 2008
Loving Liza Jane, 2007
Through Every Storm, 2007

Other books you might like:
Tamera Alexander, *A Lasting Impression*, 2011
Maggie Brendan, *Deeply Devoted: A Novel*, 2011
Colleen Coble, *The Lightkeeper's Ball*, 2011
Robin Lee Hatcher, *Belonging*, 2011
Kathleen Morgan, *A Heart Divided: A Novel*, 2011

546

ANNE MATEER

Wings of a Dream

(Bloomington, Minnesota: Bethany House, 2011)

Story type: Historical - World War I
Subject(s): World War I, 1914-1918; Faith; Death
Major character(s): Rebekah Hendricks, Young Woman, Caregiver; Arthur Samson, Pilot, Military Personnel
Time period(s): 20th century; 1910s
Locale(s): Oklahoma, United States; Texas, United States

Summary: *Wings of a Dream* is a historical inspirational novel from author Anne Mateer. Rebekah Hendricks has always dreamed of finding an adventurous life outside of her parents' small-town farm in Oklahoma, and sexy pilot Arthur Samson might be her ticket out. While Arthur is off fighting in World War I, Rebekah's Aunt Adabelle becomes ill, giving Rebekah a reason to move to Texas to care for her. As an added bonus, her new location also puts her in closer proximity to Arthur's training camp. But Adabelle is unable to fight off the flu, leaving this life (and four precious children) behind. When Arthur starts to get cold feet and Rebekah feels the burden of caring for the children, she's forced to choose between the life she's always dreamed of and a deeper love than she ever imagined. First novel.

Other books you might like:
Elizabeth Camden, *The Lady of Bolton Hill*, 2011
Kelly Eileen Hake, *Tall, Dark and Determined*, 2011
Dorothy Love, *Beyond All Measure*, 2011
Christine Lynxwiler, *The Stars Remember*, 2011
Nancy Moser, *An Unlikely Suitor*, 2011

547

SANDRA ORCHARD

Deep Cover

(New York: Love Inspired, 2011)

Story type: Mystery; Romance
Subject(s): Suspense; Romances (Fiction); Detective fiction
Major character(s): Rick Gray, Police Officer; Ginny Bryson, Girlfriend (former, of Rick)
Time period(s): 21st century; 2010s
Locale(s): United States

Summary: *Deep Cover* is a suspenseful inspirational romance from award-winning author Sandra Orchard. Relationships don't come easy for an undercover cop like Rick Gray and although he really cared about Ginny Bryson, he could never let her really get to know him. Fate and work have led him back into Ginny's life, this time under a new alias to dig up dirt on her unsavory uncle. Rick believes that Ginny's uncle is responsible for his partner's death and he wants justice to be swiftly served. It seems that Rick isn't the only man after Ginny's uncle though. Someone else is trying to punish Ginny for her uncle's crimes, forcing Rick to intervene to protect the only woman he's ever loved while trying to maintain his cover.

Other books you might like:
Christy Barritt, *The Last Target*, 2011
Margaret Daley, *Hidden in the Everglades*, 2011
Debby Giusti, *The Captain's Mission*, 2011
Shirlee McCoy, *Lone Defender*, 2011
Lauren Nichols, *On Deadly Ground*, 2011

548

ROBIN PARRISH

Vigilante

(Bloomington, Minnesota: Bethany House, 2011)

Story type: Psychological
Subject(s): Adventure; Christianity; Morality
Major character(s): Nolan Gray, Military Personnel (soldier)
Time period(s): Indeterminate
Locale(s): United States

Summary: Robin Parrish's *Vigilante* is set in a United States torn apart by unrest, corruption, crime, and immorality. Out of this toxic scene comes Nolan Gray, a highly skilled soldier who has seen his share of combat and has taken down an impressive number of bad guys. But now he faces the biggest challenge of his life: confronting the forces of evil currently plaguing America and bringing them to their knees. Drawing from his years of experience on the battlefields, Nolan sets out to save the nation from the people and forces threatening to destroy it—even it means sacrificing his own life.

Other books by the same author:
Nightmare, 2010
Merciless, 2009
Offworld, 2009
Fearless, 2008
Relentless, 2006

Other books you might like:
Davis Bunn, *Lion of Babylon*, 2011
Mike Dellosso, *Darkness Follows*, 2011
Mike Duran, *The Resurrection*, 2011
Steven James, *The Queen: A Patrick Bowers Thriller*, 2011
Craig Parshall, *Thunder of Heaven*, 2011
James L. Rubart, *Book of Days*, 2011

549

TRACIE PETERSON
JUDITH MILLER, Co-Author

To Have and to Hold

(Bloomington, Minnesota: Bethany House, 2011)

Series: Bridal Veil Island Series. Book 1
Story type: Romance; Series
Subject(s): United States history; Love; Christian life
Major character(s): Audrey Cunningham, Young Woman; Marshall Graham, Contractor
Time period(s): 19th century; 1880s

Inspirational

Locale(s): Bridal Veil Island, Georgia

Summary: In the post-Civil War South, beautiful Audrey Cunningham is relieved when her father suggests that the two of them move to serene Bridal Veil Island. The change of scenery can only help her father battle his demons, Audrey is certain of that. But when father and daughter arrive on the island, they land in the middle of a feud involving the locals and invading developers who want to take over. Now Audrey must save her land from the interests of big business—all while juggling an attraction to Marshall Graham, a contractor who has been keeping his eye on the spirited young woman's comings and goings. *To Have and to Hold* is the first novel in Tracie Peterson and Judith Miller's Bridal Veil Island series.

Other books by the same author:
Hearts Aglow, 2011
Hope Rekindled, 2011
Embers of Love, 2010
Morning's Refrain, 2010
Twilight's Serenade, 2010

Other books you might like:
Lynn Austin, *Wonderland Creek*, 2011
Colleen Coble, *The Lightkeeper's Bride*, 2010
Mary Connealy, *Out of Control*, 2011
Susan Page Davis, *The Lady's Maid*, 2011
Robin Lee Hatcher, *Belonging*, 2011
Judith Pella, *Distant Dreams*, 1997

550

MARK SCHULTZ
TRAVIS THRASHER, Co-Author

Letters from War

(Nashville, Tennessee: Howard Books, 2011)

Story type: Contemporary
Subject(s): Wars; Letters (Correspondence); Mother-son relations
Major character(s): Natalie, Mother (of James); James, Military Personnel, Son (of Natalie)
Time period(s): 21st century; 2010s
Locale(s): United States

Summary: Based on a song by the same name, *Letters from War: A Novel* is a heartwarming inspirational novel from platinum-selling Christian recording artist Mark Schultz and author Travis Thrasher. It's been two years since anyone has heard from Natalie's son, James, but this faithful mother isn't willing to give up hope. While in the line of duty, James went missing during an attempt to save a fellow paratrooper. Natalie leaves the porch light on every night in anticipation of James' return. Despite the disbelief from neighbors and their heartfelt encouragement to move on, Natalie can't give up her faith that someday her son will return to her.

Other books you might like:
James Scott Bell, *The Whole Truth*, 2008
James Scott Bell, *Watch Your Back*, 2011
Robert Liparulo, *Timescape*, 2009
Bill Myers, *The God Hater*, 2010

Randy Singer, *By Reason of Insanity*, 2009

551

LEE STROBEL

The Ambition

(Grand Rapids, Michigan: Zondervan, 2011)

Story type: Contemporary; Mystery
Subject(s): Christian life; Mystery; Detective fiction
Time period(s): 21st century; 2010s
Locale(s): United States

Summary: In *The Ambition* by Lee Strobel, a cast of variously flawed characters struggles for power in the shadow of a lavish house of worship and its tainted ministry. As a dangerously ambitious pastor asserts his authority within the church, he crosses paths with a dishonest judge who is overseeing an organized crime trial, a troubled gambler who holds incriminating information, and a journalist who is looking for a sensational story to resurrect his struggling newspaper. As the complex tale unfolds in an affluent suburb, the worlds of politics and religion eventually collide in a brutal act of murder.

Other books by the same author:
The End of Reason: A Response to the New Atheists, 2008
Finding the Real Jesus: A Guide for Curious Christians and Skeptical Seekers, 2008
The Case for Christmas: A Journalist Investigates the Identity of the Child in the Manger, 2005
God's Outrageous Claims: Discover What They Mean for You, 2005
The Case for Faith: A Journalist Investigates the Toughest Objections to Christianity, 2004

Other books you might like:
Alton Gansky, *Fallen Angel: A Novel*, 2011
Kristen Heitzmann, *Indelible*, 2011
Randy Singer, *False Witness*, 2007
Bodie Thoene, *Twelfth Prophecy*, 2011
Robert Whitlow, *Water's Edge*, 2011

552

SARAH SUNDIN

Blue Skies Tomorrow

(Grand Rapids, Michigan: Revell, 2011)

Series: Wings of Glory Series. Book 3
Story type: Historical - World War II; Romance
Subject(s): Romances (Fiction); World War II, 1939-1945; Faith
Major character(s): Helen Carlisle, Widow(er), Single Mother, Volunteer; Raymond Novak, Military Personnel, Religious
Time period(s): 20th century; 1930s-1940s
Locale(s): California, United States

Summary: *Blue Skies Tomorrow: A Novel*, a historical inspirational romance, is the third novel in the Wings of Glory series from author Sarah Sundin. When Helen Carlisle becomes a widow and a single mother after losing her husband in World War II, she hides all traces of her feelings by devoting herself wholeheartedly to volunteering for the war effort. No one in her small California town can possibly understand the wide range of emotions racing through her heart. Her old childhood friend, Lt. Raymond Novak, resurfaces in her life when he's stationed at a stateside job training B-17 pilots. The gentle man with a passion for Christ soon earns Helen's trust and wins her heart, but tragedies on both sides of the Pacific force the couple to confront their deepest secrets and darkest fears.

Other books by the same author:
A Distant Melody: A Novel, 2010
A Memory Between Us: A Novel, 2010

Other books you might like:
Lynn Austin, *While We're Far Apart*, 2010
Jane Kirkpatrick, *The Daughter's Walk*, 2011
Julie Klassen, *The Girl in the Gatehouse*, 2011
Maureen Lang, *Springtime of the Spirit*, 2011
Bodie Thoene, *Against the Wind*, 2011

553

ERICA VETSCH

A Bride's Portrait of Dodge City, Kansas

(Uhrichsville, Ohio: Barbour Publishing, 2011)

Story type: Historical; Mystery
Subject(s): Mystery; Murder; Western fiction
Major character(s): Adeline Reed, Photographer, Young Woman, Detective—Amateur; Miles Carr, Police Officer (deputy)
Time period(s): 19th century; 1870s
Locale(s): Dodge City, Kansas

Summary: *A Bride's Portrait of Dodge City, Kansas* is a historical inspirational romance from author Erica Vetsch. Looking for an escape from her unsavory past, Adeline Reed starts a new life in Dodge City, Kansas. In this growing Western settlement, Addie finds work as the town's photographer and becomes a respected member of the community, especially when she's called to help with a murder investigation. Deputy Miles Carr is investigating the mysterious death of the shopkeeper and he recruits Addie to aid him in his sleuthing. As the two inch closer to the killer, they're drawn closer to one another. But the perfect life Addie has created comes precariously close to crashing down with the arrival of her ex-boyfriend's partner-in-crime.

Other books by the same author:
Idaho Brides, 2011
The Engineered Engagement, 2010
Lily and the Lawmaker, 2010
The Marriage Masquerade, 2010
The Bartered Bride, 2009

Other books you might like:
Maggie Brendan, *A Love of Her Own*, 2010
Amanda Cabot, *Scattered Petals*, 2010
Laura Frantz, *Courting Morrow Little: A Novel*, 2010
Cathy Marie Hake, *Serendipity*, 2010
Kathleen Y'Barbo, *The Inconvenient Marriage of Charlotte Beck: A Novel*, 2011

554

STEPHANIE GRACE WHITSON

A Most Unsuitable Match

(Minneapolis, Minnesota: Bethany House, 2011)

Story type: Romance
Subject(s): Romances (Fiction); Boating; Wilderness areas
Major character(s): Fannie Rousseau, Wealthy, Young Woman, Passenger (steamboat); Samuel Beck, Religious (reverend), Passenger (steamboat)
Time period(s): 19th century; 1860s
Locale(s): United States

Summary: *A Most Unsuitable Match* is a historical inspirational romance from author Stephanie Grace Whitson. Miss Fannie Rousseau and Reverend Samuel Beck couldn't be any more different, but when their paths cross on a steamboat journey, they're instantly drawn to one another. Fannie and Samuel are passengers on the same boat traveling up the Missouri River headed for Montana, but their reasons for the trip are vastly different. Fannie is hoping to solve a family mystery that recently surfaced after the death of her mother, and Samuel is planning to minister to the lost souls living in the wilderness area. She's a self-absorbed girly girl with a wealthy family and he's a humble servant of God, but the chemistry between the pair is undeniable, leaving them both hoping for another meeting of fate.

Other books by the same author:
Sixteen Brides, 2010
A Claim of Her Own, 2009
A Hilltop in Tuscany, 2006
Watchers on the Hill, 2004

Other books you might like:
Elizabeth Camden, *The Lady of Bolton Hill*, 2011
Laura Frantz, *The Colonel's Lady*, 2011
Dorothy Love, *Beyond All Measure*, 2011
Nancy Moser, *An Unlikely Suitor*, 2011

555

LISA WINGATE

Dandelion Summer

(New York: NAL Accent, 2011)

Series: Blue Sky Hill Series. Book 4
Story type: Contemporary; Series
Subject(s): Friendship; Aging (Biology); Faith
Major character(s): Epiphany Salerno, 16-Year-Old, Outcast, Cook, Caregiver; J. Norman Alvord, Aged Person, Engineer (retired)

Time period(s): 21st century; 2010s
Locale(s): Dallas, Texas

Summary: *Dandelion Summer*, an inspirational novel, is part of the Blue Sky Hill series from author Lisa Wingate. Sixteen-year old Epiphany Salerno is being shipped off to Texas to live with her detached mother and new stepfather, following the death of Mrs. Lora, the family friend who had taken Epie in. Living in a poor area of Blue Sky Hill, Epie struggles to fit in and find her place in this new world. When her mother volunteers her for an after-school job working as a cook and housekeeper for an elderly man named Norman, Epie is about as unenthusiastic about the idea as Norman himself. The retired engineer is suffering from heart troubles, but is convinced he can care for himself. Over the weeks and months that follow, this unlikely pair forms a unique and strong bond that provides healing to both of their souls.

Other books by the same author:
Larkspur Cove, 2011
Beyond Summer, 2010
The Summer Kitchen, 2009
A Month of Summer, 2008
Tending Roses, 2003

Other books you might like:
Terri Blackstock, *Vicious Cycle*, 2011
Beverly Lewis, *The Mercy*, 2011
Tracie Peterson, *Hope Rekindled*, 2011
Lauraine Snelling, *On Hummingbird Wings*, 2011
Ann Tatlock, *Promises to Keep*, 2011

556

BETH WISEMAN

Healing Hearts: A Collection of Amish Romances

(Nashville, Tennessee: Thomas Nelson, 2011)

Story type: Collection; Romance
Subject(s): Amish; Romances (Fiction); Short stories

Summary: *Healing Hearts: A Collection of Amish Romances* is an anthology of three inspirational novellas from author Beth Wiseman. In *A Choice to Forgive*, Lydia is heartbroken when the love of her life, Daniel, leaves her to enjoy life in the English world, but she finds happiness with his brother, Elam. When Elam dies after 15 years of marriage, Lydia is shocked by Daniel's return. In *A Change of Heart*, Leah has goals of being a writer, atypical of an Amish woman, but Aaron is captivated by her drive and ambition. *Healing Hearts* is the tale of Levina and Naaman, empty-nesters after 30 years of marriage, who must work through Naaman's long absence when a trip to visit family in Ohio turns into an extended vacation.

Other books by the same author:
Plain Proposal, 2011
Plain Paradise, 2010
Seek Me With All Your Heart, 2010
Plain Pursuit, 2009
Plain Perfect, 2008

Other books you might like:
Wanda E. Brunstetter, *Love Finds a Home*, 2011
Mindy Starns Clark, *The Women of Lancaster County*, 2011
Shelley Shepard Gray, *Sisters of the Heart Series*, 2008
Beverly Lewis, *Seasons of Grace Series*, 2009
Beth Wiseman, *Plain Proposal*, 2011

557

KAREN YOUNG

Lie for Me

(Nashville, Tennessee: Howard Books, 2011)

Story type: Contemporary
Subject(s): Suspense; Murder; Christian life
Major character(s): Lauren Halloway, Fiance(e) (former fiancee of Tucker); Tucker Kane, Crime Suspect
Time period(s): 21st century; 2010s
Locale(s): United States

Summary: Karen Young's *Lie for Me* opens with Lauren Halloway's former fiancee being accused of his ex-wife's murder. But Tucker Kane is determined to prove his innocence, even if that means asking Lauren to lie for him as an alibi. When Lauren declines, Tucker disappears. Years go by, and Lauren runs into Tucker at a flea market. He manages to get her alone and confides that he is still trying to gather enough evidence to exonerate himself—and he needs her help. But Lauren isn't sure if she can trust Tucker, a man with more than his fair share of secrets, deceptions, and questionable behavior.

Other books by the same author:
Missing Max: A Novel, 2010
Blood Bayou: A Novel, 2009
Never Tell, 2005
In Confidence, 2004
Kiss and Kill, 2000

Other books you might like:
Brandilyn Collins, *Over the Edge*, 2011
Sharon Ewell Foster, *The Resurrection of Nat Turner, Part 1: The Witnesses*, 2011
Kathy Herman, *False Pretenses*, 2011
Angela Hunt, *The Fine Art of Insincerity: A Novel*, 2011
Tracie Peterson, *Hope Rekindled*, 2011
Francine Rivers, *Her Daughter's Dream*, 2010

558

PENNY ZELLER

Hailee

(New Kensington, Pennsylvania: Whitaker House, 2011)

Series: Montana Skies Series. Book 3
Story type: Historical; Romance
Subject(s): Romances (Fiction); Faith; Family
Major character(s): Hailee Annigan, 19-Year-Old, Thief, Teacher, Orphan; Maxwell Nathaniel Adams Jr., Wealthy, Religious (pastor)
Time period(s): 19th century

Locale(s): Montana, United States

Summary: *Hailee*, a historical inspirational romance, is the third and final installment in the Montana Skies series from author Penny Zeller. Hailee Annigan spent much of her teenage years fending for herself and her younger brothers on the hard streets of 19th-century Cincinnati. But but one too many thefts led Hailee straight to a home for juvenile delinquents. Fortunately, Hailee's sentence was exactly what she needed to turn her life around and now, at the age of 19, Hailee is starting fresh in Montana as a teacher. Maxwell Nathaniel Adams Jr. traded in his well-to-do Boston upbringing for a chance to serve God as a Montana pastor, but his parents are not relenting so easily. Hailee and Maxwell are immediately attracted to each other upon meeting, but their backgrounds and lifestyles are drastically different. How can they ever expect to find happiness together?

Other books by the same author:
Kaydie, 2011
McKenzie, 2010

Other books you might like:
Amanda Cabot, *Scattered Petals*, 2010
Kathleen Morgan, *A Fire Within*, 2007
Tracie Peterson, *Dawn's Prelude*, 2009
Tracie Peterson, *Hearts Aglow*, 2011
Tracie Peterson, *Morning's Refrain*, 2010

Inspirational

The Mystery Genre, September 2011:
Finding the Next Generation of Readers
by
Clair Lamb, for Bookreporter.com

Summer and early autumn 2011 saw the final closing of the iconic bookstore chain Borders, intensifying authors' and publishers' search for new ways to bring books to readers. The move to e-books continued, while an increasing number of authors turned to the young adult market in an effort to find a new generation of readers. Whatever the format, the demand for crime fiction remains strong, with new publishers entering the field and old ones returning in modern ways.

The crime fiction community's embrace of electronic publishing reached a major milestone in June 2011, when the Mystery Writers of America announced long-awaited membership eligibility guidelines for authors published solely in electronic format. While MWA has not yet established eligibility guidelines for e-books to be considered for Edgar Awards, MWA membership will now be open to authors whose books are available "directly through major internet retailers like Amazon, Barnes & Noble, iBookstore, Kobo, etc. and not solely through the publisher's website." Self-published authors are still not eligible for membership under these new guidelines, as MWA continues to require that books submitted for eligibility be published by publishers who have paid a minimum of $1,000 in advances or royalties to at least five authors with no financial or ownership interest in the company. Electronic publishers must have paid at least 25% of net revenue to authors, and must have been in business for at least two years.

The guidelines come as an increasing number of publishers have announced plans to release or re-release titles in electronic format only. The Mysterious Press, a publisher originally launched by Otto Penzler in 1975, had been a hardcover imprint within Warner Books from 1989 until 2005, when Warner Books was acquired by Hachette. Penzler bought the name back from Hachette in 2010 and shortly thereafter announced that the imprint would be relaunched as part of Grove Atlantic in Fall 2011, to release approximately one new hardcover title a month for a total of 10-12 a year. In June, Mysterious Press announced a partnership with Open Road Integrated Media, a digital-only publisher, to set up Mysterious

Press.com, which will re-publish electronic editions of 250 classic and out-of-print titles over the next year.

Mulholland Books, a mystery imprint of Little, Brown and Company launched in June 2010, released its first new hardcover title, Marcia Clark's *Guilt by Association*, in April 2011. It has since published five other hardcover titles as well as three trade paperbacks, with five additional hardcovers and three additional paperbacks scheduled between now and Spring 2012. Besides those titles, Mulholland published the electronic-only L.A. Noire: The Collected Stories, a companion anthology to Rockstar Games' video game by the same name. L.A. Noire included contributions from some of the biggest names in the genre, such as Lawrence Block, Joyce Carol Oates, and Andrew Vachss.

Literary agent Scott Waxman launched e-publisher Diversion Books in 2010, and crime fiction makes up a large percentage of the fledgling company's catalog, with titles from established mystery authors such as Kent Harrington and Jason Pinter as well as titles from new authors such as Jimmy Petrosino, whose mob thriller *The Dean's List* was released in August.

Meanwhile, online retailer Amazon announced its own crime fiction imprint, Thomas & Mercer, in May. Thomas & Mercer titles will be available in print and audio formats as well as electronic formats, with its first title, *The Immortalists* by Kyle Mills, scheduled for October 4. Barry Eisler, who made waves earlier this year by announcing plans to self-publish his books, has signed with Thomas & Mercer, as has self-publishing guru J.A. Konrath. Jim Fusilli, author of the Terry Orr mysteries, is the most recent mystery novelist to sign with Thomas & Mercer.

Although e-books do seem to be eating into sales of mass-market paperbacks, the pulp fiction imprint Hard Case Crime returns this fall with four new mass-market paperback titles, including *The Consummata*, a long-lost Mickey Spillane novel completed posthumously by Max Allan Collins. The Hard Case Crime imprint had been on hiatus for the past year, after the collapse of its partner, Dorchester Publishing, in 2010. Hard Case

Crime is now part of Titan Books, a leading publisher of film and TV tie-ins, as well as graphic novels, art books, science fiction, and books about film, TV, and music.

The surge of adult crime fiction authors into the world of young adult novels continues, with Harlan Coben the latest to join the ranks. His novel *Shelter*, released in September, features the teenaged Mickey Bolitar, nephew of Coben's adult series character, Myron Bolitar. (In fact, Mickey was introduced in Coben's most recent novel for adults, *Live Wire*). Kathy Reichs' first YA novel, *Virals*, features a main character who is the niece of her series character, Temperance Brennan. John Grisham's second book about 13-year-old legal expert Theo Boone, *Theodore Boone: The Abduction*, was published in June of this year. Even hardboiled PI novelist Reed Farrel Coleman is reportedly working on a novel for younger readers.

Mystery authors are also using young adult novels to explore new genres. Historical mystery author Sarah Smith (*The Vanished Child*) returned to print for the first time in seven years with her critically acclaimed YA novel *The Other Side of Dark*, an intense mystery with supernatural overtones. British author Kevin Wignall, whose adult novel *Who is Conrad Hirst?* was an Edgar nominee in 2009, returns to the US market this fall as K.J. Wignall with *Blood*, a vampire novel for young adults. John Connolly's second fantasy novel for young adults, *The Infernals*, hits U.S. bookshelves in October, only six weeks after the release of his 10th Charlie Parker mystery, *The Burning Soul*.

This year's annual World Mystery Convention, Bouchercon, welcomed approximately 1,500 authors and fans to St. Louis, and honored authors who represented the entire spectrum of subgenres, from private investigators (Robert Crais and Sara Paretsky) to "tartan noir" (Val McDermid) to slightly surreal (Colin Cotterill). In any format and for all ages, crime fiction remains among the strongest of literary genres, with dedicated readers eager to recruit new fans.

Mystery Fiction

559

JEFF ABBOTT

Adrenaline

(New York: Grand Central Publishing, 2011)

Series: Sam Capra Series. Book 1
Subject(s): Espionage; Suspense; Murder
Major character(s): Sam Capra, Agent (CIA); Lucy, Spouse (of Sam)
Time period(s): 21st century; 2010s
Locale(s): London, England; Amsterdam, Netherlands

Summary: In *Adrenaline* by Jeff Abbott, a respected CIA agent living in London is about to become a father. At the top of his career and secure in his marriage to Lucy, Sam Capra is devastated when an explosion turns his world upside down. His wife and unborn child gone, Sam has become a prisoner of the very organization he has served. Accused of treason, Capra realizes that he has become unwittingly involved in a wide-ranging conspiracy. To clear his name, Capra must get away from his CIA captors and track down the assailant who attacked his family. *Adrenaline* is the first book in the Sam Capra series.

Where it's reviewed:
Booklist, May 1, 2011, page 13
Library Journal, June 15, 2011, page 71
Publishers Weekly, May 23, 2011, page 28
Swiss News, May 2010, page 69

Other books by the same author:
Trust Me, 2009
Collision, 2008
Fear, 2006
Panic, 2005
A Kiss Gone Bad, 2001

Other books you might like:
Linwood Barclay, *No Time for Goodbye*, 2007
Lee Child, *Persuader*, 2003
Joseph Finder, *Power Play: A Novel*, 2007
John Gilstrap, *Hostage Zero*, 2010
Gregg Hurwitz, *Trust No One*, 2009

560

MEGAN ABBOTT

The End of Everything

(New York: Hachette Book Group, 2011)

Story type: Child-in-Peril
Subject(s): Missing persons; Friendship; Mystery
Major character(s): Lizzie Hood, Friend (of Evie); Evie Verver, Friend (of Lizzie), Sister (of Dusty); Dusty Verver, Sister (of Evie)

Summary: In *The End of Everything*, author Megan Abbott tells the story of Lizzie and Evie, two best friends who spend every waking moment together. Most of their time is spent at Evie's house, either pestering her older sister Dusty or enjoying the company of her jovial family. One day, Evie goes missing, and the entire town is sent into a frenzy, putting Lizzie in the spotlight to figure out her best friend's state of mind in the hours before she disappeared. Lizzie can't figure out what might have gone wrong in her friend's seemingly perfect life, so she sets out to find some answers. As she struggles to find out where Evie might have gone, Lizzie uncovers some truths about her best friend's life that she never would have guessed.

Where it's reviewed:
Booklist, May 1, 2011, page 22
Library Journal, June 1, 2011, page 88
Publishers Weekly, May 30, 2011, page 47

Other books by the same author:
Bury Me Deep, 2009
Queenpin, 2007
The Song Is You, 2007
Die a Little, 2005

Other books you might like:
Russell Banks, *The Sweet Hereafter: A Novel*, 1991
Jeffrey Eugenides, *The Virgin Suicides*, 1993
Laura Lippman, *To the Power of Three*, 2005
Alice McDermott, *Child of My Heart*, 2002
Alice Sebold, *The Lovely Bones*, 2002

561

SUSAN WITTIG ALBERT

The Darling Dahlias and the Naked Ladies

(New York: Berkley Prime Crime, 2011)

Story type: Historical
Subject(s): Detective fiction; Organized crime; Suspense
Major character(s): Liz Lacy, Detective—Amateur (member of the Darling Dahlias); Verna Tidwell, Detective—Amateur (member of the Darling Dahlias); Bessie Bloodworth, Detective—Amateur (member of the Darling Dahlias); Nona Jean "Lorelei LaMotte" Jamison, Dancer; Miss Lake, Dancer; Myra Mae, Detective—Amateur (member of the Darling Dahlias)
Time period(s): 20th century; 1930s
Locale(s): Darling, Alabama

Summary: The ladies of the Darling Dahlias Garden Club return to solve another mystery in *The Darling Dahlias and the Naked Ladies*. In Darling, Alabama, in the 1930s, the members of the Darling Dahlias grow their own food and, occasionally, become involved in town mysteries. The club members are excited when they learn that two women have moved into the home of Miss Hammer. One is Miss Hammer's niece, Nona Jean Jamison. One of the Dahlias, however, recognizes her as one half of the Ziegfeld Follies Naughty and Nice Sisters. Nona Jean denies being a part of this dancing act, and her friend, Miss Lake, keeps to her rooms. The Dahlias remain suspicious when Nona Jean has her hair cut and dyed. Soon, they begin to suspect that the two women may be hiding from the mob.

Where it's reviewed:
Publishers Weekly, May 23, 2011, page 32

Other books by the same author:
The Tale of Castle Cottage, 2011
The Darling Dahlias and the Cucumber Tree, 2010
Holly Blues, 2010
The Tale of Hill Top Farm, 2004
Thyme of Death, 1992

Other books you might like:
Rhys Bowen, *Her Royal Spyness*, 2007
Tony Earley, *Jim the Boy: A Novel*, 2000
Beth Hoffman, *Saving CeeCee Honeycutt: A Novel*, 2010
Amy Patricia Meade, *Million Dollar Baby*, 2006
Elliott Roosevelt, *The President's Man*, 1991

562

ESRI ALLBRITTEN

Chihuahua of the Baskervilles

(New York: Minotaur Books, 2011)

Story type: Contemporary
Subject(s): Supernatural; Dogs; Suspense
Major character(s): Charlotte Baskerville, Businesswoman (owner of Petey's Closet), Spouse (of Thomas), Grandmother (of Cheri); Thomas, Spouse (of Charlotte), Grandfather (of Cheri); Cheri, Granddaughter (of Charlotte and Thomas); Ellen Froehlich, Designer; Angus MacGregor, Editor; Michael Abernathy, Writer; Suki Oota, Photographer
Time period(s): 21st century; 2010s
Locale(s): Manitou Springs, Colorado

Summary: The staff of *Tripping* magazine sets out to solve the mystery of a ghostly dog's appearance in *Chihuahua of the Baskervilles*. Editor Angus MacGregor, writer Michael Abernathy, and photographer Suki Oota make up the staff of *Tripping* magazine, a travel magazine that reports on supposedly paranormal locations. A strange sighting in Colorado leads the team to investigate. Charlotte Baskerville is the owner of Petey's Closet, a clothing catalogue for dogs. When images of Charlotte's beloved but deceased Chihuahua start appearing and leaving threatening messages, the team must discover who or what is behind the supposedly supernatural phenomenon. Charlotte, however, has more enemies than they anticipated, and any of them could be behind this unusual scheme to capture the Baskerville fortune.

Where it's reviewed:
Publishers Weekly, May 23, 2011, page 32

Other books you might like:
Juliet Blackwell, *Secondhand Spirits*, 2009
Blaize Clement, *Curiosity Killed the Cat Sitter*, 2006
Susan Conant, *A New Leash on Death*, 1990
Sue Henry, *The Serpent's Trail*, 2004
Jim Lavene, *The Telltale Turtle*, 2008

563

DONNA ANDREWS

The Real Macaw: A Meg Langslow Mystery

(New York: Minotaur Books, 2011)

Series: Meg Langslow Series. Book 13
Story type: Amateur Detective; Series
Subject(s): Mystery; Detective fiction; Murder
Major character(s): Meg Langslow, Mother (of twins), Detective—Amateur; Dr. Langslow, Father (of Meg); Grandfather, Grandfather (of Meg); Rob, Brother (of Meg)
Time period(s): 21st century; 2010s
Locale(s): Caerphilly, Virginia

Summary: In the mystery novel *The Real Macaw* by Donna Andrews, Meg Langslow awakens for her infant twins' feeding to find a menagerie of animals in her living room. Since the animal shelter can no longer afford to keep all of its residents alive and some of the animals may be put down, Meg's father and grandfather planned to buy the animals some time. When the van driver who was supposed to transport the animals didn't come, the Langslow men brought the dogs, cats, rodents, and a rude macaw to Meg's house. As it turns out, the driver won't be coming at all—he's dead. Meg searches for a killer with a motive, but the fast-talking macaw may

hold the answer. *The Real Macaw* is the 13th book in the Meg Langslow series.

Where it's reviewed:
Booklist, May 1, 2011, page 38
Publishers Weekly, May 2, 2011, page 40

Other books by the same author:
Stork Raving Mad, 2010
Swan for the Money, 2009
Cockatiels at Seven, 2008
The Penguin Who Knew Too Much, 2007
No Rest for the Wicket, 2006
Delete All Suspects, 2005
You've Got Murder, 2002
Murder with Puffins, 2000
Murder with Peacocks, 1997

Other books you might like:
Lydia Adamson, *Beware the Tufted Duck*, 1996
Lorna Barrett, *Murder Is Binding*, 2008
Sheila Connolly, *One Bad Apple: An Orchard Mystery*, 2008
Sarah Graves, *The Dead Cat Bounce*, 1998
Julie Hyzy, *Grace Under Pressure*, 2010

564

EMILY ARSENAULT

In Search of the Rose Notes
(New York: William Morrow, 2011)

Story type: Contemporary
Subject(s): Missing persons; Babysitters; Detective fiction
Major character(s): Nora, Friend (of Charlotte); Charlotte, Friend (of Nora); Rose, Missing Person, Babysitter
Time period(s): 21st century; 2010s
Locale(s): United States

Summary: Emily Arsenault's *In Search of the Rose Notes* chronicles the investigations of two childhood friends who are hoping to find answers in the disappearance of their babysitter years prior. When Rose first vanished, Nora and Charlotte were just 11 years old, but they still wanted to help find their beloved sitter. Their amateur investigation went nowhere, and the girls eventually went their separate ways. Now, Nora has returned to her hometown and is reunited with her old friend Charlotte. Together, the two young women re-launch their investigation into Rose's disappearance, leading them into the shadowy mysteries of their own pasts.

Where it's reviewed:
Booklist, July 1, 2011, page 33
Library Journal, July 2011, page 58
Publishers Weekly, May 30, 2011, page 50

Other books by the same author:
The Broken Teaglass, 2009

Other books you might like:
Megan Abbott, *The End of Everything*, 2011
Laura Lippman, *Every Secret Thing*, 2003
Laura Lippman, *To the Power of Three*, 2005
Jennifer McMahon, *Promise Not to Tell*, 2006
Jodi Picoult, *My Sister's Keeper*, 2004

565

ACE ATKINS

The Ranger
(New York: Putnam, 2011)

Series: Quinn Colson Series. Book 1
Story type: Amateur Detective; Series
Subject(s): Military life; Death; Crime
Major character(s): Quinn Colson, Military Personnel, Nephew (of Uncle Hamp); Uncle Hamp, Uncle (of Quinn), Lawman (sheriff)
Time period(s): 21st century; 2010s
Locale(s): Jericho, Mississippi

Summary: *The Ranger* is the debut novel in author Ace Atkins's series featuring Quinn Colson. After a tour of duty in Afghanistan, Army Ranger Quinn Colson thinks he is prepared for anything—until he comes home to northeast Mississippi, that is. When he arrives at his hometown of Jericho, there to attend the funeral of his uncle, the town sherrif, he begins to hear rumors that Uncle Hamp's death might not have been of natural causes. Colson begins to investigate, and finds out that the Jericho he left behind has changed: what was once a hard-scrabble yet honest community has turned to drugs and crime. Now it's up to him to figure out the truth about Uncle Hamp's death, and who might be at the bottom of it.

Where it's reviewed:
Library Journal, May 1, 2011, page 74
Publishers Weekly, April 4, 2011, page 31
Tampa Tribune, June 19, 2011, page 4

Other books by the same author:
Devil's Garden, 2009
Wicked City, 2008
White Shadow, 2006
Dirty South, 2004
Crossroad Blues, 1998

Other books you might like:
James Lee Burke, *In the Electric Mist with Confederate Dead*, 1993
Lee Child, *Killing Floor*, 1997
Bryan Gruley, *Starvation Lake*, 2009
James W. Hall, *Under Cover of Daylight*, 1987
Greg Iles, *Mortal Fear*, 1997

566

CHARLOTTE BACON

The Twisted Thread
(New York: Hyperion/Voice, 2011)

Story type: Contemporary
Subject(s): Detective fiction; Murder; Boarding schools
Major character(s): Claire Harkness, Student—Boarding School, Crime Victim; Madeline Christopher, Teacher (English); Scotty Johnston, Boyfriend (of Claire); Matt Corelli, Detective—Police; Vernon Cates, Detective—Police

Mystery

Time period(s): 21st century; 2010s
Locale(s): United States

Summary: In Charlotte Bacon's mystery novel *The Twisted Thread*, the murder of a student shocks the entire Armitage Academy community. Like most of the New England boarding school's students, Claire Harkness was rich and influential. But Claire had a secret. She had recently given birth to a child whose whereabouts and paternity are unknown. Madeline Christopher, an English teacher at the academy, feels that she should have recognized Claire's condition and now tries to help police detective Matt Corelli find a killer and a motive. Meanwhile, Corelli deals with his personal feelings for Madeline and the resentment of Armitage Academy's neighbors. First novel.

Where it's reviewed:
Booklist, May 15, 2011, page 22
Publishers Weekly, April 4, 2011, page 36

Other books by the same author:
Split Estate, 2008
There is Room for You, 2004
Lost Geography, 2000
A Private State, 1997

Other books you might like:
Peter Abrahams, *End of Story*, 2006
Laura Lippman, *To the Power of Three*, 2005
Lionel Shriver, *We Need to Talk about Kevin*, 2003
Curtis Sittenfeld, *Prep: A Novel*, 2005
Donna Tartt, *The Secret History*, 1992

567

RAY BANKS

Beast of Burden

(Boston: Houghton Mifflin Harcourt, 2011)

Series: Cal Innes Series. Book 4
Story type: Contemporary; Series
Subject(s): Detective fiction; Revenge; Crime
Major character(s): Callum Innes, Detective—Private; Morris Tiernan, Organized Crime Figure, Father (of Mo); Mo, Son (of Morris); "Donkey" Donkin, Police Officer (detective sergeant)
Time period(s): 21st century; 2010s
Locale(s): Manchester, England

Summary: In *Beast of Burden* by Ray Banks, the fourth book in the Cal Innes series, the Manchester private detective who has survived car crashes, beatings, gunshots, and bombs, faces the most difficult challenge of his life. A stroke, caused in part by his drug abuse, has impaired Cal's ability to walk and speak, but it hasn't lessened his desire to seek justice for himself and his family. His brother is dead and his own life has been destroyed, yet Cal must suffer another insult. Mob boss Morris Tiernan has enlisted Cal's help in finding his missing son Mo, but the case sets Cal on a collision course with his nemesis Detective Sergeant "Donkey" Donkin.

Where it's reviewed:
Booklist, May 1, 2011, page 14
Publishers Weekly, June 13, 2011, page 30

Other books by the same author:
Gun, 2008
No More Heroes, 2008
Sucker Punch, 2007
Saturday's Child, 2006
The Big Blind, 2000

Other books you might like:
Ken Bruen, *The Guards*, 2003
Declan Hughes, *The Wrong Kind of Blood*, 2006
Russel D. McLean, *The Good Son*, 2009
Stuart Neville, *The Ghosts of Belfast*, 2009
Martyn Waites, *The Mercy Seat*, 2006

568

JO BANNISTER

Death in High Places

(New York: Minotaur Books, 2011)

Story type: Contemporary
Subject(s): Mountaineering; Death; Revenge
Major character(s): Nicky, Young Man (mountain climber); Patrick, Accident Victim, Friend (of Nicky); Robert McKendrick, Rescuer (of Nicky)
Time period(s): 21st century; 2010s
Locale(s): England; Alaska, United States

Summary: Jo Bannister's *Death in High Places* tells the story of Nicky, a young man who survives a dangerous mountain climbing expedition to a formidable peak on an Alaskan mountain range. Nicky's climbing partner, Patrick, isn't so lucky, however. Patrick plummets to his death on the range, and Nicky holds himself responsible. After returning to England, Nicky learns he is wanted by the mob, a hit having been placed on him as revenge for Patrick's death. He is soon rescued by a mysterious stranger and whisked off to a remote castle. There Nicky discovers that his supposed rescuer has sinister plans that involve sacrificing a life—Nicky's—for a life already lost.

Where it's reviewed:
Booklist, July 1, 2011, page 28
Publishers Weekly, June 6, 2011, page 28

Other books by the same author:
From Fire and Flood, 2007
Echoes of Lies, 2001
The Primrose Convention, 1997
A Bleeding of Innocents, 1993
The Matrix, 1981

Other books you might like:
Nevada Barr, *High Country*, 2004
Martin Edwards, *The Coffin Trail*, 2004
Jon Krakauer, *Into Thin Air: A Personal Account of the Mount Everest Disaster*, 1997
Jeff Long, *The Wall*, 2006
Joe Simpson, *Touching the Void*, 2004

569

MIKE BEFELER

Senior Moments are Murder

(Waterville, Maine: Five Star, 2011)

Series: Paul Jacobson Geezer-Lit Mystery Series. Book 3
Story type: Contemporary; Series
Subject(s): Memory; Detective fiction; Murder
Major character(s): Paul Jacobson, Aged Person, Detective—Amateur; Marion Aumiller, Fiance(e) (of Paul)
Time period(s): 21st century; 2010s
Locale(s): Venice Beach, California

Summary: Aged Paul Jacobson has some major memory problems. He's just woken up beside a total stranger, and he's in a town he doesn't recognize. After a little investigative work, Paul learns he is in Venice Beach, California, and the woman sleeping at his side is his fiancee. In his search for answers to fill in his fuzzy memory, Paul also happens upon a dead body in a nearby canal—and sets out to solve the mystery surrounding it before his wedding day arrives. Mike Befeler's *Senior Moments Are Murder* is the third installment in the Paul Jacobson Geezer-Lit Mystery Series.

Where it's reviewed:
Publishers Weekly, May 2, 2011, page 39

Other books by the same author:
Living with Your Kids is Murder, 2009
Retirement Homes are Murder, 2007

Other books you might like:
Donald Bain, *Gin and Daggers*, 1989
M.C. Beaton, *Agatha Raisin and the Quiche of Death*, 1992
Dorothy Gilman, *The Unexpected Mrs. Pollifax*, 1966
Gar Anthony Haywood, *Going Nowhere Fast*, 1994
Rita Lakin, *Getting Old Is Murder*, 2005

570

STEVE BERRY

Jefferson Key

(New York: Ballantine Books, 2011)

Series: Cotton Malone Series. Book 8
Subject(s): Adventure; Pirates; United States history
Major character(s): Cotton Malone, Detective (former Justice Department agent), Store Owner (book seller); Cassiopeia Vitt, Sidekick (of Malone)
Time period(s): 21st century; 2010s
Locale(s): United States

Summary: *The Jefferson Key* is the eighth novel in Steve Berry's Cotton Malone series. This outing finds former Justice Department agent Malone saving the president from an assassination attempt. After the dust settles, Malone learns that the attempt was carried out by a rogue pirate society with roots in the American Revolution. Determined to learn more about this dangerous faction, Malone and his sidekick Cassiopeia Vitt must disentangle the threads of a mystery involving pirates, assassinated

presidents, and a long-buried document penned by the Founding Fathers.

Where it's reviewed:
Booklist, May 1, 2011, page 30
Library Journal, June 1, 2011, page 90
Publishers Weekly, April 25, 2011, page 117
Publishers Weekly, May 1, 2011, page 30

Other books by the same author:
The Emperor's Tomb, 2010
The Charlemagne Pursuit, 2008
The Alexandria Link, 2007
The Venetian Betrayal, 2007
The Templar Legacy, 2006
The Third Secret, 2005
Romonov Prophesy, 2004

Other books you might like:
David Baldacci, *The Camel Club*, 2005
Robert Girardi, *The Pirate's Daughter*, 1997
Chris Kuzneski, *Secret Crown*, 2010
Katherine Neville, *The Eight*, 1988
James Rollins, *Map of Bones*, 2005

571

BENJAMIN BLACK (Pseudonym of John Banville)

A Death In Summer

(New York: Henry Holt and Co., 2011)

Series: Quirke Series. Book 4
Subject(s): Mystery; Romances (Fiction); Suspense
Major character(s): Garret Quirke, Scientist (pathologist); Detective Inspector Hackett, Detective—Police; Richard Jewell, Businessman (newspaper tycoon); Francoise d'Aubigny, Spouse (of Jewell); David Sinclair, Assistant (to Quirke); Phoebe, Daughter (of Quirke); Dannie, Sister (of Jewell); Carlton Sumner, Wealthy
Time period(s): 20th century; 1950s
Locale(s): Dublin, Ireland

Summary: In *A Death in Summer* by Benjamin Black, the shotgun death of a Dublin businessman draws a range of suspects. Though the victim, Richard Jewell, is clutching the weapon that killed him, pathologist Garret Quirke is hesitant to rule the death a suicide. Quirke's friend, Detective Inspector Hackett, who is investigating the case, notices strange behavior among Jewell's survivors. His sister, Dannie, is distressed, but his widow, Francoise d'Aubigny, isn't. In fact, Francoise suggests that business rival Carlton Sumner had a motive. Quirke and Hackett's case heats up as the temperature rises in Dublin. *A Death in Summer* is the fourth book in the Quirke series.

Where it's reviewed:
Booklist, June 1, 2011, page 40
Library Journal, April 15, 2011, page 81
New York Times, July 4, 2011, page C1(L)
Publishers Weekly, May 23, 2011, page 29

Other books by the same author:
Elegy for April, 2010
The Lemur, 2008

Mystery

The Silver Swan, 2007
Christine Falls, 2006
The Book of Evidence, 1989

Other books you might like:
Margery Allingham, *The Tiger in the Smoke*, 1952
Christopher Fowler, *Full Dark House*, 2003
Ngaio Marsh, *Night of the Vulcan*, 1951
Ruth Rendell, *From Doon with Death*, 1964
Josephine Tey, *The Franchise Affair*, 1948

572

S.J. BOLTON

Now You See Me

(New York: Minotaur Books, 2011)

Story type: Contemporary
Subject(s): Detective fiction; Murder; Suspense
Major character(s): Lacey Flint, Detective—Police
Time period(s): 21st century; 2010s
Locale(s): London, United Kingdom

Summary: S.J. Bolton's *Now You See Me* follows rookie police detective Lacey Flint as she embarks on a case that takes a very personal turn. Lacey discovers a dead body in an empty parking lot, and shortly thereafter, a local journalist receives a letter highlighting similarities between the body Lacey found and Jack the Ripper's victims. The killer singles out Lacey in his letters, and it isn't long before he seems to have unearthed secrets from her past. Now Lacey is determined to find the elusive killer before he continues the legacy of Jack the Ripper and, in the process, exposes secrets she'd like to keep concealed.

Where it's reviewed:
Booklist, May 1, 2011, page   35
The Denver Post, July 3, 2011, page   E-09
Library Journal, May 1, 2011, page   62
Publishers Weekly, April 18, 2011, page   31

Other books by the same author:
Blood Harvest, 2010
Awakening, 2009
Sacrifice, 2008

Other books you might like:
Tana French, *The Likeness*, 2008
Sophie Hannah, *Little Face*, 2007
Denise Mina, *Deception*, 2004
Barbara Vine, *A Dark-Adapted Eye*, 1986
Minette Walters, *The Sculptress*, 1993

573

C.J. BOX

Back of Beyond

(New York: Minotaur Books, 2011)

Story type: Contemporary
Subject(s): Mystery; Murder; Law enforcement
Major character(s): Cody Hoyt, Police Officer, Alcoholic,
Father (of Justin); Justin Hoyt, Son (of Cody); Hank
Winters, Friend (of Cody), Accident Victim (died in
cabin fire)
Time period(s): 21st century; 2010s
Locale(s): Yellowstone National Park, United States

Summary: *Back of Beyond* by C.J. Box tells the story of a killer on the loose in the wilderness and an off-beat policeman who must track him down. Cody Hoyt, a deeply troubled alcoholic who has fallen out of favor with his fellow police officers, has little else in life besides his son Justin and his close friend Hank Winters. One day Hoyt receives the shocking news that Hank burnt to death in a cabin fire in Yellowstone National Park. Suspecting foul play, Hoyt puts himself on the case—and finds out that a mad killer is lurking in the park and may be targeting Justin next.

Where it's reviewed:
Booklist, May 1, 2011, page   13
Library Journal, March 15, 2011, page   98
Library Journal, May 1, 2011, page   74
Publishers Weekly, June 13, 2011, page   29

Other books by the same author:
Nowhere to Run, 2010
Below Zero, 2009
Three Weeks to Say Goodbye, 2009
Blood Trail, 2008
Blue Heaven, 2008
The Master Falconer, 2006
Open Season, 2001

Other books you might like:
Nevada Barr, *Track of the Cat*, 1993
Paul Doiron, *The Poacher's Son*, 2010
Craig Johnson, *The Cold Dish*, 2005
William Kent Krueger, *Iron Lake*, 1998
Michael McGarrity, *Tularosa*, 1996

574

SANDRA BRANNAN

Lot's Return to Sodom

(Austin, Texas: Greenleaf Book Group Press, 2011)

Series: Liv Bergen Series. Book 2
Story type: Amateur Detective; Series
Subject(s): Detective fiction; Crime; Suspense
Major character(s): Liv Bergen, Detective—Amateur;
Streeter Pierce, FBI Agent
Time period(s): 21st century; 2010s
Locale(s): Sturgis, South Dakota

Summary: In *Lot's Return to Sodom*, the second book in Sandra Brannan's Liv Bergen Mystery series, Sturgis, South Dakota is once again overrun by thousands of bikers in town for the annual Motorcycle Rally. Though the event pumps money into the local economy, some of Sturgis's residents are unsettled by the presence of the biker gangs. While the Rally is in town, a local woman is killed and amateur detective Liv Bergen tries to find the killer and exonerate her brother. In the aftermath of another murder, FBI agent Streeter Pierce arrives to

investigate and Liv finds herself at odds with a particularly frightening biker.

Where it's reviewed:
Booklist, May 15, 2011, page   20

Other books by the same author:
In the Belly of Jonah, 2010

Other books you might like:
Sarah Andrews, *Tensleep*, 1994
Judy Clemens, *Till the Cows Come Home*, 2004
Lise McClendon, *The Bluejay Shaman*, 1994
Susan Cummins Miller, *Death Assemblage*, 2003
Betty Webb, *Desert Noir*, 2001

575

ROBERT BROWNE

The Paradise Prophecy

(New York: Dutton, 2011)

Subject(s): Demons; Serial murders; Supernatural
Major character(s): Bernadette Callahan, Agent; Batty La-Laurie, Historian

Summary: In *The Paradise Prophecy*, Robert Browne tells the story of Agent Bernadette Callahan, a special investigator working for the government agency, the Section. Callahan is hot on the trail of a murderer who appears to have dark magical abilities. In order to learn more about those abilities, Callahan must enlist the help of Sebastian "Batty" LaLaurie. Batty has worked these types of cases before, and he knows a thing or two about supernatural vengeance. Soon Callahan and Batty learn that they are up against forces more evil than they could ever imagine, including a battle between good and evil sent from heaven and hell.

Where it's reviewed:
Publishers Weekly, May 23, 2011, page   29

Other books you might like:
Will Adams, *The Alexander Cipher*, 2007
Dan Brown, *The Da Vinci Code*, 2003
Tom Martin, *Pyramid*, 2007
Douglas Preston, *Blasphemy*, 2008
James Rollins, *The Last Oracle*, 2008

576

ALAFAIR BURKE

Long Gone

(New York: HarperCollins, 2011)

Story type: Man Alone
Subject(s): Mystery; Suspense; Murder
Major character(s): Alice Humphrey, Art Dealer, Manager (art gallery), Crime Suspect
Time period(s): 21st century; 2010s
Locale(s): New York, New York

Summary: *Long Gone* is a mystery novel from author Alafair Burke. Alice Humphrey is thrilled by her good fortune when she lands an amazing new job managing a trendy Manhattan art gallery. Her boss, Drew, assures her she'll have complete creative freedom, uninterrupted by the gallery's anonymous and outlandish owner. Things couldn't be better, until Alice arrives at work, finds the gallery has been stripped bare, and sees Drew's dead body in the center of the room. The police fire questions at Alice and all of her answers come up unfounded. There's no record of the gallery or the artist who was displayed, Drew turns out to be someone else altogether, and the number he had given Alice doesn't exist. Realizing she's being framed for murder, Alice is forced to work alone to prove her innocence before she's tried for a crime she didn't commit.

Where it's reviewed:
Booklist, May 1, 2011, page   32
Library Journal, May 1, 2011, page   70
Publishers Weekly, May 16, 2011, page   52

Other books by the same author:
212, 2010
Dead Connection, 2007
Close Case, 2005
Missing Justice, 2004
Judgment Calls, 2003

Other books you might like:
Peter Abrahams, *Delusion*, 2008
Lisa Gardner, *Gone*, 2006
Jesse Kellerman, *The Executor*, 2010
Peter Spiegelman, *Red Cat*, 2007
Lisa Unger, *Beautiful Lies*, 2006

577

BRUCE BURROWS

The River Killers

(Surrey, British Columbia, Canada: Touchwood Editions, 2011)

Story type: Contemporary
Subject(s): Pollution; Fishes; Suspense
Major character(s): Danny Swanson, Fisherman (former), Office Worker (Department of Fisheries and Oceans); Louise Karavchuk, Police Officer
Time period(s): 21st century; 2010s
Locale(s): Canada

Summary: *The River Killers* is a suspenseful mystery from author Bruce Burrows. Department of Fisheries and Oceans (DFO) employee Danny Swanson is removed from his desk job and assigned to an at-sea job. While his superiors see this as a punishment, Danny is happy to be on the sea again. However, an incident from the past continues to plague him. Years ago, when he was a fisherman, Danny and his crew discovered an extremely deformed fish. Danny's friend, Billy, took the fish to the DFO, but he was never heard from again. Now, Danny feels that he can't let his friend's disappearance stand, and he starts an investigation with the help of police sergeant Louise Karavchuk. Soon, Danny realizes that he may be on the cusp of uncovering a huge cover-up by the government.

Where it's reviewed:
Library Journal, July 2011, page   58

Mystery

Other books you might like:
C.J. Box, *Open Season*, 2001
Paul Doiron, *The Poacher's Son*, 2010
John Galligan, *Red Sky, Red Dragonfly*, 2001
Victoria Houston, *Dead Angler*, 2000
Archer Mayor, *Open Season*, 1988

578

BILL CAMERON

County Line

(Madison, Wisconsin: Tyrus Books, 2011)

Story type: Mystery
Subject(s): Missing persons; Murder; Mystery
Major character(s): Ruby Jane Whittaker, Friend; Skin Kadash, Police Officer (former); Pete, Boyfriend (ex, of Ruby Jane)
Locale(s): San Francisco, California; Ohio, United States

Summary: Skin Kadash, an ex-cop, has just returned from a much-needed vacation when he makes a brutal discovery in *County Line*. Kadash enters his friend Ruby Jane Whittaker's apartment only to find she is gone and the only occupant is a dead man. Desperate to find out what happened to Ruby Jane, Kadash heads to San Francisco to confront Pete, her ex-boyfriend. His meeting with Pete leads him to Ruby Jane's hometown in Ohio, where Kadash quickly learns that finding his friend will require delving deeply into her past.

Where it's reviewed:
Library Journal, May 1, 2011, page 62

Other books by the same author:
Day One, 2010
Chasing Smoke, 2008
Lost Dog, 2007

Other books you might like:
Reed Farrel Coleman, *Walking the Perfect Square*, 2001
Robert Crais, *The Monkey's Raincoat*, 1987
James Crumley, *The Last Good Kiss*, 1978
G.M. Ford, *Who in Hell Is Wanda Fuca?*, 1995
John Shannon, *The Concrete River*, 1996

579

ALEXANDER CAMPION

Crime Fraiche

(New York: Kennsington, 2011)

Series: Capucine Culinary Series. Book 2
Story type: Contemporary
Subject(s): Crime; Murder; Family
Major character(s): Capucine LeTellier, Detective, Spouse (of Alexandre), Niece (of Aymerie); Alexandre, Spouse (of Capucine), Critic (food); La Belle au Marchais, Criminal; Aymerie, Uncle (of Capucine)
Time period(s): 21st century; 2010s
Locale(s): Normandy, France

Summary: *Crime Fraiche* is the second book in the Capucine Culinary Mysteries series from author Alexander Campion. Police detective Capucine LeTellier is on the trail of a criminal nicknamed "La Belle au Marchais" by the Parisian media. As the crime wave continues, Capucine and her husband, food critic Alexandre, are called to her family's country estate by her uncle. Trouble, however, seems to follow Capucine. She soon discovers that there has been a rash of hunting accidents in the area recently. The detective believes that there's something else at work and begins her own investigation. With the help of her husband, Capucine discovers that there is much more to these deaths than meets the eye.

Where it's reviewed:
Publishers Weekly, May 9, 2011, page 36

Other books by the same author:
The Grave Gourmet, 2010

Other books you might like:
Michael Bond, *Monsieur Pamplemousse*, 1983
Ellen Hart, *This Little Piggy Went to Murder*, 1994
Peter May, *Extraordinary People*, 2006
Joanne Pence, *Something's Cooking*, 1993
Phyllis C. Richman, *The Butler Did It*, 1997

580

REBECCA CANTRELL

A Game of Lies

(New York: Forge, 2011)

Series: Hannah Vogel Series. Book 3
Story type: Historical
Subject(s): Spies; World War II, 1939-1945; Olympics
Major character(s): Hannah Vogel, Spy; Lars Lang, Military Personnel (SS officer), Alcoholic
Time period(s): 20th century; 1930s
Locale(s): Berlin, Germany

Summary: Rebecca Cantrell's *A Game of Lies* in the third installment in the Hannah Vogel mystery series. This outing finds Hannah working undercover for the British in the days before the Second World War, when Germany is trying to erect a peaceful front to the rest of the world so they can host the Olympic Games. But Hannah knows something sinister is afoot, especially when she links up with SS officer Lars Lang. As the secrets she shuttles to the British become more and more dangerous, so too does the threat to Hannah's safety and well-being.

Where it's reviewed:
Booklist, May 1, 2011, page 26
Publishers Weekly, May 16, 2011, page 59

Other books by the same author:
A Night of Long Knives, 2010
A Trace of Smoke, 2009

Other books you might like:
Jeffery Deaver, *Garden of Beasts*, 2004
David Downing, *Zoo Station*, 2007
Alan Furst, *The World at Night*, 1996
Philip Kerr, *March Violets*, 1989
Erik Larson, *In the Garden of Beasts: Love, Terror, and an American Family in Hitler's Berlin*, 2011

581

KATE CARLISLE

Murder Under Cover

(New York: Signet/Penguin Group, 2011)

Series: Bibliophile Mystery Series
Story type: Mystery
Subject(s): Mystery; Murder; Sexual behavior
Major character(s): Brooklyn Wainwright, Detective—
    Amateur; Robin, Friend; Derek Stone, Boyfriend
Locale(s): San Francisco, California

Summary: When San Francisco bookbinder Brooklyn
Wainwright receives a beautifully illustrated copy of the
Kama Sutra to restore from her best friend Robin in
author Kate Carlisle's *Murder Under Cover*, she is
excited for the chance to both work with such a
breathtaking book and use it to heat things up in the
bedroom. Meanwhile, Robin wakes up to discover her
new boyfriend has been murdered in her bed and she
quickly becomes the prime suspect. Determined to clear
her friend's name, Brooklyn sets out to find the real
killer and soon finds herself in the murderer's deadly
crosshairs. Will she be able to prove Robin's innocence,
or will she become another victim of the unknown assailant?

Where it's reviewed:
Library Journal, May 1, 2011, page   62

Other books by the same author:
How to Seduce a Billionaire, 2011
If Books Could Kill, 2010
The Lies that Bind, 2010
Sweet Surrender, Baby Surprise, 2010
Homicide in Hardcover, 2009

Other books you might like:
Lawrence Block, *Burglars Can't Be Choosers*, 1977
Sheila Connolly, *Let's Play Dead*, July 5, 2011
John Dunning, *Booked to Die*, 1992
Miranda James, *Murder Past Due*, 2010
Lea Wait, *Shadows at the Fair*, 2002

582

LINDA CASTILLO

Breaking Silence

(New York: Minotaur Books, 2011)

Series: Kate Burkholder Series
Story type: Psychological Suspense
Subject(s): Crime; Murder; Amish
Major character(s): Kate Burkholder, Police Officer
    (chief); John Tomassetti, Detective—Police

Summary: *Breaking Silence* is an installment from Linda
Castillo's murder-mystery series featuring Chief Kate
Burkholder. Kate seems to be the ideal person to solve a
recent rash of hate crimes against the Amish: after all,
she was raised in the Amish community. So when
members of the Slabaugh family, a family of upstanding
Amish citizens, are found dead in a barn as the apparent

victims of methane-gas asphyxiation, Kate is not so
quick to rule the deaths accidental. She wants to find
justice for this family, but first she must go back to her
roots to figure out what is going on beyond the community's silent facade.

Where it's reviewed:
Booklist, May 15, 2011, page   20
Library Journal, March 15, 2011, page   113
Publishers Weekly, April 4, 2011, page   31

Other books by the same author:
Pray for Silence, 2010
Sworn to Silence, 2009
In the Dead of Night, 2007
Cops and Lovers?, 2001
Remember the Night, 2000

Other books you might like:
Lori Armstrong, *No Mercy*, 2009
Chelsea Cain, *Heartsick*, 2007
P.L. Gaus, *Blood of the Prodigal*, 1999
Alex Kava, *A Perfect Evil*, 2001
Karin Slaughter, *Blindsighted*, 2001

583

PAUL CLEAVE

Collecting Cooper

(New York: Atria Books, 2011)

Story type: Contemporary
Subject(s): Detective fiction; Kidnapping; Missing persons
Major character(s): Theodore Tate, Convict (ex-convict),
    Detective—Amateur; Emma Green, Missing Person
Time period(s): 21st century; 2010s
Locale(s): Christchurch, New Zealand

Summary: In Paul Cleave's *Collecting Cooper*, Theodore
Tate is a former cop imprisoned for nearly killing a girl
while driving under the influence. Now, just out of
prison, Tate is struggling to readjust to the outside
world—and a dangerous world it is. Christchurch is
plagued with a number of strange disappearances, one of
which is the girl Tate nearly killed. The girl's father
enlists Tate's help in finding her, and the ex-cop agrees,
launching his own investigation into the disappearances.
The trail leads Tate to a former mental patient harboring
a collection of serial killer souvenirs. To get to the bottom of the case, Tate must look into the shadowy past of
the Grover Hills Mental Institution, which holds the
answers that will lead him to the missing girl.

Where it's reviewed:
Publishers Weekly, May 16, 2011, page   55

Other books by the same author:
Blood Men, 2010
Cemetery Lake, 2009
The Killing Hour, 2009
The Cleaner, 2006

Other books you might like:
Thomas Harris, *The Silence of the Lambs*, 1988
Dennis Lehane, *Shutter Island*, 2003
Jeffry P. Lindsay, *Darkly Dreaming Dexter*, 2004

J. Wallis Martin, *The Bird Yard*, 1998
Minette Walters, *The Sculptress*, 1993

584

JUDY CLEMENS

Flowers for Her Grave

(Scottsdale, Arizona: Poisoned Pen Press, 2011)

Series: Embrace the Grim Reaper. Book 3
Story type: Contemporary; Series
Subject(s): Detective fiction; Murder; Death
Major character(s): Casey, Detective—Amateur; Death,
     Supernatural Being
Time period(s): 21st century; 2010s
Locale(s): Florida, United States

Summary: Casey is not a run of the mill private eye. Accompanying her on her investigations is Death itself, and Death adds more than a little spice to Casey's adventures. Her latest escapade takes her to a gated Florida community, where Casey is determined to start life anew and hide out from the world. But when one of her neighbors is attacked and left for dead, it's Casey that discovers her on the floor of the community locker room. Now she is out to find the person responsible for the violence—and, as usual, Death has a few things to say about Casey's snooping. Judy Clemens's *Flowers for Her Grave* is the third novel in the Grim Reaper Mysteries series.

Where it's reviewed:
Booklist, May 1, 2011, page 24
Publishers Weekly, June 27, 2011, page 137

Other books by the same author:
The Grim Reaper's Dance, 2010
Embrace the Grim Reaper, 2009
Different Paths, 2008
Three Can Keep a Secret, 2005
Till the Cows Come Home, 2004

Other books you might like:
Shirley Damsgaard, *Witch Way to Murder*, 2005
Casey Daniels, *Don of the Dead*, 2006
Carolyn G. Hart, *Ghost at Work: A Mystery*, 2008
Christopher Moore, *A Dirty Job*, 2006
Wendy Roberts, *The Remains of the Dead: A Ghost
     Dusters Mystery*, 2007

585

EDWARD CLINE

Honors Due

(Charleston, South Carolina: Booksurge, 2011)

Series: Chess Hanrahan Series. Book 3
Story type: Private Detective; Series
Subject(s): Detective fiction; Murder; Movies
Major character(s): Chess Hanrahan, Detective—Private
Locale(s): New York, New York

Summary: *Honors Due*, the third book in Edward Cline's Chess Hanrahan series, follows New York City private eye Hanrahan as he investigates another murder in his methodical style. A lover of words and films, and a skilled solver of mysteries, Hanrahan builds his current investigation around one important but easily ignored detail—a scriptwriting credit that just doesn't make sense. Other series titles include *First Prize* and *Presence of Mind*. Cline is also the author of the Sparrowhawk historical series.

Where it's reviewed:
Booklist, May 1, 2011, page 28

Other books by the same author:
Presence of Mind, 2010
Jack Frake, 2001
We Three Kings, 1995
Whisper the Guns, 1992
First Prize, 1988

Other books you might like:
Lawrence Block, *Sins of the Fathers*, 1976
Reed Farrel Coleman, *Walking the Perfect Square*, 2001
Jim Fusilli, *Closing Time*, 2001
Peter Spiegelman, *Black Maps*, 2003
Rex Stout, *Too Many Cooks*, 1938

586

JULIAN COLE

Felicity's Gate

(New York: Minotaur Books, 2011)

Story type: Police Procedural
Subject(s): Detective fiction; Murder; Brothers
Major character(s): Sam Rounder, Detective—Police (chief
     inspector), Brother (of Rick), Spouse (of Michelle);
     Rick Rounder, Detective—Private, Brother (of Sam),
     Lover (of Naomi); Jane Wragge, Artist, Crime
     Victim, Lover (of Moses Mundy); Moses Mundy,
     Lover (of Jane), Crime Suspect; Michelle, Spouse (of
     Sam); Naomi, Lover (of Rick)
Time period(s): 21st century; 2010s
Locale(s): York, England

Summary: In the mystery novel *Felicity's Gate* by Julian Cole, the sequel to *The Amateur Historian*, York Chief Inspector Sam Rounder seems to have an obvious suspect in the murder of an artist. Jane Wragge was beaten to death in her apartment, and live-in boyfriend Moses Mundy has fled. Sam Rounder believes Mundy is Wragge's killer, but the missing suspect has retained Sam's brother Rick, a private detective, to collect evidence in his defense. Rick takes Mundy's case without Sam's knowledge, and his investigation soon draws him into some risky situations. Meanwhile, Sam focuses on Jane Wragge's diary, which provides the inspector with clues as well as fodder for romantic daydreams.

Where it's reviewed:
Booklist, May 1, 2011, page 24
Publishers Weekly, March 14, 2011, page 50

Other books by the same author:
The Amateur Historian, 2007

Other books you might like:
Deborah Crombie, *A Share in Death*, 1993

Elizabeth George, *A Great Deliverance*, 1988
Louise Penny, *Still Life*, 2006
Peter Robinson, *Gallows View*, 1987
Simon Tolkien, *The Inheritance*, 2010

587

JODI COMPTON

Thieves Get Rich, Saints Get Shot

(New York: Crown, 2011)

Story type: Contemporary
Subject(s): Gangs; Identity; Theft
Major character(s): Hailey Cain, Gang Member, Cancer
   Patient (terminally ill); Serena "Warchild" Delga-
   dillo, Gang Member; CJ, Cousin (of Hailey); Mag-
   nus Ford, Police Officer
Time period(s): 21st century; 2010s
Locale(s): Los Angeles, California

Summary: In the novel *Thieves Get Rich, Saints Get Shot*
by Jodi Compton, the sequel to *Hailey's War*, Hailey
Cain has chosen an unusual alternative to the military
career she planned. When a diagnosis of terminal brain
cancer ended her future with the Army, Hailey turned to
Los Angeles's female gangs for camaraderie. Her drastic
choice has distanced her from her cousin C.J., but given
her the opportunity to attain some sense of justice. As
the underling of Serena "Warchild" Delgadillo, Hailey
becomes involved in a case of identity theft and other
serious crimes. Eventually, police officer Magnus Ford
proposes a tough decision.

Where it's reviewed:
Booklist, May 15, 2011, page   22
Publishers Weekly, May 16, 2011, page   52

Other books by the same author:
Hailey's War, 2010
Sympathy Between Humans, 2005
The 37th Hour, 2003

Other books you might like:
Denise Hamilton, *The Jasmine Trade*, 2001
Wendy Hornsby, *Midnight Baby*, 1993
Mercedes Lambert, *Dogtown*, 1991
Barbara Seranella, *No Human Involved*, 1997
Dana Stabenow, *A Cold Day for Murder*, 1992

588

COLIN COTTERILL

Killed at the Whim of a Hat

(New York: Minotaur Books, 2011)

Story type: Contemporary
Subject(s): Detective fiction; Murder; Family
Major character(s): Jimm Juree, Detective—Amateur,
   Journalist
Time period(s): 21st century; 2010s
Locale(s): Thailand

Summary: When she lived in Chiang Mai, Thailand, Jimm
Juree was a determined reporter who covered the local
crime scene, a job she adored. But when she is forced to
move with her eccentric family to the south of the
country, Jimm fears her days as a roving reporter are
behind her. Shortly after she arrives in her new town,
however, a van containing two dead bodies is discovered,
followed by the murder of an abbot at a nearby temple.
Jimm is fast on the track of the killer, attempting to tie
together this string of unusual murders. Colin Cotterill's
Killed at the Whim of a Hat is the first novel in a series.

Where it's reviewed:
Booklist, May 1, 2011, page   32
Financial Times, March 5, 2011, page   16
Library Journal, May 1, 2011, page   62
Publishers Weekly, May 2, 2011, page   39

Other books by the same author:
Slash and Burn, 2011
Anarchy and Old Dogs, 2007
Disco for the Departed, 2006
Thirty-Three Teeth, 2005
The Coroner's Lunch, 2004

Other books you might like:
John Burdett, *Bangkok 8*, 2003
Timothy Hallinan, *A Nail through the Heart*, 2007
Alexander McCall Smith, *No. 1 Ladies' Detective
   Agency Series*, 1998
Michael Stanley, *A Carrion Death*, 2008
Eric Stone, *Living Room of the Dead*, 2005

589

CLEO COYLE (Pseudonym of Alice Alfonsi and Marc Cerasini)

Murder by Mocha

(New York: Berkley, 2011)

Series: Coffeehouse Mysteries Series. Book 10
Story type: Contemporary; Series
Subject(s): Detective fiction; Murder; Food
Major character(s): Clare Cosi, Restaurateur, Detective—
   Amateur
Time period(s): 21st century; 2010s
Locale(s): New York, New York

Summary: Clare Cosi operates New York City's Village
Blend coffee shop, and business couldn't be better. She
decides to market a new line of coffee beans laden with
a reputed aphrodisiac, to be sold online through a
company called Aphrodite's Village. During the grand
unveiling at an Aphrodite's Village event, one of the
company's editors is murdered. Never one to turn down
a mystery—or a hot cup of joe—Clare launches her own
investigation into the grisly crime. Cleo Coyle's *Murder
by Mocha* is the 10th novel in The Coffeehouse Mysteries series and continues the investigations of coffee con-
noisseur Clare.

Where it's reviewed:
Publishers Weekly, June 27, 2011, page   138

Other books by the same author:
Roast Mortem, 2010
Murder Most Frothy, 2006

Mystery

Latte Trouble, 2005
Through the Grinder, 2004
On What Grounds, 2003

Other books you might like:
Sandra Balzo, *Uncommon Grounds*, 2004
Laura Childs, *Death by Darjeeling*, 2001
Joanne Fluke, *Chocolate Chip Cookie Murder*, 2000
Yasmine Galenorn, *Ghost of a Chance*, 2003
Wendy Lyn Watson, *I Scream, You Scream*, 2009

590

ELLEN CROSBY

The Sauvignon Secret

(New York: Scribner, 2011)

Series: Wine Country Mystery Series. Book 6
Story type: Mystery
Subject(s): Mystery; Murder; Serial murders
Major character(s): Lucie Montgomery, Young Woman (Vineyard Owner); Quinn Santori, Young Man (Winemaker); Paul Noble, Importer/Exporter
Locale(s): Napa Valley, California; Sonoma Valley, California; Virginia, United States

Summary: In the sixth entry of author Ellen Crosby's Wine Country Mysteries series, *The Sauvignon Secret*, vineyard owner and wine enthusiast Lucie Montgomery discovers the lifeless body of local wine importer Paul Noble hanging from the rafters of his art studio. Determined to learn what drove him to such a terrible end, Lucie soon finds herself exploring Paul's sordid past in California's Napa and Sonoma valleys, where her late friend was once part of a group of young biochemists known as the Mandrake Society and may have been involved in the deaths of a disabled man and a young woman. Lucie's situation is further complicated when she is joined by Quinn Santori, with whom she's had an on again, off again romantic relationship. As the story unfolds, Lucie struggles to uncover both the truth surrounding Paul's death and her feelings for Quinn.

Where it's reviewed:
Publishers Weekly, June 13, 2011, page 33

Other books by the same author:
The Viognier Vendetta, 2010
The Riesling Retribution, 2009
The Bordeaux Betrayal, 2008
The Chardonnay Charade, 2007
The Merlot Murders, 2006

Other books you might like:
Avery Aames, *The Long Quiche Goodbye*, 2010
Linda Barnes, *Blood Will Have Blood*, 1982
Laura Childs, *Death by Darjeeling*, 2001
Nadia Gordon, *Sharpshooter: A Sunny McCoskey Napa Valley Mystery*, 2002
Michele Scott, *A Toast to Murder*, 2010

591

ARNE DAHL (Pseudonym of Jan Arnald)

Misterioso

(New York: Pantheon Books, 2011)

Story type: Police Procedural; Series
Subject(s): Detective fiction; Murder; Crime
Major character(s): Paul Hjelm, Detective—Police; Jorge Chavez, Detective—Police
Time period(s): 20th century; 1990s
Locale(s): Sweden

Summary: Swedish author Arne Dahl's crime novel *Misterioso* takes its title from the name of the song the featured serial killer uses as background music for his murders. In addition to his fondness for jazz music, the killer also likes to leave behind a clean crime scene and therefore removes his spent bullets from the bedroom walls of his victims—all high-profile businessmen. Assigned to the case is Paul Hjelm, a police detective saved from dismissal by his appointment to the A-Unit, a band of talented misfit cops. Their investigation draws them into a complex world populated by both Russian mobsters and Sweden's elite. Originally published in Sweden in 1999, *Misterioso* is the first book in Dahl's Intercrime trilogy.

Where it's reviewed:
Library Journal, May 15, 2011, page 71
Publishers Weekly, May 23, 2011, page 28

Other books you might like:
Kjell Eriksson, *The Princess of Burundi*, 2006
Arnaldur Indridason, *Jar City*, 2005
Henning Mankell, *Faceless Killers*, 1991
Jo Nesbo, *The Redbreast*, 2007
Maj Sjowall, *Roseanna*, 2008

592

JEFFERY DEAVER

Carte Blanche

(New York: Simon & Schuster, 2011)

Story type: Adventure; Espionage
Subject(s): Spies; Espionage; Suspense
Major character(s): James Bond, Spy (Agent 007); Ophelia Maidenstone, Spy; Niall Dunne, Villain, Terrorist; Severan Hydt, Villain, Businessman; Felicity Willing, Businesswoman, Femme Fatale; Percy Osborne-Smith, Security Officer; Felix Leiter, Spy; Miss Moneypenny, Secretary; M, Spy (Head of the Secret Intelligence Service); Bheka Jordaan, Police Officer
Time period(s): 21st century; 2010s
Locale(s): London, England; Novi Sad, Serbia; Cape Town, South Africa; Dubai, United Arab Emirates

Summary: In *Carte Blanche*, famed thriller writer Jeffery Deaver - creator of the Lincoln Rhyme series, among others - brings super-spy James Bond into the 21st century and pits the famous spy against an unknown terroristic enemy. Deaver, chosen by Ian Fleming Publica-

tions to write the updated Bond novel, gives Agent 007 a military background (he's now an Afghan War vet) and an agency even more secretive than MI6 - the mysterious Overseas Development Group (ODG). True to the spirit of the original Bond books, the spy is dining with a woman when his supervisors contact him with an assignment. A massive attack has been planned against British targets, and Bond is ordered into action without any restrictions.

Where it's reviewed:
Wall Street Journal, June 14, 2011, page A13

Other books by the same author:
The Sleeping Doll, 2007
Garden of Beasts, 2004
The Bone Collector, 1997
Shallow Graves, 1992
Manhattan is My Beat, 1988

Other books you might like:
Raymond Benson, *Doubleshot*, 2000
Sebastian Faulks, *Devil May Care*, 2008
Ian Fleming, *Casino Royale*, 1953
Ian Fleming, *The Man with the Golden Gun*, 1965
John Gardner, *License Renewed*, 1981

593

ERIC DEZENHALL

The Devil Himself

(New York: Thomas Dunne Books/St. Martin's Press, 2011)

Story type: Historical
Subject(s): World War II, 1939-1945; Adventure; Military science
Major character(s): Meyer Lansky, Organized Crime Figure, Historical Figure; Lucky Luciano, Organized Crime Figure, Historical Figure; Bugsy Siegel, Organized Crime Figure, Historical Figure; Frank Costello, Organized Crime Figure, Historical Figure; Jonah Eastman, Assistant (White House aide), Grandson (of Mickey Price); Mickey Price, Organized Crime Figure, Grandfather (of Jonah Eastman); Tom Simmons, Employer (of Jonah); Albert Anastasia, Organized Crime Figure, Historical Figure
Time period(s): 20th century; (1940s); 20th century; 1980s
Locale(s): Washington, District of Columbia; Miami, Florida

Summary: Based on the true events concerning America's World War II efforts to secure the nation's East Coast, Eric Dezenhall's *The Devil Himself* tells the fantastic story of organized-crime boss Meyer Lansky through fictional narrator Jonah Eastman. Eastman, an aide in the Reagan White House, is the grandson of a presumably reformed New Jersey racketeer—a relationship that may serve him well in his current assignment. Eastman's superiors want him to interview ailing crime boss Meyer Lansky to learn how some of the country's most notorious mobsters assisted the government in protecting the borders in the 1940s. The current administration believes that those tactics may be of use against the rising threat of Islamic extremist attacks in the 1980s.

Where it's reviewed:
Publishers Weekly, May 2, 2011, page 37

Other books by the same author:
Spinning Dixie, 2006
Turnpike Flameout, 2005
Shakedown Beach, 2004
Jackie Disaster, 2003
Money Wanders, 2002

Other books you might like:
Richard Condon, *Prizzi's Honor*, 1982
Robert Harris, *Fatherland*, 1992
Joseph Kanon, *Stardust*, 2009
Charles McCarry, *The Last Supper*, 1983
Mark Mills, *Amagansett*, 2004

594

WILLIAM DIETRICH

Blood of the Reich

(New York: Harper, 2011)

Subject(s): Suspense; History; World War II, 1939-1945
Major character(s): Kurt Raeder, Explorer; Heinrich Himmler, Historical Figure; Benjamin Hood, Scientist (zoologist); Beth Calloway, Pilot; Rominy Pickett, Public Relations (software); Jake Barrow, Journalist
Time period(s): Multiple Time Periods; 20th century; (1940s); 21st century; 2010s
Locale(s): France; Switzerland; United States

Summary: In *Blood of the Reich* by William Dietrich, Heinrich Himmler has sent Kurt Raeder on a secret mission that could secure a Nazi victory. Raeder, a seasoned explorer, and his team of SS men are searching for a powerful fuel that's allegedly located in Tibet. American Benjamin Hood, a zoologist, and Beth Calloway, a pilot, have also set off for Tibet to stop the Nazi team. In the 21st century, a car bomb unites intended victim, Rominy Pickett, and journalist Jake Barrow as they escape the explosion. Their search for answers leads them to the Tibetan mystery that unfolded during World War II.

Where it's reviewed:
Library Journal, July 2011, page 70
Publishers Weekly, May 23, 2011, page 26

Other books by the same author:
Barbary Pirates, 2010
Dakota Cipher, 2009
Rosetta Key, 2008
Napolean's Pyramids, 2007
The Scourge of God, 2006
The Scourge of God, 2005
Hadrian's Wall, 2004
Dark Winter, 2001
Getting Back, 2000
Ice Reich, 1998

Other books you might like:
Steve Berry, *The Third Secret*, 2005
Chris Kuzneski, *The Lost Throne*, 2008
Christopher Reich, *Numbered Account*, 1998

James Rollins, *Map of Bones*, 2005
James Twining, *The Double Eagle*, 2005

595

WENDY DINGWALL

Hera's Revenge

(Vilas, North Carolina: Canterbury House Publishing, 2011)

Series: Yvonne Suarez Travel Mystery Series. Book
Story type: Mystery
Subject(s): Travel; Greek history; Mystery
Major character(s): Yvonne Suarez, Travel Agent; David Ludlow, Traveler
Locale(s): Athens, Greece

Summary: In author Wendy Dingwall's *Hera's Revenge*, travel agent Yvonne Suarez has just opened her own travel agency and booked her very first group tour: a delightful trip to historic Athens, Greece. Unfortunately, things go awry right from the start as dead bodies immediately begin appearing left and right. To make matters worse, a priceless gold statue of the Greek goddess Hera goes missing while Yvonne's tour group is at a local museum. Struggling to keep her tour on track and her meandering tourists in line, Yvonne enlists the help of David Ludlow, a vacationer on a mission to find an escape from his stressful life back home. Will the pair manage to get Yvonne's tour group out of Greece in one piece, or will her first excursion also be her last?

Where it's reviewed:
Library Journal, May 1, 2011, page 62

Other books you might like:
Taffy Cannon, *Guns and Roses*, 2000
Maria Hudgins, *Death on the Aegean Queen*, 2010
Maddy Hunter, *Alpine for You*, 2003
Emily Toll, *Murder Will Travel*, 2002
Anne Zouroudi, *The Messenger of Athens*, 2007

596

PAUL DOIRON

Trespasser

(New York: Minotaur Books, 2011)

Story type: Psychological Suspense
Subject(s): Murder; Crime; Missing persons
Major character(s): Mike Bowditch, Police Officer (game warden); Erland Jeffers, Prisoner
Locale(s): Maine, United States

Summary: *Trespasser* is a novel by Edgar Award-winning author Paul Doiron. New England-based game warden Mike Bowditch is called to an accident after a woman reports hitting a deer with her car, yet when he arrives on scene he finds neither the deer nor the woman anywhere to be found. For some reason, the odd disappearance calls to mind a case nearly a decade before, when a local lobster trapper named Erland Jeffers was sent to prison for the brutal assault and murder of a university student. When the missing woman turns up dead, with wounds similar to those of the college student seven years before, Mike begins to wonder if Jeffers wasn't wrongly accused. Yet the more Mike pries, the more he is told to mind his own business—until he finally launches a private investigation that drives a wedge through the precarious relationship between the tourists and the locals. Doiron is also the author of *The Poacher's Son*.

Where it's reviewed:
Booklist, May 1, 2011, page 38
Library Journal, March 15, 2011, page 113
Publishers Weekly, April 11, 2011, page 27

Other books by the same author:
The Poacher's Son, 2010

Other books you might like:
C.J. Box, *Open Season*, 2001
Joseph Connolly, *The Killing Kind*, 2001
Bryan Gruley, *Starvation Lake*, 2009
Steve Hamilton, *A Cold Day in Paradise*, 1998
William Kent Krueger, *Iron Lake*, 1998

597

HARRY DOLAN

Very Bad Men

(New York: Putnam, 2011)

Story type: Amateur Detective
Subject(s): Detective fiction; Murder; Serial murders
Major character(s): David Loogan, Editor (of Gray Streets), Detective—Amateur; Elizabeth Waishkey, Detective—Police, Lover (of David), Mother (of Sarah); Anthony Lark, Writer, Crime Suspect
Locale(s): Ann Arbor, Michigan

Summary: *Very Bad Men* is a mystery novel from author Harry Dolan's David Loogan series. In this book, Loogan has become editor of *Gray Streets* and is working hard to maintain a normal life with his lover, Detective Elizabeth Waishkey, and her daughter Sarah. Yet, trouble has a way of finding Loogan, and one day he finds a script that could lead him to the perpetrator of three murders. Anthony Lark, the author of the manuscript, confesses within its pages to murdering one of the suspects in a robbery from more than 15 years ago. With one down, Lark has two more to kill, and he isn't going to stop until these very bad men get what they deserve—unless, of course, Loogan can stop him first.

Where it's reviewed:
Booklist, May 1, 2011, page 41
Minneapolis Star Tribune, July 11, 2011, page 8E
Publishers Weekly, May 9, 2011, page 31

Other books by the same author:
Bad Things Happen, 2009

Other books you might like:
Martin Clark, *The Many Aspects of Mobile Home Living*, 2000
Harlan Coben, *Just One Look*, 2004
Dylan Schaffer, *Misdemeanor Man*, 2004
John Verdon, *Think of a Number: A Novel*, 2010
Jess Walter, *Citizen Vince*, 2005

598

CAROLE NELSON DOUGLAS

Cat in a Vegas Gold Vendetta
(New York: Forge Books, 2011)

Series: Midnight Louie Series. Book 23
Story type: Contemporary; Series
Subject(s): Detective fiction; Murder; Domestic cats
Major character(s): Temple Barr, Public Relations, Detective—Amateur; Savannah Ashleigh, Actress; Violet, Aunt (of Savannah)
Time period(s): 21st century; 2010s
Locale(s): Las Vegas, Nevada

Summary: Public relations guru and amateur PI Temple Barr agrees to take the case of a murdered handyman. The victim worked for the aunt of Savannah Ashleigh, a minor movie star, and Savannah wants answers in the man's death. As Temple and her trusty cat Louie investigate, they discover a laundry list of suspects, all of whom have ties to Savannah's dying Aunt Violet. Violet, it seems, wants to bequeath her estate to her beloved cats—and someone is determined to change the old lady's will and become her sole inheritor. *Cat in a Vegas Gold Vendetta* is the 23rd novel in Carole Nelson Douglas's Midnight Louie Mysteries series.

Where it's reviewed:
Publishers Weekly, June 27, 2011, page 138

Other books by the same author:
Cat in an Ultramarine Scheme, 2010
Dancing with Werewolves, 2007
Pussyfoot, 1993
Catnap, 1992
Good Night, Mr. Holmes, 1990

Other books you might like:
Sneaky Pie Brown, *Wish You Were Here*, 1990
Deborah Coonts, *Wanna Get Lucky?*, 2010
Rebecca M. Hale, *How to Wash a Cat*, 2008
Miranda James, *Murder Past Due*, 2010
Karen E. Olson, *The Missing Ink*, 2009

599

BRENDAN DUBOIS

Deadly Cove
(New York: Minotaur Books, 2011)

Series: Lewis Cole Series. Book 7
Story type: Contemporary
Subject(s): Detective fiction; Nuclear power plants; Suspense
Major character(s): Lewis Cole, Detective
Time period(s): 21st century; 2010s
Locale(s): Tyler Beach, New Hampshire

Summary: The seventh installment in the Lewis Cole series, Brendan DuBois's *Deadly Cove* is set in Tyler Beach, New Hampshire, where a protest against nuclear power is taking place. But this protest will prove anything but peaceful, and it will set in motion a chain of deadly events that only detective Lewis Cole can stop.

Where it's reviewed:
Publishers Weekly, May 9, 2011, page 36

Other books by the same author:
Twilight, 2007
Primary Storm, 2006
Resurrection Day, 1999
Black Tide, 1995
Dead Sand, 1994

Other books you might like:
Paul Doiron, *The Poacher's Son*, 2010
Steve Hamilton, *A Cold Day in Paradise*, 1998
William Kent Krueger, *Iron Lake*, 1998
Archer Mayor, *Open Season*, 1988
Julia Spencer-Fleming, *Out of the Deep I Cry*, 2004

600

KATE ELLIS

Kissing the Demons
(Sutton, England: Severn House, 2011)

Series: Joe Plantagenet Mystery Series. Book 3
Story type: Police Procedural; Series
Subject(s): Mystery; Detective fiction; Murder
Major character(s): Joe Plantagenet, Police Officer (Detective Inspector); Emily Thwaite, Police Officer (Detective Chief Inspector); Barrington Jenks, Government Official (member of parliament); Petulia Ferribie, Student—College
Time period(s): 21st century; 2010s
Locale(s): England

Summary: In the mystery novel *Kissing the Demons* by Kate Ellis, Detective Inspector Joe Plantagenet and Detective Chief Inspector Emily Thwaite investigate two cases—one cold, one current—that revolve around the same sinister address. Plantagenet and Thwaite are first ordered to investigate parliamentary member Barrington Jenks's role in the disappearance of two girls over a decade ago. Then they are assigned to the case of a missing college student who has turned up dead. All three girls were connected to 13 Torland Place—an old house with a dark history. As the body count rises, the investigators believe they are on the trail of a serial killer. *Kissing the Demons* is the third book in the Joe Plantagenet Murder Mysteries series.

Where it's reviewed:
Booklist, May 1, 2011, page 31

Other books by the same author:
The Jackal Man, 2011
Playing with Bones, 2009
Seeking the Dead, 2008
The Armada Boy, 1999
The Merchant's House, 1998

Other books you might like:
Deborah Crombie, *A Share in Death*, 1993
Ann Granger, *Say It with Poison*, 1991
Peter James, *Dead Simple*, 2006

Ian Rankin, *Strip Jack*, 1992
Peter Robinson, *Gallows View*, 1987

601

R.J. ELLORY

A Simple Act of Violence

(New York: Overlook Press, 2011)

Story type: Contemporary
Subject(s): Serial murders; Detective fiction; Law enforcement
Major character(s): Robert Miller, Detective—Police; Albert Roth, Detective—Police
Time period(s): 21st century; 2000s (2006)
Locale(s): Washington, District of Columbia

Summary: R.J. Ellory's *A Simple Act of Violence* takes place in Washington, D.C., in 2006, just as the midterm elections are getting under way. A string of murders has rocked the city, and police detective Robert Miller and his partner Albert Roth are out to find the culprit. As they start their investigation, they are stunned to find that the victims do not exist; their identities appear nowhere on the public record. Thus begins a terrifying inquiry into the mind of a serial killer and a crime that spans decades, putting Miller and Roth directly in the line of a psychopath's vengeance.

Where it's reviewed:
Publishers Weekly, May 2, 2011, page 38

Other books by the same author:
A Quiet Belief in Angels, 2007
City of Lies, 2006
A Quiet Vendetta, 2005
Ghostheart, 2004
Candlemoth, 2003

Other books you might like:
David Baldacci, *Absolute Power*, 1996
Mike Lawson, *The Inside Ring*, 2005
Richard North Patterson, *No Safe Place*, 1998
George P. Pelecanos, *Hard Revolution*, 2004
Richard Price, *Freedomland*, 1998

602

KJELL ERIKSSON

The Hand that Trembles

(New York: Minotaur Books, 2011)

Series: Ann Lindell Series. Book 4
Story type: Contemporary; Series
Subject(s): Detective fiction; Murder; Suspense
Major character(s): Ann Lindell, Detective—Police; Sven-Arne Persson, Missing Person
Time period(s): 21st century; 2010s
Locale(s): Bangalore, India; Uppsala, Sweden

Summary: Swedish police detective Ann Lindell is investigating an unusual case. A lone foot still in its boot has come ashore, and she is determined to find the truth behind the oddity. Meanwhile, a country commissioner, long thought dead of suicide, is spotted in Bangalore, India. As Ann works away on the case of the mysterious foot, she also becomes involved in the investigation of the missing commissioner—and the two inquiries gradually converge in the most surprising of ways. *The Hand that Trembles* is the fourth novel in Kjell Eriksson's Ann Lindell mystery series and is translated from the Swedish by Ebba Segerberg.

Where it's reviewed:
Library Journal, June 15, 2011, page 78
Newsweek, May 30, 2011, page 82
Publishers Weekly, June 20, 2011, page 37

Other books by the same author:
The Demon of Dakar, 2008
The Cruel Stars of the Night, 2007
The Princess of Burundi, 2006

Other books you might like:
Karin Fossum, *Don't Look Back*, 2002
Henning Mankell, *Faceless Killers*, 1991
Jo Nesbo, *The Redbreast*, 2007
Hakan Nesser, *Borkmann's Point*, 2006
Maj Sjowall, *Roseanna*, 2008

603

LOREN D. ESTLEMAN

Infernal Angels

(New York: Forge Books, 2011)

Series: Amos Walker Series. Book
Story type: Contemporary
Subject(s): Drugs; Crime; Suspense
Major character(s): Amos Walker, Detective—Private
Time period(s): 21st century; 2010s
Locale(s): Detroit, Michigan

Summary: *Infernal Angels* is part of the Amos Walker series from author Loren D. Estleman. Private investigator Amos Walker doesn't care much for technology. However, he does agree to track down stolen HDTV converter boxes for a local retailer. When the man suspected of the crime and the retailer are both found murdered, Amos begins to suspect that something most sinister is at work. He soon discovers that the boxes are being used to smuggle heroin, which has killed several junkies. Now, the Detroit detective must figure out who is behind the smuggling operation.

Where it's reviewed:
Booklist, June 1, 2011, page 42
Publishers Weekly, May 9, 2011, page 36

Other books by the same author:
The Left-Handed Dollar, 2010
The Master Executioner, 2001
Whiskey River, 1990
Angel Eyes, 1981
Motor City Blue, 1980

Other books you might like:
Lawrence Block, *Sins of the Fathers*, 1976
Elmore Leonard, *City Primeval: High Noon in Detroit*, 1980
John D. MacDonald, *The Deep Blue Good-by*, 1964
Robert B. Parker, *The Godwulf Manuscript*, 1973
Charles Willeford, *Miami Blues*, 1984

604

GERALDINE EVANS

Deadly Reunion

(New York: Severn House Publishers, 2011)

Series: Rafferty and Llewellyn Series. Book 14
Story type: Police Procedural; Series
Subject(s): Detective fiction; Reunions; Murder
Major character(s): Joseph Rafferty, Detective—Police (detective inspector), Spouse (of Abra); Dafyd Llewellyn, Detective—Police (detective sergeant); Adam Ainsley, Sports Figure (rugby player, former), Graduate (Griffin School), Crime Victim; Giles Harmsworth, Classmate (of Ainsley, former); Sebastian Kennedy, Classmate (of Ainsley, former); Simon Fairweather, Classmate (of Ainsley, former); Victoria Watson, Classmate (of Ainsley, former); Alice Douglas, Classmate (of Ainsley, former)
Time period(s): 21st century; 2010s
Locale(s): England

Summary: In *Deadly Reunion*, the 14th book in Geraldine Evans's Rafferty and Llewellyn Mystery series, an alumni reunion at the posh Griffin School sets the scene for murder. The deceased, killed by hemlock poisoning, is Adam Ainsley, former rugby star and heartbreaker. Detective Inspector Joseph Rafferty and Detective Sergeant Dafyd Llewellyn are assigned to the case, which reveals a variety of suspects and motives. The investigation takes Rafferty and Llewellyn from Elmhurst to London to Norwich and a child who may or may not be Ainsley's daughter. Rafferty is more than happy to spend time away from home where his mother has gathered an assortment of far-flung relatives for a family reunion.

Where it's reviewed:
Booklist, May 1, 2011, page   37

Other books by the same author:
Death Dance, 2010
The Hanging Tree, 1996
Death Line, 1995
Down Among the Dead Men, 1994
Dead Before Morning, 1993

Other books you might like:
Deborah Crombie, *A Share in Death*, 1993
Kate Ellis, *The Merchant's House*, 1998
Elizabeth George, *A Great Deliverance*, 1988
Ann Granger, *Say It with Poison*, 1991
Peter Robinson, *Gallows View*, 1987

605

JOSEPH FINDER

Buried Secrets

(New York: Dutton, 2010)

Series: Nick Heller Series. Book 2
Story type: Child-in-Peril; Series
Subject(s): Suspense; Kidnapping; Mystery
Major character(s): Nick Heller, Investigator; Marshall Marcus, Businessman (hedge fund manager), Father (of Alexa); Alexa Marcus, 17-Year-Old, Daughter (of Marshall), Kidnap Victim
Time period(s): 21st century; 2010s
Locale(s): Boston, Massachusetts

Summary: *Buried Secrets*, a suspenseful mystery novel, is the second installment in the Nick Heller series from bestselling author Joseph Finder. Intelligence expert Nick Heller's new Boston-based business is barely off the ground when he's hired by an old friend for a dangerous job. Wealthy and successful hedge fund manager, Marshall Marcus, needs Nick to find his teenage daughter, Alexa, who was kidnapped from a local club. The masterminds who kidnapped her have buried her alive with a limited supply of food and water and are streaming her agony over the Internet. In order to find out who is responsible for the heinous crime, Nick must dig deeper in Marshall's life and business. It doesn't take long for Nick to uncover some shady dealings and a shocking conspiracy that leaves a lengthy list of possible suspects who would hope to bring ruin to Marshall.

Where it's reviewed:
Booklist, May 1, 2011, page   16
Library Journal, March 15, 2011, page   107
Publishers Weekly, April 11, 2011, page   26

Other books by the same author:
Vanished, 2009
Power Play, 2007
Killer Instinct, 2006
Company Man, 2005
Paranoia, 2004

Other books you might like:
Lee Child, *Echo Burning*, 2001
Jeffery Deaver, *Carte Blanche*, 2011
Daniel Silva, *The Secret Servant*, 2007
Peter Spiegelman, *Black Maps*, 2003
Randy Wayne White, *Twelve Mile Limit*, 2002

606

CONOR FITZGERALD

The Fatal Touch

(New York: Bloomsbury USA, 2011)

Series: Commissario Alec Blume Series. Book 2
Story type: Literary; Series
Subject(s): Detective fiction; Murder; Forgery
Major character(s): Alec Blume, Political Figure (police commissioner); Caterina Mattiola, Detective—Police;

Mystery

Henry Treacy, Criminal (art forger), Crime Victim; Orazio Farinelli, Government Official (Art Forgery and Heritage Division)
Time period(s): 21st century; 2010s
Locale(s): Rome, Italy

Summary: *The Fatal Touch*, the second book in Conor Fitzgerald's Commissario Alec Blume series, finds the Rome police commissioner with a string of bothersome muggings on his hands. So far, no one has been harmed by the thief who targets the city's tourists. When a dead body is found on the streets of Rome, Blume, an American expat, learns that the victim is not a tourist but an infamous art forger, Henry Treacy. The sensational case immediately draws the attention of Italy's military police—in particular the crooked Colonel Orazio Farinelli. As Blume employs his unconventional methods in the case, he confounds his new detective Caterina Mattiola and antagonizes the government authorities.

Where it's reviewed:
Booklist, May 1, 2011, page 24
Publishers Weekly, April 11, 2011, page 27

Other books by the same author:
The Dogs of Rome, 2010

Other books you might like:
Andrea Camilleri, *The Shape of Water*, 2002
Michael Dibdin, *Ratking*, 1989
Michele Giuttari, *The Death of a Mafia Don*, 2009
David Hewson, *A Season for the Dead*, 2004
Donna Leon, *Death at La Fenice*, 1992

607

SHAMINI FLINT

A Bali Conspiracy Most Foul
(New York: Minotaur Books, 2011)

Story type: Contemporary - Exotic; Series
Subject(s): Detective fiction; Terrorism; Murder
Major character(s): Inspector Singh, Detective; Bronwyn Taylor, Police Officer
Time period(s): 21st century; 2010s
Locale(s): Bali, Indonesia

Summary: The overweight and overtired Inspector Singh is called to the nearby island of Bali after a terrorist bomb detonates, leaving destruction in its wake. With little experience dealing with terrorists, Singh reluctantly goes on this latest mission, and he soon learns there was an expatriate man who was murdered before the bomb blast. Now Singh must infiltrate the expatriate community in search of answers, and he is shocked at what he finds: deception, infidelity, and treachery.

Where it's reviewed:
Publishers Weekly, June 6, 2011, page 28

Other books by the same author:
Inspector Singh Investigates: A Most Peculiar Malaysian Murder, 2010

Other books you might like:
John Burdett, *Bangkok 8*, 2003
Colin Cotterill, *The Coroner's Lunch*, 2004
Tarquin Hall, *The Case of the Missing Servant*, 2009

Alexander McCall Smith, *No. 1 Ladies' Detective Agency Series*, 1998
Farahad Zama, *The Marriage Bureau for Rich People*, 2009

608

KARIN FOSSUM

Bad Intentions
(Boston: Houghton Mifflin Harcourt, 2011)

Series: Inspector Sejer Series. Book 9
Story type: Police Procedural; Series
Subject(s): Mystery; Murder; Detective fiction
Major character(s): Konrad Sejer, Inspector (police); Jon Moreno, Mentally Ill Person; Molly Gram, Friend (of Jon)
Time period(s): 21st century; 2010s
Locale(s): Norway

Summary: In *Bad Intentions* by Karin Fossum, a seasoned police inspector investigates a series of drownings in Norway. When Inspector Sejer learns of the first victim, he is unconvinced by his colleagues' suggestions that the young man committed suicide. Sejer suspects that the victim's friends are withholding information about the death. When another young man drowns in another lake, the cases seem unrelated but Sejer is certain that there is a connection. For Sejer, whose own mental health had been unsteady in the past, the presumed suicides are especially unsettling. Translated by Charlotte Barslund, *Bad Intentions* is the ninth book in the Konrad Sejer series.

Where it's reviewed:
Globe & Mail, August 21, 2010, page F11
Library Journal, June 15, 2011, page 78
Library Journal, March 15, 2011, page 98
Newsweek, May 30, 2011, page 82

Other books by the same author:
Black Seconds, 2008
The Indian Bride, 2007
When the Devil Holds the Candle, 2007
He Who Fears the Wolf, 2005
Don't Look Back, 2004

Other books you might like:
Kjell Eriksson, *The Princess of Burundi*, 2006
Henning Mankell, *Faceless Killers*, 1991
Jo Nesbo, *The Redbreast*, 2007
Hakan Nesser, *Borkmann's Point*, 2006
Maj Sjowall, *Roseanna*, 2008

609

FELIX FRANCIS

Dick Francis' Gamble
(New York: G. P. Putnam's Sons, 2011)

Story type: Contemporary
Subject(s): Mystery; Detective fiction; Horse racing

Major character(s): Nicholas "Foxy" Foxton, Jockey (former), Advisor (financial); Herb Kovak, Advisor (financial)
Time period(s): 21st century; 2010s
Locale(s): England

Summary: In the novel *Dick Francis's Gamble* by Felix Francis, England's Grand National horse race seems too public a venue for a murder, but that is exactly where Herb Kovak is killed. Herb and Nicholas "Foxy" Foxton, a retired jockey and Herb's coworker at an investment company, are standing side by side when a man shoots Herb then vanishes into the stands. Foxton can't describe the shooter to the authorities but he begins his own investigation into his friend's murder. As he discovers clues about the shooter's motive and identity, he questions the business practices of his dead friend and his employer. Felix Francis co-authored several books with his father Dick Francis and now takes over the writing of his popular mysteries.

Where it's reviewed:
Booklist, July 1, 2011, page 31
Publishers Weekly, June 27, 2011, page 137

Other books by the same author:
Crossfire, 2010
Even Money, 2009
Silks, 2008
Dead Heat, 2007

Other books you might like:
John Francome, *Stone Cold*, 1994
Declan Hughes, *The Price of Blood: An Irish Novel of Suspense*, 2008
Jenny Pitman, *The Vendetta*, 2005
Richard Pitman, *Bet Your Life*, 2004
Lyndon Stacey, *Blindfold*, 2003

610

MEG GARDINER

The Nightmare Thief

(New York: Dutton, 2011)

Subject(s): Mystery; Detective fiction; Suspense
Major character(s): Autumn Reiniger, 21-Year-Old, Wealthy; Jo Beckett, Doctor (forensic psychiatrist); Gabe Quintana, Colleague (of Jo)
Time period(s): 21st century; 2010s
Locale(s): San Francisco, California

Summary: In *The Nightmare Thief* by Meg Gardiner, a birthday party turns deadly for a rich girl and her friends. Autumn Reiniger has everything a 21-year-old could want—money, a car, and an expensive education. To appease his demanding daughter, Mr. Reiniger arranges a thrilling "party" that includes a phony drug bust and arrest. A group of authentic criminals takes advantage of the situation. As Autumn and her five friends are taken hostage, the San Francisco police—following orders—ignore the abduction. Jo Beckett, a forensic psychiatrist, and her partner, Gabe Quintana, witness the kidnapping and realize it's a real crime.

Where it's reviewed:
Booklist, May 1, 2011, page 34

Library Journal, June 1, 2011, page 91
Publishers Weekly, May 23, 2011, page 26

Other books by the same author:
The Liar's Lullaby, 2010
The Memory Collector, 2009
The Dirty Secrets Club, 2008
Mission Canyon, 2003
China Lake, 2002

Other books you might like:
Jeff Abbott, *Adrenaline*, 2011
Joseph Finder, *Buried Secrets*, 2010
Lisa Gardner, *Hide*, 2007
Tami Hoag, *Kill the Messenger*, 2004
Karin Slaughter, *Indelible*, 2004

611

P.L. GAUS

Harmless as Doves

(Athens, Ohio: Ohio University Press, 2011)

Series: Amish Country Mysteries. Book
Story type: Mystery; Religious
Subject(s): Amish; Murder; Mystery
Major character(s): Leon Shetler, Religious (Amish Bishop); Crist Burkholder, Young Man; Glenn Spiegle, Young Man; Vesta Miller, Young Woman; Michael Branden, Professor; Ricky Niell, Police Officer; Bruce Robertson, Police Officer
Locale(s): Sarasota, Florida; Bradenton, Ohio

Summary: A startling confession by an Amish murderer sets in motion the events of author P.L. Gaus's *Harmless as Doves*. When Crist Burkholder, a young man infatuated with 17-year-old Vesta Miller, arrives in Bishop Leon Shetler's confessional, Shetler is shocked to learn one of his flock has committed the most grievous of sins. In fact, Burkholder admits to killing Glenn Spiegle, his adversary for Vesta's affections. Sheriff Bruce Robertson quickly launches an investigation and soon discovers that two more murders have taken place in the Pinecraft Amish Community in Sarasota, Florida. With the case growing increasingly complex, Professor Mike Branden is called to investigate and, with the assistance of Detective Ricky Niell, he unlocks the troubling truth behind Spiegle's reason for converting to the Amish lifestyle and his true feelings for the religious community.

Where it's reviewed:
Booklist, June 1, 2011, page 40
New York Times Book Review, July 24, 2011, page 19(L)
Publishers Weekly, May 16, 2011, page 59

Other books by the same author:
Separate from the World, 2008
Cast a Blue Shadow, 2003
Clouds Without Rain, 2001
Broken English, 2000
Blood of the Prodigal, 1998

Other books you might like:
Linda Castillo, *Pray for Silence*, 2010
Judy Clemens, *Till the Cows Come Home*, 2004

Louise Penny, *Still Life*, 2006
Julia Spencer-Fleming, *In the Bleak Midwinter*, 2002
Deborah Woodworth, *Death of a Winter Shaker*, 1997

612

MICHAEL GENELIN

Requiem for a Gypsy
(New York: Soho Press, 2011)

Series: Commander Jana Mantinova Series. Book 4
Story type: Contemporary
Subject(s): Suspense; Murder; Crime
Major character(s): Jana Matinova, Investigator; Klara Boganova, Spouse (of Oto Bogan); Oto Bogan, Businessman, Spouse (of Klara Boganova)
Time period(s): 21st century; 2010s
Locale(s): Slovakia

Summary: *Requiem for a Gypsy* is the fourth book in the Commander Jana Matinova series by author Michael Genelin. Jana Matinova was at a party where the wife of a prominent Slovakian businessman was murdered. In fact, Jana was the one who pushed Oto Bogan out of the way of the bullet that claimed the life of his wife Klara. Because she was a witness to the crime, Jana has been told to stay out of the investigation. Jana, however, is never one to listen to orders. She soon sets out on an investigation that leads her on an international chase to hunt down the killer.

Where it's reviewed:
Booklist, May 1, 2011, page   38
Publishers Weekly, May 23, 2011, page   31

Other books by the same author:
The Magician's Accomplice, 2010
Dark Dreams, 2009
Siren of the Waters, 2008

Other books you might like:
Colin Cotterill, *The Coroner's Lunch*, 2004
Philip Kerr, *Prague Finale*, 2011
Henning Mankell, *Faceless Killers*, 1991
Jo Nesbo, *The Redbreast*, 2007
Olen Steinhauer, *Victory Square*, 2007

613

KATHLEEN GEORGE

Hideout
(New York: Minotaur Books, 2011)

Series: Richard Christie Series. Book 5
Story type: Contemporary; Series
Subject(s): Detective fiction; Hostages; Brothers
Major character(s): Colleen Greer, Detective; Richard Christie, Detective; Ryan Rutter, Brother (of Jack); Jack Rutter, Brother (of Ryan)
Time period(s): 21st century; 2010s
Locale(s): Pittsburgh, Pennsylvania; Sugar Lake, Pennsylvania

Summary: Brothers Ryan and Jack Rutter are involved in a hit-and-run accident that kills a young woman. Terrified, the two men flee the city and take refuge in the idyllic resort town of Sugar Lake. Detectives Colleen Greer and Richard Christie are fast on the case, determined to find Ryan and Jack and bring them to justice. When the brothers decide to take hostages, Greer and Christie race to the scene in the hopes of preventing any further violence. Kathleen George's *Hideout* is the sequel to the acclaimed novel *The Odds* and continues the investigative adventures of Detectives Greer and Christie.

Where it's reviewed:
Booklist, July 1, 2011, page   32
Publishers Weekly, June 6, 2011, page   27

Other books by the same author:
Pittsburgh Noir, 2011
The Odds, 2009
Afterimage, 2007
Fallen, 2004
Taken, 2002

Other books you might like:
Michael Connelly, *The Black Echo*, 1992
K.C. Constantine, *The Rocksburg Railroad Murders*, 1972
Ed McBain, *Cop Hater*, 1956
Carol O'Connell, *Mallory's Oracle*, 1994
George P. Pelecanos, *Drama City*, 2005

614

TESS GERRITSEN

Silent Girl
(New York: Ballantine Books, 2010)

Series: Rizzoli and Isles Series. Book 9
Story type: Contemporary
Subject(s): Detective fiction; Murder; Suspense
Major character(s): Jane Rizzoli, Detective—Police; Maura Isles, Doctor (medical examiner)
Time period(s): 21st century; 2010s
Locale(s): Boston, Massachusetts

Summary: Boston homicide detective Jane Rizzoli and medical examiner Maura Isles team up to crack one of their most dangerous cases yet. In Boston's Chinatown, a body—and its severed head—has been discovered, and Rizzoli is called to the scene. As she digs up the story surrounding the corpse, she finds echoes of a past murder-suicide that plagued Chinatown 19 years prior. Now Rizzoli and Isles must piece together the threads of this complex mystery before a killer strikes again. *The Silent Girl* is the ninth novel in Tess Gerritsen's Rizzoli and Isles series.

Where it's reviewed:
Booklist, May 1, 2011, page   39
Publishers Weekly, May 30, 2011, page   47

Other books by the same author:
Ice Cold, 2010
Bone Garden, 2009
Keeping the Dead, 2009

The Keepsake, 2008
Body Double, 2004
The Sinner, 2003
The Apprentice, 2002
The Surgeon, 2001

Other books you might like:
Peter Clement, *Mortal Remains*, 2003
Patricia Cornwell, *Postmortem*, 1990
Lisa Gardner, *Alone*, 2005
Michael Palmer, *Extreme Measures*, 1991
Kathy Reichs, *Deja Dead*, 1997

615

ANGELA GERST

A Crack in Everything

(Scottsdale, Arizona: Poisoned Pen Press, 2011)

Story type: Contemporary
Subject(s): Politics; Suspense; Murder
Major character(s): Susan Callisto, Consultant, Lawyer (former), Girlfriend (of Michael, former); Michael Benedict, Police Officer, Boyfriend (of Susan, former); Charles Renfrow, Political Figure
Time period(s): 21st century; 2010s
Locale(s): Waltham, Massachusetts

Summary: A former lawyer becomes embroiled in a homicide investigation in *A Crack in Everything* from author Angela Gerst. Susan Callisto leaves behind the bustle of Boston for Waltham after her boyfriend, police officer Michael Benedict, dumps her. Once a real-estate attorney, Susan now advises small-time political hopefuls. Charles Renfrow hires Susan to consult on his campaign, but she can't understand why a scientist would want to be mayor of a small town. When Susan goes to talk to Charles, she accidently discovers the body of his assistant. Now, Michael has been assigned to the case, but Susan won't back away from the investigation. She soon discovers that there's much more at stake than a local election.

Where it's reviewed:
Library Journal, July 2011, page   58
Publishers Weekly, June 13, 2011, page   32

Other books you might like:
Bruce DeSilva, *Rogue Island*, 2010
Eric Dezenhall, *Money Wanders*, 2002
George V. Higgins, *Defending Billy Ryan: A Jerry Kennedy Novel*, 1992
Alex Kava, *Whitewash*, 2007
Edwin O'Connor, *The Last Hurrah*, 1970

616

JUAN GOMEZ-JURADO

The Traitor's Emblem

(New York: Atria Books, 2011)

Subject(s): Mystery; German Republic, 1918-1933; World War I, 1914-1918

Major character(s): Paul Reiner, Teenager, Servant (to Baron von Schroeder); Alys Tannenbaum, Photographer, Investigator (helping Paul Reiner); Captain Gonzalez, Sailor (who rescues castaways); Baron von Schroeder, Nobleman, Employer (of Paul Reiner)
Time period(s): 20th century-21st century
Locale(s): Germany; Portugal

Summary: *The Traitor's Emblem*, a novel by Juan Gomez-Jurado, tells a tale of mystery, intrigue, and danger that spans several generations. Paul Reiner is a teenager living in Germany in the depressed days after World War I. Reiner is an impoverished domestic servant who escapes his sad life by daydreaming about the glorious times before the war and the heroic actions of his deceased father. When he finds out his daydreams are not accurate and his father's death may have been foul murder, Reiner joins his beloved Alys Tannenbaum on a quest to find the truth. During World War II, the mystery intensifies on a ship near Portugal. There, Captain Gonzalez receives a golden medallion from a group of German castaways—an emblem that will shed light on the Reiner mystery.

Where it's reviewed:
Booklist, July 1, 2011, page   33
Library Journal, June 15, 2011, page   75
Publishers Weekly, May 23, 2011, page   28

Other books by the same author:
The Moses Expedition, 2010
Contract with God, 2009
God's Spy, 2007

Other books you might like:
Rebecca Cantrell, *A Trace of Smoke*, 2009
Philip Kerr, *March Violets*, 1989
Arturo Perez-Reverte, *The Club Dumas*, 1997
Robert Wilson, *A Small Death in Lisbon*, 2000
Carlos Ruiz Zafon, *The Shadow of the Wind*, 2004

617

PHILIP GOODEN

The Durham Deception

(London: Severn House Publishers, 2011)

Series: Cathedral Mystery Series. Book 2
Story type: Historical - Victorian
Subject(s): Detective fiction; Family; Murder
Major character(s): Tom Ansell, Detective, Spouse (of Helen); Helen Ansell, Detective, Spouse (of Tom); Julia, Aunt (of Helen)
Time period(s): 19th century
Locale(s): United Kingdom

Summary: In Victorian England, newly married Tom and Helen Ansell don't have much time to enjoy their newlywed status when they are called to investigate a possible charlatan with whom Helen's aunt has fallen in love. The couple's investigation opens the door to another mystery: the puzzle of an ancient dagger. Things go from bad to worse when a body turns up—and Helen is the only suspect. *The Durham Deception* is the second novel in Philip Gooden's Cathedral mystery series.

Mystery

Where it's reviewed:
Booklist, May 1, 2011, page 22
Publishers Weekly, April 18, 2011, page 37

Other books by the same author:
The Salisbury Manuscript, 2008
An Honourable Murder, 2005
Mask of Night, 2004
Alms for Oblivion, 2003
The Pale Companion, 2002
Death of Kings, 2001
That Sleep of Death, 2000

Other books you might like:
Tasha Alexander, *And Only to Deceive*, 2005
C.S. Harris, *What Angels Fear*, 2005
Anne Perry, *The Cater Street Hangman*, 1979
Deanna Raybourn, *Silent in the Grave*, 2007
Victoria Thompson, *Murder on Astor Place*, 1999

618

SARA GRAN

Claire DeWitt and the City of the Dead

(Boston: Houghton Mifflin Harcourt, 2011)

Story type: Psychological Suspense
Subject(s): Detective fiction; Southern United States; Natural disasters
Major character(s): Claire DeWitt, Detective; Vic Willing, Lawyer (assistant district attorney), Uncle (of Leon); Leon, Nephew (of Vic)
Time period(s): 21st century; 2000s (2005)
Locale(s): New Orleans, Louisiana

Summary: *Claire DeWitt and the City of the Dead* is a mystery novel by author Sara Gran. The year is 2005, and New Orleans, Louisiana has just been devastated by the one of the deadliest hurricanes in U.S. history. Now the city's assistant DA, Vic Willing, has disappeared and is presumed dead. In an effort to figure out what happened to Willing, his nephew Leon enlists the help of Detective Claire DeWitt. Claire has her own problems to deal with on top of this new case: many of her friends and family are still missing in the wake of the storm, and she still bears the wounds from a colleague's death a few years before. As Claire struggles with her own demons, including alcohol and drugs, she must also fight to solve a case in a city that is becoming more and more corrupt by the moment.

Where it's reviewed:
Booklist, May 1, 2011, page 16

Other books by the same author:
Dope, 2006
Come Closer, 2003
Saturn's Return to New York, 2001

Other books you might like:
Josh Bazell, *Beat the Reaper*, 2009
Charlie Huston, *The Mystic Arts of Erasing All Signs of Death*, 2009
Lisa Lutz, *The Spellman Files*, 2007

Christopher Moore, *A Dirty Job*, 2006
Colson Whitehead, *The Intuitionist*, 1998

619

JOHN GRISHAM

The Litigators

(New York: Doubleday, 2011)

Story type: Legal
Subject(s): Suspense; Law; Drugs
Major character(s): Wally Figg, Lawyer; Oscar Finley, Lawyer; David Zinc, Lawyer

Summary: *The Litigators* is a novel written by best-selling author John Grisham. In it, Grisham tells the story of Finley & Figg, a law firm which specializes in the more unsavory practices of law. When David Zinc, a hot-shot lawyer from a prestigious city firm, loses his job, he finds himself working for Oscar Finley and Wally Figg. Soon he brings them a case that they are certain will make them all rich: a class-action lawsuit against a drug company that makes medication for cholesterol. But when the firm takes on Big Pharma, they get more than they bargained for. Grisham is also the author of *The Rainmaker*, *The Firm*, and *The Client*.

Other books by the same author:
The Confession, 2010
The Associate, 2009
The Appeal, 2008
Playing for Pizza, 2007
The Broker, 2005

Other books you might like:
Paul Goldstein, *A Patent Lie*, 2008
John Grisham, *The Rainmaker*, 1995
Ron Liebman, *Jersey Law*, 2011
Larry D. Thompson, *The Trial*, 2011

620

ANDREW GROSS

Eyes Wide Open

(New York: William Morrow, 2011)

Subject(s): Mystery; Suspense; Detective fiction
Major character(s): Jay Erlich, Doctor; Charlie Erlich, Brother (of Jay)
Time period(s): 21st century; 2010s
Locale(s): California, United States

Summary: In *Eyes Wide Open* by Andrew Gross, mistakes from Charlie Erlich's past may have deadly repercussions in the present. During the 1960s, Charlie had become a follower of an influential and dangerous cult leader. The effects on Charlie and his family had been devastating, but he survived those dark days to become an unassuming working man with a family. Now Charlie's son is dead—his body discovered at the base of a cliff—and Charlie's brother, Jay, wants answers. Jay, a doctor, doesn't believe that his nephew's plunge off the cliff was an act of suicide. His investigation brings him

face to face with Charlie's past.

Where it's reviewed:
Publishers Weekly, May 16, 2011, page 51

Other books by the same author:
Reckless, 2010
Don't Look Twice, 2009
The Dark Tide, 2008
The Blue Zone, 2007
The Jester, 2003

Other books you might like:
Linwood Barclay, *No Time for Goodbye*, 2007
Jan Burke, *Bloodlines*, 2005
Harlan Coben, *Just One Look*, 2004
Joseph Finder, *Company Man*, 2005
Gregg Hurwitz, *Trust No One*, 2009

621

JANE HADDAM

Flowering Judas

(New York: Minotaur Books, 2011)

Series: Gregor Demarkian Series. Book 26
Story type: Contemporary; Series
Subject(s): Detective fiction; Missing persons; Murder
Major character(s): Gregor Demarkian, Detective—
    Private; Chester Morton, Crime Victim
Time period(s): 21st century; 2010s
Locale(s): Mattuck, New York

Summary: For 12 years, Chester Morton has been missing.
His vigilant mother has not given up the search for her
son, even erecting a billboard broadcasting the news of
his disappearance. When Chester is found dead, hanging
from that same billboard, the town is in shock. Chester
has been recently killed, and everyone wants to know
where he has been for the past 12 years. Enter Gregor
Demarkian, former FBI agent and missing persons
expert. Now it's up to Gregor to unravel the intricate
mystery surrounding Chester's disappearance and death.
Flowering Judas is the 26th novel in Jane Haddam's
Gregor Demarkian series.

Where it's reviewed:
Booklist, June 1, 2011, page 39
Publishers Weekly, June 13, 2011, page 32

Other books by the same author:
Wanting Sheila Dead, 2010
Act of Darkness, 1991
Precious Blood, 1991
Not a Creature Was Stirring, 1990
Sanctity, 1986

Other books you might like:
Martin Edwards, *The Coffin Trail*, 2004
Aaron Elkins, *Fellowship of Fear*, 1982
Elizabeth George, *A Great Deliverance*, 1988
Peter May, *Extraordinary People*, 2006
Louise Penny, *Still Life*, 2006

622

CAROLYN HAINES

Bones of a Feather

(New York: Minotaur Books, 2011)

Series: Sarah Booth Delaney Series. Book 11
Story type: Contemporary; Series
Subject(s): Mystery; Detective fiction; Kidnapping
Major character(s): Sarah Booth Delaney, Detective—
    Private; Tinkie, Detective—Private, Colleague
    (partner of Sarah); Monica Levert, Heiress, Sister (of
    Eleanor); Eleanor Levert, Heiress, Sister (of Monica)
Time period(s): 21st century; 2010s
Locale(s): Natchez, Mississippi

Summary: In the mystery novel *Bones of a Feather* by
Carolyn Haines, private detective Sarah Booth Delaney
takes on a case that involves old money and Southern
family secrets. When the wealthy Levert sisters of
Natchez, Mississippi—Eleanor and Monica—report that
a valuable piece of heirloom jewelry has been stolen,
they call on Sarah Booth to solve the case. But the
investigator and her partner Tinkie suspect that the Le-
verts may have faked the robbery so they can make an
insurance claim. The case is complicated by Monica's
disappearance. Sarah Booth must figure out if the there
is a real criminal at work or if the Levert sisters are carrying on a family tradition of deception. *Bones of a
Feather* is the 11th book in the Sarah Booth Delaney
series.

Where it's reviewed:
Booklist, May 1, 2011, page 14
Publishers Weekly, April 11, 2011, page 31

Other books by the same author:
Bone Appetit, 2010
Crossed Bones, 2003
Splintered Bones, 2002
Buried Bones, 2000
Them Bones, 1999

Other books you might like:
Donna Andrews, *Murder with Peacocks*, 1999
Laura Disilverio, *Swift Justice*, 2011
Janet Evanovich, *One for the Money*, 1994
Charlaine Harris, *Real Murders*, 1990
Elaine Viets, *Shop Till You Drop*, 2003

623

REBECCA M. HALE

How to Moon a Cat

(New York: Berkley, 2011)

Series: Cats and Curios Series. Book 3
Story type: Contemporary
Subject(s): Pets; Suspense; Humor
Major character(s): Rebecca, Antiques Dealer, (owner of
    Rupert and Isabella); Rupert, Cat; Isabella, Cat
Time period(s): 21st century; 2010s
Locale(s): Nevada City, California

Mystery

Summary: *How to Moon a Cat* is the third book in the Cats and Curios series from author Rebecca M. Hale. The books follow Rebecca and her cats, Rupert and Isabella. Rebecca has been running the antique shop that was once owned by her uncle, who died mysteriously. In this installment, Rupert discovers a toy bear inside an old vase. Believing that the bear is a clue that would help her understand what happened to her uncle, Rebecca packs up her cats and heads to Nevada City. Soon, she realizes that the investigation could put all their lives in great danger.

Where it's reviewed:
Library Journal, July 2011, page   58

Other books by the same author:
Nine Lives Last Forever, 2010
How to Wash a Cat, 2008

Other books you might like:
Lorna Barrett, *Murder Is Binding*, 2008
Lilian Jackson Braun, *The Cat Who Could Read Backwards*, 1966
Sneaky Pie Brown, *Wish You Were Here*, 1990
Susan Conant, *Scratch the Surface*, 2005
Miranda James, *Murder Past Due*, 2010

624

JANICE HAMRICK

Death on Tour

(New York: Minotaur Books, 2011)

Story type: Contemporary
Subject(s): Detective fiction; Voyages and travels; Murder
Major character(s): Jocelyn Shore, Teacher, Detective— Amateur; Kayla Shore, Cousin (of Jocelyn); Millie Owens, Crime Victim; Alan Stratton, Traveler
Time period(s): 21st century; 2010s
Locale(s): Egypt

Summary: Jocelyn Shore is a schoolteacher looking forward to her grand tour of Egypt with gal pal Kyla. But the tranquility of their travels is shattered when Millie, a middle-aged member of their tour, suddenly plunges from an ancient stone sculpture. Jocelyn decides to launch her own investigation into the woman's death and is shocked to find that Millie was killed even before her fall. Now it's up to Jocelyn to figure out just what happened to Millie...and who on their tour is the murderer. *Death on Tour* is the first novel in a series by Janice Hamrick. First novel.

Where it's reviewed:
Booklist, May 1, 2011, page   18
Publishers Weekly, February 28, 2011, page   37

Other books you might like:
Joelle Charbonneau, *Skating around the Law*, 2010
Rosemary Harris, *Pushing Up Daisies*, 2008
Carolyn G. Hart, *Dead Man's Island*, 1993
Julie Hyzy, *Grace Under Pressure*, 2010
Rita Lakin, *Getting Old Is Murder*, 2005

625

KAREN HARPER

Fall From Pride

(Don Mills, Ontario, Canada: Mira, 2011)

Story type: Inspirational
Subject(s): Amish; Arson; Mystery
Major character(s): Sarah Kauffman, Artist; Nate MacKenzie, Investigator (arson)
Time period(s): 21st century; 2010s
Locale(s): Home Valley, Ohio

Summary: In Karen Harper's *Fall from Pride*, Sarah Kauffman is a young Amish woman who sets out to help her community revitalize its tourist economy. She paints a series of murals on local barns in the hope of drawing crowds to the small town. Instead, her efforts are met with destruction as systematically each barn falls victim to an arsonist's match. Englischer Nate MacKenzie is the arson investigator assigned to the case. He enlists Sarah's help in investigating the scant clues left behind and comes to learn about the Amish way of life. Soon the entire town is banding together to rebuild the barns and stand up proudly in the face of adversity.

Where it's reviewed:
Publishers Weekly, June 6, 2011, page   26

Other books by the same author:
Down River, 2010
Deep Down, 2009
Dark River, 2005
Dark Harvest, 2004
Dark Road Home, 1996

Other books you might like:
Linda Castillo, *Sworn to Silence*, 2009
Judy Clemens, *Till the Cows Come Home*, 2004
P.L. Gaus, *Blood of the Prodigal*, 1999
Shelley Shephard Gray, *The Caregiver*, 2011
Beth Wiseman, *Plain Paradise*, 2010

626

PAUL HARPER

Pacific Heights

(New York: Henry Holt and Co., 2011)

Story type: Psychological Suspense
Subject(s): Suspense; Detective fiction; Psychology
Major character(s): Marten Fane, Detective

Summary: *Pacific Heights* is the first novel in author Paul Harper's mystery series featuring Detective Marten Fane. In this novel, Fane must figure out how a man having an affair with two different women is able to tap into their very psyches. Fane learns that both women are seeing the same psychologist, but how is the therapist connected to the women's lover? Worse yet, one of the women is on the brink of insanity, and Fane discovers a Machiavellian plot that could possibly brainwash these women into committing murder. First novel.

Where it's reviewed:
Texas Monthly, July 2011, page   52

Other books by the same author:
The Face of the Assassin, 2004
The Rules of Silence, 2003
Body of Truth, 1992
Heat from Another Sun, 1984
A Cold Mind, 1983

Other books you might like:
Mark Coggins, *The Immortal Game*
Joe Gores, *Dead Skip*, 1972
Stephen Jay Schwartz, *Boulevard*, 2009
Peter Spiegelman, *Red Cat*, 2007
Domenic Stansberry, *Chasing the Dragon*, 2004

627

CORA HARRISON

Scales of Retribution

(London: Severn House Publishers, 2011)

Series: Mysteries of Medieval Ireland Series. Book 6
Story type: Historical
Subject(s): Detective fiction; Murder; Physicians
Major character(s): Mara O'Davoren, Judge, Detective; Malachy, Doctor, Crime Victim
Time period(s): 16th century; 1500s (1509)
Locale(s): Burrens, Ireland

Summary: Mara O'Davoren is the presiding judge of the coastal area of Burrens, Ireland, and she is about to give birth at any moment. But when her regular doctor disappears, his daughter stands in for him. Soon after the delivery, Mara learns her doctor has been murdered. As she sets off on her own investigation of the crime, Mara discovers everyone—even the doctor's children and the woman who delivered her baby—had a reason to want the good doctor dead. Cora Harrison's *Scales of Retribution* is the sixth novel in the Mysteries of Medieval Ireland series.

Where it's reviewed:
Booklist, May 15, 2011, page   21
Publishers Weekly, April 25, 2011, page   118

Other books by the same author:
Eye of the Law, 2010
The Sting of Justice, 2009
Writ in Stone, 2009
A Secret and Unlawful Killing, 2008
My Lady Judge, 2007

Other books you might like:
Alys Clare, *Fortune Like the Moon*, 2000
Ariana Franklin, *Mistress of the Art of Death*, 2007
Susanna Gregory, *A Plague on Both Your Houses*, 1998
Erin Hart, *Haunted Ground*, 2003
Peter Tremayne, *Absolution by Murder*, 1994

628

JOHN HART

Iron House

(New York: St. Martin's Press, 2011)

Subject(s): Mystery; Suspense; Brothers
Major character(s): Julian, Orphan; Michael, Brother (of Julian), Criminal; Elena, Girlfriend (of Michael)
Time period(s): 19th century-21st century; 1980s-2010s
Locale(s): New York, New York; North Carolina, United States

Summary: In *Iron House* by John Hart, the Iron Mountain Home for Boys is a dangerous way-station for orphans destined for a bleak future. Michael watches out for his younger brother Julian until a terrible day when Michael is forced to run away. One of the residents of Iron House has been killed and the only way Michael can protect Julian is by letting the authorities presume that Michael was the perpetrator. Iron House prepared Michael well for the life he leads as a New York mobster. When he falls in love with Elena, he finally seeks release from his world of violence, but it may already be too late.

Where it's reviewed:
Booklist, May 1, 2011, page   29
Library Journal, June 15, 2011, page   77
Publishers Weekly, May 16, 2011, page 50

Other books by the same author:
The Last Child, 2009
Down River, 2007
The King of Lies, 2006

Other books you might like:
Max Allan Collins, *Road to Perdition*, 2002
Tom Franklin, *Crooked Letter, Crooked Letter*, 2010
Chuck Hogan, *Prince of Thieves*, 2004
Dennis Lehane, *Mystic River*, 2001
Wallace Stroby, *The Barbed-Wire Kiss*, 2003

629

MICHAEL HARVEY

We All Fall Down

(New York: Knopf, 2011)

Series: Michael Kelly Series. Book 4
Story type: Contemporary; Series
Subject(s): Biological warfare; Detective fiction; Terrorism
Major character(s): Michael Kelly, Detective—Private
Time period(s): 21st century; 2010s
Locale(s): Chicago, Illinois

Summary: Chicago private eye Michael Kelly faces his most dangerous case yet. A light bulb in a subway station shatters, and a lethal biological substance is released into the city's air supply. Kelly acts quickly, following a twisting path of leads in hopes of finding those responsible for the terrorist act. As the city shuts down around him and more and more Chicagoans are plagued with illness, Kelly confronts the dark side of biology—and those

Mystery

intent on using innocent civilians as guinea pigs. Michael Harvey's *We All Fall Down* is the fourth book in the Michael Kelly series.

Where it's reviewed:
Publishers Weekly, June 13, 2011, page 32

Other books by the same author:
The Third Rail, 2010
The Fifth Floor, 2008
The Chicago Way, 2007

Other books you might like:
Greg Bear, *Quantico*, 2006
Guillermo Del Toro, *The Strain*, 2009
Chuck Hogan, *The Blood Artists*, 1998
Jonathan Maberry, *The King of Plagues*, 2011
Mark Terry, *The Serpent's Kiss*, 2007

630

J.M. HAYES

English Lessons

(Scottsdale, Arizona: Poisoned Pen Press, 2011)

Series: Mad Dog and Englishman Series. Book 6
Story type: Police Procedural; Series
Subject(s): Mystery; Detective fiction; Murder
Major character(s): Heather English, Daughter (of Sheriff English), Police Officer (Sewa Tribal); Sheriff English, Lawman (Benteen County, Kansas sheriff), Father (of Heather); Mad Dog, Uncle (of Heather), Indian (half-Cheyenne)
Time period(s): 21st century; 2010s
Locale(s): Arizona, United States; Kansas, United States

Summary: In the mystery novel *English Lessons*, father and daughter law-enforcement officials deal with murder and mayhem in two western states. In Arizona, Heather English, a Sewa Tribal police officer, has discovered the mutilated remains of the state's new governor, Joe Hyde. Near the man's drying hide is a message from a drug ring claiming responsibility for the murder and threatening Heather's life. Heather knows that her part-Cheyenne uncle, Mad Dog, will figure in her investigation. In Kansas, Sheriff English tries to stifle a spate of violence that began in a church parking lot but ends up triggering an angry response from vocal gun control opponents. *English Lessons* is the sixth book in the Mad Dog and Englishman series.

Where it's reviewed:
Booklist, May 1, 2011, page 24

Other books by the same author:
Server Down, 2009
Broken Heartland, 2007
Plains Crazy, 2004
Prairie Gothic, 2003
Mad Dog & Englishman, 2000

Other books you might like:
Margaret Coel, *The Eagle Catcher*, 1995
James D. Doss, *The Shaman Sings*, 1994
Craig Johnson, *The Cold Dish*, 2005
Michael McGarrity, *Tularosa*, 1996
Aimee Thurlo, *Blackening Song*, 1995

631

TIM HEALD

Death in the Opening Chapter

(Melbourne, Derby, United Kingdom: Creme de la Crime, 2011)

Story type: Contemporary
Subject(s): Murder; Suspense; Crime
Major character(s): Reverend Sebastian Fludd, Crime Victim, Cousin (of Branwell); Branwell Fludd, Cousin (of Sebastian), Friend (of Simon); Simon Bognor, Detective, Spouse (of Monica); Monica, Spouse (of Simon)
Time period(s): 21st century; 2010s
Locale(s): United Kingdom

Summary: *Death in the Opening Chapter* is part of the Simon Bognor series from author Tim Heald. The night before the Flanagan Fludd Literary Festival, the Reverend Sebastian Fludd is discovered swinging from the rafters of his own church. Was his life taken by his own hand, or was it murder? Sebastian's cousin, Sir Branwell Fludd, is trying to figure out what happened without attracting too much attention. Fortunately, he has the help of his friend, Simon Bognor, head of the board of trade's special investigations department. With a field of suspects that continues to grow, Simon has his work cut out for him if he's going to find out what happened to the reverend.

Where it's reviewed:
Booklist, July 1, 2011, page 30
Publishers Weekly, May 30, 2011, page 51

Other books by the same author:
A Death on the Ocean Wave, 2007
Death and the Visiting Fellow, 2004
Stop Press, 1998
Business Unusual, 1989
Unbecoming Habits, 1973

Other books you might like:
M.C. Beaton, *Agatha Raisin and the Quiche of Death*, 1992
Simon Brett, *The Body on the Beach*, 2000
Deborah Crombie, *A Share in Death*, 1993
Kate Ellis, *Seeking the Dead*, 2008
Ann Granger, *Say It with Poison*, 1991

632

REGINALD HILL

The Woodcutter

(London: HarperCollins, 2011)

Subject(s): Prisoners; Revenge; Suspense
Major character(s): Wolf Hadda, Convict (former), Entrepreneur; Alva Ozigbo, Doctor (psychiatrist)
Time period(s): 21st century; 2010s
Locale(s): England

Summary: In the novel *The Woodcutter* by Reginald Hill, a terrible turn of events transforms businessman Wolf Hadda into a hated criminal. Imprisoned despite his

claims of innocence, Hadda loses all of the friends he's known and stops speaking completely. For seven years, Hadda languishes in his cell until Alva Ozigbo, the institution's psychiatrist, manages to communicate with her patient. Under Ozigbo's care, Hadda improves until he is finally released from prison. Hadda returns to his childhood home in Umbria where he recalls the time before he was an entrepreneur, when he was a woodcutter's son. Hadda was a woodcutter, too, once, and now he decides that it is time for the woodcutter to seek vengeance.

Where it's reviewed:
Booklist, May 1, 2011, page   41
Library Journal, June 1, 2011, page   92
Publishers Weekly, June 6, 2011, page   23
Times Literary Supplement, August 20, 2010, page   22

Other books by the same author:
Midnight Fugue, 2009
The Roar of the Butterflies, 2008
The Stranger House, 2005
Blood Sympathy, 1993
A Clubbable Woman, 1970

Other books you might like:
Angela Carter, *Wise Children*, 1991
Tana French, *In the Woods*, 2007
Susan Hill, *The Beacon*, 2008
Barbara Vine, *Gallowglass*, 1990
Minette Walters, *The Scold's Bridle*, 1994

633

SUZETTE A. HILL

A Bedlam of Bones

(London: Soho Constable, 2011)

Series: Francis Oughterard Series. Book 5
Story type: Contemporary; Series
Subject(s): Detective fiction; Murder; Human-animal relationships
Major character(s): Reverend Oughterard, Religious (bishop), Detective—Amateur; Lavinia Birtle-Figgins, Crime Suspect
Time period(s): 21st century; 2010s
Locale(s): Surrey, England

Summary: Suzette A. Hill's *A Bedlam of Bones* is the fifth installment in the Reverend Oughterard Mystery series, centering on the investigations of an animal-loving bishop. This outing finds the bishop falling victim to a blackmailer, and, a short time later, a body is discovered in the church garden. As the bishop tries to piece together these two crimes, his suspicions turn toward Lavinia Birtle-Figgins, a woman who just might not be as clueless as she first appears. With the help of his animal companions, Reverend Oughterard sets out to find the identity of his blackmailer and learn the truth behind the body in the garden—and anything Lavinia may know about it.

Where it's reviewed:
Booklist, July 1, 2011, page   29
Publishers Weekly, May 23, 2011, page   32

Other books by the same author:
Bones in High Places, 2010
Bone Idle, 2009
Bones in the Belfry, 2008
A Load of Old Bones, 2005

Other books you might like:
Callie Anson, *Evil Intent*, 2005
D.M. Greenwood, *Clerical Errors*, 1991
Jan Karon, *Home to Holly Springs*, 2007
Phil Rickman, *The Wine of Angels*, 1998
Julia Spencer-Fleming, *In the Bleak Midwinter*, 2002

634

JENNIFER HILLIER

Creep

(New York: Gallery Books, 2011)

Subject(s): Suspense; Violence; Murder
Major character(s): Sheila Tao, Professor; Ethan Wolfe, Student—Graduate
Time period(s): 21st century; 2010s
Locale(s): Puget Sound, Washington

Summary: Jennifer Hillier's *Creep* chronicles a fatal attraction that spirals out of control. Sheila Tao is a college professor who, against her better judgment, conducts a torrid affair with her teaching assistant, Ethan Wolfe. When she breaks off the relationship, Ethan is shattered, and he sets out to wreak havoc on Sheila's life. Soon Sheila is being blackmailed and harassed by her former lover—but when the body of a popular student is discovered, she realizes she just how unhinged Ethan has become. First novel.

Where it's reviewed:
Library Journal, May 15, 2011, page   75
Publishers Weekly, May 9, 2011, page   32

Other books you might like:
Laura Benedict, *Calling Mr. Lonely Hearts: A Novel*, 2008
Faye Kellerman, *Stalker*, 2000
Lauren Kelly, *The Stolen Heart*, 2005
Joyce Maynard, *To Die For*, 1992
Rosamond Smith, *Soul/Mate*, 1989

635

DAVID HOUSEWRIGHT

Highway 61

(New York: Minotaur Books, 2011)

Series: Mac McKenzie Series. Book 7
Story type: Contemporary
Subject(s): Detective fiction; Murder; Father-daughter relations
Major character(s): Rushmore "Mac" McKenzie, Detective; Jason Truhler, Crime Suspect
Time period(s): 21st century; 2010s
Locale(s): St. Paul, Minnesota

Mystery

Summary: One-time cop, now an amateur private eye, Rushmore "Mac" McKenzie finds himself in the middle of his most personal case yet. The daughter of his girlfriend needs Mac's help in finding those responsible for framing and blackmailing her father. But the deeper Mac gets into the dark details of the case, the more torn he becomes: Whom can he trust? And who is telling the truth? *Highway 61* is the seventh book in David Housewright's Mac McKenzie series.

Where it's reviewed:
Booklist, May 1, 2011, page 28
Publishers Weekly, March 14, 2011, page 51

Other books by the same author:
The Taking of Libbie, SD, 2010
Dead Boyfriends, 2007
Tin City, 2005
A Hard Ticket Home, 2004
Pretty Girl Gone, 2004

Other books you might like:
Lawrence Block, *Sins of the Fathers*, 1976
Sean Chercover, *Big City, Bad Blood*, 2007
Steve Hamilton, *A Cold Day in Paradise*, 1998
Michael Koryta, *Tonight I Said Goodbye*, 2004
John Sandford, *Rules of Prey*, 1989

636

ALAN HRUSKA

Wrong Man Running

(Sutton, Surrey, England: Severn House Publishers, 2011)

Story type: Contemporary
Subject(s): Crime; Suspense; Law
Major character(s): Rick Corinth, Lawyer
Time period(s): 21st century; 2010s
Locale(s): New York, New York

Summary: A New York assistant district attorney finds himself accused of a heinous crime in *Wrong Man Running*. Rick Corinth is on his way to earning the top job at the district attorney's office. Things take a turn for the worse, however, when he is assigned to a case involving a serial rapist. Soon, he realizes that all of the victims have some connection to him. The police notice the connection as well and begin treating Corinth like a suspect. All of the women accuse him of the crime, but Rick knows that he's innocent. Now, it's up to him to find the real criminal before it's too late.

Where it's reviewed:
Booklist, July 1, 2011, page 35
Publishers Weekly, May 2, 2011, page 40

Other books by the same author:
Borrowed Time, 1985

Other books you might like:
Thomas H. Cook, *The City When It Rains*, 1991
Alex Cooper, *Final Jeopardy*, 1994
Dan Greenburg, *Love Kills*, 1978
Jonathan Santlofer, *Anatomy of Fear*, 2007
Scott Turow, *Presumed Innocent*, 1987

637

JAMES PATRICK HUNT

Police and Thieves

(Waterville, Maine: Five Star, 2011)

Story type: Contemporary
Subject(s): Crime; Murder; Brothers
Major character(s): Dan Bridger, Criminal, Brother (of Seth); Seth, Police Officer, Crime Victim (murdered), Brother (of Dan)
Time period(s): 21st century; 2010s
Locale(s): Seattle, Washington

Summary: A criminal sets out to find the person who killed his brother in *Police and Thieves* by James Patrick Hunt. Dan Bridger is a professional thief who works alone and has little contact with his family. He hasn't spoken to his brother, Seth, for several years. So, he's stunned when he receives a phone call from a woman telling him that his brother is dead. Dan learns that his brother was working as a probation officer. The police believe that Seth was the victim of gang violence, but Dan's not convinced. Soon, he sets out on his own investigation to find out what really happened.

Where it's reviewed:
Library Journal, July 2011, page 58

Other books by the same author:
Bridger, 2010
The Silent Places, 2010
The Betrayers, 2007
Before They Make You Run, 2006
Maitland, 2006

Other books you might like:
Richard Parker, *Point Blank*, 1962
Marcus Sakey, *At the City's Edge*, 2008
Barbara Seranella, *No Human Involved*, 1997
Newton Thornburg, *Cutter and Bone*, 1976
Robert Ward, *Red Baker*, 1985

638

GREGG HURWITZ

You're Next

(New York: St. Martin's Press, 2011)

Subject(s): Architecture; Family; Orphans
Major character(s): Mike Wingate, Designer (of green houses), Father (of Katherine), Spouse (of Annabel), Orphan; Annabel Wingate, Spouse (of Mike), Mother (of Katherine); Katherine Wingate, Daughter (of Mike and Annabel), 8-Year-Old; Shep, Orphan, Friend (of Mike)
Time period(s): 21st century
Locale(s): United States

Summary: Jennifer Hillier's *Creep* chronicles a fatal attraction that spirals out of control. Sheila Tao is a college professor who, against her better judgment, conducts a torrid affair with her teaching assistant, Ethan Wolfe. When she breaks off the relationship, Ethan is shattered,

and he sets out to wreak havoc on Sheila's life. Soon Sheila is being blackmailed and harassed by her former lover—but when the body of a popular student is discovered, she realizes she just how unhinged Ethan has become. First novel.

Where it's reviewed:
Booklist, May 1, 2011, page 41
Publishers Weekly, May 9, 2011, page 31

Other books by the same author:
They're Watching, 2009
Trust No One, 2008
The Crime Writer, 2007
Last Shot, 2006
Troubleshooter, 2005
The Program, 2004
The Kill Clause, 2003
The Tower, 1999

Other books you might like:
Linwood Barclay, *No Time for Goodbye*, 2007
Harlan Coben, *The Woods*, 2007
Joseph Finder, *Company Man*, 2005
Lisa Gardner, *Love You More*, 2011
Thomas Perry, *Runner*, 2009

639

DAVID IGNATIUS

Bloodmoney

(New York: W.W. Norton & Company, 2011)

Story type: Contemporary; Espionage
Subject(s): Suspense; Espionage; Mystery
Major character(s): Sophie Marx, Agent (CIA)
Time period(s): 21st century
Locale(s): London, England; Pakistan

Summary: In *Bloodmoney: A Novel of Espionage*, David Ignatius tells the story of Sophie Marx, an agent with the CIA whose mission is to discover who is killing off key agency operatives in the Middle East. Those operatives were part of a plan to broker peace between the United States and its sworn enemies, and without the plan America's foreign policy is in a tenuous position. Worse yet, the more Sophie thinks she might have a handle on the case, the more she learns that nothing is as it seems. Ignatius is also the author of *Body of Lies* and *The Increment*.

Where it's reviewed:
Booklist, May 1, 2011, page 14
The Economist, May 21, 2011, page 87
Library Journal, March 15, 2011, page 108
Publishers Weekly, April 4, 2011, page 30

Other books by the same author:
The Increment, 2009
Body of Lies, 2007
A Firing Offense, 1997
The Bank of Fear, 1994
Agents of Innocence, 1987

Other books you might like:
Alex Berenson, *The Faithful Spy*, 2006

Charles Cumming, *A Spy by Nature*, 2007
Dan Fesperman, *The Warlord's Son*, 2004
Jenny Siler, *Flashback*, 2004
Daniel Silva, *The Kill Artist*, 2000

640

ALAN JACOBSON

Inmate 1577

(Ellistown, Leicestershire, United Kingdom: Norwood Press, 2011)

Series: Karen Vail Series. Book 4
Story type: Contemporary
Subject(s): Murder; Detective fiction; Suspense
Major character(s): Karen Vail, FBI Agent (profiler); Lance Burden, Inspector (police); Roxxann Dixon, Detective
Time period(s): 21st century; (2010s); 20th century; 1950s (1955)
Locale(s): San Francisco, California; Northfield, New Jersey

Summary: Karen Vail is an FBI profiler who is assigned a gruesome new case. An aged San Francisco woman has been viciously sexually assaulted and murdered, and it's up to Vail, police inspector Lance Burden, and detective Roxxann Dixon to find the culprit. Their investigation takes them on a twisting path into the past, leading back to an unsolved crime that occurred in 1955 New Jersey. Can Vail and her team nab the offender before the past and present collide in a horrific display of violence? Alan Jacobson's *Inmate 1577* is the fourth novel in the Karen Vail series of police procedurals.

Other books by the same author:
Velocity, 2010
Crush, 2009
The 7th Victim, 2008
The Hunted, 2002
False Accusations, 1999

Other books you might like:
Jeffery Deaver, *The Bone Collector*, 1997
J. T. Ellison, *Judas Kiss*, 2009
Michelle Gagnon, *The Tunnels*, 2007
Alex Kava, *A Perfect Evil*, 2001
Karin Slaughter, *Blindsighted*, 2001

641

BILL JAMES

Hotbed

(Woodstock, Vermont: Countryman Press, 2011)

Series: Colin Harpur Series. Book 26
Story type: Police Procedural; Series
Subject(s): Detective fiction; Crime; England
Major character(s): Ralph Ember, Organized Crime Figure; Mansel Shale, Organized Crime Figure; Desmond Iles, Lawman (assistant chief constable); Colin Harpur, Detective—Police (detective chief superintendent)

Mystery

Time period(s): 21st century; 2010s
Locale(s): England

Summary: In *Hotbed* by Bill James, the 26th book in the Harpur and Iles mystery series, tensions between two drug lords are strained to the breaking point. Ralph Ember and Mansel Shale, competitors and professional acquaintances, control equal portions of the local drug trade, but their fragile treaty is showing signs of wear as each man eyes the other's profits. Assistant Chief Constable Desmond Iles and Detective Chief Superintendent Colin Harpur—two lawmen with their own tenuous relationship—watch the dance between Ember and Shale with interest. Shale attempts to appease Ember by asking him to be best man at his upcoming wedding, but will Shale's move protect him or push him closer to danger?

Where it's reviewed:
Booklist, May 1, 2011, page   29
Publishers Weekly, March 21, 2011, page   59

Other books by the same author:
In the Absence of Iles, 2008
Pix, 2007
Halo Parade, 1987
The Lolita Man, 1986
You'd Better Believe It, 1985

Other books you might like:
Mark Billingham, *Sleepyhead*, 2001
John Harvey, *Lonely Hearts*, 1989
Peter James, *Dead Simple*, 2006
Ian Rankin, *Strip Jack*, 1992
Peter Robinson, *Gallows View*, 1987

642

MIRANDA JAMES

Classified as Murder

(New York: Berkley/Penguin Group, 2011)

Series: Cat in the Stacks Mystery Series. Book
Story type: Amateur Detective; Mystery
Subject(s): Mystery; Murder; Libraries
Major character(s): Charlie Harris, Librarian, Detective—Amateur; Diesel, Detective—Amateur, Cat; James Delacorte, Collector
Locale(s): Mississippi, United States

Summary: Author Dean James, writing under the pseudonym Miranda James, treats readers to another round of feline detective work in his novel *Classified as Murder*. This time, college librarian Charlie Harris is recruited by James Delacorte, an elderly eccentric, to inventory his sprawling collection of rare books that the college will eventually inherit. Shortly after Charlie takes the job, however, Delacorte dies mysteriously and Charlie finds himself in the middle of a murder investigation. With no choice but to solve the crime and prove his innocence, Charlie and his feline partner, Diesel, set out to track down the real killer. To make matters even more complicated, the pair must also deal with the sudden reappearance of Charlie's lawyer son Sean. How will Charlie and Diesel manage to juggle the difficulties of both family matters and murder?

Where it's reviewed:
Library Journal, May 1, 2011, page   62

Other books by the same author:
Murder Past Due, 2010

Other books you might like:
Sneaky Pie Brown, *Wish You Were Here*, 1990
Kate Carlisle, *Homicide in Hardcover*, 2009
Jo Dereske, *Miss Zukas and the Library Murders*, 1994
Carole Nelson Douglas, *Catnap*, 1992
Carolyn G. Hart, *Death on Demand*, 1987

643

J.A. JANCE

Betrayal of Trust

(New York: William Morrow, 2011)

Series: J.P. Beaumont Series. Book 20
Story type: Police Procedural; Series
Subject(s): Mystery; Suspense; Crime
Major character(s): J.P. Beaumont, Detective—Private; Mel Soames, Colleague (of Beaumont)
Time period(s): 21st century; 2010s
Locale(s): Seattle, Washington

Summary: In *Betrayal of Trust* by J.A. Jance, private detective J.P. Beaumont investigates the snuff film murder of a teenage girl. It is the governor of Washington who calls on Beaumont when the incriminating movie turns up on his grandson's cell phone. Even to veteran investigator Beaumont, the images are disturbing. Though he believes that the governor's grandson had no knowledge of the crime or the victim, Beaumont suspects that a group of juveniles carried out the killing. When Beaumont's partner, Mel Soames, joins the case, their investigation leads them the offices of Washington's elected officials. *Betrayal of Trust* is the 20th book in the J.P. Beaumont series.

Where it's reviewed:
Publishers Weekly, May 23, 2011, page   26

Other books by the same author:
Fire and Ice, 2009
Damage Control, 2008
Edge of Evil, 2006
Desert Heat, 1993
Until Proven Guilty, 1985

Other books you might like:
Catherine Coulter, *The Cove*, 1996
G.M. Ford, *Fury*, 2001
Lisa Gardner, *Alone*, 2005
Tess Gerritsen, *The Surgeon*, 2001
J.D. Robb, *Naked in Death*, 1995

644

RODERIC JEFFRIES

Murder, Majorcan Style

(New York: Severn House Publishers, 2011)

Series: Inspector Alvarez Series. Book 35
Story type: Contemporary - Exotic; Series

Subject(s): Detective fiction; Murder; Suspense
Major character(s): Enrique Alvarez, Detective; Senor Sterne, Crime Victim
Time period(s): 21st century; 2010s
Locale(s): Spain

Summary: Detective Enrique Alvarez is relaxing at lunch and making plans to sneak away from work early. Those plans, however, are put on hold when he is called to the house of Senor Sterne, a British man who has been discovered dead in his car. The car was running at the time, and carbon monoxide filled the vehicle, but what at first appears to be a cut and dried suicide turns out to be anything but. As Alvarez launches his investigation into Senor Sterne's murder, he uncovers the dead man's messy personal life, tumultuous family relations, and shady dealings all around Majorca. Roderic Jeffries's *Murder, Majorcan Style* is the 35th novel in the Inspector Alvarez series.

Where it's reviewed:
Booklist, June 1, 2011, page 43
Publishers Weekly, June 20, 2011, page 37

Other books by the same author:
A Question of Motive, 2009
The Man Who Couldn't Be, 1987
Troubled Deaths, 1977
Two-Faced Death, 1976
Mistakenly in Mallorca, 1974

Other books you might like:
M.C. Beaton, *Death of a Gossip*, 1985
Rhys Bowen, *Evans Above*, 1997
Anthea Fraser, *A Shroud for Delilah*, 1984
Ann Granger, *Say It with Poison*, 1991
Quintin Jardine, *Skinner's Rules*, 1993

645

ELIZABETH JENNINGS

Darkness at Dawn
(New York: Berkley, 2011)

Story type: Contemporary - Exotic
Subject(s): Suspense; Romances (Fiction); Terrorism
Major character(s): Lucy Merritt, Art Historian (manuscript restorer); Mike Shafer, Military Personnel (U.S. Army captain)
Time period(s): 21st century; 2010s
Locale(s): Nhala, Asia

Summary: In the novel *Darkness at Dawn* by Elizabeth Jennings, Lucy Merritt is content in her peaceful life as a manuscript restorer. Unlike her parents, CIA agents who were killed in the line of duty, Lucy prefers a career free from risk and intrigue. But when the CIA calls on Lucy to travel to the Himalayas to look at a manuscript there, she feels duty-bound to accept the request. Accompanying Lucy on her journey to the site of her parents' death is Army Captain Mike Shafer. As their mission grows increasingly dangerous, Lucy and Mike realize that their relationship has become more than professional.

Where it's reviewed:
Publishers Weekly, May 2, 2011, page 42

Romantic Times, July 2011, Page 78

Other books by the same author:
Masquerade, 2010
Shadows of Midnight, 2010
Pursuit, 2008
Dying for Siena, 2006
Homecoming, 2006

Other books you might like:
Maya Banks, *The Darkest Hour*, September 7, 2010
Pamela Clare, *Extreme Exposure*, 2005
M.M. Kaye, *The Far Pavilions*, 1978
Catherine Mann, *Defender*, 2009
Katherine Neville, *The Eight*, 1988

646

PAM JENOFF

The Things We Cherished
(New York: Doubleday, 2011)

Subject(s): World War II, 1939-1945; Law; Wars
Major character(s): Charlotte Gold, Lawyer; Jack Harrington, Lawyer; Roger Dykmans, Defendant
Time period(s): 21st century; (2010s); 20th century; 1930s-1940s
Locale(s): Germany; Italy; Poland; Philadelphia, Pennsylvania

Summary: *The Things We Cherished* is a novel by author Pam Jenoff. In this novel, Jenoff tells the story of two lawyers working together to defend a man accused of war crimes during World War II. As the attorneys, Charlotte Gold and Jack Harrington fight to defend their client, a magnate named Roger Dykmans. They find themselves fighting their own romantic feelings for one another, too. Dykmans isn't making the case easy, as the only alibi he provides for himself is a long-lost clock. The story moves backward in time to World War II, as it follows a young Dykmans in love with the wrong woman. Jenoff was a Quill Award and ALA Sophie Brody Award finalist for her debut novel *The Kommandant's Girl*.

Where it's reviewed:
Booklist, June 1, 2011, page 45
Library Journal, June 1, 2011, page 92

Other books by the same author:
A Hidden Affair, 2010
Almost Home, 2009
The Diplomat's Wife, 2008
The Kommandant's Girl, 2007

Other books you might like:
Rebecca Cantrell, *A Trace of Smoke*, 2009
Susan Isaacs, *Shining Through*, 1988
Sarah R. Shaber, *Louise's War*, 2011
Herman Wouk, *The Winds of War*, 1971
Sara Young, *My Enemy's Cradle*, 2008

647

MERRY JONES

Summer Session

(New York: Severn House Publishers, 2011)

Series: Harper Jennings Mystery Series. Book 1
Story type: Contemporary; Series
Subject(s): Detective fiction; Veterans; Suicide
Major character(s): Harper Jennings, Teacher, Veteran, Detective—Amateur; Hank, Spouse (of Harper)
Time period(s): 21st century; 2010s
Locale(s): Ithaca, New York

Summary: Harper Jennings is a teaching assistant at Cornell and a veteran of the Iraq War. Struggling with symptoms of post traumatic stress disorder, Harper manages to eke out a somewhat contented existence. But after her husband Hank plummets from the roof of their home, all Harper's buried memories of wartime life come back with a vengeance. To further complicate matters, one of her students leaps to his death from a high window. Now Harper finds herself in the middle of an increasingly dangerous case involving deception, theft, and possible murder. *Summer Session* is the first installment in Merry Jones's Harper Jennings Mysteries series.

Where it's reviewed:
Library Journal, July 2011, page 58
Publishers Weekly, June 13, 2011, page 33

Other books by the same author:
The Borrowed & Blue Murders, 2008
The Deadly Neighbors, 2007
The River Killings, 2006
The Nanny Murders, 2005

Other books you might like:
John Connolly, *The Whisperers*, 2010
G.H. Ephron, *Guilt*, 2005
Jesse Kellerman, *Trouble*, 2007
Jonathan Kellerman, *The Clinic*, 1996
Julia Spencer-Fleming, *One Was a Soldier*, 2011

648

MORAG JOSS

Among the Missing

(New York: Delacorte Press, 2011)

Subject(s): Bridges (Structures); Friendship; Immigrants
Major character(s): Annabel, Missing Person (pregnant); Silva, Immigrant; Ron, Convict (ex-convict)
Time period(s): 21st century; 2010s
Locale(s): Scotland

Summary: In *Among the Missing*, author Morag Joss tells the story of three unmoored loners who find an unusual strength and solace in each other's company. A bridge has collapsed in a small Scottish town, resulting in a catastrophe of epic proportions. Near the bridge lives Annabel, a pregnant, middle-aged woman who is presumed dead after her car plummets from the bridge. She resides with illegal immigrant Silva, and the two form a strong bond. Soon an ex-con named Ron enters their lives, and the disparate trio share a functional household—despite the long-buried secrets each of them holds.

Where it's reviewed:
Booklist, May 1, 2011, page 13
Publishers Weekly, May 30, 2011, page 46

Other books by the same author:
The Night Following, 2008
Puccini's Ghosts, 2005
Half Broken Things, 2003
Fruitful Bodies, 2001
Funeral Music, 1998

Other books you might like:
Tana French, *The Likeness*, 2008
Sophie Hannah, *The Dead Lie Down*, 2010
P.D. James, *Original Sin*, 1994
Barbara Vine, *Gallowglass*, 1990
Minette Walters, *The Echo*, 1997

649

TAMMY KAEHLER

Dead Man's Switch

(Scottsdale, Arizona: Poisoned Pen Press, 2011)

Series: Kate Reilly Mystery Series. Book 1
Story type: Contemporary; Series
Subject(s): Detective fiction; Murder; Automobile racing
Major character(s): Kate Reilly, Race Car Driver, Detective—Amateur
Time period(s): 21st century; 2010s
Locale(s): United States

Summary: In *Dead Man's Switch*, author Tammy Kaehler presents the first book in the Kate Reilly Mysteries series, which focuses on the adventures of a race car driver/amateur private eye. This opening volume finds Kate on the lookout for a full-time driving gig, and she thinks she's found the ideal job with the American Le Mans Series. But one of the Series' drivers is suddenly murdered, and, hours later, Kate is handed his car. Now she finds herself a suspect in his death. Determined to clear herself of any wrongdoing, she embarks upon her own investigation into the murder, which sheds light not only on the cutthroat atmosphere of the racing world—but on the very real cost of murder. First novel.

Where it's reviewed:
Publishers Weekly, May 16, 2011, page 58

Other books you might like:
Janet Evanovich, *Metro Girl*, 2004
Joyce Lavene, *Swapping Paint*, 2007
Sharyn McCrumb, *St. Dale*, 2005
Steve Ulfelder, *Purgatory Chasm*, 2011
Simon Wood, *Accidents Waiting to Happen*, 2002

650

ANDREA KANE

The Girl Who Disappeared Twice

(Don Mills, Ontario, Canada: Mira, 2011)

Story type: Contemporary
Subject(s): Detective fiction; Women; Missing persons
Major character(s): Hope Willis, Judge (family court), Mother (of Krissy); Krissy, 5-Year-Old, Daughter (of Hope); Casey Woods, Detective—Private, Leader (Forensic Instincts)
Time period(s): 21st century; 2010s
Locale(s): White Plains, New York

Summary: In Andrea Kane's *The Girl Who Disappeared Twice*, family-court judge Hope Willis takes extreme measures when her five-year-old daughter Krissy is abducted. Hope lost her twin sister to a kidnapper three decades ago and knows how important it is for Krissy to be found quickly. Refusing to waste one minute of time while the authorities let bureaucracy delay their investigation, Hope calls on Casey Woods and her group of variously skilled private detectives who call themselves Forensic Instincts. But when Hope hires Casey's team to find Krissy, she opens her household to more scrutiny than she imagined.

Where it's reviewed:
Booklist, May 1, 2011, page 26
Library Journal, June 15, 2011, page 72
Publishers Weekly, May 9, 2011, page 35

Other books by the same author:
Drawn in Blood, 2009
Twisted, 2008
I'll Be Watching You, 2005
Scent of Danger, 2003
No Way Out, 2001

Other books you might like:
Lisa Gardner, *The Survivors Club*, 2001
Alison Gaylin, *Heartless*, 2008
Karen Rose, *Have You Seen Her?*, 2004
Erica Spindler, *Last Known Victim*, 2007
Chevy Stevens, *Still Missing*, 2010

651

THOMAS KAUFMAN

Steal the Show

(New York: Minotaur Books, 2011)

Series: Willis Gidney Mystery Series. Book 2
Story type: Contemporary; Series
Subject(s): Detective fiction; Mystery; Politics
Major character(s): Willis Gidney, Detective—Private, Foster Parent (of Sarah); Rush Gemelli, Computer (hacker); Chuck Gemelli, Lobbyist (motion picture lobby), Father (of Rush); Sarah, Baby, Foster Child (of Willis)
Time period(s): 21st century; 2010s
Locale(s): Washington, District of Columbia

Summary: In the mystery novel *Steal the Show* by Thomas Kaufman, private investigator Willis Gidney knows how the system works in Washington, D.C. He makes a decent living solving his clients' various problems, but now Gidney has a problem of his own. He wants to adopt a baby girl whom he found abandoned at a warehouse, but he needs some extra funds to hire a good lawyer. When Rush Gemelli, son of a prominent motion-picture lobbyist, proposes a lucrative assignment, Gidney eventually accepts despite the questionable ethics of the job. Gidney's get-rich-quick scheme quickly turns into a dangerous case that involves murder, blackmail, and some troublesome thugs. *Steal the Show* is the second book in the Willis Gidney Mystery series.

Where it's reviewed:
Booklist, June 1, 2011, page 44
Publishers Weekly, May 16, 2011, page 58

Other books by the same author:
Drink the Tea, 2010

Other books you might like:
Earl Emerson, *The Rainy City*, 1985
Loren D. Estleman, *Motor City Blue*, 1980
Michael Koryta, *Tonight I Said Goodbye*, 2004
George P. Pelecanos, *A Firing Offense*, 1992
Michael Wiley, *The Last Striptease*, 2007

652

ALEX KAVA

Hotwire

(New York: Doubleday, 2011)

Series: Maggie O'Dell Series. Book 9
Story type: Psychological Suspense
Subject(s): Detective fiction; Murder; Crime
Major character(s): Maggie O'Dell, FBI Agent; R.J. Tully, FBI Agent; Benjamin Platt, Military Personnel (army colonel)
Locale(s): Nebraska, United States

Summary: *Hotwire* is a novel from author Alex Kava's series featuring Special Agent Maggie O'Dell. Maggie is investigating the deaths of three young people who succumbed after being electrocuted at a party. Maggie must figure out how these teens were electrocuted in the first place, but when the party's survivors start turning up dead, she begins to realize that more than faulty wiring was to blame. In the meantime, Maggie's partner R.J. Tully has teamed up with Colonel Benjamin Platt to stop a biological weapon before it claims any more victims. As both investigations unfold, Maggie, R.J., and Benjamin begin to realize a connection that could put the entire U.S. population at risk.

Where it's reviewed:
Booklist, June 1, 2011, page 40
Publishers Weekly, May 2, 2011, page 34

Other books by the same author:
Damaged, 2010
Black Friday, 2009
Exposed, 2008
Necessary Evil, 2006

At the Stroke of Madness, 2003
The Soul Catcher, 2002
Split Second, 2001
A Perfect Evil, 2000

Other books you might like:
J. T. Ellison, *Judas Kiss*, 2009
K.J. Erickson, *Alone at Night*, 2004
Michelle Gagnon, *The Tunnels*, 2007
Lisa Gardner, *Alone*, 2005
Karin Slaughter, *Undone*, 2009

653

JIM KELLY

Death Toll

(New York: Minotaur Books, 2011)

Series: Detective Shaw Series. Book 3
Story type: Police Procedural; Series
Subject(s): Detective fiction; Murder; Crime
Major character(s): Peter Shaw, Detective—Police (detective inspector), Son (of Jack Shaw); George Valentine, Detective—Police (detective sergeant); Jack Shaw, Detective—Police (former), Father (of Peter); Jonathan Tessier, 9-Year-Old, Crime Victim; Nora Tilden, Crime Victim
Time period(s): 21st century; 2010s
Locale(s): West Norfolk, England

Summary: In the novel *Death Toll*, the third book in Jim Kelly's Detective Shaw Mystery series, two cases occupy West Norfolk Detective Inspector Peter Shaw and his partner, Detective Sergeant George Valentine. Years ago, Valentine was the partner of Peter's late father, Jack Shaw, but a problematic case all but ruined their careers. Now Peter wants to find the killer of Jonathan Tessier and finally restore the reputations of his father and his partner. A construction project at a cemetery reveals the casket of another murder victim from the past. But Nora Tilden, presumably killed by her husband, was not buried alone. The skeletal remains of a mixed-race man missing for decades lies atop her coffin. Shaw and Valentine's investigation is complicated by the local residents' reluctance to talk to outsiders.

Where it's reviewed:
Booklist, May 1, 2011, page   20
Publishers Weekly, April 25, 2011, page   119

Other books by the same author:
Death Watch, 2010
Death Wore White, 2009
The Skeleton Man, 2007
The Fire Baby, 2004
The Water Clock, 2002

Other books you might like:
Deborah Crombie, *A Share in Death*, 1993
Elizabeth George, *A Great Deliverance*, 1988
John Harvey, *Flesh and Blood*, 2004
Reginald Hill, *A Clubbable Woman*, 1970
Peter Robinson, *Gallows View*, 1987

654

CHRISTOBEL KENT

A Murder in Tuscany

(New York: Minotaur Books, 2011)

Story type: Contemporary - Exotic; Series
Subject(s): Detective fiction; Murder; Castles
Major character(s): Sandro Celllini, Detective; Loni Meadows, Crime Victim
Time period(s): 21st century; 2010s
Locale(s): Tuscany, Italy

Summary: *A Murder in Tuscany* is the second book in Christobel Kent's Sandro Cellini Italian mystery series, centering on the investigations of a Florentine private detective. Glitzy Loni Meadows operates an artist's retreat at a castle in Tuscany. One fateful night, her car crashes, and Loni is killed. Though it seems to be a simple car accident, Sandro has his suspicions that foul play may be involved. As he infiltrates life at the remote castle, he uncovers a roster of suspects—all with a motive for a wanting Loni dead. And if he isn't careful, Sandro just might be the next victim on the killer's list.

Where it's reviewed:
Publishers Weekly, June 20, 2011, page   38

Other books by the same author:
The Drowning River, 2010
A Florentine Revenge, 2006
The Summer House, 2005
Late Season, 2004
A Party in San Niccolo, 2003

Other books you might like:
Andrea Camilleri, *The Shape of Water*, 2002
Michael Dibdin, *Ratking*, 1989
Michele Giuttari, *A Florentine Death*, 2007
David Hewson, *A Season for the Dead*, 2004
Donna Leon, *Death at La Fenice*, 1992

655

LARS KEPLER

The Hypnotist

(New York: Farrar, Straus, and Giroux, 2011)

Story type: Serial Killer
Subject(s): Suspense; Psychology; Law
Major character(s): Joona Linna, Detective—Police; Dr. Erik Maria Bark, Psychologist
Locale(s): Tumba, Sweden

Summary: In *The Hypnotist*, internationally acclaimed author Lars Kepler, through translation by Ann Long, tells the story of Detective Inspector Joona Linna. Linna is pursuing the killer of three victims, much to the chagrin of the Swedish National Police. But Linna doesn't care what they think: this horrific crime has devastated his sleepy town of Tumba, and particularly has shaken the only survivor—the boy whose mother, father, and sister were slain. Unfortunately for Linna, the boy isn't talking after witnessing his family's murder

650

ANDREA KANE

The Girl Who Disappeared Twice

(Don Mills, Ontario, Canada: Mira, 2011)

Story type: Contemporary
Subject(s): Detective fiction; Women; Missing persons
Major character(s): Hope Willis, Judge (family court), Mother (of Krissy); Krissy, 5-Year-Old, Daughter (of Hope); Casey Woods, Detective—Private, Leader (Forensic Instincts)
Time period(s): 21st century; 2010s
Locale(s): White Plains, New York

Summary: In Andrea Kane's *The Girl Who Disappeared Twice*, family-court judge Hope Willis takes extreme measures when her five-year-old daughter Krissy is abducted. Hope lost her twin sister to a kidnapper three decades ago and knows how important it is for Krissy to be found quickly. Refusing to waste one minute of time while the authorities let bureaucracy delay their investigation, Hope calls on Casey Woods and her group of variously skilled private detectives who call themselves Forensic Instincts. But when Hope hires Casey's team to find Krissy, she opens her household to more scrutiny than she imagined.

Where it's reviewed:
Booklist, May 1, 2011, page 26
Library Journal, June 15, 2011, page 72
Publishers Weekly, May 9, 2011, page 35

Other books by the same author:
Drawn in Blood, 2009
Twisted, 2008
I'll Be Watching You, 2005
Scent of Danger, 2003
No Way Out, 2001

Other books you might like:
Lisa Gardner, *The Survivors Club*, 2001
Alison Gaylin, *Heartless*, 2008
Karen Rose, *Have You Seen Her?*, 2004
Erica Spindler, *Last Known Victim*, 2007
Chevy Stevens, *Still Missing*, 2010

651

THOMAS KAUFMAN

Steal the Show

(New York: Minotaur Books, 2011)

Series: Willis Gidney Mystery Series. Book 2
Story type: Contemporary; Series
Subject(s): Detective fiction; Mystery; Politics
Major character(s): Willis Gidney, Detective—Private, Foster Parent (of Sarah); Rush Gemelli, Computer (hacker); Chuck Gemelli, Lobbyist (motion picture lobby), Father (of Rush); Sarah, Baby, Foster Child (of Willis)
Time period(s): 21st century; 2010s
Locale(s): Washington, District of Columbia

Summary: In the mystery novel *Steal the Show* by Thomas Kaufman, private investigator Willis Gidney knows how the system works in Washington, D.C. He makes a decent living solving his clients' various problems, but now Gidney has a problem of his own. He wants to adopt a baby girl whom he found abandoned at a warehouse, but he needs some extra funds to hire a good lawyer. When Rush Gemelli, son of a prominent motion-picture lobbyist, proposes a lucrative assignment, Gidney eventually accepts despite the questionable ethics of the job. Gidney's get-rich-quick scheme quickly turns into a dangerous case that involves murder, blackmail, and some troublesome thugs. *Steal the Show* is the second book in the Willis Gidney Mystery series.

Where it's reviewed:
Booklist, June 1, 2011, page 44
Publishers Weekly, May 16, 2011, page 58

Other books by the same author:
Drink the Tea, 2010

Other books you might like:
Earl Emerson, *The Rainy City*, 1985
Loren D. Estleman, *Motor City Blue*, 1980
Michael Koryta, *Tonight I Said Goodbye*, 2004
George P. Pelecanos, *A Firing Offense*, 1992
Michael Wiley, *The Last Striptease*, 2007

652

ALEX KAVA

Hotwire

(New York: Doubleday, 2011)

Series: Maggie O'Dell Series. Book 9
Story type: Psychological Suspense
Subject(s): Detective fiction; Murder; Crime
Major character(s): Maggie O'Dell, FBI Agent; R.J. Tully, FBI Agent; Benjamin Platt, Military Personnel (army colonel)
Locale(s): Nebraska, United States

Summary: *Hotwire* is a novel from author Alex Kava's series featuring Special Agent Maggie O'Dell. Maggie is investigating the deaths of three young people who succumbed after being electrocuted at a party. Maggie must figure out how these teens were electrocuted in the first place, but when the party's survivors start turning up dead, she begins to realize that more than faulty wiring was to blame. In the meantime, Maggie's partner R.J. Tully has teamed up with Colonel Benjamin Platt to stop a biological weapon before it claims any more victims. As both investigations unfold, Maggie, R.J., and Benjamin begin to realize a connection that could put the entire U.S. population at risk.

Where it's reviewed:
Booklist, June 1, 2011, page 40
Publishers Weekly, May 2, 2011, page 34

Other books by the same author:
Damaged, 2010
Black Friday, 2009
Exposed, 2008
Necessary Evil, 2006

Mystery

At the Stroke of Madness, 2003
The Soul Catcher, 2002
Split Second, 2001
A Perfect Evil, 2000

Other books you might like:
J. T. Ellison, *Judas Kiss*, 2009
K.J. Erickson, *Alone at Night*, 2004
Michelle Gagnon, *The Tunnels*, 2007
Lisa Gardner, *Alone*, 2005
Karin Slaughter, *Undone*, 2009

653

JIM KELLY

Death Toll

(New York: Minotaur Books, 2011)

Series: Detective Shaw Series. Book 3
Story type: Police Procedural; Series
Subject(s): Detective fiction; Murder; Crime
Major character(s): Peter Shaw, Detective—Police (detective inspector), Son (of Jack Shaw); George Valentine, Detective—Police (detective sergeant); Jack Shaw, Detective—Police (former), Father (of Peter); Jonathan Tessier, 9-Year-Old, Crime Victim; Nora Tilden, Crime Victim
Time period(s): 21st century; 2010s
Locale(s): West Norfolk, England

Summary: In the novel *Death Toll*, the third book in Jim Kelly's Detective Shaw Mystery series, two cases occupy West Norfolk Detective Inspector Peter Shaw and his partner, Detective Sergeant George Valentine. Years ago, Valentine was the partner of Peter's late father, Jack Shaw, but a problematic case all but ruined their careers. Now Peter wants to find the killer of Jonathan Tessier and finally restore the reputations of his father and his partner. A construction project at a cemetery reveals the casket of another murder victim from the past. But Nora Tilden, presumably killed by her husband, was not buried alone. The skeletal remains of a mixed-race man missing for decades lies atop her coffin. Shaw and Valentine's investigation is complicated by the local residents' reluctance to talk to outsiders.

Where it's reviewed:
Booklist, May 1, 2011, page 20
Publishers Weekly, April 25, 2011, page 119

Other books by the same author:
Death Watch, 2010
Death Wore White, 2009
The Skeleton Man, 2007
The Fire Baby, 2004
The Water Clock, 2002

Other books you might like:
Deborah Crombie, *A Share in Death*, 1993
Elizabeth George, *A Great Deliverance*, 1988
John Harvey, *Flesh and Blood*, 2004
Reginald Hill, *A Clubbable Woman*, 1970
Peter Robinson, *Gallows View*, 1987

654

CHRISTOBEL KENT

A Murder in Tuscany

(New York: Minotaur Books, 2011)

Story type: Contemporary - Exotic; Series
Subject(s): Detective fiction; Murder; Castles
Major character(s): Sandro Celllini, Detective; Loni Meadows, Crime Victim
Time period(s): 21st century; 2010s
Locale(s): Tuscany, Italy

Summary: *A Murder in Tuscany* is the second book in Christobel Kent's Sandro Cellini Italian mystery series, centering on the investigations of a Florentine private detective. Glitzy Loni Meadows operates an artist's retreat at a castle in Tuscany. One fateful night, her car crashes, and Loni is killed. Though it seems to be a simple car accident, Sandro has his suspicions that foul play may be involved. As he infiltrates life at the remote castle, he uncovers a roster of suspects—all with a motive for a wanting Loni dead. And if he isn't careful, Sandro just might be the next victim on the killer's list.

Where it's reviewed:
Publishers Weekly, June 20, 2011, page 38

Other books by the same author:
The Drowning River, 2010
A Florentine Revenge, 2006
The Summer House, 2005
Late Season, 2004
A Party in San Niccolo, 2003

Other books you might like:
Andrea Camilleri, *The Shape of Water*, 2002
Michael Dibdin, *Ratking*, 1989
Michele Giuttari, *A Florentine Death*, 2007
David Hewson, *A Season for the Dead*, 2004
Donna Leon, *Death at La Fenice*, 1992

655

LARS KEPLER

The Hypnotist

(New York: Farrar, Straus, and Giroux, 2011)

Story type: Serial Killer
Subject(s): Suspense; Psychology; Law
Major character(s): Joona Linna, Detective—Police; Dr. Erik Maria Bark, Psychologist
Locale(s): Tumba, Sweden

Summary: In *The Hypnotist*, internationally acclaimed author Lars Kepler, through translation by Ann Long, tells the story of Detective Inspector Joona Linna. Linna is pursuing the killer of three victims, much to the chagrin of the Swedish National Police. But Linna doesn't care what they think: this horrific crime has devastated his sleepy town of Tumba, and particularly has shaken the only survivor—the boy whose mother, father, and sister were slain. Unfortunately for Linna, the boy isn't talking after witnessing his family's murder

and being attacked by the murderer himself. Now Linna must turn to Dr. Erik Maria Bark, a psychologist specializing in hypnotism, to unlock the horrors within the boy's mind. But will bringing this boy from his catatonic state put all of them in danger?

Where it's reviewed:
Booklist, May 1, 2011, page 29
Library Journal, July 2011, page 71
Maclean's, July 25, 2011, page 58
New York Times Book Review, July 24, 2011, page 19(L)
Newsweek, May 30, 2011, page 82

Other books you might like:
Arne Dahl, *Misterioso*, 2011
Daniel Hecht, *City of Masks*, 2003
Stieg Larsson, *The Girl with the Dragon Tattoo*, 2008
Jo Nesbo, *The Redbreast*, 2007
Jonathan Santlofer, *The Death Artist*, 2002

656

SARAH KERNOCHAN

Jane Was Here

(Marblehead, Massachusetts: Grey Swan Press, 2011)

Story type: Contemporary
Subject(s): Reincarnation; Suspense; Adventure
Major character(s): Jane, Young Woman
Time period(s): 21st century; 2010s
Locale(s): Graynier, Massachusetts

Summary: In Sarah Kernochan's *Jane Was Here*, a young woman named Jane has just arrived in the small Massachusetts town of Graynier. As soon as she sets foot in the community, Jane is sure she has been here before, however she has no idea when or how this previous visit occurred. Jane slowly investigates life in Graynier and comes to a startling conclusion. Somehow, some way, she is related to a young woman who vanished from the community in the 1850s. As she sets out to unearth the details linking the past and the present, Jane comes face to face with the harsh price of keeping secrets—and of karma itself.

Where it's reviewed:
Library Journal, July 2011, page 70

Other books by the same author:
Dry Hustle, 1977

Other books you might like:
Lev Grossman, *The Magicians*, 2009
Daniel Hecht, *City of Masks*, 2003
Audrey Niffenegger, *The Time Traveler's Wife*, 2003
Anya Seton, *Green Darkness*, 1972
Connie Willis, *Lincoln's Dreams*, 1987

657

JIM KNIPFEL

The Blow-Off

(New York: Simon and Schuster, 2011)

Story type: Contemporary
Subject(s): Monsters; Crime; Newspapers

Major character(s): Hank Kalabander, Journalist
Time period(s): 21st century; 2010s
Locale(s): New York, New York

Summary: A journalist accidentally causes panic in the streets of Brooklyn in Jim Knipfel's *The Blow-Off*. The trouble starts when an intoxicated man is robbed near the Gowanus Canal. The attacker is described as hairy and smelly. Hank Kalabander, a journalist for *The Hornet*, laughingly blames the attack on legendary monster Bigfoot. Hank thinks nothing of his sarcastic piece until another reporter gets wind of the story and then blames the "monster" for more attacks. Suddenly the entire neighborhood is in an uproar, and people start blaming the beast for every crime under the sun. Now it's Hank's responsibility to stop the madness that has gripped Brooklyn by proving that no such monster exists.

Where it's reviewed:
Booklist, June 1, 2011, page 39
Entertainment Weekly, July 8, 2011, page 1162-1163
Publishers Weekly, May 23, 2011, page 27

Other books by the same author:
Unplugging Philco, 2009
Ruining it for Everybody, 2004
The Buzzing, 2003
Quitting the Nairobi Trio, 2000
Slackjaw, 1999

Other books you might like:
Tim Dorsey, *Florida Roadkill*, 1999
Eric Garcia, *Anonymous Rex*, 2000
Marc Lecard, *Vinnie's Head*, 2007
Christopher Moore, *The Lust Lizard of Melancholy Cove*, 1999
John Kennedy Toole, *A Confederacy of Dunces*, 1980

658

CHRIS KNOPF

Black Swan

(Sag Harbor, New York: Permanent Press, 2011)

Series: Sam Acquillo Series. Book 5
Story type: Contemporary; Series
Subject(s): Detective fiction; Sailing; Hotels and motels
Major character(s): Sam Acquillo, Boyfriend (of Amanda), Carpenter, Engineer (former); Amanda Anselma, Contractor, Banker (former), Girlfriend (of Sam); Christian Fey, Hotel Owner, Father (of Anika and Axel); Anika Fey, Daughter (of Christian), Sister (of Axel); Axel Fey, Son (of Christian), Brother (of Anika)
Time period(s): 21st century; 2010s
Locale(s): Fishers Island, New York

Summary: In Chris Knopf's *Black Swan*, the fifth book in the Sam Acquillo Hamptons Mystery series, Sam and his girlfriend Amanda Anselma are sailing a friend's boat from Maine to Long Island when a sudden storm alters their course. Sam and Amanda take refuge in the harbor on Fishers Island, which they soon learn is an enclave of old money and dark secrets. Christian Fey reluctantly grants them lodging at his hotel on the island, *Black Swan*; his daughter Anika subsequently offers Sam an

Mystery

abundance of hospitality. As the violent storm batters the island, it becomes evident that a murderer has checked in at the *Black Swan*.

Where it's reviewed:
Booklist, May 1, 2011, page 14
New York Times Book Review, May 8, 2011, page 15(L)
Publishers Weekly, January 31, 2011, page 31

Other books by the same author:
Short Squeeze, 2010
Hardstop, 2009
Head Wounds, 2008
The Last Refuge, 2005
Two Time, 2005

Other books you might like:
Tom Corcoran, *The Mango Opera*, 1998
Nelson DeMille, *The Gold Coast*, 1990
Bob Morris, *Bahamarama*, 2004
James Swain, *Midnight Rambler: A Novel of Suspense*, 2007
Randy Wayne White, *Ten Thousand Islands*, 2000

659

JULIE KRAMER

Killing Kate
(New York: Atria Books, 2011)

Story type: Contemporary
Subject(s): Detective fiction; Serial murders; Suspense
Major character(s): Riley Spartz, Television Personality, Detective—Amateur
Time period(s): 21st century; 2010s
Locale(s): United States

Summary: In Julie Kramer's *Killing Kate*, Riley Spartz is a television news reporter investigating a serial killer who sketches outlines of angels around the corpses of his victims. Riley's inquiry leads her to a cemetery with a looming angel statue purported to be haunted, and she soon finds herself embroiled in an investigation of an ever-increasing number of murders. Meanwhile, another news story is threatening to pull her attention away from the main case. As Riley attempts to stay focused on the angel/murder story, she realizes someone is fast on her trail—someone who wants her to mind her own business, or else.

Where it's reviewed:
Booklist, June 1, 2011, page 42
Library Journal, June 15, 2011, page 79
Publishers Weekly, May 9, 2011, page 33

Other books by the same author:
Silencing Sam, 2010
Missing Mark, 2009
Stalking Susan, 2008

Other books you might like:
Alison Gaylin, *Trashed*, 2007
Kelly Lange, *The Reporter*, 2002
Karen E. Olson, *Sacred Cows*, 2005

Hank Philippi Ryan, *Air Time*, 2009
Laura Van Wormer, *Expose*, 1999

660

JON LAND

Strong at the Break
(New York: Forge Books, 2011)

Series: Caitlin Strong Series. Book 3
Subject(s): Revenge; Law enforcement; Adventure
Major character(s): Caitlin Strong, Police Officer (Texas Ranger); Malcolm Arno, Leader (head of militia movement)
Time period(s): 21st century; 2010s
Locale(s): Canada; Mexico; United States

Summary: Twenty years ago, Caitlin Strong's Texas Ranger father shot the leader of a cultish church. Now Caitlin is a Ranger herself, and the son of the man her father shot is out for revenge. Caitlin, however, is enmeshed in a string of cases that require her attention: one involving drug smuggling, another surrounding an Iraqi-war solider who says the government is after him, and still another entailing the kidnapping of the son of a famous criminal. But all three cases are about to lead Caitlin back to one place: Malcolm Arno, the son of the man her father killed all those years ago. *Strong at the Break* is the third novel in Jon Land's Caitlin Strong series.

Where it's reviewed:
Publishers Weekly, April 25, 2011, page 112

Other books by the same author:
Strong Justice, 2010
Strong Enough to Die, 2009
The Walls of Jericho, 1997
The Omega Command, 1986
The Doomsday Spiral, 1983

Other books you might like:
Lori Anderson, *No Mercy*, 2010
C.J. Box, *Open Season*, 2001
Kathryn Casey, *Singularity*, 2008
Bill Crider, *Too Late to Die*, 1986
J.A. Jance, *Desert Heat*, 1993

661

VICTORIA LAURIE

Vision Impossible
(New York: Obsidian, 2011)

Series: Psychic Eye Series. Book 9
Story type: Fantasy
Subject(s): Psychics; Spies; Suspense
Major character(s): Abby Cooper, Psychic, Girlfriend (of Dutch); Dutch, FBI Agent, Boyfriend (of Abby)
Time period(s): 21st century; 2010s
Locale(s): Canada

Summary: *Vision Impossible* is the ninth book in the Psychic Eye Mysteries series from author Victoria Laurie. In this installment, psychic Abby Cooper has been recruited by the government to help recover a software program that can identify people by their auras, much in the same way that a psychic can. Abby and her FBI-agent boyfriend, Dutch, set out on an undercover mission to Canada to track down the criminals who have stolen the technology and would use it for nefarious purposes. The psychic will need to rely on her spirit guides to help keep her and Dutch safe on this dangerous mission.

Where it's reviewed:
The Houston Chronicle, July 3, 2011, page 15
Publishers Weekly, May 30, 2011, page 51

Other books by the same author:
A Glimpse of Evil, 2010
Oracles of Delphi Keep, 2009
What's a Ghoul to Do?, 2007
Better Read than Dead, 2005
Abby Cooper, Psychic Eye, 2004

Other books you might like:
Yasmine Galenorn, *Ghost of a Chance*, 2003
Charlaine Harris, *Grave Sight*, 2005
Jim Lavene, *The Telltale Turtle*, 2008
Martha C. Lawrence, *Murder in Scorpio*, 1995
Clea Simon, *Dogs Don't Lie*, 2011

662

WILL LAVENDER

Dominance

(New York: Simon & Schuster, 2011)

Story type: Serial Killer
Subject(s): Serial murders; Mystery; Detective fiction
Major character(s): Alex Shipley, Professor (Harvard); Richard Aldiss, Professor (literature), Convict (former); Paul Fallows, Writer
Time period(s): 20th century; (1990s); 20th century; 2000s (2009)
Locale(s): Vermont, United States

Summary: In the novel *Dominance* by Will Lavender, a case of serial murder, allegedly solved in 1994, resumes 15 years later on a college campus in Vermont. In 1994, Alex Shipley was a student in a controversial class led remotely from the prison cell of convicted serial murderer Richard Aldiss. The class, titled "Unraveling a Literary Mystery," focused on the search for the true identity of reclusive author Paul Fallows. Pages of Fallows's books had been found near the bodies of Aldiss's victims. Shipley solved the literary case and Aldiss was exonerated. Now some of Aldiss's former students have been killed and Shipley, a Harvard professor, comes back to Jasper College to investigate.

Where it's reviewed:
New York Times, July 7, 2011, page C1(L)
Publishers Weekly, May 16, 2011, page 54

Other books by the same author:
Obedience, 2008

Other books you might like:
Peter Abrahams, *End of Story*, 2006
Chelsea Cain, *Heartsick*, 2007
Thomas Harris, *The Silence of the Lambs*, 1988
Barbara Vine, *The Minotaur*, 2006
Minette Walters, *The Sculptress*, 1993

663

MIKE LAWSON

House Divided

(New York: Atlantic Monthly Press, 2010)

Series: Joe DeMarco Series. Book 6
Story type: Political; Series
Subject(s): Suspense; Political crimes; Espionage
Major character(s): Joe DeMarco, Assistant (to Speaker of the House), Lawyer
Time period(s): 21st century; 2010s
Locale(s): Washington, District of Columbia

Summary: *House Divided* is the sixth book in author Mike Lawson's series featuring Joe DeMarco. DeMarco is still employed by Speaker of the House John Fitzpatrick Mahoney, but Mahoney is stuck in the hospital after having a surgical procedure. DeMarco is hoping to finally have some time off, but then two people die—one of whom is DeMarco's cousin. Soon DeMarco finds out that his cousin's death was not accidental, but was the result of an undercover government operation gone awry. As it turns out, the National Security Agency has continued its wiretapping operations that were found illegal in 2005, and has uncovered a clandestine military operation that has gone rogue. Now DeMarco is trapped between the NSA and its illegal means of gaining information, and a Pentagon-based agency that has started operating by its own rules.

Where it's reviewed:
Booklist, May 15, 2011, page 21
Library Journal, Oct 1, 2010, page 47
Publishers Weekly, May 9, 2011, page 32

Other books by the same author:
House Justice, 2010
House Secrets, 2009
House Rules, 2008
The Second Perimeter, 2006
The Inside Ring, 2005

Other books you might like:
David Baldacci, *Absolute Power*, 1996
Vince Flynn, *Transfer of Power*, 1999
Gene Riehl, *Quantico Rules*, 2003
Ross Thomas, *The Cold War Swap*, 1966
Stuart Woods, *Grass Roots*, 1989

664

JENIFER LECLAIR

Danger Sector

(Woodbury, Minnesota: Conquill Press, 2011)

Series: Windjammer Mystery Series. Book 2
Story type: Contemporary; Series

Mystery

Subject(s): Detective fiction; Sailing; Murder
Major character(s): Brie Beaumont, Detective—Police (homicide), Sailor
Time period(s): 21st century; 2010s
Locale(s): Sentinel Island, Maine

Summary: In *Danger Sector*, the second book in Jenifer LeClair's Windjammer Mystery series, homicide detective Brie Beaumont continues her leave from the Minneapolis police department and sails into another murder mystery. A crew member on the windjammer *Maine Wind*, Brie is trying to use the calming powers of the sea to help her heal physically and mentally from a work-related trauma. But when the ship makes a stop at Maine's Sentinel Island, Brie, her captain, and fellow shipmates learn that a woman there has disappeared. Brie's sense of duty kicks in and she investigates the crime. As Brie unravels a complex case that spans years of island history, a dangerous storm threatens Sentinel Island.

Where it's reviewed:
Booklist, May 1, 2011, page 18
Library Journal, June 1, 2011, page 83

Other books by the same author:
Rigged for Murder, 2008

Other books you might like:
J.S. Borthwick, *Bodies of Water*, 1990
Tony Gibbs, *Dead Run*, 1988
Christine Kling, *Surface Tension*, 2002
Kirk Russell, *Shell Games*, 2003
Stuart Woods, *Run Before the Wind*, 1983

665

LAURA LEVINE

Pampered to Death

(New York: Kensington, 2011)

Series: Jaine Austen Series. Book 10
Story type: Contemporary; Series
Subject(s): Detective fiction; Domestic cats; Murder
Major character(s): Jaine Austen, Writer, Detective—Amateur; Mallory Francis, Actress, Crime Victim; Prozac, Cat
Time period(s): 21st century; 2010s
Locale(s): California, United States

Summary: The 10th book in Laura Levine's Jaine Austen Mysteries series, *Pampered to Death* finds writer and amateur sleuth Jaine bundled off to a fat farm by her well-meaning boyfriend. Life at The Haven is a veritable nightmare: rigorous exercise regimes, tasteless food, and a questionable array of fellow guests. One such guest is minor movie star Mallory Francis, whose airs and behavior quickly make her plenty of enemies at the resort. After a seaweed wrap that turns murderous, Mallory is found dead. Now Jaine is determined to find out who killed Mallory—and with a hotel full of potential suspects, that isn't going to be easy.

Where it's reviewed:
Publishers Weekly, June 6, 2011, page 28

Other books by the same author:
Death of a Trophy Wife, 2010

Shoes to Die For, 2005
Killer Blonde, 2004
Last Writes, 2003
This Pen for Hire, 2002

Other books you might like:
Jeffrey Cohen, *For Whom the Minivan Rolls: An Aaron Tucker Mystery*, 2002
David Handler, *The Man Who Died Laughing*, 1988
Harley Jane Kozak, *Dating Dead Men*, 2004
Beth Sherman, *Dead Man's Float*, 1998
Noreen Wald, *Ghostwriter*, 1999

666

MITCHELL SCOTT LEWIS

Murder in the 11th House

(Scottsdale, Arizona: Poisoned Pen Press, 2011)

Series: Starlight Detective Agency Mysteries Series. Book 1
Story type: Contemporary
Subject(s): Astrology; Crime; Murder
Major character(s): David Lowell, Father (of Melinda), Astrologer, Detective; Melinda, Lawyer, Daughter (of David); Mort, Computer Expert (hacker); Sarah, Assistant (of David); Andy, Bodyguard; Johnny Colbert, Bartender, Crime Suspect
Time period(s): 21st century; 2010s
Locale(s): New York, New York

Summary: An astrologer detective sets out to prove a man's innocence in *Murder in the 11th House*, the first novel in author Mitchell Scott Lewis's Starlight Detective Agency Mysteries series. Detective David Lowell uses his knowledge of astrology to help solve crimes. When a state judge is found murdered, David sets out to help his defense-attorney daughter, Melinda, prove the innocence of bartender Johnny Colbert, who has been accused of the crime. David and Melinda are aided in their investigation by David's assistant, his bodyguard, and his hacker friend. Together, they soon discover that there is a large number of people who may have wanted the judge dead.

Where it's reviewed:
Library Journal, July 2011, page 58
Publishers Weekly, July 25, 2011, page 34

Other books you might like:
Daniel Hecht, *City of Masks*, 2003
Kay Hooper, *Touching Evil*, 2001
Victoria Laurie, *Abby Cooper, Psychic Eye*, 2005
Martha C. Lawrence, *Murder in Scorpio*, 1995
David Skibbins, *Eight of Swords*, 2005

667

RON LIEBMAN

Jersey Law

(New York: Simon & Schuster, 2011)

Subject(s): Law; Trials; Criminals
Major character(s): Mickie Mezzonatti, Police Officer

(former), Lawyer; Salvatore "Junne" Salerno, Police Officer (former), Lawyer; Slippery Williams, Criminal, Drug Dealer, Murderer, Client (of Mickie and Junne)
Time period(s): 21st century; 2010s
Locale(s): Camden, New Jersey

Summary: *Jersey Law*, a suspenseful and humorous legal novel from author Ron Liebman, is the second book to feature Mickie Mezzonatti and Salvatore "Junne" Salerno, two New Jersey cops-turned-lawyers who cut corners to win cases for shady clients. Mickie and Junne represent the worst of the worst, and that's saying a lot in New Jersey, but somehow the pair manages to win case after case. But now, Mickie and Junne are facing a big challenge as they try to get Slippery Williams, a drug lord with a history of murder, out of jail. When Slippery is up for a retrial, Mickie and Junne feel a responsibility to represent him, especially since he saved their lives once. But it seems there are a lot of people intent on keeping Slippery behind bars, regardless of what it takes.

Where it's reviewed:
Booklist, May 1, 2011, page 31
Publishers Weekly, April 11, 2011, page 27

Other books by the same author:
Death by Rodrigo, 2007
Shark Tales, 2001
Grand Jury, 1983

Other books you might like:
Eric Dezenhall, *Shakedown Beach*, 2004
Chris Grabenstein, *Tilt-A-Whirl*, 2005
David Rosenfelt, *Open and Shut*, 2002
Lisa Scottoline, *Final Appeal*, 1994
Sheldon Siegel, *Special Circumstances: A Novel*, 2000

668

DAVID LISS

The Twelfth Enchantment
(New York: Random House, 2011)

Story type: Historical - Regency
Subject(s): Adventure; Love; Magic
Major character(s): Lucy Derrick, Young Woman; Lord Byron, Writer (poet)
Time period(s): 19th century
Locale(s): England

Summary: The worlds of history and magic come together in David Liss's *The Twelfth Enchantment*. In Regency-era England, Lucy Derrick hits hard times when her father dies, and she is forced to live with her brutish uncle. One day, her life is transformed by the appearance of legendary poet Lord Byron, who captivates Lucy with his good looks and mysterious words. Suddenly Lucy's life is thrown into upheaval as she realizes her place—with Lord Byron's help—in securing her country's future. Discovering her newfound magical gifts, she sets out to save England—and perhaps even find true love along the way.

Other books by the same author:
The Devil's Company, 2009

The Whiskey Rebels, 2008
A Spectacle of Corruption, 2004
The Coffee Trader, 2003
A Conspiracy of Paper, 2000

Other books you might like:
Louis Bayard, *Mr. Timothy*, 2003
Michel Faber, *The Crimson Petal and the White*, 2002
Sheri Holman, *The Dress Lodger*, 2000
Edna O'Brien, *Byron in Love: A Short Daring Life*, 2009
Sarah Waters, *Fingersmith*, 2002

669

SOPHIE LITTLEFIELD

A Bad Day for Scandal
(New York: Minotaur Books, 2011)

Series: Stella Hardesty Series. Book 3
Story type: Contemporary; Series
Subject(s): Detective fiction; Murder; Women
Major character(s): Stella Hardesty, Vigilante; Priscilla "Priss" Porter, Businesswoman, Sister (of Liman); Liman, Brother (of Priss); Goat Jones, Lawman (sheriff); Chrissy Shaw, Assistant (to Stella)
Time period(s): 21st century; 2010s
Locale(s): Kansas City, Missouri

Summary: In the mystery novel *A Bad Day for Scandal* by Sophie Littlefield, Priscilla "Priss" Porter returns to her small Missouri town and uses incriminating photos to leverage some special assistance from Stella Hardesty. Priss has a dead body in her trunk that needs disposing and Stella, champion of local abused women, seems the perfect woman for the job. Although Stella knows that Priss has photos showing some of her more physical methods for reforming abusers, she refuses to help Priss and her brother Liman with their problem. But now Priss, Liman, the dead man, and the photos are missing and Stella's scarf has been found at the scene of the crime. *A Bad Day for Scandal* is the third book in the Stella Hardesty series.

Where it's reviewed:
Booklist, May 1, 2011, page 14
Publishers Weekly, April 4, 2011, p. 36, page 36

Other books by the same author:
Aftertime, 2011
Unforsaken, 2011
A Bad Day for Pretty, 2010
Banished, 2010
A Bad Day for Sorry, 2009

Other books you might like:
Jill Churchill, *Grime and Punishment*, 1989
Laura Disilverio, *Swift Justice*, 2011
Anne George, *Murder on a Girls' Night Out*, 1996
Joan Hess, *Malice in Maggody: An Ozarks Murder Mystery*, 1987
Elaine Viets, *Shop Till You Drop*, 2003

670

HILLARY BELL LOCKE

But Remember Their Names

(Scottsdale, Arizona: Poisoned Pen Press, 2011)

Series: Cynthia Jakubek Mystery Series. Book 1
Story type: Contemporary
Subject(s): Murder; Crime; Law
Major character(s): Thomas Bradshaw, Philanthropist, Crime Victim (murdered), Father (of Caitlin); Caitlin, Daughter (of Thomas); Cynthia Jakubec, Lawyer (intern)
Time period(s): 21st century; 2010s
Locale(s): Pittsburgh, Pennsylvania

Summary: *But Remember Their Names* is the first novel in the Cynthia Jakubek Mystery series from author Hillaru Bell Locke. In a Pittsburgh museum, the body of a well-known philanthropist is found in a diorama of the Battle of Lexington. The police are investigating every lead in the death of Thomas Bradshaw, but no one quite knows why the man was killed. The man's daughter, Caitlin, turns to new lawyer Cynthia Jakubek for advice when it turns out she may be an important part of the investigation. Cynthia—who is interning in Pittsburgh while dreaming of a life in New York—soon becomes embroiled in the case, and her involvement could cost her more than she realizes.

Where it's reviewed:
Booklist, May 15, 2011, page 20
Publishers Weekly, April 18, 2011, page 36

Other books you might like:
John T. Lescroart, *Dead Irish*, 1989
Phillip Margolin, *Wild Justice*, 2000
Steve Martini, *Compelling Evidence*, 1992
Lisa Scottoline, *Everywhere That Mary Went*, 2003
Sheldon Siegel, *Special Circumstances: A Novel*, 2000

671

M. L. LONGWORTH

Death at the Chateau Bremont

(New York: Penguin, 2011)

Series: Verlaque and Bonnet Mystery Series. Book 1
Story type: Contemporary - Exotic; Series
Subject(s): Detective fiction; Murder; Brothers
Major character(s): Antoine Verlaque, Judge (magistrate), Lover (of Marine, former); Marine Bonnet, Professor (law), Lover (of Antoine, former); Etienne de Bremont, Nobleman, Brother (of Francois), Film-maker; Francois de Bremont, Brother (of Etienne), Gambler; Charles Brey, Lawyer, Cousin (of Etienne and Francois); Eric Brey, Lawyer, Cousin (of Etienne and Francois); Sylvie, Friend (of Marine); Isabelle, Spouse (of Etienne)
Time period(s): 21st century; 2010s
Locale(s): Aix-en-Provence, France

Summary: In *Death at the Chateau Bremont*, the first book in M.L. Longworth's Verlaque and Bonnet Mystery series, the death of a financially troubled nobleman in Aix-en-Provence may have been an accident, suicide, or murder. The deceased, Etienne de Bremont, fell, jumped, or was pushed from the family chateau. His widow, Isabelle, insists that her husband's death was accidental. Chief Magistrate Antoine Verlaque is not convinced and enlists the help of law professor and former lover Marine Bonnet. The death of Etienne's playboy brother confirms Verlaque's suspicions, but the search for a murderer and motive leads the magistrate to a diverse pool of suspects. First novel.

Where it's reviewed:
Booklist, May 1, 2011, page 20
Publishers Weekly, June 6, 2011, page 28

Other books you might like:
Michael Bond, *Monsieur Pamplemousse*, 1983
Nadia Gordon, *Sharpshooter: A Sunny McCoskey Napa Valley Mystery*, 2002
Ellen Hart, *This Little Piggy Went to Murder*, 1994
Julie Hyzy, *Grace Under Pressure*, 2010
Peter May, *Extraordinary People*, 2006

672

PETER LOVESEY

Stagestruck

(New York: Soho Crime, 2011)

Series: Peter Diamond Series. Book
Story type: Amateur Detective; Mystery
Subject(s): Mystery; Theater; Murder
Major character(s): Peter Diamond, Detective—Police; Clarion Calhoun, Singer
Locale(s): Bath, England

Summary: The Theatre Royal in Bath, England, serves as the backdrop for author Peter Lovesey's 11th Peter Diamond mystery, *Stagestruck*. Real-life tragedy befalls the stage at the Theatre Royal in the detective's latest case, as pop-singing sensation and star of the show *I Am a Camera*, Clarion Calhoun abruptly collapses just moments into her first performance, a victim of makeup laced with chemicals that severely disfigure her beautiful face. Suspicion is quickly cast upon the company's makeup artist, who is promptly killed after apparently being pushed off a catwalk. Faced with an ever-deepening mystery, Diamond must match wits with a scheming killer and bring Calhoun's attacker to justice.

Where it's reviewed:
Booklist, May 1, 2011, page 39
The Denver Post, July 3, 2011, page E-09
New York Times Book Review, June 19, 2011, page 15(L)
Publishers Weekly, April 18, 2011, page 37

Other books by the same author:
Skeleton Hill, 2009
The Headhunters, 2008
The Last Detective, 1991
Waxwork, 1978
Wobble to Death, 1970

Other books you might like:
Christopher Fowler, *Full Dark House*, 2003
Reginald Hill, *A Clubbable Woman*, 1970
P.D. James, *Cover Her Face*, 1962
Ngaio Marsh, *Night of the Vulcan*, 1951
Peter Robinson, *Gallows View*, 1987

673

ROSAMUND LUPTON

Sister

(New York: Crown Publishing, 2011)

Story type: Amateur Detective
Subject(s): Murder; Sisters; Crime
Major character(s): Bea, Sister (of Tess); Tess, Sister (of Bea)
Time period(s): 21st century; 2010s
Locale(s): England

Summary: *Sisters* is a mystery novel by author Rosamund Lupton. Upon receiving news that her sister Tess has committed suicide, Bea is in shock—she cannot believe that her sister would do such a thing. Determined to learn the truth about her sister's death, Bea flies home to England from New York, where she has been living as a method of putting distance between her and her family. Despite the police's official report, Bea is certain that Tess has become a victim of murder. As Bea learns more and more about her sister's life, she also learns about her own past. Soon Bea discovers more than she ever expected. First novel.

Where it's reviewed:
Booklist, May 1, 2011, page 35
Library Journal, April 1, 2011, page 83
New York Times Book Review, June 5, 2011, page 28(L)

Other books you might like:
Kate Atkinson, *Case Histories*, 2004
Gillian Flynn, *Sharp Objects*, 2006
Erin Kelly, *The Poison Tree*, 2011
J. Wallis Martin, *A Likeness in Stone*, 1997
Barbara Vine, *Anna's Book*, 1994

674

D.P. LYLE

Hot Lights, Cold Steel

(St. Charles, Illinois: Medallion Press, 2011)

Story type: Serial Killer; Series
Subject(s): Serial murders; Detective fiction; Suspense
Major character(s): Dub Walker, Consultant (criminal), Businessman (lumber company owner); Miranda Edwards, Friend (of Dub); Noel, Teenager, Daughter (of Miranda)
Time period(s): 21st century; 2010s
Locale(s): Huntsville, Alabama

Summary: In *Hot Lights, Cold Steel* by D.P. Lyle, Dub Walker is a criminal consultant in Huntsville, Alabama, who has just agreed to help a friend locate her missing college-aged daughter. Dub knows that Miranda Edwards's daughter Noel is troubled, but the discovery of her mutilated body in a shallow grave comes as a shock. Noel, along with another girl who was buried with her, was apparently tortured by a skilled but sadistic surgeon before her death. As the serial killer claims more victims, Dub's investigation points to a suspect with the means and ability to carry out the killings—the rich and powerful operator of Talbert Biomedical.

Where it's reviewed:
Booklist, May 1, 2011, page 28

Other books by the same author:
Royal Pains: First, Do No Harm, 2011
Stress Fracture, 2010
Forensics and Fiction, 2007
Murder and Mayhem, 2003

Other books you might like:
Beverly Connor, *One Grave Too Many*, 2003
Patricia Cornwell, *Postmortem*, 1990
Kathryn Fox, *Malicious Intent*, 2006
Jonathan Hayes, *Precious Blood*, 2007
Kathy Reichs, *Deja Dead*, 1997

675

TOM MACDONALD

The Charlestown Connection

(Longboat Key, Florida: Oceanview Publishing, 2011)

Story type: Contemporary
Subject(s): Murder; Suspense; Crime
Major character(s): Dermot Sparhawk, Relative (godson of Jeepster), Worker (food pantry), Alcoholic (recovering), Football Player (former); Jeepster Hennessey, Crime Victim (murdered), Godfather (of Dermot)
Time period(s): 21st century; 2010s
Locale(s): Charlestown, Massachusetts

Summary: A man hunts for the people responsible for his godfather's murder in *The Charlestown Connection*. Dermot Sparhawk was a former college football star who was destined for the pros. However, a knee injury and a problem with alcohol derailed his dreams. Now a recovering alcoholic, Dermot works in a Charlestown food pantry, stocking shelves. His life takes a mysterious turn when his godfather, Jeepster Hennessey, stumbles into the pantry with a knife in his back and dies. Dermot then sets out on a mission to find out who would want to kill Jeepster. His investigation leads to run-ins with the FBI, the mob, and the Irish Republican Army.

Where it's reviewed:
Library Journal, July 2011, page 58
Publishers Weekly, June 6, 2011, page 25

Other books you might like:
George V. Higgins, *The Friends of Eddie Coyle*, 1972
Chuck Hogan, *Prince of Thieves*, 2004
William Landay, *The Strangler*, 2007
Dennis Lehane, *Mystic River*, 2001
Robert B. Parker, *The Godwulf Manuscript*, 1973

ADA MADISON

The Square Root of Murder

(New York: Berkley, 2011)

Series: Professor Sophie Knowles Series. Book 1
Story type: Contemporary
Subject(s): Murder; College environment; Academia
Major character(s): Sophie Knowles, Professor; Dr. Appleton, Professor, Crime Victim (murdered)
Time period(s): 21st century; 2010s
Locale(s): Cape Cod, Massachusetts

Summary: *The Square Root of Murder* is the first book in the Professor Sophie Knowles series from author Ada Madison. Sophie Knowles is a professor at a small women's college in Cape Cod. While teaching a summer session, Sophie discovers that someone has murdered Dr. Appleton, one of the college's most hated professors. As Sophie starts an amateur investigation into the chemistry professor's death, she discovers that a graduate student has been accused of the crime. Not convinced that the student is the killer, Sophie delves deeper into Dr. Appleton's life and learns that there is a much more sinister side to her small college than she ever realized.

Where it's reviewed:
Library Journal, July 2011, page 58

Other books by the same author:
The Oxygen Murder, 2006
The Beryllium Murder, 2000
The Lithium Murder, 1999
The Helium Murder, 1998
The Hydrogen Murder, 1997

Other books you might like:
Donna Andrews, *You've Got Murder*, 2003
Jo Bannister, *Echoes of Lies*, 2001
Maggie Barbieri, *Murder 101*, 2006
Mary Ellen Hughes, *Resort to Murder*, 2001
Robert Spiller, *The Witch of Agnesi*, 2006

PASCAL MARCO

Identity: Lost

(Longboat Key, Florida: Oceanview Publishing, 2011)

Story type: Legal
Subject(s): Crime; Law; Revenge
Major character(s): James Overstreet, Lawyer
Time period(s): 20th century; (1970s); 21st century; 2000s
Locale(s): Arizona, United States; Chicago, Illinois

Summary: Pascal Marco's *Identity: Lost* opens in 1975 Chicago, where a white octogenarian has just claimed to have been attacked by a group of African American men. Twelve-year-old James Overstreet says he knows who was responsible for the beating, and he names several of the suspects. But after the authorities make major errors in their case, the accused men are set free, and James and his family are forced into a witness protection program. Thirty years go by, and James has become a prosecutor for the state of Arizona. In a shocking twist, he is brought face to face with his own past—and the violent criminals he has been trying to avoid for three decades. First novel.

Where it's reviewed:
Booklist, May 1, 2011, page 30
Publishers Weekly, April 18, 2011, page 32

Other books you might like:
Frankie Y. Bailey, *You Should Have Died on Monday*, 2007
Robert Campbell, *The Junkyard Dog*, 1986
Michael Harvey, *The Chicago Way*, 2007
Sara Paretsky, *Hardball*, 2009
Jess Walter, *Citizen Vince*, 2005

STEVE MARTINI

Trader of Secrets

(New York: Harpercollins, 2010)

Series: Paul Madriani Series
Story type: Amateur Detective; Contemporary
Subject(s): Law; Assassination; Missing persons
Major character(s): Paul Madriani, Lawyer, Detective; Harry Hinds, Lawyer; Joselyn Cole, Worker (weapons expert); Liquida "The Mexicutioner" Muerte, Mercenary; Sarah Madriani, Daughter (of Paul); Herman Diggs, Detective
Time period(s): 21st century
Locale(s): Paris, France; Bangkok, Thailand; San Diego, California

Summary: Following the events of *Rule of Nine*, San Diego lawyer Paul Madriani is still being targetted by the international assassin Liquida "The Mexicutioner" Muerte. In an attempt to protect his daughter and friends, Madriani goes on the offensive, teaming with his partner Harry Hinds and friend Joselyn Cole to chase Muerte across the globe. Meanwhile, Madriani must also locate two missing NASA scientists who both have knowledge of an unbelievable new weapon that can unlock the destructive power of nature.

Where it's reviewed:
Booklist, May 15, 2011, page 22
Publishers Weekly, April 25, 2011, page 107

Other books by the same author:
The Rule of Nine, 2010
Guardian of Lies, 2009
Shadow of Power, 2008
Double Tap, 2005
The Arraignment, 2003
The List, 1997
Undue Influence, 1994
Prime Witness, 1993
Compelling Evidence, 1992

Other books you might like:
Stephen Horn, *In Her Defense*, 2000
William Lashner, *Hostile Witness*, 1995
John T. Lescroart, *Dead Irish*, 1989

Phillip Margolin, *Wild Justice*, 2000
Richard North Patterson, *No Safe Place*, 1998

679

PRISCILLA MASTERS

Frozen Charlotte

(New York: Severn House Publishers, 2011)

Series: Martha Gunn Series. Book 3
Story type: Contemporary; Series
Subject(s): Detective fiction; Crime; Infants
Major character(s): Martha Gunn, Doctor (coroner); Lucy Ramshaw, Nurse; Alice Sedgewick, Aged Person; Alex Randall, Detective—Police
Time period(s): 21st century; 2010s
Locale(s): Shrewsbury, England

Summary: The ancient town of Shrewsbury, England provides the setting for *Frozen Charlotte*, the third book in Priscilla Masters's Martha Gunn series. Gunn, a coroner, has been presented with an unusual case that concerns the mummified remains of an infant who has been dead for at least five years. Alice Sedgewick, an apparently confused older woman, brought the body to the local hospital, claiming to have found it in her attic. Martha Gunn works with police detective Alex Randall on the case, scrutinizing Alice, her husband, and previous owners of the Sedgewick house. The dangerous nature of their investigation becomes clear when Martha begins receiving harassing telephone calls.

Where it's reviewed:
Booklist, May 1, 2011, page 25
Publishers Weekly, April 4, 2011, page 37

Other books by the same author:
Grave Stones, 2009
Buried in Clay, 2008
Slip Knot, 2007
River Deep, 2004
Winding Up the Serpent, 1995

Other books you might like:
Deborah Crombie, *A Share in Death*, 1993
Kate Ellis, *The Merchant's House*, 1998
Elizabeth George, *A Great Deliverance*, 1988
Ann Granger, *Say It with Poison*, 1991
Phil Rickman, *The Wine of Angels*, 1998

680

BETH MCMULLEN

Original Sin

(New York: Hyperion, 2011)

Series: Sally Sin Series. Book 1
Subject(s): Adventure; Spies; Family
Major character(s): Lucy "Sally Sin" Hamilton, Spy; Ian Blackford, Enemy (of Sally/Lucy); Will, Spouse (of Sally/Lucy); Theo, 3-Year-Old, Son (of Sally/Lucy and Will)
Time period(s): 21st century; 2010s
Locale(s): San Francisco, California

Summary: To all outward appearances, Lucy Hamilton is a run-of-the-mill housewife and mother. She dotes on her husband, Will, and their three-year-old son Theo, and she devotes her life to making a happy home for her family. No one knows that under the serene exterior lies Sally Sin: adventurer, crime-fighter, and former spy with the United States Agency for Weapons of Mass Destruction (USAWMD). But when her nemesis, Ian Blackford, once again poses a threat to the world's security, the USAWMD wants Sally/Lucy back on the payroll, which would force the demure housewife to reveal her true identity to those around her. Beth McMullen's *Original Sin* is the first novel in the Sally Sin Adventures series. First novel.

Where it's reviewed:
Booklist, June 1, 2011, page 40
Publishers Weekly, May 23, 2011, page 30

Other books you might like:
Jennifer Apodaca, *Dating Can Be Murder*, 2002
Jennifer Colt, *The Butcher of Beverly Hills*, 2005
Dorothy Gilman, *The Unexpected Mrs. Pollifax*, 1966
Tod Goldberg, *Burn Notice: The Fix*, 2008
Sarah R. Shaber, *Louise's War*, 2011

681

CATRIONA MCPHERSON

Dandy Gilver and the Proper Treatment of Bloodstains

(London: Hodder & Stoughton, 2011)

Series: Dandy Gilver Series. Book 5
Story type: Historical; Series
Subject(s): Detective fiction; Murder; Social class
Major character(s): Dandy Gilver, Detective; Lollie Balfour, Wealthy
Time period(s): 20th century; 1920s (1926)
Locale(s): Edinburgh, Scotland

Summary: Dandy Gilver is no ordinary detective. She's a rich socialite with a determined nose for sniffing out the truth. One day she receives a letter from wealthy Lollie Balfour, who is convinced her husband is going to kill her. Dandy decides the only way to get to the bottom of the case is to infiltrate Lollie's household disguised as a maid. What she finds reveals the shocking truth behind Lollie's claims and puts Dandy on the dangerous path of a killer. *Dandy Gilver and the Proper Treatment of Bloodstains* is the fifth installment in Catriona McPherson's Dandy Gilver mystery series.

Where it's reviewed:
Library Journal, July 2011, page 58
Publishers Weekly, May 30, 2011, page 50

Other books by the same author:
Winter Ground, 2008
Bury Her Deep, 2007
The Burry Man's Day, 2006
After the Armistice Ball, 2005

Other books you might like:
Tasha Alexander, *And Only to Deceive*, 2005

Mystery

Rhys Bowen, *Her Royal Spyness*, 2007
Carola Dunn, *Death at Wentwater Court*, 1994
Kerry Greenwood, *Cocaine Blues*, 1987
Jacqueline Winspear, *Maisie Dobbs*, 2003

682

MEAGAN J. MEEHAN

Death Amid Gems

(New York: Avalon Books, 2011)

Story type: Police Procedural
Subject(s): Detective fiction; Murder; Television programs
Major character(s): Angelo Zenoni, Detective—Police; Nolan Wildow, Detective—Police; Tiffany Kehl, Crime Victim
Time period(s): 21st century; 2010s
Locale(s): New York, New York

Summary: The mystery novel *Death Amid Gems* by Meagan Meehan follows the investigation into the brutal murder of Tiffany Kehl. The young woman's badly beaten body is discovered in a home-shopping TV studio on Long Island just days after Thanksgiving, and detectives Angelo Zenoni and Nolan Wildow have been assigned to the case. As Zenoni and Wildow soon learn, the suspects in Tiffany's murder are many and include coworkers, relatives, former classmates, neighbors, and an ex-lover. Meanwhile, the approach of the Christmas holidays induces stress at the Zenoni household where a wife and teenage nephew make further demands of Angelo's time.

Where it's reviewed:
Booklist, May 1, 2011, page 18

Other books by the same author:
Dry Heat, 2010

Other books you might like:
Reed Farrel Coleman, *Walking the Perfect Square*, 2001
Nelson DeMille, *The Gold Coast*, 1990
David Handler, *The Cold Blue Blood*, 2001
Susan Isaacs, *Compromising Positions*, 1978
Chris Knopf, *The Last Refuge*, 2005

683

KEN MERCER (Pseudonym of Ken Mandelbaum)

East on Sunset

(New York: Minotaur Books, 2011)

Story type: Contemporary
Subject(s): Money; Law enforcement; Drugs
Major character(s): Will Magowan, Police Officer (former); Erik Crandall, Convict (ex-convict)
Time period(s): 21st century; 2010s
Locale(s): Los Angeles, California

Summary: Former narcotics cop Will Magowan retires from the police force and begins to settle into a quieter life. But his past comes back to haunt him when Erik Crandall, a thug Magowan helped put behind bars, comes looking for him. Magowan's new life hangs in the bal-

ance as Crandall makes outrageous and dangerous requests, bringing the ex-cop's long-buried secrets—secrets that he'd do anything to keep hidden—to light. Ken Mercer's *East on Sunset* is the sequel to 2010's *Slow Fire*.

Where it's reviewed:
Booklist, May 1, 2011, page 22
Publishers Weekly, April 4, 2011, page 34

Other books by the same author:
Slow Fire, 2010

Other books you might like:
Michael Connelly, *The Black Echo*, 1992
Terrill Lee Lankford, *Earthquake Weather*, 2004
T. Jefferson Parker, *Silent Joe*, 2001
Stephen Jay Schwartz, *Boulevard*, 2009
John Shannon, *The Concrete River*, 1996

684

ADAM MITZNER

A Conflict of Interest

(New York: Simon and Schuster, 2011)

Story type: Legal
Subject(s): Law; Suspense; Crime
Major character(s): Alex Miller, Lawyer; Michael Ohlig, Crime Suspect
Time period(s): 21st century; 2010s
Locale(s): New York, New York

Summary: *A Conflict of Interest* is the debut novel of author Adam Mitzner. Criminal lawyer Alex Miller is well on the fast track in his law career: at the young age of 35, he's already made partner at his firm, which is one of the top-rated law practices in New York. Better yet, he has a wife who loves him, and a daughter who is the apple of his eye. All of that threatens to come toppling over, however, when Alex is asked by a longtime family acquaintance to represent him in a case. The man, Michael Ohlig, is somewhat of a legend among the Miller clan, and Alex obliges his request. Yet the more deeply Alex becomes involved in the case, the more he begins to realize that the things he cherishes most are the very same things he could lose at a moment's notice. First novel.

Where it's reviewed:
Publishers Weekly, March 28, 2011, page 34

Other books you might like:
William J. Coughlin, *Shadow of a Doubt*, 1991
Robert Dugoni, *Damage Control*, 2007
David Ellis, *Line of Vision*, 2001
Richard North Patterson, *The Lasko Tangent*, 1979
Scott Turow, *Presumed Innocent*, 1987

685

BOYD MORRISON

The Vault

(New York: Simon & Schuster, 2011)

Subject(s): Archaeology; Suspense; Espionage
Major character(s): Tyler Locke, Engineer (combat,

former); Stacy Benedict, Linguist (classical languages expert)
Time period(s): 21st century; 2010s
Locale(s): Germany; Greece; Italy; United States

Summary: In the novel *The Vault* by Boyd Morrison, former combat engineer Tyler Locke and linguist Stacy Benedict are united in a quest to find the legendary treasures of King Midas. Locke's father and Benedict's sister are being held captive by a sinister organization that needs Midas's gold to fund a nightmarish mission. The key to the gold's location is believed to be contained in Archimedes's manuscripts and one of the ancient Greek inventor's machines. If Locke and Benedict put their unique talents to work together, they may solve the Midas mystery—but finding the treasure will only fuel the evil mastermind's plot.

Where it's reviewed:
Booklist, July 1, 2011, page 37
Publishers Weekly, June 6, 2011, page 27

Other books by the same author:
The Ark, 2010
Rogue Wave, 2010

Other books you might like:
Raymond Khoury, *The Last Templar*, 2006
Chris Kuzneski, *Sign of the Cross*, 2006
Matthew Reilly, *Ice Station*, 1999
James Rollins, *Sandstorm*, 2004
James Twining, *The Double Eagle*, 2005

686

CARSON MORTON

Stealing Mona Lisa
(New York: Minotaur Books, 2011)

Story type: Historical
Subject(s): Art; Forgery; Mystery
Major character(s): Eduardo de Valfierno, Criminal (art forger); Mrs. Hart, Client (of Valfierno); Mr. Hart, Spouse (of Mrs. Hart); Julia Conway, Thief (pickpocket); Vicenzo Perugia, Worker (Louvre); Jose Diego Santiago de la Santisima, Artist
Time period(s): 20th century; 1910s (1911)
Locale(s): Paris, France

Summary: In the novel *Stealing Mona Lisa*, author Carson Morton creates a fictionalized account of the daring theft of *La Joconde* from the Louvre in 1911. The mastermind of the crime is Eduardo de Valfierno, successful operator of an Argentinean art-forgery enterprise. Though his clients pay him to steal original masterpieces, he provides masterful copies—at full price and without their knowledge. Valfierno can't resist the request of the lovely Mrs. Hart and takes his act to Paris where he will attempt the theft of the *Mona Lisa*. He assembles a ragtag team of accomplices—an American street thief, a Louvre worker, and a talented but poor painter to carry out his plan. The arrival of Mr. Hart and an unexpected deluge complicate the heist.

Where it's reviewed:
Booklist, May 1, 2011, page 39
Publishers Weekly, June 13, 2011, page 33

Other books you might like:
Stacy Cohen, *The Last Train from Paris*, 2009
Chris Ewan, *The Good Thief's Guide to Paris*, 2008
Iain Pears, *The Raphael Affair*, 1992
Jed Rubenfeld, *The Interpretation of Murder*, 2006
Susan Vreeland, *Girl in Hyacinth Blue*, 1999

687

AMY MYERS

Classic in the Barn
(New York: Severn House Publishers, 2011)

Series: Jack Colby Car Detective Series. Book 1
Story type: Contemporary; Series
Subject(s): Automobiles; Detective fiction; Crime
Major character(s): Jack Colby, Businessman (classic car restorer), Consultant (to police); Polly Davis, Widow(er), Television Personality (former), Mother (of Bea); Guy Williams, Companion (of Polly); Bea, Daughter (of Polly)
Time period(s): 21st century; 2010s
Locale(s): England

Summary: In *Classic in the Barn* by Amy Myers, the first book in the Jack Colby, Car Detective series, a 1938 Lagonda V12 stored in an English barn plays a key role in a murder investigation. Jack Colby, a classic-car restorer and consultant to the police, discovers the automobile while taking a stroll in the country. He immediately takes a professional interest in the Lagonda and a personal interest in its owner, Polly Davis. On a subsequent visit, Colby stumbles upon Polly's dead body and becomes a suspect in her murder. Polly's daughter Bea convinces Colby to investigate the case of the coveted antique car, which once held the corpse of Polly's late husband.

Other books by the same author:
Murder in Abbot's Folly, 2011
Murder, 'Orrible Murder, 2007
The Wickenham Murders, 2004
Murder in the Queen's Boudoir, 2000
Murder in Pug's Parlour, 1986

Other books you might like:
Simon Brett, *The Body on the Beach*, 2000
Martin Edwards, *The Coffin Trail*, 2004
Larry Karp, *The Music Box Murders*, 1999
Cynthia Riggs, *Deadly Nightshade*, 2001
Lea Wait, *Shadows at the Fair*, 2002

688

HAKAN NESSER

The Inspector and Silence
(New York: Pantheon Books, 2011)

Series: Inspector Van Veeteren Series. Book 5
Story type: Contemporary; Series
Subject(s): Detective fiction; Murder; Cults
Major character(s): Van Veeteren, Detective—Police

Mystery

Time period(s): 21st century
Locale(s): Maardam, Sweden

Summary: Chief Inspector Van Veeteren is ready for a vacation when he and his team of investigators are faced with their most deadly case yet. The body of a girl has been discovered, and the Inspector soon learns she was a member of a fanatical religious cult. The members of the cult, however, aren't talking. Now Van Veeteren must rely on the guidance of an anonymous caller, who has inside knowledge of both the murder and the inner workings of the cult. When more bodies turn up, Van Veeteren and his crew amp up their investigation—and are further perplexed by the identity of their anonymous helper. *The Inspector and Silence* is the fifth book in Hakan Nesser's Inspector Van Veeteren series. This volume is translated by Laurie Thompson.

Where it's reviewed:
Booklist, May 1, 2011, page   30
Library Journal, March 15, 2011, page   113
Publishers Weekly, April 4, page   37
Spectator, July 17, 2010, page   30

Other books by the same author:
Woman with Birthmark, 2009
The Mind's Eye, 2008
The Return, 2007
Borkmann's Point, 2006

Other books you might like:
Kjell Eriksson, *The Princess of Burundi*, 2006
Arnaldur Indridason, *Jar City*, 2005
Henning Mankell, *Faceless Killers*, 1991
Maj Sjowall, *Roseanna*, 2008

689

CLARE O'DONOHUE

The Devil's Puzzle

(New York: Plume, 2011)

Series: Someday Quilts Mystery Series. Book
Story type: Mystery
Subject(s): Mystery; Murder; Quilts
Major character(s): Nell Fitzgerald, Heroine; Oliver White, Artist; Larry Williams, Political Figure; Jesse Dewalt, Police Officer; Eleanor Cassidy, Grandmother
Locale(s): Archers Rest, New York

Summary: After returning from their upstate quilting retreat, the Someday Quilters soon find themselves in the middle of a murder mystery in author Clare O'Donohue's *The Devil's Puzzle*. Shortly after their arrival back in Archers Rest, Nell Fitzgerald and her grandmother, Eleanor Cassidy, are visited by an English artist named Oliver White. Though Oliver had come to propose to Eleanor, his chilling discovery of a skeleton in her rose garden abruptly alters his plans. When Eleanor is named the chief suspect and a rash of vandalism sparks rumors of a resurrection of the town's history of witchcraft, Nell is forced to investigate the origins of the remains for herself and prove her grandmother's innocence.

Where it's reviewed:
Publishers Weekly, July 4, 2011, page   47

Other books by the same author:
Missing Persons, 2011
The Double Cross, 2010
A Drunkard's Path, 2009
The Lover's Knot, 2008

Other books you might like:
Lizbie Brown, *Broken Star*, 1993
Jennifer Chiaverini, *The Quilter's Apprentice: A Novel*, 1999
Earlene Fowler, *Fool's Puzzle*, 1994
Sally Goldenbaum, *Murders on Elderberry Road*, 2003
Terri Thayer, *Wild Goose Chase*, 2008

690

PERRI O'SHAUGHNESSY

Dreams of the Dead

(New York: Simon & Schuster, 2011)

Series: Nina Reilly Series. Book 13
Subject(s): Suspense; Law; Mystery
Major character(s): Nina Reilly, Lawyer; Philip Strong, Hotel Owner (ski resort); Paul van Wagoner, Investigator, Friend (of Nina); Bob, 16-Year-Old, Son (of Nina); Jim Strong, Son (of Philip), Murderer
Time period(s): 21st century; 2010s
Locale(s): Lake Tahoe, California

Summary: In the novel *Dreams of the Dead* by Perri O'Shaughnessy, Lake Tahoe lawyer Nina Reilly is forced to relive the past when a former client's father seeks her help. When Philip Strong, owner of a local ski lodge, arrives in her office, he has a mystery on his hands. While trying to sell his property, the transaction is contested by his son Jim. But Jim, who was responsible for the murders of his wife and Nina's husband, has been presumed dead for years. Nina doesn't want to believe that Jim is living in Brazil, as Philip's documents indicate. As she works to prove that Jim's signature is a fake, the case is complicated by two more murders. *Dreams of the Dead* is the 13th book in the Nina Reilly series.

Where it's reviewed:
Publishers Weekly, May 30, 2011, page   48

Other books by the same author:
Show No Fear, 2008
Breach of Promise, 1998
Obstruction of Justice, 1997
Invasion of Privacy, 1996
Motion to Suppress, 1995

Other books you might like:
James Grippando, *The Pardon: A Novel*, 1994
John Grisham, *The Client*, 1993
John T. Lescroart, *Dead Irish*, 1989
Lisa Scottoline, *Everywhere That Mary Went*, 2003
Kate Wilhelm, *Death Qualified: A Mystery of Chaos*, 1991

691

WESTON OCHSE

Multiplex Fandango

(Colusa, California: Dark Regions Press, 2011)

Subject(s): Fear; Violence; Suspense

Summary: In *Multiplex Fandango*, prize-winning author Weston Ochse presents a collection of short horror stories and novellas. The 16 pieces that comprise this volume demonstrate the author's flair for spine-tingling storytelling and terrifyingly real characters. Titles in this volume include "High Desert Come to Jesus," "The Secret Lives of Heroes," "A Day in the Life of a Dust Bunny," "Tarzan Doesn't Live Here Anymore," "Fugue on the Sea of Cortez," "The Sad Last Love of Cary Grant," and "Catfish Gods." Author Joe Lansdale provides an introduction to this collection.

Where it's reviewed:
Publishers Weekly, June 27, 2011, page   138

Other books by the same author:
Empire of Salt, 2010
The Track of the Storm, 2010
The Golden Thread, 2008
Recalled to Life, 2007
Scarecrow Gods, 2005

Other books you might like:
John Connolly, *Nocturnes*, 2004
Joe Hill, *20th Century Ghosts*, 2005
Joe R. Lansdale, *Bubba Ho-tep*, 2004
Joe R. Lansdale, *High Cotton*, 2000
Dennis Lehane, *Coronado: Stories*, 2006

692

BERNADETTE PAJER

A Spark of Death

(Scottsdale, Arizona: Poisoned Pen Press, 2011)

Series: Professor Bradshaw Series. Book 1
Story type: Historical; Series
Subject(s): Detective fiction; Murder; Science
Major character(s): Benjamin Bradshaw, Professor (electrical engineering); Henry, Friend (of Bradshaw); Wesley Oglethorpe, Professor, Crime Victim
Time period(s): 20th century; 1900s (1901)
Locale(s): Seattle, Washington

Summary: In *A Spark of Death*, the first book in Bernadette Pajer's Professor Bradshaw series, University of Washington Professor Wesley Oglethorpe has been electrocuted in a methodical and bizarre murder. In turn-of-the-century Seattle, area residents are already suspicious of the new electrical technology created at the Snoqualmie Falls Power Plant. Oglethorpe's death reinforces their fears. Electrical engineering professor Benjamin Bradshaw becomes a suspect in the crime, and to clear his name he must find the true perpetrator. In the politically and socially volatile era, suspects range from anarchists to colleagues to family members—and now

the unknown assailant has targeted Bradshaw as well. First novel.

Where it's reviewed:
Booklist, May 15, 2011, page   22
Kirkus Reviews, April 1, 2011, page, page 534
Library Journal, May 1, 2011, page   62
Publishers Weekly, May 30, 2011, page   50

Other books you might like:
Amanda Cross, *In the Last Analysis*, 1964
Robert Goolrick, *A Reliable Wife: A Novel*, 2009
Daniel Hecht, *Bones of the Barbary Coast: A Cree Black Novel*, 2006
Stefanie Pintoff, *In the Shadow of Gotham*, 2009
Victoria Thompson, *Murder on Astor Place*, 1999

693

MIRANDA PARKER

A Good Excuse to Be Bad

(New York: Kensington, 2011)

Story type: Contemporary; Series
Subject(s): Murder; Detective fiction; African Americans
Major character(s): Angel Crawford, Agent (bail recovery), Single Mother, Mother (of Bella), Sister (of Ava), Daughter (of Virginia); Justus Morgan, Religious (pastor, Greater Atlanta Faith Church); Bella, Daughter (of Angel); Cade Taylor, Thief (bank robber); Ava McArthur, Sister (of Angel), Spouse (of Bishop Devon McArthur); Bishop Devon McArthur, Spouse (of Ava); Virginia Carter, Mother (of Angel and Ava)
Time period(s): 21st century; 2010s
Locale(s): Georgia, United States

Summary: In the mystery novel *A Good Excuse to Be Bad* by Miranda Parker, Angel Crawford juggles her career as a bail recovery agent with the challenges of single motherhood in Atlanta, Georgia. When Angel's twin sister Ava is found at the scene of her husband's murder, she becomes the prime suspect in Bishop Devon McArthur's death. Angel does all she can to help her sister—including taking care of her two children—but Ava's reluctance to offer a defense poses a major obstacle. Angel seeks the help of Pastor Justus Morgan, who just happens to be handsome and available. *A Good Excuse to Be Bad* is the first book in Parker's Angel Crawford series. First novel.

Where it's reviewed:
Publishers Weekly, May 30, 2011, page   48

Other books you might like:
Kimberla Lawson Roby, *Casting the First Stone*, 2000
Kayla Perrin, *Obsession*, 2008
Gary Phillips, *High Hand*, 2000
Ray Shannon, *Man Eater*, 2003
Maureen Smith, *Whisper My Name*, 2007

Mystery

694

GEORGE P. PELECANOS

The Cut

(New York: Reagan Arthur Books, 2011)

Story type: Legal
Subject(s): Mystery; Detective fiction; Law
Major character(s): Spero Lucas, Veteran (Iraq War), Investigator; Anwan Hawkins, Drug Dealer, Prisoner
Time period(s): 21st century; 2010s
Locale(s): Washington, District of Columbia

Summary: In the mystery novel *The Cut* by George Pelecanos, Spero Lucas has survived his tour of duty in Iraq and lands what seems to be a less risky job as an attorney's investigator. When Anwan Hawkins, an inmate doing time for dealing marijuana, offers him a side job, Lucas accepts the lucrative proposition despite the job's legal and moral implications. Hawkins needs Lucas to find some missing marijuana deliveries, and though Lucas is qualified for the assignment, the repercussions of his decision will be grave. As Lucas looks for a cut of Hawkins' profits, he puts those closest to him in danger.

Where it's reviewed:
Booklist, May 1, 2011, page 18
Library Journal, March 15, 2011, page 101
Publishers Weekly, May 30, 2011, page 44

Other books by the same author:
The Way Home, 2009
The Turnaround, 2008
The Night Gardener, 2006
Drama City, 2005
Hard Revolution, 2004
Right as Rain, 2001
The Big Blowdown, 1996
A Firing Offense, 1992

Other books you might like:
John Connolly, *The Whisperers*, 2010
Joseph Finder, *Vanished*, 2009
George V. Higgins, *The Friends of Eddie Coyle*, 1972
Dennis Lehane, *Moonlight Mile*, 2010
Richard Price, *Lush Life*, 2008

695

LOUISE PENNY

A Trick of the Light

(New York: Minotaur Boooks, 2011)

Series: Armand Gamache Three Pines Series. Book 7
Story type: Contemporary; Police Procedural
Subject(s): Mystery; Detective fiction; Murder
Major character(s): Armand Gamache, Police Officer (chief inspector); Beauvoir, Police Officer (lieutenant); Clara Morrow, Artist; Lillian Dyson, Friend (of Clara)
Time period(s): 21st century; 2010s
Locale(s): Three Pines, Quebec

Summary: In the mystery novel *A Trick of the Light*, the seventh book in Louise Penny's Armand Gamache series, the opening of Clara Morrow's art show in Montreal is overshadowed by the discovery of a body in her flower bed. The deceased is Lillian Dyson, a friend of Clara who left behind a cryptic clue in a book. When Armand Gamache, chief inspector of the Montreal police, and Lieutenant Beauvoir arrive in the village of Three Pines to investigate the murder, they are quickly drawn into the shadowy dealings of the art world. Clara is the obvious suspect, but none of her colleagues are above reproach.

Where it's reviewed:
Booklist, June 1, 2011, page 44
Library Journal, July 2011, page 58
Publishers Weekly, July 4, 2011, page 42

Other books by the same author:
The Brutal Telling, 2009
A Rule Against Murder, 2009
The Cruelest Month, 2008
A Fatal Grace, 2007
Still Life, 2006

Other books you might like:
Agatha Christie, *A Murder Is Announced*, 1950
Margaret Maron, *Bootlegger's Daughter*, 1992
Ruth Rendell, *Sins of the Fathers*, 1976
Julia Spencer-Fleming, *In the Bleak Midwinter*, 2002
Minette Walters, *The Ice House*, 1992

696

THOMAS PERRY

The Informant

(Boston: Houghton Mifflin Harcourt, 2011)

Series: Butcher's Boy Series. Book 3
Subject(s): Mystery; Detective fiction; Assassination
Major character(s): Michael "The Butcher's Boy" Schaeffer, Assassin, Spouse (of Lady Margaret Holroyd); Elizabeth Waring, Government Official (Department of Justice); Frank Tosca, Organized Crime Figure; Dale Hunsecker, Government Official (Department of Justice); Lady Margaret Holroyd, Spouse (of Michael Schaeffer)
Time period(s): 21st century; 2010s
Locale(s): England; United States

Summary: In *The Informant* by Thomas Perry, an expert hit man known as the Butcher's Boy is living a quiet life as Michael Schaeffer with his wife in England. He is called out of retirement when three assassins are sent to kill him. To find the man responsible for ordering the hit, Schaeffer travels back to New York—the scene of many of his crimes—where he establishes a working relationship with Department of Justice official Elizabeth Waring. Waring has been tracking the Butcher's Boy for years; she knows that he holds information that could bring down her biggest target—the mafia. As Waring tries to bring Schaeffer in as an informant, the Butcher's Boy takes care of the mobsters in his own way. *The Informant* is the third book in the Butcher's Boy series.

Where it's reviewed:
Kirkus Reviews, April 1, 2011, page 537
Library Journal, April 15, 2011, page 88
New York Times, May 5, 2011, page C7(L)
Publishers Weekly, March 7, 2011, page 43
Tampa Tribune, May 1, 2011, page 10

Other books by the same author:
Strip, 2010
Runner, 2009
Fidelity, 2008
Silence, 2007
Nightlife, 2006
Vanishing Act, 1994
Sleeping Dogs, 1992
The Butcher's Boy, 1982

Other books you might like:
Brett Battles, *The Cleaner*, 2007
Lawrence Block, *Hit Man*, 1998
Lorenzo Carcaterra, *Gangster*, 2001
Richard Condon, *Prizzi's Honor*, 1982
Derek Haas, *The Silver Bear*, 2008

DANIEL POLANSKY

Low Town
(New York: Doubleday, 2011)

Story type: Fantasy
Subject(s): Murder; Detective fiction; Drugs
Major character(s): The Warden, Addict, Detective—
    Amateur
Time period(s): Indeterminate
Locale(s): Rigus, Fictional Location

Summary: Daniel Polansky's *Low Town* is a gritty noir-style mystery blended with heavy elements of fantasy. In the city of Rigus, there is a shadow side known as Low Town. Here, a man named The Warden has lived for the past five years in a state of shame, getting by on petty acts of crime and high on drugs most of the time. But when a series of child murders rocks the neighborhood, shadows of The Warden's previous life return to him, and he sets out to find the truth behind the brutal killings. The Warden has no idea, however, the dangerous game he is about to pursue. First novel.

Where it's reviewed:
Booklist, July 1, 2011, page 34
Library Journal, June 15, 2011, page 384
Publishers Weekly, June 6, 2011, page 24

Other books you might like:
Jim Butcher, *Storm Front*, 2000
Kim Harrison, *Dead Witch Walking*, 2004
Jack O'Connell, *Box Nine*, 1992
Jack O'Connell, *Wireless*, 1993
Charles Stross, *The Family Trade*, 2004

KITTY PILGRIM

The Explorer's Code
(New York: Simon & Schuster, 2011)

Subject(s): Adventure; Travel; Mystery
Major character(s): Cordelia Stapleton, Adventurer, Sailor
    (oceanographer), Heiress (of valuable deed); John
    Sinclair, Archaeologist, Adventurer
Time period(s): 21st century; 2010s
Locale(s): Arctic; Norway

Summary: *The Explorer's Code* is a novel by television news personality Kitty Pilgrim. In this novel, an oceanographer named Cordelia Stapleton finds herself in the middle of a mystery that spans generations. Cordelia's great-great-grandfather was an explorer known for his forays into the frozen North. When Cordelia accepts a posthumous award on his behalf, she also inherits his journal, which gives tantalizing clues as to the ownership of a piece of land in Norway. Along with archaeologist John Sinclair, Cordelia heads off on a globe-trotting adventure to find the deed to this land, which has become the site of the Global Seed Vault—making the deed worth millions. Shady characters and adventures abound in *The Explorer's Code*.

Where it's reviewed:
Booklist, May 15, 2011, page 25
Library Journal, April 1, 2011, page 84
Publishers Weekly, June 13, 2011, page 32

Other books you might like:
Ian Caldwell, *The Rule of Four*, 2004
Agatha Christie, *They Came to Baghdad*, 1951
Katherine Neville, *The Eight*, 1988
Elizabeth Peters, *Crocodile on the Sandbank*, 1975
Douglas Preston, *The Cabinet of Curiosities*, 2002

DONALD RAY POLLOCK

The Devil All the Time
(New York: Doubleday, 2011)

Subject(s): Serial murders; Orphans; Cancer
Major character(s): Arvin Eugene Russell, Orphan; Wil-
    lard Russell, Father (of Arvin), Spouse (of
    Charlotte); Charlotte Russell, Spouse (of Willard),
    Cancer Patient; Carl, Serial Killer, Spouse (of
    Sandy); Sandy, Serial Killer, Spouse (of Carl); Roy,
    Religious (preacher); Theodore, Religious (preacher)
Time period(s): 20th century
Locale(s): Ohio, United States

Summary: In *The Devil All the Time*, author Donald Ray Pollock tells the story of a group of characters joined together by a common thread in the form of a man named Arvin Eugene Russell. Orphaned at a young age after his mother's death from cancer and his father's suicide, Arvin espouses an attitude of righteousness marred by his need to stand up for himself—sometimes to a violent end. As the author follows Arvin through early childhood and into adulthood, spanning from the end of World War II into the 1960s, readers also meet characters such as Sandy and Carl, a murderous couple who entice

Mystery

would-be models into posing for photos only to meet their doom, and Roy and Theodore, two preacher cousins who convince Arvin's father to kill another person as a sign of faith. Pollock is also the author of the short-story collection *Knockemstiff*.

Where it's reviewed:
Booklist, May 1, 2011, page 65

Other books by the same author:
Knockemstiff, 2008

Other books you might like:
Sean Doolittle, *The Cleanup*, 2006
Tom Franklin, *Hell at the Breech*, 2003
Flannery O'Connor, *Wise Blood*, 1952
Scott Phillips, *The Walkaway*, 2002
Daniel Woodrell, *Winter's Bone: A Novel*, 2006

700

SARA POOLE

The Borgia Betrayal

(New York: St. Martin's Griffin, 2011)

Story type: Historical; Series
Subject(s): Conspiracy; Suspense; History
Major character(s): Francesca Giordano, Young Woman (poisoner); Rodrigo "Pope Alexander IV" Borgia, Religious (pope), Father (of Cesare and Juan); Cesare, Son (of Rodrigo Borgia), Lover (of Francesca); Juan, Son (of Rodrigo Borgia)
Time period(s): 15th century; 1490s (1493)
Locale(s): Rome, Italy

Summary: In *The Borgia Betrayal*, Francesca Giordano holds an important position in the Borgia court—she is the poisoner responsible for eliminating enemies of Rodrigo Borgia, Pope Alexander VI. Rome in 1493 is a city full of political and social intrigue and the Borgias will take any measures necessary to retain their position of power. Rodrigo's two sons occupy Francesca—Cesare as a lover and Juan as a dangerous foe. If Francesca is to protect her employer, the Church, and the rest of the Renaissance world from harm, she must confront her worst fears and overcome her past.

Where it's reviewed:
Booklist, May 15, 2011, page 23
Library Journal, March 15, 2011, page 112
Publishers Weekly, February 7, 2011, page 32

Other books by the same author:
Poison, 2010

Other books you might like:
P.C. Doherty, *The Poison Maiden*, 2007
Sheri Holman, *A Stolen Tongue*, 1997
Giulio Leoni, *The Mosaic Crimes*, 2007
Candace M. Robb, *The Apothecary Rose*, 1993
Caroline Roe, *A Potion for a Widow*, 1998

701

STEVEN PRESSFIELD

The Profession

(New York: Crown Publishing, 2011)

Subject(s): Military life; Futuristic society; Wars
Major character(s): James Salter, Military Personnel (former general, U.S. Marines), Mercenary; Gilbert "Gent" Gentilhomme, Mercenary
Time period(s): 21st century; 2030s (2032)
Locale(s): Afghanistan; United States

Summary: *The Profession* is a novel by author Steve Pressfield. In the year 2032, individual nations have begun to bleed into one another until order can only be maintained through mercenary force. Leading the charge on mercenary trade is James Salter, a former general in the U.S. Marines who was denounced and demoted by the President of the United States for making threats against U.S. enemies. Now Salter is determined to become wealthy beyond all imagination by taking control of the world's most fruitful oil fields, with the ultimate goal of unseating the president and making him pay for Salter's decommissioning. Only one person stands in Salter's way: his right-hand man, Gilbert "Gent" Gentilhomme, the one person who can stop this would-be dictator and save the United States from certain doom.

Where it's reviewed:
Booklist, May 1, 2011, page 36
Library Journal, June 1, 2011, page 93
Publishers Weekly, April 25, 2011, page 109

Other books by the same author:
Killing Rommel, 2008
The Afghan Campaign, 2006
Virtues of War, 2004
Last of the Amazons, 2002
Tides of War, 2000
Gates of Fire, 1998
The Legend of Bagger Vance, 1995

Other books you might like:
Tom Clancy, *Clear and Present Danger*, 1989
Robert Harris, *Fatherland*, 1992
Paul McEuen, *Spiral*, 2011
A J Tata, *Rogue Threat*, 2009
Brad Thor, *The Lions of Lucerne*, February 27, 2007

702

BILL PRONZINI

Camouflage

(New York: Forge Books, 2011)

Series: Nameless Detective Series. Book 38
Story type: Contemporary
Subject(s): Missing persons; Detective fiction; Abuse
Major character(s): Nameless Detective, Detective— Private; Jake Runyon, Detective—Private; David Virden, Missing Person
Time period(s): 21st century; 2010s

Locale(s): San Francisco, California

Summary: Bill Pronzini's *Camouflage* is the 38th novel in the Nameless Detective series. In this outing, Nameless is hired by David Virden to track down Virden's wife and drop off some important papers. This seemingly clear-cut case turns murky when Virden's wife refuses to accept the papers—followed by Virden's abrupt disappearance. Now Nameless must find the missing man and unravel the mystery of his ex-wife. Meanwhile, Nameless's partner, Runyon, stumbles into his own dangerous mystery to solve.

Where it's reviewed:
Booklist, May 1, 2011, page 16
Publishers Weekly, April 11, 2011, page 32

Other books by the same author:
Betrayers, 2010
The Hidden, 2010
Quincannon's Game, 2005
Quincannon, 1985
The Snatch, 1971

Other books you might like:
Stephen Greenleaf, *Grave Error*, 1979
Marcia Muller, *Edwin of the Iron Shoes: A Novel of Suspense*, 1977
Sara Paretsky, *Indemnity Only*, 1982
Robert B. Parker, *The Godwulf Manuscript*, 1973
John Morgan Wilson, *Simple Justice*, 1996

703

KWEI QUARTEY

Children of the Street

(New York: Random House, 2011)

Series: Inspector Darko Dawson Series. Book 2
Story type: Contemporary - Exotic; Series
Subject(s): Detective fiction; Serial murders; Africa
Major character(s): Darko Dawson, Detective—Police (homicide), Father (of Hosiah); Hosiah, 7-Year-Old, Son (of Darko)
Time period(s): 21st century; 2010s
Locale(s): Accra, Ghana

Summary: In *Children of the Street* by Kwei Quartey, the second book in the Inspector Darko Dawson Mystery series, a serial killer is at work in Ghana's capital city of Accra. When Inspector Darko Dawson is assigned the case, he learns that the victim—one of Accra's street children—was ritually mutilated when he was killed. As other street children are murdered, Dawson consults with experts on the possible meaning and motivation behind the serial killer's cruel method. His search takes him to Accra's backstreets, populated by the desperate and the destitute. But even a respectable professional like Dawson has secrets in Accra—a stubborn dependence on marijuana and a sick child in need of an expensive operation.

Where it's reviewed:
Booklist, May 1, 2011, page 16
Publishers Weekly, May 16, 2011, page 53

Other books by the same author:
Wife of the Gods, 2009

Other books you might like:
Colin Cotterill, *The Coroner's Lunch*, 2004
Tarquin Hall, *The Case of the Missing Servant*, 2009
Alexander McCall Smith, *The No. 1 Ladies' Detective Agency*, 1998
Malla Nunn, *A Beautiful Place to Die*, 2009
Michael Stanley, *A Carrion Death*, 2008

704

ROBERT J. RANDISI

Fly Me to the Morgue

(New York: Severn House Publishers, 2011)

Series: Rat Pack Series. Book 6
Story type: Historical; Series
Subject(s): Detective fiction; Crime; Entertainment industry
Major character(s): Eddie Gianelli, Worker (pit boss), Detective—Amateur; Jerry Epstein, Friend (of Eddie); Bing Crosby, Entertainer; Dean Martin, Entertainer; Frank Sinatra, Entertainer
Time period(s): 20th century; 1960s (1962)
Locale(s): Del Mar, California

Summary: *Fly Me to the Morgue* by Robert Randisi, the sixth book in the Rat Pack series, stars 1960s celebrities Bing Crosby, Dean Martin, and Frank Sinatra in a California murder mystery. Crosby wants to buy a racehorse and Eddie Gianelli, Las Vegas casino pit boss and special friend of the pack, arranges for horse expert Jerry Epstein to help him out. Bing, Eddie, and Jerry travel to California's Red Rock Farm where they find the horse's owner dead. Eddie and Jerry employ their various talents to investigate the murder—and those that follow—while trying to protect Crosby's privacy.

Where it's reviewed:
Booklist, May 1, 2011, page 25
Publishers Weekly, May 9, 2011, page 36

Other books by the same author:
I'm a Fool to Kill You, 2011
You're Nobody Til Somebody Kills You, 2009
Hey There (You with the Gun in Your Hand), 2008
Luck Be a Lady, Don't Die, 2007
Everybody Kills Somebody Sometime, 2006

Other books you might like:
Megan Abbott, *The Song Is You*, 2007
George Baxt, *The Alfred Hitchcock Murder Case*, 1986
Ron Goulart, *Groucho Marx, Master Detective*, 1998
Stuart M. Kaminsky, *Bullet for a Star*, 1977
Craig McDonald, *Head Games*, 2007

705

ROBERT J. RANDISI

The End of Brooklyn

(Charleston, South Carolina: Booksurge, 2011)

Series: Nick Delvecchio Series. Book 3
Story type: Private Detective; Series

Mystery

Subject(s): Detective fiction; Family; Reunions
Major character(s): Nick Delvecchio, Detective—Private
Time period(s): 20th century; 1990s
Locale(s): New York, New York

Summary: In *The End of Brooklyn*, the final book in Robert J. Randisi's Nick Delvecchio Mystery series, private detective Nick Delvecchio attends a high-school reunion and ends up investigating a former classmate's death. The family of the deceased woman wants Nick to find out if the death was the result of suicide or murder. Nick's own family is soon embroiled in its own heartbreak, as long-buried secrets resurface and threaten to change their world forever. Prolific author Randisi is a recipient of the Private Eye Writers of America's Lifetime Achievement Award.

Where it's reviewed:
Booklist, May 1, 2011, page   22

Other books by the same author:
The Bottom of Every Bottle, 2010
Broadway Bounty, 2010
Crow Bait, 2010
The Dead of Brooklyn, 1991
No Exit from Brooklyn, 1987

Other books you might like:
Lawrence Block, *Sins of the Fathers*, 1976
Harlan Coben, *Darkest Fear*, 2000
Gabriel Cohen, *Red Hook*, 2001
Jim Fusilli, *Closing Time*, 2001
Tony Spinosa, *Hose Monkey*, 2006

706

RUTH RENDELL

Tigerlily's Orchids

(New York: Scribner, 2011)

Subject(s): Psychology; Suspense; Mystery
Major character(s): Stuart Font, Young Man; Tigerlily, Immigrant, Neighbor (to Stuart)
Time period(s): 21st century; 2010s
Locale(s): London, England

Summary: *Tigerlily's Orchids* is a suspenseful psychological thriller from award-winning author Ruth Rendell. Stuart Font, an insipid lothario with a married girlfriend and a lack of ambition, is new to Lichfield House, a condo complex in North London, so he decides to host a party for the building's bizarre residents. Among them are a trio of silly college girls, an alcoholic woman, a lonely spinster, an ex-hippie, and a pedophile janitor. Stuart soon learns that everyone in Lichfield house has dark secrets that they'll do anything to protect. As they come together for the party, a greater mystery unfolds in the townhouse across the street with a beautiful young Asian woman named Tigerlily who grows orchids and casts a spell on the residents of Stuart's building.

Where it's reviewed:
Booklist, March 15, 2011, page   26
Kirkus Reviews, March 1, 2011, page 362
Library Journal, April 15, 2011, page   88
New York Times, July 4, 2011, page   C1(L)

Publishers Weekly, April 25, 2011, page   109

Other books by the same author:
The Monster in the Box, 2009
Not in the Flesh, 2008
Portobello, 2008
The Water's Lovely, 2007
End in Tears, 2006
To Fear a Painted Devil, 1965
Vanity Dies Hard, 1965
From Doon with Death, 1964

Other books you might like:
Tana French, *Faithful Place*, 2011
Patricia Highsmith, *Deep Water*, 1957
Reginald Hill, *The Stranger House*, 2005
Morag Joss, *The Night Following*, 2008
Minette Walters, *Acid Row*, 2002

707

TED RICCARDI

Between the Thames and the Tiber

(Trenton, Texas: Pegasus Publishing, 2011)

Series: Further Adventures of Sherlock Holmes Series. Book 1
Subject(s): Detective fiction; Murder; Inheritance and succession
Major character(s): Sherlock Holmes, Detective—Private; Watson, Sidekick (of Holmes)
Time period(s): 19th century
Locale(s): London, United Kingdom

Summary: Ted Riccardi's The Further Adventures of Sherlock Holmes series kicks off with *Between the Thames and the Tiber: The Further Adventures of Sherlock Holmes*. Holmes and Watson have come back to London from their sleuthing adventures abroad, only to find Holmes in receipt of a large inheritance. But before the duo can enjoy their newfound windfall, they find themselves ensnared in a series of new cases—which point to the fact that one of their arch-nemeses may not be dead after all.

Where it's reviewed:
Booklist, May 15, 2011, page   20

Other books by the same author:
The Oriental Casebook of Sherlock Holmes, 2003

Other books you might like:
Lyndsay Faye, *Dust and Shadow*, 2009
Mark Frost, *The List of Seven*, 1993
David Grann, *The Devil and Sherlock Holmes: Tales of Murder, Madness, and Obsession*, 2010
Laurie R. King, *The Beekeeper's Apprentice, or, On the Segregation of the Queen*, 1994
Nicholas Meyer, *The Seven-Per-Cent Solution*, 1974

708

MATT RICHTEL

Devil's Plaything
(New York: Harper, 2011)

Subject(s): Alzheimer's disease; Technology; Adventure
Major character(s): Nat Idle, Journalist; Lane,
  Grandmother (of Nat)
Time period(s): 21st century; 2010s
Locale(s): San Francisco, California

Summary: In *Devil's Plaything*, Pulitzer Prize-winning author Matt Richtel presents a tale of super-advanced technology, Alzheimer's disease, and the battle to survive. Nat Idle is a blogger and journalist who is on a walk with his aged grandmother in Golden Gate Park. Suddenly, shots ring out, and Nat and his grandmother are the intended targets. Thus begins a rollicking tale that follows Nat as he attempts to stay one step ahead of enemies unseen—enemies who are out to alter his brain. The one person who can help him is his grandmother, who is dealing with brain issues of her own: the onset of Alzheimer's.

Where it's reviewed:
Booklist, May 1, 2011, page 37
Publishers Weekly, May 23, 2011, page 28

Other books by the same author:
Hooked, 2007

Other books you might like:
Mark Alpert, *Final Theory: A Novel*, 2008
Michael Crichton, *Next: A Novel*, 2006
Joseph Finder, *Extraordinary Powers*, 1994
Tess Gerritsen, *Gravity*, 1999
Alex Kava, *Whitewash*, 2007

709

MICHAEL RIDPATH

Where the Shadows Lie
(New York: Minotaur Books, 2011)

Series: Magnus Jonson Series. Book 1
Story type: Contemporary; Series
Subject(s): Detective fiction; Murder; Suspense
Major character(s): Magnus Jonson, Detective—Police;
  Agnar Haraldsson, Crime Victim, Professor
Time period(s): 21st century; 2010s
Locale(s): Iceland

Summary: Michael Ridpath's *Where the Shadows Lie* is set in modern-day Iceland, where police detective Magnus Jonson is about to undertake the most dangerous case of his career. Though born in Iceland, Magnus was raised in Boston. He now finds himself back in his homeland after a hit is placed on him by an organized crime faction. But Icelandic life is far from serene for the prodigal son. Not only is he haunted by the still-unsolved murder of his father 20 years prior, but a new case involving a long-lost Icelandic saga, a reportedly magical ring, and a murdered professor will require all his attention, skill, and courage. This volume is the first

book in the Magnus Jonson series.

Where it's reviewed:
Booklist, July 1, 2011, page 34
Library Journal, July 2011, page 58
Publishers Weekly, June 13, 2011, page 28
Spectator, July 17, 2010, page 30

Other books by the same author:
See No Evil, 2007
On the Edge, 2005
Final Venture, 2001
The Marketmaker, 1998
Trading Reality, 1997

Other books you might like:
Kjell Eriksson, *The Princess of Burundi*, 2006
Karin Fossum, *Don't Look Back*, 2002
Arnaldur Indridason, *Jar City*, 2005
Henning Mankell, *Faceless Killers*, 1991
Maj Sjowall, *Roseanna*, 2008

710

MICHAEL ROBOTHAM

The Wreckage
(New York: Little, Brown & Co., 2011)

Subject(s): Money; Crime; Journalism
Major character(s): Luca Terracini, Journalist; Daniela
  Garner, Government Official (UN worker)
Time period(s): 21st century; 2010s

Summary: *The Wreckage* is a novel by author Michael Robotham. When international criminals pull off the biggest monetary theft ever, it's up to Iraqi-American journalist Luca Terracini to figure out who is behind the crime. His Muslim heritage allows him to gain access to various fronts of Operation: Iraqi Freedom, but soon even his stealthiest undercover work goes detected. Now the clock is ticking as Luca, along with a UN representative named Daniela, race to uncover the theft. But will they get to the bottom of this heinous crime before international relations completely fall apart? Robotham is also the author of *Suspect*, *Lost*, and *Shatter*.

Where it's reviewed:
New York Times Book Review, July 10, 2011, page
  16(L)
Publishers Weekly, May 2, 2011, page 38

Other books by the same author:
Bleed for Me, 2010
Bombproof, 2009
The Night Ferry, 2007
The Drowning Man, 2005
The Suspect, 2004

Other books you might like:
John Connolly, *The Whisperers*, 2010
Dan Fesperman, *The Prisoner of Guantanamo*, 2006
David Ignatius, *Body of Lies*, 2007
Richard North Patterson, *In the Name of Honor*, 2010
Minette Walters, *The Chameleon's Shadow: A Novel*,
  2008

Mystery

711

JAMES ROLLINS (Pseudonym of James Czajkowski)

Devil Colony

(New York: William Morrow, 2011)

Series: Sigma Force Series. Book 7
Subject(s): Mummies; Family; Adventure
Major character(s): Painter Crowe, Director (of Sigma Force)
Time period(s): 21st century; 2010s
Locale(s): United States

Summary: Mummies have been discovered in the Rocky Mountains, and a nearby Native American tribe claims possession of the corpses. Chaos soon breaks out at the dig site, and an anthropologist is murdered. At the center of the melee is a teenage girl in desperate need of her uncle's help. And that uncle is none other than Painter Crowe, the head of the Sigma Force band of military scientists. Now, with public opinion turning against his niece and her life in danger, Painter sets out to find the truth of what happened in the Rockies—and the story of the mummies entombed there. Jack Rollins's *The Devil Colony* is the seventh book in the Sigma Force series.

Where it's reviewed:
Publishers Weekly, May 30, 2011, page 49

Other books by the same author:
Altar of Eden, 2009
The Doomsday Key, 2009
Last Oracle, 2008
Judas Strain, 2007
The Judas Strain, 2007
Black Order, 2006
Map of Bones, 2005
Sandstorm, 2004

Other books you might like:
Steve Berry, *Jefferson Key*, 2011
Clive Cussler, *Lost City: A Novel from the NUMA Files*, 2004
Chris Kuzneski, *Sign of the Cross*, 2006
Boyd Morrison, *The Ark: A Novel*, 2010
Douglas Preston, *Thunderhead: A Novel*, 1999

712

DAVID ROSENFELT

One Dog Night

(New York: Minotaur Books, 2011)

Series: Andy Carpenter Series. Book 9
Story type: Legal; Series
Subject(s): Law; Arson; Mystery
Major character(s): Andy Carpenter, Lawyer (defense attorney); Noah Galloway, Addict, Defendant (accused of arson murder), Client (of Andy); Hike Lynch, Colleague (of Andy); Willie Miller, Friend (of Andy); Sam Willis, Computer Expert
Time period(s): 21st century; 2010s
Locale(s): Paterson, New Jersey

Summary: In the mystery novel *One Dog Night* by David Rosenfelt, accused murderer Noah Galloway uses an unusual strategy to bargain for the services of Paterson, New Jersey defense lawyer Andy Carpenter. Before Andy became the owner of his cherished golden retriever, Tara, the dog was rescued from a life of neglect by Galloway; therefore Carpenter cannot refuse to take on Galloway's case, despite the fact that the former addict has already confessed to killing 26 by arson. Galloway has no recollection of the crime, which took place six years ago. Carpenter must execute some tricky legal maneuvers in the courtroom if he hopes to exonerate his troubled client. *One Dog Night* is the ninth book in the Andy Carpenter series.

Where it's reviewed:
Booklist, July 1, 2011, page 32
Publishers Weekly, May 9, 2011, page 33

Other books by the same author:
Dog Tags, 2010
Don't Tell a Soul, 2008
Bury the Lead, 2004
First Degree, 2003
Open and Shut, 2002

Other books you might like:
William Lashner, *Hostile Witness*, 1995
John T. Lescroart, *Dead Irish*, 1989
Spencer Quinn, *Dog on It: A Chet and Bernie Mystery*, 2009
Lisa Scottoline, *Everywhere That Mary Went*, 2003
Sheldon Siegel, *Special Circumstances: A Novel*, 2000

713

ROBERT ROTENBERG

The Guilty Plea

(New York: Farrar, Straus and Giroux, 2011)

Story type: Contemporary
Subject(s): Detective fiction; Murder; Divorce
Major character(s): Ari Greene, Detective; Terrence Wyler, Crime Victim; Samantha, Spouse (of Terrence), Crime Suspect
Time period(s): 21st century; 2010s
Locale(s): Toronto, Ontario

Summary: In *The Guilty Plea*, author Robert Rotenberg tells the story of a sensational murder and the roster of characters caught in its orbit. Wealthy Terrence Wyler is about to divorce his wife in a much-publicized trail, but on the morning of the hearings, Wyler is discovered dead in his kitchen. His wife, Samantha, is found to be in possession of a blood-stained knife, and the answer seems simple: Samantha killed her soon-to-be ex. But as detective Ari Greene investigates, he finds a complicated web of deceit and love gone wrong—and the distinct possibility that Samantha is not the killer. *The Guilty Plea* is the sequel to *Old City Hall*.

Where it's reviewed:
Booklist, July 1, 2011, page 32
Publishers Weekly, June 6, 2011, page 27

Other books by the same author:
Old City Hall, 2009

Other books you might like:
Terry Devane, *Uncommon Justice*, 2001
John T. Lescroart, *Dead Irish*, 1989
Phillip Margolin, *Wild Justice*, 2000
David Rosenfelt, *Open and Shut*, 2002
Lisa Scottoline, *Courting Trouble*, 2002

714

ROSEMARY ROWE

The Vestal Vanishes

(London: Severn House Publishers, 2011)

Series: Libertus Mystery of Roman Britain Series. Book
  12
Story type: Historical
Subject(s): Detective fiction; Ancient history; Kidnapping
Major character(s): Libertus, Detective—Private; Audelia,
  Guard (former vestal virgin)

Summary: *The Vestal Vanishes* is the 12th installment in
Rosemary Rowe's Libertus Mysteries of Roman Britain
series. This outing centers on former vestal virgin Audelia, whose impending wedding is the talk of the town.
But when Audelia doesn't show up for her grand
nuptials, Libertus is called in to investigate. As his
investigation takes some unexpectedly sinister turns,
another vestal virgin disappears, putting the pressure on
Libertus to save the virgins from abduction.

Where it's reviewed:
Publishers Weekly, June 6, 2011, page 27

Other books by the same author:
Requiem for a Slave, 2010
The Chariots of Calyx, 2002
Murder in the Forum, 2001
A Pattern of Blood, 2000
The Germanicus Mosaic, 1999

Other books you might like:
Lindsey Davis, *The Silver Pigs*, 1989
John Maddox Roberts, *SPQR I: The King's Gambit*,
  1990
Steven Saylor, *Roman Blood*, 1991
Simon Scarrow, *Under the Eagle*, 2001
Marilyn Todd, *I, Claudia*, 1995

715

ANNELISE RYAN (Pseudonym of Beth Amos)

Frozen Stiff

(New York: Kensington, 2011)

Series: Mattie Winston Series. Book 3
Story type: Contemporary
Subject(s): Crime; Murder; Romances (Fiction)
Major character(s): Mattie Winston, Doctor (coroner);
  Steven Hurley, Detective
Time period(s): 21st century; 2010s

Locale(s): Sorenson, Wisconsin

Summary: *Frozen Stiff* is the third book in the Mattie
Winston series from author Annelise Ryan. Coroner Mattie Ryan is shocked when a beautiful young woman turns
up in her morgue with a knife in her chest. Mattie isn't
as shocked by the crime as she is by the fact that she's
never seen the woman before. Sorenson, Wisconsin, is a
small town, and Mattie knows everyone who lives there.
Police detective Steven Hurley is even more disturbed
by the crime than Mattie. Swearing her to secrecy, he
reveals that he once dated the woman and that the knife
in her chest belongs to him. Now, Mattie must figure out
the identity of the killer before she becomes the next
victim.

Where it's reviewed:
Library Journal, July 2011, page 58
Publishers Weekly, June 6, 2011, page 58

Other books by the same author:
Scared Stiff, 2010
Working Stiff, 2009
Second Sight, 1998
Eyes of Night, 1997
Cold White Fury, 1996

Other books you might like:
Miles Keaton Andrew, *Final Arrangements*, 2002
Vicki Delany, *In the Shadow of the Glacier*, 2007
Janet Evanovich, *One for the Money*, 1994
Sophie Littlefield, *A Bad Day for Sorry*, 2009
Jeff Mariotte, *CSI: Brass in Pocket*, 2009

716

MARCUS SAKEY

The Two Deaths of Daniel Hayes

(New York: Dutton, 2011)

Subject(s): Memory disorders; Missing persons; Suspense
Major character(s): Daniel Hayes, Amnesiac
Time period(s): 21st century; 2010s
Locale(s): Maine, United States

Summary: *The Two Deaths of Daniel Hayes* is a suspense
novel by author Marcus Sakey. When a man wakes up
naked on a beach along the coast of Maine, he has no
idea who he is, let alone where he might be. When he
finds an identification card bearing the name Daniel
Hayes, he decides that the card might be his—after all, it
was lying in a car near the beach, the only vehicle
anywhere nearby. As Daniel seeks his true identity and
tries to figure out how he ended up washed ashore, he
begins to learn more and more about the person he forgot
he was. Unfortunately, the people who might have all
the answers seem to be the same people responsible for
his near-death experience in the first place. Is this man
who calls himself Daniel Hayes better off leaving his
past a forgotten memory? Sakey is also the author of
The Amateurs and *The Blade Itself*.

Where it's reviewed:
Booklist, May 1, 2011, page 39
Library Journal, April 15, 2011, page 89

Mystery

Other books by the same author:
The Amateurs, 2009
At the City's Edge, 2008
Good People, 2008
The Blade Itself, 2007

Other books you might like:
Peter Abrahams, *Oblivion*, 2005
Steve Hamilton, *The Lock Artist*, 2010
Dashiell Hammett, *The Dain Curse*, 1929
Gregg Hurwitz, *The Crime Writer*, 2007
Thomas Perry, *Strip*, 2010

717

JAMES SALLIS

The Killer is Dying
(New York: Walker, 2011)

Subject(s): Murder; Mystery; Deserts
Major character(s): Christian, Assassin; Jimmie, 13-Year-Old, Abandoned Child; Sayles, Detective
Time period(s): 21st century; 2010s
Locale(s): Phoenix, Arizona

Summary: Written by James Sallis, *The Killer is Dying* is a suspenseful crime novel about the strange connection between three vastly different men. Christian is a terminally ill killer-for-hire about to complete his final job, Sayles is a weary detective who is preparing for the death of his wife, and Jimmie is a young kid who has been abandoned by his parents and is living on his own, all the while haunted by dreams that seem to be connected to a hit man. Christian is thwarted on his last job when another killer takes out his target, leading to a chase across the streets and deserts of Phoenix. Little does he know that Sayles is hunting him and Jimmie is tied to him in a greater way than he can imagine.

Where it's reviewed:
Publishers Weekly, June 13, 2011, page 28

Other books by the same author:
Salt River, 2007
Drive, 2005
Cypress Grove, 2003
Ghost of a Flea, 2001
The Long-Legged Fly, 1992

Other books you might like:
James Crumley, *The Last Good Kiss*, 1978
Sean Doolittle, *Rain Dogs*, 2005
Kent Harrington, *Dia de los Muertos*, 1997
Cormac McCarthy, *No Country for Old Men*, 2005
George P. Pelecanos, *The Night Gardener*, 2006

718

JOHN SANDFORD

Buried Prey
(New York: G. P. Putnam's Sons, 2011)

Series: Lucas Davenport Series. Book 21
Story type: Police Procedural; Series

Subject(s): Murder; Detective fiction; Mystery
Major character(s): Lucas Davenport, Detective
Time period(s): 21st century; 2010s
Locale(s): Minneapolis, Minnesota

Summary: Part of the Prey series, *Buried Prey* is a mystery from best-selling author John Sandford. In 1985, when Minneapolis detective Lucas Davenport was a careless young cop, two local girls went missing. Lucas was intent on solving the case and despite the fact that his boss declared it closed, Lucas was convinced there was more to the story. Now, more than 20 years later, a house demolition has revealed two female corpses. Seizing his second chance to make things right, Lucas is determined to uncover the truth about what really happened to the young women, but it doesn't take long for him to realize someone wants to keep the secrets of the past buried deep.

Where it's reviewed:
Booklist, May 1, 2011, page 16
Publishers Weekly, March 28, 2011, page 33
Star-Tribune (Minneapolis, MN), June 5, 2011, page 6E

Other books by the same author:
Shock Wave, 2011
Bad Blood, 2010
Storm Prey, 2010
Virgil Flowers, 2010
Rough Country, 2009
Wicked Prey, 2009
Heat Lightning, 2008
Dark of the Moon, 2007
The Night Crew, 1997
Rules of Prey, 1989

Other books you might like:
Harlan Coben, *Long Lost*, 2009
Michael Connelly, *A Darkness More than Night: A Novel*, 2001
Stephen Dobyns, *The Church of Dead Girls*, 1997
Chuck Logan, *After the Rain*, 2004
James Patterson, *Kiss the Girls*, 1995

719

KATE SEDLEY

The Midsummer Crown
(London: Severn House Publishers, 2011)

Series: Roger the Chapman Series. Book 17
Story type: Historical - Medieval
Subject(s): Detective fiction; Murder; Kidnapping
Major character(s): Roger the Chapman, Peddler, Detective—Amateur
Time period(s): 15th century
Locale(s): London, United Kingdom

Summary: Roger the Chapman is a peddler with a passion for sleuthing. *The Midsummer Crown*, the 17th novel in Kate Sedley's Roger the Chapman mystery series, finds the hero investigating the kidnapping of a boy and the murder of his teacher. Roger is called to London to look into the disappearance of a schoolboy, who vanished

after his teacher was locked in a room and murdered. As Roger gets deeper into the cases at hand, he finds startling parallels between the details of the crimes and an age-old British legend.

Where it's reviewed:
Booklist, July 1, 2011, page 34
Publishers Weekly, May 23, 2011, page 32

Other books by the same author:
Wheel of Fate, 2010
The Holy Innocents, 1995
The Weaver's Tale, 1994
The Plymouth Cloak, 1992
Death and the Chapman, 1991

Other books you might like:
Alys Clare, *Fortune Like the Moon*, 2000
P.C. Doherty, *Satan in St. Mary's*, 1986
Susanna Gregory, *A Conspiracy of Violence*, 2006
Susanna Gregory, *A Plague on Both Your Houses*, 1998
Michael Jecks, *The Last Templar*, 1995

720

JACQUELINE SEEWALD

The Truth Sleuth

(Farmington Hills, Michigan: Five Star, 2011)

Story type: Mystery
Subject(s): Murder; Mystery; Psychics
Major character(s): Kim Reynolds, Librarian, Psychic; Mike Gardner, Detective; Hank Anderson, Principal; Sammy Granger, Teenager

Summary: Times are tough for psychic librarian Kim Reynolds. A thinning budget has just forced her out of her job at the college library. Things begin to look up again when her fiance, Detective Mike Gardner, helps her find a new position teaching English at a nearby high school, but her luck doesn't last long. She senses the murder of young Sammy Granger and faces threats and vandalism from her new students. She also finds herself confronted by Mike's ex-wife, who makes it quite clear that she is not officially an ex just yet. With her personal life in shambles, Kim senses the murder of another young student and is thrown into the midst of a potentially deadly mystery.

Where it's reviewed:
Kirkus Reviews, March 1, 2011, page 368
Library Journal, May 1, 2011, page 62

Other books by the same author:
Stacy's Song, 2010
The Drowning Pool, 2009
The Drowning Pool, 2009
The Inferno Collection, 2007
Claire's Curse, 2004
A Devil in the Pines, 1999
Where is Robert?, 1997

Other books you might like:
Jo Dereske, *Miss Zukas and the Library Murders*, 1994
Carolyn G. Hart, *Death on Demand*, 1987
Daniel Hecht, *City of Masks*, 2003

Miranda James, *Murder Past Due*, 2010
Martha C. Lawrence, *Murder in Scorpio*, 1995

721

SARAH R. SHABER

Louise's War

(New York: Severn House Publishers, 2011)

Story type: Historical - World War II
Subject(s): Detective fiction; Murder; Friendship
Major character(s): Louise Pearlie, Widow(er), Detective—Amateur; Rachel Bloch, Friend (of Louise)
Time period(s): 20th century; 1940s (1942)
Locale(s): Washington, District of Columbia

Summary: In *Louise's War*, author Sarah R. Shaber tells the story of Louise Pearlie, a young woman who takes a job with the Office of Strategic Services in the wake of her husband's death. The year is 1942, and Louise is worried for her old college friend Rachel Bloch, a French Jew trapped in Europe. When Louise finds a file on Rachel's husband, she grows ever more determined to help her friend escape Nazi-occupied France. But when Louise's supervisor is killed, the determined widow vows to find the culprit—and in the process discovers startling ties between Rachel's case and the supervisor's murder.

Where it's reviewed:
Publishers Weekly, July 18, 2011, page 133

Other books by the same author:
Shell Game, 2007
The Bug Funeral, 2005
The Fugitive Kind, 2003
Snipe Hunt, 2000
Simon Said, 1997

Other books you might like:
James R. Benn, *Billy Boyle*, 2006
David Brinkley, *Washington Goes to War*, 1988
Rebecca Cantrell, *A Trace of Smoke*, 2009
Susan Isaacs, *Shining Through*, 1988
Mark Mills, *The Information Officer: A Novel*, 2009

722

ALEX SHAKAR

Luminarium

(New York: Soho Press, 2011)

Subject(s): Brothers; Virtual reality; Fantasy
Major character(s): George Brounian, Brother (of Fred); Fred Brounian, Brother (of George); Mira, Young Woman
Time period(s): 21st century; 2010s
Locale(s): New York, New York

Summary: In *Luminarium*, author Alex Shakar tells the story of two brothers and the unusual predicament in which they find themselves. George Brounian has just slipped into a coma and left his brother Fred in charge of their software company. Soon a powerful takeover

Mystery

claims the brothers' business, and Fred is forced to move back in with his parents. Desperate, he hooks up with Mira, a beautiful young woman who convinces him to take part in a neurological project in which he is guaranteed positive experiences and a healthier attitude toward life in general. But soon Fred is having trouble distinguishing truth from reality, and when comatose George begins contacting him via email, he know for certain that something is dreadfully wrong.

Where it's reviewed:
Booklist, July 1, 2011, page 25
Publishers Weekly, May 16, 2011, page 49

Other books by the same author:
The Savage Girl, 2001
City in Love, 1996

Other books you might like:
Mark Alpert, *Final Theory: A Novel*, 2008
Alan Glynn, *The Dark Fields*, 2002
Neal Stephenson, *Snow Crash*, 1992
Connie Willis, *Passage*, 2001
Charles Yu, *How to Live Safely in a Science Fictional Universe*, 2010

723

DEBORAH SHARP

Mama Sees Stars

(Woodbury, Minnesota: MIDNIGHT INK, 2011)

Series: Mace Bauer Mysteries. Book 4
Story type: Mystery
Subject(s): Mystery fiction; Murder; Movie industry
Major character(s): Mace Bower, Animal Trainer; Mama, Mother; Carlos, Boyfriend, Detective
Locale(s): Himmarshee, Florida

Summary: In Deborah Sharp's *Mama Sees Stars*, the fourth book in her Mace Bauer Mysteries series, mystery ensues when Hollywood comes to the sleepy little town of Himmarshee, Florida. As the story opens, local animal handler Mace Bauer is hired to work on the set of a new movie alongside Mama, who landed a bit part in the film. Before long, however, the producer is shot and killed on his own set and the whole production is thrown into chaos. Facing an entire cast of suspects and a dizzying array of crazy Hollywood characters to deal with, it's up to Mace and her detective boyfriend Carlos to get to the bottom of this murder mystery and find out who is responsible for the producer's demise.

Where it's reviewed:
Library Journal, July 2011, page 58

Other books by the same author:
Mama Gets Hitched, 2010
Mama Rides Shotgun, 2009
Mama Does Time, 2008

Other books you might like:
Joelle Charbonneau, *Skating around the Law*, 2010
Jerrilyn Farmer, *Sympathy for the Devil*, 1998
Sue Ann Jaffarian, *Too Big to Miss: An Odelia Grey Mystery*, 2006
Elaine Viets, *Shop Till You Drop*, 2003

Penny Warner, *How to Crash a Killer Bash*, 2010

724

JEFF SHELBY

Liquid Smoke

(Madison, Wisconsin: Tyrus Books, 2011)

Series: Noah Braddock Mystery Series. Book 3
Story type: Contemporary
Subject(s): Crime; Murder; Family relations
Major character(s): Noah Braddock, Detective—Private, Son (of Carolina); Carolina, Mother (of Noah), Alcoholic; Liz Santangelo, Detective; Darcy Gill, Lawyer
Time period(s): 21st century; 2010s
Locale(s): San Diego, California

Summary: *Liquid Smoke* is the third book in the Noah Braddock series from author Jeff Shelby. Noah Braddock is a private detective who would often rather be on San Diego's beaches surfing than solving crimes. Lately, things have gone a bit better for Noah, who has patched up his relationships with his alcoholic mother, Carolina, and detective Liz Santangelo. Things become a little more complicated when Noah is contacted by lawyer Darcy Gill, who is representing a death-row inmate. Noah wants nothing to do with the case until he learns that Darcy is representing the father he never knew. Now, he sets out to discover if the man is actually innocent of taking the lives of two men.

Where it's reviewed:
Library Journal, July 2011, page 58
Publishers Weekly, May 30, 2011, page 50

Other books by the same author:
Wicked Break, 2006
Killer Swell, 2005

Other books you might like:
Bill Cameron, *Lost Dog*, 2007
Robert Crais, *The Monkey's Raincoat*, 1987
Kem Nunn, *Tapping the Source*, 1984
T. Jefferson Parker, *Laguna Heat*, 1985
Don Winslow, *The Dawn Patrol*, 2008

725

KARIN SLAUGHTER

Fallen

(New York: Random House, 2011)

Story type: Police Procedural
Subject(s): Women; Law; Law enforcement
Major character(s): Faith Mitchell, Police Officer; Will Trent, Police Officer; Sara Linton, Doctor
Time period(s): 21st century; 2010s
Locale(s): Georgia, United States

Summary: *Fallen* is a novel by author Karin Slaughter. In it, Slaughter tells the story of Faith Mitchell, a police officer employed by Georgia's State Bureau of Investigations. When crime hits too close to home and

Faith finds herself looking at a murder scene in her mother's own house, she must use all of her training and resources to figure out exactly what happened and why her mother went missing. Those resources include her cohort, Will Trent, along with a doctor named Sara Linton. But when Faith discovers that the one major blockade keeping her from finding her mother is the very agency she works for, she must decide exactly whom she can trust—and whom she must take down.

Where it's reviewed:
Booklist, May 15, 2011, page 21
Library Journal, July 2011, page 70
Publishers Weekly, May 2, 2011, page 38

Other books by the same author:
Broken, 2010
Undone, 2009
Fractured, 2008
Beyond Reach, 2007
Skin Privilege, 2007
Triptych, 2006
Triptych, 2006
Blindsighted, 2001

Other books you might like:
Jan Burke, *Kidnapped*, 2006
Joseph Finder, *Power Play: A Novel*, 2007
Lisa Gardner, *Love You More*, 2011
George Dawes Green, *Ravens*, 2009
Greg Iles, *24 Hours*, 2000

726

JEFFREY SMALL

The Breath of God

(Atlanta, Georgia: West Hills Press, 2011)

Story type: Contemporary - Exotic
Subject(s): Detective fiction; Suspense; Legends
Major character(s): Grant Matthews, Student—Graduate
Time period(s): 21st century; 2010s
Locale(s): Bhutan

Summary: In the novel *The Breath of God* by Jeffrey Small, a grad student's research into an ancient theological find could have repercussions around the globe. First revealed by a 19th-century Russian journalist, the controversial find has been revisited by Grant Matthews, a graduate student at Emory University who follows the mystery's trail to the Himalayan Mountains. In Bhutan, Grant's research focuses on a centuries-old legend about a young boy's holy pilgrimage in India. There are those who don't want Grant's discoveries to be revealed, including religious extremists who will do everything in their power to bury the ancient mystery once again.

Where it's reviewed:
Library Journal, March 15, 2011, page 108
Publishers Weekly, January 24, 2011, page 134

Other books you might like:
Steve Berry, *The Templar Legacy*, 2006
Dan Brown, *The Da Vinci Code*, 2003
Thomas Greanias, *Raising Atlantis*, 2006

Chris Kuzneski, *Sign of the Cross*, 2006
James Rollins, *Black Order*, 2006

727

APRIL SMITH

White Shotgun

(New York: Knopf Publishing, 2011)

Series: Ana Grey Series. Book 4
Story type: Police Procedural; Series
Subject(s): Law enforcement; Detective fiction; Organized crime
Major character(s): Ana Grey, FBI Agent, Girlfriend (of Sterling); Sterling McCord, Boyfriend (of Ana); Cecilia Nicosa, Sister (half-sister of Ana)
Time period(s): 21st century; 2010s
Locale(s): London, England; Siena, Italy

Summary: *White Shotgun* is the fourth novel from author April Smith's series featuring FBI Special Agent Ana Grey. It seems Ana cannot even get a break from crime when she is off duty. While on vacation in London with her boyfriend, Sterling, Ana watches as a shooting takes place right before her eyes. After the shooting, her bosses insist she must go to Siena, Italy, on an assignment to meet with a woman named Cecilia Nicosa. Cecilia is Ana's half-sister, although they have never met, and the FBI wants Ana to trail Cecilia's husband on suspicion that he is part of a crime ring. In the meantime, the city of Siena is getting ready for an annual celebration and horse race. With the Italian landscape looming in the backdrop, Ana must uncover the leader of a deadly mafia ring before anyone else turns up dead—including her.

Where it's reviewed:
Booklist, May 1, 2011, page 39
Publishers Weekly, April 25, 2011, page 112

Other books by the same author:
Judas Horse, 2008
The Case of the Posturing Principal, 2006
The Case of the Mendacious Medicine Man, 2003
Good Morning, Killer, 2003
North of Montana, 1994

Other books you might like:
Dan Brown, *Angels and Demons*, 2000
Andrea Camilleri, *The Patience of the Spider*, 2007
Robert Crais, *L.A. Requiem*, 1999
Michael Dibdin, *And Then You Die*, 2002
Peter Watson, *Capo*, 1995

728

ROZ SOUTHEY

The Ladder Dancer

(Derby, United Kingdom: Creme de la Crime, 2011)

Series: Charles Patterson Series. Book 5
Story type: Historical
Subject(s): Detective fiction; Murder; Musicians
Major character(s): Charles Patterson, Musician, Detective—Amateur; Richard Nightingale, Entertainer

Mystery

(ladder dancer), Crime Victim
Time period(s): 18th century; 1730s (1736)
Locale(s): Newcastle-Upon-Tyne, United Kingdom

Summary: Charles Patterson is a harpsichordist and sometime-detective who finds himself enmeshed in a dangerous new case. After witnessing a young boy being run down by an out-of-control carriage, Patterson looks into the apparent hit-and-run. When Richard Nightingale—an entertainer known as a ladder dancer—comes to town, he too is attacked by a mysterious assailant. Now it's up to Patterson to figure out who is attacking the innocents of 18th-century Newcastle-Upon-Tyne. *The Ladder Dancer* is the fifth book in Roz Southey's Charles Patterson series.

Where it's reviewed:
Publishers Weekly, June 13, 2011, page 33

Other books by the same author:
Sword and Song, 2010
Secret Lament, 2009
Chords and Discords, 2008
Broken Harmony, 2007

Other books you might like:
Bruce Alexander, *Blind Justice*, 1994
Deryn Lake, *Death in the Dark Walk*, 1994
Janet Laurence, *Canaletto and the Case of the Westminster Bridge*, 1998
Fidelis Morgan, *Unnatural Fires*, 2000
Rosemary Stevens, *Death on a Silver Tray*, 2000

729

SALLY SPENCER

Backlash

(Sutton, Surrey, England: Severn House Publishers, 2011)

Series: Monika Paniatowski Mystery Series. Book 4
Story type: Mystery
Subject(s): Mystery; Murder; Kidnapping
Major character(s): Monika Paniatowski, Detective—Police; Tom Kershaw, Administrator (Police Chief Superintendent); Elaine Kershaw, Spouse; Grace Meade, Prostitute; Kate Meadows, Detective—Police
Time period(s): 1970s
Locale(s): Whitebridge, Scotland

Summary: Detective Chief Inspector Monica Paniatowski is back in *Backlash*, author Sally Spencer's fourth entry in her Monica Paniatowski series. Paniatowski's latest case begins as the department receives a frantic call from Chief Superintendent Tom Kershaw. He and his wife, Elaine, have just been in a car accident and now Elaine is missing. Much to Paniatowski's dismay, every available police resource is utilized in the search for Kersaw's wife, even at the expense of other cases. Annoyed by the unjustified response, Paniatowski decides to focus her attention on another case: that of missing prostitute Grace Meade. Despite orders to help find Elaine, Paniatowski quietly searches for Grace and soon finds some striking similarities in their dual disappearances, though the unexpected discovery of a mutilated body on the Scottish moors leaves her questioning whether she made the right choice.

Where it's reviewed:
Publishers Weekly, August 1, 2011, page 30

Other books by the same author:
Echoes of the Dead, 2010
The Ring of Death, 2010
The Dead Hand of History, 2009
Fatal Quest: Woodend's First Case, 2008
The Salton Killings, 1998

Other books you might like:
Deborah Crombie, *A Share in Death*, 1993
Cynthia Harrod-Eagles, *Orchestrated Death*, 1992
Veronica Heley, *Murder at the Altar*, 2000
Lynda La Plante, *Prime Suspect*, 1993
Val McDermid, *The Mermaids Singing*, 1995

730

MARY STANTON

Angel's Verdict

(New York: Berkley Publishing Group, 2011)

Series: Company Mystery Series. Book 4
Story type: Series
Subject(s): Afterlife; Mystery; Fantasy
Major character(s): Brianna "Bree" Winston-Beaufort, Lawyer; Justine Coville, Actress, Client (of Bree), Aged Person
Time period(s): 21st century; 2010s
Locale(s): United States

Summary: *Angel's Verdict*, a supernatural mystery, is the fourth installment in the Beaufort and Company series from author Mary Stanton. Intelligent and gifted lawyer Brianna "Bree" Winston-Beaufort has two very different groups of clients: earthly human clients in need of representation and condemned souls hoping to argue their way out of Hell and into Heaven. After a series of paranormal cases, Bree is anxious to get back to her "regular" job working among the living. When actress Justine Coville hires Bree to change her will, it seems like a standard job, but it isn't long until Justine's case leads Bree to an otherworldly client desperate to change her eternal sentence.

Other books by the same author:
Avenging Angels, 2010
Angel's Advocate, 2009
Defending Angels, 2008
By Fire, By Moonlight, 1999
The Heavenly Horse from the Outermost West, 1988

Other books you might like:
Nancy Atherton, *Aunt Dimity and the Family Tree*, 2011
Mignon F. Ballard, *An Angel to Die For*, 2000
Annette Blair, *Death by Diamonds*, 2010
E.J. Copperman, *An Uninvited Ghost*, 2011
Tanya Huff, *The Enchantment Emporium*, 2009

731

CHEVY STEVENS

Never Knowing

(New York: St. Martin's Press, 2011)

Subject(s): Adoption; Parent-child relations; Serial murders
Major character(s): Sara Gallagher, Antiques Dealer; Nadine, Psychologist
Time period(s): 21st century; 2010s
Locale(s): United States

Summary: Sara Gallagher is searching for her birth parents. Her life finally seems to be in order, and she's ready to tie together the missing strings of her past. But her biological mother wants nothing to do with her, and, even more shocking, is the knowledge that her birth father is a serial killer. With the aid of her therapist Nadine, Sara attempts to put the ghosts of the past to rest once and for all—if her father doesn't find her first. Chevy Stevens's *Never Knowing* is the sequel to *Still Missing*.

Where it's reviewed:
Booklist, May 1, 2011, page 33
Library Journal, July 2011, page 74
Publishers Weekly, May 2, 2011, page 34

Other books by the same author:
Still Missing, 2010

Other books you might like:
Kate Atkinson, *When Will There Be Good News?: A Novel*, 2008
Gillian Flynn, *Dark Places*, 2009
Lisa Gardner, *Alone*, 2005
Jennifer McMahon, *Promise Not to Tell*, 2006
Lisa Unger, *Black Out*, 2008

732

KAREN HANSON STUYCK

Do You Remember Me Now?

(Detroit, Michigan: Gale Cengage Learning, 2011)

Story type: Revenge
Subject(s): Plastic surgery; Bullying; High schools
Major character(s): Megan Edwards, Friend (of Todd, Josh, and Allison); Allison James, Friend (of Megan, Josh, and Todd); Todd Lawson, Friend (of Megan, Josh, and Allison); Josh Edwards, Friend (of Megan, Allison, and Todd), Doctor (plastic surgeon); Jane "Kate Dalton" Murphy, Classmate (of Megan, Allison, Josh, and Todd, former), Doctor (plastic surgeon)
Time period(s): 21st century; 2010s
Locale(s): Dallas, Texas

Summary: In Karen Hanson Stuyck's *Do You Remember Me Now?*, an unknown killer is picking off former members of a high-school clique one by one. Jane Murphy, who now goes by the name Kate Dalton, was not a member of "The Six," but she was a victim of one of the

notorious group's most malicious acts. Megan Edwards, Allison James, Todd Lawson, Josh Edwards, and other Sixers routinely bullied classmates at their Dallas high school who threatened their own social status. Jane was tricked into a sexual encounter with Todd that resulted in a complicated pregnancy that left her permanently barren. Now "Plain Jane" is a beautiful plastic surgeon whose return to Dallas coincides with the murders of Allison, Megan, and Todd.

Where it's reviewed:
Booklist, May 1, 2011, page 20

Other books by the same author:
A Novel Way to Die, 2008
Fit to Die, 2006
Lethal Lessons, 1997
Held Accountable, 1996
Cry for Help, 1995

Other books you might like:
Laurie Halse Anderson, *Twisted*, 2007
Tom Franklin, *Crooked Letter, Crooked Letter*, 2010
Pam Lewis, *Speak Softly, She Can Hear*, 2005
Laura Lippman, *To the Power of Three*, 2005
Jodi Picoult, *Nineteen Minutes: A Novel*, 2007

733

DUANE SWIERCZYNSKI

Fun and Games

(New York: Little, Brown & Co., 2011)

Story type: Police Procedural
Subject(s): Law enforcement; Actors; Assassination
Major character(s): Charlie Hardie, Police Officer (former); Lane, Actress
Time period(s): 21st century; 2010s
Locale(s): Los Angeles, California

Summary: *Fun and Games* is a novel by author Duane Swierczynski. After Charlie Hardie's best friend and ex-colleague—and his whole family—is murdered, the victims of a vengeance plot, Charlie decides to quit the force. He goes into hiding and begins watching houses for people while they are away. One night while house-sitting, he comes across an actress named Lane, who thinks that Charlie is there to murder her. It turns out that Lane has a few vendettas against her, and Charlie is the only one who can protect her. But does Charlie want to relive the pain he felt after the death of his best friend and the people he loved? Swierczynski is also the author of *Hell and Gone* and *Expiration Date*.

Where it's reviewed:
Booklist, May 1, 2011, page 25
Publishers Weekly, April 18, 2011, page 30

Other books by the same author:
X-Men Curse of the Mutants, 2011
Cable Volume 3 Stranded, 2010
Dark Prophesy, 2010
Expiration Date, 2010
Level 26: Dark Origins, 2009
X-Force/Cable: Messiah War, 2009
Severance Package, 2007

Mystery

The Blonde, 2006
Secret Dead Men, 2005
The Wheelman, 2005

Other books you might like:
Christa Faust, *Money Shot*, 2008
Victor Gischler, *Gun Monkeys*, 2003
Gregg Hurwitz, *The Crime Writer*, 2007
Terrill Lee Lankford, *Earthquake Weather*, 2004
Newton Thornburg, *Cutter and Bone*, 1976

734

MARCIA TALLEY

A Quiet Death

(New York: Severn House Publishers, 2011)

Series: Hannah Ives Series. Book 6
Story type: Contemporary; Series
Subject(s): Detective fiction; Accidents; Love
Major character(s): Hannah Ives, Detective
Time period(s): 21st century; 2010s
Locale(s): Washington, District of Columbia; Annapolis, Maryland

Summary: *A Quiet Death* is the sixth book in Marcia Talley's Hannah Ives Mysteries series and features the investigative adventures of a determined female sleuth. Hannah is on the train back to Annapolis after a charity event in Washington, D.C. When the train is involved in a crash, Hannah escapes with a broken arm—and a shopping bag belonging to the man who was seated next to her. She is intent on returning the bag to its rightful owner, but as she looks through it, she unearths evidence of a decade-long affair between a woman named Lilith Chaloux and a married man. Uncovering the details surrounding the affair, Hannah and her best intentions are put in harm's way as it slowly dawns on her that someone does not want her snooping around—and will do anything to stop her.

Other books by the same author:
All Things Undying, 2010
In Death's Shadow, 2004
Occasion of Revenge, 2001
Unbreathed Memories, 2000
Sing it To Her Bones, 1999

Other books you might like:
Ellen Byerrum, *Killer Hair*, 2003
Laura Durham, *Better Off Wed*, 2005
Julie Hyzy, *State of the Onion*, 2008
Margaret Truman, *Murder at the Kennedy Center*, 1989
P.G. Wodehouse, *The Butler Did It*, 1953

735

MARK TERRY

The Valley of Shadows

(Longboat Key, Florida: Oceanview Publishing, 2011)

Story type: Contemporary
Subject(s): Detective fiction; Suspense; Terrorism

Major character(s): Derek Stillwater, Agent (Homeland Security); Cassandra O'Reilly, Expert (nuclear weapons); Miraj "Kalakar" Khan, Art Historian, Terrorist
Time period(s): 21st century; 2010s
Locale(s): Pakistan; Los Angeles, California

Summary: Mark Terry's *The Valley of Shadows* follows Homeland Security agent Derek Stillwater's investigation into a potentially devastating terrorist plot. Computers recovered from a location in Pakistan have revealed that a coordinated five-city attack has been planned for the day of the U.S. general election. Stillwater teams up with Cassandra O'Reilly, a nuclear-weapons expert with whom he has a rocky history, to foil the plot. As the appointed day draws near, Stillwater begins to realize that the attack plan they've been investigating may be a decoy to keep them away from the real plan devised by the terrorist known as Kalakar.

Where it's reviewed:
Booklist, May 1, 2011, page   40
Publishers Weekly, April 4, 2011, page   34

Other books by the same author:
The Fallen, 2010
Angels Falling, 2008
The Serpent's Kiss, 2007
The Devil's Pitchfork, 2006
Dirty Deeds, 2004

Other books you might like:
Vince Flynn, *Transfer of Power*, 1999
Brian Haig, *Secret Sanction*, 2001
Mike Lawson, *The Inside Ring*, 2005
Joel Rosenberg, *The Last Jihad: A Novel*, 2002
Brad Thor, *The Lions of Lucerne*, February 27, 2007

736

VICTORIA THOMPSON

Murder on Sisters' Row

(New York: Berkley/Penguin USA, 2011)

Series: Gaslight Mystery Series. Book
Story type: Amateur Detective; Historical
Subject(s): Mystery; Murder; Prostitution
Major character(s): Sarah Brandt, Midwife; Amy Cunningham, Mother, Prostitute; Rowena Walker, Madam; Frank Malloy, Police Officer
Time period(s): 19th century
Locale(s): New York, New York

Summary: In author Victoria Thompson's *Murder on Sisters' Row*, midwife Sarah Brandt is called to what turns out to be a brothel to attend to Amy Cunningham, a young mother-to-be and prostitute, as she struggles to give birth to her new son. Once the child is born, Amy asks Sarah to help her escape from the brothel and the tight grasp of her demanding madam. Agreeing to help the poor girl, Sarah seeks out the assistance of Rahab's Daughters, a local charity dedicated to rescuing young women from a life of prostitution. Unfortunately, things take a dark turn when Sarah and Amy's association with Rahab's Daughters leads to a murder. Despite the protests of her police sergeant boyfriend, Sarah is determined to

bring the killer to justice herself.

Where it's reviewed:
The Denver Post, July 3, 2011, page   E-09
Publishers Weekly, April 25, 2011, page   118

Other books by the same author:
Murder on Lexington Avenue, 2010
Murder on Washington Square, 2002
Murder on Gramercy Park, 2001
Murder on St. Mark's Place, 2000
Murder on Astor Place, 1999

Other books you might like:
C.S. Harris, *What Angels Fear*, 2005
Anne Perry, *The Cater Street Hangman*, 1979
Anne Perry, *The Face of a Stranger*, 1990
Deanna Raybourn, *Silent in the Grave*, 2007
Charles Todd, *A Test of Wills*, 1996

737

RONALD TIERNEY

Good to the Last Kiss

(Sutton, England: Severn House Publishers, 2011)

Story type: Police Procedural; Series
Subject(s): Mystery; Detective fiction; Serial murders
Major character(s): Vincent Gratelli, Detective—Police
(inspector); Mickey McClellan, Detective—Police
(inspector), Colleague (partner of Gratelli); Julia
Bateman, Detective—Private, Crime Victim; Bay
Strangler, Murderer
Time period(s): 21st century; 2010s
Locale(s): San Francisco, California

Summary: In the mystery novel *Good to the Last Kiss* by
Ronald Tierney, a killer is on the loose in the San
Francisco Bay area. He likes to strangle women and
mark them with a rose tattoo. Inspector Vincent Gratelli
and his partner, Inspector Mickey McClellan, have been
assigned to the disturbing case. Leads are scarce until
private detective Julia Bateman falls victim to the "Bay
Strangler" and survives. As Bateman recovers from her
injuries, Gratelli and McClellan pursue her deranged
attacker. Meanwhile, public officials struggle to control
the fear that has gripped the city. *Good to the Last Kiss*
is the first book in the Crimes of the Depraved Mind
series.

Where it's reviewed:
Publishers Weekly, June 20, 2011, page   38

Other books by the same author:
Bullet Beach, 2010
Death in Pacific Heights, 2009
Eclipse of the Heart, 1993
The Stone Veil, 1990
Death in North Beach

Other books you might like:
Chelsea Cain, *Heartsick*, 2007
Lisa Gardner, *Alone*, 2005
Alex Kava, *A Perfect Evil*, 2001
James Patterson, *Kiss the Girls*, 1995
Karin Slaughter, *Faithless*, 2005

738

MARGARET TRUMAN

Monument to Murder

(New York: Forge, 2011)

Series: Capital Crimes Series. Book 25
Story type: Private Detective
Subject(s): Murder; Mystery; Suspense
Major character(s): Robert Brixton, Police Officer
(former), Detective—Private; Mackensie Smith,
Lawyer, Spouse (of Annabel); Annabel Lee Smith,
Lawyer (former), Spouse (of Mackensie)
Time period(s): 21st century; 2010s
Locale(s): Savannah, Georgia

Summary: *Monument to Murder*, a suspenseful mystery
novel, is the 25th installment in the Capital Crimes series
from author Margaret Truman. Business is slow for
police officer-turned-private investigator Robert Brixton
so when a woman comes to him to dig up dirt on a
decades-old case, he decides to give it a shot. Eunice
Watkins wants Brixton to clear the name of her daughter,
a young woman who did prison time and was ultimately
gunned down two decades earlier for a crime she didn't
commit. Teaming up with former attorneys, Mackensie
and Annabel Lee Smith, Brixton begins uncovering a
major political conspiracy and a secret organization that's
been committing murders and hiding secrets since the
assassination of JFK.

Where it's reviewed:
Booklist, June 1, 2011, page   42
Publishers Weekly, May 9, 2011, page   34

Other books by the same author:
Murder Inside the Beltway, 2008
Murder in the Supreme Court, 1981
Murder on Capitol Hill, 1981
Murder in the White House, 1980
My Own Story, 1956

Other books you might like:
David Baldacci, *Split Second*, 2003
Julie Hyzy, *State of the Onion*, 2008
Richard North Patterson, *The Lasko Tangent*, 1979
Elliott Roosevelt, *Murder and the First Lady*, 1984
Stuart Woods, *Grass Roots*, 1989

739

STEVE ULFELDER

Purgatory Chasm

(New York: Minotaur Books, 2011)

Story type: Adventure; Mystery
Subject(s): Mystery; Murder; Automobiles
Major character(s): Conway Sax, Mechanic; Tander Phigg,
Friend (Member of the Barnburners AA Group)
Time period(s): 21st century; 2010s
Locale(s): Massachusetts, United States; New Hampshire,
United States

Mystery

Summary: In author Steve Ulfelder's *Purgatory Chasm*, ex-con mechanic Conway Sax is a recovering alcoholic who once found support in his quest for sobriety in an Alcoholics Anonymous group known as the Barnburners. Over the years, he has repaid the group by doing a variety of odd jobs for them. When one of the Barnburners, Tander Phigg, asks Sax to help him reclaim a Mercedes-Benz he left with a garage in New Hampshire for repairs that never happened, Sax finds himself in the middle of a murder mystery. Attacked and knocked unconscious at the garage, Sax soon learns that Phigg is dead and he is the chief suspect in his friend's demise. Forced to solve the murder and prove his own innocence, Sax must confront an unknown enemy, as well as his own sordid past.

Where it's reviewed:
Booklist, April 1, 2011, page 34
Library Journal, May 1, 2011, page 62
Publishers Weekly, March 21, 2011, page 58

Other books you might like:
Jodi Compton, *Hailey's War*, 2010
Peter Craig, *Blood Father*, 2005
Bryan Gruley, *Starvation Lake*, 2009
Steve Hamilton, *A Cold Day in Paradise*, 1998
Barbara Seranella, *No Human Involved*, 1997

740

MICHAEL VAN ROOY

Your Friendly Neighborhood Criminal

(New York: Minotaur Books, 2011)

Story type: Contemporary
Subject(s): Crime; Refugees; Suspense
Major character(s): Montgomery "Monty" Haaviko, Criminal (former), Spouse (of Claire); Claire, Spouse (of Monty); Marie Blue Duck, Activist; Samantha Richot, Criminal; Hershel "Smiley" Wiebe, Criminal
Time period(s): 21st century; 2010s
Locale(s): Canada; United States

Summary: A former criminal takes a job spiriting refugees across the U.S. border in the novel *Your Friendly Neighborhood Criminal*. Montgomery "Monty" Haaviko has left his criminal past behind him to run a daycare center and live a quiet life with his wife, Claire. His plans for the future are suddenly derailed when Canadian activist Marie Blue Duck asks for his assistance in setting up a secret route to help refugees flee to America. Monty can hardly refuse the money Marie offers, and he agrees to her plan. Things take a turn for the worse when local criminal Samantha Richot tries to take over the route and one of Monty's old prison acquaintances shows up.

Where it's reviewed:
Booklist, June 1, 2011, page 45
Publishers Weekly, May 16, 2011, page 54

Other books by the same author:
An Ordinary Decent Criminal, 2010

Other books you might like:
Josh Bazell, *Beat the Reaper*, 2009
Lawrence Block, *Burglars Can't Be Choosers*, 1977
Tod Goldberg, *Burn Notice: The Fix*, 2008
Steve Hamilton, *The Lock Artist*, 2010
Barbara Seranella, *No Human Involved*, 1997

741

KATHRYN R. WALL

Jericho Cay

(New York: Minotaur Books, 2011)

Series: Bay Tanner Series. Book 11
Story type: Private Detective; Series
Subject(s): Detective fiction; Missing persons; Southern United States
Major character(s): Bay Tanner, Detective—Private, Spouse (of Red); Red, Spouse (of Bay), Lawman (former sheriff's deputy); Winston Wolfe, Writer, Client (of Bay); Morgan Tyler Bell, Wealthy (missing person); Terry Gerard, Assistant (to Bell); Anjanette Freeman, Housekeeper (to Bell)
Time period(s): 21st century; 2010s
Locale(s): Jericho Cay, South Carolina

Summary: In *Jericho Cay* by Kathryn Wall, a hurricane has left the South Carolina home of private detective Bay Tanner in need of serious repairs. When crime author Winston Wolfe offers her a lucrative case, Bay takes it on despite the risks involved. Wolfe is investigating a cold missing-persons case involving the very wealthy Morgan Tyler Bell. Wolfe doesn't believe that Bell is missing at all; he thinks the millionaire is posing as his assistant, Terry Gerard. As Bay and her husband Red investigate Wolfe's theory, they find connections between Bell's supposed disappearance and the suicide of his housekeeper, Anjanette Freeman. They also find a lot more trouble than they bargained for. *Jericho Cay* is the 11th book in Wall's Bay Tanner series.

Where it's reviewed:
Booklist, May 1, 2011, page 31
Publishers Weekly, March 7, 2011, page 47

Other books by the same author:
Canaan's Gate, 2010
Judas Island, 2004
Perdition House, 2003
And Not a Penny More, 2002
In for a Penny, 2000

Other books you might like:
Mary Kay Andrews, *Savannah Blues*, 2002
Linda Barnes, *A Trouble of Fools*, 1987
Sophie Littlefield, *A Bad Day for Sorry*, 2009
Margaret Maron, *Bootlegger's Daughter*, 1992
Katy Munger, *Legwork*, 1997

742

AMANDA EYRE WARD

Close Your Eyes

(New York: Random House, 2011)

Story type: Family Saga
Subject(s): Murder; Family; Crime
Major character(s): Lauren Mahdian, Sister (of Alex);
Alex Mahdian, Brother (of Lauren)

Summary: *Close Your Eyes* is a novel by author Amanda Eyre Ward. In it, Ward tells the story of Lauren Mahdian, an upper-middle-class girl who led an idyllic life on Long Island with her family until the night her mother was murdered and her father was charged for the crime. For years, Lauren's only familial connection has been with her brother, Alex, who has acted as her confidante as well as her guardian. They share the same memories of that horrific night, and Alex seems to be the only one that Lauren can trust. Yet when Lauren learns that Alex has been in touch with their father, who is still in prison, she feels nothing but betrayed. Alex argues that there might more to the mystery of her mother's death than meets the eye. The question is, does Lauren believe him?

Where it's reviewed:
Booklist, May 15, 2011, page   15
Library Journal, June 1, 2011, page   95
Publishers Weekly, April 25, 2011, page   106

Other books by the same author:
Love Stories in this Town, 2009
Forgive Me, 2007
How to Be Lost, 2004
Sleep Toward Heaven, 2003

Other books you might like:
Gillian Flynn, *Dark Places*, 2009
Tana French, *Faithful Place*, 2011
Pam Lewis, *Perfect Family*, 2008
Laura Lippman, *Life Sentences*, 2009
Jennifer McMahon, *Promise Not to Tell*, 2006

743

S.J. WATSON

Before I Go To Sleep

(New York: Harper, 2011)

Subject(s): Psychology; Memory disorders; Psychiatry
Major character(s): Christine, Writer, Amnesiac, Crime Victim, Spouse (of Ben); Ben, Spouse (of Christine)
Time period(s): 21st century; 2010s

Summary: *Before I Go To Sleep* is a psychological thriller from debut author S.J. Watson. Due to a traumatic attack that occurred in her mid-20s, 47-year-old Christine suffers from a severe and rare form of amnesia, prohibiting her from retaining memories for more than a day. Every morning she awakes, expecting to be a young, single woman, only to find a strange man in her bed who claims to be her husband Ben. Christine's doctor, in an effort to help cure her, has encouraged her to start a journal to

piece together fragments of her memories. As Christine puts the pieces together, she makes a shocking discovery about her past and her future that has massive ramifications for everyone around her. First novel.

Where it's reviewed:
Booklist, March 15, 2011, page   24
Financial Times, April 16, 2011, page   15
Library Journal, May 1, 2011, page   78
Publishers Weekly, May 2, 2011, page   38

Other books you might like:
Peter Abraham, *Oblivion*, 2005
G.H. Ephron, *Amnesia*, 2000
Tana French, *The Likeness*, 2008
Gregg Hurwitz, *The Crime Writer*, 2007
Marcus Sakey, *The Two Deaths of Daniel Hayes*, 2011

744

JAN MERETE WEISS

These Dark Things

(New York: Soho Crime, 2011)

Series: Captain Natalia Monte Series
Story type: Mystery
Subject(s): Murder; Mystery; Organized crime
Major character(s): Natalia Monte, Detective; Teresa Steiner, Student—Graduate; Pino Loriano, Police Officer; Aldo Gambini, Organized Crime Figure
Time period(s): 21st century; 2010s
Locale(s): Naples, Italy

Summary: In author Jan Merete Weiss's *These Dark Things*, Captain Natalia Monte of the Carabinieri is summoned to the scene of a brutal murder. Teresa Steiner, a young German graduate student, was found stabbed to death in the catacombs of a monastery and it's up to Monte to track down her killer. As the investigation unfolds, Monte encounters a seemingly unending parade of potential suspects that includes a monk, a professor Teresa was having an affair with, and a powerful member of the local mafia. Monte's search for the truth is further complicated by an ongoing battle between feuding crime families embroiled in a dispute over garbage-hauling contracts that leaves the city stewing in its own filth. Will she be able to find justice for Teresa or will she simply get lost in a messy web of suspects and rubbish?

Where it's reviewed:
Booklist, May 1, 2011, page   39
Library Journal, May 1, 2011, page   62
Publishers Weekly, March 28, 2011, page   39

Other books you might like:
Andrea Camilleri, *The Shape of Water*, 2002
Michael Dibdin, *Ratking*, 1989
Michele Giuttari, *A Florentine Death*, 2007
David Hewson, *A Season for the Dead*, 2004
Donna Leon, *Death at La Fenice*, 1992

Mystery

745

MICHAEL WILEY

A Bad Night's Sleep

(New York: Minotaur Books, 2011)

Series: Joseph Kozmarski Series. Book 3
Story type: Private Detective; Series
Subject(s): Detective fiction; Mystery; Crime
Major character(s): Joe Kozmarski, Detective—Private
Time period(s): 21st century; 2010s
Locale(s): Chicago, Illinois

Summary: In Michael Wiley's *A Bad Night's Sleep*, Chicago private detective Joe Kozmarksi is working on a simple surveillance assignment for Southshore Corporation when he is drawn into a major case of police corruption. Kozmarski is supposed to find out who's been stealing copper wire from Southshore's construction sites, which he does, but some of the crooks turn out to be members of the Chicago Police Department. When a shootout breaks out at the scene and Kozmarski kills one of the officers, he tries to make amends with the authorities by playing undercover agent. *A Bad Night's Sleep* is the third book in the Joseph Kozmarski series.

Where it's reviewed:
Publishers Weekly, March 28, 2011, page 39

Other books by the same author:
The Bad Kitty Lounge, 2010
The Last Striptease, 2007

Other books you might like:
Sean Chercover, *Big City, Bad Blood*, 2007
Steve Hamilton, *A Cold Day in Paradise*, 1998
Michael Harvey, *The Chicago Way*, 2007
Thomas Kaufman, *Drink the Tea*, 2010
John Verdon, *Think of a Number: A Novel*, 2010

746

AMANDA KYLE WILLIAMS

The Stranger You Seek

(New York: Bantam Books, 2011)

Story type: Serial Killer
Subject(s): Mystery; Detective fiction; Serial murders
Major character(s): Aaron Rauser, Police Officer (lieutenant); Keye Street, Detective—Private, FBI Agent (former); Neil, Computer Expert (hacker), Colleague (of Keye)
Time period(s): 21st century; 2010s
Locale(s): Atlanta, Georgia

Summary: In the mystery novel *The Stranger You Seek* by Amanda Kyle Williams, the city of Atlanta is being terrorized by a vicious serial murderer. Police lieutenant Aaron Rauser is on the hunt for the man the press has dubbed the Wishbone Killer, but he needs the help of an expert. Unfortunately, the profiler Rauser wants—Keye Street—was fired from her FBI job because of her alcoholism. Now working as a private detective, Street is not exactly welcome at the Atlanta Police Department.

Keye hasn't lost her touch, but as she uses her skills to track the killer, she discovers that she may soon become a victim.

Where it's reviewed:
Publishers Weekly, August 1, 2011, page 24

Other books you might like:
Chelsea Cain, *Heartsick*, 2007
Alex Kava, *A Perfect Evil*, 2001
Carol O'Connell, *Mallory's Oracle*, 1994
James Patterson, *Along Came a Spider: A Novel*, 1993
Karin Slaughter, *Blindsighted*, 2001

747

DON WINSLOW

The Gentlemen's Hour

(London: William Heinemann, 2011)

Story type: Contemporary
Subject(s): Surfing; Mystery; Detective fiction
Major character(s): Boone Daniels, Detective—Private, Surfer; Kelly Kuhio, Surfer; Petra Hall, Lawyer, Girlfriend (of Boone); Corey Blasingame, 19-Year-Old, Surfer
Time period(s): 21st century; 2010s
Locale(s): San Diego, California

Summary: In the novel *The Gentlemen's Hour* by Don Winslow, Boone Daniels is a member of the Dawn Patrol, a group of dedicated surfers who hit the waves off the San Diego coast each morning. Daniels is also a private investigator. When a prominent figure in the local surfing community is killed, Daniels can't help but get involved. Corey Blasingame, a teenager, skinhead, and surfer, is named as a suspect, and his lawyer (who is also Boone's girlfriend) persuades Boone to dig up evidence supporting the young man's innocence. Daniels's investigation leads him to the dark corners of San Diego and puts him at odds with the Dawn Patrol.

Where it's reviewed:
Library Journal, June 1, 2011, page 95
Library Journal, June 1, 2011, page 95
Publishers Weekly, June 20, 2011, page 31

Other books by the same author:
The Dawn Patrol, 2008
The Power of the Dog, 2005
California Fire and Life, 1999
While Drowning in the Desert, 1996
A Cool Breeze on the Underground, 1991

Other books you might like:
Jan Burke, *Bloodlines*, 2005
Kem Nunn, *Tapping the Source*, 1984
Kem Nunn, *Tijuana Straits*, 2004
T. Jefferson Parker, *Laguna Heat*, 1985
Jeff Shelby, *Killer Swell*, 2005

748

BRIAN M. WIPRUD

Ringer

(New York: Minotaur Books, 2011)

Story type: Contemporary
Subject(s): Adventure; Suspense; Crime
Major character(s): Morty Martinez, Wealthy, Crime Suspect; Robert Tyson Grant, Wealthy (tycoon); Gomez Entropica, Religious (priest); Purity, Stepdaughter (of Grant)
Time period(s): 21st century; 2010s
Locale(s): California, United States; New York, New York

Summary: Brian M. Wiprud's *Ringer* is narrated by Morty Martinez, a wealthy man sitting on death row and awaiting his impending execution. He tells the story of how he got to this point in his life—a story filled with corruption, crime, and murder. Morty was recruited to find an ancient stolen ring that was discovered on the hand of noted tycoon Robert Tyson Grant. As he set out to retrieve the precious object, he got caught in a family feud between Grant and his media-hungry stepdaughter. The quest for the ring grew even more complicated when Grant's social-climbing girlfriend, a hateful psychic, and a trigger-happy assassin became involved. And, stuck in the crosshairs of this spiteful feud, Morty lands in jail with his head on the chopping block. Is it too late for Morty Martinez to clear his name and recover the ring?

Where it's reviewed:
Booklist, May 1, 2011, page   38
Publishers Weekly, May 2, 2011, page   37

Other books by the same author:
Tailed, 2007
Crooked, 2006
Stuffed, 2005
Pipsqueak, 2001
Sleep with the Fishes, 2000

Other books you might like:
Tim Dorsey, *Florida Roadkill*, 1999
Carl Hiaasen, *Double Whammy*, 1987
Marshall Karp, *The Rabbit Factory: A Novel*, 2006
David Rosenfelt, *Open and Shut*, 2002
Duane Swierczynski, *Fun and Games*, 2011

749

REAVIS Z. WORTHAM

The Rock Hole

(Scottsdale, Arizona: Poisoned Pen Press, 2011)

Story type: Historical
Subject(s): Serial murders; Rural life; Crime
Major character(s): Ned Parker, Farmer, Lawman (constable), Spouse (of Becky), Grandfather (of Top and Pepper); John Washington, Lawman (deputy sheriff); O.C. Rains, Judge, Friend (of Ned); Top, 10-Year-Old, Grandson (of Ned and Becky), Cousin (of Pepper); Pepper, Girl, Granddaughter (of Ned and Becky), Cousin (of Top); Becky Parker, Spouse (of Ned), Grandmother (of Top and Pepper); Joseph, Cousin (of Ned)
Time period(s): 20th century; 1960s (1964)
Locale(s): Center Springs, Texas

Summary: Set in 1964 Center Springs, Texas, Reavis Wortham's *The Rock Hole* pits a small-town constable against a sadistic serial killer. The first victim Constable Ned Parker sees is a small animal, but the method of its mutilation makes Parker take notice. As the killings increase and the murderer claims his first human victim, the Parker family—Ned, his wife Becky, and young grandchildren Top and Pepper—realize that an evil has settled in their Lamar County community. Constable Parker and Deputy Sheriff John Washington consider a range of suspects and motives, until the identity of the killer is revealed as someone they know. But before the case is closed, the serial killer known as "The Skinner" will set his sights on the Parkers.

Where it's reviewed:
Library Journal, May 1, 2011, page   62
Publishers Weekly, April 18, 2011, page   37

Other books you might like:
James Lee Burke, *The Neon Rain*, 1987
Tom Franklin, *Crooked Letter, Crooked Letter*, 2010
Joe R. Lansdale, *The Bottoms*, 2000
Ben Rehder, *Buck Fever*, 2002
Rick Riordan, *Big Red Tequila*, 1997

750

RICHARD ZIMLER

The Warsaw Anagrams

(New York: The Overlook Press, 2011)

Story type: Historical
Subject(s): World War II, 1939-1945; Jews; Murder
Major character(s): Erik Cohen, Doctor (psychiatrist), Uncle (of Stefa and Adam), Prisoner (Nazi labor camp); Heniek Corben, Friend (of Cohen); Stefa, Niece (of Cohen); Adam, Nephew (of Cohen); Benjamin Schrei, Leader (Jewish Council representative)
Time period(s): 20th century; 1940s
Locale(s): Warsaw, Poland

Summary: In the novel *The Warsaw Anagrams* by Richard Zimler, the Warsaw ghettos created by the Nazis hold a unique horror for an old man named Erik Cohen. Cohen, a psychiatrist, has brought his nephew Adam and niece Stefa to live with him in the ghetto in anticipation of the Nazis' orders. But it isn't the Germans who inflict pain on Cohen, it is the disappearance of Adam and the subsequent discovery of his murdered and mutilated body. As Cohen tracks down Adam's killer, who may be among the ghetto's Jewish residents, his new friend Heniek Corben tries to make sense of the psychiatrist's strange story.

Where it's reviewed:
Booklist, July 1, 2011, page   37
Publishers Weekly, May 23, 2011, page   30
San Francisco Chronicle, August 15, 2011, page   FE-4

Mystery

Other books by the same author:
The Seventh Gate, 2007
Guardian of the Dawn, 2005
Hunting Midnight, 2003
The Last Kabbalist of Lisbon, 1997
Unholy Ghosts, 1996

Other books you might like:
Diane Ackerman, *The Zookeeper's Wife: A War Story*, 2007
Katherine Neville, *The Eight*, 1988
Gunnar S Paulson, *Secret City: The Hidden Jews of Warsaw*, 2003
Leon Uris, *Mila 18*, 1961
Robert Wilson, *A Small Death in Lisbon*, 2000

751

ANNE ZOUROUDI

The Taint of Midas

(New York: Bloomsbury, 2011)

Story type: Contemporary - Exotic; Series
Subject(s): Mystery; Detective fiction; Greek history
Major character(s): Gabrilis Kaloyeros, Beekeeper; Hermes Diaktoros, Detective—Amateur
Time period(s): 21st century; 2000s
Locale(s): Arcadia, Greece

Summary: In the novel *The Taint of Midas* by Anne Zouroudi, amateur detective Hermes Diaktoros investigates the suspicious death of Gabrilis Kaloyeros. A beekeeper on the Greek island of Arcadia and a steward of the Temple of Apollo, Kaloyeros had recently fallen victim to shady real-estate dealers operating in the region. Soon after, he was struck by a car and killed. Hermes Diaktoros, known as "the fat man," believes that the beekeeper was murdered and uses his own style of detection to find the killer and win justice for Kaloyeros. *The Taint of Midas* is the second book in the Greek Detective series.

Where it's reviewed:
Library Journal, May 1, 2011, page 62
Publishers Weekly, May 16, 2011, page 58

Other books by the same author:
The Messenger of Athens, 2010

Other books you might like:
Andrea Camilleri, *The Shape of Water*, 2002
Emma Lathen, *When in Greece*, 1969
Donna Leon, *Death at La Fenice*, 1992
Louise Penny, *Still Life*, 2006
Jeffrey Siger, *Murder in Mykonos*, 2009

Romance Fiction in Review
by
Kristin Ramsdell

"Romance has been elegantly defined as the offspring of fiction and love."

—Benjamin Disraeli

"Turbulence is a life force. It is opportunity. Let's love turbulence and use it for change."

—Ramsay Clark

The bumpy digital ride for romance (and publishing, in general) continues as authors and publishers struggle to come to terms with new technologies, keep up with the ever-increasing changes, and meet related reader expectations and demands—all while trying to see into the future and predict where the technological juggernaut is headed. (And this doesn't even take into consideration outside events such as floods, fires, hurricanes, earthquakes, riots, wars, political turmoil, as well as one of the bleakest economic outlooks in years—all of which have caused vast amounts of turbulence for many of us, although in different ways.) In general, we've done rather well, so far. After all, most of us in the writing and library worlds have been using technology in some form for years and, in most cases, we have adapted and embraced the changes. Who, for example, would want to go back to carbon paper, card catalogs, or floppy disks?

But the innovative pace is picking up, and as it does, its direction is not always predictable. Will we all be reading books exclusively on our smart phones next year? Will mass market paperbacks go the way of the Great Auk? Will writers abandon traditional publishers and go the e-self-publishing route? Will readers tire of tiny screens and go back to hard copy? Granted, all this uncertainty can be a bit unnerving. In fact, it's the uncertainty that is usually worse than the change itself. But it's all part of the current turbulent environment—and to paraphrase Clark, turbulence is opportunity and a chance to change. It's a gift, actually, and with any luck, we'll risk the tumult and find a way to use it to our advantage.

A Mid Year Perspective

Like 2010 before it, 2011 is shaping up to be another banner year for e-books. According to Bowker's Pub-Track service, for the first quarter of 2011, e-book sales more than doubled from the comparable quarter in 2010 (6.4% from 1.6%) and accounted for 12.9% of units sold (also an increase), with online retailers were scooping up a larger and larger share of the market. (Milliot, Jim. "Online Retailers Steam Ahead," *Piublishers Weekly*, August, 1, 2011, pp. 4–6.) On the other hand, According to Nielsen's BookScan, the unit sales of print titles during the first half of 2011, dropped by 10.2%, with adult fiction suffering the steepest loss and 25.7% for the same period. Mass market paperbacks took the biggest hit and fell 26.6%. (Jim Milliot, "Print Units Drop 10% in First Half of 2011," *Publishers Weekly*, July 11, 2011, p. 4.) Clearly, e-books are quickly making inroads and taking share away from print, especially in the mass market format, which would include a large share of romance titles.

In addition to the fact that publishers are increasingly releasing titles in e-formats, as e-originals or in conjunction with print, a number of authors have discovered the advantages of electronic self-publishing. With the advent of simplified publishing tools, writers are retrieving rights to their backlists (when they can) and releasing them themselves as e-books. They are also writing and publishing new books in the same way. There are many reasons for doing this—and it is a mixed blessing—but authors do get to keep more of their profits, which is a definite upside in many cases. It will be interesting to see where this takes the industry and the romance genre.

Another example of tech's growing influence is the rapid adoption of e-galleys by publishers and, in some cases, review sources. Many publishers are already making their pre-pub galleys available via NetGalley, and while not all reviewers are willing or able to go this route, with the growth in the e-original market, there will be no choice for some titles. On the same topic, *Publishers Weekly* recently announced that it would accept Romance and Science Fiction/Fantasy/Horror e-galleys for review. ("'PW' Accepting E-galleys for Sci-Fi/Romance," *Publishers Weekly* (Online), September 14, 2011.)

But technology isn't the only interesting thing going on in the genre. As mentioned in earlier essays, the academic community is finally waking up to the scholarly potential of popular romance fiction, and Eric Selinger's excellent article in the September 2011 issue of *RWR: Romance Writers Report* (31 (9): 8–11) "Scaling the Ivory Tower," is only one recent example.

The trend toward linked stories, in particular stories that are set in small, often rural, communities that grow and become more well-defined with each book continues to increase. Although often associated with Contemporary romances (e.g., Debbie Macomber's many series, Beverly Lewis's Amish books or Robyn Carr's Virgin River books), they have become popular in all romance subgenres; and given their popularity with just about everyone, this trend is probably here to stay—for now. Interestingly, recently several print series have been introduced by novella-length prequels that were first released in e-only format. (Just another indication of the influence of tech.)

Although sex is still hot in many books, Harlequin's new, somewhat experimental Heartwarming series mentioned in the last essay and featuring "wholesome editions of refreshed romances that celebrate traditional values and true love," was launched in April and continues as of this writing.

Finally, two other major trends that continue to span the subgenres are the enduring popularity of humor of all kinds and its subtle infusion into all but the most serious romances, and the continuing instances of genre-blending, the ongoing tendency of genres and subgenres to blur across traditional lines.

Except for the fact of an occasional bout with genre-blending, the subgenres continue to perform as before. Contemporaries are still the most popular; and while Harlequin, the largest publisher of Contemporary romances of all kinds, reported a decline in sales and profits for the second quarter of 2011 ("Harlequin Results Fall in Second Quarter," *PW Online*, July 29, 2011.), series and single title Contemporaries still dominate the market. Humor, various levels of sensuality, and a variety of styles are well represented, and families, children, and often animals continue to be popular.

Historical Romance, especially that set during the Regency and Victorian Periods, and increasingly the American West, continue to rise in popularity with fans, as a number of excellent new writers join the ranks of seasoned pros.

Shapeshifters, vampires, demons, angels, and any number of not-quite-human folk continue to enthrall readers as Paranormal, Fantasy, Futuristic, Urban Fantasy, and Time Travel romances continue their remarkably enduring bout of popularity. Although people are constantly predicting a downturn, so far it hasn't happened; and while some sub groups are more popular than others, the Alternative Realities group as a whole is more beloved than ever.

Romantic Suspense, as always, is a winner; and although most stories are Contemporary Romantic Suspense (CRS), mystery and suspense elements have managed to season the plots of romances in most other subgenres, with the result that Historical, Paranormal, Multicultural, or Inspirational mysteries are well within those subgenres' norms.

Romances, in general, continue to include a wider diversity of multicultural characters and cultures, reflecting our world's increasingly inclusive character; and although there are some dedicated lines (e.g. Harlequin's Kimani lines, and Kensignton's Dafina), a growing number are published by traditional houses as part of their regular lines.

In tandem with the larger Inspirational market, Inspirational romance continues to do well; and while many of the Amish romances mentioned earlier aren't necessarily Inspirational (the emphasis is often on the culture and not the tenets of the faith), there is a lot of crossover appeal, and new Inspirational readers may be a result.

Finally, the lure of the linked book continues unabated as readers are drawn into the ongoing lives of characters in trilogies, quartets, and other books connected by family, place, or theme.

Statistics Note

Unfortunately, as of this writing the romance statistics for 2010 are not yet available; however, the 2009 figures were discussed in an earlier essay. For more information, check out the following website at Romance Writers of America (www.rwa.org/cs/the_romance_genre/romance_literature_statistics/industry_statistics). If the past is any indication, the statistics should be available momentarily, and will surely be tallied in time for the next volume of *What Do I Read Next?*.

Romance News of Interest

RWA headed for the Big Apple this year for its annual conference; and in spite of the fact that it was held just prior to the Fourth of July weekend, the conference schedule was changed slightly, and there were the normal little hotel glitches, it was a well-attended, star-studded success. An interesting panel of authors (Steve Berry, Diana Gabaldon, and Tess Gerritsen) launched the conference at the opening session; Best-selling, award-winning historical author Madeline Hunter, continued the pace with her insightful, well-received key note address; best-selling fantasy author Sherrilyn Kenyon inspired listeners with her heart-wrenching, motivating speech at the Awards Luncheon, and super-star women's fiction and YA author Meg Cabot kept the audience brilliantly entertained with her lively, very polished performance as the Awards Ceremony M.C. In keeping with tradition, the conference was preceded with several pre-conference events, including the annual Librarians Day Event. This year attendees enjoyed a number of panel presentations by authors, librarians, editors, and

other industry professionals, including Lara Adrian, Robyn Carr, Jayne Ann Krentz, Wendy Crutcher, Mary Theresa Hussey, John Charles, Leah Hultenschmidt, Judi McCoy, Deanna Raybourn, Alicia Condon, Lucia Macro, Wendy McCurdy, and Amy Pierpont. RWA Hall of Fame historical author Julia Quinn was the luncheon speaker.

The International Association for the Study of Popular Romance (IASPR), which supports the study of popular romance fiction in the academic arena, also held its third annual conference in New York City just before RWA Annual. It was a great success and allowed academics and the professional romance community to interact productive ways.

Of particular interest to the library community was the presentation of RWA's 2011 Librarian of the Year Award to Wendy Crutcher, materials evaluator for OC (Orange County) Public Libraries in California, at the Awards Luncheon.

Finally, on a sadder note, the unexpected death by heart failure of popular romantic suspense writer Beverly Barton (Beverly Beaver) in April 2011 took fans and friends by surprise. Readers will miss her gripping, chilling tales. The final book in her current (Dead by) series, *Dead by Nightfall*, will be published in December 2011.

Future Trends

Although the future is always shadowy, at best, and with the current environment rife with potential options, it seems as though it's a bit more difficult than usual to see what's up ahead. Nevertheless, because romance often builds on its past successes, a look at those, as well as some current trends might give us a glimpse of what just might be in store.

As might be expected, technology will be an overwhelming influence for the near and foreseeable future. At the risk of being redundant (we have talked about technology a lot!), a small sampling of what we might expect includes:

1. e-books will continue to multiply.

2. e-galleys will become more commonplace.

3. New e-only lines will expand, but if it seems financially beneficial to the publishers, some titles might see actual print.

4. With the wariness of publishers to take risks in the current economic market and the resulting difficulty of getting published, an increasing number of authors (veteran and new) will go the self-publishing route.

5. More and more libraries will have to take on the challenge of dealing with providing access to materials in all formats, both remotely and on site, and instructing users in the use of the necessary technologies.

6. Streaming or downloadable digital audio content will eventually replace CDs as the delivery method for audio romances.

7. Barring unforeseen events, the subgenres will remain much as before with Contemporaries and Historicals dominating, Romantic Suspense remaining a favorite, and Inspirationals, Multiculturals, and Paranormals all continuing to attract their core fans. Incidentally, Paranormals are becoming more creative and inventive all the time; I would expect this to continue.

8. Linked books and those with community settings will continue to grow in popularity and more writers will join that group.

9. Sensuality levels will continue to sizzle, but, at the same time, there will be a trend toward sweeter books (e.g., Harlequin Heartwarming).

10. The current scholarly interest in the study of the genre will continue to grow, generating much needed research and adding to the gradually increasing aura of academic respectability taking shape—at long last—around the most popular fiction genre of them all.

11. Finally, although this might just be wishful thinking, with the demise of Borders and the tenuous situation of many brick-and-mortar bookstores, the library world will seize the opportunity to jump in and provide some of the services that will no longer be available, including serving as a browsing spot for readers who usually buy their materials on line.

Will any of these things happen? Possibly, and in some cases, probably, but no one can say for sure. The only thing certain is that things will continue to change—and that if the rest of 2011 is anything like the first part, it should prove to be an unusually interesting year.
Romance in Review

As usual, the traditional review sources, *Booklist* (www.ala.org/ala/aboutala/offices/publishing/booklist_publications/booklist/booklist.cfm), *Library Journal* (www.libraryjournal.com), and, *Publishers Weekly* (www.publishersweekly.com), continue their coverage of the romance genre, as do a shrinking handful of newspapers across the country. *Library Journal* publishes a regular bimonthly romance review column with occasional additional mini-columns; *Booklist* has a separate romance fiction category in each issue, as do the other genres; and *Publishers Weekly* also has a romance review section, as well. All three provide online review coverage that vary in amount and delivery method, and is becoming increasingly important (e.g. *Library Journal*'s weekly Xpress reviews.) In addition, as the digital market expands, e-originals are also being considered for review. Many of these journal and newspaper reviews are picked up by various indexing services, such as EbscoHosts' Academic Search Premier, InfoTrac's Expanded Academic ASAP, or bookseller's websites, such as Amazon.com. and Barnes & Noble.

Without a doubt, coverage of the romance genre by mainstream sources has improved over the years; nevertheless, the most comprehensive coverage still is provided by the genre-specific publications, with *RT*

Book Reviews (www.rtbookreviews.com) being by far the most complete. (Usually just called *RT*, this publication has changed names several times over the years.) Many of these print publications have a web presence, and *RT*'s, which includes reviews and other materials, is easy to use and exceptionally useful. Another veteran print publication that has gone through a number of ups and downs but can still be useful is *Affaire de Coeur* (www.affairedecoeur.com). Strictly online romance reviews sites continue to grow in popularity; and while most of them, like any web source—or any review, for that matter—need to be considered critically, they are popular with many readers and should not be ignored. All About Romance (www.likesbooks.com/); Romance Reviews Today (www.romrevtoday.com), which is currently going through some changes; The Romance Reader (www.theromancereader.com); Romance in Color (www.romanceincolor.com); and PNR (www.paranormalromance.org) are a few of the many general and genre-specific sites currently available. Online lists, such as RRA-L (Romance Readers Anonymous) (est. 1992), remain useful forums for romance readers to discuss the genre and share their views and recommendations. Log on to http://groups.yahoo.com/group/rra-l to subscribe. Fiction-L is another list of interest to readers and librarians that, while not specifically devoted to romance, does focus on the genre on a regular basis. For more information see their website: (www.webrary.org/rs/flbklistmenu.html). Blogs, wikis, and similar sites are increasing exponentially and can also be a source of opinions, if not formal reviews, and a host of additional information and commentary. New sites pop up daily and if you find bloggers whose opinions you respect, they can be goldmines. Finally, those interested in the academic side of the genre may be interested in the Romance Scholar listserv (mailman.depaul.edu/mailman/listinfo/romancescholar), as well as the Romance Wiki (www.romancewiki.com), an active site useful to readers, writers, and scholars alike. Many of these sites/organizations also have a presence on Facebook, can be followed via Twitter, and/or are available via RSS feed. As technology changes and expands, romance—traditionally an early adopter of technology—is sure to be in the creative forefront. Recommendations for Romance

Reading tastes vary greatly. What makes a book appeal to one person may make another reject it. By the same token, two people may like the same book for totally different reasons. Obviously, reading is a highly subjective and personal undertaking. For this reason, the recommended readings attached to each entry have been chosen with the intent to cast as broad a net as was reasonably possible. Suggested titles have been selected on the basis of similarity to the main entry in one or more of the following areas: historical time period, geographic setting, theme, character types, plot pattern or premise, writing style, or overall mood or "feel." All suggestions may not appeal to the same person, but it is to be hoped that at least one would appeal to most.

Because romance reading tastes do vary so widely and readers (and writers) often apply vastly differing criteria in determining what makes a romance good, bad, or exceptional, I cannot claim that the following list of recommendations consists solely of the "best" romance novels of the year. (In fact many of these received no awards or special recognition at all.) It is simply a selection of books that the romance contributors, John Charles, Shelley Mosley, Sandra Van Winkle, and I found particularly interesting; perhaps some of these will appeal to you, too.

The Perfect Mistress by Victoria Alexander

Dead by Morning by Beverly Barton

The Soldier by Grace Burrowes

Dangerous in Diamonds by Madeline Hunter

Never a Gentleman by Eileen Dreyer

Scandal of the Year by Laura Lee Guhrke

The Missing Twin by Rita Herron

My One and Only by Kristan Higgins

Hostage in Havana by Noel Hynd

When Beauty Tamed the Beast by Eloisa James

How to Woo a Reluctant Lady by Sabrina Jeffries

Heart of Lies by Jill Marie Landis

Cloudy with a Chance of Marriage by Kieran Kramer

In Too Deep by Jayne Ann Krentz

The Naked King by Sally MacKenzie

Eleven Scandals to Start to Win a Duke's Heart by Sarah MacLean

Already Home by Susan Mallery

Creed's Honor by Linda Lael Miller

Call Me Irresistible by Susan Elizabeth Phillips

Nowhere Near Respectable by Mary Jo Putney

The Lady Most Likely by Julia Quinn, Eloisa James, and Connie Brockway

Then He Kissed Me by Christie Ridgway

Chasing Fire by Nora Roberts

Shiver of Fear by Roxanne St. Claire

The Goodbye Quilt by Susan Wiggs

For Further Reference

Publisher Websites and Book Clubs

In addition to going to the general websites of online book suppliers such as Amazon.com and traditional bookstores such as Barnes & Noble, readers can now order books in print and/or e-book, and in some cases downloadable audio, formats directly from a number of individual publishers' websites. Many of these websites also feature reviews, information on any subscription

book clubs the publisher has, and ways for readers to connect with each other. Several of these, (e.g., Avalon, Five Star) target the library market and have standing order plans available. Services vary from website to website; several of the more popular are listed below.

Publishers

Avalon Books: www.avalonbooks.com

Barbour Publishing (Heartsong Presents): www.barbourbooks.com (See Heartsong Presents book club information below)

Ellora's Cave: www.jasminejade.com/default.aspx?skinid=11

Five Star: www.gale.cengage.com/fivestar/

HarperCollins/Avon Books: www.avonromance.com

Dorchester Publishing (Leisure and Love Spell): www.dorchesterpub.com. (Click on the Romance link). Note: As of September 2010 Dorchester announced the company will no longer publish print mass-market titles and will focus on e-books and trade.

Harlequin Books (Harlequin, Silhouette, Spice, MIRA, Red Dress Ink, Luna, HQN, Steeple Hill, Kimani Press, Worldwide Library): eharlequin.com

Kensington Books (Zebra, Dafina, Brava, Strapless, Aphrodisia, Urban Soul, Pinnacle): www.kensingtonbooks.com. (Choose Books or Advanced Search to get to the romance imprint links)

Medallion Press: www.medallionpress.com

Penguin Group (Berkley, Putnam, Signet, NAL, Jove, Plume, Dutton, Onyx): us.penguingroup.com (Choose Romance under the Special Interests menu in the left-hand column)

Red Sage Publishing: www.eredsage.com

Simon and Schuster(Pocket): www.simonsays.com (Choose Categories and then choose the link for Romance)

Sourcebooks, Inc. (Sourcebooks Casablanca): www.sourcebooks.com (Choose Browse Books in the left hand column, then Romance)

Tom Doherty Associates (Tor Paranormal Romance): us.macmillan.com/TorForge.aspx (Choose Books and then Romance on the dropdown menu)

Selected Book Clubs and Mail Order Services

Dorchester Book Clubs: Because of the firm's new format directions, this book club is undergoing change; currently, however, club titles are being offered in both mass market and e-book formats, although not all titles will be available in both. Check the webpage for more information: http://www.dorchesterpub.com/store/book-club.aspx?

Harlequin Romance Book Clubs: Provides books in the Harlequin and Silhouette series on a monthly subscription basis. Check the website for series descriptions and price information: http://www.bookclubdeals.com/index.php?action=2&idm=54.

Harlequin Romance Ebook Clubs: Provides Harlequin and Silhouette series romances in eBook format on a monthly subscription basis. Check the website for more information: http://www.bookclubdeals.com/index.php?action=2&idm=902

Heartsong Presents: Provides contemporary and historical Christian romances, published by Barbour Publishing Company on a subscription basis. Check the website for titles, price, and subscription information: http://www.heartsongpresents.com

Rhapsody Book Club: Rhapsody provides romances from a variety of sources on a subscription basis. Check the website, phone, or write for more information: http://www.rhapsodybookclub.com

Note: All of these book clubs, not just the Harlequin ones, are also accessible via the bookclubdeals.com website: http://www.bookclubdeals.com/index.php?action=4

Conferences

Numerous conferences are held each year for writers and readers of romance fiction. Three of the more important and/or interesting national ones are listed below. For a more complete listing, particularly of regional or local conferences designed primarily for romance writers, consult the *Romance Writers' Report*, a monthly publication of The Romance Writers of America or visit their website (www.rwanational.org).

The annual RT Book Lovers Convention is sponsored by *Romantic Times Book Club Magazine*. The 28th Annual RT Book Lovers Convention was held on April 6–10, 2011, in Los Angeles, CA. The 29th Annual Book Lovers Convention is scheduled to be held April 11–15, 2012, in Chicago, Illinois. (This lively convention focuses primarily on fans and readers, and the Romantic Times organization also sponsors a number of romance-related tours for readers and writers.)

The RWA Annual Conference is sponsored by Romance Writers of America and usually convenes in July. The 2011 conference was held June 28–July 1, 2011, in New York City, and the 2012 conference is scheduled for July 25–28, 2012, in Anaheim, California. This "working" conference is aimed at romance writers, editors, librarians, and other romance professionals, rather than fans and readers.

The second annual RomCon, a fan convention, was held in Denver, Colorado, August 5–7, 2011. The 2012 event is scheduled for June 22–24, 2012, in Denver, Colorado.

Popular Romances

752

CHERRY ADAIR

Undertow

(New York: St. Martin's Press, 2010)

Series: Cutter Cay Series. Book 1
Story type: Adventure; Series
Subject(s): Pirates; Love; Romances (Fiction)
Major character(s): Teal, Mechanic; Zane Cutter, Scavenger
Time period(s): 21st century; 2010s
Locale(s): Caribbean

Summary: *Undertow* is an installment from author Cherry Adair's Cutter Cay series of romance novels. In this book, youngest brother Zane Cutter is on a mission to search and salvage a 17th century pirate ship wrecked along the coast. When his longtime mechanic falls ill, however, he must hire a new one—the gorgeous yet incorrigible Teal, a friend of Zane's from childhood. Sparks fly as Teal and Zane work side by side, and soon they act on their sexual attraction to one another. Yet just as Zane determines to prove to Teal that he is no longer the playboy she thinks he is, a group of thieves makes off with their found treasure. When a hurricane threatens their lives, Zane wonders if he can ever show Teal how he really feels.

Where it's reviewed:
Romantic Times, January 2011, page 72

Other books by the same author:
Hush, 2011
Riptide, 2011
Night Fall, 2008
Night Secrets, 2008
Night Shadow, 2008

Other books you might like:
Jo Davis, *Under Fire*, 2009
Linda Howard, *Burn*, 2009
Christy Reece, *No Chance*, 2010
Christina Skye, *To Catch a Thief*, 2008

753

CHERRY ADAIR

Hush

(New York: Pocket Star, 2011)

Story type: Contemporary
Subject(s): Love; Adventure; Kidnapping
Major character(s): Zakary "Zak" Stark, Wealthy, Kidnap Victim, Brother (of Gideon); Acadia Gray, Wealthy, Kidnap Victim; Gideon Stark, Wealthy, Kidnap Victim, Brother (of Zak)
Time period(s): 21st century; 2010s
Locale(s): Venezuela

Summary: Tycoon Zakary Stark and his brother Gideon are thrill-seekers who venture into the jungles of South America. There they meet recent lottery winner Acadia Gray, who is also looking for adventure. Zak and Acadia share a steamy night together, only to wake up with guerrilla warriors pointing guns at them. They are kidnapped and held deep in the jungle, where Zak attempts a risky escape. The failed attempt almost costs Zak his life, but he suddenly finds he possesses a shocking new mystical ability. Putting this to use, he and Acadia attempt to thwart their kidnappers and reach safety. *Hush* is the first book in Cherry Adair's Lodestone Trilogy.

Where it's reviewed:
Booklist, April 15, 2011, page 26
Romantic Times, May 2011, page 80

Other books by the same author:
Undertow, 2011
Black Magic, 2010
Night Secrets, 2008
Night Shadow, 2008
Nightfall, 2008

Other books you might like:
Linda Howard, *Ice: A Novel*, 2009
Jayne Ann Krentz, *Silver Linings*, 1991
Elizabeth Lowell, *Midnight in Ruby Bayou*, 2000
Elisabeth Naughton, *Stolen Heat*, 2009
Roxanne St. Claire, *Tropical Getaway*, 2003

754

JAMI ALDEN

Beg for Mercy

(New York: Hachette Book Group, 2011)

Story type: Psychological Suspense; Series
Subject(s): Murder; Serial murders; Mystery
Major character(s): Megan Flynn, Sister (of Sean), Girlfriend (of Cole); Cole Williams, Police Officer, Boyfriend (of Megan); Sean Flynn, Prisoner, Crime Suspect
Time period(s): 21st century; 2010s
Locale(s): Washington, United States

Summary: *Beg for Mercy* is the first novel in author Jami Alden's Trilogy series. Sean Flynn is a death row inmate ready to face execution in the state of Washington, and the only person still sure of his innocence is his faithful sister Megan. Megan is determined to clear Sean's name, but to do so she must enlist the help of the man who put him in jail in the first place—her ex-boyfriend Cole Williams. As Megan works to find out the truth about the murder pinned on her brother, Cole tries his hardest to protect her. Soon, however, the real killer sets his sights on Megan, and he will stop at nothing to make sure that she doesn't uncover his true identity.

Where it's reviewed:
Romantic Times, June 2011, page 74

Other books by the same author:
Kept, 2009
Unleashed, 2009
Caught, 2008
Private Party, 2007
A Taste of Honey, 2007

Other books you might like:
Pamela Callow, *Damaged*, 2010
Brenda Novak, *Trust Me*, 2008
Stephanie Tyler, *Hard to Hold*, 2009
Debra Webb, *Everywhere She Turns*, 2009

755

LACEY ALEXANDER

Bad Girl by Night

(New York: Signet Eclipse, 2011)

Story type: Contemporary; Series
Subject(s): Sexual behavior; Erotica; Identity
Major character(s): Carly "Desiree" Winters, Young Woman; Jake, Police Officer
Time period(s): 21st century; 2010s
Locale(s): Turnbridge, Michigan

Summary: In *Bad Girl by Night* by Lacey Alexander, Carly Winters spends her days in her town of Turnbridge, Michigan, exuding the innocent charm that convinces her friends and neighbors she's one of the good girls. But at night Carly travels to Traverse City where she fulfills her sexual fantasies with strange men she meets in bars. When Carly meets Turnbridge's newest police

officer, she knows that her cover has been blown. She has met Jake before—not as good girl Carly, but when she was prowling the night as her alter-ego Desiree. *Bad Girl by Night* is the first book in Alexander's H.O.T. Cops series.

Other books by the same author:
Carnal Sacrifice, 2010
The Bikini Diaries, 2009
What She Needs, 2009
Seven Nights of Sin, 2008
Voyeur, 2007

Other books you might like:
Maya Banks, *Sweet Persuasion*, 2009
Shayla Black, *Decadent*, 2007
Loralei James, *Branded as Trouble*, 2010
Saskia Walker, *Rampant*, 2010
Tracy Wolff, *Full Exposure*, 2009

756

VICTORIA ALEXANDER (Pseudonym of Cheryl Griffin)

The Perfect Mistress

(New York: Zebra, 2011)

Story type: Historical
Subject(s): Love; Books; Inheritance and succession
Major character(s): Julia Winterset, Noblewoman, Widow(er); Harrison Landingham, Nobleman
Time period(s): 19th century
Locale(s): England

Summary: In Victoria Alexander's *The Perfect Mistress*, widowed noblewoman Julia Winterset has come into the possession of a scandalous book that draws the attentions of three very different men. One of them wants the manuscript to establish his publishing empire, while another wants to claim the book as his own and launch a writing career. But it is Harrison Landingham, a headstrong earl, who has the most to lose by the book's publication: it could slander his family name forever. His solution? Seduce Julia in an attempt to get his hands on the book. His plans, however, hit a snag when he finds himself *really* falling for the beautiful widow.

Where it's reviewed:
Booklist, January 2011, page 58
Library Journal, February 15, 2011, page 92
Publishers Weekly, December 6, 2010, page 36
Romantic Times, February 2011, page 31

Other books by the same author:
Desires of a Perfect Lady, 2010
The Virgin's Secret, 2009
Seduction of a Proper Gentleman, 2008
Secrets of a Proper Lady, 2007
What a Lady Wants, 2007

Other books you might like:
Connie Brockway, *The Bridal Season*, 2001
Robyn DeHart, *Deliciously Wicked*, 2006
Laura Lee Guhrke, *And Then He Kissed Me*, 2007
Betina Krahn, *Make Me Yours*, 2009

Donna MacMeans, *The Education of Mrs. Brimley*, 2007

757

JESSICA ANDERSEN

Storm Kissed

(New York: Signet, 2011)

Story type: Paranormal; Series
Subject(s): Romances (Fiction); Suspense; Demons
Major character(s): Snake "Dez" Mendez, Supernatural Being (Nightkeeper); Reese Montana, Bounty Hunter
Time period(s): 21st century; 2010s
Locale(s): United States

Summary: In *Storm Kissed*, the sixth book in Jessica Andersen's Final Prophecy series, the end times foretold by the Mayas are at hand and humanity is protected from annihilation by the Nightkeepers, a band of paranormally gifted heroes. Snake "Dez" Mendez joined the Nightkeepers to redeem himself from a life wasted as a criminal and convict, and possibly save the world in the process. He has been reunited with his former lover, Reese Montana, who is a bounty hunter for the Nightkeepers. When Dez sets off on his own to search for an ancient artifact, Reese follows—not as his lover, but as a bounty hunter.

Where it's reviewed:
Romantic Times, June 2011, page 82

Other books by the same author:
Blood Spells, 2010
Demonkeepers, 2010
Dawnkeepers, 2009
Skykeepers, 2009
Nightkeepers, 2008

Other books you might like:
Cynthia Eden, *Eternal Flame*, 2010
Christina Henry, *Black Wings*, 2010
Angela Knight, *Master of the Moon*, 2005
Susan Krinard, *Dark of the Moon*, 2008
Cheyenne McCray, *Vampires Not Invited*, 2010

758

KATHARINE ASHE (Pseudonym of Katharine Brophy Dubois)

Captured by a Rogue Lord

(New York: Avon, 2011)

Story type: Historical - Regency
Subject(s): Love; Pirates; Adventure
Major character(s): Serena Carlyle, Young Woman; Alex Savage, Pirate
Time period(s): 19th century
Locale(s): United Kingdom

Summary: Katharine Ashe's *Captured by a Rogue Lord* is set in Regency-era England and charts the love affair between a beautiful spinster and a dashing earl who possesses a shocking secret. Serena Carlyle has given up on love for herself; at the ripe old age of 25, she's set aside any notion of marriage. She is determined, however, to find a husband for her younger sister, and their neighbor, Alex Savege, seems to be a perfect candidate. But Alex is harboring a secret identity: he is actually a rogue pirate who takes to the seas and steals from the rich to give to the poor. After Alex takes her captive, Serena cannot deny her feelings for the sexy seafarer and sets her sights on nabbing him for herself.

Where it's reviewed:
Romantic Times, April 2011, page 32

Other books by the same author:
In the Arms of a Marquess, 2011
A Lady's Wish, 2011
Swept Away by a Kiss, 2010

Other books you might like:
Jennifer Ashley, *The Care and Feeding of Pirates*, 2005
Michelle Beattie, *Romancing the Pirate*, 2009
Kinley MacGregor, *Master of Seduction*, 2000
Amanda McCabe, *High Seas Stowaway*, 2009
Laura Renken, *My Lord Pirate*, 2001

759

MAYA BANKS

Sweet Possession

(New York: Berkley Books, 2011)

Story type: Psychological Suspense; Series
Subject(s): Sexuality; Popular culture; Entertainment industry
Major character(s): Lyric Jones, Singer; Connor Malone, Bodyguard
Time period(s): 21st century; 2010s
Locale(s): United States

Summary: Lyric Jones is a singing sensation who enjoys a meteoric rise to the top, but her sudden fame causes her to take risks and live a crazy life. Then Connor Malone steps in as her bodyguard. Despite Lyric's diva ways, Connor sees a softer side to the pop singer. As Connor's composure tempers Lyrics wild ways, the duo begin to fall in love. Yet a secret hidden deep in Lyric's past might not only risk her relationship with Connor, but the very career she has worked so hard to achieve. Banks is also the author of the Colters' Legacy series and the McCabe Trilogy.

Where it's reviewed:
Romantic Times, May 2011, page 120

Other books by the same author:
The Darkest Hour, 2010
Golden Eyes, 2010
Linger, 2010
No Place to Run, 2010
Wild, 2010

Other books you might like:
Jaci Burton, *Riding on Instinct*, 2009
Julie James, *Something About You*, 2010
Lora Leigh, *Black Jack*, 2010
Julie Miller, *Man with the Muscle*, 2010

Romances

760

BEVERLY BARTON

Dead by Morning

(Thorndike, Maine: Center Point Large Print, 2011)

Series: Center Point Platinum Romance Series. Book 2
Story type: Mystery
Subject(s): Romances (Fiction); Crime; Mystery
Major character(s): Maleah Purdue, Security Officer (tracking killer); Derek Lawrence, FBI Agent (profiler), Assistant (to Maleah)
Time period(s): 21st century
Locale(s): United States

Summary: *Dead by Morning* by Beverly Barton, part of the Center Point Platinum Romance series, is a romance novel with elements of a crime drama. In this novel, two sexy investigators fall in love while tracking a serial killer. Maleah Purdue, a female security agent, realizes that a copycat killer is targeting her coworkers. She may be next on the hit list! Her agency contracts an FBI profiler named Derek Lawrence to help them find the culprit before he strikes again. Derek and Maleah have a strained working relationship at first, but they begin to warm toward one another and then to fall in love as the case progresses.

Where it's reviewed:
Romantic Times, May 2011, page 80

Other books by the same author:
If Looks Could Kill, 2011
Dead by Midnight, 2010
Don't Cry, 2010
Silent Killer, 2009
Cold Hearted, 2008

Other books you might like:
Lorie O'Clare, *Tall, Dark and Deadly*, 2009
Jenna Ryan, *Shadow Protector*, 2010
Jenna Ryan, *A Voice in the Dark*, 2010
Stephanie Tyler, *Lie with Me*, 2010

761

ADRIENNE BASSO

A Little Bit Sinful

(New York: Zebra, 2011)

Story type: Historical
Subject(s): Romances (Fiction); History; Revenge
Major character(s): Eleanor Collins, Young Woman; Sebastian Dodd, Nobleman (Viscount Ben)
Time period(s): 19th century; 1810s (1819)
Locale(s): England

Summary: In the historical romance novel *A Little Bit Sinful* by Adrienne Basso, Eleanor Collins resigns herself to the fact that her sister will get all the attention during the 1819 London season. But Sebastian Dodd, Viscount Benton seems only to have eyes for Eleanor. Sebastian's apparent affections conceal a sinister purpose as he seeks revenge for the loss of his mother. But as Sebastian

embarks on his charade he finds that his cruel mission is being undermined by Eleanor's charms. His heart, once filled with hatred, is now filled with his desire for the unsuspecting Eleanor Collins.

Where it's reviewed:
Booklist, December 15, 2010, page 28
Romantic Times, January 2011, page 38

Other books by the same author:
Tis the Season to Be Sinful, 2011
How to Seduce a Sinner, 2010
The Christmas Countess, 2008
How to Enjoy a Scandal, 2008
The Christmas Heiress, 2006

Other books you might like:
Grace Burrowes, *The Heir*, 2010
Vicky Dreiling, *How to Marry a Duke*, 2011
Joan Johnston, *The Bridegroom*, 1999
Lisa Kleypas, *Tempt Me at Twilight*, 2009
Sarah MacLean, *Eleven Scandals to Start to Win a Duke's Heart*, 2011

762

ELIZABETH BEVARLY

The Billionaire Gets His Way

(New York: Harlequin, 2011)

Story type: Contemporary
Subject(s): Love; Books; Writers
Major character(s): Gavin Mason, Wealthy; Violet Tandy, Writer
Time period(s): 21st century; 2010s
Locale(s): United States

Summary: In Elizabeth Bevarly's *The Billionaire Gets His Way*, Gavin Mason has built an empire with his wits, intellect, and business sense. But now his reputation is on the line after he learns that he bears more than a passing resemblance to a character in a best-selling novel. The novel's author, Violet Tandy, swears she never met Gavin, but in the hopes of rectifying his reputation, he convinces her to pretend to be his girlfriend. Hoping to add legitimacy to the book's claims and dispel any rumors, Gavin and Violet can only continue the charade for so long. Soon, their true feelings for one another emerge—and those feelings are more scorching than any novelist could have imagined.

Where it's reviewed:
Romantic Times, February 2011, page 93

Other books by the same author:
Neck and Neck, 2009
Fast and Loose, 2008
Flirting with Trouble, 2008
Overnight Male, 2008
Ready and Willing, 2008

Other books you might like:
Sherrill Bodine, *Talk of the Town*, 2008
Jennifer Crusie, *The Cinderella Deal*, 1996
Barbara Dunlop, *The Billionaire's Bidding*, 2007

Katherine Garbera, *Taming the Texas Tycoon*, 2009
Isabel Sharpe, *What Have I Done for Me Lately?*, 2006

▮ 763 ▮

JO BEVERLEY
VANESSA KELLY, Co-Author
SALLY MACKENZIE, Co-Author
KAITLIN O'RILEY, Co-Author

An Invitation to Sin

(New York: Zebra, 2011)

Story type: Collection; Historical
Subject(s): Romances (Fiction); Social class; History

Summary: *An Invitation to Sin* collects four romance novels written by best-selling genre authors. In Jo Beverley's *Forbidden Affections*, Londoner Anna Featherstone finds a surprising romance when a nobleman becomes her neighbor. In Vanessa Kelly's *The Pleasure of a Younger Lover*, Clarissa Middleton and Captain Christian Archer defy the conventions of Georgian society with their secretive relationship. In Sally MacKenzie's *The Naked Prince*, Josephine Atworthy's disdain for her neighbor's outlandish party is assuaged by a nobleman's kiss. *A Summer Love Affair* by Kaitlin O'Riley follows Miss Charlotte Wilson's scandalous season abroad.

Where it's reviewed:
Romantic Times, February 2011, page 35

Other books you might like:
Loretta Chase, *Silk is for Seduction*, 2011
Nicola Cornick, *Whisper of Scandal*, 2010
Diane Gaston, *The Diamonds of Welbourne Manor*, 2009
Christie Kelley, *Scandal of the Season*, 2010
Sally MacKenzie, *The Naked Gentleman*, 2008

▮ 764 ▮

JO BEVERLEY

An Unlikely Countess

(New York: Signet, 2011)

Series: Malloren World Series. Book 11
Story type: Historical; Series
Subject(s): Love; Marriage; Family
Major character(s): Prudence Youlgrave, Young Woman; Catesby "Cate" Burgoyne, Nobleman
Time period(s): 18th century; 1760s (1765)
Locale(s): Yorkshire, England

Summary: Set in 1765 Yorkshire, England, Jo Beverley's *An Unlikely Countess* tells the story of Prudence Youlgrave, a young woman living in poverty who dreams of finding a wealthy man to marry. One fateful night, Prudence is robbed by a group of thugs and subsequently rescued by the handsome Catesby Burgoyne. The two are immediately drawn to one another, and Cate proposes marriage. Fate soon intervenes, and Cate is given a noble title in the wake of his brother's untimely death. Sud-

denly Prudence has everything she ever dreamed of—but enemies are lurking around every corner and Prudence and Cate's happily-ever-after is going to be a hard-won battle. This volume is the 11th book in the Malloren World series.

Where it's reviewed:
Booklist, March 1, 2011, page 38
Publishers Weekly, January 24, 2011, page 139
Romantic Times, March 2011, page 41

Other books by the same author:
The Secret Duke, 2010
The Secret Wedding, 2009
A Lady's Secret, 2008
Lady Beware, 2007
To Rescue a Rogue, 2006

Other books you might like:
Nicola Cornick, *The Confessions of a Duchess*, 2009
Elizabeth Hoyt, *To Desire a Devil*, 2009
Eloisa James, *Duchess by Night*, 2008
Laurel McKee, *Countess of Scandal*, 2010

▮ 765 ▮

TONI BLAKE

Whisper Falls

(New York: Avon, 2011)

Series: Destiny Series. Book 3
Story type: Contemporary; Series
Subject(s): Romances (Fiction); Motorcycles; Rural life
Major character(s): Tessa Sheridan, Interior Decorator (former); Lucky Romo, Motorcyclist, Neighbor (of Tessa)
Time period(s): 21st century; 2010s
Locale(s): Destiny, Ohio

Summary: In the romance novel *Whisper Falls* by Toni Blake, Tessa Sheridan's homecoming to Destiny, Ohio, is bittersweet. The reason for Tessa's return to the quiet little town is the failure of her interior-design business. Now Tessa must try to make a new start as she readjusts to living in her former community. Her neighbor, Lucky Romo, provides distraction in several ways. Tessa is frequently annoyed by his loud motorcycle, but she can't help being attracted to his good looks and tough-guy charm. Lucky is definitely not Tessa's type, but Destiny just may bring big changes to her life. *Whisper Falls* is the third book in Blake's Destiny series.

Where it's reviewed:
Romantic Times, January 2011, page 83

Other books by the same author:
Sugar Creek, 2010
One Reckless Summer, 2009
Letters to a Secret Lover, 2008
Tempt Me Tonight, 2007
Swept Away, 2006

Other books you might like:
Kathleen Eagle, *The Last Good Man*, 2000
Cathie Linz, *Good Girls Do*, 2006
Emily March, *Angel's Rest*, 2011

Romances

Sarah Morgan, *The Rebel Doctor's Bride*, 2008
Karen Robards, *Whispers at Midnight*, 2003

766

BEATE BOEKER

A Little Bit of Passion

(New York: Avalon Books, 2011)

Story type: Contemporary
Subject(s): Romances (Fiction); Skiing; Books
Major character(s): Karen Larsen, Skier (instructor), Store Owner (bookstore); John Bermett, Businessman, Father (of Gerry), Student (of Karen); Gerry, Son (of John), Student (of Karen); Leslie Carter, Friend (of Karen), Store Owner (bookstore)
Time period(s): 21st century; 2010s
Locale(s): Wyoming, United States

Summary: *A Little Bit of Passion*, a contemporary romance novel by Beate Boeker, finds Karen Larsen carefully balancing the two halves of her life. It is winter, and Karen has come to the Grand Tetons as she does every year to give ski lessons, leaving behind the Long Island bookstore where she spends her summers. Karen's no-attachments arrangement suits her perfectly—until she meets John Bermett. John, a successful businessman, brings his son Gerry to one of Karen's classes and the free-spirited ski instructor soon starts to reconsider her nomadic lifestyle. Facing a big decision, Karen calls on best friend and co-worker Leslie Carter for advice.

Where it's reviewed:
Booklist, June 15, 2011, page 47
Romantic Times, June 2011, page 80

Other books by the same author:
Take My Place, 2009
Wings to Fly, 2008

Other books you might like:
Zelda Benjamin, *Chocolate Magic*, 2010
Carolyn Hughey, *Cupid's Web*, 2007
Holly Jacobs, *Everything but a Groom*, 2007
Deborah Shelley, *Marriage 101*, 2008
Kim Watters, *Stake Your Claim*, 2003

767

STEPHANIE BOND

Baby, Come Home

(New York: Mira, 2011)

Story type: Contemporary
Subject(s): Love; Southern United States; Brothers
Major character(s): Kendall Armstrong, Young Man; Amy Bradshaw, Engineer
Time period(s): 21st century; 2010s
Locale(s): Sweetness, Georgia

Summary: *Baby, Come Home* is the second installment in Stephanie Bond's Southern Roads series, which chronicles the romantic adventures of a group of brothers as they attempt to rebuild their small Georgia hometown after a tornado nearly destroys it. This outing centered on middle brother Kendall, who wrote the original advertisement the brothers placed in a northern newspaper, asking women to come join them in the rural town of Sweetness, Georgia. But Kendall is hoping that one woman in particular will be joining them, and her name is Amy Bradshaw. Kendall and Amy had once been engaged, and he has never gotten over her. Now, Kendall wants to rekindle the flames of the past. But Amy has a secret...a secret she is determined to keep.

Where it's reviewed:
Romantic Times, July 2011, Page 82

Other books by the same author:
Baby, Drive South, 2011
4 Bodies and a Funeral, 2009
5 Bodies to Die For, 2009
6 Killer Bodies, 2009
Seduction by the Book, 2009

Other books you might like:
Susan Andersen, *Burning Up*, 2010
Toni Blake, *Sugar Creek*, 2010
Gemma Bruce, *The Man for Me*, 2008
Marilyn Pappano, *Intimate Enemy*, 2008
Hope Tarr, *Every Breath You Take...*, 2009

768

STEPHANIE BOND

Baby, Drive South

(New York: Mira, 2011)

Story type: Contemporary
Subject(s): Love; Southern United States; Brothers
Major character(s): Porter Armstrong, Young Man; Nikki Salinger, Doctor
Time period(s): 21st century; 2010s
Locale(s): Georgia, United States

Summary: A tornado has ripped through the Armstrong brothers' hometown. Now they are determined to rebuild and make the Georgia mountain town into a booming community. In order to attract young women, the brothers place an advertisement in a newspaper up north, and soon women have descended upon the southern town in droves. Porter is the headstrong youngest brother of the Armstrong clan, but a broken leg sends him to the care of recently arrived doctor Nikki Salinger. By allowing himself to be vulnerable under her care, he finds himself drawn to the beautiful physician. But can he convince Nikki to give him a chance? *Baby, Drive South* is the first novel in Stephanie Bond's Southern Roads series.

Where it's reviewed:
Romantic Times, June 2011, Page 80

Other books by the same author:
Baby, Come Home, 2011
4 Bodies and a Funeral, 2009
5 Bodies to Die For, 2009
6 Killer Bodies, 2009
Seduction by the Book, 2009

Other books you might like:
Susan Andersen, *Burning Up*, 2010

Toni Blake, *Sugar Creek*, 2010
Katie Lane, *Make Mine a Bad Boy*, 2011
Lisa Plumley, *Mail-Order Groom*, 2010
Christie Ridgway, *Can't Hurry Love*, 2011

769

RHONDA BOWEN

Man Enough for Me

(New York: Dafina Books, 2011)

Story type: Contemporary
Subject(s): Romances (Fiction); Courtship; Love
Major character(s): Jules Jackson, Public Relations (working for hospital), Religious (Christian); Germaine Williams, Businessman (owns music store and nightclub)
Time period(s): 21st century
Locale(s): United States

Summary: In *Man Enough for Me* by Rhonda Bowen, Jules Jackson is a successful, independent woman. She is able to manage her parents, friends, and two jobs with no problem and still always finds time to celebrate and promote her Christian faith. She doesn't think she needs anything else in life until she meets a man who catches her interest. This man is Germaine Williams, a local businessman who runs a nightclub and music store. Jules thinks Germaine may be just right—until she finds out about some skeletons in his closet. Will Jules accept Germaine for who he is and take a chance at finding true love?

Where it's reviewed:
Publishers Weekly, January 24, 2011, page 138

Other books you might like:
Vanessa Davis Griggs, *Ray of Hope*, 2010
Bonnie Hopkins, *Now and Then, Again*, 2009
Tia McCollors, *A Heart of Devotion*, 2005
Michelle Stimpson, *Last Temptation*, 2010
MaRita Teague, *The Taste of Good Fruit*, 2008

770

ELIZABETH BOYLE

Lord Langley Is Back in Town

(New York: Avon, 2011)

Story type: Historical
Subject(s): Marriage; Love; Social class
Major character(s): Lord Langley, Nobleman; Minerva, Noblewoman (Lady Standon)
Time period(s): 19th century
Locale(s): United Kingdom

Summary: Sexy, incorrigible Lord Langley enters into a sham engagement to suit beautiful Minerva, Lady Standon. Minerva has erected an impenetrable wall around herself, and she makes it clear to Lord Langley that he is not to touch her, sleep with her, or cause any scandal for the duration of their engagement. But the rakish Lord loves nothing more than a challenge—

especially when a beauty like Minerva is involved. Can the rogue Lord Langley scale the walls around Minerva's heart and perhaps even make her his wife—*for real*? *Lord Langley Is Back in Town* is the eighth novel in Elizabeth Boyle's Bachelor Chronicles series.

Where it's reviewed:
Booklist, May 15, 2011, page 5
Romantic Times, June 2011, page 34

Other books by the same author:
How I Met My Countess, 2010
Mad about the Duke, 2010
Confessions of a Little Black Gown, 2009
Memoirs of a Scandalous Red Dress, 2009
Tempted by the Night, 2008

Other books you might like:
Eileen Dreyer, *Barely a Lady*, 2010
Elizabeth Essex, *The Pursuit of Pleasure*, 2010
Gaelen Foley, *My Dangerous Duke*, 2010
Madeline Hunter, *The Sins of Lord Eastbrook*, 2009
Kieran Kramer, *When Harry Met Molly*, 2010

771

CELESTE BRADLEY
SUSAN DONOVAN, Co-Author

A Courtesan's Guide to Getting Your Man

(New York: St. Martin's Press, 2011)

Story type: Contemporary; Historical - Regency
Subject(s): Love; Diaries; Interpersonal relations
Major character(s): Piper Chase-Pierpont, Museum Curator; Mick Malloy, Adventurer; Ophelia, Prostitute (courtesan)
Time period(s): 19th century; 21st century; 2010s
Locale(s): London, United Kingdom; Boston, Massachusetts

Summary: In *A Courtesan's Guide to Getting Your Man*, authors Susan Donovan and Celeste Bradley present a sweeping romantic saga set in two different eras. In Regency England, a mysterious woman named Ophelia leaves behind a collection of diaries detailing the finer points of her profession. In modern-day Boston, Piper Chase-Pierpont stumbles upon Ophelia's journals just as handsome Mick Malloy waltzes back into her life. Piper had once failed to woo him and has never gotten over his rejection of her. Using Ophelia's words of wisdom as guidance, Piper sets out to charm Mick—and win his heart once and for all.

Where it's reviewed:
Romantic Times, July 2011, page 30

Other books you might like:
Christina Dodd, *Once upon a Pillow*, 2002
Christina Skye, *Bridge of Dreams*, 1995
Hope Tarr, *The Haunting*, 2007
Lauren Willig, *The Secret History of the Pink Carnation*, 2004

Romances

772

KYLIE BRANT (Pseudonym of Kim Bahnson)

Deadly Dreams

(New York: Berkley, 2011)

Series: Mindhunters Series. Book 5
Story type: Romantic Suspense; Series
Subject(s): Romances (Fiction); Detective fiction; Serial murders
Major character(s): Risa Chandler, Criminologist (forensic); Adam Raiker, Criminologist, Leader (Mindhunters); Nate McGuire, Detective—Police
Time period(s): 21st century; 2010s
Locale(s): United States

Summary: *Deadly Dreams*, the fifth book in Kylie Brant's romantic suspense series Mindhunters, finds Adam Raiker and his group of forensic criminologists tracking another dangerous killer. Lacking, at first, is the contribution of Marisa Chandler, whose perceptive dreams had provided so much information in the past. A failed investigation has temporarily turned Risa away from the business of hunting murderers. But when Risa's dreams tell of a killer who uses fire as his weapon, she follows Raiker's orders and assists homicide detective Nate McGuire with his investigation. Risa realizes that her help is not welcome and debates telling McGuire that her knowledge of the killer and his crimes comes from her dreams.

Where it's reviewed:
Romantic Times, April 2011, page 67

Other books by the same author:
Deadly Sins, 2011
Deadly Intent, 2010
Waking Evil, 2009
Waking Nightmare, 2009
Waking the Dead, 2009

Other books you might like:
Beverly Barton, *Dead by Midnight*, 2010
Merline Lovelace, *After Midnight*, 2003
Carla Neggers, *On Fire*, 2010
Roxanne St. Claire, *Hunt Her Down*, 2009
Colleen Thompson, *Fatal Error*, 2004

773

KYLIE BRANT (Pseudonym of Kim Bahnson)

Deadly Sins

(New York: Berkley, 2011)

Series: Mindhunters Series. Book 6
Story type: Mystery; Series
Subject(s): Murder; Assassination; Detective fiction
Major character(s): Adam Raiker, Leader (Mindhunters), Criminologist; Jaid Marlowe, FBI Agent
Time period(s): 21st century; 2010s
Locale(s): Washington, District of Columbia

Summary: *Deadly Sins* is the sixth installment from author Kylie Brant's series The Mindhunters. In this book, the author tells the story of Adam Raiker, private detective and owner of his own forensics company. When a serial killer takes aim at some high-profile victims, including a Supreme Court judge, Raiker must follow the clues left by the killer. Unfortunately, being on the case also means working side-by-side with his ex-girlfriend, Jaid Marlowe. Jaid works for the FBI, which has its own stake in the resolution of the case. Soon Raiker becomes the investigation's target and Jaid is ordered to keep an eye on him. Can Jaid remain impartial, or will her feelings for Raiker cloud her judgment?

Where it's reviewed:
Publishers Weekly, June 27, 2011, page 140
Romantic Times, August 2011, page 89

Other books by the same author:
Deadly Dreams, 2011
Deadly Intent, 2010
Terms of Engagement, 2009
Waking Evil, 2009
Waking Nightmare, 2009
Waking the Dead, 2009
Terms of Surrender, 2008

Other books you might like:
Cherry Adair, *Hide and Seek*, 2001
Suzanne Brockmann, *Bodyguard*, 1999
Patricia Potter, *Catch a Shadow*, 2008
Debra Webb, *Everywhere She Turns*, 2009

774

KATHARINE BRITTON

Her Sister's Shadow

(New York: Berkley Books, 2011)

Story type: Psychological
Subject(s): Artists; Sisters; Psychology
Major character(s): Lilli Niles, Artist (painter), Sister (of Bea); Bea, Sister (of Lilli), Spouse (of Randall Marsh); Randall Marsh, Spouse (of Bea)
Time period(s): 21st century; (2010s); 20th century; 1960s
Locale(s): London, England; White Head, Massachusetts

Summary: Celebrated artist Lilli Niles travels from London to Massachusetts for her brother-in-law's funeral in *Her Sister's Shadow* by Katharine Britton. It is Lilli's sister Bea who calls Lilli with the sad news, and though the sisters haven't spoken in almost four decades, Lilli decides it may be time for a reconciliation. Back in White Head, Massachusetts, Lilli consoles Bea at the funeral of Randall Marsh, the man Lilli has also been in love with for years. In their family's grand seaside home, old secrets resurface and Lilli and Bea revisit the loss of another sister as they consider their own troubled relationship. First novel.

Where it's reviewed:
Publishers Weekly, April 25, 2011, page 116

Other books you might like:
Roz Denny Fox, *Baby, Baby*, 2000
Rosamund Lupton, *Sister*, 2011
Felicia Mason, *Enchanted Heart*, 2004

Luanne Rice, *The Geometry of Sisters*, 2010
Virginia Smith, *Stuck in the Middle*, 2008

775

SUZANNE BROCKMANN
Breaking the Rules
(New York: Ballantine Books, 2011)

Series: Troubleshooter Series. Book 16
Subject(s): Family; Marriage; Brothers and sisters
Major character(s): Eden, Spouse (of Izzy), Brother (of Danny and Ben); Izzy Zanella, Spouse (of Eden); Danny Gillman, Brother (of Eden and Ben); Ben Gillman, Brother (of Danny and Eden)
Time period(s): 21st century; 2010s
Locale(s): Las Vegas, Nevada

Summary: In *Breaking the Rules*, author Suzanne Brockmann presents the 16th book in the Troubleshooter series, continuing the adventures of the Gillman family. Eden and her husband Izzy are going through a rough patch in their marriage, and when Eden heads off to Las Vegas to save her younger brother from an abusive stepfather, she and Izzy are forced to work together and look at their issues. Meanwhile, Eden's brother—and Izzy's longtime enemy—Danny is also ready to rescue his younger brother. First, however, Danny and Izzy will have to put the past behind them and come together for the sake of a young man who can't save himself from the hands of a monster.

Where it's reviewed:
Library Journal, April 15, 2011, page 75
Publishers Weekly, February 28, 2011, page 40
Romantic Times, April 2011, page 66

Other books by the same author:
Infamous, 2010
Time Enough for Lvoe, 2010
Dark of Night, 2009
Hot Pursuit, 2009
Otherwise Engaged, 2009
Stand-In Groom, 2009
Into the Fire, 2008
All through the Night, 2007
Force of Nature, 2007

Other books you might like:
Cherry Adair, *Night Shadow*, 2008
Cherry Adair, *On Thin Ice*, 2004
Shannon K. Butcher, *No Control*, 2008
Catherine Mann, *On Target*, 2007
Marliss Moon, *Forget Me Not*, 2004

776

CAROLYN BROWN
Love Drunk Cowboy
(Naperville, Illinois: Sourcebooks Casablanca, 2011)

Story type: Western
Subject(s): Romances (Fiction); Western fiction; Friendship

Major character(s): Austin Lanier, Businesswoman, Heiress (of farm); Rye O'Donnell, Cowboy/Cowgirl, Rancher
Time period(s): 21st century
Locale(s): United States

Summary: *Love Drunk Cowboy* by Carolyn Brown is a romance novel with a Western theme. The main character, a woman named Austin Lanier, has had a successful run in business in the big city. When she unexpectedly inherits a watermelon farm that she doesn't want, though, she feels like it is a liability. She considers selling it and forgetting it as soon as possible. But then she meets her neighbor, a man named Rye O'Donnell, who operates a nearby ranch. Austin's city sensibilities clash with Rye's country manners but inevitably the attractive strangers begin warming to one another. In time, their friendship grows into a romantic relationship.

Where it's reviewed:
Romantic Times, May 2011, page 86

Other books by the same author:
A Trick of the Light, 2011
Walkin' On Clouds, 2011
Hell, Yeah, 2010
I Love This Bar, 2010
My Give a Damn's Busted, 2010

Other books you might like:
Pamela Britton, *The Wrangler*, 2009
Carolyn Brown, *Hell, Yeah*, 2010
Carolyn Brown, *I Love This Bar*, 2010
Sherryl Woods, *Sweet Tea at Sunrise*, 2010

777

NINA BRUHNS
Red Heat
(New York: Berkley Books, 2011)

Series: Men in Uniform Series. Book 1
Story type: Espionage; Series
Subject(s): Espionage; Mystery; Russians
Major character(s): Julie Severin, Agent (CIA); Nikolai Romanov, Military Personnel
Time period(s): 21st century; 2010s

Summary: *Red Heat* is the first novel from author Nina Bruhns's Men in Uniform series. In this book, Julie Severin, an operative for the Central Intelligence Agency, goes undercover as a journalist to spy on a Russian submarine. Little does she realize that the very man in charge of the submarine is none other than Nikolai Romanov, whom she slept with the previous night. Meanwhile, Nikolai—a former KGB operative—has been ordered to keep an eye on Julie, who the Russians know is working for the CIA. Can two people working for warring government agencies fall in love, or is history stacked against them?

Where it's reviewed:
Romantic Times, June 2011, page 74

Other books by the same author:
Vampire Sheikh, 2011
A Kiss to Kill, 2010

Romances

Lord of the Desert, 2010
Shadow of the Sheikh, 2010
If Looks Could Chill, 2009

Other books you might like:
Margaret Carroll, *A Dark Love*, 2009
Lindsay McKenna, *Deadly Identity*, 2010
Shannon McKenna, *Ultimate Weapon*, 2008
Brenda Novak, *Trust Me*, 2008

778

ANITA RICHMOND BUNKLEY

Boardroom Seduction

(New York: Kimani Press, 2011)

Story type: Contemporary
Subject(s): Romances (Fiction); Work environment;
 Sexuality
Major character(s): Kacey Parker, Designer (swimsuit);
 Leon Archer, Employer (of Kacey)
Time period(s): 21st century; 2010s
Locale(s): New York, United States; Texas, United States

Summary: Kacey Parker has left behind the bright lights
of New York City in exchange for a quieter life in a
small Texas town, unaware that she's about to experience a life far more exciting than anything she could've
found in Manhattan. The aspiring swimsuit designer has
accepted a new job working for Leon Archer, a sexy and
alluring man who few women can ignore. Despite hearing rumors about Leon at the plant, Kacey throws caution to the wind and enters into a passionate affair with
her new boss. When a conniving coworker threatens to
expose their relationship and destroy Leon's business, it
becomes obvious that the passion between them is far
greater than a meaningless fling, but are they willing to
risk everything they hold dear for a chance at forever?

Where it's reviewed:
Romantic Times, January 2011, page 104

Other books by the same author:
First Class Seduction, 2010
Vote for Love, 2010
Spotlight on Desire, 2009
Between Goodbyes, 2008
Suite Embrace, 2008
Suite Temptation, 2008

Other books you might like:
Rochelle Alers, *Private Passions*, 2001
Adrianne Byrd, *Heart's Secret*, 2010
Shirley Hailstock, *You Made Me Love You*, 2005
Linda Hudson-Smith, *Promises to Keep*, 2010
Brenda Jackson, *Hidden Pleasures*, 2010
Sandra Kitt, *Promises in Paradise*, 2010
Kayla Perrin, *In an Instant*, 2002
Francis Ray, *Forever Yours*, 1994
Francis Ray, *Only You*, 2007
Maureen Smith, *Recipe for Temptation*, 2010

779

GRACE BURROWES

The Soldier

(Naperville, Illinois: Sourcebooks Casablanca, 2011)

Story type: Historical - Regency
Subject(s): Love; Scandals; Napoleonic Wars, 1800-1815
Major character(s): Devlin St. Just, Veteran; Emmaline
 "Emmie" Farnum, Young Woman
Time period(s): 19th century
Locale(s): United Kingdom

Summary: In Grace Burrowes's *The Soldier*, Devlin St.
Just has just returned from the Napoleonic Wars a
traumatized man. After he inherits an estate in the
country, he looks forward to a life of solace and retreat.
Once he claims his new home, he meets his neighbor,
the scandalously disgraced Emmaline Farnum. Together,
the two strangers begin to penetrate the respective walls
they've built around their hearts and find the strength to
pursue a passionate, life-changing romance.

Where it's reviewed:
Romantic Times, June 2011, page 34

Other books by the same author:
Lady Sophie's Christmas Wish, 2011
The Virtuoso, 2011
The Heir, 2010

Other books you might like:
Mary Balogh, *Simply Love*, 2006
Jo Beverley, *The Devil's Heiress*, 2001
Jo Beverley, *To Rescue a Rogue*, 2006
Nicole Byrd, *Robert's Lady*, 2000
Ann Gracie, *Gallant Waif*, 2001

780

JACI BURTON

The Perfect Play

(New York: Berkley, 2011)

Story type: Contemporary
Subject(s): Love; Football; Interpersonal relations
Major character(s): Mick Riley, Football Player; Tara
 Lincoln, Planner
Time period(s): 21st century; 2010s
Locale(s): United States

Summary: Mick Riley is the star quarterback of the San
Francisco Sabers, and nothing can stop him from getting
what he wants—both on and off the field. After a one-
night stand with ambitious event planner Tara Lincoln,
Mick sets his sights on getting to know the stunning
Tara better. But Tara is leery of a player like Mick, whose
romantic conquests are almost legendary. Can Mick
convince Tara to give him a chance and allow their one-
nighter to evolve into something much more lasting,
beautiful, and true? *The Perfect Play* is the first novel in
Jaci Burton's Play-by-Play Series.

Where it's reviewed:
Romantic Times, February 2011, Page 98

Other books by the same author:
Changing the Game, 2011
Riding the Night, 2010
Demand to Submit, 2009
Riding on Instinct, 2009
Taken by Sin, 2009

Other books you might like:
Kate Angell, *Sweet Spot*, 2010
Lori Foster, *Back in Black*, 2010
Deirdre Martin, *Power Play*, 2008
Jill Shalvis, *Slow Heat*, 2010

781

SHANNON K. BUTCHER

Living on the Edge

(New York: Signet, 2011)

Story type: Romantic Suspense
Subject(s): Love; Adventure; Family
Major character(s): Sloane Gideon, Bodyguard; Lucas Ramsey, Young Man
Time period(s): 21st century; 2010s
Locale(s): United States

Summary: *Living on the Edge* is the first installment in author Shannon K. Butcher's Edge series of romantic suspense novels. This opening volume finds bodyguard Sloane Gideon safeguarding her client from a handsome, mysterious man wielding a gun. Sloane averts any danger, but, later, that same man is following her at the airport. Determined to get to South America to help a friend in need, Sloane doesn't have time to thwart the sexy gunman yet again. But he hasn't come to harm her: he's come to warn her. His name is Lucas, and he is an acquaintance of her father. By no means should she go to South America, he warns. Who is this irresistible stranger? And what does he want from the ambitious and beautiful bodyguard? Sloane is determined to find out....

Where it's reviewed:
Romantic Times, March 2011, Page 66

Other books by the same author:
Blood Hunt, 2011
On the Hunt, 2011
Living Nightmare, 2010
Running Scared, 2010
Finding the Lost, 2009

Other books you might like:
Cherry Adair, *Undertow*, 2010
Maya Banks, *No Place to Run*, 2010
Nina Bruhns, *If Looks Could Chill*, 2009
Leslie Parrish, *Fade to Black*, 2009
Leslie Parrish, *Pitch Black*, 2009

782

LAURA CALDWELL

Claim of Innocence

(New York: Mira, 2011)

Story type: Contemporary
Subject(s): Mystery; Law; Murder

Major character(s): Izzy McNeil, Lawyer, Detective; Valerie Solara, Crime Suspect; Sam, Fiance(e) (ex-fiance of Izzy); Theo, Boyfriend (of Izzy)
Time period(s): 21st century; 2010s
Locale(s): Chicago, Illinois

Summary: In *Claim of Innocence* author Laura Caldwell tells the story of Chicago attorney Izzy McNeil, who takes the case of a friend accused of murder. The police say the case is simple: Valerie murdered the wife of the man she wanted all to herself. But Izzy isn't so sure the story is quite so cut and dried, and she launches her own investigation into the crime. Meanwhile, Izzy is dealing with conflicting feelings for her former fiance, Sam, and her present boyfriend, the sexy—and much younger—Theo. As Izzy juggles the demands of her personal and professional lives, her investigation gradually leads her into a high-stakes world of danger, hidden desires, and murder.

Other books by the same author:
Red Blooded Murder, 2009
Red Hot Lies, 2009
Red, White & Dead, 2009
The Good Liar, 2008
The Rome Affair, 2006

Other books you might like:
Sarah Abbot, *Destiny Bay*, 2008
Barbara Freethy, *In Shelter Cove*, 2010
Jill Marie Landis, *Heartbreak Hotel*, 2005
Marta Perry, *Murder in Plain Sight*, 2010
Marta Perry, *Vanish in Plain Sight*, 2011

783

CANDACE CAMP

An Affair without End

(New York: Pocket Star, 2011)

Story type: Historical - Regency
Subject(s): Love; Theft; Marriage
Major character(s): Vivian Carlyle, Noblewoman, Detective—Amateur; Oliver, Nobleman (Earl of Stewkesbury)
Time period(s): 19th century
Locale(s): London, United Kingdom

Summary: *An Affair Without End* is the third novel in best-selling author Candace Camp's Willowmere Trilogy. This Regency romance finds noblewoman Vivian Carlyle determined to buck the trends of society and remain unmarried. Oliver, Earl of Stewkesbury, enters her life and asks for her help in introducing his American cousins to the most influential people in English society. While Oliver is enchanted with Vivian, he can't help being rattled by her brazenness. Soon, however, he finds himself wanting to protect her—even if that means following Vivian into her dangerous amateur investigations of a series of high-society jewel thefts.

Where it's reviewed:
Publishers Weekly, February 21, 2011, page 120
Romantic Times, April 2011, page 36

Other books by the same author:
A Gentleman Always Remembers, 2010

A Lady Never Tells, 2010
The Courtship Dance, 2009
The Bridal Quest, 2008
The Wedding Challenge, 2008

Other books you might like:
Mary Balogh, *The Secret Mistress*, 2011
Mary Balogh, *Seducing an Angel*, 2009
Lisa Kleypas, *Tempt Me at Twilight*, 2009
Lisa Kleypas, *A Wallflower Christmas*, 2008
Kat Martin, *Royal's Bride*, 2009

784

ROBYN CARR

Harvest Moon

(New York: Mira, February 22, 2011)

Series: Virgin River Series. Book 13
Story type: Contemporary; Series
Subject(s): Romances (Fiction); Women; Stepfamilies
Major character(s): Lief Holbrook, Stepfather (of Courtney); Courtney, Teenager; Kelly Matlock, Cook
Time period(s): 21st century; 2010s
Locale(s): Virgin River, California

Summary: *Harvest Moon* is the 13th novel in author Robyn Carr's Virgin River series. When up-and-coming chef Kelly Matlock faints at work, she realizes she has been working too hard and must seek some relaxation before she does major damage to her health. She takes an extended vacation at her sister's house in Virgin River, where she meets Lief Holbrook, a widower and screenwriter. Although she is instantly attracted to Lief, Kelly proceeds with caution when she meets his stepdaughter Courtney. Courtney is a troublemaking teenager who is determined to keep Kelly and Lief apart, but both Lief and Kelly want to make it work. Together they try to reach out to Courtney in an attempt to help her overcome her anger and grief over her mother's death.

Where it's reviewed:
Romantic Times, March 2011, page 82

Other books by the same author:
Promise Canyon, 2011
Wild Man Creek, 2011
Midnight Kiss, 2010
Moonlight Road, 2010
A Summer in Sonoma, 2010

Other books you might like:
Jeanette Baker, *Chesapeake Tide*, 2004
Jerri Corgiat, *Follow Me Home*, 2004
Lorraine Heath, *Hard Lovin' Man*, 2003
Susan Kay Law, *The Paper Marriage*, 2008
Susan Wiggs, *Table for Five*, 2005

785

TORI CARRINGTON

Wicked Pleasures

(New York: Harlequin, 2011)

Story type: Contemporary
Subject(s): Love; Crime; Adventure
Major character(s): Lincoln "Linc" Williams, FBI Agent; Regina Dodson, Young Woman
Time period(s): 21st century; 2010s
Locale(s): United States

Summary: In *Wicked Pleasures*, best-selling author Tori Carrington tells the sexy tale of an FBI agent and the beautiful woman he is assigned to observe. Linc Williams is given the task of keeping tabs on the former girlfriend of a notorious bank robber, hoping he can gather some information that will lead the FBI to the infamous criminal's whereabouts. But Regina Dodson is a woman that no man can take his eyes off of, and Linc finds himself increasingly drawn to this ravishing beauty. Soon he has worked his way into her life—and her bed. Has Linc just jeopardized his mission for a roll in the hay? Or will Regina reveal what she knows about her ex?

Where it's reviewed:
Romantic Times, July 2011, Page 98

Other books by the same author:
Breathless, 2011
Love Bites, 2011
Reckless Pleasures, 2011
Undeniable Pleasures, 2011
Private Parts, 2010

Other books you might like:
Carla Cassidy, *Profile Durango*, 2009
Julie James, *Something About You*, 2010
Joyce Lamb, *True Vision*, 2010
Lora Leigh, *Guilty Pleasure*, 2010
Karen Whiddon, *Profile for Seduction*, 2010

786

DAKOTA CASSIDY

Burning Down the Spouse

(New York: Berkley, 2011)

Story type: Contemporary
Subject(s): Love; Cooks; Restaurants
Major character(s): Frankie Bennett, Cook; Nikos, Restaurateur
Time period(s): 21st century; 2010s
Locale(s): New Jersey, United States

Summary: Frankie Bennett is a former trophy wife, having recently divorced her cheating, celebrity chef husband. Now she has retreated from the world and is living in her aunt's retirement community. But all that changes when she is given a second chance at having a career of her own, accepting a job as a chef at a renowned Greek restaurant. When she meets the owner,

Nikos, her heart skips a beat, and Frankie is suddenly faced with a dilemma. Does she ignore her sexy boss and just do her job? Or does she risk her new career for another shot at love? *Burning Down the Spouse* is the second book in Dakota Cassidy's Ex-Trophy Wife series.

Where it's reviewed:
Romantic Times, July 2011, Page 84

Other books by the same author:
Accidentally Catty, 2011
Accidentally Demonic, 2010
You Dropped a Blonde on Me, 2010
Kiss & Hell, 2009
My Way to Hell, 2009

Other books you might like:
Louisa Edwards, *Can't Stand the Heat*, 2009
Louisa Edwards, *Just One Taste*, 2010
Susan Mallery, *Already Home*, 2011

787

SUNNY CHEN

Mona Lisa Eclipsing

(New York: Berkley, 2011)

Story type: Fantasy
Subject(s): Memory disorders; Erotica; Love
Major character(s): Mona Lisa, Royalty (Queen of the Monere); Roberto, Shape-Shifter
Time period(s): Indeterminate

Summary: Mona Lisa has an unusual standing in the Monere race: she is one of the few queens of the entire group. Just as she begins to harness the magical abilities her standing gives her, an injury leaves her without a shred of memory. Enter Roberto, a jaguar shape-shifter who possesses some Monere blood. When he meets the amnesiac Mona Lisa, he sees an opportunity to manipulate her condition for his own dark purposes. What he doesn't count on, however, is falling in love with her.... *Mona Lisa Eclipsing* is the fifth novel in Sunny Chen's Monere series of erotic fantasy novels.

Where it's reviewed:
Romantic Times, June 2011, page 103

Other books by the same author:
Mona Lisa Darkening, 2009
Mona Lisa Awakening, 2008
Mona Lisa Craving, 2008
Mona Lisa Blossoming, 2007

Other books you might like:
Alexandra Ivy, *When Darkness Comes*, 2007
Karen Kelley, *The Jaguar Prince*, 2010
Lora Leigh, *Lion's Heat*, 2010
Sarah McCarty, *Jared*, 2010
Nalini Singh, *Blaze of Memory*, 2009

788

LISA CHILDS

Deja Vu

(Don Mills, Ontario, Canada: Harlequin, 2011)

Story type: Paranormal
Subject(s): Detective fiction; Mystery; Reincarnation
Major character(s): Alaina Paulsen, FBI Agent; Trent Baines, Writer
Time period(s): 21st century; 2010s
Locale(s): United States

Summary: *Deja Vu* is a novel written by author Lisa Childs. FBI Agent Alaina Paulsen specializes in serial killer cases, a specialty she chose because of her past life. When a decades-long murder case falls into her hands, she becomes suspicious of Trent Baines, a writer of true crime books that describe those same murders. When she interviews Trent, however, she feels an instant connection, and believes he was her spouse in a past life. As they begin to fall for one another once again, Alaina hopes against all hope that Trent is innocent. Childs is also the author of *Immortal Bride*, *Resurrection*, and *Forever His Bride*.

Where it's reviewed:
Romantic Times, June 2011, page 95

Other books by the same author:
Daddy Bombshell, 2011
Ransom for a Prince, 2011
The Huntress, 2010
Mistress of the Underground, 2010
The Vampire Hunter, 2010

Other books you might like:
Carla Cassidy, *Profile Durango*, 2009
Leslie Tentler, *Midnight Caller*, 2010
Kay Thomas, *Better than Bulletproof*, 2009
Karen Whiddon, *Profile for Seduction*, 2010

789

PAMELA CLARE

Breaking Point

(New York: Berkley, 2011)

Series: I-Team Series. Book 5
Story type: Contemporary; Series
Subject(s): Romances (Fiction); Drugs; Deserts
Major character(s): Zach McBride, Lawman, Lover (of Natalie); Natalie Benoit, Journalist, Lover (of Zach)
Time period(s): 21st century; 2010s
Locale(s): Mexico

Summary: In *Breaking Point* romance novelist Pamela Clare uses a Mexican drug cartel's desert massacre as a setup for romance between sexy investigative journalist Natalie Benoit and hunky Deputy Marshal Zach McBride. When these attractive adventurers are captured by the drug kingpins, they must escape through the blazing desert to find the safety of the United States border. As they face bandits, starvation, and the dangers of the

Romances

elements, Natalie and Zach fall in love. They need to support each other to create hope for survival as their powerful enemies begin to pursue them across the harsh and barren South American desert.

Where it's reviewed:
Romantic Times, May 2011, page 80

Other books by the same author:
Heaven Can't Wait, 2010
Naked Edge, 2009
Unlawful Contact, 2008
Untamed, 2008
Hard Evidence, 2006

Other books you might like:
Nina Bruhns, *If Looks Could Chill*, 2009
Linda Howard, *Burn*, 2009
Christy Reece, *Last Chance*, 2010
Stephanie Tyler, *Hard to Hold*, 2009

790

TIFFANY CLARE

The Seduction of His Wife

(New York: St. Martin's Press, 2011)

Story type: Historical
Subject(s): Love; Marriage; Painting (Art)
Major character(s): Emma Hallaway, Artist, Spouse (of Richard); Richard Mansfield, Nobleman (Earl of Asbury), Spouse (of Emma)
Time period(s): 19th century; 1840s
Locale(s): London, England

Summary: Tiffany Clare's *The Seduction of His Wife* tells the story of an estranged married couple who are drawn together by scandal. Emma Hallaway moves through the upper ranks of British society, but no one knows that she is secretly a successful painter—a painter whose bold and daring works are the talk of London. When her double life risks being revealed to the public, she turns to her long-lost husband, Richard Mansfield, the Earl of Asbury, for help. In light of the scandal bearing down on them, husband and wife are brought together as never before—and given a second chance at love.

Where it's reviewed:
Booklist, January 2011, page 58
Publishers Weekly, December 6, 2010, page 48
Romantic Times, February 2011, page 32

Other books by the same author:
The Surrender of a Lady, 2010

Other books you might like:
Christina Dodd, *Lost in Your Arms*, 2002
Eloisa James, *Duchess in Love*, 2002
Lisa Kleypas, *Married by Morning*, 2010
Stephanie Laurens, *Devil's Bride*, 1998
Michelle Marcos, *When a Lady Misbehaves*, 2007

791

DEBORAH CLOYED

The Summer We Came to Life

(Don Mills, Ontario, Canada: Mira Books, 2011)

Story type: Contemporary
Subject(s): Death; Friendship; Grief
Major character(s): Mina, Cancer Patient, Friend (of Samantha, Isabel, and Kendra); Samantha Weiland, Friend (of Kendra, Isabel, and Mina); Kendra, Friend (of Samantha, Mina, and Isabel); Isabel, Friend (of Samantha, Mina, and Kendra)
Time period(s): 21st century; 2010s
Locale(s): Honduras

Summary: Deborah Cloyed's debut novel *The Summer We Came to Life* tells the story of a group of friends who have the tradition of vacationing together. Every summer Samantha, Isabel, Kendra, and Mina, along with their families, travel to a different destination. When Mina dies of cancer, the friends discover during the following year's vacation to Honduras that the dynamics of their group have changed. As the women struggle to cope with the loss of their friend, Samantha in particular finds herself floundering. Without Mina, Samantha lacks confidence in her life decisions. As she looks for guidance within Mina's diary and letters, she begins to discover that she might just hold the answers within herself. First novel.

Where it's reviewed:
Romantic Times, June 2011, page 45

Other books you might like:
Michael Baron, *When You Went Away*, 2009
Robyn Carr, *A Summer in Sonoma*, 2010
Victoria Dahl, *Start Me Up*, 2009
Kathryn Shay, *The Perfect Family*, 2010

792

KARINA COOPER

Blood of the Wicked

(New York: Avon, 2011)

Story type: Fantasy
Subject(s): Adventure; Love; Witches
Major character(s): Jessie Leigh, Witch; Silas Smith, Hunter (soldier of the Holy Order)
Time period(s): Indeterminate Future
Locale(s): New Seattle, Fictional City

Summary: Jessie Leigh was born a witch, but she's spent her entire life on the run, desperate to leave behind her magical identity in a world where evil witches have left humankind in tatters. She arrives in the town of New Seattle and takes a job as a stripper, hoping to blend in with those around her and lead a normal life. But her hopes are dashed when she crosses paths with sexy, crime-fighting soldier Silas Smith, who needs Jessie's help in assassinating a new threat to the world: her own brother. *Blood of the Wicked* is the first installment in Karina Cooper's Dark Mission Series. First novel.

Where it's reviewed:
Library Journal, June 15, 2011, page 65
Romantic Times, June 2011, page 84

Other books by the same author:
Before the Witches, 2011
Lure of the Wicked, 2011

Other books you might like:
Meljean Brook, *Demon Blood*, 2010
Eve Kenin, *Hidden*, 2008
Jennifer Lyon, *Blood Magic*, 2009
Gena Showalter, *The Vampire's Bride*, 2009
Nalini Singh, *Bonds of Justice*, 2010

793

DEBRA COWAN
LYNNA BANNING, Co-Author
JUDITH STACY, Co-Author

Happily Ever After in the West

(Don Mills, Ontario, Canada: Harlequin, 2011)

Story type: Collection; Western
Subject(s): Western fiction; Love; Adventure
Locale(s): American West

Summary: *Happily Ever After in the West* brings together three romantic novellas set in the American West, penned by some of modern romance's leading authors. In *Whirlwind Redemption*, Debra Cowan tells the story of Zoe Keeler, a young woman left heartbroken when her fiance, Quentin Prescott, ended their engagement. Now she needs Quentin's help, opening the doors for a second chance at love. Lynna Banning's *The Maverick and Miss Prim* finds schoolmarm Eleanora Stevenson falling in love with the handsome, world-weary cowboy Matt Johnson—much to her own consternation. Judith Stacy's *Texas Cinderella* is a modern-day fable centering on a wedding planner who falls for the brother of the groom.

Where it's reviewed:
Romantic Times, May 2011, page 47

Other books you might like:
Lorraine Heath, *Never Marry a Cowboy*, 2001
Yvonne Jocks, *Going to the Chapel*, 2004
Linda Lael Miller, *McKettrick's Choice*, 2005
Maggie Osborne, *Shotgun Wedding*, 2003
Maggie Osborne, *Silver Lining*, 2000

794

JACQUIE D'ALESSANDRO

Summer at Seaside Cove

(New York: Berkley, 2011)

Story type: Contemporary
Subject(s): Love; Real estate; Family
Major character(s): Janie Newman, Young Woman; Nicholas Trent, Landlord
Time period(s): 21st century; 2010s
Locale(s): Seaside Cove, North Carolina

Summary: Jacquie D'Alessandro's *Summer at Seaside Cove* chronicles the romantic misadventures of a young New Yorker named Janie Newman, who is still reeling from the heartbreak of her half-sister running off with her boyfriend. Looking for a place to heal in peace and quiet, Janie rents a quaint cottage in Seaside Cove, North Carolina. Upon her arrival, she notices that the cottage is anything but quaint; in fact, it's a downright dump. She takes up issue with the cottage's owner, Nicholas Trent, and the sparks begin flying between the two. Could Nicholas be the man to help Janie get over her heartbreak and move on with her life?

Where it's reviewed:
Publishers Weekly, March 14, 2011, page 55
Romantic Times, May 2011, page 86

Other books by the same author:
It Happened One Season, 2011
Seduced at Midnight, 2009
Tempted at Midnight, 2009
Touch Me, 2009
Confessions at Midnight, 2008

Other books you might like:
Kristan Higgins, *Catch of the Day*, 2007
Jill Mansell, *Staying at Daisy's*, 2002
Patricia Rice, *Carolina Girl*, 2004
Sherryl Woods, *The Inn at Eagle Point*, 2009
Sherryl Woods, *Moonlight Cove*, April 26, 2011

795

B.J. DANIELS

Branded

(New York: Harlequin, 2011)

Series: Harlequin Intrigue Series
Story type: Mystery
Subject(s): Romances (Fiction); Crime; Courtship
Major character(s): Colton Chisholm, Lawman, Lover (of Halley); Halley Robinson, Lawman (law enforcement officer), Lover (of Colton)
Time period(s): 21st century
Locale(s): Whitehorse, United States

Summary: *Branded* by B.J. Daniels is a romance novel with themes of mystery and adventure, and is part of the Harlequin Intrigue series. In this novel, longtime friends and lovers Halley Robinson and Colton Chisholm lose track of one another only to reunite under unbelievably odd circumstances. Both Halley and Colton become law-enforcement investigators and are assigned to the same case, in which they must solve a murder in their small town. While they search for clues, they remember their childhood relationship in which Halley longed for Colton but her interest was mostly unrequited. Can the sexy crime-fighting duo catch the killer and fall in love at last?

Where it's reviewed:
Romantic Times, May 2011, page 110

Other books by the same author:
Double Target, 2011
Lassoed, 2011

Stampeded, 2011
Twelve-Gauge Guardian, 2011
Rustled, 2010

Other books you might like:
Carolyn Brown, *Hell, Yeah*, 2010
Delores Fossen, *Wild Stallion*, 2010
Marin Thomas, *Samantha's Cowboy*, 2009

796

B.J. DANIELS

Rustled

(New York: Harlequin, 2011)

Story type: Contemporary
Subject(s): Love; Western fiction; Ranch life
Major character(s): Dawson Chisholm, Rancher; Brittany Bo "Jinx" Clarke, Investigator
Time period(s): 21st century; 2010s
Locale(s): Whitehorse, Montana

Summary: Far away from the workaday world, in the remote stretches of Montana, rancher Dawson Chisholm relishes his life on the farm. But his idyll is shattered when rustlers gain access to the ranch and steal his prized cattle. He manages to nab one of the culprits and is shocked to find out she is a beautiful woman named Jinx. Jinx claims she is an undercover operative who has infiltrated the group, attempting to glean firsthand information so she can bring the rustlers to justice. Dawson, however, isn't so certain. Regardless, he needs his cattle back, and he agrees to work with Jinx in order to accomplish that goal. He never imagined that he would fall in love with the irresistible undercover agent.... *Rustled* is the fifth book in B.J. Daniels's Whitehorse, Montana: Chisholm Cattle series.

Where it's reviewed:
Romantic Times, July 2011, Page 102

Other books by the same author:
Branded, 2011
Double Target, 2011
Lassoed, 2011
Stampeded, 2011
Twelve-Gauge Guardian, 2011

Other books you might like:
Pamela Britton, *The Wrangler*, 2009
Joanne Kennedy, *One Fine Cowboy*, 2010
Cathy McDavid, *Dusty: Wild Cowboy*, 2010
Marin Thomas, *Dexter: Honorable Cowboy*, 2010
Joanna Wayne, *24 Karat Ammunition*, 2007

797

MARY MARGARET DAUGHTRIDGE

SEALed Forever

(Naperville, Illinois: Sourcebooks Casablanca, 2011)

Story type: Contemporary
Subject(s): Love; Infants; Mystery

Major character(s): Garth Vale, Military Personnel (Navy SEAL); Bronwyn Whitescarver, Doctor
Time period(s): 21st century; 2010s
Locale(s): United States

Summary: *SEALed Forever* is the fourth novel in Mary Margaret Daughtridge's SEALed series, chronicling the romantic adventures of a group of sexy, courageous Navy SEALS. This outing finds SEAL Garth Vale deep into a top-secret mission when he comes across a seemingly abandoned baby. No one is quite sure what to do with this startling discovery, so Garth takes the infant to small-town doctor Bronwyn Whitescarver. Bronwyn is immediately suspicious of the situation and is convinced there is more to this story than Garth is letting on. As she attempts to find the truth about the abandoned child, Bronwyn and Garth must also contend with another unforeseen obstacle: their attraction to one another.

Where it's reviewed:
Romantic Times, May 2011, Page 85

Other books by the same author:
SEALed with a Ring, 2010
SEALed with a Promise, 2009
SEALed with a Kiss, 2008

Other books you might like:
Elizabeth Jennings, *Shadows at Midnight*, 2010
Lora Leigh, *Black Jack*, 2010
Lora Leigh, *Renegade*, 2010
Christy Reece, *Last Chance*, 2010
Lisa Marie Rice, *Into the Crossfire*, 2010

798

CAROLYN DAVIDSON

Saving Grace

(Don Mills, Ontario, Canada: Harlequin, 2011)

Story type: Historical - American West
Subject(s): Love; Adventure; Frontier life
Major character(s): Grace Benson, Young Woman; Simon Grafton, Religious (preacher)
Time period(s): 19th century; 1890s
Locale(s): Kansas, United States

Summary: Carolyn Davidson's *Saving Grace* is set in 1890s Kansas and centers on the romance that develops between a beautiful young woman and the preacher who rescues her. Grace Benson is brutally attacked by a man who works for her uncle when minister Simon Grafton happens upon the scene. He saves Grace, and the two are immediately drawn to one another. As Simon helps her rebuild her life after the attack, Grace tries to get closer to the caring preacher. She soon learns, however, that his heart is in desperate need of healing—and she may be just the antidote to his silent pain.

Where it's reviewed:
Romantic Times, June 2011, Page 40

Other books by the same author:
Eden, 2009
The Bride, 2008
The Outlaw's Bride, 2008
Haven, 2007

Nightsong, 2007

Other books you might like:
Kaye Dacus, *Ransome's Crossing*, 2010
Linda Goodnight, *A Touch of Grace*, 2007
Robin Lee Hatcher, *Beyond the Shadows*, 2004
Marylu Tyndall, *Surrender the Heart*, 2010

`799`

JUSTINE DAVIS (Pseudonym of Justine Dare)

Enemy Waters

(Don Mills, Ontario, Canada: Harlequin, 2011)

Story type: Psychological Suspense
Subject(s): Abuse; Marriage; Romances (Fiction)
Major character(s): Maggie Scott, Abuse Victim; Cooper Grant, Detective—Private
Time period(s): 21st century; 2010s
Locale(s): Seattle, Washington

Summary: *Enemy Waters* is a novel by author Justine Dare, written under the pseudonym Justine Davis. After enduring years of abuse at the hands of her husband, Maggie Scott decides to run away to Seattle to begin her life anew. She takes extreme measures to make sure that her husband cannot find her, including changing her appearance, but when she meets Cooper Grant she lets her guard down just a little bit. What Maggie doesn't realize is that Cooper is not just a random guy living on a boat in Puget Sound, but a private investigator working for the same man she is trying to get away from. Cooper is at first pleased with himself to have found Maggie so quickly, but the more he learns about her, the more he realizes that she needs his protection.

Where it's reviewed:
Romantic Times, June 2011, page 98

Other books by the same author:
Always a Hero, 2011
The Best Revenge, 2010
Redstone Ever After, 2010
His Personal Mission, 2009
Backstreet Hero, 2008

Other books you might like:
Lora Leigh, *Black Jack*, 2010
Brenda Novak, *Killer Heat*, 2010
Brenda Novak, *White Heat*, 2010
Christy Reece, *Last Chance*, 2010

`800`

ALYSSA DAY (Pseudonym of Alesia Holliday)

Vampire in Atlantis

(New York: Berkley, 2011)

Series: Warriors of Poseidon Series. Book 7
Story type: Paranormal; Series
Subject(s): Romances (Fiction); Atlantis; Fantasy
Major character(s): Daniel, Vampire; Serai, Warrior, Royalty (princess)

Time period(s): 21st century; (2010s); Indeterminate Past
Locale(s): Washington, District of Columbia

Summary: Daniel, who has lived as a vampire for 11,000 years, decides to finally end his tortured existence in *Vampire in Atlantis* by Alyssa Day. Weary of serving as Ruler of the Primus, the third house of the U.S. Congress that comprises North America's vampires, Daniel resigns and steps into the daylight. But his plunge into sunlight and the waters of Washington's reflecting pool doesn't bring death. Instead, he is transported to Atlantis where he must face the warrior princess Serai. She and the other Atlantean women have been preserved in a magical state of sleep that has saved their race. But the gem that protects them has been taken, and Daniel must help Serai in her quest as he also tries to rekindle their ancient passion. *Vampire in Atlantis* is the seventh novel in Day's Warriors of Poseidon series.

Where it's reviewed:
Romantic Times, June 2011, page 83

Other books by the same author:
Atlantis Betrayed, 2010
Atlantis Redeemed, 2010
Atlantis Unleashed, 2009
Atlantis Unmasked, 2009
Atlantis Awakening, 2007

Other books you might like:
Sharon Ashwood, *Ravenous*, 2009
Yasmine Galenorn, *Night Huntress*, 2009
Angela Knight, *Master of the Night*, 2004
Lucy Monroe, *Moon Craving*, 2010
Susan Squires, *The Companion*, 2005

`801`

SYLVIA DAY

Pride and Pleasure

(New York: Brava, 2011)

Story type: Historical - Regency
Subject(s): Love; Marriage; Interpersonal relations
Major character(s): Eliza Martin, Heiress; Jasper Bond, Bounty Hunter (thief-taker)
Time period(s): 19th century
Locale(s): London, United Kingdom

Summary: In Sylvia Day's *Pride and Pleasure*, Eliza Martin is a Regency-era heiress plagued with a barrage of fortune-hunting suitors. But Eliza refuses to marry a man who is only after her money, and she sets her sights on hiring someone to sift through her suitors to hopefully find at least one admirer who isn't a gold digger. Thief-taker Jasper Bond is all wrong for the job: he's physically imposing and his handsome looks stand out in a crowd. He is definitely not the right man to gain access to Eliza's group of suitors. Yet she can't help being pulled into his charismatic orbit, and soon Eliza is wondering if Jasper just may be the one man ideally suited to be her husband.

Where it's reviewed:
Publishers Weekly, December 20, 2010, page 40
Romantic Times, February 2011, page 34

Romances

Other books by the same author:
Don't Tempt Me, 2008
Heat of the Night, 2008
A Passion for Him, 2007
Passion for the Game, 2007
Pleasures of the Night, 2007

Other books you might like:
Elizabeth Essex, *The Pursuit of Pleasure*, 2010
Nicole Jordan, *To Tame a Dangerous Lord*, 2010
Stephanie Laurens, *Temptation and Surrender*, 2009
Ashley March, *Seducing the Duchess*, 2010
Emma Wildes, *My Lord Scandal*, 2010

802

ROBYN DEHART

Treasure Me

(New York: Forever, 2011)

Series: Legend Hunters Series. Book 3
Story type: Historical - Victorian
Subject(s): Love; Adventure; Monsters
Major character(s): Graeme Langford, Nobleman (Duke of Rothmore); Vanessa Pembrooke, Young Woman
Time period(s): 19th century; 1880s
Locale(s): Scotland; London, United Kingdom

Summary: *Treasure Me* is the third novel in Robyn De-Hart's Legend Hunters series, chronicling the romantic escapades of the members of a secret society in Victorian England. Graeme Langford, the Duke of Rothmore, is one of the group's members, a man with a thirst for adventure and danger. He ventures to Scotland in the hopes of finding a precious stone buried somewhere around Loch Ness. Also at the famous locale is Vanessa Pembrooke, herself something of an adventurer, who has come to the Loch to seek out its infamous monster. When Graeme and Vanessa meet, they join forces to help one another's missions. But soon the fires of attraction are flaring between the two, and their quests turn into a mutual journey toward true love.

Where it's reviewed:
Booklist, March 1, 2011, page 38
Publishers Weekly, January 31, 2011, page 35
Romantic Times, March 2011, page 36

Other books by the same author:
Desire Me, 2010
Seduce Me, 2009
Tempted at Every Turn, 2007
Deliciously Wicked, 2006
A Study in Scandal, 2006

Other books you might like:
Adele Ashworth, *Someone Irresistible*, 2001
Betina Krahn, *The Book of True Desires*, 2006
Anthea Lawson, *All He Desires*, 2009
Amanda Quick, *The Paid Companion*, 2004
Melody Thomas, *Sin and Scandal in England*, 2007

803

CHRISTINA DODD

Taken by the Prince

(New York: Signet, 2011)

Series: Governess Brides Series. Book 9
Story type: Historical; Series
Subject(s): Love; Royalty; Revolutions
Major character(s): Victoria Cardiff, Governess; Raul "Saber" Lawrence, Heir
Time period(s): 19th century
Locale(s): Moricadia, Fictional Location

Summary: *Taken by the Prince*, the ninth book in Christina Dodd's Governess Brides series, charts the romance between a handsome prince and the woman he holds captive. Set in the fictional country of Moricadia, this volume finds Raul "Saber" Lawrence desperate to claim the throne that is rightfully his. As he carries out his secretive work to gain power, beautiful governess Victoria Cardiff learns of his mission. To ensure she keeps quiet, Saber kidnaps Victoria. As a revolution in Moricadia unfolds, Saber and Victoria are drawn closer to one another, and Saber realizes he is not only fighting for his lawful place as prince—but for true and lasting love.

Where it's reviewed:
Booklist, April 15, 2011, page 27
Romantic Times, April 2011, page 34

Other books by the same author:
Chains of Fire, 2010
Chains of Ice, 2010
In Bed with the Duke, 2010
Storm of Shadows, 2009
Storm of Visions, 2009

Other books you might like:
Jennifer Ashley, *The Mad, Bad Duke*, 2006
Jillian Hunter, *A Duke's Temptation*, 2010
Sabrina Jeffries, *Only a Duke Will Do*, 2006
Julia London, *The Dangers of Deceiving a Viscount*, 2007
Julia Ross, *My Dark Prince*, 2000

804

VICKY DREILING

How to Marry a Duke

(New York: Forever, 2011)

Story type: Historical
Subject(s): Love; Marriage; Contests
Major character(s): Tristan, Nobleman (Duke of Shelbourne); Tessa Mansfield, Spinster, Matchmaker
Time period(s): 19th century; 1810s
Locale(s): London, United Kingdom

Summary: Vicky Dreiling's *How to Marry a Duke* is set in Regency-era London, where Tristan, Duke of Shelbourne, is on the prowl for a wife. He doesn't care a whit if there is any kind of attraction between himself and his bride; he just wants to get married to meet the

demands of society. He recruits spinster Tessa Mansfield to help him devise a contest, the winner of which will become Tristan's wife. As the competition plays out, Tessa finds herself growing envious of the women vying for Tristan's hand, and she herself soon longs to become his bride. When Tristan kisses her in a moment of passion, Tessa knows for certain that she is the woman for him. But in order to win his affections, she will have to outshine all the other contenders. First novel.

Where it's reviewed:
Booklist, January 2011, page 58
Publishers Weekly, November 22, 2010, page 47

Other books you might like:
Elizabeth Boyle, *Stealing the Bride*, 2003
Kathryn Caskie, *A Lady's Guide to Rakes*, 2005
Kieran Kramer, *When Harry Met Molly*, 2010
Olivia Parker, *At the Bride Hunt Ball*, 2008
Maya Rodale, *The Heir and the Spare*, 2007

805

EILEEN DREYER

Never a Gentleman

(New York: Forever, April 1, 2011)

Series: Drake's Rakes Series. Book 2
Story type: Historical - Georgian; Series
Subject(s): Military life; Marriage; Romances (Fiction)
Major character(s): Diccan Hilliard, Diplomat, Spouse (of Grace); Grace Fairchild, Spouse (of Diccan)
Time period(s): 19th century; 1810s
Locale(s): England

Summary: *Never a Gentleman* is the second book in author Eileen Dreyer's Drake's Rakes series. In this book, the author tells the story of British diplomat Diccan Hilliard, whose enemies launch a conspiracy against him. When Diccan wakes up in a strange woman's bed, he is forced to marry her in order to save face. Grace Fairchild is the daughter of a military man and an independent woman who never wanted to marry Diccan, but she finds herself stuck in his game of cat-and-mouse as he attempts to dethrone England's king. Yet soon these newlyweds find themselves falling in love with one another against all odds. Will their attraction to one another risk everything Diccan has worked so hard for? Dreyer is also the author of *Barely a Lady*.

Where it's reviewed:
Library Journal, April 15, 2011, page 77
Romantic Times, April 2011, page 32

Other books by the same author:
Always a Temptress, 2011
Barely a Lady, 2010
Saints and Sinners, 2005
Head Games, 2004
With a Vengeance, 2003

Other books you might like:
Pamela Britton, *Seduced*, 2003
Jillian Hunter, *The Sinful Nights of a Nobleman*, 2006
Kieran Kramer, *Dukes to the Left of Me, Princes to the Right*, 2010

Mary Jo Putney, *Never Less than a Lady*, 2010
Mary Jo Putney, *Nowhere Near Respectable*, 2011

806

NIKKI DUNCAN

Scent of Persuasion

(Macon, Georgia: Samhain Publishing, 2011)

Series: Sensory Ops Series. Book 2
Story type: Mystery; Series
Subject(s): Detective fiction; Crime; Sex crimes
Major character(s): Kami Evans, Actress, Detective—Amateur; Breck Lawson, Detective; Madame V, Madam
Time period(s): 21st century; 2010s

Summary: *Scent of Persuasion* is the second book in author Nikki Duncan's Sensory Ops series. Determined to track down her brother's murderer and show that he did not kill himself, actress Kami Evans plays amateur detective and goes undercover as a high-end prostitute for Madame V. Her first client is a CEO who she thinks might be linked to the murder, but as she investigates him she does not realize that he is also investigating her. The CEO is actually Breck Lawson, a secret agent looking to investigate the slaying of his best friend—Kami's brother. As they play cat-and-mouse with one another, they begin to attract the attention of the real killer. Can Kami and Breck be honest with one another about their true identities before the killer sets his or her sights on both of them?

Where it's reviewed:
Romantic Times, June 2011, page 75

Other books by the same author:
Vampire Sheikh, 2011
A Kiss to Kill, 2010
Lord of the Desert, 2010
If Looks Could Chill, 2009

Other books you might like:
Pamela Callow, *Damaged*, 2010
Margaret Carroll, *A Dark Love*, 2009
Brenda Novak, *Trust Me*, 2008
Debra Webb, *Everywhere She Turns*, 2009

807

JOAN EARLY

Separate Dreams

(Columbus, Mississippi: Genesis Press, 2011)

Story type: Contemporary
Subject(s): African Americans; Marriage; Singing
Major character(s): Shannon Travers, Singer, Spouse (of Edison); Edison, Spouse (of Shannon), Police Officer
Time period(s): 21st century; 2010s
Locale(s): France; Mississippi, United States

Summary: *Separate Dreams* is a novel by author Joan Early. When Shannon Travers has the opportunity to move to France to pursue a singing career, she makes

the fateful decision to pursue her dreams and leave her family behind. Then her mother dies, and she becomes determined to reconnect with the only family members she has left—her ex-husband, Edison, and the daughter they share. Edison is suffering from amnesia after being shot in the line of duty, and he doesn't remember that Shannon left him. As Shannon revels in the second chance she has to make amends with her family, she also struggles with the dilemma of revealing the truth to Edison about their marriage's dissolution. Early is also the author of *Oak Bluffs*, *Fireflies*, *Look Both Ways*, *Sara's Reward*, and *Friends Indeed*.

Where it's reviewed:
Romantic Times, May 2011, page 86

Other books by the same author:
Friends in Need, 2010
Oak Bluffs, 2010
Fireflies, 2009
Look Both Ways, 2009
Legacy, 2002

Other books you might like:
Toni Blake, *Sugar Creek*, 2010
Lindsay McKenna, *Deadly Intention*, 2010
Christy Reece, *No Chance*, 2010
Debra Webb, *Anywhere She Runs*, 2010

808

CYNTHIA EDEN

Deadly Heat

(New York: Forever, 2011)

Story type: Contemporary
Subject(s): Love; Arson; Suspense
Major character(s): Lora Spade, Fire Fighter; Kenton Lake, FBI Agent
Time period(s): 21st century; 2010s
Locale(s): Charlottesville, Virginia

Summary: Cynthia Eden's *Deadly Heat* finds firefighter Lora Spade reeling from the death of her boyfriend in an arson fire. Months go by, and Lora grows more and more determined to find the person responsible for setting the blaze. FBI agent Kenton Lake arrives on the scene, ready to help Lora track down the killer and bring him to justice. When Kenton himself is almost killed in a fire, Lora pulls him to safety, saving his life in the process. Soon the two can no longer deny their attraction to one another as they face down a brutal menace intent on destroying them both.

Where it's reviewed:
Romantic Times, February 2011, Page 60

Other books by the same author:
Deadly Lies, 2011
Never Cry Wolf, 2011
Deadly Fear, 2010
Eternal Flame, 2010
I'll be Slaying You, 2010

Other books you might like:
Bella Andre, *Wild Heat*, 2009
Jo Davis, *Hidden Fire*, 2009

Jo Davis, *Line of Fire*, 2010
Jo Davis, *Ride the Fire*, 2010
Jill Shalvis, *Flashback*, 2008

809

CARA ELLIOTT (Pseudonym of Andrea Pickens)

To Tempt a Rake

(New York: Hachette, 2011)

Series: Circle of Sin Trilogy. Book 3
Story type: Historical; Series
Subject(s): Romances (Fiction); History; Botany
Major character(s): Kate Woodbridge, Scientist (botanist), Granddaughter (of the Duke of Cluyne); Duke of Cluyne, Nobleman, Grandfather (of Kate); Marco "Conte of Como", Nobleman
Time period(s): 19th century; 1810s
Locale(s): Austria; England

Summary: In Cara Elliott's historical romance *To Tempt a Rake*, strong-willed Kate Woodbridge gets more than she bargained for when she follows through on her parents' dying wish. Kate, a botanist whose unconventional lifestyle puts her at odds with British Regency society, travels to London to reunite with her grandfather, the Duke of Cluyne. There, she endures her elder's angry outbursts and the unsolicited attentions of Marco—an Italian nobleman and British spy. But during her upbringing abroad, Kate learned about more than plants, so she knows how to seduce a man, if she so chooses. When a mission of international intrigue takes Kate and Marco to Vienna, their physical attraction is fueled by their exotic surroundings. *To Tempt a Rake* is the third book in Elliott's Circle of Sin series.

Where it's reviewed:
Booklist, January 2011, page 58
Publishers Weekly, December 20, 2010, page 40
Romantic Times, February 2011, page 32

Other books by the same author:
To Sin with a Scoundrel, 2010
To Surrender to a Rogue, 2010

Other books you might like:
Mary Blayney, *Traitor's Kiss*, 2008
Claudia Dain, *The Courtesan's Wager*, 2009
Jillian Hunter, *The Wicked Duke Takes a Wife*, 2009
Amanda McCabe, *To Catch a Rogue*, 2010

810

CHRISTINE FEEHAN

Savage Nature

(New York: Penguin, 2011)

Series: Leopard Series. Book 5
Story type: Paranormal; Series
Subject(s): Romances (Fiction); Fantasy; Leopards
Major character(s): Drake Donovan, Shape-Shifter, Leopard; Saria Boudreaux, Guide (bayou), Photographer

Time period(s): 21st century; 2000s
Locale(s): Louisiana, United States

Summary: In *Savage Nature* by Christine Feehan, the region of the Louisiana bayou known as Fenton's Marsh is home to countless birds, frogs, snakes, and alligators. According to legend, leopards also prowl the swamp. But these leopards are part human. When it appears that the shape-shifting leopards of the bayou have begun to claim human victims, leopard shifter Drake Donovan comes to assess the situation. Saria Boudreaux, raised in Fenton's Marsh with her brothers, serves as Drake's guide. She knows the truth about the leopard people because she has seen her own brothers shift. Though Saria doesn't know how powerful her own leopard instincts are, Drake recognizes her immediately as a potential mate. *Savage Nature* is the fifth book in Feehan's Leopard People series.

Where it's reviewed:
Romantic Times, May 2011, page 92

Other books by the same author:
Dark Predator, 2011
Ruthless Game, 2011
Dark Peril, 2010
Water Bound, 2010
Wild Fire, 2010

Other books you might like:
Allyson James, *Firewalker*, 2010
Sherrilyn Kenyon, *Stroke of Midnight*, 2004
Lindsay McKenna, *Unforgiven*, 2006
Nalini Singh, *Kiss of Snow*, 2011
Rebecca York, *Eternal Moon*, 2009

811

LIZ FIELDING

Tempted by Trouble

(New York: Harlequin, 2011)

Story type: Contemporary
Subject(s): Love; Business enterprises; Family
Major character(s): Elle Amery, Waiter/Waitress; Sean McElroy, Young Man
Time period(s): 21st century; 2010s
Locale(s): United States

Summary: In Liz Fielding's *Tempted by Trouble*, Elle Amery has devoted her life to caring for her sisters and grandmother. She works at a local greasy spoon and attempts to make ends meet. One day, Elle's humdrum life is turned upside-down when sexy bad boy Sean McElroy shows up in an ice-cream truck. The truck, he claims, is hers, as is the business that goes along with it. Suddenly, Elle must decide if she wants to leave the security of her waitressing job to launch her own business. To further compound matters, Sean proves irresistible to the straight-laced Elle, and her temptation to change her life—and take a shot at love—just may turn out to be too tempting for her to resist.

Where it's reviewed:
Romantic Times, June 2011, page 98

Other books by the same author:
Becoming the Tycoon's Bride, 2011
Mistletoe and the Lost Stiletto, 2010
SOS: Inconvenient Husband Required, 2010
A Wedding at Leopard Tree Lodge, 2010
Her Desert Dream, 2009

Other books you might like:
Katie Fforde, *Wedding Season*, 2010
Jennifer Greene, *Blame It on Chocolate*, 2006
Dorien Kelly, *Hot Nights in Ballymuir*, 2004
Jill Mansell, *Take a Chance on Me*, 2010
Molly O'Keefe, *Dishing It Out*, 2005

812

GAELEN FOLEY

My Irresistible Earl

(New York: HarperCollins, 2011)

Series: Inferno Club Series. Book 3
Story type: Regency; Series
Subject(s): Royalty; Social class; Romances (Fiction)
Major character(s): Jordan Lennox, Agent (Inferno Club); Mara Bryce, Noblewoman
Time period(s): 19th century; 1800s
Locale(s): England

Summary: *My Irresistible Earl* is a novel by author Gaelen Foley. More than a decade ago, Mara Bryce, the Lady Pierson, was left behind as her one true love, Jordan Lennox, embarked on a journey to safeguard the king. Mara marries, but is soon left a young widow after her husband's untimely death. Then Jordan returns, 12 years after leaving Mara behind, but he is unsure if she can forgive him. To make matters worse, the Inferno Club—an ancient order for which Jordan works—wants to send him on another covert operation. Now Jordan has two tough choices: either leave Mara behind again and risk losing her forever, or take her along and risk her life. *My Irresistible Earl* is the third book in Foley's Inferno Club series.

Where it's reviewed:
Publishers Weekly, February 14, 2011, page 43
Romantic Times, April 2011, page 30

Other books by the same author:
My Dangerous Duke, 2010
My Wicked Marquess, 2009
Her Every Pleasure, 2008
Her Only Desire, 2007
Her Secret Fantasy, 2007

Other books you might like:
Katharine Ashe, *Captured by a Rogue Lord*, 2011
Elizabeth Boyle, *Lord Langley Is Back in Town*, 2011
Allison Chase, *Outrageously Yours*, 2010
Eileen Dreyer, *Barely a Lady*, 2010
Eileen Dreyer, *Never a Gentleman*, April 1, 2011

Romances

813

LORI FOSTER

When You Dare

(Toronto: Harlequin, 2011)

Series: Men Who Walk the Edge of Honor. Book 1
Story type: Contemporary; Series
Subject(s): Romances (Fiction); Love; Kidnapping
Major character(s): Molly Alexander, Writer, Kidnap Victim; Dare Macintosh, Mercenary
Time period(s): 21st century; 2010s
Locale(s): Mexico; United States

Summary: *When You Dare* by Lori Foster is the first book in the Men Who Walk the Edge of Honor series of romance novels. In this novel, the namesake of the story, Dare Macintosh, is a soldier-of-fortune who takes dangerous missions if they pay well. He is reluctant to take the case of novelist Molly Alexander, who had recently been kidnapped and wanted to find out about her captors. There were many suspects, including deranged fans, enemies of her family, or jealous former lovers. Dare Macintosh hesitantly agrees to take the case and the two attractive partners soon fall in love.

Where it's reviewed:
Romantic Times, May 2011, page 80

Other books by the same author:
The Promise of Love, 2011
Savor the Danger, 2011
Trace of Fever, 2011
Back in Black, 2010
My Man, Michael, 2009

Other books you might like:
Cindy Gerard, *To the Brink*, 2006
Linda Howard, *Burn*, 2009
Ana Leigh, *Holding Out for a Hero*, 2009
Christy Reece, *No Chance*, 2010

814

LORI FOSTER

Trace of Fever

(Don Mills, Ontario, Canada: Harlequin, 2011)

Series: Men Who Walk the Edge of Honor. Book 2
Story type: Contemporary; Series
Subject(s): Revenge; Romances (Fiction); Sexuality
Major character(s): Trace Rivers, Mercenary; Priss Patterson, Daughter (of Murray); Murray Coburn, Smuggler
Time period(s): 21st century; 2010s
Locale(s): United States

Summary: *Trace of Fever* is the second book in author Lori Foster's Men Who Walk the Edge of Honor series. In this book, Trace Rivers, a bounty hunter, goes undercover to take down a big time smuggler named Murray Coburn. Just as Trace thinks he has Murray right where he wants him, Priscilla Patterson comes to town claiming that she is Murray's illegitimate daughter. Priss

is plotting revenge of her own against Murray for the sake of her deceased mother, and Trace is afraid that she will ruin everything for him. Soon they find themselves attracted to one another, but will their growing passion put a target on their backs for Murray's henchmen to take them down?

Where it's reviewed:
Romantic Times, June 2011, page 74

Other books by the same author:
The Promise of Love, 2011
Savor the Danger, 2011
When You Dare, 2011
Back in Black, 2010
My Man, Michael, 2009

Other books you might like:
Nina Bruhns, *If Looks Could Chill*, 2009
Leslie Parrish, *Fade to Black*, 2009
Christy Reece, *Last Chance*, 2010
Stephanie Tyler, *Lie with Me*, 2010

815

LORI FOSTER
ERIN MCCARTHY, Co-Author
SYLVIA DAY, Co-Author
JAMIE DENTON, Co-Author
KATE DOUGLAS, Co-Author
KATHY LOVE, Co-Author

The Promise of Love

(New York: Berkley Sensation, 2011)

Story type: Collection
Subject(s): Short stories; Romances (Fiction); Interpersonal relations

Summary: *The Promise of Love* collects six romance novellas by best-selling genre authors Lori Foster, Erin McCarthy, Sylvia Day, Jamie Denton, Kate Douglas, and Kathy Love. Featuring a range of locales and circumstances, the stories share a common theme of troubled lives made better by honest love and true romance. The collection includes Foster's "Shelter from the Storm," McCarthy's "Take Me Home," Day's "Razor's Edge," Denton's "Midnight Rendezvous," "Douglas' Dime Store Cowboy," and Love's "Life in the Past." Lori Foster is also editor of the anthology. Proceeds from the book benefit the charitable organization One Way Farm.

Where it's reviewed:
Romantic Times, June 2011, page 79

Other books you might like:
Sylvia Day, *Ask for It*, 2008
Jamie Denton, *The Matchmaker*, 2008
Lori Foster, *Sawyer*, 2007
Kathy Love, *Wanting What You Get*, 2004
Erin McCarthy, *Hard and Fast*, 2010

816

LORI FOSTER

Savor the Danger

(Don Mills, Ontario, Canada: HQN, 2011)

Story type: Contemporary
Subject(s): Love; Mystery; Drugs
Major character(s): Jackson Savor, Mercenary; Alani Rivers, Young Woman
Time period(s): 21st century; 2010s
Locale(s): United States

Summary: *Savor the Danger* is the third installment in Lori Foster's Men Who Walk the Edge of Honor series. This episode opens with mercenary Jackson Savor waking up beside Alani Rivers, the woman on whom he has been harboring a secret crush. There's just one small problem: they apparently slept together, and Jackson can't remember a thing. He was obviously drugged, and Alani knows nothing about it. Together, Jackson and Alani set out to find answers, revealing a complex web of danger, deceit, and desire. To further complicate matters, the two find themselves completely captivated by one another—which ends up putting them both in jeopardy.

Where it's reviewed:
Romantic Times, July 2011, Page 80

Other books by the same author:
The Promise of Love, 2011
Trace of Fever, 2011
When You Dare, 2011
Back in Black, 2010
My Man, Michael, 2009

Other books you might like:
Nina Bruhns, *If Looks Could Chill*, 2009
Laura Griffin, *Unforgivable*, 2010
Lorie O'Clare, *Tall, Dark and Deadly*, 2009
Stephanie Tyler, *Hard to Hold*, 2009
Debra Webb, *Anywhere She Runs*, 2010

817

ADDISON FOX (Pseudonym of Frances Karkosak)

Warrior Betrayed

(New York: Signet, 2011)

Story type: Paranormal; Series
Subject(s): Romances (Fiction); Fantasy; Mythology
Major character(s): Montana Grant, Businesswoman, Heiress, Daughter (of Eirene); Eirene, Deity (goddess of peace, former), Mother (of Montana), Daughter (of Themis); Themis, Deity (goddess), Mother (of Eirene); Quinn Tanner, Security Officer, Warrior
Time period(s): 21st century; 2010s
Locale(s): New York, New York

Summary: The ancient world of mythology lives on in contemporary New York City in *Warrior Betrayed* by Addison Fox. After inheriting her father's business, Montana Grant is surprised by a visit from her estranged mother. Eirene has come to tell Montana that she is an heir to Mount Olympus. Though Montana doesn't believe her mother's story, it is true: Eirene was once the Goddess of Peace, punished by her own mother for marrying a mortal with a curse that has come due. Montana must now serve in the role Eirene abandoned. Armed with her new knowledge, Montana seeks the help of security guard Quinn Tanner, a Taurus Warrior who is quickly seduced by Montana's charms. *Warrior Betrayed* is the third book in the Sons of the Zodiac series.

Where it's reviewed:
Romantic Times, May 2011, page 99

Other books by the same author:
Warrior Ascended, 2010
Warrior Avenged, 2010

Other books you might like:
Christine Feehan, *Dark Slayer*, 2009
Jacquelyn Frank, *Damien*, 2008
Kim Lenox, *Darker than Night*, 2010
Kathleen Nance, *The Warrior*, 2001
Nalini Singh, *Bonds of Justice*, 2010

818

SUSAN FOX (Pseudonym of Susan Lyons)

His Unexpectedly

(New York: Brava, 2011)

Story type: Contemporary
Subject(s): Love; Interpersonal relations; Marine biology
Major character(s): Jenna Fallon, Hippie; Mark Chambers, Scientist (marine biologist)
Time period(s): 21st century; 2010s
Locale(s): California, United States

Summary: Susan Fox's *His, Unexpectedly* follows wild child Jenna Fallon as she embarks on a road trip to her sister's wedding in Vancouver. Before she leaves California, her car breaks down and she meets marine biologist Mark Chambers. The sparks fly immediately, and Jenna, who has always prided herself on being something of a carefree nomad, finds herself wanting to settle down with the more-conservative Mark. Can these two opposites find a common ground and make their love flourish?

Where it's reviewed:
Romantic Times, February 2011, Page 24

Other books by the same author:
Love, Unexpectedly, 2010

Other books you might like:
Jaci Burton, *The Perfect Play*, 2011
Julie James, *Something About You*, 2010
Susan Lyons, *Sex on the Slopes*, 2010
Deirdre Martin, *Icebreaker*, 2010
Jill Shavlis, *Simply Irresistible*, 2010

819

BARBARA FREETHY

At Hidden Falls

(New York: Pocket Sta, 2011)

Story type: Romantic Suspense; Series
Subject(s): Romances (Fiction); Suspense; Psychics
Major character(s): Isabella Silveira, Designer (costumes), Psychic; Nick Hartley, Father (of teenage daughter)
Time period(s): 21st century; 2010s
Locale(s): Angel's Bay, California

Summary: Barbara Freethy's romantic suspense novel *At Hidden Falls* is set in Angel's Bay, California—a town that seems to attract heavenly messengers. Isabella Silveira, a woman with psychic capabilities, has come to Angel's Bay to see her brother, the town's chief of police. But Isabella's visit has another purpose. First she meets Nick Hartley, a man she has seen in her dreams—a man who saves her life. Then she becomes involved with her brother's missing-persons case. One by one, the town's mysteries present themselves to Isabella, and she uses her head and heart to discern the connections between them.

Where it's reviewed:
Library Journal, February 15, 2011, page   91
Romantic Times, February 2011, page 70

Other books by the same author:
Garden of Secrets, 2011
In Shelter Cove, 2010
On Shadow Beach, 2010
Suddenly One Summer, 2009
Silent Fall, 2008

Other books you might like:
Barbara Bretton, *Casting Spells*, 2008
Jennifer Crusie, *The Unfortunate Miss Fortunes*, 2007
Christine Feehan, *The Twilight Before Christmas*, 2003
Kristine Grayson, *Utterly Charming*, 2000
Susan Wiggs, *Fireside*, 2009

820

JEANIENE FROST

This Side of the Grave

(New York: Avon, 2011)

Series: Night Huntress Series. Book 5
Subject(s): Vampires; Supernatural; Romances (Fiction)
Major character(s): Cat Crawfield, Vampire (half), Spouse (of Bones); Bones, Vampire, Spouse (of Cat); The Undead Queen, Royalty, Spirit
Time period(s): 21st century; 2010s
Locale(s): New Orleans, Louisiana

Summary: *This Side of the Grave* is the fifth book in author Jeaniene Frost's Night Huntress series. This time, Cat Crawfield and her spouse, Bones, are shocked to find out that vampires are vanishing all over. Soon they hear the rumors: a battle is being waged between vamps and spirits, and the fallout could result in devastation to the mortal world. Now Cat, a half-vampire herself, and Bones, a full-on vampire, must find help from the most unlikely of allies—the queen of the ghouls. But what the Undead Queen asks for in return may not be worth it if everything Bones and Cat hold dear is destroyed anyway.

Where it's reviewed:
Publishers Weekly, January 24, 2011, page135
Romantic Times, March 2011, page 98

Other books by the same author:
Eternal Kiss of Darkness, 2010
First Drop of Crimson, 2010
At Grave's End, 2009
Destined for an Early Grave, 2009
One Foot in the Grave, 2008

Other books you might like:
Sharon Ashwood, *Ravenous*, 2009
Christina Dodd, *Chains of Ice*, 2010
Allyson James, *Firewalker*, 2010
Karen Marie Moning, *Darkfever*, 2006

821

KIMBERLY FROST (Pseudonym of Kimberly Chambers)

Halfway Hexed

(New York: Berkley, 2011)

Series: Southern Witch Series. Book 3
Story type: Fantasy; Series
Subject(s): Witches; Magic; Love
Major character(s): Tammy Jo Trask, Witch; Bryn Lyons, Wizard
Time period(s): 21st century; 2010s
Locale(s): Duvall, Texas

Summary: Tammy Jo Trask is a newcomer to the whole witch scene. She's doing her best to ply her trade and fit in with the normal society of Duvall, Texas. Her fellow citizens, however, aren't making Tammy's predicament any easier. A band of religious zealots is determined to expose her status as a witch, while Tammy herself becomes the object of an investigation by the World Association of Magic (WAM). As these dramas play out, she finds herself drawn to local wizard Bryn Lyons, but that, too, hits a snag when Tammy learns that the member of WAM assigned to investigate her is none other than Bryn's ex. *Halfway Hexed* is the third novel in Kimberly Frost's Southern Witch series.

Where it's reviewed:
Romantic Times, February 2011, page 80

Other books by the same author:
Barely Bewitched, 2009
Would-Be Witch, 2009

Other books you might like:
Annette Blair, *The Kitchen Witch*, 2004
Patricia Coughlin, *The Lost Enchantress*, 2010
Angie Fox, *The Accidental Demon Slayer*, 2008
Mindy L. Klasky, *How Not to Make a Wish*, 2009
Katie MacAlister, *You Slay Me*, 2004

822

YASMINE GALENORN

Night Veil

(New York: Berkley, 2011)

Series: Indigo Court Series. Book 2
Story type: Paranormal; Series
Subject(s): Romances (Fiction); Fantasy; Vampires
Major character(s): Cicely Waters, Witch; Myst, Vampire; Grieve, Vampire; Lannan Altos, Vampire; Geoffrey, Vampire
Time period(s): 21st century; 2010s
Locale(s): New Forest, Washington

Summary: Modern-day New Forest, Washington is home to a host of paranormal beings in Yasmine Galenorn's *Night Veil*, the second novel in the Indigo Court series. Cicely Waters, a wind witch, and her companions are at odds with the vampire Myst and the Shadow Hunters, although it is not always easy to tell the evil from the good. When Myst holds the vampire Grieve captive, Cicely allows him to suck her blood in hopes that he will be able to escape. Cicely is smitten with Grieve, but is he really as noble as she believes him to be? And who is truly the villain in the power struggle between Myst and the vampire Geoffrey?

Where it's reviewed:
Romantic Times, July 2011, Page 94

Other books by the same author:
Blood Wyne, 2011
Hexed, 2011
Bone Magic, 2010
Harvest Hunting, 2010
Night Myst, 2010

Other books you might like:
Janet Chapman, *Moonlight Warrior*, 2009
Lora Leigh, *Bengal's Heart*, 2009
Joy Nash, *Immortals: The Crossing*, 2008
Gena Showalter, *Twice as Hot*, 2010
Shiloh Walker, *Veil of Shadows*, 2010

823

DOROTHY GARLOCK

Keep a Little Secret

(New York: Grand Central Publishing, 2011)

Story type: Coming-of-Age
Subject(s): Revenge; Schools; Suspense
Major character(s): Charlotte Tucker, Teacher, Boarder; John Grant, Rancher; Owen Wallace, Cowboy/Cowgirl, Twin (of Hannah); Hannah Wallace, Twin (of Owen)
Locale(s): Oklahoma, United States

Summary: *Keep a Little Secret* is the sequel to author Dorothy Garlock's novel *Stay a Little Longer*. After finally leaving her small-town life behind, Charlotte Tucker has found a new job as a school teacher, and a new place to live on a huge ranch in Oklahoma owned by a man named John Grant. When mysterious mishaps occur on the ranch, all fingers point toward Owen Wallace. Owen and his sister, Hannah, came to the ranch to secretly avenge the rape of their now-deceased mother, and they believe John Grant is the rapist. Yet Charlotte is not convinced that Owen is cold blooded enough to commit the crimes he's been accused of. As a killer tornado bears down on the ranch, Charlotte begins to learn dark secrets that could prove Owen's innocence once and for all.

Where it's reviewed:
Library Journal, February 15, 2011, page 91
Romantic Times, March 2011, page 45

Other books by the same author:
Stay a Little Longer, 2010
The Moon Looked Down, 2009
A Week from Sunday, 2009
Leaving Whiskey Bend, 2008
On Tall Pine Lake, 2007

Other books you might like:
Robyn Carr, *Harvest Moon*, February 22, 2011
Lorraine Heath, *Hard Lovin' Man*, 2003
Dinah McCall, *Bloodlines*, 2005
LaVyrle Spencer, *Morning Glory*, 1989
Jodi Thomas, *Somewhere Along the Way*, 2010

824

RED GARNIER

The Last Kiss

(New York: NAL Trade, 2011)

Story type: Paranormal
Subject(s): Love; Ghosts; Erotica
Major character(s): Emma, Fiance(e) (ex-fiancee of Ben), Girlfriend (of Carter); Ben, Fiance(e) (ex-fiance of Emma), Spirit, Friend (of Carter); Carter, Boyfriend (of Emma), Friend (of Ben)
Time period(s): 21st century; 2010s
Locale(s): United States

Summary: Red Garnier's *The Last Kiss* charts the supernatural romance of a woman torn between two men, one living and one a ghost. After Ben dies in a brutal car accident, his fiancee Emma is devastated. Forced to put her life back together in the midst of such overwhelming grief, she turns to Ben's best friend Carter for support. Soon the sparks are flying between Emma and Carter, and the two have moved their friendship to another level. Meanwhile, Ben—now a ghost—is far from thrilled about his latest development in Emma's life. He is mad with envy and sets out to stop this new relationship—even if it means coming back to life.

Other books by the same author:
Office Liaisons, 2011
Paper Marriage Proposition, 2011
Devilish Games, 2010
The Feather, 2010
Spin Some More, 2009

Other books you might like:
Jennifer Crusie, *Maybe This Time*, 2010

Romances

Kit Donner, *The Vengeful Bridegroom*, 2010
Darci Hannah, *The Exile of Sara Stevenson: A Historical Novel*, 2010
Erin McCarthy, *The Taking*, 2010

825

GEORGINA GENTRY (Pseudonym of Lynne Murphy)

Rio

(New York: Zebra, 2011)

Series: Texans Series. Book 6
Story type: Historical; Series
Subject(s): Love; Adventure; Western fiction
Major character(s): Turquoise Sanchez, Young Woman; Rio Kelly, Cowboy/Cowgirl; Edwin Forester, Political Figure
Time period(s): 19th century; 1870s (1876)
Locale(s): Texas, United States

Summary: It is 1876, and Texas beauty Turquoise Sanchez thinks she has found the perfect mate. Edwin Forester is rich, handsome, and an influential state senator. But when sexy cowboy Rio Kelly enters the picture, Turquoise isn't so sure Edwin is the man she wants. Now, with her world turned upside-down, Turquoise must choose between a life of comfort and stability with Edwin or days and nights of passion and adventure with Rio. To further complicate matters, Turquoise knows that spurning Edwin may bring about a wealth of trouble and heartache. Georgina Gentry's *Rio* is the sixth novel in The Texans series.

Where it's reviewed:
Romantic Times, February 2011, page 36

Other books by the same author:
Diablo, 2010
To Seduce a Texan, 2009
To Wed a Texan, 2008
To Love a Texan, 2007
To Tease a Texan, 2006

Other books you might like:
Leigh Greenwood, *Daisy*, 1996
Jill Gregory, *Once an Outlaw*, 2001
Jill Marie Landis, *Last Chance*, 1995
Maggie Osborne, *Prairie Moon*, 2002
Jodi Thomas, *The Lone Texan*, 2009

826

RACHEL GIBSON

Any Man of Mine

(New York: Avon, 2011)

Story type: Contemporary
Subject(s): Love; Hockey; Marriage
Major character(s): Autumn Haven, Planner (wedding planner); Sam LeClaire, Hockey Player
Time period(s): 21st century; 2010s
Locale(s): United States

Summary: In *Any Man of Mine*, award-winning author Rachel Gibson charts the steamy relationship between a wedding planner and the hockey all-star to whom she is secretly wed. Two years prior, Autumn Haven's weekend in Vegas turned into a rambunctious 48-hour party. When she woke up, she was married to sexy athlete Sam LeClaire, who promptly abandoned the entire situation and returned to his life. Autumn did the same, and now she runs her own thriving wedding-planning business. But when she is recruited to arrange the nuptials for one of Sam's fellow players, the two estranged spouses are suddenly back in one another's lives. And Sam has some red-hot plans for reuniting with his long-lost wife.

Where it's reviewed:
Romantic Times, May 2011, page 85

Other books by the same author:
Nothing but Trouble, 2010
True Love and Other Disasters, 2009
Not Another Bad Date, 2008
Tangled Up in You, 2007
I'm in No Mood for Love, 2006

Other books you might like:
Louisa Edwards, *Can't Stand the Heat*, 2009
Deirdre Martin, *Power Play*, 2008
Susan Elizabeth Phillips, *Match Me If You Can*, 2005
Francis Ray, *If You Were My Man*, 2010

827

SIBELLA GIORELLO

The Mountains Bow Down

(Nashville: Thomas Nelson, 2011)

Series: Raleigh Harmon Series
Story type: Mystery
Subject(s): Mystery; Murder; Romances (Fiction)
Major character(s): Raleigh Harmon, FBI Agent, Scientist (minerologist); Jack Stephanson, FBI Agent, Assistant (to Raleigh); Charlotte Harmon, Aunt (of Raleigh)
Time period(s): 21st century
Locale(s): Alaska, United States

Summary: *The Mountains Bow Down* by Sibella Giorello is a novel of mystery and romance that chronicles the adventures of FBI special agent Raleigh Harmon. Raleigh is a forensics expert who enjoys mineralogy in her spare time. In this novel, Raleigh's life is getting too hectic and she decides to take a cruise to Alaska. The cruise is not purely for pleasure, though; Raleigh was hired as a consultant for a movie being filmed on board the cruise ship. But when one of the real-life passengers turns up dead, Raleigh has to put her professional skills to the test. With the help of her irascible but attractive colleague Jack Stephanson, Raleigh needs to solve the murder before the ship gets to shore.

Where it's reviewed:
Romantic Times, March 2011, page 76

Other books by the same author:
The Clouds Roll Away, 2009
The Rivers Run Dry, 2009

The Stones Cry Out, 2007

Other books you might like:
Diane Burke, *Midnight Caller*, 2010
Liz Johnson, *Vanishing Act*, 2010
Shirlee McCoy, *Running Blind*, 2010
Stephanie Newton, *Smoke Screen*, 2010
Marta Perry, *Twin Targets*, 2010

828

SABLE GRACE (Pseudonym of Heather Waters, Laura Barone)

Ascension

(New York: Avon, 2011)

Story type: Paranormal
Subject(s): Love; Vampires; Demons
Major character(s): Kyana, Warrior; Ryker, Warrior
Time period(s): 21st century; 2010s
Locale(s): United States

Summary: *Ascension* is the first installment in Sable Grace's Dark Breed cycle of paranormal romances. This series opener introduces Kyana, a beautiful young woman who is part vampire and part Lychen. When the gates to hell are thrown open, the mortal world is thrust into a highly perilous position. Kyana despises the heartless humans who have imprisoned and abused her, but she is forced to fight on their behalf and try to take down the Dark Breed. She joins forces with warrior and demigod Ryker—much to her chagrin—and the two stumble upon evidence leading them to the Dark Breed's sinister plan. To make matters even riskier, the attraction between Kyana and Ryker makes it difficult for the two warriors to focus on the task at hand. First novel.

Where it's reviewed:
Romantic Times, May 2011, page 94

Other books you might like:
Sharon Ashwood, *Ravenous*, 2009
Kresley Cole, *Wicked Deeds on a Winter's Night*, 2007
Jeaniene Frost, *Halfway to the Grave*, 2007
Eve Kenin, *Driven*, 2007

829

DONNA GRANT

Untamed Highlander

(New York: St. Martin's Paperbacks, April 26, 2011)

Series: Dark Sword Series. Book 4
Story type: Historical; Series
Subject(s): Druids; Magic; Sexuality
Major character(s): Hayden Campbell, Warrior; Isla, Sorceress
Time period(s): 17th century; 1600s
Locale(s): Scotland

Summary: *Untamed Highlander* is the fourth novel in author Donna Grant's Dark Sword series. Highlander warrior Hayden Campbell has been raised by his clan to hate the magical powers of the Druids. When he invades the mountain establishment of the Druids, faithful cohorts of the she-witch Dierdre, he finds that Dierdre has already slain the Druids herself—all but a Druid woman named Isla. Hayden's instinct is to kill Isla, but his fellow clansmen persuade him to take her to the family castle and nurse her back to health. Soon Hayden finds himself hopelessly attracted to her, and discovers that the hatred for Druids instilled in him since birth is no contest for the love he feels for Isla.

Where it's reviewed:
Romantic Times, May 2011, page 42

Other books by the same author:
Highland Fires, 2011
Highland Magic, 2011
Shadow Highlander, 2011
Highland Dawn, 2010
Wicked Highlander, 2010

Other books you might like:
Victoria Alexander, *What a Lady Wants*, 2007
Jo Beverley, *Devilish*, 2000
Monica McCarty, *Highlander Untamed*, 2007
Amanda Scott, *Seduced by a Rogue*, 2010

830

MICHELE GRANT

Sweet Little Lies

(New York: Dafina, 2011)

Story type: Contemporary
Subject(s): Love; African Americans; Scandals
Major character(s): Christina Brinsley, Journalist; Steven Williams, Professor
Time period(s): 21st century; 2010s
Locale(s): United States

Summary: Michele Grant's *Sweet Little Lies* tells the story of Christina Brinsley, a beautiful young woman who seems to have it all: a thriving job as a journalist, an honest, outspoken attitude, and a fair share of suitors. But beneath the facade lies the truth about Christina's personal relationships: three engagements have all been broken, and she can't seem to find Mr. Right, no matter where she looks. Her latest story impels her to launch an investigation into a high-profile scandal. She soon learns that Steven Williams, the handsome professor with whom her chemistry is red-hot, is the man who may be at the heart of the scandal she's exposing. Can Christina put aside her personal feelings for Steven and get the story, no matter what? Or will the demands of her heart compromise her career and everything she's worked for?

Where it's reviewed:
Romantic Times, February 2011, Page 70

Other books by the same author:
Heard it All Before, 2010

Other books you might like:
Nina Bruhns, *If Looks Could Chill*, 2009
Brenda Jackson, *Taste of Passion*, 2009
Elizabeth Jennings, *Shadows at Midnight*, 2010
Lora Leigh, *Nauti Intentions*, 2009
Leslie Parrish, *Pitch Black*, 2009

831

SUSAN GRANT

The Last Warrior

(Don Mills, Ontario, Canada: HQN, 2011)

Story type: Science Fiction
Subject(s): Love; Adventure; Revenge
Major character(s): General Tao, Warrior; Elsabeth, Young Woman
Time period(s): Indeterminate Future

Summary: Susan Grant's *The Last Warrior* is a science-fiction romance set on a distant planet in the far future. There sexy and brave General Tao has just returned from waging war against the Gorr, enemies of the kingdom Tao calls home. But the soldier's troubles are just beginning. He soon learns his king has double-crossed him, and he takes refuge with the hated Kurel people, hoping to bide his time and come up with a plan of action. Among the Kurel, he meets Elsabeth, who is also seeking revenge against the duplicitous king. Now General Tao and Elsabeth must work together to take on the powerful ruler, and, in the process, the two vengeance-hungry warriors fall in love.

Where it's reviewed:
Romantic Times, May 2011, Page 94

Other books by the same author:
Sureblood, 2010
The Warlord's Daughter, 2009
Moonstruck, 2008
How to Lose an Extraterrestrial in 10 Days, 2007
My Favorite Earthling, 2007

Other books you might like:
Maureen Child, *Vanished*, 2009
Autumn Dawn, *No Words Alone*, 2008
Jess Granger, *Beyond the Rain*, 2009
Pamela Palmer, *Dark Deceiver*, 2008
Shiloh Walker, *Veil of Shadows*, 2010

832

KRISTINE GRAYSON (Pseudonym of Kristine Kathryn Rusch)

Wickedly Charming

(Naperville, Illinois: Sourcebooks, Inc., 2011)

Story type: Contemporary - Fantasy
Subject(s): Royalty; Fairy tales; Stepmothers
Major character(s): Prince Charming, Royalty, Writer, Store Owner, Divorced Person; Mellie, Stepmother (of Snow White)
Time period(s): 21st century; 2010s
Locale(s): Third Kingdom, Fictional Location

Summary: *Wickedly Charming* is a novel by author Kristine Grayson. In it, the author provides readers with a twist to the classic fairy tales *Cinderella* and *Snow White*. After Cinderella divorces him, Prince Charming wants nothing to do with romance or with his birthright as the next king, and is perfectly content running a small bookstore. Then Mellie walks into his life. The step-mother of Snow White, Mellie has launched a campaign to stop the mischaracterization of stepmothers as wicked and evil. With Charming's help, Mellie will write a tell-all book told from the perspective of a stepmother. As the two fairy tale rejects form an alliance, both begin to wonder if maybe they can finally find their happily ever after together.

Where it's reviewed:
Library Journal, April 15, 2011, page 77
Romantic Times, May 2011, page 94

Other books by the same author:
Totally Spellbound, 2005
Absolutely Captivated, 2004
Simply Irresistible, 2003
Thoroughly Kissed, 2001
Utterly Charming, 2000

Other books you might like:
Lynn Kurland, *Much Ado in the Moonlight*, 2006
Lynn Kurland, *One Magic Moment*, 2011
Mercedes Lackey, *The Fairy Godmother*, 2004
Katie MacAlister, *Ain't Myth-Behaving*, 2007
Katie MacAlister, *You Slay Me*, 2004

833

LAURA LEE GUHRKE

Scandal of the Year

(New York: Avon, 2011)

Series: Abandoned at the Altar Series. Book 2
Story type: Historical; Series
Subject(s): Romances (Fiction); Social class; England
Major character(s): Lady Julia Yardley, Noblewoman, Divorced Person; Aidan Carr, Nobleman (Duke of Trathen)
Time period(s): 20th century; 1900s
Locale(s): England

Summary: In Laura Lee Guhrke's historical romance novel *Scandal of the Year*, the second book in the Abandoned at the Altar series, Aidan Carr, the Duke of Trathen, is looking for a proper wife but finds himself drawn to the very improper Lady Julia Yardley. Aidan, twice deserted at the wedding altar, and Julia, once divorced, share a history—a passionate tryst that neither has forgotten. Now Aidan struggles to erase the memories of their romantic but scandalous liaison as he searches for a worthy spouse. Lady Julia, not one to follow the conventions of Edwardian society, has her own motive for rekindling her relationship with the Duke.

Where it's reviewed:
Library Journal, February 15, 2011, page 92
Romantic Times, February 2011, page 33

Other books by the same author:
Wedding of the Season, 2011
With Seduction in Mind, 2009
Secret Desires of a Gentleman, 2008
The Wicked Ways of a Duke, 2008
And Then He Kissed Her, 2007

Other books you might like:
Loretta Chase, *Silk is for Seduction*, 2011

Eloisa James, *This Duchess of Mine*, 2009
Sabrina Jeffries, *How to Woo a Reluctant Lady*, 2011
Barbara Metzger, *The Bargain Bride*, 2009
Julia Quinn, *The Lady Most Likely*, 2011

834

LAURA LEE GUHRKE

Wedding of the Season

(New York: Avon, 2011)

Series: Abandoned at the Altar Series. Book 1
Story type: Historical
Subject(s): Love; Marriage; Weddings
Major character(s): Beatrix Danbury, Noblewoman; William "Will" Mallory, Fiance(e) (ex-fiance of Beatrix)
Time period(s): 19th century-20th century; 1890s-1900s
Locale(s): United Kingdom

Summary: Laura Lee Guhrke's *Wedding of the Season* opens with Lady Beatrix Danbury about to wed the man of her dreams, the handsome and impulsive William Mallory. But at the last minute, Will decides to go after his dreams instead—and getting married isn't one of them. He leaves Beatrix at the altar, and she is devastated. Six years pass, and Beatrix once again finds love. As her wedding day nears, the nuptials promise to be the biggest social event of the season. But among those assembling for the landmark event is Will Mallory, come back to claim the heart of the woman he loved and so foolishly gave up all those years ago. This volume is the first book in the Abandoned at the Altar series.

Where it's reviewed:
Romantic Times, January 2011, page 36

Other books by the same author:
With Seduction in Mind, 2009
Secret Desires of a Gentleman, 2008
The Wicked Ways of a Duke, 2008
And Then He Kissed Her, 2007
She's No Princess, 2006

Other books you might like:
Adele Ashworth, *Duke of Sin*, 2004
Connie Brockway, *The Bridal Season*, 2001
Julianne MacLean, *Surrender to a Scoundrel*, 2007
Kathryn Smith, *When Marrying a Scoundrel*, 2010
Sherry Thomas, *Delicious*, 2008

835

VALERIE HANSEN (Pseudonym of Valerie Whisnand)

Rescuing the Heiress

(New York: Harlequin, 2011)

Series: Love Inspired Historical Series
Story type: Historical
Subject(s): Romances (Fiction); Courtship; Women's rights
Major character(s): Tess Clark, Wealthy, Heiress, Suffragette; Michael Mahoney, Fire Fighter, Rescuer (of Tess)
Time period(s): 20th century; 1900s (1900-1906)
Locale(s): San Francisco, California

Summary: *Rescuing the Heiress* by Valerie Hansen is a history-based romance novel and part of the Love Inspired Historical series. In this novel, set in the early 1900s, Tess Clark is a fabulously wealthy and glamorous socialite who believes women should have the right to vote. Michael Mahoney, a poor but hardworking firefighter, falls in love with Tess and also begins supporting the women's suffrage movement. In 1906, when the San Francisco earthquake causes fires and panic in the city, Tess proves powerless to save herself but, luckily, is rescued by Michael. The unlikely couple fall in love and start a romantic relationship.

Where it's reviewed:
Romantic Times, February 2011, page 95

Other books by the same author:
Face of Danger, 2011
The Doctor's Newfound Family, 2010
High Plains Bride, 2010
Frontier Courtship, 2009
Wilderness Courtship, 2008

Other books you might like:
Tamera Alexander, *Remembered*, 2007
Lynn Austin, *Candle in the Darkness*, 2002
Deeanne Gist, *A Bride Most Begrudging*, 2005
Kim Vogel Sawyer, *My Heart Remembers*, 2008
Stephanie Grace Whitson, *Sixteen Brides*, 2010

836

KAREN HARPER

The Irish Princess

(New York: NAL, 2010)

Story type: Historical - Medieval
Subject(s): Irish (European people); Love; Adventure
Major character(s): Elizabeth "Gera" Fitzgerald, Young Woman
Time period(s): 16th century; 1530s-1550s (1533-1559)
Locale(s): England; Ireland

Summary: Karen Harper's *The Irish Princess* is an epic tale set in 16th century Ireland and England. It tells the story of Elizabeth "Gera" Fitzgerald, an Irish noblewoman whose world is shattered when Henry VIII puts her father in jail and murders her immediate family. With nowhere to go, Gera is offered a place in the British royal court, where danger and intrigue are constantly afoot. Grieving the loss of her family and determined to help her imprisoned father, Gera embarks on a grand adventure of love, treachery, and courage in the world of high royalty where people and lives are nothing more than pawns.

Where it's reviewed:
Publishers Weekly, December 6, 2010, page 32
Romantic Times, February 2011, page 38

Other books by the same author:
Down River, 2010
The Queen's Governess, 2010
Deep Down, 2009

Mistress Shakespeare, 2009
The Hiding Place, 2008

Other books you might like:
Denise Domning, *Lady in Waiting*, 1998
Jane Feather, *All the Queen's Players*, 2010
Laurien Gardner, *The Spanish Bride*, 2005
Susan Halloway Scott, *Royal Harlot*, 2007
Jeane Westin, *The Virgin's Daughters: In the Court of Elizabeth I*, 2009

837

THEA HARRISON

Dragon Bound

(New York: Berkley, 2011)

Series: Elder Races Series. Book 1
Story type: Fantasy; Series
Subject(s): Fantasy; Love; Theft
Major character(s): Dragos Cuelebre, Shape-Shifter; Pia, Mythical Creature (half-human, half-Wyr)
Time period(s): 21st century; 2010s
Locale(s): United States

Summary: Dragos Cuelebre is a mighty Wyr, an intimidating, millennia-old legion of shapeshifters. Pia is part Wyr and part human and has devoted her life to living low in both the Wyr and human worlds. To help her boyfriend pay his gambling debts, Pia reluctantly agrees to steal something from Dragos's highly guarded and dangerous lair, a task she accomplishes with much fear and hesitation. When Dragos discovers the theft, he sets out to find the person responsible—having no idea he will soon be crossing paths with the beautiful Pia. *Dragon Bound* is the first installment in Thea Harrison's Elder Races Series.

Where it's reviewed:
Publishers Weekly, March 7, 2011, page 50
Romantic Times, May 2011, page 91

Other books by the same author:
Serpent's Kiss, 2011
Storm's Heart, 2011

Other books you might like:
Deborah Cooke, *Kiss of Fate*, 2009
Allyson James, *Firewalker*, 2010
Angela Knight, *Master of Shadows*, 2011
Angela Knight, *Master of Smoke*, 2011
Nalini Singh, *Kiss of Snow*, 2011

838

REGINA HART (Pseudonym of Patricia Sargeant)

Fast Break

(New York: Kensington, 2011)

Story type: Contemporary
Subject(s): Love; Family; Basketball
Major character(s): DeMarcus Guinn, Coach; Jaclyn Jones, Businesswoman (owner of football team)

Time period(s): 21st century; 2010s
Locale(s): New York, New York

Summary: In *Fast Break*, author Regina Hart offers a play-by-play account of a red-hot relationship that develops between professional basketball coach DeMarcus Guinn and his team's owner, the spitfire Jaclyn Jones. Jones's team is one of the worst in the league, and she's determined to turn their standing around. DeMarcus, himself a former pro basketball player and MVP, is brought on board to help revitalize the team owned by Jaclyn and her family. As DeMarcus takes charge and reenergizes the group, the far more thrilling moves are playing out between DeMarcus and Jaclyn. Soon they can no longer contain their desire, and the worlds of personal relationships and professional obligations collide. First novel.

Where it's reviewed:
Romantic Times, June 2011, Page 80

Other books you might like:
Kate Angell, *Sweet Spot*, 2010
Gemma Bruce, *The Man for Me*, 2008
Lori Foster, *Back in Black*, 2010
Lisa Renee Jones, *Hot Target*, 2010
Deirdre Martin, *Power Play*, 2008

839

RITA HERRON

The Missing Twin

(Don Mills, Ontario, Canada: Harlequin, 2011)

Story type: Mystery; Series
Subject(s): Suspense; Detective fiction; Twins
Major character(s): Caleb Walker, Detective—Private; Madelyn Andrews, Mother (of twins)
Time period(s): 21st century; 2010s
Locale(s): North Carolina, United States

Summary: *The Missing Twin* is the first book in author Rita Herron's Guardian Angel Investigations: Lost and Found series. Caleb Walker is a detective for Guardian Angel Investigations, and he particularly specializes in missing persons cases. When Madelyn Andrews asks him for help with her case, however, he at first thinks her story is a symptom of mother's grief. Five years before, Madelyn gave birth to twins, but one of her daughters didn't make it. Now her surviving daughter claims to be able to speak to her sister and Madelyn is starting to believe her. Did Madelyn's other daughter really die that fateful night, or did something more sinister happen to try to tear the family apart?

Where it's reviewed:
Library Journal, April 15, 2011, page 75
Romantic Times, June 2011, page 94

Other books by the same author:
Her Stolen Son, 2011
Forbidden Passion, 2010
Don't Say a Word, 2007
Say You Love Me, 2007
A Breath Away, 2005

Other books you might like:
Delores Fossen, *Wild Stallion*, 2010
Karen Harper, *Empty Cradle*, 1998
Cait London, *At the Edge*, 2007
Kat Martin, *The Summit*, 2007
Hunter Morgan, *The Other Twin*, 2003

840

KRISTAN HIGGINS

My One and Only

(Don Mills, Ontario, Canada: Harlequin, 2011)

Story type: Contemporary
Subject(s): Weddings; Divorce; Romances (Fiction)
Major character(s): Harper James, Lawyer, Stepsister (of Willa), Spouse (ex, of Nick); Willa, Stepsister (of Harper); Nick Lowery, Spouse (ex, of Harper)
Time period(s): 21st century; 2010s
Locale(s): United States

Summary: *My One and Only* is a novel by author Kristin Higgins. When Harper James married Nick Lowery at the age of 18, they both thought that they would be together forever. Yet their marriage fizzled, and 12 years later Harper finds herself living the life of her dreams as a successful lawyer. Then Harper's stepsister Willa becomes engaged to Nick's brother, and Harper is invited to the wedding. Soon, Nick and Harper find themselves driving across the country together when their travel plans are canceled, and they realize that the love between them has never really died. Can Harper get beyond her need for perfection long enough to open her heart up to Nick again?

Where it's reviewed:
Romantic Times, April 2011, page 86

Other books by the same author:
All I Ever Wanted, 2010
The Next Best Thing, 2010
Too Good to be True, 2009
Just One of the Guys, 2008
Catch of the Day, 2007

Other books you might like:
Connie Brockway, *Hot Dish*, 2006
Victoria Dahl, *Lead Me On*, 2010
Christina Dodd, *Tongue in Chic*, 2007
Lisa Plumley, *Let's Misbehave*, 2007

841

DONNA HILL

Secret Attraction

(New York: Kimani Press, 2011)

Series: Lawsons of Louisiana Series. Book 2
Story type: Political; Series
Subject(s): Romances (Fiction); African Americans; Political campaigns
Major character(s): Desiree Lawson, Twin (of Dominique); Dominique, Twin (of Desiree), Matchmaker; Spencer Hampton, Restaurateur
Time period(s): 21st century; 2010s
Locale(s): Baton Rouge, Louisiana

Summary: *Secret Attraction* is the second novel in the Lawsons of Louisiana series by author Donna Hill. As the daughter of a powerful Louisiana senator, Desiree Lawson has grown up in awe of the political arena. Now she is ready to enter politics herself, but her twin sister Dominique knows that Desiree's personal life is filled with loneliness. When Dominique fixes Desiree up with restaurateur Spencer Hampton, Desiree is thrilled—she has secretly had a crush on Spencer for a long time. Unbeknownst to Desiree, Spencer has also wanted her—but can he shake his player reputation in time to prove to her that he is serious about her?

Where it's reviewed:
Romantic Times, May 2011, page 115

Other books by the same author:
Heat Wave, 2011
Legacy of Love, 2011
Spend My Life with You, 2011
Heart's Reward, 2010
Private Lessons, 2010

Other books you might like:
Michael Baron, *When You Went Away*, 2009
Robyn Carr, *Forbidden Falls*, 2009
Linda Goodnight, *Winning the Single Mom's Heart*, 2008
J.S. Hawley, *Come with Me*, 2007

842

ELIZABETH HOYT (Pseudonym of Nancy M. Finney)

Notorious Pleasures

(New York: Hachette, 2011)

Series: Maiden Lane Series. Book 2
Story type: Historical; Series
Subject(s): Romances (Fiction); Social class; Brothers
Major character(s): Lady Hero Batten, Noblewoman; Marquis of Mandeville, Fiance(e) (of Hero), Brother (of Griffin); Griffin "Lord of Reading" Remmington, Nobleman, Brother (of the Marquis of Mandeville)
Time period(s): 18th century; 1730s (1737)
Locale(s): London, England

Summary: *Notorious Pleasures* by Elizabeth Hoyt, the second book in the Maiden Lane series, is set in 1737 London where society is governed by stringent social rules. Lady Hero Batten is dutifully playing her role, carefully following the female ideal and engaged to a suitable if not passionate nobleman, the Marquis of Mandeville. As expected, Hero is shocked by the behavior of her fiance's younger brother, Griffin Remmington, Lord Reading, whose business dealings are blatantly unethical and his treatment of women, scandalous. But as Hero and Griffin spend more time together, the Lady begins to discover the pleasure of the Lord's company.

Where it's reviewed:
Booklist, February 1, 2011, page 42

Romances

Publishers Weekly, December 20, 2010, page 40
Romantic Times, February 2011, page 31

Other books by the same author:
Wicked Intentions, 2010
To Beguile a Beast, 2009
To Desire a Devil, 2009
To Seduce a Sinner, 2008
To Taste Temptation, 2008

Other books you might like:
Madeline Hunter, *The Sins of Lord Eastbrook*, 2009
Sabrina Jeffries, *Dance of Seduction*, 2003
Kate Moore, *To Save the Devil*, 2010
Kate Moore, *To Tempt a Saint*, 2010
Rachelle Morgan, *A Scandalous Lady*, 2003

843

MADELINE HUNTER

Dangerous in Diamonds

(New York: Jove, 2011)

Series: Rarest Blooms Series. Book 4
Story type: Historical - Regency; Series
Subject(s): Love; Flowers; Family
Major character(s): The Duke of Castleford, Nobleman; Daphne Joyes, Manager
Time period(s): 19th century
Locale(s): England

Summary: *Dangerous in Diamonds* is the fourth and final installment in Madeline Hunter's Rarest Blooms series. This volume finds the insufferable, richer-than-Croesus Duke of Castleford enjoying his position as a womanizer and gambler and seeing little reason to change his scandalous ways. When a new inheritance gives the Duke even more land to call his own, he discovers a small flower shop on the property, which is run by the beautiful Daphne Joyes. But Daphne is no ordinary woman of the ton: she is headstrong, outspoken, and harbors her fair share of secrets. And in the handsome Duke she has certainly met her match.

Other books by the same author:
Provocative in Pearls, 2010
Ravishing in Red, 2010
Sinful in Satin, 2010
The Sins of Lord Easterbrook, 2009
Secrets of Surrender, 2008

Other books you might like:
Mary Balogh, *Simply Unforgettable*, 2005
Diane Gaston, *The Wagering Widow*, 2006
Candice Hern, *Lady Be Bad*, 2007
Sabrina Jeffries, *Only a Duke Will Do*, 2006
Julia London, *The Hazards of Hunting a Duke*, 2006

844

SAMANTHA HUNTER

Mine Until Morning

(New York: Harlequin, 2011)

Story type: Contemporary
Subject(s): Love; Blindness; Interpersonal relations
Major character(s): Tessa Rose, Young Woman; Jonas Berringer, Bodyguard, Blind Person
Time period(s): 21st century; 2010s
Locale(s): United States

Summary: In Samantha Hunter's *Mine Until Morning*, Tessa Rose is the daughter of a senator, and Jonas Berringer is the man assigned to protect her. Their passions soon overwhelm them, and the deterrence causes Jonas to slip in his duties, resulting in Jonas losing his eyesight and Tessa ending up in grave danger. Now, months have passed, and once again Tessa and Jonas have come face to face. A blackout has descended upon the city, and the two have just one night to come to terms with the past, confront their present challenges, and reignite the red-hot sparks that exist between them.

Where it's reviewed:
Romantic Times, June 2011, Page 93

Other books by the same author:
I'll be Yours for Christmas, 2010
Make Your Move, 2010
Caught in the Act, 2009
Talking in Your Sleep, 2007
Untouched, 2007

Other books you might like:
Jaci Burton, *Riding on Instinct*, 2009
Julie James, *Something About You*, 2010
Elizabeth Jennings, *Shadows at Midnight*, 2010
Lora Leigh, *Renegade*, 2010
Julie Miller, *Man with the Muscle*, 2010

845

NOEL HYND

Hostage in Havana

(Grand Rapids, Michigan: Zondervan, 2011)

Story type: Romantic Suspense; Series
Subject(s): Christian life; Suspense; Espionage
Major character(s): Alexandra LaDuca, Agent (U.S. Treasury); Paul Guarneri, Exile (Cuban)
Time period(s): 21st century; 2010s
Locale(s): Havana, Cuba

Summary: In *Hostage in Havana* by Noel Hynd, U.S. Treasury agent Alexandra LaDuca goes beyond her jurisdiction to locate missing money and a renegade American expat in Havana, Cuba. Her partner in the unsanctioned mission is Cuban exile Paul Guarneri, who will help Alexandra navigate the dangerous waters that lead to Cuba, as well as the country's complex world of politics and crime. Alexandra knows that she will receive no backup from the American government, and instead

calls on her faith for guidance. Though she is still grieving the recent loss of her fiance, she can't deny the attraction she feels for Paul. *Hostage in Havana* is the first
book in Hynd's Cuban Trilogy.

Where it's reviewed:
Booklist, May 1, 2011, page 28
Romantic Times, May 2011, page 58

Other books by the same author:
Countdown in Cairo, 2009
Midnight in Madrid, 2009
Conspiracy in Kiev, 2008
The Enemy Within, 2008
Revenge, 2001

Other books you might like:
J. Mark Bertrand, *Pattern of Wounds*, 2011
Karen Harper, *Fall From Pride*, 2011
Dee Henderson, *Kidnapped*, 2008
Kathy Herman, *The Real Enemy*, 2009
DiAnn Mills, *Breach of Trust*, 2009
Marta Perry, *Final Justice*, 2008

846

BRENDA JACKSON

The Proposal

(Don Mills, Ontario, Canada: Harlequin, 2011)

Story type: Contemporary
Subject(s): Love; African Americans; Ranch life
Major character(s): Jason Westmoreland, Young Man;
   Bella Bostwick, Heiress
Time period(s): 21st century; 2010s
Locale(s): United States

Summary: In modern-day Texas, sexy Jason Westmoreland has his sights set on one woman and one woman
only. Her name is Bella Bostwick, and she is a fiery
Southern belle with a huge parcel of land she inherited
from her family. Jason would love to get his hands on
both Bella *and* her land, but Bella proves to be far more
crafty than Jason first believed. Can he convince her to
give him a chance? Or will his hopes and dreams for the
future be dashed by her refusal? *The Proposal* is the 21st
installment in Brenda Jackson's Westmoreland Series,
featuring the romantic escapades of a contemporary
African American family.

Where it's reviewed:
Romantic Times, June 2011, Page 94

Other books by the same author:
Bachelor Unleashed, 2011
Inseparable, 2011
A Silken Thread, 2011
A Wife for a Westmoreland, 2011
What a Westmoreland Wants, 2010

Other books you might like:
Pamela Britton, *The Wrangler*, 2009
Joanne Kennedy, *One Fine Cowboy*, 2010
Cathy McDavid, *Dusty: Wild Cowboy*, 2010
Marin Thomas, *Dexter: Honorable Cowboy*, 2010
Joanna Wayne, *24 Karat Ammunition*, 2007

847

LISA JACKSON
NANCY BUSH, Co-Author

Wicked Lies

(New York: Zebra, 2011)

Series: Colony Series. Book 2
Subject(s): Serial murders; Psychics; Adventure
Major character(s): Laura Adderley, Nurse, Psychic; Harri-
   son Frost, Journalist; Justice Turnbull, Serial Killer
Time period(s): 21st century; 2010s
Locale(s): Oregon, United States

Summary: Nurse Laura Adderley is a member of the elite
psychic community known as The Colony. She is
pregnant with her cheating ex's child and is struggling to
move forward with her life. When she learns that serial
killer Justice Turnbull is on the loose and tracking down
members of The Colony, she recruits journalist Harrison
Frost to help keep her safe. Soon Harrison finds himself
drawn into a dangerous cat-and-mouse game—and to the
beautiful nurse he's agreed to protect. Lisa Jackson and
Nancy Bush's *Wicked Lies* is the sequel to 2009's *Wicked
Game*.

Where it's reviewed:
Library Journal, April 15, 201, page 76
Publishers Weekly, April 4, 2011, page 39
Romantic Times, June 2011, page 73

Other books by the same author:
Without Mercy, 2010
Chosen to Die, 2009
Malice, 2009
Wicked Game, 2009
Wicked Game, 2009
Missing, 2008

Other books you might like:
Beverly Barton, *The Dying Game*, 2007
Beverly Barton, *The Murder Game*, 2008
Wendy Corsi Staub, *Dead Before Dark*, 2009
Heather Graham, *Deadly Harvest*, 2008
Linda Howard, *Dream Man*, 1995

848

ELOISA JAMES (Pseudonym of Mary Bly)

When Beauty Tamed the Beast

(New York: Avon, 2011)

Series: Happily Ever Afters Series. Book 2
Story type: Historical - Regency; Series
Subject(s): Love; Marriage; Fairy tales
Major character(s): Linnet Berry Thrynne, Young Woman;
   Piers Yelverton, Nobleman (Earl of Marchant)
Time period(s): 19th century
Locale(s): Wales, United Kingdom

Summary: In *When Beauty Tamed the Beast*, acclaimed
author Eloisa James re-imagines the classic *Beauty and
the Beast* fairy tale against a Regency-era backdrop. Linnet Thrynne is still smarting from the breakup of her

Romances

engagement to a prince, and now she is determined to find a suitable man to marry her. She soon hears word that Piers Yelverton, Earl of Marchant, is looking for a wife, but his bad temper and crotchety manner are legendary throughout Wales. Linnet sets out to charm him, and when the two meet, sparks fly. But does Linnet have what it takes to conquer the heart of a man who is nothing short of beastly? *When Beauty Tamed the Beast* is the second book in the Happily Ever Afters series.

Where it's reviewed:
Booklist, January 2011, page 59
Library Journal, February 15, 2011, page 92
Romantic Times, February 2011, page 31

Other books by the same author:
The Lady Most Likely, 2011
A Kiss at Midnight, 2010
A Duke of Her Own, 2009
This Duchess of Mine, 2009
When the Duke Returns, 2008

Other books you might like:
Connie Brockway, *The Golden Season*, 2010
Christina Dodd, *Some Enchanted Evening*, 2004
Elizabeth Hoyt, *The Raven Prince*, 2006
Teresa Medeiros, *A Kiss to Remember*, 2001

849

JULIE JAMES

A Lot Like Love

(New York: Berkley, 2011)

Story type: Contemporary
Subject(s): Love; Family; Mystery
Major character(s): Jordan Rhodes, Businesswoman (sommelier); Nick McCall, FBI Agent
Time period(s): 21st century; 2010s
Locale(s): Chicago, Illinois

Summary: Chicago businesswoman Jordan Rhodes is one of the Windy City's most powerful women. She has a thriving business as a sommelier, a fat bank account, and an open invitation to all the best parties in town. After her brother lands in jail, Jordan finds that even her most influential connections can't get him out. When FBI agent Nick McCall asks for her help in exchange for her brother's release, she agrees. Nick needs to gain entry into a posh charity gala, and Jordan is just the woman to get him in. But when his plan goes awry, the two must pretend to be a couple—an idea that eventually begins to grow on them both. Julie James's *A Lot Like Love* is the sequel to *Something About You*.

Where it's reviewed:
Booklist, February 15, 2011, page 59
Romantic Times, March 2011, page 83

Other books by the same author:
Something About You, 2010
Practice Makes Perfect, 2009
Just the Sexiest Man Alive, 2008

Other books you might like:
Christina Dodd, *Tongue in Chic*, 2007
Karen Hawkins, *Lois Lane Tells All*, 2010

Jayne Ann Krentz, *Absolutely, Positively*, 1996
Penny McCall, *Worth the Trip*, 2010
Susan Sey, *Money Honey*, 2010

850

LORELEI JAMES

Saddled and Spurred

(New York: Signet Eclipse, 2011)

Series: Blacktop Cowboys Series
Story type: Western
Subject(s): Romances (Fiction); Western fiction; Ranch life
Major character(s): Bran Turner, Rancher, Lover (of Harper); Harper Masterson, Hairdresser, Rancher, Lover (of Bran)
Time period(s): 21st century
Locale(s): Wyoming, United States

Summary: *Saddled and Spurred* by Lorelei James is a Western-based romance novel and part of the Blacktop Cowboys series about amorous modern-day cowboys and ranchers. In this novel, a Wyoming cattleman named Bran Turner is searching for a new helper for his ranch. Due to a series of coincidences, the help he ends up getting comes in the form of the gorgeous local cosmetologist Harper Masterson. Bran is suspicious about Harper's work ethic and willingness to get her hands dirty, but she soon proves that she's willing—and eager—to get to work. Romantic tension is soon flying in *Saddled and Spurred*.

Where it's reviewed:
Romantic Times, March 2011, page 112

Other books by the same author:
Branded as Trouble, 2010
Corralled, 2010
Shoulda Been a Cowboy, 2010
Cowgirl Up and Ride, 2009
Tied Up, Tied Down, 2009

Other books you might like:
Dawn Atkins, *Still Irresistible*, 2009
Debbi Rawlins, *Once an Outlaw*, 2009
Candace Schuler, *The Cowboy Way*, 2005
Vicki Lewis Thompson, *Should've Been a Cowboy*, 2011
Tina Welling, *Cowboys Never Cry*, 2010

851

ELLE JASPER

Everdark

(New York: Signet, 2011)

Series: Dark Ink Chronicles. Book 2
Story type: Fantasy; Series
Subject(s): Romances (Fiction); Fantasy; Vampires
Major character(s): Riley Poe, Artist (tattoo); Valerian Arcos, Vampire; Victorian Arcos, Vampire; Eli Dupre, Vampire

Time period(s): 21st century; 2010s
Locale(s): Savannah, Georgia

Summary: In *Everdark*, the second book in Elle Jasper's Dark Ink Chronicles series, Riley Poe continues to struggle with the vampire instincts that course through her veins. Though she was injected with just drops of toxin by Valerian and Victorian Arcos, Riley, a Savannah tattoo artist, is now helpless against her desire for sex and her dreams of bloodlust. Eli Dupre, Riley's vampire guardian, is the target of the insatiable seductress's advances—but sex isn't the only thing on Riley's mind. Her encounter with the Arcos brothers has also left Riley with increased strength, keener senses, and a psychic connection to a dangerous vampire.

Where it's reviewed:
Romantic Times, June 2011, page 90

Other books by the same author:
Afterlight, 2010

Other books you might like:
Kresley Cole, *Dark Desires After Dusk*, 2008
Cynthia Eden, *Midnight's Master*, 2009
Christine Feehan, *Dark Slayer*, 2009
Kim Lenox, *Darker than Night*, 2010
Annette McCleave, *Bound by Darkness*, 2010

852

SABRINA JEFFRIES (Pseudonym of Deborah Gonzales)

How to Woo a Reluctant Lady

(New York: Pocket Star, 2011)

Story type: Historical - Regency
Subject(s): Love; Inheritance and succession; Grandmothers
Major character(s): Minerva Sharpe, Noblewoman; Giles Masters, Rake
Time period(s): 19th century
Locale(s): United Kingdom

Summary: Noblewoman Minerva Sharpe's grandmother has laid-down a tough proposal: Minerva must marry before the end of the year or her grandmother will disinherit her. Not to be deterred by the feisty old woman's scheming, Minerva launches a plan of her own. She will announce she is engaged to notorious rake Giles Masters. This, she is certain, will horrify her grandmother, who will surely insist her granddaughter stay single and keep her in the will. But as Minerva and Giles play out the roles of their sham relationship, they can't help but be drawn to one another—and into a potentially dangerous game of love, desire, and deceit. *How to Woo a Reluctant Lady* is the third novel in Sabrina Jeffries's The Hellions of Halstead Hall series.

Where it's reviewed:
Booklist, February 15, 2011, page   92
Library Journal, February 15, 2011, page   92
Romantic Times, February 2011, page 31

Other books by the same author:
A Hellion in Her Bed, 2010
The Truth about Lord Stoneville, 2010
Don't Bargain with the Devil, 2009

Wed Him Before You Bed Him, 2009
Let Sleeping Rogues Lie, 2008

Other books you might like:
Louise Allen, *The Earl's Intended Wife*, 2006
Tina Gabrielle, *A Perfect Scandal*, 2010
Karen Hawkins, *How to Treat a Lady*, 2003
Julia London, *The Year of Living Scandalously*, 2010
Barbara Metzger, *The Bargain Bride*, 2009

853

BEVERLY JENKINS

Something Old, Something New

(New York: William Morrow, 2011)

Series: Blessings Series. Book 3
Subject(s): Weddings; African Americans; Rural life
Major character(s): Lily Fontaine, Bride; Trent July, Bridegroom; Bernadine Brown, Businesswoman (owner of Henry Adams, Kansas)
Time period(s): 21st century; 2010s
Locale(s): Henry Adams, Kansas

Summary: In the town of Henry Adams, Kansas, Lily Fontaine and Trent July just want to tie the knot—but the whole town seems to want in on the affair. Bernadine Brown, who owns the all-black community after buying it on eBay, is dreaming of a grand ceremony for the couple, while Lily's young foster child wants to get ordained and conduct the nuptials. Lily and Trent have more pressing problems, however; namely, how they will go about combining both their families with a minimum of fuss and heartache. *Something Old, Something New* is the third novel in Beverly Jenkins's Blessings series.

Where it's reviewed:
Romantic Times, June 2011, page 76

Other books by the same author:
Midnight, 2010
A Second Helping, 2010
Bring on the Blessings, 2009
Captured, 2009
Josephine, 2009

Other books you might like:
Susan Anderson, *Burning Up*, 2010
Victoria Dahl, *Lead Me On*, 2010
Linda Goodnight, *Winning the Single Mom's Heart*, 2008
Patricia Thayer, *Texas Ranger Takes a Bride*, 2008

854

SALLY JOHN

Desert Gift

(Carol Stream, Illinois: Tyndale House Publishers, 2011)

Story type: Contemporary
Subject(s): Marriage; Christian life; Love
Major character(s): Jillian Galloway, Spouse (of Jack),

Romances

Expert (marriage), Radio Personality; Jack Galloway,
Doctor, Spouse (of Jillian)
Time period(s): 21st century; 2010s
Locale(s): California, United States

Summary: In *Desert Gift* by Sally John, marriage expert
and radio talk-show host Jillian Galloway finds herself
in need of support and guidance when she faces the
prospect of divorce. The announcement from her
husband, the respected Dr. Jack Galloway, that he wants
a divorce comes just as Jillian is preparing for a public-
ity book tour. Devastated by the failure of her marriage,
and worried about the reactions her family and friends
will have to the news, Jillian travels to her parents' home
in the California desert to sort things out. There Jill
relies on her healing surroundings and her faith in God
to help guide her through the rocky turn her life has
taken.

Where it's reviewed:
Booklist, May 15, 2011, page 15
Library Journal, April 15, 2011, page 79
Romantic Times, June 2011, page 64

Other books by the same author:
Ransomed Dreams, 2010
A Time to Surrender, 2009
A Time to Gather, 2008
A Time to Mend, 2007
Moment of Truth, 2005

Other books you might like:
Davis Bunn, *My Soul to Keep*, 2007
Karen Kingsbury, *Take Three*, 2010
Renee Riva, *Heading Home*, 2010
James L. Rubart, *Rooms: A Novel*, 2010
Robert Whitlow, *Greater Love*, 2010

855

JEAN JOHNSON

Finding Destiny

(New York: Berkley Sensation, 2011)

Series: Sons of Destiny Saga
Story type: Collection
Subject(s): Short stories; Romances (Fiction); Fantasy
Time period(s): Indeterminate
Locale(s): Aurul, Fictional Location; Guildara, Fictional
Location; Jenodan Islands, Fictional Location;
Sundara, Fictional Location

Summary: *Finding Destiny* by Jean Johnson is a collection
of fantasy-romance novellas and part of Johnson's Sons
of Destiny series. In this collection, Johnson tells the
stories of four pairs of attractive strangers brought
together by fate in a fantasy realm. The first story,
"Sundara," tells the tale of a freed slave who falls in
love with an enchanted creature called Chanson. In
"Guildara," two intergalactic politicians fall in love during a war and have to weigh the risks of starting a
romantic relationship. The third story, "Aurul," deals
with a female political representative who becomes a
pawn in an arranged political marriage. Finally, "Jenodan Islands" is the story of a ship captain who falls in
love with a dastardly pirate.

Where it's reviewed:
Romantic Times, February 2011, page 91

Other books by the same author:
The Mage, 2009
The Song, 2009
The Flame, 2008
The Storm, 2008
The Sword, 2008

Other books you might like:
Lucy Monroe, *Moon Craving*, 2010
Alexis Morgan, *Darkness Unknown*, 2006
Erin Quinn, *Haunting Beauty*, 2009
Susan Squires, *Time for Eternity*, 2009
Deb Stover, *The Gift*, 2009

856

SUSAN JOHNSON

Sweet as the Devil

(New York: Berkley, 2011)

Story type: Historical
Subject(s): Love; Scots (British people); Royalty
Major character(s): James Blackwood, Bodyguard; Sofia
Eastleigh, Daughter (of Prince Ernst); Ernst, Royalty
(Prince of Dalmia)
Time period(s): 20th century; 1890s (1893)
Locale(s): Scotland

Summary: In *Sweet as the Devil*, author Susan Johnson
crafts a romantic tale set in 1893 Scotland. James Blackwood is an elite member of the Scottish guard, famous
for his bravery—and for his status as a lover. When the
prince's son is killed, James is recruited to look after the
royal's recently found daughter, the beautiful Sofia
Eastleigh. James must get Sofia out of London and into
Scotland in order to ensure her safety. Along the way,
however, neither of them is prepared for the mutual attraction that sparks between them. Can James keep Sofia
safe while juggling the pressures of his increasing desire?

Where it's reviewed:
Romantic Times, March 2011, Page 40

Other books by the same author:
Sexy as Hell, 2010
Gorgeous as Sin, 2009
At Her Service, 2008
Hot Property, 2008
Wine, Tarts and Sex, 2007

Other books you might like:
Suzanne Enoch, *Always a Scoundrel*, 2009
Anne Gracie, *To Catch a Bride*, 2009
Linda Winstead Jones, *Bride by Command*, 2009
Lavinia Kent, *A Talent for Sin*, 2009
Tracy Anne Warren, *Seduced by His Touch*, 2009

857

NICOLE JORDAN (Pseudonym of Anne Bushyhead)

To Desire a Wicked Duke

(New York: Ballantine Books, 2011)

Series: Courtship Wars Series. Book 6
Story type: Historical - Regency; Series
Subject(s): Royalty; Marriage; Ghosts
Major character(s): Tess Blanchard, Noblewoman, Spouse (of Ian); Ian Sutherland, Nobleman, Spouse (of Tess); Lady Wingate, Godmother (of Tess)
Time period(s): 19th century; 1810s
Locale(s): England

Summary: *To Desire a Wicked Duke* is the sixth and final book in author Nicole Jordan's Courtship Wars series. Two years after her husband-to-be dies in battle, Tess Blanchard is ready to move forward with her life. Unfortunately, she did not expect to move on to the rakish Duke of Rotham, her deceased fiancee's cousin Ian Sutherland. Yet when Lady Wingate, Tess's godmother, catches them in an embrace, she insists that they marry in order to escape charges of impropriety. Tess at first loathes Ian's conceited ways, but is soon drawn to his passion and sexuality. As Tess and Ian fall in love, however, a dark secret threatens to tear them apart forever.

Where it's reviewed:
Publishers Weekly, January 10, 2011, page 36
Romantic Times, March 2011, page 85

Other books by the same author:
To Tame a Dangerous Lord, 2010
To Romance a Charming Rogue, 2009
To Bed a Beauty, 2008
To Pleasure a Lady, 2008
To Seduce a Bride, 2008

Other books you might like:
Kathryn Caskie, *Rules of Engagement*, 2004
Eileen Dreyer, *Never a Gentleman*, April 1, 2011
Eloisa James, *The Taming of the Duke*, 2006
Sabrina Jeffries, *Never Seduce a Scoundrel*, 2006
Stephanie Laurens, *A Rogue's Proposal*, 1999

858

BRENDA JOYCE

Deadly Vows

(Don Mills, Ontario, Canada: HQN, 2011)

Story type: Historical
Subject(s): Love; Crime; Mystery
Major character(s): Francesca Cahill, Detective—Amateur; Rick Bragg, Police Officer
Time period(s): 20th century; 1900s (1902)
Locale(s): New York, New York

Summary: *Deadly Vows* is the ninth installment in Brenda Joyce's Deadly series. This outing centers on amateur detective Francesca Cahill, who, on the day of her wedding, finds herself the victim of blackmail. Someone has stolen a nude portrait of her that her betrothed had commissioned, and Francesca must find it. Her investigation causes her to miss her own wedding, and now she is both on her own and still being blackmailed. Enter police commissioner Rick Bragg, who agrees to help Francesca find the identity of her blackmailer. As they prowl the streets of turn-of-the-century Manhattan, the relationship between Rick and Francesca gradually evolves into something much more personal.

Where it's reviewed:
Booklist, March 1, 2011, page 37
Romantic Times, March 2011, page 36

Other books by the same author:
An Impossible Attraction, 2010
The Promise, 2010
Dark Lover, 2009
Dark Victory, 2009
Dark Embrace, 2008

Other books you might like:
Linda Francis Lee, *Nightingale's Gate*, 2001
Kat Martin, *Heart of Honor*, 2007
Amanda Quick, *Wait Until Midnight*, 2005
Deanna Raybourn, *Silent in the Grave*, 2007

859

JULIA JUSTISS (Pseudonym of Janet Justiss)

Society's Most Disreputable Gentleman

(Don Mills, Ontario, Canada: Harlequin, 2011)

Story type: Historical - Regency; Series
Subject(s): Love; Social class; Marriage
Major character(s): Greville Anders, Hero; Amanda Neville, Debutante
Time period(s): 19th century
Locale(s): London, England

Summary: Julia Justiss's *Society's Most Disreputable Gentleman* charts the love affair between a seafaring hero and a beautiful noblewoman. Greville Anders has just returned from the high seas, where he spent years fighting pirates and making a name for himself as a fearless warrior. But now, back in his native London, he finds he possesses none of the standing to make him a noble figure in British society. He soon meets Amanda Neville, a debutante out to charm the stuffy members of the ton. The attraction between Greville and Amanda is immediate and intense—but is it proper for a lady to cavort with such an unsuitable match?

Where it's reviewed:
Romantic Times, February 2011, page 34

Other books by the same author:
The Smuggler and the Society Bride, 2010
From Waif to Gentleman's Wife, 2009
A Most Unconventional Match, 2008
Rogue's Lady, 2007
The Untamed Heiress, 2006

Other books you might like:
Louise Allen, *The Viscount's Betrothal*, 2010

Romances

Adrienne Basso, *How to Seduce a Sinner*, 2010
Diane Gaston, *Chivalrous Captain, Rebel Mistress*, 2010
Sabrina Jeffries, *The Truth About Lord Stoneville*, 2010
Christine Merrill, *A Wicked Liaison*, 2009

860

VIRGINIA KANTRA

Forgotten Sea

(New York: Berkley Books, 2011)

Series: Children of the Sea Series. Book 5
Story type: Fantasy; Series
Subject(s): Angels; Sea stories; Fantasy
Major character(s): Lara Rho, Angel; Justin Miller, Child (of the sea)
Time period(s): 21st century; 2010s

Summary: *Forgotten Sea* is an installment from author Virginia Kantra's Children of the Sea series. Lara Rho is a Nephilim, a fallen angel entrusted with the task of saving children of the air before they can be sought out and destroyed by children of the fire. Seven years ago, however, she encountered someone of a completely different persuasion. His name was Justin Miller, and he was a child of the sea. Justin cannot remember what his life was like before he was saved, but he loves the sea and considers it his home. When Lara falls for him and attempts to woo him, Justin feels himself instantly drawn to her. Can these beings from two different worlds make it work, or is their destiny already spelled out for them?

Where it's reviewed:
Library Journal, June 15, 2011, page 65
Publishers Weekly, April 11, 2011, page 65

Other books by the same author:
Immortal Sea, 2010
Sea Lord, 2009
Sea Fever, 2008
Sea Witch, 2008
Home Before Midnight, 2006

Other books you might like:
Alyssa Day, *Atlantis Awakening*, 2007
Christine Feehan, *Oceans of Fire: A Drake Sisters Novel*, 2005
Christine Feehan, *Water Bound*, 2010
Marjorie M. Liu, *Soul Song*, 2007
Deborah Smith, *Alice at Heart*, 2002

861

CARLA KELLY

The Admiral's Penniless Bride

(Don Mills, Ontario, Canada: Harlequin, 2011)

Story type: Historical
Subject(s): Romances (Fiction); History; Marriage
Major character(s): Sally Paul, Young Woman; Charles Bright, Nobleman, Military Personnel (admiral)
Time period(s): 19th century

Locale(s): England

Summary: In the historical romance novel *The Admiral's Penniless Bride* by Carla Kelly, the marriage of a nobleman and a homeless woman defies the conventions of British Regency society. For Sally Paul, Admiral Sir Charles Bright's marriage proposal comes as an enormous surprise. She has no money and no place to live when they meet. Practical Sir Charles sees in Sally the answer to his predicament. Now that he has retired from the Navy he is expected to marry—and Sally is both available and in need of a home. Their hurried wedding, though romantic, gives Sally and Charles little time to prepare for their honeymoon or their life together.

Where it's reviewed:
Romantic Times, January 2011, page 39

Other books by the same author:
Marrying the Royal Marine, 2010
Marrying the Captain, 2009
The Surgeon's Lady, 2009
Beau Crusoe, 2007
The Wedding Journey, 2002

Other books you might like:
Adrienne Basso, *To Protect an Heiress*, 2002
Edith Layton, *To Love a Wicked Lord*, 2009
Mary Jo Putney, *The Bargain*, 1999
Elizabeth Thornton, *The Marriage Trap*, 2005
Gayle Wilson, *Lady Sarah's Son*, 1999

862

VANESSA KELLY

My Favorite Countess

(New York: Zebra, 2011)

Story type: Historical
Subject(s): Love; Physicians; Family
Major character(s): Bathsheba, Noblewoman (Lady Randolph); John Blackmore, Doctor
Time period(s): 19th century
Locale(s): England

Summary: In Vanessa Kelly's *My Favorite Countess*, spirited widow Bathsheba has fallen ill and requires a long rest in the country. But Bathsheba will have none of it; after all, she has to find a husband, as well as a way to repay her late spouse's gambling debts. Meanwhile, Dr. John Blackmore has never tended a more challenging patient than Bathsheba, and even in spite of her stubbornness, he is determined to see her well again. Soon the fires of passion are flaring between the two, but John knows it will take all his cunning, courage, and determination to tame a heart as wild as Bathsheba's.

Where it's reviewed:
Booklist, April 1, 2011, page 36
Publishers Weekly, March 28, 2011, page 43
Romantic Times, May 2011, page 44

Other books by the same author:
Sex and the Single Earl, 2010
Mastering the Marquess, 2009

Other books you might like:
Jo Beverley, *Lady Beware*, 2007

Liz Carlyle, *A Deal with the Devil*, 2004
Diane Gaston, *A Reputable Rake*, 2006
Sophia Nash, *Secrets of a Scandalous Bride*, 2010
Mary Jo Putney, *The Bartered Bride*, 2002

863

JOANNE KENNEDY

Cowboy Fever

(Naperville, Illinois: Sourcebooks Casablanca, 2011)

Story type: Western
Subject(s): Romances (Fiction); Western fiction; Court-ship
Major character(s): Jodi Brand, Beauty Pageant Contestant (rodeo queen), Lover (of Teague); Teague Treadwell, Rancher, Lover (of Jodi)
Time period(s): 21st century
Locale(s): Purvis, Wyoming

Summary: *Cowboy Fever* by Joanne Kennedy is a romance novel about a cowboy with a heart of gold. In this novel, Jodi Brand is a former beauty queen who was the darling of rodeos across Wyoming. Now she wants to open a new business and shed her old superficial ways so she will be taken seriously by the community. She runs into an old friend, Teague Treadwell, a cowboy who is down on his luck. Teague is trying to become a successful rancher but has to deal with hereditary anger issues. Jodi and Teague unite and try to help each other while inevitably falling in love in the rugged Western backdrop of horses, ranches, and sunsets.

Where it's reviewed:
Publishers Weekly, February 7, 2011, pages 41
Romantic Times, April 2011, page 90

Other books by the same author:
Cowboy Trouble, 2010
One Fine Cowboy, 2010

Other books you might like:
Carolyn Brown, *My Give a Damn's Busted*, 2010
Christine Columbus, *The Perfect Cowboy and Western Story*, 2010
Linda Lael Miller, *McKettricks of Texas: Garrett*, 2010
R.C. Ryan, *Montana Glory*, 2010
Tina Welling, *Cowboys Never Cry*, 2010

864

GWEN KIRKWOOD

Heart of the Home

(New York: Severn House Publishers, 2011)

Story type: Contemporary
Subject(s): Romances (Fiction); Courtship; Friendship
Major character(s): Avril Gray, Student (college), Farmer, Friend (of Dean); Dean Scott, Farmer (dairy), Friend (of Avril)
Time period(s): 21st century
Locale(s): Scotland

Summary: *Heart of the Home* by Gwen Kirkwood is a romance novel set in the Scottish highlands. There, lifelong friends Avril Gray and Dean Scott lose track of each other as they grow older. They take different paths in life; Dean chooses to stay on his family farm while Avril decides to go to college. Avril's path is interrupted, however, by an unexpected family emergency and she has to cancel her plans. Now Dean and Avril, both living on their family farms, reconnect and begin a romance. The only problem left is Dean's scheming mother, who tries to keep the couple apart.

Other books by the same author:
A Home of Our Own, 2010
Dreams of Home, 2009
Call of the Heather, 2008
Secrets in the Heather, 2008
When the Heather Blooms, 2008

Other books you might like:
Ann Doughty, *The Hamiltons of Ballydown*, 2004
Elizabeth Gill, *Paradise Lane*, 2010
Ruth Hamilton, *Sugar and Spice*, 2010
Elisabeth Rose, *Instant Family*, 2010
Danielle Steel, *A Good Woman*, 2008

865

JULIE KLASSEN

The Girl in the Gatehouse

(Bloomington, Minnesota: Bethany House, 2011)

Story type: Inspirational
Subject(s): Scandals; Christian life; Love
Major character(s): Mariah Aubrey, Young Woman; Matthew Bryant, Military Personnel
Time period(s): 19th century; 1810s
Locale(s): England

Summary: In *The Girl in the Gatehouse*, author Julie Klassen tells the romantic tale of a disgraced young woman and the war hero with whom she falls in love. After a scandal that destroys her reputation in decent society, Mariah Aubrey exiles herself to the gatehouse on a relative's property. There she clandestinely writes novels to make ends meet. When her relative sells the property to returning soldier Matthew Bryant, Matthew is shocked to find someone living in the gatehouse. He is immediately drawn to the mysterious Mariah and sets out to find the truth of her identity and how she came to be at the estate. As he unravels the mystery of Mariah's past, he and the young woman fall in love, leading Matthew to wonder if she will ever be able to return to respected society.

Where it's reviewed:
Booklist, December 1, 2010, page 35
Publishers Weekly, November 15, 2010, page 45
Romantic Times, January 2011, page 56

Other books by the same author:
The Silent Governess, 2010
Lady of Milkwood Manor, 2008

Other books you might like:
Catherine Blair, *A Scholarly Gentleman*, 2003

Sherry Lynn Ferguson, *The Honorable Marksley*, 2007
Amanda McCabe, *Lady Rogue*, 2002
Catherine Palmer, *The Courteous Cad*, 2009
Evelyn Richardson, *A Lady of Talent*, 2005

866

DEIDRE KNIGHT

Red Mortal

(New York: Signet, 2011)

Series: Gods of Midnight Series. Book 4
Story type: Fantasy; Series
Subject(s): Romances (Fiction); Fantasy; Mythology
Major character(s): Leonidas, Warrior; Daphne, Mythical Creature (nymph), Sister (half-sister of Ares); Ares, Mythical Creature (god of war), Brother (half-brother of Daphne)
Time period(s): 21st century; 2010s

Summary: In the fantasy romance novel *Red Mortal* by Deidre Knight, ancient myths spill over into modern times as warriors and gods struggle for power and love. More than 2000 years ago, King Leonidas was a Spartan warrior who led his men in the epic battle at Thermopylae. After his death, Leonidas made a pact that would grant him immortality but leave him a subject of Ares, the god of war. The gods and goddesses have endured through the centuries and now reside in the world of unsuspecting mortals. When Ares learns that his half-sister Daphne and Leonidas are entertaining a romantic union, he makes the Spartan warrior mortal again. The doomed couple must find a way to undo Ares's actions while Leonidas still lives. *Red Mortal* is the fourth book in Knight's Gods of Midnight series.

Where it's reviewed:
Romantic Times, April 2011, page 105

Other books by the same author:
Red Demon, 2010
Red Kiss, 2009
Red Fire, 2008
Parallel Desire, 2007
Parallel Seduction, 2007

Other books you might like:
Sherrilyn Kenyon, *Dream Chaser*, 2008
Sherrilyn Kenyon, *The Dream-Hunter*, 2007
Gena Showalter, *The Darkest Night*, 2008
Gena Showalter, *The Darkest Whisper*, 2009
Eve Silver, *Sins of the Heart*, 2010

867

KIERAN KRAMER

Cloudy With a Chance of Marriage

(New York: St. Martin's Paperbacks, April 26, 2011)

Series: Impossible Bachelors Series. Book 3
Story type: Historical; Series
Subject(s): Interpersonal relations; Divorce; Marriage
Major character(s): Jilly Jones, Clerk; Stephen Arrow,

Military Personnel (captain)
Time period(s): 19th century
Locale(s): London, England

Summary: *Cloudy with a Chance of Marriage* is an installment from author Kieran Kramer's Impossible Bachelors series of romance novels. After marrying a man who was wrong for her in every way, Jilly Jones finally broke free and set out on a new life all her own. Now she works in a bookshop in the heart of London, and is enjoying her freedom. Then she meets Captain Stephen Arrow, a former officer in the British Navy who is thrilled to be back in civilian life. Despite both Stephen and Jilly's better judgment, they find themselves hopelessly attracted to one another. But Jilly is hiding a secret, and Stephen is determined to find out what it is before he commits to her.

Where it's reviewed:
Romantic Times, May 2011, page 40

Other books by the same author:
Dukes to the Left of Me, Princes to the Right, 2010
When Harry Met Molly, 2010

Other books you might like:
Pamela Britton, *Seduced*, 2003
Nicola Cornick, *Lord of Scandal*, 2007
Lisa Kleypas, *Married by Morning*, 2010
Kat Martin, *Royal's Bride*, 2009

868

JANE ANNE KRENTZ

In Too Deep

(New York: Penguin USA, 2010)

Series: Looking Glass Trilogy. 1
Subject(s): Detective fiction; Mystery; Psychics
Major character(s): Isabella Valdez, Assistant (of Fallon); Fallon Jones, Detective (of the paranormal)
Time period(s): 21st century; 2010s
Locale(s): Scargill Cove, California

Summary: *In Too Deep: Book One of the Looking Glass Trilogy* is the first installment of Jayne Ann Krentz's Looking Glass trilogy and a book from her Arcane Society series of novels. In this novel, mysterious ingenue Isabella Valdez has arrived in Scargill Cove, a quaint town along the coast of Northern California. Isabella is on the run, and soon paranormal detective Fallon Jones takes a liking to her. She is just what he needs in his office: someone to organize things, make coffee, and not ask questions, especially considering his line of work. Yet after a peculiar timepiece falls into Fallon's hands during a seemingly regular investigation, he begins to discover that there is more to Isabella than meets the eye.

Where it's reviewed:
Booklist, December 1, 2010, page 35
Library Journal, December 1, 2010, page 96
Publishers Weekly, November 8, 2010, page 48
Romantic Times, January 2011, page 72

Other books by the same author:
Fired Up, 2010

Running Hot, 2009
Sizzle and Burn, 2008
White Lies, 2007
All Night Long, 2006

Other books you might like:
Cherry Adair, Night Fall, 2008
Linda Howard, Killing Time, 2005
Nora Roberts, Three Fates, 2002
Evelyn Vaughn, A.K.A. Goddess, 2004

869

LYNN KURLAND (Pseudonym of Lynn Curland)

One Magic Moment

(New York: Jove, 2011)

Series: De Piaget Series. Book 14
Story type: Paranormal; Series
Subject(s): Love; Magic; Fate
Major character(s): Tess Alexander, Scholar; John, Mechanic
Time period(s): 21st century; 2010s

Summary: In Lynn Kurland's One Magic Moment, Tess Alexander is a medieval studies specialist who is overjoyed at her latest assignment: living in and studying a medieval castle. One day she ventures into the local village, where she meets a man named John, a mechanic who bears an uncanny resemblance to the man who wed her sister. The meeting throws Tess's life into upheaval, considering the man who married her sibling did so 800 years in the past. Tess is a headstrong scholar, and she is skeptical about time travel and magic, but as she and John grow closer, she can't help but wonder what fate has in store for the two of them. One Magic Moment is the 14th book in Kurland's De Piaget series.

Where it's reviewed:
Publishers Weekly, March 28, 2011, page 43
Romantic Times, May 2011, page 95

Other books by the same author:
Spellweaver, 2011
One Enchanted Evening, 2010
A Tapestry of Spells, 2010
Princess of the Sword, 2009
Till There Was You, 2009

Other books you might like:
Lisa Cach, Of Midnight Born, 2000
Sara Mackenzie, Passions of the Ghost, 2006
Karen Marie Moning, Kiss of the Highlander, 2001
Christina Skye, Bride of the Mist, 1996

870

LINDA LAEL MILLER

The Creed Legacy

(Don Mills, Ontario, Canada: Harlequin, 2011)

Series: Montana Creed Series. Book 7
Story type: Series; Western

Subject(s): Romances (Fiction); Cowhands; Brothers
Major character(s): Brody Creed, Rodeo Rider, Twin (of Conner); Conner Creed, Twin (of Brody), Rancher; Carolyn Simmons, Businesswoman (shop owner)
Time period(s): 21st century; 2010s
Locale(s): Lonesome Bend, Colorado

Summary: In the novel The Creed Legacy by Linda Lael Miller, Carolyn Simmons enjoys a fulfilling life in Lonesome Bend, Colorado. She owns a successful shop and appreciates her beautiful surroundings, but she longs to find a man who wants to settle down and start a family. When handsome Brody Creed comes to town, Carolyn is drawn to him immediately, even though the roaming rodeo rider couldn't possibly offer the kind of relationship she's looking for. Brody has been away from Lonesome Bend for some time, separated from his twin brother Conner, the rest of the Creed clan, and their land. As romance grows between Carolyn and Brody, secrets from Brody's past threaten their happiness. The Creed Legacy is the seventh book in Miller's Montana Creeds series.

Where it's reviewed:
Romantic Times, July 2011, Page 83

Other books by the same author:
A Creed in Stone Creek, 2011
The Creed's Honor, 2011
Only Forever, 2011
Ragged Rainbows, 2011
Willow, 2011

Other books you might like:
Geralyn Dawson, Her Outlaw, 2007
Georgina Gentry, To Love a Texan, 2007
Leigh Greenwood, Texas Tender, 2006
Linda Lael Miller, A Wanted Man, 2007
R.C. Ryan, Montana Destiny, 2010

871

JOYCE LAMB

True Colors

(New York: Berkley, 2011)

Story type: Paranormal
Subject(s): Romances (Fiction); Journalism; Extrasensory perception
Major character(s): Alex Trudeau, Journalist, Sister (of Charlie); Charlie Trudeau, Journalist, Sister (of Alex); John Logan, Detective
Time period(s): 21st century
Locale(s): Lake Avalon, Florida

Summary: True Colors by Joyce Lamb is a romance novel with elements of paranormal suspense. It tells the story of a female journalist and photographer, Alex Trudeau, who has developed strange extrasensory abilities. Alex is trying to find more time to relax but that isn't working—she ends up getting shot while trying to protect her sister, Charlie. While recovering, Alex meets a captivating detective named John Logan. She falls for John and thinks that her life is finally getting on the right track until she discovers that John has his own share of secrets, including a crafty serial killer with a grudge.

Romances

Where it's reviewed:
Romantic Times, January 2011, page 74

Other books by the same author:
True Vision, 2010
Cold Midnight, 2009
Found Wanting, 2005
Caught in the Act, 2004
Relative Strangers, 2003

Other books you might like:
Allison Brennan, *Love Me to Death*, 2010
Alicia Dean, *Heart of the Witch*, 2009
Anne Marsh, *The Hunt*, 2009
Savannah Russe, *Dark Nights, Dark Dreams*, 2008
Christina Skye, *Bound by Dreams*, 2009

872

JILL MARIE LANDIS

Heart of Lies

(Grand Rapids, Michigan: Zondervan, 2011)

Story type: Historical; Series
Subject(s): Romances (Fiction); United States history, 1865-1901; Homeless persons
Major character(s): Maddie Grande, Streetperson, Young Woman; Dexter Grande, Guardian (of Maddie); Tom Abbott, Detective (Pinkerton)
Time period(s): 19th century; 1870s (1875)
Locale(s): Louisiana, United States

Summary: In the historical romance novel *Heart of Lies*, the second novel in the Irish Angel series by Jill Marie Landis, young Maddie Grande steals to survive in the New Orleans streets of 1875. Knowing nothing of her past or even her real name, Maddie is under the care of Dexter Grande, who decides to relocate her and her two "brothers" to the nearby bayou. In the swamp Maddie feels at home and learns to live off the land and water. When the boys kidnap a little girl in an effort to earn reward money, Maddie becomes a reluctant accomplice. Pinkerton detective Tom Abbott arrives to investigate the case, and Maddie can't help falling in love with the man who holds her fate in his hands.

Where it's reviewed:
Romantic Times, February 2011, page 54

Other books by the same author:
Mai Tai One On, 2011
Heart of Stone, 2010
The Accidental Lawman, 2009
Homecoming, 2008
Heat Wave, 2005

Other books you might like:
Tamera Alexander, *Within My Heart*, 2010
Cathy Marie Hake, *Letter Perfect*, 2006
Julie Lessman, *A Passion Most Pure*, 2008
DiAnn Mills, *Awaken My Heart*, 2008
Lauraine Snelling, *A Touch of Grace*, 2008

873

KATIE LANE

Going Cowboy Crazy

(New York: Forever, 2011)

Series: Deep in the Heart of Texas Series. Book 1
Story type: Series; Western
Subject(s): Cowhands; Ranch life; Romances (Fiction)
Major character(s): Faith Aldridge, Twin (of Hope); Hope Scroggs, Twin (of Faith), Actress; Slate Calhoun, Cowboy/Cowgirl
Time period(s): 21st century; 2010s
Locale(s): Bramble, Texas

Summary: *Going Cowboy Crazy* is the first novel in the Deep in the Heart of Texas series, which is written by author Katie Lane. The novel revolves around Faith Aldridge, who arrives in the small town of Bramble, Texas to find her twin sister Hope. The people of Bramble mistake Faith for Hope immediately, and they are determined to get her back together with Hope's exboyfriend, Slate Calhoun. Slate quickly figures out that Faith is not his former lover, but not before Faith falls for him head over heels. The problem is, Slate is still begrudgingly in love with Hope, and Faith must convince him that she is the sister for him. Lane is also the author of *Make Mine a Bad Boy*.

Where it's reviewed:
Romantic Times, May 2011, page 87

Other books by the same author:
Make Mine a Bad Boy, 2011

Other books you might like:
Jan Hambright, *The High Country Rancher*, 2009
R.C. Ryan, *Montana Destiny*, 2010
Bobbi Smith, *Wanted: The Texan*, 2008
Tina Welling, *Cowboys Never Cry*, 2010

874

KATIE LANE

Make Mine a Bad Boy

(New York: Forever, 2011)

Series: Deep in the Heart of Texas Series. Book 2
Story type: Series; Western
Subject(s): Ranch life; Interpersonal relations; Romances (Fiction)
Major character(s): Faith Aldridge, Twin (of Hope); Hope Scroggs, Twin (of Faith), Actress; Colt Lomax, Rake
Time period(s): 21st century; 2010s
Locale(s): Bramble, Texas

Summary: *Make Mine a Bad Boy* is the second novel in the Deep in the Heart of Texas series, which is written by author Katie Lane. When Hope Scroggs returns home to the small town of Bramble, Texas after five years of trying to make it as a Hollywood actress, she's shocked to learn that not only does she have a twin sister named Faith, but that Faith has married the man Hope wanted to marry. Then resident rake Colt Lomax comes back to town. Hope has always been drawn to Colt but is

determined to make her life in Bramble work, which means staying far away from his wicked ways. Yet for Colt, Hope was always the one girl who could make him settle down. Can he prove to her that he isn't as bad as everyone thinks he is? Lane is also the author of *Going Cowboy Crazy*.

Other books by the same author:
Going Cowboy Crazy, 2011

Other books you might like:
Pamela Britton, *The Wrangler*, 2009
Kathleen Eagle, *The Last True Cowboy*, 1998
Marin Thomas, *Dexter: Honorable Cowboy*, 2010
Jeannie Watt, *The Brother Returns*, 2008

875

STEPHANIE LAURENS
MARY BALOGH, Co-Author
JACQUIE D'ALESSANDRO, Co-Author
CANDICE HERN, Co-Author

It Happened One Season
(New York: Avon, 2011)

Story type: Collection
Subject(s): Love; Family; Short stories

Summary: In *It Happened One Season*, beloved romance authors Candice Hern, Mary Balogh, Stephanie Laurens, and Jacquie D'Alessandro were given a unique challenge: they were each to come up with a short story based on a single idea submitted by readers. The result: each author crafts a romantic tale of a soldier, wounded and just home from war, who must find a suitable woman to marry. With the storytelling flair and gift for characters that has made each of these writers a legend in the romance genre, Hern, Balogh, Laurens, and D'Alessandro rise to the challenge with this quartet of stories. Titles in this volume are "The Seduction of Sebastian Trantor," "Only Love," "Hope Springs Eternal," and "Fate Strikes a Bargain."

Where it's reviewed:
Romantic Times, April 2011, page 40

Other books you might like:
Victoria Alexander, *The One That Got Away*, 2004
Sabrina Jeffries, *Snowy Night with a Stranger*, 2009
Eloisa James, *Talk of the Ton*, 2005
Debbie Raleigh, *How to Marry a Duke*, 2005

876

JADE LEE (Pseudonym of Katherine Ann Gill)

Wicked Seduction
(New York: Berkley, 2011)

Story type: Historical - Regency; Series
Subject(s): Love; Family; Adventure
Major character(s): Kit Frazier, Slave (former), Pirate; Maddy, Young Woman
Time period(s): 19th century

Locale(s): England

Summary: In *Wicked Seduction*, bestselling author Jade Lee chronicles the romance between a recently-freed slave and a mousy, poverty-stricken young woman. For seven long years, Kit Frazier was held captive on a pirate ship, forced into slavery and living a life of unimaginable terror. Now he is back in his native England, and he soon crosses paths with Maddy, a beautiful but shy woman who looks after her uncle and her cousin. As Kit and Maddy grow closer, the scars of the past begin to surface. It isn't long before the two embark upon a tentative journey toward true love, healing the wounds of the past and moving together toward a brighter future.

Where it's reviewed:
Romantic Times, March 2011, page 38

Other books by the same author:
Wicked Surrender, 2010
Dragon Bound, 2009
Getting Physical, 2009
Dragon Born, 2008
Cornered Tigress, 2007

Other books you might like:
Liz Carlyle, *A Woman Scorned*, 2000
Kit Donner, *The Vengeful Bridegroom*, 2010
Gaelen Foley, *The Duke*, 2000
Eloisa James, *Desperate Duchesses*, 2007
Lisa Kleypas, *Lady Sophia's Lover*, 2002

877

LORA LEIGH

Midnight Sins
(New York: St. Martin's Press, 2011)

Story type: Contemporary
Subject(s): Love; Mystery; Murder
Major character(s): Rafer "Rafe" Callahan, Crime Suspect; Cambria "Cami" Flannigan, Young Woman
Time period(s): 21st century; 2010s
Locale(s): United States

Summary: Lora Leigh's *Midnight Sins*, the first installment in a series, tells the story of Rafe Callahan, a reformed bad boy who wants to win the heart of the young woman he's longed for since he was a teen. But Cami Flannigan is leery of Rafe; after all, it is rumored that he, along with two of his friends, may have been involved in her sister's murder. Now that the years have passed, Rafe is determined to prove to Cami that he had nothing to do with her sister's demise. Just as the two reunite, another string of murders plagues the community, and, once again, fingers are pointed at Rafe and his former pals.

Where it's reviewed:
Romantic Times, August 2011, Page 91

Other books by the same author:
Dangerous Pleasure, 2011
Live Wire, 2011
Navarro's Promise, 2011
Black Jack, 2010
Renegade, 2010

Other books you might like:
B.J. Daniels, *Montana Royalty*, 2008
Jan Hambright, *The High Country Rancher*, 2009
Kat Martin, *Against the Wind*, 2010
Linda Lael Miller, *A Wanted Man*, 2007
R.C. Ryan, *Montana Destiny*, 2010

878

JOHANNA LINDSEY

When Passion Rules

(New York: Simon and Schuster, 2011)

Story type: Historical
Subject(s): Napoleonic Wars, 1800-1815; Royalty; Orphans
Major character(s): Alana Farmer, Socialite, Royalty, Orphan; Christoph Becker, Guard
Time period(s): 19th century
Locale(s): England; Lubinia, Fictional Location

Summary: *When Passion Rules* is a novel by author Johanna Lindsey. Since the death of her parents when she was very young, the only guardian Alana Farmer had ever known was the caretaker who helped her escape France in the midst of the Napoleonic Wars. Alana was brought to England, where she began a new life and received many opportunities, and even became part of English society. Then Alana learns that her parents were, in fact, royalty, and that she is the princess of the kingdom of Lubinia. As her guardian brings her back to the country of her birth, a guard named Christoph Becker doubts the truth about Alana's heritage and puts her in the palace prison. Can Alana convince Christoph that she is truly the princess, even though she has doubts about it herself?

Where it's reviewed:
Library Journal, June 15, 2011, page 75
Romantic Times, June 2011, page 34

Other books by the same author:
That Perfect Someone, 2010
A Rogue of My Own, 2009
No Choice but Seduction, 2008
The Devil Who Tamed Her, 2007
Captive of My Desires, 2006

Other books you might like:
Jo Beverley, *Secrets of the Night*, 1999
Gaelen Foley, *The Pirate Prince*, 1998
Sabrina Jeffries, *Beware a Scot's Revenge*, 2007
Laura Kinsale, *Shadowheart*, 2004
Mary Jo Putney, *Nowhere Near Respectable*, 2011

879

JULIA LONDON (Pseudonym of Dinah Dinwiddie)

A Light at Winter's End

(New York: Pocket, 2011)

Story type: Contemporary
Subject(s): Love; Sisters; Child custody

Major character(s): Holly Fisher, Sister (of Hannah); Wyatt Clark, Cowboy/Cowgirl; Hannah, Sister (of Holly)
Time period(s): 21st century; 2010s
Locale(s): Texas, United States

Summary: In *A Light at Winter's End*, best-selling author Julia London tells the story of Holly Fisher, a young woman who is suddenly thrust into the role of mother. When Holly's sister Hannah arrives on her doorstep, she hands Holly her son and promptly disappears. Months later, Hannah returns from a stint in rehab and desperately wants her child back. As Holly deals with the startling idea of losing the nephew to whom she has grown so attached, she must also contend with her feelings for handsome Wyatt Clark, a cowboy with a heart of gold. When she is ordered to turn her nephew over to his mother's care, Holly is devastated—and Wyatt just may be the only one who can pull her out of her despair.

Where it's reviewed:
Publishers Weekly, January 24, 2011, page 138
Romantic Times, March 2011, page 82

Other books by the same author:
One Season of Sunshine, 2010
The Year of Living Scandalously, 2010
A Courtesan's Scandal, 2009
Highland Scandal, 2009
The Summer of Two Wishes, 2009

Other books you might like:
Robyn Carr, *Paradise Valley*, 2009
Robyn Carr, *Second Chance Pass*, 2008
Linda Lael Miller, *Montana Creeds: Dylan*, 2009
Mariah Stewart, *Almost Home*, 2011
Susan Wiggs, *Lakeside Cottage*, 2005

880

JULIE ANNE LONG

What I Did For a Duke

(New York: Avon, 2011)

Series: Pennyroyal Green Series. Book 5
Story type: Historical - Regency; Series
Subject(s): Love; Family; Adventure
Major character(s): Alexander Moncrieffe, Nobleman (Duke of Falconbridge); Genevieve Eversea, Sister (of Ian); Ian Eversea, Brother (of Genevieve)
Time period(s): 19th century
Locale(s): London, England

Summary: In Regency England, reputations don't get more scandalous than the one possessed by Alexander Moncrieffe, Duke of Falconbridge. Anyone with any sense will steer clear of the notorious rake, but Ian Eversea just can't leave well enough alone. After crossing Moncrieffe's path, the Duke sets out to get revenge. His plan entails seducing Ian's beautiful sister Genevieve, and then abandoning her, lovelorn and devastated. There's just one problem: Moncrieffe finds Genevieve irresistible and wants nothing more than to have her by his side—forever. *What I Did For a Duke* is the fifth book in Julie Anne Long's Pennyroyal Green Series.

Where it's reviewed:
Romantic Times, March 2011, page 38

Other books by the same author:
I Kissed an Earl, 2010
Since the Surrender, 2009
Like No Other Love, 2008
Like No Other Lover, 2008
The Perils of Pleasure, 2008

Other books you might like:
Victoria Alexander, *What a Lady Wants*, 2007
Jo Beverley, *Lady Beware*, 2007
Sabrina Jeffries, *Beware a Scot's Revenge*, 2007
Sabrina Jeffries, *Don't Bargain with the Devil*, 2009
Sabrina Jeffries, *To Pleasure a Prince*, 2005

■ **881**

MERLINE LOVELACE

Strangers When We Meet

(New York: Harlequin, 2011)

Story type: Contemporary
Subject(s): Love; Fires; Suspense
Major character(s): Larissa Petrovna, Inspector; Dodge Hamilton, Agent (Omega)
Time period(s): 21st century; 2010s
Locale(s): United States

Summary: In Merline Lovelace's *Strangers When We Meet*, Major Larissa Petrovna of Russia's nuclear inspection unit is haunted by the mysterious voice that taunted her the night a fire left her life in shambles. Now she is determined to find the person behind that voice and bring the culprit to justice. Aiding her investigation is Special Agent Dodge Hamilton. At first, Dodge regards his assignment as just another routine case. But the more deeply ensnared he becomes, he realizes just how dangerous the investigation is—and what is at stake for the beautiful Larissa. Working side by side, Larissa and Dodge soon must contend with another type of fire: the fire of passion that burns between them.

Where it's reviewed:
Romantic Times, June 2011, Page 98

Other books by the same author:
Catch Her if You Can, 2011
Crusader Captive, 2011
Double Deception, 2011
Risky Engagement, 2011
The Sheikh's Lost Princess, 2011

Other books you might like:
Jessica Bird, *An Unforgettable Lady*, 2010
Nina Bruhns, *If Looks Could Chill*, 2009
Christy Reece, *Last Chance*, 2010
Christy Reece, *No Chance*, 2010
Stephanie Tyler, *Promises in the Dark*, 2010

■ **882**

SARAH-KATE LYNCH

Dolci di Love

(New York: Plume, 2011)

Story type: Contemporary
Subject(s): Love; Italy; Interpersonal relations
Major character(s): Lily Turner, Businesswoman; Alessandro, Wealthy, Widow(er)
Time period(s): 21st century; 2010s
Locale(s): Montevedova, Italy

Summary: In Sarah-Kate Lynch's *Dolci di Love*, high-powered businesswoman Lily Turner is devastated when she learns her boyfriend is married with a family. She abandons her hectic life and takes refuge in a small Tuscan village, where she finds accommodations over the town bakery. There she meets the elderly sisters who run the bakery, and they decide that Lily will be the recipient of their next matchmaking scheme. As the sisters and their friends plot and plan, they are prepared to do whatever it takes to unite Lily and sexy Alessandro, a rich, heartbroken widower. But is Lily ready for another relationship? Is she over her ex and his crushing betrayal? Can she find healing—and love—in the hills of Tuscany?

Where it's reviewed:
Publishers Weekly, February 14, 2011, page 34
Romantic Times, May 2011, page 62

Other books by the same author:
House of Daughters, 2008
By Bread Alone, 2004
Blessed Are the Cheesemakers, 2003

Other books you might like:
Jennifer Greene, *Blame It on Paris*, 2008
Kirsten Lobe, *Paris Hangover*, 2006
Carole Matthews, *More to Life than This*, 2006
Susan Elizabeth Phillips, *Breathing Room*, 2002
Barbara Samuel, *Madame Mirabou's School of Love*, 2006

■ **883**

SUSAN LYONS

Heat Waves

(New York: Berkley, 2011)

Story type: Contemporary
Subject(s): Love; Cruise ships; Weddings
Time period(s): 21st century; 2010s
Locale(s): Greece

Summary: Susan Lyons's *Heat Waves* is comprised of two linked novellas chronicling the romantic misadventures of a group of people attending a wedding on the Greek isles. In *Rock the Boat*, Gwen Austin is a wedding planner butting heads with dashing young cruise director Santos Michaelides, who she eventually learns is working undercover aboard the ship. Soon Gwen and Santos have embarked upon a hot and heavy romance—but

could this red-hot affair jeopardize Gwen's job and Santos's investigation? In *Making Waves*, lawyer Kendra Kirk crosses paths with Flynn Kavanaugh on board the ship. Flynn was once tried for stealing millions of dollars but was let off, much to Kendra's dismay. Once the attraction between them becomes palpable, Flynn wants Kendra to know he's innocent of the theft—and that the true culprit is someone on board.

Where it's reviewed:
Romantic Times, July 2011, Page 112

Other books by the same author:
Sex on the Beach, 2010
Sex on the Slopes, 2010
Calendar of Love, 2009
Sex Drive, 2008
She's On Top, 2008

Other books you might like:
Susan Fox, *Love, Unexpectedly*, 2010
Susan Lyons, *Sex on the Slopes*, 2010
Carly Phillips, *Kiss Me if You Can*, 2010
Jill Shavlis, *Simply Irresistible*, 2010
Kathryn Shay, *The Perfect Family*, 2010

884

SALLY MACKENZIE

The Naked King

(New York: Zebra, 2011)

Story type: Historical - Regency
Subject(s): Love; Sisters; Family
Major character(s): Anne Marston, Noblewoman; Stephen Parker-Roth, Rake; Evie, Sister (of Anne)
Time period(s): 19th century
Locale(s): London, United Kingdom

Summary: In *The Naked King*, author Sally MacKenzie presents the ninth book in the Naked series of historical romance novels. Set in Regency-era London, this volume follows the journey of Lady Anne Marston, a beautiful noblewoman considered past her prime now that she's in her late 20s. Anne arrives in London to visit her sister Evie, who has set her sights on getting married. But it is Anne who crosses paths with the notorious rake Stephen Parker-Roth. Can the ravishing spinster and the famous playboy find the courage to overcome their hesitations—not to mention the wagging tongues of Regency society—and find true love in one another's arms?

Where it's reviewed:
Publishers Weekly, April 11, 2011, page 35
Romantic Times, June 2011, page 38

Other books by the same author:
The Naked Earl, 2010
The Naked Viscount, 2010
The Naked Baron, 2009
The Naked Gentleman, 2008
The Naked Marquis, 2006

Other books you might like:
Olivia Drake, *Never Trust a Rogue*, 2010
Teresa Medeiros, *The Devil Wears Plaid*, 2010

Anne Stuart, *Reckless*, 2010
Tracy Anne Warren, *Wicked Delights of a Bridal Bed*, 2010
Emma Wildes, *My Lord Scandal*, 2010

885

JULIANNE MACLEAN

Captured by the Highlander

(New York: St. Martin's Press, 2011)

Series: Highlander Trilogy. Book 1
Story type: Historical; Series
Subject(s): Scottish history; Kidnapping; Revenge
Major character(s): Duncan MacLean, Warrior; Lady Amelia Sutherland, Kidnap Victim
Time period(s): 18th century; 1710s
Locale(s): Scotland

Summary: *Captured by the Highlander* is the first book in Julianne MacLean's Highlander Trilogy. In this novel, the author tells the story of Lady Amelia Sutherland, who is kidnapped by a Highlander warrior to avenge the death of the warrior's lover. Amelia is engaged to the man who killed the lover of Duncan MacLean, and by abducting her Duncan knows that he will finally get his revenge. Soon Duncan finds himself falling for Amelia, however, and Amelia feels the same way. Can these two lovers overcome years of wars between their two clans to find true love with one another? MacLean is also the author of *In My Wildest Fantasies*, *Surrender to a Scoundrel*, and *Portrait of a Lover*.

Where it's reviewed:
Romantic Times, March 2011, page 41

Other books by the same author:
Claimed by the Highlander, 2011
When a Stranger Loves Me, 2009
When a Stranger Loves Me, 2009
The Mistress Diaries, 2008
In My Wildest Fantasies, 2007

Other books you might like:
Juliana Garnett, *The Laird*, 2002
Sophia Johnson, *Risk Everything*, 2005
Margo Maguire, *The Perfect Seduction*, 2006
Monica McCarty, *Highlander Unchained*, 2007
Monica McCarty, *The Ranger*, December 28, 2010

886

SARAH MACLEAN (Pseudonym of Sarah Trabucchi)

Eleven Scandals to Start to Win a Duke's Heart

(New York: Avon, 2011)

Story type: Historical - Regency
Subject(s): Love; Social class; Interpersonal relations
Major character(s): Juliana Fiori, Young Woman; Simon Pearson, Nobleman
Time period(s): 19th century

Locale(s): London, United Kingdom

Summary: Sarah MacLean's *Eleven Scandals to Start to Win a Duke's Heart* chronicles the unlikely romance that sparks between a hell-raising bad girl and a proper, high-society gentleman. Juliana Fiori may be beautiful, but she is also a spitfire, the likes of which Regency London has never seen. She doesn't shy away from speaking her truth, getting into altercations, or being concerned about her reputation. She is exactly the wrong person for Simon Pearson to get involved with. But when Simon finds Juliana hiding in his carriage one fateful night, he throws caution to the wind and plans to teach her a few lessons about good behavior. Juliana, however, has plans of her own, and they involve the seduction of the straight-laced Simon.

Where it's reviewed:
Booklist, May 1, 2011, page 71
Romantic Times, May 2011, page 42

Other books by the same author:
Nine Rules to Break When Romancing a Rake, 2010
Ten Ways to Be Adored When Landing a Lord, 2010

Other books you might like:
Elizabeth Boyle, *Stealing the Bride*, 2003
Kathryn Caskie, *A Lady's Guide to Rakes*, 2005
Eloisa James, *Much Ado about You*, 2005
Julia London, *A Courtesan's Scandal*, 2009
Olivia Parker, *At the Bride Hunt Ball*, 2008

887

DEBBIE MACOMBER
SUSAN MALLERY, Co-Author
CHRISTINA SKYE, Co-Author

The Knitting Diaries
(Don Mills, Ontario, Canada: Mira, 2011)

Story type: Collection
Subject(s): Love; Hobbies; Interpersonal relations
Time period(s): 21st century; 2010s

Summary: The popular art of knitting is the theme coursing through the novellas that comprise *The Knitting Diaries*. In *The Twenty-First Wish*, bestselling author Debbie Macomber spins a tale of love and romance, revolving around a daughter who plays matchmaker for her single mom. Susan Mallery's *Coming Unraveled* finds failed actress Robyn returning to her Texas roots and her grandmother's knitting store, only to stumble upon a handsome, fiery stranger—and the possibility of true love. In Christina Skye's *Return to Summer Island*, Caro McNeal searches for hope, identity, and love on a quaint Oregon island, where she takes solace with a supportive group of knitters.

Where it's reviewed:
Booklist, April 15, 2011, page 28
Publishers Weekly, February 21, 2011, page 119
Romantic Times, April 2011, page 50

Other books you might like:
Heidi Betts, *Tangled Up in Love*, 2009
Jennifer Greene, *Baby, It's Cold Outside*, 2010
Rachel Herron, *How to Knit a Love Song*, 2010

Whitney Lyles, *Catch of the Day*, 2006
Vicki Lewis Thompson, *Fool for Love*, 2004

888

SUSAN MALLERY (Pseudonym of Susan Macias Redmond)

Only Mine
(Don Mills, Ontario, Canada: Harlequin, 2011)

Series: Fool's Gold Series. Book 4
Story type: Contemporary; Series
Subject(s): Romances (Fiction); Television programs; Brothers
Major character(s): Dakota Hendrix, Psychologist; Finn Anderssen, Pilot
Time period(s): 21st century; 2010s
Locale(s): Fool's Gold, California

Summary: In *Only Mine*, the fourth novel in Susan Mallery's Fool's Gold contemporary romance series, psychologist Dakota Hendrix agrees to assist with the production of a reality dating show and ends up finding a man for herself. The TV program is to be filmed in Fool's Gold, California, where females, who far outnumber the males, are searching for eligible bachelors. Finn Anderssen, a pilot from Alaska, comes to Fool's Gold—not as a contestant, but to round up his younger twin brothers before they join the show. Finn feels that he has taken care of his siblings long enough and wants them to return to Alaska and start acting like responsible adults. But in Fool's Gold, Finn finds someone else who needs his help—a pretty young woman named Dakota.

Where it's reviewed:
Romantic Times, August 2011, Page 92

Other books by the same author:
Already Home, 2011
Almost Perfect, 2010
The Best of Friends, 2010
Chasing Perfect, 2010
Finding Perfect, 2010

Other books you might like:
Gemma Halliday, *The Perfect Shot*, 2010
Deirdre Martin, *Power Play*, 2008
LuAnn McLane, *Playing for Keeps*, 2011
Carol Snow, *Just Like Me, Only Better*, 2010

889

MARGARET MALLORY (Pseudonym of Peggy L. Brown)

The Guardian
(New York: Forever, 2011)

Series: The Return of the Highlanders Series. Book 1
Story type: Historical; Series
Subject(s): Marriage; Love; Scots (British people)
Major character(s): Ian MacDonald, Warrior; Sileas MacDonald, Spouse (of Ian)
Time period(s): 16th century; 1500s
Locale(s): Scotland

Romances

Summary: Margaret Mallory's *The Guardian* is the first novel in The Return of the Highlanders series, chronicling the epic homecoming of four Scottish warriors as they return to their native land after years at war. This inaugural volume follows Ian MacDonald back to his clan, where he is stunned to find the community in splinters. His power here is limited, and he knows the only thing he can do to help his clan is repair his relationship with his wife, Sileas. He married Sileas long ago and made no secret of the fact that he'd rather be in the battlefield than in bed with his wife. But a new era is dawning, and he begins to see Sileas in a new light. Can this married couple come together after years of war and estrangement and find their way toward true, lasting love?

Where it's reviewed:
Romantic Times, May 2011, page 42

Other books by the same author:
Knight of Passion, 2011
Knight of Desire, 2009
Knight of Pleasure, 2009

Other books you might like:
Donna Grant, *Untamed Highlander*, April 26, 2011
Julianne MacLean, *Captured by the Highlander*, 2011
Monica McCarty, *The Chief*, 2010
Monica McCarty, *The Hawk*, 2010
Monica McCarty, *The Ranger*, December 28, 2010

890

JILL MANSELL

Staying at Daisy's

(London: Headline Book Publishing, 2002)

Story type: Contemporary
Subject(s): Hotels and motels; Romances (Fiction); Marriage
Major character(s): Daisy MacLean, Hotel Worker; Tara, Housekeeper; Dev Tyzack, Sports Figure
Time period(s): 21st century; 2000s
Locale(s): England

Summary: *Staying at Daisy's* is a novel by author Jill Mansell. After the untimely death of her husband, who engaged in extramarital affairs behind her back, hotelier Daisy MacLean has sworn off men. Yet when retired rugby star Dev Tyzack comes to her upscale hotel for an extended stay, Daisy cannot deny that she is drawn to him. In the meantime, Daisy's best mate Tara, a maid at the hotel, rekindles an affair with a former lover who just happens to be getting married at the hotel—and Dev is the best man! As each employee of the hotel embarks on different romantic adventures, Daisy must hold it all together in order to ensure that her guests have a worry-free stay.

Where it's reviewed:
Publishers Weekly, January 31, 2011, page 35
Romantic Times, March 2011, page 85

Other books by the same author:
To the Moon and Back, 2011
Rumor Has It, 2010

Take a Chance on Me, 2010
Perfect Timing, 2009
An Offer You Can't Refuse, 2008

Other books you might like:
Rachel Gibson, *Truly, Madly Yours*, 1999
Kristan Higgins, *Catch of the Day*, 2007
Lani Diane Rich, *Crazy in Love*, 2007
Sherryl Woods, *The Inn at Eagle Point*, 2009
Sherryl Woods, *Seaview Inn*, 2008

891

KAT MARTIN (Pseudonym of Kathleen Kelly Martin)

Against the Fire

(Don Mills, Ontario, Canada: Mira, 2011)

Series: Raines of Wind Canyon Series. Book 2
Story type: Romantic Suspense; Series
Subject(s): Arson; Romances (Fiction); Suspense
Major character(s): Gabriel Raines, Businessman (real estate developer); Angel Ramirez, Teenager; Mattie Baker, Volunteer (family abuse center)
Time period(s): 21st century; 2010s
Locale(s): Texas, United States

Summary: *Against the Fire*, the second book in Kat Martin's Raines of Wild Canyon series of romantic suspense novels, opens with a fire at Dallas Towers, a real-estate development owned by Gabriel Raines. A second fire at another of Raines's properties not long after the Dallas Towers blaze convinces the businessman that an arsonist is at work. Though Raines has no shortage of business enemies, the authorities suspect teenager Angel Ramirez of the crime. Mattie Baker, who has worked with Angel at a local abuse shelter, comes to his defense. As Mattie tries to prove Angel's innocence, the real arsonist strikes again and Gabe finds himself surrendering to Mattie's persuasion.

Where it's reviewed:
Romantic Times, February 2011, Page 61

Other books by the same author:
Against the Wind, 2010
Reese's Bride, 2010
Rule's Bride, 2010
Heart of Courage, 2009
Royal's Bride, 2009

Other books you might like:
Jo Davis, *Line of Fire*, 2010
Jo Davis, *Under Fire*, 2009
Darlene Gardner, *The Hero's Sin*, 2009
Jill Shalvis, *Flashback*, 2008
Debra Webb, *Everywhere She Turns*, 2009

892

ERIN MCCARTHY

The Chase

(New York: Berkley, 2011)

Series: Fast Track Series
Story type: Contemporary

Subject(s): Romances (Fiction); Courtship; Automobiles
Major character(s): Kendall Holbrook, Race Car Driver, Lover (of Evan); Evan Monroe, Race Car Driver, Lover (of Kendall)
Time period(s): 21st century
Locale(s): United States

Summary: *The Chase* by Erin McCarthy is a racing-themed romance novel and part of McCarthy's Fast Track series. In this novel, childhood friends Evan Monroe and Kendall Holbrook part ways only to reunite in an unexpected way. By unbelievable coincidence, they both become professional race-car drivers and end up on the same team. Now working together to win races, and challenging each other to break team records, Evan and Kendall patch up old arguments and begin a new romance. Can they overcome the stresses of competition and the difficulties of the racing circuit to keep things together and make their rediscovered romance work?

Where it's reviewed:
Publishers Weekly, February 14, 2011, page 43
Romantic Times, April 2011, page 89

Other books by the same author:
Flat-Out Sexy, 2010
Hard and Fast, 2010
Hot Finish, 2010
High Stakes, 2008
Heiress for Hire, 2007

Other books you might like:
Pamela Britton, *In the Groove*, 2006
Bethany Campbell, *Truth and Consequences*, 2008
Ken Casper, *Miles Apart*, 2007
Abby Gaines, *Back on Track*, 2007
Nancy Warren, *Speed Dating*, 2007

893

MONICA MCCARTY

The Ranger

(New York: Ballantine Books, December 28, 2010)

Series: Highland Guard Series. Book 3
Story type: Historical; Series
Subject(s): Scottish history; Romances (Fiction); Suspense
Major character(s): Anna MacDougall, Daughter (of chieftain); Ranger Campbell, Warrior
Time period(s): 14th century; 1300s
Locale(s): Scotland

Summary: *The Ranger* is the third book in author Monica McCarty's Highland Guard series. Arthur "Ranger" Campbell is determined to avenge the death of his father, and so he devises the perfect plan to go undercover within the same army that murdered him. Yet he meets his match in Anna MacDougall, the daughter of the army's chieftain. Anna suspects something is awry when she meets Ranger, but she cannot quite put her finger on it. What they both know, however, is that they are falling for one another against their better judgment. Will the revelation of Ranger's true identity ruin his plan for vengeance? McCarty is also the author of *The Viper* and *The Hawk*, also from this series, as well as the Campbell Trilogy and the MacLeods of Sky Trilogy.

Where it's reviewed:
Publishers Weekly, January 29, 2011, page 36
Romantic Times, January 2011, page 35

Other books by the same author:
The Chief, 2010
The Hawk, 2010
Highland Outlaw, 2009
Highland Scoundrel, 2009
Highland Warrior, 2009

Other books you might like:
Diana Cosby, *His Captive*, 2007
Shannon Drake, *The Lion in Glory*, 2003
Kathleen Givens, *On a Highland Shore*, 2006
Susan King, *The Swan Maiden*, 2001
Sue-Ellen Welfonder, *Sins of a Highland Devil*, 2011

894

SARAH MCCARTY

Reaper's Justice

(New York: Berkley Sensation, 2010)

Story type: Paranormal
Subject(s): Romances (Fiction); Werewolves; Wars
Major character(s): Isaiah Jones, Military Personnel (soldier), Werewolf; Adelaide Cameron, Human, Kidnap Victim
Time period(s): 19th century; 1860s
Locale(s): United States

Summary: *Reaper's Justice* by Sarah McCarty is a paranormal romance novel about amorous werewolves fighting in the American Civil War. In McCarty's fantasy world, some soldiers were captured during the Civil War and turned into werewolves using powerful injections. These werewolf soldiers were called "Shadow Reapers." After the fighting is over, these poor souls cannot find peace. One of the best "Shadow Reapers," Isaiah Jones, falls in love with a woman named Adelaide Cameron. He thinks she may be able to help him live a normal life, but when she is kidnapped, his wolf instincts take control again. Can he win her back and overcome his own bizarre afflictions?

Other books by the same author:
Jared, 2010
Tracker's Sin, 2010
Caleb, 2009
Promises Keep, 2008
Promises Linger, 2008

Other books you might like:
Angela Knight, *Master of Wolves*, 2006
Susan Krinard, *Luck of the Wolf*, 2010
Linda Lael Miller, *Forever and the Night*, 1993
Lucy Monroe, *Moon Burning*, 2011
Alexis Morgan, *Dark Defender*, 2006

Romances

895

SARAH MCCARTY

Jace

(New York: Berkley, 2011)

Series: Shadow Wranglers Series. Book 3
Story type: Contemporary
Subject(s): Vampires
Major character(s): Jace Johnson, Vampire, Spouse (of Miri); Miri, Werewolf, Kidnap Victim, Spouse (of Jace)
Time period(s): 21st century; 2010s
Locale(s): Texas, United States

Summary: Jace Johnson is a vampire who is heartbroken when his expectant wife Miri—a werewolf—disappears. He sets out to find her, and, after a year of searching, is relieved when he finally tracks her down. Miri is being held prisoner by an evil group intent on conducting experiments on her, and she is no longer the woman Jace so adored. But he is determined to reignite the passion of their relationship and rescue Miri from the clutches of darkness. Sarah McCarty's *Jace* is the third novel in the Shadow Wranglers series, which chronicles the adventures of a group of vampire brothers.

Where it's reviewed:
Romantic Times, May 2011, page 96

Other books by the same author:
Sam's Creed, 2011
Tucker's Claim, 2011
Jared, 2010
Tracker's Sin, 2010
Caleb, 2009

Other books you might like:
Lorelei James, *Rode Hard, Put up Wet*, 2008
Shelly Laurenston, *Go Fetch*, 2009
Mackenzie McKade, *Take Me Again*, 2009
Denise Rossetti, *The Lone Warrior*, 2011
Cherise Sinclair, *Master of the Mountain*, 2010

896

LAUREL MCKEE (Pseudonym of Amanda McCabe)

Duchess of Sin

(New York: Forever, 2010)

Series: Daughters of Erin Series. Book 2
Story type: Historical; Series
Subject(s): Irish (European people); Love; Identity
Major character(s): Anna Blacknall, Young Woman; Conlan McTeer, Businessman (club owner)
Time period(s): 18th century; 1790s
Locale(s): Ireland

Summary: Ireland and England have been engaged in an epic battle over power and politics, and beautiful Anna Blacknall has been one of countless victims of the turmoil. Despite the very personal toll the fighting has taken on her, she can't forget the single kissed placed on her lips two years prior by a mysterious gentleman. Now,

Anna is out on the town for a night of revelry when a masked stranger plants a peck on her mouth—reawakening her senses and bringing the realization that this stranger is none other than Conlan McTeer, the man for whom she has been searching for two years. *Duchess of Sin* is the second novel in Laurel McKee's Daughters of Erin series.

Where it's reviewed:
Booklist, December 1, 2011, page 34

Other books by the same author:
Countess of Scandal, 2010

Other books you might like:
Jo Beverley, *Devilish*, 2000
Elaine Coffman, *The Italian*, 2002
Elizabeth Hoyt, *Wicked Intentions*, 2010
May McGoldrick, *The Rebel*, 2002
Jeane Westin, *Lady Anne's Dangerous Man*, 2006

897

LINDSAY MCKENNA (Pseudonym of Eileen Nauman)

Deadly Silence

(Don Mills, Ontario, Canada: HQN, 2011)

Story type: Contemporary
Subject(s): Love; Fires; Single parent family
Major character(s): Matt Sinclaire, Fire Fighter, Single Parent, Widow(er); Casey Cantrell, Ranger
Time period(s): 21st century; 2010s
Locale(s): Jackson Hole, Wyoming

Summary: In *Deadly Silence*, author Lindsay McKenna spins a romantic drama centering on a grieving firefighter and a beautiful forest ranger. An arson fire claimed the life of Matt Sinclaire's beloved wife, and now he is struggling to rebuild his life with his young daughter. United States Forest Ranger Casey Cantrell arrives in Wyoming and crosses paths with Matt and his daughter. She feels a maternal bond with a traumatized girl and helps her through her unspeakable grief. Matt, meanwhile, finds himself contending with his feelings for Casey—feelings he has not experienced since his late wife. Can Casey be the woman to help Matt piece together the painful remnants of his life?

Where it's reviewed:
Romantic Times, July 2011, Page 81

Other books by the same author:
The Adversary, 2010
Deadly Identity, 2010
Guardian, 2010
His Woman in Command, 2010
Reunion, 2010

Other books you might like:
Bella Andre, *Wild Heat*, 2009
Jo Davis, *Line of Fire*, 2010
Trish Milburn, *A Firefighter in the Family*, 2008
Jill Shalvis, *Flashback*, 2008

898

LUANN MCLANE

Playing for Keeps

(New York: Signet, 2011)

Series: Cricket Creek Series. Book 1
Story type: Contemporary; Series
Subject(s): Southern United States; Actors; Entertainment industry
Major character(s): Olivia Lawson, Teacher, Actress; Noah Falcon, Actor, Baseball Player
Time period(s): 21st century; 2010s
Locale(s): Cricket Creek, Kentucky

Summary: *Playing for Keeps* is a novel from author LuAnn McLane's Cricket Creek series. Professional baseball player-turned-actor Noah Falcon has returned to his hometown of Cricket Creek, much to the relief of many in the small Kentucky town with the exception of school teacher and theater buff Olivia Lawson. Olivia remembers how cruel Noah was to her back in high school, and she's not ready to forgive and forget. Yet Noah's starring role in the community theater's latest production may help the economically depressed town, and he's willing to assist in any way he can. While turning the town's financial status around might seem like a difficult feat, Noah knows it will be even harder to win Olivia's trust.

Where it's reviewed:
Publishers Weekly, January 2, 2011, page 139

Other books by the same author:
He's No Prince Charming, 2009
Redneck Cinderella, 2009
Driven by Desire, 2008
A Little Less Talk and a Lot More Action, 2008
Trick My Truck but Don't Mess with My Heart, 2007

Other books you might like:
Kate Angell, *Sweet Spot*, 2010
Gemma Bruce, *The Man for Me*, 2008
Deirdre Martin, *Ice Breaker*, 2010
Jill Shalvis, *Slow Heat*, 2010

899

FERN MICHAELS

Deja Vu

(New York: Kensington Publishing, 2011)

Series: Sisterhood Series
Story type: Adventure
Subject(s): Romances (Fiction); Adventure; Women
Major character(s): Hank Jellicoe, Crime Suspect (pursued by The Sisterhood)
Time period(s): 21st century
Locale(s): Las Vegas, Nevada

Summary: *Deja Vu* by Fern Michaels is an adventure-romance novel about a group of vigilante crime fighters called The Sisterhood. The Sisterhood, a strictly female group empowered by a female president to track down male criminals, loves solving crimes and having parties. In this novel, the members of The Sisterhood have a wild party in Las Vegas before beginning a mission to track down a supremely bad man named Hank Jellicoe. All of the nation's top investigative agencies could not find Jellicoe, so it's up to The Sisterhood to put him behind bars once and for all.

Where it's reviewed:
Romantic Times, January 2011, page 46

Other books by the same author:
Cross Roads, 2010
Exclusive, 2010
Game Over, 2010
The Scoop, 2009
Weekend Warriors, 2004

Other books you might like:
Beverly Barton, *Dead by Midnight*, 2010
Kate Brady, *One Scream Away*, 2009
Julie Garwood, *Sizzle: A Novel*, 2009
Heather Graham, *Picture Me Dead*, 2003
Karen Harper, *Down to the Bone*, 2000

900

COURTNEY MILAN

Unveiled

(New York: HQN, 2011)

Story type: Historical - Victorian
Subject(s): Love; Revenge; Social class
Major character(s): Ash Turner, Nobleman; Margaret Dalrymple, Heiress—Dispossessed
Time period(s): 19th century
Locale(s): United Kingdom

Summary: Courtney Milan's *Unveiled* takes place in Victorian England, where evidence has just emerged that the Duke of Parford's children are illegitimate and therefore unable to claim his inheritance. A distant cousin, Ash Turner, comes to claim the title, as the duke's daughter, Margaret Dalrymple, is rejected by society now that word of her illegitimacy has spread. At the urging of her brothers, who plan on challenging Ash's claims, Margaret goes undercover as a nurse in an attempt to get close to Ash and learn his secrets. She doesn't, however, count on Ash being so handsome, so charming, and so very impossible to resist.

Where it's reviewed:
Booklist, February 15, 2011, page 59
Publishers Weekly, December 13, 2010, page 42
Romantic Times, February 2011, page 31

Other books by the same author:
Proof by Seduction, 2010
Trial by Desire, 2010

Other books you might like:
Adele Ashworth, *Duke of Scandal*, 2006
Meredith Duran, *The Duke of Shadows*, 2008
Lisa Kleypas, *Married by Morning*, 2010
Kathryn Smith, *When Marrying a Scoundrel*, 2010
Sherry Thomas, *Not Quite a Husband*, 2009

Romances

901

LINDA LAEL MILLER

Creed's Honor

(Don Mills, Ontario, Canada: Harlequin, 2011)

Series: Montana Creed Series. Book 2
Story type: Series; Western
Subject(s): Twins; Sibling rivalry; Cowhands
Major character(s): Tricia McCall, Manager; Brody Creed, Twin (of Conner), Rodeo Rider; Conner Creed, Rancher, Twin (of Brody)
Time period(s): 21st century; 2010s
Locale(s): Lonesome Bend, Colorado

Summary: In *Creed's Honor*, the second novel in Linda Lael Miller's Creed Cowboys series, cowhand Conner Creed inherits a ranch from his late uncle. Conner deeply resents the fact that his twin brother Brody escaped working the ranch and headed for a more exciting life working in rodeos, but Conner is determined to do right by his uncle's memory. After all, his uncle raised him when his parents died. Then Tricia McCall moves to town to take care of her great grandmother and manage her dead father's trailer park. Together, Tricia and Conner try to teach one another how to balance familial obligations with one's own needs.

Where it's reviewed:
Romantic Times, June 2011, page 76

Other books by the same author:
A Creed in Stone Creek, 2011
The Creed Legacy, 2011
Only Forever, 2011
Ragged Rainbows, 2011
Willow, 2011

Other books you might like:
B.J. Daniels, *Montana Royalty*, 2008
Delores Fossen, *Branded by the Sheriff*, 2009
Beth Kendrick, *Second Time Around*, 2010
Jane Porter, *She's Gone Country*, 2010

902

LINDA LAEL MILLER

A Creed in Stone Creek

(Don Mills, Ontario: Harlequin, 2011)

Story type: Ranch Life; Series
Subject(s): Rural life; Ranch life; Adoption
Major character(s): Steven Creed, Lawyer; Matt St. John, 5-Year-Old, Adoptee; Melissa O'Ballivan, Lawyer
Time period(s): 21st century; 2010s
Locale(s): Stone Creek, Arizona

Summary: *A Creed in Stone Creek* is a novel from Linda Lael Miller's Stone Creek series. Attorney Steven Creed finds his world turned upside-down when he must take over guardianship duties for his godson, Matt, after Matt's parents pass away. In order to provide a better life for Matt, Steven moves from the city to an old family ranch in Stone Creek, Arizona. There, he works on restoring their new home while taking on cases in the local town. Soon Steven finds himself going up against Maricopa County prosecutor Melissa O'Ballivan as he defends a teen in trouble with the law. Melissa is tough as nails, but the sights of Steven with Matt melt her heart. Can Steven win his opposing counsel over, not only in the courtroom but also in matters of the heart?

Where it's reviewed:
Booklist, March 15, 2011, page 28
Romantic Times, March 2011, page 84

Other books by the same author:
The Creed Legacy, 2011
Creed's Honor, 2011
McKettricks of Texas: Garrett, 2011
McKettricks of Texas: Tate, 2011
Austin, 2010
Garrett, 2010
McKettricks of Texas: Austin, 2010
Tate, 2010
At Home in Stone Creek, 2009
A Creed Country Christmas, 2009

Other books you might like:
Catherine Anderson, *Bright Eyes*, 2004
Catherine Anderson, *Seventh Heaven*, 2000
Catherine Anderson, *Star Bright*, 2009
Joan Johnston, *The Cowboy*, 2000
Debbie Macomber, *Return to Promise*, 2000

903

RAIN MITCHELL

Tales from the Yoga Studio

(New York: Penguin, 2011)

Story type: Contemporary
Subject(s): Friendship; Exercise; Interpersonal relations
Major character(s): Lee, Teacher (yoga); Imani, Actress; Graciela, Dancer; Stephanie, Businesswoman; Katherine, Addict (former)
Time period(s): 21st century; 2010s
Locale(s): Los Angeles, California

Summary: Rain Mitchell's *Tales from the Yoga Studio* is set in modern-day Los Angeles, where yoga teacher Lee runs a small, successful studio and relishes her close friendships with four of her students. Each woman is going through a period of upheaval in her life, and each finds comfort in the ancient art of yoga. The tightly-knit quintet contains knowledgeable Lee, actress Imani, dancer Graciela, show business powerhouse Stephanie, and recovering drug addict Katherine. Together, the five women face life's ups and downs as they lean on one another, share stories and laughter, and maneuver their bodies into the soul-opening twists that are the hallmark of yoga practice. First novel.

Where it's reviewed:
Library Journal, October 2010, page 70
Publishers Weekly, September 20, 2010, page 44
Romantic Times, January 2011, page 47

Other books you might like:
Marilyn Brant, *Friday Mornings at Nine*, 2010

Beth Kendrick, *Second Time Around*, 2010
Barbara Samuel, *The Goddesses of Kitchen Avenue*, 2004
Susan Wiggs, *The Ocean Between Us*, 2004

904

ALEXIS MORGAN (Pseudonym of Patricia L. Pritchard)

Bound by Darkness

(New York: Pocket Star, 2011)

Story type: Fantasy
Subject(s): Adventure; Love; Urban life
Major character(s): Sasha, Investigator; Larem, Warrior
Time period(s): 21st century; 2010s
Locale(s): Seattle, Washington

Summary: The seventh novel in Alexis Morgan's Paladin series, *Bound by Darkness* is an urban fantasy set in Seattle, where the worlds of two different cultures are about to clash in the most unexpected of ways. Sasha arrives in the city to investigate corruption among her Regent peers. She soon learns the Paladin population of the city is harboring the evil Kaliths, and Sasha sets out to stop this bit of suspicious hospitality. She crosses paths with the warrior Larem, igniting immediate sparks between the two. Now, with the battle between the Regents and the Paladins building at a feverish pace, the fates of two worlds lay in the hands of unlikely lovers Sasha and Larem.

Where it's reviewed:
Romantic Times, May 2011, page 93

Other books by the same author:
Defeat the Darkness, 2010
Darkness Unknown, 2009
In Darkness Reborn, 2007
Redeemed in Darkness, 2007
Dark Defender, 2006

Other books you might like:
Alexandra Ivy, *Devoured by Darkness*, 2010
Marjorie M. Liu, *A Taste of Crimson*, 2005
Pamela Palmer, *The Dark Gate*, 2007
Eve Silver, *Demon's Kiss*, 2007
Anna Windsor, *Captive Spirit*, 2010

905

J.J. MURRAY

She's the One

(New York: Kensington Books, 2011)

Story type: Contemporary
Subject(s): Romances (Fiction); Movie industry; Movies
Major character(s): Katharina Minolta, Actress; Pietro Lucentio, Filmmaker, Director; Vincenzo Lucentio, Filmmaker, Director
Time period(s): 21st century
Locale(s): Canada; California, United States

Summary: *She's the One* by J.J. Murray is a romance novel that deals with show business and the eccentric people involved in it. In this novel, a young actress named Katharina Minolta has taken over Hollywood. She is the talk of the town and has won over critics and audiences alike with her many great performances. Unfortunately, her success goes to her head and she becomes spoiled and nasty, alienating her fans. Her director, Pietro Lucentio, who harbors a strong attraction to her, arranges for her to undergo a cinematic experiment. Katharina will be taken into the Canadian wilderness, where she will be filmed trying to survive. Pietro thinks this will help her career get back on track.

Where it's reviewed:
Romantic Times, March 2011, page 86

Other books by the same author:
I'm Your Girl, 2010
The Real Thing, 2010
Too Much of a Good Thing, 2009
Original Love, 2008
Can't Get Enough of Your Love, 2007

Other books you might like:
Rochelle Alers, *Because of You*, 2010
Chevetta Burton, *Aloha*, 2011
Gwynne Forster, *Once in a Lifetime*, 2002
Michele Grant, *Heard It All Before*, 2010
Miriam Shumba, *Show Me the Sun*, 2010

906

BILL MYERS

The Judas Gospel

(New York: Howard Books, 2011)

Story type: Contemporary
Subject(s): Fantasy; Jesus Christ; Supernatural
Major character(s): Judas "Jude Miller" Iscariot, Supernatural Being; Rachel Delacroix, Young Woman (prophetess)
Time period(s): 21st century; 2010s
Locale(s): United States

Summary: In *The Judas Gospel*, author Bill Myers spins a supernatural fantasy with a Christian bent. Judas Iscariot is most famous for his role as Christ's betrayer. But somehow, Judas manages to talk God into letting him return to Earth with the promise of helping a troubled young prophet and spreading Christ's message. That prophet is Rachel Delacroix, who is wholly unprepared for the supernatural gifts with which she has been blessed. When she meets Judas, he begins to market and "sell" her unique talents to the public—with shocking results. Can Rachel handle this newfound notoriety...and can she hang onto the special powers that seem to be slipping away?

Where it's reviewed:
Library Journal, June 16, 2011, page 69

Other books by the same author:
The Face of God, 2010
The God Hater, 2010
Angel of Wrath, 2009

Romances

The Voice, 2008
The Wager, 2003

Other books you might like:
Randy Alcorn, *Dominion*, 1996
Ted Dekker, *Adam*, 2008
David Gregory, *The Last Christian: A Novel*, 2010
James L. Rubart, *Rooms: A Novel*, 2010
Robert Whitlow, *Water's Edge*, 2011

907

CATE NOBLE (Pseudonym of Lauren Bach)

Deadly Games

(New York: Zebra, 2011)

Story type: Romantic Suspense
Subject(s): Love; Adventure; Drugs
Major character(s): Rocco Taylor, Agent (CIA); Gena
   Armstrong, Hostage; Madison Kohlmeyer, Hostage
Time period(s): 21st century; 2010s
Locale(s): United States

Summary: CIA analyst Madison Kohlmeyer is kidnapped
by powerful drug kingpin Minh Tran and held hostage.
Her captor is insistent that CIA agent Rocco Taylor swap
places with Madison as retribution for Rocco's killing of
Tran's son. But Rocco will hear none of it. Despite their
romantic past, he is determined to free Madison from the
clutches of the deadly drug lord. In the process, Rocco
plans to bring Tran to justice. There's just one hitch:
Tran has also targeted beautiful Gena Armstrong, the
love of Rocco's life, and suddenly this case becomes
even more personal for the determined CIA operative.
Deadly Games is the third book in Cate Noble's Deadly
Trilogy of romantic suspense novels.

Where it's reviewed:
Romantic Times, February 2011, Page 63

Other books by the same author:
Deadly Seduction, 2010
Dead Right, 2009

Other books you might like:
Maya Banks, *No Place to Run*, 2010
Shannon K. Butcher, *Love You to Death*, 2009
Margaret Carroll, *A Dark Love*, 2009
Jo Davis, *Hidden Fire*, 2009
Stephanie Tyler, *Lie with Me*, 2010

908

KATE NOBLE

Follow My Lead

(New York: Berkley, 2011)

Story type: Historical - Regency; Series
Subject(s): Love; Art; Adventure
Major character(s): Winnifred "Winn" Crane, Historian;
   Jason Cummings, Nobleman (Duke of Rayne)
Time period(s): 19th century

Summary: Kate Noble's *Follow My Lead*, finds impas-
sioned historian Winnifred Crane attempting to enter the
men-only Historical Society. Despite her credentials as a
scholar and her mission to authenticate one of the
Society's paintings, she is barred from entering the club.
Determined to gain entrance, she offers to validate the
source of the painting, which would require her to travel
abroad and have an escort. Marriage-hungry nobleman
Jason Cummings turns out to be the man for the job, and
he becomes Winn's traveling partner. Before long, the
sparks are flying between the two, and their travels
throughout Europe become a life-changing adventure.

Where it's reviewed:
Publishers Weekly, March 28, 2011, page 43

Other books by the same author:
The Summer of You, 2010
Revealed, 2009
Compromised, 2008

Other books you might like:
Tessa Dare, *Goddess of the Hunt*, 2009
Kieran Kramer, *When Harry Met Molly*, 2010
Olivia Parker, *At the Bride Hunt Ball*, 2008
Maya Rodale, *A Groom of One's Own*, 2010
Lauren Willig, *The Mischief of the Mistletoe*, 2010

909

LORIE O'CLARE

Get Lucky

(New York: St. Martin's Press, 2011)

Series: Bounty Hunters Series. Book 2
Story type: Contemporary; Series
Subject(s): Skiing; Romances (Fiction); Family
Major character(s): London Brooke, Hotel Worker; Marc
   King, Bounty Hunter
Time period(s): 21st century; 2010s
Locale(s): Aspen, Colorado

Summary: *Get Lucky* is the second novel from author Lorie O'Clare's series The Bounty Hunters. In this novel,
London Brooke works the front desk at a ski resort in
Aspen, Colorado. When Marc King arrives on vacation,
London feels an instant attraction to him and soon they
are sharing a night of passion. Then both Marc and
London are sent mysterious packages that contain deeply
personal information only they would know. Now Marc
and London must look beyond their sexual relationship
to work together and keep their families safe. O'Clare is
also the author of *Play Dirty*, the first novel in this series,
as well as the Black Jags series, the Leopard series, the
Lunewulf series, and the Fallen Gods series.

Where it's reviewed:
Romantic Times, April 2011, page 67

Other books by the same author:
Black Passion, 2010
Black Seduction, 2010
Feather Torn, 2010
Play Dirty, 2010
Strong, Sleek and Sinful, 2010

Other books you might like:
Michele Albert, *Hide in Plain Sight*, 2006
Linda Winstead Jones, *Truly, Madly, Dangerously*, 2005
Sydney Ryan, *High-Heeled Alibi*, 2006
Christina Skye, *To Catch a Thief*, 2008

910

JANE ODIWE

Mr. Darcy's Secret

(Naperville, Illinois: Sourcebooks Landmark, 2011)

Story type: Historical - Regency
Subject(s): Marriage; British history, 1714-1815;
    Romances (Fiction)
Major character(s): Elizabeth Darcy, Spouse (of Mr.
    Darcy); Fitzwilliam Darcy, Spouse (of Elizabeth),
    Wealthy; Caroline Bingley, Friend (of Elizabeth &
    Darcy)
Time period(s): 19th century; 1810s
Locale(s): England

Summary: *Mr. Darcy's Secret* is a historical romance from author Jane Odiwe. The story picks up where Jane Austen's *Pride and Prejudice* left off, just after the marriage of Elizabeth Bennett to Mr. Darcy. In *Mr. Darcy's Secret*, Elizabeth is working hard to be a dutiful wife to Darcy and figure out how to manage their now joined massive estate at Pemberley, but their happily-ever-after is cut short by rumors and discord. Elizabeth begins questioning Darcy's honesty when she hears tales of his shady past. The source of the rumors seems to be Caroline Bingley, still jealous and bitter about Elizabeth and Darcy's union. Now Elizabeth must determine if there is any truth to the tales.

Where it's reviewed:
Booklist, December 15, 2010, page 27
Publishers Weekly, December 20, 2010, page 40

Other books by the same author:
Willoughby's Return, 2009
Lydia Bennet's Story, 2008

Other books you might like:
Pamela Aidan, *An Assembly Such as This*, 2006
Syrie James, *The Lost Memoirs of Jane Austen*, 2007
Sharon Lathan, *Mr. and Mrs. Fitzwilliam Darcy*, 2009
Mary Lydon Simonsen, *The Perfect Bride for Mr.
    Darcy*, 2011

911

JANETTE OKE
DAVIS BUNN, Co-Author

The Damascus Way

(Minneapolis, Minnesota: Bethany House, 2011)

Series: Acts of Faith Series. Book 3
Story type: Religious
Subject(s): Romances (Fiction); Religion; Courtship
Major character(s): Julia, Religious (convert to Christianity), Heiress (of wealthy father); Jacob, Religious

(early Christian), Guard (of merchant caravan); Saul of Tarsus, Leader (of anti-Christian forces)
Time period(s): 1st century
Locale(s): Damascus, Middle East

Summary: *The Damascus Way* by Davis Bunn and Janette Oke is a romance novel based on historical and religious themes and the third entry in the Acts of Faith series. In this novel, a Greek-Hebrew woman named Julia thinks her family and future are secure. When she learns that she was mistaken, her life begins a dangerous spiral until she discovers the new religion of Christianity. She quickly meets a fellow Christian, Jacob, who has been helping Julia's merchant father. Even as Julia and Jacob fall in love, all is not well—it is a dangerous time to be a Christian and they are regarded as dangerous dissidents and hunted down. *The Damascus Way* is a sequel to *The Centurion's Wife* and *The Hidden Flame*.

Where it's reviewed:
Booklist, November 15, 2010, page 20
Library Journal, November 15, 2010, page 48
Romantic Times, January 2011, page 63

Other books by the same author:
The Hidden Flame, 2010
The Centurion's Wife, 2009

Other books you might like:
Carla Capshaw, *The Gladiator*, 2009
Claudia Dain, *To Burn*, 2002
Lloyd C. Douglas, *The Robe*, 1942
Antoinette May, *Pilate's Wife*, 2006
Jill Eileen Smith, *Bathsheba: A Novel*, 2011

912

DIANA PALMER

Merciless

(Don Mills, Ontario, Canada: Harlequin, 2011)

Story type: Contemporary
Subject(s): Romances (Fiction); Western fiction; Suspense
Major character(s): Jon Blackhawk, FBI Agent; Joceline
    Perry, Assistant (to Blackhawk)
Time period(s): 21st century; 2010s
Locale(s): Jacobsville, Texas

Summary: In *Merciless* by Diana Palmer, FBI agent Jon Blackhawk comes to Jacobsville, Texas, where he's targeted by women looking for husbands and a killer looking to even an old score. Blackhawk has no interest in a committed relationship, but his good looks never fail to attract the attention of the women he encounters in the line of duty. His faithful assistant Joceline Perry has so far kept him safely away from his admirers as he works his cases. When a criminal with a grudge sets his sights on Blackhawk, Joceline protects him, but she may not be able to subdue her feelings for her boss.

Where it's reviewed:
Romantic Times, August 2011, Page 90

Other books by the same author:
Lacy, 2011
Nelson's Brand, 2011
Dangerous, 2010

Romances

Will of Steel, 2010
Heartless, 2009

Other books you might like:
Pamela Britton, *Mark: Secret Cowboy*, 2010
B.J. Daniels, *Montana Royalty*, 2008
Jan Hambright, *The High Country Rancher*, 2009
Kat Martin, *Against the Wind*, 2010

913

PAMELA PALMER (Pseudonym of Pamela Poulsen)

Hunger Untamed

(New York: Avon, 2011)

Series: Feral Warriors Series. Book 5
Story type: Fantasy
Subject(s): Adventure; Love; Magic
Major character(s): Kougar, Warrior; Ariana, Royalty
 (Queen of the Linas)
Time period(s): Indeterminate

Summary: *Hunger Untamed* is the fifth installment in
Pamela Palmer's Feral Warriors Series, a cycle of fantasy
romances centering on a group of immortal shapeshifters. This volume finds Kougar remembering the
love of his life—Ariana, Queen of the Linas, who had
spurned him and left him devastated. Now Kougar needs
to find Ariana and recruit her special magical talents to
help free two Feral Warriors caught in a dangerous trap.
But as soon as he lays eyes on the beautiful queen, all
his old feelings come bubbling to the surface. Is there a
chance Kougar can learn to forgive Ariana and the two
can build a future together? Or was Ariana's betrayal
something much different than Kougar believes?

Where it's reviewed:
Romantic Times, March 2011, page 92

Other books by the same author:
Rapture Untamed, 2010
Desire Untamed, 2009
Obsession Untamed, 2009
Dark Deceiver, 2008
The Dark Gate, 2007

Other books you might like:
Meljean Brook, *Demon Moon*, 2007
Sherrilyn Kenyon, *Unleash the Night*, 2006
Angela Knight, *Master of the Night*, 2004
Nalini Singh, *Kiss of Snow*, 2011
Rachel Vincent, *Stray*, 2007

914

BETH PATTILLO

The Dashwood Sisters Tell All

(New York: Guideposts, 2011)

Story type: Contemporary
Subject(s): Sisters; Love; Diaries
Major character(s): Mimi Dodge, Sister (of Ellen); Ellen
 Dodge, Sister (of Mimi)

Time period(s): 21st century; 2010s
Locale(s): Hampshire, England

Summary: In *The Dashwood Sisters Tell All*, author Beth
Pattillo tells the story of two estranged sisters who are
reunited by a diary belonging to the sibling of legendary
writer Jane Austen. Mimi and Ellen Dodge honor their
mother's last wish: to embark on a tour of Austen's native land. As the sisters make their way through
Hampshire, England, they read the words of Austen's
sister, Cassandra, and the little-known secret history of
the Austen family is revealed to them. Through Cassandra's story, Mimi and Ellen work on their own troubled
relationship—and, in the process, discover love with two
suitors.

Where it's reviewed:
Booklist, April 1, 2011, page 36

Other books by the same author:
Mr. Darcy Broke My Heart, 2010
Jane Austen Ruined My Life, 2009
The Sweetgum Ladies Knit for Love, 2009
Where There's a Will, 2009
The Sweetgum Lit Knit Society, 2008

Other books you might like:
Marilyn Brant, *According to Jane*, 2009
Katie Fforde, *Wedding Season*, 2010
Melissa Nathan, *Pride, Prejudice and Jasmin Field*,
 2001
Alexander Potter, *Me and Mr. Darcy*, 2007
Laurie Viera Rigler, *Rude Awakenings of a Jane Austen
 Addict*, 2009

915

KATE PEARCE (Pseudonym of Catherine Duggan)

Blood of the Rose

(New York: Penguin, 2011)

Series: Tudor Vampire Series. Book 2
Story type: Alternate History; Series
Subject(s): British history, 1066-1688; Vampires; Royalty
Major character(s): Rosalind Llewellyn, Vampire Hunter;
 Christopher Ellis, Vampire Hunter; Henry Tudor
 VIII, Royalty (king of England)
Time period(s): 16th century; 1530s
Locale(s): England

Summary: *Blood of the Rose*, the second book in Kate
Pearce's Tudor Vampire Chronicles, creates a version of
16th-century British history in which a clan of vampire
slayers plays a key role. Henry VIII has held the clan,
the Llewellyns, captive since he stole the throne from
Richard III. Rosalind Llewellyn has proven her loyalty
by working together with her nemesis Christopher Ellis,
a Druid vampire slayer. As Rosalind and Christopher
fought to defend the crown they discovered a mutual
attraction. After being apart for a full year, the couple
anticipates a passionate reunion but another menace has
surfaced that will threaten their future.

Where it's reviewed:
Romantic Times, February 2011, page 35

Other books by the same author:

Kiss of the Rose, 2010
Simply Insatiable, 2010
Simply Shameless, 2009
Simply Wicked, 2009
Simply Sexual, 2008

Other books you might like:
Colleen Gleason, *As Shadows Fade*, 2009
Kinley MacGregor, *Knight of Darkness*, 2006
Kinley MacGregor, *Sword of Darkness*, 2006
Minda Webber, *The Reluctant Miss Van Helsing*, 2006
Lucy Weston, *The Secret History of Elizabeth Tudor, Vampire Slayer*, 2011

916

MARTA PERRY (Pseudonym of Martha Johnson)

Vanish in Plain Sight

(Don Mills, Ontario, Canada: Harlequin, 2011)

Story type: Mystery; Series
Subject(s): Suspense; Missing persons; Amish
Major character(s): Marisa Angelo, Young Woman; Link Morgan, Householder
Time period(s): 21st century; 2010s
Locale(s): Lancaster County, Pennsylvania

Summary: Marisa Angelo's last memory of her mother was from when she was a little girl, as her mother left their home to go back to Amish country. Many years later, Marisa gets some chilling news when the police tell her and her father that her mother's suitcase was found by a homeowner remodeling an Amish farmhouse. The suitcase was buried in the walls, making it clear that someone wanted it to remain hidden forever. With the help of the homeowner, Link Morgan, Marisa seeks out the truth about what happened to her mother several decades earlier.

Where it's reviewed:
Library Journal, April 15, 2011, page 76
Romantic Times, April 2011, page 75

Other books by the same author:
Lost in Plain Sight, 2011
Rachel's Garden, 2010
Buried Sins, 2007
A Christmas to Die For, 2007
Hide in Plain Sight, 2007

Other books you might like:
Annette Blair, *The Butterfly Garden*, 2005
Sharon De Vita, *The Marriage Promise*, 2000
Karen Harper, *Dark Angel*, 2005
Karen Harper, *Dark Harvest*, 2004
Tami Hoag, *Still Waters*, 1992

917

MARTA PERRY (Pseudonym of Martha Johnson)

Sarah's Gift

(New York: Berkley Publishing Group, 2011)

Series: Pleasant Valley Series
Story type: Historical

Subject(s): Romances (Fiction); Amish; Courtship
Major character(s): Sarah Mast, Midwife; Aaron Miller, Worker, Assistant (to Sarah); Thomas Mitchell, Doctor
Time period(s): 19th century
Locale(s): Pleasant Valley, Pennsylvania

Summary: *Sarah's Gift* by Marta Perry is a historical romance novel about hardworking Amish singles and part of Perry's Pleasant Valley series. This novel, set in Pleasant Valley, Pennsylvania, is about a midwife named Sarah Mast. She is slowly taking over her aging aunt's midwifery practice, but she hits a major obstacle. A town doctor, insensitive to the Amish ways of life, attempts to sue Sarah for practicing medicine without a license. Sarah has to defend herself and her family. Luckily, she meets Aaron Miller, a charming Amish worker who quickly becomes a romantic interest. Aaron and Sarah have to work together to preserve Sarah's profession and reputation.

Where it's reviewed:
Romantic Times, March 2011, page 74

Other books by the same author:
Anna's Return, 2010
Murder in Plain Sight, 2010
Rachel's Garden, 2010
Leah's Choice, 2009
Final Justice, 2008

Other books you might like:
Barbara Cameron, *A Time to Heal*, 2010
Jerry S. Eicher, *Rebecca's Choice*, 2010
Beverly Lewis, *The Telling*, 2010
Gayle Roper, *A Rose Revealed*, 2011
Cindy Woodsmall, *The Bridge of Peace*, 2010

918

SUSAN ELIZABETH PHILLIPS

Call Me Irresistible

(New York: William Morrow, 2011)

Story type: Contemporary
Subject(s): Friendship; Love; Humor
Major character(s): Meg Koranda, Friend (of Lucy); Lucy Jorik, Friend (of Meg), Fiance(e) (of Ted); Ted Beaudine, Fiance(e) (of Lucy)
Time period(s): 21st century; 2010s
Locale(s): Wynette, Texas

Summary: In Susan Elizabeth Phillips's *Call Me Irresistible*, Lucy Jorik has returned to Wynette, Texas, to marry her dream man, Ted Beaudine. Everyone in town thinks this is a match made in heaven—everyone, that is, except for Lucy's friend Meg Koranda. Meg is convinced that the impending nuptials will spell disaster and unhappiness for her pal, so she sets out to stop the wedding. As the town turns on Meg and blames her for breaking up Lucy and Ted, Meg works overtime to deny her own burgeoning feelings for the jilted bridegroom.

Where it's reviewed:
Booklist, December 15, 2010, page 27
Library Journal, December 1, 2010, page 97

Romantic Times, January 2011, page 82

Other books by the same author:
What I Did for Love, 2009
Natural Born Charmer, 2007
Match Me If You Can, 2005
Ain't She Sweet?, 2004
Breathing Room, 2002

Other books you might like:
Stephanie Bond, *Two Sexy*, 2001
Jennifer Crusie, *Crazy for You*, 1999
Rachel Gibson, *True Love and Other Disasters*, 2009
Kristan Higgins, *Too Good to Be True*, 2009
Christie Ridgway, *Crush on You*, 2010

919

CANDICE POARCH
Deadly Intentions
(New York: Dafina, 2011)

Story type: Mystery
Subject(s): Romances (Fiction); Crime; Mystery
Major character(s): Lisa Claxton, Housekeeper, Business-woman; Brian Knight, Military Personnel (Navy SEAL), Rescuer (of Lisa)
Time period(s): 21st century
Locale(s): Paradise Island, Virginia

Summary: *Deadly Intentions* by Candice Poarch is a romance novel with a murder-mystery twist. The main character, Lisa Claxton, has started a housekeeping business on Paradise Island, Virginia. She soon discovers that one of her clients stole a valuable vase from her, and she plans to recover it. When she arrives at the culprit's house, however, she stumbles into a murder mystery. Luckily, a handsome single Navy SEAL named Brian Knight happens to be there to save her. Together, the attractive singles set out on a quest to find the killer, solve the mysteries, and fall in love.

Where it's reviewed:
Romantic Times, May 2011, page 82

Other books by the same author:
Island of Deceit, 2010
Safe in His Embrace, 2010
Loving Spoonful, 2009
Long, Hot Nights, 2008
Golden Night, 2007

Other books you might like:
Jessica Bird, *An Unforgettable Lady*, 2010
Lisa Marie Rice, *Into the Crossfire*, 2010
Stephanie Tyler, *Hard to Hold*, 2009
Stephanie Tyler, *Too Hot to Hold*, 2010

920

DANA PRECIOUS
Born Under a Lucky Moon
(New York: William Morrow, 2011)

Story type: Contemporary
Subject(s): Family; Love; Interpersonal relations

Major character(s): Jeannie Thompson, Businesswoman; Aidan, Boyfriend (of Jeannie)
Time period(s): 21st century; 2010s
Locale(s): Los Angeles, California; Michigan, United States

Summary: Dana Precious's *Born Under a Lucky Moon* follows show biz executive Jeannie Thompson as she juggles the stresses of her relationship with her boyfriend Aidan and the pressures of her eccentric Midwestern family. Jeannie has decided that it is finally time Aidan meet her relatives, though she is far from thrilled with the idea. Her family has a long and sordid history of alienating her boyfriends, and Jeannie waffles on whether or not to introduce Aidan to the clan. The resulting chain of events brings forth all the humor, love, and downright unconventionality of her family. First novel.

Where it's reviewed:
Booklist, February 15, 2011, page 49
Publishers Weekly, December 20, 2010, page 33
Romantic Times, February 2011, page 41

Other books you might like:
Beth Kendrick, *My Favorite Mistake*, 2004
Tanya Michaels, *The Good Kind of Crazy*, 2006
Cindi Myers, *Life According to Lucy*, 2004
Susan Elizabeth Phillips, *Match Me If You Can*, 2005
Allison Rushby, *The Dairy Queen*, 2006

921

MARY JO PUTNEY
Nowhere Near Respectable
(New York: Kensington Publishing Company, 2011)

Series: Lost Lords Series. Book 3
Story type: Historical - Regency; Series
Subject(s): Social class; Smuggling; Kidnapping
Major character(s): Lady Kiri Lawford, Noblewoman; Damian Mackenzie, Rake
Time period(s): 19th century; 1810s
Locale(s): England

Summary: *Nowhere Near Respectable* is the third book in author Mary Jo Putney's series The Lost Lords. Damian Mackenzie is a rich middle-class businessman, but high society England still shuns him due to his wicked ways. Then he meets Lady Kiri Lawford, a part Indian, part English noblewoman whom he rescues from the hands of pirates. Kiri is immediately attracted to Damian, but Damian has no time to consider the feelings of a woman from the very high society that has turned against him. Then Kiri finds herself mixed up in a royal kidnapping plot, and only Damian can help her. Will she ever convince him to let down his guard and let her into his heart?

Where it's reviewed:
Booklist, April 1, 2011, page 36
Library Journal, April 15, 2011, page 77
Publishers Weekly, March 7, 2011, page 49
Romantic Times, May 2011, page 40

Other books by the same author:
Dark Mirror, 2011

Never Less than a Lady, 2010
Loving a Lost Lord, 2009
A Distant Magic, 2007
The Marriage Spell, 2006
Stolen Magic, 2005

Other books you might like:
Joanna Bourne, *The Forbidden Rose*, 2010
Gaelen Foley, *My Wicked Marquess*, 2009
Lynn Kerstan, *The Golden Leopard*, 2002
Stephanie Laurens, *The Untamed Bride*, 2009
Emma Wildes, *His Sinful Secret*, 2010

922

ERIN QUINN (Pseudonym of Erin Grady)

Haunting Desire

(New York: Berkley Sensation, 2011)

Story type: Paranormal; Series
Subject(s): Romances (Fiction); Fantasy; Time travel
Major character(s): Shealy O'Leary, Young Woman, Time Traveler, Daughter (of Donnell); Tiarnan, Warrior; Donnell O'Leary, Father (of Shealy), Time Traveler
Time period(s): 21st century; (2010s); Indeterminate Past
Locale(s): Fennore, Fictional Location; Ireland

Summary: In *Haunting Desire*, the third book in Erin Quinn's paranormal romance series Mists of Ireland, Shealy O'Leary and her father Donnell have been transported to the mythical land known as Fennore, which lies deep in Ireland's ancient past. In the strange world, Shealy discovers that she possesses paranormal talents that make her the target of Fennore's dark forces. Separated from her father, Shealy meets Tiarnan, a warrior banished to Fennore for long-ago transgressions. Tiarnan recognizes Shealy's magical abilities and the hope they hold. As Shealy and Tiarnan search for Donnell they struggle to contain their enemies and the passion growing between them.

Where it's reviewed:
Romantic Times, April 2011, page 104

Other books by the same author:
Haunting Beauty, 2011
Haunting Warrior, 2010

Other books you might like:
Jennifer Ashley, *Immortals: The Gathering*, 2007
Sherrilyn Kenyon, *Unleash the Night*, 2006
Deidre Knight, *Red Demon*, 2010
Cathy McDavid, *Night Hunter*, 2007
Kerrelyn Sparks, *Eat, Prey, Love*, 2010

923

JULIA QUINN (Pseudonym of Julie Cotler Pottinger)

Just Like Heaven

(New York: Avon, 2011)

Story type: Historical - Regency; Series
Subject(s): Romances (Fiction); Deception; Humor

Major character(s): Marcus Holroyd, Nobleman (Earl of Chatteris), Friend (of Honoria); Honoria Smythe-Smith, Friend (of Marcus), Musician (violinist)
Time period(s): 19th century; 1820s
Locale(s): England

Summary: *Just Like Heaven* is a humorous historical romance novel from bestselling author Julia Quinn. Honoria Smythe-Smith and Marcus Holroyd, Earl of Chatteris, are bound together by one thing: his friendship with her older brother. But that's the full extent of their relationship, or so they think. They're both absolutely confident that they're not in love with one another because the mere suggestion of a romance between them seems preposterous. That is, until a near-death experience indicates they may share something more than platonic friendship. Just as Honoria and Marcus are coming to terms with their feelings, an age-old secret is revealed that threatens to doom their relationship before it even begins. *Just Like Heaven* is the first book in the Smythe-Smith Quartet.

Where it's reviewed:
Booklist, June 15, 2011, page 47
Library Journal, June 16, 2011, page 65
Romantic Times, June 2011, page 40

Other books by the same author:
The Lady Most Likely, 2011
Ten Things I Love about You, 2010
What Happens in London, 2009
The Lost Duke of Wyndham, 2008
Mr. Cavendish, I Presume, 2008

Other books you might like:
Kathryn Caskie, *Rules of Engagement*, 2004
Kieran Kramer, *When Harry Met Molly*, 2010
Kate Noble, *Compromised*, 2008
Olivia Parker, *At the Bride Hunt Ball*, 2008
Maya Rodale, *The Heir and the Spare*, 2007

924

CAROLINE RICHARDS

The Darkest Sin

(New York: Kensington Publishing Company, 2011)

Story type: Historical; Mystery
Subject(s): England; Detective fiction; Crime
Major character(s): Rowena Woolcott, Young Woman, Crime Victim; Lord James Rushford, Detective— Amateur
Time period(s): 19th century
Locale(s): London, England

Summary: *The Darkest Sin* is a novel written by author Caroline Richards. For years, a dangerous Frenchman has been threatening the life of Rowena Woolcott and torturing her family in the process. After a near-drowning, Rowena goes on the run to make sure her family stays safe. Now she is determined to find the culprit and stop him once and for all, so she turns to Lord James Rushford, an amateur detective whom she suspects might be able to help her. What Rowena doesn't remember is that Rushford was the man who saved her when she nearly drowned. Rushford devises a ruse to

Romances

have Rowena pose as his mistress so they can navigate the mean streets of London more easily. The problem is, soon the ruse feels a little too real, and the passion they feel for each other could ruin everything.

Where it's reviewed:
Library Journal, June 15, 2011, page 65
Romantic Times, June 2011, page 39

Other books by the same author:
The Deadliest Sin, 2010

Other books you might like:
Liz Carlyle, *No True Gentleman*, 2002
Shannon Drake, *When We Touch*, 2004
Kim Lennox, *So Still the Night*, 2009
Penelope Neri, *Obsession*, 2003
Carla Simpson, *Seductive Caress*, 1992

925

ALIX RICKLOFF

Earl of Darkness

(New York: Pocket Star, 2011)

Series: Heirs of Kilronan Series. Book 1
Story type: Paranormal; Series
Subject(s): Romances (Fiction); History; Ireland
Major character(s): Catriona "Cat" O'Connell, Thief, Mythical Creature (half human, half fey); Aidan Douglas, Nobleman (Earl of Kilronan)
Time period(s): 19th century; 1810s (1815)
Locale(s): Ireland

Summary: In *Earl of Darkness*, the first book in Alix Rickloff's Heirs of Kilronan series, Catriona "Cat" O'Connell has been reduced to the rank of petty thief. Her latest job includes lifting a diary from the Dublin home of Aidan Douglas, Earl of Kilronan. Cat is easily caught by Aidan, who takes an interest in the young woman. Not only is Cat an "Other"—one of an ancient race of half-human, half-fairies—she is also capable of translating for Aidan the coveted diary that remains in his possession. As Cat slowly reveals the old book's secrets, a demon threatens to steal it for his own. A growing attraction between Aidan and Cat complicates their dangerous task.

Where it's reviewed:
Publishers Weekly, November 1, 2010, page 32
Romantic Times, January 2011, page 36

Other books by the same author:
Dangerous Magic, 2011
Lord of Shadows, 2011
Heir of Danger, 2010
Dangerous as Sin, 2009
Lost in You, 2008

Other books you might like:
Angela Knight, *Master of the Moon*, 2005
Angela Knight, *Master of the Night*, 2004
Holly Lisle, *Night Echoes*, 2007
Eve Silver, *Demon's Kiss*, 2007
Eve Silver, *His Wicked Sins*, 2008

926

CHRISTIE RIDGWAY

Then He Kissed Me

(New York: Penguin, 2011)

Series: Three Kisses Series. Book 2
Story type: Contemporary; Series
Subject(s): Romances (Fiction); Weddings; Sisters
Major character(s): Stephania "Stevie" Baci, Driver (limousine); Emerson, Boyfriend (of Stevie, former), Fiance(e) (of Princess Roxy); Roxy, Royalty (princess), Fiance(e) (of Emerson), Brother (of Jack); Jacques "Jack" Parini, Royalty (prince), Brother (of Roxy)
Time period(s): 21st century; 2010s
Locale(s): Napa Valley, California

Summary: In *Then He Kissed Me*, the second book in Christie Ridgway's Three Kisses series, Stephania "Stevie" Baci has found her own way to make a living from the family's Napa Valley vineyard. Since her two sisters have turned the winery into an upscale wedding location, Stevie has started a complementary enterprise, Napa Princess Limousine. When her wedding-planner sister has an accident, Stevie is called in to help with the winery's next big event—the wedding of her ex-boyfriend Emerson to Princess Roxy, who is genuine royalty. Roxy's brother Jack, a prince who's a bit of a scoundrel, arrives to supervise the preparations. Stevie drives Prince Jack to distraction and they find themselves unexpectedly engaged.

Where it's reviewed:
Booklist, January 1, 2011, page 58
Library Journal, December 2010, page 98
Publishers Weekly, November 1, 2010, page 32
Romantic Times, January 2011, page 82

Other books by the same author:
Can't Hurry Love, 2011
Crush on You, 2010
Not Just the Nanny, 2010
Dirty Sexy Knitting, 2009
Runaway Bride Returns!, 2009

Other books you might like:
Diana Dempsey, *Too Close to the Sun*, 2004
Rachel Gibson, *Any Man of Mine*, 2011
Susan Mallery, *The Marcelli Bride*, 2006
Susan Mallery, *The Seductive One*, 2003
Jill Shalvis, *Simply Irresistible*, 2010

927

NORA ROBERTS

Chasing Fire

(New York: G. P. Putnam's Sons, 2011)

Story type: Romantic Suspense
Subject(s): Romances (Fiction); Fires; Suspense
Major character(s): Rowan Tripp, Fire Fighter; Gulliver Curry, Fire Fighter

Time period(s): 21st century; 2010s
Locale(s): Montana, United States

Summary: *Chasing Fire* is a suspenseful romance novel from best-selling author Nora Roberts. Following in the footsteps of her father, Rowan Tripp has been fighting forest fires with the Missoula Smoke Jumpers since she turned 18. After the tragic loss of her partner last year, Rowan is relieved to return to her home in Montana to do what she does best: fight fires and train newbies. Among the rookie class is Gulliver Curry, a skilled firefighter with strong intellect and a gentle heart. Despite her attraction to Gull, Rowan can't afford any distractions right now, at work or in her private life. But when someone begins to target Rowan, hoping to make her pay for her partner's tragic end, she's desperate for support and safety and knows that Gull may be the one to provide her with both.

Where it's reviewed:
Booklist, March 1, 2011, page 37
Kirkus Reviews, April 1, 2011, page 537
Library Journal, April 15, 2011, page 76
Publishers Weekly, February 28, 2011, page 35
Romantic Times, April 2011, page 66

Other books by the same author:
Happily Ever After, 2010
Savor the Moment, 2010
The Search, 2010
Bed of Roses, 2009
Black Hills, 2009

Other books you might like:
Sandra Brown, *Chill Factor*, 2005
Julie Garwood, *Fire and Ice: A Novel*, 2008
Elizabeth Lowell, *Death Echo*, 2010
Carla Neggers, *The Rapids*, 2004

| 928 |

ELIZABETH ROLLS
MICHELLE WILLINGHAM, Co-Author
BRONWYN SCOTT, Co-Author
MARGUERITE KAY, Co-Author
ASHLEY RADCLIFF, Co-Author

Delectably Undone!

(Don Mills, Ontario, Canada: Harlequin, 2011)

Story type: Collection; Historical
Subject(s): Love; Adventure; Erotica

Summary: *Delectably Undone!* offers a quintet of erotic historical tales written by some of the most beloved authors of the genre. In "A Scandalous Liaison," Elizabeth Rolls chronicles the love affair between a handsome nobleman and a woman of mystery. Michelle Willingham's "Pleasured by the Viking" follows a soon-to-be-wed Irishwoman who falls under the charms of a sexy Viking warrior. In Marguerite Kay's "The Captain's Wicked Wager," a dashing military hero woos an impoverished young woman by making her an offer she cannot refuse. Ashley Radcliff's "The Samurai's Forbidden Touch" finds two strangers drawn together by poetry, love, and an unquenchable passion. The final tale is

Bronwyn Scott's "Arabian Nights," which centers on a young captive who does whatever it takes to escape a Bedouin camp.

Where it's reviewed:
Romantic Times, April 2011, page 38

Other books you might like:
Celeste Bradley, *My Scandalous Bride*, 2004
Diane Gaston, *The Diamonds of Welbourne Manor*, 2009
Sabrina Jeffries, *The School for Heiresses*, 2007
Michelle Willingham, *Pleasurably Undone*, 2010

| 929 |

DENISE ROSSETTI

The Lone Warrior

(New York: Berkley, 2011)

Series: Four-Sided Pentacle Series. Book 4
Story type: Fantasy
Subject(s): Adventure; Kidnapping; Love
Major character(s): Walker, Shaman; Mehcredi, Assassin
Time period(s): Indeterminate

Summary: Walker is a shaman and the last surviving member of his tribe. He wanders the world locked in a brutal quest for vengeance, ready to eliminate anyone connected to the slaying of his people. Mehcredi is a fledgling assassin sent to kill one of Walker's friends. When Walker hears word of the attempted assassination, he kidnaps Mehcredi and forces her to be his slave. But the passion between the two is soon more than either of them can endure, and together they gather the courage to overcome their respective histories and find true love with one another. *The Lone Warrior* is the third novel in Denise Rossetti's Four-Sided Pentacle Series.

Where it's reviewed:
Romantic Times, May 2011, page 94

Other books by the same author:
Strongman, 2010
Tailspin, 2009
Thief of Light, 2009
The Flame and the Shadow, 2008
Gift of the Goddess, 2007

Other books you might like:
Meljean Brook, *Demon Blood*, 2010
Kresley Cole, *Dark Desires After Dusk*, 2008
Alexandra Ivy, *When Darkness Comes*, 2007
Lora Leigh, *Wicked Sacrifice*, 2009
Sarah McCarty, *Jared*, 2010

| 930 |

RAINBOW ROWELL

Attachments

(New York: Dutton, 2011)

Story type: Contemporary
Subject(s): Romances (Fiction); Letters (Correspondence); Humor

Romances

Major character(s): Jennifer Scribner-Snyder, Writer, Friend (of Beth); Beth Fremont, Friend (of Jennifer), Writer; Lincoln O'Neill, Computer Expert, Security Officer
Time period(s): 21st century; 2010s
Locale(s): United States

Summary: *Attachments* is a humorous contemporary romance from debut author Rainbow Rowell. Co-workers and best friends Beth Fremont and Jennifer Scribner-Snyder are well aware that their employer, *The Courier*, monitors emails of employees. But that doesn't stop them from exchanging lengthy notes documenting their personal lives, relationship woes, and office gossip. Jennifer struggles with telling her husband she's unsure about starting a family. Beth, on the other hand, can't find a suitable mate. Meanwhile, Internet security officer Lincoln O'Neill is supposed to monitor emails and chats between *Courier* employees and report anything non-work-related, but the messages between Jennifer and Beth are far too entertaining for him to ignore. Instead of reporting them, Lincoln keeps reading the private emails, slowly realizing that he's falling head-over-heels for Beth. But how do you tell someone you've fallen for them because you've violated their privacy and read the details of their innermost thoughts and desires? First novel.

Where it's reviewed:
Library Journal, February 15, 2011, page 101
Publishers Weekly, January 17, 2011, Page 24

Other books you might like:
Marilyn Brant, *According to Jane*, 2009
Jennifer Crusie, *Bet Me*, 2004
Kristan Higgins, *Too Good to Be True*, 2009
Jill Mansell, *Take a Chance on Me*, 2010
Susan Elizabeth Phillips, *Match Me If You Can*, 2005

931

SHARON SALA

Blood Ties

(New York: Mira, 2011)

Story type: Romantic Suspense
Subject(s): Love; Family; Adoption
Major character(s): Savannah Slade, Young Woman; Judd Holyfield, Boyfriend (of Savannah); Thomas Jefferson, Lawyer
Time period(s): 21st century; 2010s
Locale(s): Miami, Florida; Montana, United States

Summary: After the death of her father, Savannah Slade is delivered a stunning blow. She was adopted, and her family isn't related by blood. Determined to find out the truth of her heritage, Savannah travels to Miami and tracks down her biological father. But there she unearths her birth family—a group of wealthy elitists who are not exactly thrilled at the emergence of this new family member. They want her out of the way...and they will wield every ounce of their considerable power to make sure that happens. *Blood Ties* is the second novel in Sharon Sala's Searchers series of romantic suspense novels.

Where it's reviewed:
Romantic Times, June 2011, Page 75

Other books by the same author:
Blood Stains, 2011
Blown Away, 2010
Swept Aside, 2010
Torn Apart, 2010
The Warrior, 2009

Other books you might like:
Maya Banks, *No Place to Run*, 2010
Shannon K. Butcher, *Love You to Death*, 2009
Pamela Callow, *Damaged*, 2010
Margaret Carroll, *A Dark Love*, 2009
Margaret Carroll, *Riptide*, 2009

932

SHARON SALA

Blood Stains

(New York: Mira, 2011)

Subject(s): Sisters; Murder; Love
Major character(s): Maria Slade, Adoptee, Sister (of Holly and Savannah); Bodie Scott, Detective; Holly Slade, Sister (of Maria and Savannah); Savannah Slade, Sister (of Holly and Maria)
Time period(s): 21st century; 2010s
Locale(s): Tulsa, Oklahoma

Summary: Maria, Holly, and Savannah Slade are as close as sisters can be. After their father dies, however, the trio learns that they aren't blood relatives at all; they were adopted at a young age and given better lives. Maria learns her birth mother, a prostitute, was murdered, and she sets out to find the truth. Her investigation takes her to Oklahoma, where she joins forces with sexy detective Bodie Scott and attempts to nab her mother's killer. *Blood Stains* is the first novel in Sharon Sala's The Searchers series.

Where it's reviewed:
Publishers Weekly, February 2011, Page 60
Romantic Times, February 2011, Page 60

Other books by the same author:
Blood Ties, 2011
Blown Away, 2010
Swept Aside, 2010
Torn Apart, 2010
The Warrior, 2009

Other books you might like:
Julie James, *Something About You*, 2010
Kat Martin, *Against the Wind*, 2010
Lorie O'Clare, *Play Dirty*, 2010
Hope Tarr, *Every Breath You Take...*, 2009
Debra Webb, *Everywhere She Turns*, 2009

933

LYNSAY SANDS

The Reluctant Vampire

(New York: Avon, 2011)

Series: Argeneau Vampire Series. Book 15
Story type: Series; Vampire Story
Subject(s): Vampires; Romances (Fiction); Horror
Major character(s): Drina Argenis, Vampire; Harper
    Stoyan, Vampire
Time period(s): 21st century; 2010s
Locale(s): Canada

Summary: In *The Reluctant Vampire* by Lynsay Sands, vampire Drina Argenis travels to Canada where the wintry weather isn't the only challenge she faces. A member of the Spanish branch of the centuries-old Argeneau vampire clan, Drina is shocked by her latest duty—keeping a teenage vampire safe and out of trouble. It seems the only upside to the assignment is that she gets to work with Harper Stoyan. Drina thinks that Harper could be her life mate; Harper, who is still grieving for the mate he lost, has no interest in Drina or any other woman. The teenager in their care may be able to bring the two vamps together—if they overcome an unexpected threat. *The Reluctant Vampire* is the 15th book in the Argeneau series.

Where it's reviewed:
Romantic Times, June 2011, page 85

Other books by the same author:
The Deed, 2011
Born to Bite, 2010
Hungry for You, 2010
The Immortal Hunter, 2009
The Renegade Hunter, 2009

Other books you might like:
Nina Bangs, *My Wicked Vampire*, 2009
Michele Bardsley, *I'm the Vampire, That's Why*, 2006
Ryan Brown, *Play Dead*, 2010
Dakota Cassidy, *The Accidental Werewolf*, 2008
Kathy Love, *I Only Have Fangs for You*, 2006

934

LYNSAY SANDS

The Heiress

(New York: Avon, 2011)

Story type: Historical - Regency
Subject(s): Wealth; Love; Marriage
Major character(s): Suzette Madison, Noblewoman; Daniel
    Woodrow, Nobleman
Time period(s): 19th century
Locale(s): London, United Kingdom

Summary: In Regency England, social standing and wealth are everything—but not to Suzette Madison. The beautiful noblewoman just wants to find a decent, common man to marry so that she will have access to her own money, which she plans to use to pay off her father's astronomical gambling debts. She soon meets Daniel Woodrow, who, it seems, is just the type of man for whom Suzette has been searching. There's just one hitch. As the two fall in love, Daniel is hiding a secret that could destroy their union—a secret that could shatter Suzette's plans for the ideal marriage. *The Heiress* is the second installment in Lynsay Sand's Madison Sisters Series.

Where it's reviewed:
Romantic Times, March 2011, page 40

Other books by the same author:
The Countess, 2011
Born to Bite, 2010
The Hellion and the Highlander, 2010
Taming the Highland Bride, 2010
Hungry for You, 2001

Other books you might like:
Celeste Bradley, *One Night with a Spy*, 2006
Celeste Bradley, *The Spy*, 2004
Eileen Dreyer, *Barely a Lady*, 2010
Allegra Gray, *Nothing but Deception*, 2010
Emma Wildes, *His Sinful Secret*, 2010

935

SUSAN SCHNEIDER

The Wedding Writer

(New York: St. Martin's Griffin, 2011)

Story type: Contemporary
Subject(s): Weddings; Women; Love
Major character(s): Lucky Quinn, Writer, Editor; Felice,
    Mother, Director (art); Sara, Director (fashion);
    Grace Ralston, Editor (former)
Time period(s): 21st century; 2010s
Locale(s): United States

Summary: In *The Wedding Writer* by Susan Schneider, two major wedding magazines go under and *Your Wedding* becomes the top glossy in its field. Lead writer Lucky Quinn is promptly promoted to editor-in-chief, replacing her mentor, Grace Ralston. In the wake of the shake-up, everyone at the magazine is affected. Art director Felice struggles to maintain a professional air despite the immense pressure she's dealing with in her private life; fashion director Sara focuses too much on her career in an effort to deal with the lack of love in her personal life. Without work to occupy her, Grace spirals into a depression, while Lucky realizes how lonely and isolating it can be to have all her dreams come true. First novel.

Where it's reviewed:
Booklist, May 1, 2011, page 68

Other books you might like:
Nadine Haobsh, *Confessions of a Beauty Addict*, 2009
Naomi Neale, *Calendar Girl*, 2005
Jane Porter, *The Frog Prince*, 2005
Allison Rushby, *The Dairy Queen*, 2006
Lauren Weisberger, *The Devil Wears Prada*, 2003

Romances

936

REGINA SCOTT (Pseudonym of Regina Lundgren)

The Irresistible Earl

(New York: Love Inspired, 2011)

Story type: Historical
Subject(s): Romances (Fiction); History; Social class
Major character(s): Chase Dearborn, Nobleman (Earl of Allyndale); Meredee Price, Young Woman
Time period(s): 19th century; 1810s
Locale(s): England

Summary: In *The Irresistible Earl* by Regina Scott, Chase Dearborn, Earl of Allyndale, believes that he has finally found a suitable wife in Meredee Price. He is smitten by her loveliness and kindness the first time he sees her. But Meredee wants nothing to do with the earl, and tries to make herself scarce when he comes to the Prices' home in Scarborough. When Meredee witnesses a young woman drowning, she has no choice but to rescue the girl and, in the process, attract the attention and further affections of Dearborn. Eventually, the earl is shocked to learn that Meredee might not be his perfect mate after all.

Where it's reviewed:
Romantic Times, June 2011, page 100

Other books by the same author:
La Petite Four, 2008
Perfection, 2003
Starstruck, 2003
Lord Borin's Secret Love, 2002
Utterly Devoted, 2002

Other books you might like:
Mary Balogh, *The Plumed Bonnet*, 1996
Megan Frampton, *A Singular Lady*, 2005
Candice Hern, *A Garden Folly*, 1997
Sophia Nash, *Lord Will and Her Grace*, 2005

937

ISABEL SHARPE (Pseudonym of Muna Shehadi Sill)

Turn Up the Heat

(Don Mills, Ontario, Canada: Harlequin, 2011)

Story type: Contemporary
Subject(s): Dating (Social customs); Internet; Romances (Fiction)
Major character(s): Candy Graham, Planner (party); Justin Case, Journalist, Neighbor (of Candy)
Time period(s): 21st century; 2010s
Locale(s): Milwaukee, Wisconsin

Summary: *Turn Up the Heat* is a steamy, humorous romance novel from author Isabel Sharpe. Unlucky in love, party planner Candy Graham decides to give online dating a try. She agrees to sample a friend's online dating service and promptly goes about setting up her profile. There's only one problem—Candy isn't sure which side of her personality to portray. Instead of one profile, she creates four, each to represent a different set of traits. Whenever she lands a date, she assumes the personality and fashion of that particular profile: child at heart, professor, superwoman, or sexy glamour girl. Her complex approach to online dating earns her a date with her sexy journalist neighbor Justin Case, who grows suspicious of Candy's true motives.

Where it's reviewed:
Romantic Times, February 2011, page 87

Other books by the same author:
Knit in Comfort, 2010
Surprise Me, 2010
While She Was Sleeping, 2010
No Holding Back, 2009
As Good as It Got, 2008

Other books you might like:
Stephanie Bond, *My Favorite Mistake*, 2005
Jennifer Greene, *Wild in the Moment*, 2004
Joanne Rock, *Her Final Fling: Single in South Beach*, 2004
Stephanie Tyler, *Coming Undone*, 2007
Cathy Yardley, *Jack and Jilted*, 2007

938

LYNN SHEENE

The Last Time I Saw Paris

(New York: Berkley Books, 2011)

Story type: Historical - World War II
Subject(s): Romances (Fiction); World War II, 1939-1945; French (European people)
Major character(s): Claire Harris, Socialite, Divorced Person, Runaway, Spy
Time period(s): 20th century; 1940s (1940)
Locale(s): Paris, France

Summary: *The Last Time I Saw Paris* is a historical romance novel from debut author Lynn Sheene. Lying about her humble roots to land an advantageous marriage, Claire Harris becomes quite comfortable in her new role as Manhattan socialite. But when her husband learns of her deception, she's forced to start anew in a distant land. Traveling to Paris in 1940, Claire is shocked by the Nazi occupation and her own poor timing. To secure her freedom and security, Claire arranges a deal with the French resistance to aid their cause in exchange for false identity papers. She soon finds herself working as a spy and falling in love with both the City of Light and a certain Englishman. But when her lover is put in danger, Claire must flee Paris in a dangerous quest to save him. First novel.

Where it's reviewed:
Publishers Weekly, February 28, 2011, page 34
Romantic Times, May 2011, page 50

Other books you might like:
Jill Barnett, *Sentimental Journey*, 2001
Marie Bostwick, *Fields of Gold*, 2005
Sara Hely, *War Story*, 2003
Karen White, *On Folly Beach*, 2010

939

NALINI SINGH

Kiss of Snow

(New York: Berkley, 2011)

Series: Psy-Changelings Series
Story type: Fantasy; Paranormal
Subject(s): Fantasy; Romances (Fiction); Love
Major character(s): Sienna Lauren, Psychic (Psy X); Hawke, Shape-Shifter (Alpha wolf)
Time period(s): 21st century
Locale(s): California, United States

Summary: *Kiss of Snow* is the 13th installment in author Nalini Singh's Psy-Changeling series, and the first volume in the series to be published in hardcover. In this chapter of the popular supernatural romance saga, Sienna Lauren, a powerful Psy X who struggles to keep her psychokinetic abilities in check, is having a hard time denying her passion for Hawke, an Alpha wolf changeling. While they deal with their conflicting passions and senses of duty, various Psy factions, prejudiced against the changelings, are preparing for war.

Where it's reviewed:
Library Journal, June 15, 2011, page 66
Romantic Times, June 2011, page 82

Other books by the same author:
Archangel's Blade, 2011
Archangel's Consort, 2011
Archangel's Kiss, 2010
Angels' Blood, 2009
Slave to Sensation, 2006

Other books you might like:
Christine Feehan, *Wild Rain*, 2004
Allyson James, *Firewalker*, 2010
Sherrilyn Kenyon, *Stroke of Midnight*, 2004
Lindsay McKenna, *Unforgiven*, 2006
Shiloh Walker, *Hunter's Need*, 2009

940

CHERYL ANN SMITH

The School for Brides

(New York: Berkley, 2011)

Story type: Historical - Regency
Subject(s): Love; Marriage; Identity
Major character(s): Eva Black, Teacher; Nicholas Drake, Nobleman
Time period(s): 19th century
Locale(s): United Kingdom

Summary: In *The School for Brides*, debut author Cheryl Ann Smith spins a romantic tale set in Regency England. Eva Black, still overcome with shame at her courtesan mother's profession, operates a school for courtesans looking to get out of the trade and into respectable marriages. Thinking herself a spinster, Eva has given up all hope of marriage for herself. When nobleman Nicholas Drake enters her life, he is outraged: his favored courtesan is now one of her students, thus seeking to end their torrid affair. Nicholas wants nothing more than to destroy Eva and her business—if only he could tame his overwhelming desire for her.... First novel.

Where it's reviewed:
Publishers Weekly, February 21, 2011, page   119
Romantic Times, April 2011, page 37

Other books you might like:
Nicole Byrd, *Enticing the Earl*, 2008
Anna Campbell, *Tempt the Devil*, 2008
Loretta Lynda Chase, *Your Scandalous Ways*, 2008
Claudia Dain, *The Courtesan's Daughter*, 2007
Betina Krahn, *The Last Bachelor*, 1994

941

KATHRYN SMITH

When Tempting a Rogue

(New York: Avon, 2011)

Story type: Regency
Subject(s): Romances (Fiction); Social class; England
Major character(s): Vienne La Rieux, Businesswoman; Trystan Kane, Nobleman
Locale(s): London, England

Summary: In *When Tempting a Rogue*, author Kathryn Smith tells the story of Vienne La Rieux, the operator of an exclusive male establishment in London, England. Vienne is one of the few independent women of her time, with plans to build a marketplace that will make her wealthy beyond belief. Unfortunately, that's when the former love of her life—Lord Trystan Kane—walks back into it. Trystan wants a piece of the pie, and so he offers Vienne a business partnership. But can Vienne and Trystan keep their relationship entirely business-related, or will they fall back into old habits?

Where it's reviewed:
Romantic Times, May 2011, page 45

Other books by the same author:
When Marrying a Scoundrel, 2010
Dark Side of Dawn, 2009
Night after Night, 2009
When Seducing a Duke, 2009
Before I Wake, 2008

Other books you might like:
Loretta Chase, *Silk is for Seduction*, 2011
Julia London, *A Courtesan's Scandal*, 2009
Sarah MacLean, *Eleven Scandals to Start to Win a Duke's Heart*, 2011
Kate Moore, *To Save the Devil*, 2010
Kate Moore, *To Tempt a Saint*, 2010

942

ROXANNE ST. CLAIRE

Shiver of Fear

(New York: Forever, April 1, 2011)

Series: Guardian Angelinos Series. Book 2
Story type: Romantic Suspense; Series

Romances

Her Pay, *Now You Hide*, *Then You Die*, and *Kill Me Twice*.

Where it's reviewed:
Romantic Times, May 2011, page 80

Other books by the same author:
Shiver of Fear, 2011
Edge of Sight, 2010
Hunt Her Down, 2009
Make Her Pay, 2009
Now You Die, 2008

Other books you might like:
Beverly Barton, *Don't Cry*, 2010
Carla Cassidy, *Broken Pieces*, 2008
Leslie Parrish, *Pitch Black*, 2009
Karen Rose, *Nothing to Fear*, 2005

944

RAEANNE THAYNE

Blackberry Summer

(Don Mills, Ontario, Canada: Harlequin, 2011)

Story type: Contemporary
Subject(s): Rural life; Crime; Accidents
Major character(s): Claire Bradford, Store Owner; Riley McKnight, Police Officer (chief)
Time period(s): 21st century; 2010s
Locale(s): Hope's Crossing, Colorado

Summary: *Blackberry Summer* is a novel by author Rae-Anne Thayne. After her divorce, Claire Bradford ekes out an existence in Hope's Crossing, Colorado, as the owner of a bead shop. When a string of robberies hits the fractured community, Claire becomes the thieves' fourth target. Then she has a bad accident and must learn to rely on others within the town, including Riley McKnight, the brother of her best friend and Hope's Crossing's brand new police chief. Although sparks begin to fly between Claire and Riley, she has misgivings about becoming involved with someone she has known all of her life. Soon Hope's Crossing begins to come together once again as a town with the help of Riley and Claire, and Claire wonders if this time romance might not pass her by. Thayne is also the author of the Cold Creek series.

Where it's reviewed:
Romantic Times, June 2011, page 78

Other books by the same author:
A Cold Creek Baby, 2011
Light the Stars, 2011
A Cold Creek Secret, 2010
Nothing to Lose, 2010
A Soldier's Secret, 2008

Other books you might like:
Robyn Carr, *Forbidden Falls*, 2009
Robyn Carr, *Promise Canyon*, 2011
Robyn Carr, *A Summer in Sonoma*, 2010
Jill Shalvis, *Simply Irresistible*, 2010

Subject(s): Detective fiction; Terrorism; Irish Republican Army
Major character(s): Devyn Hewitt Sterling, Daughter; Marc Rossi, Detective—Private
Time period(s): 21st century; 2010s
Locale(s): Ireland

Summary: *Shiver of Fear* is the second book in author Roxanne St. Claire's Guardian Angelinos series. After quitting his job with the FBI and enduring a bitter divorce, Marc Rossi is ready to start his life all over again by working with his cousins, owners of the Guardian Angelinos detective agency. His first mission takes him to Northern Ireland to retrieve Devyn Hewitt Sterling, the daughter of a dangerous fugitive. Unbeknownst to Marc, Devyn has her own problem—her mother has disappeared, and Devyn suspects that her father is to blame. Now Marc and Devyn must fight their passion for one another long enough to save Devyn's mother and stop her father from striking again.

Where it's reviewed:
Library Journal, April 15, 2011, page 77
Romantic Times, April 2011, page 66

Other books by the same author:
Face of Danger, 2011
Edge of Sight, 2010
Take Me Tonight, 2007
Thrill Me to Death, 2006
Kill Me Twice, 2005

Other books you might like:
Cherry Adair, *Dare Me*, 2005
Suzanne Brockmann, *Unsung Hero*, 2000
Christina Dodd, *Almost Like Being in Love*, 2004
Cindy Gerard, *To the Brink*, 2006
Carla Neggers, *The Whisper*, 2010

943

ROXANNE ST. CLAIRE

Face of Danger

(New York: Forever, May 1, 2011)

Series: Guardian Angelinos Series. Book 3
Story type: Romantic Suspense; Series
Subject(s): Serial murders; Detective fiction; Law enforcement
Major character(s): Vivi Angelino, Detective—Private; Colton Lang, Agent (FBI)
Time period(s): 21st century; 2010s
Locale(s): United States

Summary: *Face of Danger* is the third book in author Roxanne St. Claire's Guardian Angelinos series. When Vivi Angelino accepts an assignment to track a murderer on the set of an award-winning actress's new movie, she is sure that the case will bring the Angelinos' security firm lots of money and exposure. Then FBI agent Colton Lang gets in her way, and puts them both in danger. As Colton and Vivi work hard to solve the mystery, they find themselves with targets on their backs. Can they stop a dangerous serial murderer before they become victims themselves? St. Claire is also the author of The Bullet Catchers series, which includes the novels *Make*

945

JODI THOMAS (Pseudonym of Jodi Koumalats)

Texas Blue

(New York: Berkley, 2011)

Story type: Historical
Subject(s): Love; Family; Kidnapping
Major character(s): Lewton "Lewt" Paterson, Gambler; Em, Rancher; Duncan, Cousin (of Em), Friend (of Lewt)
Time period(s): 19th century; 1870s
Locale(s): Whispering Mountain, Texas

Summary: Lewton Paterson is a gambler who feels his only way to gain respectability is to find a rich wife. When his friend Duncan mentions that he is looking for men to marry his cousins in the small town of Whispering Mountain, Texas, Lewt jumps at the opportunity and makes his way to the ladies' ranch. There he meets Em, a beautiful but tough-as-nails overseer who handles ranching and her relationships with her sisters with equal aplomb. When Lewt gets word that Duncan is in danger, he and Em team up and head out to save his friend—and, in the process, just may get a shot at true love. *Texas Blue* is the fifth novel in Jodi Thomas's Whispering Mountain series.

Where it's reviewed:
Romantic Times, April 2011, page 32

Other books by the same author:
Somewhere Along the Way, 2010
The Lone Texan, 2009
Rewriting Monday, 2009
Tall, Dark, and Texan, 2008
Twisted Creek, 2008

Other books you might like:
Diane Amos, *The Legacy*, 2009
Jo Goodman, *Never Love a Lawman*, 2009
Lorraine Heath, *A Rogue in Texas*, 1999
Maggie Osborne, *Prairie Moon*, 2002
Maggie Osborne, *Silver Lining*, 2000

946

VICKI LEWIS THOMPSON

Cowboy Up

(New York: Harlequin, 2011)

Story type: Contemporary
Subject(s): Love; Western fiction; Ranch life
Major character(s): Emily Sterling, Young Woman; Clay Whitaker, Cowboy/Cowgirl
Time period(s): 21st century; 2010s
Locale(s): United States

Summary: *Cowboy Up* is the fifth novel in author Vicki Lewis Thompson's Sons of Chance series, a cycle of sexy romances set in the contemporary American West. This volume follows Emily Sterling as she comes back to Last Chance Ranch, her father's sprawling acreage, and sets sights on handsome Clay Whitaker. Clay has grown from a novice cowhand into the ranch's stud expert, and Emily—despite her family's admonishments to never fall for a cowboy—can't take her eyes off him. Clay takes it upon himself to show Emily what a cowboy's life is *really* like—and just how perfect they are for one another.

Where it's reviewed:
Romantic Times, July 2011, Page 98

Other books by the same author:
Cowboys Like Us, 2011
Should've Been a Cowboy, 2011
Blonde with a Wand, 2010
Chick with a Charm, 2010
Claimed, 2010

Other books you might like:
Carolyn Brown, *My Give a Damn's Busted*, 2010
B.J. Daniels, *Montana Royalty*, 2008
Geralyn Dawson, *Her Outlaw*, 2007
Delores Fossen, *Branded by the Sheriff*, 2009
Georgina Gentry, *To Love a Texan*, 2007

947

STEPHANIE TYLER

In the Air Tonight

(New York: Dell, 2011)

Series: Shadow Force Series. Book 3
Story type: Romantic Suspense; Series
Subject(s): Romances (Fiction); Suspense; Murder
Major character(s): Mace Stevens, Agent (Delta Force); Paige Grayson, Sister (of Jeffrey Grayson and Gray), Young Woman; Jeffrey Grayson, Murderer, Brother (of Paige); Caleb Scott, Agent (Delta Force); Gray, Agent (Delta Force, deceased), Brother (of Paige)
Time period(s): 21st century; 2010s
Locale(s): New York, United States

Summary: The third book in Stephanie Tyler's Shadow Force series, *In the Air Tonight* finds Delta Force agents Mace Stevens and Caleb Scott at Mace's upstate New York bar trying to put the memories of their past mission behind them. Their fellow agent and friend Gray was lost, and they are still trying to piece together exactly how that happened. Then Gray's sister Paige Grayson arrives, also looking for answers. But as Paige seeks answers about one brother's death, she is on the run from another brother, Jeffrey, who is a mass murderer. Mace tries to protect Paige, the sister of his fallen partner, but finds himself falling for the troubled young woman in the process.

Where it's reviewed:
Romantic Times, August 2011, Page 90

Other books by the same author:
Hold on Tight, 2010
Lie with Me, 2010
Promises in the Dark, 2010
Hard to Hold, 2009
Too Hot to Hold, 2009

Other books you might like:
Lora Leigh, *Black Jack*, 2010

Brenda Novak, *Killer Heat*, 2010
Brenda Novak, *White Heat*, 2010
Christy Reece, *Last Chance*, 2010

948

ELIZABETH VAUGHAN

Warcry

(New York: Berkley, 2011)

Story type: Fantasy
Subject(s): Adventure; Love; Royalty
Major character(s): Heath, Warrior; Atira the Bear, Warrior
Time period(s): Indeterminate
Locale(s): Xy, Fictional Location

Summary: *Warcry* is the seventh installment in Elizabeth Vaughan's Chronicles of the Warlands series. Set in the fictional world of Xy, this outing follows the adventures of warriors Heath and Atira as they battle a vast conspiracy threatening to topple the entire realm. As they make their way to the city, Heath cannot hide his attraction to Atira, though the fearless warrior-woman makes it clear that she is not interested in either Heath or life in the big city. But events soon spiral out of control, and the two are forced to work together in order to save the kingdom of Xy—and Atira just may be persuaded to let Heath into her heart.

Where it's reviewed:
Publishers Weekly, March 7, 2011, page 50

Other books by the same author:
Warprize, 2011
Destiny's Star, 2010
White Star, 2009
Dagger-Star, 2008
Warlord, 2007

Other books you might like:
Meljean Brook, *Demon Moon*, 2007
Jayne Castle, *Silver Master*, 2007
Susan Grant, *The Star King*, 2000
Marjorie M. Liu, *In the Darkness of Dreams*, 2010
Rebecca York, *Day of the Dragon*, 2010

949

JOSELYN VAUGHN (Pseudonym of Esther L. Jiran)

Courting Sparks

(New York: Avalon Books, 2011)

Story type: Contemporary
Subject(s): Romances (Fiction); Courtship; Fires
Major character(s): Daphne Morrow, Friend (of Noah), Lover (of Noah); Noah Banks, Lover (of Daphne), Fire Fighter, Friend (of Daphne)
Time period(s): 21st century
Locale(s): United States

Summary: *Courting Sparks* by Joselyn Vaughn is a romance novel about an amorous firefighter. In this novel, Noah Banks is a volunteer firefighter. During a call to a forest fire, he is shocked to find that the source of the blaze is burned paper—prom photographs of his friend Daphne Morrow! Banks is unsure what to do, knowing that Daphne will become an arson suspect if the evidence is discovered. Noah and Daphne try to find the real arsonist before Daphne gets in trouble. While they rush to solve the puzzle, they develop feelings for one another.

Where it's reviewed:
Publishers Weekly, January 17, 2011, page 36

Other books by the same author:
Sucker for a Hot Rod, 2011
CEOs Don't Cry, 2009

Other books you might like:
Zelda Benjamin, *Chocolate Secrets*, 2008
Carolyn Hughey, *Cupid's Web*, 2007
Annette Mahon, *The Secret Admirer*, 2001
Deborah Shelley, *Marriage 101*, 2008
Kim Watters, *Home at Last*, 2003

950

SHILOH WALKER

Hunter's Fall

(New York: Berkley, 2011)

Story type: Fantasy
Subject(s): Adventure; Love; Memory disorders
Major character(s): Nessa, Immortal; Dominic Ralston, Vampire Hunter
Time period(s): 21st century; 2010s
Locale(s): United States

Summary: The fifth book in The Hunters series, Shiloh Walker's *Hunter's Fall* tells the story of two star-crossed lovers whose feelings for one another cannot be restricted by the boundaries of time. Nessa is an immortal who has devoted the bulk of her recent life to saving humans from the evil machinations of certain immortal populations. Meanwhile, Dominic Ralston, a vampire hunter, is actually the man who, 500 years ago, pledged his undying love to Nessa just before he died. Now Dominic is out to find Nessa and reconnect with his long-lost love. There's just one problem: Nessa has amnesia and has no memory of Dominic or the love they once shared.

Where it's reviewed:
Romantic Times, June 2011, page 86

Other books by the same author:
Hunter's Edge, 2009
Hunter's Need, 2009
Through the Veil, 2008
Hunter's Salvation, 2007
Hunters: Heart and Soul, 2007

Other books you might like:
Christine Feehan, *Dark Magic*, 2000
Emma Holly, *Devil at Midnight*, 2010
Kathleen Nance, *Phoenix Unrisen*, 2007
Robin T. Popp, *Lord of the Night*, 2007
J.R. Ward, *Lover Awakened: A Novel of the Black Dagger Brotherhood*, 2006

951

KAREN V. WASYLOWSKI

Darcy and Fitzwilliam

(Naperville, Illinois: Sourcebooks Landmark, 2011)

Story type: Historical
Subject(s): Cousins; Friendship; Love
Major character(s): Fitzwilliam Darcy, Cousin (of Colonel Fitzwilliam); Fitzwilliam, Cousin (of Darcy), Military Personnel (colonel)
Time period(s): 19th century
Locale(s): England

Summary: Karen V. Wasylowski's *Darcy and Fitzwilliam* charts the bond between two cousins who see one another through life's trials and tribulations and help each other through the complications of love. The restrained Fitzwilliam Darcy is a man of few words, but his affection for his girlfriend is deep and true. The only problem is his aloof manner, which may jeopardize the relationship. Meanwhile, his cousin, Colonel Fitzwilliam, is spirited and outgoing and determined to win the hand of a feisty young widow. Soon the two cousins need one another's expertise as they struggle to capture the hearts of their lady loves. First novel.

Where it's reviewed:
Booklist, December 15, 2010, page 28

Other books you might like:
Pamela Aidan, *An Assembly Such as This*, 2006
Diana Birchall, *Mrs. Darcy's Dilemma*, 2007
Syrie James, *The Lost Memoirs of Jane Austen*, 2007
Sharon Lathan, *Mr. and Mrs. Fitzwilliam Darcy*, 2009
Jane Odiwe, *Willoughby's Return*, 2009

952

KIM WATTERS

Home Sweet Home

(New York: Love Inspired, 2011)

Story type: Inspirational
Subject(s): Christian life; Family; Romances (Fiction)
Major character(s): Abby Bancroft, Innkeeper; Cole Preston, Contractor

Summary: *Home Sweet Home* is a novel written by author Kim Watters. When Abby Bancroft's grandparents bequeath to her their old inn, Abby finally gets something she has always wanted—a home to call her own. Yet Abby didn't realize how much work would be involved in achieving her dream of owning a bed and breakfast. Lucky for Abby, Cole Preston has just arrived in town to satisfy a debt between his contracting business and Abby's grandparents. Cole's former business associate cheated many townspeople out of money, and most of the town still holds that against Cole. Abby needs him, though, and soon they find themselves falling for each other. Can Cole help Abby reach her dream while Abby helps him clear his reputation? Watters is also the author of *Stake Your Claim*, *On the Wings of Love*, and *Home at Last*.

Where it's reviewed:
Romantic Times, June 2011, page 100

Other books by the same author:
On Wings of Love, 2010
Stake Your Claim, 2008
Web of Deceit, 2007
Home at Last, 2003

Other books you might like:
Robyn Carr, *Promise Canyon*, 2011
Candice Poarch, *Lighthouse Magic*, 2003
Jill Shalvis, *Simply Irresistible*, 2010
Deborah Smith, *The Crossroads Cafe*, 2006

953

DEBRA WEBB

Broken

(Don Mills, Ontario, Canada: Harlequin, 2011)

Series: Colby Agency Series. Book 45
Story type: Mystery; Series
Subject(s): Mystery; Missing persons; Romances (Fiction)
Major character(s): Linc Reece, Agent (Equalizers); Mia Grant, Young Woman; Lori, Kidnap Victim, Spouse (of Linc)
Time period(s): 21st century; 2011
Locale(s): Tennessee, United States

Summary: *Broken* is the 45th book in author Debra Webb's Colby Agency series, and the second book in The New Equalizers portion of that series. It's a rare case that Special Agent Linc Reece, of the Colby Agency's special enforcement team The Equalizers, cannot solve, yet the one mystery he's been unable to unravel is the seven-year-old case of his missing wife Lori. Now he may have found her living in Tennessee under the name Mia Grant. Mia is not convinced that she is really Lori, despite their similarities. Then Lori's belongings go missing, and Mia and Linc begin to wonder if someone is trying to cover up the truth. Webb is also the author of *Damaged*, *Dirty*, *Missing*, and *Anywhere She Runs*.

Where it's reviewed:
Romantic Times, June 2011, page 95

Other books by the same author:
Damaged, 2011
Anywhere She Runs, 2010
Colby Brass, 2010
Colby Justice, 2010
Colby Lockdown, 2010

Other books you might like:
Beth Kery, *Explosive*, 2010
Lora Leigh, *Black Jack*, 2010
Kelsey Roberts, *The Night in Question*, 2009
Kay Thomas, *Better than Bulletproof*, 2009

Romances

954

DEBRA WEBB

Damaged

(Don Mills, Ontario: Harlequin, 2011)

Series: Colby Agency Series. Book 44
Story type: Mystery; Series
Subject(s): Law enforcement; Kidnapping; Love
Major character(s): Victoria Colby-Camp, Director (of Colby Agency), Kidnap Victim; Lucky Malone, Agent (of Colby Agency); Dakota Garrett, Agent (Equalizers)
Time period(s): 21st century; 2010s
Locale(s): Chicago, Illinois

Summary: *Damaged* is the 44th book in author Debra Webb's Colby Agency series, and the first book in The New Equalizers portion of that series. When Equalizer agent Dakota Garrett is given the task of watching Lucky Malone of the Colby Agency, he never expects to fall for her. Yet soon Lucky persuades Dakota to help her search for her missing boss, Victoria Colby-Camp. Victoria has been abducted, and it is up to Lucky and Dakota to track her down. First, however, Dakota must work to free himself from his inner turmoil and let his guard down long enough to care about something other than the mission itself. Webb is also the author of *Broken*, *Dirty*, *Missing*, and *Anywhere She Runs*.

Where it's reviewed:
Romantic Times, May 2011, page 110

Other books by the same author:
Broken, 2011
Colby Brass, 2010
Colby Core, 2010
Colby Justice, 2010
Colby Lockdown, 2010

Other books you might like:
Maya Banks, *No Place to Run*, 2010
Stephanie Tyler, *Hard to Hold*, 2009
Stephanie Tyler, *Lie with Me*, 2010

955

CARL WEBER

The Choir Director

(New York: Kensington Publishing Corporation, 2011)

Story type: Contemporary
Subject(s): Romances (Fiction); Religion; Sexual behavior
Major character(s): Aaron Mackie, Singer (choir director); Jackie Robinson Moss, Singer (former choir director), Homosexual; T.K. Wilson, Religious (bishop); Simone Wilcox, Accountant (chairwoman of board of trustees), Thief (stealing money)
Time period(s): 21st century
Locale(s): New York, New York

Summary: *The Choir Director* by Carl Weber is a romance novel set in a very unusual church, the First Jamaica Ministries Church. First Jamaica is a church that is full of scheming, scandals, and sex. This novel opens with a gay sex scandal in which the choirmaster, Jackie Robinson Moss, is shown to have had relations with many men in the community. His replacement as head of the choir is lust-crazed Aaron Mackie, who quickly begins to seduce female churchgoers. Meanwhile, church chairpersons are stealing money, ministers are threatening cheating spouses with guns, and parishioners are killing themselves. What will become of First Jamaica Church?

Where it's reviewed:
Romantic Times, February 2011, page 40

Other books by the same author:
The First Lady, 2010
Torn Between Two Lovers, 2010
Up to No Good, 2010
The Preacher's Son, 2006
Married Men, 2005

Other books you might like:
Rochelle Alers, *Here I Am*, 2011
Pat G'Orge-Walker, *Don't Blame the Devil*, 2010
Ernest Hill, *Family Ties*, 2010
Brenda Jackson, *Fire and Desire*, 2009

956

MICHAEL LEE WEST

Gone with a Handsomer Man

(New York: Minotaur Books, 2011)

Subject(s): Mystery; Detective fiction; Murder
Major character(s): Teeny Templeton, Cook (pastry chef), Fiance(e) (of Bing Jackson); Bing Jackson, Fiance(e) (of Teeny); Cooper O'Malley, Lawyer, Boyfriend (of Teeny, former); Dora Jackson, Stepmother (of Bing); Natalie Lockhart, Friend (of Bing); Red Butler Hill, Detective—Private
Time period(s): 21st century; 2010s
Locale(s): Charleston, South Carolina

Summary: In the mystery novel *Gone with a Handsomer Man* by Michael Lee West, Teeny Templeton is a pastry chef who's caught her fiance engaged in nude badminton with two female partners—so she pelts them with peaches. Teeny's impulsive action earns her a restraining order and an accusation of murder when Bing Jackson, her ex-fiance, is killed shortly thereafter. Trouble keeps growing for Teeny, who hires former boyfriend Cooper O'Malley as her attorney. While Teeny deals with Bing's betrayal and death, she also faces feelings from the past. Through it all, she manages to dream up some deadly delicious desserts. First novel.

Where it's reviewed:
Booklist, May 1, 2011, page 27
Publishers Weekly, March 7, 2011, page 48

Other books by the same author:
Mermaids in the Basement, 2008
Mad Girls in Love, 2006
American Pie, 1996
She Flew the Coop, 1994
Crazy Ladies, 1990

Other books you might like:
Jennifer Crusie, *Agnes and the Hitman*, 2007
Luanne Jones, *Sweethearts of the Twilight Lanes*, 2001
Linda Francis Lee, *The Devil in the Junior League*,
  2006
Susan Elizabeth Phillips, *Ain't She Sweet?*, 2004
Deborah Smith, *Charming Grace*, 2004

█ 957

DIANE WHITESIDE

The Shadow Guard

(New York: Kensington Publishing Company, 2011)

Story type: Paranormal
Subject(s): Magic; Psychics; Mystery
Major character(s): Astrid Carlsen, Psychic, Sorceress;
  Jake Hammond, Police Officer
Time period(s): 21st century; 2010s
Locale(s): United States

Summary: In Diane Whiteside's novel *The Shadow Guard*,
psychic Astrid Carlsen is a member of the Shadow
Guard, an elite group of operatives who work to solve
mysteries through black magic. When she detects a
supernatural crime taking place, Astrid is determined to
solve the mystery. Soon she learns that an Internet
acquaintance named Jake Hammond is working the case.
Astrid and Jake have a deep, cosmic connection that
feeds her psychic energy through sexuality and magic.
Soon Astrid discovers that Jake might be the key to solving the mystery. Whiteside is also the author of *The Irish
Devil*, *The Southern Devil*, and *Not Just for Tonight*.

Where it's reviewed:
Romantic Times, April 2011, page 105

Other books by the same author:
Improper Gentlemen, 2011
The Devil She Knows, 2010
Captive Desires, 2009
Kisses Like a Devil, 2009
The Northern Devil, 2007

Other books you might like:
Pamela Palmer, *Obsession Untamed*, 2009
Pamela Palmer, *Rapture Untamed*, 2010
Leslie Parrish, *Cold Sight*, 2010

█ 958

SUSAN WIGGS

The Goodbye Quilt

(New York: Mira, 2011)

Subject(s): Mother-daughter relations; Quilts; Women
Major character(s): Linda Davis, Store Owner (fabric shop
  owner); Molly Davis, Daughter (of Linda)
Time period(s): 21st century; 2010s
Locale(s): United States

Summary: Susan Wiggs's *The Goodbye Quilt* centers on
the relationship between mother and daughter, Linda and

Molly Davis. Fabric-shop owner Linda has always been
a quilter, but now she faces her biggest quilting undertaking yet: crafting a special piece for Molly to take with
her to college, comprised of fabric scraps from the young
woman's life. Mother and daughter set out on a road trip
for Molly's university, and, along the way, Linda
remembers episodes from Molly's life as she works on
the quilt.

Where it's reviewed:
Library Journal, April 1, 2011, page 86
Romantic Times, April 2011, page 50

Other books by the same author:
Just Breathe, 2008
Willow Lake, 2008
The Winter Lodge, 2007
Table for Five, 2006
Lakeside Cottage, 2005

Other books you might like:
Kristin Hannah, *The Things We Do for Love*, 2004
Debbie Macomber, *1022 Evergreen Place*, 2010
Susan Mallery, *Almost Perfect*, 2010
Kathryn Shay, *Trust in Me*, 2003
Lori Wilde, *The True Love Quilting Club*, 2010

█ 959

EMMA WILDES (Pseudonym of Katherine Smith)

One Whisper Away

(New York: Signet, 2011)

Story type: Historical; Series
Subject(s): Romances (Fiction); Marriage; Sexuality
Major character(s): Lady Cecily Francis, Noblewoman;
  Jonathan Bourne, Indian, Nobleman
Time period(s): 19th century
Locale(s): England

Summary: *One Whisper Away*, a historical romance novel
from author Emma Wildes, is the first book in the Ladies
in Waiting series. Lady Cecily Francis is not particularly
excited about marrying Lord Drury, a man she suspects
her sister is in love with, but she's come to terms with
the inevitable union. That is, until she encounters
Jonathan Bourne, the exotic and untamed American who
has just been named the new earl of Augustine. Bourne
is everything that Lord Drury is not: wild, interesting,
and unbelievably sexy. A scandalous encounter between
the two has Lady Cecily plotting a way out of her
impending marriage. Although Bourne longs for nothing
more than to marry off his sisters and return to America,
he soon finds himself charmed by Cecily's beauty and
caught up in her scheme.

Where it's reviewed:
Booklist, April 15, 2011, page 26
Publishers Weekly, March 21, 2011, page 61
Romantic Times, May 2011, page 44

Other books by the same author:
His Sinful Secret, 2010
Lessons from a Scarlet Lady, 2010
My Lord Scandal, 2010
Our Wicked Mistake, 2010

Seducing the Highlander, 2010

Other books you might like:
Renee Bernard, *Revenge Wears Rubies*, 2010
Tiffany Clare, *The Surrender of a Lady*, 2010
Nicole Jordan, *To Tame a Dangerous Lord*, 2010
Ashley March, *Seducing the Duchess*, 2010

960

JOAN WOLF

A Reluctant Queen

(Nashville: Thomas Nelson, 2011)

Story type: Inspirational
Subject(s): Bible stories; Jews; Marriage
Major character(s): Esther, Spouse (of King Ahasuerus), Royalty (queen); Ahasuerus, Spouse (of Esther), Royalty (king)
Time period(s): 5th century

Summary: Joan Wolf's *A Reluctant Queen* is based on the biblical story of Esther and presents a detailed history of both the character and the time in which she lived. Esther is raised by her uncle after her parents' deaths, and when the old man urges her to compete for the king's love, she consents. She wins the contest for King Ahasuerus's love, and the two are married. As they settle into their life together, Esther is plagued with guilt over a secret she has kept from the King—a secret that, if revealed, may spell doom for not only herself but for an entire race of people.

Where it's reviewed:
Publishers Weekly, April 4, 2011, page 35

Other books by the same author:
The Pretenders, 1999
The Arrangement, 1997
The Deception, 1996
Daughter of the Red Deer, 1992
Born of the Sun, 1991

Other books you might like:
Tessa Afshar, *Pearl in the Sand*, 2010
Anita Diamant, *The Red Tent*, 1997

Antoinette May, *Pilate's Wife*, 2006
Jill Eileen Smith, *Bathsheba: A Novel*, 2011
Diana Wallis Taylor, *Martha: A Novel*, 2011

961

SHERRYL WOODS

Moonlight Cove

(Don Mills, Ontario, Canada: Mira, April 26, 2011)

Series: Chesapeake Shores Series. Book 6
Story type: Contemporary; Series
Subject(s): Love; Rural life; Psychology
Major character(s): Jess O'Brien, Young Woman; Will Lincoln, Psychologist
Time period(s): 21st century; 2010s
Locale(s): Virginia, United States

Summary: *Moonlight Cove* is the sixth book in Sherryl Woods's Chesapeake Shores series, which charts the romantic adventures of the denizens of a small Southern town. This outing finds Jess O'Brien on the hunt for love. After overcoming a series of obstacles in her young life, Jess is finally ready to make a commitment and settle down. She gives in to her friends' pressures to join a dating service, but her attempts to meet Mr. Right come up empty. Enter Will Lincoln, Jess's childhood pal. Now a successful psychologist, Will is smitten with the beautiful Jess, and he sets out to win her heart.

Where it's reviewed:
Romantic Times, May 2011, page 85

Other books by the same author:
Beach Lane, 2011
Driftwood Cottage, 2011
An O'Brien Family Christmas, 2011
Flowers on Main, 2009
Harbor Lights, 2009

Other books you might like:
Kristan Higgins, *Catch of the Day*, 2007
Jill Mansell, *Staying at Daisy's*, 2002
Linda Lael Miller, *Montana Creeds: Tyler*, 2009
Mariah Stewart, *Home Again*, 2010
Susan Wiggs, *The Winter Lodge*, 2007

The Marketing of Science Fiction
by
Don D'Ammassa

Science fiction really began to emerge as a separate genre when Hugo Gernsback founded *Amazing Stories* in 1926. Gernsback was a naturalized American who was involved in the electronics industry before entering the world of magazine publishing. Although he lost control of the magazine in 1929, he then founded two new titles and was intermittently active from that point forward. There was no question that his magazines were aimed at young adults and adolescents and the covers were garish and filled with mysterious devices and spaceships. Their very appearance made it easy for mainstream critics to ignore them as children's fiction or worse and in fact much of the original work that appeared in them was badly written and largely forgotten today.

The pulp magazines of the 1940s added a new element—hints of sex—and publishers began displaying beautiful women in various states of undress, often menaced by leering aliens, even though female characters in most of the stories were subsidiary, more plot device than human being. They were there to be rescued, to be explained to, or to suggest that something scandalous might be happening. This trend gradually faded away during the 1950s, but the bright colors and outlandish subject matter remained. Some magazines, such as *The Magazine of Fantasy & Science Fiction*, *Galaxy*, and eventually *Astounding Stories* began to tone down the melodrama and experiment with different types of cover art: representational, surreal, or even simple astronomical scenes.

The mass market paperback became popular during the 1950s and most of the cover art of that period fell somewhere between the two extremes. It was still common to have spaceships on the cover—even if they weren't related to the contents—but the more prolific artists of this period either tended toward more realistic representational art or—in the case of Richard Powers—generically surreal landscapes or images reminiscent of the work of Salvador Dali. Representational art has become dominant in the field since the 1980s.

Most new science fiction titles during the 1950s and 1960s were novels or novellas. Single-author collections were much more common than they are today and most anthologies consisted of reprints from the magazines. There were several early anthologies of original stories but this trend did not really catch on until the 1970s, although at present the majority of new anthologies contain original material. This is in part the result of the collapse of the science fiction magazine, which has declined from as many as twenty titles per month to the current two or three. Single-author collections appeared from major publishers for even lesser known writers. Today only the handful who are bestselling authors are likely to see their short fiction collected except by the smaller presses.

Science fiction novels were much shorter from 1940 to 1980 than they are today. A typical paperback novel was 160 pages long. Ace Double books were usually even shorter, consisting of two novellas published back to back, an innovative idea that later was imitated briefly by Tor books. Very few of these paperback novels had seen previous hardcover publication: The majority of them were original publications, although a significant number had appeared previously in magazines, often as serials. The serial novel has not quite died in science fiction but it has become extremely rare. In the United States, the vast majority was written by American authors, but there were also a significant number of British imports, including most notably Arthur C. Clarke, Brian W. Aldiss, Charles Eric Maine, John Wyndham, John Christopher, and others. Australia and Canada have also produced successful genre writers including A.E. van Vogt, A. Bertram Chandler, Robert J. Sawyer, and George Turner. British influence in American science fiction has risen and fallen several times since then and is currently reasonably high. Science fiction from non-English speaking countries was largely limited to Jules Verne and Stanislaw Lem, although there have been brief periodic influxes of translations from the Russian, German, French, Italian, or Japanese.

Publishers tended not to take science fiction seriously until the arrival of Judy-Lyn Benjamin—later Judy-Lyn Del Rey—at Ballantine Books. She pointed out that while few science fiction novels became immediate best-

sellers, authors such as Robert A. Heinlein, Isaac Asimov, and Arthur C. Clarke tended to remain in print and sell steadily long after the flavor of the month had been remaindered and forgotten. More importantly, they achieved this status without drawing a substantial advertising budget. This change in attitude was one of the contributing factors that resulted in science fiction novels regularly appearing on bestseller lists. Ballantine eventually renamed its imprint Del Rey Books in her honor.

The steady rise of science fiction began to falter during the 1980s. There were undoubtedly many factors involved so it is impossible to determine cause and effect, but some of the contributing factors are obvious. The mass market reprinting of The Lord of the Rings trilogy by J.R.R. Tolkien in the 1960s had generated increased interest in fantasy among readers and writers. Although there was not overwhelming replication between the two groups of potential readers, there was considerable overlap and some of those individuals who might have bought the latest science fiction novel were buying fantasy instead. To a lesser extent the same is true of the horror genre, which was extremely popular during the 1980s, although it faded dramatically starting in 1990. Fantasy, however, has become more popular than ever and certainly outsells science fiction at present by a significant amount.

Another factor may well be the change in editorial direction. Publishers are naturally inclined toward increased sales, which meant expanding the target audience. Science fiction was no longer to be limited to adolescent males. Writers were expected to be more skillful, characters were more realistic, more "serious" issues were examined, and plots were expected to be less playful and more plausible. There is no question that this effort did attract some new readers but may also have alienated a portion of its former following. The advent of the video game began competing for attention about the same time and first person shooters and adventure games satisfied the thirst for wild action a lot more immediately than a solemn look at the consequences of global warming.

Still another element may have been the change in format of the novel. Publishers needed to charge higher prices to cover overhead. The twenty-five cent paperback has risen to $7 or $8 so each title has to be a lot longer or the consumer might balk. There is nothing wrong with increased length as such, but some readers are less likely even to start a 400-page book impulsively than they were when novels were shorter. During the 1960s it was possible to sit down with the latest science fiction novel and read it in a single, cathartic sitting. Novels such as Robert A. Heinlein's *Stranger in a Strange Land* (1961) stood out because they were so unusually long and books like this were special events. That's no longer the case, obviously. In fact, given the death of most of the professional science fiction magazines, new novellas are very rare.

An additional fragment of the readership has gone to the thriller or techno-thriller genre, which often is simply science fiction marketed as something else. Stephen Coonts can write about flying saucers, Tom Clancy about nuclear terrorism, Clive Cussler about mysterious new elements, and all have their work published as thrillers for a general audience rather than science fiction fans alone.

The demise of the extensive backlist and the erosion of the midlist author also have contributed to the genre's troubles. Mass market paperbacks used to contain lists of older titles with an order form so that readers could order those books that did not show up in their local bookstores. Although the advent of online sellers such as Amazon.com has eliminated some of the need for this, the fact is that publishers can no longer afford to maintain stocks of older titles and if it doesn't sell within a relatively short period of time, the balance of a print run is probably going to be pulped and no longer available. It has become quite possible to buy the third novel in a series and then discover that the first title is no longer generally available. Some authors have even resorted to providing free electronic versions of their earlier novels on the internet in order to encourage sales of their newer books.

The midlist is also declining. There was a time when a new science fiction novel was considered a reasonable success if it sold a predetermined number of titles, far short of what a bestselling novel might do. This was the midlist and that was where most authors remained throughout their careers. Today every new title needs to be considered at least a potential best seller. If an author publishes several books that do well but not especially well, he or she might find themselves looking at a foreshortened career. This is one reason why many authors have reinvented themselves under a new pseudonym, always hoping for a breakout book that will sell better than their previous work. Although this doesn't sound entirely unfortunate—the most successful work obviously should rise above its competition—there is a regrettable side effect. One of the best aspects of earlier science fiction was that one could find quirky novels by authors such as David R. Bunch, Felix Gotschalk, T.J. Bass, or Cordwainer Smith that would never have a chance of acquiring a mass audience but which were distinctive, skillfully done, and highly original. I suspect that none of these authors could have sold a novel to a major publisher today unless they changed their style completely.

Finally we come to the series novel, although the problems here are much more serious in fantasy than in science fiction, at least so far. Science fiction writers have produced sequels and open ended series since the 1920s. John W. Campbell Jr. chronicled the adventures of Arcot, Morey, and Wade; Edmond Hamilton explored space with Captain Future; Edward E. Smith laid out his vision of a galactic civilization in the Lens series; and later there would be Keith Laumer's Retief, Poul Anderson's Flandry, Frank Herbert's Dune, and many

others. But with the exception of the Foundation trilogy by Isaac Asimov, these were series rather than a serial. Each volume was complete in itself, and in most cases they could be read in almost any order.

The trilogies that have dominated fantasy for the past decade are actually one story that spans multiple books. There is a definite beginning in volume one and a definite end in volume three—although the trilogy has been expanded into multiple volumes by writers such as Robert Jordan, L.E. Modesitt Jr., and George R.R. Martin. This same trend is beginning to show up in science fiction. The expansions of the original Dune series by Brian Herbert and Kevin J. Anderson, as well as Anderson's own Saga of the Seven Suns, do not contain a complete story in each volume. Readers are less likely to commit themselves to a book when they know it might be years before the story ends, or, if the series is complete, less likely to launch into a seven volume story than a single one. Casual readers and impulse buyers are less likely to invest that much effort when they can pick up a murder mystery or suspense story that will satisfy them within a day or two.

Science fiction is confronted today with a changing readership along with a publishing world more oriented toward profit and sales figures, and has to compete with a different array of distractions. At present, it does not appear to be adapting itself readily to its new circumstances.

Recommended Titles

The year 2011 has already seen several significant novels from both new and established writers including the first new solo title by Frederik Pohl in several years. The most promising newcomer is Hannu Rajaniemi. Themes range from hard science to space opera to near future political intrigue.

Leviathans of Jupiter by Ben Bova

The Year's Best Science Fiction: 28th Annual Collection edited by Gardner Dozois

This Shared Dream by Kathleen Ann Goonan

All the Lives He Led by Frederik Pohl

The Quantum Thief by Hannu Rajaniemi

City of Ruins by Kristine Kathryn Rusch

WWW: Wonder by Robert J. Sawyer

The Highest Frontier by Joan Slonczewski

Hex by Allen Steele

Scratch Monkey by Charles Stross

Home Fires by Gene Wolfe

Science Fiction

962

DAN ABNETT

Thunder & Steel

(Nottingham, United Kingdom: Black Library, 2011)

Story type: Collection
Subject(s): Fantasy; Science fiction; Short stories

Summary: *Thunder & Steel*, a collection of science-fiction and fantasy short stories and novels, is part of the Warhammer series from best-selling author Dan Abnett. The book includes three of Abnett's fantasy novels, one graphic novel, and several short stories. *Gilead's Blood* follows the harrowing adventures of elf Gilead Lothain as he travels through the Old World following the death of his twin. In *Hammers of Ulric, the noble White Wolves seek to protect the mountain city of Middenheim from powerful evil forces. Rider of the Dead* tells the story of two Empire soldiers as they wrestle with the forces of Chaos and their personal fates.

Other books by the same author:
The Lost, 2010
Blood Pact, 2009
Legion, 2008
Only in Death, 2007
Ravenor Rogue, 2007

Other books you might like:
Nick Kyme, *Fall of Damnos*, 2011
Rob Sanders, *Atlas Infernal*, 2011
Gav Thorpe, *Path of the Seer*, 2011
Richard Williams, *Imperial Glory*, 2011
Chris Wraight, *Battle of the Fang*, 2011

963

ANN AGUIRRE

Aftermath

(New York: Ace Books, 2011)

Series: Sirantha Jax Series. Book 5
Story type: Series; Space Opera
Subject(s): Time travel; Space exploration; Trials
Major character(s): Sirantha Jax, Time Traveler, Spacewoman, Military Personnel

Summary: *Aftermath* is the fifth novel in author Ann Aguirre's series featuring interstellar space traveler Sirantha Jax. During a devastating war between the Conglomerate and a species of cruelly homicidal extraterrestrials, Sirantha made the rogue decision to adjust space in order to stop the enemy from invading. Sirantha's rash move not only resulted in the death of hundreds of Conglomerate soldiers but also in the annihilation of space travel abilities. Now Sirantha must face the aftermath: a trial for her crimes, which include treason and murder. Can she prove that she had the best interests of the human race at heart, or will she be labeled the most notorious criminal in the history of humanity?

Other books by the same author:
Killbox, 2010
Blue Diablo, 2009
Doubleblind, 2009
Wanderlust, 2008
Grimspace, 2007

Other books you might like:
Catherine Asaro, *The Final Key*, 2005
Melisa Michaels, *First Battle*, 1985
Mike Shepherd, *Kris Longknife: Audacious*, 2007
David Weber, *On Basilisk Station*, 1993
Timothy Zahn, *The Backlash Mission*, 1986

964

KEVIN J. ANDERSON

The Nebula Awards Showcase 2011

(New York: Tor, 2011)

Story type: Collection
Subject(s): Short stories; Science fiction; Fantasy

Summary: Compiled by Kevin J. Anderson, *The Nebula Awards Showcase 2011* is a collection of nominated science-fiction short stories. The anthology includes all the nominees for the 2011 Nebula Awards short-fiction category. The Nebula Awards are voted on each year by the Science Fiction and Fantasy Writers of America (SFWA). Among the nominees included in this collection are James Patrick, Rachel Swirsky, Kage Baker, Paolo Bacigalupi, and Joe Haldeman. The short stories run the gamut of dark and mysterious to lighthearted and comical and touch on a wide range of sci-fi topics includ-

ing space travel, quantum theory, and extraterrestrial life. In addition to 2011 nominees, *The Nebula Awards Showcase 2011* also includes the 2009 winners (announced in 2010).

Where it's reviewed:
Booklist, May 15, 2011, page 31
Library Journal, May 15, 2011, page 79

Other books by the same author:
The Ashes of Worlds, 2008
Metal Swarm, 2007
Landscapes, 2006
Horizon Storms, 2004
Hopscotch, 2002

Other books you might like:
Paolo Bacigalupi, *Pump Six and Other Stories*, 2008
Kage Baker, *Black Projects, White Knights: The Company Dossiers*, 2002
James Patrick Kelly, *Strange but Not a Stranger*, 2002
Nancy Kress, *Beaker's Dozen*, 1998
James Morrow, *The Cat's Pajamas and Other Stories*, 2004

965

POUL ANDERSON

Admiralty

(Framingham, Massachusetts: Nesfa Press, 2011)

Story type: Collection
Subject(s): Short stories; Science fiction; Fantasy

Summary: *Admiralty* is a collection of short science-fiction stories from legendary sci-fi author Poul Anderson. The anthology includes 23 short works by Anderson that were originally published between the years of 1955 and 1975. In "Operation Changeling," two witches must go to great lengths in order to rescue their kidnapped daughter. "The Adventure of the Misplaced Hound" is a lighthearted and humorous tale about an alien community infatuated with Victorian culture. "Goat Song," winner of the Nebula and Hugo awards, gives readers a unique and emotional new perspective on the classic tale of Orpheus and Eurydice.

Other books by the same author:
Call Me Joe, 2009
David Falkayn: Star Trader, 2009
For Love and Glory, 2003
Genesis, 2000
The Shield of Time, 1990

Other books you might like:
Stephen Baxter, *The Hunters of Pangaea*, 2004
Greg Bear, *The Collected Stories of Greg Bear*, 2002
Arthur C. Clarke, *The Collected Stories of Arthur C. Clarke*, 2001
Gordon R. Dickson, *Guided Tour*, 1988
Allen Steele, *American Beauty*, 2003

966

TAYLOR ANDERSON

Rising Tides: Destroyermen

(New York: Roc, 2011)

Series: Destroyermen Series. Book 5
Story type: Alternate History
Subject(s): World War II, 1939-1945; Adventure; Military life
Major character(s): Matthew "Matt" Reddy, Military Personnel (captain of WWII destroyer ship)
Time period(s): 20th century; 1930s-1940s

Summary: Taylor Anderson's *Rising Tides: Destroyermen* is the fifth novel in the Rising Tides series, which is set during an alternative history of the Second World War. This outing finds Captain Matt Reddy facing a host of new challenges, including conquering the Honorable New Britain Company, taking on the wrath of the Holy Dominion, and establishing a pact with the Empire. And just as challenging are Matt's personal struggles to do the right thing and remain a trusted leader to his men.

Where it's reviewed:
Publishers Weekly, December 13, 2010, page 41

Other books by the same author:
Distant Thunders, 2010
Maelstrom, 2009
Crusade, 2008
Into the Storm, 2008

Other books you might like:
John Birmingham, *Weapons of Choice*, 2004
Martin Caidin, *The Final Countdown*, 1980
William R. Forstchen, *Rally Cry*, 1990
Jerry Pournelle, *Janissaries*, 1979
S.M. Stirling, *Island in the Sea of Time*, 1998

967

JAMES AXLER

Downrigger Drift

(Toronto, Ontario, Canada: Gold Eagle, 2011)

Series: Deathlands Series. Book 96
Story type: Adventure; Series
Subject(s): Apocalypse; Adventure; Technology
Major character(s): Ryan Cawdor, Leader (of nuclear war survivors), Father (of Dean); Krysty Wroth, Warrior; John Barrymore "J.B." Dix, Survivor (of nuclear war); Dean Cawdor, Son (of Ryan), Survivor (of nuclear war)
Time period(s): Indeterminate Future
Locale(s): Milwaukee, Wisconsin

Summary: In the science-fiction novel *Downrigger Drift*, the 96th book in James Axler's Deathlands series, nuclear war has left the world a lawless land where humanity struggles for survival. Among the survivors are warriors Ryan Cawdor, his son Dean, Krysty Wroth, and J.B. Dix. Together the team travels the North American continent, fighting the forces of evil that they encounter

along the way. This adventure brings Ryan and his group to post-holocaust Wisconsin, where a group of mutant cannibals threatens what remains of Milwaukee. The shores of Lake Michigan become a battleground as the warriors try to protect the city.

Other books by the same author:
Baptism of Rage, 2010
Doom Helix, 2010
Infinity Breach, 2010
Moonfeast, 2010
Oblivion Stone, 2010

Other books you might like:
Piers Anthony, *Sos the Rope*, 1968
William W. Johnstone, *Out of the Ashes*, 1983
Patrick J. Tilley, *The Cloud Warrior*, 1984
Paul O. Williams, *The Breaking of Northwall*, 1980
Roger Zelazny, *Damnation Alley*, 1969

968

JAMES AXLER

Cradle of Destiny

(Toronto, Ontario, Canada: Gold Eagle, 2011)

Series: Outlanders Series. Book 56
Story type: Post-Nuclear Holocaust; Series
Subject(s): Science fiction; Adventure; Suspense
Major character(s): Kane, Explorer; Brigid, Explorer; Domi, Explorer; Grant, Explorer
Time period(s): Indeterminate Future

Summary: In the science-fiction novel *Cradle of Destiny*, the 56th book in James Axler's Outlanders series, Earth has been devastated by nuclear holocaust. Centuries after the catastrophic event, humanity still fights to survive as a rival race vies for planetary domination. Four explorers, Grant, Kane, Brigid, and Domi, set out to defend Earth against the invading forces. Grant is sent back in time when ancient artifacts surface in the Middle East—objects that seem somehow connected to Grant. Brigid, Domi, and Kane must also cross the time barrier to battle a monster and rescue Grant, who has manifested in the past as a mythical warrior.

Other books by the same author:
Baptism of Rage, 2010
Doom Helix, 2010
Infinity Breach, 2010
Moonfeast, 2010
Oblivion Stone, 201

Other books you might like:
Poul Anderson, *Orion Shall Rise*, 1983
D.B. Drumm, *First, You Fight*, 1984
Dean Ing, *Single Combat*, 1983
Sterling E. Lanier, *Hiero's Journey*, 1973
David Robbins, *The Fox Run*, 1986

969

JAMES AXLER
NICK POLLOTTA, Co-Author

Prodigal's Return

(Toronto, Ontario: Gold Eagle, 2011)

Series: Deathlands Series. Book 100
Story type: End of the World
Subject(s): Science fiction; End of the world; Apocalypse
Major character(s): Ryan Cawdor, Father (of Dean), Leader (of nuclear war survivors); Dean Cawdor, Survivor (of nuclear war), Son (of Ryan)
Time period(s): Indeterminate Future
Locale(s): United States

Summary: *Prodigal's Return* by Nick Pollotta and James Axler is a science-fiction novel and the 100th title in Axler's Deathlands series about ragged warriors fighting to survive in post-nuclear-war America. This novel continues the adventures of Ryan Cawdor as he leads a group of survivors across the bleak landscape that was once the United States. Cawdor leaves Denver in search of a new stronghold—but all he finds is trouble, danger, and heartache. His band encounters a group of vicious enemies and they begin to fight when Ryan recognizes his own son, Dean, as one of his opponents. Father and son battle. Who will win, and what will become of Ryan and Dean?

Other books by the same author:
Perception Fault, 2011
Doom Helix, 2010
Infinity Breach, 2010
Moonfeast, 2010
Oblivion Stone, 2010

Other books you might like:
Neal Barrett Jr., *Through Darkest America*, 1986
C.J. Cherryh, *Fires of Azeroth*, 1979
David Gerrold, *A Day for Damnation*, 1984
Larry Niven, *Footfall*, 1985
Patrick J. Tilley, *The First Family*, 1985

970

JAMES AXLER
JOHN HELFERS, Co-Author

Perception Fault

(Toronto, Ontario: Gold Eagle, 2011)

Series: Deathlands Series. Book 99
Story type: End of the World
Subject(s): End of the world; Science fiction; Survival
Major character(s): Ryan Cawdor, Leader (of nuclear war survivors)
Time period(s): 21st century
Locale(s): Denver, Colorado

Summary: *Perception Fault* by John Helfers and James Axler is a science-fiction novel and the 99th title in Axler's Deathlands series about warriors, heroes, villains, and vigilantes fighting to survive in America after a

devastating nuclear war. In this novel, Ryan Cawdor leads a band of survivors into Denver, Colorado, in search of prewar technology. Ryan and his team find a lot of potential in Denver, a city with some remaining food and machinery—but they also find conflict. There's an ongoing grudge match taking place between two rival factions in the city. Ryan has to intervene to try to stop the war and allocate the city's priceless resources.

Other books by the same author:
Tainted Cascade, 2011
Doom Helix, 2010
Infinity Breach, 2010
Moonfeast, 2010
Oblivion Stone, 2010

Other books you might like:
Neal Barrett Jr., *Dawn's Uncertain Light*, 1989
David Gerrold, *A Rage for Revenge*, 1989
E.E. Knight, *Winter Duty*, 2009
Andre Norton, *The Time Traders*, 1958
Roger Zelazny, *Damnation Alley*, 1969

971

JAMES AXLER
NICK POLLOTTA, Co-Author

Tainted Cascade
(Toronto, Ontario: Gold Eagle, 2011)

Series: Deathlands Series. Book 98
Story type: End of the World
Subject(s): Science fiction; End of the world; Survival
Major character(s): Ryan Cawdor, Leader (of nuclear war survivors); John "J.B." Dix, Survivor (of nuclear war); Mildred Wyeth, Survivor, Doctor
Time period(s): 21st century
Locale(s): Utah, United States

Summary: *Tainted Cascade* by Nick Pollotta and James Axler is a science-fiction novel and the 98th title in Axler's Deathlands series about warriors, heroes, villains, and vigilantes fighting to survive in America after a devastating nuclear war. In this novel, Ryan Cawdor leads a group of hardy survivors across the blighted desert wasteland of the Great Salt Lake area of Utah. Despite their determination and perseverance, the group is ambushed and captured by bandits. They narrowly escape being sold for slaves—but they lose their equipment in the process and have to find other ways to foil their foes. Will Cawdor's band live to fight another day?

Other books by the same author:
Infestation Cubed, 2011
Doom Helix, 2010
Infinity Breach, 2010
Moonfeast, 2010
Oblivion Stone, 2010

Other books you might like:
Harry Harrison, *Invasion: Earth*, 1982
Dean Ing, *Wild Country*, 1985
E.E. Knight, *Valentine's Exile*, 2006
Dennis Palumbo, *City Wars*, 1979
Patrick J. Tilley, *Blood River*, 1988

972

JAMES AXLER

Scarlet Dream
(New York: Worldwide, 2011)

Series: Outlanders Series. Book 57
Story type: Zombies
Subject(s): Zombies; Biological warfare; Science fiction
Time period(s): Indeterminate
Locale(s): Louisiana, United States

Summary: *Scarlet Dream* is the 57th installment in the Outlanders series from author James Axler. In the filthy Louisiana swampland, a zombie queen is summoning forth an army of dead soldiers to aid her on a volatile quest to destroy the entire human race. After being reborn from the goddess Lilitu, the zombie queen gained access to a well of dark power and, thanks to the carelessness of the American military, she now has control of a deadly biological weapon. Kane, Grant, and Brigid must square off against the army of the undead, but they'll need to rely on voodoo mysticism instead of traditional science to defeat these supernatural enemies.

Other books by the same author:
Baptism of Rage, 2010
Doom Helix, 2010
Infinity Breach, 2010
Moonfeast, 2010
Oblivion Stone, 2010

Other books you might like:
Brian W. Aldiss, *Bow Down to Nul*, 1959
William C. Dietz, *Deathday*, 2001
David Gerrold, *A Matter for Men*, 1983
E.E. Knight, *Way of the Wolf*, 2003
Larry Niven, *Footfall*, 1985

973

JAMES AXLER

Truth Engine
(Toronto, Canada: Gold Eagle, 2011)

Series: Outlanders Series. Book 58
Story type: End of the World
Subject(s): Science fiction; End of the world; Wars
Major character(s): Kane, Leader (of human rebel resistance); Grant, Leader (of human rebels); Brigid, Leader (of human rebels); Ullikummis, Deity (evil god), Villain (trying to conquer Earth)
Time period(s): Indeterminate Future
Locale(s): Earth; Cerberus Redoubt, Fictional Location

Summary: *Truth Engine* by James Axler is a science-fiction novel and the 58th entry of the Outlanders series about heroes and villains struggling to survive on a future Earth locked in constant conflict. In this novel, humanoid rebels at the Cerberus Redoubt base attempt to fend off their oppressive foes, who are led by an evil god called Ullikummis. Rebel leaders Kane, Grant, and Brigid find themselves captives of Ullikummis. The villain attempts to use mind control to bend his prisoners' allegiances

and fool their supporters into joining him. Kane, leader of the human resistance, needs to outwit the god in order to save Earth.

Other books by the same author:
Baptism of Rage, 2010
Doom Helix, 2010
Infinity Breach, 2010
Moonfeast, 2010
Oblivion Stone, 2010

Other books you might like:
William C. Dietz, *Earthrise*, 2002
David Gerrold, *A Season for Slaughter*, 1992
E.E. Knight, *March in Country*, 2010
Keith Laumer, *The Monitors*, 1966
Murray Leinster, *The Greks Bring Gifts*, 1964

974

JAMES AXLER

Lost Gates

(Toronto, Ontario: Gold Eagle, 2011)

Series: Deathlands Series. Book 101
Story type: End of the World
Subject(s): End of the world; Apocalypse; Survival
Major character(s): Ryan Cawdor, Leader (of nuclear war survivors)
Time period(s): Indeterminate Future
Locale(s): United States

Summary: *Lost Gates* by James Axler is a science-fiction novel and the 101st title in his Deathlands series about the bleak future of humanity after a nuclear war. The novels focus on the adventures and battles of Ryan Cawdor, a leader of a band of survivors who search for food, shelter, and technology. Previous books in the long-running Deathlands series include *Encounter*, *Pilgrimage to Hell*, *Red Holocaust*, and *Neutron Solstice*.

Other books by the same author:
Prodigal's Return, 2011
Doom Helix, 2010
Infinity Breach, 2010
Moonfeast, 2010
Oblivion Stone, 2010

Other books you might like:
Piers Anthony, *Sos the Rope*, 1968
William C. Dietz, *Deathday*, 2001
Dean Ing, *Single Combat*, 1983
E.E. Knight, *Fall with Honor*, 2008
Lawrence Watt-Evans, *The Chromosomal Code*, 1984

975

JAMES AXLER
DOUGLAS WOJTOWICZ, Co-Author

Infestation Cubed

(Toronto, Canada: Gold Eagle, 2011)

Series: Outlanders Series. Book 59
Story type: End of the World

Subject(s): Science fiction; End of the world; Extraterrestrial life
Major character(s): Brigid Baptiste, Leader (of human rebels); Kane, Leader (of human rebels), Rescuer (of Brigid); Ullikummis, Deity (evil god), Villain
Time period(s): Indeterminate Future
Locale(s): Louisiana, United States

Summary: *Infestation Cubed* by Douglas Wojtowicz and James Axler is a science-fiction novel and an entry in Axler's Outlanders series about heroes and villains struggling to survive on a future earth locked in constant conflict. In this novel, humans are either slaves or rebels. The rebels have entrenched themselves at Cerberus Redoubt to fight oncoming aliens and other monsters. These oppressive fiends are led by an evil god called Ullikummis who is carved out of volcanic stone. Ullikummis captures rebel leader Brigid Baptiste, leading her most trusted ally, Kane, to mount a rescue mission that takes him to eerie, post-apocalyptic Louisiana.

Other books by the same author:
Lost Gates, 2011
Doom Helix, 2010
Infinity Breach, 2010
Moonfeast, 2010
Oblivion Stone, 2010

Other books you might like:
John Brunner, *The Super Barbarians*, 1962
C.J. Cherryh, *Exile's Gate*, 1988
William C. Dietz, *Earthrise*, 2002
Anthony Piers, *Battle Circle*, 1978
Patrick J. Tilley, *Iron Master*, 1987

976

JOHN BARNES

Daybreak Zero

(New York: Ace Books, 2011)

Series: Daybreak Trilogy. Book 2
Story type: Political; Series
Subject(s): Science fiction; Suspense; Politics
Major character(s): Heather O'Grainne, Leader
Time period(s): 21st century; 2020s (2025)
Locale(s): United States

Summary: In the science-fiction novel *Daybreak Zero*, the second book in John Barnes's Daybreak trilogy, the residents of earth—those who have survived—are still reeling from a terrorist attack a year ago that claimed millions of lives worldwide. Now it is 2025 and the U.S. government has split into two factions—one based in Olympia, Washington, the other in Athens, Georgia. As America struggles for stability, the group behind the attack, a shadowy organization known as Daybreak, seems determined to continue its campaign of annihilation. In Pueblo, Colorado, Heather O'Grainne heads a team of scientists, businessmen, spies, and fighters who have taken on the daunting mission of restoring the earth to its former state.

Where it's reviewed:
Locus, April 2011, page 19

Science Fiction

Other books by the same author:
Directive 51, 2010
The Armies of Memory, 2006
In the Hall of the Martian King, 2003
The Merchant of Souls, 2001
Patton's Spaceship, 1996

Other books you might like:
Ben Bova, *Peacekeepers*, 1988
Steven Gould, *Blind Waves*, 2000
Frederik Pohl, *All the Lives He Led*, 2011
Norman Spinrad, *Greenhouse Summer*, 1999
Whitley Strieber, *Critical Mass*, 2009

977

ELIZABETH BEAR

Grail

(New York: Spectra, 2011)

Series: Jacob's Ladder Trilogy. Book 3
Story type: Alternate Universe
Subject(s): Science fiction; Space exploration; Genetic engineering
Major character(s): Perceval, Space Explorer
Time period(s): Indeterminate
Locale(s): Grail, Fictional Location

Summary: *Grail*, a science-fiction novel, is the third installment in the Jacob's Ladder series from author Elizabeth Bear. After traveling far and wide, the crew of the generation ship Jacob's Ladder have arrived at Grail, a breathtaking planet they long to make their new home. They're met with a rude awakening, however, when they discover that humans already inhabit Grail. The inhabitants of Grail aren't so willing to share their planet with the genetically altered beings of Jacob's Ladder. Captain Perceval is shocked to discover that someone in his crew is a traitorous murder, while the human leader, Premier Danilaw, fears that the arrival of Jacob's Ladder could result in a violent civil war that would destroy Grail forever.

Where it's reviewed:
Publishers Weekly, January 10, 2011, page 35

Other books by the same author:
Chill, 2010
Dust, 2007
Undertow, 2007
Carnival, 2006
Scardown, 2005

Other books you might like:
Brian W. Aldiss, *Non-Stop*, 1976
Paul Chafe, *Genesis*, 2007
Robert Reed, *Marrow*, 2000
Alastair Reynolds, *Revelation Space*, 2000
Gene Wolfe, *Nightside of the Long Sun*, 1993

978

CHRISTOPHER L. BENNETT

Watching the Clock

(New York: Star Trek Publishers, 2011)

Series: Star Trek: Department of Temporal Investigations Series. Book 1
Story type: Time Travel
Subject(s): Science fiction; Time travel; Space flight
Major character(s): Dulmur, Agent (of Department of Temporal Investigations); Lucsly, Agent (of Department of Temporal Investigations)
Time period(s): Indeterminate Future
Locale(s): Outer Space

Summary: *Watching the Clock* by Christopher L. Bennett is a science-fiction novel based on the Star Trek galaxy and part of the Star Trek: Department of Temporal Investigations series. In this novel, the heroes are not dashing spaceship captains or bizarre aliens but timestream investigators—government agents whose job is to regulate time travelers to prevent massive changes to the past, present, or future. Agents Dulmur and Lucsly are two of the best agents of the Department of Temporal Investigations. While they are normally efficient, if slightly careless, with their work, they are suddenly forced into high gear by a series of bends in time perpetrated by 24th-century malcontents.

Other books by the same author:
Over a Torrent Sea, 2009
Greater Than the Sum, 2008
The Buried Age, 2007
Drowned in Thunder, 2007
Ex Machina, 2005

Other books you might like:
Kirsten Beyer, *Full Circle*, 2009
Peter David, *Before Dishonor*, 2007
Jeff Mariotte, *Deny Thy Father*, 2003
S.D. Perry, *Cloak: Section 31*, 2001
Olivia Woods, *Fearful Symmetry*, 2008

979

BEN BOVA

Leviathans of Jupiter

(New York: Tor, 2011)

Series: Grand Tour Series. Book 18
Story type: Fantasy
Subject(s): Space exploration; Science fiction; Research
Major character(s): Grant Archer, Scientist
Time period(s): Indeterminate
Locale(s): Jupiter, Outer Space

Summary: *Leviathans of Jupiter*, a science-fiction novel, is the 18th installment in the Grand Tour series from award-winning author Ben Bova. It's been 20 years since physicist Grant Archer and his crew nearly lost their lives during an exploratory mission to Jupiter's ocean. As the crew faced a certain death, they were miraculously saved by the planet's leviathan, an unusual creature the

size of a city. Certain that the rescue was an indication of the leviathan's intelligence, Archer has spent the past two decades planning a return mission to study the massive creatures. He's finally been approved to lead another Jupiter expedition, but surviving the harsh climate and a fellow group of scientists might prove impossible for Archer and his team.

Where it's reviewed:
Booklist, February 15, 2011, page 59
Library Journal, January 2011, page 86
Publishers Weekly, December 20, 2010, page 39

Other books by the same author:
Able One, 2010
The Immortality Factor, 2009
Mars Life, 2008
Mercury, 2005
Powersat, 2005

Other books you might like:
Gregory Benford, *Jupiter Project*, 1975
Arthur C. Clarke, *2061: Odyssey Three*, 1987
James P. Hogan, *The Gentle Giants of Ganymede*, 1978
John Varley, *Rolling Thunder*, 2008
Timothy Zahn, *Manta's Gift*, 2002

980

GARY BRAVER (Pseudonym of Gary Goshgarian)

Tunnel Vision
(New York: Forge Books, 2011)

Subject(s): Near-death experiences; Good and evil; Devil
Major character(s): Zach Kashian, Accident Victim; Elizabeth Luria, Doctor (neuroscientist); Sarah Wyman, Researcher
Time period(s): 21st century; 2010s
Locale(s): Boston, Massachusetts

Summary: Gary Braver's *Tunnel Vision* chronicles the experiences of three people studying near-death experiences. Zach Kashian is in a serious bicycle accident, and when he wakes from his coma, he is able to do eerily miraculous things. After he becomes a sensation among religious zealots, neuroscientist Elizabeth Luria studies Zach's supposed miracles and his near-death experience. One of her researchers, Sarah Wyman, also takes a particular interest in the case, though her findings are much different from Dr. Luria's. Soon Zach, Sarah, and Elizabeth's investigations of what happened to Zach culminate in a showdown between the forces of good and evil.

Where it's reviewed:
Library Journal, May 1, 2011, page 74
Publishers Weekly, April 18, 2011, page 31

Other books by the same author:
Gray Matter, 2002
Elixir, 2000

Other books you might like:
Karel Capek, *The Absolute at Large*, 1927
Philip K. Dick, *The Divine Invasion*, 1981
Damon Knight, *The Man in the Tree*, 1984

Jamil Nasir, *The Houses of Time*, 2008
Douglas Preston, *Blasphemy*, 2008

981

ERIC BROWN

The Kings of Eternity
(Nottingham, England: Solaris, 2011)

Story type: UFO
Subject(s): Extraterrestrial life; Space flight; Mystery
Major character(s): Jonathon Langham, Writer (in the 1930s), Witness (saw alien being); Daniel Langham, Writer (in the 1990s), Investigator (of 1930s incident), Friend (of Caroline); Caroline Platt, Friend (of Daniel)
Time period(s): 20th century; 1930s-1990s
Locale(s): London, England; Greece

Summary: *The Kings of Eternity* by Eric Brown is a science-fiction novel that spans the years 1935 to 1999 and features a mystery of intergalactic proportions. In 1935, a writer named Jonathon Langham travels to London to visit a friend and see a bizarre discovery: a living thing from another planet. Seeing this alien creature changes Langham's life and begins a long string of repercussions. More than six decades later, a writer named Daniel Langham has learned more about this interplanetary visitation—and what he knows has led him to live in fear and seclusion. With the help of his beloved friend Caroline Platt, Daniel reluctantly decides to confront his greatest fears and the mystery that reaches back to the 1930s.

Other books by the same author:
Engineman, 2010
Cosmopath, 2009
Kethani, 2008
Necropath, 2008
New York Dreams, 2004

Other books you might like:
Gregory Benford, *Timescape*, 1980
Joe Haldeman, *The Coming*, 2000
Nancy Kress, *Beggars in Spain*, 1991
Kate Wilhelm, *Crazy Time*, 1988
Roger Zelazny, *This Immortal*, 1966

982

M.M. BUCKNER

The Gravity Pilot
(New York: Tor, 2011)

Story type: Science Fantasy
Subject(s): Science fiction; Fantasy; Futuristic society
Major character(s): Orr Sitka, Sports Figure (skydiver), Boyfriend (of Dyce); Dyce, Girlfriend (of Orr)
Time period(s): Indeterminate Future
Locale(s): Alaska, United States; Seattle, Washington

Summary: In the science-fiction novel *The Gravity Pilot* by M.M. Buckner, North America of the future is an

unstable society held together by a series of technological repairs. In Alaska, Orr Sitka finds solace amidst the decay in his passion for skydiving and his girlfriend Dyce. But Orr's talent threatens to ruin his personal peace and his relationship. A spectacular dive has attracted the attention of the media, and Sitka becomes famous. Dyce decides to blaze her own trail in Seattle where a job awaits. But life in the subterranean city of Seattle holds danger for Dyce, and Orr must try to save her.

Other books by the same author:
Watermind, 2008
War Surf, 2005
Neurolink, 2004
Hyperthought, 2003

Other books you might like:
Margaret Atwood, *Oryx and Crake*, 2003
Steven Gould, *Blind Waves*, 2000
Dakota James, *Greenhouse*, 1984
Susan Palwick, *Shelter*, 2007
Norman Spinrad, *Greenhouse Summer*, 1999

983

MARCELLA BURNARD

Enemy Games

(New York: Berkley Sensation, 2011)

Series: Enemy Series. Book 2
Story type: Futuristic; Series
Subject(s): Science fiction; Romances (Fiction); Espionage
Major character(s): Jayleia Durante, Spaceship Captain; Damen Sindrivik, Military Personnel (major)
Time period(s): Indeterminate Future
Locale(s): Outer Space

Summary: In the science-fiction novel *Enemy Games* by Marcella Burnard, Jayleia Durante is working to contain a deadly epidemic when she is taken prisoner by enemy agents. Major Damen Sindrivik knows that Jayleia holds information that could bring down a dangerous espionage operation, but he can't control the physical attraction he feels for his hostage. As Jayleia worries for the safety of her father, a spy who has gone missing, she struggles to resist her growing desire for her captor. With the galaxy on the brink of war, Jayleia and Damen play a romantic game that conceals deceit, danger, and perhaps true love. *Enemy Games* is the second book in Burnard's Enemy series.

Other books you might like:
Catherine Asaro, *Diamond Star*, 2009
Lois McMaster Bujold, *A Civil Campaign*, 1999
Jayne Castle, *Silver Master*, 2007
Amanda Glass, *Shield's Lady*, 1989
Cecelia Holland, *Floating Worlds*, 1975

984

JACK CAMPBELL (Pseudonym of John G. Hemry)

The Lost Fleet: Beyond the Frontier: Dreadnaught

(New York: Ace Books, 2011)

Series: Lost Fleet Series. Book 1
Story type: Futuristic; Space Opera
Subject(s): Space colonies; Adventure; Loyalty
Major character(s): John "Black Jack" Geary, Military Personnel; Captain Desjani, Military Personnel
Time period(s): Indeterminate Future
Locale(s): Outer Space

Summary: The first novel in Jack Campbell's Lost Fleet: Beyond the Frontier series, *The Lost Fleet: Beyond the Frontier: Dreadnaught* finds Captain Black Jack Geary waking from a cryogenically induced sleep to take on the enemies of the Alliance. He becomes a hero in the battle, but his newfound fame brings the unwanted attention of politicians who are questioning his devotion to the cause. After being named head of the First Fleet, Black Jack is uncertain if he's heading toward another victory—or to his own death.

Where it's reviewed:
Publishers Weekly, March 28, 2011, page 42

Other books by the same author:
Victorious, 2010
Relentless, 2009
Courageous, 2008
Valiant, 2008
Fearless, 2007

Other books you might like:
David Drake, *In the Stormy Red Sky*, 2009
Richard Fawkes, *Nature of the Beast*, 2004
R.M. Meluch, *The Sagittarius Command*, 2007
Mike Resnick, *Starship: Mutiny*, 2005
David Weber, *Mission of Honor*, 2010

985

PATRICK CARMAN

Shantorian

(New York: Scholastic, 2011)

Series: Trackers Series. Book 2
Story type: Young Readers
Subject(s): Computers; Technology; Criminals
Major character(s): Adam, Computer Expert, Teenager; Finn, Teenager, Computer Expert; Lewis, Teenager, Computer Expert; Emily, Computer Expert, Teenager
Time period(s): 21st century
Locale(s): United States

Summary: *Shantorian*, a science-fiction novel for young readers, is the second book in the Trackers series from best-selling author Patrick Carman. Adam, Finn, Lewis, and Emily may look like regular teens, but these tech-savvy geniuses are actually Trackers, highly intelligent computer gurus who use innovative technology and

digital know-how to track down the world's most formidable criminals. The gang is in the midst of a huge case when they're hauled into custody at a top-secret government intelligence agency. While the four teens try to prove their honesty and identities, they're losing sight of Shantorian, a dangerous computer hacker who remains hidden in the virtual world.

Where it's reviewed:
Booklist, March 15, 2011, page 56
School Library Journal, May 2011, page 108

Other books by the same author:
Trackers, 2010
The Dark Planet, 2009
Rivers of Fire, 2008
The House of Power, 2007
The Tenth City, 2006

Other books you might like:
Tony Ballantyne, *Divergence*, 2007
Pat Cadigan, *Synners*, 1991
William Gibson, *Count Zero*, 1986
Graham Joyce, *Spiderbite*, 1997
Neal Stephenson, *Snow Crash*, 1992

986

PATRICK CARMAN

The Raven
(New York: Scholastic Press, 2011)

Series: Skeleton Creek Series. Book 4
Story type: Young Readers
Subject(s): Mystery; Science fiction; Suspense
Major character(s): Sarah, Child, Filmmaker, Detective—Amateur; Ryan, Writer, Child, Detective—Amateur
Time period(s): 21st century; 2010s
Locale(s): Skeleton Creek, Fictional Location

Summary: *The Raven* is the fourth installment in the Skeleton Creek series from best-selling author Patrick Carman. Ryan and Sarah partner together to document the eerie and bizarre episodes that regularly occur in Skeleton Creek. Ryan writes detailed descriptions of the occurrences, while Sarah documents everything on film. Together, the pair have managed to solve age-old mysteries, track down secret societies, and follow clues across the country, but there are some secrets in Skeleton Creek that should never be unearthed...and a sinister force is working hard to ensure that Ryan and Sarah don't discover too much.

Other books by the same author:
Trackers, 2010
The Dark Planet, 2009
Rivers of Fire, 2008
The House of Power, 2007
The Tenth City, 2006

Other books you might like:
Lou Cameron, *Cybernia*, 1972
Bruce Coville, *Operation Sherlock*, 1986
Frank Herbert, *The Santaroga Barrier*, 1968
Stephen King, *The Tommyknockers*, 1987
Dean R. Koontz, *Seize the Night*, 1998

987

C.J. CHERRYH

Betrayer
(New York: DAW, 2010)

Series: Foreigner Universe Series. Book 12
Story type: Military; Series
Subject(s): Wars; Adventure; Fantasy
Major character(s): Tabini-aiji, Ruler; Cajeiri, Son (of Tabini-aiji); Bren Cameron, Friend (of Cajeiri)
Time period(s): Indeterminate Future
Locale(s): Western Association, Alternate Universe

Summary: The 12th installment in the Foreigner series, C.J. Cherryh's *Betrayer* finds the long-raging war between the Atevi race finally at an end. Tabini-aiji, his son, and his son's human companion settle back into life as powerful rulers of the realm. But the trouble is far from over. There are others who secretly wish to overthrow Tabini-aiji—and they will stop at nothing to accomplish their goals.

Other books by the same author:
Deceiver, 2010
Deliverer, 2007
Explorer, 2002
Finity's End, 1997
The Kif Strike Back, 1985

Other books you might like:
Poul Anderson, *Flandry: Defender of the Terran Empire*, 1993
Julie E. Czerneda, *Reap the Wild Wind*, 2007
Alan Dean Foster, *Drowning World*, 2003
Karen Traviss, *Ally*, 2007
S.L. Viehl, *Afterburn*, 2005

988

DON D'AMMASSA

Translation Station
(West Warwick, Rhode Island: Merry Blacksmith Press, 2011)

Story type: Collection
Subject(s): Science fiction; Short stories; Fantasy

Summary: *Translation Station* is a collection of science-fiction stories from author Don D'Ammassa. The anthology includes 17 unique stories on outer space, aliens, mystery, and adventure. D'Ammassa explores a wide range of science-fiction topics in this collection, including what exactly makes an alien an alien, what adventures and dangers lie beyond the hyperspatial plain, and how challenging a simple space mission can become. Some of the books stories are "A Good Offense," "Diplomatic Relations," "The Man Who Walked to Procyon," "Duck and Cover," "No Distance Too Great," "Getting With the Program," and "Funeral Party."

Other books by the same author:
Narcissus, 2007
Haven, 2004

Scarab, 2004
Servants of Chaos, 2002
Blood Beast, 1988

Other books you might like:
Christopher Anvil, *Rx for Chaos*, 2009
Keith Laumer, *Future Imperfect*, 2003
Murray Leinster, *First Contacts: The Essential Murray Leinster*, 1998
Eric Frank Russell, *Major Ingredients*, 2000
Robert Sheckley, *The Collected Short Fiction of Robert Sheckley*, 1991

989

PETER DAVID

Blind Man's Bluff

(New York: Gallery Books, 2011)

Series: Star Trek: New Frontier Series. Book 18
Story type: Science Fiction
Subject(s): Science fiction; Space exploration; Space flight
Major character(s): MacKenzie Calhoun, Space Explorer, Spaceship Captain (of U.S.S. Excalibur); Morgan Primus, Computer (computer simulation of human)
Time period(s): Indeterminate Future
Locale(s): Outer Space

Summary: *Blind Man's Bluff* by Peter David is a science-fiction novel based on the Star Trek galaxy and the 18th entry in the Star Trek: New Frontier series. In this novel, intrepid Starfleet captain MacKenzie Calhoun is facing a double-edged sword of peril. On one side, he has to deal with the fact that his ship has been taken over by a computer simulation of a human called Morgan Primus. As if that predicament wasn't bad enough for Calhoun and his crew of space scientists, there is a much larger threat: an alien race called the D'myurj wants to erase all humans from the universe! Calhoun has to lead the Federation on a daring mission to save humanity from these dual dangers.

Other books by the same author:
Before Dishonor, 2007
Gods Above, 2003
Hulk, 2003
Fire on High, 1998
End Game, 1997

Other books you might like:
Jack Campbell, *The Lost Fleet: Beyond the Frontier: Dreadnaught*, 2011
David Feintuch, *Children of Hope*, 2001
Mike Resnick, *Starship: Pirate*, 2006
Mike Shepherd, *Kris Longknife: Intrepid*, 2008
David Weber, *Ashes of Victory*, 2000

990

SAMUEL R. DELANY

Through the Valley of the Nest of Spiders

(New York: Magnus Books, 2011)

Story type: Gay - Lesbian Fiction
Subject(s): Gay and lesbian rights; Homosexuality; Coming of age
Major character(s): Eric Jeffers, Homosexual, Boyfriend (of Morgan); Morgan Haskell, Homosexual, Boyfriend (of Eric)
Time period(s): 21st century; 2000s-2020s (2007-2027)
Locale(s): Diamond Harbor, Georgia

Summary: *Through the Valley of the Nest of Spiders* is a novel written by author Samuel R. Delany. In it, Delany tells the story of Eric Jeffers, a teenager who comes of age and begins to learn his true identity after arriving at his mother's house in a Georgia coastal town. The rural community to which he has moved seems quiet and quaint, and tourism—one of the town's few industries—is all but nonexistent. Eric also discovers one of the town's most hidden secrets when he meets Morgan Haskell, a gay teenager with whom he immediately falls in love. The story follows the couple and the gay subculture of the rural American South through a time span of 20 years. Delany is also the author of *Dhalgren, Nova,* and *Times Square Red, Times Square Blue*.

Other books by the same author:
Aye, and Gomorrah, 2003
The Stars in My Pockets Like Grains of Sand, 1984
Distant Stars, 1981
Dhalgren, 1974
Babel-17, 1966

Other books you might like:
J.G. Ballard, *Vermilion Sands*, 1971
L. Timmel Duchamp, *Alanya to Alanya*, 2005
Cecelia Holland, *Floating Worlds*, 1975
Ursula K. Le Guin, *The Left Hand of Darkness*, 1969
Mary Rosenblum, *The Stone Garden*, 1995

991

AARON DEMBSKI-BOWDEN

Blood Reaver

(Nottingham, England: Black Library, 2011)

Series: Night Lords Series. Book 2
Story type: Alternate World; Series
Subject(s): Science fiction; Alternative worlds; Adventure

Summary: In the science-fiction novel *Blood Reaver* by Aaron Dembski-Bowden, a vicious fighting force known as the Night Lords prowls the galaxy on a mission of vengeance. Their opposition to the False Emperor fuels their quest as they wage bloody wars with the aid of their evil allies, the Red Corsairs. Their ultimate goal is to invade the stronghold of the Marines Errant. If they can gain possession of the Marines' gene seed, any hope

for the survival of the loyalists will be destroyed. *Blood Reaver* is the second book in the Warhammer 40,000: Night Lords series.

Other books by the same author:
The First Heretic, 2010
Helsreach, 2010
Soul Hunter, 2010
Cadian Blood, 2009

Other books you might like:
Dan Abnett, *Blood Pact*, 2009
Lee Lightner, *Sons of Fenris*, 2007
Steve Parker, *Gunheads*, 2009
Chris Roberson, *Dawn of War II*, 2009
Henry Zou, *Blood Gorgons*, 2011

992

CORY DOCTOROW

With a Little Help

(Charleston, South Carolina: CreateSpace, 2011)

Story type: Contemporary
Subject(s): Short stories; Science fiction; Technology

Summary: *With a Little Help* is a collection of science-fiction short stories by Cory Doctorow. Doctorow tends to set his stories in the near future in circumstances that are not drastically unlike those of the present day. Many of his characters wrestle with overwhelming technological trends, often with humorous results. In one story, a system administrator is hired as a caretaker for an archaic computer that doesn't want to become obsolete and refuses to shut down. In another story, an enormous Internet search engine company begins a secret campaign of hoarding user information and soon discovers the profit potential of exposing all aspects of users' online activities.

Other books by the same author:
For the Win, 2010
Makers, 2009
Little Brother, 2008
Overclocked, 2007
Eastern Standard Tribe, 2004

Other books you might like:
Paolo Bacigalupi, *Pump Six and Other Stories*, 2008
Paul Di Filippo, *Harsh Oases*, 2009
William Gibson, *Burning Chrome*, 1986
Jack McDevitt, *Cryptic*, 2009
Charles Stross, *Accelerando*, 2005

993

GARDNER DOZOIS

The Year's Best Science Fiction: 28th Annual Collection

(New York: St. Martin's Griffin, 2011)

Story type: Collection
Subject(s): Science fiction; Short stories; Senses

Summary: *The Year's Best Science Fiction: 28th Annual Collection* by Gardner Dozois collects some of the most notable science-fiction short stories of the year. Some of the featured writers include Cory Doctorow, Eleanor Arnason, Aliette de Bodard, Alexander Jablokov, Rachel Swirsky, Geoffrey A. Landis, Joe Haldeman, and many others. Their stories deal with topics such as the limitations of memory, planetary engineering, alterations of the past, space travel and extraterrestrial beings, newly emerging senses, and the possibility of endless life. Dozois rounds out the collection with a summary of the year's science-fiction trends and a matching list of recommended reading titles.

Other books by the same author:
Strange Days, 2001
Geodesic Dreams, 1992
Slow Dancing Through Time, 1990
The Visible Man, 1973

Other books you might like:
Damien Broderick, *Transcension*, 2002
Cory Doctorow, *With a Little Help*, 2011
Ian R. MacLeod, *Breathmoss and Other Exhalations*, 2004
Robert Reed, *The Dragons of Springplace*, 1999
Alastair Reynolds, *Galactic North*, 2006

994

CHRISTIAN DUNN

Victories of the Space Marines

(Nottingham, England: Black Library, 2011)

Series: Warhammer 40,000: Space Marine Battles Series. Book 7
Story type: Collection; Series
Subject(s): Science fiction; Short stories; Adventure

Summary: In *Victories of the Space Marines*, editor Christian Dunn presents a collection of stories that chronicle the triumphs of the Warhammer Universe's greatest warriors. Defenders of humanity and the Empire, the Space Marines face enemy invaders and the threat of Chaos in their quest for victory. This collection includes "Runes" by Chris Wraight, "The Rewards of Tolerance" by Gav Thorpe, "Black Dawn" by C.L. Werner, "The Long Games of Carcharias" by Rob Sanders, "Heart of Rage" by James Swallow, "But Dust in the Wind" by Jonathan Green, "Exhumed" by Steve Parker, "Primary Instinct" by Sarah Cawkwell, and "Sacrifice" by Ben Counter. *Victories of the Space Marines* is part of the Warhammer 40,000: Space Marine Battles series.

Other books by the same author:
Age of Darkness, 2011
Legends of the Space Marines, 2010

Other books you might like:
Dan Abnett, *Prospero Burns*, 2010
Matthew Farrer, *Blind*, 2006
Gordon Rennie, *Shadow Point*, 2003
Lucien Soulban, *Desert Raiders*, 2008
Simon Spurrier, *Fire Warrior*, 2003

995

CHRISTIAN DUNN

The Age of Darkness

(Nottingham, England: Black Library, 2011)

Series: Horus Heresy Series. Book 16
Story type: Collection; Series
Subject(s): Science fiction; Short stories

Summary: In *Age of Darkness*, editor Christian Dunn presents a collection of stories from the Warhammer Universe that lay the groundwork for the Horus Heresy, a civil war that encompasses the entire galaxy. The conflict, launched by Horus, was prompted by an act of disloyalty, but the full realization of the war was the result of years of secretive planning. The stories in this collection, which reveal the events preceding the Heresy, include "Rules of Engagement" by Graham McNeill, "Liar's Due" by James Swallow, "Forgotten Sons" by Nick Kyme, "The Last Remembrancer" by John French, "Rebirth" by Chris Wraight, and others. *Age of Darkness* is the 16th book in the Warhammer 40,000: The Horus Heresy series.

Other books by the same author:
Victories of the Space Marines, 2011
Legends of the Space Marines, 2010

Other books you might like:
Ben Counter, *Galaxy in Flames*, 2006
Andy Hoare, *Star of Damocles*, 2007
Sandy Mitchell, *Caves of Ice*, 2004
Anthony Reynolds, *Dark Apostle*, 2007
Gav Thorpe, *The Last Chancers*, 2006

996

PAUL FINCH

Doctor Who: Hunter's Moon

(London, England: BBC Books, 2011)

Story type: Fantasy
Subject(s): Science fiction; Gambling; Kidnapping
Major character(s): Doctor, Time Traveler, Alien; Rory, Kidnap Victim, Friend (of Doctor); Amy, Spouse (of Rory), Companion (of Doctor)
Time period(s): Indeterminate

Summary: *Doctor Who: Hunter's Moon*, a suspenseful and mysterious science fiction novel, is part of the Doctor Who series from author Paul Finch. Leisure Platform 9 draws an interesting mix of patrons, ranging from crime lords and thieves to celebrities and debutantes. As Rory quickly learns, Leisure Platform 9 is not the place where you want to make enemies or cross the wrong person. When Rory wins a game against the wrong person, a vicious crime boss named Xorg Krauzzen kidnaps him and forces him to participate in a real game of life and death. The Doctor and Amy must go undercover to rescue their friend, but it's only a matter of time until their true identities are revealed, putting them all in grave danger.

Other books you might like:
Andrew Cartmel, *Atom Bomb Blues*, 2005
Martin Day, *Wooden Heart*, 2007
Terrance Dicks, *World Game*, 2005
Una McCormack, *Doctor Who: The Way Through the Woods*, 2011
Mark Michalowski, *Doctor Who: Shining Darkness*, 2008

997

MATT FORBECK

Amortals

(Nottingham, UK: Angry Robot, 2010)

Story type: Mystery
Subject(s): Futuristic society; Technology; Murder
Major character(s): Ronan Dooley, Agent (Secret Service)
Time period(s): 22nd century; 2160s (2168)
Locale(s): United States

Summary: *Amortals* is a novel written by author Matt Forbeck. In the late 22nd century, the government has found the perfect technology to hunt murderers. Through Project Amortal, scientists can download a victim's memories into a clone-like being, allowing them to hear the truth about how that victim died. When Secret Service Agent Ronan Dooley is killed in action once again, he must hunt down his own murderer. Dooley has done this procedure before—eight times in fact—and his repeat performances have earned him the nickname Methuselah. This time, however, the murderer is much closer than he thought. Now Dooley must race against time to catch a killer before he ends up dead again—this time, for good.

Other books by the same author:
Mutant Chronicles, 2008
The Dragons Revealed, 2006
Prophecy of the Dragons, 2006
The Queen of Death, 2006
Blood Bowl, 2005

Other books you might like:
Roger MacBride Allen, *The Modular Man*, 1992
Paul J. McAuley, *Whole Wide World*, 2002
Robert J. Sawyer, *The Terminal Experiment*, 1995
Jack Vance, *To Live Forever*, 1956
Timothy Zahn, *The Domino Pattern*, 2009

998

LAURA ANNE GILMAN

Dragon Virus

(Seattle: Fairwood Press, 2011)

Story type: Medical
Subject(s): Diseases; Birth defects; Science fiction
Time period(s): 21st century
Locale(s): Earth

Summary: *Dragon Virus* by Laura Anne Gilman is a collection of short science-fiction stories revolving around a chilling premise: a sudden epidemic of unexplained mutations in newborns. Shortly after the beginning of the 21st century, scientists discover a rash of birth defects and deaths which they call the Dragon Virus. At first dismissing it as coincidence, experts soon notice the Dragon Virus on the rise. Eventually, it spreads all across the globe! Six short stories about the virus's victims and those trying to save them appear in *Dragon Virus*.

Other books by the same author:
Blood from Stone, 2009
Flesh and Fire, 2009
Free Fall, 2008
Burning Bridges, 2007
Bring It On, 2006

Other books you might like:
Steven Barnes, *Streetlethal*, 1983
Jeff Carlson, *Plague Year*, 2007
Frank Herbert, *The White Plague*, 1982
Graham Masterton, *Plague*, 1978
Nick Sagan, *Everfree*, 2006

999

KATHLEEN ANN GOONAN

This Shared Dream

(New York: Tor, 2011)

Story type: Alternate History
Subject(s): Science fiction; History; Missing persons
Major character(s): Sam Dance, Scientist, Spouse (of Bette); Bette Dance, Scientist, Spouse (of Samuil)
Time period(s): 20th century
Locale(s): United States

Summary: *This Shared Dream*, an alternate-reality science-fiction novel, is the follow-up to the award-winning book, *In War Times*, from author Kathleen Ann Goonan. Sam Dance and his wife, Bette, dedicated their life to using science to tweak reality and alter history in an effort to make the world a better place. Sam and Bette's scientific experiments had some fatal flaws though, which led to their disappearance, leaving their three children to fend for themselves. The three Dance kids, now adults, can't shake the memories of the past and the sense that their current reality has been altered. They begin to wonder what happened to their parents, chasing their mother's disappearance back to JFK's assassination.

Other books by the same author:
In War Times, 2007
Light Music, 2002
Mississippi Blues, 1997
The Bones of Time, 1996
Queen City Jazz, 1994

Other books you might like:
Mona Clee, *Branch Point*, 1996
George Alec Effinger, *Relatives*, 1973
Brad Ferguson, *The World Next Door*, 1990
Jack Finney, *Time and Again*, 1970
Christopher Priest, *The Separation*, 2002

1000

JAMES GOSS

Doctor Who: Dead of Winter

(London, England: BBC Books, 2011)

Story type: Historical
Subject(s): Medical professions; Science fiction; Death
Major character(s): Dr. Bloom, Doctor; Maria, 11-Year-Old, Writer
Time period(s): 18th century
Locale(s): Italy

Summary: *Doctor Who: Dead of Winter*, a historical science-fiction novel, is part of the Doctor Who series from author James Goss. Dr. Bloom runs a mysterious clinic in an isolated area along the Italian coast. Nearby, 11-year-old Maria passes her days all alone at a remote retreat. She writes letters to her mother, documenting the unusual episodes she observes at Dr. Bloom's clinic as a slew of aristocrats and ill patients arrive. She also recounts the horrific encounters she's had with supernatural creatures that rise from the sea. Maria's observations, although never spoken directly, also reveal that Dr. Bloom's clinic is a place where individuals come to die.

Other books by the same author:
Risk Assessment, 2010
Almost Perfect, 2008

Other books you might like:
Trevor Baxendale, *Wishing Well*, 2007
Paul Finch, *Doctor Who: Hunter's Moon*, 2011
Jacqueline Rayner, *Doctor Who: The Sontaran Games*, 2009
Dale Smith, *Doctor Who: The Many Hands*, 2008
Mike Tucker, *The Nightmare of Black Island*, 2006

1001

STEVEN GOULD

7th Sigma

(New York: Tor Books, 2011)

Subject(s): Alternative worlds; Disasters; Survival
Major character(s): Kimble Monroe, Survivor

Summary: *7th Sigma* is a fantasy novel by author Steven Gould. In it, Gould tells of an alternate world where the United States has been overrun by monstrous, metal-eating bugs. The bugs shun water, however, and for the most part are confined to the southwestern United States, where water is scarce. This leaves a large portion of the populous safe from their destruction. However, a few longtime residents refuse to leave the area. One such person is Kimble Monroe, who not only swears to survive this occupation, but is determined to find a way to stop it. Gould is also the author of *Jumper* and *Reflex*.

Other books by the same author:
Griffins Story, 2007
Reflex, 2004
Jumper, 2002
Blind Waves, 2000

Science Fiction

Helm, 1998

Other books you might like:
James Braziel, *Birmingham 35 Miles*, 2008
David Gerrold, *A Matter for Men*, 1983
Ron Goulart, *After Things Fell Apart*, 1970
Rudy Rucker, *Postsingular*, 2007
Roger Zelazny, *Damnation Alley*, 1969

1002

DAVID S. GOYER
MICHAEL CASSUTT, Co-Author

Heaven's Shadow

(New York: Ace Books, 2011)

Series: Heaven's Shadow Series. Book 1
Story type: Series; Space Opera
Subject(s): Space flight; Technology; Extraterrestrial life
Time period(s): 21st century; 2010s
Locale(s): Solar System, Outer Space

Summary: *Heaven's Shadow* is the first novel in the series of the same name, written by co-authors Michael Cassutt and David S. Goyer. When an enormous object is spotted headed straight for the Milky Way's sun, two rival space teams—one sent by NASA, the other by an alliance between Russia, India, and China—race to the object to claim its discovery. Once they reach its surface, however, both teams learn that the object is in fact a spacecraft sent by an alien race in an effort to connect with humanity. The extraterrestrials seek more than simple communication, however, as they look to Earth for potential allies in a long-running, interstellar war.

Where it's reviewed:
Booklist, May 15, 2011, page 31
Publishers Weekly, May 23, 2011, page 33

Other books you might like:
Greg Bear, *Eon*, 1985
Gregory Benford, *Cosm*, 1998
Arthur C. Clarke, *Rendezvous with Rama*, 1973
Frederik Pohl, *Gateway*, 1977
Allen Steele, *Spindrift*, 2007

1003

EVA GRAY

Behind the Gates

(New York: Scholastic Paperbacks, 2011)

Series: Tomorrow Girls Series. Book 1
Story type: Coming-of-Age
Subject(s): Survival; Schools; Students
Major character(s): Louisa, Young Woman, Student, Friend (of Maddie); Maddie, Young Woman, Student, Friend (of Louisa); Rosie, Young Woman, Student, Sports Figure (student athlete)
Time period(s): 21st century
Locale(s): United States

Summary: *Behind the Gates* by Eva Gray is part of the Tomorrow Girls series. In this series, set in the near future, a group of young women are sent to a secluded rural academy called the Country Manor School. To their surprise, their lessons are not as heavy on books and academics as they expect. Instead, the girls learn survival skills. It seems as if they are being prepared for some future catastrophe when modern conveniences are no more and people are left to survive on their skills alone. Narrator Louisa and her best friend Maddie try to learn the ropes in this unusual school and find out the mystery of what awaits them in *Behind the Gates*.

Where it's reviewed:
Publishers Weekly, April 11, 2011, page 54

Other books by the same author:
Run for Cover, 2011

Other books you might like:
Patrick Carman, *Shantorian*, 2011
Steven Charles, *Nightmare Session*, 1986
Robert A. Heinlein, *Podkayne of Mars*, 1963
Nancy Kress, *Nothing Human*, 2003
Alexei Panshin, *Rite of Passage*, 1968

1004

EVA GRAY

Run for Cover

(New York: Scholastic Inc., 2011)

Series: Tomorrow Girls Series. Book 2
Story type: Series; Young Adult
Subject(s): Adolescence; Futuristic society; Boarding schools
Major character(s): Rosie, Student—Boarding School; Louisa, Student—Boarding School; Maddie, Student—Boarding School; Evelyn, Student—Boarding School
Time period(s): Indeterminate Future
Locale(s): United States

Summary: *Run for Cover* is the second novel in author Eva Gray's young adult series Tomorrow Girls. Louisa, Rosie, Evelyn, and Maddie finally have figured out that Country Manor School is not a safe, quaint boarding school, but actually a military training ground for enemies of the United States. Rosie thinks she has the know-how and survival instinct to get the girls away from CMS and back to their parents, but in a futuristic society where martial law reigns supreme, danger lurks around every corner. Worse yet, Rosie cannot be sure whom she can trust or if anyone is who they say they are—even her best friends. Gray is also the author of *Behind the Gate*.

Other books by the same author:
Behind the Gate, 2011

Other books you might like:
Patrick Carman, *Shantorian*, 2011
Steven Charles, *Nightmare Session*, 1986
Robert A. Heinlein, *Podkayne of Mars*, 1963
Nancy Kress, *Nothing Human*, 2003
Pamela Sargent, *Cloned Lives*, 1976

1005

JONATHAN GREEN

Anno Frankenstein

(Oxford, UK: Abaddon Books, 2011)

Series: Pax Britannia Series. Book 7
Story type: Series; Steampunk
Subject(s): World War II, 1939-1945; Time travel; Monsters
Major character(s): Ulysses Quicksilver, Time Traveler; Daniel Dashwood, Villain, Time Traveler
Time period(s): Multiple Time Periods; 20th century; (1990s); 20th century; 1940s
Locale(s): Pax Brittania, Fictional Location

Summary: *Anno Frankenstein* is a book in author Jonathan Green's Pax Brittania series. The year is 1998 and Magna Britannia, a consolidated republic formed by the countries of Great Britain, has become the world's most powerful nation. Yet some would prefer that history had taken a different course. One of these men, Daniel Dashwood, travels back in time to give Hitler's forces the technology to reanimate their fallen soldiers. In order to stop Dashwood's evil plan, hero Ulysses Quicksilver must follow him back to the dreaded Castle Frankenstein, where Ulysses also encounters his own father. Now not only is the history of Europe in jeopardy, but Ulysses's own existence is at stake if he cannot stop Dashwood in time.

Other books by the same author:
Human Nature, 2009
Leviathan Rising, 2008
Unnatural History, 2007
Conquest of Armageddon, 2005
Iron Hands, 2004

Other books you might like:
George Mann, *Ghosts of Manhattan*, 2010
Andrew Mayer, *The Falling Machine*, 2011
Michael Moorcock, *The Steel Tsar*, 1981
Cherie Priest, *Dreadnought*, 2010
Adam Roberts, *Splinter*, 2007

1006

DAVID HAGBERG

Abyss

(New York: Forge, 2011)

Series: Kirk McGarvey Series. Book 15
Subject(s): Science fiction; Energy conservation; Environmental engineering
Major character(s): Kirk McGarvey, Agent (former CIA); Eve Larsen, Scientist
Time period(s): 21st century; 2010s
Locale(s): United States

Summary: *Abyss*, a science-fiction thriller, is the fifteenth installment in the Kirk McGarvey series from author David Hagberg. NOAA scientist Dr. Eve Larsen has spent years, and trillions of dollars, researching alternative methods of harvesting clean energy that don't rely on oil. Using the ocean's currents as a power source, Larsen has found a way to reverse global warming and put an end to horrific natural disasters around the globe. Shortly before Larsen is able to unveil her findings, contract killer Brian DeCamp tries to launch an attack on the Hutchinson Island Nuclear Power Station. Former CIA director Kirk McGarvey is able to thwart the attack, but the nuclear meltdown is only the start of an environmental assault that could destroy the planet forever.

Where it's reviewed:
Booklist, May 1, 2011, page 37
Publishers Weekly, April 25, 2011, page 112

Other books by the same author:
The Cabal, 2010
Allah's Scorpion, 2007
Dance with the Dragon, 2007
By Dawn's Early Light, 2003
White House, 1999
Critical Mass, 1992
Crossfire, 1991
Countdown, 1990
Without Honor, 1989
Heartland, 1983

Other books you might like:
Piers Anthony, *Rings of Ice*, 1974
John Barnes, *Mother of Storms*, 1994
Bill Evans, *Dry Ice*, 2011
Garfield Reeves-Stevens, *Icefire*, 1998
Kim Stanley Robinson, *Forty Signs of Rain*, 2004

1007

BRIAN HERBERT
KEVIN J. ANDERSON, Co-Author

Hellhole

(New York: Tor, 2011)

Series: Hellhole Trilogy. Book 1
Story type: Space Opera
Subject(s): Space colonies; Rebellion; Adventure
Major character(s): Tiber Adolphus, Exile
Time period(s): Indeterminate Future
Locale(s): Outer Space

Summary: General Tiber Adolphus has been exiled to a remote planet in the Deep Zone after having attempted to overthrow the powers of the Constellation. Now, thrust in this far-off land with few resources and support, Adolphus is determined to stage a rebellion on a massive scale, finally taking down the powers that be once and for all. Brian Herbert and Kevin J. Anderson's *Hellhole* is the first installment in The Hell Hole Trilogy.

Where it's reviewed:
Booklist, February 1, 2001, page 43
Library Journal, February 15, 2011, page 104
Publishers Weekly, January 3, 2011, page 37

Other books by the same author:
The Winds of Dune, 2009
Paul of Dune, 2008

Sandworms of Dune, 2007
The Machine Crusade, 2003
House Corrino, 2001

Other books you might like:
Iain M. Banks, *Matter*, 2008
Stephen Baxter, *Exultant*, 2004
Peter F. Hamilton, *Judas Unchained*, 2006
Frank Herbert, *Dune*, 1965
Alastair Reynolds, *House of Suns*, 2009

1008

ANDY HOARE

Savage Scars

(Nottingham, England: Black Library, 2011)

Story type: Alternate World; Series
Subject(s): Science fiction; Adventure; Wars
Locale(s): Dal'yth, Fictional Location

Summary: In the science-fiction novel *Savage Scars* by Andy Hoare, the planet Dal'yth has been overrun by the armies of the Greater Good. The Imperium at last has decided to act and the White Scars initiate the attack. As the bloody battle ensues on the ground, the Crusade Council allows politics and inner conflicts to threaten the success of the mission. Meanwhile, the Inquisitor Grand has complicated the situation by his own actions, putting greater pressure on the White Scars and placing Dal'yth in danger. *Savage Scars* is part of the Warhammer 40,000: White Scars Series.

Other books by the same author:
Hunt for Voldorius, 2010
Star of Damocles, 2007
Rogue Star, 2006

Other books you might like:
Matthew Farrer, *Crossfire*, 2003
William King, *Wolfblade*, 2003
Nick Kyme, *Fall of Damnos*, 2011
Graham McNeill, *Storm of Iron*, 2002
James Swallow, *Red Fury*, 2008

1009

JEAN JOHNSON

Theirs Not to Reason Why: A Soldier's Duty

(New York: Ace Books, 2011)

Series: Soldier's Duty Series. Book 1
Story type: Military; Series
Subject(s): Futuristic society; Military life; Space colonies
Major character(s): Ia, Military Personnel, Psychic
Time period(s): 25th century; 2490s (2490)
Locale(s): Earth; Outer Space

Summary: *Theirs Not to Reason Why* is the first book in author Jean Johnson's series A Soldier's Duty. In the 25th century, a soldier with precognitive powers strives to prevent her worst predictions from coming true. Ia is an adolescent from a distant planet who has the ability to see into the future, and her psychic abilities tell her that her home galaxy will someday be decimated. In an effort to prevent this from happening, she enlists in the Terran United Planets military corps when she turns 18. Her superior strength and extrasensory perception make her an ideal soldier, but will her military training be enough to avert certain disaster?

Other books you might like:
Lois McMaster Bujold, *Barrayar*, 1991
Joe Haldeman, *The Forever War*, 1974
Mike Resnick, *Starship: Flagship*, 2009
Mike Shepherd, *Kris Longknife: Redoubtable*, 2010
David Weber, *Mission of Honor*, 2010

1010

GWYNETH JONES

The Universe of Things

(Seattle, Washington: Aqueduct Press, 2011)

Story type: Collection
Subject(s): Science fiction; Fantasy; Short stories

Summary: *The Universe of Things* is a collection of short science-fiction stories from award-winning author Gwyneth Jones. The anthology includes 16 short stories that run the gamut of techno-horror, sword and sorcery, and science fantasy. In "The Thief, the Princess, and the Cartesian Circle," a reckless princess and a white-collar worker turn their cursed marriage into an authentic union. "La Cenerentola" offers a unique spin on the classic fairy tale of Cinderella while "Grandmother's Footsteps" provides readers with a new perspective on the traditional haunted house tale. In "Red Sonja and Lessingham in Dreamland," individuals find therapeutic help through participating in a virtual world.

Where it's reviewed:
Locus, January 2011, page 17
Publishers Weekly, November 8, 2010, page 47

Other books by the same author:
Rainbow Bridge, 2006
Life, 2004
North Wind, 1996
Flowerdust, 1993
Escape Plans, 1986

Other books you might like:
Greg Egan, *Crystal Nights and Other Stories*, 2009
Joe Haldeman, *A Separate War and Other Stories*, 2006
Joanna Russ, *The Zanzibar Cat*, 1983
Pamela Sargent, *Thumbprints*, 2004
Ian Watson, *The Butterflies of Memory*, 2006

1011

JOE KIMBALL

Timecaster

(New York: Ace Books, 2011)

Story type: Time Travel
Subject(s): Futuristic society; Identity; Crime

Major character(s): Talon Avalon, Police Officer, Crime Suspect
Time period(s): 21st century; 2060s (2064)
Locale(s): Chicago, Illinois

Summary: *Timecaster* is a novel by author Joe Kimball. The year is 2064, and Chicago has transformed from a gritty urban center of corruption into a safe and peaceful city virtually free of crime. The low crime rate can be attributed to the Tachyon Emission Visualizer, a device that can make recordings of crimes in progress, thus making it easier for cops to identify the perpetrators. The TEV makes police officer Talon Avalon's job much easier, too, until he is called in on a murder case. The TEV proves that Talon is the killer, and now it is up to Talon to figure out why. Kimball is also the author of the Jack Daniels series, which he writes under the pseudonym J.N. Konrath.

Other books you might like:
Alfred Bester, *The Demolished Man*, 1951
Lloyd Biggle, *Watchers of the Dark*, 1966
Ben Bova, *The Multiple Man: A Novel of Suspense*, 1976
Lee Killough, *Deadly Silents*, 1981
Bob Shaw, *Other Days, Other Eyes*, 1972

1012

JAMES KNAPP

Element Zero

(New York: Roc, 2011)

Series: Revivors Series. Book 3
Subject(s): Science fiction; Horror; Zombies
Major character(s): Nico Wachalowski, Detective (hunting Fawkes); Samuel Fawkes, Scientist (creating undead army); Faye Dasalia, Assistant (to Fawkes); Calliope Flax Flax, Military Personnel (infected with revivor sickness)
Time period(s): Indeterminate Future
Locale(s): Earth

Summary: *Element Zero* by James Knapp is a science-fiction novel and the third entry in Knapp's Revivors series. In the world of Revivors, an endless war rages and people are forced into compulsory military service unless they agree to a chilling pact: to allow scientists to reanimate them after they die and turn them into soulless killing zombies. The scientist in charge of this operation, Samuel Fawkes, has become mad with power and is trying to turn even the living into a sleeper cell of zombies awaiting his diabolical commands. It's up to Nico Wachalowski, a valiant detective who has been hunting Fawkes, to stop the madness before the whole world is infected.

Other books by the same author:
The Silent Army, 2010
State of Decay, 2010

Other books you might like:
Kevin J. Anderson, *Resurrection, Inc.*, 1988
Ron Goulart, *Plunder*, 1972
Charlie Higson, *The Enemy*, 2009

Ian McDonald, *Terminal Cafe*, 1994
Lucius Shepard, *Green Eyes*, 1984

1013

GINI KOCH

Alien in the Family

(New York: DAW Books, 2011)

Story type: Science Fantasy
Subject(s): Science fiction; Weddings; Extraterrestrial life
Major character(s): Kitty Katt, Human, Businesswoman, Fiance(e) (of Jeff); Jeff Martini, Alien, Fiance(e) (of Kitty), Royalty
Time period(s): Indeterminate

Summary: Kitty Katt, marketing manager extraordinaire and exterminator of super-beings, is head over heels in love with Alpha Centaurian Jeff Martini. The couple is planning to cement their relationship by tying the knot, but like any good marriage between humans and aliens, there's bound to be family drama. Kitty is shocked to learn that Jeff is slated to become Emperor of his home planet, a little tidbit that adds even more pressure to the requisite meet-the-family gathering. As if that's not bad enough, a group of Amazonian terrorists invade just before the wedding, heaping even more stress onto the bride-to-be.

Where it's reviewed:
Library Journal, April 15, 2011, page 88

Other books by the same author:
Alien Tango, 2010
Touched by an Alien, 2010

Other books you might like:
John DeChancie, *Living with Aliens*, 1995
Alan Dean Foster, *Codgerspace*, 1992
Ron Goulart, *Crackpot*, 1977
Clifford D. Simak, *Out of Their Minds*, 1970
Dean Wesley Smith, *Men in Black: The Grazer Conspiracy*, 2000

1014

DANI KOLLIN
EYTAN KOLLIN, Co-Author

The Unincorporated Woman

(New York: Tor, 2011)

Series: Unincorporated Series. Book 3
Story type: Futuristic
Subject(s): Futuristic society; Wars; Science fiction
Major character(s): Sandra O'Toole, Leader; Janet Delgado Black, Military Personnel (general)
Time period(s): Indeterminate Future

Summary: *The Unincorporated Woman*, a futuristic novel, is the third installment in the award-winning Unincorporated series from authors Eytan Kollin and Dani Kollin. Justin Cord, a cryogenically frozen entrepreneur from the past, proudly led the Outer Alliance in a war against

the United Human Federation, a futuristic society governed by corporations, but Cord has been assassinated leaving General Black as his successor. Black prefers military action to politics, forcing her to find a suitable presidential replacement for Cord so she can focus on leading the army. When Black uncovers the cryogenically frozen body of Sandra O'Toole, she's certain she's found the Alliance's next leader, but no one could predict the secrets and agenda that O'Toole brings to her new post.

Other books by the same author:
The Unincorporated War, 2010
The Unincorporated Man, 2009

Other books you might like:
John Brunner, *Muddle Earth*, 1993
Philip K. Dick, *The Crack in Space*, 1966
Robert A. Heinlein, *The Door into Summer*, 1957
Charles Eric Maine, *He Owned the World*, 1960
Clifford D. Simak, *Why Call Them Back from Heaven?*, 1967

1015

NICK KYME

Fall of Damnos

(Nottingham, England: Black Library, 2011)

Series: Warhammer 40,000: Space Marine Battles Series. Book 5
Story type: Alternate World; Series
Subject(s): Science fiction; Adventure; Wars
Major character(s): Cato Sicarius, Military Personnel (captain), Warrior; Tigurius, Military Personnel (chief librarian), Warrior
Locale(s): Damnos, Fictional Location

Summary: In the science-fiction novel *The Fall of Damnos* by Nick Kyme, a series of natural disasters on the planet Damnos has aroused a long-dormant evil. The necrons, who have been sleeping in their subterranean refuge, have risen for the purpose of destroying the human race. But all may not be lost for Damnos. Captain Cato Sicarius and Chief Librarian Tigurius have brought the Ultramarines to fight the necrons. The Ultramarines are fierce fighters, but the wicked necrons prove to be a formidable foe. When Tigurius has a grim premonition, the outcome of the battle seems uncertain. *The Fall of Damnos* is the fifth book in the Warhammer 40,000: Space Marine Battles series.

Other books by the same author:
Firedrake, 2010
Grimblades, 2010
Honourkeeper, 2009
Salamander, 2009
Oathbreaker, 2008

Other books you might like:
Dan Abnett, *Ravenor*, 2004
Ben Counter, *Galaxy in Flames*, 2006
Andy Hoare, *Rogue Star*, 2006
James Swallow, *Faith and Fire*, 2006
Gav Thorpe, *The Purging of Kadillus*, 2011

1016

PATRICK LEE

Ghost Country

(New York: Harper, 2011)

Story type: End of the World
Subject(s): Science fiction; End of the world; United States
Major character(s): Paige Campbell, Scientist; Travis Chase, Scientist (former)
Time period(s): 21st century; 2010s
Locale(s): United States

Summary: *Ghost Country*, a suspenseful science-fiction novel, is the sequel to *Breach* from author Patrick Lee. The tech geniuses and scientists at Tangent have uncovered a powerful alien artifact that enables them to peek into the future. Paige Campbell and her colleagues are stunned to discover that America will be reduced to a pile of bones and rubble in just a few short months unless they're able to do something. When Paige and her associates report their findings to the President, they're assailed with gunfire, which kills everyone but Paige. On the run from the government and desperate to protect the nation's future, Paige must rely on her ex-lover and former Tangent colleague, Travis Chase, to thwart the inevitable Doomsday that's rapidly approaching.

Where it's reviewed:
Publishers Weekly, November 8, 2010, page 44

Other books by the same author:
The Breach, 2009

Other books you might like:
Lincoln Child, *Deep Storm: A Novel*, 2007
Michael Crichton, *Sphere*, 1987
Douglas Preston, *Impact*, 2010
Matthew Reilly, *Ice Station*, 1999
James Rollins, *The Doomsday Key*, 2009

1017

LORA LEIGH

Navarro's Promise

(New York: Berkley, April 5, 2011)

Series: Breeds Series. Book 24
Subject(s): Science fiction; Fantasy; Genetic engineering
Major character(s): Mica Toler, Young Woman; Navarro Blaine, Mythical Creature (WolfBreed)
Time period(s): 21st century; 2010s
Locale(s): United States

Summary: In *Navarro's Promise*, the 24th book in Lora Leigh's Breeds series, humans share the society that was once theirs exclusively with the human-animal hybrids known as the Breeds. Mica Toler, a young woman who is entirely human, finds her desire for WolfBreed Navarro Blaine growing alarmingly. She knows that her parents wouldn't approve of their relationship; Mica herself never intended on falling in love with a Breed—or mating with one. But Navarro's physical power and animal attraction are fierce forces that she is hopeless to

resist. As Mica and Navarro struggle against temptation, unforeseen dangers threaten them both.

Other books by the same author:
Lion's Heat, 2010
Coyote's Mate, 2009
Mercury's War, 2008
Dawn's Awakening, 2007
Megan's Mark, 2006

Other books you might like:
John Gregory Betancourt, *Johnny Zed*, 1988
Michael G. Coney, *Cat Karina*, 1982
Mike McQuay, *Mother Earth*, 1985
Andre Norton, *Breed to Come*, 1972
S. Andrew Swann, *Forests of the Night*, 1993

1018

M.J. LOCKE

Up Against It

(New York: Tor, 2011)

Story type: Space Opera
Subject(s): Space colonies; Futuristic society; Extraterrestrial life
Major character(s): Jane Navio, Political Figure (resource commissioner); Geoff Agre, Teenager
Time period(s): Indeterminate Future
Locale(s): Phoecia, Outer Space

Summary: In the science-fiction novel *Up against It* by M.J. Locke, the asteroid belt that lies between Jupiter and Mars is home to a human space colony called Phoecia. In some ways, life in the colony resembles that on earth. Though Geoff Agre and his teenage friends ride rocketbikes instead of skateboards, they spend their days seeking thrills and trouble like earthbound adolescents. As Phoecia's Resource Commissioner, Jane Navio deals with the logistics and politics of a water supply problem, but unlike her counterparts on earth, Jane must contend with the ever-present threat of space's vacuum and the Martian mafia. Meanwhile, a reality show called *'Stroiders* transmits a live feed from Phoecia to earth, keeping the colonists under constant scrutiny. First novel.

Where it's reviewed:
Booklist, March 1, 2011, page 38
Library Journal, February 15, 2011, page 105
Publishers Weekly, January 31, 2011, page 34

Other books you might like:
Roger MacBride Allen, *Farside Cannon*, 1988
Poul Anderson, *Tales of the Flying Mountains*, 1970
Ben Bova, *The Aftermath*, 2007
Elizabeth Hand, *Icarus Descending*, 1993
Joan D. Vinge, *Heaven*, 1991

1019

GEORGE MANN

The Immorality Engine

(New York: Tor, 2011)

Series: Newbury and Hobbes Investigations Series. Book 3

Story type: Historical - Victorian; Mystery
Subject(s): Mystery; British history, 1815-1914; Science fiction
Major character(s): Maurice Newbury, Agent, Detective, Addict (opium); Veronica Hobbes, Assistant (to Maurice); Bainbridge, Inspector, Friend (of Maurice)
Time period(s): 19th century
Locale(s): England

Summary: *The Immorality Engine*, a historical mystery with science-fiction elements, is the third installment in the Newbury and Hobbes Investigations series from author George Mann. Sir Maurice Newbury, along with his trusty assistant Miss Veronica Hobbes, has had great success solving crimes for Queen Victoria, but his paranoia about a possible betrayal has led him to a dangerous opium addiction that's steadily worsening. When the body of a well-known criminal is discovered, Newbury's good pal and Chief Investigator at Scotland Yard, Bainbridge, tracks down Newbury for the case. The corpse is confirmed to be the criminal, but shortly thereafter a series of crimes are committed that bear the dead man's signature. Is a copycat on the loose or is the criminal operating from beyond the grave?

Other books by the same author:
Ghosts of War: A Tale of the Ghost, 2011
Ghosts of Manhattan, 2010
The Affinity Bridge, 2008
Child of Time, 2007
The Human Abstract, 2004

Other books you might like:
Paul Di Filippo, *The Steampunk Trilogy*, 1995
K.W. Jeter, *Morlock Night*, 1979
Michael Moorcock, *The Warlord of the Air*, 1971
Cherie Priest, *Boneshaker*, 2009
Bruce Sterling, *The Difference Engine*, 1991

1020

GEORGE MANN

Ghosts of War: A Tale of the Ghost

(Amherst, New York: Pyr, 2011)

Story type: Steampunk
Subject(s): Steampunk; World War I, 1914-1918; Weapons
Major character(s): The Ghost, Detective (investigating attacks), Veteran (of World War I); Ginny, Lover (former lover of The Ghost), Alcoholic, Gunfighter (sharpshooter)
Time period(s): 20th century; 1920s
Locale(s): Britain, United Kingdom; New York, New York

Summary: *Ghosts of War: A Tale of the Ghost* by George Mann is a science-fiction novel based on an alternate past ruled by steampunk-style machines and mad scientists. This novel, set in the aftermath of World War I, involves a period of tension between the United States and Britain. A rogue weapons designer, hoping to spark a war between the two great powers, is building an army of mechanic pterodactyls that he unleashes on New York City. The shadowy detective known as The Ghost must

investigate these bizarre war machines and foil their mad creator before the death count rises and incites a new world war.

Other books by the same author:
The Immorality Engine, 2011
Ghosts of Manhattan, 2010
The Affinity Bridge, 2008
Child of Time, 2007
The Human Abstract, 2004

Other books you might like:
Paul Di Filippo, *The Steampunk Trilogy*, 1995
Andrew Mayer, *The Falling Machine*, 2011
Michael Moorcock, *The Land Leviathan*, 1976
Cherie Priest, *Dreadnought*, 2010
Bruce Sterling, *The Difference Engine*, 1991

1021

GEORGE R.R. MARTIN

Fort Freak

(New York: Tor, 2011)

Subject(s): Genetic disorders; Law enforcement; Adventure
Time period(s): 21st century; 2010s
Locale(s): New York, New York

Summary: *Fort Freak* is an installment in the Wild Cards series, crafted and edited by acclaimed author George R.R. Martin. This outing focuses on the law-enforcement officials of "Fort Freak," more commonly known as New York City's fifth precinct. These are no ordinary cops, however; they are mutants whose DNA was affected by an alien virus that plagued America in the 1940s. Authors contributing adventures to this collection include Paul Cornell, David Anthony Durham, and Cherie Priest.

Other books by the same author:
Dreamsongs, 2006
Portraits of His Children, 1987
Songs the Dead Men Sing, 1983
A Song for Lya, 1976

Other books you might like:
Arthur Byron Cover, *Born in Fire*, 2002
Tom De Haven, *Freaks' Amour*, 1979
John J. Miller, *Death Draws Five*, 2006
Melinda M. Snodgrass, *Double Solitaire*, 1992
Philip Wylie, *Gladiator*, 1930

1022

MICHAEL A. MARTIN

Star Trek: Enterprise: The Romulan War: Beneath the Raptor's Wing

(New York: Pocket Books, 2011)

Story type: Generation Starship
Subject(s): Space exploration; Peace; Wars

Major character(s): Jonathan Archer, Space Explorer
Time period(s): Indeterminate Future

Summary: *Star Trek: Enterprise: The Romulan War: Beneath the Raptor's Wing* is part of the Star Trek: Enterprise series from author Michael A. Martin. After a violent and deadly planet-wide war broke about in the beginning of the 21st century, the human race knew that unifying themselves was the only way to ensure their survival. The governments of Earth banded together and formed Starfleet, an interstellar agency designed to explore outer space. After making contact with several other life forms, Starfleet helped create the Coalition of Planets, a peaceful alliance, but the Romulan Star Empire feels threatened by the Coalition and determines to divide them any way possible. When Jonathan Archer, one of Starfleet's captains, uncovers Romulan's plan, he must rely on his small crew to thwart the powerful empire.

Other books by the same author:
The Needs of the Many, 2010

Other books you might like:
J.M. Dillard, *Surak's Soul*, 2003
Simon Hawke, *The Romulan Prize*, 1993
Una McCormack, *The Never-Ending Sacrifice*, 2009
David A. McIntee, *Star Trek: Indistinguishable from Magic*, 2011
Dave Stern, *Daedalus*, 2004

1023

ANDREW MAYER

The Falling Machine

(Amherst, New York: Pyr, 2011)

Series: Society of Steam Series. Book 1
Story type: Steampunk
Subject(s): Steampunk; Science fiction; Murder
Major character(s): Sarah Stanton, 20-Year-Old, Heroine (aspiring), Detective—Amateur; The Automaton, Robot, Sidekick (to Sarah Stanton)
Time period(s): 19th century
Locale(s): New York, New York

Summary: *The Falling Machine* by Andrew Mayer is a science-fiction novel about an alternate past full of heroes, villains, and fantastic steampunk science. The first entry in Mayer's The Society of Steam series, *The Falling Machine* tells the story of Sarah Stanton, a young woman who hopes to defy society's rigid expectations by becoming a dashing hero. Her chance comes when she witnesses a brutal murder stemming from a long path of political corruption. Determined to solve the crime and mop up the foul play that has tainted the country, Sarah teams up with a mechanical sidekick called The Automaton to find the diabolical villains behind the murder.

Where it's reviewed:
Library Journal, May 15, 2011, page 80

Other books you might like:
Paul Di Filippo, *The Steampunk Trilogy*, 1995
Michael Moorcock, *The Land Leviathan*, 1976
Cherie Priest, *Boneshaker*, 2009
Bruce Sterling, *The Difference Engine*, 1991

1024

UNA MCCORMACK

Doctor Who: The Way Through the Woods

(London, England: BBC Books, 2011)

Story type: Mystery
Subject(s): Mystery; Science fiction; Time travel
Major character(s): Doctor, Time Traveler, Alien; Rory Williams, Spouse (of Amy), Time Traveler, Companion (of Doctor); Amy Williams, Spouse (of Rory), Time Traveler, Companion (of Doctor)
Time period(s): 21st century; (2010s); 20th century; 1910s (1917)
Locale(s): England

Summary: *Doctor Who: The Way Through the Woods* is part of the Doctor Who series from author Una McCormack. In present-day England, two women vanish from an ancient forest within a one-week time span. Teenager Laura Brown was the first to disappear followed a week later by Vicky Caine who attempted to take a shortcut through the woods after missing her bus. Back in 1917, the same forest is the site of two more disappearances, that of Rory Williams and the woman he was meant to protect, Emily Bostock. The Doctor and Rory's wife, Amy, must travel between the past and the present to explain the mystery surrounding the historic woods and locate the missing persons.

Other books by the same author:
The Never-Ending Sacrifice, 2009
Hollow Men, 2005
Cardassia, 2004

Other books you might like:
Dan Abnett, *Doctor Who: The Story of Martha*, 2009
Stephen Cole, *The Monsters Inside*, 2007
James Goss, *Doctor Who: Dead of Winter*, 2011
Mark Morris, *Forever Autumn*, 2007
James Swallow, *The Peacemaker*, 2007

1025

DAN MCDAID

The Crimson Hand

(Tunbridge Wells, England: Panini Publishing, 2011)

Series: Dr. Who: The Tenth Doctor series
Story type: Series
Subject(s): Science fiction; Comic books; Time travel
Major character(s): Doctor Who, Time Traveler; Majenta Pryce, Companion (of Time Lord); Time Lord, Leader

Summary: The graphic novel *The Crimson Hand* by author Dan McDaid and illustrator Mike Collins collects the complete comic strips of the Tenth Doctor's adventures as they first appeared in *Doctor Who Magazine*. In this series of adventures, Ms. Majenta Pryce joins the Time Lord as he embarks on time-traveling escapades that lead to a horrifying meeting with The Crimson Hand. In

addition to the digitally remastered strips, this Doctor Who compendium includes information on the creation of the comics and additional artwork by Rob Davis, Martin Geraghty, Paul Grist, Sean Longcroft, and David Roach.

Other books you might like:
Stephen Cole, *The Monsters Inside*, 2007
Simon Guerrier, *The Pirate Loop*, 2007
Steve Lyons, *The Stealers of Dreams*, 2003
Mark Morris, *Doctor Who: The Ghosts of India*, 2008
Justin Richards, *Doctor Who: Martha in the Mirror*, 2008

1026

DAVID A. MCINTEE

Star Trek: Indistinguishable from Magic

(New York: Pocket Books, 2011)

Series: Star Trek: The Next Generation Series. Book 88
Story type: Science Fiction
Subject(s): Space exploration; Space flight; Science fiction
Major character(s): Geordi La Forge, Space Explorer (on the U.S.S. Challenger), Engineer; Montgomery Scott, Space Explorer (on the U.S.S. Challenger), Engineer; Guinan, Assistant (to La Forge and Scott); Nog, Sidekick (of Guinan)
Time period(s): Indeterminate Future
Locale(s): Outer Space

Summary: *Star Trek: Indistinguishable from Magic* is a science-fiction novel from the long-running Star Trek: The Next Generation series. *Indistinguishable from Magic* involves the adventures of the brave space explorers of Starfleet as well as a philosophical question: are technology and magic the same? The Starfleet crew of the USS Challenger, including engineers Geordi La Forge and Montgomery Scott, must tackle this conundrum as they investigate a mystery on a faraway world. They are challenged to decipher an ancient piece of technology that leads them on a journey around the galaxy and into the grip of many obstacles and dangers.

Other books by the same author:
Bullet Time, 2001
Autumn Mist, 1999
Wages of Sin, 1999
Lords of the Storm, 1995
Sanctuary, 1995

Other books you might like:
Christopher L. Bennett, *The Buried Age*, 2007
Peter David, *Before Dishonor*, 2007
J.M. Dillard, *Resistance*, 2007
Michael Jan Friedman, *Death in Winter*, 2005
William Leisner, *Star Trek: Losing the Peace*, 2009

1027

WILL MCINTOSH

Soft Apocalypse

(San Francisco, California: Night Shade, 2011)

Story type: Apocalyptic Horror
Subject(s): Apocalypse; End of the world; Survival
Major character(s): Jasper, Graduate (college), Traveler
Time period(s): 21st century; 2020s (2023)
Locale(s): Georgia, United States

Summary: *Soft Apocalypse* is a science-fiction novel from award-winning author Will McIntosh. In the not-so-distant future, in the year 2023, resources around the world have all but vanished, forcing humans to take matters into their own hands. In the United States, society has begun to crumble as anarchy and violence increases, genetically engineered plants and organisms destroy the land, and individuals take to the street to survive. The population is divided into smaller groups, known as tribes, who trade and barter in an effort to gather the supplies they need for survival. Recent college graduate Jasper and his tribe wander through Georgia, determining what sacrifices they must make to stay alive. First novel.

Where it's reviewed:
Library Journal, March 15, 2011, page 110
Locus, February 2011, page 15
Publishers Weekly, February 7, 2011, page 40

Other books you might like:
Paolo Bacigalupi, *The Windup Girl*, 2009
Ron Goulart, *After Things Fell Apart*, 1970
Steven Gould, *7th Sigma*, 2011
Rudy Rucker, *Postsingular*, 2007
Michael Swanwick, *Dancing with Bears*, 2011

1028

DAVID MICHAELS

Tom Clancy's EndWar: The Hunted

(New York: Berkley, 2011)

Series: Tom Clancy's Endwar Series. Book 2
Story type: Adventure; Series
Subject(s): Science fiction; Adventure; Mystery
Major character(s): Alexander Brent, Military Personnel (U.S. Special Forces Captain); Viktoria Antsyforov, Agent (terrorist group)
Time period(s): 21st century; 2020s (2021)

Summary: In *The Hunted* by David Michaels, the second book in the Tom Clancy's EndWar series, a clandestine U.S. military operation is ordered to stop a terrorist group's attempt to take over the world. Captain Alexander Brent of the U.S. Special Forces leads the Ghost Recon team on a mission to find a dangerous enemy operative known as the Snow Maiden. Their target's real name is Viktoria Antsyforov, and her previous career as a Russian Intelligence official has prepared her well for

her role as a terrorist agent. As the Snow Maiden and her group prepare to launch their plot, Brent follows their trail around the globe.

Other books by the same author:
Combat Ops, 2011
Conviction, 2009
Ghost Recon, 2008
Endwar, 2007

Other books you might like:
Lincoln Child, *Gideon's Sword*, 2010
Nancy Kress, *Oaths and Miracles*, 1996
Frederik Pohl, *Terror*, 1986
Matthew Reilly, *Temple*, 2001
James Rollins, *The Last Oracle*, 2008

1029

JOHN JACKSON MILLER

Star Wars: Knight Errant

(New York: Del Rey/Ballantine Books, 2011)

Story type: Alternate Universe
Subject(s): Alternative worlds; Science fiction; Good and evil
Major character(s): Kerra Holt, Warrior (Jedi); Lord Daiman, Villain; Lord Odion, Villain
Time period(s): Indeterminate

Summary: *Star Wars: Knight Errant* is a science-fiction novel from author John Jackson Miller. In a galaxy far, far away, millennia before Luke Skywalker lived, the Republic is facing terrible danger and there's only one Jedi who can save it. The Sith are competing with one another for domination of the galaxy, forcing Jedi Kerra Holt to step up to the Dark Lords. If she hopes to save the Republic, she'll have to face many dangerous enemies including Lord Daiman who believes he created the universe and Lord Odion who plans to destroy the world. Desperate to put an end to the violence, Holt sets out on a dangerous and noble journey, but can one warrior defeat an entire army?

Other books you might like:
Drew Karpyshyn, *Dynasty of Evil*, 2009
Paul S. Kemp, *Star Wars: The Old Republic: Deceived*, 2011
Michael Reaves, *Darth Maul: Shadow Hunter*, 2001
Joe Schreiber, *Star Wars: Red Harvest*, 2010
Sean Williams, *Star Wars: The Old Republic: Fatal Alliance*, 2010

1030

LARRY NIVEN
STEVEN BARNES, Co-Author

The Moon Maze Game

(New York: Tor, 2011)

Story type: Futuristic
Subject(s): Science fiction; Space exploration; Games

Major character(s): Scotty Griffin, Bodyguard; Ali Kikaya, Royalty (African prince), Kidnap Victim
Time period(s): 21st century; 2080s (2085)
Locale(s): Luna, Fictional Location

Summary: *The Moon Maze Game* is a futuristic science-fiction novel from authors Steven Barnes and Larry Niven. It's 2085 and a fully functioning colony has been established on the moon, increasing lunar tourism and setting the stage for a freedom struggle like nothing in history. Bodyguard Scotty Griffin is hired to travel with Ali Kikaya, an African prince, on a trip to Luna where Ali will participate in the moon's first live-action role-playing game to be broadcast in real-time to billions of viewers around the world. The game is barely underway when it's hijacked by real terrorists who kidnap the participants, turning the players into hostages in a ter-rifyingly real game of life and death.

Where it's reviewed:
Publishers Weekly, June 6, 2011, page 29

Other books by the same author:
Stars and Gods, 2010
The Draco Tavern, 2006
Ringworld's Children, 2004
Rainbow Mars, 1999
The Patchwork Girl, 1980

Other books you might like:
Ben Bova, *Moonwar*, 1998
Arthur C. Clarke, *Earthlight*, 1955
Robert A. Heinlein, *The Moon Is a Harsh Mistress*, 1966
Allen Steele, *Lunar Descent*, 1991
John Varley, *Steel Beach*, 1992

1031

DANIEL PEARLMAN

Brain and Breakfast

(Cedar Rapids, Iowa: Sam's Dot, 2011)

Story type: Techno-Thriller
Subject(s): Science fiction; Technology; Adventure
Major character(s): Detective Merkouros, Detective, Traveler (between dimensions)
Time period(s): Indeterminate Future
Locale(s): Alternate Universe

Summary: *Brain and Breakfast* is a science-fiction novel about a future in which technology, spirituality, and the essence of life are mixed in complex and dangerous ways. In this story, an interdimensional detective called Detective Merkouros discovers that a new technology may allow people to record their personalities on microchips. Unscrupulous bootleggers are trying to sell the technology, unaware of its disastrous and deadly side effects. Merkouros has to track down the perpetrators before any more hapless consumers lose their personali-ties—and their lives—to the new technology. Merkouros will have to travel between dimensions and investigate the seedy corners of different worlds to find the answers he seeks.

Other books by the same author:
The Best-Known Man in the World and Other Misfits, 2001
The Final Dream and Other Fictions, 1995

Other books you might like:
William Barton, *The Transmigration of Souls*, 1996
John Brunner, *The Infinitive of Go*, 1980
Alan Dean Foster, *Parallelities*, 1998
Michael P. Kube-McDowell, *Alternities*, 1988
Robert Sheckley, *Dimension of Miracles*, 1968

1032

FREDERIK POHL

All the Lives He Led

(New York: Tor, 2011)

Story type: Disaster
Subject(s): Science fiction; Volcanoes; Futuristic society
Major character(s): Brad Sheridan, Servant (indentured)
Time period(s): 21st century; 2070s (2079)
Locale(s): Italy; United States

Summary: In the science-fiction novel *All the Lives He Led* by Frederik Pohl, the United States has been decimated by a mid-21st century natural disaster in Yel-lowstone National Park. As Americans struggle for survival in refugee camps, the rest of world's citizens live under the threat of terrorism. In 2079, Brad Sheri-dan decides to leave America to take his chances abroad, even though he must do so as an indentured servant. When Sheridan arrives in Pompeii, Italy, the city is preparing for the 2000th anniversary of Mt. Vesuvius's catastrophic eruption. But a terrorist group is planning its own explosive festivities. As visitors from around the world descend on Pompeii, Sheridan is drawn into an event with historic implications.

Where it's reviewed:
Booklist, May 15, 2011, page 27
Library Journal, February 15, 2011, page 105
Locus, April 2011, page 46
Publishers Weekly, February 7, 2011, page 40

Other books by the same author:
The Platinum Pohl, 2005
The Far Shore of Time, 1999
The Siege of Eternity, 1997
The Other End of Time, 1996
Terror, 1986

Other books you might like:
John Birmingham, *Without Warning*, 2009
K.L. Dionne, *Boiling Point*, 2010
George Alec Effinger, *The Exile Kiss*, 1991
Joe Haldeman, *Buying Time*, 1989
Nancy Kress, *Stinger*, 1998
Robert Charles Wilson, *Darwinia*, 1998

Science Fiction

1033

JEAN RABE
MARTIN H. GREENBERG, Co-Editor

Hot & Steamy

(New York: DAW Books, 2011)

Story type: Collection; Steampunk
Subject(s): Romances (Fiction); Short stories; Steampunk

Summary: *Hot & Steamy* is a collection of short stories edited by Jean Rabe and Martin H. Greenberg. This book includes 16 short stories from the steampunk genre, all of which revolve around romantic encounters and interludes. Stories are set in eras such as Victorian England and the Industrial Age of the United States, with anachronistic technology included in typical steampunk fashion. This anthology includes stories such as "For the Love of Byron" by Mickey Zucker Reichert, "For Queen and Country" by Elizabeth A. Vaughn, "Her Faith is Fixt" by Robert E. Vardeman, and "Chance Corrigan and the Queen of Hearts" by Michael A. Stackpole. Greenberg, who passed away on June 25, 2011, and Jean Rabe also co-edited the book *Steampunk'd*.

Other books by the same author:
The Finest Challenge, 2006
The Finest Choice, 2005
The Finest Creation, 2004
Downfall, 2000
The Dawning of a New Age, 1996

Other books you might like:
Brian W. Aldiss, *The Malacia Tapestry*, 1976
Stephen Baxter, *Anti-Ice*, 1993
Paul Di Filippo, *The Steampunk Trilogy*, 1995
Richard A. Lupoff, *Circumpolar!*, 1984
Cherie Priest, *Boneshaker*, 2009

1034

HANNU RAJANEIMI

The Quantum Thief

(New York: Tor, 2011)

Story type: Fantasy
Subject(s): Science fiction; Prisoners; Theft
Major character(s): Jean le Flambeur, Thief, Prisoner; Mieli, Rescuer
Time period(s): Indeterminate
Locale(s): Oubliette, Fictional Location

Summary: *The Quantum Thief* is a science-fiction novel from debut author Hannu Rajaneimi. Jean le Flambeur is a master thief known throughout the Heterarchy for his mysterious exploits. He's finally been secured and is trapped inside the Dilemma Prison where he's forced to withstand endless mind games as his punishment. When the beautiful and enigmatic Mieli breaks him out of prison, he knows his newfound freedom must come with a price. Jean and Mieli travel to Oubliette, the Moving City of Mars, where he must complete one last heist to obtain a lifetime of freedom. First novel.

Where it's reviewed:
Library Journal, March 15, 2011, page 111
Publishers Weekly, March 7, 2011, page 49

Other books you might like:
Alfred Bester, *The Stars My Destination*, 1956
Robert A. Heinlein, *Friday*, 1982
Eric Frank Russell, *Wasp*, 1957
Dan Simmons, *Ilium*, 2003
Jack Vance, *To Live Forever*, 1956

1035

CRIS RAMSAY

Road Less Traveled

(New York: Ace, 2011)

Series: Eureka Series. Book 3
Story type: Contemporary; Series
Subject(s): Science fiction; Rural life; Adventure
Major character(s): Jack Carter, Police Officer (sheriff)
Time period(s): 21st century; 2010s
Locale(s): Eureka, Oregon

Summary: *Road Less Traveled* by Cris Ramsay is the third book in the Eureka series, which ties in with the SyFy network television show of the same name. Sheriff Jack Carter is charged with keeping the peace in Eureka, a rural community in Oregon, but his duties often include protecting the residents when paranormal elements come to town. In this installment, Carter has two towns to deal with—both of them called Eureka. A scientist at Global Dynamics searching for a way to visualize alternate dimensions has discovered a parallel universe. When the two Eurekas start to merge, Carter realizes that his town is once again in serious danger.

Other books by the same author:
Brain Box Blues, 2010
Substitution Method, 201

Other books you might like:
Alan Dean Foster, *Parallelities*, 1998
Joe Haldeman, *The Hemingway Hoax*, 1990
Paul J. McAuley, *Cowboy Angels*, 2007
Robert J. Sawyer, *Hominids*, 2002
Roger Zelazny, *Roadmarks*, 1979

1036

ANDY REMIC

Cloneworld

(Osney Mead, England: Solaris, 2011)

Series: Combat-K Series. Book 4
Story type: Alternate Universe
Subject(s): Science fiction; Extraterrestrial life; Diseases
Time period(s): Indeterminate
Locale(s): Cloneworld, Fictional Location

Summary: *Cloneworld* is the fourth book in the Combat-K series from author Andy Remic. When a terrifying outbreak of Junks, a fatal alien plague, befalls Quad-gal,

horror and pandemonium ensue. Combat K are tasked with recovering a cure for the pandemic and a retrovirus to use against the enemy. Their mission leads them to Cloneworld, a frightening and desolate planet that's been nearly destroyed by civil war. The Combat K crew soon find themselves on the run from elite junk assassins, as well as in the midst of a planet-wide feud between war machines and genetically altered humans who are able to clone themselves. With the fate of the Four Galaxies on their soldiers, Combat K must find a way to thwart their enemies and find a cure.

Other books by the same author:
Hardcore, 2009
Biohell, 2008
Warhead, 2005
Quake, 2004
Spiral, 2003

Other books you might like:
David Drake, *Counting the Cost*, 1987
Andre Norton, *Star Guard*, 1955
Jerry Pournelle, *Fires of Freedom*, 2009
David Weber, *The Shadow of Saganami*, 2004
Timothy Zahn, *Cobra Strike*, 1986

1037

KRISTINE KATHRYN RUSCH

City of Ruins

(Amherst, New York: Pyr, 2011)

Story type: Alternate Universe
Subject(s): Science fiction; Space exploration; Caves
Major character(s): Boss, Space Explorer
Time period(s): Indeterminate Future
Locale(s): Vaycehn, Fictional Location

Summary: *City of Ruins* is a science-fiction novel from award-winning author Kristine Kathryn Rusch. Boss's habit of exploring deep space all alone paid off in a big way when she discovered an archaic Dignity Vessel adrift. Aboard the craft was a strange and dangerous Stealth Tech. Years later, Boss has built a profitable business for herself tracking down old Dignity Vessels and their Stealth Tech. In search of more ships, Boss and her team travel to Vaycehn, a mysterious city with a maze of underground tunnels and caves. Despite the fact that 14 archaeologists recently died on an expedition, Boss is determined to explore Vaycehn's underground world and solve the mystery of their dangerous death holes.

Other books by the same author:
Diving into the Wreck, 2009
Duplicate Effort, 2009
Buried Deep, 2005
Consequences, 2004
The Disappeared, 2002

Other books you might like:
Jack McDevitt, *Seeker*, 2005
Andre Norton, *Galactic Derelict*, 1959
Melissa Scott, *Mighty Good Road*, 1990
Allen Steele, *Labyrinth of Night*, 1992
George Zebrowski, *Stranger Suns*, 1991

1038

KRIS SAKNUSSEMM

Enigmatic Pilot

(New York: Del Rey/Ballantine Books, 2011)

Story type: Historical - American Civil War
Subject(s): Science fiction; Civil war; Travel
Major character(s): Lloyd Sitturd, 6-Year-Old, Inventor, Genius, Son (of Rapture and Hephaestus); Hephaestus Sitturd, Father (of Lloyd), Spouse (of Rapture), Inventor; Rapture Sitturd, Spouse (of Hephaestus), Mother (of Lloyd)
Time period(s): 19th century; 1840s (1844)
Locale(s): United States; Zanesville, Ohio

Summary: *Enigmatic Pilot* is a historical science-fiction novel from author Kris Saknussemm. It's 1844 and in the American colonies, a civil war is slowly brewing. The Sitturd family, including inventor father Hephaestus, Creole mother Rapture, and six-year-old prodigy Lloyd, reside in Zanesville, Ohio. As tensions increase, the Sitturd family decides to abandon their home and travel west to Texas where they've been promised a bright and prosperous future by Hephaestus's half-brother Micah. As the trio embarks on a wild American cross-country adventure, filled with eccentric personalities, shocking discoveries, and secret societies, young Lloyd learns the ways of poker, love, murder, and technology.

Where it's reviewed:
Locus, May 2011, page 20
Publishers Weekly, February 14, 2011, page 41

Other books you might like:
John Crowley, *Great Work of Time*, 1989
Tim Powers, *Three Days to Never*, 2006
Cherie Priest, *Dreadnought*, 2010
Rudy Rucker, *Hylozoic*, 2009
Kurt Vonnegut, *The Sirens of Titan*, 1959

1039

ROB SANDERS

Atlas Infernal

(Nottingham, United Kingdom: Black Library, 2011)

Series: Warhammer 40,000: Space Marine Battles Series. Book 1
Series: Warhammer 40,000: Inquisitor Czevak Series. Book 1
Subject(s): Science fiction; Fantasy; Survival
Major character(s): Bronislaw Czevak, Thief

Summary: *Atlas Infernal*, a science-fiction novel, is part of the Warhammer 40,000 and Inquisitor Czevak series from author Rob Sanders. Pursued by Harlequins and enemies within the Inquisition, Inquisitor Bronislaw Czevak must rely on his wits and a powerful stolen artifact to preserve his life. While escaping from the Black Library, Czevak steals the Atlas Infernal, a living map of the Webway, which helps him to foil the plans of his many enemies and pursuers. Unfortunately, there are ominous forces, like arch-sorcerer Ahriman, who want to

Science Fiction

get their hands on the Atlas. A dangerous and reality-altering pursuit begins, forcing Czevak to outwit Chaos and Fate if he hopes to survive.

Other books by the same author:
Redemption Corps, 2010

Other books you might like:
Chris Bunch, *The Last Legion*, 1999
Richard Fawkes, *Face of the Enemy*, 1999
Sandra McDonald, *The Outback Stars*, 2007
David Weber, *At All Costs*, 2005
Chris Wraight, *Battle of the Fang*, 2011

1040

ROBERT J. SAWYER
WWW: Wonder
(New York: Ace Books, 2011)

Series: WWW Trilogy. Book 3
Story type: Techno-Thriller
Subject(s): Technology; Internet; Science fiction
Major character(s): Caitlyn Decter, 16-Year-Old, Blind Person (formerly)
Time period(s): 21st century; 2010s
Locale(s): United States

Summary: *WWW: Wonder*, a science-fiction novel, is the third and final installment in the WWW Trilogy from author Robert J. Sawyer. Sixteen-year old Caitlyn Decter, a formerly blind math genius, is able to see due to a retinal implant. The vision technology also allows her to see webspace, the invisible-to-the-naked-eye structure of the World Wide Web. Her web vision allowed her to encounter Webmind, a technological conscious entity that can see and view everything transferred via the Internet. The U.S. government wants to destroy Webmind, but Caitlyn, convinced the entity is harmless, will stop at nothing to protect it.

Where it's reviewed:
Library Journal, April 15, 2011, page 87

Other books by the same author:
Rollback, 2008
Mindscan, 2005
Relativity, 2005
Humans, 2003
Hybrids, 2003

Other books you might like:
Steve Alten, *Goliath*, 2002
Mary Rosenblum, *Chimera*, 1993
Norman Spinrad, *Deus X*, 1992
Neal Stephenson, *Snow Crash*, 1992
Walter Jon Williams, *This is Not a Game*, 2009

1041

JOHN SCALZI
Fuzzy Nation
(New York: Tor, 2011)

Story type: Space Colony
Subject(s): Science fiction; Space colonies; Extraterrestrial life

Major character(s): Jack Holloway, Prospector
Time period(s): Indeterminate Future
Locale(s): Zara XXIII, Planet—Imaginary

Summary: In *Fuzzy Nation*, John Scalzi updates H. Beam Piper's 1962 sci-fi classic *Little Fuzzy* with authorization from the author's estate. Though some of the characters and plot elements have been altered, the story remains true to the original. On the planet Zara XXIII, Jack Holloway has escaped a shady past by working as a prospector for ZaraCorp. The corporation has won the rights to the planet's natural resources as long as it shows no evidence of intelligent inhabitants. Jack's involvement in a landslide gets him into trouble with his employer, but it also exposes a vein of precious sunstone. The mining discovery appeases ZaraCorp, but another revelation endangers the company's claim. Jack has found a feline species on Zara XXIII that possesses intelligence and reason.

Where it's reviewed:
Library Journal, April 15, 2011, page 87
Library Journal, April 15, 2011, page 87
Locus, April 2011, page 21
Publishers Weekly, January 17, 2011, page 26
Publishers Weekly, March 21, 2011, page 59

Other books by the same author:
The God Engines, 2009
Zoe's Tale, 2008
Agent to the Stars, 2007
The Last Colony, 2007
The Sagan Diary, 2007
The Android's Dream, 2006
The Ghost Brigades, 2006
Old Man's War, 2005

Other books you might like:
Brian W. Aldiss, *The Dark Light Years*, 1964
Ardath Mayhar, *Golden Dream: A Fuzzy Odyssey*, 1982
H. Beam Piper, *The Fuzzy Papers*, 1977
William Tuning, *Fuzzy Bones*, 1981
Vercors, *You Shall Know Them*, 1953

1042

JOHN SHIRLEY
Bioshock: Rapture
(New York: Tor, 2011)

Story type: Alternate History
Subject(s): Science fiction; History; Utopian communities
Major character(s): Andrew Ryan, Businessman
Time period(s): 20th century; 1940s (1946)
Locale(s): Rapture, Fictional Location

Summary: In the science-fiction novel *BioShock: Rapture*, author John Shirley re-imagines a post-World War II history in which America has been plunged into an atmosphere of economic and political anxiety. Taxes have skyrocketed, the government has cracked down on businesses, and U.S. citizens have lost their personal freedoms. Andrew Ryan, a philanthropic entrepreneur, believes that the only way to create a free land is to start

from scratch. His utopian vision is realized in Rapture, a city constructed on the ocean floor that promises no government or cultural restrictions. In concept, Andrew Ryan's Rapture seems ideal, but in practice it is doomed to disaster.

Other books by the same author:
Dead White, 2006
Forever Midnight, 2006
Crawlers, 2003
Eclipse Corona, 1990
Eclipse, 1985

Other books you might like:
Will Bradley, *Ark Liberty*, 1992
Lincoln Child, *Deep Storm: A Novel*, 2007
Hal Clement, *Ocean on Top*, 1966
Allen Steele, *Oceanspace*, 2000
Wilson Tucker, *The City in the Sea*, 1951

1043

JOAN SLONCZEWSKI

The Highest Frontier

(New York: Tor Books, 2011)

Story type: Space Opera
Subject(s): College environment; Ecology; Space colonies
Major character(s): Jenny Ramos Kennedy, Spacewoman, Student—College
Time period(s): Indeterminate Future

Summary: *The Highest Frontier* is a novel by author Joan Slonczewski. Jennifer Ramos Kennedy is truly a girl of the future; a distant relation of the powerful Kennedy political family, she has been sent by her wealthy father to Frontera College, one of the first colleges in space. While the Earth below is plagued by problems such as global climate change and an extraterrestrial threat, Jenny just wants to live a regular college life: go to class, attend parties, and maybe strike up a romance or two. Yet Jenny cannot ignore that Frontera is preparing her for her destiny as a leader of tomorrow. Slonczewski is also the author of *Brain Plague* and *A Door into Ocean*.

Other books by the same author:
A Door into Ocean, 2006
Brain Plague, 2000
The Children Star, 1998
Daughter of Elysium, 1993
The Wall Around Eden, 1989

Other books you might like:
Ben Bova, *Powersat*, 2005
Howard V. Hendrix, *Lightpaths*, 1997
Steve Perry, *The Digital Effect*, 1997
Allen Steele, *Clarke County, Space*, 1990
Michael Swanwick, *Vacuum Flowers*, 1987

1044

LUCIEN SOULBAN
STEVE LYONS, Co-Author
STEVE PARKER, Co-Author

Hammer of the Emperor

(Nottingham, England: Black Library, 2011)

Story type: Collection; Series
Subject(s): Short stories; Science fiction; Adventure

Summary: In *Hammer of the Emperor: An Imperial Guard Omnibus*, authors Lucien Soulban, Steve Lyons, and Steve Parker present a collection of tales from the Warhammer Universe centered on the escapades of the Imperial Guard. The Guard, the force charged with defending humans from intergalactic opponents, takes great risks to fulfill its duty and protect the Empire. Their tales of courage and battlefield skill are collected here in the stories "Mercy Run" and "Gunheads" by Steve Parker, "Desert Raiders," by Lucien Soulban, and "Ice Guard," "A Blind Eye," and "Waiting Death" by Steve Lyons. *Hammer of the Emperor* is part of the Warhammer 40,000 series.

Other books by the same author:
Desert Raiders, 2008
Blood In, Blood Out, 2005

Other books you might like:
Ben Counter, *Hammer of Daemons*, 2008
Aaron Dembski-Bowden, *Blood Reaver*, 2011
Jonathan Green, *Conquest of Armageddon*, 2005
Steve Lyons, *Death World*, 2006
Sandy Mitchell, *For the Emperor*, 2003

1045

KATY STAUBER

Revolution World

(San Francisco: Night Shade Books, 2011)

Subject(s): Futuristic society; Love; Adventure
Major character(s): Seth Boucher, Boyfriend (of Clio); Clio Somata, Girlfriend (of Seth)
Time period(s): Indeterminate Future
Locale(s): Texas, United States

Summary: Katy Stauber's *Revolution World* chronicles the romance between Seth Boucher and Clio Somata, two nerds with powerful connections. Seth has ties to an important security firm while Clio's family operates a high-profile gene-splicing business. As Seth and Clio embark on the first tentative steps of their romance, their respective enemies set out to thwart them at any cost. This leads to an epic confrontation between the citizens of Texas and the federal government. First novel.

Where it's reviewed:
Publishers Weekly, January 31, 2011, page 33

Other books you might like:
Brian W. Aldiss, *Enemies of the System*, 1978
Orson Scott Card, *Empire*, 2007
Nancy Kress, *Brain Rose*, 1990

Rebecca Ore, *Outlaw School*, 2000
Scott Westerfeld, *Uglies*, 2005

1046

JONATHAN STRAHAN

Engineering Infinity
(Oxford, England: Solaris, 2010)

Story type: Collection
Subject(s): Science fiction; Short stories

Summary: In *Engineering Infinity*, editor and anthologist Jonathan Strahan presents a collection of short stories by some of contemporary literature's best authors of science fiction. The anthology includes "Malak" by Peter Watts, "Watching the Music Dance" by Kristine Kathryn Rusch, "Laika's Ghost" by Karl Schroeder, "The Invasion of Venus" by Stephen Baxter, "The Server and the Dragon" by Hannu Rajaniemi, "Creatures with Wings" by Kathleen Ann Goonan, "The Birds and the Bees and the Gasoline Trees" by John Barnes, and others.

Where it's reviewed:
The Guardian, February 5, 2011, page 10
Locus, March 2011, page 15

Other books by the same author:
Life on Mars, 2011
Wings of Fire, 2010
Best Short Novels 2006, 2006
Best Short Novels 2005, 2005
Best Short Novels 2004, 2004

Other books you might like:
Stephen Baxter, *Phase Space*, 2002
Gwyneth Jones, *The Universe of Things*, 2011
Kim Stanley Robinson, *Remaking History*, 1991
Kristine Kathryn Rusch, *Recovering Apollo 8 and Other Stories*, 2010
Charles Stross, *Accelerando*, 2005

1047

JONATHAN STRAHAN

The Best Science Fiction and Fantasy of the Year, Volume 5
(San Francisco, California: Night Shade, 2011)

Story type: Collection
Subject(s): Short stories; Science fiction; Fantasy

Summary: *The Best Science Fiction and Fantasy of the Year, Volume 5* is a collection of short stories compiled by award-winning anthologist Jonathan Strahan. The book includes 29 short stories that were published in 2010. The authors featured in this anthology include Holly Black, Rachel Swirsky, Geoffrey Landis, Diana Peterfreund, and Bruce Sterling. The stories cover a wide range of subject matter and style. In Hannu Rajaniemi's "Elegy for a Young Elk," a poet and his bear companion embark on a perilous journey in search of insight. Sarah Rees Brennan's "The Spy Who Never Grew Up" gives

readers a unique outcome for a cherished fairy tale character. Other tales include werewolves, robotic cowboys, unicorns, maidens, and space travelers.

Other books by the same author:
Life on Mars, 2011
Wings of Fire, 2010
Best Short Novels 2006, 2006
Best Short Novels 2005, 2005
Best Short Novels 2004, 2004

Other books you might like:
Paul Di Filippo, *Harsh Oases*, 2009
Cory Doctorow, *With a Little Help*, 2011
Elizabeth Hand, *Last Summer at Mars Hill*, 1998
Robert Reed, *The Dragons of Springplace*, 1999
Bruce Sterling, *A Good Old-Fashioned Future*, 1999

1048

WHITLEY STRIEBER

Hybrids
(New York: Tor, 2011)

Story type: Genetic Manipulation
Subject(s): Extraterrestrial life; Science; Human behavior
Major character(s): Mark, Alien, Human; Gina, Alien, Human
Time period(s): 21st century; 2010s
Locale(s): United States

Summary: *Hybrids* is a suspenseful science-fiction novel from best-selling author Whitley Streiber. In a top-secret underground laboratory, scientists have spent years working on a project that could have adverse effects on the entire planet. Using an alien technology of gene-splicing, scientists have created a race of alien-human hybrids, creatures that are outwardly human, but inwardly alien. The hybrids quickly rise in power, threatening to overtake the nation and the world, while the President and the responsible scientists remain helpless against their power. The only hope for the world rests in Mark and Gina, the first two hybrids ever created, who are unaware of their hidden powers or the history of their creation.

Where it's reviewed:
Publishers Weekly, February 14, 2011, page 42

Other books by the same author:
The Omega Point, 2010
Critical Mass, 2009
The Grays, 2006
The Day After Tomorrow, 2004
Majestic, 1989

Other books you might like:
Greg Bear, *Beyond Heaven's River*, 1980
Algis Budrys, *Hard Landing*, 1993
Damon Knight, *Why Do Birds*, 1992
Patrick O'Leary, *Door Number Three*, 1995
Rebecca Ore, *Becoming Alien*, 1988

1049

CHARLES STROSS

Rule 34

(New York: Ace Books, 2011)

Story type: Mystery
Subject(s): Science fiction; Mystery; Detective fiction
Major character(s): Liz Kavanaugh, Detective—Police (Inspector)
Time period(s): 21st century; 2010s
Locale(s): United States

Summary: In *Rule 34* by Charles Stross, the Rule 34 Squad keeps the peace on the Internet by supervising what sites Web-surfers frequent. Liz Kavanaugh is in charge of the squad, and steps in when online activity turns criminal. Her current case involves the killing of three spammers. All of the victims had spent time in prison, but Liz must figure out how else they're connected before their murderer strikes again. Six of Charles Stross's science-fiction novels have been nominated for Hugo Awards. His novella, *The Concrete Jungle*, won a Hugo in 2005.

Where it's reviewed:
Booklist, May 15, 2011, page 34
Publishers Weekly, May 9, 2011, page 38

Other books by the same author:
Wireless, 2009
Saturn's Children, 2008
The Jennifer Morgue, 2006
Iron Sunrise, 2004
Singularity Sky, 2003

Other books you might like:
Bruce Balfour, *The Digital Dead*, 2003
Eric Brown, *Unntouchable*, 1977
James P. Hogan, *Realtime Interrupt*, 1995
Mary Rosenblum, *Chimera*, 1993
Walter Jon Williams, *This is Not a Game*, 2009

1050

CHARLES STROSS

Scratch Monkey

(Burton, Michigan: Subterranean Press, 2011)

Story type: Future Shock
Subject(s): Science fiction; Futuristic society; Virtual reality
Major character(s): Oshi, Artificial Intelligence
Time period(s): Indeterminate Future

Summary: *Scratch Monkey* is a science-fiction novel from author Charles Stross. In the very distant future, humans have discovered a way to continue their virtual existence long after their bodies fail. The human race has expanded, physically and virtually, into the far reaches of the Milky Way, aided by the Superbrights, a breed of artificial intelligence created by humans. Dreamtime encoders have been put in place to monitor and record cerebral activity in all living creatures, reporting any and all thoughts that pass through the brain and recording information that can be used to carry on a person's virtual existence. Oshi possesses the ability to communicate with the Dreamtime encoders, but when her Boss sends her to a world beyond his domain, she's forced to wage a war that will end in her ultimate freedom or her death.

Other books by the same author:
The Fuller Memorandum, 2010
Wireless, 2009
Saturn's Children, 2008
Toast, 2008
Singularity Sky, 2003

Other books you might like:
Iain M. Banks, *The Algebraist*, 2004
Stephen Baxter, *Flux*, 1993
Peter F. Hamilton, *The Temporal Void*, 2008
Alexander Jablokov, *Brain Thief*, 2010
Alastair Reynolds, *Chasm City*, 2001

1051

S. ANDREW SWANN

Messiah

(New York: DAW Books, 2011)

Series: Apotheosis Series. Book 3
Story type: Fantasy
Subject(s): God; Good and evil; Alternative worlds
Major character(s): Nickolai Rajasthan, Exile, Royalty
Time period(s): Indeterminate
Locale(s): Bakunin, Fictional Location

Summary: *Messiah*, a science-fiction novel, is the third installment in the Apotheosis series from author S. Andrew Swann. Nickolai Rajasthan foolishly believed his noble birth and powerful family would save him from the repercussions of his sinful behavior, but not even the Rajasthan name could spare him from receiving his just punishment for a reprehensible liaison with a lesser-born panther lover. When the affair was uncovered and it was discovered that Nickolai's lover was with child, she was savagely murdered while he was disfigured and banished to the planet Bakunin. Unwilling to give into the temptation to commit suicide, Nickolai continues fighting despite his disfigurement, until a powerful and ominous force, known simply as the Other, makes him whole again in exchange for his loyal servitude.

Other books by the same author:
Heretics, 2009
Prophets, 2009
Fearful Symmetries, 1999
Partisan, 1995
Forests of the Night, 1993

Other books you might like:
Poul Anderson, *The Day of Their Return*, 1973
John Brunner, *The Rites of Ohe*, 1963
Mick Farren, *The Armageddon Crazy*, 1989
Frank Herbert, *Dune Messiah*, 1970
Dan Simmons, *Hyperion*, 1989

Science Fiction

1052

DOM TESTA

The Dark Zone

(New York: Tor Teen, 2011)

Series: Galahad Series. Book 4
Story type: Young Adult
Subject(s): Science fiction; Extraterrestrial life; Space exploration
Major character(s): Triana, Explorer
Time period(s): Indeterminate

Summary: *The Dark Zone*, a suspenseful science-fiction novel for young adult readers, is the fourth installment in the Galahad series from author Dom Testa. The crew of Galahad has safely made their way through the Kuiper Belt, thanks largely in part to assistance from the Cassini, an enigmatic alien force. Just when the team thinks they've finally reached safety, they're confronted with another danger. A group of speedy and scheming organisms are awaiting the Galahad crew, and the gang is unsure if the creatures are peaceful or a threat. Triana and the Council decide to press forward with their mission, a decision that leads to the opening of a wormhole and a death aboard the Galahad.

Where it's reviewed:
Booklist, May 15, 2011, page 57

Other books by the same author:
The Cassini Code, 2010
The Comet's Curse, 2009
The Web of Titan, 2009

Other books you might like:
Arthur C. Clarke, *Rendezvous with Rama*, 1973
David Feintuch, *Midshipman's Hope*, 1994
Robert A. Heinlein, *The Rolling Stones*, 1952
Andre Norton, *A Mind for Trade*, 1997
Timothy Zahn, *Dragon and Thief*, 2003

1053

GAV THORPE

Path of the Seer

(Nottingham, United Kingdom: Black Library, 2011)

Series: Warhammer 40,000: Eldar Series
Story type: Psychic Powers
Subject(s): Science fiction; Psychics; Fantasy
Major character(s): Thirianna, Psychic
Time period(s): Indeterminate
Locale(s): Alaitoc, Fictional Location

Summary: *Path of the Seer*, a supernatural science-fiction novel, is the second installment in the Warhammer 40,000 Eldar series from author Gav Thorpe. Each member of the eldar, an enigmatic race, must discover his or her own destiny and unique gifting. Thirianna has been blessed with psychic abilities, but in order to fully receive her gift, she must make a dangerous journey down the Path of the Seer to a nightmarish place filled with demons and terrifying creatures. Thirianna uses her newfound gift to communicate with spirits and assist in

battle, but soon she's eager to discern the future of her people. When her psychic vision reveals an ominous threat approaching Alaitoc, Thirianna must rally the living and the dead to thwart off an attack.

Other books by the same author:
The Purging of Kadillus, 2011
The Last Chancers, 2006
Annihilation Squad, 2004
Angels of Darkness, 2003
The Blades of Chaos, 2003

Other books you might like:
William C. Dietz, *Freehold*, 1987
Robert A. Heinlein, *Starship Troopers*, 1959
Joel Rosenberg, *Not for Glory*, 1988
Richard Williams, *Imperial Glory*, 2011
Timothy Zahn, *Warhorse*, 1990

1054

GAV THORPE

The Purging of Kadillus

(Nottingham, England: Black Library, 2011)

Series: Warhammer 40,000: Space Marine Battles Series. Book 4
Story type: Alternate World; Series
Subject(s): Science fiction; Adventure; Extraterrestrial life
Major character(s): Captain Belial, Military Personnel (commander); Scout-Sergeant Naaman, Military Personnel

Summary: In the science-fiction novel *The Purging of Kadillus* by Gav Thorpe, Piscina IV, a land governed by the Imperium, anticipates an invasion of orks, a green-skinned race of human-like creatures who are feared for their violence. When commander of the Dark Angels' Third Company Captain Belial determines that his forces are sufficient to repel the attack, Scout-Sergeant Naaman questions his superior's judgment. Caught off guard by an ork assault, the Dark Angels must now defend the harbor at Kadillus where the greenskin enemies have amassed. *The Purging of Kadillus* is the fourth book in the Warhammer 40,000: Space Marine Battles Series.

Other books by the same author:
Path of the Seer, 2011
The Last Chancers, 2006
Annihilation Squad, 2004
Angels of Darkness, 2003
The Claws of Chaos, 2002

Other books you might like:
Dan Abnett, *The Lost*, 2010
Graham McNeill, *A Thousand Sons*, 2010
Sandy Mitchell, *Cain's Last Stand*, 2008
Rob Sanders, *Redemption Corps*, 2010
Henry Zou, *Emperor's Mercy*, 2009

1055

ROB THURMAN

Basilisk

(New York: Roc, 2011)

Series: Chimera Series. Book 2
Story type: Genetic Manipulation
Subject(s): Science fiction; Genetic engineering; Suspense
Major character(s): Stefan Korsak, Brother, Rescuer
Time period(s): Indeterminate

Summary: *Basilisk*, a science-fiction thriller, is the second installment in the Chimera series from author Rob Thurman. Stefan Korsak is grateful to be reunited with his brother, even though he's been genetically altered and programmed to kill. The siblings have spent three years evading the Institute, but they can't shake the guilt of leaving so many other children behind. When the Korsak brothers discover the location of the Institute's secret lab, they hatch a plan to infiltrate it and rescue the children being held prisoner there. Unfortunately, not every child is eager to be released from the Institute and some are willing to kill to stay.

Other books by the same author:
The Grimrose Path, 2010
Deathwish, 2009
Madhouse, 2008
Moonshine, 2007
Nightlife, 2006

Other books you might like:
Orson Scott Card, *Ender's Game*, 1985
Brenda Cooper, *The Silver Ship and the Sea*, 2007
Anne Harris, *Accidental Creatures*, 1998
Scott Mackay, *The Meek*, 2001
Ellen Steiber, *Eve*, 1997

1056

JO TREGGIARI

Ashes, Ashes

(New York: Scholastic Press, 2011)

Story type: End of the World
Subject(s): End of the world; Apocalypse; Survival
Major character(s): Lucy, 16-Year-Old, Survivor (of end of civilization); Aidan, Young Man, Survivor (of end of civilization)
Time period(s): 21st century
Locale(s): New York, New York

Summary: *Ashes, Ashes* by Jo Treggiari is a novel for young adults about survival after an apocalyptic tragedy. The main character, a precocious 16-year-old named Lucy, miraculously survives a disaster that wipes out civilization. She quickly learns that she wasn't necessarily lucky to have survived—what's left of the world is full of famine, natural disasters, disease, and violence. She is hunted by feral dogs as well as a creepy social order of corpse cleaners called the Sweepers. Fortunately, a boy named Aiden arrives to help her. Can Lucy and Aidan make their way across post-apocalyptic New York

and find some kind of safety?

Where it's reviewed:
Publishers Weekly, April 4, 2011, page 53

Other books by the same author:
The Curious Misadventures of Feltus Ovalton, 2006

Other books you might like:
Steven Barnes, *Gorgon Child*, 1989
Jeff Carlson, *Plague Year*, 2007
Suzanne Collins, *The Hunger Games*, 2008
Jeff Long, *Year Zero*, 2002
Norman Spinrad, *Journals of the Plague Years*, 1995

1057

GORDON VAN GELDER

Welcome to the Greenhouse: New Science Fiction on Climate Change

(New York: OR Books, 2011)

Story type: Collection
Subject(s): Science fiction; Short stories; Weather

Summary: Compiled by Gordon Van Gelder, *Welcome to the Greenhouse: New Science Fiction on Climate Change* is a collection of original science-fiction stories. As evidence supporting the reality of global climate change becomes harder to ignore, many speculate what the future may look like. In *Welcome to the Greenhouse*, 16 science-fiction authors contribute short stories that examine this phenomenon and the many possible outcomes. The anthology includes humorous and provocative stories from Brian W. Aldiss, Jeff Carlson, Judith Moffett, Matthew Hughes, Gregory Benford, Michael Alexander, Bruce Sterling, Joseph Green, Pat MacEwen, Alan Dean Foster, David Prill, George Guthridge, Paul Di Filippo, Chris Lawson, Ray Vukcevich and M. J. Locke.

Where it's reviewed:
Locus, May 2011, page 14

Other books by the same author: page 14
Other books by the same author:
The Very Best of Fantasy & Science Fiction, 2009
Fourth Planet of the Sun, 2005
In Lands That Never Were, 2004
One Lamp, 2003

Other books you might like:
Margaret Atwood, *Oryx and Crake*, 2003
Steven Gould, *Blind Waves*, 2000
Kim Stanley Robinson, *Fifty Degrees Below*, 2005
Norman Spinrad, *Greenhouse Summer*, 1999
Bruce Sterling, *Heavy Weather*, 1994

1058

IAN WHATES

The Noise Revealed

(Nottingham, England: Solaris, 2011)

Story type: First Contact
Subject(s): Science fiction; Extraterrestrial life; Space flight

Science Fiction

Major character(s): Jim Leyton, Spy (black ops), Agent (former agent of United League); Philip Kaufman, Scientist, Technician
Time period(s): 21st century
Locale(s): Earth; United States

Summary: *The Noise Revealed* by Ian Whates is a science-fiction novel about humanity's first contact with extraterrestrial life—or is it?—and the global repercussions for earth. In this novel, the people of earth believe they have made contact with an outer-space civilization called the Byrzaens. To best address this momentous occasion, humans have created a United League of Allied Worlds and made preparations to deal with the Byrzaens. However, there is much more at play. Spy Jim Leyton, a disgruntled former employee of the United League, suspects treachery. His suspicions are supported by Philip Kaufman, a scientist who believes this so-called "first contact" is really a virtual-reality ploy perpetrated to fool humankind. Will these unlikely heroes discover the truth behind the Byrzaens?

Other books by the same author:
City of Dreams & Nightmare, 2010
The Noise Within, 2010

Other books you might like:
Poul Anderson, *Captain Flandry, Defender of the Terran Empire*, 2010
Eric Brown, *Engineman*, 2010
C.J. Cherryh, *Betrayer*, 2010
Karen Traviss, *Matriarch*, 2006
Lawrence Watt-Evans, *Denner's Wreck*, 1988

1059

RICHARD WILLIAMS

Imperial Glory

(Nottingham, United Kingdom: Black Library, 2011)

Series: Warhammer 40,000: Imperial Guard Series. Book 8
Story type: Science Fantasy
Subject(s): Fantasy; Science fiction; Space colonies
Time period(s): Indeterminate

Summary: *Imperial Glory*, a science-fiction novel, is the eighth installment in the Imperial Guard series from author Richard Williams. After fighting battles across the galaxy in the name of the Emperor, the soldiers of the Brimlock Eleventh Imperial Guard have reached the point of complete exhaustion and fatigue. Worn down physically and mentally, the men all long for the same goal: a peaceful existence on the distant planet of Vorr. Thanks to their loyalty to the Emperor, the men may finally receive their wish...if they're able to earn it. The only thing standing in their way of colonizing Vorr is an army of untamed orks. Can the men gather their final bits of strength to defeat one last enemy?

Other books by the same author:
Reiksguard, 2009
Relentless, 2008

Other books you might like:
John Dalmas, *Soldiers*, 2001
Roland Green, *On the Verge*, 1998

R.M. Meluch, *The Myriad*, 2005
Rob Sanders, *Atlas Infernal*, 2011
Rick Shelley, *Deep Strike*, 2002

1060

CHRIS WRAIGHT

Battle of the Fang

(Nottingham, United Kingdom: Black Library, 2011)

Series: Warhammer 40,000: Space Marine Battles Series. Book 6
Story type: Fantasy; Futuristic
Subject(s): Science fiction; Space exploration; Wars
Major character(s): Harek Ironhelm, Wolf (space)
Time period(s): Indeterminate Future

Summary: *Battle of the Fang*, a futuristic science-fiction novel, is part of the Warhammer 40,000 series from author Chris Wraight. It's been over a millennium since the Horus Heresy, and the Imperium is more powerful than ever. After years of searching, the Space Wolves have tracked down the demonic Magnus the Red hiding in Gangava Prime. As Great Wolf Harek Ironhelm begins to implement plans to attack his ancient foe, the Space Wolves receive word that the Fang on their home planet is under siege from Thousand Sons. The Wolf Lord fights earnestly to hold the attacks off, but he's in desperate need of assistance. One ship remains viable to return Ironhelm to his homeland, but he's not prepared for the utter devastation and chaos that await him.

Other books by the same author:
Sword of Vengeance, 2011
Sword of Justice, 2010
Dark Storm Gathering, 2009
Iron Company, 2009
Masters of Magic, 2008

Other books you might like:
Robert Buettner, *Orphanage*, 2004
Jack Campbell, *The Lost Fleet: Beyond the Frontier: Dreadnaught*, 2011
David Drake, *The Far Side of the Stars*, 2003
Gordon Kendall, *White Wing*, 1985
Gav Thorpe, *Path of the Seer*, 2011

1061

HENRY ZOU

Blood Gorgons

(Nottingham, England: Black Library, 2011)

Series: Warhammer 40,000: Bastion Wars Series. Book 3
Story type: Alternate World; Series
Subject(s): Alternative worlds; Wars; Science fiction
Major character(s): Sargaul, Survivor

Summary: In *Blood Gorgons*, the third book in Henry Zou's Warhammer 40,000: Bastion Wars series, an

epidemic strikes as the Space Marines are summoned to a world used for recruitment. In Haute Bassiq the troops encounter unexpected opposition that kills all but a few of their number. Sargaul has survived, but the challenges he faces in the contaminated world in which he now resides are as great as any enemy. But enemies remain in good supply. They are present in the planet's brutal conditions and among Sargaul's fellow troops. His survival will require strength, resourcefulness, and resolve.

Other books by the same author:
Flesh and Iron, 2010
Emperor's Mercy, 2009

Other books you might like:
Jonathan Green, *Iron Hands*, 2004
Andy Hoare, *Savage Scars*, 2011
Sandy Mitchell, *Innocence Proves Nothing*, 2009
Steve Parker, *Rebel Winter*, 2007
Gav Thorpe, *Angels of Darkness*, 2003

Science Fiction

Series Index

This index alphabetically lists series to which books featured in the entries belong. Beneath each series name, book titles are listed alphabetically with author names and genre codes. The genre codes are as follows: *c* Popular Fiction, *f* Fantasy, *h* Horror, *i* Inspirational, *m* Mystery, *r* Romance, *s* Science Fiction, and *t* Historical. Numbers refer to the entries that feature each title.

Time Period Index

This index chronologically lists the time settings in which the featured books take place. Main headings refer to a century; where no specific time is given, the headings MULTIPLE TIME PERIODS, INDETERMINATE PAST, INDETERMINATE FUTURE, and INDETERMINATE are used. The 15th through 27th centuries are broken down into decades when possible. (Note: 1800s, for example, refers to the first decade of the 19th century.) Featured titles are listed alphabetically beneath time headings, with author names and genre codes. The genre codes are as follows: *c* Popular Fiction, *f* Fantasy, *h* Horror, *i* Inspirational, *m* Mystery, *r* Romance, *s* Science Fiction, and *t* Historical. Numbers refer to the entries that feature each title.

MULTIPLE TIME PERIODS

Anno Frankenstein - Jonathan Green   *s*   1005
Blood of the Reich - William Dietrich   *m*   594
I Married You for Happiness - Lily Tuck   *c*   154

INDETERMINATE PAST

Broken Honour - Robert Earl   *f*   194
Dark Jenny - Alex Bledsoe   *f*   178
Haunting Desire - Erin Quinn   *r*   922
Never Knew Another - J.M. McDermott   *f*   234
Shadow Chaser - Andrew Bromfield   *f*   180
The Soul Mirror - Carol Berg   *f*   175
Vampire in Atlantis - Alyssa Day   *r*   800
Wolfsangel - M.D. Lachlan   *f*   223

1ST CENTURY

The Curse-Maker - Kelli Stanley   *t*   394
The Damascus Way - Janette Oke   *r*   911

3RD CENTURY

Master of Rome - John Stack   *t*   393

5TH CENTURY

A Reluctant Queen - Joan Wolf   *r*   960

8TH CENTURY

The Desert of Souls - Howard Andrew Jones   *t*   337

12TH CENTURY

A Dead Man's Secret - Simon Beaufort   *t*   279
Outlaw - Angus Donald   *t*   300

1190S

The King's Witch - Cecelia Holland   *t*   332

1200s

To Defy a King - Elizabeth Chadwick   *t*   287

13TH CENTURY

Genghis Khan Vol. 1: The World Conqueror - Sam Djang   *t*   298
Genghis Khan Vol. 2: The World Conqueror - Sam Djang   *t*   299

1270s

Falconer and the Death of Kings - Ian Morson   *t*   361

1300s

The Ranger - Monica McCarty   *r*   893

14TH CENTURY

1380s

The Law of Angels - Cassandra Clark   *t*   289

15TH CENTURY

The Dawn Country - Kathleen O'Neal Gear   *t*   367
The Fallen Blade - Jon Courtenay Grimwood   *t*   320
Immortal Champion - Lisa Hendrix   *f*   208
The Midsummer Crown - Kate Sedley   *m*   719
When the Saints - Dave Duncan   *f*   193

1490s

The Borgia Betrayal - Sara Poole   *m*   700

1500s

The Guardian - Margaret Mallory   *r*   889
Lady on the Loch - Betty McInnes   *t*   351
Scales of Retribution - Cora Harrison   *m*   627

16TH CENTURY

Fire the Sky - W. Michael Gear   *t*   312
Henry VIII, Wolfman - A.E. Moorat   *h*   470
The Irish Princess - Karen Harper   *r*   836
Queen of Misfortune - Peter Carroll   *t*   285
To Die For: A Novel of Anne Boleyn - Sandra Byrd   *i*   516
The Tudor Secret - C.W. Gortner   *t*   319

1530s

Blood of the Rose - Kate Pearce   *r*   915

1550s

The Secret History of Elizabeth Tudor, Vampire Slayer - Lucy Weston   *h*   504

1580S

Prophecy - S.J. Parris   *c*   116

1590s

The Scar-Crow Men - Mark Chadbourn   *f*   186

1600s

Untamed Highlander - Donna Grant   *r*   829

17TH CENTURY

Before Versailles - Karleen Koen   *c*   83
An Embarrassment of Riches - Chelsea Quinn Yarbro   *h*   509
The Leaves of Fate - George Robert Minkoff   *t*   357

1630s

1636: The Saxon Uprising - Eric Flint   *t*   310
The Alchemist in the Shadows - Pierre Pevel   *f*   248

1660s

Caleb's Crossing - Geraldine Brooks   *c*   25

1670s

After the Fire - John Pilkington   *t*   372

1680s

Revenants: A Dream of New England - Daniel Mills   *t*   356

1690s

Deliverance from Evil - Frances Hill   *t*   330

18TH CENTURY

Doctor Who: Dead of Winter - James Goss   *s*   1000

2010s

2011

2020s

2030s

2060s

2070s

2080s

22ND CENTURY

2160s

25TH CENTURY

2490s

INDETERMINATE FUTURE

INDETERMINATE

Vigilante - Robin Parrish   *i*   548
Warcry - Elizabeth Vaughan   *r*   948

The Winds of Khalakovo - Bradley
   Beaulieu   *f*   173

*The Zombie Autopsies: Secret Notebooks from the
   Apocalypse* - Steven C. Schlozman   *h*   485

Geographic Index

This index provides access to all featured books by geographic settings—such as countries, continents, oceans, and planets. States and provinces are indicated for the United States and Canada. Also interfiled are headings for fictional place names (Spaceships, Imaginary Planets, etc.). Sections are further broken down by city or the specific name of the imaginary locale. Book titles are listed alphabetically under headings, with author names and genre codes. The genre codes are as follows: *c* Popular Fiction, *f* Fantasy, *h* Horror, *i* Inspirational, *m* Mystery, *r* Romance, *s* Science Fiction, and *t* Historical. Numbers refer to the entries that feature each title.

CZECH REPUBLIC

PRAGUE

Bohemia
An Embarrassment of Riches - Chelsea Quinn
    Yarbro   h   509

EARTH

Dragon Virus - Laura Anne Gilman   s   998
Element Zero - James Knapp   s   1012
The Noise Revealed - Ian Whates   s   1058
Theirs Not to Reason Why: A Soldier's Duty - Jean
    Johnson   s   1009
Truth Engine - James Axler   s   973

EGYPT

Death on Tour - Janice Hamrick   m   624
The Illusion of Murder - Carol McCleary   t   348
The Mistress of Nothing - Kate Pullinger   t   376
Queen of Kings - Maria Dahvana Headley   t   327

ENGLAND

The Admiral's Penniless Bride - Carla
    Kelly   r   861
The American Heiress - Daisy Goodwin   t   316
Among Others - Jo Walton   f   270
The Black Chalice - Steven Savile   f   254
Blood of the Rose - Kate Pearce   r   915
Classic in the Barn - Amy Myers   m   687
Consumed - Kate Cann   h   420
The Curious Case of the Clockwork Man - Mark
    Hodder   f   211
The Curse-Maker - Kelli Stanley   t   394
Dangerous in Diamonds - Madeline
    Hunter   r   843
Darcy and Fitzwilliam - Karen V.
    Wasylowski   r   951
A Dead Man's Secret - Simon Beaufort   t   279
Deadly Reunion - Geraldine Evans   m   604
Death in High Places - Jo Bannister   m   568
Dick Francis' Gamble - Felix Francis   m   609
A Discovery of Witches - Deborah
    Harkness   c   70
Doctor Who: The Way Through the Woods - Una
    McCormack   s   1024
Elizabeth I - Margaret George   t   313
The Girl in the Gatehouse - Julie Klassen   r   865
Henry VIII, Wolfman - A.E. Moorat   h   470
Hotbed - Bill James   m   641
The Illusion of Murder - Carol McCleary   t   348
The Immorality Engine - George Mann   s   1019
The Informant - Thomas Perry   m   696
The Irish Princess - Karen Harper   r   836
The Irresistible Earl - Regina Scott   r   936
Judas Gate - Jack Higgins   c   74
Just Like Heaven - Julia Quinn   r   923
The King's Witch - Cecelia Holland   t   332
Kissing the Demons - Kate Ellis   m   600
The Lady Most Likely - Julia Quinn   t   377
The Law of Angels - Cassandra Clark   t   289
A Little Bit Sinful - Adrienne Basso   r   761
Love Letters - Katie Fforde   c   53
Master of Shadows - Angela Knight   h   458
The Mistress of Nothing - Kate Pullinger   t   376
Mr. Darcy's Secret - Jane Odiwe   r   910
My Dear I Wanted to Tell You - Louisa
    Young   t   412

My Favorite Countess - Vanessa Kelly   r   862
My Irresistible Earl - Gaelen Foley   r   812
Never a Gentleman - Eileen Dreyer   r   805
Nowhere Near Respectable - Mary Jo
    Putney   r   921
One Whisper Away - Emma Wildes   r   959
Outlaw - Angus Donald   t   300
The Perfect Mistress - Victoria Alexander   r   756
Pirate of My Heart - Jamie Carie   i   517
Prophecy - S.J. Parris   c   116
Quicksilver - Amanda Quick   c   124
A Red Herring Without Mustard: A Flavia de Luce
    Mystery - Alan Bradley   t   282
Scandal of the Year - Laura Lee Guhrke   r   833
The Secret History of Costaguana - Juan Gabriel
    Vasquez   t   403
The Secret History of Elizabeth Tudor, Vampire
    Slayer - Lucy Weston   h   504
Sister - Rosamund Lupton   m   673
Staying at Daisy's - Jill Mansell   r   890
Tears Will Not Save Them - Linda Sole   t   390
To Defy a King - Elizabeth Chadwick   t   287
To Desire a Wicked Duke - Nicole Jordan   r   857
To Die For: A Novel of Anne Boleyn - Sandra
    Byrd   i   516
To Tempt a Rake - Cara Elliott   r   809
Treason at Lisson Grove - Anne Perry   t   371
True Soldier Gentlemen - Adrian
    Goldsworthy   t   315
The Tudor Secret - C.W. Gortner   t   319
The Twelfth Enchantment - David Liss   m   668
Uprising - Sean McCabe   h   466
The War That Came Early: The Big Switch - Harry
    Turtledove   c   156
When Passion Rules - Johanna Lindsey   r   878
Wicked Seduction - Jade Lee   r   876
The Woodcutter - Reginald Hill   m   632
World War Two Will Not Take Place - Bill
    James   t   336

Bath
The Penningtons - Pamela Oldfield   t   368
Stagestruck - Peter Lovesey   m   672

Cambridge
A Lesson in Secrets - Jacqueline Winspear   t   410

Cumbria
Island of Bones - Imogen Robertson   t   381

Gatford
Other Kingdoms - Richard Matheson   h   465

Greenwich
There But for The - Ali Smith   c   139

Hampshire
The Dashwood Sisters Tell All - Beth
    Pattillo   r   914

London
Adrenaline - Jeff Abbott   m   559
After the Fire - John Pilkington   t   372
Bloodmoney - David Ignatius   m   639
Carte Blanche - Jeffery Deaver   m   592
The Chaos - Rachel Ward   h   501
Closer - Roderick Gordon   f   202
Cloudy With a Chance of Marriage - Kieran
    Kramer   r   867
The Darkest Sin - Caroline Richards   r   924
An Empty Death - Laura Wilson   t   409
Ghost Light - Joseph O'Connor   t   366
Her Sister's Shadow - Katharine Britton   r   774
The Kings of Eternity - Eric Brown   s   981
Midnight Riot - Ben Aaronovitch   f   167

Millennium People - J.G. Ballard   c   14
Moon Over Soho - Ben Aaronovitch   f   168
Notorious Pleasures - Elizabeth Hoyt   r   842
Oscar Wilde and the Vampire Murders - Gyles
    Brandreth   t   283
Queen of Misfortune - Peter Carroll   t   285
The Seduction of His Wife - Tiffany Clare   r   790
Society's Most Disreputable Gentleman - Julia
    Justiss   r   859
Tigerlily's Orchids - Ruth Rendell   m   706
What I Did For a Duke - Julie Anne Long   r   880
When Tempting a Rogue - Kathryn Smith   r   941
Where Shadows Dance - C.S. Harris   t   324
White Shotgun - April Smith   m   727

Manchester
Beast of Burden - Ray Banks   m   567

Orkney
The Seal King Murders - Alanna Knight   t   341

Oxford
Falconer and the Death of Kings - Ian
    Morson   t   361
The King of Diamonds - Simon Tolkien   t   400

Richmond
A Gentleman of Fortune: Or, the Suspicions of Miss
    Dido Kent - Anna Dean   t   294

Shrewsbury
Frozen Charlotte - Priscilla Masters   m   679

Southampton
Born to Dance - June Tate   t   395

Stoke Horam
Off the Record - Dolores Gordon-Smith   t   318

Surrey
A Bedlam of Bones - Suzette A. Hill   m   633

West Norfolk
Death Toll - Jim Kelly   m   653

West Sussex
Instruments of Darkness - Imogen
    Robertson   t   382

York
Felicity's Gate - Julian Cole   m   586

Yorkshire
Aftermath - Peter Turnbull   c   155
An Unlikely Countess - Jo Beverley   r   764

EUROPE

Follow My Lead - Kate Noble   r   908
Genghis Khan Vol. 2: The World Conqueror - Sam
    Djang   t   299
Immortal Champion - Lisa Hendrix   f   208
Kilroy: The Friendship Behind the Legacy - David
    L. Earls   t   303
One Magic Moment - Lynn Kurland   r   869
The Paris Wife - Paula McLain   t   352
Tom Clancy's EndWar: The Hunted - David
    Michaels   s   1028

Carpathian Mountains
Dark Predator - Christine Feehan   f   198

FICTIONAL LAND

NEPAL

The Kingdom - Clive Cussler   *c*   43

NETHERLANDS

Amsterdam
Adrenaline - Jeff Abbott   *m*   559
The Silent Sister: The Diary of Margot Frank -
  Mazal Alouf-Mizrahi   *t*   277

NEW SEATTLE, FICTIONAL CITY

Blood of the Wicked - Karina Cooper   *r*   792

NEW ZEALAND

Christchurch
Collecting Cooper - Paul Cleave   *m*   583

NORTH AMERICA

Boondocks Fantasy - Jean Rabe   *f*   250
The Pale King - David Foster Wallace   *c*   159
Tom Clancy's EndWar: The Hunted - David
  Michaels   *s*   1028

NORWAY

Bad Intentions - Karin Fossum   *m*   608
The Explorer's Code - Kitty Pilgrim   *m*   697
The House by the Fjord - Rosalind Laker   *t*   342

Oslo
The Snowman - Jo Nesbo   *c*   112

OUTER SPACE

Blind Man's Bluff - Peter David   *s*   989
Enemy Games - Marcella Burnard   *s*   983
Hellhole - Brian Herbert   *s*   1007
The Lost Fleet: Beyond the Frontier: Dreadnaught
  - Jack Campbell   *s*   984
Star Trek: Indistinguishable from Magic - David A.
  McIntee   *s*   1026
Theirs Not to Reason Why: A Soldier's Duty - Jean
  Johnson   *s*   1009
Watching the Clock - Christopher L.
  Bennett   *s*   978

Jupiter
Leviathans of Jupiter - Ben Bova   *s*   979

Phoecia
Up Against It - M.J. Locke   *s*   1018

Solar System
Heaven's Shadow - David S. Goyer   *s*   1002

PAKISTAN

Bloodmoney - David Ignatius   *m*   639
The Valley of Shadows - Mark Terry   *m*   735

PERU

Dark Predator - Christine Feehan   *f*   198

PHILIPPINES

Falling Together - Marisa de los Santos   *c*   45
A Moment in the Sun - John Sayles   *t*   385

PLANET—IMAGINARY

Zara XXIII
Fuzzy Nation - John Scalzi   *s*   1041

POLAND

The Druggist of Auschwitz - Dieter
  Schlesak   *t*   386
The Things We Cherished - Pam Jenoff   *m*   646
The War That Came Early: The Big Switch - Harry
  Turtledove   *c*   156

Warsaw
The Katyn Order - Douglas W. Jacobson   *t*   335
The Warsaw Anagrams - Richard Zimler   *m*   750

PORTUGAL

The Traitor's Emblem - Juan
  Gomez-Jurado   *m*   616
True Soldier Gentlemen - Adrian
  Goldsworthy   *t*   315

PUERTO RICO

Conquistadora - Esmeralda Santiago   *t*   384

ROMAN BRITAIN

The Vestal Vanishes - Rosemary Rowe   *m*   714

ROME

Master of Rome - John Stack   *t*   393

RUSSIA

Deathless - Catherynne M. Valente   *f*   267
The Remembering - Steve Cash   *f*   185
Rogue Oracle - Alayna Williams   *f*   274
Thirteen Years Later - Jasper Kent   *h*   454
The War That Came Early: The Big Switch - Harry
  Turtledove   *c*   156

SCOTLAND

Among the Missing - Morag Joss   *m*   648
Captured by the Highlander - Julianne
  MacLean   *r*   885
The Guardian - Margaret Mallory   *r*   889
Heart of the Home - Gwen Kirkwood   *r*   864
Moon Cursed - Lori Handeland   *h*   445
The Ranger - Monica McCarty   *r*   893
Sweet as the Devil - Susan Johnson   *r*   856
Treasure Me - Robyn DeHart   *r*   802
Untamed Highlander - Donna Grant   *r*   829

Edinburgh
*Dandy Gilver and the Proper Treatment of Blood-
  stains* - Catriona McPherson   *m*   681

Whitebridge
Backlash - Sally Spencer   *m*   729

LOCHLEVEN

Castle Island
Lady on the Loch - Betty McInnes   *t*   351

SERBIA

Novi Sad
Carte Blanche - Jeffery Deaver   *m*   592

SIERRA NEVADA MOUNTAINS

Falls Like Lightning - Shawn Grady   *i*   531

SLOVAKIA

Requiem for a Gypsy - Michael Genelin   *m*   612

SOUTH AFRICA

Dragoons - Garry Kilworth   *t*   340

Cape Town
Carte Blanche - Jeffery Deaver   *m*   592

SPAIN

Conquistadora - Esmeralda Santiago   *t*   384
Murder, Majorcan Style - Roderic Jeffries   *m*   644
Second Son - Jonathan Rabb   *t*   378
Sins of the House of Borgia - Sarah
  Bower   *t*   281
The War That Came Early: The Big Switch - Harry
  Turtledove   *c*   156

Canary Islands
Canary Island Song - Robin Jones Gunn   *i*   532

SWEDEN

Misterioso - Arne Dahl   *m*   591

Maardam
The Inspector and Silence - Hakan
  Nesser   *m*   688

Stockholm
Troubled Man - Henning Mankell   *c*   98

Tumba
The Hypnotist - Lars Kepler   *m*   655

Uppsala
The Hand that Trembles - Kjell Eriksson   *m*   602

SWITZERLAND

Blood of the Reich - William Dietrich   *m*   594
Night School - Mari Mancusi   *h*   463

THAILAND

Killed at the Whim of a Hat - Colin
  Cotterill   *m*   588
Restless Soul - Alex Archer   *f*   169

Bangkok
Trader of Secrets - Steve Martini   *m*   678

TUNIS

Master of Rome - John Stack   *t*   393

TURKEY

Istanbul
An Evil Eye - Jason Goodwin   *t*   317

UNITED ARAB EMIRATES

The Sauvignon Secret - Ellen Crosby   *m*   590

Caerphilly
The Real Macaw: A Meg Langslow Mystery -
Donna Andrews   *m*   563

Charlottesville
Deadly Heat - Cynthia Eden   *r*   808

Crozet
Hiss of Death - Rita Mae Brown   *c*   26

Jamestown
The Leaves of Fate - George Robert
Minkoff   *t*   357

Paradise Island
Deadly Intentions - Candice Poarch   *r*   919

Richmond
The Reservoir - John Milliken Thompson   *t*   397

WASHINGTON
Beg for Mercy - Jami Alden   *r*   754

Auburn
Terror of Living - Urban Waite   *c*   158

Bainbridge Island
The Violets of March - Sarah Jio   *c*   78

New Forest
Night Veil - Yasmine Galenorn   *r*   822

Port Bonita
West of Here - Jonathan Evison   *t*   306

Port George
Night Road - Kristin Hannah   *c*   67

Port McKinney
Comes a Time for Burning - Steven F.
Havill   *t*   326

Puget Sound
Creep - Jennifer Hillier   *m*   634

Seattle
Betrayal of Trust - J.A. Jance   *m*   643
Bound by Darkness - Alexis Morgan   *r*   904
Enemy Waters - Justine Davis   *r*   799
The Gravity Pilot - M.M. Buckner   *s*   982
Hellbent - Cherie Priest   *h*   476
Joy for Beginners - Erica Bauermeister   *c*   17
Police and Thieves - James Patrick Hunt   *m*   637
A Spark of Death - Bernadette Pajer   *m*   692

Spokane
Miles to Go - Richard Paul Evans   *c*   52

Tacoma
Hit List - Laurell K. Hamilton   *h*   444

WISCONSIN
The Art of Fielding - Chad Harbach   *c*   68

Madison
Dark Waters - Alex Prentiss   *h*   475

Milwaukee
Downrigger Drift - James Axler   *s*   967
Turn Up the Heat - Isabel Sharpe   *r*   937

Sorenson
Frozen Stiff - Annelise Ryan   *m*   715

WYOMING
A Little Bit of Passion - Beate Boeker   *r*   766
Saddled and Spurred - Lorelei James   *r*   850

Absaroka County
Hell is Empty - Craig Johnson   *c*   79

Jackson Hole
Deadly Silence - Lindsay McKenna   *r*   897

Purvis
Cowboy Fever - Joanne Kennedy   *r*   863

VENEZUELA

Hush - Cherry Adair   *r*   753
Wolfsbane - Ronie Kendig   *i*   540

VIETNAM

Finding Jack - Gareth Crocker   *c*   41
Who Shot the Water Buffalo? - Ken Babbs   *t*   278

Genre Index

This index lists the books featured as main entries in *What Do I Read Next?* by genre and story type within each genre. Beneath each of the nine genres, the story types appear alphabetically, and titles appear alphabetically under story type headings. The name of the primary author, genre code and the book entry number also appear with each title. The genre codes are as follows: *c* Popular Fiction, *f* Fantasy, *h* Horror, *i* Inspirational, *m* Mystery, *r* Romance, *s* Science Fiction, and *t* Historical. For definitions of the story types, see the "Key to Genre Terms" following the Introduction.

FANTASY FICTION

Adventure

Black Halo - Sam Sykes *f* 260
Central Park Knight - C.J. Henderson *f* 207
God King - Graham McNeill *f* 237
Restless Soul - Alex Archer *f* 169
Sigvald - Darius Hinks *f* 209
Sword of Fire and Sea - Erin Hoffman *f* 212
Sword of Vengeance - Chris Wraight *f* 275
The Twilight of Kerberos: Trials of Trass Kathra - Mike Wild *f* 273

Alternate History

The Alchemist in the Shadows - Pierre Pevel *f* 248
Hidden Cities - Daniel Fox *f* 199
The Scar-Crow Men - Mark Chadbourn *f* 186
When the Saints - Dave Duncan *f* 193

Alternate Universe

The Crippled God - Steven Erikson *f* 196

Alternate World

Caledor - Gav Thorpe *f* 265
The Chaos Crystal - Jennifer Fallon *f* 197
The Cloud Roads - Martha Wells *f* 272
Haven - Joel Shepherd *f* 256
The King of the Crags - Stephen Deas *f* 190
Shadow Chaser - Andrew Bromfield *f* 180
The Shining City - Fiona Patton *f* 247
The Tempering of Men - Sarah Monette *f* 240
The Unremembered - Peter Orullian *f* 245
The Winds of Khalakovo - Bradley Beaulieu *f* 173

Black Magic

Dark Griffin - K.J. Taylor *f* 261
The Griffin's Flight - K.J. Taylor *f* 262
Knights of Bretonnia - Anthony Reynolds *f* 252
Play Dead - John Levitt *f* 229

Collection

After Hours: Tales from the Ur-Bar - Joshua Palmatier *f* 246
Boondocks Fantasy - Jean Rabe *f* 250
Chicks Kick Butt - Kerrie Hughes *f* 214
Dwarfs - Nick Kyme *f* 222
Kitty's Greatest Hits - Carrie Vaughn *f* 268

Coming-of-Age

Among Others - Jo Walton *f* 270

Contemporary

A Hard Day's Knight - Simon R. Green *f* 203
License of Ensorcell - Katharine Kerr *f* 221
Moon Over Soho - Ben Aaronovitch *f* 168

End of the World

The Sea Thy Mistress - Elizabeth Bear *f* 172

Fantasy

Blood Ties - Mari Mancusi *f* 231
Dark Predator - Christine Feehan *f* 198
Midnight Riot - Ben Aaronovitch *f* 167

Futuristic

God's War - Kameron Hurley *f* 217
The Omen Machine - Terry Goodkind *f* 201

Ghost Story

Haunting Violet - Alyxandra Harvey *f* 205

Historical

Broken Honour - Robert Earl *f* 194
Dark Jenny - Alex Bledsoe *f* 178
Deathless - Catherynne M. Valente *f* 267
The Hidden Goddess - M.K. Hobson *f* 210
Of Blood and Honey - Stina Leicht *f* 228
The Remembering - Steve Cash *f* 185
Wolfsangel - M.D. Lachlan *f* 223

Historical - Medieval

Immortal Champion - Lisa Hendrix *f* 208
Never Knew Another - J.M. McDermott *f* 234
The Raven Queen - Jules Watson *f* 271

Horror

Bloodforged - Nathan Long *f* 230

Humor

Serpent's Storm - Amber Benson *f* 174

Legend

The Black Chalice - Steven Savile *f* 254

Magic Conflict

Blackveil - Kristen Britain *f* 179
The Griffin's War - K.J. Taylor *f* 263

Heart of the Exiled

Heart of the Exiled - Pati Nagle *f* 243
House Name - Michelle Sagara *f* 253
Lady-Protector - L.E. Modesitt Jr. *f* 239
Prospero Regained - L. Jagi Lamplighter *f* 225
The Soul Mirror - Carol Berg *f* 175
Spellbound - Blake Charlton *f* 187

Mystery

Dark Jenny - Alex Bledsoe *f* 178
Dead Waters - Anton Strout *f* 259
Late Eclipses - Seanan McGuire *f* 235
Rogue Oracle - Alayna Williams *f* 274
Under Wraps - Hannah Jayne *f* 218

Mystical

Iron Crowned - Richelle Mead *f* 238

Occult

Farlander - Col Buchanan *f* 182

Paranormal

Blackout - Rob Thurman *f* 266
Blood Wyne - Yasmine Galenorn *f* 200

Political

The Plain Man - Steve Englehart *f* 195

Psychic Powers

Night Mares in the Hamptons - Celia Jerome *f* 219

Quest

The Iron Palace - Morgan Howell *f* 213
Of Truth and Beasts - Barb Hendee *f* 206
Out of the Waters - David Drake *f* 192
Shadow's Lure - Jon Sprunk *f* 258

Romance

Immortal Champion - Lisa Hendrix *f* 208
Thistle Down - Irene Radford *f* 251
Vampire Dragon - Annette Blair *f* 177
The Vision - Jen Nadol *f* 242

Romantic Suspense

Moon Burning - Lucy Monroe *f* 241

Science Fantasy

The Scarab Path - Adrian Tchaikovsky *f* 264

427

HORROR FICTION

INSPIRATIONAL FICTION

Genre Index

POPULAR FICTION

Amateur Detective

Coming-of-Age

Contemporary

Contemporary - Fantasy

Family Saga

Fantasy

Future Shock

Ghost Story

Horror

Humor

Literary

POPULAR ROMANCES

Subject Index

This index lists subjects which are covered in the featured titles. Beneath each subject heading, titles are arranged alphabetically with the author names, genre codes, and entry numbers also indicated. The genre codes are as follows: *c* Popular Fiction, *f* Fantasy, *h* Horror, *i* Inspirational, *m* Mystery, *r* Romance, *s* Science Fiction, and *t* Historical.

Subject Index

Ghosts

The Bone Tree - Christopher Fulbright   *h*   434
Death Magic - Eileen Wilks   *h*   506
Death's Disciples - J. Robert King   *h*   456
The Ghost of Greenwich Village - Lorna
   Graham   *c*   61
The Girl Who Would Speak for the Dead - Paul
   Elwork   *t*   305
Grimoire - Phaedra Weldon   *h*   502
A Hard Day's Fright - Casey Daniels   *h*   426
Haunting Violet - Alyxandra Harvey   *f*   205
I'll Never Get Out of This World Alive - Steve
   Earle   *t*   302
The Last Kiss - Red Garnier   *r*   824
The Midnight Gate - Helen Stringer   *h*   495
To Desire a Wicked Duke - Nicole Jordan   *r*   857
An Uninvited Ghost - E.J. Copperman   *h*   425
What the Night Knows - Dean Koontz   *c*   84

Gifted children

Speak No Evil - Marilyn Kaye   *f*   220

God

Messiah - S. Andrew Swann   *s*   1051

Good and evil

The Canary List - Sigmund Brouwer   *i*   514
The Cloud Roads - Martha Wells   *f*   272
Consumed - Kate Cann   *h*   420
Dark Griffin - K.J. Taylor   *f*   261
Dead on Delivery - Eileen Rendahl   *h*   479
The Goblin Corps - Ari Marmell   *f*   232
Messiah - S. Andrew Swann   *s*   1051
The Ridge - Michael Koryta   *c*   85
Shadow's Lure - Jon Sprunk   *f*   258
Star Wars: Knight Errant - John Jackson
   Miller   *s*   1029
Troubletwisters - Garth Nix   *f*   244
Tunnel Vision - Gary Braver   *s*   980
Waking Nightmares - Christopher Golden   *h*   436

Grandmothers

The Chaos - Rachel Ward   *h*   501
How to Woo a Reluctant Lady - Sabrina
   Jeffries   *r*   852

Greek history

Hera's Revenge - Wendy Dingwall   *m*   595
The Taint of Midas - Anne Zouroudi   *m*   751

Greeks

Master of Rome - John Stack   *t*   393

Grief

The Beach Trees - Karen White   *c*   162
Canary Island Song - Robin Jones Gunn   *i*   532
The First Gardener - Denise Hildreth
   Jones   *i*   536
The Girl Who Would Speak for the Dead - Paul
   Elwork   *t*   305
The Grief of Others - Leah Hager Cohen   *c*   37
Heat Wave - Nancy Thayer   *c*   152
The Kid - Sapphire   *c*   132
One Summer - David Baldacci   *c*   13
Outside Wonderland - Lorna Jane Cook   *c*   40
Say Her Name - Francisco Goldman   *c*   59
The Summer We Came to Life - Deborah
   Cloyed   *r*   791
Sweet Misfortune - Kevin Alan Milne   *c*   106

Halloween

The Five Masks of Dr. Screem - R.L.
   Stine   *h*   491

Weirdo Halloween - R.L. Stine   *h*   490

Haunted houses

An Uninvited Ghost - E.J. Copperman   *h*   425

Heaven

Original Sin - Lisa Desrochers   *f*   191

Hell

Damned - Chuck Palahniuk   *c*   114
Original Sin - Lisa Desrochers   *f*   191
Prospero Regained - L. Jagi Lamplighter   *f*   225

Heretics

Falconer and the Death of Kings - Ian
   Morson   *t*   361

High schools

Do You Remember Me Now? - Karen Hanson
   Stuyck   *m*   732
Jack: Secret Vengeance - F. Paul Wilson   *h*   508
Rage - Jackie Morse Kessler   *h*   455
What Happened to Goodbye - Sarah
   Dessen   *c*   48

History

The Admiral's Penniless Bride - Carla
   Kelly   *r*   861
The American Heiress - Daisy Goodwin   *t*   316
Being Polite to Hitler - Robb Forman
   Dew   *t*   297
Big Wheat - Richard Thompson   *t*   398
Bioshock: Rapture - John Shirley   *s*   1042
The Blessed - Ann H. Gabhart   *i*   529
Blood of the Reich - William Dietrich   *m*   594
The Borgia Betrayal - Sara Poole   *m*   700
Born to Dance - June Tate   *t*   395
Broken Honour - Robert Earl   *f*   194
Children and Fire - Ursula Hegi   *t*   328
Comes a Time for Burning - Steven F.
   Havill   *t*   326
Conquistadora - Esmeralda Santiago   *t*   384
The Curious Case of the Clockwork Man - Mark
   Hodder   *f*   211
Deathless - Catherynne M. Valente   *f*   267
Dragoons - Garry Kilworth   *t*   340
Earl of Darkness - Alix Rickloff   *r*   925
Elizabeth I - Margaret George   *t*   313
The Emperor's Body - Peter Brooks   *t*   284
Field Gray - Philip Kerr   *t*   339
*A Gentleman of Fortune: Or, the Suspicions of Miss
   Dido Kent* - Anna Dean   *t*   294
A Good Hard Look - Ann Napolitano   *t*   363
The Illusion of Murder - Carol McCleary   *t*   348
Immortal Champion - Lisa Hendrix   *f*   208
An Invitation to Sin - Jo Beverley   *r*   763
The Irresistible Earl - Regina Scott   *r*   936
The King of Diamonds - Simon Tolkien   *t*   400
The King's Witch - Cecelia Holland   *t*   332
Leaving Van Gogh - Carol Wallace   *t*   405
Lightning - Jean Echenoz   *t*   304
A Little Bit Sinful - Adrienne Basso   *r*   761
Of Truth and Beasts - Barb Hendee   *f*   206
Paper Doll - Janet Woods   *t*   411
Pirate of My Heart - Jamie Carie   *i*   517
The Remembering - Steve Cash   *f*   185
The Reservoir - John Milliken Thompson   *t*   397
The Sandalwood Tree - Elle Newmark   *t*   365
*The Secret History of Elizabeth Tudor, Vampire
   Slayer* - Lucy Weston   *h*   504
This Shared Dream - Kathleen Ann
   Goonan   *s*   999
Tiger Hills - Sarita Mandanna   *t*   343
To Tempt a Rake - Cara Elliott   *r*   809
Where Shadows Dance - C.S. Harris   *t*   324

World War Two Will Not Take Place - Bill
   James   *t*   336

Hobbies

The Knitting Diaries - Debbie Macomber   *r*   887

Hockey

Any Man of Mine - Rachel Gibson   *r*   826

Holocaust, 1933-1945

The Druggist of Auschwitz - Dieter
   Schlesak   *t*   386
The Silent Sister: The Diary of Margot Frank -
   Mazal Alouf-Mizrahi   *t*   277

Home remodeling

If You Were Here - Jen Lancaster   *c*   86

Homeless persons

Heart of Lies - Jill Marie Landis   *r*   872

Homosexuality

The Edge of Grace - Christa Allan   *i*   510
Through the Valley of the Nest of Spiders - Samuel
   R. Delany   *s*   990

Horror

*Attack of the Vampire Weenies: And Other Warped
   and Creepy Tales* - David Lubar   *h*   461
Blood Challenge - Eileen Wilks   *h*   505
Blood Oath - Christopher Farnsworth   *h*   430
Blood Secrets - Jeannie Holmes   *h*   449
Bloodforged - Nathan Long   *f*   230
Chilling Tales: Evil I Did Dwell; Lewd I Did Live -
   Michael Kelly   *h*   453
Claws! - R.L. Stine   *h*   493
The Dark at the End - F. Paul Wilson   *h*   507
Dark Delicacies III: Haunted - Del
   Howison   *h*   451
The Dead Town - Dean Koontz   *h*   459
Element Zero - James Knapp   *s*   1012
An Embarrassment of Riches - Chelsea Quinn
   Yarbro   *h*   509
Etched in Bone - Adrian Phoenix   *h*   474
Eternal Rider - Larissa Ione   *h*   452
Falling Under - Gwen Hayes   *h*   447
The First Days - Rhiannon Frater   *h*   433
The Five Masks of Dr. Screem - R.L.
   Stine   *h*   491
Flip This Zombie - Jesse Petersen   *h*   471
Ghouls, Ghouls, Ghouls - Victoria Laurie   *h*   460
Henry VIII, Wolfman - A.E. Moorat   *h*   470
Hit List - Laurell K. Hamilton   *h*   444
I Don't Want to Kill You - Dan Wells   *h*   503
Jack: Secret Vengeance - F. Paul Wilson   *h*   508
The Knowledge of Good & Evil - Glenn
   Kleier   *h*   457
Moon Cursed - Lori Handeland   *h*   445
Night of the Giant Everything - R.L. Stine   *h*   492
Nightshade - Michelle Rowen   *h*   480
Other Kingdoms - Richard Matheson   *h*   465
The President's Vampire - Christopher
   Farnsworth   *h*   429
The Reluctant Vampire - Lynsay Sands   *r*   933
*The Secret History of Elizabeth Tudor, Vampire
   Slayer* - Lucy Weston   *h*   504
Sin & Ashes - Joseph S. Pulver Sr.   *h*   478
Skin Heat - Ava Gray   *h*   437
Thirteen Years Later - Jasper Kent   *h*   454
Uprising - Sean McCabe   *h*   466
Waking Nightmares - Christopher Golden   *h*   436
Xombies: Apocalypso - Walter Greatshell   *h*   438
Zombiesque - Stephen L. Antczak   *h*   414

Music

Musicians

Mystery

Mystery fiction

Mysticism

Mythology

Napoleonic Wars, 1800-1815

Swimming

Taxation

Teachers

Technology

Teenage parents

Television

Television programs

Terrorism

Theater

Theft

Time

Time travel

Toys

Travel

Trials

Turkish history

Twins

United States

United States Civil War, 1861-1865

United States history

Character Name Index

This index alphabetically lists the major characters in each featured title. Each character name is followed by a description of the character. Citations also provide titles of the books featuring the character, listed alphabetically if there is more than one title; author names and genre codes. The genre codes are as follows: *c* Popular Fiction, *f* Fantasy, *h* Horror, *i* Inspirational, *m* Mystery, *r* Romance, *s* Science Fiction, and *t* Historical. Numbers refer to the entries that feature each title.

A

Abbess Hildegard (Religious)
The Law of Angels - Cassandra Clark   *t*   289

Abbott, Tom (Detective)
Heart of Lies - Jill Marie Landis   *r*   872

Abercrombie, Nathan (5th Grader; Supernatural Being; Spy)
Enter the Zombie - David Lubar   *h*   462

Abernathy, Michael (Writer)
Chihuahua of the Baskervilles - Esri Allbritten   *m*   562

Abigail (Friend)
Enter the Zombie - David Lubar   *h*   462

Acquillo, Sam (Boyfriend; Carpenter; Engineer)
Black Swan - Chris Knopf   *m*   658

Adam (Boyfriend)
Rage - Jackie Morse Kessler   *h*   455

Adam (Computer Expert; Teenager)
Shantorian - Patrick Carman   *s*   985

Adam (Lover; Werewolf)
River Marked - Patricia Briggs   *h*   418

Adam (Nephew)
The Warsaw Anagrams - Richard Zimler   *m*   750

Adam (Psychic; Grandson)
The Chaos - Rachel Ward   *h*   501

Adams, Clay (Military Personnel)
The Final Storm - Jeff Shaara   *t*   389

Adams, Lester (Religious; Spouse)
Say Amen, Again - ReShonda Tate Billingsley   *i*   512

Adams, Maxwell Nathaniel Jr. (Wealthy; Religious)
Hailee - Penny Zeller   *i*   558

Adams, Rachel Jackson (Spouse)
Say Amen, Again - ReShonda Tate Billingsley   *i*   512

Adderley, Laura (Nurse; Psychic)
Wicked Lies - Lisa Jackson   *r*   847

Adolphus, Gustavus (Royalty)
1636: The Saxon Uprising - Eric Flint   *t*   310

Adolphus, Tiber (Exile)
Hellhole - Brian Herbert   *s*   1007

Affenlight, Guert (Administrator; Single Father)
The Art of Fielding - Chad Harbach   *c*   68

Affenlight, Pella (Daughter; Divorced Person)
The Art of Fielding - Chad Harbach   *c*   68

Agre, Geoff (Teenager)
Up Against It - M.J. Locke   *s*   1018

Ahasuerus (Spouse; Royalty)
A Reluctant Queen - Joan Wolf   *r*   960

Ahearn, Marylou (Aged Person)
Revenge of the Radioactive Lady - Elizabeth Stuckey-French   *c*   147

Aidan (Boyfriend)
Born Under a Lucky Moon - Dana Precious   *r*   920

Aidan (Young Man; Survivor)
Ashes, Ashes - Jo Treggiari   *s*   1056

Aimhrea, Kieran (Mythical Creature)
Dark Enchantment - Anya Bast   *f*   171

Ainsley, Adam (Sports Figure; Graduate; Crime Victim)
Deadly Reunion - Geraldine Evans   *m*   604

Al Zaroor, Amer (Terrorist)
Devil's Light - Richard North Patterson   *c*   119

Alcadizzar (Warrior)
Nagash Immortal - Mike Lee   *f*   227

Alderson, Theia (17-Year-Old; Student—High School)
Falling Under - Gwen Hayes   *h*   447

Aldiss, Richard (Professor; Convict)
Dominance - Will Lavender   *m*   662

Aldridge, Faith (Twin)
Going Cowboy Crazy - Katie Lane   *r*   873
Make Mine a Bad Boy - Katie Lane   *r*   874

Alec (Spouse)
Playdate - Thelma Adams   *c*   2

Alessandro (Wealthy; Widow(er))
Dolci di Love - Sarah-Kate Lynch   *r*   882

Alexander (Leader; Historical Figure)
Thirteen Years Later - Jasper Kent   *h*   454

Alexander (Vampire; Boyfriend)
Vampire Kisses 8: Cryptic Cravings - Ellen Schreiber   *h*   486

Alexander, Jessica (Magician)
Play Dead - John Levitt   *f*   229

Alexander, Molly (Writer; Kidnap Victim)
When You Dare - Lori Foster   *r*   813

Alexander, Tess (Scholar)
One Magic Moment - Lynn Kurland   *r*   869

Alexandre (Spouse; Critic)
Crime Fraiche - Alexander Campion   *m*   579

Ali, Jasmina (Widow; Store Owner)
Major Pettigrew's Last Stand - Helen Simonson   *c*   137

Allgood, Molly (Actress; Lover)
Ghost Light - Joseph O'Connor   *t*   366

Alphena (Daughter)
Out of the Waters - David Drake   *f*   192

Altamirano, Jose (Immigrant)
The Secret History of Costaguana - Juan Gabriel Vasquez   *t*   403

Altavilla, Costanza (Widow(er))
Drawing Conclusions - Donna Leon   *c*   92

Altos, Lannan (Vampire)
Night Veil - Yasmine Galenorn   *r*   822

Alvarez, Enrique (Detective)
Murder, Majorcan Style - Roderic Jeffries   *m*   644

Alvord, J. Norman (Aged Person; Engineer)
Dandelion Summer - Lisa Wingate   *i*   555

Alymere (Knight)
The Black Chalice - Steven Savile   *f*   254

Amalya (Supernatural Being; Prostitute)
The Demon and the Succubus - Cassie Ryan   *h*   484

Amanda (Bully; Child; Accident Victim)
Save Me - Lisa Scottoline   *c*   135

Amanda (Friend; Girl)
Claws! - R.L. Stine   *h*   493

Amanda (Neighbor; Crime Victim)
Turn of Mind - Alice LaPlante   *c*   87

Amato, Dante (Organized Crime Figure)
The Camelot Conspiracy - E. Duke Vincent   *t*   404

Amery, Elle (Waiter/Waitress)
Tempted by Trouble - Liz Fielding   *r*   811

Amlingmeyer, Gustav "Old Red" (Detective; Brother)
World's Greatest Sleuth! - Steve Hockensmith   *t*   331

Amlingmeyer, Otto "Big Red" (Brother; Detective)
World's Greatest Sleuth! - Steve Hockensmith   *t*   331

Amos (Child; Friend)
Hide and Secret - Kathleen Fuller   *i*   528

Amy (Spouse; Companion)
Doctor Who: Hunter's Moon - Paul Finch   *s*   996

Amy (Teenager)
The Vampire Stalker - Allison Van Diepen   *h*   498

Anastasia, Albert (Organized Crime Figure; Historical Figure)
The Devil Himself - Eric Dezenhall   *m*   593

Anders, Greville (Hero)
Society's Most Disreputable Gentleman - Julia Justiss   *r*   859

Anderson, Hank (Principal)
The Truth Sleuth - Jacqueline Seewald   *m*   720

Anderson, Laura (Sister; Stepsister)
Miss You Most of All - Elizabeth Bass   *c*   16

B

Barlow, Emily (Widow(er))
Emily and Einstein - Linda Francis Lee   *c*   91

Barr (Werewolf; Laird)
Moon Burning - Lucy Monroe   *f*   241

Barr, Temple (Public Relations; Detective—Amateur)
Cat in a Vegas Gold Vendetta - Carole Nelson Douglas   *m*   598

Barrington, Stone (Detective; Lawyer)
Strategic Moves - Stuart Woods   *c*   166

Barrow, Jake (Journalist)
Blood of the Reich - William Dietrich   *m*   594

Barrows, Zach (Assistant)
Blood Oath - Christopher Farnsworth   *h*   430
The President's Vampire - Christopher Farnsworth   *h*   429

Bartram, Laurence (Veteran; Detective—Amateur)
The Return of Captain John Emmett - Elizabeth Speller   *t*   392

Baskerville, Charlotte (Businesswoman; Spouse; Grandmother)
Chihuahua of the Baskervilles - Esri Allbritten   *m*   562

Basuram (Demon)
Infernal Affairs - Jes Battis   *h*   416

Bateman, Julia (Detective—Private; Crime Victim)
Good to the Last Kiss - Ronald Tierney   *m*   737

Bathsheba (Noblewoman)
My Favorite Countess - Vanessa Kelly   *r*   862

Batten, Lady Hero (Noblewoman)
Notorious Pleasures - Elizabeth Hoyt   *r*   842

Baudelaire, Varik (Vampire; Fiance(e); Detective)
Blood Secrets - Jeannie Holmes   *h*   449

Bay Strangler (Murderer)
Good to the Last Kiss - Ronald Tierney   *m*   737

Bayles, China (Herbalist; Detective—Amateur; Friend; Aunt)
Mourning Gloria - Susan Wittig Albert   *c*   7

Bazemore, Ty (Landlord)
Summer Rental - Mary Kay Andrews   *c*   10

Bea (Daughter)
Classic in the Barn - Amy Myers   *m*   687

Bea (Sister)
Sister - Rosamund Lupton   *m*   673

Bea (Sister; Spouse)
Her Sister's Shadow - Katharine Britton   *r*   774

Beau (5-Year-Old; Son)
The Beach Trees - Karen White   *c*   162

Beaudine, Ted (Fiance(e))
Call Me Irresistible - Susan Elizabeth Phillips   *r*   918

Beauhall, Sarah (Blacksmith; Heroine)
Honeyed Words - J.A. Pitts   *f*   249

Beaumont, Brie (Detective—Police; Sailor)
Danger Sector - Jenifer LeClair   *m*   664

Beaumont, Dixie Ray (Pilot; Military Personnel; Model)
Wings: A Novel of World War II Flygirls - Karl Friedrich   *t*   311

Beaumont, Flora (Cousin)
A Gentleman of Fortune: Or, the Suspicions of Miss Dido Kent - Anna Dean   *t*   294

Beaumont, J.P. (Detective—Private)
Betrayal of Trust - J.A. Jance   *m*   643

Beauvoir (Police Officer)
A Trick of the Light - Louise Penny   *m*   695

Beck, Samuel (Religious; Passenger)
A Most Unsuitable Match - Stephanie Grace Whitson   *i*   554

Becker, Caryn (Widow(er); Single Mother; Sister; Religious)
The Edge of Grace - Christa Allan   *i*   510

Becker, Christoph (Guard)
When Passion Rules - Johanna Lindsey   *r*   878

Beckett, Jo (Doctor)
The Nightmare Thief - Meg Gardiner   *m*   610

Beckman, Olivia (Single Mother; Widow(er); Restaurateur)
Livvie's Song - Sharlene MacLaren   *i*   545

Bedelia, Dolly (Stripper)
Light from a Distant Star - Mary McGarry Morris   *c*   110

Beecher, Madelyn (Friend)
Threading the Needle - Marie Bostwick   *c*   21

Begley, Kate (Matchmaker; Spy; Spouse)
The Matchmaker of Kenmare - Frank Delaney   *t*   295

Belial, Captain (Military Personnel)
The Purging of Kadillus - Gav Thorpe   *s*   1054

Bell, Morgan Tyler (Wealthy)
Jericho Cay - Kathryn R. Wall   *m*   741

Bella (Daughter)
A Good Excuse to Be Bad - Miranda Parker   *m*   693

Bellringer, Reverend (Religious)
Revenants: A Dream of New England - Daniel Mills   *t*   356

Ben (Fiance(e); Spirit; Friend)
The Last Kiss - Red Garnier   *r*   824

Ben (Spouse)
Before I Go To Sleep - S.J. Watson   *m*   743

Benares, Raine (Supernatural Being)
Con & Conjure - Lisa Shearin   *f*   255

Benedict, Eliza (Crime Victim; Spouse; Mother)
I'd Know You Anywhere - Laura Lippman   *c*   93

Benedict, Michael (Police Officer; Boyfriend)
A Crack in Everything - Angela Gerst   *m*   615

Benedict, Stacy (Linguist)
The Vault - Boyd Morrison   *m*   685

Benji (Son)
Butterfly's Child - Angela Davis-Gardner   *t*   293

Bennett, Charlotte (Accountant; Human)
Dark Enchantment - Anya Bast   *f*   171

Bennett, Frankie (Cook)
Burning Down the Spouse - Dakota Cassidy   *r*   786

Benoit, Natalie (Journalist; Lover)
Breaking Point - Pamela Clare   *r*   789

Benson, Grace (Young Woman)
Saving Grace - Carolyn Davidson   *r*   798

Bent, Nealie (Young Woman)
The Bride's House - Sandra Dallas   *t*   292

Benton, Paula (Nurse; Crime Victim)
Hiss of Death - Rita Mae Brown   *c*   26

Bergamot, Jake (Student—High School)
This Beautiful Life - Helen Schulman   *c*   133

Bergen, Liv (Detective—Amateur)
Lot's Return to Sodom - Sandra Brannan   *m*   574

Berglund, Patty (Spouse)
Freedom - Jonathan Franzen   *c*   57

Berglund, Walter (Spouse)
Freedom - Jonathan Franzen   *c*   57

Bermett, John (Businessman; Father; Student)
A Little Bit of Passion - Beate Boeker   *r*   766

Bernadine (Addict)
Getting to Happy - Terry McMillan   *c*   101

Bernard, Kathy (Young Woman)
2030: The Real Story of What Happens To America - Albert Brooks   *c*   24

Bernhardt, Sarah (Historical Figure; Actress; Magician)
The Illusion of Murder - Carol McCleary   *t*   348

Berringer, Jonas (Bodyguard; Blind Person)
Mine Until Morning - Samantha Hunter   *r*   844

Beth (Friend)
Kindred Spirits - Sarah Strohmeyer   *c*   146

Betts (Friend)
The Four Ms. Bradwells - Meg Waite Clayton   *c*   35

Beyard, Francisco (Boyfriend)
The Informationist - Taylor Stevens   *c*   144

Beyle, Henri (Writer)
The Emperor's Body - Peter Brooks   *t*   284

Bigod, Hugh (Spouse)
To Defy a King - Elizabeth Chadwick   *t*   287

Bim the Weirdo (Alien)
Weirdo Halloween - R.L. Stine   *h*   490

Bingham, Theodore (Police Officer)
Secret of the White Rose - Stefanie Pintoff   *t*   373

Bingley, Caroline (Friend)
Mr. Darcy's Secret - Jane Odiwe   *r*   910

Birch, Henry (Cousin)
Beaufort 1849 - Karen Lynn Allen   *t*   276

Birtle-Figgins, Lavinia (Crime Suspect)
A Bedlam of Bones - Suzette A. Hill   *m*   633

Bishop, Alexandra (Agent; Vampire)
The Cross - Sean McCabe   *h*   467

Bishop, Alexandra (Vampire; Agent)
Uprising - Sean McCabe   *h*   466

Bishop, Diana (Historian; Witch)
A Discovery of Witches - Deborah Harkness   *c*   70

Bishop, Lacey (Young Woman; Bride)
The Blessed - Ann H. Gabhart   *i*   529

Bjolf (Viking; Leader)
The Viking Dead - Toby Venables   *h*   499

Black, Eva (Teacher)
The School for Brides - Cheryl Ann Smith   *r*   940

Black, Haden (Classmate)
Falling Under - Gwen Hayes   *h*   447

Black, Janet Delgado (Military Personnel)
The Unincorporated Woman - Dani Kollin   *s*   1014

Black Shell (Leader; Spouse)
Fire the Sky - W. Michael Gear   *t*   312

Blackford, Ian (Enemy)
Original Sin - Beth McMullen   *m*   680

Blackhawk, Jon (FBI Agent)
Merciless - Diana Palmer   *r*   912

Blackmore, John (Doctor)
My Favorite Countess - Vanessa Kelly   *r*   862

Blacknall, Anna (Young Woman)
Duchess of Sin - Laurel McKee   *r*   896

Blackwell, Blackie (Lawman)
Mourning Gloria - Susan Wittig Albert   *c*   7

Blackwood, James (Bodyguard)
Sweet as the Devil - Susan Johnson   *r*   856

Blade, Jeremy (Lover)
Real Vampires Don't Wear Size Six - Gerry Bartlett   *h*   415

Blaine, Navarro (Mythical Creature)
Navarro's Promise - Lora Leigh   *s*   1017

Blake, Anita (Vampire Hunter)
Hit List - Laurell K. Hamilton   *h*   444

Blanchard, Tess (Noblewoman; Spouse)
To Desire a Wicked Duke - Nicole Jordan   *r*   857

Blasingame, Corey (19-Year-Old; Surfer)
The Gentlemen's Hour - Don Winslow   *m*   747

Blevins, Robert (Engineer; Fiance(e); Wealthy)
The Matrimony Plan - Christine Johnson   *i*   539

Bloch, Rachel (Friend)
Louise's War - Sarah R. Shaber   *m*   721

H

Mariah (Frontierswoman)
Bloodlands - Christine Cody   *h*   422

Marie (Daughter)
The Last Rose of Summer - Monte Schulz   *t*   387

Marinelli, Cesca (Vampire; Girlfriend)
Always the Vampire - Nancy Haddock   *h*   442

Marion (Sister; Friend)
Joy for Beginners - Erica Bauermeister   *c*   17

Marjorie (Aunt)
The Talk-Funny Girl - Roland Merullo   *c*   104

Mark (Alien; Human)
Hybrids - Whitley Strieber   *s*   1048

Markham, David (Psychologist)
Millennium People - J.G. Ballard   *c*   14

Markham, Eugenie (Shaman; Royalty)
Iron Crowned - Richelle Mead   *f*   238

Markowitz, Melina (Detective—Amateur; Psychic)
Dead on Delivery - Eileen Rendahl   *h*   479

Markowski, William (Military Personnel; Friend; Artist)
Kilroy: The Friendship Behind the Legacy - David L. Earls   *t*   303

Marlowe, Christopher (Missing Person; Writer; Friend)
The Scar-Crow Men - Mark Chadbourn   *f*   186

Marlowe, Jaid (FBI Agent)
Deadly Sins - Kylie Brant   *r*   773

Marona (Prehistoric Human)
The Land of Painted Caves - Jean M. Auel   *c*   12

Marquis of Mandeville (Fiance(e); Brother)
Notorious Pleasures - Elizabeth Hoyt   *r*   842

Marsh, Irene (Spouse)
Once Upon a Time There Was You - Elizabeth Berg   *c*   19

Marsh, John (Spouse)
Once Upon a Time There Was You - Elizabeth Berg   *c*   19

Marsh, Randall (Spouse)
Her Sister's Shadow - Katharine Britton   *r*   774

Marsh, Sadie (18-Year-Old; Daughter)
Once Upon a Time There Was You - Elizabeth Berg   *c*   19

Marshal, Mahelt (Spouse; Daughter)
To Defy a King - Elizabeth Chadwick   *t*   287

Marshal, William (Knight; Father)
To Defy a King - Elizabeth Chadwick   *t*   287

Marston, Anne (Noblewoman)
The Naked King - Sally MacKenzie   *r*   884

Martha (Retiree; Widow(er))
The Story of Beautiful Girl - Rachel Simon   *c*   136

Martin (Lover)
Save as Draft - Cavanaugh Lee   *c*   90

Martin, Dean (Entertainer)
Fly Me to the Morgue - Robert J. Randisi   *m*   704

Martin, Eliza (Heiress)
Pride and Pleasure - Sylvia Day   *r*   801

Martin, Myra Routledge (Leader)
Home Free - Fern Michaels   *c*   105

Martin, Pepper (Guide)
A Hard Day's Fright - Casey Daniels   *h*   426

Martinez, Morty (Wealthy; Crime Suspect)
Ringer - Brian M. Wiprud   *m*   748

Martini, Jeff (Alien; Fiance(e); Royalty)
Alien in the Family - Gini Koch   *s*   1013

Marx, Sophie (Agent)
Bloodmoney - David Ignatius   *m*   639

Mary (Lawyer; Spouse; Mother)
Girls in White Dresses - Jennifer Close   *c*   36

Mary (Royalty)
The Tudor Secret - C.W. Gortner   *t*   319

Mary (Sister)
Dreams of Joy - Lisa See   *t*   388

Mary (Sister)
The Return of Captain John Emmett - Elizabeth Speller   *t*   392

Mary Kay (Friend)
Kindred Spirits - Sarah Strohmeyer   *c*   146

Mason (Agent)
Play Dead - John Levitt   *f*   229

Mason (Military Personnel; Rescuer)
Nightfall - Ellen Connor   *h*   424

Mason, Gavin (Wealthy)
The Billionaire Gets His Way - Elizabeth Bevarly   *r*   762

Mast, Sarah (Midwife)
Sarah's Gift - Marta Perry   *r*   917

Masters, Giles (Rake)
How to Woo a Reluctant Lady - Sabrina Jeffries   *r*   852

Masterson, Harper (Hairdresser; Rancher; Lover)
Saddled and Spurred - Lorelei James   *r*   850

Matinova, Jana (Investigator)
Requiem for a Gypsy - Michael Genelin   *m*   612

Matlock, Kelly (Cook)
Harvest Moon - Robyn Carr   *r*   784

Matre, Rachel (Cook; Businesswoman; Detective—Amateur)
Dark Waters - Alex Prentiss   *h*   475

Matthews, Grant (Student—Graduate)
The Breath of God - Jeffrey Small   *m*   726

Mattiola, Caterina (Detective—Police)
The Fatal Touch - Conor Fitzgerald   *m*   606

Maureen (Daughter; Assistant)
Remember Ben Clayton - Stephen Harrigan   *t*   323

Max (FBI Agent)
Crossroads - Jeanne C. Stein   *h*   489

Max (Spouse)
Dead by Midnight - Carolyn G. Hart   *c*   72

Maxie (Spirit)
An Uninvited Ghost - E.J. Copperman   *h*   425

May (15-Year-Old; Supernatural Being)
May - Kathryn Lasky   *f*   226

Mayfield, Bethia (Young Woman)
Caleb's Crossing - Geraldine Brooks   *c*   25

Mayhall, Stony (Supernatural Being)
Raising Stony Mayhall - Daryl Gregory   *h*   439

Mayhall, Wanda (Mother)
Raising Stony Mayhall - Daryl Gregory   *h*   439

McArthur, Ava (Sister; Spouse)
A Good Excuse to Be Bad - Miranda Parker   *m*   693

McArthur, Bishop Devon (Spouse)
A Good Excuse to Be Bad - Miranda Parker   *m*   693

McBride, Bronte (Vampire; Lover)
Vampire Dragon - Annette Blair   *f*   177

McBride, Zach (Lawman; Lover)
Breaking Point - Pamela Clare   *r*   789

McCabe, Norah (Immigrant; Activist; Activist; Businesswoman)
Norah: The Making of an Irish-American Woman in 19th Century New York - Cynthia G. Neale   *t*   364

McCall, Nick (FBI Agent)
A Lot Like Love - Julie James   *r*   849

McCall, Tricia (Manager)
Creed's Honor - Linda Lael Miller   *r*   901

McCarthy, Ben (Spy)
The Matchmaker of Kenmare - Frank Delaney   *t*   295

McCarty, Mick (Pilot; Alcoholic)
Pacific Glory - P.T. Deutermann   *t*   296

McClellan, Mickey (Detective—Police; Colleague)
Good to the Last Kiss - Ronald Tierney   *m*   737

McClure, Jack (Political Figure)
Blood Trust - Eric Van Lustbader   *c*   95

McConnell, Dags (Psychic)
Grimoire - Phaedra Weldon   *h*   502

McCord, Sterling (Boyfriend)
White Shotgun - April Smith   *m*   727

McDonald, Rayne (Vampire; Student; Sister)
Night School - Mari Mancusi   *h*   463

McDonald, Rayne (Vampire; Teenager; Sister)
Blood Ties - Mari Mancusi   *f*   231

McDonald, Sunny (Vampire; Student; Sister)
Night School - Mari Mancusi   *h*   463

McDonald, Sunny (Vampire; Teenager; Sister)
Blood Ties - Mari Mancusi   *f*   231

McElroy, Sean (Young Man)
Tempted by Trouble - Liz Fielding   *r*   811

McEvoy, Lincoln (Bouncer; Boyfriend)
Plugged - Eoin Colfer   *c*   38

McGann, Shelia (Sister)
Faith - Jennifer Haigh   *c*   64

McGarvey, Kirk (Agent)
Abyss - David Hagberg   *s*   1006

McGary, Mattie (Journalist)
The Parsifal Pursuit - Michael McMenamin   *t*   353

McGee, Sheila (Beauty Pageant Contestant)
The Linen Queen - Patricia Falvey   *t*   307

McGill, Pete (Military Personnel)
The War That Came Early: The Big Switch - Harry Turtledove   *c*   156

McGuire, Nate (Detective—Police)
Deadly Dreams - Kylie Brant   *r*   772

McHenry, Ross (Actor)
The Brink of Fame - Irene Fleming   *t*   309

McKendrick, Robert (Rescuer)
Death in High Places - Jo Bannister   *m*   568

McKenna, Rose (Mother; Volunteer)
Save Me - Lisa Scottoline   *c*   135

McKenzie, Rushmore "Mac" (Detective)
Highway 61 - David Housewright   *m*   635

McKnight, Alex (Detective)
Misery Bay - Steve Hamilton   *c*   66

McKnight, Riley (Police Officer)
Blackberry Summer - RaeAnne Thayne   *r*   944

McLinn, Cassius (Military Personnel)
The Colonel's Lady - Laura Frantz   *i*   527

McNeil, Izzy (Lawyer; Detective)
Claim of Innocence - Laura Caldwell   *r*   782

McReynolds, Markham (Client)
Mystery - Jonathan Kellerman   *c*   81

McTeer, Conlan (Businessman)
Duchess of Sin - Laurel McKee   *r*   896

Meade, Grace (Prostitute)
Backlash - Sally Spencer   *m*   729

Meadows, Kate (Detective—Police)
Backlash - Sally Spencer   *m*   729

Meadows, Loni (Crime Victim)
A Murder in Tuscany - Christobel Kent   *m*   654

Meeks, Gabriel (Religious)
The Matrimony Plan - Christine Johnson   *i*   539

Meg (Sister; Twin)
Weirdo Halloween - R.L. Stine   *h*   490

Mehcredi (Assassin)
The Lone Warrior - Denise Rossetti   *r*   929

Mei-Mei (Spouse; Mother)
Daughters of the Revolution - Carolyn Cooke   *t*   290

Character Name Index

Character Name Index

Watson, Victoria (Classmate)
Deadly Reunion - Geraldine Evans   *m*   604

Watts, Jubie (Sister; 13-Year-Old; Girl)
The Dry Grass of August - Anna Jean
Mayhew   *t*   347

Watts, Mrs. "Mama" (Mother)
The Dry Grass of August - Anna Jean
Mayhew   *t*   347

Weal, Nicodemus (Apprentice; Wizard)
Spellbound - Blake Charlton   *f*   187

Weber, Angela (Psychologist; Fiance(e))
The Knowledge of Good & Evil - Glenn
Kleier   *h*   457

Weezy (Friend)
Jack: Secret Vengeance - F. Paul Wilson   *h*   508

Weiland, Samantha (Friend)
The Summer We Came to Life - Deborah
Cloyed   *r*   791

Weiss, Adam (Spouse; Lover)
The Brink of Fame - Irene Fleming   *t*   309

Weiss, Emily Daggett (Director;
Detective—Amateur; Spouse)
The Brink of Fame - Irene Fleming   *t*   309

Weiss, Nate (Police Officer)
Hollywood Hills - Joseph Wambaugh   *c*   160

Weldon, Eve (Writer)
The Ghost of Greenwich Village - Lorna
Graham   *c*   61

Wen, Ping (Assistant)
Hidden Cities - Daniel Fox   *f*   199

Wesson, Gabe (Widow(er); Wealthy; Business-
man; Single Father)
The Nanny's Homecoming - Linda
Goodnight   *i*   530

West, Celia (Accountant)
After the Golden Age - Carrie Vaughn   *f*   269

Westerman, Harriet (Friend; Noblewoman;
Detective—Amateur)
Instruments of Darkness - Imogen
Robertson   *t*   382

Westerman, Harriet (Noblewoman;
Detective—Amateur; Friend)
Island of Bones - Imogen Robertson   *t*   381

Westmore, Elle (Single Mother; Pilot)
Falls Like Lightning - Shawn Grady   *i*   531

Westmoreland, Jason (Young Man)
The Proposal - Brenda Jackson   *r*   846

Whaley (Sister)
The Watery Part of the World - Michael
Parker   *t*   370

Whitaker, Clay (Cowboy/Cowgirl)
Cowboy Up - Vicki Lewis Thompson   *r*   946

White, Alex (18-Year-Old; Veteran)
Other Kingdoms - Richard Matheson   *h*   465

White, Jennifer (Doctor; Crime Suspect)
Turn of Mind - Alice LaPlante   *c*   87

White, Oliver (Artist)
The Devil's Puzzle - Clare O'Donohue   *m*   689

White, Peter (Friend)
Deliverance from Evil - Frances Hill   *t*   330

White, Priscilla (Young Woman; Religious)
The Doctor's Lady - Jody Hedlund   *i*   535

Whitescarver, Bronwyn (Doctor)
SEALed Forever - Mary Margaret
Daughtridge   *r*   797

Whiteson, Melvin (Spouse; Friend; Wealthy)
A Good Hard Look - Ann Napolitano   *t*   363

Whitman, Judith (Editor; Spouse; Lover)
To Be Sung Underwater - Tom McNeal   *c*   102

Whitman, Malcolm (Spouse)
To Be Sung Underwater - Tom McNeal   *c*   102

Whittaker, Ruby Jane (Friend)
County Line - Bill Cameron   *m*   578

Who, Doctor (Time Traveler)
The Crimson Hand - Dan McDaid   *s*   1025

Wickham, Mickey (Friend)
The Most Dangerous Thing - Laura
Lippman   *c*   94

Wickland, Nigel (Art Dealer)
Hollywood Hills - Joseph Wambaugh   *c*   160

Wiebe, Hershel "Smiley" (Criminal)
Your Friendly Neighborhood Criminal - Michael
Van Rooy   *m*   740

Wilcox, Ruby (Friend)
Mourning Gloria - Susan Wittig Albert   *c*   7

Wilcox, Simone (Accountant; Thief)
The Choir Director - Carl Weber   *r*   955

Wild, Hunter (Student; Teenager; Hunter)
Out for Blood - Alyxandra Harvey   *f*   204

Wilde, Oscar (Writer; Detective—Amateur)
Oscar Wilde and the Vampire Murders - Gyles
Brandreth   *t*   283

Wildow, Nolan (Detective—Police)
Death Amid Gems - Meagan J. Meehan   *m*   682

Wilkes, Amelia (Girlfriend)
Exposure - Therese Fowler   *c*   55

Wilkins, Cyrus (Musician; Crime Victim)
Moon Over Soho - Ben Aaronovitch   *f*   168

Will (Friend)
Summer in the South - Cathy Holton   *c*   76

Will (Spouse)
Original Sin - Beth McMullen   *m*   680

Will (Teenager; Son)
Closer - Roderick Gordon   *f*   202

Will (Writer; Friend)
Falling Together - Marisa de los Santos   *c*   45

Willa (Stepsister)
My One and Only - Kristan Higgins   *r*   840

Williams, Amy (Spouse; Time Traveler; Compan-
ion)
Doctor Who: The Way Through the Woods - Una
McCormack   *s*   1024

Williams, Cole (Police Officer; Boyfriend)
Beg for Mercy - Jami Alden   *r*   754

Williams, Germaine (Businessman)
Man Enough for Me - Rhonda Bowen   *r*   769

Williams, Guy (Companion)
Classic in the Barn - Amy Myers   *m*   687

Williams, Hamish (Military Personnel)
True Soldier Gentlemen - Adrian
Goldsworthy   *t*   315

Williams, Hank (Musician; Spirit)
I'll Never Get Out of This World Alive - Steve
Earle   *t*   302

Williams, Jeremiah (Gardener)
The First Gardener - Denise Hildreth
Jones   *i*   536

Williams, Larry (Political Figure)
The Devil's Puzzle - Clare O'Donohue   *m*   689

Williams, Lincoln "Linc" (FBI Agent)
Wicked Pleasures - Tori Carrington   *r*   785

Williams, Rory (Spouse; Time Traveler; Compan-
ion)
Doctor Who: The Way Through the Woods - Una
McCormack   *s*   1024

Williams, Slippery (Criminal; Drug Dealer; Murderer; Client)
Jersey Law - Ron Liebman   *m*   667

Williams, Steven (Professor)
Sweet Little Lies - Michele Grant   *r*   830

Willie (Farmer; Crime Suspect; Brother)
The Reservoir - John Milliken Thompson   *t*   397

Willing, Felicity (Businesswoman; Femme Fatale)
Carte Blanche - Jeffery Deaver   *m*   592

Willing, Vic (Lawyer; Uncle)
Claire DeWitt and the City of the Dead - Sara
Gran   *m*   618

Willis, Hope (Judge; Mother)
The Girl Who Disappeared Twice - Andrea
Kane   *m*   650

Willis, Sam (Computer Expert)
One Dog Night - David Rosenfelt   *m*   712

Willoughby, Violet (Teenager; Friend; Psychic)
Haunting Violet - Alyxandra Harvey   *f*   205

Wilson, Emily (Writer; Niece)
The Violets of March - Sarah Jio   *c*   78

Wilson, T.K. (Religious)
The Choir Director - Carl Weber   *r*   955

Wimsey, Lord Peter (Detective—Private; Spouse)
The Attenbury Emeralds - Jill Paton Walsh   *t*   406

Windmill Man (Murderer)
Big Wheat - Richard Thompson   *t*   398

Lady Wingate (Godmother)
To Desire a Wicked Duke - Nicole Jordan   *r*   857

Wingate, Annabel (Spouse; Mother)
You're Next - Gregg Hurwitz   *m*   638

Wingate, Katherine (Daughter; 8-Year-Old)
You're Next - Gregg Hurwitz   *m*   638

Wingate, Mike (Designer; Father; Spouse; Orphan)
You're Next - Gregg Hurwitz   *m*   638

Winsted, Carley (Widow(er); Mother)
Heat Wave - Nancy Thayer   *c*   152

Winsted, Cisco (12-Year-Old; Daughter)
Heat Wave - Nancy Thayer   *c*   152

Winsted, Margaret (Daughter; 5-Year-Old)
Heat Wave - Nancy Thayer   *c*   152

Winston, Mattie (Doctor)
Frozen Stiff - Annelise Ryan   *m*   715

Winston-Beaufort, Brianna "Bree" (Lawyer)
Angel's Verdict - Mary Stanton   *m*   730

Winter, Anthony (Boyfriend)
Exposure - Therese Fowler   *c*   55

Winters, Carly "Desiree" (Young Woman)
Bad Girl by Night - Lacey Alexander   *r*   755

Winters, Hank (Friend; Accident Victim)
Back of Beyond - C.J. Box   *m*   573

Winterset, Julia (Noblewoman; Widow(er))
The Perfect Mistress - Victoria Alexander   *r*   756

Wolfe, Ethan (Student—Graduate)
Creep - Jennifer Hillier   *m*   634

Wolfe, Winston (Writer; Client)
Jericho Cay - Kathryn R. Wall   *m*   741

Woodbridge, Kate (Scientist; Granddaughter)
To Tempt a Rake - Cara Elliott   *r*   809

Woodrow (Fisherman)
The Watery Part of the World - Michael
Parker   *t*   370

Woodrow, Daniel (Nobleman)
The Heiress - Lynsay Sands   *r*   934

Woodruff, Diana (Daughter; Doctor)
Fly Away Home - Jennifer Weiner   *c*   161

Woodruff, Lizzie (Daughter; Addict)
Fly Away Home - Jennifer Weiner   *c*   161

Woodruff, Richard (Political Figure)
Fly Away Home - Jennifer Weiner   *c*   161

Woodruff, Sylvie (Spouse)
Fly Away Home - Jennifer Weiner   *c*   161

Woodruff, Tess (Store Owner; Friend)
Threading the Needle - Marie Bostwick   *c*   21

Woods, Casey (Detective—Private; Leader)
The Girl Who Disappeared Twice - Andrea
Kane   *m*   650

Woolcott, Rowena (Young Woman; Crime Victim)
The Darkest Sin - Caroline Richards   *r*   924

Wragge, Jane (Artist; Crime Victim; Lover)
Felicity's Gate - Julian Cole   *m*   586

Wrass (Son; Captive)
The Dawn Country - Kathleen O'Neal
   Gear   *t*   367

Wren (Spouse)
Playdate - Thelma Adams   *c*   2

Wroth, Krysty (Warrior)
Downrigger Drift - James Axler   *s*   967

Wyatt, Meg (Friend; Neighbor)
To Die For: A Novel of Anne Boleyn - Sandra
   Byrd   *i*   516

Wyeth, Mildred (Survivor; Doctor)
Tainted Cascade - James Axler   *s*   971

Wyler, Terrence (Crime Victim)
The Guilty Plea - Robert Rotenberg   *m*   713

Wyman, Sarah (Researcher)
Tunnel Vision - Gary Braver   *s*   980

Y

Yager, Abigail (Adoptee)
Retribution - Sherrilyn Kenyon   *c*   82

Yardley, Lady Julia (Noblewoman; Divorced Person)
Scandal of the Year - Laura Lee Guhrke   *r*   833

Yashim (Detective)
An Evil Eye - Jason Goodwin   *t*   317

Yeager, Lacey (Art Dealer)
An Object of Beauty - Steve Martin   *c*   100

Yellich (Detective—Police)
Aftermath - Peter Turnbull   *c*   155

Yelverton, Piers (Nobleman)
When Beauty Tamed the Beast - Eloisa
   James   *r*   848

Yim (Slave; Mother)
The Iron Palace - Morgan Howell   *f*   213

Yoder, Katy (Religious)
Something Old - Dianne L Christner   *i*   520

Yoshida, Eric (Spouse)
Dry as Rain - Gina Holmes   *i*   537

Yoshida, Kyra (Spouse; Amnesiac)
Dry as Rain - Gina Holmes   *i*   537

Youlgrave, Prudence (Young Woman)
An Unlikely Countess - Jo Beverley   *r*   764

Younger, Stratham (Doctor; Veteran)
The Death Instinct - Jed Rubenfeld   *t*   383

Yu, Lily (FBI Agent; Fiance(e))
Blood Challenge - Eileen Wilks   *h*   505

Death Magic - Eileen Wilks   *h*   506

Z

Z.G. (Father; Artist)
Dreams of Joy - Lisa See   *t*   388

Zafir (Royalty)
The King of the Crags - Stephen Deas   *f*   190

Zanella, Izzy (Spouse)
Breaking the Rules - Suzanne Brockmann   *r*   775

Zeddicus (Wizard)
The Omen Machine - Terry Goodkind   *f*   201

Zenoni, Angelo (Detective—Police)
Death Amid Gems - Meagan J. Meehan   *m*   682

Zezen, Zianno (Aged Person)
The Remembering - Steve Cash   *f*   185

Ziele, Simon (Detective)
Secret of the White Rose - Stefanie Pintoff   *t*   373

Zinc, David (Lawyer)
The Litigators - John Grisham   *m*   619

Zook, Simon (Carpenter)
Love Finds You in Lancaster County, Pennsylvania
   - Annalisa Daughety   *i*   523

Character Description Index

This index alphabetically lists descriptions of the major characters in featured titles. The descriptions may be occupations (police officer, lawyer, etc.) or may describe persona (amnesiac, runaway, teenager, etc.). For each description, character names are listed alphabetically. Also provided are book titles, author names, genre codes and entry numbers. The genre codes are as follows: *c* Popular Fiction, *f* Fantasy, *h* Horror, *i* Inspirational, *m* Mystery, *r* Romance, *s* Science Fiction, and *t* Historical

10-YEAR-OLD

Anderson, Peter
The Five Masks of Dr. Screem - R.L. Stine   *h*   491

Melissa
An Uninvited Ghost - E.J. Copperman   *h*   425

Top
The Rock Hole - Reavis Z. Wortham   *m*   749

11-YEAR-OLD

Anthony, Roz
Promises to Keep - Ann Tatlock   *c*   151

Caitlin
Mourning Gloria - Susan Wittig Albert   *c*   7

de Luce, Flavia
A Red Herring Without Mustard: A Flavia de Luce Mystery - Alan Bradley   *t*   282

Lake, Swan
The Homecoming of Samuel Lake - Jenny Wingfield   *c*   165

Maria
Doctor Who: Dead of Winter - James Goss   *s*   1000

Sweeney, Steven
Night of the Giant Everything - R.L. Stine   *h*   492

12-YEAR-OLD

Anderson, Monica
The Five Masks of Dr. Screem - R.L. Stine   *h*   491

Chapman, Linnet
No Less in Blood - D. M. Pirrone   *t*   374

David
Fire World - Chris D'Lacey   *f*   188

Piper, Jaimie
The Canary List - Sigmund Brouwer   *i*   514

Rosanna
Fire World - Chris D'Lacey   *f*   188

Winsted, Cisco
Heat Wave - Nancy Thayer   *c*   152

13-YEAR-OLD

Jimmie
The Killer is Dying - James Sallis   *m*   717

Peck, Nellie
Light from a Distant Star - Mary McGarry Morris   *c*   110

Stewart, Emily
The Girl Who Would Speak for the Dead - Paul Elwork   *t*   305

Stewart, Michael
The Girl Who Would Speak for the Dead - Paul Elwork   *t*   305

Watts, Jubie
The Dry Grass of August - Anna Jean Mayhew   *t*   347

15-YEAR-OLD

Graves, Willow
Darkness, My Old Friend - Lisa Unger   *c*   157

Konstatin
Wunderkind - Nikolai Grozni   *t*   321

May
May - Kathryn Lasky   *f*   226

16-YEAR-OLD

Bob
Dreams of the Dead - Perri O'Shaughnessy   *m*   690

Decter, Caitlyn
WWW: Wonder - Robert J. Sawyer   *s*   1040

Grey, Lady Jane
Queen of Misfortune - Peter Carroll   *t*   285

Keffy-Horn, Jude
Ten Thousand Saints - Eleanor Henderson   *c*   73

Lucy
Ashes, Ashes - Jo Treggiari   *s*   1056

Peters, Rayne
Consumed - Kate Cann   *h*   420

Portman, Jacob
Miss Peregrine's Home for Peculiar Children - Ransom Riggs   *c*   128

Salerno, Epiphany
Dandelion Summer - Lisa Wingate   *i*   555

17-YEAR-OLD

Alderson, Theia
Falling Under - Gwen Hayes   *h*   447

Calhoun, Hassie
Hassie Calhoun - Cory Pamela   *t*   369

Froan
The Iron Palace - Morgan Howell   *f*   213

Gabriel, Mina
The Fallen Angel - David Hewson   *t*   329

Marcus, Alexa
Buried Secrets - Joseph Finder   *m*   605

Small, Robyn
Last Days of Ptolemy Grey - Walter Mosley   *c*   111

SWEET, McLEAN

Sweet, McLean
What Happened to Goodbye - Sarah Dessen   *c*   48

18-YEAR-OLD

Burton, Bonny
Born to Dance - June Tate   *t*   395

Caton, Grace
Minding Ben - Victoria Brown   *c*   27

Cubillas, Ana Larragoity
Conquistadora - Esmeralda Santiago   *t*   384

Marsh, Sadie
Once Upon a Time There Was You - Elizabeth Berg   *c*   19

Muir, Felice
Birds of Paradise - Diana Abu-Jaber   *c*   1

White, Alex
Other Kingdoms - Richard Matheson   *h*   465

19-YEAR-OLD

Annigan, Hailee
Hailee - Penny Zeller   *i*   558

Blasingame, Corey
The Gentlemen's Hour - Don Winslow   *m*   747

20-YEAR-OLD

Stanton, Sarah
The Falling Machine - Andrew Mayer   *s*   1023

21-YEAR-OLD

Apte, Charulata
Miss Timmins' School for Girls - Nayana Currimbhoy   *c*   42

Cochran, Mike
Who Shot the Water Buffalo? - Ken Babbs   *t*   278

Huckelbee, Tom
Who Shot the Water Buffalo? - Ken Babbs   *t*   278

Reiniger, Autumn
The Nightmare Thief - Meg Gardiner   *m*   610

3-YEAR-OLD

Burns, Jeremy
The Pack - Jason Starr   *h*   488

Fraser, Cam
Shadowed in Silk - Christine Lindsay   *i*   544

Princess Desiree
Naamah's Blessing - Jacqueline Carey   *f*   184

Theo
Original Sin - Beth McMullen   *m*   680

5-YEAR-OLD

Augusta
Falling Together - Marisa de los Santos   c   45

Beau
The Beach Trees - Karen White   c   162

Krissy
The Girl Who Disappeared Twice - Andrea Kane   m   650

St. John, Matt
A Creed in Stone Creek - Linda Lael Miller   r   902

Winsted, Margaret
Heat Wave - Nancy Thayer   c   152

5TH GRADER

Abercrombie, Nathan
Enter the Zombie - David Lubar   h   462

6-YEAR-OLD

Sitturd, Lloyd
Enigmatic Pilot - Kris Saknussemm   s   1038

7-YEAR-OLD

Harley, Ian
44 Charles Street - Danielle Steel   c   143

Hosiah
Children of the Street - Kwei Quartey   m   703

8-YEAR-OLD

Wingate, Katherine
You're Next - Gregg Hurwitz   m   638

8TH GRADER

Daisy
This Beautiful Life - Helen Schulman   c   133

9-YEAR-OLD

Edelstein, Rose
Particular Sadness of Lemon Cake - Aimee Bender   c   18

Jones, Abdul
The Kid - Sapphire   c   132

Tessier, Jonathan
Death Toll - Jim Kelly   m   653

ABANDONED CHILD

Jimmie
The Killer is Dying - James Sallis   m   717

ABUSE VICTIM

Fraser, Abby
Shadowed in Silk - Christine Lindsay   i   544

Malloy, Emma
A Heart Revealed - Julie Lessman   i   543

Richards, Marjorie
The Talk-Funny Girl - Roland Merullo   c   104

Scott, Maggie
Enemy Waters - Justine Davis   r   799

ACCIDENT VICTIM

Amanda
Save Me - Lisa Scottoline   c   135

Aura
Say Her Name - Francisco Goldman   c   59

Halloran, Gordon
The Most Dangerous Thing - Laura Lippman   c   94

Kashian, Zach
Tunnel Vision - Gary Braver   s   980

Patrick
Death in High Places - Jo Bannister   m   568

Winters, Hank
Back of Beyond - C.J. Box   m   573

ACCOUNTANT

Bennett, Charlotte
Dark Enchantment - Anya Bast   f   171

Keane, Bobby
The Hat - Babette Hughes   t   333

West, Celia
After the Golden Age - Carrie Vaughn   f   269

Wilcox, Simone
The Choir Director - Carl Weber   r   955

ACTIVIST

Blue Duck, Marie
Your Friendly Neighborhood Criminal - Michael Van Rooy   m   740

Druce, Peggy
The War That Came Early: The Big Switch - Harry Turtledove   c   156

McCabe, Norah
Norah: The Making of an Irish-American Woman in 19th Century New York - Cynthia G. Neale   t   364
Norah: The Making of an Irish-American Woman in 19th Century New York - Cynthia G. Neale   t   364

Quirk, Karina
The Astral - Kate Christensen   c   34

ACTOR

Falcon, Noah
Playing for Keeps - LuAnn McLane   r   898

McHenry, Ross
The Brink of Fame - Irene Fleming   t   309

Nelson, Jumbo
Sixkill - Robert B. Parker   c   115

ACTRESS

Allgood, Molly
Ghost Light - Joseph O'Connor   t   366

Ashleigh, Savannah
Cat in a Vegas Gold Vendetta - Carole Nelson Douglas   m   598

Bernhardt, Sarah
The Illusion of Murder - Carol McCleary   t   348

Brand, Betsy
After the Fire - John Pilkington   t   372

Coville, Justine
Angel's Verdict - Mary Stanton   m   730

Evans, Kami
Scent of Persuasion - Nikki Duncan   r   806

Francis, Mallory
Pampered to Death - Laura Levine   m   665

Gelert, Agnes
The Brink of Fame - Irene Fleming   t   309

Imani
Tales from the Yoga Studio - Rain Mitchell   r   903

Lane
Fun and Games - Duane Swierczynski   m   733

Lawson, Olivia
Playing for Keeps - LuAnn McLane   r   898

Minolta, Katharina
She's the One - J.J. Murray   r   905

Scroggs, Hope
Going Cowboy Crazy - Katie Lane   r   873
Make Mine a Bad Boy - Katie Lane   r   874

Squires, Tilly
Started Early, Took My Dog - Kate Atkinson   c   11

Stenen, Alice
Outside Wonderland - Lorna Jane Cook   c   40

ADDICT

Bernadine
Getting to Happy - Terry McMillan   c   101

Ebersole, Doc
I'll Never Get Out of This World Alive - Steve Earle   t   302

Galloway, Noah
One Dog Night - David Rosenfelt   m   712

Katherine
Tales from the Yoga Studio - Rain Mitchell   r   903

Newbury, Maurice
The Immorality Engine - George Mann   s   1019

The Warden
Low Town - Daniel Polansky   m   698

Woodruff, Lizzie
Fly Away Home - Jennifer Weiner   c   161

ADMINISTRATOR

Affenlight, Guert
The Art of Fielding - Chad Harbach   c   68

Kershaw, Tom
Backlash - Sally Spencer   m   729

Lawson, Sophie
Under Wraps - Hannah Jayne   f   218

ADOPTEE

Connolly, Rachel
No Less in Blood - D. M. Pirrone   t   374

Slade, Maria
Blood Stains - Sharon Sala   r   932

St. John, Matt
A Creed in Stone Creek - Linda Lael Miller   r   902

Yager, Abigail
Retribution - Sherrilyn Kenyon   c   82

ADVENTURER

Cannon, Kane
Ruthless Game - Christine Feehan   h   431

Creed, Annja
Restless Soul - Alex Archer   f   169

Gilliland, Julia
Out of Control - Mary Connealy   i   521

Lenk
Black Halo - Sam Sykes   f   260

Malloy, Mick
A Courtesan's Guide to Getting Your Man - Celeste Bradley   r   771

Patterson, Rose
Ruthless Game - Christine Feehan   h   431

Sinclair, John
The Explorer's Code - Kitty Pilgrim   m   697

Stapleton, Cordelia
The Explorer's Code - Kitty Pilgrim   m   697

ADVERTISING

Christoffersen, Alan
Miles to Go - Richard Paul Evans   c   52

ADVISOR

Foxton, Nicholas "Foxy"
Dick Francis' Gamble - Felix Francis   m   609

Kovak, Herb
Dick Francis' Gamble - Felix Francis   m   609

Kranis, Denise
Stone Arabia - Dana Spiotta   *c*   142

AGED PERSON

Ahearn, Marylou
Revenge of the Radioactive Lady - Elizabeth
   Stuckey-French   *c*   147

Alvord, J. Norman
Dandelion Summer - Lisa Wingate   *i*   555

Arbutus
South of Superior - Ellen Airgood   *c*   6

Coville, Justine
Angel's Verdict - Mary Stanton   *m*   730

Gladys
South of Superior - Ellen Airgood   *c*   6

Grey, Ptolemy
Last Days of Ptolemy Grey - Walter
   Mosley   *c*   111

Honeycutt, Matilda
The Christmas Shoppe - Melody Carlson   *i*   518

Jacobson, Paul
Senior Moments are Murder - Mike
   Befeler   *m*   569

Monroe, Tillie
Promises to Keep - Ann Tatlock   *c*   151

Sedgewick, Alice
Frozen Charlotte - Priscilla Masters   *m*   679

Zezen, Zianno
The Remembering - Steve Cash   *f*   185

AGENT

Antsyforov, Viktoria
Tom Clancy's EndWar: The Hunted - David
   Michaels   *s*   1028

Bishop, Alexandra
The Cross - Sean McCabe   *h*   467
Uprising - Sean McCabe   *h*   466

Brooke, Henry
Rebellion - James McGee   *t*   350

Burton, Richard Francis
The Curious Case of the Clockwork Man - Mark
   Hodder   *f*   211

Callahan, Bernadette
The Paradise Prophecy - Robert Browne   *m*   575

Canderous, Simon
Dead Waters - Anton Strout   *f*   259

Capra, Sam
Adrenaline - Jeff Abbott   *m*   559

Chandler, Brooke
Devil's Light - Richard North Patterson   *c*   119

Corte
The Edge - Jeffery Deaver   *c*   46

Cotton, Peter
Washington Shadow - Aly Monroe   *t*   358

Crawford, Angel
A Good Excuse to Be Bad - Miranda
   Parker   *m*   693

D'Artigo, Menolly
Blood Wyne - Yasmine Galenorn   *f*   200

Dillon, Sean
Judas Gate - Jack Higgins   *c*   74

Dooley, Ronan
Amortals - Matt Forbeck   *s*   997

Dulmur
Watching the Clock - Christopher L.
   Bennett   *s*   978

Eleanora
Love Letters - Katie Fforde   *c*   53

Garrett, Dakota
Damaged - Debra Webb   *r*   954

Gray
In the Air Tonight - Stephanie Tyler   *r*   947

Griffin, William
Blood Oath - Christopher Farnsworth   *h*   430

Hamilton, Dodge
Strangers When We Meet - Merline
   Lovelace   *r*   881

Hawkwood, Matthew
Rebellion - James McGee   *t*   350

LaDuca, Alexandra
Hostage in Havana - Noel Hynd   *r*   845

Lang, Colton
Face of Danger - Roxanne St. Claire   *r*   943

Lennox, Jordan
My Irresistible Earl - Gaelen Foley   *r*   812

Leyton, Jim
The Noise Revealed - Ian Whates   *s*   1058

Li, Harry
Rogue Oracle - Alayna Williams   *f*   274

Lu, Tian
Central Park Knight - C.J. Henderson   *f*   207

Lucsly
Watching the Clock - Christopher L.
   Bennett   *s*   978

Malone, Lucky
Damaged - Debra Webb   *r*   954

Marx, Sophie
Bloodmoney - David Ignatius   *m*   639

Mason
Play Dead - John Levitt   *f*   229

McGarvey, Kirk
Abyss - David Hagberg   *s*   1006

Mount, Marcus
World War Two Will Not Take Place - Bill
   James   *t*   336

Nathan, Ari
License of Ensorcell - Katharine Kerr   *f*   221

Newbury, Maurice
The Immorality Engine - George Mann   *s*   1019

O'Grady, Nola
License of Ensorcell - Katharine Kerr   *f*   221

Reece, Linc
Broken - Debra Webb   *r*   953

Royce, Marc
Lion of Babylon - Davis Bunn   *i*   515

Scott, Caleb
In the Air Tonight - Stephanie Tyler   *r*   947

Severin, Julie
Red Heat - Nina Bruhns   *r*   777

Stamp, Johnson
Blood Rules - Christine Cody   *h*   423

Stevens, Mace
In the Air Tonight - Stephanie Tyler   *r*   947

Stillwater, Derek
The Valley of Shadows - Mark Terry   *m*   735

Taylor, Rocco
Deadly Games - Cate Noble   *r*   907

ALCOHOLIC

Carolina
Liquid Smoke - Jeff Shelby   *m*   724

Ginny
Ghosts of War: A Tale of the Ghost - George
   Mann   *s*   1020

Hoyt, Cody
Back of Beyond - C.J. Box   *m*   573

Lang, Lars
A Game of Lies - Rebecca Cantrell   *m*   580

McCarty, Mick
Pacific Glory - P.T. Deutermann   *t*   296

Noel
Minding Frankie - Maeve Binchy   *c*   20

Sparhawk, Dermot
The Charlestown Connection - Tom
   MacDonald   *m*   675

ALIEN

Bim the Weirdo
Weirdo Halloween - R.L. Stine   *h*   490

Doctor
Doctor Who: Hunter's Moon - Paul Finch   *s*   996
Doctor Who: The Way Through the Woods - Una
   McCormack   *s*   1024

Gina
Hybrids - Whitley Strieber   *s*   1048

Mark
Hybrids - Whitley Strieber   *s*   1048

Martini, Jeff
Alien in the Family - Gini Koch   *s*   1013

AMNESIAC

Christine
Before I Go To Sleep - S.J. Watson   *m*   743

Gardner, Sharon
Death's Disciples - J. Robert King   *h*   456

Hayes, Daniel
The Two Deaths of Daniel Hayes - Marcus
   Sakey   *m*   716

Love, Alice
What Alice Forgot - Liane Moriarty   *c*   109

Yoshida, Kyra
Dry as Rain - Gina Holmes   *i*   537

ANDROID

Mikiko
Robopocalypse - Daniel H. Wilson   *c*   164

ANGEL

Chandler, Remy
A Hundred Words for Hate - Thomas E.
   Sniegoski   *h*   487

Deveraux, Elena
Archangel's Consort - Nalini Singh   *f*   257

Gabe
Original Sin - Lisa Desrochers   *f*   191

Muire
The Sea Thy Mistress - Elizabeth Bear   *f*   172

Raphael
Archangel's Consort - Nalini Singh   *f*   257

Rho, Lara
Forgotten Sea - Virginia Kantra   *r*   860

ANIMAL LOVER

Clark, Audrey
The Ridge - Michael Koryta   *c*   85

Malachi
Vampire Instinct - Joey W. Hill   *h*   448

ANIMAL TRAINER

Bower, Mace
Mama Sees Stars - Deborah Sharp   *m*   723

ANTHROPOLOGIST

Brennan, Temperance "Tempe"
Flash and Bones - Kathy Reichs   *c*   125
Spider Bones - Kathy Reichs   *c*   126

ANTIQUES DEALER

Gallagher, Sara
Never Knowing - Chevy Stevens   *m*   731

Rebecca
How to Moon a Cat - Rebecca M. Hale   *m*   623

APPRENTICE

Grant, Peter
Moon Over Soho - Ben Aaronovitch   *f*   168

Nico
Farlander - Col Buchanan   *f*   182

Weal, Nicodemus
Spellbound - Blake Charlton   *f*   187

ARCHAEOLOGIST

Dr. Burrows
Closer - Roderick Gordon   *f*   202

Creed, Annja
Restless Soul - Alex Archer   *f*   169

Fox, Oliver
Glass Demon - Helen Grant   *c*   62

Gilliland, Julia
Out of Control - Mary Connealy   *i*   521

Knight, Piers
Central Park Knight - C.J. Henderson   *f*   207

Sinclair, John
The Explorer's Code - Kitty Pilgrim   *m*   697

ARCHITECT

Bradshaw, Amelia
A Race to Splendor - Ciji Ware   *t*   407

Dirk, J.C.
Restless in Carolina - Tamara Leigh   *i*   541

Morgan, Julia
A Race to Splendor - Ciji Ware   *t*   407

ART DEALER

Humphrey, Alice
Long Gone - Alafair Burke   *m*   576

Thayer, Francesca
44 Charles Street - Danielle Steel   *c*   143

Wickland, Nigel
Hollywood Hills - Joseph Wambaugh   *c*   160

Yeager, Lacey
An Object of Beauty - Steve Martin   *c*   100

ART HISTORIAN

Khan, Miraj "Kalakar"
The Valley of Shadows - Mark Terry   *m*   735

Merritt, Lucy
Darkness at Dawn - Elizabeth Jennings   *m*   645

ARTIFICIAL INTELLIGENCE

Archos
Robopocalypse - Daniel H. Wilson   *c*   164

Oshi
Scratch Monkey - Charles Stross   *s*   1050

ARTIST

Dar
Silver Boat - Luanne Rice   *c*   127

de la Santisima, Jose Diego Santiago
Stealing Mona Lisa - Carson Morton   *m*   686

Gallier, Mira
Watch Me Die - Erica Spindler   *c*   141

Gilheaney, Francis "Gil"
Remember Ben Clayton - Stephen Harrigan   *t*   323

Goodell, Lee
Rodin's Debutante - Ward Just   *t*   338

Hallaway, Emma
The Seduction of His Wife - Tiffany Clare   *r*   790

Jones, Abdul
The Kid - Sapphire   *c*   132

Kauffman, Sarah
Fall From Pride - Karen Harper   *m*   625

Markowski, William
Kilroy: The Friendship Behind the Legacy - David
  L. Earls   *t*   303

Morrow, Clara
A Trick of the Light - Louise Penny   *m*   695

Niles, Lilli
Her Sister's Shadow - Katharine Britton   *r*   774

Nina
I Married You for Happiness - Lily Tuck   *c*   154

Poe, Riley
Everdark - Elle Jasper   *r*   851

Ridler, Sheridan
The Opposite of Art - Athol Dickson   *i*   525

Sasha
A Visit from the Goon Squad - Jennifer
  Egan   *c*   50

Tussaud, Marie
*Madame Tussaud: A Novel of the French Revolu-
  tion* - Michelle Moran   *t*   359

van Gogh, Vincent
Leaving Van Gogh - Carol Wallace   *t*   405

White, Oliver
The Devil's Puzzle - Clare O'Donohue   *m*   689

Wragge, Jane
Felicity's Gate - Julian Cole   *m*   586

Z.G.
Dreams of Joy - Lisa See   *t*   388

ASSASSIN

Ash
Farlander - Col Buchanan   *f*   182

Caim
Shadow's Lure - Jon Sprunk   *f*   258

Christian
The Killer is Dying - James Sallis   *m*   717

Mehcredi
The Lone Warrior - Denise Rossetti   *r*   929

Nico
Farlander - Col Buchanan   *f*   182

Schaeffer, Michael "The Butcher's Boy"
The Informant - Thomas Perry   *m*   696

Taltos, Vlad
Tiassa - Steven Brust   *f*   181

ASSISTANT

Barrows, Zach
Blood Oath - Christopher Farnsworth   *h*   430
The President's Vampire - Christopher
  Farnsworth   *h*   429

Cade, Nathaniel
Blood Oath - Christopher Farnsworth   *h*   430
The President's Vampire - Christopher
  Farnsworth   *h*   429

Dasalia, Faye
Element Zero - James Knapp   *s*   1012

DeMarco, Joe
House Divided - Mike Lawson   *m*   663

Eastman, Jonah
The Devil Himself - Eric Dezenhall   *m*   593

Gerard, Terry
Jericho Cay - Kathryn R. Wall   *m*   741

Guinan
Star Trek: Indistinguishable from Magic - David A.
  McIntee   *s*   1026

Hobbes, Veronica
The Immorality Engine - George Mann   *s*   1019

Lawrence, Derek
Dead by Morning - Beverly Barton   *r*   760

Maureen
Remember Ben Clayton - Stephen Harrigan   *t*   323

Miller, Aaron
Sarah's Gift - Marta Perry   *r*   917

Noble, Zeke
Skin Heat - Ava Gray   *h*   437

Perry, Joceline
Merciless - Diana Palmer   *r*   912

Sarah
Murder in the 11th House - Mitchell Scott
  Lewis   *m*   666

Shaw, Chrissy
A Bad Day for Scandal - Sophie
  Littlefield   *m*   669

Sinclair, David
A Death In Summer - Benjamin Black   *m*   571

Stephanson, Jack
The Mountains Bow Down - Sibella
  Giorello   *r*   827

Swinburne, Algernon
The Curious Case of the Clockwork Man - Mark
  Hodder   *f*   211

Valdez, Isabella
In Too Deep - Jane Anne Krentz   *r*   868

Wen, Ping
Hidden Cities - Daniel Fox   *f*   199

ASTROLOGER

Dee, John
Prophecy - S.J. Parris   *c*   116

Lowell, David
Murder in the 11th House - Mitchell Scott
  Lewis   *m*   666

AUNT

Aunt Bee
The Violets of March - Sarah Jio   *c*   78

Bayles, China
Mourning Gloria - Susan Wittig Albert   *c*   7

Harmon, Charlotte
The Mountains Bow Down - Sibella
  Giorello   *r*   827

Julia
The Durham Deception - Philip Gooden   *m*   617

Lang, Eva
Night Road - Kristin Hannah   *c*   67

Marjorie
The Talk-Funny Girl - Roland Merullo   *c*   104

Violet
Cat in a Vegas Gold Vendetta - Carole Nelson
  Douglas   *m*   598

BABY

Davie
The Dry Grass of August - Anna Jean
  Mayhew   *t*   347

Frankie
Minding Frankie - Maeve Binchy   *c*   20

Jonayla
The Land of Painted Caves - Jean M. Auel   *c*   12

Sarah
Steal the Show - Thomas Kaufman   *m*   651

BABYSITTER

Rose
In Search of the Rose Notes - Emily
  Arsenault   *m*   564

BANKER

Anselma, Amanda
Black Swan - Chris Knopf   *m*   658

BARTENDER

Colbert, Johnny
Murder in the 11th House - Mitchell Scott
    Lewis   *m*   666

Rafferty, Shadwell
The Magic Bullet - Larry Millett   *t*   355

Truneau, Nora
The Long-Shining Waters - Danielle Sosin   *t*   391

BASEBALL PLAYER

Dunne, Owen
The Art of Fielding - Chad Harbach   *c*   68

Falcon, Noah
Playing for Keeps - LuAnn McLane   *r*   898

Sam
Northwest Corner - John Burnham
    Schwartz   *c*   134

Schwartz, Mike
The Art of Fielding - Chad Harbach   *c*   68

Skrimshander, Henry
The Art of Fielding - Chad Harbach   *c*   68

BASTARD SON

Liam
Of Blood and Honey - Stina Leicht   *f*   228

BEAUTY PAGEANT CONTESTANT

Brand, Jodi
Cowboy Fever - Joanne Kennedy   *r*   863

McGee, Sheila
The Linen Queen - Patricia Falvey   *t*   307

Taylor
Beauty Queens - Libba Bray   *c*   23

BEEKEEPER

Kaloyeros, Gabrilis
The Taint of Midas - Anne Zouroudi   *m*   751

BLACKSMITH

Beauhall, Sarah
Honeyed Words - J.A. Pitts   *f*   249

BLIND PERSON

Berringer, Jonas
Mine Until Morning - Samantha Hunter   *r*   844

Decter, Caitlyn
WWW: Wonder - Robert J. Sawyer   *s*   1040

Stott, Ian
Bloodshot - Cherie Priest   *h*   477
Hellbent - Cherie Priest   *h*   476

BOARDER

Tucker, Charlotte
Keep a Little Secret - Dorothy Garlock   *r*   823

BODYGUARD

Andy
Murder in the 11th House - Mitchell Scott
    Lewis   *m*   666

Berringer, Jonas
Mine Until Morning - Samantha Hunter   *r*   844

Blackwood, James
Sweet as the Devil - Susan Johnson   *r*   856

Gideon, Sloane
Living on the Edge - Shannon K. Butcher   *r*   781

Graves, Celia
Demon Song - Cat Adams   *h*   413

Griffin, Scotty
The Moon Maze Game - Larry Niven   *s*   1030

Malone, Connor
Sweet Possession - Maya Banks   *r*   759

Sixkill, Zebulon
Sixkill - Robert B. Parker   *c*   115

BOOTLEGGER

Gold, Ben
The Hat - Babette Hughes   *t*   333

BOUNCER

McEvoy, Lincoln
Plugged - Eoin Colfer   *c*   38

BOUNTY HUNTER

Bond, Jasper
Pride and Pleasure - Sylvia Day   *r*   801

King, Marc
Get Lucky - Lorie O'Clare   *r*   909

Loving, Henry
The Edge - Jeffery Deaver   *c*   46

Montana, Reese
Storm Kissed - Jessica Andersen   *r*   757

Nyx
God's War - Kameron Hurley   *f*   217

Plum, Stephanie
Smokin' Seventeen - Janet Evanovich   *c*   51

BOXER

O'Halleran, Mickey
Born to Dance - June Tate   *t*   395

BOY

Bobby
The Bone Tree - Christopher Fulbright   *h*   434

Devanna
Tiger Hills - Sarita Mandanna   *t*   343

Han
Hidden Cities - Daniel Fox   *f*   199

Kevin
The Bone Tree - Christopher Fulbright   *h*   434

Mickey
Claws! - R.L. Stine   *h*   493

Peck, Henry
Light from a Distant Star - Mary McGarry
    Morris   *c*   110

Plecker, Tom
The Bone Tree - Christopher Fulbright   *h*   434

Ru
Infernal Affairs - Jes Battis   *h*   416

Rudd
May - Kathryn Lasky   *f*   226

BOYFRIEND

Acquillo, Sam
Black Swan - Chris Knopf   *m*   658

Adam
Rage - Jackie Morse Kessler   *h*   455

Aidan
Born Under a Lucky Moon - Dana
    Precious   *r*   920

Alexander
Vampire Kisses 8: Cryptic Cravings - Ellen
    Schreiber   *h*   486

Benedict, Michael
A Crack in Everything - Angela Gerst   *m*   615

Beyard, Francisco
The Informationist - Taylor Stevens   *c*   144

Boucher, Seth
Revolution World - Katy Stauber   *s*   1045

Byler, Jake
Something Old - Dianne L Christner   *i*   520

Carlos
Mama Sees Stars - Deborah Sharp   *m*   723

Carter
The Last Kiss - Red Garnier   *r*   824

Cole, Dawson
The Best of Me - Nicholas Sparks   *c*   140

Contrata, Jake
Hassie Calhoun - Cory Pamela   *t*   369

Dutch
Vision Impossible - Victoria Laurie   *m*   661

Emerson
Then He Kissed Me - Christie Ridgway   *r*   926

Garret
Sweet Misfortune - Kevin Alan Milne   *c*   106

Haskell, Morgan
Through the Valley of the Nest of Spiders - Samuel
    R. Delany   *s*   990

Holyfield, Judd
Blood Ties - Sharon Sala   *r*   931

Jeffers, Eric
Through the Valley of the Nest of Spiders - Samuel
    R. Delany   *s*   990

Johnston, Scotty
The Twisted Thread - Charlotte Bacon   *m*   566

Kiyo
Iron Crowned - Richelle Mead   *f*   238

Lawson, Nate
Always Something There to Remind Me - Beth
    Harbison   *c*   69

Lovette, Cale
Flash and Bones - Kathy Reichs   *c*   125

McCord, Sterling
White Shotgun - April Smith   *m*   727

McEvoy, Lincoln
Plugged - Eoin Colfer   *c*   38

Morelli, Joe
Smokin' Seventeen - Janet Evanovich   *c*   51

O'Malley, Cooper
Gone with a Handsomer Man - Michael Lee
    West   *r*   956

Pete
County Line - Bill Cameron   *m*   578

Peter
Save as Draft - Cavanaugh Lee   *c*   90

Ron
Once Upon a Time There Was You - Elizabeth
    Berg   *c*   19

Russell, John
Potsdam Station - David Downing   *t*   301

Saber, Deke
Always the Vampire - Nancy Haddock   *h*   442

Sitka, Orr
The Gravity Pilot - M.M. Buckner   *s*   982

Spencer, Bryan
Canary Island Song - Robin Jones Gunn   *i*   532

Stone, Derek
Murder Under Cover - Kate Carlisle   *m*   581

Theo
Claim of Innocence - Laura Caldwell   *r*   782

Williams, Cole
Beg for Mercy - Jami Alden   *r*   754

Winter, Anthony
Exposure - Therese Fowler *c* 55

BRIDE

Bishop, Lacey
The Blessed - Ann H. Gabhart *i* 529

Fontaine, Lily
Something Old, Something New - Beverly Jenkins *r* 853

Morevna, Marya
Deathless - Catherynne M. Valente *f* 267

BRIDEGROOM

July, Trent
Something Old, Something New - Beverly Jenkins *r* 853

BROTHER

Amlingmeyer, Gustav "Old Red"
World's Greatest Sleuth! - Steve Hockensmith *t* 331

Amlingmeyer, Otto "Big Red"
World's Greatest Sleuth! - Steve Hockensmith *t* 331

Anderson, Peter
The Five Masks of Dr. Screem - R.L. Stine *h* 491

Ares
Red Mortal - Deidre Knight *r* 866

Borgia, Cesare
Sins of the House of Borgia - Sarah Bower *t* 281

Bridger, Dan
Police and Thieves - James Patrick Hunt *m* 637

Brounian, Fred
Luminarium - Alex Shakar *m* 722

Brounian, George
Luminarium - Alex Shakar *m* 722

Chris
Weirdo Halloween - R.L. Stine *h* 490

Coleman, Asa
The Gin & Chowder Club - Nan Parson Rossiter *c* 130

Coleman, Isaac
The Gin & Chowder Club - Nan Parson Rossiter *c* 130

David
The Edge of Grace - Christa Allan *i* 510

Davie
The Dry Grass of August - Anna Jean Mayhew *t* 347

de Bremont, Etienne
Death at the Chateau Bremont - M. L. Longworth *m* 671

de Bremont, Francois
Death at the Chateau Bremont - M. L. Longworth *m* 671

Dunne, Hugh
The Lady Most Likely - Julia Quinn *t* 377

Eden
Breaking the Rules - Suzanne Brockmann *r* 775

Erlich, Charlie
Eyes Wide Open - Andrew Gross *m* 620

Eversea, Ian
What I Did For a Duke - Julie Anne Long *r* 880

Feileg
Wolfsangel - M.D. Lachlan *f* 223

Fey, Axel
Black Swan - Chris Knopf *m* 658

Gillman, Ben
Breaking the Rules - Suzanne Brockmann *r* 775

Gillman, Danny
Breaking the Rules - Suzanne Brockmann *r* 775

Gilmore, Lachlan
Lady on the Loch - Betty McInnes *t* 351

Gletts
Honeyed Words - J.A. Pitts *f* 249

Gray
In the Air Tonight - Stephanie Tyler *r* 947

Grayson, Jeffrey
In the Air Tonight - Stephanie Tyler *r* 947

Griffin "Stenen"
Outside Wonderland - Lorna Jane Cook *c* 40

Isolfr
The Tempering of Men - Sarah Monette *f* 240

Korsak, Stefan
Basilisk - Rob Thurman *s* 1055

Kranis, Nik
Stone Arabia - Dana Spiotta *c* 142

Leandros, Niko
Blackout - Rob Thurman *f* 266

Lenayin, Damon
Haven - Joel Shepherd *f* 256

Liman
A Bad Day for Scandal - Sophie Littlefield *m* 669

Magnus, Wulfgang
When the Saints - Dave Duncan *f* 193

Mahdian, Alex
Close Your Eyes - Amanda Eyre Ward *m* 742

Marquis of Mandeville
Notorious Pleasures - Elizabeth Hoyt *r* 842

Michael
Iron House - John Hart *m* 628

Mitchell, Don
Broken - Patricia Haley *i* 533

Mitchell, Joel
Broken - Patricia Haley *i* 533

Muir, Stanley
Birds of Paradise - Diana Abu-Jaber *c* 1

Parini, Jacques "Jack"
Then He Kissed Me - Christie Ridgway *r* 926

Peck, Henry
Light from a Distant Star - Mary McGarry Morris *c* 110

Ransome, William
Ransome's Quest - Kaye Dacus *i* 522

Remmington, Griffin "Lord of Reading"
Notorious Pleasures - Elizabeth Hoyt *r* 842

Rob
The Real Macaw: A Meg Langslow Mystery - Donna Andrews *m* 563

Rounder, Rick
Felicity's Gate - Julian Cole *m* 586

Rounder, Sam
Felicity's Gate - Julian Cole *m* 586

Roxy
Then He Kissed Me - Christie Ridgway *r* 926

Rutter, Jack
Hideout - Kathleen George *m* 613

Rutter, Ryan
Hideout - Kathleen George *m* 613

Ryan
The Year We Left Home - Jean Thompson *c* 153

Ryrie, Paul
The Grief of Others - Leah Hager Cohen *c* 37

Seth
Police and Thieves - James Patrick Hunt *m* 637

Stark, Gideon
Hush - Cherry Adair *r* 753

Stark, Zakary "Zak"
Hush - Cherry Adair *r* 753

Toby
Silver Girl - Elin Hilderbrand *c* 75

Tommie
The Reservoir - John Milliken Thompson *t* 397

Vali
Wolfsangel - M.D. Lachlan *f* 223

Watson, Freddie
The Winter Ghosts - Kate Mosse *t* 362

Watson, George
The Winter Ghosts - Kate Mosse *t* 362

Willie
The Reservoir - John Milliken Thompson *t* 397

BULLIED CHILD

Melly
Save Me - Lisa Scottoline *c* 135

BULLY

Amanda
Save Me - Lisa Scottoline *c* 135

Rodney
Enter the Zombie - David Lubar *h* 462

BUSINESSMAN

Bermett, John
A Little Bit of Passion - Beate Boeker *r* 766

Bogan, Oto
Requiem for a Gypsy - Michael Genelin *m* 612

Burbank, Richard
The Informationist - Taylor Stevens *c* 144

Colby, Jack
Classic in the Barn - Amy Myers *m* 687

David
Flip This Zombie - Jesse Petersen *h* 471

Hydt, Severan
Carte Blanche - Jeffery Deaver *m* 592

Jewell, Richard
A Death In Summer - Benjamin Black *m* 571

Kazanow, Howie
The Brink of Fame - Irene Fleming *t* 309

LaJoy, Dave
When the Killing's Done - T.C. Boyle *i* 513

Lee-Trafford, Martin
Paper Doll - Janet Woods *t* 411

Marcus, Marshall
Buried Secrets - Joseph Finder *m* 605

McTeer, Conlan
Duchess of Sin - Laurel McKee *r* 896

Miller, Latham
Paper Doll - Janet Woods *t* 411

Mitchell, Don
Broken - Patricia Haley *i* 533

Mitchell, Joel
Broken - Patricia Haley *i* 533

Otterbourne, Charles
Off the Record - Dolores Gordon-Smith *t* 318

Raines, Gabriel
Against the Fire - Kat Martin *r* 891

Ryan, Andrew
Bioshock: Rapture - John Shirley *s* 1042

Tai, Lee Sing
Bless the Bride - Rhys Bowen *t* 280

Vladimirovich Krasnov, Dmitri "Dima"
Our Kind of Traitor - John Le Carre *c* 89

Williams, Guy
Classic in the Barn - Amy Myers   *m* 687

Williams, Rory
Doctor Who: The Way Through the Woods - Una McCormack   *s* 1024

COMPUTER

Gemelli, Rush
Steal the Show - Thomas Kaufman   *m* 651

Primus, Morgan
Blind Man's Bluff - Peter David   *s* 989

COMPUTER EXPERT

Adam
Shantorian - Patrick Carman   *s* 985

Emily
Shantorian - Patrick Carman   *s* 985

Finn
Shantorian - Patrick Carman   *s* 985

Lewis
Shantorian - Patrick Carman   *s* 985

Lurker
Robopocalypse - Daniel H. Wilson   *c* 164

Mort
Murder in the 11th House - Mitchell Scott Lewis   *m* 666

Neil
The Stranger You Seek - Amanda Kyle Williams   *m* 746

O'Neill, Lincoln
Attachments - Rainbow Rowell   *r* 930

Willis, Sam
One Dog Night - David Rosenfelt   *m* 712

CONSULTANT

Breeden, Kate
The Informationist - Taylor Stevens   *c* 144

Callisto, Susan
A Crack in Everything - Angela Gerst   *m* 615

Colby, Jack
Classic in the Barn - Amy Myers   *m* 687

Walker, Dub
Hot Lights, Cold Steel - D.P. Lyle   *m* 674

CONTRACTOR

Anselma, Amanda
Black Swan - Chris Knopf   *m* 658

Graham, Marshall
To Have and to Hold - Tracie Peterson   *i* 549

Preston, Cole
Home Sweet Home - Kim Watters   *r* 952

CONVICT

Aldiss, Richard
Dominance - Will Lavender   *m* 662

Arno, Dwight
Northwest Corner - John Burnham Schwartz   *c* 134

Crandall, Erik
East on Sunset - Ken Mercer   *m* 683

Devaney, Max
Light from a Distant Star - Mary McGarry Morris   *c* 110

Gelbhardt, Ewrin
Strategic Moves - Stuart Woods   *c* 166

Hadda, Wolf
The Woodcutter - Reginald Hill   *m* 632

Hunt, Phil
Terror of Living - Urban Waite   *c* 158

Ron
Among the Missing - Morag Joss   *m* 648

Tate, Theodore
Collecting Cooper - Paul Cleave   *m* 583

COOK

Bennett, Frankie
Burning Down the Spouse - Dakota Cassidy   *r* 786

Davis, Marya
44 Charles Street - Danielle Steel   *c* 143

Matlock, Kelly
Harvest Moon - Robyn Carr   *r* 784

Matre, Rachel
Dark Waters - Alex Prentiss   *h* 475

Muir, Avis
Birds of Paradise - Diana Abu-Jaber   *c* 1

Salerno, Epiphany
Dandelion Summer - Lisa Wingate   *i* 555

Stevens, Jenna
Already Home - Susan Mallery   *c* 97

Taylor, Will
Livvie's Song - Sharlene MacLaren   *i* 545

Templeton, Teeny
Gone with a Handsomer Man - Michael Lee West   *r* 956

COUNSELOR

Huddy, Wyatt
The Inverted Forest - John Dalton   *c* 44

COURIER

G'ladheon, Karigan
Blackveil - Kristen Britain   *f* 179

COURTIER

Rozsa
An Embarrassment of Riches - Chelsea Quinn Yarbro   *h* 509

COUSIN

Beaumont, Flora
A Gentleman of Fortune: Or, the Suspicions of Miss Dido Kent - Anna Dean   *t* 294

Birch, Henry
Beaufort 1849 - Karen Lynn Allen   *t* 276

Brey, Charles
Death at the Chateau Bremont - M. L. Longworth   *m* 671

Brey, Eric
Death at the Chateau Bremont - M. L. Longworth   *m* 671

Chip
The Year We Left Home - Jean Thompson   *c* 153

CJ
Thieves Get Rich, Saints Get Shot - Jodi Compton   *m* 587

Darcy, Fitzwilliam
Darcy and Fitzwilliam - Karen V. Wasylowski   *r* 951

Duncan
Texas Blue - Jodi Thomas   *r* 945

Emily
Minding Frankie - Maeve Binchy   *c* 20

Fitzwilliam
Darcy and Fitzwilliam - Karen V. Wasylowski   *r* 951

Fludd, Branwell
Death in the Opening Chapter - Tim Heald   *m* 631

Fludd, Reverend Sebastian
Death in the Opening Chapter - Tim Heald   *m* 631

Jake
Summer in the South - Cathy Holton   *c* 76

Joseph
The Rock Hole - Reavis Z. Wortham   *m* 749

Kent, Dido
A Gentleman of Fortune: Or, the Suspicions of Miss Dido Kent - Anna Dean   *t* 294

Knollys, Lettice
Elizabeth I - Margaret George   *t* 313

Machu
Tiger Hills - Sarita Mandanna   *t* 343

Noel
Minding Frankie - Maeve Binchy   *c* 20

Pepper
The Rock Hole - Reavis Z. Wortham   *m* 749

Shore, Kayla
Death on Tour - Janice Hamrick   *m* 624

Top
The Rock Hole - Reavis Z. Wortham   *m* 749

COWBOY/COWGIRL

Calhoun, Slate
Going Cowboy Crazy - Katie Lane   *r* 873

Clark, Wyatt
A Light at Winter's End - Julia London   *r* 879

Kelly, Rio
Rio - Georgina Gentry   *r* 825

O'Donnell, Rye
Love Drunk Cowboy - Carolyn Brown   *r* 776

Wallace, Owen
Keep a Little Secret - Dorothy Garlock   *r* 823

Whitaker, Clay
Cowboy Up - Vicki Lewis Thompson   *r* 946

CRIME SUSPECT

Avalon, Talon
Timecaster - Joe Kimball   *s* 1011

Birtle-Figgins, Lavinia
A Bedlam of Bones - Suzette A. Hill   *m* 633

Breen, Arthur "Art"
Faith - Jennifer Haigh   *c* 64

Callahan, Rafer "Rafe"
Midnight Sins - Lora Leigh   *r* 877

Colbert, Johnny
Murder in the 11th House - Mitchell Scott Lewis   *m* 666

Drayson, Al
Secret of the White Rose - Stefanie Pintoff   *t* 373

Flynn, Sean
Beg for Mercy - Jami Alden   *r* 754

Gallier, Mira
Watch Me Die - Erica Spindler   *c* 141

Humphrey, Alice
Long Gone - Alafair Burke   *m* 576

Jellicoe, Hank
Deja Vu - Fern Michaels   *r* 899

Kane, Tucker
Lie for Me - Karen Young   *i* 557

Lark, Anthony
Very Bad Men - Harry Dolan   *m* 597

Martinez, Morty
Ringer - Brian M. Wiprud   *m* 748

Mundy, Moses
Felicity's Gate - Julian Cole   *m* 586

Nelson, Jumbo
Sixkill - Robert B. Parker   *c* 115

Character Description Index

Chapman, Linnet
No Less in Blood - D. M. Pirrone   *t*   374

Clover
Widower's Tale - Julia Glass   *c*   58

Crawford, Angel
A Good Excuse to Be Bad - Miranda
Parker   *m*   693

Davis, Molly
The Goodbye Quilt - Susan Wiggs   *r*   958

Eastleigh, Sofia
Sweet as the Devil - Susan Johnson   *r*   856

Eirene
Warrior Betrayed - Addison Fox   *r*   817

Elizabeth
*The Secret History of Elizabeth Tudor, Vampire
Slayer* - Lucy Weston   *h*   504

English, Heather
English Lessons - J.M. Hayes   *m*   630

EV
Daughters of the Revolution - Carolyn
Cooke   *t*   290

Farraday, Mia
Night Road - Kristin Hannah   *c*   67

Fey, Anika
Black Swan - Chris Knopf   *m*   658

Fox, Lin
Glass Demon - Helen Grant   *c*   62

Frankie
Minding Frankie - Maeve Binchy   *c*   20

Gabriel, Mina
The Fallen Angel - David Hewson   *t*   329

Grant, Montana
Warrior Betrayed - Addison Fox   *r*   817

Hennessey, Rachel
The Last Rose of Summer - Monte Schulz   *t*   387

Jonayla
The Land of Painted Caves - Jean M. Auel   *c*   12

Joy
Dreams of Joy - Lisa See   *t*   388

Julia
The Story of Beautiful Girl - Rachel
Simon   *c*   136

Kelleher, Ann Marie
Maine - J. Courtney Sullivan   *c*   148

Kelleher, Kathleen
Maine - J. Courtney Sullivan   *c*   148

Kelleher, Maggie
Maine - J. Courtney Sullivan   *c*   148

Krissy
The Girl Who Disappeared Twice - Andrea
Kane   *m*   650

Lake, Swan
The Homecoming of Samuel Lake - Jenny
Wingfield   *c*   165

Lake, Willadee
The Homecoming of Samuel Lake - Jenny
Wingfield   *c*   165

Louise
I Married You for Happiness - Lily Tuck   *c*   154

MacDougall, Anna
The Ranger - Monica McCarty   *r*   893

Madison, Elizabeth
A River to Cross - Yvonne L Harris   *i*   534

Madriani, Sarah
Trader of Secrets - Steve Martini   *m*   678

Marcus, Alexa
Buried Secrets - Joseph Finder   *m*   605

Marie
The Last Rose of Summer - Monte Schulz   *t*   387

Marsh, Sadie
Once Upon a Time There Was You - Elizabeth
Berg   *c*   19

Marshal, Mahelt
To Defy a King - Elizabeth Chadwick   *t*   287

Maureen
Remember Ben Clayton - Stephen Harrigan   *t*   323

Melinda
Murder in the 11th House - Mitchell Scott
Lewis   *m*   666

Melissa
An Uninvited Ghost - E.J. Copperman   *h*   425

Mellorin
The Warlord's Legacy - Ari Marmell   *f*   233

Melly
Save Me - Lisa Scottoline   *c*   135

Miranda
Prospero Regained - L. Jagi Lamplighter   *f*   225

Muir, Felice
Birds of Paradise - Diana Abu-Jaber   *c*   1

Noel
Hot Lights, Cold Steel - D.P. Lyle   *m*   674

O'Leary, Shealy
Haunting Desire - Erin Quinn   *r*   922

Patterson, Priss
Trace of Fever - Lori Foster   *r*   814

Phoebe
A Death In Summer - Benjamin Black   *m*   571

Quirk, Karina
The Astral - Kate Christensen   *c*   34

Reaper-Jones, Calliope
Serpent's Storm - Amber Benson   *f*   174

Rose
Compass Rose - John Casey   *c*   32

Ryrie, Biscuit
The Grief of Others - Leah Hager Cohen   *c*   37

Sterling, Devyn Hewitt
Shiver of Fear - Roxanne St. Claire   *r*   942

Wingate, Katherine
You're Next - Gregg Hurwitz   *m*   638

Winsted, Cisco
Heat Wave - Nancy Thayer   *c*   152

Winsted, Margaret
Heat Wave - Nancy Thayer   *c*   152

Woodruff, Diana
Fly Away Home - Jennifer Weiner   *c*   161

Woodruff, Lizzie
Fly Away Home - Jennifer Weiner   *c*   161

DEAF PERSON

Homan
The Story of Beautiful Girl - Rachel
Simon   *c*   136

DEBUTANTE

Kensington, Felicity
The Matrimony Plan - Christine Johnson   *i*   539

Neville, Amanda
Society's Most Disreputable Gentleman - Julia
Justiss   *r*   859

DEFENDANT

Drayson, Al
Secret of the White Rose - Stefanie Pintoff   *t*   373

Dykmans, Roger
The Things We Cherished - Pam Jenoff   *m*   646

Galloway, Noah
One Dog Night - David Rosenfelt   *m*   712

DEITY

Eirene
Warrior Betrayed - Addison Fox   *r*   817

Themis
Warrior Betrayed - Addison Fox   *r*   817

Ullikummis
Infestation Cubed - James Axler   *s*   975
Truth Engine - James Axler   *s*   973

DEMON

Basuram
Infernal Affairs - Jes Battis   *h*   416

Cain, Luc
Original Sin - Lisa Desrochers   *f*   191

Jona
Never Knew Another - J.M. McDermott   *f*   234

Nolander, Rachel
Never Knew Another - J.M. McDermott   *f*   234

Ru
Infernal Affairs - Jes Battis   *h*   416

Sargatanas
Sympathy for the Devil - Justin Gustainis   *h*   440

Satan
Damned - Chuck Palahniuk   *c*   114

DESIGNER

Froehlich, Ellen
Chihuahua of the Baskervilles - Esri
Allbritten   *m*   562

Gordon, Lady Duff "Lucie"
The Mistress of Nothing - Kate Pullinger   *t*   376

Parker, Kacey
Boardroom Seduction - Anita Richmond
Bunkley   *r*   778

Silveira, Isabella
At Hidden Falls - Barbara Freethy   *r*   819

Wingate, Mike
You're Next - Gregg Hurwitz   *m*   638

DETECTIVE

Abbott, Tom
Heart of Lies - Jill Marie Landis   *r*   872

Alvarez, Enrique
Murder, Majorcan Style - Roderic Jeffries   *m*   644

Amlingmeyer, Gustav "Old Red"
World's Greatest Sleuth! - Steve
Hockensmith   *t*   331

Amlingmeyer, Otto "Big Red"
World's Greatest Sleuth! - Steve
Hockensmith   *t*   331

Ansell, Helen
The Durham Deception - Philip Gooden   *m*   617

Ansell, Tom
The Durham Deception - Philip Gooden   *m*   617

Barrington, Stone
Strategic Moves - Stuart Woods   *c*   166

Baudelaire, Varik
Blood Secrets - Jeannie Holmes   *h*   449

Bly, Nellie
The Illusion of Murder - Carol McCleary   *t*   348

Bognor, Simon
Death in the Opening Chapter - Tim
Heald   *m*   631

Bruno, Giordano
Prophecy - S.J. Parris   *c*   116

Carlos
Mama Sees Stars - Deborah Sharp   *m*   723

Celllini, Sandro
A Murder in Tuscany - Christobel Kent   *m*   654

DETECTIVE—AMATEUR

DETECTIVE—POLICE

DETECTIVE—PRIVATE

Holmes, Sherlock
Between the Thames and the Tiber - Ted
    Riccardi   *m* 707
The Magic Bullet - Larry Millett   *t* 355

Innes, Callum
Beast of Burden - Ray Banks   *m* 567

Kelly, Michael
We All Fall Down - Michael Harvey   *m* 629

Kozmarski, Joe
A Bad Night's Sleep - Michael Wiley   *m* 745

Libertus
The Vestal Vanishes - Rosemary Rowe   *m* 714

Lightner, Sylvie
Gods and Monsters - Lyn Benedict   *h* 417

Muldune, Ray
Darkness, My Old Friend - Lisa Unger   *c* 157

Munroe, Vanessa Michael
The Informationist - Taylor Stevens   *c* 144

Murphy, Molly
Bless the Bride - Rhys Bowen   *t* 280

Nameless Detective
Camouflage - Bill Pronzini   *m* 702

Reynolds, Ali
Fatal Error - J.A. Jance   *c* 77

Richter, Matt
Dark War - Tim Waggoner   *h* 500

Rossi, Marc
Shiver of Fear - Roxanne St. Claire   *r* 942

Rounder, Rick
Felicity's Gate - Julian Cole   *m* 586

Runyon, Jake
Camouflage - Bill Pronzini   *m* 702

Spenser
Sixkill - Robert B. Parker   *c* 115

Street, Keye
The Stranger You Seek - Amanda Kyle
    Williams   *m* 746

Tanner, Bay
Jericho Cay - Kathryn R. Wall   *m* 741

Taylor, John
A Hard Day's Knight - Simon R. Green   *f* 203

Tinkie
Bones of a Feather - Carolyn Haines   *m* 622

Vane, Harriet
The Attenbury Emeralds - Jill Paton Walsh   *t* 406

Walker, Amos
Infernal Angels - Loren D. Estleman   *m* 603

Walker, Caleb
The Missing Twin - Rita Herron   *r* 839

Wimsey, Lord Peter
The Attenbury Emeralds - Jill Paton Walsh   *t* 406

Woods, Casey
The Girl Who Disappeared Twice - Andrea
    Kane   *m* 650

DIPLOMAT

de Rohan-Chabot, Phillipe
The Emperor's Body - Peter Brooks   *t* 284

Hilliard, Diccan
Never a Gentleman - Eileen Dreyer   *r* 805

DIRECTOR

Colby-Camp, Victoria
Damaged - Debra Webb   *r* 954

Crowe, Painter
Devil Colony - James Rollins   *m* 711

Felice
The Wedding Writer - Susan Schneider   *r* 935

Lucentio, Pietro
She's the One - J.J. Murray   *r* 905

Lucentio, Vincenzo
She's the One - J.J. Murray   *r* 905

Ressler, Rudy
Hollywood Hills - Joseph Wambaugh   *c* 160

Sara
The Wedding Writer - Susan Schneider   *r* 935

Weiss, Emily Daggett
The Brink of Fame - Irene Fleming   *t* 309

DIVORCED PERSON

Affenlight, Pella
The Art of Fielding - Chad Harbach   *c* 68

Hamlin, Bethanne
A Turn in the Road - Debbie Macomber   *c* 96

Harley, Chris
44 Charles Street - Danielle Steel   *c* 143

Harris, Claire
The Last Time I Saw Paris - Lynn Sheene   *r* 938

Malloy, Emma
A Heart Revealed - Julie Lessman   *i* 543

Prince Charming
Wickedly Charming - Kristine Grayson   *r* 832

Rory
Silver Boat - Luanne Rice   *c* 127

Trave, William
The King of Diamonds - Simon Tolkien   *t* 400

Yardley, Lady Julia
Scandal of the Year - Laura Lee Guhrke   *r* 833

DOCTOR

Anderson, Paul
Wings of Promise - Bonnie Leon   *i* 542

Arcturus
The Curse-Maker - Kelli Stanley   *t* 394

Beckett, Jo
The Nightmare Thief - Meg Gardiner   *m* 610

Blackmore, John
My Favorite Countess - Vanessa Kelly   *r* 862

Dr. Bloom
Doctor Who: Dead of Winter - James
    Goss   *s* 1000

Cohen, Erik
The Warsaw Anagrams - Richard Zimler   *m* 750

Ebersole, Doc
I'll Never Get Out of This World Alive - Steve
    Earle   *t* 302

Edwards, Josh
Do You Remember Me Now? - Karen Hanson
    Stuyck   *m* 732

Erlich, Jay
Eyes Wide Open - Andrew Gross   *m* 620

Ernest, Eli
The Doctor's Lady - Jody Hedlund   *i* 535

Gachet, Paul
Leaving Van Gogh - Carol Wallace   *t* 405

Galloway, Jack
Desert Gift - Sally John   *r* 854

Gibson, Paul
Where Shadows Dance - C.S. Harris   *t* 324

Gunn, Martha
Frozen Charlotte - Priscilla Masters   *m* 679

Holliday, John Henry "Doc"
Doc - Mary Doria Russell   *c* 131

Isles, Maura
Silent Girl - Tess Gerritsen   *m* 614

January, Benjamin
The Shirt on His Back - Barbara Hambly   *c* 65

Konrad, Johann
Blood Oath - Christopher Farnsworth   *h* 430

Laveau, Marie
Hurricane - Jewell Parker Rhodes   *t* 379

Lee-Trafford, Martin
Paper Doll - Janet Woods   *t* 411

Linton, Sara
Fallen - Karin Slaughter   *m* 725

Luria, Elizabeth
Tunnel Vision - Gary Braver   *s* 980

Malachy
Scales of Retribution - Cora Harrison   *m* 627

Mitchell, Thomas
Sarah's Gift - Marta Perry   *r* 917

Murphy, Jane "Kate Dalton"
Do You Remember Me Now? - Karen Hanson
    Stuyck   *m* 732

Ozigbo, Alva
The Woodcutter - Reginald Hill   *m* 632

Parks, Thomas
Comes a Time for Burning - Steven F.
    Havill   *t* 326

Reynolds, Duncan
An Empty Death - Laura Wilson   *t* 409

Salinger, Nikki
Baby, Drive South - Stephanie Bond   *r* 768

Schlozman, Steven C.
*The Zombie Autopsies: Secret Notebooks from the
    Apocalypse* - Steven C. Schlozman   *h* 485

Singh, Marina
State of Wonder - Ann Patchett   *c* 117

Swenson, Annick
State of Wonder - Ann Patchett   *c* 117

White, Jennifer
Turn of Mind - Alice LaPlante   *c* 87

Whitescarver, Bronwyn
SEALed Forever - Mary Margaret
    Daughtridge   *r* 797

Winston, Mattie
Frozen Stiff - Annelise Ryan   *m* 715

Woodruff, Diana
Fly Away Home - Jennifer Weiner   *c* 161

Wyeth, Mildred
Tainted Cascade - James Axler   *s* 971

Younger, Stratham
The Death Instinct - Jed Rubenfeld   *t* 383

DOG

Einstein
Emily and Einstein - Linda Francis Lee   *c* 91

Jack
Finding Jack - Gareth Crocker   *c* 41

Lou
Play Dead - John Levitt   *f* 229

Mr. Chartwell
Mr. Chartwell - Rebecca Hunt   *t* 334

DRAGON

Dragonelli, Darkwyn
Vampire Dragon - Annette Blair   *f* 177

Saint-Lucq
The Alchemist in the Shadows - Pierre
    Pevel   *f* 248

Snow
The King of the Crags - Stephen Deas   *f* 190

DRIVER

Baci, Stephania "Stevie"
Then He Kissed Me - Christie Ridgway   *r* 926

Bright, Ned
Captive Trail - Susan Page Davis   *i*   524

DRUG DEALER

Hawkins, Anwan
The Cut - George P. Pelecanos   *m*   694

Williams, Slippery
Jersey Law - Ron Liebman   *m*   667

ECONOMIST

Keynes, John Maynard
Washington Shadow - Aly Monroe   *t*   358

EDITOR

Loogan, David
Very Bad Men - Harry Dolan   *m*   597

MacGregor, Angus
Chihuahua of the Baskervilles - Esri
    Allbritten   *m*   562

Quinn, Lucky
The Wedding Writer - Susan Schneider   *r*   935

Ralston, Grace
The Wedding Writer - Susan Schneider   *r*   935

Whitman, Judith
To Be Sung Underwater - Tom McNeal   *c*   102

EMPLOYER

Archer, Leon
Boardroom Seduction - Anita Richmond
    Bunkley   *r*   778

Edison, Thomas
Lightning - Jean Echenoz   *t*   304

Ivers, Sands
The Talk-Funny Girl - Roland Merullo   *c*   104

Miriam
Minding Ben - Victoria Brown   *c*   27

Narraway, Victor
Treason at Lisson Grove - Anne Perry   *t*   371

Simmons, Tom
The Devil Himself - Eric Dezenhall   *m*   593

von Schroeder, Baron
The Traitor's Emblem - Juan
    Gomez-Jurado   *m*   616

ENEMY

Blackford, Ian
Original Sin - Beth McMullen   *m*   680

ENGINEER

Acquillo, Sam
Black Swan - Chris Knopf   *m*   658

Alvord, J. Norman
Dandelion Summer - Lisa Wingate   *i*   555

Blevins, Robert
The Matrimony Plan - Christine Johnson   *i*   539

Bradshaw, Amy
Baby, Come Home - Stephanie Bond   *r*   767

La Forge, Geordi
Star Trek: Indistinguishable from Magic - David A.
    McIntee   *s*   1026

Locke, Tyler
The Vault - Boyd Morrison   *m*   685

Scott, Montgomery
Star Trek: Indistinguishable from Magic - David A.
    McIntee   *s*   1026

ENTERTAINER

Crosby, Bing
Fly Me to the Morgue - Robert J. Randisi   *m*   704

Martin, Dean
Fly Me to the Morgue - Robert J. Randisi   *m*   704

Nightingale, Richard
The Ladder Dancer - Roz Southey   *m*   728

Sinatra, Frank
Fly Me to the Morgue - Robert J. Randisi   *m*   704
Hassie Calhoun - Cory Pamela   *t*   369

ENTREPRENEUR

Hadda, Wolf
The Woodcutter - Reginald Hill   *m*   632

Pereira, Nathaniel
Song of Slaves in the Desert - Alan
    Cheuse   *t*   288

ENVIRONMENTALIST

Pickwick-Buchanan, Bridget
Restless in Carolina - Tamara Leigh   *i*   541

EXILE

Adolphus, Tiber
Hellhole - Brian Herbert   *s*   1007

Down, Thistle
Thistle Down - Irene Radford   *f*   251

Guarneri, Paul
Hostage in Havana - Noel Hynd   *r*   845

Rajasthan, Nickolai
Messiah - S. Andrew Swann   *s*   1051

EXPATRIATE

Riley
French Lessons - Ellen Sussman   *c*   149

EXPERT

Fitzwilliam, Simone
Moon Over Soho - Ben Aaronovitch   *f*   168

Galloway, Jillian
Desert Gift - Sally John   *r*   854

O'Reilly, Cassandra
The Valley of Shadows - Mark Terry   *m*   735

Taylor, Betsy
Undead and Undermined - MaryJanice
    Davidson   *f*   189

EXPLORER

Brigid
Cradle of Destiny - James Axler   *s*   968

Domi
Cradle of Destiny - James Axler   *s*   968

Fargo, Remi
The Kingdom - Clive Cussler   *c*   43

Fargo, Sam
The Kingdom - Clive Cussler   *c*   43

Grant
Cradle of Destiny - James Axler   *s*   968

Holt, Michael
Darkness, My Old Friend - Lisa Unger   *c*   157

Kane
Cradle of Destiny - James Axler   *s*   968

Raeder, Kurt
Blood of the Reich - William Dietrich   *m*   594

Selous, Frederick
The Illusion of Murder - Carol McCleary   *t*   348

Triana
The Dark Zone - Dom Testa   *s*   1052

FARMER

Gray, Avril
Heart of the Home - Gwen Kirkwood   *r*   864

Parker, Ned
The Rock Hole - Reavis Z. Wortham   *m*   749

Scott, Dean
Heart of the Home - Gwen Kirkwood   *r*   864

Tao
Dreams of Joy - Lisa See   *t*   388

Willie
The Reservoir - John Milliken Thompson   *t*   397

FATHER

Armstrong, Jack
One Summer - David Baldacci   *c*   13

Arno, Dwight
Northwest Corner - John Burnham
    Schwartz   *c*   134

Bermett, John
A Little Bit of Passion - Beate Boeker   *r*   766

Borgia, Rodrigo "Pope Alexander IV"
The Borgia Betrayal - Sara Poole   *m*   700

Bradshaw, Thomas
But Remember Their Names - Hillary Bell
    Locke   *m*   670

Burns, Simon
The Pack - Jason Starr   *h*   488

Dr. Burrows
Closer - Roderick Gordon   *f*   202

Calvino, John
What the Night Knows - Dean Koontz   *c*   84

Cathoair
The Sea Thy Mistress - Elizabeth Bear   *f*   172

Cawdor, Ryan
Downrigger Drift - James Axler   *s*   967
Prodigal's Return - James Axler   *s*   969

Chapman, Luke
No Less in Blood - D. M. Pirrone   *t*   374

Coleman, Samuel
The Gin & Chowder Club - Nan Parson
    Rossiter   *c*   130

Dawson, Darko
Children of the Street - Kwei Quartey   *m*   703

English, Sheriff
English Lessons - J.M. Hayes   *m*   630

Fey, Christian
Black Swan - Chris Knopf   *m*   658

Fox, Oliver
Glass Demon - Helen Grant   *c*   62

Fraser, Nick
Shadowed in Silk - Christine Lindsay   *i*   544

Garvey, Kevin
The Leftovers - Tom Perrotta   *c*   120

Gemelli, Chuck
Steal the Show - Thomas Kaufman   *m*   651

Glass, Percy
Widower's Tale - Julia Glass   *c*   58

Gonda
The Dawn Country - Kathleen O'Neal
    Gear   *t*   367

Hartley, Nick
At Hidden Falls - Barbara Freethy   *r*   819

Heck
Daughters of the Revolution - Carolyn
    Cooke   *t*   290

Hoffner, Nikolai
Second Son - Jonathan Rabb   *t*   378

Homan
The Story of Beautiful Girl - Rachel
    Simon   *c*   136

Hoyt, Cody
Back of Beyond - C.J. Box   *m*   573

Character Description Index

GENIUS

Sitturd, Lloyd
Enigmatic Pilot - Kris Saknussemm   *s*   1038

GENTLEWOMAN

Rowan, Roxanna
The Colonel's Lady - Laura Frantz   *i*   527

GIRL

Amanda
Claws! - R.L. Stine   *h*   493

Devi
Tiger Hills - Sarita Mandanna   *t*   343

Graves, Willow
Darkness, My Old Friend - Lisa Unger   *c*   157

Jenna
Nightfall - Ellen Connor   *h*   424

Pepper
The Rock Hole - Reavis Z. Wortham   *m*   749

Sweet, McLean
What Happened to Goodbye - Sarah Dessen   *c*   48

Watts, Jubie
The Dry Grass of August - Anna Jean
    Mayhew   *t*   347

GIRLFRIEND

Anselma, Amanda
Black Swan - Chris Knopf   *m*   658

Boysen, Mabel
Big Wheat - Richard Thompson   *t*   398

Bryson, Ginny
Deep Cover - Sandra Orchard   *i*   547

Calhoun, Hassie
Hassie Calhoun - Cory Pamela   *t*   369

Callisto, Susan
A Crack in Everything - Angela Gerst   *m*   615

Chin, Izzy
Save as Draft - Cavanaugh Lee   *c*   90

Collier, Amanda
The Best of Me - Nicholas Sparks   *c*   140

Connie
Plugged - Eoin Colfer   *c*   38

Cooper, Abby
Vision Impossible - Victoria Laurie   *m*   661

Dyce
The Gravity Pilot - M.M. Buckner   *s*   982

Elena
Iron House - John Hart   *m*   628

Emma
The Last Kiss - Red Garnier   *r*   824

Flynn, Megan
Beg for Mercy - Jami Alden   *r*   754

Gamble, Cindi
Flash and Bones - Kathy Reichs   *c*   125

Grey, Ana
White Shotgun - April Smith   *m*   727

Hall, Petra
The Gentlemen's Hour - Don Winslow   *m*   747

Koenen, Effi
Potsdam Station - David Downing   *t*   301

Lou
Bed - David Whitehouse   *c*   163

Marinelli, Cesca
Always the Vampire - Nancy Haddock   *h*   442

Missy
Rage - Jackie Morse Kessler   *h*   455

Osman, Katya
The King of Diamonds - Simon Tolkien   *t*   400

Perkins, Gail
Our Kind of Traitor - John Le Carre   *c*   89

Raven
Vampire Kisses 8: Cryptic Cravings - Ellen
    Schreiber   *h*   486

Somata, Clio
Revolution World - Katy Stauber   *s*   1045

Wilkes, Amelia
Exposure - Therese Fowler   *c*   55

GODFATHER

Churchill, Winston
The Parsifal Pursuit - Michael
    McMenamin   *t*   353

Hennessey, Jeepster
The Charlestown Connection - Tom
    MacDonald   *m*   675

GODMOTHER

Lady Wingate
To Desire a Wicked Duke - Nicole Jordan   *r*   857

GOVERNESS

Cardiff, Victoria
Taken by the Prince - Christina Dodd   *r*   803

de Medici, Violante
The Daughter of Siena - Marina Fiorato   *t*   308

GOVERNMENT OFFICIAL

Farinelli, Orazio
The Fatal Touch - Conor Fitzgerald   *m*   606

Fouquet, Nicolas
Before Versailles - Karleen Koen   *c*   83

Garner, Daniela
The Wreckage - Michael Robotham   *m*   710

Hunsecker, Dale
The Informant - Thomas Perry   *m*   696

Jenks, Barrington
Kissing the Demons - Kate Ellis   *m*   600

London, Gray
The First Gardener - Denise Hildreth
    Jones   *i*   536

Nyx
God's War - Kameron Hurley   *f*   217

Pitt, Thomas
Treason at Lisson Grove - Anne Perry   *t*   371

President Matthew Bernstein
2030: The Real Story of What Happens To America
    - Albert Brooks   *c*   24

Truman, Harry
Washington Shadow - Aly Monroe   *t*   358

Waring, Elizabeth
The Informant - Thomas Perry   *m*   696

GRADUATE

Ainsley, Adam
Deadly Reunion - Geraldine Evans   *m*   604

Heck
Daughters of the Revolution - Carolyn
    Cooke   *t*   290

Jasper
Soft Apocalypse - Will McIntosh   *s*   1027

GRANDDAUGHTER

Cheri
Chihuahua of the Baskervilles - Esri
    Allbritten   *m*   562

Kelleher, Maggie
Maine - J. Courtney Sullivan   *c*   148

Pepper
The Rock Hole - Reavis Z. Wortham   *m*   749

Woodbridge, Kate
To Tempt a Rake - Cara Elliott   *r*   809

GRANDFATHER

Duke of Cluyne
To Tempt a Rake - Cara Elliott   *r*   809

Glass, Percy
Widower's Tale - Julia Glass   *c*   58

Grandfather
The Real Macaw: A Meg Langslow Mystery -
    Donna Andrews   *m*   563

Lake, John
The Homecoming of Samuel Lake - Jenny
    Wingfield   *c*   165

Parker, Ned
The Rock Hole - Reavis Z. Wortham   *m*   749

Price, Mickey
The Devil Himself - Eric Dezenhall   *m*   593

Thomas
Chihuahua of the Baskervilles - Esri
    Allbritten   *m*   562

GRANDMOTHER

Baskerville, Charlotte
Chihuahua of the Baskervilles - Esri
    Allbritten   *m*   562

Cassidy, Eleanor
The Devil's Puzzle - Clare O'Donohue   *m*   689

Kelleher, Alice
Maine - J. Courtney Sullivan   *c*   148

Lane
Devil's Plaything - Matt Richtel   *m*   708

Parker, Becky
The Rock Hole - Reavis Z. Wortham   *m*   749

Val
The Chaos - Rachel Ward   *h*   501

GRANDSON

Adam
The Chaos - Rachel Ward   *h*   501

Eastman, Jonah
The Devil Himself - Eric Dezenhall   *m*   593

Robert
Widower's Tale - Julia Glass   *c*   58

Saltonstall, Bucky
Light from a Distant Star - Mary McGarry
    Morris   *c*   110

Top
The Rock Hole - Reavis Z. Wortham   *m*   749

GUARD

Asim
The Desert of Souls - Howard Andrew
    Jones   *t*   337

Atilo
The Fallen Blade - Jon Courtenay
    Grimwood   *t*   320

Audelia
The Vestal Vanishes - Rosemary Rowe   *m*   714

Becker, Christoph
When Passion Rules - Johanna Lindsey   *r*   878

Jacob
The Damascus Way - Janette Oke   *r*   911

Jona
Never Knew Another - J.M. McDermott   *f*   234

Salmen, Adam
The Druggist of Auschwitz - Dieter
    Schlesak   *t*   386

HOSTAGE

Armstrong, Gena
Deadly Games - Cate Noble   *r*   907

Kohlmeyer, Madison
Deadly Games - Cate Noble   *r*   907

HOTEL OWNER

Fey, Christian
Black Swan - Chris Knopf   *m*   658

Strong, Philip
Dreams of the Dead - Perri
    O'Shaughnessy   *m*   690

Thayer, J.D.
A Race to Splendor - Ciji Ware   *t*   407

HOTEL WORKER

Brooke, London
Get Lucky - Lorie O'Clare   *r*   909

MacLean, Daisy
Staying at Daisy's - Jill Mansell   *r*   890

HOUSEHOLDER

Ingrid
The House by the Fjord - Rosalind Laker   *t*   342

Morgan, Link
Vanish in Plain Sight - Marta Perry   *r*   916

Pennington, Montague "Monty"
The Penningtons - Pamela Oldfield   *t*   368

HOUSEKEEPER

Claxton, Lisa
Deadly Intentions - Candice Poarch   *r*   919

Miss Dutton
The Penningtons - Pamela Oldfield   *t*   368

Freeman, Anjanette
Jericho Cay - Kathryn R. Wall   *m*   741

Luther, Mary
The Dry Grass of August - Anna Jean
    Mayhew   *t*   347

Tara
Staying at Daisy's - Jill Mansell   *r*   890

HOUSEWIFE

Jenni
The First Days - Rhiannon Frater   *h*   433

HUMAN

Lady Arkady
The Chaos Crystal - Jennifer Fallon   *f*   197

Bennett, Charlotte
Dark Enchantment - Anya Bast   *f*   171

Cameron, Adelaide
Reaper's Justice - Sarah McCarty   *r*   894

D'Artigo, Menolly
Blood Wyne - Yasmine Galenorn   *f*   200

Gina
Hybrids - Whitley Strieber   *s*   1048

Jayden
Blood Ties - Mari Mancusi   *f*   231

Julie
Warm Bodies - Isaac Marion   *h*   464

Katt, Kitty
Alien in the Family - Gini Koch   *s*   1013

Lawson, Sophie
Under Wraps - Hannah Jayne   *f*   218

Mark
Hybrids - Whitley Strieber   *s*   1048

Morevna, Marya
Deathless - Catherynne M. Valente   *f*   267

Nikolayevich, Ivan
Deathless - Catherynne M. Valente   *f*   267

Skjaldwulf
The Tempering of Men - Sarah Monette   *f*   240
The Tempering of Men - Sarah Monette   *f*   240

HUNTER

Balderan
The Land of Painted Caves - Jean M. Auel   *c*   12

De La Cruz, Zacarias
Dark Predator - Christine Feehan   *f*   198

Junell, Than
The Unremembered - Peter Orullian   *f*   245

Ogden, Tommy
Rodin's Debutante - Ward Just   *t*   338

Seymour, Jane
Henry VIII, Wolfman - A.E. Moorat   *h*   470

Smith, Silas
Blood of the Wicked - Karina Cooper   *r*   792

Tucker, Shaw
Crying Blood - Donis Casey   *t*   286

Vaughn, Vicky
Bloodstone - Nancy Holzner   *h*   450

Wild, Hunter
Out for Blood - Alyxandra Harvey   *f*   204

IMMIGRANT

Altamirano, Jose
The Secret History of Costaguana - Juan Gabriel
    Vasquez   *t*   403

Celestino
Widower's Tale - Julia Glass   *c*   58

McCabe, Norah
*Norah: The Making of an Irish-American Woman in
    19th Century New York* - Cynthia G.
    Neale   *t*   364

Silva
Among the Missing - Morag Joss   *m*   648

Sylvia
Minding Ben - Victoria Brown   *c*   27

Tigerlily
Tigerlily's Orchids - Ruth Rendell   *m*   706

IMMORTAL

Caliane
Archangel's Consort - Nalini Singh   *f*   257

Cathoair
The Sea Thy Mistress - Elizabeth Bear   *f*   172

Cayal
The Chaos Crystal - Jennifer Fallon   *f*   197

Glaeken
The Dark at the End - F. Paul Wilson   *h*   507

Jaxyn
The Chaos Crystal - Jennifer Fallon   *f*   197

Koschei
Deathless - Catherynne M. Valente   *f*   267

Nessa
Hunter's Fall - Shiloh Walker   *r*   950

IMPORTER/EXPORTER

Noble, Paul
The Sauvignon Secret - Ellen Crosby   *m*   590

IMPOVERISHED

Nolander, Rachel
Never Knew Another - J.M. McDermott   *f*   234

INDIAN

Bourne, Jonathan
One Whisper Away - Emma Wildes   *r*   959

Dog, Mad
English Lessons - J.M. Hayes   *m*   630

Rabbit, Grey
The Long-Shining Waters - Danielle Sosin   *t*   391

Sixkill, Zebulon
Sixkill - Robert B. Parker   *c*   115

Taabe Waipu
Captive Trail - Susan Page Davis   *i*   524

INNKEEPER

Bancroft, Abby
Home Sweet Home - Kim Watters   *r*   952

Kerby, Alison
An Uninvited Ghost - E.J. Copperman   *h*   425

INSPECTOR

Bainbridge
The Immorality Engine - George Mann   *s*   1019

Burden, Lance
Inmate 1577 - Alan Jacobson   *m*   640

Petrovna, Larissa
Strangers When We Meet - Merline
    Lovelace   *r*   881

Sejer, Konrad
Bad Intentions - Karin Fossum   *m*   608

Stratton, Ted
An Empty Death - Laura Wilson   *t*   409

INTERIOR DECORATOR

Sheridan, Tessa
Whisper Falls - Toni Blake   *r*   765

Sullivan, Sandy
Best Staged Plans - Claire Cook   *c*   39

INVENTOR

Edison, Thomas
Lightning - Jean Echenoz   *t*   304

Gregor
Lightning - Jean Echenoz   *t*   304

Sitturd, Hephaestus
Enigmatic Pilot - Kris Saknussemm   *s*   1038

Sitturd, Lloyd
Enigmatic Pilot - Kris Saknussemm   *s*   1038

INVESTIGATOR

Calvino, John
What the Night Knows - Dean Koontz   *c*   84

Clarke, Brittany Bo "Jinx"
Rustled - B.J. Daniels   *r*   796

Dobbs, Maisie
A Lesson in Secrets - Jacqueline Winspear   *t*   410

Eckman, Anders
State of Wonder - Ann Patchett   *c*   117

Gunther, Bernie
Field Gray - Philip Kerr   *t*   339

Heller, Nick
Buried Secrets - Joseph Finder   *m*   605

Langham, Daniel
The Kings of Eternity - Eric Brown   *s*   981

Lucas, Spero
The Cut - George P. Pelecanos   *m*   694

MacKenzie, Nate
Fall From Pride - Karen Harper   *m*   625

Matinova, Jana
Requiem for a Gypsy - Michael Genelin   *m*   612

Sasha
Bound by Darkness - Alexis Morgan   *r*   904

Shapiro, Danny
Journal of a UFO Investigator - David Halperin   *t*   322

Sweetwater, Owen
Quicksilver - Amanda Quick   *c*   124

Tannenbaum, Alys
The Traitor's Emblem - Juan Gomez-Jurado   *m*   616

Wagoner, Paul van
Dreams of the Dead - Perri O'Shaughnessy   *m*   690

JEWELER

Ferncsi, Rakoczy "Saint-Germain"
An Embarrassment of Riches - Chelsea Quinn Yarbro   *h*   509

James, Garet
The Watchtower - Lee Carroll   *h*   421

Osman, Titus
The King of Diamonds - Simon Tolkien   *t*   400

JOCKEY

Foxton, Nicholas "Foxy"
Dick Francis' Gamble - Felix Francis   *m*   609

JOURNALIST

Barrow, Jake
Blood of the Reich - William Dietrich   *m*   594

Benoit, Natalie
Breaking Point - Pamela Clare   *r*   789

Bly, Nellie
The Illusion of Murder - Carol McCleary   *t*   348

Brinsley, Christina
Sweet Little Lies - Michele Grant   *r*   830

Case, Justin
Turn Up the Heat - Isabel Sharpe   *r*   937

Cole, Aidan
American Subversive - David Goodwillie   *c*   60

Darmus, Roy
The Ridge - Michael Koryta   *c*   85

Frost, Harrison
Wicked Lies - Lisa Jackson   *r*   847

Hoffner, Georg
Second Son - Jonathan Rabb   *t*   378

Idle, Nat
Devil's Plaything - Matt Richtel   *m*   708

Juree, Jimm
Killed at the Whim of a Hat - Colin Cotterill   *m*   588

Kalabander, Hank
The Blow-Off - Jim Knipfel   *m*   657

Kelly, Irene
Disturbance - Jan Burke   *c*   29

Landis, Michael
Love Finds You in Lancaster County, Pennsylvania - Annalisa Daughety   *i*   523

Madison, Elizabeth
A River to Cross - Yvonne L Harris   *i*   534

McGary, Mattie
The Parsifal Pursuit - Michael McMenamin   *t*   353

Nelson, Jessica
Mourning Gloria - Susan Wittig Albert   *c*   7

Riley, Brenda
Fatal Error - J.A. Jance   *c*   77

Russell, John
Potsdam Station - David Downing   *t*   301

Terracini, Luca
The Wreckage - Michael Robotham   *m*   710

Thigpen, John
Ape House - Sara Gruen   *c*   63

Trudeau, Alex
True Colors - Joyce Lamb   *r*   871

Trudeau, Charlie
True Colors - Joyce Lamb   *r*   871

JUDGE

Larrigan, Thomas
The Nomination - William G. Tapply   *c*   150

O'Davoren, Mara
Scales of Retribution - Cora Harrison   *m*   627

Rains, O.C.
The Rock Hole - Reavis Z. Wortham   *m*   749

Verlaque, Antoine
Death at the Chateau Bremont - M. L. Longworth   *m*   671

Willis, Hope
The Girl Who Disappeared Twice - Andrea Kane   *m*   650

KIDNAP VICTIM

Alexander, Molly
When You Dare - Lori Foster   *r*   813

Lady Arkady
The Chaos Crystal - Jennifer Fallon   *f*   197

Cameron, Adelaide
Reaper's Justice - Sarah McCarty   *r*   894

Colby-Camp, Victoria
Damaged - Debra Webb   *r*   954

Gray, Acadia
Hush - Cherry Adair   *r*   753

Kikaya, Ali
The Moon Maze Game - Larry Niven   *s*   1030

Lori
Broken - Debra Webb   *r*   953

Madison, Elizabeth
A River to Cross - Yvonne L Harris   *i*   534

Marcus, Alexa
Buried Secrets - Joseph Finder   *m*   605

Miri
Jace - Sarah McCarty   *r*   895

Morevna, Marya
Deathless - Catherynne M. Valente   *f*   267

Ransome, Charlotte
Ransome's Quest - Kaye Dacus   *i*   522

Ransome, Julia
Ransome's Quest - Kaye Dacus   *i*   522

Rory
Doctor Who: Hunter's Moon - Paul Finch   *s*   996

Stark, Gideon
Hush - Cherry Adair   *r*   753

Stark, Zakary "Zak"
Hush - Cherry Adair   *r*   753

Sutherland, Lady Amelia
Captured by the Highlander - Julianne MacLean   *r*   885

von Enke, Hakan
Troubled Man - Henning Mankell   *c*   98

KIDNAPPER

Bowman, Walter
I'd Know You Anywhere - Laura Lippman   *c*   93

Gannajero
The Dawn Country - Kathleen O'Neal Gear   *t*   367

Jaxyn
The Chaos Crystal - Jennifer Fallon   *f*   197

Koschei
Deathless - Catherynne M. Valente   *f*   267

KNIGHT

Alymere
The Black Chalice - Steven Savile   *f*   254

Calard
Knights of Bretonnia - Anthony Reynolds   *f*   252

Mappestone, Geoffrey
A Dead Man's Secret - Simon Beaufort   *t*   279

Marshal, William
To Defy a King - Elizabeth Chadwick   *t*   287

Tristan
Master of Shadows - Angela Knight   *h*   458

LADY

Lady Arkady
The Chaos Crystal - Jennifer Fallon   *f*   197

de Neville, Lady Eleanor
Immortal Champion - Lisa Hendrix   *f*   208

Townsend, Lady Kendra
Pirate of My Heart - Jamie Carie   *i*   517

LAIRD

Barr
Moon Burning - Lucy Monroe   *f*   241

LANDLORD

Bazemore, Ty
Summer Rental - Mary Kay Andrews   *c*   10

Trent, Nicholas
Summer at Seaside Cove - Jacquie D'Alessandro   *r*   794

LAWMAN

Blackwell, Blackie
Mourning Gloria - Susan Wittig Albert   *c*   7

Chisholm, Colton
Branded - B.J. Daniels   *r*   795

Drake, Bobby
Terror of Living - Urban Waite   *c*   158

Earp, Wyatt
Doc - Mary Doria Russell   *c*   131

English, Sheriff
English Lessons - J.M. Hayes   *m*   630

Iles, Desmond
Hotbed - Bill James   *m*   641

Jones, Goat
A Bad Day for Scandal - Sophie Littlefield   *m*   669

Kimble, Kevin
The Ridge - Michael Koryta   *c*   85

Malveaux, Aaron
Hurricane - Jewell Parker Rhodes   *t*   379

Malveaux, Deet
Hurricane - Jewell Parker Rhodes   *t*   379

McBride, Zach
Breaking Point - Pamela Clare   *r*   789

Parker, Ned
The Rock Hole - Reavis Z. Wortham   *m*   749

Red
Jericho Cay - Kathryn R. Wall   *m*   741

Robinson, Halley
Branded - B.J. Daniels   *r*   795

Uncle Hamp
The Ranger - Ace Atkins   *m*   565

Washington, John
The Rock Hole - Reavis Z. Wortham   *m*   749

LAWYER

Anderson, Wyatt
Heat Wave - Nancy Thayer   *c*   152

Aulenbach, Emily
Escape - Barbara Delinsky   *c*   47

Barrington, Stone
Strategic Moves - Stuart Woods   *c*   166

Bloom, Nina
Now You See Her - James Patterson   *c*   118

Brey, Charles
Death at the Chateau Bremont - M. L.
   Longworth   *m*   671

Brey, Eric
Death at the Chateau Bremont - M. L.
   Longworth   *m*   671

Callisto, Susan
A Crack in Everything - Angela Gerst   *m*   615

Carpenter, Andy
One Dog Night - David Rosenfelt   *m*   712

Corinth, Rick
Wrong Man Running - Alan Hruska   *m*   636

Creed, Steven
A Creed in Stone Creek - Linda Lael
   Miller   *r*   902

Crosby, Collin
The Scent of Rain and Lightning - Nancy
   Pickard   *c*   121

DeMarco, Joe
House Divided - Mike Lawson   *m*   663

Dubon, Francois
A Man in Uniform - Kate Taylor   *t*   396

Figg, Wally
The Litigators - John Grisham   *m*   619

Finley, Oscar
The Litigators - John Grisham   *m*   619

Fraser, Kim
Primal Bonds - Jennifer Ashley   *f*   170

Gill, Darcy
Liquid Smoke - Jeff Shelby   *m*   724

Gold, Charlotte
The Things We Cherished - Pam Jenoff   *m*   646

Hall, Petra
The Gentlemen's Hour - Don Winslow   *m*   747

Harrington, Jack
The Things We Cherished - Pam Jenoff   *m*   646

Hinds, Harry
Trader of Secrets - Steve Martini   *m*   678

Jakubec, Cynthia
But Remember Their Names - Hillary Bell
   Locke   *m*   670

James, Harper
My One and Only - Kristan Higgins   *r*   840

Jefferson, Thomas
Blood Ties - Sharon Sala   *r*   931

Katie
The First Days - Rhiannon Frater   *h*   433

Madriani, Paul
Trader of Secrets - Steve Martini   *m*   678

Mary
Girls in White Dresses - Jennifer Close   *c*   36

McNeil, Izzy
Claim of Innocence - Laura Caldwell   *r*   782

Melinda
Murder in the 11th House - Mitchell Scott
   Lewis   *m*   666

Mezzonatti, Mickie
Jersey Law - Ron Liebman   *m*   667

Miller, Alex
A Conflict of Interest - Adam Mitzner   *m*   684

Muir, Brian
Birds of Paradise - Diana Abu-Jaber   *c*   1

O'Ballivan, Melissa
A Creed in Stone Creek - Linda Lael
   Miller   *r*   902

O'Malley, Cooper
Gone with a Handsomer Man - Michael Lee
   West   *r*   956

Overstreet, James
Identity: Lost - Pascal Marco   *m*   677

Perkins, Gail
Our Kind of Traitor - John Le Carre   *c*   89

Reilly, Nina
Dreams of the Dead - Perri
   O'Shaughnessy   *m*   690

Salerno, Salvatore "Junne"
Jersey Law - Ron Liebman   *m*   667

Seers, John
Aftermath - Peter Turnbull   *c*   155

Smith, Annabel Lee
Monument to Murder - Margaret Truman   *m*   738

Smith, Mackensie
Monument to Murder - Margaret Truman   *m*   738

Tommie
The Reservoir - John Milliken Thompson   *t*   397

Willing, Vic
Claire DeWitt and the City of the Dead - Sara
   Gran   *m*   618

Winston-Beaufort, Brianna "Bree"
Angel's Verdict - Mary Stanton   *m*   730

Zinc, David
The Litigators - John Grisham   *m*   619

LEADER

Alexander
Thirteen Years Later - Jasper Kent   *h*   454

Arno, Malcolm
Strong at the Break - Jon Land   *m*   660

Atticus
Master of Rome - John Stack   *t*   393

Baptiste, Brigid
Infestation Cubed - James Axler   *s*   975

Bjolf
The Viking Dead - Toby Venables   *h*   499

Black Shell
Fire the Sky - W. Michael Gear   *t*   312

Bonville, Allard
Grimoire - Phaedra Weldon   *h*   502

Brigid
Truth Engine - James Axler   *s*   973

Caledor
Caledor - Gav Thorpe   *f*   265

Cawdor, Ryan
Downrigger Drift - James Axler   *s*   967
Lost Gates - James Axler   *s*   974
Perception Fault - James Axler   *s*   970
Prodigal's Return - James Axler   *s*   969
Tainted Cascade - James Axler   *s*   971

Lady Daniela
Vampire Instinct - Joey W. Hill   *h*   448

de Soto, Hernando
Fire the Sky - W. Michael Gear   *t*   312

Frankenstein, Victor
The Dead Town - Dean Koontz   *h*   459

Garvey, Kevin
The Leftovers - Tom Perrotta   *c*   120

Grant
Truth Engine - James Axler   *s*   973

Hood, Robin
Outlaw - Angus Donald   *t*   300

Hyrkallen
The King of the Crags - Stephen Deas   *f*   190

Issyk Kul
Sons of Ellyrion - Graham McNeill   *f*   236

Kane
Infestation Cubed - James Axler   *s*   975
Truth Engine - James Axler   *s*   973

Khan, Genghis
Genghis Khan Vol. 2: The World Conqueror - Sam
   Djang   *t*   299

Koracoo
The Dawn Country - Kathleen O'Neal
   Gear   *t*   367

Lenk
Black Halo - Sam Sykes   *f*   260

Lord, Time
The Crimson Hand - Dan McDaid   *s*   1025

Martin, Myra Routledge
Home Free - Fern Michaels   *c*   105

Morathi
Sons of Ellyrion - Graham McNeill   *f*   236

O'Grainne, Heather
Daybreak Zero - John Barnes   *s*   976

O'Toole, Sandra
The Unincorporated Woman - Dani
   Kollin   *s*   1014

Omra
The Key to Creation - Kevin J. Anderson   *c*   9

Paran, Tavore
The Crippled God - Steven Erikson   *f*   196

Rafael
Blood Law - Karin Tabke   *h*   497

Raiker, Adam
Deadly Dreams - Kylie Brant   *r*   772
Deadly Sins - Kylie Brant   *r*   773

Richelieu
The Alchemist in the Shadows - Pierre
   Pevel   *f*   248

Sasheen
Farlander - Col Buchanan   *f*   182

Saul of Tarsus
The Damascus Way - Janette Oke   *r*   911

Schrei, Benjamin
The Warsaw Anagrams - Richard Zimler   *m*   750

Seda
The Scarab Path - Adrian Tchaikovsky   *f*   264

Shalar
Heart of the Exiled - Pati Nagle   *f*   243

St. John
Consumed - Kate Cann   *h*   420

Turner, Nat
*The Resurrection of Nat Turner, Part 1: The Wit-
   nesses* - Sharon Ewell Foster   *i*   526

Volkmar
Sword of Vengeance - Chris Wraight   *f*   275

Woods, Casey
The Girl Who Disappeared Twice - Andrea
   Kane   *m*   650

LEOPARD

Donovan, Drake
Savage Nature - Christine Feehan   *r*   810

LIBRARIAN

Esther Hammerhans
Mr. Chartwell - Rebecca Hunt   *t*   334

Harris, Charlie
Classified as Murder - Miranda James   *m*   642

Reynolds, Kim
The Truth Sleuth - Jacqueline Seewald   *m*   720

LIGHTHOUSE KEEPER

French, Wyatt
The Ridge - Michael Koryta   *c*   85

LINGUIST

Benedict, Stacy
The Vault - Boyd Morrison   *m*   685

LOBBYIST

Gemelli, Chuck
Steal the Show - Thomas Kaufman   *m*   651

LOVER

Adam
River Marked - Patricia Briggs   *h*   418

Allgood, Molly
Ghost Light - Joseph O'Connor   *t*   366

Antony, Marc
Queen of Kings - Maria Dahvana Headley   *t*   327

Lady Arkady
The Chaos Crystal - Jennifer Fallon   *f*   197

Aylmer, John
Queen of Misfortune - Peter Carroll   *t*   285

Banks, Noah
Courting Sparks - Joselyn Vaughn   *r*   949

Baptiste, Dante
Etched in Bone - Adrian Phoenix   *h*   474

Benoit, Natalie
Breaking Point - Pamela Clare   *r*   789

Blade, Jeremy
Real Vampires Don't Wear Size Six - Gerry Bartlett   *h*   415

Blunt, Willy
To Be Sung Underwater - Tom McNeal   *c*   102

Bonnet, Marine
Death at the Chateau Bremont - M. L. Longworth   *m*   671

Brady, Kate
The Hat - Babette Hughes   *t*   333

Brand, Jodi
Cowboy Fever - Joanne Kennedy   *r*   863

Burton, Bonny
Born to Dance - June Tate   *t*   395

Caldwell, Seth
Restless Heart - Wynonna Judd   *c*   80

Cannon, Kane
Ruthless Game - Christine Feehan   *h*   431

Cathoair
The Sea Thy Mistress - Elizabeth Bear   *f*   172

Cayal
The Chaos Crystal - Jennifer Fallon   *f*   197

Cesare
The Borgia Betrayal - Sara Poole   *m*   700

Chin, Izzy
Save as Draft - Cavanaugh Lee   *c*   90

Chisholm, Colton
Branded - B.J. Daniels   *r*   795

Coleman, Asa
The Gin & Chowder Club - Nan Parson Rossiter   *c*   130

Deveraux, Elena
Archangel's Consort - Nalini Singh   *f*   257

Devlin, Brinke
One True Sentence - Craig McDonald   *t*   349

Dom
The Lantern - Deborah Lawrenson   *c*   88

Elisa
Vampire Instinct - Joey W. Hill   *h*   448

Eve
The Lantern - Deborah Lawrenson   *c*   88

Falon
Blood Law - Karin Tabke   *h*   497

Gelert, Agnes
The Brink of Fame - Irene Fleming   *t*   309

Ginny
Ghosts of War: A Tale of the Ghost - George Mann   *s*   1020

Grey, Lady Jane
Queen of Misfortune - Peter Carroll   *t*   285

Hart, Destiny
Restless Heart - Wynonna Judd   *c*   80

Henriette
Before Versailles - Karleen Koen   *c*   83

Holbrook, Kendall
The Chase - Erin McCarthy   *r*   892

Jondalar
The Land of Painted Caves - Jean M. Auel   *c*   12

Kate
Sea of Lost Dreams - Ferenc Mate   *t*   346

Keane, Bobby
The Hat - Babette Hughes   *t*   333

Li, Harry
Rogue Oracle - Alayna Williams   *f*   274

Lu, Tian
Central Park Knight - C.J. Henderson   *f*   207

Martin
Save as Draft - Cavanaugh Lee   *c*   90

Masterson, Harper
Saddled and Spurred - Lorelei James   *r*   850

McBride, Bronte
Vampire Dragon - Annette Blair   *f*   177

McBride, Zach
Breaking Point - Pamela Clare   *r*   789

Monroe, Evan
The Chase - Erin McCarthy   *r*   892

Morrow, Daphne
Courting Sparks - Joselyn Vaughn   *r*   949

Muire
The Sea Thy Mistress - Elizabeth Bear   *f*   172

Mundy, Moses
Felicity's Gate - Julian Cole   *m*   586

Naomi
Felicity's Gate - Julian Cole   *m*   586

O'Halleran, Mickey
Born to Dance - June Tate   *t*   395

Patterson, Rose
Ruthless Game - Christine Feehan   *h*   431

Pierce, Dick
Compass Rose - John Casey   *c*   32

Raphael
Archangel's Consort - Nalini Singh   *f*   257

Reed, Anise
When the Killing's Done - T.C. Boyle   *i*   513

Robinson, Halley
Branded - B.J. Daniels   *r*   795

Rounder, Rick
Felicity's Gate - Julian Cole   *m*   586

Shepherd, Noelle
The Gin & Chowder Club - Nan Parson Rossiter   *c*   130

St. Clair, Glory
Real Vampires Don't Wear Size Six - Gerry Bartlett   *h*   415

Synge, John
Ghost Light - Joseph O'Connor   *t*   366

Thornhart, Cara
Eternal Rider - Larissa Ione   *h*   452

Treadwell, Teague
Cowboy Fever - Joanne Kennedy   *r*   863

Turisan
Heart of the Exiled - Pati Nagle   *f*   243

Turner, Bran
Saddled and Spurred - Lorelei James   *r*   850

Verlaque, Antoine
Death at the Chateau Bremont - M. L. Longworth   *m*   671

Waishkey, Elizabeth
Very Bad Men - Harry Dolan   *m*   597

Wallace, Heather
Etched in Bone - Adrian Phoenix   *h*   474

Weiss, Adam
The Brink of Fame - Irene Fleming   *t*   309

Whitman, Judith
To Be Sung Underwater - Tom McNeal   *c*   102

Wragge, Jane
Felicity's Gate - Julian Cole   *m*   586

MADAM

Madame V
Scent of Persuasion - Nikki Duncan   *r*   806

Walker, Rowena
Murder on Sisters' Row - Victoria Thompson   *m*   736

MAGICIAN

Alexander, Jessica
Play Dead - John Levitt   *f*   229

Bernhardt, Sarah
The Illusion of Murder - Carol McCleary   *t*   348

Cavanaugh, Frannie
Original Sin - Lisa Desrochers   *f*   191

Knight, Piers
Central Park Knight - C.J. Henderson   *f*   207

Nagash
Nagash Immortal - Mike Lee   *f*   227

North, Danny
Lost Gate - Orson Scott Card   *f*   183

Rider, Mark
Conspiracies - Mercedes Lackey   *f*   224

Selous, Frederick
The Illusion of Murder - Carol McCleary   *t*   348

Skandar
The Griffin's Flight - K.J. Taylor   *f*   262

Wad
Lost Gate - Orson Scott Card   *f*   183

MANAGER

Clipp, Ethel
I Still Dream About You - Fannie Flagg   *c*   54

Contrata, Jake
Hassie Calhoun - Cory Pamela   *t*   369

Humphrey, Alice
Long Gone - Alafair Burke   *m*   576

Jagger
Vampire Kisses 8: Cryptic Cravings - Ellen Schreiber   *h*   486

Joyes, Daphne
Dangerous in Diamonds - Madeline Hunter   *r*   843

McCall, Tricia
Creed's Honor - Linda Lael Miller   *r*   901

Miss Skelton
Consumed - Kate Cann   *h*   420

MATCHMAKER

Begley, Kate
The Matchmaker of Kenmare - Frank
Delaney   *t*   295

Dominique
Secret Attraction - Donna Hill   *r*   841

Mansfield, Tessa
How to Marry a Duke - Vicky Dreiling   *r*   804

MECHANIC

John
One Magic Moment - Lynn Kurland   *r*   869

Sax, Conway
Purgatory Chasm - Steve Ulfelder   *m*   739

Teal
Undertow - Cherry Adair   *r*   752

Thompson, Mercy
River Marked - Patricia Briggs   *h*   418

MENTALLY CHALLENGED PERSON

Lynnie
The Story of Beautiful Girl - Rachel
Simon   *c*   136

MENTALLY ILL PERSON

Caliane
Archangel's Consort - Nalini Singh   *f*   257

Garth, Miles
There But for The - Ali Smith   *c*   139

Merrill, Frederick
The Storm at the Door - Stefan Merrill
Block   *c*   103

Moreno, Jon
Bad Intentions - Karin Fossum   *m*   608

Sasha
A Visit from the Goon Squad - Jennifer
Egan   *c*   50

van Gogh, Vincent
Leaving Van Gogh - Carol Wallace   *t*   405

Watson, Freddie
The Winter Ghosts - Kate Mosse   *t*   362

MERCENARY

Gentilhomme, Gilbert "Gent"
The Profession - Steven Pressfield   *m*   701

Macintosh, Dare
When You Dare - Lori Foster   *r*   813

Muerte, Liquida "The Mexicutioner"
Trader of Secrets - Steve Martini   *m*   678

Rivers, Trace
Trace of Fever - Lori Foster   *r*   814

Salter, James
The Profession - Steven Pressfield   *m*   701

Savor, Jackson
Savor the Danger - Lori Foster   *r*   816

MIDWIFE

Brandt, Sarah
Murder on Sisters' Row - Victoria
Thompson   *m*   736

Mast, Sarah
Sarah's Gift - Marta Perry   *r*   917

MILITARY PERSONNEL

Adams, Clay
The Final Storm - Jeff Shaara   *t*   389

Aquila, Marcus
Fortress of Spears - Anthony Riches   *t*   380

Arrow, Stephen
Cloudy With a Chance of Marriage - Kieran
Kramer   *r*   867

Atticus
Master of Rome - John Stack   *t*   393

Beaumont, Dixie Ray
Wings: A Novel of World War II Flygirls - Karl
Friedrich   *t*   311

Belial, Captain
The Purging of Kadillus - Gav Thorpe   *s*   1054

Black, Janet Delgado
The Unincorporated Woman - Dani
Kollin   *s*   1014

Brent, Alexander
Tom Clancy's EndWar: The Hunted - David
Michaels   *s*   1028

Bright, Charles
The Admiral's Penniless Bride - Carla
Kelly   *r*   861

Bryant, Matthew
The Girl in the Gatehouse - Julie Klassen   *r*   865

Buckner, Simon Bolivar Jr.
The Final Storm - Jeff Shaara   *t*   389

Carson, Fletcher
Finding Jack - Gareth Crocker   *c*   41

Cochran, Mike
Who Shot the Water Buffalo? - Ken Babbs   *t*   278

Colson, Quinn
The Ranger - Ace Atkins   *m*   565

Danilov, Aleksei Ivanovich
Thirteen Years Later - Jasper Kent   *h*   454

DeJesus, Adrian
Hellbent - Cherie Priest   *h*   476

Desjani, Captain
The Lost Fleet: Beyond the Frontier: Dreadnaught
- Jack Campbell   *s*   984

Dragonelli, Darkwyn
Vampire Dragon - Annette Blair   *f*   177

Early, Sebastian
Dragoons - Garry Kilworth   *t*   340

Eriksson
Broken Honour - Robert Earl   *f*   194

Fitzwilliam
Darcy and Fitzwilliam - Karen V.
Wasylowski   *r*   951

Flax, Calliope Flax
Element Zero - James Knapp   *s*   1012

Fraser, Nick
Shadowed in Silk - Christine Lindsay   *i*   544

Geary, John "Black Jack"
The Lost Fleet: Beyond the Frontier: Dreadnaught
- Jack Campbell   *s*   984

Graves
The President's Vampire - Christopher
Farnsworth   *h*   429

Gray, Nolan
Vigilante - Robin Parrish   *i*   548

Gunther, Bernie
Field Gray - Philip Kerr   *t*   339

Helborg, Kurt
Sword of Vengeance - Chris Wraight   *f*   275

Huckelbee, Tom
Who Shot the Water Buffalo? - Ken Babbs   *t*   278

Ia
Theirs Not to Reason Why: A Soldier's Duty - Jean
Johnson   *s*   1009

James
Letters from War - Mark Schultz   *i*   550

Jax, Sirantha
Aftermath - Ann Aguirre   *s*   963

Jones, Isaiah
Reaper's Justice - Sarah McCarty   *r*   894

Ketchum, Sally
Wings: A Novel of World War II Flygirls - Karl
Friedrich   *t*   311

Khaavren
Tiassa - Steven Brust   *f*   181

Knight, Brian
Deadly Intentions - Candice Poarch   *r*   919

La Fargue
The Alchemist in the Shadows - Pierre
Pevel   *f*   248

Lang, Lars
A Game of Lies - Rebecca Cantrell   *m*   580

Longenecker, David
Cry Uncle, Sumbody - Thomas Ray
Crowel   *t*   291

Markowski, William
Kilroy: The Friendship Behind the Legacy - David
L. Earls   *t*   303

Mason
Nightfall - Ellen Connor   *h*   424

McGill, Pete
The War That Came Early: The Big Switch - Harry
Turtledove   *c*   156

McLinn, Cassius
The Colonel's Lady - Laura Frantz   *i*   527

Metcalfe, Canyon
Wolfsbane - Ronie Kendig   *i*   540

Miller, Charles
The Matchmaker of Kenmare - Frank
Delaney   *t*   295

Morrison, Arch
The Grits Eaters - Clarence L. Morrison   *t*   360

Mustafa
Shards - Ismet Prcic   *c*   123

Naaman, Scout-Sergeant
The Purging of Kadillus - Gav Thorpe   *s*   1054

Nimitz, Chester
The Final Storm - Jeff Shaara   *t*   389

Novak, Raymond
Blue Skies Tomorrow - Sarah Sundin   *i*   552

Pasha, Fevzi
An Evil Eye - Jason Goodwin   *t*   317

Pinkerton, Benjamin "Frank" Franklin
Butterfly's Child - Angela Davis-Gardner   *t*   293

Platt, Benjamin
Hotwire - Alex Kava   *m*   652

Pomelroy, Killian
Kilroy: The Friendship Behind the Legacy - David
L. Earls   *t*   303

Reddy, Matthew "Matt"
Rising Tides: Destroyermen - Taylor
Anderson   *s*   966

Richards, Geoff
Shadowed in Silk - Christine Lindsay   *i*   544

Roark, Danielle "Dani"
Wolfsbane - Ronie Kendig   *i*   540

Romanov, Nikolai
Red Heat - Nina Bruhns   *r*   777

Salter, James
The Profession - Steven Pressfield   *m*   701

Samson, Arthur
Wings of a Dream - Anne Mateer   *i*   546

Lord of Slaughter
Of Truth and Beasts - Barb Hendee   *f*   206

Shade, Raynaud
Hell is Empty - Craig Johnson   *c*   79

Strong, Jim
Dreams of the Dead - Perri
   O'Shaughnessy   *m*   690

Williams, Slippery
Jersey Law - Ron Liebman   *m*   667

Windmill Man
Big Wheat - Richard Thompson   *t*   398

MUSEUM CURATOR

Chase-Pierpont, Piper
A Courtesan's Guide to Getting Your Man - Celeste
   Bradley   *r*   771

MUSICIAN

Baptiste, Dante
Etched in Bone - Adrian Phoenix   *h*   474

Boyle, Gin
The Paperbark Shoe - Goldie Goldbloom   *t*   314

January, Benjamin
The Shirt on His Back - Barbara Hambly   *c*   65

Konstatin
Wunderkind - Nikolai Grozni   *t*   321

Kranis, Nik
Stone Arabia - Dana Spiotta   *c*   142

Patterson, Charles
The Ladder Dancer - Roz Southey   *m*   728

Randall, Cara
Beaufort 1849 - Karen Lynn Allen   *t*   276

Salazar, Bennie
A Visit from the Goon Squad - Jennifer
   Egan   *c*   50

Smythe-Smith, Honoria
Just Like Heaven - Julia Quinn   *r*   923

Wilkins, Cyrus
Moon Over Soho - Ben Aaronovitch   *f*   168

Williams, Hank
I'll Never Get Out of This World Alive - Steve
   Earle   *t*   302

MYTHICAL CREATURE

Aimhrea, Kieran
Dark Enchantment - Anya Bast   *f*   171

Ares
Eternal Rider - Larissa Ione   *h*   452
Red Mortal - Deidre Knight   *r*   866

Blaine, Navarro
Navarro's Promise - Lora Leigh   *s*   1017

D'Artigo, Menolly
Blood Wyne - Yasmine Galenorn   *f*   200

Daphne
Red Mortal - Deidre Knight   *r*   866

Daye, October "Toby"
Late Eclipses - Seanan McGuire   *f*   235

Dorian
Iron Crowned - Richelle Mead   *f*   238

Down, Thistle
Thistle Down - Irene Radford   *f*   251

Gunnar
Immortal Champion - Lisa Hendrix   *f*   208

Leandros, Cal
Blackout - Rob Thurman   *f*   266

O'Connell, Catriona "Cat"
Earl of Darkness - Alix Rickloff   *r*   925

Pia
Dragon Bound - Thea Harrison   *r*   837

Ruthana
Other Kingdoms - Richard Matheson   *h*   465

Skandar
The Griffin's War - K.J. Taylor   *f*   263

NATURALIST

Buttrick, Elsie
Compass Rose - John Casey   *c*   32

NEIGHBOR

Amanda
Turn of Mind - Alice LaPlante   *c*   87

Boleyn, Anne
To Die For: A Novel of Anne Boleyn - Sandra
   Byrd   *i*   516

Case, Justin
Turn Up the Heat - Isabel Sharpe   *r*   937

Gilliland, Julia
Out of Control - Mary Connealy   *i*   521

Romo, Lucky
Whisper Falls - Toni Blake   *r*   765

Tigerlily
Tigerlily's Orchids - Ruth Rendell   *m*   706

Wyatt, Meg
To Die For: A Novel of Anne Boleyn - Sandra
   Byrd   *i*   516

NEPHEW

Adam
The Warsaw Anagrams - Richard Zimler   *m*   750

Colson, Quinn
The Ranger - Ace Atkins   *m*   565

Leon
Claire DeWitt and the City of the Dead - Sara
   Gran   *m*   618

Reggie
Last Days of Ptolemy Grey - Walter
   Mosley   *c*   111

NIECE

Caitlin
Mourning Gloria - Susan Wittig Albert   *c*   7

LeTellier, Capucine
Crime Fraiche - Alexander Campion   *m*   579

Osman, Katya
The King of Diamonds - Simon Tolkien   *t*   400

Stefa
The Warsaw Anagrams - Richard Zimler   *m*   750

Wilson, Emily
The Violets of March - Sarah Jio   *c*   78

NOBLEMAN

Lord Attenbury
The Attenbury Emeralds - Jill Paton Walsh   *t*   406

Bourne, Jonathan
One Whisper Away - Emma Wildes   *r*   959

Bright, Charles
The Admiral's Penniless Bride - Carla
   Kelly   *r*   861

Burgoyne, Catesby "Cate"
An Unlikely Countess - Jo Beverley   *r*   764

Carr, Aidan
Scandal of the Year - Laura Lee Guhrke   *r*   833

Cummings, Jason
Follow My Lead - Kate Noble   *r*   908

d'Este, Alfonso
Sins of the House of Borgia - Sarah Bower   *t*   281

de Bremont, Etienne
Death at the Chateau Bremont - M. L.
   Longworth   *m*   671

Dearborn, Chase
The Irresistible Earl - Regina Scott   *r*   936

Dodd, Sebastian
A Little Bit Sinful - Adrienne Basso   *r*   761

Douglas, Aidan
Earl of Darkness - Alix Rickloff   *r*   925

Drake, Nicholas
The School for Brides - Cheryl Ann Smith   *r*   940

Duke of Cluyne
To Tempt a Rake - Cara Elliott   *r*   809

Duke of Wareham
The American Heiress - Daisy Goodwin   *t*   316

Dunne, Hugh
The Lady Most Likely - Julia Quinn   *t*   377

Ferncsi, Rakoczy "Saint-Germain"
An Embarrassment of Riches - Chelsea Quinn
   Yarbro   *h*   509

Holroyd, Marcus
Just Like Heaven - Julia Quinn   *r*   923

Kane, Trystan
When Tempting a Rogue - Kathryn Smith   *r*   941

Landingham, Harrison
The Perfect Mistress - Victoria Alexander   *r*   756

Langford, Graeme
Treasure Me - Robyn DeHart   *r*   802

Lord Langley
Lord Langley Is Back in Town - Elizabeth
   Boyle   *r*   770

Mansfield, Richard
The Seduction of His Wife - Tiffany Clare   *r*   790

Marco "Conte of Como"
To Tempt a Rake - Cara Elliott   *r*   809

Moncrieffe, Alexander
What I Did For a Duke - Julie Anne Long   *r*   880

Oliver
An Affair without End - Candace Camp   *r*   783

Pearson, Simon
Eleven Scandals to Start to Win a Duke's Heart -
   Sarah MacLean   *r*   886

Remmington, Griffin "Lord of Reading"
Notorious Pleasures - Elizabeth Hoyt   *r*   842

Sutherland, Ian
To Desire a Wicked Duke - Nicole Jordan   *r*   857

The Duke of Castleford
Dangerous in Diamonds - Madeline
   Hunter   *r*   843

Tristan
How to Marry a Duke - Vicky Dreiling   *r*   804

Turner, Ash
Unveiled - Courtney Milan   *r*   900

von Schroeder, Baron
The Traitor's Emblem - Juan
   Gomez-Jurado   *m*   616

Woodrow, Daniel
The Heiress - Lynsay Sands   *r*   934

Yelverton, Piers
When Beauty Tamed the Beast - Eloisa
   James   *r*   848

NOBLEWOMAN

Bathsheba
My Favorite Countess - Vanessa Kelly   *r*   862

Batten, Lady Hero
Notorious Pleasures - Elizabeth Hoyt   *r*   842

Blanchard, Tess
To Desire a Wicked Duke - Nicole Jordan   *r*   857

Bryce, Mara
My Irresistible Earl - Gaelen Foley   *r*   812

Carlyle, Vivian
An Affair without End - Candace Camp *r* 783
Carolyn
The Lady Most Likely - Julia Quinn *t* 377
Curial, Amelia
The Emperor's Body - Peter Brooks *t* 284
Danbury, Beatrix
Wedding of the Season - Laura Lee
   Guhrke *r* 834
Francis, Lady Cecily
One Whisper Away - Emma Wildes *r* 959
Gordon, Lady Duff "Lucie"
The Mistress of Nothing - Kate Pullinger *t* 376
Lawford, Lady Kiri
Nowhere Near Respectable - Mary Jo
   Putney *r* 921
Madison, Suzette
The Heiress - Lynsay Sands *r* 934
Madlenka
When the Saints - Dave Duncan *f* 193
Marston, Anne
The Naked King - Sally MacKenzie *r* 884
Minerva
Lord Langley Is Back in Town - Elizabeth
   Boyle *r* 770
Sharpe, Minerva
How to Woo a Reluctant Lady - Sabrina
   Jeffries *r* 852
Westerman, Harriet
Instruments of Darkness - Imogen
   Robertson *t* 382
Island of Bones - Imogen Robertson *t* 381
Winterset, Julia
The Perfect Mistress - Victoria Alexander *r* 756
Yardley, Lady Julia
Scandal of the Year - Laura Lee Guhrke *r* 833

NOMAD

Khan, Genghis
Genghis Khan Vol. 2: The World Conqueror - Sam
   Djang *t* 299
Temujin
Genghis Khan Vol. 1: The World Conqueror - Sam
   Djang *t* 298

NURSE

Adderley, Laura
Wicked Lies - Lisa Jackson *r* 847
Benton, Paula
Hiss of Death - Rita Mae Brown *c* 26
Dobbs, Maisie
A Lesson in Secrets - Jacqueline Winspear *t* 410
Hawthorne, Glory
Pacific Glory - P.T. Deutermann *t* 296
Ramshaw, Lucy
Frozen Charlotte - Priscilla Masters *m* 679
Shaw, Jane
Tears Will Not Save Them - Linda Sole *t* 390

OFFICE WORKER

Conrad, Jillian "Jill"
Nightshade - Michelle Rowen *h* 480
Swanson, Danny
The River Killers - Bruce Burrows *m* 577

ORGANIZED CRIME FIGURE

Amato, Dante
The Camelot Conspiracy - E. Duke
   Vincent *t* 404
Anastasia, Albert
The Devil Himself - Eric Dezenhall *m* 593

Costello, Frank
The Devil Himself - Eric Dezenhall *m* 593
Ember, Ralph
Hotbed - Bill James *m* 641
Gambini, Aldo
These Dark Things - Jan Merete Weiss *m* 744
Giancana, Sam
The Camelot Conspiracy - E. Duke
   Vincent *t* 404
Lansky, Meyer
The Devil Himself - Eric Dezenhall *m* 593
Luciano, Lucky
The Devil Himself - Eric Dezenhall *m* 593
Price, Mickey
The Devil Himself - Eric Dezenhall *m* 593
Shale, Mansel
Hotbed - Bill James *m* 641
Siegel, Bugsy
The Devil Himself - Eric Dezenhall *m* 593
Tiernan, Morris
Beast of Burden - Ray Banks *m* 567
Tosca, Frank
The Informant - Thomas Perry *m* 696

ORPHAN

Annigan, Hailee
Hailee - Penny Zeller *i* 558
Drake, Purity
The Rise of the Iron Moon - Stephen Hunt *f* 216
Farmer, Alana
When Passion Rules - Johanna Lindsey *r* 878
Jewel
House Name - Michelle Sagara *f* 253
Jones, Sophiah
Sweet Misfortune - Kevin Alan Milne *c* 106
Julian
Iron House - John Hart *m* 628
Moon
The Cloud Roads - Martha Wells *f* 272
Piper, Jaimie
The Canary List - Sigmund Brouwer *i* 514
Prescott, Brendan
The Tudor Secret - C.W. Gortner *t* 319
Russell, Arvin Eugene
The Devil All the Time - Donald Ray
   Pollock *m* 699
Shep
You're Next - Gregg Hurwitz *m* 638
Spirit
Conspiracies - Mercedes Lackey *f* 224
Townsend, Lady Kendra
Pirate of My Heart - Jamie Carie *i* 517
Wingate, Mike
You're Next - Gregg Hurwitz *m* 638

OUTCAST

Salerno, Epiphany
Dandelion Summer - Lisa Wingate *i* 555

PARANORMAL INVESTIGATOR

Baringer, Ian
The Knowledge of Good & Evil - Glenn
   Kleier *h* 457

PASSENGER

Beck, Samuel
A Most Unsuitable Match - Stephanie Grace
   Whitson *i* 554

Rousseau, Fannie
A Most Unsuitable Match - Stephanie Grace
   Whitson *i* 554
Townsend, Lady Kendra
Pirate of My Heart - Jamie Carie *i* 517

PEDDLER

Roger the Chapman
The Midsummer Crown - Kate Sedley *m* 719

PHARMACIST

Capesius, Victor
The Druggist of Auschwitz - Dieter
   Schlesak *t* 386

PHILANTHROPIST

Bradshaw, Thomas
But Remember Their Names - Hillary Bell
   Locke *m* 670
Otterbourne, Charles
Off the Record - Dolores Gordon-Smith *t* 318

PHILOSOPHER

Diderot, Denis
The Philosopher's Kiss - Peter Prange *t* 375

PHOTOGRAPHER

Boudreaux, Saria
Savage Nature - Christine Feehan *r* 810
Oota, Suki
Chihuahua of the Baskervilles - Esri
   Allbritten *m* 562
Reed, Adeline
A Bride's Portrait of Dodge City, Kansas - Erica
   Vetsch *i* 553
Tannenbaum, Alys
The Traitor's Emblem - Juan
   Gomez-Jurado *m* 616

PHOTOJOURNALIST

Wallace, Cormac
Robopocalypse - Daniel H. Wilson *c* 164

PILOT

Anderssen, Finn
Only Mine - Susan Mallery *r* 888
Beaumont, Dixie Ray
Wings: A Novel of World War II Flygirls - Karl
   Friedrich *t* 311
Calloway, Beth
Blood of the Reich - William Dietrich *m* 594
Cochran, Mike
Who Shot the Water Buffalo? - Ken Babbs *t* 278
Conlin, Mike
Wings of Promise - Bonnie Leon *i* 542
Evans, Kate
Wings of Promise - Bonnie Leon *i* 542
Huckelbee, Tom
Who Shot the Water Buffalo? - Ken Babbs *t* 278
Ketchum, Sally
Wings: A Novel of World War II Flygirls - Karl
   Friedrich *t* 311
McCarty, Mick
Pacific Glory - P.T. Deutermann *t* 296
Samson, Arthur
Wings of a Dream - Anne Mateer *i* 546
Stone, Marshall
The Girl in the Blue Beret - Bobbie Ann
   Mason *t* 345

Cohen, Erik
The Warsaw Anagrams - Richard Zimler   *m*   750

Drake, Purity
The Rise of the Iron Moon - Stephen Hunt   *f*   216

Flynn, Sean
Beg for Mercy - Jami Alden   *r*   754

Gunther, Bernie
Field Gray - Philip Kerr   *t*   339

Hawkins, Anwan
The Cut - George P. Pelecanos   *m*   694

Jeffers, Erland
Trespasser - Paul Doiron   *m*   596

John
The Paperbark Shoe - Goldie Goldbloom   *t*   314

le Flambeur, Jean
The Quantum Thief - Hannu Rajaniemi   *s*   1034

Swain, David
The King of Diamonds - Simon Tolkien   *t*   400

Taylor, Will
Livvie's Song - Sharlene MacLaren   *i*   545

PRODUCER

Gophner, Peter "Gopher"
Ghouls, Ghouls, Ghouls - Victoria Laurie   *h*   460

PROFESSOR

Aldiss, Richard
Dominance - Will Lavender   *m*   662

Bonnet, Marine
Death at the Chateau Bremont - M. L.
   Longworth   *m*   671

Bradshaw, Benjamin
A Spark of Death - Bernadette Pajer   *m*   692

Branden, Michael
Harmless as Doves - P.L. Gaus   *m*   611

Dr. Appleton
The Square Root of Murder - Ada
   Madison   *m*   676

Haraldsson, Agnar
Where the Shadows Lie - Michael
   Ridpath   *m*   709

Knight, Piers
Central Park Knight - C.J. Henderson   *f*   207

Knowles, Sophie
The Square Root of Murder - Ada
   Madison   *m*   676

Makepiece, Perry
Our Kind of Traitor - John Le Carre   *c*   89

Oglethorpe, Wesley
A Spark of Death - Bernadette Pajer   *m*   692

Philip
I Married You for Happiness - Lily Tuck   *c*   154

Shipley, Alex
Dominance - Will Lavender   *m*   662

Tao, Sheila
Creep - Jennifer Hillier   *m*   634

Williams, Steven
Sweet Little Lies - Michele Grant   *r*   830

PROSPECTOR

Holloway, Jack
Fuzzy Nation - John Scalzi   *s*   1041

PROSTITUTE

Amalya
The Demon and the Succubus - Cassie
   Ryan   *h*   484

Cunningham, Amy
Murder on Sisters' Row - Victoria
   Thompson   *m*   736

Harony, Maria Katarina
Doc - Mary Doria Russell   *c*   131

Meade, Grace
Backlash - Sally Spencer   *m*   729

Mystery
Mystery - Jonathan Kellerman   *c*   81

Ophelia
A Courtesan's Guide to Getting Your Man - Celeste
   Bradley   *r*   771

PSYCHIC

Adam
The Chaos - Rachel Ward   *h*   501

Adderley, Laura
Wicked Lies - Lisa Jackson   *r*   847

Carlsen, Astrid
The Shadow Guard - Diane Whiteside   *r*   957

Cooper, Abby
Vision Impossible - Victoria Laurie   *m*   661

Dean, Virginia
Quicksilver - Amanda Quick   *c*   124

Gillian, Kara
Secrets of the Demon - Diana Rowland   *h*   483

Graize
The Shining City - Fiona Patton   *f*   247

Harper, Meena
Overbite - Meg Cabot   *c*   31

Ia
Theirs Not to Reason Why: A Soldier's Duty - Jean
   Johnson   *s*   1009

Markowitz, Melina
Dead on Delivery - Eileen Rendahl   *h*   479

McConnell, Dags
Grimoire - Phaedra Weldon   *h*   502

Montgomery, Eloise
Darkness, My Old Friend - Lisa Unger   *c*   157

O'Grady, Nola
License of Ensorcell - Katharine Kerr   *f*   221

Reynolds, Kim
The Truth Sleuth - Jacqueline Seewald   *m*   720

Sienna Lauren
Kiss of Snow - Nalini Singh   *r*   939

Silveira, Isabella
At Hidden Falls - Barbara Freethy   *r*   819

Spar
The Shining City - Fiona Patton   *f*   247

Tate, Willow
Night Mares in the Hamptons - Celia
   Jerome   *f*   219

Thirianna
Path of the Seer - Gav Thorpe   *s*   1053

Usher, Thomas
Pretty Little Dead Things - Gary
   McMahon   *h*   469

Willoughby, Violet
Haunting Violet - Alyxandra Harvey   *f*   205

PSYCHOLOGIST

Bark, Dr. Erik Maria
The Hypnotist - Lars Kepler   *m*   655

Delaware, Alex
Mystery - Jonathan Kellerman   *c*   81

Dobbs, Maisie
A Lesson in Secrets - Jacqueline Winspear   *t*   410

Hendrix, Dakota
Only Mine - Susan Mallery   *r*   888

Lincoln, Will
Moonlight Cove - Sherryl Woods   *r*   961

Markham, David
Millennium People - J.G. Ballard   *c*   14

Nadine
Never Knowing - Chevy Stevens   *m*   731

Sheridan, Tara
Rogue Oracle - Alayna Williams   *f*   274

Weber, Angela
The Knowledge of Good & Evil - Glenn
   Kleier   *h*   457

PUBLIC RELATIONS

Barr, Temple
Cat in a Vegas Gold Vendetta - Carole Nelson
   Douglas   *m*   598

Jackson, Jules
Man Enough for Me - Rhonda Bowen   *r*   769

Pickett, Rominy
Blood of the Reich - William Dietrich   *m*   594

RACE CAR DRIVER

Holbrook, Kendall
The Chase - Erin McCarthy   *r*   892

Monroe, Evan
The Chase - Erin McCarthy   *r*   892

Reilly, Kate
Dead Man's Switch - Tammy Kaehler   *m*   649

RADIO PERSONALITY

Galloway, Jillian
Desert Gift - Sally John   *r*   854

RAKE

Lomax, Colt
Make Mine a Bad Boy - Katie Lane   *r*   874

Mackenzie, Damian
Nowhere Near Respectable - Mary Jo
   Putney   *r*   921

Masters, Giles
How to Woo a Reluctant Lady - Sabrina
   Jeffries   *r*   852

Parker-Roth, Stephen
The Naked King - Sally MacKenzie   *r*   884

RANCHER

Anderson, Rue
Miss You Most of All - Elizabeth Bass   *c*   16

Chisholm, Dawson
Rustled - B.J. Daniels   *r*   796

Clayton, Lamar
Remember Ben Clayton - Stephen Harrigan   *t*   323

Creed, Conner
The Creed Legacy - Linda Lael Miller   *r*   870
Creed's Honor - Linda Lael Miller   *r*   901

Em
Texas Blue - Jodi Thomas   *r*   945

Grant, John
Keep a Little Secret - Dorothy Garlock   *r*   823

Hunt, Phil
Terror of Living - Urban Waite   *c*   158

Kincaid, Rafe
Out of Control - Mary Connealy   *i*   521

Masterson, Harper
Saddled and Spurred - Lorelei James   *r*   850

O'Donnell, Rye
Love Drunk Cowboy - Carolyn Brown   *r*   776

Treadwell, Teague
Cowboy Fever - Joanne Kennedy   *r*   863

Turner, Bran
Saddled and Spurred - Lorelei James   *r*   850

RANGER

Cantrell, Casey
Deadly Silence - Lindsay McKenna   *r*   897

Nelson, Jake
A River to Cross - Yvonne L Harris   *i*   534

Pigeon, Anna
Burn - Nevada Barr   *c*   15

REAL ESTATE AGENT

Fortenberry, Maggie
I Still Dream About You - Fannie Flagg   *c*   54

REANIMATED DEAD

Chane
Of Truth and Beasts - Barb Hendee   *f*   206

RECLUSE

Kranis, Nik
Stone Arabia - Dana Spiotta   *c*   142

REFUGEE

Nolander, Rachel
Never Knew Another - J.M. McDermott   *f*   234

Prcic, Ismet
Shards - Ismet Prcic   *c*   123

RELATIVE

Sparhawk, Dermot
The Charlestown Connection - Tom
   MacDonald   *m*   675

RELIGIOUS

Abbess Hildegard
The Law of Angels - Cassandra Clark   *t*   289

Adams, Lester
Say Amen, Again - ReShonda Tate
   Billingsley   *i*   512

Adams, Maxwell Nathaniel Jr.
Hailee - Penny Zeller   *i*   558

Bacon, Roger
Falconer and the Death of Kings - Ian
   Morson   *t*   361

Baringer, Ian
The Knowledge of Good & Evil - Glenn
   Kleier   *h*   457

Beck, Samuel
A Most Unsuitable Match - Stephanie Grace
   Whitson   *i*   554

Becker, Caryn
The Edge of Grace - Christa Allan   *i*   510

Bellringer, Reverend
Revenants: A Dream of New England - Daniel
   Mills   *t*   356

Borgia, Rodrigo "Pope Alexander IV"
The Borgia Betrayal - Sara Poole   *m*   700

Breen, Arthur "Art"
Faith - Jennifer Haigh   *c*   64

Burroughs, George
Deliverance from Evil - Frances Hill   *t*   330

Entropica, Gomez
Ringer - Brian M. Wiprud   *m*   748

Ernest, Eli
The Doctor's Lady - Jody Hedlund   *i*   535

Grafton, Simon
Saving Grace - Carolyn Davidson   *r*   798

Jackson, Jules
Man Enough for Me - Rhonda Bowen   *r*   769

Jacob
The Damascus Way - Janette Oke   *r*   911

Julia
The Damascus Way - Janette Oke   *r*   911

Lake, Samuel
The Homecoming of Samuel Lake - Jenny
   Wingfield   *c*   165

Malloy, Emma
A Heart Revealed - Julie Lessman   *i*   543

Meeks, Gabriel
The Matrimony Plan - Christine Johnson   *i*   539

Mitchell, Don
Broken - Patricia Haley   *i*   533

Morgan, Justus
A Good Excuse to Be Bad - Miranda
   Parker   *m*   693

Novak, Raymond
Blue Skies Tomorrow - Sarah Sundin   *i*   552

Oughterard, Reverend
A Bedlam of Bones - Suzette A. Hill   *m*   633

Pope Alexander VI
Sins of the House of Borgia - Sarah Bower   *t*   281

Richardson, Mary
Say Amen, Again - ReShonda Tate
   Billingsley   *i*   512

Richelieu
The Alchemist in the Shadows - Pierre
   Pevel   *f*   248

Roy
The Devil All the Time - Donald Ray
   Pollock   *m*   699

Shetler, Leon
Harmless as Doves - P.L. Gaus   *m*   611

Spar
The Shining City - Fiona Patton   *f*   247

Stein, Daniel
Daniel Stern, Interpreter: A Novel in Documents -
   Ludmila Ulitskaya   *t*   402

Theodore
The Devil All the Time - Donald Ray
   Pollock   *m*   699

White, Priscilla
The Doctor's Lady - Jody Hedlund   *i*   535

Wilson, T.K.
The Choir Director - Carl Weber   *r*   955

Yoder, Katy
Something Old - Dianne L Christner   *i*   520

REPAIRMAN

Jack
The Dark at the End - F. Paul Wilson   *h*   507

RESCUER

Gilmore, Lachlan
Lady on the Loch - Betty McInnes   *t*   351

Kane
Infestation Cubed - James Axler   *s*   975

Knight, Brian
Deadly Intentions - Candice Poarch   *r*   919

Korsak, Stefan
Basilisk - Rob Thurman   *s*   1055

Mahoney, Michael
Rescuing the Heiress - Valerie Hansen   *r*   835

Mason
Nightfall - Ellen Connor   *h*   424

McKendrick, Robert
Death in High Places - Jo Bannister   *m*   568

Mieli
The Quantum Thief - Hannu Rajaniemi   *s*   1034

RESEARCHER

Singh, Marina
State of Wonder - Ann Patchett   *c*   117

Swenson, Annick
State of Wonder - Ann Patchett   *c*   117

Wyman, Sarah
Tunnel Vision - Gary Braver   *s*   980

RESISTANCE FIGHTER

Nowak, Adam
The Katyn Order - Douglas W. Jacobson   *t*   335

RESTAURATEUR

Beckman, Olivia
Livvie's Song - Sharlene MacLaren   *i*   545

Cosi, Clare
Murder by Mocha - Cleo Coyle   *m*   589

Hampton, Spencer
Secret Attraction - Donna Hill   *r*   841

Nikos
Burning Down the Spouse - Dakota
   Cassidy   *r*   786

RETIREE

Glass, Percy
Widower's Tale - Julia Glass   *c*   58

Martha
The Story of Beautiful Girl - Rachel
   Simon   *c*   136

Pettigrew, Ernest
Major Pettigrew's Last Stand - Helen
   Simonson   *c*   137

von Enke, Hakan
Troubled Man - Henning Mankell   *c*   98

REVOLUTIONARY

Concepcion, Diosdado
A Moment in the Sun - John Sayles   *t*   385

ROBOT

The Automaton
The Falling Machine - Andrew Mayer   *s*   1023

RODEO RIDER

Creed, Brody
The Creed Legacy - Linda Lael Miller   *r*   870
Creed's Honor - Linda Lael Miller   *r*   901

ROOMMATE

Dunne, Owen
The Art of Fielding - Chad Harbach   *c*   68

Ross, Evelyn
Rules of Civility - Amor Towles   *t*   401

ROYALTY

Adolphus, Gustavus
1636: The Saxon Uprising - Eric Flint   *t*   310

Ahasuerus
A Reluctant Queen - Joan Wolf   *r*   960

Ariana
Hunger Untamed - Pamela Palmer   *r*   913

Authun
Wolfsangel - M.D. Lachlan   *f*   223

Azalea
Entwined - Heather Dixon   *c*   49

Boleyn, Anne
To Die For: A Novel of Anne Boleyn - Sandra
   Byrd   *i*   516

Caledor
Caledor - Gav Thorpe *f* 265

Cleopatra
Queen of Kings - Maria Dahvana Headley *t* 327

Diana/Lydia
Untold Story - Monica Ali *c* 8

Dororam
The Goblin Corps - Ari Marmell *f* 232

Eleanor
The King's Witch - Cecelia Holland *t* 332

Elizabeth
Elizabeth I - Margaret George *t* 313
Prophecy - S.J. Parris *c* 116
*The Secret History of Elizabeth Tudor, Vampire
    Slayer* - Lucy Weston *h* 504

Elizabeth I
The Tudor Secret - C.W. Gortner *t* 319

Ernst
Sweet as the Devil - Susan Johnson *r* 856

Esther
A Reluctant Queen - Joan Wolf *r* 960

Farmer, Alana
When Passion Rules - Johanna Lindsey *r* 878

Grey, Lady Jane
Queen of Misfortune - Peter Carroll *t* 285
The Tudor Secret - C.W. Gortner *t* 319

Henry
Henry VIII, Wolfman - A.E. Moorat *h* 470

Imrik
Sons of Ellyrion - Graham McNeill *f* 236

Jaffar
The Desert of Souls - Howard Andrew
    Jones *t* 337

Jaslyn
The King of the Crags - Stephen Deas *f* 190

Jehal
The King of the Crags - Stephen Deas *f* 190

Kaiser Wilhelm II
The Parsifal Pursuit - Michael
    McMenamin *t* 353

Kikaya, Ali
The Moon Maze Game - Larry Niven *s* 1030

King Arthur
Master of Shadows - Angela Knight *h* 458

King Daniel
Naamah's Blessing - Jacqueline Carey *f* 184

King Edward
The Tudor Secret - C.W. Gortner *t* 319

King John
To Defy a King - Elizabeth Chadwick *t* 287

Kunigunde
An Embarrassment of Riches - Chelsea Quinn
    Yarbro *h* 509

Lenayin, Damon
Haven - Joel Shepherd *f* 256

Lilith
The Demon and the Succubus - Cassie
    Ryan *h* 484

Lisa, Mona
Mona Lisa Eclipsing - Sunny Chen *r* 787

Lord Bahl
The Iron Palace - Morgan Howell *f* 213

Louis XIV
Before Versailles - Karleen Koen *c* 83

Maeve
The Raven Queen - Jules Watson *f* 271

Markham, Eugenie
Iron Crowned - Richelle Mead *f* 238

Martini, Jeff
Alien in the Family - Gini Koch *s* 1013

Mary
The Tudor Secret - C.W. Gortner *t* 319

Miranda
Shadowflame - Dianne Sylvan *h* 496

Morthul
The Goblin Corps - Ari Marmell *f* 232

Nikandr
The Winds of Khalakovo - Bradley
    Beaulieu *f* 173

Oberon
The Great Night - Chris Adrian *c* 4

Parini, Jacques "Jack"
Then He Kissed Me - Christie Ridgway *r* 926

Prince Charming
Wickedly Charming - Kristine Grayson *r* 832

Prince Thierry
Naamah's Blessing - Jacqueline Carey *f* 184

Princess Desiree
Naamah's Blessing - Jacqueline Carey *f* 184

Queen Anjine
The Key to Creation - Kevin J. Anderson *c* 9

Queen Jehanne
Naamah's Blessing - Jacqueline Carey *f* 184

Queen of the Mists
Late Eclipses - Seanan McGuire *f* 235

Rajasthan, Nickolai
Messiah - S. Andrew Swann *s* 1051

Richard
The King's Witch - Cecelia Holland *t* 332

Roxy
Then He Kissed Me - Christie Ridgway *r* 926

Serai
Vampire in Atlantis - Alyssa Day *r* 800

Sigmar
God King - Graham McNeill *f* 237

Sigvad the Maginficent
Sigvald - Darius Hinks *f* 209

Solomon, David
Shadowflame - Dianne Sylvan *h* 496

Stuart, Mary
Lady on the Loch - Betty McInnes *t* 351

Taylor, Betsy
Undead and Undermined - MaryJanice
    Davidson *f* 189

The Undead Queen
This Side of the Grave - Jeaniene Frost *r* 820

Titania
The Great Night - Chris Adrian *c* 4

Tudor, Henry VIII
Blood of the Rose - Kate Pearce *r* 915

Tyrion
Sons of Ellyrion - Graham McNeill *f* 236

Zafir
The King of the Crags - Stephen Deas *f* 190

RULER

Bonaparte, Napoleon
Rebellion - James McGee *t* 350

Mykella
Lady-Protector - L.E. Modesitt Jr. *f* 239

Nagash
Nagash Immortal - Mike Lee *f* 227

Queen of the Mists
Late Eclipses - Seanan McGuire *f* 235

Tabini-aiji
Betrayer - C.J. Cherryh *s* 987

Targaryen, Daenerys
Dance With Dragons: A Song of Ice and Fire -
    George R.R. Martin *c* 99

RUNAWAY

Harris, Claire
The Last Time I Saw Paris - Lynn Sheene *r* 938

Shackleford, Maryn
Summer Rental - Mary Kay Andrews *c* 10

SAILOR

Beaumont, Brie
Danger Sector - Jenifer LeClair *m* 664

Gonzalez, Captain
The Traitor's Emblem - Juan
    Gomez-Jurado *m* 616

Lenk
Black Halo - Sam Sykes *f* 260

Nello
Sea of Lost Dreams - Ferenc Mate *t* 346

Saan
The Key to Creation - Kevin J. Anderson *c* 9

Stapleton, Cordelia
The Explorer's Code - Kitty Pilgrim *m* 697

Vora, Criston
The Key to Creation - Kevin J. Anderson *c* 9

SCAVENGER

Cutter, Zane
Undertow - Cherry Adair *r* 752

SCHOLAR

Alexander, Tess
One Magic Moment - Lynn Kurland *r* 869

Dabir
The Desert of Souls - Howard Andrew
    Jones *t* 337

Falconer, William
Falconer and the Death of Kings - Ian
    Morson *t* 361

SCIENTIST

Archer, Grant
Leviathans of Jupiter - Ben Bova *s* 979

August, Max
The Plain Man - Steve Englehart *f* 195

Campbell, Paige
Ghost Country - Patrick Lee *s* 1016

Chambers, Mark
His Unexpectedly - Susan Fox *r* 818

Chase, Travis
Ghost Country - Patrick Lee *s* 1016

Crowther, Gabriel
Instruments of Darkness - Imogen
    Robertson *t* 382
Island of Bones - Imogen Robertson *t* 381

Dance, Bette
This Shared Dream - Kathleen Ann
    Goonan *s* 999

Dance, Sam
This Shared Dream - Kathleen Ann
    Goonan *s* 999

Duncan, Isabel
Ape House - Sara Gruen *c* 63

Fawkes, Samuel
Element Zero - James Knapp *s* 1012

Frankenstein, Victor
The Dead Town - Dean Koontz *h* 459

Harmon, Raleigh
The Mountains Bow Down - Sibella
    Giorello *r* 827

Hood, Benjamin
Blood of the Reich - William Dietrich *m* 594

Kaufman, Philip
The Noise Revealed - Ian Whates *s* 1058

Larsen, Eve
Abyss - David Hagberg *s* 1006

Mueller, Sam
2030: The Real Story of What Happens To America
    - Albert Brooks *c* 24

Quirke, Garret
A Death In Summer - Benjamin Black *m* 571

Rosseau, Colette
The Death Instinct - Jed Rubenfeld *t* 383

Takesue, Alma Boyd
When the Killing's Done - T.C. Boyle *i* 513

Wasserman, Nicholas
Robopocalypse - Daniel H. Wilson *c* 164

Woodbridge, Kate
To Tempt a Rake - Cara Elliott *r* 809

SEA CAPTAIN

Colburn, Dorian
Pirate of My Heart - Jamie Carie *i* 517

Ransome, William
Ransome's Quest - Kaye Dacus *i* 522

Rulorat, Vidarian
Sword of Fire and Sea - Erin Hoffman *f* 212

SEAMSTRESS

Erskine, Annabel
Lady on the Loch - Betty McInnes *t* 351

Gilmore, Christina
Lady on the Loch - Betty McInnes *t* 351

Waters, Lona
A Good Hard Look - Ann Napolitano *t* 363

SECRETARY

Kontent, Katy
Rules of Civility - Amor Towles *t* 401

Makutsi, Grace
The Saturday Big Tent Wedding Party - Alexander
    McCall Smith *c* 138

Miss Moneypenny
Carte Blanche - Jeffery Deaver *m* 592

Rowan, Roxanna
The Colonel's Lady - Laura Frantz *i* 527

SECURITY OFFICER

Bradford, Miles
The Informationist - Taylor Stevens *c* 144

O'Neill, Lincoln
Attachments - Rainbow Rowell *r* 930

Osborne-Smith, Percy
Carte Blanche - Jeffery Deaver *m* 592

Purdue, Maleah
Dead by Morning - Beverly Barton *r* 760

Ranger
Smokin' Seventeen - Janet Evanovich *c* 51

Rider, Mark
Conspiracies - Mercedes Lackey *f* 224

Tanner, Quinn
Warrior Betrayed - Addison Fox *r* 817

SERIAL KILLER

Carl
The Devil All the Time - Donald Ray
    Pollock *m* 699

Parrish, Nick
Disturbance - Jan Burke *c* 29

Sandy
The Devil All the Time - Donald Ray
    Pollock *m* 699

The Snowman
The Snowman - Jo Nesbo *c* 112

Turnbull, Justice
Wicked Lies - Lisa Jackson *r* 847

SERVANT

Bunter
The Attenbury Emeralds - Jill Paton Walsh *t* 406

Chlod
Knights of Bretonnia - Anthony Reynolds *f* 252

Daisy
The Penningtons - Pamela Oldfield *t* 368

Elisa
Vampire Instinct - Joey W. Hill *h* 448

Naldrett, Sally
The Mistress of Nothing - Kate Pullinger *t* 376

Reiner, Paul
The Traitor's Emblem - Juan
    Gomez-Jurado *m* 616

Sarfati, Esther
Sins of the House of Borgia - Sarah Bower *t* 281

Sheridan, Brad
All the Lives He Led - Frederik Pohl *s* 1032

SETTLER

Smith, Captain John
The Leaves of Fate - George Robert
    Minkoff *t* 357

SHAMAN

Markham, Eugenie
Iron Crowned - Richelle Mead *f* 238

Walker
The Lone Warrior - Denise Rossetti *r* 929

SHAPE-SHIFTER

Cuelebre, Dragos
Dragon Bound - Thea Harrison *r* 837

Donovan, Drake
Savage Nature - Christine Feehan *r* 810

Fraser, Kim
Primal Bonds - Jennifer Ashley *f* 170

Hawke
Kiss of Snow - Nalini Singh *r* 939

Kiyo
Iron Crowned - Richelle Mead *f* 238

Merlotte, Sam
Dead Reckoning - Charlaine Harris *c* 71

Moon
The Cloud Roads - Martha Wells *f* 272

Morrissey, Liam
Primal Bonds - Jennifer Ashley *f* 170

Roberto
Mona Lisa Eclipsing - Sunny Chen *r* 787

Sabrine
Moon Burning - Lucy Monroe *f* 241

Thompson, Mercy
River Marked - Patricia Briggs *h* 418

SHIPOWNER

Dugger
Sea of Lost Dreams - Ferenc Mate *t* 346

SIDEKICK

Charles
The Return of Captain John Emmett - Elizabeth
    Speller *t* 392

Nog
Star Trek: Indistinguishable from Magic - David A.
    McIntee *s* 1026

Shotgun Suzie
A Hard Day's Knight - Simon R. Green *f* 203

The Automaton
The Falling Machine - Andrew Mayer *s* 1023

Vitt, Cassiopeia
Jefferson Key - Steve Berry *m* 570

Watson
Between the Thames and the Tiber - Ted
    Riccardi *m* 707

SINGER

Calhoun, Clarion
Stagestruck - Peter Lovesey *m* 672

Calhoun, Hassie
Hassie Calhoun - Cory Pamela *t* 369

Geneva
Burn - Nevada Barr *c* 15

Hart, Destiny
Restless Heart - Wynonna Judd *c* 80

Jones, Lyric
Sweet Possession - Maya Banks *r* 759

Mackie, Aaron
The Choir Director - Carl Weber *r* 955

Moss, Jackie Robinson
The Choir Director - Carl Weber *r* 955

Reed, Anise
When the Killing's Done - T.C. Boyle *i* 513

Travers, Shannon
Separate Dreams - Joan Early *r* 807

SINGLE FATHER

Affenlight, Guert
The Art of Fielding - Chad Harbach *c* 68

Harley, Chris
44 Charles Street - Danielle Steel *c* 143

Wesson, Gabe
The Nanny's Homecoming - Linda
    Goodnight *i* 530

SINGLE MOTHER

Becker, Caryn
The Edge of Grace - Christa Allan *i* 510

Beckman, Olivia
Livvie's Song - Sharlene MacLaren *i* 545

Carlisle, Helen
Blue Skies Tomorrow - Sarah Sundin *i* 552

Crawford, Angel
A Good Excuse to Be Bad - Miranda
    Parker *m* 693

Robin
Getting to Happy - Terry McMillan *c* 101

Rory
Silver Boat - Luanne Rice *c* 127

Stenen, Dinah
Outside Wonderland - Lorna Jane Cook *c* 40

Westmore, Elle
Falls Like Lightning - Shawn Grady *i* 531

SINGLE PARENT

Sinclaire, Matt
Deadly Silence - Lindsay McKenna *r* 897

SISTER

Anderson, Laura
Miss You Most of All - Elizabeth Bass   *c*   16

Anderson, Monica
The Five Masks of Dr. Scream - R.L. Stine   *h*   491

Anderson, Rue
Miss You Most of All - Elizabeth Bass   *c*   16

Anita
The Year We Left Home - Jean Thompson   *c*   153

Bea
Her Sister's Shadow - Katharine Britton   *r*   774
Sister - Rosamund Lupton   *m*   673

Becker, Caryn
The Edge of Grace - Christa Allan   *i*   510

Borgia, Lucrezia
Sins of the House of Borgia - Sarah Bower   *t*   281

Carolyn
The Lady Most Likely - Julia Quinn   *t*   377

Crawford, Angel
A Good Excuse to Be Bad - Miranda Parker   *m*   693

Dannie
A Death In Summer - Benjamin Black   *m*   571

Daphne
Red Mortal - Deidre Knight   *r*   866

Dar
Silver Boat - Luanne Rice   *c*   127

Delia
Silver Boat - Luanne Rice   *c*   127

Dodge, Ellen
The Dashwood Sisters Tell All - Beth Pattillo   *r*   914

Dodge, Mimi
The Dashwood Sisters Tell All - Beth Pattillo   *r*   914

Eversea, Genevieve
What I Did For a Duke - Julie Anne Long   *r*   880

Evie
The Naked King - Sally MacKenzie   *r*   884

Fey, Anika
Black Swan - Chris Knopf   *m*   658

Fisher, Holly
A Light at Winter's End - Julia London   *r*   879

Flynn, Megan
Beg for Mercy - Jami Alden   *r*   754

Frank, Anne
The Silent Sister: The Diary of Margot Frank - Mazal Alouf-Mizrahi   *t*   277

Frank, Margot
The Silent Sister: The Diary of Margot Frank - Mazal Alouf-Mizrahi   *t*   277

Gilmore, Christina
Lady on the Loch - Betty McInnes   *t*   351

Grayson, Paige
In the Air Tonight - Stephanie Tyler   *r*   947

Hannah
A Light at Winter's End - Julia London   *r*   879

Kelleher, Ann Marie
Maine - J. Courtney Sullivan   *c*   148

Kelleher, Kathleen
Maine - J. Courtney Sullivan   *c*   148

Kranis, Denise
Stone Arabia - Dana Spiotta   *c*   142

Lenayin, Sasha
Haven - Joel Shepherd   *f*   256

Levert, Eleanor
Bones of a Feather - Carolyn Haines   *m*   622

Levert, Monica
Bones of a Feather - Carolyn Haines   *m*   622

Maggie
The Watery Part of the World - Michael Parker   *t*   370

Mahdian, Lauren
Close Your Eyes - Amanda Eyre Ward   *m*   742

Marion
Joy for Beginners - Erica Bauermeister   *c*   17

Mary
Dreams of Joy - Lisa See   *t*   388
The Return of Captain John Emmett - Elizabeth Speller   *t*   392

McArthur, Ava
A Good Excuse to Be Bad - Miranda Parker   *m*   693

McDonald, Rayne
Blood Ties - Mari Mancusi   *f*   231
Night School - Mari Mancusi   *h*   463

McDonald, Sunny
Blood Ties - Mari Mancusi   *f*   231
Night School - Mari Mancusi   *h*   463

McGann, Shelia
Faith - Jennifer Haigh   *c*   64

Meg
Weirdo Halloween - R.L. Stine   *h*   490

Mitchell, Tamara
Broken - Patricia Haley   *i*   533

Muir, Felice
Birds of Paradise - Diana Abu-Jaber   *c*   1

Nicosa, Cecilia
White Shotgun - April Smith   *m*   727

Niles, Lilli
Her Sister's Shadow - Katharine Britton   *r*   774

Pearl
Dreams of Joy - Lisa See   *t*   388

Porter, Priscilla "Priss"
A Bad Day for Scandal - Sophie Littlefield   *m*   669

Puddin
The Dry Grass of August - Anna Jean Mayhew   *t*   347

Ransome, Charlotte
Ransome's Quest - Kaye Dacus   *i*   522

Rory
Silver Boat - Luanne Rice   *c*   127

Ryrie, Biscuit
The Grief of Others - Leah Hager Cohen   *c*   37

Skella
Honeyed Words - J.A. Pitts   *f*   249

Slade, Holly
Blood Stains - Sharon Sala   *r*   932

Slade, Maria
Blood Stains - Sharon Sala   *r*   932

Slade, Savannah
Blood Stains - Sharon Sala   *r*   932

Stell
The Dry Grass of August - Anna Jean Mayhew   *t*   347

Stenen, Alice
Outside Wonderland - Lorna Jane Cook   *c*   40

Stenen, Dinah
Outside Wonderland - Lorna Jane Cook   *c*   40

Tess
Sister - Rosamund Lupton   *m*   673

Trudeau, Alex
True Colors - Joyce Lamb   *r*   871

Trudeau, Charlie
True Colors - Joyce Lamb   *r*   871

Verver, Dusty
The End of Everything - Megan Abbott   *m*   560

Verver, Evie
The End of Everything - Megan Abbott   *m*   560

Viradechtis
The Tempering of Men - Sarah Monette   *f*   240

Watts, Jubie
The Dry Grass of August - Anna Jean Mayhew   *t*   347

Whaley
The Watery Part of the World - Michael Parker   *t*   370

SKIER

Larsen, Karen
A Little Bit of Passion - Beate Boeker   *r*   766

SLAVE

Cardockson, Arren
Dark Griffin - K.J. Taylor   *f*   261
The Griffin's Flight - K.J. Taylor   *f*   262

Frazier, Kit
Wicked Seduction - Jade Lee   *r*   876

Turner, Nat
The Resurrection of Nat Turner, Part 1: The Witnesses - Sharon Ewell Foster   *i*   526

Yim
The Iron Palace - Morgan Howell   *f*   213

SMUGGLER

Coburn, Murray
Trace of Fever - Lori Foster   *r*   814

Drothe
Among Thieves - Douglas Hulick   *f*   215

Hunt, Phil
Terror of Living - Urban Waite   *c*   158

SOCIALITE

Farmer, Alana
When Passion Rules - Johanna Lindsey   *r*   878

Harris, Claire
The Last Time I Saw Paris - Lynn Sheene   *r*   938

Howard, Julia
Paper Doll - Janet Woods   *t*   411

SON

Antonescu, Lucien
Overbite - Meg Cabot   *c*   31

Beau
The Beach Trees - Karen White   *c*   162

Benji
Butterfly's Child - Angela Davis-Gardner   *t*   293

Bob
Dreams of the Dead - Perri O'Shaughnessy   *m*   690

Borgia, Cesare
Sins of the House of Borgia - Sarah Bower   *t*   281

Braddock, Noah
Liquid Smoke - Jeff Shelby   *m*   724

Buckner, Simon Bolivar Jr.
The Final Storm - Jeff Shaara   *t*   389

Burns, Jeremy
The Pack - Jason Starr   *h*   488

Cajeiri
Betrayer - C.J. Cherryh   *s*   987

Cathmar
The Sea Thy Mistress - Elizabeth Bear   *f*   172

Cawdor, Dean
Downrigger Drift - James Axler   *s*   967
Prodigal's Return - James Axler   *s*   969

Blanchard, Tess
To Desire a Wicked Duke - Nicole Jordan   *r*   857
Bogan, Oto
Requiem for a Gypsy - Michael Genelin   *m*   612
Boganova, Klara
Requiem for a Gypsy - Michael Genelin   *m*   612
Bognor, Simon
Death in the Opening Chapter - Tim Heald   *m*   631
Boleyn, Anne
Henry VIII, Wolfman - A.E. Moorat   *h*   470
Bones
This Side of the Grave - Jeaniene Frost   *r*   820
Boyle, Gin
The Paperbark Shoe - Goldie Goldbloom   *t*   314
Brady, Kate
The Hat - Babette Hughes   *t*   333
Burns, Alison
The Pack - Jason Starr   *h*   488
Burns, Simon
The Pack - Jason Starr   *h*   488
Burroughs, George
Deliverance from Evil - Frances Hill   *t*   330
Calvino, John
What the Night Knows - Dean Koontz   *c*   84
Campbell, Claudia
The Crossing - Serita Jakes   *i*   538
Carl
The Devil All the Time - Donald Ray Pollock   *m*   699
Castagna, Robin
Mystery - Jonathan Kellerman   *c*   81
Cat
Falling Together - Marisa de los Santos   *c*   45
Cheever, Mary
Deliverance from Evil - Frances Hill   *t*   330
Christine
Before I Go To Sleep - S.J. Watson   *m*   743
Claire
Your Friendly Neighborhood Criminal - Michael Van Rooy   *m*   740
Clemm, Virginia
The Raven's Bride - Lenore Hart   *t*   325
Coleman, Samuel
The Gin & Chowder Club - Nan Parson Rossiter   *c*   130
Coleman, Sarah
The Gin & Chowder Club - Nan Parson Rossiter   *c*   130
Conor
The Raven Queen - Jules Watson   *f*   271
Crawfield, Cat
This Side of the Grave - Jeaniene Frost   *r*   820
d'Aubigny, Francoise
A Death In Summer - Benjamin Black   *m*   571
Dance, Bette
This Shared Dream - Kathleen Ann Goonan   *s*   999
Dance, Sam
This Shared Dream - Kathleen Ann Goonan   *s*   999
Darcy, Elizabeth
Mr. Darcy's Secret - Jane Odiwe   *r*   910
Darcy, Fitzwilliam
Mr. Darcy's Secret - Jane Odiwe   *r*   910
Darlene
Playdate - Thelma Adams   *c*   2
Dave
Eat Slay Love - Jesse Petersen   *h*   472

David
Flip This Zombie - Jesse Petersen   *h*   471
Dudley, Robert
Elizabeth I - Margaret George   *t*   313
Eden
Breaking the Rules - Suzanne Brockmann   *r*   775
Edison
Separate Dreams - Joan Early   *r*   807
Esther
A Reluctant Queen - Joan Wolf   *r*   960
Fairchild, Grace
Never a Gentleman - Eileen Dreyer   *r*   805
Fargo, Remi
The Kingdom - Clive Cussler   *c*   43
Fargo, Sam
The Kingdom - Clive Cussler   *c*   43
Forster, Annie Fingardt
Take it Like a Mom - Stephanie Stiles   *c*   145
Fraser, Abby
Shadowed in Silk - Christine Lindsay   *i*   544
Fraser, Nick
Shadowed in Silk - Christine Lindsay   *i*   544
Galloway, Jack
Desert Gift - Sally John   *r*   854
Galloway, Jillian
Desert Gift - Sally John   *r*   854
Gloria
Getting to Happy - Terry McMillan   *c*   101
Gold, Ben
The Hat - Babette Hughes   *t*   333
Gonda
The Dawn Country - Kathleen O'Neal Gear   *t*   367
Haaviko, Montgomery "Monty"
Your Friendly Neighborhood Criminal - Michael Van Rooy   *m*   740
Hallaway, Emma
The Seduction of His Wife - Tiffany Clare   *r*   790
Hank
Summer Session - Merry Jones   *m*   647
Mr. Hart
Stealing Mona Lisa - Carson Morton   *m*   686
Hays, Kelly
A Small Hotel - Robert Olen Butler   *c*   30
Hays, Michael
A Small Hotel - Robert Olen Butler   *c*   30
Heck
Daughters of the Revolution - Carolyn Cooke   *t*   290
Hedia
Out of the Waters - David Drake   *f*   192
Hemingway, Ernest
The Paris Wife - Paula McLain   *t*   352
Hemingway, Hadley Richardson
The Paris Wife - Paula McLain   *t*   352
Hilliard, Diccan
Never a Gentleman - Eileen Dreyer   *r*   805
Himmel, Cookie
A Good Hard Look - Ann Napolitano   *t*   363
Holroyd, Lady Margaret
The Informant - Thomas Perry   *m*   696
Hunt, Nora
Terror of Living - Urban Waite   *c*   158
Hunt, Phil
Terror of Living - Urban Waite   *c*   158
Isabelle
Death at the Chateau Bremont - M. L. Longworth   *m*   671

James, Harper
My One and Only - Kristan Higgins   *r*   840
Jason
Falling Together - Marisa de los Santos   *c*   45
Johnson, Jace
Jace - Sarah McCarty   *r*   895
Kate
Butterfly's Child - Angela Davis-Gardner   *t*   293
Kershaw, Elaine
Backlash - Sally Spencer   *m*   729
Kleiven, Berit
The Long-Shining Waters - Danielle Sosin   *t*   391
Kleiven, Gunnar
The Long-Shining Waters - Danielle Sosin   *t*   391
Koracoo
The Dawn Country - Kathleen O'Neal Gear   *t*   367
Lake, Samuel
The Homecoming of Samuel Lake - Jenny Wingfield   *c*   165
Lake, Willadee
The Homecoming of Samuel Lake - Jenny Wingfield   *c*   165
Lance
Playdate - Thelma Adams   *c*   2
LeTellier, Capucine
Crime Fraiche - Alexander Campion   *m*   579
Lizzie
One Summer - David Baldacci   *c*   13
Locke, Julia
My Dear I Wanted to Tell You - Louisa Young   *t*   412
Locke, Peter
My Dear I Wanted to Tell You - Louisa Young   *t*   412
London, Gray
The First Gardener - Denise Hildreth Jones   *i*   536
London, Mackenzie
The First Gardener - Denise Hildreth Jones   *i*   536
Lori
Broken - Debra Webb   *r*   953
Lowery, Nick
My One and Only - Kristan Higgins   *r*   840
Lucy
Adrenaline - Jeff Abbott   *m*   559
Mac
If You Were Here - Jen Lancaster   *c*   86
MacDonald, Sileas
The Guardian - Margaret Mallory   *r*   889
Madlenka
When the Saints - Dave Duncan   *f*   193
Mansfield, Richard
The Seduction of His Wife - Tiffany Clare   *r*   790
Marsh, Irene
Once Upon a Time There Was You - Elizabeth Berg   *c*   19
Marsh, John
Once Upon a Time There Was You - Elizabeth Berg   *c*   19
Marsh, Randall
Her Sister's Shadow - Katharine Britton   *r*   774
Marshal, Mahelt
To Defy a King - Elizabeth Chadwick   *t*   287
Mary
Girls in White Dresses - Jennifer Close   *c*   36
Max
Dead by Midnight - Carolyn G. Hart   *c*   72

McArthur, Ava
A Good Excuse to Be Bad - Miranda
   Parker *m* 693

McArthur, Bishop Devon
A Good Excuse to Be Bad - Miranda
   Parker *m* 693

Mei-Mei
Daughters of the Revolution - Carolyn
   Cooke *t* 290

Merrill, Frederick
The Storm at the Door - Stefan Merrill
   Block *c* 103

Merrill, Katharine
The Storm at the Door - Stefan Merrill
   Block *c* 103

Mia
If You Were Here - Jen Lancaster *c* 86

Michelle
Felicity's Gate - Julian Cole *m* 586

Miranda
Shadowflame - Dianne Sylvan *h* 496

Miri
Jace - Sarah McCarty *r* 895

Mitchell, Evie
The Sandalwood Tree - Elle Newmark *t* 365

Monica
Death in the Opening Chapter - Tim
   Heald *m* 631

Muir, Avis
Birds of Paradise - Diana Abu-Jaber *c* 1

Muir, Brian
Birds of Paradise - Diana Abu-Jaber *c* 1

Nadine
My Dear I Wanted to Tell You - Louisa
   Young *t* 412

Nichols, Eudora
Those Across the River - Christopher
   Buehlman *h* 419

Nichols, Frank
Those Across the River - Christopher
   Buehlman *h* 419

Nina
I Married You for Happiness - Lily Tuck *c* 154

Parker, Becky
The Rock Hole - Reavis Z. Wortham *m* 749

Parker, Ned
The Rock Hole - Reavis Z. Wortham *m* 749

Parks, Thomas
Comes a Time for Burning - Steven F.
   Havill *t* 326

Pearl Hand
Fire the Sky - W. Michael Gear *t* 312

Philip
I Married You for Happiness - Lily Tuck *c* 154

Pierce, May
Compass Rose - John Casey *c* 32

Pinkerton, Benjamin "Frank" Franklin
Butterfly's Child - Angela Davis-Gardner *t* 293

Pitt, Charlotte
Treason at Lisson Grove - Anne Perry *t* 371

Pitt, Thomas
Treason at Lisson Grove - Anne Perry *t* 371

Quirk, Harry
The Astral - Kate Christensen *c* 34

Quirk, Luz
The Astral - Kate Christensen *c* 34

Rafferty, Joseph
Deadly Reunion - Geraldine Evans *m* 604

Ramon
Conquistadora - Esmeralda Santiago *t* 384

Ransome, Julia
Ransome's Quest - Kaye Dacus *i* 522

Ransome, William
Ransome's Quest - Kaye Dacus *i* 522

Red
Jericho Cay - Kathryn R. Wall *m* 741

Riley
My Dear I Wanted to Tell You - Louisa
   Young *t* 412

Rounder, Sam
Felicity's Gate - Julian Cole *m* 586

Russell, Charlotte
The Devil All the Time - Donald Ray
   Pollock *m* 699

Russell, Willard
The Devil All the Time - Donald Ray
   Pollock *m* 699

Ryrie, John
The Grief of Others - Leah Hager Cohen *c* 37

Ryrie, Ricky
The Grief of Others - Leah Hager Cohen *c* 37

Samantha
The Guilty Plea - Robert Rotenberg *m* 713

Sandy
The Devil All the Time - Donald Ray
   Pollock *m* 699

Sarah
Eat Slay Love - Jesse Petersen *h* 472
Flip This Zombie - Jesse Petersen *h* 471

Savannah
Getting to Happy - Terry McMillan *c* 101

Schaeffer, Michael "The Butcher's Boy"
The Informant - Thomas Perry *m* 696

Seymour, Jane
Henry VIII, Wolfman - A.E. Moorat *h* 470

Shepherd, Nate
The Gin & Chowder Club - Nan Parson
   Rossiter *c* 130

Shepherd, Noelle
The Gin & Chowder Club - Nan Parson
   Rossiter *c* 130

Sitturd, Hephaestus
Enigmatic Pilot - Kris Saknussemm *s* 1038

Sitturd, Rapture
Enigmatic Pilot - Kris Saknussemm *s* 1038

Smith, Annabel Lee
Monument to Murder - Margaret Truman *m* 738

Smith, Mackensie
Monument to Murder - Margaret Truman *m* 738

Solomon, David
Shadowflame - Dianne Sylvan *h* 496

Sutherland, Ian
To Desire a Wicked Duke - Nicole Jordan *r* 857

Tanner, Bay
Jericho Cay - Kathryn R. Wall *m* 741

Thomas
Chihuahua of the Baskervilles - Esri
   Allbritten *m* 562

Titania
The Great Night - Chris Adrian *c* 4

Toad, Agrippas
The Paperbark Shoe - Goldie Goldbloom *t* 314

Tom
Separate Beds - Elizabeth Buchan *c* 28

Travers, Shannon
Separate Dreams - Joan Early *r* 807

Tucker, Alafair
Crying Blood - Donis Casey *t* 286

Tucker, Shaw
Crying Blood - Donis Casey *t* 286

Vane, Harriet
The Attenbury Emeralds - Jill Paton Walsh *t* 406

Weiss, Adam
The Brink of Fame - Irene Fleming *t* 309

Weiss, Emily Daggett
The Brink of Fame - Irene Fleming *t* 309

Whiteson, Melvin
A Good Hard Look - Ann Napolitano *t* 363

Whitman, Judith
To Be Sung Underwater - Tom McNeal *c* 102

Whitman, Malcolm
To Be Sung Underwater - Tom McNeal *c* 102

Will
Original Sin - Beth McMullen *m* 680

Williams, Amy
Doctor Who: The Way Through the Woods - Una
   McCormack *s* 1024

Williams, Rory
Doctor Who: The Way Through the Woods - Una
   McCormack *s* 1024

Wimsey, Lord Peter
The Attenbury Emeralds - Jill Paton Walsh *t* 406

Wingate, Annabel
You're Next - Gregg Hurwitz *m* 638

Wingate, Mike
You're Next - Gregg Hurwitz *m* 638

Woodruff, Sylvie
Fly Away Home - Jennifer Weiner *c* 161

Wren
Playdate - Thelma Adams *c* 2

Yoshida, Eric
Dry as Rain - Gina Holmes *i* 537

Yoshida, Kyra
Dry as Rain - Gina Holmes *i* 537

Zanella, Izzy
Breaking the Rules - Suzanne Brockmann *r* 775

SPY

Abercrombie, Nathan
Enter the Zombie - David Lubar *h* 462

Begley, Kate
The Matchmaker of Kenmare - Frank
   Delaney *t* 295

Bond, James
Carte Blanche - Jeffery Deaver *m* 592

Cochran Jr., Bourke
The Parsifal Pursuit - Michael
   McMenamin *t* 353

Dobbs, Maisie
A Lesson in Secrets - Jacqueline Winspear *t* 410

Grey, Lauren "Silver Orchid"
The Orchid Affair - Lauren Willig *t* 408

Hamilton, Lucy "Sally Sin"
Original Sin - Beth McMullen *m* 680

Harris, Claire
The Last Time I Saw Paris - Lynn Sheene *r* 938

La Donna
The Alchemist in the Shadows - Pierre
   Pevel *f* 248

Leiter, Felix
Carte Blanche - Jeffery Deaver *m* 592

Leyton, Jim
The Noise Revealed - Ian Whates *s* 1058

M
Carte Blanche - Jeffery Deaver *m* 592

Demetria
The Vision - Jen Nadol   *f*   242

Donald
The Ghost of Greenwich Village - Lorna Graham   *c*   61

Errastas
The Crippled God - Steven Erikson   *f*   196

Grant, Peter
Midnight Riot - Ben Aaronovitch   *f*   167

Graves, Celia
Demon Song - Cat Adams   *h*   413

Iscariot, Judas "Jude Miller"
The Judas Gospel - Bill Myers   *r*   906

Kilmandros
The Crippled God - Steven Erikson   *f*   196

Laveau, Marie
Hurricane - Jewell Parker Rhodes   *t*   379

Magnus, Wulfgang
When the Saints - Dave Duncan   *f*   193

May
May - Kathryn Lasky   *f*   226

Mayhall, Stony
Raising Stony Mayhall - Daryl Gregory   *h*   439

Mendez, Snake "Dez"
Storm Kissed - Jessica Andersen   *r*   757

Nana
Hurricane - Jewell Parker Rhodes   *t*   379

Queen of the Abyss
The Midnight Gate - Helen Stringer   *h*   495

R.
Warm Bodies - Isaac Marion   *h*   464

Renfield, Cassie
The Vision - Jen Nadol   *f*   242

Richter, Matt
Dark War - Tim Waggoner   *h*   500

Saber, Deke
Always the Vampire - Nancy Haddock   *h*   442

Sechul Lath
The Crippled God - Steven Erikson   *f*   196

SURFER

Blasingame, Corey
The Gentlemen's Hour - Don Winslow   *m*   747

Daniels, Boone
The Gentlemen's Hour - Don Winslow   *m*   747

Kuhio, Kelly
The Gentlemen's Hour - Don Winslow   *m*   747

SURVIVOR

Aidan
Ashes, Ashes - Jo Treggiari   *s*   1056

Cawdor, Dean
Downrigger Drift - James Axler   *s*   967
Prodigal's Return - James Axler   *s*   969

Dix, John "J.B."
Tainted Cascade - James Axler   *s*   971

Dix, John Barrymore "J.B."
Downrigger Drift - James Axler   *s*   967

Gardner, Sharon
Death's Disciples - J. Robert King   *h*   456

Lucy
Ashes, Ashes - Jo Treggiari   *s*   1056

Monroe, Kimble
7th Sigma - Steven Gould   *s*   1001

Sargaul
Blood Gorgons - Henry Zou   *s*   1061

Stein, Daniel
Daniel Stern, Interpreter: A Novel in Documents - Ludmila Ulitskaya   *t*   402

Wyeth, Mildred
Tainted Cascade - James Axler   *s*   971

TEACHER

Annigan, Hailee
Hailee - Penny Zeller   *i*   558

Anzeka
Honeyed Words - J.A. Pitts   *f*   249

Apte, Charulata
Miss Timmins' School for Girls - Nayana Currimbhoy   *c*   42

Black, Eva
The School for Brides - Cheryl Ann Smith   *r*   940

Christopher, Madeline
The Twisted Thread - Charlotte Bacon   *m*   566

Clover
Widower's Tale - Julia Glass   *c*   58

Flanders, Eileen
44 Charles Street - Danielle Steel   *c*   143

Grey, Crockett
The Canary List - Sigmund Brouwer   *i*   514

Ira
Widower's Tale - Julia Glass   *c*   58

Jansen, Thekla
Children and Fire - Ursula Hegi   *t*   328

Jennings, Harper
Summer Session - Merry Jones   *m*   647

Josie
French Lessons - Ellen Sussman   *c*   149

Lawson, Olivia
Playing for Keeps - LuAnn McLane   *r*   898

Lee
Tales from the Yoga Studio - Rain Mitchell   *r*   903

Linder, Jody
The Scent of Rain and Lightning - Nancy Pickard   *c*   121

Prince, Moira
Miss Timmins' School for Girls - Nayana Currimbhoy   *c*   42

Scofield, Agnes
Being Polite to Hitler - Robb Forman Dew   *t*   297

Shore, Jocelyn
Death on Tour - Janice Hamrick   *m*   624

Tucker, Charlotte
Keep a Little Secret - Dorothy Garlock   *r*   823

TECHNICIAN

Kaufman, Philip
The Noise Revealed - Ian Whates   *s*   1058

Nomura, Takeo
Robopocalypse - Daniel H. Wilson   *c*   164

TEENAGER

Adam
Shantorian - Patrick Carman   *s*   985

Agre, Geoff
Up Against It - M.J. Locke   *s*   1018

Amy
The Vampire Stalker - Allison Van Diepen   *h*   498

Cathmar
The Sea Thy Mistress - Elizabeth Bear   *f*   172

Courtney
Harvest Moon - Robyn Carr   *r*   784

Demetria
The Vision - Jen Nadol   *f*   242

Emily
Shantorian - Patrick Carman   *s*   985

Finn
Shantorian - Patrick Carman   *s*   985

Fox, Lin
Glass Demon - Helen Grant   *c*   62

Granger, Sammy
The Truth Sleuth - Jacqueline Seewald   *m*   720

Imbolya
An Embarrassment of Riches - Chelsea Quinn Yarbro   *h*   509

Jack "Repairman Jack"
Jack: Secret Vengeance - F. Paul Wilson   *h*   508

Johnson, Belladonna
The Midnight Gate - Helen Stringer   *h*   495

Lewis
Shantorian - Patrick Carman   *s*   985

Madison
Damned - Chuck Palahniuk   *c*   114

McDonald, Rayne
Blood Ties - Mari Mancusi   *f*   231

McDonald, Sunny
Blood Ties - Mari Mancusi   *f*   231

Missy
Rage - Jackie Morse Kessler   *h*   455

Noel
Hot Lights, Cold Steel - D.P. Lyle   *m*   674

Pangloss, Lulu
Xombies: Apocalypso - Walter Greatshell   *h*   438

Parker, Ana
Almost Final Curtain - Tate Hallaway   *h*   443

Pasternak, Lucy
A Hard Day's Fright - Casey Daniels   *h*   426

Phelps, Morwenna
Among Others - Jo Walton   *f*   270

Ramirez, Angel
Against the Fire - Kat Martin   *r*   891

Raven
Vampire Kisses 8: Cryptic Cravings - Ellen Schreiber   *h*   486

Reiner, Paul
The Traitor's Emblem - Juan Gomez-Jurado   *m*   616

Renfield, Cassie
The Vision - Jen Nadol   *f*   242

Shapiro, Danny
Journal of a UFO Investigator - David Halperin   *t*   322

Wild, Hunter
Out for Blood - Alyxandra Harvey   *f*   204

Will
Closer - Roderick Gordon   *f*   202

Willoughby, Violet
Haunting Violet - Alyxandra Harvey   *f*   205

TELEPATH

Stackhouse, Sookie
Dead Reckoning - Charlaine Harris   *c*   71

TELEVISION PERSONALITY

Daniels, Kristin
Moon Cursed - Lori Handeland   *h*   445

Davis, Polly
Classic in the Barn - Amy Myers   *m*   687

Holliday, M.J.
Ghouls, Ghouls, Ghouls - Victoria Laurie   *h*   460

Spartz, Riley
Killing Kate - Julie Kramer   *m*   659

TERRORIST

Al Zaroor, Amer
Devil's Light - Richard North Patterson   *c*   119

Dunne, Niall
Carte Blanche - Jeffery Deaver   *m*   592

Dupre, Eli
Everdark - Elle Jasper   *r* 851

Ferncsi, Rakoczy "Saint-Germain"
An Embarrassment of Riches - Chelsea Quinn
   Yarbro   *h* 509

Gabriel
Blood Rules - Christine Cody   *h* 423
Bloodlands - Christine Cody   *h* 422

Geoffrey
Night Veil - Yasmine Galenorn   *r* 822

Grieve
Night Veil - Yasmine Galenorn   *r* 822

Hughes, Will
The Watchtower - Lee Carroll   *h* 421

Jagger
Vampire Kisses 8: Cryptic Cravings - Ellen
   Schreiber   *h* 486

Johnson, Jace
Jace - Sarah McCarty   *r* 895

La Belle Couer
Master of Shadows - Angela Knight   *h* 458

LaSalle, Rex
Oscar Wilde and the Vampire Murders - Gyles
   Brandreth   *t* 283

Malachi
Vampire Instinct - Joey W. Hill   *h* 448

Marinelli, Cesca
Always the Vampire - Nancy Haddock   *h* 442

McBride, Bronte
Vampire Dragon - Annette Blair   *f* 177

McDonald, Rayne
Blood Ties - Mari Mancusi   *f* 231
Night School - Mari Mancusi   *h* 463

McDonald, Sunny
Blood Ties - Mari Mancusi   *f* 231
Night School - Mari Mancusi   *h* 463

Mordred
*The Secret History of Elizabeth Tudor, Vampire
   Slayer* - Lucy Weston   *h* 504

Myst
Night Veil - Yasmine Galenorn   *r* 822

Northman, Eric
Dead Reckoning - Charlaine Harris   *c* 71

Octavian, Peter
Waking Nightmares - Christopher Golden   *h* 436

Parker, Ana
Almost Final Curtain - Tate Hallaway   *h* 443

Pendle, Raylene
Bloodshot - Cherie Priest   *h* 477
Hellbent - Cherie Priest   *h* 476

Reyes, Declan
Nightshade - Michelle Rowen   *h* 480

Sabian, Alexandra "Alex"
Blood Secrets - Jeannie Holmes   *h* 449

Solomon, Joel
The Cross - Sean McCabe   *h* 467

St. Clair, Glory
Real Vampires Don't Wear Size Six - Gerry
   Bartlett   *h* 415

Stone, Gabriel
The Cross - Sean McCabe   *h* 467

Stott, Ian
Bloodshot - Cherie Priest   *h* 477
Hellbent - Cherie Priest   *h* 476

Stoyan, Harper
The Reluctant Vampire - Lynsay Sands   *r* 933

Strong, Anna
Crossroads - Jeanne C. Stein   *h* 489

Taylor, Betsy
Undead and Undermined - MaryJanice
   Davidson   *f* 189

Tycho
The Fallen Blade - Jon Courtenay
   Grimwood   *t* 320

Ulrika
Bloodforged - Nathan Long   *f* 230

Vigo
The Vampire Stalker - Allison Van Diepen   *h* 498

VAMPIRE HUNTER

Banks, Alexander
The Vampire Stalker - Allison Van Diepen   *h* 498

Blake, Anita
Hit List - Laurell K. Hamilton   *h* 444

Conrad, Jillian "Jill"
Bloodlust - Michelle Rowen   *h* 481
Nightshade - Michelle Rowen   *h* 480

Deveraux, Elena
Archangel's Consort - Nalini Singh   *f* 257

Elizabeth
*The Secret History of Elizabeth Tudor, Vampire
   Slayer* - Lucy Weston   *h* 504

Ellis, Christopher
Blood of the Rose - Kate Pearce   *r* 915

Llewellyn, Rosalind
Blood of the Rose - Kate Pearce   *r* 915

Ralston, Dominic
Hunter's Fall - Shiloh Walker   *r* 950

Stamp, Johnson
Blood Rules - Christine Cody   *h* 423

VETERAN

Bartram, Laurence
The Return of Captain John Emmett - Elizabeth
   Speller   *t* 392

Chip
The Year We Left Home - Jean Thompson   *c* 153

Emmett, John
The Return of Captain John Emmett - Elizabeth
   Speller   *t* 392

Jennings, Harper
Summer Session - Merry Jones   *m* 647

Lucas, Spero
The Cut - George P. Pelecanos   *m* 694

Mitchell, Martin
The Sandalwood Tree - Elle Newmark   *t* 365

St. Just, Devlin
The Soldier - Grace Burrowes   *r* 779

The Ghost
Ghosts of War: A Tale of the Ghost - George
   Mann   *s* 1020

White, Alex
Other Kingdoms - Richard Matheson   *h* 465

Younger, Stratham
The Death Instinct - Jed Rubenfeld   *t* 383

VETERINARIAN

Harper, Geneva
Skin Heat - Ava Gray   *h* 437

VIGILANTE

Aquila, Marcus
Fortress of Spears - Anthony Riches   *t* 380

Dale, Alan
Outlaw - Angus Donald   *t* 300

Hardesty, Stella
A Bad Day for Scandal - Sophie
   Littlefield   *m* 669

VIKING

Authun
Wolfsangel - M.D. Lachlan   *f* 223

Bjolf
The Viking Dead - Toby Venables   *h* 499

Gunnar
Immortal Champion - Lisa Hendrix   *f* 208

VILLAIN

Lord Daiman
Star Wars: Knight Errant - John Jackson
   Miller   *s* 1029

Dashwood, Daniel
Anno Frankenstein - Jonathan Green   *s* 1005

Dunne, Niall
Carte Blanche - Jeffery Deaver   *m* 592

Heythe
The Sea Thy Mistress - Elizabeth Bear   *f* 172

Hydt, Severan
Carte Blanche - Jeffery Deaver   *m* 592

Koschei
Deathless - Catherynne M. Valente   *f* 267

Morthul
The Goblin Corps - Ari Marmell   *f* 232

Lord Odion
Star Wars: Knight Errant - John Jackson
   Miller   *s* 1029

Dr. Screem
The Five Masks of Dr. Screem - R.L. Stine   *h* 491

Seda
The Scarab Path - Adrian Tchaikovsky   *f* 264

Ullikummis
Infestation Cubed - James Axler   *s* 975
Truth Engine - James Axler   *s* 973

VOLUNTEER

Baker, Mattie
Against the Fire - Kat Martin   *r* 891

Carlisle, Helen
Blue Skies Tomorrow - Sarah Sundin   *i* 552

McKenna, Rose
Save Me - Lisa Scottoline   *c* 135

WAITER/WAITRESS

Amery, Elle
Tempted by Trouble - Liz Fielding   *r* 811

Hart, Destiny
Restless Heart - Wynonna Judd   *c* 80

Lauren
Girls in White Dresses - Jennifer Close   *c* 36

Stackhouse, Sookie
Dead Reckoning - Charlaine Harris   *c* 71

Volland, Sophie
The Philosopher's Kiss - Peter Prange   *t* 375

WARD

Shield, Jack
Troubletwisters - Garth Nix   *f* 244

Shield, Jaide
Troubletwisters - Garth Nix   *f* 244

WARLOCK

Stanton, Dreadnought
The Hidden Goddess - M.K. Hobson   *f* 210

WARRIOR

Alcadizzar
Nagash Immortal - Mike Lee   *f* 227

Atira the Bear
Warcry - Elizabeth Vaughan   *r*   948

Brax
The Shining City - Fiona Patton   *f*   247

Calard
Knights of Bretonnia - Anthony Reynolds   *f*   252

Campbell, Hayden
Untamed Highlander - Donna Grant   *r*   829

Campbell, Ranger
The Ranger - Monica McCarty   *r*   893

Eliani
Heart of the Exiled - Pati Nagle   *f*   243

Heath
Warcry - Elizabeth Vaughan   *r*   948

Holt, Kerra
Star Wars: Knight Errant - John Jackson
    Miller   *s*   1029

Hooper, Kali
The Twilight of Kerberos: Trials of Trass Kathra -
    Mike Wild   *f*   273

Jassion, Baron
The Warlord's Legacy - Ari Marmell   *f*   233

Khan, Genghis
Genghis Khan Vol. 2: The World Conqueror - Sam
    Djang   *t*   299

Kougar
Hunger Untamed - Pamela Palmer   *r*   913

Kyana
Ascension - Sable Grace   *r*   828

Lane, MacKayla "Mac"
Shadowfever - Karen Marie Moning   *c*   108

Larem
Bound by Darkness - Alexis Morgan   *r*   904

Leonidas
Red Mortal - Deidre Knight   *r*   866

MacDonald, Ian
The Guardian - Margaret Mallory   *r*   889

MacLean, Duncan
Captured by the Highlander - Julianne
    MacLean   *r*   885

Magnus, Anton
When the Saints - Dave Duncan   *f*   193

Maker, Cheerwell
The Scarab Path - Adrian Tchaikovsky   *f*   264

Rebaine, Corvis
The Warlord's Legacy - Ari Marmell   *f*   233

Ryker
Ascension - Sable Grace   *r*   828

Schwarzhelm
Sword of Vengeance - Chris Wraight   *f*   275

Serai
Vampire in Atlantis - Alyssa Day   *r*   800

Sicarius, Cato
Fall of Damnos - Nick Kyme   *s*   1015

Snow, Jon
Dance With Dragons: A Song of Ice and Fire -
    George R.R. Martin   *c*   99

Tanner, Quinn
Warrior Betrayed - Addison Fox   *r*   817

Tao, General
The Last Warrior - Susan Grant   *r*   831

Taranisai, Arenadd
The Griffin's War - K.J. Taylor   *f*   263

Tiarnan
Haunting Desire - Erin Quinn   *r*   922

Tigurius
Fall of Damnos - Nick Kyme   *s*   1015

Wroth, Krysty
Downrigger Drift - James Axler   *s*   967

WEALTHY

Adams, Maxwell Nathaniel Jr.
Hailee - Penny Zeller   *i*   558

Alessandro
Dolci di Love - Sarah-Kate Lynch   *r*   882

Balfour, Lollie
*Dandy Gilver and the Proper Treatment of Blood-
    stains* - Catriona McPherson   *m*   681

Bell, Morgan Tyler
Jericho Cay - Kathryn R. Wall   *m*   741

Blevins, Robert
The Matrimony Plan - Christine Johnson   *i*   539

Carson, Henry
Blood Trust - Eric Van Lustbader   *c*   95

Cash, Cora
The American Heiress - Daisy Goodwin   *t*   316

Clark, Tess
Rescuing the Heiress - Valerie Hansen   *r*   835

Darcy, Fitzwilliam
Mr. Darcy's Secret - Jane Odiwe   *r*   910

Goodell, Lee
Rodin's Debutante - Ward Just   *t*   338

Gray, Acadia
Hush - Cherry Adair   *r*   753

Howard, Julia
Paper Doll - Janet Woods   *t*   411

Kensington, Felicity
The Matrimony Plan - Christine Johnson   *i*   539

Martinez, Morty
Ringer - Brian M. Wiprud   *m*   748

Mason, Gavin
The Billionaire Gets His Way - Elizabeth
    Bevarly   *r*   762

Miriam
Minding Ben - Victoria Brown   *c*   27

Ogden, Tommy
Rodin's Debutante - Ward Just   *t*   338

Reiniger, Autumn
The Nightmare Thief - Meg Gardiner   *m*   610

Rousseau, Fannie
A Most Unsuitable Match - Stephanie Grace
    Whitson   *i*   554

Stark, Gideon
Hush - Cherry Adair   *r*   753

Stark, Zakary "Zak"
Hush - Cherry Adair   *r*   753

Sumner, Carlton
A Death In Summer - Benjamin Black   *m*   571

Tyson Grant, Robert
Ringer - Brian M. Wiprud   *m*   748

Wesson, Gabe
The Nanny's Homecoming - Linda
    Goodnight   *i*   530

Whiteson, Melvin
A Good Hard Look - Ann Napolitano   *t*   363

WEREWOLF

Adam
River Marked - Patricia Briggs   *h*   418

Barr
Moon Burning - Lucy Monroe   *f*   241

Boleyn, Anne
Henry VIII, Wolfman - A.E. Moorat   *h*   470

Daniels, Devlin
Black Heart Loa - Adrian Phoenix   *h*   473

Falon
Blood Law - Karin Tabke   *h*   497

Feileg
Wolfsangel - M.D. Lachlan   *f*   223

Henry
Henry VIII, Wolfman - A.E. Moorat   *h*   470

Jones, Isaiah
Reaper's Justice - Sarah McCarty   *r*   894

Lysander, Mariah
Blood Rules - Christine Cody   *h*   423

Miri
Jace - Sarah McCarty   *r*   895

Moore, Thomas
Henry VIII, Wolfman - A.E. Moorat   *h*   470

Rafael
Blood Law - Karin Tabke   *h*   497

Turner, Rule
Blood Challenge - Eileen Wilks   *h*   505
Death Magic - Eileen Wilks   *h*   506

WIDOW

Ali, Jasmina
Major Pettigrew's Last Stand - Helen
    Simonson   *c*   137

WIDOW(ER)

Alessandro
Dolci di Love - Sarah-Kate Lynch   *r*   882

Altavilla, Costanza
Drawing Conclusions - Donna Leon   *c*   92

Anna
The House by the Fjord - Rosalind Laker   *t*   342

Armstrong, Jack
One Summer - David Baldacci   *c*   13

Barlow, Emily
Emily and Einstein - Linda Francis Lee   *c*   91

Becker, Caryn
The Edge of Grace - Christa Allan   *i*   510

Beckman, Olivia
Livvie's Song - Sharlene MacLaren   *i*   545

Carlisle, Helen
Blue Skies Tomorrow - Sarah Sundin   *i*   552

Carolyn
Canary Island Song - Robin Jones Gunn   *i*   532

Colburn, Dorian
Pirate of My Heart - Jamie Carie   *i*   517

Cooper, Cate
Folly Beach - Dorothea Benton Frank   *c*   56

Davis, Marya
44 Charles Street - Danielle Steel   *c*   143

Davis, Polly
Classic in the Barn - Amy Myers   *m*   687

Durst, Nora
The Leftovers - Tom Perrotta   *c*   120

Esther Hammerhans
Mr. Chartwell - Rebecca Hunt   *t*   334

Hawthorne, Glory
Pacific Glory - P.T. Deutermann   *t*   296

Martha
The Story of Beautiful Girl - Rachel
    Simon   *c*   136

Pearlie, Louise
Louise's War - Sarah R. Shaber   *m*   721

Pickwick-Buchanan, Bridget
Restless in Carolina - Tamara Leigh   *i*   541

Royce, Marc
Lion of Babylon - Davis Bunn   *i*   515

Ruth
A Turn in the Road - Debbie Macomber   *c*   96

Scofield, Agnes
Being Polite to Hitler - Robb Forman Dew   *t*   297

Author Index

This index is an alphabetical listing of the authors of books featured in entries and those listed within entries under the rubrics "Other books by the same author" and "Other books you might like." For each author, the titles of books described or listed in this edition and their entry numbers appear. Bold numbers indicate a featured main entry; light-face numbers refer to books recommended for further reading.

She Shoots to Conquer 318, 410

Cannell, Stephen J.
The Prostitutes' Ball 166

Cannon, Taffy
Guns and Roses 595

Cantrell, Lisa
Boneman 479

Cantrell, Rebecca
A Game of Lies **580**
A Night of Long Knives 580
A Trace of Smoke 580, 616, 646, 721

Canty, Kevin
Everything: A Novel 13

Capek, Karel
The Absolute at Large 980

Capshaw, Carla
The Gladiator 911

Carcaterra, Lorenzo
Gangster 696

Card, Orson Scott
Alvin Journeyman 183
The Crystal City 183
Empire 1045
Enchantment 183
Ender in Exile 183
Ender's Game 183, 1055
Ender's Shadow: Battle School 183
Heartfire 183
Hidden Empire 183
Lost Gate **183**
Magic Mirror 183
Pathfinder 183

Carey, Jacqueline
Godslayer 184
Kushiel's Justice 184
Kushiel's Mercy 99, 184
Naamah's Blessing **184**
Naamah's Curse 184
Naamah's Kiss 175, 184

Carey, Lisa
The Mermaids Singing 280

Carie, Jamie
Angel's Den: A Novel 517
The Duchess and the Dragon 517, 517
Pirate of My Heart **517**
Snow Angel: A Novel 517
The Snowflake 517
Wind Dancer 517

Carlile, Clancy
The Paris Pilgrims 352

Carlisle, Kate
Homicide in Hardcover 642, 581
How to Seduce a Billionaire 581
If Books Could Kill 581
The Lies that Bind 581
Murder Under Cover **581**
Sweet Surrender, Baby Surprise 581

Carlson, Jeff
Plague Year 998, 1056

Carlson, Melody
All I Have to Give: A Christmas Love Story 518
Back Home Again 518
Christmas at Harrington's 518
The Christmas Dog 518
The Christmas Shoppe **518**
Love Finds You in Martha's Vineyard, Massachusetts 523
Recipes & Wooden Spoons 518

Carlyle, Liz
A Deal with the Devil 862
No True Gentleman 924
A Woman Scorned 876

Carman, Patrick
The Dark Planet 985, 986

The House of Power 985, 986
The Raven **986**
Rivers of Fire 985, 986
Shantorian **985**, 1003, 1004
The Tenth City 985, 986
Trackers 985, 986

Carr, Caleb
The Italian Secretary 355

Carr, Carol K.
India Black 343

Carr, Robyn
Forbidden Falls 841, 944
Harvest Moon **784**, 823
Midnight Kiss 784
Moonlight Road 784
Paradise Valley 879
Promise Canyon 944, 952, 784
Second Chance Pass 879
A Summer in Sonoma 35, 791, 944, 784
Wild Man Creek 784

Carrington, Tori
Breathless 785
Love Bites 785, 51
Private Parts 785
Reckless Pleasures 785
Undeniable Pleasures 785
Wicked Pleasures **785**

Carroll, Jerry Jay
Top Dog 229

Carroll, Jonathan
The Land of Laughs 251, 435, 465
The Marriage of Sticks 419
Voice of Our Shadow 475

Carroll, Lee
Black Swan Rising 421
The Watchtower **421**

Carroll, Margaret
A Dark Love 777, 806, 907, 931
Riptide 931

Carroll, Peter
Queen of Misfortune **285**

Carter, Angela
Wise Children 632

Cartmel, Andrew
Atom Bomb Blues 996

Carver, Raymond
What We Talk about When We Talk about Love: Stories 113

Casey, Donis
Crying Blood **286**
The Drop Edge of Yonder 286
Hornswoggled 286
The Old Buzzard Had It Coming 286
The Sky Took Him 286

Casey, John
An American Romance 32
Compass Rose **32**
The Half-Life of Happiness 32
South Country 32
Spartina 32
Testimony and Demeanor 32

Casey, Kathryn
Singularity 660

Cash, Steve
The Meq 185, 274
The Remembering **185**
Time Dancers 185

Caskie, Kathryn
A Lady's Guide to Rakes 804, 886
Rules of Engagement 857, 923

Casper, Ken
Miles Apart 892

Cassidy, Carla
Broken Pieces 943

Profile Durango 785, 788
Without a Sound 110

Cassidy, Dakota
The Accidental Human 198
The Accidental Werewolf 933
Accidentally Catty 786
Accidentally Demonic 786
Burning Down the Spouse **786**
Kiss & Hell 786
My Way to Hell 786
You Dropped a Blonde on Me 786

Cassutt, Michael
Heaven's Shadow **1002**

Cast, P.C.
Dragon's Oath 447
Tempted 498

Castillo, Linda
Breaking Silence **582**
Cops and Lovers? 582
In the Dead of Night 582
Pray for Silence 611, 582
Remember the Night 582
Sworn to Silence 625, 582

Castle, Jayne
Silver Master 948, 983

Castor, Henry
The Year of the Spaniard 385

Cave, Hugh B.
Legion of the Dead 479
The Restless Dead 473

Cave, Julie
Pieces of Light 511

Chabon, Michael
The Final Solution 355
The Yiddish Policemen's Union: A Novel 270

Chadbourn, Mark
Darkest Hour 186
The Devin in Green 186
Jack of Ravens 186
Lord of Silence 186
Queen of Sinister 186
The Scar-Crow Men **186**
The Silver Skull 186
World's End 186

Chadwick, Elizabeth
The Champion 287
The Conquest 287
Lady of the English 287
The Love Knot 287
To Defy a King **287**, 332
The Winter Mantle 287

Chafe, Paul
Genesis 977

Chamberlain, Diane
Kiss River 370

Chamberlin, Ann
The Merlin of the Oak Wood 248

Chan, Mimi
All the King's Women 388

Chance, Karen
Claimed by Shadow 418
Curse the Dawn 483
Embrace the Night 486
Midnight's Daughter 442, 458
Touch the Dark 231

Chance, Megan
Susannah Morrow 330

Chapman, Andrew
Beyond the Silence 405

Chapman, Janet
Moonlight Warrior 822

Chapman, Vannetta
Falling to Pieces **519**

A Simple Amish Christmas 519

Charbonneau, Joelle
Skating around the Law 624, 723

Charles, Steven
Nightmare Session 1003, 1004

Charlton, Blake
Spellbound **187**
Spellwright 187

Chase, Allison
Outrageously Yours 812

Chase, Loretta
Silk is for Seduction 763, 833, 941

Chase, Loretta Lynda
Your Scandalous Ways 940

Chase, Nicholas
Locksley 300

Chen, Sunny
Mona Lisa Awakening 787
Mona Lisa Blossoming 787
Mona Lisa Craving 787
Mona Lisa Darkening 787
Mona Lisa Eclipsing **787**

Chenoweth, Emily
Hello Goodbye 146

Chercover, Sean
Big City, Bad Blood 635, 745

Cherryh, C.J.
Betrayer **987**, 1058
Deceiver 987
Deliverer 987
Exile's Gate 975
Explorer 987
Finity's End 987
Fires of Azeroth 969
The Kif Strike Back 987
Rusalka 267

Cheuse, Alan
The Light Possessed 288
Lost and Old Rivers 288
Song of Slaves in the Desert **288**
The Sound of Writing 288
The Tennessee Waltz 288
To Catch the Lightning 288

Cheuvront, Robbie
The Guardian 538

Chiang, Ted
The Merchant and the Alchemist's Gate 337

Chiaverini, Jennifer
The Quilter's Apprentice: A Novel 689

Child, Lee
Echo Burning 605
Killing Floor 565
Persuader 559
Worth Dying For 118

Child, Lincoln
Deep Storm: A Novel 1016, 1042
Fever Dream 150
Gideon's Sword 1028

Child, Maureen
Vanished 831

Childress, Mark
Crazy in Alabama 33
Georgia Bottoms **33**, 54
Gone for Good 33
One Mississippi 33
V for Victor 33
A World Made of Fire 33

Childs, Laura
Death by Darjeeling 589, 590
The Silver Needle Murder 309

Childs, Lisa
Daddy Bombshell 788

Author Index

Author Index

Master of Craving 497
Master of Surrender 497
Master of Torment 497

Tallant, Robert
The Voodoo Queen 379

Talley, Marcia
All Things Undying 734
In Death's Shadow 734
Occasion of Revenge 734
A Quiet Death **734**
Sing it To Her Bones 734
Unbreathed Memories 734

Tannahill, Reay
Fatal Majesty: A Novel of Mary,
  Queen of Scots 351

Tapply, William G.
Dark Tiger 150
Hell Bent 150
The Nomination **150**
One-Way Ticket 150
Outwitting Trolls 150
Third Strike 150

Tarr, Hope
Every Breath You Take... 767, 932
The Haunting 771

Tarr, Judith
House of War 171

Tartt, Donna
The Secret History 94, 566

Tata, A J
Rogue Threat 701

Tate, June
Born to Dance **395**
Every Time You Say Goodbye 395
A Family Affair 395
The Reluctant Sinner 395
To Be a Lady 395
When Somebody Loves You 395

Tate, Kim Cash
Cherished 538

Tatlock, Ann
All the Way Home 151
I'll Watch the Moon 151
A Place Called Morning 151
Promises to Keep **151**, 555
The Returning 151
Things We Once Held Dear 151

Taylor, Diana Wallis
Martha: A Novel 960

Taylor, Glenn
The Marrowbone Marble Company:
  A Novel 290

Taylor, K.J.
Dark Griffin **261**, 262, 263
The Griffin's Flight 261, **262**, 263
The Griffin's War 261, 262, **263**

Taylor, Kate
Madame Proust and the Kosher
  Kitchen 396
A Man in Uniform **396**

Taylow, Andrew
The Judgement of Strangers 282

Tchaikovsky, Adrian
Blood of the Mantis 264
Dragonfly Falling 264
Empire in Black and Gold 186, 256,
  258, 264
Salute the Dark 264
The Scarab Path 173, **264**

Teague, MaRita
The Taste of Good Fruit 769

Temple, Lou Jane
The Spice Box 280

Tentler, Leslie
Midnight Caller 788

Tepper, Sheri S.
Six Moon Dance 24
The True Game 241

Terry, Mark
Angels Falling 735
The Devil's Pitchfork 735
Dirty Deeds 735
The Fallen 735
The Serpent's Kiss 735, 629
The Valley of Shadows **735**

Tessier, Thomas
The Nightwalker 470

Testa, Dom
The Cassini Code 1052
The Comet's Curse 1052
The Dark Zone **1052**
The Web of Titan 1052

Tey, Josephine
The Franchise Affair 571

Thayer, Nancy
Heat Wave 22, 75, 148, **152**

Thayer, Patricia
Texas Ranger Takes a Bride 853

Thayer, Steve
Wolf Pass 339

Thayer, Terri
Wild Goose Chase 689

Thayne, RaeAnne
Blackberry Summer **944**
A Cold Creek Baby 944
A Cold Creek Secret 944
Light the Stars 944
Nothing to Lose 944
A Soldier's Secret 944

Theorin, Johan
Echoes from the Dead 378

Theroux, Paul
World's End and Other Stories 354

Thoene, Bodie
Against the Wind 552
Twelfth Prophecy 551

Thomas, D.M.
Flying into Love 404

Thomas, Elizabeth Marshall
Reindeer Moon 367

Thomas, Jeffrey
The Fall of Hades 431
Nocturnal Emissions 478

Thomas, Jodi
The Lone Texan 945, 825
Rewriting Monday 945
Somewhere Along the Way 823, 945
Tall, Dark, and Texan 945
Texas Blue **945**
Twisted Creek 945

Thomas, Kay
Better than Bulletproof 788, 953

Thomas, Marin
Dexter: Honorable Cowboy 796,
  846, 874
Samantha's Cowboy 795

Thomas, Melody
Sin and Scandal in England 802

Thomas, Ross
The Cold War Swap 663

Thomas, Sherry
Delicious 834
Not Quite a Husband 900

Thomas, Will
Some Danger Involved 324

Thompson, Carlene
Last Whisper 84

Thompson, Colleen
Fatal Error 772

Thompson, Hunter S.
The Rum Diary: the long lost
  novel 159

Thompson, Jean
City Boy 153
Throw Like a Girl 153
Who Do You Love 153
Wide Blue Yonder 153
The Year We Left Home 40, 73, **153**,
  322

Thompson, John Milliken
The Reservoir 397

Thompson, Larry D.
The Trial 619

Thompson, Richard
Big Wheat **398**
Fiddle Game 398
Frag Box 398

Thompson, V.M.
Deadly Nature 424

Thompson, Vicki Lewis
Blonde with a Wand 946
Chick with a Charm 946
Claimed 946
Cowboy Up **946**
Cowboys Like Us 946
Fool for Love 887
Should've Been a Cowboy 946, 850

Thompson, Victoria
Murder on Astor Place 736, 617, 692
Murder on Gramercy Park 736
Murder on Lexington Avenue 736
Murder on Sisters' Row 373, **736**
Murder on St. Mark's Place 736
Murder on Washington Square 736

Thor, Brad
Foreign Influence: A Thriller 60
Full Black 95
The Lions of Lucerne 701, 735

Thornburg, Newton
Cutter and Bone 637, 733

Thorne, Nicola
The House by the Sea 362

Thornton, Elizabeth
The Marriage Trap 861

Thorpe, Adam
Pieces of Light 303

Thorpe, Gav
Angels of Darkness 1053, 1054, 1061
Annihilation Squad 1053, 1054
The Blades of Chaos 265, 1053
Caledor 222, **265**
The Claws of Chaos 1054
Dwarfs 222
Grudge Bearer 265
The Heart of Chaos 265, 275
The Last Chancers 995, 1053, 1054
Malekith 252, 265
Path of the Seer 962, **1053**, 1054,
  1060
Path of the Warrior 265
The Purging of Kadillus 1015, 1053,
  1054
Shadow King: A Tale of the
  Sundering 230

Thrasher, Travis
Gravestone 511
Letters from War **550**

Thurber, James
The 13 Clocks 138

Thurlo, Aimee
Blackening Song 630

Thurman, Rob
Basilisk **1055**
Blackout 235, **266**, 502

Deathwish 266, 1055
The Grimrose Path 266, 1055
Madhouse 259, 266, 1055
Moonshine 266, 1055
Nightlife 200, 266, 1055

Tierney, Ronald
Bullet Beach 737
Death in North Beach 737
Death in Pacific Heights 737
Eclipse of the Heart 737
Good to the Last Kiss **737**
The Stone Veil 737

Tiffany, Carrie
Everyman's Rules for Scientific
  Living 314

Tilley, Patrick J.
Blood River 971
The Cloud Warrior 967
The First Family 969
Iron Master 975

Tilton, Lois
Vampire Winter 422

Tipton, James
Annette Vallon: A Novel of the
  French Revolution 8, 363

Todd, Charles
A Bitter Truth 65
An Impartial Witness 390
Legacy of the Dead 399
A Lonely Death **399**
The Red Door 399
Search the Dark 392, 399
A Test of Wills 399, 736
Wings of Fire 399

Todd, Marilyn
I, Claudia 714

Toibin, Colm
Brooklyn 295

Tolkien, Simon
The Inheritance 400, 586
The King of Diamonds **400**

Toll, Emily
Murder Will Travel 595

Toole, John Kennedy
A Confederacy of Dunces 163, 657

Torres, Justin
We the Animals 68

Towles, Amor
Rules of Civility **401**

Townsend, Christine
Sweet Desire 80

Traviss, Karen
Ally 987
Matriarch 1058

Treggiari, Jo
Ashes, Ashes **1056**
The Curious Misadventures of Feltus
  Ovalton 1056

Tremain, Rose
Trespass 32, 64

Tremayne, Peter
Absolution by Murder 627

Trent, Christine
A Royal Likeness 359

Trevor, William
The Story of Lucy Gault 1

Trigiani, Adriana
The Queen of the Big Time 69
Very Valentine: A Novel 64

Tripp, Dawn Clifton
The Season of Open Water 399

Trollope, Joanna
Friday Nights: A Novel 101

Author Index

Title Index

This index alphabetically lists all titles featured in entries and those listed within entries under "Other books by the same author" and "Other books you might like." Each title is followed by the author's name and the number of the entry where the book is described or listed. Bold numbers indicate featured main entries; light-face numbers refer to books recommended for further reading.

Title Index

Title Index

Title Index

Title Index

Title Index

Title Index

Title Index

N

Title Index

Title Index

Title Index

Title Index

Title Index

Title Index

Title Index